A SELECT LIBRARY

OF

NICENE AND POST-NICENE FATHERS

OF

THE CHRISTIAN CHURCH.

𝔖𝔢𝔠𝔬𝔫𝔡 𝔖𝔢𝔯𝔦𝔢𝔰.

TRANSLATED INTO ENGLISH WITH PROLEGOMENA AND EXPLANATORY NOTES

UNDER THE EDITORIAL SUPERVISION OF

PHILIP SCHAFF, D.D., LL.D.,   AND   **HENRY WACE, D.D.,**

*Professor of Church History in the Union Theological
Seminary, New York.*

*Principal of King's College,
London.*

*IN CONNECTION WITH A NUMBER OF PATRISTIC SCHOLARS OF EUROPE
AND AMERICA.*

VOLUME III.

THEODORET, JEROME, GENNADIUS, RUFINUS:

HISTORICAL WRITINGS, ETC.

T&T CLARK
EDINBURGH

WM. B. EERDMANS PUBLISHING COMPANY
GRAND RAPIDS, MICHIGAN

British Library Cataloguing in Publication Data
Nicene & Post-Nicene Fathers. — 2nd series
1. Fathers of the church
I. Schaff, Philip   II. Mace, Henry
230'.11   BR60.A62

T&T Clark ISBN 0 567 09412 X

Eerdmans ISBN 0-8028-8117-3

Reprinted, July 1989

Photolithoprinted by Eerdmans Printing Company
Grand Rapids, Michigan, United States of America

CONTENTS OF VOLUME III

PREFACE

THIS volume contains the following works:

I. THEODORET: *Church History, Dialogues, and Letters.* Translated, with ample Prolegomena and explanatory notes, by the Rev. BLOMFIELD JACKSON, M.A., Rector of St. Bartholomew's, Cripplegate, London.

II. JEROME and GENNADIUS: *Lives of Illustrious Men.* Translated, with introduction and notes, by ERNEST CUSHING RICHARDSON, Ph.D., Librarian of Princeton College.

III. RUFINUS: *Apology against Jerome,* and JEROME: *Apology in reply to Rufinus;* RUFINUS: *Commentary on the Apostles' Creed,* and *Prefaces* to his translations of the Clementine Recognitions, the Sayings of Xystus, Eusebius's Church History, and several of Origen's works; translated, with notes, and an introduction on the Life and Works of Rufinus by the Hon. and Rev. WM. HENRY FREMANTLE, M.A., Canon of Canterbury.

The English reader has now, in the first three volumes of this Library, a complete collection of the *historical* writings of the Fathers, whose permanent value, as sources, is universally acknowledged. Several of them have never before appeared in English.

The unavoidable delay in the publication of the third volume has been very annoying to the general editors and publishers, but the subscribers will be amply compensated by the addition of the writings of Rufinus, which were not promised in the prospectus.

It is encouraging that this difficult and costly enterprise is beginning to be duly appreciated by competent judges on both sides of the Atlantic. It is especially gratifying to read from a thorough patristic scholar of the Anglican Church such a hearty commendation of the first volume (the work of two young American divines), as appeared in "The Church Quarterly Review" for April, 1892. We share in his hope (p. 125) that the labors of Dr. McGiffert and Dr. Richardson will stimulate a new and critical edition of all the historical works of Eusebius, after the model set by Bishop Lightfoot in his *Apostolic Fathers*, and that one of the English University Presses will consider it an honor to undertake the expense of publication.

PHILIP SCHAFF.

NEW YORK, July 12, 1892.

THE ECCLESIASTICAL HISTORY, DIALOGUES, AND LETTERS

OF

THEODORET

TRANSLATED WITH NOTES

BY

THE REV. BLOMFIELD JACKSON, M.A.,

Vicar of St. Bartholomew's, Moor Lane, and Fellow of King's College, London.

TRANSLATOR'S PREFACE

THE following translation has been made from the edition published in Migne's Patrologia. The plan originally proposed was, in the case of the History, to make a revision of an existing translation. This was, however, after a brief trial, abandoned, and the translation has throughout been made entirely fresh. The Letters, so far as the translator is aware, have never been published in English before. The notes indicate with sufficient clearness to whom he is indebted for such elucidation of the text as he may have been enabled to furnish. Conscious of its imperfections, and not confident that revision can have removed all blemishes and errors, he yet puts forth this English version of the History, Dialogues, and Letters of Theodoret, Bishop of Cyrus, in the hope that he may not have done great injustice to their holy and learned author.

LONDON, July, 1892.

Πρὸς τῶν κρατούντων ἐσμέν.
— *Æschylus.*

CONTENTS

——————

CHRONOLOGICAL TABLES TO ACCOMPANY THE HISTORY AND LIFE OF THEODORET.

323.	Defeat and relegation of Licinius.	*Theod. i. 1;* Soc. i. 4; Soz. i. 8; Eus. x. 9.
324.	Execution of Licinius. Macarius, bishop of Jerusalem, Silvester of Rome, and Alexander of Alexandria.	*Theod. i. 2;* Soc. i. 9; Soz. i. 2.
	Colluthus condemned at Alexandria.	*Theod. i. 3.*
325.	20th year of Constantine I. COUNCIL OF NICÆA (May 20—Aug. 25).	*Theod. i. 6;* Soc. i. 8; Soz. i. 17.
	Birth of Gallus (Cæsar).	*Theod. iii. 1.*
	Birth of Gregory of Nazianzus.	
	Eustathius of Berœa elected bishop of Antioch.	*Theod. i. 3;* Soz. i. 2.
	Constantine writes a letter ordering the building and reparation of churches.	*Theod. i. 14.*
	Also a letter to Macarius, bishop of Jerusalem, about the Church of the Holy Sepulchre.	*Theod. i. 16;* Soc. i. 9.
326.	Alexander, bishop of Alexandria, died in January (perhaps April), and Athanasius succeeds, probably on June 8th. The Festal Index gives 328.	*Theod. i. 25;* Soc. i. 15; Soz. ii. 17.
327.	?Consecration of Frumentius to the Abyssinian bishopric.	*Theod. i. 22;* Soc. i. 19; Soz. ii. 24.
328.	Arian Council of Antioch, and deposition of Eustathius: but the date is much controverted. Possibly 330 or 331.	*Theod. i. 20;* Soc. i. 24; Soz. ii. 19.
329.	Incident of Ischyras and Macarius.	*Theod. ii. 6;* Soc. i. 27.
	Birth of Basil of Cæsarea, " the Great."	
330.	Byzantium dedicated as Constantinople, May 11th.	*cf. Theod. i. 18;* Soc. i. 16; Soz. i. 3.
331.	Birth of Julian.	
	Perhaps the deposition of Eustathius.	
333.	Constantine's letter to Sapor II.	*Theod. i. 24.*
335.	Division of the empire between Constantine, Constantius, and Constans, sons, and Dalmatius and Hannibalianus, nephews, of the emperor.	
	Dedication of the Great Church at Jerusalem.	*Theod. i. 29;* Soc. i. 28; Soz. ii. 26.
	Anthony summoned to Alexandria.	*Theod. iv. 24.*
	Councils of Tyre and Jerusalem; first exile of Athanasius.	*Theod. i. 28–29;* Soc. i. 28; Soz. ii. 25.
336.	Athanasius at Treves.	*Theod. i. 29;* Soc. i. 35; Soz. ii. 28.
	Death of Arius.	*Theod. i. 13;* Soc. i. 38; Soz. ii. 29.
	Death (? Clinton gives 340) of Alexander of Constantinople.	*Theod. i. 19.*
337.	Death of Constantine I. Whitsunday.	*Theod. i. 30;* Soc. i. 39; Soz. ii. 34.
338.	Athanasius' restoration recommended by Constantine II.	*Theod. ii. 1;* Soc. ii. 3; Soz. iii. 2.
340.	Constantine II. defeated and slain near Aquileia.	*Theod. ii. 3;* Soc. ii. 5; Soz. iii. 2.
	Constantius at war with Persia.	
	Death of Eusebius of Cæsarea, the historian.	
	Paul and Eusebius of Nicomedia rivals at Constantinople.	*Theod. i. 19;* Soc. ii. 7; Soz. iii. 4.
	Athanasius withdraws to Rome.	
	Gregory at Alexandria.	*Theod. ii. 3;* Soc. ii. 11; Soz. iii. 6.
	Arian Synod of the Dedication of the Great Church at Antioch, commonly dated 341.	*Theod. ii. 3;* Soc. ii. 10; Soz. iii. 5.
342.	Constantius orders expulsion of Paul from Constantinople.	*Theod. ii. 4;* Soc. ii. 7; Soz. iii. 4.
343.	Persecution in Persia.	
343-4 or 347.	(See note on p. 67.) Council of Sardica.	*Theod. ii. 6;* Soc. ii. 14; Soz. iii. 11.
	Athanasius received at Milan by Constans.	
345.	Murder of Gregory.	*Theod. ii. 9.*
345 or 346.	Deposition of Stephen of Antioch.	*Theod. ii. 8;* Soc. ii. 26; Soz. iii. 20.
	Return of Athanasius, October 21.	*Theod. ii. 3;* Soc. ii. 33; Soz. iii. 70.

347.	Birth of John Chrysostom.	
349.	Council at Jerusalem (Mansi. ii. 171 u.), under bp. Maximus, in favour of Athanasius. 1st Council of Sirmium.	
350.	Revolt of Magnentius.	*Theod. ii. 12;* Soc. ii. 25.
	Constans killed February 27.	*Theod. ii. 9;* Soc. ii. 25; Soz. iv. 1.
351.	Constantius, sole emperor, defeats Magnentius at Mursa.	
	2nd Council of Sirmium.	
352.	Liberius succeeds Julius in the See of Rome	*Theod. ii. 12.*
	Paul of Constantinople strangled.	*Theod. ii. 4;* Soc. ii. 26; Soz. iv. 2.
353.	Suicide of Magnentius.	
355.	Council of Milan.	*Theod. ii. 12;* Soc. ii. 36; Soz. iv. 9.
356.	Intrusion of George at Alexandria.	*Theod. ii. 10;* Soc. ii. 14; Soz. iv. 30.
357.	Deposition of Cyril of Jerusalem by Acacius.	*Theod. ii. 22;* Soc. ii. 42; Soz. iv. 25.
	3rd Council of Sirmium.	
358.	Return of Liberius.	*Theod. ii. 14;* Soc. ii. 42; Soz. iv. 15.
359.	Synod of the Isaurian Seleucia.	*Theod. ii. 22;* Soc. ii. 39; Soz. iv. 22.
	Birth of Gratianus.	
	Council of Ariminum.	*Theod. ii. 15;* Soc. ii. 37; Soz. iv. 17.
300.	Synod of Nica.	*Theod. ii. 16.*
	3rd Council of Constantinople. (Semi Arian.)	
361.	Nov. 3 Death of Constantius. ⎫ Accession of Julian. ⎭	*Theod. iii. 1;* Soc. ii. 47; Soz. v. 1.
362.	Murder of George of Alexandria.	
	Athanasius returns Feb. 22, but goes into 4th exile in October.	*Theod. iii. 5;* Soc. iii. 4; Soz. vi. 6.
363.	Julian's baffled attempt to rebuild the Temple.	*Theod. iii. 15;* Soc. iii. 70; Soz. v. 22.
	Julian's Persian expedition and death, June 26.	*Theod. iii. 20;* Soc. iii. 17; Soz. vi. 1.
	Accession of Jovian, June 27.	
364.	Death of Jovian.	*Theod. iv. 4;* Soc. iii. 26; Soz. vi. 3.
	Accession of Valentinian. Valens *Augustus.*	
366.	Liberius, bp. of Rome, dies and is succeeded by Damasus.	*Theod. ii. 17;* Soc. iv. 29; Soz. vi. 23.
367.	Gratianus, son of Valentinian, declared Augustus. æt. s. 8.	*Theod. v. 1.*
	5th exile of Athanasius.	
370.	Basil becomes bishop of Cæsarea.	*Theod. iv. 16;* Soc. iv. 26; Soz. vi. 16.
372.	Gregory of Nazianzus becomes bishop of Sasima.	*Theod. v. 7;* Soc. iv. 26; Soz. vi. 17.
373.	Death of Athanasius, May 2.	*Theod. iv. 17;* Soc. iv. 20; Soz. vi. 19.
	Death of Ephraim Syrus, June 19.	*Theod. iv. 26;* Soz. iii. 16.
374.	Auxentius of Milan dies.	*Theod. iv. 5;* Soc. iv. 30; Soz. i. 24.
	Ambrose archbishop of Milan.	*Theod. iv. 6.*
375.	Gratian emperor of the West.	*Theod. v. 1;* Soc. iv. 31; Soz. vi. 36.
378.	Death of Valens.	*Theod. iv. 32;* Soc. iv. 37; Soz. vi. 40.
379.	Theodosius named *Augustus,* Jan. 19.	*Theod. v. 5;* Soc. v. 2; Soz. vii. 2.
	Gregory of Nazianzus at Constantinople.	*Theod. v. 8;* Soc. v. 6; Soz. vii. 7.
381.	COUNCIL OF CONSTANTINOPLE.	*Theod. v. 8;* Soc. v. 8; Soz. vii. 7.
383.	Death of Gratian. Rebellion of Maximus.	*Theod. v. 12;* Soc. v. 11; Soz. vii. 13.
386.	Birth of Theodoret, according to the less probable date of Garnerius.	
387.	Sedition at Antioch.	*Theod. v. 19;* Soc. v. 15; Soz. vii. 23.
388.	Defeat and death of Maximus.	
	Death of Cyril of Jerusalem.	
390.	Destruction of the Serapeum.	*Theod. v. 22;* Soc. v. 16; Soz. vii. 15.
	Massacre at Thessalonica.	*Theod. v. 17.*
	Death of Gregory of Nazianzus.	
392.	Death of Valentinian II. Eugenius set up as Emperor.	*Theod. v. 24.*
393.	BIRTH OF THEODORET, according to the more probable date of Tillemont.	
394.	Theodosius defeats Eugenius.	*Theod. v. 24;* Soc. v. 25; Soz. vii. 24.
395.	Death of Theodosius. Accession of Honorius and Arcadius.	*Theod. v. 25;* Soc. v. 26; Soz. vii. 25.
398.	John Chrysostom becomes bishop of Constantinople.	*Theod. v. 27;* Soc. vi. 2; Soz. viii. 2.
400.	Revolt of Gainas.	*cf. Theod. v. 33;* Soc. vi. 6; Soz. viii. 4.
401.	Roman legions withdrawn from Britain.	
403.	Synod of " the Oak."	*Theod. v. 34;* Soc. vi. 15; Soz. viii. 19.
404.	Death of the empress Eudoxia.	
	Chrysostom ordered to quit Constantinople.	*Theod. v. 34 ;* Soc. vi. 18; Soz. viii. 24.
407.	Death of Chrysostom.	*Theod. v. 34.*
408.	Death of Arcadius. Accession of Theodosius II.	*Theod. v. 36.*
410.	Sack of Rome by Alaric.	

412.	Cyril becomes patriarch of Alexandria.	*Theod. v. 35.*
415.	Murder of Hypatia at Alexandria.	
	Theodoret loses his parents and retires to Nicerte.	*Theod. Epp. CXIII, CXIX.*
418.	Council of Carthage.	
423.	Death of Honorius.	
	Theodoret becomes bishop of Cyrus.	
425.	Accession of Valentinian III.	
428.	Nestorius becomes bishop of Constantinople.	
	Vandals in Africa.	*Theod. Epp. XXIX–XXXVI.*
429.	Death of Theodotus, patriarch of Antioch, fixed by Theodoretus as the term of his History.	*Theod. v. 39.*
430.	Letters of Celestine of Rome and Cyril of Alexandria to John of Antioch on the Western condemnation of Nestorius.	
	Death of St. Augustine.	
431.	COUNCIL OF EPHESUS. (3rd GENERAL.)	
432.	Council of Orientals at Berœa. (St. Patrick's mission.)	
433.	Peace between Cyril and the Orientals.	
434 (c).	Friendly correspondence between Theod. and Cyril.	*Theod. Ep. LXXXIII.*
438.	Translation of the relics of Chrysostom to Constantinople.	*Theod. v. 36;* Soc. vii. 45.
	Cyril denounces Diodorus and Theodore of Mopsuestia: renewal of hostilities with Theodoret.	
440.	Accession of Isdigerdes II., the last event referred to in the Ecc. History.	*Theod. v. 38.*
444.	Death of Cyril of Alexandria.	*Theod. Ep. CLXXX.*
	Accession of Dioscorus.	
446 (c).	Composition of the "Dialogues."	
448.	Dioscorus deposes Irenæus of Tyre.	
449.	(March 30.) Edict confining Theodoret within the limits of his diocese.	
	(Aug.) Assembly of the "Latrocinium" at Ephesus.	
450.	(July 29.) Death of Theodosius II.	
	Accession of Pulcheria and Marcian.	
451.	COUNCIL OF CHALCEDON. (4th GENERAL.)	
453.	Death of Theodoret, according to Tillemont.	
458.	Probable date of the death, according to Garnerius.	

PROLEGOMENA

THE LIFE AND WRITINGS OF THE BLESSED THEODORETUS, BISHOP OF CYRUS.

I. — PARENTAGE, BIRTH, AND EDUCATION.

At Antioch at the close of the fourth century there were living a husband and wife, opulent and happy in the enjoyment of all the good things of this life, one thing only excepted. They were childless. Married at seventeen, the young bride lived for several years in the enjoyment of such pleasures as wealth and society could give. At the age of twenty-three she was attacked by a painful disease in one of her eyes, for which neither the books of older authorities nor later physiological discoveries could suggest a remedy. One of her domestic servants, compassionating her distress, informed her that the wife of Pergamius, at that time in authority in the East, had been healed of a similar ailment by Petrus, a famous Galatian solitary who was then living in the upper story of a tomb in the neighbourhood, to which access could only be obtained by climbing a ladder. The afflicted lady, says the story which her son himself repeats,[1] hastened to climb to the recluse's latticed cell, arrayed in all her customary elaborate costume, with earrings, necklaces, and the rest of her ornaments of gold, her silk robe blazing with embroidery, her face smeared with red and white cosmetics, and her eyebrows and eyelids artificially darkened. "Tell me," said the hermit, on beholding his brilliant visitor, "tell me, my child, if some skilful painter were to paint a portrait according to his art's strict rules and offer it for exhibition, and then up were to come some dauber dashing off his pictures on the spur of the moment, who should find fault with the artistic picture, lengthen the lines of brows and lids, make the face whiter and heighten the red of the cheeks, what would you say? Do you not think the original painter would be hurt at this insult to his art and these needless additions of an unskilled hand." These arguments, we learn, led eventually to the improvement of the young Antiochene gentlewoman both in piety and good taste and her eye is said to have been restored to health by the imposition of the sign of the cross. Not impossibly the discontinuance of the use of cosmetics may have helped, if not caused, the cure.

Six years longer the husband and wife lived together a more religious life, but still unblessed with children. Among the ascetic solitaries whom the disappointed husband begged to aid him in his prayers was one Macedonius, distinguished, from the simplicity of his diet, as "the barley eater." In answer to his prayers, it was believed, a son was at last granted to the pious pair.[2] The condition of the boon being that the boy should be devoted to the divine service, he was appropriately named at his birth "Theodoretus," or "Given by God."[3] Of the exact date of this birth, productive of such important consequences to the history and literature of the Church, no precise knowledge is attainable. The less probable year is 386 as given by Garnerius,[4] the more probable and now generally accepted year 393 follows the computation of Tillemont.[5]

---

[1] Relig. Hist. 1188 et seq.   [2] Relig. Hist, 1214.
[3] The Hebrew equivalents of this very general designation are Nathaniel and Matthew. Modern English custom has travelled back to the Greek for its Theodore, Theodora, but Dieudonné and Diodati are familiar in French and Italian.
[4] Garnier the French Jesuit Father, was born in Paris in 1612, and died in 1681. His " Auctarium Theodoreti Episcopi Cyrensis," with dissertations, was published in 1684.
[5] According to this reckoning Theodoret would be fifty-six at the time of the letter to Leo, written 449, in which he speaks of his old age, and about thirty at his consecration as bishop in 423.
W. Möller in Herzog's Encyclopedia of Prot. Theol. (Ed. 1885. xv. 402) gives 390.

While yet in his swaddling bands the little Theodoret began to receive training appropriate to his high career,[1] and, as he himself tells us, with the pardonable exaggeration of enthusiasm, was no sooner weaned than he began to learn the apostolic teaching. Among his earliest impressions were the lessons and exhortations of Peter of Galatia, to whom his mother owed so much, and of Macedonius " the barley eater," who had helped to save the Antiochenes in the troubles that arose about the statues.[2] Of the latter[3] Theodoret quotes the earnest charges to a holy life, and in his modesty expresses his sorrow that he had not profited better by the solitary's solemn entreaties. If however Macedonius was indeed quite ignorant of the Scriptures,[4] it may have been well for the boy's education to have been not wholly in his hands. It is not impossible that he may have had a childish recollection of Chrysostom, who left Antioch in 398. To Peter he used to pay a weekly visit, and records[5] how the holy man would take him on his knees and feed him with bread and raisins. A treasure long preserved in the household of Theodoret's parents was half Peter's girdle, woven of coarse linen, which the old man had one day wound round the loins of the boy. Frequently proved an unfailing remedy in various cases of family ailment, its very reputation led to its loss, for all the neighbours used to borrow it to cure their own complaints, and at last an unkind or careless friend omitted to return it.[6]

When a stripling Theodoret was blessed by the right hand of Aphraates the monk, of whom he relates an anecdote in his Ecclesiastical History,[7] and when his beard was just beginning to grow was also blessed by the ascetic Zeno.[8] At this period he was already a lector[9] and was therefore probably past the age of eighteen. By this time his general education would be regarded as more or less complete, and to these earlier years may be traced the acquaintance which he shows with the writings of Homer, Thucydides, Plato, Euripides, and other Greek classics. Lighter literature, too, will not have been excluded from his reading, if we accept the genuineness of the famous letter on the death of Cyril,[10] and may infer that the dialogues of Lucian are more likely to have amused the leisure hours of a lad at school and college than have intruded on the genuine piety and marvellous industry of the Bishop of Cyrus.

Theodoret was familiar with Greek, Syriac, and Hebrew, but is said to have been unacquainted with Latin.[11] Such I presume to be an inference from a passage in one of his works[12] in which he tells us " The Romans indeed had poets, orators, and historians, and we are informed by those who are skilled in both languages that their reasonings are closer than the Greeks' and their sentences more concise. In saying this I have not the least intention of disparaging the Greek language which is in a sense mine,[13] or of making an ungrateful return to it for my education, but I speak that I may to some extent close the lips and lower the brows of those who make too big a boasting about it, and may teach them not to ridicule a language which is illuminated by the truth." But it is not clear from these words that Theodoret had no acquaintance with Latin. His admiration for orthodox Western theology as well as his natural literary and social curiosity would lead him to learn it. In the Ecclesiastical History (III. 16) there is a possible reference to Horace.

Theodoret's chief instructor in Theology was the great light of the school of Antioch, Theodorus, known from the name of the see to which he was appointed in 392, "Mopsuestia," or " the hearth of Mopsus," in Cilicia Secunda. He also refers to his obligations

---

[1] Ep. LXXXI.   [2] Ecc. Hist. v. 19. p. 146.   [3] Relig. Hist. 1215.   [4] cf. Ecc. Hist. p. 146.   [5] Relig. Hist. 1188.
[6] The confidence of Theodoret in the wonder working powers of half Peter's girdle may be taken as a crucial instance of what detractors of the individual and of the age would call his foolish credulity. But an unsound process of reasoning from *post hoc* to *propter hoc* is not confined to any particular period, and it is not impossible that the scientists of the thirty-fourth century may smile benevolently at some of the cherished remedies of the nineteenth.
[7] Cf. p. 127.   [8] Relig. Hist. 1203.   [9] Vide n. p. 34.
[10] Vide p. 346. To what is said there may be added the following remarks from Dr. Salmon's " *Infallibility of the Church*," p. 303, n. "The letter from which these passages are taken was read as Theodoret's at the fifth General Council (fifth Session) and there accepted as his. But on questions of this kind Councils are not infallible; and the letter contains a note of spuriousness in purporting to be addressed to John, bishop of Antioch, who died before Cyril. I own that the suggestion that for 'John' we ought to read 'Domnus' does not suffice to remove suspicion from my mind. But it is solely for the reason just stated that I feel no confidence in accepting the letter as Theodoret's. Newman's opinion that it is incredible Theodoret could have written so 'atrocious' a letter is one which it is amazing should be held by any one familiar with the controversial amenities of the time. Our modern urbanity is willing to bury party animosities in the grave; but in the fifth century Swift's translation would be thought the only proper one of the maxim' *De mortuis nil nisi bonum*,' 'when scoundrels die let all bemoan them.' Certainly the man who half a dozen years after Chrysostom's death spoke of him as Judas Iscariot had no right to expect to be politely treated after his own death by one whom he had relentlessly persecuted."
Glubokowski, whose great work on Theodoret now in progress is unfortunately a sealed volume to the majority of readers on account of its being written in the author's native Russian, is of opinion that the letter is spurious. See also Schröckh Kircheges. xviii. 370. I am myself unable to see the force of the *internal* evidence of spuriousness. It may have been half playful, and never meant for publication.
[11] Cf. Can. Venables Dict. Christ. Biog. iv. 906.   [12] *Græcarum affectionum curatio* 843.
[13] To a Syrian it would not be literally the mother tongue, but was possibly acquired in infancy.

to Diodorus of Tarsus.[1]   Accepting 393 as the date of his birth and 392 as that of Theodore's appointment to his see, it would seem that the younger theologian must have been rather a reader than a hearer as well of Theodore as of Diodore.   But Theodore expounded Scripture in many churches of the East.[2]   The friendship of Theodoret for Nestorius may have begun when the latter was a monk in the convent of St. Euprepius at the gates of Antioch. It is recorded [3] that on one occasion Theodore gave offence while preaching at Antioch by refusing to give to the blessed Virgin the title Θεοτόκος.   He afterwards retracted this refusal for the sake of peace.   The original objection and subsequent consent have a curious significance in view of the subsequent careers of his two famous pupils.   Of the school of Antioch as distinguished from that of Alexandria it may be said broadly that while the latter shewed a tendency to syntheticism and to unity of conception, the former, under the influence of the Aristotelian philosophy, favoured analytic processes.[4]   And while the general bent of the school of thinkers among whom Theodoret was brought up inclined to a recognition of a distinction between the two natures in the Person of Christ, there was much in the special teaching of its great living authority which was not unlikely to lead to such division of the Person as was afterwards attributed to Nestorius. [5]   Such were the influences under which Theodoret grew up.

On the death of his parents he at once distributed all the property that he inherited from them, and embraced a life of poverty,[6] retiring, at about the age of three and twenty, to Nicerte, a village three miles from Apamea, and seventy-five from Antioch, in the monastery of which he passed seven calm and happy years, occasionally visiting neighbouring monasteries and perhaps during this period paying the visit to Jerusalem which left an indelible impression on his memory.   " With my own eyes," he writes,[7] "I have seen that desolation.   The prediction rang in my ears when I saw the fulfilment before my eyes and I lauded and worshipped the truth."   Of the peace of Theodoret's earlier manhood Dr. Newman [8] says in a sentence less open to criticism than another which shall be quoted further on, " There he laid deep within him that foundation of faith and devotion, and obtained that vivid apprehension of the world unseen and future which lasted him as a secret spring of spiritual strength all through the conflict and sufferings of the years that followed."

II. — Episcopate at Cyrus.

Cyrus or Cyrrhus was a town of the district of Syria called after it Cyrestica.   The capital of Cyrestica was Gindarus, which Strabo describes [9] as being in his time a natural nest of robbers.   Cyrus lies on a branch of the river Œnoparas, now Aphreen, and the site is still known as Koros.   A tradition has long obtained that it received the name of Cyrus from the Jews in honour of their great benefactor, but this is more than doubtful. The form Cyrus may have arisen from a confusion with a Cyrus in Susiana.[10]   The Cyrestica is a fertile plain lying between the spurs of the Alma Dagh and the Euphrates, irrigated by three streams and blessed with a rich soil.   The diocese, which was subject to the Metropolitan of Hierapolis, contained some sixteen hundred square miles [11] and eight hundred distinct parishes each with its church.[12]   But Cyrus itself was a wretched little place [13] scantily inhabited.   Before it was beautified by the munificence of Theodoret it contained no buildings of any dignity or grace.   The people of the town as well as of the diocese seem to have been poor in orthodoxy as well as in pocket, and the rich soil of the district grew a plentiful crop of the tares of Arianism, Marcionism, Eunomianism and Judaism.[14]

Such was the diocese to which Theodoret, in spite of his honest *nolo episcopari*,[15] was consecrated at about the age of thirty, A.D. 423.   Of the circumstances of this consecration we have no evidence.   Garnerius conjectures that he must have been ordained deacon by Alexander who succeeded Porphyrius at Antioch.   He was probably appointed, if not consecrated, to succeed Isidorus at Cyrus, by Theodotus the successor of Alexander on the patriarchal throne of Antioch.   In this diocese certainly for five and twenty years, perhaps for five and thirty, with occasional intervals he worked night and day with unflagging patience and perseverance for the good of the people committed to his care, and in the cause of his Master and of the truth.   The ecclesiastic of these early

[1] Ep. xvi.   [2] John of Antioch Fac. ii. 2.
[3] Cyril. Alex. Ep. LXIX.   [7] *Græc. Affect. Cur.* 1099.   [11] Ep. XLII.   [15] Ep. LXXXI.
[4] Glubokowski p. 63.   [8] *Historical Sketches* iii. 319.   [12] Ep. CXIII.
[5] e.g. Theodorus, Migne 776.   [9] Strabo xvi. c.751.   [13] Ep. CXXXVIII.
[6] Ep. CXIII.   [10] Glubokowski p. 31. Tillemont v. 217.   [14] Epp. LXXXI, CXIII.

times is sometimes imagined to have been a morose and ungenial ascetic, wasting his energies in unprofitable hair-splitting, and taking little or no interest in the every day needs of his contemporaries. In marked contrast with this imaginary bishop stands out the kindly figure of the real bishop of Cyrus, as the modest statements and hints supplied by his own letters enable us to recall him.

As an administrator and man of business he was munificent and efficient. Stripped, as we have already learnt, of his family property by his own act and will, he must have been dependent in his diocese on the revenues of his see. From these, which cannot have been small, he was able to spend large sums on public works. Cyrus was adorned with porticoes, with two great bridges, with baths, and with an aqueduct, all at Theodoret's expense.[1] On assuming the administration of his diocese he took measures, he tells us,[2] to secure for Cyrus "the necessary arts," and from these three words we need not hesitate to infer that architects, engineers, masons, sculptors, and carpenters, would be attracted "from all quarters" to the bishop's important works. And for this increased population it is interesting to note that Theodoret provided competent practitioners in medicine and surgery, in which it would seem he was not himself unskilled.[3] His keen interest in the temporal needs of his people is shewn by the efforts he made to obtain relief for them from the cruel pressure of exorbitant taxation.[4] So unendurable was the tale of imposts under which they groaned that in many cases they were deserting their farms and the country, and he earnestly appeals to the empress Pulcheria and to his friend Anatolius to help them.[5] The tender sympathy felt by him for all those afflicted in body and estate, as well as in mind, is shewn in his letters on behalf of Celestinianus, or Celestiacus, a gentleman of position at Carthage, who had suffered cruelly during the attack of the Vandals,[6] and in the admirable and touching letters of consolation addressed to survivors on the deaths of relatives. That these should have been religiously preserved need excite no surprise.[7] Of the terms on which he lived with his neighbours we can form some idea from the justifiable boast contained in his letter to Nomus. In the quarter of a century of his episcopate, he writes, he never appeared in court either as prosecutor or defendant; his clergy followed his admirable example; he never took an obol or a garment from any one; not one of his household ever received so much as a loaf or an egg; he could not bear to think that he had any property beyond his few poor clothes.[8] Yet he was always ready to give where he would not receive, and in addition to all the diocesan and literary work which he conscientiously performed, he spent more time than he could well afford in all sorts of extra diocesan business which his position thrust in his way.

As a shepherd of souls he was unceasing in his efforts to win heathen, heretics and Jews to the true faith. His diocese, when he assumed its government, was a very hotbed of heresy.[9] Nevertheless in the famous letter to Leo[10] he could boast that not a tare was left to spoil the crop. His fame as a preacher was great and wide, and makes us the more regret that of the discourses which in turn roused, cheered, and blamed, so little should survive. The eloquence, so to say, of his extant writings, gives indications of the force of spoken utterances not less marked by learning and literary skill. Two of his letters give vivid pictures of the enthusiasm of oriental auditories in Antioch, once so populous and so keen in theological interest, where now, amid a people numbering only about a fiftieth part of their predecessors of the fifth century, there is not a single church. We see the patriarch John in a frenzy of gladness at Theodoret's sermons, clapping his hands and springing again and again from his chair;[11] we see the heads of the congregation receiving the bishop of Cyrus with frantic delight as he came down from the pulpit, flinging their arms round him, kissing now his head, now his breast, now his hands, now his knees, and hear them exclaiming, "This is the Voice of the Apostle!"[12] But Theodoret had to encounter sometimes the fury of opposition. Again and again in his campaign against heretics and unbelievers he was stoned, wounded, and brought nigh unto death.[13] "He from whom no secrets are hid knows all the bruises my body has received, aimed at me by ill-named heretics, and what fights I have fought in most of the cities of the East against Jews, heretics, and heathen."[14]

---

[1] Epp. LXXIX. LXXXI.   [2] Ep. CXV.   [3] Epp. CXIV, CXV, and Dial. p. 217 cf. also de Prov. 518 et seqq.
[4] Epp. XLII, XLIII, XLV.   [5] Epp. XLIII. and XLV.   [6] Epp. XXIX.-XXXVI.
[7] cf. Epp. VII. VIII. XIV. XV. XVII. XVIII. LXV. LXIX.   [8] Ep. LXXXI.
[9] " In a diocese such as his, lying as it were in a corner of the world, not reached by the public posts, isolated by the great river to the east and the mountain chains to the west, peopled by half-leavened heathen, Christianity assumed many strange forms, sometimes hardly recognisable caricatures of the truth." Canon Venables. Dict. Christ. Biog. iv. 906.
[10] Epp. CXIII.   [11] Ep. LXXXIII.   [12] Ep. CXLVII.   [13] Epp. LXXXI and CXIII.   [14] Ep. CXIII.

III. — Relations with Nestorius and to Nestorianism.

Nestorius, patriarch of Constantinople, was bound by ties of close friendship both to Theodoret and to John, patriarch of Antioch. In August, 430, the western bishops, under the presidency of the Pope Celestine, assembled in council at Rome, condemned Nestorius, and threatened him with excommunication. Shortly afterwards a council of Orientals at Alexandria, summoned by Cyril, endorsed this condemnation and despatched it to Constantinople. Then John received from Celestine and Cyril letters announcing their common action. When the couriers conveying these communications reached Antioch they found John surrounded by Theodoret and other bishops who were assembled possibly for the ordination of Macarius, the new bishop of Laodicea. John took counsel with his brother bishops, and a letter was despatched in their common name to Nestorius, exhorting him to accept the term Θεοτόκος, round which the whole war waged; pointing out the sense in which it could not but be accepted by every loyal Christian, and imploring him not to embroil Christendom for a word. This letter has been generally attributed to Theodoret. But while the conciliatory sage of Cyrus was endeavouring to formulate an Eirenicon, the ardent Egyptian made peace almost impossible by the publication of his famous anathematisms. John and his friends were distressed at the apparent unorthodoxy of Cyril's condemnation of Nestorius, and asked Theodoret to refute Cyril.[1] The strong language employed in Letter CL. conveys an idea of the heat of the enthusiasm with which Theodoret entered on the task, and his profound conviction that Cyril, in blind zeal against imaginary error on the part of Nestorius, was himself falling headlong into the Apollinarian pit. An eager war of words now waged over Nestorius between Cyril and Theodoret, each denouncing the other for supposed heresy on the subject of the incarnation; and, with deep respect for the learning and motives of Theodoret, we may probably find a solution of much that he said and did in the fact that he misunderstood Nestorius as completely as he did Cyril.[2] Cyril, nursed in the synthetic principles of the Alexandrian school, could see only the unity of the two natures in the one Person. To him, to distinguish, as the analysis of Theodoret distinguished, between God the Word and Christ the Man, was to come perilously near a recognition of two Christs, keeping up as it were a mutual dialogue of speech and action. But Cyril's unqualified assertion that there is one Christ, and that Christ is God, really gave no ground for the accusation that to him the manhood was an unreality. Yet he and Theodoret were substantially at one. Theodoret's failure to apprehend Cyril's drift was no doubt due less to any want of intelligence on the part of the Syrian than to the overbearing bitterness of the fierce Egyptian.

On the other hand Theodoret's loyal love for Nestorius led him to give his friend credit for meaning what he himself meant. While he was driven to contemplate the doctrines of Cyril in their most dangerous exaggeration, he shrank from seeing how the Nestorian counter statement might be dangerously exaggerated. Theodoret, as Dr. Bright remarks,[3] "uses a good deal of language which is *prima facie* Nestorian; his objections are pervaded by an *ignoratio elenchi*, and his language is repeatedly illogical and inconsistent; but he and Cyril were essentially nearer to each other in belief than at the time they would have admitted, for Theodoret virtually owns the personal oneness and explains the phrase 'God assumed man' by 'He assumed manhood.'" Cyril "in his letter to Euoptius earnestly disclaims both forms of Apollinarianism — the notion of a mindless manhood in Christ and the notion of a body formed out of Godhead. In his reply (on Art iv.) he admits the language appropriate to each nature."

Probably both the Egyptian and the Syrian would have found no difficulty in subscribing the language of our own judicious divine; "a kind of mutual commutation there is whereby those concrete names, *God* and *Man*, when we speak of Christ, do take interchangeably one another's room, so that for truth of speech it skilleth not whether we say that the Son of God hath created the world and the Son of Man by his death hath saved it or else that the Son of Man did create, and the Son of God died to save the world. Howbeit, as oft as we attribute to God what the manhood of Christ claimeth, or to man what his Deity hath right unto, we understand by the name of God and the name of Man neither the one nor the other nature, but the whole person of Christ, in whom both natures are. When the Apostle saith of the Jews that they crucified the Lord of Glory, and when the Son of Man being on earth affirmeth that the Son of Man was in heaven at

---

[1] Vide the Anathematisms and Theodoret's refutation in the Prolegomena.
[2] cf. Glubokowski p. 98. [3] Dict. Christ Biog. i. 767.

the same instant, there is in these two speeches that mutual circulation before mentioned. In the one there is attributed to God or the Lord of Glory death, whereof divine nature is not capable; in the other ubiquity unto man, which human nature admitteth not. Therefore by the Lord of Glory we must needs understand the whole person of Christ, who being Lord of Glory, was indeed crucified, but not in that nature for which he is termed the Lord of Glory. In like manner by the Son of Man the whole person of Christ must necessarily be meant, who being man upon earth, filled heaven with his glorious presence, but not according to that nature for which the title of Man is given him. Without this caution the Fathers whose belief was divine and their meaning most sound, shall seem in their writing one to deny what another constantly doth affirm. Theodoret disputeth with great earnestness that *God* cannot be said to suffer. But he thereby meaneth Christ's *divine nature* against Apollinarius, which held even Deity itself passible. Cyril on the other side against Nestorius as much contendeth that whosoever will deny *very God* to have suffered death doth forsake the faith. Which notwithstanding to hold were heresy, if the name of God in this assertion did not import as it doth the person of Christ, who being verily God suffered death, but in the flesh, and not in that substance for which the name of God is given him." [1]

As to the part played by Theodoret throughout the whole controversy we may conclude that though he had to own himself beaten intellectually, yet the honours of the moral victory remain with him rather than with his illustrious opponent. Not for the last time in the history of the Church a great duel of dialectic issued in a conclusion wherein of the champion who was driven to say, " I was wrong," the congregation of the faithful has yet perforce felt that he was right.

The end is well known. Theodosius summoned the bishops to Ephesus at the Pentecost of 431. There arrived Cyril with fifty supporters early in June; there arrived Theodoret with his Metropolitan Alexander of Hierapolis, in advance of the rest of the Orientals. The Cyrillians were vainly entreated to wait for John of Antioch and his party, and opened the Council without them. When they arrived they would not join the Council, and set up their own " Conciliabulum " apart. Under the hot Levantine sun of July and August the two parties denounced one another on the one side for not accepting the condemnation of Nestorius, which the Cyrillians had passed in the beginning of their proceedings, on the other for the informality and injustice of the condemnation. Then deputies from the Orientals, of whom Theodoret was one, hurried to Constantinople, but were allowed to proceed no further than Chalcedon. The letters written by Theodoret at this time to his friends among the bishops and at the court, and his petitions to the Emperor,[2] leave a vivid impression of the zeal, vigour and industry of the writer, as well as of the extraordinary literary readiness which could pour out letter after letter, memorial after memorial, amid all the excitement of controversy, the weariness of travel, the sojourning in strange and uncomfortable quarters, and the tension of anxiety as to an uncertain future.

Though Nestorius was deposed his friends protested that they would continue true to him, and Theodoret was one of the synod held at Tarsus, and of another at Antioch, in which the protest against Cyril's action was renewed. But the oriental bishops were now themselves undergoing a process of scission,[3] John of Antioch and Acacius of Berœa heading the peacemakers who were anxious to come to terms with Cyril, while Alexander of Hierapolis led the irreconcilables. Intellectually Theodoret shrank from concession, but his moral instincts were all in favour of peace. He himself drew up a declaration of faith which was presented by Paul of Emesa to Cyril, which Cyril accepted. But still true to his friend, Theodoret refused to accept the deposition of Nestorius and his individual condemnation, and it was not till several years had elapsed that, moved less by the threat of exile and forfeiture, as the imperial penalty for refusing to accept the position, than by the entreaties of his beloved flock and of his favourite ascetic solitaries that he would not leave them, Theodoret found means of attaching a meaning to the current anathemas on Nestorianism, not, as he said, on Nestorius, which allowed him to submit. He even entered into friendly correspondence with Cyril.[4] But the truce was hollow. Cyril was indignant to find that Theodoret still maintained his old opinions. At last the protracted quarrel was ended by Cyril's death in June, 444.

On the famous letter over which so many battles of criticism have been fought we

---

[1] Hooker. Ecc. Pol. v. liii. 4.   [2] Epp., clvii., clviii., clxvii,, clxviii., clxix., clxx.
[3] Hefele. Hist. Consc. iii. 127.   Can. Venables. Dict. Christ. Biog. iv. 910.   [4] Ep. lxxxiii.

have already spoken. If it was really written by Theodoret, to which opinion my own view inclines,[1] there is no reason why we should damn it as "a coarse and ferocious invective." If genuine, it was clearly a piece of grim pleasantry dashed off in a moment of excitement to a personal friend, and never intended for the publicity which has drawn such severe blame upon its writer.

But though the death of Cyril might appear to bring relief to the Church and Empire as well as to his individual opponents, it was by no means a ground of unmixed gratification to Theodoret.[2] Dioscorus, who succeeded to the Patriarchate of Alexandria, however Theodoret in the language of conventional courtesy may speak of the new bishop's humble mindedness,[3] inherited none of the good qualities of Cyril and most of his faults. Theodoret, naturally viewed with suspicion and dislike as the friend and supporter of Nestorius, gave additional ground for ill-will and hostility by action which brought him into individual conflict with Dioscorus. He accepted the synodical letters issued at Constantinople at the time of Proclus, and so seemed to lower the dignity of the apostolic sees of Antioch and Alexandria;[4] he also warmly resented the tyrannical treatment of his friend Irenæus, bishop of Tyre.[5] Irenæus had indeed in the earlier days of his banishment to Petra after his first condemnation in 435 attacked Theodoret for not being thoroughly Nestorian, but Theodoret was able to claim Irenæus as not objecting to the crucial term θεοτόκος,[6] reasonably understood, and accepted him as unquestionably orthodox. When therefore Dioscorus, the Archimandrite Eutyches, and his godson the eunuch Chrysaphius attacked Domnus for consecrating Irenæus to the Metropolitan see of Tyre, Theodoret indignantly protested and counselled Domnus as to how he had best reply.[7] But Dioscorus and his party had now the ear, and guided the fingers, of the imperial weakling at Constantinople, and the deposition of Irenæus (Feb. 17, 448) was followed after a year's successful intrigues by the autograph edict of Theodosius confining Theodoret within the limits of his own diocese as a vexatious and turbulent busybody.

IV. — UNDER THE BAN OF THEODOSIUS AND OF THE LATROCINIUM.

Theodoret was at Antioch when Count Rufus brought him the edict. His friends would have detained him, but he hurried away.[8] On reaching Cyrus he wrote to his friend Anatolius warmly protesting against the cruel and unjust action taken against him, and informing the patrician that Euphronius, a military officer, had travelled hard on the track of Rufus to ask for a written acknowledgment of the receipt of the edict of relegation.[9] The letters written at this crisis by the indignant pen of the maligned scholar and saint[10] have a peculiar value, at once biographical, literary, and theological. To Eusebius bishop of Ancyra he sends an important catalogue of his works. To Dioscorus, the chief of the cabal against him, he sends a summary of his views on the incarnation and the nature of our Lord, couched in such terms as might perhaps in earlier days have shortened his great controversy with Cyril. But the opponents of Theodoret were not in a mood to be moved by any formulation of the terms of his faith. Dioscorus received the letter with insult, and publicly joined in the shout of anathema which he permitted to be raised against his hated brother.[11] The condemnation of Eutyches by Flavian's Constantinopolian Synod had roused the Eutychian party to leave no stone unturned to secure its reversal and crush it and all who upheld it. Of the latter Theodoret was the most prominent, the ablest and perhaps the holiest. Hence he was the natural representative and personification of the doctrines that Dioscorus sought to decry and degrade.[12] The sixth Council of Ephesus of evil fame met in the Church of St. Mary the Virgin on August 8, 449. Eutyches was acquitted. Flavian was condemned. Ibas of Edessa, Domnus of Antioch, and Theodoret of Cyrus were deprived of their sees. The disgraceful scenes of violence which marked every stage of this shameful ecclesiastical gathering have been described again and again with the vivid detail[13] rendered possible by the exactitude of contemporary

---

[1] Glubokowski p. 163 thinks it spurious. [2] Glubokowski, p. 163.
[3] Ep. LX. [6] Ep. CX. [9] Ep. LXXIX.
[4] Ep. LXXXVI. [7] Ep. CX. [10] Epp. LXXIX. LXXX. LXXXI. LXXXII. LXXXIII.
[5] Epp. III. XII. XVI. XXXV. [8] Epp. LXXIX and LXXX. [11] Ep. LXXXVI.
[12] "Theodoret's condemnation was the chief object aimed at in summoning" the Latrocinium. He was "the bugbear of the whole Eutychian party and consequently condemned in advance." Canon Venables, Dict. Christ. Biog. iv. 913 and Martin Brigandage à Ephèse p. 192.
[13] See specially Gibbon Chap. xlvii. Milman Hist. Lat. Christ. Book II. Chap. iv. Stanley, *Christian Institutions*, Chap. xvi. 4 and Canon Bright Art. Dioscorus in Dict. Christ. Biog. General Councils, it may be remarked, have been depreciated and ridiculed by historians of two kinds; the anti-Christian, such as Gibbon, who have been glad of the opportunity of bringing discredit on the Church; and the Roman, such as Cardinal Newman, who are aware that the authority of Councils is not always reconcileable with the asserted authority of the Bishop of their favourite see. ("Even those councils which were œcumenical have nothing to boast of in regard to the Fathers, taken individually, which compose them. They appear as the

narrative, but, inasmuch as Theodoret was condemned in his absence we are concerned here less with the manner in which his condemnation was brought about than with the steps he took to protest against and to reverse it.

To the prisoner of Cyrus courier after courier would bring intelligence of the riots and tricks of the council. At last came news of the crowning wrong. On the indictment of an Antiochene presbyter named Pelagius, Theodoret was condemned as an enemy of God, a disseminator of poison, a false teacher deserving to be burnt. In support of the accusation was quoted the careful theological statement addressed by Theodoret to the monks in the Euphratensis and the Osrhoene which appears as Letter CLI., as well as citations from his works at large. Dioscorus described the absent defendant as a blasphemous enemy of God and the Emperor whose life had been spent in damning souls. Theodoret was sentenced not merely to deposition from his see but to degradation from the priesthood and to excommunication, and his books were ordered to be burnt.[1] So the great council ended with the deposition of Flavian of Constantinople, Eusebius of Dorylæum, Daniel of Carræ, Irenæus of Tyre, Aquilinus of Biblus, and Domnus of Antioch as well as of Theodoret.[2] Eutyches the heretic Archimandrite was restored and the brutal Dioscorus seemed master of Christendom. One word of manly Latin had broken in on the supple suffrages of the servile orientals, the "*Contradicitur*" of Hilarius the representative of the Church of Rome.

To that church, and to its illustrious bishop, Theodoret naturally turned in his hour of need. He implored his friend Anatolius to get him permission to plead his own cause in person in the West, or if not to let him retire to his old home at Nicerte.[3] The latter alternative was conceded. In this retreat he received many proofs of the affectionate regard of his friends and offers of more practical help than his modest necessities demanded.[4] Thence products of his facile pen travelled far and wide. The whole series of letters written at this period gives touching testimony to the gentle and forgiving spirit of the sorely tried bishop. There is nothing of the bitterness and fierce anger which appear sometimes in the earlier controversy with Cyril. He is refined, not soured, by adversity, and, though he never approached nearer to canonization than the acquisition of the inferior title of Blessed, he appears in these dark days as no unworthy specimen of the suffering saint.[5] The chief interest of these letters is in truth moral spiritual and theological. This, however, has been obscured by the ecclesiastical interest which has been given them by the unwarranted attempt to represent Theodoret's letter to Leo as an " appeal " to the see of Rome in the later and technical sense of the word. Whether St. Hilary of Arles ever did or did not give the lie to his short life of strenuous protest against the growing aggrandizement of the see of Rome, there is no doubt that before his death at the age of 41 in 449 his suffragans had been released by Leo from allegiance to a Metropolitan disobedient to the Roman chair, and that Valentinian had issued an edict confirming Leo's claims and making the

antagonist host in a battle, not as the shepherds of their people." Hist. Sketches, p. 335.) And it must be conceded that so far as outward circumstances went the Latrocinium was as good a council as any other. As is pointed out by Dean Milman, " It is difficult to discover in what respect, either in the legality of its convocation or the number and dignity of the assembled prelates, consists its inferiority to more received and honoured councils. Two imperial commissioners attended to maintain order in the council and peace in the city Dioscorus the patriarch of Alexandria by the Imperial command assumed the presidency. The Bishops who formed the Synod of Constantinople were excluded as parties in the transaction, but Flavianus took his place with the Metropolitans of Antioch and Jerusalem and no less than three hundred and sixty bishops and ecclesiastics. Three ecclesiastics, Julian a bishop, Renatus a presbyter, and Hilarius a deacon were to represent the bishop of Rome. The Abbot Barsumas (this was an innovation) took his seat in the Council as a kind of representative of the monks." Milman, Lat. Christ. Book II. Chap. iv. The fact is that the great Councils of the Early Church are like the great men of the Early Church. Some have authority and some have not. But their authority does not depend upon formal circumstances or outward position. They have authority because the inspired common sense of the Church has seen and valued the truth and wisdom of their utterances. Athanasius, Arius, Cyril, and Nestorius, were all great churchmen. Athanasius and Cyril stand out against the background of centuries as champions of the faith. Arius and Nestorius are counted as heretics. Character does not outweigh doctrine. Nestorius is unsound in the faith though he was an amiable and virtuous man; Cyril is an authority of orthodoxy though his personal qualities were not saintly. Of all the councils that according to Ammianus Marcellinus hamstrung the postal resources of the Empire, take Nicæa, Tyre, and the two Ephesian councils of 431 and 449. Nicæa and the earlier Ephesian are accepted by the Church Catholic. Tyre and the later Ephesian, though both were sum moned at the will of princes and attended by a large concourse of bishops, are rejected. Why? The earlier Ephesian in the disorder and violence of its proceedings was as disgraceful as the Tyrian and the later Ephesian. The councils of Nicæa and of Ephesus, called the first and the third œcumenical councils, are vindicated by the assent of the wisest of the Church. The dictum *securus judicat orbis terrarum* here holds good, and is seen to be identical with the ultimate foundation of the great Aristotelian definition " defined by reason, and as the wise man would define." And such is also the practical outcome of the statement of Article XXI. of the Church of England.
    cf. the striking passage of Augustine (Cont. Maximin. Arian. ii. 14). " *Sed nunc nec ego Nicænum, nec tu debes Ariminense, tanquam præjudicaturus, proferre consilium. Nec ego hujus auctoritate, nec tu illius detineris. Scripturarum auctoritatibus, non quorumque propriis, sed utrisque communibus testibus, res cum re, causa cum causa, ratio cum ratione concertet.*" On the first four accepted œcumenical councils Dr. Salmon (*Infallibility of the Church*, p. 287) remarks, " Gregory the Great says that he venerates these four as the four Gospels, and describes them as the four square stones on which the structure of faith rests. Yet the hard struggle each of these councils had to make and the number of years which the struggle lasted before its decrees obtained general acceptance, show that they obtain their authority because of the truth which they declared and it was not because of their authority that the decrees were recognised as true."
    [1] Canon Venables Dict. Christ. Biog. Actes du Brigandage, pp. 193, 195.   [2] Evagrius i. 10.
    [3] Ep. CXIX.   [4] Ep. CXXIII.   [5] Epp. CXIII. to CXXXIII. and CLXXXI.

authority of the Bishop of Rome supreme in the West.[1] It would be useful to maintainers of the Roman supremacy if they could adduce instances of any assertion or acceptance of similar authority in the East. So it has been said that Theodoret appealed to the Pope.[2] In a sense this is of course perfectly true. Theodoret did appeal to the Pope. But the whole superstructure of papal supremacy, so far as Theodoret is concerned, is really based upon a poor paronomasia. The bishop of Cyrus "appealed" to the bishop of Rome as any bishop believing himself to lie under an unjust sentence might appeal to any other bishop, and as Theodoret did appeal to other bishops. It is quite true that the church of Rome had many claims to honour and regard, as Theodoret himself felicitously and opportunely points out, and that the present occupant of its throne was a man of unblemished orthodoxy and of commanding personal dignity. But to recognise these facts is a long way from ad- mitting that this very dignified see had either *de facto* or *de jure* any coercive jurisdiction over the Metropolitans of Alexandria or of Hierapolis, to the latter of whom Cyrus was subordinate. Theodoret himself quotes the crucial passage in St. Matthew's gospel[3] ap- parently without any idea that the "Petra" means all the successors of the "Petrus."[4] What Theodoret asked from Leo was not the sentence of a superior but the sympathy and support of an influential brother. What made it so peculiarly important that he should gain the ear and the approval of Leo was that Rome had been wholly unconcerned in the intrigue which condemned him. He could have had no more idea of papal authority in the later *ultramontane* sense than he could of the decrees of the Vatican Council. Bound as he was to do his utmost to vindicate not so much his own position and doctrinal soundness, as the truth now trampled on by the combined factions of Alexandria and the court, he naturally turned to Leo as alike the most respected and most independent bishop of his age.[5]

Leo, however, could do little or nothing to help him. Theodosius, completely under the influence of Chrysaphius and Dioscorus, was quite satisfied as to the proper constitution and equity of the Latrocinium.

V. — THEODORET AND CHALCEDON.

Now, not for the last time in history, an important part was played by a horse. In July, 450, Theodosius, while hunting in the neighbourhood of his capital, was thrown from the saddle into a stream, hurt his spine, and a few days afterwards died.[6] With him died the cause of Eutyches and of Chrysaphius. The eunuch was promptly executed, and at last a Council was conceded to reconsider and rectify the crimes and blunders of the Latrocinium.[7] But the Empress and her venerable husband did not wait for the Council to undo some of the wrong done to Theodoret, and the large place he filled in the eyes and estimation of the oriental world is shewn by the interest shewn at Constantinople in his behalf.[8] The decree of relegation appears to have been rescinded, and he was free to present himself at the synod. On the first assembling of the five hundred bishops,[9] under the

---

[1] Cf. Milman Lat. Christ. Book ii. Chap. iv; Const. Valentin. iii Aug. apud S. Leon. op. epist. xi.

[2] Garnerius, the Jesuit, in his dissertation on the life of Theodoret writes : " When Theodoret got news of his deposition he determined to send envoys to the apostolic see, that is to the head of all the churches in the world, to plead his cause before the righteous judgment seat of St. Leo," and in his summary of his own chapter he says " Theodoret appeals to the apostolic see."

[3] Matt. xvi. 18.   [4] Ep. CXLVI.

[5] cf. Glubokowski. pp. 237, 239. Du Pin. iv. 83. Cardinal Newman, in his very bright and sympathetic sketch of Theodoret, (Hist. Sketches ii. 308 ed. 1891) writes the following remarkable sentence. "This, at least, he has in common with St. Chrysostom that both of them were deprived of their episcopal rank by a council, both appealed to the holy see, and by the holy see both were cleared and restored to their ecclesiastical dignities." It would be difficult in the compass of so short a sentence to combine more statements so completely misleading. To say that Chrysostom and Theodoret both ap- pealed to the "holy see" is as much an anachronism as to say that they appealed to the Court of the Vatican or to the Dome of St. Peter's. In their day there was no holy see, that is to say, κατ' ἐξοχήν. All sees were holy sees, just as all bishops were styled your holiness. Rome, it is true, was the only apostolical see in the West, but it was not the only apostolical see, and whatever official precedence it could claim over Antioch, Jerusalem, and Alexandria, was due to its being the see of the old imperial capital, a precedence expressly ordered at Chalcedon to be shared with the new Rome on the Bosphorus. As to the "appeal," we have seen what it meant in the case of Theodoret. It meant the same in the case of Chrysostom. Cut to the quick at the cruel and brutal treatment of his friends after his banishment from Constantinople in the summer of 404 he pleaded his cause in letters sent as well to Venerius of Milan and Chromatius of Aquileia as to Innocent of Rome. Innocent very properly espoused his cause, declared his deposition void, and did his best to move Honorius to move Arcadius to con- voke a council. The cruel story of the long martyrdom of bitter exile and the death in the lonely chapel at Comana is a terri- ble satire on the restoration to ecclesiastical dignities. The unwary reader of " the historical sketch " might imagine the famous John of the mouth of gold brought back in triumph to Constantinople by the authority of the pope in 404 as he had been by the enthusiasm of his flock in 403, and Arcadius and Eudoxia cowering before the power of Holy Church like Henry IV. at Canossa in 1077. The true picture of the three years of agony which preceded the old man's passage to the better world in 407 is a painful contrast to contemplate (Pallad. Dial. 1-3. Theodoret V. 34. Sozomen viii. 26, 27, 28.) Of Theodoret's restoration to " ecclesiastical dignity," and Leo's part in it, we shall see further on.

[6] cf. the deaths of William I. and William III. of England.

[7] Though Marcian's independence of western dictation was shewn in the summoning of the bishops not to a place in Italy, as Leo had hoped and urged, but to Chalcedon, the beautiful Asiatic suburb of Constantinople.

[8] Epp. CXXXIX, CXL.

[9] Accounts of the numbers vary. Marcellinus says 630. There were more than 400 signatures.

presidency of the imperial Commissioners,[1] the minutes of the Latrocinium were read; the presence of Dioscorus was protested against by the Roman representation as having dared to hold a synod unauthorized by Rome; and the claim of Theodoret to sit and vote, allowed both by the imperial Commissioners and by the westerns, since Leo [2] had accepted him as an orthodox bishop, was vehemently resisted by the Eutychians. He entered, but at first did not vote, and his enemies at last succeeded in wringing from him a personal anathema not only of Nestorianism, but of Nestorius. The scenes reported in detail are too characteristic alike of the earlier Councils and of Theodoret to be omitted.

" The illustrious Presidents and the honorable Assessors ordered that the most religious bishop Theodoret should enter, that he might be a partaker of the Council, because the holy Archbishop Leo had restored the bishopric to him; and the most sacred and pious Emperor determined that he was to be present at the Holy Council. And on the entrance of the most religious Theodoret, the most religious bishops of Egypt, Illyricum and Palestine called out: ' Have mercy upon us ! The faith is destroyed. The Canons cast him out. Cast out the teacher of Nestorius.' The most religious bishops of the East and those of Pontus, Asia, and Thrace shouted out: ' We had to sign a blank paper ; we were scourged, and so we signed. Cast out the Manichæans; cast out the enemies of Flavian; cast out the enemies of the faith.' Dioscorus, the most religious bishop of Alexandria said: ' Why is Cyril being cast out, who is anathematized by Theodoret?' The Eastern and Pontic and Asian and Thracian most religious bishops shouted out: ' Cast out Dioscorus the murderer. Who does not know the deeds of Dioscorus?' The Egyptian and the Illyrian and the Palestinian most religious bishops shouted out: ' Long years to the Empress !' The Eastern and the most religious bishops with them shouted out: ' Cast out the murderers !' The Egyptians and the most religious bishops with them shouted out: ' The Empress has cast out Nestorius. Long years to the orthodox Empress ! The Council will not receive Theodoret.' Theodoret, the most religious bishop, came up into the midst and said: ' I have offered petitions to the most godlike, most religious and Christ-loving masters of the world, and I have related the disasters which have befallen me, and I claim that they shall be read.' The most illustrious Presidents and the most honourable Assessors said: ' Theodoret, the most religious bishop, having received his proper place from the holy Archbishop of the renowned Rome, now occupies the place of an accuser. Wherefore, that there be no confusion in our proceedings, allow the things which have had a beginning to be finished. No prejudice will accrue to anyone from the appearance of the most religious Theodoret. Every argument for you and for him, if you desire to make one on one side or the other is of course reserved.' And after Theodoret, the most religious bishop, had sat down in the midst, the Eastern, and the most religious bishops who were with them, shouted out: ' He is worthy ! He is worthy !' The Egyptians and the most religious bishops who were with them shouted out: ' Do not call him a bishop ! He is not a bishop ! Cast out the fighter against God ! Cast out the Jew !' The Easterns and the most religious bishops who were with them shouted out: ' The orthodox for the Council ! Cast out the rebels ! Cast out the murderers !' The Egyptians and the most religious bishops who were with them shouted out: ' Cast out the fighter against God ! Cast out the insulter of Christ ! Long years to the Empress ! Long years to the Emperor ! Long years to the orthodox Emperor ! Theodoret has anathematized Cyril.' The Easterns and the most religious bishops who were with them shouted out: ' Cast out the murderer Dioscorus !' The Egyptians and the most religious bishops with them shouted out: ' Long years to the Assessors ! He has not the right of speech. He is expelled from the whole Synod !' Basil, the most religious bishop of Trajanopolis, in the province of Rhodope, rose up and said: ' Theodoret has been condemned by us.' The Egyptians and the most religious bishops with them shouted out: ' Theodoret has accused Cyril. We cast out Cyril if we receive Theodoret. The Canons cast out Theodoret. God has turned away from him.' The most illustrious Presidents and the most honourable Assessors said: ' The vulgar cries are not worthy of bishops, nor will they assist either side. Suffer, therefore, the reading of all the documents.' The Egyptians and the most

---

[1] Perhaps of the Emperor himself. (Breviar. Hist. Eutych.) The representatives of the imperial government sat in the centre of the Cancelli; on their right were Dioscorus, Juvenal of Jerusalem, and the Palestinian bishops; on their left Paschasinus of Lilybæum, (Marsala) Lucentius of Asculum (Ascoli) with Boniface, a Roman presbyter, the three representatives of Leo, Anatolius of Constantinople, Maximus of Antioch, and the orientals. Paschasinus signed as "*synodo præsidens*," but he did not either locally or effectively preside.

[2] The acts of the Council of Chalcedon refer to Theodoret having been righted by the bishop of "the illustrious city of Rome;" "the archbishop of the senior city of Rome." The primacy is that of the ancient capital.

religious bishops with them shouted out: 'Cast out one man, and we will all hear. We shout out in the cause of Religion. We say these things for the sake of the orthodox Faith.' The most illustrious Presidents and the honourable Assessors said: 'Rather acquiesce, in God's name, that the hearing of the documents should take place, and concede that all shall be read in proper order.' And at last they were silent, and Constantine, the most holy Secretary and Magistrate of the Divine Synod, read these documents."[1]

One more sad incident must be given — the demand made at the eighth session that Theodoret should pronounce a curse on his ancient friend. "The most reverend bishops all stood before the rails of the most holy altar, and shouted "Theodoret must now anathematize Nestorius." Theodoret, the most reverend bishop, passed into the midst, and said: "I have made my petition to the most divine and religious Emperor, and I have laid documents before the most reverend bishops occupying the place of the most sacred Archbishop Leo; and if you think fit, they shall be read to you, and you will know what I think.' The most reverend bishops shouted 'We want nothing to be read — only anathematize Nestorius.' Theodoret, the most reverend bishop, said: 'I was brought up by the orthodox, I was taught by the orthodox, I have preached orthodoxy, and not only Nestorius and Eutyches, but any man who thinks not rightly, I avoid and count him an alien.' The most reverend bishops shouted out: 'Speak plainly; anathema to Nestorius and his doctrine — anathema to Nestorius and to those who defend him.' Theodoret, the most reverend bishop said: 'Of a truth I say nothing except so far as I know it to be pleasing to God. First I will convince you that I am here, not because I care for my city, not because I covet rank. Because I have been falsely accused, I come to satisfy you that I am orthodox, and that I anathematize Nestorius and Eutyches, and every one who says that there are two Sons.' Whilst he was speaking, the most reverend bishops shouted out: 'Speak plainly; anathematize Nestorius and those who think with him.' Theodoret, the most reverend bishop, said: 'Unless I set forth at length my faith I cannot speak. I believe'— And whilst he spoke the most reverend bishops shouted: 'He is a heretic! He is a Nestorian! Away with the heretic! Anathema to Nestorius and to any one who does not confess that the Holy Virgin Mary is the Parent of God, and who divides the only begotten Son to two Sons.' Theodoret, the most reverend bishop, said, 'Anathema to Nestorius and to whoever denies that the Holy Virgin Mary is the Parent of God, and who divides the only begotten Son into two Sons. I have subscribed the definition of faith, and the epistle of the most holy Archbishop Leo.'"[2]

VI. — RETIREMENT AFTER CHALCEDON, AND DEATH.

Some doubt hangs over the question whether after his vindication at Chalcedon Theodoret resumed his labours at Cyrus, or occupied himself with literary work in the congenial seclusion of Nicerte. Garnerius makes it about the time of his quitting Chalcedon that Sporacius charged him with the duty of writing on the Heresies,[3] and if so his five books on this subject would seem to have constituted the first fruit of his comparative leisure. Sporacius[4] he styles his "Christ-loving Son," and no doubt owed something to the aid of the influential "Comes domesticorum," who was present at Chalcedon, when the question of his admission to the Council was being agitated. To this period has also been referred his commentary on the Octateuch.[5] On Dr. Newman's statement that Theodoret made over the charge of his diocese to Hypatius (one of his chorepiscopi, who had been entrusted with his appeal to Pope Leo) and retired into his monastery, and there regaining the peace which he had enjoyed in youth, passed from the peace of the Church to the peace of eternity, Canon Venables[6] remarks that there is no authority for so pleasing a picture, and that Tillemont[7] contradicts it altogether. Garnerius quotes his congratulation to Sabinianus[8] on leaving Perrha as suggestive of what conduct he might have preferred.

It is at least certain that during this period he received a long and sympathetic letter from

---

[1] Labbe, iv., 102, 103.
[2] Labbe iv. 621. Bertram (Theod. Ep. Cyr. doctrina christologica, 1883) thinks Theodoret changed his views; Möller Herzog XV. s.v.) that he retained them, though necessarily modified in expression by stress of circumstances.
[3] Præf. Hæret Fab.   [4] Ep. XCVII.
[5] Photius Cod. 204. The Octateuch comprises the first eight books of the Old Testament.
[6] Dict. Christ. Biog. iv. 916.   [7] xv., 311.   [8] Ep. CXXVI.

Leo, from which it is clear that the Roman bishop reposed great confidence in him.[1]   It is characteristic of one in whom the mere man was merged in the theologian and ecclesiastic that, as of the year of his birth, so of the year of his death, we have no specific information, and are compelled to form our conclusions on evidence which though valuable, is not overwhelming.   Theodorus Lector, the composer of the Historia Tripartita, in the 6th century, states[2] that Theodoret prepared a sepulchral urn for the burial of the famous ascetic Jacobus; that he predeceased Jacobus; but that Jacobus was buried in it.[3]   Evagrius[4] mentions Jacobus Syrus as still living when the Emperor Leo sent his Circular Letter to the bishops in 458, though then he must have been in extreme old age.   And Gennadius, who lived not long after Theodoret, says that he died in the reign of Leo.   The evidence is not strong.   Theodoret may have died some years before Jacob.   But Gennadius probably knew.   On the whole we may conclude that there is some probability that Theodoret survived till 458; none that he lived longer.   Like Lucius Cary, Viscount Falkland, to whom, in his isolation, Dean Stanley[5] compares him, Theodoret must have expired with the cry of " Peace, Peace," in his heart, if not on his lips.   Garnerius is careful to prove that he died in " the peace of the Church," and appeals in support of this contention to the laudatory testimony of Popes Vigilius, Pelagius I., Pelagius II., and Gregory the Great. The peace of the Church, in the narrower sense, has not always been accorded to holy men and women who have assuredly departed this life in the faith and fear of their Lord.   In its truer and holier connotation it coincides with a state in which we trust we may contemplate the godly old man of Cyrus, forgetting the storms that had beaten now and again on the life he was leaving behind him, and stepping quietly into the calm of the windless haven of souls, — the Peace not of man, but of God.

VII. — The Condemnation of " the Three Chapters."

A sketch of the life of Theodoret might well be supposed to terminate with his death. But it can hardly be regarded as complete without a brief supplementary notice of the posthumous controversy which has contributed to his fame in ecclesiastical history.   The Council of Chalcedon was designed to give rest to the Church, and to undo a great wrong, and catholic common sense has since vindicated its decisions.   But it was not to be supposed that the opinions and passions which had achieved a combined triumph at Ephesus in 449 would die away and disappear in consequence of the imperial and synodical action of 451.   The face of the world was changing.   The vandal Genseric captured and pillaged Rome.   The Teutonic races were pushing to a foremost place, and accepting first of all an Arian Christianity.   Clovis represented orthodoxy almost alone.   Theodoric, the Arian Ostrogoth, mastered Italy.   Then the turning tide saw Rome once again a city of sole empire, but not the chief city.   The victories of Belisarius made of Rome a suburb of Constantinople, and empire and theology swayed and were swayed by the policy of Justinian and the palace plots of Theodora.   All through monophysitism had had its friends and defenders.   Metropolitans, monks, and mobs had anathematized one another for nearly a century.   At Alexandria Dioscorus had won almost a local canonization, and the patriarch Timotheus, nicknamed " the Cat," had left a strong monophysite party, consolidated under Peter the Stutterer as the " acephali."[6]   At Antioch Peter the Fuller had anathematized all who refused to accept the Shibboleth he appended to the Trisagion, " who wast crucified on our account."   Leo, Marcian's successor, on the Eastern throne, had followed Marcian's theology, and Zeno, Leo; but the usurper Basiliscus had seen elements of strength in a bold bid for monophysite support.   Zeno, on the fall of Basiliscus, had attempted to atone the disunited sections of Christendom by the henoticon, or edict of unity, but the henoticon had been for years a watchword of division.   Anastasius had favoured the Eutychians.   And in his reign Theodoret had been twice condemned, at the synods of Constantinople and Sidon, in 499 and 512.[7]

Justin I., the unlettered barbarian, supported the Chalcedonians, but in 544 Belisarius

---

[1] Leo. Ep. cxx., and Migne Theod. iv. 1193. Chagrined at the decision of the Council that Constantinople was to enjoy honorary precedence next after old Rome and practical equality and independence, in that the metropolitans of Pontus, Asia, and Thrace were to be ordained by the patriarch of Constantinople, Leo manages to write to Theodoret, *par parenthèse*, of the Roman See as one " *quam cæteris omnium Dominus statuit præsidere.*"   If in " *statuit* " Leo had meant to refer to a Divine Providence overruling history, and in " *præsidere* " to the fact that Rome was for many years the capital of the world, his remark would have been open to little objection.   But he meant something quite different.
[2] Collect. Book i.   Ed. Migne p. 566.
[3] There seems no authority for the statement of Garnerius (Hist. Theod. xiii) repeated in Smith's Dict. Chris. Biog. that Jacobus and Theodoret shared it.   [4] de Scrip. Ecc. 89.
[5] *Christian Institutions.*   Chap. xvi.   [6] Ἀκέφαλοι = headless, i.e., without bishop.
[7] Victor: Turon: and Mansi, viii. 371.   Mansi, viii. 197-200.

had made the Eutychian Vigilius bishop of Rome. When Justinian aspired to become a second Constantine, and give theological as well as civil law to the world, it was proposed to condemn in a fifth œcumenical council certain so-called Nestorian writings, on the plea that such a condemnation might reconcile the opponents of Chalcedon. The writings in question were the Letter of Ibas of Edessa to Maris, praising Theodore of Mopsuestia ; the works of Theodore himself, and the writings of Theodoret against Cyril. These three literary monuments were known as " the Three Chapters." [1] Of the controversy of the Three Chapters it has been said that it " filled more volumes than it was worth lines." [2] The Council satisfied nobody. Pope Vigilius, detained at Constantinople and Marmora with something of the same violence with which Napoleon I. detained Pius VI. at Valence, declined to preside over a gathering so exclusively oriental. The West was outraged by the constitution of the synod, irrespective of its decisions. The Monophysites were disappointed that the credit of Chalcedon should be even nominally saved by the nice distinction which damned the writings, but professed complete agreement with the council which had refused to damn the writers. The orthodox wanted no slur cast upon Chalcedon, and, however fenced, the condemnation of the Three Chapters indubitably involved such a slur. Practically, the decrees of the fourth and fifth councils are mutually inconsistent, and it is impossible to accept both. Theodoret was reinstated at Chalcedon in spite of what he had written, and what he had written was anathematized at Constantinople in spite of his reinstatement.

The xiii Canon of the fifth Council runs as follows, " if any one defends the impious writings of Theodoret which he published against the true faith, against the first holy synod of Ephesus and against the holy Cyril and his twelve chapters; and all that he wrote in defence of the impious Theodorus and Nestorius, and others who held the same opinions as the aforesaid Theodorus and Nestorius, defending them and their impiety, and accordingly calling impious the doctors of the church who confess the union according to hypostasis of God the Word in the flesh; and does not anathematize these writings and those who have held or do hold similar opinions, above all those who have written against the true faith and the holy Cyril and his twelve chapters, and have remained to the day of their death in such impiety; let him be anathema."

In this condemnation the works certainly included are Theodoret's " Objections to Cyril's Chapters," some of his letters, and, among his lost works, the " Pentalogium," namely five books on the Incarnation written against Cyril and his supporters at Ephesus, of which fragments are preserved, and two allocutions against Cyril delivered at Chalcedon in 431, of which portions exist in the acts of the fifth Council, and do not exhibit Theodoret at his best.

The Council has at least preserved to us an interesting little record of the survival at Cyrus of the memory of her great bishop, for it appears that at the seventh collation, held at the end of May, notice was taken of an enquiry ordered by Justinian respecting a statue or portrait of Theodoret which was said to have been carried in procession into his cathedral town, by Andronicus a presbyter and George a deacon. [1] A more important tribute to his memory is the fact that, though it officially anathematized writings some of which, composed in the thick of the fight, and soiled with its indecorous dust, Theodoret himself may well have regretted and condemned, the Council advisedly abstained from directly condemning a bishop whose character and person were protected by the notorious iniquity of the robber council that had deposed him, the friendship of the illustrious Leo, and the solemn vindication of the church in Synod at Chalcedon, as well as by his own confession of the faith, his repudiation of the errors of Nestorius, and the stainless beauty and pious close of his long life.

No better reconciliation between Chalcedon and Constantinople can be proffered than that which Garnerius quotes from the letter said to have been written by Gregory the Great, though sent in the name of Pelagius II, to the Illyrians on the fifth council, " It is the part of unwarrantable rashness to defend those writings of Theodoret which it is noto-

---

[1] Dean Milman (Lat. Christ. iv, 4), following in the wake of Gibbon, remarks that "the church was not now disturbed by the sublime, if inexplicable, dogmas concerning the nature of God, the Persons of the Trinity, or the union of the divine and human nature of Christ, concerning the revelations of Scripture, or even the opinions of the ancient fathers. The orthodoxy or heterodoxy of certain writings by bishops, but recently dead, became the subject of imperial edicts, of a fifth so-called Œcumenic Council, held at Constantinople, and a religious war between the East and the West," but it was on their explanation of sublime if inexplicable dogmas that the orthodoxy or heterodoxy of these bishops depended, and so far as the subject matter of dispute is concerned, the position in 553 was not very different from that of 451. In both cases the church was moved at once by honest conviction and partisan passion ; the state was influenced partly by a healthy desire to promote peace through-out the empire, partly by the meaner ambition of posing as theological arbitrator.

[2] Gibbon, chap. xlvii. Schaff Hist. Christ. iii, 770.

rious that Theodoret himself condemned in his subsequent profession of the right faith. So long as we at once accept himself and repudiate the erroneous writings which have long remained unknown we do not depart in any way from the decision of the sacred synod, because so long as we only reject his heretical writings, we, with the synod, attack Nestorius, and with the synod express our veneration for Theodoret in his right confession. His other writings we not only accept, but use against our foes." [1]

VIII. — The Works of Theodoret.

Of authorities for the works of Theodoret we may first cite himself. In four of his letters he mentions his own writings; viz.: in lxxxii, to Eusebius of Ancyra; in cxiii, to Leo of Rome; in cxvi, to the Presbyter Renatus; and in cxlv, to the monks at Constantinople. Of these the first was written in 445 and the last three in 449 and a reference to them will show the works mentioned. It is to be noticed [3] that no allusion is made to the refutation of the twelve chapters; to the defence of Diodorus of Tarsus and Theodorus of Mopsuestia, nor to the Dialogues, though all are held to have been written before the Latrocinium. It may have been, as Garnerius conjectures, that Theodoret did not judge it politic at this time to call attention to these particular works, but the assumption is not based on strong grounds, and Theodoret never appears as one unwilling to avow his convictions, which indeed, were perfectly well known.

Gennadius, presbyter of Marseilles, who died in 496, writes " Theodoretus, bishop of Cyrus, is said to have written many works: those, however, which have come to my knowledge are the following; of the Incarnation of the Lord, against the presbyter Eutyches, and Dioscorus, bishop of Alexandria, who deny that there was in Christ human flesh, — powerful writings wherein he proves, as well by argument as by scriptural evidence, that Christ had very flesh of the substance of His mother, which He took from the Virgin, and very Godhead, which by eternal generation He received, in being generated, from God the father begetting Him. There exist also his books of Ecclesiastical History, which he wrote in imitation of Eusebius of Cæsarea, beginning from the end of the books of Eusebius down to his own time, viz.: from the twentieth year of Constantine down to the reign of Leo I, in whose reign he died." [4]

Photius, in the ninth century, says that he has read the Ecclesiastical History; twenty-seven books against Heresies, among which he reckons the "Eranistes;" five books "Hæreticarum Fabularum;" five in praise of Chrysostom; with Commentaries on Daniel, the Octateuch, Kings, Chronicles, and the Twelve Minor Prophets.

Nicephorus Callistus Xanthopulus in the fourteenth century, Hist. Ecc. xiv. 54, writes: "Theodoretus, Syrian by birth, was a follower of the great Chrysostom, whom he set before him as a model of style. His own was flowing and copious, eloquent and easy, and not destitute of Attic grace." He mentions expositions of difficult passages of the Old Testament; Commentaries on the Prophets and the Psalms; the "de Providentia;" a volume "On the Apostles;" the Confutation of heresies, called "the battle between truth and falsehood;" the refutation of Cyril's "Twelve Chapters;" the Ecclesiastical History; the "Philotheus," a History of the Lovers of God; three books on the divine doctrines, and five hundred (?) letters.

The following is the catalogue of extant works as given by Sirmondus and followed by Garnerius.

(i.)   *Exegetical.*   Questions on the Octateuch, the Books of Kings and Chronicles; the Interpretation of the Psalms, Canticles, the Four Greater, and the Twelve Lesser Prophets; an exposition of all the Epistles of St. Paul, including the Hebrews.

(ii.)   *Historical.*   The Ecclesiastical History, and the "Philotheus," or Religious History.

(iii.)   *Controversial.*   The Eranistes, or Dialogues, and the Hæreticarum Fabularum Compendium.

(iv.)   *Theological.*   The Græcarum Affectionum Curatio, the Discourse on Charity, and the De Providentia.

(v.)   *Epistolary.*   The Letters.

(vi.)   To these may be added the Refutation of the Twelve Chapters, and the following given in the Auctarium of Garnerius.

---

[1] Labbe. Act. Conc. Const. v. Coll. vii.   [2] Pelag. Papæ. 736 ed. Migne.   [3] Cf. Garnerius in Migne's Theodoret V. 255.   [4] The last record in the History appears to be of A.D. 440, cf. p. 159. Eusebius ends, and Theodoret begins, with the defeat of Licinius in 323. Constantine began to reign in 306.

(1.) Prolegomena and extracts from Commentaries on the Psalms.
(2.) Part of a Commentary on St. Luke.
(3.) Sermon on the Nativity of St. John the Baptist.
(4.) Portions of Sermons on St. Chrysostom.
(5.) Homily preached at Chalcedon in 431.
(6.) Fragments of the Pentalogium, extracted from Marius Mercator,[1] who attributed the work to the instigation of the devil.

Lost works.[2]

(1.) The Pentalogium, of which fragments are preserved in the Auctarium.
(2.) Opus mysticum, sive mysteriorum fidei expositiones, lib. xii.
(3.) Works "de theologia et Incarnatione," identified by Garnier with three Dialogues against the Macedonians, and two against the Apollinarians, erroneously attributed to Athanasius.
(4.) Adversus Marcionem.
(5.) Adversus Judæos (? the Commentary on Daniel).
(6.) Responsiones ad quæsitus magorum Persarum.
(7.) Five sermons on St. Chrysostom.
(8.) Two allocutions spoken at Chalcedon against Cyril in 431.
(9.) Sermon preached at Antioch on the death of Cyril.
(10.) Works on Sabellius and the Trinity, of which portions are given by Baluz.
Misc. iv.

IX. — CONTENTS AND CHARACTER OF THE EXTANT WORKS.

(a) The character of the Commentary on the Octateuch and the Books of Kings and Chronicles is indicated by the Title "εἰς τὰ ᾿άπορα τῆς θείας Γραφῆς κατ᾽ ᾿εκλογήν," or "On selected difficulties in Holy Scripture." These questions are treated, with occasional deflexions into allegory, from the historico-exegetical point of view of the Syrian School,[3] of which Diodorus of Tarsus and Theodore of Mopsuestia were distinguished representatives. On Diodorus Socrates[4] remarks, "he composed many works, relying on the bare letter of Scripture, and avoiding their speculative aspect." This might be said of Diodorus' great pupil too. Nevertheless, though generally following a line of interpretation in broad contrast with that of Origen, Theodoret quotes Origen as well as Diodore and Theodore of Mopsuestia as authorities. Of the 182 "questions" on Genesis and Exodus the following may be taken as specimens.

Question viii. "What spirit moved upon the waters?" Theodoret's conclusion is that the wind is indicated.

Question x. "Why did the author add, 'And God saw that it was good'?" To persuade the thankless not to find fault with what the divine judgment pronounces good.

Question xix. "To whom did God say 'let us make man in our image and likeness'?" The reply, carefully elaborated, is that here is an indication of the Trinity.

Question xx. "What is meant by 'image'?"
Here long extracts from Diodorus, Theodorus, and Origen are given.

Question xxiv. "Why did God plant paradise, when He intended straightway to drive out Adam thence?"
God condemns none of foreknowledge. And besides, He wished to shew the saints the Kingdom prepared for them from the foundation of the world.[5]

Question xl. "What is the meaning of the statement 'The man is become as one of us'?" Theodoret thinks this is said ironically. God had forbidden Adam to take of the fruit of the tree of life, not because he grudged man immortal life, but to check the course of sin. So death is a means of cure, not a punishment.

Question xlvii. "Whom did Moses call sons of God?" A long argument replies, the sons of Seth.

Question lxxxi suggests an ingenious excuse for Jacob. "Did not Jacob lie when he said, I am Esau thy firstborn?" He had bought the precedence of primogeniture, and therefore spoke the truth when he called himself firstborn.

---

[1] A writer, supposed to be a layman, whose works were discovered in two MSS. at the end of the seventeenth century. One is in the Vatican, the other was found in the Cathedral Library of Beauvais. Marius wrote fully on the Nestorian Controversy, and with acrimony against Theodoret.
[2] As catalogued by Canon Venables from Cave (Hist. Lit. i. 405 ff.) Dict. Christ. Biog. iv. 918.
[3] cf. Gieseler i. 200, who refers to Münter in Staüdlins Archiv. für Kirchengesch. i. 1. 13.
[4] vi., 3.   [5] Matt. xxv. 34.

Exodus. "Question xii. What is the meaning of the phrase 'I will harden Pharaoh's heart'?" This is answered at great length.

The information given in these notes, as we might call them, is theological, exegetic, and explanatory of peculiar terms, and is often of interest and value. On the fourteen Books of Questions and Answers Canon Venables,[1] quoting Ceillier, remarks that the whole form a literary and historical commentary of great service for the right comprehension of the text, characterized by honesty and common sense, and seldom straining or evading the meaning to avoid dangerous conclusions.

(b) On the Psalms and the rest of the Books of the Old Testament the Commentary is no longer in the catechetical form, but is styled Interpretation.[2]

The Psalmist, Theodoret observes,[3] in many places predicts the passion and resurrection of our Lord, and to attentive readers causes real delight by the variety of his prophesying. In view of some recent discussions concerning the authorship of certain Psalms it is interesting to find the enthusiast for orthodoxy in the 5th century writing "It has been contended by some critics that the Psalms are not all the work of David, but are to be ascribed in some cases to other writers. Accordingly, from the titles, some have been attributed to Idithum, some to Etham, some to the sons of Core, some to Asaph, by men who have learned from the Chronicles that these writers were prophets.[4] On this point I make no positive statement. What difference indeed does it make to me whether all the Psalms are David's, or some were the composition of others, when it is clear that all were written by the active operation of the Holy Spirit?"

The importance of the commentary on the Psalms may be estimated by the fact that it is longer than all the catechetical commentary on the preceding Books combined.

The interpretation on the Canticles follows spiritual, as distinguished from literal, lines. The lover is Jesus Christ; — the bride, the Church. From the prologue it appears that Theodoret held all the Old Testament to have been re-written, under divine inspiration, by Ezra. This is regarded as the earliest of the exegetical works.

The original commentary on Isaiah has been lost. The only existing portions are passages collected from the Greek catenæ by Sirmond and edited in his edition, but the opinion has been entertained[5] that these passages should be referred to Theodore of Mopsuestia who also commented on Isaiah, and who is sometimes confused with Theodoret by the compilers of the Greek catenæ.

The commentary on Jeremiah includes Baruch and the Lamentations.[6]

(c) The epistles of St. Paul, among which Theodoret reckons the Epistle to the Hebrews, are the only portions of the New Testament on which we possess our author's commentaries. On them the late Bishop Lightfoot writes, "Theodoret's commentaries on St. Paul are superior to his other exegetical writings, and have been assigned the palm over all patristic expositions of Scripture. See Schröckh xviii. p. 398. sqq., Simon, p. 314 sqq. Rosenmüller iv. p. 93 sqq., and the monograph of Richter, de Theodoreto Epist. Paulin. interprete (Lips. 1822.) For appreciation, terseness of expression and good sense, they are perhaps unsurpassed, and, if the absence of faults were a just standard of merit, they would deserve the first place; but they have little claim to originality, and he who has read Chrysostom and Theodore of Mopsuestia will find scarcely anything in Theodoret which he has not seen before. It is right to add however that Theodoret modestly disclaims any such merit. In his preface he apologises for attempting to interpret St. Paul after two such men who are 'luminaries of the world:' and he professes nothing more than to gather his stores 'from the blessed fathers.' In these expressions he alludes doubtless to Chrysostom and Theodore."[7]

As a specimen of the mode of treatment of a crucial passage, of interest in view of the writer's relations to the Nestorian and Eutychian controversies, the notes on I. Cor. xv. 27, 28 may be quoted. "This is a passage which Arians and Eunomians have been wont to be constantly adducing with the notion that they are thereby belittling the dignity of the only-begotten. They ought to have perceived that the divine apostle has written nothing in this passage about the Godhead of the only-begotten. He is exhorting us to believe in the resurrection of the flesh, and endeavours to prove the resurrection of the flesh by the resurrection of the Lord. It is obvious that like is conformed to like. On this account he calls Him 'the first fruits of them that have fallen asleep,' and styles Him

---

[1] Dict. Christ. Biog. iv. 916,;   [2] ἑρμηνεία.   [3] In Ps. Ed. Migne 604, 605.
[4] cf. I. Chron. vi. 44., xv. 17, 19, and Art. Jeduthun in Dict. Bib.
[5] Garnerius. Theod. Ed. Migne 1, 274.   [6] cf. note on page 327.   [7] Lightfoot. Epist. Gal. ed. 1866, p. 226.

'Man,' and by comparison with Adam proves that by Him the general resurrection will come to pass, with the object of persuading objectors, by shewing the resurrection of one of like nature, to believe that all mankind will share His resurrection. It must therefore be recognised that the natures of the Lord are two : and that divine Scripture names Him sometimes from the human, and sometimes from the divine. If it speaks of God, it does not deny the manhood : if it mentions man it at the same time confesses the Godhead. It is impossible always to speak of Him in terms of sublimity, on account of the nature which He received from us, for if even when lowly terms are employed some men deny the assumption of the flesh, clearly still more would have been found infected with this unsoundness, had no lowly terms been used. What then is the meaning of 'then is subjected'? This expression is applicable to sovereigns exercising sovereignty now, for if He then is subjected He is not yet subjected. So they are all in error who blaspheme and try to make subject Him who has not yet submitted to the limits of subjection. We must wait, and learn the mode of the subjection. But we have gone through long discussions on these points in our contests with them. It is enough now to indicate briefly the Apostle's aim. He is writing to the Corinthians who have only just been set free from the fables of heathendom. Their fables are full of violence and iniquity. Not to name others, and pollute my lips, they worship parricide gods, and say that sons revolted against their fathers, drove them from their realm, and seized their sovereignty. So after saying great things of Christ, in that He shall destroy all rule and authority and power, and shall put an end to death, and hath subdued all things under his feet; lest starting from those fables of theirs they should expect Him to treat His father like the Dæmons whom they adore; after mentioning, as was necessary, the subjugation of all things the apostle adds 'The Son Himself shall be subject to Him that did put all things under Him.' For not only shall He not subject the Father to Himself, but shall Himself accept the subjection becoming to a son. So the divine apostle, suspecting the mischief arising from the pagan mythology, uses expressions of lowliness because such terms are helpful. But let objectors tell us the form of that subjection. If they are willing to consider the truth, He shewed obedience when He was made man, and wrought out our salvation. How then shall He then be subjected, and how shall He then deliver the kingdom to God the Father? If the case be viewed in this way, it will appear that God the Father does not hold the kingdom now. So full of absurdity are their arguments. But He makes what is ours His own, since we are called His body, and He is called our Head. 'He took our iniquities and bore our diseases.'[1] So He says in the Psalm 'my God, my God, look upon me, why hast Thou forsaken me. The words of my transgressions are far from my health.'[2] And yet He did no sin, neither was guile found in His mouth. But a mouth is made of our nature, in that He was made the first fruits of the nature. So He appropriates our frequent disobedience and the then subjection, and, when we are subjected after our delivery from corruption He is said to be subjected. What follows leads us on to this sense. For after the words 'then shall the son be subject to Him that did put all things under Him,' the Apostle adds 'that God may be all in all.' He is everywhere now in accordance with His essence, for His Nature is uncircumscribed, as says the divine apostle, ' in Him we live and move and have our being.'[3] But, as regards His good pleasure, He is not in all, for 'the Lord taketh pleasure in them that fear Him, in those that hope in his mercy.'[4] But in these He is not wholly. For no one is pure of uncleanness,[5] and In thy sight shall no man living be justified[6] and 'If thou Lord shouldst mark iniquities O Lord who shall stand?' Therefore the Lord taketh pleasure wherein they do right and taketh not pleasure wherein they err. But in the life to come where corruption ceases and immortality is given passions have no place ; and after these have been quite driven out no kind of sin is committed for the future. Thus hereafter God shall be all in all, when all have been released from sin and turned to Him and are incapable of any inclination to the worse. And what in this place the divine Apostle has said of God in another passage he has laid down of Christ. His words are these. 'Where there is neither Jew nor Greek, circumcision nor uncircumcision, barbarian, Scythian . . . but Christ is all and in all.'[7] He would not have applied to the Son what is attributable to the Father had he not of divine grace learnt that He is of equal honour with Him."[8]

On the meaning of the passage about them that are baptized for the dead it is curious to

[1] Is. liii. 4. [3] Acts xvii. 28. [5] [7] Coloss. iii. 11.
[2] Ps. xxii. 1. [4] Ps. cxlvii. 11. [6] Psalm cxliii. 2. [8] Theodor. Ed. Migne iii. 271. Seqq.

find only one interpretation curtly proffered in apparent unconsciousness of any other being known or possible. Theodoret's words are " He, says the apostle, who is baptized is buried with the Lord, that as he has been sharer in the death so he may be sharer in the resurrection. But if the body is dead and does not rise why then is he baptized?" The dead for which a man is baptized seems to be regarded as his own dead body i.e., dead in trespasses and sin and subject to corruption.

(d) Of the historical works, (i) the Ecclesiastical History needs less description, in that a translation in extenso is given in the text. Its style and spirit speak for themselves. Photius[2] well describes it as " clear, lofty, and concise."

Gibbon,[3] referring to the three ecclesiastical historians of this period speaks of " Socrates, the more curious Sozomen, and the learned Theodoret." Of learning, industry, and veracity the proofs are patent in the book itself. The chief fault of the work is its want of chronological arrangement.[4] A minor shortcoming is what may be called a lack of perspective; a fulness of detail is sometimes conceded to mere episode and parenthesis, while characters and events of high and crucial importance would scarcely be known to be so, were we dependent for our estimation of them on Theodoret alone. Valesius inclines to the opinion that his opening words about supplying things omitted[5] refer to Socrates and Sozomen, and compares him in his composition of a history after those writers (there is just a possibility that he might have completed the parallel by referring to a third predecessor — Rufinus) to St. John filling up the gaps left by the synoptists.[6] But this view is open to question. Theodoret names no previous writers but Eusebius. A special importance attaches to his account of such events and persons as his local knowledge enables him to give with completeness of detail, as for instance, all that relates to Antioch and its bishops. Garnerius is of opinion that the work might with propriety be entitled A History of the Arian Heresy; all other matter introduced he views as merely episodic.' He also quotes the letter[8] of Gregory the great in which the Roman bishop states that " the apostolic see refuses to receive the History of 'Sozomenus' (sic) inasmuch as it abounds with lies, and praises Theodore of Mopsuestia, maintaining that he was up to the day of his death, a great Doctor." "Sozomen" is supposed to be a slip of the pen, or of the memory, for "Theodoret." But, if this be so, " multa mentitur " is an unfair description of the errors of the historian. Fallible he was, and exhibits failure in accuracy, especially in chronology, but his truthfulness of aim is plain.[9]

(ii) The Religious History, several times referred to in the Ecclesiastical History, and therefore an earlier composition, contains the lives of thirty-three famous ascetics, of whom three were women. The " curious intellectual problem "[10] of the readiness with which Theodoret, a disciple of the " prosaic and critical " school of Antioch, accepts and repeats marvellous tales of the miracles of his contemporary hermits, has been invested with fresh interest in our own time by the apparent sympathy and similar belief of Dr. Newman, who asks " What made him drink in with such relish what we reject with such disgust? Was it that, at least, some miracles were brought home so absolutely to his sensible experience that he had no reason for doubting the others which came to him second-hand? This certainly will explain what to most of us is sure to seem the stupid credulity of so well-read, so intellectual an author."[11] Cardinal Newman evidently implies that the evidence was irresistible, even to a keen and trained intelligence. Probably in many cases the explanation is to be found, as has been already suggested in the remarks on Theodoret's birth, in the ready acceptance of the current views of the age and place as to cause and effect. Theodoret believed in the marvels of his monks. Matthew Hale believed in

1 Here Theodoret agrees in the main with Chrysostom and Theophylact, vide Reff. in Alford ad loc.

2 " Unquestionably the right view of this controverted passage is that of the Greek Fathers, Chrysostom, Theophylact, Theodoret, and others. In reading their comments it is quite clear that they found no more difficulty in St. Paul's elliptical use of the Greek υπερ than we do in Shakespere's use of the English ' for.' They did not hesitate in their homilies to expound that the phrase ' for the dead ' meant ' with an interest in the resurrection of the dead,' or that ' for ' by itself meant even so much as ' in expectation of the resurrection.' Speaker's Commentary, iii. 373.

3 Chap. xxi. n.

4 Ceillier (x. 42) repeats the charge of distinct errors in chronology in (a) the statement that Arius died in 325 instead of in 336; (b) the extension of the exile of Athanasius by four months; (c) the election of Ambrose at the beginning of the reign of Valentinian, instead of ten years later; (d) the troubles at Antioch placed after instead of before those at Thessalonica; (e) the siege of Nisibis in 350 confounded with that of 359. As to (a) the truth is that Theodoret is guilty rather of vagueness than of a misstatement. (Vide I. capp. xiii, xiv.) The objection to (b) the two years and four months exile of Athanasius is due to Valerius (obs. Ecc. i). Canon Bright (Dict. Christ. Biog. i. 187) agrees with Theodoret (cf. Newman Hist. Tracts xii and Hefele, Conciliengesch. i. 467.) In (c) Theodoret is vague, in (d) wrong. According to Valerius Volagesus, and not Jacobus, was bishop of Nisibis in 350.   5 τῆς ἐκκλησιαστικῆς ἱστορίας τὰ παραλειπόμενα.

6 Valesii annotationes — Theod: Migne III. 1522. Valesius is the Latinized form of Henri de Valois, French historiographer royal, who edited Ammianus Marcellinus and the Greek Ecclesiastical historians. He died in 1692.

7 Theod. Ed. Migne. V. 282.   8 Ep. XXXIV.

9 " Baronius obviously approves of Gregory's remark about Theodoret's lies, that is his errors in the order of events, and out of Book iv. produces no less than fifteen blunders, to say nothing of those in iii and v." Garner. loc. cit. 280, 281.

10 Canon Venables Dict. Christ. Biog. iv. 918.   11 Historical Sketches iii. 314.

witchcraft. Neither, that is, was some centuries removed from his own age. Neither
need be accused of stupid credulity. The enthusiasm which led him to reckon on finding
the noble army of martyrs a very present help in time of trouble because he had a little
bottle of their oil, probably that burned at their graves, slung over his bed; and his
assurance that the old cloak of Jacobus, folded for his pillow, was a more than adamantine
bulwark against the wiles of the devil, indicate no more than an exaggerated reliance on
the power of material memorials to affect the imagination.[1] And it is curious to remark
that with all this acceptance of the cures effected by ascetics, Theodoret made a
provision of medical skill for his flock at Cyrus.[2]

(e) The works reckoned as theological, as distinct from the controversial, are three:
(i) The twelve discourses entitled Ἑλληνικῶν θεραπευτικὴ παθημάτων, or " *Græcarum affectionum
curatio, seu evangelicæ veritatis ex gentilium philospohia cognitio.*' They contain an
elaborate apology for Christian philosophy, with a refutation of the attacks of paganism
against the doctrines of the gospel, and may have been designed, as Garnerius conjectures, to serve as an antidote against whatever might still survive of the influence of
Julian and his writings. Here we see at once our author's " genius and erudition "
(Mosheim). In these orations he exhibits a wide acquaintance with Greek literature,
and we find cited, or referred to, among other writers, Homer, Hesiod, Alcman,
Theognis, Xenophanes, Pindar, Heraclitus, Zeno, Parmenides, Empedocles, Euripides,
Herodotus, Xenophon, Plato, Aristotle, Demosthenes, Diodorus Siculus, Plutarch, and
Porphyry. Homer and Plato are largely quoted. Basnage,[3] indeed, contested their
genuineness, but without weakening their position among Theodoret's accepted works.
They have seemed to some to encourage undue honour to and invocation of saints and
martyrs[4] but their author seems to anticipate later exaggeration of their reverence by the
distinction, " We ascribe Godhead to nothing visible. Them that have been distinguished
in virtue we honour as excellent men, but we worship none but the God and Father of
all, His Word, and the Holy Spirit."[5] (ii). The Discourses against paganism were
followed by ten on Divine Providence, a work justly eulogized as exhibiting Theodoret's
literary power in its highest form. Of it Garnerius, who is by no means disposed
to bestow indiscriminate laudation on the writer, remarks that nothing was ever published on this subject more eloquent or more admirable, either by Theodoret, or by
any other.[6] The discourses may not improbably have been delivered in public at
Antioch, and have been the occasion of the enthusiastic admiration described as shewn
by the patriarch John.[7] In them he presses the argument of the divine guidance of the
world from the constitution of the visible creation, and specially of the body of man.
The preacher draws many illustrations from the animal world and shews himself to be
an intelligent observer. The pursuit of righteousness is proved not to be vain, even though
the achieved result is not seen until the resurrection, and it is argued that from the beginning God has not cared for one chosen race alone but for all mankind. The crowning
evidence of divine providence is in the incarnation. " I have taught you " — so the great orations conclude—" the universal providence of God. You behold His unfathomable loving
kindness; — His boundless mercy; cease then to strive against Him that made you; learn
to do honour to your benefactor, and requite his mighty benefits with grateful utterance.
Offer to God the sacrifice of praise; defile not your tongue with blasphemy, but make it
the instrument of worship for which it was designed. Such divine dispensations as are
plain, reverence; about such as are hidden make no ado, but wait for knowledge in the
time to come. When we shall put off the senses, then we shall win perfect knowledge.
Imitate not Adam who dared to pluck the forbidden fruit; lay not hold of hidden things,
but leave the knowledge of them to their own fit season. Obey the words of the wise
man — say not What is this? For what purpose is this! 'For all things were made for
good.'[8] Gathering then from every source occasion for praise, and mingling one melody,
offer it with me to the Creator, the giver of good, and Christ the Saviour, our very God.
To them be glory and worship and honour for endless age on age. Amen."

(iii) The Discourse on Divine Love. This love, says Theodoret, is the source of the
holy life of the ascetics. For his own part he would not accept the kingdom of heaven
without it, or with it, were such a thing possible, shrink from the pains of hell. It was

[1] Theod. Ed. Migne. iii. 1244. Schröckh. xviii. 362.   [2] Ep. CXV.
[3] *Histoire de l'Église.* II. 1225. Jacques de Beauval Basnage † 1723.
[4] Schröckh Kirchengesch., Vol. xviii. 410.   [5] Græc. Cur. Aff. Ed. Migne 754.
[6] " *On y voit toute la beauté du génie de Théodoret; du choix dans les pensées, de la noblesse dans les expressions, de
l'élégance et de la netteté dans le style, de la suite et de la force dans les raisonnements.*" Ceillier x. 88 (Remi Ceillier † 1761.
His "*Histoire Générale des auteurs sacrés*" was published in Paris 1729-1763.)   [7] Ep. lxxxiii.   [8] cf. Ecclus. xxxix. 27.

really love, he says, which led to Peter's denial; he need not have denied if he could have
borne to keep aloof, but love goaded him to be near his Lord.

(f.) The controversial works are

(i.) The "Eranistes," or Dialogues, of which the translation is included in the
text. They contain a complete refutation of the Eutychian position, and the quotations
in them are in several cases valuable as giving portions of the writing of Fathers not elsewhere preserved. They are supposed to have been written shortly after the death of Cyril
in 444, and are intended at once to vindicate Theodoret's own orthodoxy, and to expose
the errors of the party protected by Dioscorus.

(ii.) The Hæreticarum Fabularum Compendium, (Αἱρετικῆς κακομυι.ιας ἐπιτομή) was composed at the request of Sporacius, one of the representatives of Marcian at Chalcedon, and
is, as its title indicates, an account of past or present heresies. It is divided into five
Books, which treat of the following heretics.

I. Simon Magus, Menander, Saturnilus,[1] Basilides, Isidorus, Carpocrates, Epiphanes,
Prodicus, Valentinus, Secundus, Marcus the Wizard, the Ascodruti,[2] the Colorbasii, the
Barbelioti,[3] the Ophites, the Cainites, the Antitacti, the Perati, Monoimus, Hermogenes,
Tatianus, Severus, Bardesanes, Harmoniu Florinus, Cerdo, Marcion, Apelles, Potitus,
Prepo, and Manes.

II. The Ebionites, the Nazarenes, Cerinthus, Artemon, Theodotus, the Melchise-
deciani, the Elkesites, Paul of Samosata, Sabellius, Marcellus, Photinus.

III. The Nicolaitans, the Montanists, Noetus of Smyrna, the Tessarescædecatites
(i.e. Quartodecimani) Novatus, Nepos.

IV. Arius, Eudoxius, Eunomius, Aetius, the Psathyriani, the Macedoniani, the Donatists, the Meletians, Appollinarius, the Audiani, the Messaliani, Nestorius, Eutyches.

V. The last book is an "Epitome of the Divine Decrees."

This catalogue, it has been remarked, does not include Origenism and Pelagianism.[4]
But though Theodoret did not sympathize with Origen's school of scriptural interpretation, there was no reason why he should damn him as unsound in the faith. And the
controversy between Jerome and Rufinus as to Origen was a distinctively western controversy. So was Pelagianism a western heresy, with which Theodoret was not brought
into immediate contact.

The fourth book is obviously the most important, as treating of heresies of which the
writer would have contemporary knowledge. And special interest has attached to the
chapter on Nestorius, who is condemned not merely for erroneous opinion on the incarnation and person of Christ, but as a timeserver and pretender, seeking rather to be thought,
than to be, a Christian. Garnerius indeed doubts the genuineness of the chapter, and
Schulze, in defending it, points out the similarity of its line of argument to that employed in
the treatise "against Nestorius," which is very generally regarded as spurious. It may
have been added after Chalcedon, when the writer had been forced into the denunciation of
his old friend. But the expressions used alike of the incarnation and of Nestorius seem
somewhat in contrast with other writings of Theodoret. Schröckh[5] inclines to the view in
which Ceillier concurs, that this damning account of Nestorius was really written by his
old champion, and accounts for the harshness of condemnation by the influence of the
clamours of Chalcedon and the induration which old age sometimes brings on tender
spirits. It can only be said that if this is Theodoret, it is Theodoret at his worst.

The heads of the Epitome of Divine Decrees are the following twenty-nine: Of the
Father; of the Son; of the Holy Ghost; of Creation; of Matter; of Æons; of Angels; of
Dæmons; of Man; of Providence; of the Incarnation of the Saviour; that the Lord took a
body; that He took a soul as well as His body; that the human nature which He took was
perfect; that He raised the nature which He took; that He is good and just; that He gave
the Old and the New Testament; of Baptism; of Resurrection; of Judgment; of Promises;
of the Second Advent (Ἐπιφάνεια) of the Saviour; of Antichrist; of Virginity; of Marriage;
of Second Marriage; of Fornication; of Repentance; of Abstinence.

The short chapter on the Incarnation has a special value in view of the author's connection with the Nestorian Controversy. "It is worth while," he writes in it, "to exhibit what we hold concerning the Incarnation, for this exposition proclaims more clearly

---

[1] Σατορνεῖλος or Σατορνῖλος in Hippolytus, Epiphanius, and Theodoret; but Σατορνῖνος (Saturninus) in Irenæus and
Eusebius.
[2] A Galatian sect. Jerome has "Ascodrobi," Epiphanius (Hær. 416) identifies "Tascodrugitæ," with Cataphrygians or
Montanists, and says they were so called from the habit of putting their finger to their nose when praying.
[3] In Epiphanius (i. 85, B) Barbelitæ. Barbelo was a mythologic personage; — The sect gnostic.
[4] Ceillier x. 84.   [5] xviii. 416.

the providence of the God of all. In his forged fables Valentinus maintained a distinction between the only-begotten and the Word, and further between the Christ within the pleroma and Jesus, and also the Christ who is without. He said that Jesus became man, by putting on the Christ that is without, and assuming a body of the substance of the soul ; and that He made a passage only through the Virgin, having assumed nothing of the nature of man. Basilides in like manner distinguished between the only-begotten, the Word and the Wisdom. Cerdon, on the other hand, Marcion, and Manes, said that the Christ appeared as man, though he had nothing human. Cerinthus maintained that Jesus was generated of Joseph and Mary after the common manner of men, but that the Christ came down from on high on Jesus. The Ebionites, the Theodotians, the Artemonians, and Photinians said that the Christ was bare man born of the Virgin. Arius and Eunomius taught that He assumed a body, but that the Godhead discharged the function of the soul. Apollinarius held that the body of the Saviour had a soul,[1] but had not the reasonable soul ; for, according to his views, intelligence was superfluous, God the Word being present. I have stated the opinions taught by the majority of heresies with the wish of making plain the truth taught by the church. Now the church makes no distinction between (τὸν αὐτὸν ὀνομάζει) the Son, the only begotten, God the Word, the Lord the Saviour, and Jesus Christ. ' Son,' ' only begotten,' ' God the Word,' and ' Lord,' He was called before the Incarnation ; and is so called also after the Incarnation ; but after the Incarnation the same (Lord) was called Jesus Christ, deriving the titles from the facts. ' Jesus ' is interpreted to mean the Saviour, whereof Gabriel is witness in his words to the Virgin ' Thou shalt call His name Jesus, for He shall save His people from their sins.'[2] But He was styled ' Christ' on account of the unction of the Spirit. So the Psalmist David says ' Therefore God, thy God, hath anointed thee with the oil of gladness above thy fellows.'[3] And through the Prophet Isaiah the Lord Himself says ' The spirit of the Lord is upon me, because the Lord hath anointed me.'[4] Thus the Lord Himself taught us to understand the prophecy, for when He had come into the synagogue, and opened the book of the Prophets, He read the passage quoted, and said to those present ' This day is the Scripture fulfilled in your ears.'[5] The great Peter, too, preached in terms harmonious with the prophets, for in his explanation of the mystery to Cornelius he said ' That word ye know which was published throughout all Judæa, and began from Galilee after the Baptism which John preached ; how God anointed Jesus Christ with the Holy Ghost and with power.'[6] Hence it is clear that He is called Christ on account of the unction of the spirit. But he was anointed not as God, but as man. And as in His human nature He was anointed, after the Incarnation He was called also ' Christ.' But yet there is no distinction between God the Word and the Christ, for God the Word incarnate was named Christ Jesus. And He was incarnate that He might renew the nature corrupted by sin. The reason of His taking all the nature which had sinned was that He might heal all. For He did not take the nature of the body using it as a veil of His Godhead, according to the wild teaching of Arius and Eunomius ; for it had been easy for Him even without a body to be made visible as He was seen of old by Abraham, Jacob and the rest of the saints. But he wished the very nature that had been worsted to beat down the enemy and win the victory. For this reason He took both a body and a reasonable soul. For Holy Scripture does not divide man in a threefold division, but states that this living being consists of a body and a soul.[7] For God after forming the body out of the dust breathed into it the soul and shewed it to be two natures not three. And the same Lord in the Gospels says, ' Fear not them which kill the body but are not able to kill the soul,'[8] and many similar passages may be found in divine Scripture. And that He did not assume man's nature in its perfection, contriving it as a veil for His Godhead, according to the heretics' fables, but achieving victory by means of the first fruits for the whole race, is truly witnessed and accurately taught by the divine apostle, for in His Epistle to the Romans, when unveiling the mystery of the Incarnation, he writes ' Wherefore as by one man sin entered into the world, and death by sin ; and so death passed upon all men, for that all have sinned : for until the law sin was in the world : but sin is not imputed when there is no law. Nevertheless death reigned from Adam to Moses, even over them who had not sinned after the similitude of Adam's transgression, who is the figure of Him that is to come.'[9]

---

[1] ἐμψυχον.
[2] Matt. i. 21.
[3] Ps. xlv. 7.

[4] Is, lxi. 1.
[5] Luke iv. 21.
[6] Acts x. 37, 38.

[7] cf. note on pp. 132 and 194.
[8] Matt. x. 2S.
[9] Rom. v.12, 13, 14.

(iii.) The refutations of the Twelve Chapters of Cyril are translated in the Prolegomena.[1]

In the Epistle of Cyril to Celestinus and the Commonitorium datum Posidonio [2] Cyril shows what sense he wishes to fix on the utterances of Nestorius. " The faith, or rather the ' cacodoxy' of Nestorius, has this force; he says that God the Word, prescient that he who was to be born of the Holy Virgin would be holy and great, therefore chose him and arranged that he should be generated of the Virgin without a husband and conferred on him the privilege of being called by His own names, and raised him so that even though after the incarnation he is called the only begotten Word of God, he is said to have been made man because He was always with him as with a holy man born of the Virgin. And as He was with the prophets so, says Nestorius, was He by a greater conjunction (συνάφεια). On this account Nestorius always shrinks from using the word union (ἕνωσις) and speaks of ' conjunction,' as of some one without, and, as He says to Joshua ' as I was with Moses so will I be with thee.' [3] But, to conceal his impiety, Nestorius says that He was with him from the womb. Wherefore he does not say that Christ was very God, but that Christ was so called of God's good pleasure; and, if he was called Lord, so again Nestorius understands him to be Lord because the divine Word conceded him the boon of being so named. Nor does he say as we do that the Son of God died and rose again on our behalf. The man died and the man rose, and this has nothing to do with God the Word. And in the mysteries what lies (i.e. on the Holy Table) (τὸ προκείμενον) is a man's body; but we believe that it is flesh of the Word, having power to quicken because it is made flesh and blood of the Word that quickeneth all things."

Nestorius was not unnaturally indignant at this misrepresentation of his words, and complains of Cyril for leaving out important clauses and introducing additions of his own.[4] Cyril succeeded in pressing upon Celestinus the idea that Nestorius, who had vigorously opposed the Pelagians, was really in sympathy with them, and so secured the condemnation of his opponent at Rome and at Alexandria, and published his twelve anathemas to complete his own vindication. These were answered by Theodoret on behalf of the eastern church in 431. In 433 formal peace was made, so far as the theological, as apart from the personal, dispute was concerned, by the acceptance by both John of Antioch and Cyril of the formula, slightly modified, which Theodoret himself had drawn up at Ephesus two years before.[5] It is as follows: " We confess our Lord Jesus Christ, the Son of God, the only begotten, to be perfect God and perfect man, of a reasonable soul and body, begotten before the ages of the Father, as touching His godhead, and in the last days on account of us and our salvation (born) of the Virgin Mary as touching His manhood; that He is of one substance with the Father as touching His godhead, of one substance with us as touching His manhood; for there is made an union of two natures; wherefore we confess one Christ, one Son, one Lord. According to this meaning of the unconfounded union we confess the holy Virgin to be 'θεοτόκος,' on account of God the Word being made flesh and becoming man, and of this conception uniting to Himself the temple taken of her. We acknowledge that theologians use the words of evangelists and apostles about the Lord some in common, as of one person, and some distinctively, as of two natures, and deliver the divine as touching the Godhead of the Christ, and the lowly as touching His manhood." [6]

This is substantially what Theodoret says again and again. This satisfied Cyril. This would probably have been accepted by Nestorus too.[7] What then was it, apart from the odium theologicum, which kept Nestorius and Cyril apart? Below the apparent special pleading and word-jugglery on the surface of the controversy lay the principle that in the Christ God and man were one; the essence of the atonement or reconciliation lying in the complete union of the human and the divine in the one Person; the "I" in the " I am" of the Temple and the " I thirst" of the Cross being really the same. "God and man is one Christ." The position which the Cyrillians viewed with alarm was a reduction of this unity to a mere partnership or alliance; — God dwelling in Jesus of Nazareth as He dwells in all good men, only to a greater degree; — the eternal Word being in close contact with the son of Mary (συνάφεια). So, whatever may have been the unhappy faction-fights with which the main issue was confused, there was in truth a great crisis, a great question for decision; was Jesus of Nazareth an unique personality,

---

[1] Page 26.　　　　　　　　　　　　　　[2] Mansi. T. IV. 1012 Seqq. Migne Pat. LXXVII. 85.
[3] Jos. i. 5.　　　[4] Gieseler Vol. I. p. 231.　　　[5] Gieseler i. 235.　　　[6] Synod. c. 17. Mansi V. p. 773.
[7] In Walch's Hist. Ketz. V. 778, there is a good summary of Nestorius' views: he thinks the dispute a mere logomachy. So also Luther, and after him Basnage, Dupin, Jablonski. Vide reff. in Gieseler i. 236.

or only one more in the goodly fellowship of prophets? Was He God, or was He not? There can be little doubt as to the answer Nestorius would have given. There can be none as to that of Theodoret. But on the part of Cyril there was the quite mistaken conviction that Theodoret was practically contending for two Christs. On the other hand Theodoret erroneously identified Cyril with the confusion of the substance and practical patripassianism which he scathes in the "Eranistes," and which the common sense of Christendom has condemned in Eutyches.

(g) To Nicephorus Callistus in the 15th century five hundred of Theodoret's letters were known,[1] and he is eloquent in their praise. Now, the collection, including several by other writers, comprises only one hundred and eighty one. The value of their contributions to the history of the times as well as of their writer will be evident on their study. The order in which they are published is preserved in the translation for the sake of reference. A chronological order would have obvious advantages, but this in many cases could only be conjectural. Where the indications of time are fairly plain the probable date is suggested in a note. The letters are divided into (a) dogmatic, (b) consolatory, (c) festal, (d) commendatory, (e) congratulatory, (f) commenting on passing events. Of them Schulze writes "Nihil eo in genere scribendi perfectius; nam quæ sunt epistolarum virtutes, brevitas, perspicuitas, elegantia, urbanitas, modestia, observantia decori, et ingeniosa prudensque ac erudita simplicitas, in epistolis Theodoreti admirabiliter ita elucent ut scribentibus exempla esse possint." "They not only" says Schröckh,[2] "vindicate the admiration of Nicephorus, but are specially attractive on account of their exhibition of the writer's simplicity, modesty, and love of peace."

From the study of these letters "we rise," writes Canon Venables,[3] "with a heightened estimate of Theodoret himself, his intellectual power, his theological precision, his warmhearted affection for his friends, and the Christian virtues with which, notwithstanding some weaknesses and an occasional bitterness for which, however distressing, his persecutions offered some palliation, his character was adorned."

The reputation of Theodoret in the Church is a growing reputation, and the practical canonization which he has won in the heart of Christendom is a testimony to the power and worth of character and conduct. Though never officially dignified by a higher ecclesiastical title than "Beatus" he is yet to Marcellinus "Episcopus sanctus Cyri"[4] and to Photius[5] "divinus vir." His earnest, sometimes bitter, conflict with the great intellect and strong will of Cyril, and apparent discomfiture in the war which raged, often with dire confusion, up and down the long lines of definition, have not succeeded in robbing him of one of the highest places among the Fathers of whom the Church is proudest. He exhibits, each in a lofty and conspicuous form, all the qualities which mark a great and good churchman. His theological writings would have won high fame in a recluse. His administration of his diocese, as we learn it from his modest letters, would have gained him the character of an excellent bishop, even had he been no scholar. His temper in controversy, though occasionally breaking out into the fiery heat of the oriental, is for the most part in happy contrast with that of his opponents. His devotion to his duty is undeniable, and his industry astonishing. It is impossible not to feel as we read his writings that he is no self-seeker arguing for victory. He believes that the fate of the Church rests on the fidelity of Christians to the Nicene Confession, and in his championship of this creed, and his opposition to all that seems to him to threaten its adulteration or defeat, he knows no awe of prince or court. Owning but one Lord, he is true through evil and good report to Him, and his figure stands out large, bright, and gracious across the centuries, against a background of intrigue and controversy sometimes very dark, as of a patient and faithful soldier and servant of Christ.[6] If his shortcomings were those of his own age, — and in an age of virulent strife and of denial of all mercy to opponents his memory rises as a comparative monument of moderation, — his graces were the graces of all the ages.[7] Were it customary, or even possible, in our own church and time to maintain the ancient custom of reciting before the Holy Table the names approved as of good men and true in the past history of the Holy Society, in the long catalogue of the faithful departed for whom worshippers bless the name of their common Lord, a place must indubitably be kept for Theodoretus, bishop of Cyrus.

---

[1] Ecc. Hist. xiv. 54.   [2] xviii. 427.   [3] Dict. Christ. Biog. iv. 918.
[4] Marc. 466. Ceiller x. 25.   [5] Cod. xxiv., p. 527.
[6] *La vie sainte et édifiante que Théodoret mena dès sa première jeunesse; les travaux apostoliques dont il honora son épiscopat; son zèle pour la conversion des ennemis de l'église; les persecutions qu'il souffrait pour le nom de Jésus Christ; son amour pour la solitude, pour la pauvreté et pour les pauvres; l'esprit de charité qu'il a fait paraître dans toutes les occasions; la généreuse liberté dans la confession de la vérité; sa profonde humilité qui paraît dans tous ses écrits; le succès dont Dieu bénit ses soins et ses mouvements pour le salut des hommes, l'ont rendu venerable dans l'église. Les anciens l'ont qualifié saint, et apellé un homme divin; mais la qualité qu'ils lui donnent ordinairement c'est celle de bienheureux."* Ceillier
[7] of Schröckb xxiii 256

MANUSCRIPTS AND EDITIONS OF SEPARATE WORKS.

The editions of the Ecclesiastical History are the most numerous, though of several others there are many. Of the collected works the following are the principal.

(i)   Editio princeps, of Paulus Manutius, Latin Version only.   Rome 1556.

(ii)   J. Birckman, fol. 2 voll. Latin only Cologne 1573.

(iii)   J. Sirmond, 4 voll. fol. Greek and Latin, Paris 1642.

To this the Auctarium of J. Garnier, with his dissertations was added in 1684.

(iv)   John Lewis Schulze, Greek and Latin, based upon the preceding, in 5 voll. Halle, 1774.

(v)   Migne's edition of the foregoing.   Paris 1860.

(The last-named is the Edition used for the translation in this work.)

The MSS. authority for the works of Theodoret is strong.   The afore-named editions are based on MS. in the libraries of Augsburg, Florence, Rome and Naples.

To works on Theodoret mentioned in the notes may be added : —

S. Küpper, Ausgew, Schriften des sel. Theodoret aus dem Urtext übers.

E. Binder, Études sur Theodoret.   Geneva, 1844.

Specht, Theodor von Mopsuestia, und Theodoret von Cyrus.   Munich, 1871.

THE ANATHEMAS OF CYRIL IN OPPOSITION TO NESTORIUS.

(Mansi T. IV. p. 1067–1082, Migne Cat. 76, col. 391. The anathemas of Nestorius against Cyril are to be found in Hardouin i. 1297.)

I. If any one refuses to confess that the Emmanuel is in truth God, and therefore that the holy Virgin is Mother of God (θεοτόκος), for she gave birth after a fleshly manner to the Word of God made flesh ; let him be anathema.

II. If any one refuses to confess that the Word of God the Father is united in hypostasis to flesh, and is one Christ with His own flesh, the same being at once both God and man, let him be anathema.

III. If any one in the case of the one Christ divides the hypostases after the union, conjoining them by the conjunction alone which is according to dignity, independence, or prerogative, and not rather by the concurrence which is according to natural union, let him be anathema.

IV. If any one divides between two persons or hypostases the expressions used in the writings of evangelists and apostles, whether spoken by the saints of Christ or by Him about Himself, and applies the one as to a man considered properly apart from the Word of God, and the others as appropriate to the divine and the Word of God the Father alone, let him be anathema.

V. If any one dares to maintain that the Christ is man bearing God, and not rather that He is God in truth, and one Son, and by nature, according as the Word was made flesh, and shared blood and flesh in like manner with ourselves, let him be anathema.

VI. If any one dares to maintain that the Word of God the Father was God or Lord of the Christ, and does not rather confess that the same was at once both God and man, the Word being made flesh according to the Scriptures, let him be anathema.

VII. If any one says that Jesus was energized as man by God the Word, and that He was invested with the glory of the only begotten as being another beside Him, let him be anathema.

VIII. If any one dares to maintain that the ascended man ought to be worshipped together with the divine Word, and be glorified with Him, and with Him be called God as one with another (in that the continual use of the preposition " with " in composition makes this sense compulsory), and does not rather in one act of worship honour the Emmanuel and praise Him in one doxology, in that He is the Word made flesh, let him be anathema.

IX. If any one says that the one Lord Jesus Christ is glorified by the Spirit, using the power that works through Him as a foreign power, and receiving from Him the ability to operate against unclean spirits, and to complete His miracles among men ; and does not rather say that the Spirit is His own, whereby also He wrought His miracles, let him be anathema.

X. Holy Scripture states that Christ is High Priest and Apostle of our confession,[1] and offered Himself on our behalf for a sweet-smelling savour to God and our Father.[2] If, then, any one says that He, the Word of God, was not made our High Priest and Apostle when He was made flesh and man after our manner; but as being another, other than Himself, properly man made of a woman ; or if any one says that He offered the offering on His own behalf, and not rather on our behalf alone ; for He that knew no sin would not have needed an offering, let him be anathema.

XI. If any one confesses not that the Lord's flesh is giver of life,[3] and proper to the Word of God Himself, but (states) that it is of another than Him, united indeed to Him in dignity, yet as only possessing a divine indwelling ; and not rather, as we said, giver of life, because it is proper to the Word of Him who hath might to engender all things alive, let him be anathema.

XII. If any one confesses not that the Word of God suffered in flesh, and was crucified in flesh, and tasted death in flesh, and was made firstborn of the dead, in so far as He is life and giver of life, as God ; let him be anathema.

---

[1] Heb. iii. 1, R. V.   [2] cf. Eph. v. 2.   [3] ζωοποιόν. cf. τὸ κύριον τὸ ζωοποιόν of the Creed of Constantinople.

COUNTER-STATEMENTS OF THEODORET.

(Opp. Ed. Schulze. V. i. seq. Migne, Lat. 76. col. 391.)

Against I. — But all we who follow the words of the evangelists state that God the Word was not made flesh by nature, nor yet was changed into flesh; for the Divine is immutable and invariable. Wherefore also the prophet David says, " Thou art the same, and thy years shall not fail." [1] And this the great Paul, the herald of the truth, in his Epistle to the Hebrews, states to have been spoken of the Son. [2] And in another place God says through the Prophet, " I am the Lord: I change not." [3] If then the Divine is immutable and invariable, it is incapable of change or alteration. And if the immutable cannot be changed, then God the Word was not made flesh by mutation, but took flesh and tabernacled in us, according to the word of the evangelist. This the divine Paul expresses clearly in his Epistle to the Philippians in the words, " Let this mind be in you which was also in Christ Jesus: who, being in the form of God, thought it not robbery to be equal with God: but made Himself of no reputation and took upon Him the form of a servant." [4] Now it is plain from these words that the form of God was not changed into the form of a servant, but, remaining what it was, took the form of the servant. So God the Word was not made flesh, but assumed living and reasonable flesh. He Himself is not naturally conceived of the Virgin, fashioned, formed, and deriving beginning of existence from her; He who is before the ages, God, and with God, being with the Father and with the Father both known and worshipped; but He fashioned for Himself a temple in the Virgin's womb, and was with that which was formed and begotten. Wherefore also we style that holy Virgin θεοτόκος, not because she gave birth in natural manner to God, but to man united to the God that had fashioned Him. Moreover if He that was fashioned in the Virgin's womb was not man but God the Word Who is before the ages, then God the Word is a creature of the Holy Ghost. For that which was conceived in her, says Gabriel, is of the Holy Ghost. [5] But if the only begotten Word of God is uncreate and of one substance and co-eternal with the Father it is no longer a formation or creation of the Spirit. And if the Holy Ghost did not fashion God the Word in the Virgin's womb, it follows that we understand the form of the servant to have been fashioned, formed, conceived, and generated. But since the form was not stripped of the form of God, but was a Temple containing God the Word dwelling in it, according to the words of Paul " For it pleased the Father that in him should all fulness dwell " " bodily," [6] we call the Virgin not mother of man (ἀνθρωποτόκος) but mother of God (θεοτόκος), applying the former title to the fashioning and conception, but the latter to the union. For this cause the child who was born is called Emmanuel, neither God separated from human nature nor man stripped of Godhead. For Emmanuel is interpreted to mean " God with us ", according to the words of the Gospels; and the expression " God with us " at once manifests Him Who for our sakes was assumed out of us, and proclaims God the Word Who assumed. Therefore the child is called Emmanuel on account of God Who assumed, and the Virgin θεοτόκος on account of the union of the form of God with the conceived form of a servant. For God the Word was not changed into flesh, but the form of God took the form of a servant.

Against II. — We, in obedience to the divine teaching of the apostles, confess one Christ; and, on account of the union, we name the same both God and man. But we are wholly ignorant of the union according to hypostasis [7] as being strange and foreign to the divine Scriptures and the Fathers who have interpreted them. And if the author of these statements means by the union according to hypostasis that there was a mixture of flesh and Godhead, we shall oppose his statement with all our might, and shall confute his blasphemy, for the mixture is of necessity followed by confusion; and the admission of confusion destroys the individuality of each nature. Things that are undergoing mixture do not remain what they were, and to assert this in the case of God the Word and of the seed of

---

[1] Ps. ci. 28.
[2] Heb. i. 12.
[3] Mal. iii. 6.
[4] Phil. ii. 5, 6,7.
[5] Matt. . 23.
[6] Coloss. i. 19, and ii. 9.
[7] cf. n. p. 72.

David would be most absurd. We must obey the Lord when He exhibits the two natures and says to the Jews, " Destroy this temple and in three days I will raise it up." [1] But if there had been mixture then God had not remained God, neither was the temple recognised as a temple; then the temple was God and God was temple. This is involved in the theory of the mixture. And it was quite superfluous for the Lord to say to the Jews, " Destroy this temple and in three days I will raise it up." He ought to have said, Destroy me and in three days I shall be raised, if there had really been any mixture and confusion. As it is, He exhibits the temple undergoing destruction and God raising it up. Therefore the union according to hypostasis, which in my opinion they put before us instead of mixture, is superfluous. It is quite sufficient to mention the union, which both exhibits the properties of the natures and teaches us to worship the one Christ.

Against III. — The sense of the terms used is misty and obscure. Who needs to be told that there is no difference between conjunction and concurrence? The concurrence is a concurrence of the separated parts; and the conjunction is a conjunction of the distinguished parts. The very clever author of the phrases has laid down things that agree as though they disagreed. It is wrong, he says, to conjoin the hypostases by conjunction; they ought to be conjoined by concurrence, and that a natural concurrence. Possibly he states this not knowing what he says; if he knows, he blasphemes. Nature has a compulsory force and is involuntary; as for instance, if I say we are naturally hungry, we do not feel hunger of free-will but of necessity; and assuredly paupers would have left off begging if the power of ceasing to be hungry had lain in their own will; we are naturally thirsty; we naturally sleep; we naturally breathe; and all these actions, I repeat, belong to the category of the involuntary, and he who is no longer capable of them necessarily ceases to exist. If then the concurrence in union of the form of God and the form of a servant was natural, then God the Word was united to the form of the servant under the compulsion of necessity, and not because He put in force His loving kindness, and the Lawgiver of the Universe will be found to be a follower of the laws of necessity. Not thus have we been taught by the blessed Paul; on the contrary, we have been taught that He took the form of a servant and " emptied Himself;" [2] and the expression " emptied Himself" indicates the voluntary act. If then He was united by purpose and will to the nature assumed from us, the addition of the term natural is superfluous. It suffices to confess the union, and an union is understood of things distinguished, for if there were no division an union could never be apprehended. The apprehension then of the union implies previous apprehension of the division. How then can he say that the hypostases or natures ought not to be divided? He knows all the while that the hypostasis of God the Word was perfect before the ages; and that the form of the servant which was assumed by It was perfect; and this is the reason why he said hypostases and not hypostasis. If therefore either nature is perfect, and both came together, it is obvious that after the form of God had taken the form of a servant, piety compels us to confess one son and Christ; while to speak of the united hypostases or natures as two, so far from being absurd, follows the necessity of the case. For if in the case of the one man we divide the natures, and call the mortal nature body, but the immortal nature soul, and both man, much more consonant is it with right reason to recognise the properties alike of the God who took and of the man who was taken. We find the blessed Paul dividing the one man into two where he says in one passage, " Though our outward man perish yet the inward man is renewed," [3] and in another " For I delight in the law of God after the inward man." [4] And again " that Christ may dwell in the inner man." [5] Now if the apostle divides the natural conjunction of the synchronous natures, with what reason can the man who describes the mixture to us by means of other terms indite us as impious when we divide the properties of the natures of the everlasting God and of the man assumed at the end of days?

Against IV. — These statements, too, are akin to the preceding. On the assumption that there has been a mixture, he means that there is a distinction of terms as used both in the holy Gospels and in the apostolic writings. And he uses this language while glorifying himself that he is at war at once with Arius and Eunomius and the rest of the heresiarchs. Let then this exact professor of theology tells us how he would confute the blasphemy of the heretics, while applying to God the Word what is uttered humbly and appropriately by the form of the servant. They indeed while thus doing lay down that the Son of God is inferior, a creature, made, and a servant. To whom then are we, hold-

---

[1] John ii. 19.   [3] II. Cor. iv. 16.   [5] Ephes. iii. 17. Greek as in A.V. " in your hearts."
[2] Phil. ii. 7.   [4] Rom. vii. 22.

ing as we do the opposite opinion to theirs, and confessing the Son to be of one substance and co-eternal with God the Father, Creator of the Universe, Maker, Beautifier, Ruler, and Governor, All-wise, Almighty, or rather Himself, Power, Life and Wisdom, to refer the words "My God, my God why hast thou forsaken me;"[1] or "Father if it be possible let this cup pass from me;"[2] or "Father save me from this hour;"[3] or "That hour no man knoweth, not even the Son of Man;"[4] and all the other passages spoken and written in lowliness by Him and by the holy apostles about Him? To whom shall we apply the weariness and the sleep? To whom the ignorance and the fear? Who was it who stood in need of angelic succour? If these belong to God the Word, how was wisdom ignorant? How could it be called wisdom when affected by the sense of ignorance? How could He speak the truth in saying that He had all that the Father hath,[5] when not having the knowledge of the Father? For He says, "The Father alone knoweth that day."[6] How could He be the unchanged image of Him that begat Him if He has not all that the Begetter hath? If then He speaks the truth when saying that He is ignorant, any one might suppose this of Him. But if He knoweth the day, but says that He is ignorant with the wish to hide it, you see in what a blasphemy the conclusion issues. For the truth lies and could not properly be called truth if it has any quality opposed to truth. But if the truth does not lie, neither is God the Word ignorant of the day which He Himself made, and which He Himself fixed, wherein He purposes to judge the world, but has the knowledge of the Father as being unchanged image. Not then to God the Word does the ignorance belong, but to the form of the servant who at that time knew as much as the indwelling Godhead revealed. The same position may be maintained about other similar cases. How for instance could it be reasonable for God the Word to say to the Father, "Father if it be possible let this cup pass from me, nevertheless not as I will but as Thou wilt"?[7] The absurdities which necessarily thence follow are not a few. First it follows that the Father and the Son are not of the same mind, and that the Father wishes one thing and the Son another, for He said, "Nevertheless not as I will but as Thou wilt." Secondly we shall have to contemplate great ignorance in the Son, for He will be found ignorant whether the cup can or cannot pass from Him; but to say this of God the Word is utter impiety and blasphemy. For exactly did He know the end of the mystery of the œconomy Who for this very reason came among us, Who of His own accord took our nature, Who emptied Himself. For this cause too He foretold to the Holy Apostles, "Behold we go up to Jerusalem; and the Son of Man shall be betrayed . . . into the hands of the Gentiles to mock and to scourge and to crucify Him, and the third day He shall rise again."[8] How then can He Who foretold these things, and, when Peter deprecated their coming to pass, rebuked him, Himself deprecate their coming to pass, when He clearly knows all that is to be? Is it not absurd that Abraham many generations ago should have seen His day and have been glad,[9] and that Isaiah in like manner, and Jeremiah, and Daniel, and Zechariah, and all the fellowship of the prophets, should have foretold His saving passion, and He Himself be ignorant, and beg release from and deprecate it, though it was destined to come to pass for the salvation of the world? Therefore these words are not the words of God the Word, but of the form of the servant, afraid of death because death was not yet destroyed.[10] Surely God the Word permitted the utterance of these expressions allowing room for fear, that the nature of Him that had to be born may be plain, and to prevent our supposing the Son of Abraham and David to be an unreality or appearance. The crew of the impious heretics has given birth to this blasphemy through entertaining these sentiments. We shall therefore apply what is divinely spoken and acted to God the Word; on the other hand what is said and done in humility we shall connect with the form of a servant, lest we be tainted with the blasphemy of Arius and Eunomius.

Against V. — We assert that God the Word shared like ourselves in flesh and blood, and in immortal soul, on account of the union relating to them; but that God the Word was made flesh by any change we not only refuse to say, but accuse of impiety those who do, and it may be seen that this is contrary to the very terms laid down. For if the Word was

---

[1] Matt. xxvii. 48.   [2] Matt. xxvi. 39.   [3] John xii. 27.
[4] Matt. xxiv. 36 and Mk. xiii. 22. There is no manuscript authority for the variation Son "of Man."
[5] John xvi. 15.   [6] Matt. xxiv. 36.   [7] Matt. xxvi. 39.   [8] Matt. xx. 18, 19.   [9] John viii. 26.
[10] For the view that the cup deprecated by the Saviour was death there is no direct Scriptural authority, and to adopt the exegesis of Theodoret and of many others would be to place the divine humanity of the Messiah on a lower level than that not merely of many a martyr and patriot but of many men unconscious of martyr's or patriot's high calling, who have nevertheless faced death and pain with calm and cheerful fortitude. The bitterness of the cup which the Saviour prayed might if possible pass from Him seems rather to have lain in the culmination of the sin of the race and nation with which His love for men had identified Him; the greed, the treachery, the meanness, the cruelty, the disloyalty, shewn by the Sons of Israel to the Son of David, by the sons of men to the Son of Man.

changed into flesh He did not share with us in flesh and blood: but if He shared in flesh and blood He shared as being another besides them: and if the flesh is anything other besides Him, then He was not changed into flesh. While therefore we use the term sharing[1] we worship both Him that took and that which was taken as one Son. But we reckon the distinction of the natures. We do not object to the term man bearing God, as employed by many of the holy Fathers, one of whom is the great Basil, who uses this term in his argument to Amphilochius about the Holy Ghost, and in his interpretation of the fifty-ninth psalm. But we call Him man bearing God, not because He received some particular divine grace, but as possessing all the Godhead of the Son united. For thus says the blessed Paul in his interpretation, " Beware lest any man spoil you through philosophy and vain deceit, after the tradition of men, after the rudiments of the world, and not after Christ. For in Him dwelleth all the fulness of the Godhead bodily." [2]

Against VI. — The blessed Paul calls that which was assumed by God the Word " form of a servant," [3] but since the assumption was prior to the union, and the blessed Paul was discoursing about the assumption when he called the nature which was assumed " form of a servant," after the making of the union the name of " servitude " has no longer place. For seeing that the Apostle when writing to them that believed in Him said, " So thou art not a servant but a son " [4] and the Lord said to His disciples, " Henceforth I will not call you servants but friends ; " [5] much more the first fruits of our nature, through whom even we were guerdoned with the boon of adoption, would be released from the title of servant. We therefore confess even " the form of the servant " to be God on account of the form of God united to it ; and we bow to the authority of the prophet when he calls the babe also Emmanuel, and the child which was born, " Angel of great counsel, wonderful Counsellor, mighty God, powerful, Prince of peace, and Father of the age to come." [6] Yet the same prophet, even after the union, when proclaiming the nature of that which was assumed, calls him who is of the seed of Abraham " servant " in the words " Thou art my servant O Israel and in thee will I be glorified ; " [7] and again, " Thus says the Lord that formed me from the womb to be his servant ; " [8] and a little further on, " Lo I have given thee for a covenant of the people, for a light to the Gentiles, that thou mayest be my salvation unto the end of the earth." [9] But what was formed from the womb was not God the Word but the form of the servant. For God the Word was not made flesh by being changed, but He assumed flesh with a rational soul.

Against VII. — If the nature of man is mortal, and God the Word is life and giver of life, and raised up the temple which had been destroyed by the Jews, and carried it into heaven, how is not the form of the servant glorified through the form of God? For if being originally and by nature mortal it was made immortal through its union with God the Word, it therefore received what it had not ; and after receiving what it had not, and being glorified, it is glorified by Him who gave. Wherefore also the Apostle exclaims, " According to the working of His mighty power which he wrought in Christ when He raised Him from the dead." [10]

Against VIII. — As I have often said, the doxology which we offer to the Lord Christ is one, and we confess the same to be at once God and man, as the method of the union has taught us ; but we shall not shrink from speaking of the properties of the natures. For God the Word did not undergo change into flesh, nor yet again did the man lose what he was and undergo transmutation into the nature of God. Therefore we worship the Lord Christ, while we maintain the properties of either nature.

Against IX. — Here he has plainly had the hardihood to anathematize not only those who at the present time hold pious opinions, but also those who were in former days heralds of truth ; aye even the writers of the divine gospels, the band of the holy Apostles, and, in addition to these, Gabriel the archangel. For he indeed it was who first, even before the conception, announced the birth of the Christ according to the flesh ; saying in reply to Mary when she asked, " How shall this be, seeing I know not a man ? " " The Holy Ghost shall come upon thee and the power of the Highest shall overshadow thee ; therefore also that holy thing that shall be born of thee shall be called the Son of God." [11] And to Joseph he said, " Fear not to take unto thee Mary thy wife, for that which is conceived in her is of the Holy Ghost." [12] And the Evangelist says, " When as his mother Mary was espoused to Joseph . . . she was found with child of the Holy Ghost." [1]

---

[1] κοινωνία, in the sense of participation.   [2] Coloss. ii. 8. 9.   [3] Phil. ii. 7.   [4] Gal. iv. 7.
[5] John xv. 15.   [6] Isaiah vii. 14 and ix. 6. lxx. Alex.   [7] Isaiah xlix. 3.   [8] Isaiah xlix. 5.
[9] Isaiah xlix. 6 " covenant of the people " being imported from lxii. 6.   [10] Ephes. i, 19, 20.   [11] Luke 1. 34, 35.
[12] Matt. i. 20.   [13] Matt. i. 18.

And the Lord Himself when He had come into the synagogue of the Jews and had taken the prophet Isaiah, after reading the passage in which he says, " The spirit of the Lord is upon me because He hath anointed me " and so on, added, " This day is this scripture fulfilled in your ears." [1] And the blessed Peter in his sermon to the Jews said, " God anointed Jesus of Nazareth with the Holy Ghost." [2] And Isaiah many ages before had predicted, " There shall come forth a rod out of the stem of Jesse, and a branch shall grow out of his roots ; and the spirit of the Lord shall rest upon him, the spirit of wisdom and understanding, the spirit of counsel and might, the spirit of knowledge and of the fear of the Lord ; " [3] and again, " Behold my servant whom I uphold, my beloved in whom my soul delighteth. I will put my spirit upon him : he shall bring forth judgment to the Gentiles." [4] This testimony the Evangelist too has inserted in his own writings. And the Lord Himself in the Gospels says to the Jews, " If I with the spirit of God cast out devils, no doubt the kingdom of God is come upon you." [5] And John says, " He that sent me to baptize with water, the same said unto me, Upon whom thou shalt see the Spirit descending and remaining on Him, the same is He which baptizeth with the Holy Ghost." [6] So this exact examiner of the divine decrees has not only anathematized prophets, apostles, and even the archangel Gabriel, but has suffered his blasphemy to reach even the Saviour of the world Himself. For we have shewn that the Lord Himself after reading the passage " The spirit of the Lord is upon me because He hath anointed me," said to the Jews, " This day is this scripture fulfilled in your ears." And to those who said that He was casting out devils by Beelzebub He replied that He was casting them out by the Spirit of God. But we maintain that it was not God the Word, of one substance and co-eternal with the Father, that was formed by the Holy Ghost and anointed, but the human nature which was assumed by Him at the end of days. We shall confess that the Spirit of the Son was His own if he spoke of it as of the same nature and proceeding from the Father, and shall accept the expression as consistent with true piety. But if he speaks of the Spirit as being of the Son, or as having its origin through the Son we shall reject this statement as blasphemous and impious. For we believe the Lord when He says, " The spirit which proceedeth from the Father ; " [7] and likewise the very divine Paul saying, " We have received not the spirit of the world, but the spirit which is of God." [8]

Against X. — The unchangeable nature was not changed into nature of flesh, but assumed human nature and set it over the common high priests, as the blessed Paul teaches in the words, " For every high priest taken from among men is ordained for men in things pertaining to God, that he may offer both gifts and sacrifices for sins : who can have compassion on the ignorant and on them that are out of the way ; for that he himself also is encompassed with infirmity. And by reason hereof he ought, as for the people so also for himself." [9] And a little further on interpreting this he says, " As was Aaron so also was the Christ." [10] Then pointing out the infirmity of the assumed nature he says, " Who in the days of His flesh, when He had offered up prayers and supplication with strong crying and tears unto Him that was able to save Him from death, and was heard for His godly fear, though He was a son yet learned obedience by the things that He suffered : and having been made perfect He became unto all that obey Him the author of eternal salvation ; named of God a high priest of the order of Melchisedec." [11] Who then is He who was perfected by toils of virtue and who was not perfect by nature? Who is He who learnt obedience by experience, and before his experience was ignorant of it? Who is it that lived with godly fear and offered supplication with strong crying and tears, not able to save Himself but appealing to Him that is able to save Him and asking for release from death? Not God the Word, the impassible, the immortal, the incorporeal, whose memory is joy and release from tears, " For he has wiped away tears from off all faces," [12] and again the prophet says, " I remembered God and was glad," [13] Who crowneth them that live in godly fear, " Who knoweth all things before they be," [14] " Who hath all things that the Father hath ; " [15] Who is the unchangeable image of the Father," [16] " Who sheweth the Father in himself." [17] It is on the contrary that which was assumed by Him of the seed of David, mortal, passible, and afraid of death ; although this itself afterwards destroyed the power of death through union with the God who had assumed it ; [18] which walked through all righteousness and said to John, " Suffer it to be so now for thus it becometh us to fulfil all righteousness." [19]

1 Luke iv. 17, 21.	6 John i. 33.	11 Hebrews v. 7, 10.	16 Col. i. 15.
2 Acts x. 38.	7 John x. 5, 26.	12 Isaiah xxv. 8.	17 John xiv. 7.
3 Isaiah xi. 1, 2.	8 I Cor. ii. 12.	13 Psalms 77, 3, lxx.	18 Heb. ii. 14.
4 Isaiah xlii. 1.	9 Hebrews v. 1-3.	14 Hist. Susann : 42.	19 Matt. iii. 15.
5 Matt. xii. 28.	10 Hebrews v. 4 and 5.	15 John xvi. 15.	

This took the name of the priesthood of Melchisedec, for it put on infirmity of nature; — not the Almighty God the Word. Wherefore also, a little before, the blessed Paul said, "We have not a high priest which cannot be touched with the feeling of our infirmities, but was in all points tempted like as we are yet without sin." [1] It was the nature taken from us for our sakes which experienced our feelings without sin, not He that on account of our salvation assumed it. And in the beginning of this part of his subject he teaches us in the words "Consider the apostle and high priest of our profession, Jesus, who was faithful to Him that appointed Him as also Moses was faithful in all His house." [2] But no one holding the right faith would call the unmade the uncreate, God the Word coeternal with the Father, a creature; but on the contrary, Him of David's seed Who being free from all sin was made our high priest and victim, after Himself offering Himself on our behalf to God having in Himself the Word, God of God, united to Himself and inseparably conjoined.

Against XI. — In my opinion he appears to give heed to the truth, in order that, by concealing his unsound views by it, he may not be detected in asserting the same dogmas as the heretics. But nothing is stronger than truth, which by its own rays uncovers the darkness of falsehood. By the aid of its illumination we shall make his heterodox belief plain. In the first place he has nowhere made mention of intelligent flesh, nor confessed that the assumed man was perfect, but everywhere in accordance with the teaching of Apollinarius he speaks of flesh. Secondly, after introducing the conception of the mixture under other terms, he brings it into his arguments; for there he clearly states the flesh of the Lord to be soulless. For, he says, if any one states that the flesh of the Lord is not proper flesh of the very Word who is of God the Father, but that it is of another beside Him, let him be anathema. Hence it is plain that he does not confess God the Word to have assumed a soul, but only flesh, and that He Himself stands to the flesh in place of soul. We on the contrary assert that the flesh of the Lord having in it life [3] was life-giving and reasonable, on account of the life-giving Godhead united to it. And he himself unwillingly confesses the difference between the two natures, speaking of flesh, and "God the Word" and calling it "His own flesh." Therefore God the Word was not changed into nature of flesh, but has His own flesh, the assumed nature, and has made it life-giving by the union.

Against XII. — Passion is proper to the passible; the impassible is above passions. It was then the form of the servant that suffered, the form of God of course dwelling with it, and permitting it to suffer on account of the salvation brought forth of the sufferings, and making the sufferings its own on account of the union. Therefore it was not the Christ [4] who suffered, but the man assumed of us by God. Wherefore also the blessed Isaiah exclaims in his prophecy, "A man of sorrows and acquainted with grief." [5] And the Lord Christ Himself said to the Jews, "Why seek ye to kill me, a man that hath told you the truth?" [6] But what is threatened with death is not the very life, but he that hath a mortal nature. And giving this lesson in another place the Lord said to the Jews, "Destroy this temple, and in three days I will raise it up." [7] Therefore what was destroyed was the (temple descended) from David, and, after its destruction, it was raised up by the only begotten Word of God, impassibly begotten of the Father before the ages.

---

[1] Heb. iv. 15. [2] Heb. iii. 1-2. [3] 'ἔμψυχον.
[4] For "the Christ" we might expect here "the Word," for that the Christ suffered is the plain statement of Scripture (I. Pet. ii. 21). But Theodoret uses the name Christ of the eternal word, e.g. *de Providentia* x. 661. "When you hear Christ mentioned, understand the only-begotten Son the Word, begotten of His Father before the ages, clad in human nature."
[5] Is. liii. 3. [6] John vii. 19. d. viii. 40. [7] John ii. 9.

DYNASTY OF CONSTANTINE.

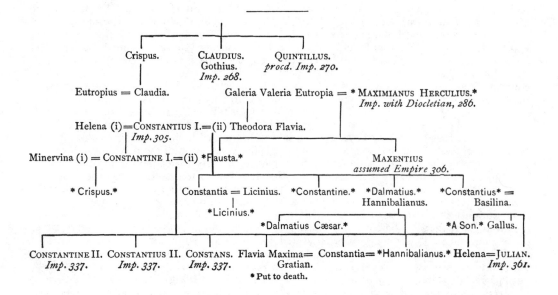

DYNASTIES OF VALENTINIAN AND THEODOSIUS.

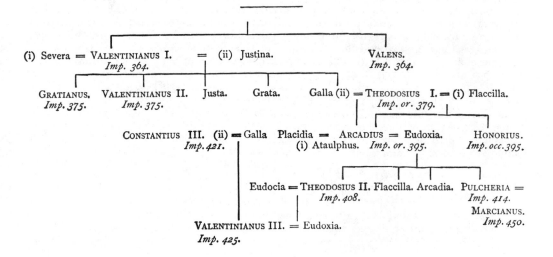

THE ECCLESIASTICAL HISTORY OF THEODORET

BOOK I

PROLOGUE.

Design of the History.

WHEN artists paint on panels and on walls the events of ancient history, they alike delight the eye, and keep bright for many a year the memory of the past. Historians substitute books for panels, bright description for pigments, and thus render the memory of past events both stronger and more permanent, for the painter's art is ruined by time. For this reason I too shall attempt to record in writing events in ecclesiastical history hitherto omitted, deeming it indeed not right to look on without an effort while oblivion robs [1] noble deeds and useful stories of their due fame. For this cause too I have been frequently urged by friends to undertake this work. But when I compare my own powers with the magnitude of the undertaking, I shrink from attempting it. Trusting, however, in the bounty of the Giver of all good, I enter upon a task beyond my own strength.

Eusebius of Palestine [2] has written a history of the Church from the time of the holy Apostles to the reign of Constantine, the prince beloved of God. I shall begin my history from the period at which his terminates [3].

CHAPTER I.

Origin of the Arian Heresy.

AFTER the overthrow of the wicked and impious tyrants, Maxentius, Maximinus, and Licinius, the surge which those destroyers, like hurricanes, had roused was hushed to sleep; the whirlwinds were checked, and the Church henceforward began to enjoy a settled calm. This was established for her by Constantine, a prince deserving of all praise, whose calling, like that of the divine Apostle, was not of men, nor by man, but from heaven. He enacted laws prohibiting sacrifices to idols, and commanding churches [1] to be erected. He appointed Christians to be governors of the provinces, ordering honour to be shown to the priests, and threatening with death those who dared to insult them. By some the churches which had been destroyed were rebuilt; others erected new ones still more spacious and magnificent. Hence, for us, all was joy and gladness, while our enemies were overwhelmed with gloom and despair. The temples of the idols were closed; but frequent assemblies were held, and festivals celebrated, in the churches. But the devil, full of all envy and wickedness, the destroyer of mankind, unable to bear the sight of the Church sailing on with favourable winds, stirred up plans of evil counsel, eager to sink the vessel steered by the Creator and Lord of the Universe. When he began to perceive that the error of the Greeks had been made manifest, that the various tricks of the demons had been detected, and that the greater number of men worshipped the Creator, instead of adoring, as heretofore, the creature, he did not dare to declare open war against our God and Saviour; but having found some who, though dignified with the name of Christians,

---

[1] συλαω. Cf. 2 Cor. xi. 8.
[2] Cf. Basil de Spir. Sanct., 29. "ὁ παλαιστῖνος" means "of Cæsarea," his see, to distinguish him from his namesake, Bishop of Nicomedia.
[3] The last event mentioned by Eusebius is the defeat of Licinius, who was put to death A.D. 324.

[1] ἐκκλησία. The use of the word in 1 Cor. xi. 18 indicates a transition stage between "Assembly" and "Building." The brethren met "in assembly:" soon they met in a church. Cf. Aug. Ep. 190, 5. 19: "*ut nomine ecclesiæ, id est populi qui continetur, significemus locum qui continet.*" Chrysost. Hom. xxix. in Acta: οἱ πρόγονοι τὰς ἐκκλησίας ᾠκοδόμησαν.

were yet slaves to ambition and vainglory, he made them fit instruments for the execution of his designs, and by their means drew others back into their old error, not indeed by the former method of setting up the worship of the creature, but by bringing it about that the Creator and Maker of all should be reduced to a level with the creature. I shall now proceed to relate where and by what means he sowed these tares.

Alexandria is an immense and populous city, charged with the leadership not only of Egypt, but also of the adjacent countries, the Thebaid and Libya. After Peter[2], the victorious champion of the faith, had, during the sway of the aforesaid impious tyrants, obtained the crown of martyrdom, the Church in Alexandria was ruled for a short time by Achillas[3]. He was succeeded by Alexander[4], who proved himself a noble defender of the doctrines of the gospel. At that time, Arius, who had been enrolled in the list of the presbytery, and entrusted with the exposition of the Holy Scriptures, fell a prey to the assaults of jealousy, when he saw that the helm of the high priesthood was committed to Alexander. Stung by this passion, he sought opportunities for dispute and contention; and, although he perceived that Alexander's irreproachable conduct forbade his bringing any charges against him, envy would not allow him to rest. In him the enemy of the truth found an instrument whereby to stir and agitate the angry waters of the Church, and persuaded him to oppose the apostolical doctrine of Alexander. While the Patriarch, in obedience to the Holy Scriptures, taught that the Son is of equal dignity with the Father, and of the same substance with God who begat Him, Arius, in direct opposition to the truth, affirmed that the Son of God is merely a creature or created being, adding the famous dictum, "There once was a time when He was not[5];" with other opinions which may be learned from his own writings. He taught these false doctrines perseveringly, not only in the church, but also in general meetings and assemblies; and he even went from house to house, endeavouring to make men the slaves of his error. Alexander, who was strongly attached to the doctrines of the Apostles, at first tried by exhortations and counsels to convince him of his error; but when he saw him playing the madman[6] and making public declaration of his impiety, he deposed him from the order of the presbytery,

for he heard the law of God loudly declaring, "*If thy right eye offend thee, pluck it out, and cast it from thee[7].*"

CHAPTER II.

List of the principal Bishops.

OF the church of Rome at this period Silvester[1] held the reins. His predecessor in the see was Miltiades[2], the successor of that Marcellinus[3] who had so nobly distinguished himself during the persecution.

In Antioch, after the death of Tyrannus[4], when peace began to be restored to the churches, Vitalis[5] received the chief authority, and restored the church in the "Palæa[6]" which had been destroyed by the tyrants. He was succeeded by Philogonius[7], who completed all that was wanting in the work of restoration: he had, during the time of Licinius, signalised himself by his zeal for religion.

After the administration of Hermon[8], the government of the church in Jerusalem was committed to Macarius[9], a man whose character was equal to his name, and whose mind was adorned by every kind of virtue.

At this same period also, Alexander, illustrious for his apostolical gifts, governed the church of Constantinople[10].

It was at this time that Alexander, bishop of Alexandria, perceiving that Arius, enslaved by the lust of power, was assembling those who had been taken captive by his blasphemous doctrines, and was holding private meetings, communicated an account of his heresy by letter to the rulers of the principal churches. That the authenticity of my history may not be suspected, I shall now insert in my narrative the letter which he wrote to his namesake, containing, as it does, a clear account of all the facts I have mentioned. I shall also subjoin the letter of Arius, together with the other letters which are necessary to the completeness of this narrative, that they may at once testify to the truth of my work, and make the course of events more clear.

The following letter was written by Alexander of Alexandria, to the bishop of the same name as himself.

---

7 ἐὰν . . . σκανδαλίζῃ, St. Matt. v. 29 and xviii. 9; εἰ . . σκανδαλίζει, cf. Mark ix. 43.
1 Bp. of Rome, from Jan. 31, A.D. 314, to Dec. 31, A.D. 335.
2 Otherwise Melchiades. July 2, A.D. 310, to Jan. 10, A.D. 314.
3 Jan. 30, A.D. 296, to Oct. 25, A.D. 304. Accused of apostasy, under Diocletian.
4 Bishop of Antioch during the persecution of Diocletian, καθ' ὃν ἤκμασεν ἡ τῶν ἐκκλησιῶν πολιορκία. Eus. H.E. vii. 32.
5 21st Bp. of Antioch, A.D. 312—A.D. 318.
6 The ancient part of the city of Antioch.
7 A.D. 319—323.　　　　8 A.D. 302—311.
9 Macarius = Blessed. A.D. 311—? 334. Vide Chapters iv. and xvii.　　　10 Circa ? A.D. 313 or 317—340.

---

2 Succeeded Theonas as Archbishop of Alexandria, A.D. 300. Beheaded by order of Maximinus, A.D. 311. Euseb. vii. 32.
3 Patriarch of Alexandria, A.D. 311—312. Promoted Arius to the priesthood. Soz. i. 15.　　4 Patriarch, A.D. 312—326.
5 ἦν ποτε ὅτε οὐκ ἦν.　　6 κορυβαντιῶντα.

CHAPTER III.

The Epistle of Alexander, Bishop of Alexandria, to Alexander, Bishop of Constantinople.

" To his most revered and likeminded brother Alexander, Alexander sendeth greeting in the Lord.

" Impelled by avarice and ambition, evil-minded persons have ever plotted against the wellbeing of the most important dioceses. Under various pretexts, they attack the religion of the Church ; and, being maddened by the devil, who works in them, they start aside from all piety according to their own pleasure, and trample under foot the fear of the judgment of God. Suffering as I do from them myself, I deem it necessary to inform your piety, that you may be on your guard against them, lest they or any of their party should presume to enter your diocese (for these cheats are skilful in deception), or should circulate false and specious letters, calculated to delude one who has devoted himself to the simple and undefiled faith.

" Arius and Achillas have lately formed a conspiracy, and, emulating the ambition of Colluthus, have gone far beyond him [1]. He indeed sought to find a pretext for his own pernicious line of action in the charges he brought against them. But they, beholding his making a trade of Christ for lucre [2], refused to remain any longer in subjection to the Church ; but built for themselves caves, like robbers, and now constantly assemble in them, and day and night ply slanders there against Christ and against us. They revile every godly apostolical doctrine, and in Jewish fashion have organized a gang to fight against Christ, denying His divinity, and declaring Him to be on a level with other men. They pick out every passage which refers to the dispensation of salvation, and to His humiliation for our sake ; they endeavour to collect from them their own impious assertion, while they evade all those which declare His eternal divinity, and the unceasing [3] glory which He possesses with the Father. They maintain the ungodly doctrine entertained by the Greeks and the Jews concerning Jesus Christ ; and thus, by every means in their power, hunt for their applause. Everything which outsiders ridicule

in us they officiously practise. They daily excite persecutions and seditions against us. On the one hand they bring accusations against us before the courts, suborning as witnesses certain unprincipled women whom they have seduced into error. On the other they dishonour Christianity by permitting their young women to ramble about the streets. Nay, they have had the audacity to rend the seamless garment of Christ, which the soldiers dared not divide.

" When these actions, in keeping with their course of life, and the impious enterprise which had been long concealed, became tardily known to us, we unanimously ejected them from the Church which worships the divinity of Christ. They then ran hither and thither to form cabals against us, even addressing themselves to our fellow-ministers who were of one mind with us, under the pretence of seeking peace and unity with them, but in truth endeavouring by means of fair words, to sweep some among them away into their own disease. They ask them to write a wordy letter, and then read the contents to those whom they have deceived, in order that they may not retract, but be confirmed in their impiety, by finding that bishops agree with and support their views. They make no acknowledgment of the evil doctrines and practices for which they have been expelled by us, but they either impart them without comment, or carry on the deception by fallacies and forgeries. Thus concealing their destructive doctrine by persuasive and meanly truckling language, they catch the unwary, and lose no opportunity of calumniating our religion. Hence it arises that several have been led to sign their letter, and to receive them into communion, a proceeding on the part of our fellow-ministers which I consider highly reprehensible; for they thus not only disobey the apostolical rule, but even help to inflame their diabolical action against Christ. It is on this account, beloved brethren, that without delay I have stirred myself up to inform you of the unbelief of certain persons who say that " There was a time when the Son of God was not [4];" and " He who previously had no existence subsequently came into existence ; and when at some time He came into existence He became such as every other man is." God, they say, created all things out of that which was non-existent, and they include in the number of creatures, both rational and irrational, even the Son of God. Consistently with this doctrine they, as a necessary consequence, affirm that He

---

[1] Alexander's words seem to imply that Colluthus began his schismatical proceedings in assuming to exercise episcopal functions before the separation of Arius from the Church, and that one cause of his wrong action was impatience at the mild course at first adopted by Alexander towards Arius. The Council of Alexandria held in A.D. 324 under Hosius, decided that he was only a Presbyter.

[2] χριστεμπορία. The word χριστέμπορος is applied in the "Didache" to lazy consumers of alms. Cf. Ps. Ignat. ad Trall. : οὐ χριστιανοὶ ἀλλὰ χριστέμποροι, Ps. Ignat. ad Mag. ix., and Bp. Lightfoot's note.

[3] Readings vary between ἄλεκτος = indescribable, and ἄληκτος = ceaseless. Cf. Ἀληκτώ, the Fury.

[4] Ἦν ποτε ὅτε οὐκ ἦν ὁ υἱὸς τοῦ θεοῦ. καὶ Γέγονεν ὕστερον ὁ πρότερον μὴ ὑπάρχων τοιοῦτος γενόμενος ὅτε καί ποτε γέγονεν οἷος καὶ πᾶς πέφυκεν ἄνθρωπος.

is by nature liable to change, and capable both of virtue and of vice, and thus, by their hypothesis of his having been created out of that which was non-existent, they overthrow the testimony of the Divine Scriptures, which declare the immutability of the Word and the Divinity of the Wisdom of the Word, which Word and Wisdom is Christ. 'We are also able,' say these accursed wretches, ' to become like Him, the sons of God ; for it is written,—*I have nourished and brought up children*[5].' When the continuation of this text is brought before them, which is, '*and they have rebelled against Me*,' and it is objected that these words are inconsistent with the Saviour's nature, which is immutable, they throw aside all reverence, and affirm that God foreknew and foresaw that His Son would not rebel against Him, and that He therefore chose Him in preference to all others. They likewise assert that He was not chosen because He had by nature any thing superior to the other sons of God ; for no man, say they, is son of God by nature, nor has any peculiar relation to Him. He was chosen, they allege, because, though mutable by nature, His painstaking character suffered no deterioration. As though, forsooth, even if a Paul and a Peter made like endeavours, their sonship would in no respects differ from His.

"To establish this insane doctrine they insult the Scriptures, and bring forward what is said in the Psalms of Christ, ' *Thou hast loved righteousness and hated iniquity, therefore thy God hath anointed thee with the oil of gladness above thy fellows*[6].' Now that the Son of God was not created out of the non-existent[7], and that there never was a time in which He was not, is expressly taught by John the Evangelist, who speaks of Him as ' *the only begotten Son which is in the bosom of the Father*[8].' This divine teacher desired to show that the Father and the Son are inseparable ; and, therefore, he said, ' that the Son is in the bosom of the Father.' Moreover, the same John affirms that the Word of God is not classed among things created out of the non-existent, for, he says that ' *all things were made by Him*[9],' and he also declares His individual personality[10] in the following words : ' *In the beginning was the Word, and the Word was with God, and the Word was God. . . . All things were made by Him, and without Him was not any thing made that was made*[11].' If, then, all things were made by

Him, how is it that He who thus bestowed existence on all, could at any period have had no existence himself? The Word, the creating power, can in no way be defined as of the same nature as the things created, if indeed He was in the beginning, and all things were made by Him, and were called by Him out of the non-existent into being. ' *That which is*[12]' must be of an opposite nature to, and essentially different from, things created out of the non-existent. This shows, likewise, that there is no separation between the Father and the Son, and that the idea of separation cannot even be conceived by the mind ; while the fact that the world was created out of the non-existent involves a later and fresh genesis of its essential nature[13], all things having been endowed with such an origin of existence by the Father through the Son. John, the most pious apostle, perceiving that the word 'was' applied to the Word of God[14] was far beyond and above the intelligence of created beings, did not presume to speak of His generation or creation, nor yet dared to name the Maker and the creature in equivalent syllables. Not that the Son of God is unbegotten, for the Father alone is unbegotten ; but that the ineffable personality of the only-begotten God

---

[5] Isai. i. 2. υἱοὺς ἐγέννησα καὶ ὕψωσα, as in Sept. Vulg., *filios enutrivi et exaltavi.* Revd., marg., " made great and exalted."
[6] Ps. xlv. 7, as in Sept., except that ἀδικίαν is substituted for ἀνομίαν.
[7] Οὔτε ἐξ οὐκ ὄντων γεγένηται.
[8] John i. 18.　[9] John i. 3.　[10] ὑπόστασιν.
[11] John i. 1, 3.

[12] τὸ ὄν, the self-existent of philosophy.
[13] The history of the word ὑπόστασις is of crucial value in the study of the Arian controversy. Its various usages may be classified as (i) *Classical ;* (ii) *Scriptural ;* (iii) *Ecclesiastical.* The correlative substantive of the verb ὑφίστημι, I make to stand under, [from ὑπό = sub. under, and ἵστημι, |STA] ; it means primarily a *standing under.* Hence, materially, it means in (i) Classical Greek, sediment, prop. foundation : substances as opposed to their reflexions, substantial nature, as of timber [Theoph. C. P. 5. 16. 4]. So naturally grew the signification of ground of hope, actual existence ; and, in the later philosophy, it had come to be employed instead of οὐσία for the noetic substratum "underlying" the phænomena. (ii) Scriptural. In the N.T. it is found five times, twice in 2 Cor. and thrice in Heb. (α) 2 Cor. ix. 4, and (β) xi. 17. "Confidence" of boasting. (γ) Heb. i. 3, ὁ χαρακτὴρ τῆς ὑποστάσεως, A.V. the express image of His " person." R.V., the very image of His "substance.' (δ) Heb. iii. 14, "Confidence." (ε) Heb. xi. 1, A.V. "substance" of things hoped for. R.V. Assurance of things hoped for. (iii) Ecclesiastical. The earlier ecclesiastical use, like the later philosophical, identified it with οὐσία, and so the Nicene Confession anathematized those who maintained the Son to be of a different substance or essence from the Father (ὑποστάσεως ἢ οὐσίας). In the version of Hilary of Poictiers (*de Synodis*, § 84 ; Op. ii. 510) οὐσία is translated by " substantia," the etymological equivalent of ὑπόστασις, except in the phrase quoted, when " substantia aut essentia" represents οὐσία by its own etymological equivalent " essentia." Thus in A.D. 325 to have contended for τρεῖς ὑποστάσεις would have been heretical. But as the subtilty of controversy required greater nicety of phrase, it was laid down (Basil the Great, Ep. 38) that while οὐσία is an universal denoting that which is common to the individuals of a species, ὑπόστασις makes an individual that which it is, and constitutes personal existence. Hence μία ὑπόστασις became Sabellian, and τρεῖς οὐσίαι Arian, while τρεῖς ὑποστάσεις was orthodox. cf. Theod. Dial. i. 7. Eranistes loq. "Is there any distinction between οὐσία and ὑπόστασις ?"
Orthodoxus. "In extra-Christian philosophy there is not ; for οὐσία signifies τὸ ὄν, that which is, and ὑπόστασις that which subsists. But according to the doctrine of the Fathers there is the same difference between οὐσία and ὑπόστασις as between the common and the particular ; the race, and the species or individual." . . "The Divine οὐσία (substance) means the Holy Trinity ; but the ὑπόστασις indicates any πρόσωπον (person) as of the Father, the Son, or of the Holy Ghost. For we who follow the definitions of the Fathers assert ὑπόστασις, πρόσωπον and ἰδιότης (substantial nature, person, or individuality) to mean the same thing." Vide also Newman's *Arians of the Fourth Century*, Appendix, Note iv. fourth Edition.
[14] "In the beginning *was* the word." John i. 1.

is beyond the keenest conception of the evangelists and perhaps even of angels. Therefore, I do not think men ought to be considered pious who presume to investigate this subject, in disobedience to the injunction, ' *Seek not what is too difficult for thee, neither enquire into what is too high for thee* [15].' For if the knowledge of many other things incomparably inferior is beyond the capacity of the human mind, and cannot therefore be attained, as has been said by Paul, ' *Eye hath not seen, nor ear heard, neither have entered into the heart of man, the things which God hath prepared for them that love Him* [16],' and as God also said to Abraham, that the stars could not be numbered by him [17]; and it is likewise said, ' *Who shall number the grains of sand by the sea-shore, or the drops of rain* [18] ?' how then can any one but a madman presume to enquire into the nature of the Word of God? It is said by the Spirit of prophecy, ' *Who shall declare His generation* [19] ?' And, therefore, our Saviour in His kindness to those men who were the pillars of the whole world, desiring to relieve them of the burden of striving after this knowledge, told them that it was beyond their natural comprehension, and that the Father alone could discern this most divine mystery; ' *No man,*' said He, ' *knoweth the Son but the Father, and no man knoweth the Father save the Son* [20].' It was, I think, concerning this same subject that the Father said, ' *My secret is for Me and for Mine* [21].'

" But the insane folly of imagining that the Son of God came into being out of that which had no being, and that His sending forth took place in time, is plain from the words ' which had no being,' although the foolish are incapable of perceiving the folly of their own utterances. For the phrase ' He was not' must either have reference to time, or to some interval in the ages. If then it be true that all things were made by Him, it is evident that every age, time, all intervals of time, and that ' when ' in which ' was not' has its place, were made by Him. And is it not absurd to say that there was a time when He who created all time, and ages, and seasons, with which the ' was not' is confused, was not? For it would be the height of ignorance, and contrary indeed to all reason, to affirm that the cause of any created thing can be posterior to that caused by it. The interval during which they say the Son was still unbegotten of the Father was, according to their opinion, prior to the wisdom of God, by whom all things were created.

They thus contradict the Scripture which declares Him to be ' the *firstborn of every creature* [22].' In consonance with this doctrine, Paul with his usual mighty voice cries concerning Him ; ' *whom He hath appointed heir of all things, by whom also He made the worlds* [23].' ' *For by Him were all things created that are in heaven, and that are in earth, visible and invisible, whether they be thrones, or dominions, or principalities, or powers: all things were created by Him and for Him: and He is before all things* [24].' Since the hypothesis implied in the phrase ' out of the non-existent' is manifestly impious, it follows that the Father is always Father. And He is Father from the continual presence of the Son, on account of whom He is called [25] Father. And the Son being ever present with Him, the Father is ever perfect, wanting in no good thing, for He did not beget His only Son in time, or in any interval of time, nor out of that which had no previous existence.

" Is it not then impious to say that there was a time when the wisdom of God was not? Who saith, ' *I was by Him as one brought up with Him: I was daily His delight* [26] ?' Or that once the power of God was not, or His Word, or anything else by which the Son is known, or the Father designated, defective? To assert that the brightness of the Father's glory ' once did not exist,' destroys also the original light of which it is the brightness [27]; and if there ever was a time in which the image of God was not, it is plain that He Whose image He is, is not always : nay, by the non-existence of the express image of God's Person, He also is taken away of whom this is ever the express image. Hence it may be seen, that the Sonship of our Saviour has not even anything in common with the sonship of men. For just as it has been shown that the nature of His existence cannot be expressed by language, and infinitely surpasses in excellence all things to which He has given being, so His Sonship, naturally partaking in His paternal Divinity, is unspeakably different from the sonship of those who, by His appointment, have been adopted as sons. He is by nature immutable, perfect, and all-sufficient, whereas men are liable to change, and need His help. What further advance can be made by the

---

[15] Ecclus. iii. 21.
[16] 1 Cor. ii. 9.
[17] Gen. xv. 5.
[18] Ecclus. i. 2.
[19] Isai. liii. 8.
[20] Matt. xi. 27.
[21] Is. xxiv. 16 : "My leanness, my leanness, woe unto me." A.V. " *Secretum meum mihi.*" Vulg.

[22] Col. i. 15.
[23] Heb. i. 2. Vide Alford. proleg. to Ep. to Heb., " Nowhere except in the Alexandrian Church does there seem to have existed any idea that the Epistle was St. Paul's." " At Alexandria the conventional habit of quoting the Epistle as St. Paul's gradually prevailed over critical suspicion and early tradition."
[24] Col. i. 16, 17.
[25] χρηματίζω = (i) to have dealings with ; (ii) to deal with an oracle or divine power ; (iii) to get a name for dealing, and so to *be called.* Cf. Matt. ii. 12 ; Acts xi. 26.
[26] Prov. viii. 30.
[27] Heb. i. 3. ὤν ἀπαύγασμα τῆς Δόξης καὶ χαρακτὴρ τῆς ὑποστάσεως αὐτοῦ.

wisdom of God[28]? What can the Very Truth, or God the Word, add to itself? How can the Life or the True Light in any way be bettered? And is it not still more contrary to nature to suppose that wisdom can be susceptible of folly? that the power of God can be united with weakness? that reason itself can be dimmed by unreasonableness, or that darkness can be mixed with the true light? Does not the Apostle say, ' *What communion hath light with darkness? and what concord hath Christ with Belial*[29]?' and Solomon, that ' *the way of a serpent upon a rock*[30]' was ' *too wonderful*' for the human mind to comprehend, which 'rock,' according to St. Paul, is Christ[31]. Men and angels, however, who are His creatures, have received His blessing, enabling them to exercise themselves in virtue and in obedience to His commands, that thus they may avoid sin. And it is on this account that our Lord, being by nature the Son of the Father, is worshipped by all; and they who have put off the spirit of bondage, and by brave deeds and advance in virtue have received the spirit of adoption through the kindness of Him Who is the Son of God by nature, by adoption also become sons.

"His true, peculiar, natural, and special Sonship was declared by Paul, who, speaking of God, says, that ' *He spared not His own Son, but delivered Him up for us*[32],' who are not by nature His sons. It was to distinguish Him from those who are not ' *His own*,' that he called Him ' *His own son.*' It is also written in the Gospel, ' *This is My beloved Son in whom I am well pleased*[33];' and in the Psalms the Saviour says, ' *The Lord said unto Me, Thou art My Son*[34].' By proclaiming natural sonship He shows that there are no other natural sons besides Himself.

" And do not these words, I begot thee 'from the womb before the morning[35],' plainly show the natural sonship of the paternal birth[36] of One whose lot it is, not from diligence of conduct, or exercise in moral progress, but by individuality of nature? Hence it ensues that the filiation of the only-begotten Son of the Father is incapable of fall; while the adoption of reasonable beings who are not His sons by nature, but merely on account of fitness of character, and by the bounty of God, may fall away, as it is written in the word, ' *The sons of God saw the daughters of men, and took them as wives*,' and so forth[37]. And

God, speaking by Isaiah, said, ' *I have nourished and brought up children, and they have rebelled against Me*[38].'

" I have many things to say, beloved, but because I fear that I shall cause weariness by further admonishing teachers who are of one mind with myself, I pass them by. You, having been taught of God, are not ignorant that the teaching at variance with the religion of the Church which has just arisen, is the same as that propagated by Ebion[39] and Artemas[40], and rivals that of Paul of Samosata, bishop of Antioch, who was excommunicated by a council of all the bishops. Lucianus[41], his successor, withdrew himself from communion with these bishops during a period of many years.

" And now amongst us there have sprung up, 'out of the non-existent' men who have greedily sucked down the dregs of this impiety, offsets of the same stock: I mean Arius and Achillas, and all their gang of rogues. Three bishops[42] of Syria, appointed no one knows how, by consenting to them, fire them to more fatal heat. I refer their sentence to your decision. Retaining in their memory all that they can collect concerning the suffering, humiliation, emptying of Himself[43], and so-called poverty, and everything of which the Saviour for our sake accepted the acquired name, they bring forward those passages to disprove His eternal existence and divinity, while they forget all those which declare His glory and nobility and abiding with the Father; as for instance, ' *I and My Father are one*[44].' In these words the Lord does not proclaim Himself to be the Father, neither does He represent two natures as one; but that the essence of the Son of the Father preserves accurately the likeness of the Father, His nature taking off the impress of likeness to Him in all things, being the exact image of the Father and the express stamp of the prototype. When, therefore, Philip, desirous of seeing the Father, said to Him, ' *Lord, show us the Father*,' the Lord with abundant plainness said to him, ' *He that hath seen Me hath seen the Father*[45],' as though the Father

---

[28] Contrast the advance of the manhood. Luke ii. 52, "πρού-κοπτε," the word used in the text.
[29] 2 Cor. vi. 14, 15.　　[30] Prov. xxx. 19.　　[31] 1 Cor. x. 4.
[32] Rom. viii. 32.　　[33] Matt. iii. 17.　　[34] Ps. ii. 7.
[35] Ps. cx. 3.　Sept. ἐκ γαστρὸς πρὸ Ἑωσφόρου ἐγέννησά σε.
[36] The readings vary between γεννήσεως, γενέσεως, and μαιεύσεως (cf. Plat. Theæt. 150 B), which is adopted by Valesius.
[37] Gen. vi. 2.

[38] Isa. i. 2.
[39] The imaginary name for the founder of Ebionism, first started by Tertullian. אֶבְיוֹן = poor.
[40] Artemas, or Artemon, a philosophizing denier of Christ's divinity, excommunicated by Pope Zephyrinus (A.D. 202—21).
[41] Lucianus, the presbyter of Antioch, who became the head of the theological school of that city in which the leaders of the Arian heresy were trained, after the deposition of Paulus refused to hold communion with his three successors in the patriarchate, Domnus, Timæus, and Cyril. During the episcopate of the last named he once more entered into communion with the church of Antioch. On the importance of Lucianus as founder of the Arians, Vide Newman's *Arians of the Fourth Century*, Chap. I. Sec. i. and cf. the letter of Arius post. Chap. iv.
[42] Eusebius of Cæsarea, Theodotus of Laodicea, and Paulinus of Tyre. See Arius' letter to Eusebius of Nicomedia, ch. iv.
[43] κένωσις, cf. Phil. ii. 7.
[44] John x. 30.　　[45] John xiv. 9.

were beheld in the spotless and living mirror of His image. The same idea is conveyed in the Psalms, where the saints say, '*In Thy light we shall see light* [46].' It is on this account that '*he who honoureth the Son, honoureth the Father* [47].' And rightly, for every impious word which men dare to utter against the Son is spoken also against the Father.

"After this no one can wonder at the false calumnies which I am about to detail, my beloved brethren, propagated by them against me, and against our most religious people. They not only set their battle in array against the divinity of Christ, but ungratefully insult us. They think it beneath them to be compared with any of those of old time, nor do they endure to be put on a par with the teachers we have been conversant with from childhood. They will not admit that any of our fellow-ministers anywhere possess even mediocrity of intelligence. They say that they themselves alone are the wise and the poor, and discoverers of doctrines, and to them alone have been revealed those truths which, say they, have never entered the mind of any other individuals under the sun. O what wicked arrogance! O what excessive folly! What false boasting, joined with madness and Satanic pride, has hardened their impious hearts! They are not ashamed to oppose the godly clearness of the ancient scriptures, nor yet does the unanimous piety of all our fellow-ministers concerning Christ blunt their audacity. Even devils will not suffer impiety like this; for even they refrain from speaking blasphemy against the Son of God.

"These then are the questions I have to raise, according to the ability I possess, with those who from their rude resources throw dust on the Christ, and try to slander our reverence for Him. These inventors of silly tales assert that we, who reject their impious and unscriptural blasphemy concerning the creation of Christ from the non-existent, teach that there are two unbegotten Beings. For these ill-instructed men contend that one of these alternatives must hold; either He must be believed to have come out of the non-existent, or there are two unbegotten Beings. In their ignorance and want of practice in theology they do not realize how vast must be the distance between the Father who is uncreate, and the creatures, whether rational or irrational, which He created out of the non-existent; and that the only-begotten nature of Him Who is the Word of God, by Whom the Father created the universe out of the non-existent, standing, as it were, in the middle between the two, was

begotten of the self-existent Father, as the Lord Himself testified when He said, '*Every one that loveth the Father, loveth also the Son that is begotten of Him* [48].'

"We believe, as is taught by the apostolical Church, in an only unbegotten Father, Who of His being hath no cause, immutable and invariable, and Who subsists always in one state of being, admitting neither of progression nor of diminution; Who gave the law, and the prophets, and the gospel; of patriarchs and apostles, and of all saints, Lord: and in one Lord Jesus Christ, the only-begotten Son of God, begotten not out of that which is not, but of the Father, Who is; yet not after the manner of material bodies, by severance or emanation, as Sabellius [49] and Valentinus [50] taught; but in an inexpressible and inexplicable manner, according to the saying which we quoted above, '*Who shall declare His generation* [51]?' since no mortal intellect can comprehend the nature of His Person, as the Father Himself cannot be comprehended, because the nature of reasonable beings is unable to grasp the manner in which He was begotten of the Father [52].

"But those who are led by the Spirit of truth have no need to learn these things of me, for the words long since spoken by the Saviour yet sound in our ears, '*No one knoweth who the Father is but the Son, and no one knoweth who the Son is but the Father* [53].' We have learnt that the Son is immutable and unchangeable, all-sufficient and perfect, like the Father, lacking only His "unbegotten." He is the exact and precisely similar image of His Father. For it is clear that the image fully contains everything by which the greater likeness exists, as the Lord taught us when He said, '*My Father is greater than I* [54].' And in accordance with this we believe that the Son always existed of the Father; for he is the *brightness of His glory*, and the express *image of His Father's Person* [55].' But let no one be led by the word '*always*' to imagine that the Son is unbegotten, as is thought by some who have their intellects blinded: for to say that He was, that He has always been, and that before all ages, is not to say that He is unbegotten.

"The mind of man could not possibly invent a term expressive of what is meant by being unbegotten. I believe that you are of this opinion; and, indeed, I feel confident in your orthodox view that none of these terms in any way signify the unbegotten. For all the terms

---

46 Ps. xxxvi. 9.　　　　47 John v. 23.

48 1 John v. 1.
49 Condemned A.D. 261 by Council held at Alexandria.
50 Taught in Rome in A.D. 140, and died in Cyprus in A.D. 160.
51 Isa. liii. 8.　　52 ἡ πατρικὴ θεογονία.　　53 Matt. xi. 27 : observe the slight variation.　54 John xiv. 28.　55 Heb. i. 3.

appear to signify merely the extension of time, and are not adequate to express the divinity and, as it were, the primæval being of the only-begotten Son. They were used by the holy men who earnestly endeavoured to clear up the mystery, and who asked pardon from those who heard them, with a reasonable excuse for their failure, by saying 'as far as our comprehension has reached.' But if those who allege that what was '*known in part*' has been '*done away*[56]' for them, expect from human lips anything beyond human powers, it is plain that the terms 'was,' and 'ever,' and 'before all ages,' fall far short of this expectation. But whatever, they may mean, it is not the same as 'the unbegotten.' Therefore His own individual dignity must be reserved to the Father as the Unbegotten One, no one being called the cause of His existence : to the Son likewise must be given the honour which befits Him, there being to Him a generation from the Father which has no beginning ; we must render Him worship, as we have already said, only piously and religiously ascribing to Him the 'was' and the 'ever,' and the 'before all ages ;' not however rejecting His divinity, but ascribing to Him a perfect likeness in all things to His Father, while at the same time we ascribe to the Father alone His own proper glory of 'the unbegotten,' even as the Saviour Himself says, '*My Father is greater than I*[57].'

"And in addition to this pious belief respecting the Father and the Son, we confess, as the Sacred Scriptures teach us, one Holy Ghost, who moved the saints of the Old Testament, and the divine teachers of that which is called the New. We believe in one only Catholic Church, the apostolical, which cannot be destroyed even though all the world were to take counsel to fight against it, and which gains the victory over all the impious attacks of the heterodox ; for we are emboldened by the words of its Master, '*Be of good cheer, I have overcome the world*[58].' After this, we receive the doctrine of the resurrection from the dead, of which Jesus Christ our Lord became the first-fruits ; Who bore a Body, in truth, not in semblance, derived from Mary the mother of God[59] ; in the fulness of time sojourning among the race, for the remission of sins : who was crucified and died, yet for all this suffered no diminution of His Godhead. He rose from the dead, was taken into heaven, and sat down at the right hand of the Majesty on high.

" In this epistle I have only mentioned these things in part, deeming it, as I have said, wearisome to dwell minutely on each article, since they are well known to your pious diligence. These things we teach, these things we preach ; these are the dogmas of the apostolic Church, for which we are ready to die, caring little for those who would force us to forswear them ; for we will never relinquish our hope in them, though they should try to compel us by tortures.

"Arius and Achillas, together with their fellow foes, have been expelled from the Church, because they have become aliens from our pious doctrine : according to the blessed Paul, who said, '*If any of you preach any other gospel than that which you have received, let him be accursed, even though he should pretend to be an angel from heaven*[60], and '*But if any man teach otherwise, and consent not to wholesome words, even the words of our Lord Jesus Christ, and to the doctrine which is according to godliness, he is proud, knowing nothing*[61],' and so forth. Since, then, they have been condemned by the brotherhood, let none of you receive them, nor attend to what they say or write. They are deceivers, and propagate lies, and they never adhere to the truth. They go about to different cities with no other intent than to deliver letters under the pretext of friendship and in the name of peace, and by hypocrisy and flattery to obtain other letters in return, in order to deceive a few '*silly women who are laden with sins*[62].' I beseech you, beloved brethren, to avoid those who have thus dared to act against Christ, who have publicly held up the Christian religion to ridicule, and have eagerly sought to make a display before judicial tribunals, who have endeavoured to excite a persecution against us at a period of the most entire peace, and who have enervated the unspeakable mystery of the generation of Christ. Unite unanimously in opposition to them, as some of our fellow-ministers have already done, who, being filled with indignation, wrote to me against them, and signed our formulary[63].

" I have sent you these letters by my son Apion, the deacon ; being those of (the ministers in) all Egypt and the Thebaid, also of those of Libya, and the Pentapolis, of Syria, Lycia, Pamphylia, Asia, Cappadocia, and in the other adjoining countries. Whose example you likewise, I trust, will follow. Many kindly attempts have been made by me to gain back those who have been led astray, but no remedy has proved more efficacious in restoring the laity who have been deceived by them and leading them to repentance, than

---

[56] 1 Cor. xiii. 10.   [57] John xiv. 28.
[58] John xvi. 33.   [59] ἐκ τῆς Θεοτόκου Μαρίας.

[60] Gal. i. 9.   [61] 1 Tim. vi. 3, 4.   [62] 2 Tim. iii. 6.
[63] Τόμος. (i) a cut or slice ; (ii) a portion of a roll, volume, or " tome."

the manifestation of the union of our fellow-ministers. Salute one another, with the brotherhood that is with you. I pray that you may be strong in the Lord, my beloved, and that I may receive the fruit of your love to Christ.

"The following are the name of those who have been anathematized as heretics : among the presbyters, Arius ; among the deacons, Achillas, Euzoius, Aïthales, Lucius, Sarmates, Julius, Menas, another Arius, and Helladius."

Alexander wrote in the same strain to Philogonius [64], bishop of Antioch, to Eustathius [65], who then ruled the church of the Berœans, and to all those who defended the doctrines of the Apostles. But Arius could not endure to keep quiet, but wrote to all those whom he believed to agree with him in opinion. His letter to Eusebius, bishop of Nicomedia, is a clear proof that the divine Alexander wrote nothing that was false concerning him. I shall here insert his letter, in order that the names of those who were implicated in his impiety may become generally known.

CHAPTER IV.

The Letter of Arius to Eusebius, Bishop of Nicomedia.

"To his very dear lord, the man of God, the faithful and orthodox Eusebius, Arius, unjustly persecuted by Alexander the Pope [1], on account of that all-conquering truth of which you also are a champion, sendeth greeting in the Lord.

"Ammonius, my father, being about to depart for Nicomedia, I considered myself bound to salute you by him, and withal to inform that natural affection which you bear towards the brethren for the sake of God and His Christ, that the bishop greatly wastes and persecutes us, and leaves no stone unturned [2] against us. He has driven us out of the city as atheists, because we do not concur in what he publicly preaches, namely, God always, the Son always ; as the Father so the Son ; the Son co-exists unbegotten with God ; He is everlasting ; neither by thought nor by any interval does God precede the Son ; always God, always Son ; he is begotten of the unbegotten ; the Son is of God Himself. Eusebius,

your brother bishop of Cæsarea, Theodotus, Paulinus, Athanasius, Gregorius, Aëtius, and all the bishops of the East, have been condemned because they say that God had an existence prior to that of His Son ; except Philogonius, Hellanicus, and Macarius, who are unlearned men, and who have embraced heretical opinions. Some of them say that the Son is an eructation, others that He is a production, others that He is also unbegotten. These are impieties to which we cannot listen, even though the heretics threaten us with a thousand deaths. But we say and believe, and have taught, and do teach, that the Son is not unbegotten, nor in any way part of the unbegotten ; and that He does not derive His subsistence from any matter ; but that by His own will and counsel He has subsisted before time, and before ages, as perfect God, only begotten and unchangeable, and that before He was begotten, or created, or purposed, or established, He was not. For He was not unbegotten. We are persecuted, because we say that the Son has a beginning, but that God is without beginning. This is the cause of our persecution, and likewise, because we say that He is of the non-existent [3]. And this we say, because He is neither part of God, nor of any essential being [4]. For this are we persecuted ; the rest you know. I bid thee farewell in the Lord, remembering our afflictions, my fellow-Lucianist [5], and true Eusebius [6]."

Of those whose names are mentioned in this letter, Eusebius was bishop of Cæsarea [7], Theo-

---

3 ἐξ οὐκ ὄντων ἐστιν.

4 ἐξ ὑποκειμένου τινός. Aristotle, Metaph. vi. 3, 1, defines τὸ ὑποκείμενον as that καθ' οὗ τὰ ἄλλα λέγεται. . . . μάλιστα δὲ δοκεῖ εἶναι οὐσία τὸ ὑποκείμενον πρῶτον.

5 Arius and Eusebius had been fellow disciples of Lucianus the Priest of Antioch martyred under Maximinus in A.D. 311 or 312. Vide note on page 38.

6 Arius plays on the name Eusebius, εὐσεβής, pious.

7 From the phrase, "ὁ ἀδελφός σου ὁ ἐν Καισαρείᾳ," it has been inferred by some that the two Eusebii were actually brothers. Eusebius of Nicomedia, in the letter of Chapter V., calls the Palestinian δεσπότης ; but this alone would not be fatal to the brotherhood, for Seneca (*Ep. Mor.* 104), calls his brother Gallio *dominus*. The phrase of Arius is not worth much against the silence of every one else. Vid. Dict. Christ. Biog. Article, Eusebius.

Theodotus, bishop of Laodicea, in Syria, (not the Phrygian Laodicea of the Apocalypse), was a Physician of the body as well as of the soul (*Euseb.* H.E. vii. 32).

Paulinus, bishop first of Tyre, and then of Antioch for six months, died in A.D. 329. (*Philost.* H.E. iii. 15, cf. Bishop Lightfoot in Dict. Christian Biog. Article, Eusebius of Cæsarea).

Athanasius, bishop of Anazarbus, an important town of Cilicia Campestris, is accused of dangerous Arianism by his great namesake. (*Athan. de Synod*, 584).

Gregorius succeeded Eusebius of Nicomedia at Berytus (Beyrout), on the translation of the latter to Nicomedia.

Aetius, Bishop of Lydda, (the Lydda of the Acts, on the plain of Sharon, now Ludd, the city of El-Khudr, who is identified with St. George), died soon after the Arian Synod of Antioch, A.D. 330 (*Philost.* H.E. iii. 12), and is to be distinguished from the arch-Arian Aetius, Julian's friend, who survived' till A.D. 367 (*Phil.* H.E. ix. 6).

Philogonius was raised to the episcopate *per saltum*, like St. Ambrose (*Chrysost. Orat.* 71, tom. v. p. 507), he preceded the Arian Paulinus.

Hellanicus was present at Nicæa, but was driven from the See of Tripolis, in Phœnicia, by the Arians (*Athan. Hist. Ar. ad Mon.* § 5).

---

64 Vide supra.

65 Bp. first of Berœa in Syria and then of Antioch, c. 324—331. Berœa, the Helbon of Ezekiel (xxvii. 18) is now Aleppo or Haleb.

1 On the name " Pope," vide Dict. Christ. Ant., s.v. 1st, it was applied to the teachers of converts, 2ndly, to Bishops and Abbots, and was, 3rdly, confined to the Patriarchs of Alexandria, Antioch, Jerusalem, Constantinople, and to the Bp. of Rome ; 4thly, it was claimed by the Bp. of Rome exclusively.

2 πάντα κάλων κινεῖ. Cf. Luc. Scyth. ii. The common proverb was πάντα ἐξιέναι κάλων, to let out every reef. Ar. Eq. 756 Eur. Med. 278, &c.

dotus of Laodicea, Paulinus of Tyre, Athanasius of Anazarbus, Gregorius of Berytus, and Aetius of Lydda. Lydda is now called Diospolis. Arius prided himself on having these men of one mind with himself. He names as his adversaries, Philogonius, bishop of Antioch, Hellanicus, of Tripolis, and Macarius, of Jerusalem. He spread calumnies against them because they said that the Son is eternal, existing before all ages, of equal honour and of the same substance with the Father.

When Eusebius received the epistle, he too vomited forth his own impiety, and wrote to Paulinus, chief [8] of the Tyrians, in the following words.

CHAPTER V.

The Letter of Eusebius, Bishop of Nicomedia, to Paulinus, Bishop of Tyre.

"To my lord Paulinus, Eusebius sendeth greeting in the Lord.

"The zeal of my lord Eusebius in the cause of the truth, and likewise your silence concerning it, have not failed to reach our ears. Accordingly, if, on the one hand, we rejoiced on account of the zeal of my lord Eusebius; on the other we are grieved at you, because even the silence of such a man appears like a defeat of our cause. Hence, as it behoves not a wise man to be of a different opinion from others, and to be silent concerning the truth, stir up, I exhort you, within yourself the spirit of wisdom to write, and at length begin what may be profitable to yourself and to others, specially if you consent to write in accordance with Scripture, and tread in the tracks of its words and will.

"We have never heard that there are two unbegotten beings, nor that one has been divided into two, nor have we learned or believed that it has ever undergone any change of a corporeal nature; but we affirm that the unbegotten is one, and one also that which exists in truth by Him, yet was not made out of His substance, and does not at all participate in the nature or substance of the unbegotten, entirely distinct in nature and in power, and made after perfect likeness both of character and power to the maker. We believe that the mode of His beginning not only cannot be expressed by words but even in thought, and is incomprehensible not only to man, but also to all beings superior to man. These opinions we advance, not as having derived them from our own imagination, but as having deduced them from Scripture, whence we learn that the Son was created, established, and begotten in the same substance and in the same immutable and inexpressible nature as the Maker; and so the Lord says, ' *God created me in the beginning of His way; I was set up from everlasting; before the hills was I brought forth* [1].'

"If He had been from Him or of Him, as a portion of Him, or by an emanation of His substance, it could not be said that He was created or established; and of this you, my lord, are certainly not ignorant. For that which is of the unbegotten could not be said to have been created or founded, either by Him or by another, since it is unbegotten from the beginning. But if the fact of His being called the begotten gives any ground for the belief that, having come into being of the Father's substance, He also has from the Father likeness of nature, we reply that it is not of Him alone that the Scriptures have spoken as begotten, but that they also thus speak of those who are entirely dissimilar to Him by nature. For of men it is said, ' *I have begotten and brought up sons, and they have rebelled against me* [2];' and in another place, ' *Thou hast forsaken God who begat thee* [3];' and again it is said, '*Who begat the drops of dew* [4]?' This expression does not imply that the dew partakes of the nature of God, but simply that all things were formed according to His will. There is, indeed, nothing which is of His substance, yet every thing which exists has been called into being by His will. He is God; and all things were made in His likeness, and in the future likeness of His Word, being created of His free will. All things were made by His means by God. All things are of God.

"When you have received my letter, and have revised it according to the knowledge and grace given you by God, I beg you will write as soon as possible to my lord Alexander. I feel confident that if you would write to him, you would succeed in bringing him over to your opinion. Salute all the brethren in the Lord. May you, my lord, be preserved by the grace of God, and be led to pray for us."

It is thus that they wrote to each other, in order to furnish one another with weapons against the truth [5]. And so when the blasphemous doctrine had been disseminated in the churches of Egypt and of the East, disputes and contentions arose in every city, and in every village, concerning theological dogmas. The common people looked on, and became judges

---

Macarius is praised by Athanasius (*Orat. I. adv. Arian.* p. 291). On a possible "passage of arms" between him and Eusebius of Cæsarea at Nicæa, vide Stanley, *Eastern Church*, Lect. V. Cf. *post*, cap. xvii.
8 ἡγούμενος.

1 Prov. viii. 22—26 Sept.   2 Isa. i 2.
3 Deut. xxxii. 18.   4 Job xxxviii. 28.
5 Arius first published his heresy, A.D. 319.

of what was said on either side, and some applauded one party, and some the other. These were, indeed, scenes fit for the tragic stage, over which tears might have been shed. For it was not, as in bygone days, when the church was attacked by strangers and by enemies, but now natives of the same country, who dwelt under one roof, and sat down at one table, fought against each other not with spears, but with their tongues. And what was still more sad, they who thus took up arms against one another were members of one another, and belonged to one body.

CHAPTER VI.

General Council of Nicæa.

THE emperor, who possessed the most profound wisdom, having heard of these things, endeavoured, as a first step, to stop up their fountain-head. He therefore despatched a messenger renowned for his ready wit to Alexandria with letters, in the endeavour to extinguish the dispute, and expecting to reconcile the disputants. But his hopes having been frustrated, he proceeded to summon the celebrated council of Nicæa[1]; and pledged his word that the bishops and their officials should be furnished with asses, mules, and horses for their journey at the public expense. When all those who were capable of enduring the fatigue of the journey had arrived at Nicæa, he went thither himself, with both the wish of seeing the multitude of bishops, and the yearning desire of maintaining unanimity amongst them. He at once arranged that all their wants should be liberally supplied. Three hundred and eighteen bishops were assembled. The bishop of Rome[2], on account of his very advanced age, was absent, but he sent two presbyters[3] to the council, with authority to agree to what was done.

At this period many individuals were richly endowed with apostolical gifts ; and many, like the holy apostle, bore in their bodies the marks of the Lord Jesus Christ[4]. James, bishop of Antioch, a city of Mygdonia, which is called Nisibis by the Syrians and Assyrians, raised the dead and restored them to life, and performed many other wonders which it would be superfluous to mention again in detail in this history, as I have already given an account of them in my work, entitled "Philotheus[5]." Paul, bishop of

Neo-Cæsarea, a fortress situated on the banks of the Euphrates, had suffered from the frantic rage of Licinius. He had been deprived of the use of both hands by the application of a red-hot iron, by which the nerves which give motion to the muscles had been contracted and rendered dead. Some had had the right eye dug out, others had lost the right arm. Among these was Paphnutius of Egypt. In short, the Council looked like an assembled army of martyrs. Yet this holy and celebrated gathering was not entirely free from the element of opposition ; for there were some, though so few as easily to be reckoned, of fair surface, like dangerous shallows, who really, though not openly, supported the blasphemy of Arius.

When they were all assembled[6], the emperor ordered a great hall to be prepared for their accommodation in the palace, in which a sufficient number of benches and seats were placed ; and having thus arranged that they should be treated with becoming dignity, he desired the bishops to enter in, and discuss the subjects proposed. The emperor, with a few attendants, was the last to enter the room ; remarkable for his lofty stature, and worthy of admiration for personal beauty, and for the still more marvellous modesty which dwelt on his countenance. A low stool was placed for him in the middle of the assembly, upon which, however, he did not seat himself until he had asked the permission of the bishops. Then all the sacred assembly sat down around him. Then forthwith rose first the great Eustathius, bishop of Antioch, who, upon the translation of Philogonius, already referred to, to a better life, had been compelled reluctantly to become his successor by the unanimous suffrages of the bishops, priests, and of the Christ-loving laity. He crowned the emperor's head with the flowers of panegyric, and commended the diligent attention he had manifested in the regulation of ecclesiastical affairs.

The excellent emperor next exhorted the Bishops to unanimity and concord ; he recalled to their remembrance the cruelty of the late tyrants, and reminded them of the honourable peace which God had, in his reign and by his means, accorded them. He pointed out how dreadful it was, aye, very dreadful, that at the very time when their enemies were destroyed, and when no one dared to oppose them, they should fall upon one another, and make their amused adversaries laugh, especially as they were debating about holy

---

Originally named Antigonea, after its founder ; then Nicæa after the Queen of Lysimachus ; now Isnik.
[2] Sylvester.   [3] Vitus and Vincentius.
[4] Cf. Gal. vi. 17. The "stigmata" here meant are the marks of persecution.
[5] i.e. The Φιλόθεος ἱστορία, or "Religious History," a work containing the lives of celebrated ascetics, composed before the Ecclesiastical History. For Dr. Newman's explanation of its apparent credulity, Vide Hist. Sketches, iii. 314, and compare his

Apologia pro Vita sua, on his own acceptance of the marvellous, Appendix, p. 57.
[6] On the circumstances and scene of the opening of the Council consult Stanley's Eastern Church, Lecture IV.

things, concerning which they had the written teaching of the Holy Spirit. "For the gospels" (continued he), "the apostolical writings, and the oracles of the ancient prophets, clearly teach us what we ought to believe concerning the divine nature. Let, then, all contentious disputation be discarded; and let us seek in the divinely-inspired word the solution of the questions at issue." These and similar exhortations he, like an affectionate son, addressed to the bishops as to fathers, labouring to bring about their unanimity in the apostolical doctrines. Most members of the synod, won over by his arguments, established concord among themselves, and embraced sound doctrine. There were, however, a few, of whom mention has been already made, who opposed these doctrines, and sided with Arius; and amongst them were Menophantus, bishop of Ephesus, Patrophilus, bishop of Scythopolis, Theognis, bishop of Nicæa, and Narcissus, bishop of Neronias, which is a town of the second Cilicia, and is now called Irenopolis; also Theonas, bishop of Marmarica, and Secundus, bishop of Ptolemais in Egypt[7]. They drew up a formulary of their faith, and presented it to the council. As soon as it was read it was torn to pieces, and was declared to be spurious and false. So great was the uproar raised against them, and so many were the reproaches cast on them for having betrayed religion, that they all, with the exception of Secundus and Theonas, stood up and took the lead in publicly renouncing Arius. This impious man, having thus been expelled from the Church, a confession of faith which is received to this day was drawn up by unanimous consent; and, as soon as it was signed, the council was dissolved.

CHAPTER VII.

Confutation of Arianism deduced from the Writings of Eustathius and Athanasius.

THE above-named bishops, however, did not consent to it in sincerity, but only in appearance. This was afterwards shewn by their plotting against those who were foremost in zeal for religion, as well as by what these latter have written about them. For instance, Eustathius, the famous bishop of Antioch, who has been already mentioned, when explaining the text in the Proverbs, ' The Lord created me in the beginning of His way, before His works of old[1],' wrote against them, and refuted their blasphemy.

[2] "I WILL now proceed to relate how these different events occurred. A general council was summoned at Nicæa, and about two hundred and seventy bishops were convened. There were, however, so many assembled that I cannot state their exact number, neither, indeed, have I taken any great trouble to ascertain this point. When they began to inquire into the nature of the faith, the formulary of Eusebius was brought forward, which contained undisguised evidence of his blasphemy. The reading of it before all occasioned great grief to the audience, on account of its departure from the faith, while it inflicted irremediable shame on the writer. After the Eusebian gang had been clearly convicted, and the impious writing had been torn up in the sight of all, some amongst them by concert, under the pretence of preserving peace, imposed silence on all the ablest speakers. The Ariomaniacs, fearing lest they should be ejected from the Church by so numerous a council of bishops, sprang forward to anathematize and condemn the doctrines condemned, and unanimously signed the confession of faith. Thus having retained possession of their episcopal seats through the most shameful deception, although they ought rather to have been degraded, they continue, sometimes secretly, and sometimes openly, to patronize the condemned doctrines, plotting against the truth by various arguments. Wholly bent upon establishing these plantations of tares, they shrink from the scrutiny of the intelligent, avoid the observant, and attack the preachers of godliness. But we do not believe that these atheists can ever thus overcome the Deity. For though they ' gird themselves ' they ' shall be broken in pieces,' according to the solemn prophecy of Isaiah[3]."

These are the words of the great Eustathius. Athanasius, his fellow combatant, the champion of the truth, who succeeded the celebrated Alexander in the episcopate, added the following, in a letter addressed to the Africans.

"The bishops convened in council being

---

[7] Menophantus was one of the disciples of Lucianus (*Philos. H.E.* ii. 14). He accepted the Nicene decision, but was excommunicated by the Sardican Fathers. Cf. Book II. Chap. 6.

Patrophilus, bishop of Scythopolis, the Bethshan of Scripture, was an ardent and persistent Arian. Theodoret mentions his share in the deposition of Eustathius (I. 20). Theognis was sentenced to banishment on account of the Arian sympathies he displayed at Nicæa, but escaped by a feigned acceptance.

Narcissus of Irenopolis, a town of Cilicia Secunda, took an active part in the Arian movement: Athanasius says that he was thrice degraded by different synods, and is the worst of the Eusebians (*Ath. Ap. de fuga*, sec. 28).

Marmarica is not a town, but a district. It lay west of Egypt, about the modern Barca.

There were two cities in Egypt named Ptolemais, one in Upper Egypt below Abydos; one a port of the Red Sea.

After the time of Constantine, Cilicia was divided into three districts; Cilicia Prima, with Tarsus for chief town; Secunda, with Anazarbus; Tertia, with Seleuceia.

[1] Prov. viii. 22, lxx. Κύριος ἔκτισέ με ἀρχὴν ὁδῶν αὑτοῦ εἰς ἔργα αὑτοῦ.

[2] At this point, according to Valesius, a quotation from the homily of Eustathius on the above text from Proverbs viii. 22, begins. On Eustathius, see notes on Chapters III. and XX.

[3] Is. viii. 9, lxx. ἐὰν γὰρ πάλιν ἰσχύσητε πάλιν ἡττηθήσεσθε.

desirous of refuting the impious assertions invented by the Arians, that the Son was created out of that which was non-existent[4], that He is a creature and created being[5], that there was a period in which He was not[6], and that He is mutable by nature, and being all agreed in propounding the following declarations, which are in accordance with the holy Scriptures; namely, that the Son is by nature only-begotten of God, Word, Power, and sole Wisdom of the Father; that He is, as John said, 'the true God[7],' and, as Paul has written, 'the brightness of the glory, and the express image of the person of the Father[8],' the followers of Eusebius, drawn aside by their own vile doctrine, then began to say one to another, Let us agree, for we are also of God; *'There is but one God, by whom are all things*[9];' *'Old things are passed away; behold, all things are become new, and all things are of God*[10].' They also dwelt particularly upon what is contained in 'The Shepherd[11]:' 'Believe above all that there is one God, who created and fashioned all things, and making them to be out of that which is not.'

"But the bishops saw through their evil design and impious artifice, and gave a clearer elucidation of the words 'of God,' and wrote, that the Son is of the substance of God; in order that while the creatures, which do not in any way derive their existence of or from themselves, are said to be of God, the Son alone is said to be of the substance of the Father; this being peculiar to the only-begotten Son, the true Word of the Father. This is the reason why the bishops wrote, that He is of the substance of the Father.

"But when the Arians, who seemed few in number, were again interrogated by the Bishops as to whether they admitted 'that the Son is not a creature, but Power, and sole Wisdom, and eternal unchangeable[12] Image of the Father; and that He is very God,' the Eusebians were noticed making signs to one another to shew that these declarations were equally applicable to us. For it is said, that we are *'the image and glory of God*[13];' and *'for always we who live*[14]:' there are, also, they said, many powers; for it is written —*'All the power of God went out of the land of Egypt*[15].' The canker-worm and the locust are said to be *'a great power*[16].' And elsewhere it is written, *'The God of powers is with us, the God of Jacob is our helper*[17].' To which may be added that we are God's own not simply, but because the Son called us *'brethren*[18].' The declaration that Christ is 'the true God' does not distress us, for, having come into being, He is true.

"Such was the corrupt opinion of the Arians; but on this the bishops, having detected their deceitfulness in this matter, collected from Scripture those passages which say of Christ that He is the glory, the fountain, the stream, and the express image of the person; and they quoted the following words: *'In thy light we shall see light*[19];' and likewise, *'I and the Father are one*[20].' They then, with still greater clearness, briefly declared that the Son is of one substance with the Father; for this, indeed, is the signification of the passages which have been quoted. The complaint of the Arians, that these precise words are not to be found in Scripture, is proved groundless by their own practice, for their own impious assertions are not taken from Scripture; for it is not written that the Son is of the non-existent, and that there was a time when He was not: and yet they complain of having been condemned by expressions which, though not actually in Scripture, are in accordance with true religion. They themselves, on the other hand, as though they had found their words on a dunghill, uttered things verily of earth. The bishops, on the contrary, did not find their expressions for themselves; but, received their testimony from the fathers, and wrote accordingly. Indeed, there were bishops of old time, nearly one hundred and thirty years ago, both of the great city of Rome and of our own city[21], who condemned those who asserted that the Son is a creature, and that He is not of one substance with the Father. Eusebius, the bishop of Cæsarea, was acquainted with these facts; he, at one time, favoured the Arian heresy, but he afterwards signed the confession of faith of the Council of Nicæa. He wrote to the people of his diocese, maintaining that the word 'consubstantial' was 'used by illustrious bishops and learned writers as a term for expressing the divinity of the Father and of the Son[22].'"

So these men concealed their unsoundness through fear of the majority, and gave their

---

4 Ἐξ οὐκ ὄντων.   5 Κτίσμα καὶ ποίημα.
6 Ποτε ὅτε οὐκ ἦν.   7 1 Joh.v. 20.
8 Heb. i. 3. Cf. p. 37, note xxvii.
9 1 Cor. viii. 6.   10 2 Cor. v. 17, 18.
11 Herm. Pastor. Vis. v. Mand. i.
12 ἀπαράλλακτος, cf. James i. 17, Παρ' ᾦ οὐκ ἔνι παραλλαγή.
13 1 Cor. xi. 7.
14 2 Cor. iv. 11. ἀεὶ γὰρ ἡμεῖς οἱ ζῶντες. The ἀεί of St. Paul qualifies not "οἱ ζῶντες" but the παραδιδόμεθα which follows, "For we who live are ever being delivered to death."
15 Exod. xii. 41, "The Hosts of the Lord," A.V. ἐξῆλθε πᾶσα ἡ δύναμις Κυρίου, Sept.

16 Joel ii. 25, "My great army," A.V.
17 "The Lord of hosts is with us, the God of Jacob is our refuge," Ps. xlvi. 7.
18 Heb. ii. 11.   19 Ps. xxxvi. 9.   20 Joh. x. 30.
21 Alexandria. The allusion, according to Valesius, is to Dionysius, Bishop of Rome, 259–269, and to Dionysius, Bishop of Alexandria. The Letter of Athanasius to the Africans was written, according to Baronius, in 369. So τριῶν may suit the chronology better than τριάκοντα.
22 Ath. Ep. ad Afros 5 and 6.

assent to the decisions of the council, thus drawing upon themselves the condemnation of the prophet, for the God of all cries unto them, " *This people honour Me with their lips, but in their hearts they are far from Me* [23]." Theonas and Secundus, however, did not like to take this course, and were excommunicated by common consent as men who esteemed the Arian blasphemy above evangelical doctrine. The bishops then returned to the council, and drew up twenty laws to regulate the discipline of the Church.

CHAPTER VIII.

Facts relating to Meletius the Egyptian, from whom originated the Meletian schism, which remains to this day.—Synodical Epistle respecting him.

AFTER Meletius[1] had been ordained bishop, which was not long before the Arian controversy, he was convicted of certain crimes· by the most holy Peter, bishop of Alexandria, who also received the crown of martyrdom. After being deposed by Peter he did not acquiesce in his deposition, but filled the Thebaid and the adjacent part of Egypt with tumult and disturbance, and rebelled against the primacy of Alexandria. A letter was written by the council to the Church of Alexandria, stating what had been decreed against his revolutionary practices. It was as follows :—

Synodical Epistle.

" To the Church of Alexandria which, by the grace of God, is great and holy, and to the beloved brethren in Egypt, Libya, and Pentapolis, the bishops who have been convened to the great and holy council of Nicæa, send greeting in the Lord.

" The great and holy council of Nicæa having been convened by the grace of God, and by the most religious emperor, Constantine, who summoned us from different provinces and cities, we judge it requisite that a letter be sent from the whole Holy Synod to inform you also what questions have been mooted and debated, and what has been decreed and established.

" In the first place, the impious doctrines of Arius were investigated before our most religious emperor Constantine ; and his impiety was unanimously anathematized, as well as the blasphemous language and views

which he had propounded, alleging that the Son of God was out of what was not, that before He was begotten He was not, that there was a period in which He was not, and that He can, according to His own free-will, be capable either of virtue or of vice. The holy council anathematized all these assertions, and even refused so much as to listen to such impious and foolish opinions, and such blasphemous expressions. The final decision concerning him you already know, or will soon hear ; but we will not mention it now, lest we should appear to trample upon a man who has already received the recompense due to his sins. Such influence has his impiety obtained as to involve Theonas, bishop of Marmarica, and Secundus, bishop of Ptolemais, in his ruin, and they have shared his punishment.

" But after Egypt had, by the grace of God, been delivered from these false and blasphemous opinions, and from persons who dared to raise discord and division among a hitherto peaceable people, there yet remained the question of the temerity of Meletius, and of those ordained by him. We now inform you, beloved brethren, of the decrees of the council on this subject. It was decided by the holy council, that Meletius should be treated with clemency, though, strictly speaking, he was not worthy of even the least concession. He was permitted to remain in his own city, but was divested of all power, whether of nomination or of ordination, neither was he to shew himself in any province or city for these purposes : but only to retain the bare name of his office. Those who had received ordination at his hands were to submit to a more religious re-ordination ; and were to be admitted to communion on the terms of retaining their ministry, but of ranking in every diocese and church below those who had been ordained before them by Alexander, our much-honoured fellow-minister Thus they would have no power of choosing or nominating others to the ministry, according to their pleasure, or indeed of doing anything without the consent of the bishops of the Catholic and Apostolic Church, who are under Alexander. But they who, by the grace of God, and in answer to your prayers, have been detected in no schism, and have continued spotless in the Catholic and Apostolic Church, are to have the power of electing, and of nominating men worthy of the clerical office, and are permitted to do whatsoever is in accordance with law and the authority of the Church. If it should happen, that any of those now holding an office in the Church should die, then let those recently admitted be advanced to the honours of the deceased, provided only that

---

23 Isai. xxix. 13.
[1] Meletius (Μελέτιος), Bishop of Lycopolis, in Upper Egypt, was accused of apostasy. During the Patriarch Peter's withdrawal under persecution he intruded into the see of Alexandria. He was deposed in 306.

they appear worthy, and that the people choose them, and that the election be confirmed and ratified by the catholic bishop of Alexandria. The same privilege has been conceded to all the others. With respect to Meletius, however, an exception has been made, both on account of his former insubordination, and of the rashness and impetuosity of his disposition; for if the least authority were accorded to him, he might abuse it by again exciting confusion. These are the chief points which relate to Egypt, and to the holy Church of Alexandria. Whatever other canons were made, or dogmas decreed, you will hear of them from Alexander, our most-honoured fellow-minister and brother, who will give you still more accurate information, because he himself directed, as well as participated in, every thing that took place.

"We also give you the good news that, according to your prayers, the celebration of the most holy paschal feast was unanimously rectified, so that our brethren of the East, who did not previously keep the festival at the same time as those of Rome, and as yourselves, and, indeed, all have done from the beginning, will henceforth celebrate it with you. Rejoice, then, in the success of our undertakings, and in the general peace and concord, and in the extirpation of every heresy, and receive with still greater honour and more fervent love, Alexander, our fellow-minister and your bishop, who imparted joy to us by his presence, and who, at a very advanced age, has undergone so much fatigue for the purpose of restoring peace among you. Pray for us all, that what has been rightly decreed may remain steadfast, through our Lord Jesus Christ, being done, as we trust, according to the good pleasure of God and the Father in the Holy Ghost, to whom be glory for ever and ever. Amen."

Notwithstanding the endeavours of that divine assembly of bishops to apply this medicine to the Meletian disease, vestiges of his infatuation remain even to this day; for there are in some districts bodies of monks who refuse to follow sound doctrine, and observe certain vain points of discipline, agreeing with the infatuated views of the Jews and the Samaritans.

CHAPTER IX.

The Epistle of the Emperor Constantine, concerning the matters transacted at the Council, addressed to those Bishops who were not present.

The great emperor also wrote an account of the transactions of the council to those bishops who were unable to attend. And I consider it worth while to insert this epistle in my work, as it clearly evidences the piety of the writer.

"CONSTANTINUS AUGUSTUS to the Churches.

"Viewing the common public prosperity enjoyed at this moment, as the result of the great power of divine grace, I am desirous above all things that the blessed members of the Catholic Church should be preserved in one faith, in sincere love, and in one form of religion, towards Almighty God. But, since no firmer or more effective measure could be adopted to secure this end, than that of submitting everything relating to our most holy religion to the examination of all, or most of all, the bishops, I convened as many of them as possible, and took my seat among them as one of yourselves; for I would not deny that truth which is the source of my greatest joy, namely, that I am your fellow-servant. Every point obtained its due investigation, until the doctrine pleasing to the all-seeing God, and conducive to unity, was made clear, so that no room should remain for division or controversy concerning the faith.

"The commemoration of the most sacred paschal feast being then debated, it was unanimously decided, that it would be well that it should be everywhere celebrated upon the same day. What can be more fair, or more seemly, than that that festival by which we have received the hope of immortality should be carefully celebrated by all, on plain grounds, with the same order and exactitude? It was, in the first place, declared improper to follow the custom of the Jews in the celebration of this holy festival, because, their hands having been stained with crime, the minds of these wretched men are necessarily blinded. By rejecting their custom, we establish and hand down to succeeding ages one which is more reasonable, and which has been observed ever since the day of our Lord's sufferings. Let us, then, have nothing in common with the Jews, who are our adversaries. For we have received from our Saviour another way. A better and more lawful line of conduct is inculcated by our holy religion. Let us with one accord walk therein, my much-honoured brethren, studiously avoiding all contact with that evil way. They boast that without their instructions we should be unable to commemorate the festival properly. This is the highest pitch of absurdity. For how can they entertain right views on any point who, after having compassed the death of the Lord, being out of their minds, are guided not by sound reason, but by an unrestrained passion, wherever their innate madness carries them. Hence it follows that they have so far lost sight of truth, wandering as far as possible from the correct revisal, that they celebrate a second Passover in the same year. What motive can we have for following those who are thus confessedly unsound and in dire error? For we could never tolerate celebrating the Passover twice in one year. But, even if all these facts did not exist, your own sagacity would prompt you to watch with diligence and with prayer, lest your pure minds should appear to share in the customs of a people so utterly depraved. It must also be borne in mind, that upon so important a point as the celebration of a feast of such sanctity, discord is wrong. One day has our Saviour set apart for a commemoration of our deliverance, namely, of His most holy Passion. One hath He wished His Catholic Church to be, whereof the members, though dispersed throughout the most various parts of the world, are yet nourished by one spirit, that is, by the divine will. Let your pious sagacity reflect how evil and improper it is, that days devoted by some to fasting, should be spent by others in convivial feasting; and that after the paschal feast, some are rejoicing in festivals and relaxations, while others give themselves up to the appointed fasts. That this impropriety should be rectified, and that all these diversities of commemoration should be resolved into one form, is the will of divine Providence, as I am convinced you will all perceive. Therefore, this irregularity must be corrected, in order that we may no more have any thing in common with those parricides and the murderers of our Lord. An orderly and excellent form of commemoration is observed in all the churches of the western, of the southern, and of the northern parts of the world, and by some of the eastern; this form being universally commended, I engaged that you would be ready to adopt it likewise, and thus gladly accept the rule unanimously adopted in the city of Rome, throughout Italy, in all Africa, in Egypt, the Spains, the Gauls, the Britains, Libya, Greece, in the dioceses of Asia, and of Pontus, and in Cilicia, taking into your consideration not only that the churches of the places above-mentioned are greater in point of number, but also that it is most pious that all should unanimously agree in that course which accurate reasoning seems to demand, and which has no single point in common with the perjury of the Jews.

" Briefly to summarize the whole of the preceding, the judgment of all is, that the holy Paschal feast should be held on one and the same day; for, in so holy a matter, it is not becoming that any difference of custom should exist, and it is better to follow the opinion which has not the least association with error and sin. This being the case, receive with gladness the heavenly gift and the plainly divine command; for all that is transacted in the holy councils of the bishops is to be referred to the Divine will. Therefore, when you have made known to all our beloved brethren the subject of this epistle, regard yourselves bound to accept what has gone before, and to arrange for the regular observance of this holy day, so that when, according to my long-cherished desire, I shall see you face to face, I may be able to celebrate with you this holy festival upon one and the same day; and may rejoice with you all in witnessing the cruelty of the devil destroyed by our efforts, through Divine grace, while our faith and peace and concord flourish throughout the world. May God preserve you, beloved brethren."

CHAPTER X.

The daily wants of the Church supplied by the Emperor, and an account of his other virtues.

THUS did the emperor write to the absent. To those who attended the council, three hundred and eighteen in number, he manifested great kindness, addressing them with much gentleness, and presenting them with gifts. He ordered numerous couches to be prepared for their accommodation and entertained them all at one banquet. Those who were most worthy he received at his own table, distributing the rest at the others. Observing that some among them had had the right eye torn out, and learning that this mutilation had been undergone for the sake of religion, he placed his lips upon the wounds, believing that he would extract a blessing from the kiss. After the conclusion of the feast, he again presented other gifts to them. He then wrote to the governors of the provinces, directing that provision-money should be given in every city to virgins and widows, and to those who were consecrated to the divine service; and he measured the amount of their annual allowance more by the impulse of his own generosity than by their need. The third part of the sum is distributed to this day. Julian impiously withheld the whole. His successor[1] conferred the sum which is now dispensed, the famine which then prevailed having lessened the resources of the state. If the pensions were formerly triple in amount to what they are at present, the generosity of the emperor can by this fact be easily seen.

I do not account it right to pass over the following circumstance in silence. Some quarrelsome individuals wrote accusations against

---

[1] Jovian.

certain bishops, and presented their indictments to the emperor. This occurring before the establishment of concord, he received the lists, formed them into a packet which he sealed with his ring, and ordered them to be kept safely. After the reconciliation had been effected, he brought out these writings, and burnt them in their presence, at the same time declaring upon oath that he had not read a word of them. He said that the crimes of priests ought not to be made known to the multitude, lest they should become an occasion of offence, and lead them to sin without fear. It is reported also that he added that if he were to detect a bishop in the very act of committing adultery, he would throw his imperial robe over the unlawful deed, lest any should witness the scene, and be thereby injured. Thus did he admonish all the priests, as well as confer honours upon them, and then exhorted them to return each to his own flock.

CHAPTER XI.

I shall here insert the letter respecting the faith, written by Eusebius, bishop of Cæsarea, as it describes the effrontery of the Arians, who not only despise our fathers, but reject their own: it contains a convincing proof of their madness. They certainly honour Eusebius, because he adopted their sentiments, but yet they openly contradict his writings. He wrote this epistle to some of the Arians, who were accusing him, it seems, of treachery. The letter itself explains the writer's object.

Epistle of Eusebius, Bishop of Cæsarea, which he wrote from Nicæa when the great Council was assembled.

"You will have probably learnt from other sources what was decided respecting the faith of the church at the general council of Nicæa, for the fame of great transactions generally outruns the accurate account of them: but lest rumours not in strict accordance with the truth should reach you, I think it necessary to send to you, first, the formulary of faith originally proposed by us, and, next, the second, published with additions made to our terms. The following is our formulary, which was read in the presence of our most pious emperor, and declared to be couched in right and proper language.

The Faith put forth by us.

"'As in our first catechetical instruction, and at the time of our baptism, we received from the bishops who were before us and as we have learnt from the Holy Scriptures, and, alike as presbyters, and as bishops, were wont to believe and teach; so we now believe and thus declare our faith. It is as follows:—

"'We believe in one God, Father Almighty, the Maker of all things, visible and invisible; and in one Lord Jesus Christ, the Word of God, God of God, Light of Light, Life of Life, Only-begotten Son, First-born of every creature, begotten of the Father before all worlds; by Whom all things were made; Who for our salvation was incarnate, and lived among men [1]. He suffered and rose again the third day, and ascended to the Father; and He will come again in glory to judge the quick and the dead. We also believe in one Holy Ghost.

"'We believe in the being and continual existence of each of these; that the Father is in truth the Father; the Son in truth the Son; the Holy Ghost in truth the Holy Ghost; as our Lord, when sending out His disciples to preach the Gospel, said, '*Go forth and teach all nations, baptizing them into the name of the Father, and of the Son, and of the Holy Ghost* [2].' We positively affirm that we hold this faith, that we have always held it, and that we adhere to it even unto death, condemning all ungodly heresy. We testify, as before God the Almighty and our Lord Jesus Christ, that we have thought thus from the heart, and from the soul, ever since we have known ourselves; and we have the means of showing, and, indeed, of convincing you, that we have always during the past thus believed and preached.'

"When this formulary had been set forth by us, there was no room to gainsay it; but our beloved emperor himself was the first to testify that it was most orthodox, and that he coincided in opinion with it; and he exhorted the others to sign it, and to receive all the doctrine it contained, with the single addition of the one word—'consubstantial.' He explained that this term implied no bodily condition or change [3], for that the Son did not derive His existence from the Father either by means of division or of abscission, since an immaterial, intellectual, and incorporeal nature could not be subject to any bodily condition or change [3]. These things must be understood as bearing a divine and mysterious signification. Thus reasoned our wisest and most religious emperor. The addition of the word consubstantial has given occasion for the composition of the following formulary:—

---

[1] "πολιτευσάμενον." Cf. Phil. i. 27, and iii. 20, and Acts xxiii. 1.
[2] Matt. xxviii. 19.   [3] πάθη, πάθος.

The Creed published by the Council.

" 'We believe in one God, Father Almighty, Maker of all things visible and invisible. And in one Lord Jesus Christ, the Son of God, begotten of the Father; only-begotten, that is, of the substance of the Father, God of God, Light of Light, Very God of very God, begotten not made, being of one substance with the Father: by Whom all things were made both in heaven and on earth: Who for us men, and for our salvation, came down from heaven, and was incarnate, and was made man; He suffered, and rose again the third day; He ascended into heaven, and is coming to judge both quick and dead. And we believe in the Holy Ghost. The holy Catholic and Apostolic Church anathematizes all who say that there was a time when the Son of God was not; that before He was begotten He was not; that He was made out of the non-existent; or that He is of a different essence and of a different substance[4] from the Father; and that He is susceptible of variation or change.'

" When they had set forth this formulary, we did not leave without examination that passage in which it is said that the Son is of the substance of the Father, and consubstantial with the Father. Questions and arguments thence arose, and the meaning of the terms was exactly tested. Accordingly they were led to confess that the word consubstantial signifies that the Son is of the Father, but not as being a part of the Father. We deemed it right to receive this opinion; for that is sound doctrine which teaches that the Son is of the Father, but not part of His substance. From the love of peace, and lest we should fall from the true belief, we also accept this view, neither do we reject the term 'consubstantial.' For the same reason we admitted the expression, 'begotten, but not made;' for they alleged that the word 'made' applies generally to all things which were created by the Son, to which the Son is in no respect similar; and that consequently He is not a created thing, like the things made by Him, but is of a substance superior to all created objects. The Holy Scriptures teach Him to be begotten of the Father, by a mode of generation which is incomprehensible and inexplicable to all created beings. So also the term 'of one

substance with the Father,' when investigated, was accepted not in accordance with bodily relations or similarity to mortal beings. For it was also shown that it does not either imply division of substance, nor abscission, nor any modification or change or diminution in the power of the Father, all of which are alien from the nature of the unbegotten Father. It was concluded that the expression '*being of one substance with the Father*,' implies that the Son of God does not resemble, in any one respect, the creatures which He has made; but that to the Father alone, who begat Him, He is in all points perfectly like: for He is of the essence and of the substance[4] of none save of the Father. This interpretation having been given of the doctrine, it appeared right to us to assent to it, especially as we were aware that of the ancients some learned and celebrated bishops and writers have used the term 'consubstantial' with respect to the divinity of the Father and of the Son.

" These are the circumstances which I had to communicate respecting the published formulary of the faith. To it we all agreed, not without investigation, but, after having subjected the views submitted to us to thorough examination in the presence of our most beloved emperor, for the above reasons we all acquiesced in it. We also allowed that the anathema appended by them to their formulary of faith should be accepted, because it prohibits the use of words which are not scriptural; through which almost all the disorder and troubles of the Church have arisen. And since no passage of the inspired Scripture uses the terms 'out of the non-existent,' or that 'there was a time when He was not,' nor indeed any of the other phrases of the same class, it did not appear reasonable to assert or to teach such things. In this opinion, therefore, we judged it right to agree; since, indeed, we had never, at any former period, been accustomed to use such terms[5]. Moreover, the condemnation of the assertion that before He was begotten He was not, did not appear to involve any incongruity, because all assent to the fact that He was the Son of God before He was begotten according to the flesh. And here our emperor, most beloved by God,

---

4 ὑποστάσεως and οὐσίας.

5 The genuineness of the following sentence is doubted. It is not found in Socrates or in Epiphanius. But it is not unreasonably held by Valesius that Socrates, who seems to have undertaken to clear the character of Eusebius of all heretical taint, purposely suppressed the passage as inconsistent with orthodoxy. Soc. i. 8. Dr. Newman writes of this passage, "It is remarkable as shewing his (Constantine's) utter ignorance of doctrines which were never intended for discussion among the unbaptized heathen, or the secularized Christian, that, in spite of bold avowal of the orthodox faith in detail" (i.e. in his letter to Arius), "yet shortly after he explained to Eusebius one of the Nicene declarations in a sense which even Arius would scarcely have allowed, expressed as it is almost after the manner of Paulus. "Arians," 3rd ed., p. 256.

began to reason concerning His divine origin, and His existence before all ages. He was virtually in the Father without generation [6], even before He was actually begotten, the Father having always been the Father, just as He has always been a King and a Saviour, and, virtually, all things, and has never known any change of being or action.

"We have thought it requisite, beloved brethren, to transmit you an account of these circumstances, in order to show you what examination and investigation we bestowed on all the questions which we had to decide; and also to prove how at one time we resisted firmly, even to the last hour, when doctrines improperly expressed offended us, and, at another time, we, without contention, accepted the articles which contained nothing objectionable, when after a thorough and candid investigation of their signification, they appeared perfectly comformable with what had been confessed by us in the formulary of faith which we had published."

CHAPTER XII.

Confutation of the blasphemies of the Arians of our time, from the writings of Eusebius, Bishop of Cæsarea.

EUSEBIUS clearly testifies that the aforesaid term "consubstantial" is not a new one, nor the invention of the fathers assembled at the council; but that, from the very first [1] it has been handed down from father to son. He states that all those then assembled unanimously received the creed then published; and he again bears testimony to the same fact in another work, in which he highly extols the conduct of the great Constantine. He writes as follows [2] : —

"The emperor having delivered this discourse in Latin, it was translated into Greek by an interpreter, and then he gave liberty of speech to the leaders of the council. Some at once began to bring forward complaints against their neighbours, while others had recourse to recriminations and reproaches. Each party had much to urge, and at the beginning the debate waxed very violent. The emperor patiently and attentively listened to all that was advanced, and gave full attention to what was urged by each party in turn. He calmly endeavoured to reconcile the conflicting parties; addressing them mildly in Greek, of which language he was not ignorant, in a sweet and gentle manner. Some he convinced by argu-

ment, others he put to the blush; he commended those who had spoken well, and excited all to unanimity; until, at length, he reduced them all to oneness of mind and opinion on all the disputed points, so that they all agreed to hold the same faith, and to celebrate the festival of Salvation upon the same day. What had been decided was committed to writing, and was signed by all the bishops."

Soon after the author thus continues the narrative :—

"When matters had been thus arranged, the emperor gave them permission to return to their own dioceses. They returned with great joy, and have ever since continued to be of the one opinion, agreed upon in the presence of the emperor, and, though once widely separated, now united together, as it were, in one body. Constantine, rejoicing in the success of his efforts, made known these happy results by letter to those who were at a distance. He ordered large sums of money to be liberally distributed both among the inhabitants of the country and of the cities, in order that the twentieth anniversary of his reign might be celebrated with public festivities."

Although the Arians impiously gainsay the statements of the other fathers, yet they ought to believe what has been written by this father, whom they have been accustomed to admire. They ought, therefore, to receive his testimony to the unanimity with which the confession of faith was signed by all. But, since they impugn the opinions of their own leaders, they ought to become acquainted with the most foul and terrible manner of the death of Arius and with all their powers to flee from the impious doctrine of which he was the parent. As it is likely that the mode of his death is not known by all, I shall here relate it.

CHAPTER XIII.

Extract from the Letter of Athanasius on the Death of Arius [1].

AFTER Arius had remained a long time in Alexandria, he endeavoured riotously to obtrude himself again into the assemblies of the Church, professing to renounce his impiety, and promising to receive the confession of faith drawn up by the fathers. But not succeeding in obtaining the confidence of the divine Alexander, nor of Athanasius, who followed [2] Alexander alike in the patriarchate and in

---

6 Here it has been proposed to read for ἀγεννήτως, without generation, which does not admit of an orthodox interpretation, ἀειγεννήτως, i.e. by eternal generation.
1 ἄνωθεν. Cf. St. Luke i. 3. Plat. Phil. 44 D. &c.
2 Euseb. *Vit. Constant.* lib. iii. c. 13.

1 The letter was written to Serapion, Bishop of Thmuis, not Tmi el Emdid, in Egypt. St. Anthony left one of his sheepskins to Serapion, the other to Athanasius. Cf. Jer. *de Vir. illust.* 99.
2 Athanasius, chosen alike by the designation of the dying Alexander, by popular acclamation, and by the election of the Bishops of the Province, was, in spite of his reluctance and retirement, consecrated, A.D. 326.

piety, he, helped and encouraged by Eusebius, bishop of Nicomedia, betook himself to Constantinople. The intrigues upon which he then entered, and their punishment by the righteous Judge are all best narrated by the excellent Athanasius, in his letter to Apion [3]. I shall therefore now insert this passage in my work. He writes :—

"I was not at Constantinople when he died ; but Macarius, the presbyter, was there, and from him I learnt all the circumstances. The emperor Constantine was induced by Eusebius and his party to send for Arius. Upon his arrival, the emperor asked him whether he held the faith of the Catholic church. Arius then swore that his faith was orthodox, and presented a written summary of his belief; concealing, however, the reasons of his ejection from the Church by the bishop Alexander, and making a dishonest use of the language of Holy Scripture. When, therefore, he had declared upon oath that he did not hold the errors for which he had been expelled from the Church by Alexander, Constantine dismissed him, saying, 'If thy faith is orthodox, thou hast well sworn ; but if thy faith is impious and yet thou hast sworn, let God from heaven judge thee.' When he quitted the emperor, the partizans of Eusebius, with their usual violence, desired to conduct him into the church ; but Alexander, of blessed memory, bishop of Constantinople, refused his permission, alleging that the inventor of the heresy ought not to be admitted into communion. Then at last the partizans of Eusebius pronounced the threat: 'As, against your will, we succeeded in prevailing on the emperor to send for Arius, so now, even if you forbid it, shall Arius join in communion [4] with us in this church to-morrow.' It was on Saturday that they said this. The bishop Alexander, deeply grieved at what he had heard, went into the church and poured forth his lamentations, raising his hands in supplication to God, and throwing himself on his face on the pavement in the sanctuary [5], prayed. Macarius went in with him, prayed with him, and heard his prayers. He asked one of two things. 'If Arius,' said he, 'is to be joined to the Church to-morrow, let me Thy servant depart, and do not destroy the pious with the impious. If Thou wilt spare Thy Church, and

I know that Thou dost spare her, look upon the words of the followers of Eusebius, and give not over Thy heritage to destruction and to shame. Remove Arius, lest if he come into the Church, heresy seem to come in with him, and impiety be hereafter deemed piety.' Having thus prayed, the bishop left the church deeply anxious, and then a horrible and extraordinary catastrophe ensued. The followers of Eusebius had launched out into threats, while the bishop had recourse to prayer. Arius, emboldened by the protection of his party, delivered many trifling and foolish speeches, when he was suddenly compelled by a call of nature to retire, and immediately, as it is written, '*falling headlong, he burst asunder in the midst* [6],' and gave up the ghost, being deprived at once both of communion and of life. This, then, was the end of Arius [7]. The followers of Eusebius were covered with shame, and buried him whose belief they shared. The blessed Alexander completed the celebration, rejoicing with the Church in piety and orthodoxy, praying with all the brethren and greatly glorifying God. This was not because he rejoiced at the death of Arius—God forbid ; for '*it is appointed unto all men once to die* [8],' but because the event plainly transcended any human condemnation. For the Lord Himself passing judgment upon the menaces of the followers of Eusebius, and the prayer of Alexander, condemned the Arian heresy, and shewed that it was unworthy of being received into the communion of the Church ; thus manifesting to all that, even if it received the countenance and support of the emperor, and of all men, yet by truth itself it stood condemned."

These were the first fruits, reaped by Arius, of those pernicious seeds which he had himself sown, and formed the prelude to the punishments that awaited him hereafter. His impiety was condemned by his punishment.

I shall now turn my narrative to the piety of the emperor. He addressed a letter to all the subjects of the Roman empire, exhorting them to renounce their former errors, and to embrace the doctrines of our Saviour, and trying to guide them to this truth. He stirred up the bishops in every city to build churches, and encouraged them not only by his letter, but also by presenting them with large sums of money, and defraying all the expenses of building. This his own letter sets forth, which was after this manner :—

---

[3] The name does not vary in the MSS. of Theodoretus, but Schulze would alter it to Serapion on the authority of the MSS. of Athanasius.

[4] συναχθήσεται. The word σύναξις, originally equivalent to συναγωγή, and little used before the Christian era, means sometimes the gathering of the congregation, sometimes the Holy Communion. Vide Suicer s.v. Here the meaning is determined by parallel authority. (Cf. Soc. I. 38.)

[5] ἱερατεῖον. The sacrarium or chancel, called also τὸ ἅγιον. Cf. Book V. cap. 17, where Ambrosius rebukes Theodosius for entering within the rails.

[6] Acts i. 18.

[7] We are not necessarily impaled on Gibbon's dilemma of poison or miracle. There are curious instances of sudden death under similar circumstances, e.g. that of George Valla of Piacenza, at Venice, *circa* 1500. Vide Bayle's Dict. s.v.

[8] Heb. ix. 27.

CHAPTER XIV.

Letter written by the Emperor Constantine respecting the building of Churches[1].

"CONSTANTINUS AUGUSTUS, the great and the victorious, to Eusebius.

"I am well aware, and am thoroughly convinced, my beloved brother, that as the servants of our Saviour Christ have been suffering up to the present time from nefarious machinations and tyrannical persecutions, the fabrics of all the churches must have either fallen into utter ruin from neglect, or, through apprehension of the impending iniquity, have been reduced below their proper dignity. But now that freedom is restored, and that dragon[2], through the providence of God, and by our instrumentality, thrust out from the government of the Empire, I think that the divine power has become known to all, and that those who hitherto, from fear or from incredulity or from depravity, have lived in error, will now, upon becoming acquainted with Him who truly is, be led into the true and correct manner of life. Exert yourself, therefore, diligently in the reparation of the churches under your own jurisdiction, and admonish the principal bishops, priests, and deacons of other places to engage zealously in the same work; in order that all the churches which still exist may be repaired or enlarged, and that new ones may be built wherever they are required. You, and others through your intervention, can apply to magistrates[3] and to provincial governments[4], for all that may be necessary for this purpose; for they have received written injunctions to render zealous obedience to whatever your holiness may command. May God preserve you, beloved brother."

Thus the emperor wrote to the bishops in each province respecting the building of churches. From his letter to Eusebius of Palestine, it is easily learnt what measures he adopted to obtain copies of the Holy Bible[5].

CHAPTER XV.

The Epistle of Constantine concerning the preparation of copies of the Holy Scriptures.

"CONSTANTINUS AUGUSTUS, the great and the victorious, to Eusebius.

"In the city[1] which bears our name, a great number of persons have, through the providential care of God the Saviour, united themselves to the holy Church. As all things there are in a state of rapid improvement, we deemed it most important that an additional number of churches should be built. Adopt joyfully the mode of procedure determined upon by us, which we have thought expedient to make known to your prudence, namely, that you should get written, on fine parchment, fifty volumes[2], easily legible and handy for use; these you must have transcribed by skilled calligraphers, accurately acquainted with their art. I mean, of course, copies of the Holy Scriptures, which, as you know, it is most necessary that the congregation of the Church should both have and use. A letter has been sent from our clemency to the catholicus[3] of the diocese, in order that he may be careful that everything necessary for the undertaking is supplied. The duty devolving upon you is to take measures to ensure the completion of these manuscripts within a short space of time. When they are finished, you are authorised by this letter to order two public carriages for the purpose of transmitting them to us; and thus the fair manuscripts will be easily submitted to our inspection. Appoint one of the deacons of your church to take charge of this part of the business; when he comes to us, he shall receive proofs of our benevolence. May God preserve you, beloved brother."

What has been already said is enough to shew, nay to clearly prove, how great zeal the emperor manifested on the matters of religion. I will, however, add his noble acts with regard to the Sepulchre of our Saviour. For having learnt that the idolaters, in their frantic rage, had heaped earth over the Lord's tomb, eager thus to destroy all remembrance of His Salvation, and had built over it a temple to the goddess of unbridled lust, in mockery of the Virgin's birth, the emperor ordered the foul shrine to be demolished, and the soil polluted with abominable sacrifices to be carried away

---

1 This letter, according to Du Pin, was written A.D. 324 or 325.
2 Either Maxentius or Licinius.
3 ἡγεμονεύω, used in Luke ii. 2, of Quirinus, and iii. 1, of Pontius Pilate, but Theodoretus employs it and its correlatives of both civil and ecclesiastical authorities.
4 ἐπαρχικὴ τάξις ; ἐπαρχία occurs Acts xxiii. 34, of Cilicia, and in xxv. 1, of Judæa, the province of the Procurator Festus, but in the time of Constantine the ἔπαρχοι were civil præfects, without any military command, governing four great ἐπαρχίαι, viz. (i) Thrace, Egypt, and the East, (ii) Illyricum, Macedonia, and Greece, (iii) Italy and Africa, and (iv) Gaul, Spain, and Britain. (Zos. ii. 33.) On the accurate use of titles in the N.T. vide Bp. Lightfoot in Appendix to Essays on Supernatural Religion.
5 τὰ ἱερὰ βιβλία, or, "the holy books:" The Books, par excellence, were about this time becoming The Book, whence Biblia Sacra as a singular.

---

1 Constantinople was dedicated A.D. 330 on the site of the ancient Byzantium.
2 σωμάτια. The Codex Sinaiticus has been thought to be one of these.
3 i.e. the "Comes fisci," or officer managing the revenues of the Province. Dioecesis is used in civil sense by Cicero, Ep. Fam. 3; 8, 4, and Ammianus (17, 7, 6), mentions the compliment paid by Constantius II. to his empress Eusebia, by naming a "Diocese" of the Empire after her.

and thrown out far from the city, and a new temple of great size and beauty to be erected on the site. All this is clearly set forth in the letter which he wrote to the president [4] of the church of Jerusalem, Macarius, whom we have already mentioned as a member of the great Nicene Council, and united with his brethren in withstanding the blasphemies of Arius. The following is the letter.

CHAPTER XVI.

Letter from the Emperor to Macarius, Bishop of Jerusalem, concerning the building of the Holy Church.

"CONSTANTINUS, the victorious and the great, to Macarius.

"The grace of our Saviour is so wonderful, that no words are adequate to express the present marvel. The fact that the monument of His most holy sufferings should have remained concealed beneath the earth, during so long a course of years, until the time when, on the death of the common enemy of all, it was destined to shine forth on His liberated servants, surpasses every other subject of admiration. If all the wise men throughout the world were collected into one place, and were to endeavour to express themselves worthily of it, they could not approach within an infinite distance of it; for this miracle is as much beyond all human power of belief, as heavenly things by their nature are mightier than human. Hence it is my first and only object that, as by new miracles the faith in the truth is daily confirmed, so the minds of us all may be more earnestly devoted to the holy law, wisely, zealously, and with one accord. As my design is, I think, now generally known, I desire that you, above all, should be assured that my most intense anxiety is to decorate with beautiful edifices that consecrated spot, which by God's command I have relieved from the burden of the foul idol which encumbered it. For from the beginning He declared it holy, and has rendered it still more holy from the time that He brought to light the proof and memorial of the sufferings of our Lord.

I trust, then, to your sagacity to take every necessary care, not only that the basilica itself surpass all others; but that all its arrangements be such that this building may be incomparably superior to the most beautiful structures in every city throughout the world. We have entrusted our friend Dracilianus [1], who discharges the functions of the most illustrious præfect of the province, with the superintendence of the work of the erection and decoration of the walls. He has received our orders to engage workmen and artisans, and to provide all that you may deem requisite for the building. Let us know, by letter, when you have inspected the work, what columns or marbles you consider would be most ornamental, in order that whatever you may inform us is necessary for the work may be conveyed thither from all quarters of the world. For that which is of all places the most wonderful, ought to be decorated in accordance with its dignity. I wish to learn from you whether you think that the vaulted roof of the basilica ought to be panelled [2], or to be adorned in some other way; for if it is to be panelled it may also be gilt. Your holiness must signify to the aforesaid officers, as soon as possible, what workmen and artificers, and what sums of money, are requisite; and let me know promptly not only about the marbles and columns, but also about the panelled ceiling, if you decide that this will be the most beautiful mode of construction. May God preserve you, beloved brother [3]."

CHAPTER XVII.

Helena [1], Mother of the Emperor Constantine.—Her zeal in the Erection of the Holy Church.

THE bearer of these letters was no less illustrious a personage than the mother of the emperor, even she who was glorious in her offspring, whose piety was celebrated by all; she who brought forth that great luminary and nurtured him in piety. She did not shrink from the fatigue of the journey on account of her extreme old age, but undertook it a little before her death, which occurred in her eightieth year [2].

---

[2] λακωναρία, fr. Lat. lacunar, (lacuna lacus √LAK) = fretted ceiling. Cf. Hor. Od. II. xviii. 2.

[3] On the traditional site of the Holy Sepulchre, and the buildings on it, vide Stanley's "Sinai and Palestine," pp. 457 and seqq., and Canon Bright in Dict. Christ. Ant., article "Holy Sepulchre."

[1] Flavia Julia Helena, the first wife of Constantius Chlorus, born of obscure parents in Bithynia, †A.D. 328. "Stabulariam hanc primo fuisse adserunt, sic cognitam Constantio seniori." (Ambr. de obitu Theod. § 42, p. 295.) The story of her being the daughter of a British Prince, and born at York or Colchester, is part of the belief current since William of Malmesbury concerning Constantine's British Origin, which is probably due to two passages of uncertain interpretation in the Panegyrici: (a) Max. et Const. iv., "liberavit ille (Constantius) Britannias servitute, tu etiam nobiles, illic oriendo, fecisti." (b) Eum. Pan. Const. ix., "O fortunata et nunc omnibus beatior terris Britannia, quæ Constantinum Cæsarem prima vidisti." But is this said of birth or accession? Cf. Gibbon, chap. xiv.

[2] Crispus and Fausta were put to death in 326. "If it was not in order to seek expiation for her son's crimes, and consolation for her own sorrows, that Helen made her famous journey to the Holy Land, it was immediately consequent upon them." Stanley, Eastern Church, p. 211.

---

[4] πρόεδρος. Cf. Thuc. iii. 25. The πρυτάνεις in office in the Athenian ἐκκλησία were so called. In our author a common synonym for Bishop. προεδρια = sedes = see.

[1] Vide note 4 on chap. xiv.

When the empress beheld the place where the Saviour suffered, she immediately ordered the idolatrous temple, which had been there erected [3], to be destroyed, and the very earth on which it stood to be removed. When the tomb, which had been so long concealed, was discovered, three crosses were seen buried near the Lord's sepulchre. All held it as certain that one of these crosses was that of our Lord Jesus Christ, and that the other two were those of the thieves who were crucified with Him. Yet they could not discern to which of the three the Body of the Lord had been brought nigh, and which had received the outpouring of His precious Blood. But the wise and holy Macarius, the president of the city, resolved this question in the following manner. He caused a lady of rank, who had been long suffering from disease, to be touched by each of the crosses, with earnest prayer, and thus discerned the virtue residing in that of the Saviour. For the instant this cross was brought near the lady, it expelled the sore disease, and made her whole.

The mother of the emperor, on learning the accomplishment of her desire, gave orders that a portion of the nails should be inserted in the royal helmet, in order that the head of her son might be preserved from the darts of his enemies [4]. The other portion of the nails she ordered to be formed into the bridle of his horse, not only to ensure the safety of the emperor, but also to fulfil an ancient prophecy; for long before Zechariah, the prophet, had predicted that "*There shall be upon the bridles of the horses Holiness unto the Lord Almighty* [5]."

She had part of the cross of our Saviour conveyed to the palace [6]. The rest was enclosed in a covering of silver, and committed to the care of the bishop of the city, whom she exhorted to preserve it carefully, in order that it might be transmitted uninjured to posterity [7]. She then sent everywhere for workmen and for materials, and caused the most spacious and most magnificent churches to be erected.

It is unnecessary to describe their beauty and grandeur; for all the pious, if I may so speak, hasten thither and behold the magnificence of the buildings [8].

This celebrated and admirable empress performed another action worthy of being remembered. She assembled all the women who had vowed perpetual virginity, and placing them on couches, she herself fulfilled the duties of a handmaid, serving them with food and handing them cups and pouring out wine, and bringing a basin and pitcher, and pouring out water to wash their hands.

After performing these and other laudable actions, the empress returned to her son, and not long after, she joyfully entered upon the other and a better life, after having given her son much pious advice and her fervent parting blessing. After her death, those honours were rendered to her memory which her steadfast and zealous service to God deserved [9].

CHAPTER XVIII.

The unlawful Translation of Eusebius, Bishop of Nicomedia.

THE Arian party did not desist from their evil machinations. They had only signed the confession of faith for the purpose of disguising themselves in sheeps'-skins, while they were acting the part of wolves. The holy Alexander, of Byzantium, for the city was not yet called Constantinople, who by his prayer had pierced Arius to the heart, had, at the period to which we are referring, been translated to a better life. Eusebius, the propagator of impiety, little regarding the definition which, only a short time previously, he with the other bishops had agreed upon, without delay quitted Nicomedia and seized upon the see of Constantinople, in direct violation of that canon [1] which prohibits bishops and presbyters from being translated from one city to another. But that those who carry their infatuation so far as to deny the divinity of the only-begotten Son of God, should likewise violate the other laws, cannot excite surprise. Nor was this the first occasion

3 i.e. of Venus, said to have been erected by Hadrian to pollute a spot hallowed by Christians.

4 The tradition which identifies the nail in Constantine's helmet with the iron band in the famous crown of Queen Theodolinda at Monza dates from the sixteenth century.

5 Zech. xiv. 20. ἔσται τὸ ἐπὶ τὸν χαλινὸν τοῦ ἵππου Ἅγιον τῷ Κυρίῳ τῷ παντοκράτορι. lxx.

6 This portion Socrates says (i. 17) was enclosed by Constantine in a statue placed on a column of porphyry in his forum at Constantinople.

7 Carried away from Jerusalem by Chosroes II. in 614, it was recovered, says the legend, by Heraclius in 628. The feast of the "Exaltation of the Cross" on Sept. 14th, combines the Commemoration of the Vision of Constantine, the exaltation of the relic at Jerusalem, and its triumphal entry after its exile under Chosroes. In later years it was, as is well known, supposed to have a miraculous power of self-multiplication, and such names as St. Cross at Winchester, Santa Croce at Florence, and Vera Cruz in Mexico illustrate its cultus. Paulinus of Nola, at the beginning of the fifth century, sending a piece to Sulpicius Severus, says that though bits were frequently taken from it, it grew no smaller (Ep. xxxi.).

8 May 3rd has been kept since the end of the eighth century in honour of the "Invention of the Cross," and the Commemoration of the ancient "Ellinmas" was retained in the reformed Anglican Calendar.

9 Tillemont puts her death in 328. Eusebius (V. Const. iii. 47), says she was carried ἐπὶ τὴν βασιλεύουσαν πόλιν, by which he generally means Rome, but Socrates (i. 17) writes, εἰς τὴν βασιλεύουσαν νέαν Ῥώμην, i.e. Constantinople. There is a chapel in her honour in the church of the Ara Cœli at Rome, but her traditional burial-place is a mile and a half beyond the Porta Maggiore, on the Via Labicana, and thence came the porphyry sarcophagus called St. Helena's, which was placed by Pius VI. in the Hall of the Greek Cross in the Vatican.

1 i.e. Apost. Can. xiv., which forbids translation without an "εὔλογος αἰτία, or prospect of more spiritual gain in saving souls; and guards the application of the rule by the proviso that neither the bishop himself, nor the παροικία desiring him, but many bishops, shall decide the point." Dict. Christ. Ant. i. 226.

that he made this innovation ; for, having been originally entrusted with the see of Berytus, he leapt from thence to Nicomedia. Whence he was expelled by the synod, on account of his manifest impiety, as was likewise Theognis, bishop of Nicæa. This is related a second time in the letters of the emperor Constantine ; and I shall here insert the close of the letter which he wrote to the Nicomedians.

CHAPTER XIX.

Epistle of the Emperor Constantine against Eusebius and Theognis, addressed to the Nicomedians.

"WHO has taught these doctrines to the innocent multitude ? It is manifestly Eusebius, the co-operator in the cruelty of the tyrants. For that he was the creature [1] of the tyrant has been clearly shown ; and, indeed, is proved by the slaughter of the bishops, and by the fact that these victims were true bishops. The relentless persecution of the Christians proclaims this fact aloud.

"I shall not here say anything of the insults directed against me, by which the conspiracies of the opposite faction were mainly carried out. But he went so far as to send spies to watch me, and scarcely refrained from raising troops in aid of the tyrant. Let not any one imagine that I allege what I am not prepared to prove. I am in possession of clear evidence ; for I have caused the bishops and presbyters belonging to his following to be seized. But I pass over all these facts. I only mention them for the purpose of making these persons ashamed of their conduct, and not from any feeling of resentment.

"There is one thing I fear, one thing which causes me anxiety, and that is to see you charged as accomplices ; for you are influenced by the doctrines of Eusebius, and have thus been led away from the truth. But your cure will be speedy, if, after obtaining a bishop who holds pure and faithful doctrines, you will but look unto God. This depends upon you alone ; and you would, no doubt, have thus acted long ago, had not the aforesaid Eusebius come here, strongly supported by those then in power, and overturned all discipline.

"As it is necessary to say something more about Eusebius, your patience will remember that a council was held in the city of Nicæa, at which, in obedience to my conscience, I was present, being actuated by no other motive than the desire of producing unanimity among all, and

before all else of proving and dispelling the mischief which originated from the infatuation of Arius of Alexandria, and was straightway strengthened by the absurd and pernicious machinations of Eusebius. But, beloved and much-honoured brethren, you know not how earnestly and how disgracefully Eusebius, although convicted by the testimony of his own conscience, persevered in the support of the false doctrines which had been universally condemned. He secretly sent persons to me to petition on his behalf, and personally intreated my assistance in preventing his being ejected from his bishopric, although his crimes had been fully detected. God, who, I trust, will continue His goodness towards you and towards me, is witness to the truth of what I say. I was then myself deluded and deceived by Eusebius, as you shall well know. In everything he acted according to his own desire, his mind being full of every kind of secret evil.

"Omitting the relation of the rest of his misdeeds, it is well that you should be informed of the crime which he lately perpetrated in concert with Theognis, the accomplice of his folly. I had sent orders for the apprehension of certain individuals in Alexandria who had deserted our faith, and by whose means the firebrand of dissension was kindled. But these good gentlemen, forsooth, bishops, whom, by the clemency of the council, I had reserved for penitence, not only received them under their protection, but also participated in their evil deeds. Hence I came to the determination to punish these ungrateful men, by apprehending and banishing them to some far-distant region.

"It is now your duty to look unto God with that same faith which it is clear that you have ever held, and in which it is fitting you should abide. So let us have cause of rejoicing in the appointment of pure, orthodox, and beneficent bishops. If any one should make mention of those destroyers, or presume to speak in their praise, let him know that his audacity will be repressed by the authority which has been committed to me as the servant of God. May God preserve you, beloved brethren !"

The above-mentioned bishops were then deposed and banished. Amphion [2] was entrusted with the church of Nicomedia, and Chrestus [3] with that of Nicæa. But the exiled bishops, employing their customary artifices, abused the benevolence of the emperor, renewed the

---

[1] πρόσφυξ, originally a protected "runaway," then protégé or client.

[2] Athanasius, *Disp. prima Cont. Ar.*, mentions an Amphion, orthodox bishop of Epiphania in Cilicia Secunda. That he is the same as the Amphion of the text is asserted by Baronius and doubted by Tillemont. Dict. Christ. Biog. s.v.

[3] In 328, Chrestus and Amphion retired on the recantation of Theognis and Eusebius, whose βιβλίον μετανοίας, or act of retractation, is given in Soc. i. xiv.

previous contests, and regained their former power.

CHAPTER XX.

The artful Machinations of Eusebius and his followers against the Holy Eustathius, Bishop of Antioch.

EUSEBIUS, as I have already stated, seized the diocese of Constantinople by force. And thus having acquired great power in that city, frequently visiting and holding familiar intercourse with the emperor, he gained confidence and formed plots against those who were foremost in the support of the truth. He at first feigned a desire of going to Jerusalem, to see the celebrated edifices there erected: and the emperor, who was deceived by his flattery, allowed him to set out with the utmost honour, providing him with carriages, and the rest of his equipage and retinue. Theognis, bishop of Nicæa, who, as we have before said, was his accomplice in his evil designs, travelled with him. When they arrived at Antioch, they put on the mask of friendship, and were received with the utmost deference. Eustathius, the great champion of the faith, treated them with fraternal kindness. When they arrived at the holy places, they had an interview with those who were of the same opinions as themselves, namely, Eusebius, bishop of Cæsarea, Patrophilus, bishop of Scythopolis, Aetius, bishop of Lydda, Theodotus, bishop of Laodicea, and others who had imbibed the Arian sentiments; they made known the plot they had hatched to them, and went with them to Antioch. The pretext for their journey was, that due honour might be rendered to Eusebius; but their real motive was their war against religion. They bribed a low woman, who made a traffic of her beauty, to sell them her tongue, and then repaired to the council, and when all the spectators had been ordered to retire, they introduced the wretched woman. She held a babe in her arms, of which she loudly and impudently affirmed that Eustathius was the father. Eustathius, conscious of his innocence, asked her whether she could bring forward any witness to prove what she had advanced. She replied that she could not: yet these equitable judges admitted her to oath, although it is said in the law, that "*at the mouth of two or three witnesses shall the matter be established*[1];" and the apostle says, "*against an elder receive not any accusation but before two or three witnesses*[2]." But they despised these divine laws, and admitted the accusation against this great man without any witnesses. When the woman had again declared upon oath that Eustathius was the father of the babe, these truth-loving judges condemned him as an adulterer. When the other bishops, who upheld the apostolical doctrines, being ignorant of all these intrigues, openly opposed the sentence, and advised Eustathius not to submit to it, the originators of the plot promptly repaired to the emperor, and endeavoured to persuade him that the accusation was true, and the sentence of deposition just; and they succeeded in obtaining the banishment of this champion of piety and chastity, as an adulterer and a tyrant. He was conducted across Thrace to a city of Illyricum[3].

CHAPTER XXI.

Bishops of Heretical opinions ordained in Antioch after the Banishment of St. Eustathius[1].

EULALIUS was first consecrated in place of Eustathius. But Eulalius surviving his elevation only a short period, it was intended that Eusebius of Palestine should be translated to this bishopric. Eusebius, however, refused the appointment, and the emperor forbade its being conferred on him. Next Euphronius was put forward, who also dying, after a lapse of only one year and a few months, the see was conferred on Flaccillus[2]. All these bishops secretly clung to the Arian heresy. Hence it was that most of those individuals, whether of the clergy or of the laity, who valued the true religion, left the churches and formed assemblies among themselves. They were called Eustathians, since it was after the banishment of Eustathius that they began to hold their meetings. The wretched woman above-mentioned was soon after attacked by a severe and protracted illness, and then avowed the imposture in which she had been engaged, and made known the whole plot, not only to two or three, but to a very large number of priests. She confessed that she had been bribed to bring this false and impudent charge, but yet that her

3 Jerome says Trajanopolis, but Eustathius died at Philippi, *circa* 337. Athanasius, who calls Eustathius "a confessor and sound in the faith" (Hist. Ar. § 4), says the false charge which had most weight with Constantine was that the bishop of Antioch had slandered the Empress Helena. Sozomen (II. 19) records the patience with which Eustathius suffered, and sums up his character as that of "a good and true man, specially remarkable for eloquence, to which his extant writings testify, admirable as they are alike for the dignity of their style of ancient cast, the sound wisdom of their sentiments, the beauty of their language, and grace of expression." The sole survivor of his works is an attack on Origen's interpretation of Scripture.

1 Socrates, H E. i. 24, says that on the deposition of Eustathius "ἐφεξῆς ἐπὶ ἔτη ὀκτὼ λέγεται τὸν ἐν Ἀντιοχείᾳ θρόνον τῆς ἐκκλησίας σχολάσαι ὀψὲ δὲ . . . χειροτονεῖται Εὐφρόνιος." Cf. Soz. H.E. ii. 19. There is much confusion about this succession of bishops. Jerome (Chron. ii. p. 92) gives the names of the Arian bishops thrust in succession into the place of Eustathius, as Eulalius, Eusebius, Eufronius, Placillus. "Perhaps Eulalius was put forward for the vacant see, like Eusebius, but never actually appointed." Bp. Lightfoot, Dict. Christ. Biog. ii. 315.

2 This name is variously given as Placillus (Jerome), Placitus (Soz.), Flaccillus (Ath. and Eus.), and in different versions of Theodoret are found Φλάκιτος, Πλακέντιος, and Φάλκιος.

1 Deut. xix. 15.   2 1 Tim. v. 19.

oath was not altogether false, as a certain Eustathius, a coppersmith, was the father of the babe. Such were some of the crimes perpetrated in Antioch by this most excellent faction.

CHAPTER XXII.
Conversion of the Indians[1].

AT this period, the light of the knowledge of God was for the first time shed upon India. The courage and the piety of the emperor had become celebrated throughout the world; and the barbarians, having learnt by experience to choose peace rather than war, were able to enjoy intercourse with one another without fear. Many persons, therefore, set out on long journeys; some for the desire of making discoveries, others from a spirit of commercial enterprise. About this period a native of Tyre[2], acquainted with Greek philosophy, desiring to penetrate into the interior of India, set off for this purpose with his two young nephews. When he had accomplished the object of his wishes, he embarked for his own country. The ship being compelled to put in to land in order to obtain a fresh supply of water, the barbarians fell upon her, drowned some of the crew, and took the others prisoners. The uncle was among the number of those who were killed, and the lads were conducted to the king. The name of the one was Ædesius, and of the other Frumentius. The king of the country, in course of time, perceiving their intelligence, promoted them to the superintendence of his household. If any one should doubt the truth of this account, let him recal to mind the history of Joseph in the kingdom of Egypt, and also the history of Daniel, and of the three champions of the truth, who, from being captives, became princes of Babylon. The king died; but these young men remained with his son, and were advanced to still greater power. As they had been brought up in the true religion, they exhorted the merchants who visited the country to assemble, according to the custom of Romans[3], to take part in the divine liturgy. After a considerable time they solicited the king to reward their services by permitting them to return to their own country. They obtained his permission, and safely reached Roman territory. Ædesius directed his course towards Tyre,

but Frumentius, whose religious zeal was greater than the natural feeling of affection for his relatives, proceeded to Alexandria, and informed the bishop of that city that the Indians were deeply anxious to obtain spiritual light. Athanasius then held the rudder of that church; he heard the story, and then "Who," said he, "better than you yourself can scatter the mists of ignorance, and introduce among this people the light of Divine preaching?" After having said this, he conferred upon him the episcopal dignity, and sent him to the spiritual culture of that nation. The newly-ordained bishop left this country, caring nothing for the mighty ocean, and returned to the untilled ground of his work. There, having the grace of God to labour with him, he cheerfully and successfully played the husbandman, catching those who sought to gainsay his words by works of apostolic wonder, and thus, by these marvels, confirming his teaching, he continued each day to take many souls alive[4].

CHAPTER XXIII.
Conversion of the Iberians[1].

FRUMENTIUS thus led the Indians to the knowledge of God. Iberia, about the same time, was guided into the way of truth by a captive woman[2]. She continued instant in prayer, allowing herself no softer bed than a sack spread upon the ground, and accounted fasting her highest luxury. This austerity was rewarded by gifts similar to those of the Apostles. The barbarians, who were ignorant of medicine, were accustomed, when attacked by disease, to go to one another's houses, in order to ask those who had suffered in a similar way, and had got well, by what means they had been cured. In accordance with this custom, a mother who had a sick child, repaired to this admirable woman, to enquire if she knew of any cure for the disease. The latter took the child, placed it

---

[1] Περὶ τῆς Ἰνδῶν πίστεως. The term "India" is used vaguely, partly from the old belief that Asia and Africa joined somewhere south of the Indian Ocean. Here the Indians are Abyssinians.

[2] The version adopted by Rufinus, the earliest extant authority for this story, is followed, in the main, by Socrates, Sozomen, and Theodoret. The Tyrian traveller is named Meropius.

[3] The words of Sozomen (ii. 24) corresponding with the passage in which Rufinus (i. 9) speaks of meeting 'romano ritu orationis caussa,' are ᾗ ῥωμαίοις ἔθος ἐκκλησιάζειν, i.e. to assemble to worship after the manner of civilized citizens of the Empire, and not like savages. The expression has nothing to do with the customs of the Church of Rome, in the later sense of the word, as has sometimes been represented. Cf. Soc. I. 19, τὰς χριστιανικὰς ἐκτελεῖν εὐχάς.

[4] "The king, if we identify the narrative with the Ethiopian version of the story, must have been the father of the Abreha and Atzbeha of the Ethiopian annals" "Frumentius received the title of Abbana, or Abba Salama" (cf. Absalom), "the Father of Peace." "The bishopric of Auxume" (Axum, about 100 miles S. W. of Massowah) "assumed a metropolitan character." (Dict. of Christ. Biog., Art. Ethiopian Church). Constantius afterwards wrote to the Ethiopian Prince to ask him to replace Frumentius by Theophilus, an Arian, but without success (Ath. Ap. ad Const. 31).

[1] This story, like the preceding, is copied or varied by Sozomen, Socrates, and our author, from the version found also in Rufinus. Iberia, the modern Georgia, was conquered by Pompey, and ceded by Jovian.

[2] The Evangelizer of Georgia is honoured on Dec. 15th (Guerin Pet. Bolland, xiv. 306) as "Sainte Chrétienne," and it is doubtful whether the name Nina, in which she appears in the Armeno-gregorian Calendar for June 11 (Neale, Eastern Church, ii. 799), may not be a title. "Nina" is probably a name of rank, and perhaps is connected with our nun (Neale, i. 61). Moses of Chorene (ii. 83) gives the name "Nunia." Rufinus (i. 10) states that he gives the story as he heard it from King Bacurius at Jerusalem. On the various legends of St. Nina and her work, vide S. C. Malan, Hist. of Georgian Church pp. 17—33.

upon her bed, and prayed to the Creator of the world to be propitious to it, and cure the disease. He heard her prayer, and made it whole. This extraordinary woman hence obtained great celebrity; and the queen, who was suffering from a severe disease, hearing of her by report, sent for her. The captive held herself in very low estimation, and would not accept the invitation of the queen. But the queen, forced by her sore need, and careless of her royal dignity, herself ran to the captive. The latter made the queen lie down upon her mean bed, and once again applied to her disease the efficacious remedy of prayer. The queen was healed, and offered as rewards for her cure, gold, silver, tunics, and mantles, and such gifts as she thought worthy of possession, and such as royal munificence should bestow. The holy woman told her that she did not want any of these, but that she would deem her greatest reward to be the queen's knowledge of true religion. She then, as far as in her lay, explained the Divine doctrines, and exhorted her to erect a church in honour of Christ who had made her whole. The queen then returned to the palace, and excited the admiration of her consort, by the suddenness of her cure; she then made known to him the power of that God whom the captive adored, and besought him to acknowledge the one only God, and to erect a church to Him, and to lead all the nation to worship Him. The king was greatly delighted with the miracle which had been performed upon the queen, but he would not consent to erect a church. A short time after he went out hunting, and the loving Lord made a prey of him as He did of Paul; for a sudden darkness enveloped him and forbade him to move from the spot; while those who were hunting with him enjoyed the customary sunlight, and he alone was bound with the fetters of blindness. In his perplexity he found a way of escape, for calling to mind his former unbelief, he implored the help of the God of the captive woman, and immediately the darkness was dispelled. He then went to the marvellous captive, and asked her to shew him how a church ought to be built. He who once filled Bezaleel with architectural skill, graciously enabled this woman to devise the plan of a church. The woman set about the plan, and men began to dig and build. When the edifice was completed, the roof put on, and every thing supplied except the priests, this admirable woman found means to obtain these also. For she persuaded the king to send an embassy to the Roman emperor asking for teachers of religion. The king accordingly despatched an embassy for the purpose. The

emperor Constantine, who was warmly attached to the cause of religion, when informed of the purport of the embassy, gladly welcomed the ambassadors, and selected a bishop endowed with great faith, wisdom, and virtue, and presenting him with many gifts, sent him to the Iberians, that he might make known to them the true God. Not content with having granted the requests of the Iberians, he of his own accord undertook the protection of the Christians in Persia; for, learning that they were persecuted by the heathens, and that their king himself, a slave to error, was contriving various cunning plots for their destruction, he wrote to him, entreating him to embrace the Christian religion himself, as well as to honour its professors. His own letter will render his earnestness in the cause the plainer.

CHAPTER XXIV.

Letter written by the Emperor Constantine to Sapor [1], the King of Persia, respecting the Christians.

"In protecting the holy faith I enjoy the light of truth, and by following the light of truth I attain to fuller knowlege of the faith. Therefore, as facts prove, I recognize that most holy worship as teaching the knowledge of the most holy God. This service I profess. With the Power of this God for my ally, beginning at the furthest boundaries of the ocean, I have, one after another, quickened every part of the world with hope. Now all the peoples once enslaved by many tyrants, worn by their daily miseries, and almost extinct, have been kindled to fresh life by receiving the protection of the State.

"The God I reverence is He whose emblem my dedicated troops bear on their shoulders, marching whithersoever the cause of justice leads them, and rewarding me by their splendid victories. I confess that I reverence this God with eternal remembrance. Him, who dwelleth in the highest heavens, I contemplate with pure and unpolluted mind. On Him I call on bended knees, shunning all abominable blood, all unseemly and illomened odours, all fire or incantation [2], and all pollution by which unlawful and shameful error has destroyed whole nations and hurled them down to hell.

"God does not permit those gifts which, in His beneficent Providence, He has bestowed

---

[1] Sapor II. (Shapur) Postumus, the son of Hormisdas II., was one of the greatest of the Sassanidæ. He reigned from A.D. 310 to 381, and fought with success against Constantius II. and Julian, "augendi regni cupiditate supra homines flagrans." Amm. Marc. xviii. 4.

[2] The reading of Basil. Gr. and Lat., and Pini Codex, ἐπῳδῇ for γεώδη, is approved by Schulze, and may indicate a side-hit at the Magian fire-worship. But the adjectival form ἐπῳδῆς for ἐπῳδός is doubtful.

upon men for the supply of their wants to be perverted according to every man's desire. He only requires of men a pure mind and a spotless soul, and by these He weighs their deeds of virtue and piety. He is pleased with gentleness[3] and modesty; He loves the meek[4], and hates those who excite contentions; He loves faith, chastises unbelief; He breaks all power of boasting[5], and punishes the insolence of the proud[6]. Men exalted with pride He utterly overthrows, and rewards the humble[7] and the patient[8] according to their deserts. Of a just sovereignty He maketh much, strengthens it by His aid, and guards the counsels of Princes with the blessing of peace.

"I know that I am not in error, my brother, when I confess that this God is the Ruler and the Father of all men, a truth which many who preceded me upon the imperial throne were so deluded by error as to attempt to deny. But their end was so dreadful that they have become a fearful warning to all mankind, to deter others from similar iniquity[9]. Of these I count that man one whom the wrath of God, like a thunderbolt, drove hence into your country, and who made notorious the memorial of his shame which exists in your own land[10]. Indeed it appears to have been well ordered that the age in which we live should be distinguished by the open and manifest punishments inflicted on such persons. I myself have witnessed the end of those who have persecuted the people of God by unlawful edicts. Hence it is that I more especially thank God for having now, by His special Providence, restored peace to those who observe His law, in which they exalt and rejoice.

---

3 Cf. 2 Cor. x. i.   4 Cf. Matt. xi. 29.   5 Cf. Jas. iv. 16.
6 Cf. Luke i. 51.   7 Cf. Luke i. 52.   8 Cf. 2 Tim. ii. 24.
9 The imperial writer may have had in his mind Tiberius, whose miserable old age was probably ended by murder; Caius, stabbed by his own guard; Claudius, poisoned by his wife; Nero, driven to shameful suicide; Vitellius, beaten to death by a brutal mob; Domitian, assassinated by his wife and freedmen; Commodus, murdered by his courtiers; and Pertinax by his guards; Caracalla, murdered; Heliogabalus, murdered; Alexander Severus, Maximinus, Gordianus, murdered; Decius, killed in war; Gallus, Æmilianus, Gallienus, all murdered; Aurelianus, Probus, Carus, murdered. On the other hand Trajan, Marcus Aurelius, and Diocletian, who persecuted the Church with less or more severity, died peaceful deaths.
10 Valerianus, proclaimed Emperor in Rhœtia, A.D. 254, was defeated in his campaign against the Persians, and treated with indignity alive and dead. After being made to crouch as a footstool for his conqueror to tread on when mounting on horseback, he was flayed alive, A.D. 260, and his tanned skin nailed in a Persian temple as a "memorial of his shame." Cf. Const. Orat. xxiv. Gibbon's catholic scepticism includes the humiliation of Valerianus. "The tale," he says, "is moral and pathetic, but the truth of it may very fairly be called in question." (Decline and Fall, Chap. X.). But the passage in the text, in which the allusion has not always been perceived, and the parallel reference in the Emperor's oration, indicate the belief of a time little more than half a century after the event. Lactantius (de Morte Persecutorum V.), was probably about ten years old when Valerianus was defeated, and, if so, gives the testimony of a contemporary. Orosius (vii. 22) and Agathias (iv. p. 133) would only copy earlier writers, but the latter states that for the fact of Sapor's thus treating Valerianus there is "abundant historical testimony." Cf. Tillemont, Hist. Emp. iii. pp. 314, 315.

"I am led to expect future happiness and security whenever God in His goodness unites all men in the exercise of the one pure and true religion. You may therefore well understand how exceedingly I rejoice to hear that the finest provinces of Persia are adorned abundantly with men of this class; I mean Christians; for it is of them I am speaking. All then is well with you and with them, for you will have the Lord of all merciful and beneficent to you. Since then you are so mighty and so pious, I commend the Christians to your care, and leave them in your protection. Treat them, I beseech you, with the affection that befits your goodness. Your fidelity in this respect will confer on yourself and on us inexpressible benefits."

This excellent emperor felt so much solicitude for all who had embraced the true religion, that he not only watched over those who were his own subjects, but also over the subjects of other sovereigns. For this reason he was blessed with the special protection of God, so that although he held the reins of the whole of Europe and of Africa, and the greater part of Asia, his subjects were all well disposed to his rule, and obedient to his government. Foreign nations submitted to his sway, some by voluntary submission, others overcome in war. Trophies were everywhere erected, and the emperor was styled Victorious.

The praises of Constantine have, however, been proclaimed by many other writers. We must resume the thread of our history. This emperor, who deserves the highest fame, devoted his whole mind to matters worthy of the apostles, while men who had been admitted to the sacerdotal dignity not only neglected to edify the church, but endeavoured to uproot it from the very foundations. They invented all manner of false accusations against those who governed the church in accordance with the doctrines taught by the apostles, and did their best to depose and banish them. Their envy was not satisfied by the infamous falsehood which they had invented against Eustathius, but they had recourse to every artifice to effect the overthrow of another great bulwark of religion. These tragic occurrences I shall now relate as concisely as possible.

CHAPTER XXV.

An account of the plot formed against the Holy Athanasius.

ALEXANDER, that admirable bishop, who had successfully withstood the blasphemies of Arius, died five months after the council of Nicæa, and was succeeded in the episcopate of the church of Alexandria by Athanasius. Trained from his youth in sacred studies, Athanasius had attracted general admiration in each ecclesiastical office that he filled. He had, at the general council, so defended the doctrines of the apostles, that while he won the approbation of all the champions of the truth, its opponents learned to look on their antagonist as a personal foe and public enemy. He had attended the council as one of the retinue of Alexander, then a very young man, although he was the principal deacon [1].

When those who had denied the only-begotten Son of God heard that the helm of the Church of Alexandria had been entrusted to his hands, knowing as they did by experience his zeal for the truth, they thought that his rule would prove the destruction of their authority. They, therefore, resorted to the following machinations against him. In order to avert suspicion, they bribed some of the adherents of Meletius, who, although deposed by the council of Nicæa, had persevered in exciting commotions in the Thebaid and in the adjacent part of Egypt, and persuaded them to go to the emperor, and to accuse Athanasius of levying a tax upon Egypt [2], and giving the gold collected to a certain man who was preparing to usurp the imperial power [3]. The emperor being deceived by this story, Athanasius was brought to Constantinople. Upon his arrival he proved that the accusation was false, and had the charge given him by God restored to him. This is shown by a letter from the emperor to the Church of Alexandria, of which I shall transcribe only the concluding paragraph.

A Portion of the Letter from the Emperor Constantine to the Alexandrians.

"BELIEVE me, my brethren, the wicked men were unable to effect anything against your bishop. They surely could have had no other design than to waste our time, and to leave themselves no place for repentance in this life. Do you, therefore, help yourselves, and love that which wins your love [4]; and exert all your power in the expulsion of those who wish to destroy your concord. Look unto God, and love one another. I joyfully welcomed Athanasius your bishop; and I have conversed with him as with one whom I know to be a man of God."

CHAPTER XXVI.

Another plot against Athanasius.

THE calumniators of Athanasius, however, did not desist from their attempts. On the contrary, they devised so bold a fiction against him, that it surpassed every invention of the ancient writers of the tragic or comic stage. They again bribed individuals of the same party, and brought them before the emperor, vociferously accusing that champion of virtue of many abominable crimes. The leaders of the party were Eusebius, Theognis, and Theodorus, bishop of Perinthus, a city now called Heraclea [1]. After having accused Athanasius of crimes which they described as too shocking to be tolerated, or even listened to, they persuaded the emperor to convene a council at Cæsarea in Palestine, where Athanasius had many enemies, and to command that his cause should be there tried. The emperor, utterly ignorant of the plot that had been devised, was persuaded by them to give the required order.

But the holy Athanasius, well aware of the malevolence of those who were to try him, refused to appear at the council. This served as a pretext to those who opposed the truth to criminate him still further; and they accused him before the emperor of contumacy and arrogance. Nor were their hopes altogether frustrated; for the emperor, although exceedingly forbearing, became exasperated by their representations, and wrote to him in an angry manner, commanding him to repair to Tyre. Here the council was ordered to assemble, from the suspicion, as I think, that Athanasius had an apprehension of Cæsarea on account of its bishop. The emperor wrote also to the council in a style consistent with his devoted piety. His letter is as follows.

CHAPTER XXVII.

Epistle of the Emperor Constantine to the Council of Tyre [1].

"CONSTANTINUS AUGUSTUS to the holy council assembled in Tyre.

"In the general prosperity which distinguishes the present time, it seems right that the Catholic Church should likewise be exempt

---

[1] "τοῦ χοροῦ τῶν διακόνων ἡγούμενος." The youth of Athanasius indicates a variety in the qualifications for the archidiaconate, for he can hardly have been the senior deacon. Cf. Dict. Christian Ant., Art. "Archdeacon.'

[2] In order to provide στιχάρια or variegated vestments. Ath. Apol. cont. Ar. V. ¿ 60. The possibility of such charges indicates the importance of the Patriarchate.

[3] Philumenus. Ath. Ap. cont. Ar. V. ¿ 60.

[4] τὸ φίλτρον τὸ ὑμέτερον. Athanasius (Apol. cont. Ar. V. ¿ 62) quotes the phrase as ἡμέτερον, "our love."

[1] Perinthus, on the Propontis, also known as Heraclea, and now Erekli, was once a flourishing town. Theodorus was deposed at Sardica. On his genuine writings, vide Jer. de Vir. Ill. c. 90, and on a Commentary on the Psalter, published in 1643, and attributed to him, vide Dict. Christ. Biog. iv. 934.

[1] The Council of Tyre met A.D. 335, on the date, vide Bp. Lightfoot in Dict. Christ. Biog. iii. 316, note. "The scenes at the Council of Tyre form the most picturesque and the most shameful chapter in the Arian controversy." Id.

from trouble, and that the servants of Christ should be freed from every reproach.

"But certain individuals instigated by the mad desire of contention, not to say leading a life unworthy of their profession, are endeavouring to throw all into disorder. This appears to me to be the greatest of all possible calamities. I beseech you, therefore, in post haste, as the phrase goes, to assemble together, without any delay, in formal synod ; so that you may support those who require your assistance, heal the brethren who are in danger, restore unanimity to the divided members, and rectify the disorders of the Church while time permits ; and thus restore to those great provinces the harmony which, alas ! the arrogance of a few men has destroyed. I believe every one would admit that you could not perform anything so pleasing in the sight of God, so surpassing all my prayers as well as your own, or so conducive to your own reputation, as to restore peace.

"Do not ye therefore delay, but when you have come together with all that sincerity and fidelity which our Saviour demands of all His servants, almost in words that we can hear, endeavour with redoubled eagerness to put a fitting end to these dissensions.

"Nothing shall be omitted on my part to further the interests of our religion. I have done all that you recommended in your letters. I have sent to those bishops whom you specified, directing them to repair to the council for the purpose of deliberating with you upon ecclesiastical matters. I have also sent Dionysius [2], a man of consular rank, to counsel those who are to sit in synod with you, and to be himself an eye witness of your proceedings, and particularly of the order and regularity that is maintained. If any one should dare on the present occasion also to disobey our command, and refuse to come to the council, which, however, I do not anticipate, an officer will be despatched immediately to send him into banishment by imperial order, that he may learn not to oppose the decrees enacted by the emperor for the support of truth.

"All that now devolves upon your holinesses is to decide with unanimous judgment, without partiality or prejudice, in accordance with the ecclesiastical and apostolical rule, and to devise suitable remedies for the offences which may have resulted from error; in order that the Church may be freed from all reproach, that my anxiety may be diminished, that peace may be restored to those now at variance, and that your renown may be increased. May God preserve you, beloved brethren."

The bishops accordingly repaired to the council of Tyre. Amongst them were those who were accused of holding heterodox doctrines ; of whom Asclepas, bishop of Gaza, was one. The admirable Athanasius also attended. I shall first dwell on the tragedy of the accusation, and shall then relate the proceedings of this celebrated tribunal.

CHAPTER XXVIII.

The Council of Tyre.

ARSENIUS was a bishop of the Meletian faction. The men of his party put him in a place of concealment, and charged him to remain there as long as possible. They then cut off the right hand of a corpse, embalmed it, placed it in a wooden case, and carried it about everywhere, declaring that it was the hand of Arsenius, who had been murdered by Athanasius. But the all-seeing eye did not permit Arsenius to remain long in concealment. He was first seen alive in Egypt ; then in the Thebaid ; afterwards he was led by Divine Providence to Tyre, where the hand of tragic fame was brought before the council. The friends of Athanasius hunted him up, and brought him to an inn, where they compelled him to lie hid for a time. Early in the morning the great Athanasius came to the council.

First of all a woman of lewd life was brought in, who deposed in a loud and impudent manner that she had vowed perpetual virginity, but that Athanasius, who had lodged in her house, had violated her chastity. After she had made her charge, the accused came forward, and with him a presbyter worthy of all praise, by name Timotheus. The court ordered Athanasius to reply to the indictment ; but he was silent, as if he had not been Athanasius. Timotheus, however, addressed her thus : "Have I, O woman, ever conversed with you, or have I entered your house?" She replied with still greater effrontery, screaming aloud in her dispute with Timotheus, and, pointing at him with her finger, exclaimed, "It was you who robbed me of my virginity; it was you who stripped me of my chastity ;" adding other indelicate expressions which are used by shameless women. The devisers of this calumny were put to shame, and all the bishops who were privy to it, blushed.

The woman was now being led out of the Court, but the great Athanasius protested that instead of sending her away they ought to examine her, and learn the name of the hatcher of the plot. Hereupon his accusers yelled and shouted that he had perpetrated other viler crimes, of which it was utterly impossible that he could by any art or ingenuity

---

[2] Athanasius (Apol. cont. Ar. VI. § 72) describes him as acting with gross partiality.

be cleared; and that eyes, not ears, would decide on the evidence. Having said this, they exhibited the famous box and exposed the embalmed hand to view. At this sight all the spectators uttered a loud cry. Some believed the accusation to be true; the others had no doubt of the falsehood, and thought that Arsenius was lurking somewhere or other in concealment. When at length, after some difficulty, a little silence was obtained, the accused asked his judges whether any of them knew Arsenius. Several of them replying that they knew him well, Athanasius gave orders that he should be brought before them. Then he again asked them, "Is this the right Arsenius? Is this the man I murdered? Is this the man those people mutilated after his murder by cutting off his right hand?" When they had confessed that it was the same individual, Athanasius pulled off his cloak, and exhibited two hands, both the right and the left, and said, "Let no one seek for a third hand, for man has received two hands from the Creator and no more."

Even after this plain proof the calumniators and the judges who were privy to the crime, instead of hiding themselves, or praying that the earth might open and swallow them up, raised an uproar and commotion in the assembly, and declared that Athanasius was a sorcerer, and that he had by his magical incantations bewitched the eyes of men. The very men who a moment before had accused him of murder now strove to tear him in pieces and to murder him. But those whom the emperor had entrusted with the preservation of order saved the life of Athanasius by dragging him away, and hurrying him on board a ship [1].

When he appeared before the emperor, he described all the dramatic plot which had been got up to ruin him. The calumniators sent bishops attached to their faction into Mareotis, viz., Theognis, bishop of Nicæa, Theodorus, bishop of Perinthus, Maris, bishop of Chalcedon, Narcissus of Cilicia [2], with others of the same sentiments. Mareotis is a district near Alexandria, and derives its name from the lake Maria [3]. Here they invented other falsehoods, and, forging the reports of the trial, mixed up the charges which had been shown to be false with fresh accusations, as if they had been true, and despatched them to the emperor.

CHAPTER XXIX.

Consecration of the Church of Jerusalem.— Banishment of St. Athanasius.

ALL the bishops who were present at the council of Tyre, with all others from every quarter, were commanded by the emperor to proceed to Ælia [1] to consecrate the churches which he had there erected. The emperor despatched also a number of officials of the most kindly disposition, remarkable for piety and fidelity, whom he ordered to furnish abundant supplies of provisions, not only to the bishops and their followers, but to the vast multitudes who flocked from all parts to Jerusalem. The holy altar was decorated with imperial hangings and with golden vessels set with gems. When the splendid festival was concluded, each bishop returned to his own diocese. The emperor was highly gratified when informed of the splendour and magnificence of the function, and blessed the Author of all good for having thus granted his petition.

Athanasius having complained of his unjust condemnation, the emperor commanded the bishops against whom this complaint was directed to present themselves at court. Upon their arrival, they desisted from urging any of their former calumnies, because they knew how clearly they could be refuted; but they made it appear that Athanasius had threatened to prevent the exportation of corn. The emperor believed what they said, and banished him to a city of Gaul called Treves [2]. This occurred in the thirtieth year of the emperor's reign [3].

CHAPTER XXX.

Will of the blessed Emperor Constantine.

A YEAR and a few months afterwards [1] the emperor was taken ill at Nicomedia, a city of Bithynia, and, knowing the uncertainty of human life, he received the holy rite of baptism [2], which he had intended to have deferred until he could be baptized in the river Jordan.

He left as heirs of the imperial throne his three sons, Constantine, Constantius, and Constans [3], the youngest.

He ordered that the great Athanasius should

---

[1] Here comes in the famous scene of the sudden apparition of Athanasius before Constantine. "The Emperor is entering Constantinople in state. A small figure darts across his path in the middle of the square, and stops his horse. The Emperor, thunderstruck, tries to pass on; he cannot guess who the petitioner can be. It is Athanasius, who comes to insist on justice, when thought to be leagues away at the Council of Tyre." Stanley, Eastern Church, Lect. VII.

[2] Bishop of Neronias, or Irenopolis. Cf. p. 44, note.

[3] Marëa or Maria, a town and lake of Lower Egypt, giving its name to the district: now lake Marrout.

[1] Ælia Capitolina, the name given to Jerusalem on its restoration by (Ælius) Hadrianus.

[2] Augusta Treverorum, Treveri, Trier, or Treves, on the Moselle, was now the official Capital of Gaul.

[3] i.e. A.D. 336.

[1] A.D. 337.

[2] At the hand of Eusebius of Nicomedia.

[3] Vide Pedigree, in the Prolegomena. Constantine II. received Gaul, Britain, Spain, and a part of Africa: Constantius the East, and Constans Illyricum, Italy, and the rest of Africa. In 340 Constans defeated his brother, who was slain near Aquileia, and became master of the West.

return to Alexandria, and expressed this decision in the presence of Eusebius, who did all he could to dissuade him.

CHAPTER XXXI.

Apology for Constantine.

IT ought not to excite astonishment that Constantine was so far deceived as to send so many great men into exile ; for he believed the assertions of bishops of high fame and reputation, who skilfully concealed their malice. Those who are acquainted with the Sacred Scriptures know that the holy David, although he was a prophet, was deceived ; and that too not by a priest, but by one who was a menial, a slave, and a rascal. I mean Ziba, who deluded the king by lies against Mephibosheth, and thus obtained his land [1]. It is not to condemn the prophet that I thus speak ; but that I may defend the emperor, by showing the weakness of human nature, and to teach that credit should not be given only to those who advance accusations, even though they may appear worthy of credit ; but that the other party ought also to be heard, and that one ear should be left open to the accused.

---

[1] Our Author is of the same opinion as Sir George Grove, as against Professor Blunt, on the character of Mephibosheth. Dict. Bib. ii. 326.

CHAPTER XXXII.

The end of the Holy Emperor Constantine.

The emperor was now translated from his earthly dominions to a better kingdom [1].

THE body of the emperor was enclosed in a golden coffin, and was carried to Constantinople by the governors of the provinces, the military commanders, and the other officers of state, preceded and followed by the whole army, all bitterly deploring their loss; for Constantine had been as an affectionate father to them all. The body of the emperor was allowed to remain in the palace until the arrival of his sons, and high honours were rendered to it. But these details require no description here, as a full account has been given by other writers. From their works, which are easy of access, may be learnt how greatly the Ruler of all honours His faithful servants. If any one should be tempted to unbelief, let him look at what occurs now near the tomb and the statue of Constantine [2], and then he must admit the truth of what God has said in the Scriptures, " *Them that honour Me I will honour, and they that despise Me shall be lightly esteemed* [3]."

---

[1] Whitsunday, A.D. 337.
[2] Valesius explains this allusion by quoting the Arian Philostorgius (ii. 17), who says that "the statue of Constantine, standing on its porphyry column, was honoured with sacrifices, illuminations, and incense." The accusation of idolatrous worship may be disregarded. Cf. Chron. Alex. 665, 667.   [3] 1 Sam. ii. 30.

END OF THE FIRST BOOK

BOOK II

CHAPTER I.

Return of St. Athanasius.

THE divine Athanasius returned to Alexandria, after having remained two years and four months at Treves [1]. Constantine, the eldest son of Constantine the Great, whose imperial sway extended over Western Gaul, wrote the following letter to the church of Alexandria.

Epistle of the Emperor Constantine, the son of Constantine the Great, to the Alexandrians.

"CONSTANTINUS CÆSAR to the people of the Catholic Church of Alexandria.

"I think that it cannot have escaped your pious intelligence that Athanasius, the interpreter of the venerated law, was opportunely sent into Gaul, in order that, so long as the savagery of these bloodthirsty opponents was threatening peril to his sacred head, he might be saved from suffering irremediable wrongs. To avoid this imminent peril, he was snatched from the jaws of his foes, to remain in a city under my jurisdiction, where he might be abundantly supplied with every necessary. Yet the greatness of his virtue, relying on the grace of God, led him to despise all the calamities of adverse fortune. Constantine, my lord and my father, of blessed memory, intended to have reinstated him in his former bishopric, and to have restored him to your piety; but as the emperor was arrested by the hand of death before his desires were accomplished, I, being his heir, have deemed it fitting to carry into execution the purpose of this sovereign of divine memory. You will learn from your bishop himself, when you see him, with how much respect I have treated him. Nor indeed is it surprising that he should have been thus treated by me. I was moved to this line of conduct by his own great virtue, and the thought of your affectionate longing for his return. May Divine Providence watch over you, beloved brethren!"

Furnished with this letter, St. Athanasius returned [2] from exile, and was most gladly welcomed both by the rich and by the poor, by the inhabitants of cities, and by those of the provinces. The followers of the madness of Arius were the only persons who felt any vexation at his return. Eusebius, Theognis, and those of their faction resorted to their former machinations, and endeavoured to prejudice the ears of the young emperor against him.

I shall now proceed to relate in what manner Constantius swerved from the doctrines of the Apostles.

CHAPTER II.

Declension of the Emperor Constantius from the true Faith.

CONSTANTIA, the widow of Licinius, was the half-sister of Constantine [1]. She was intimately acquainted with a certain priest who had imbibed the doctrines of Arius. He did not openly acknowledge his unsoundness; but, in the frequent conversations which he had with her, he did not refrain from declaring that Arius had been unjustly calumniated. After the death of her impious husband, the renowned Constantine did everything in his power to solace her, and strove to prevent her from experiencing the saddest trials of widowhood. He attended her also in her last illness [2], and rendered her every proper attention. She then presented the priest whom I mentioned to the emperor, and entreated him to receive

---

[1] From Feb. 336 to June 338. The "Porta Nigra" and the ruins of the Baths still shew relics of the splendour of the imperial city. The exile was generously treated. Maximinus, the bishop of Treves, was orthodox and friendly. (Ath. *ad Episc. Ægypt.* § 8.) On the conclusion of the term of his relegation to Treves Constantine II. took him in the imperial suite to Viminacium, a town on the Danube, not far from the modern Passarovitz. Here the three emperors met. Athanasius continued his journey to Alexandria *via* Constantinople and the Cappadocian Cæsarea. (Ath. *Hist. Ar.* § 8 and *Apol. ad Const.* § 5.)

[2] In Nov. 338. His clergy thought it the happiest day of their lives. Ath. *Ap. Cont. Ar.* § 7.
[1] Vide Pedigree. Philostorgius (ii. 16) said the will was given to Eusebius of Nicomedia. Valesius (on Soc. i. 25) thinks that if the story had been true Athanasius would have recorded it, with the name of the Presbyter.
[2] A.D. 327—328.

him under his protection. Constantine acceded to her request, and soon after fulfilled his promise. But though the priest was permitted the utmost freedom of speech, and was most honourably treated, he did not venture to reveal his corrupt principles, for he observed the firmness with which the emperor adhered to the truth. When Constantine was on the point of being translated to an eternal kingdom, he drew up a will, in which he directed that his temporal dominions should be divided among his sons. None of them was with him when he was dying, so he entrusted the will to this priest alone, and desired him to give it to Constantius, who, being at a shorter distance from the spot than his brothers, was expected to arrive the first. These directions the priest executed, and thus by putting the will into his hands, became known to Constantius, who accepted him as an intimate friend, and commanded him to visit him frequently. Perceiving the weakness of Constantius, whose mind was like reeds driven to and fro by the wind, he became emboldened to declare war against the doctrines of the gospel. He loudly deplored the stormy state of the churches, and asserted it to be due to those who had introduced the unscriptural word "consubstantial" into the confession of faith, and that all the disputes among the clergy and the laity had been occasioned by it. He calumniated Athanasius and all who coincided in his opinions, and formed designs for their destruction, being used as their fellow-worker by Eusebius [3], Theognis, and Theodorus, bishop of Perinthus.

The last-named, whose see is generally known by the name of Heraclea, was a man of great erudition, and had written an exposition of the Holy Scriptures [4].

These bishops resided near the emperor, and frequently visited him; they assured him that the return of Athanasius from banishment had occasioned many evils, and had excited a tempest which had shaken not only Egypt, but also Palestine, Phœnicia, and the adjacent countries [5].

CHAPTER III.

Second Exile of St. Athanasius.—Ordination and Death of Gregorius.

WITH these and similar arguments, the bishops assailed the weak-minded emperor, and persuaded him to expel Athanasius from his church. But Athanasius obtained timely intimation of their design, and departed to the west [1]. The friends of Eusebius had sent false accusations against him to Julius, who was then bishop of Rome [2]. In obedience to the laws of the church, Julius summoned the accusers and the accused to Rome, that the cause might be tried [3]. Athanasius, accordingly, set out for Rome, but the calumniators refused to go because they saw that their falsehood would easily be detected [4]. But perceiving that the flock of Athanasius was left without a pastor, they appointed over it a wolf instead of a shepherd. Gregorius, for this was his name, surpassed the wild beasts in his deeds of cruelty towards the flock: but at the expiration of six years he was destroyed by the sheep themselves. Athanasius went to Constans (Constantine, the eldest brother, having fallen in battle), and complained of the plots laid against him by the Arians, and of their opposition to the apostolical faith [5]. He reminded him of his father, and how he attended in person the great and famous council which he had summoned; how he was present at its debates, took part in framing its decrees, and confirmed them by law. The emperor was moved to emulation by his father's zeal, and promptly wrote to his brother, exhorting him to preserve inviolate the religion of their father, which they had inherited; "for," he urged, "by piety he made his empire great, destroyed the tyrants of Rome, and subjugated the foreign nations on every side." Constantius was led by this letter to summon the bishops from the east and from the west to Sardica [6], a city of Illyricum, and the metropolis of Dacia, that they might deliberate on the means of removing

---

[1] Easter, A.D. 340. The condemnation was confirmed at the Council of Antioch, A.D. 341.
[2] They were met by a deputation of Athanasians, bringing the encyclical of the Egyptian Bishops in favour of the accused. *Apol. Cont. Ar.* § 3.
[3] On the bearing of these communications with Rome on the question of Papal jurisdiction, vide Salmon, *Infallibility of the Church*, p. 405. Cf. Wladimir Guettée, *Histoire de l'Eglise*, III. p. 112.
[4] The innocence of Athanasius was vindicated at the Council held at Rome in Nov. A.D. 341.
[5] For the violent resentment of the Alexandrian Church at the obtrusion of Gregorius, an Ultra-Arian, and apparently an illustration of the old proverb of the three bad Kappas, "Καππάδοκες, Κρῆτες, Κίλικες, τρία κάππα κάκιστα," for he was a Cappadocian—vide Ath. *Encyc.* 3, 4, *Hist. Ar.* 10. The sequence of events is not without difficulty, and our author gives here little help. Athanasius was in Alexandria in the spring of 340, when Gregorius made his entry, and started for Rome at or about Easter. Constantine II. was defeated and slain by the troops of his brother Constans, in the neighbourhood of Aquileia, and his corpse found in the river Alsa, in April, 340. Athanasius remained at Rome till the summer of 343, when he was summoned to Milan by Constans (*Ap. ad Const.* 3, 4).
    Results of his visit to Rome were the adherence of Latin Christianity to the orthodox opinion (Cf. Milman, *Hist. of Lat. Christianity*, vol. i. p. 78), and the introduction of Monachism into the West. Vide Robertson's *Ch. Hist.* ii. 6.
[6] Now Sophia, in Bulgaria. The centre of Mœsia was called Dacia Cis-Danubiana, when the tract conquered by Trajan was abandoned.

---

[3] Of Nicomedia, now transferred to the see of Constantinople.
[4] Vide note on p. 61.
[5] The ground of objection to the return was (i) that Athanasius had been condemned by a Council—that of Tyre, and (ii) that he was restored by the authority of the state alone. The first intention was to get the Arian Pistus advanced to the patriarchate.

the other troubles of the church, which were many and pressing.

CHAPTER IV.

Paulus, Bishop of Constantinople.

PAULUS[1], bishop of Constantinople, who faithfully maintained orthodox doctrines, was accused by the unsound Arians of exciting seditions, and of such other crimes as they usually laid to the charge of all those who preached true piety. The people, who feared the machinations of his enemies, would not permit him to go to Sardica. The Arians, taking advantage of the weakness of the emperor, procured from him an edict of banishment against Paulus, who was, accordingly, sent to Cucusus, a little town formerly included in Cappadocia, but now in Lesser Armenia. But these disturbers of the public peace were not satisfied with having driven the admirable Paulus into a desert. They sent the agents of their cruelty to despatch him by a violent death. St. Athanasius testifies to this fact in the defence which he wrote of his own flight. He uses the following words[2]: "They pursued Paulus, bishop of Constantinople, and having seized him at Cucusus, a city of Cappadocia, they had him strangled, using as their executioner Philippus the prefect, who was the protector of their heresy, and the active agent of their most atrocious projects[3]."

Such were the murders to which the blasphemy of Arius gave rise. Their mad rage against the Only-begotten was matched by cruel deeds against His servants.

CHAPTER V.

The Heresy of Macedonius.

THE Arians, having effected the death of Paulus, or rather having despatched him to the kingdom of heaven, promoted Macedonius[1] in his place, who, they imagined, held the same sentiments, and belonged to the same faction as themselves, because he, like them, blasphemed the Holy Ghost. But, shortly after, they deposed him also, because he refused to call Him a creature Whom the Holy Scriptures affirm to be the Son of God. After his separation from them, he became the leader of a sect of his own. He taught that the Son of God is not of the same substance as the Father, but that He is like Him in every particular. He also openly affirmed that the Holy Ghost is a creature. These circumstances occurred not long afterwards as we have narrated them.

CHAPTER VI.

Council held at Sardica.

Two hundred and fifty bishops assembled at Sardica[1], as is proved by ancient records. The great Athanasius, Asclepas, bishop of Gaza, already mentioned[2], and Marcellus[3], bishop of Ancyra, the metropolis of Galatia, who also held this bishopric at the time of the council of Nicæa, all repaired thither. The calumniators, and the chiefs of the Arian faction, who had previously judged the cause of Athanasius, also attended. But when they found that the members of the synod were staunch in their adherence to sound doctrine, they would not even enter the council, although they had been summoned to it, but fled away, both accusers and judges. All these circumstances are far more clearly explained in a letter drawn up by the council; and I shall therefore now insert it.

Synodical Letter from the Bishops assembled at Sardica, addressed to the other Bishops.

"THE holy council assembled at Sardica, from Rome, Spain, Gaul, Italy, Campania, Calabria, Africa, Sardinia, Pannonia, Mœsia, Dacia, Dardania, Lesser Dacia, Macedonia, Thessaly, Achaia, Epirus, Thrace, Rhodope, Asia, Caria, Bithynia, the Hellespont, Phrygia, Pisidia, Cappadocia, Pontus, the lesser Phrygia, Cilicia, Pamphylia, Lydia, the Cyclades, Egypt, the Thebaid, Libya, Galatia, Palestine and Arabia, to the bishops throughout the world, our fellow-ministers in the catholic and apostolic Church, and our beloved brethren in the Lord. Peace be unto you.

"The madness of the Arians has often led them to the perpetration of violent atrocities

---

[1] A native of Thessalonica; he had been secretary to his predecessor Alexander.

[2] Ath. *de fug.* § 3. Cf. *Hist. Ar. ad Mon.* 7.

[3] Flavius Philippus, prætorian præfect of the East, is described by Socrates (II. 16), as δεύτερος μετὰ βασιλέα. Paulus was removed from Constantinople in 342, and not slain till 350. Philippus died in disappointment and misery. *Dict. Christ. Biog.* iv. 356.

[1] On the vicissitudes of the see of Constantinople, after the death of Alexander, in A.D. 336, vide Soc. ii. 6 and Soz. iii. 3. Paulus was murdered in 350 or 351, and the "shortly after" of the text means nine years, Macedonius being replaced by Eudoxius of Antioch, in 360. On how far the heresy of the "Pneumatomachi," called Macedonianism, was really due to the teaching of Macedonius, vide Robertson's *Church Hist.* II. iv. for reff.

[1] The Council met in 343, according to Hefele; 344, according to Mansi, on the authority of the Festal Letters of Athanasius. Summoned by both Emperors, it was presided over by Hosius. The accounts of the numbers present vary. Some authorities adhere to the traditional date, 347. Soc. ii. 20; Soz. iii. 11.

[2] Vide I. xxvii.

[3] Perhaps present at the Synod of Ancyra (Angora), in A.D. 315. Died, A.D. 374. Marcellus played the man at Nicæa, and was accused by the Arians of Sabellianism, and deposed. He was distrusted as a trimmer, but could boast "se communione Julii et Athanasii, Romanæ et Alexandrinæ urbis pontificum, esse munitum" (*Jer. de vir. ill.* c. 86). Cardinal Newman thinks Athanasius attacked him in the IVth Oration against the Arians. Vide *Dict. Christ. Biog.* iii. 808.

against the servants of God who keep the true faith ; they introduce false doctrines themselves, and persecute those who uphold orthodox principles. So violent were their attacks on the faith, that they reached the ears of our most pious emperors. Through the co-operation of the grace of God, the emperors have summoned us from different provinces and cities to the holy council which they have appointed to be held in the city of Sardica, in order that all dissensions may be terminated, all evil doctrines expelled, and the religion of Christ alone maintained amongst all people. Some bishops from the east have attended the council at the solicitation of our most religious emperors, principally on account of the reports circulated against our beloved brethren and fellow-ministers, Athanasius, bishop of Alexandria, Marcellus, bishop of Ancyra in Galatia, and Asclepas, bishop of Gaza. Perhaps the calumnies of the Arians have already reached you, and they have endeavoured thus to forestall the council, and make you believe their groundless accusations of the innocent, and prevent any suspicion being raised of the depraved heresy which they uphold. But they have not long been permitted so to act. The Lord is the Protector of the churches ; for them and for us all He suffered death, and opened for us the way to heaven.

"The adherents of Eusebius. Maris, Theodorus, Theognis, Ursacius, Valens, Menophantus, and Stephanus, had already written to Julius, the bishop of Rome, and our fellow-minister, against our aforesaid fellow-ministers, Athanasius, bishop of Alexandria, Marcellus, bishop of Ancyra in Galatia, and Asclepas, bishop of Gaza. Some bishops of the opposite party wrote also to Julius, testifying to the innocence of Athanasius, and proving that all that had been asserted by the followers of Eusebius was nothing more than lies and slander. The refusal of the Arians to obey the summons of our beloved brother and fellow-ruler, Julius, and also the letter written by that bishop, clearly prove the falseness of their accusation. For, had they believed that what they had done and represented against our fellow-minister admitted of justification, they would have gone to Rome. But their mode of procedure in this great and holy council is a manifest proof of their fraud. Upon their arrival at Sardica, they perceived that our brethren, Athanasius, Marcellus, Asclepas, and others, were there also ; they were therefore afraid to come to the test, although they had been summoned, not once or twice only, but repeatedly. There were they waited for by the assembled bishops, particularly by the venerable Hosius, one worthy of all honour and respect, on account of his advanced age, his adherence

to the faith, and his labours for the church. All urged them to join the assembly and avail themselves of the opportunity of proving, in the presence of their fellow-ministers, truth of the charges they had brought against them in their absence, both by word and by letter. But they refused to obey the summons, as we have already stated, and so by their excesses proved the falsity of their statements, and all but proclaimed aloud the plot and schemes they had formed. Men confident of the truth of their assertions are always ready to stand to them openly. But as these accusers would not appear to substantiate what they had advanced, any future allegations which they may by their usual artifices bring against our fellow-ministers, will only be regarded as proceeding from a desire of slandering them in their absence, without the courage to confront them openly.

"They fled, beloved brethren, not only because their charges were slander, but also because they saw men arrive with serious and manifold accusations against themselves. Chains and fetters were produced. Some were present whom they had exiled : others came forward as representatives of those still kept in exile. There stood relations and friends of men whom they had put to death. Most serious of all, bishops also appeared, one of whom [4] exhibited the irons and the chains with which they had laden him. Others testified that death followed their false charges. For their infatuation had led them so far as even to attempt the life of a bishop ; and he would have been killed had he not escaped from their hands. Theodulus [5], our fellow-minister, of blessed memory, passed hence with their calumny on his name ; for, through it, he had been condemned to death. Some showed the wounds which had been inflicted on them by the sword ; others deposed that they had been exposed to the miseries of famine.

"All these depositions were made, not by a few obscure individuals, but by whole churches ; the presbyters of these churches giving evidence that the persecutors had armed the military against them with swords, and the common people with clubs ; had employed judicial threats, and produced spurious documents. The letters written by Theognis, for the purpose of prejudicing the emperor against our fellow-ministers, Athanasius, Marcellus, and Asclepas, were read and attested by those who had formerly been the deacons

---

4 Probably Lucius, Bishop of Hadrianople, who had been deposed by the Arians, and appealed to Julius, who wished to right him. Still kept out by the Arians, he appealed to the Council of Sardica, apd, in accordance with its decree, Constantius ordered his restoration (Soc. ii. 26). Cf. Chap. XII.
5 Bishop of Trajanopolis (Ath. *Hist. Ar.* 19).

of Theognis. It was also proved that they had stripped virgins naked, had burnt churches, and imprisoned our fellow-ministers, and all because of the infamous heresy of the Ariomaniacs. For thus all who refused to make common cause with them were treated.

"The consciousness of having committed all these crimes placed them in great straits. Ashamed of their deeds, which could no longer be concealed, they repaired to Sardica, thinking that their boldness in venturing thither would remove all suspicion of their guilt. But when they perceived the presence of those whom they had falsely accused, and of those who had suffered from their cruelty; and that likewise several had come with irrefragable accusations against them, they would not enter the council. Our fellow-ministers, on the other hand, Athanasius, Marcellus, and Asclepas, took every means to induce them to attend, by tears, by urgency, by challenge, promising not only to prove the falsity of their accusations, but also to show how deeply they had injured their own churches. But they were so overwhelmed by the consciousness of their own evil deeds, that they took to flight, and by this flight clearly proved the falsity of their accusations, as well as their own guilt.

"But though their calumny and perfidy, which had indeed been apparent from the beginning, were now clearly perceived, yet we determined to examine the circumstances of the case according to the laws of truth, lest they should, from their very flight, derive pretexts for renewed acts of deceitfulness.

"Upon carrying this resolution into effect, we proved by their actions that they were false accusers, and that they had formed plots against our fellow-ministers. Arsenius, whom they declared had been put to death by Athanasius, is still alive, and takes his place among the living. This fact alone is sufficient to show that their other allegations are false.

"Although they spread a report everywhere that a chalice had been broken by Macarius, one of the presbyters of Athanasius, yet those who came from Alexandria, from Mareotis, and from other places, testified that this was not the fact; and the bishops in Egypt wrote to Julius, our fellow-minister, declaring that there was not the least suspicion that such a deed had been done. The judicial facts which the Arians assert they possess against Macarius have been all drawn up by one party; and in these documents the depositions of pagans and of catechumens were included. One of these catechumens, when interrogated, replied that he was in the church on the entry of Macarius. Another deposed that Ischyras, whom they had talked about so much, was

then lying ill in his cell. Hence it appears that the mysteries could not have been celebrated at that time, as the catechumens were present, and as Ischyras was absent; for he was at that very time confined by illness. Ischyras, that wicked man who had falsely affirmed that Athanasius had burnt some of the sacred books, and had been convicted of the crime, now confessed that he was ill in bed when Macarius arrived; hence the falsehood of his accusation was clearly demonstrated. His calumny was, however, rewarded by his party; they gave him the title of a bishop, although he was not yet even a presbyter. For two presbyters came to the synod, who some time back had been attached to Meletius, and were afterwards received back by the blessed Alexander, bishop of Alexandria, and are now with Athanasius, protesting that he had never been ordained a presbyter, and that Meletius had never had any church, or employed any minister in Mareotis. Yet, although he had never been ordained a presbyter, they promote him to a bishopric, in order that his title may impose upon those who hear his false accusations[6].

"The writings of our fellow-minister, Marcellus, were also read, and plainly evinced the duplicity of the adherents of Eusebius; for what Marcellus had simply suggested as a point of inquiry, they accused him of professing as a point of faith. The statements which he had made, both before and after the inquiry, were read, and his faith was proved to be orthodox. He did not affirm, as they represented, that the beginning of the Word of God was dated from His conception by the holy Mary, or that His kingdom would have an end. On the contrary, he wrote that His kingdom had had no beginning, and would have no end. Asclepas, our fellow-minister, produced the reports drawn up at Antioch in the presence of the accusers, and of Eusebius, bishop of Cæsarea, and proved his innocence by the sentence of the bishops who had presided as judges.

"It was not then without cause, beloved brethren, that, although so frequently summoned, they would not attend the council; it was not without cause that they took to flight. The reproaches of conscience constrained them to make their escape, and thus, at the same time, to demonstrate the groundlessness of their calumnies, and the truth of those accusations which were advanced and

---

6 The strange story of Ischyras is gathered from notices in the *Apol. c. Arian.* Without ordination, he started a small conventicle of some half-dozen people, and the Alexandrian Synod of 324 condemned his pretensions. The incident of the text may be assigned to 329. He afterwards faced both ways, to Athanasius and the Eusebians, and was recognised by them as a bishop. *Dict. Christ. biog.* iii. 302.

proved against them. Besides all the other grounds of complaint, it may be added that all those who had been accused of holding the Arian heresy, and had been ejected in consequence, were not only received, but advanced to the highest dignities by them. They raised deacons to the presbyterate, and thence to the episcopate ; and in all this they were actuated by no other motive than the desire of propagating and diffusing their heresy, and of corrupting the true faith.

" Next to Eusebius, the following are their principal leaders ; Theodorus, bishop of Heraclea, Narcissus, bishop of Neronias in Cilicia, Stephanus, bishop of Antioch, Georgius[7], bishop of Laodicea, Acacius[8], bishop of Cæsarea in Palestine, Menophantus, bishop of Ephesus in Asia, Ursacius, bishop of Singidunum[9] in Mœsia, and Valens, bishop of Mursa[10] in Pannonia. These bishops forbade those who came with them from the east to attend the holy council, or to unite with the Church of God. On their road to Sardica they held private assemblies at different places, and formed a compact cemented by threats, that, when they arrived in Sardica, they would not join the holy council, nor assist at its deliberations ; arranging that, as soon as they had arrived they should present themselves for form's sake, and forthwith betake themselves to flight. These facts were made known to us by our fellow-ministers, Macarius of Palestine[11], and Asterius of Arabia[12], who came with them to Sardica, but refused to share their unorthodoxy. These bishops complained before the holy council of the violent treatment they had received from them, and of the want of right principles evinced in all their transactions. They added that there were many amongst them who still held orthodox opinions, but that these were prevented from going to the council ; and that sometimes threats, sometimes promises, were resorted to, in order to retain them in that party. For this reason they were compelled to reside together in one house ; and never allowed, even for the shortest space of time, to be alone.

" It is not right to pass over in silence and without rebuke the calumnies, the imprison-ments, the murders, the stripes, the forged letters, the indignities, the stripping naked of virgins, the banishments, the destruction of churches, the acts of incendiarism, the translation of bishops from small towns to large dioceses, and above all, the ill-starred Arian heresy, raised by their means against the true faith. For these causes, therefore, we declare the innocence and purity of our beloved brethren and fellow-ministers, Athanasius, bishop of Alexandria, Marcellus, bishop of Ancyra in Galatia, and Asclepas, bishop of Gaza, and of all the other servants of God who are with them ; and we have written to each of their dioceses, in order that the people of each church may be made acquainted with the innocence of their respective bishops, and that they may recognise them alone and wait for their return. Men who have come down on their churches like wolves[13], such as Gregorius in Alexandria, Basilius in Ancyra, and Quintianus[14] in Gaza, we charge them not even to call bishops, nor yet Christians, nor to have any communion with them, nor to receive any letters from them, nor to write to them.

" Theodorus, bishop of Heraclea in Europe, Narcissus, bishop of Neronias in Cilicia, Acacius, bishop of Cæsarea in Palestine, Stephanus, bishop of Antioch, Ursacius, bishop of Singidunum in Mœsia, Valens, bishop of Mursa in Pannonia, Menophantus, bishop of Ephesus, and Georgius, bishop of Laodicea (for though fear kept him from leaving the East, he has been deposed by the blessed Alexander, bishop of Alexandria, and has imbibed the infatuation of the Arians), have on account of their various crimes been cast forth from their bishoprics by the unanimous decision of the holy council. We have decreed that they are not only not to be regarded as bishops, but to be refused communion with us. For those who separate the Son from the substance and divinity of the Father, and alienate the Word from the Father, ought to be separated from the Catholic Church, and alienated from all who bear the name of Christians. Let them then be anathema to you, and to all the faithful, because they have corrupted the word of truth. For the apostle's precept enjoins, if any one should bring to you another gospel than that which ye have received, *let him be accursed*[15]. Command that no one hold communion with them ; for light can have no fellowship with darkness. Keep far off from them ; for what concord has Christ with Belial ? Be careful, beloved brethren, that you neither write to them nor receive their

---

7 Georgius succeeded the Arian Theodotus, of whom mention has already been made (p. 42), in the see of the Syrian Laodicea (Latakia). Athanasius (*de fug.* § 26), speaks of his "dissolute life, condemned even by his own friends."

8 Known as ὁ μονόφθαλμος, "The one-eyed." He succeeded the Historian Eusebius in the see of Cæsarea in 340, and the Nicomedian Eusebius as a leader of the Arian Court party in 342.

9 Now Belgrade.

10 Now Esseg on the Drave. Here Constantius defeated Magnentius, A.D. 351.

11 Bishop of Petra in Palestine. (*Tomus ad Antioch.* 10.) There is some confusion in the names of the sees, and a doubt whether there were really two Petras. Cf. Reland, *Palestine*, p. 298, Le Quien, *East. Christ.* iii. 665, 666.

12 Bishop of Petra in Arabia. (Ath. *Hist. Ar.* 18, *Apol. cont. Ar.* 48).

13 Cf. Acts xx. 29.

14 Thrust on the see of Gaza by the Arians on the deposition of Asclepas (Soz. iii. 8, 12).

15 Gal. i. 8.

letters. Endeavour, beloved brethren and fellow-ministers, as though present with us in spirit at the council, to give your hearty consent to what is enacted, and affix to it your written signature, for the sake of preserving unanimity of opinion among all our fellow-ministers throughout the world [16].

"We declare those men excommunicate from the Catholic Church who say that Christ is God, but not the true God; that He is the Son, but not the true Son; and that He is both begotten and made; for such persons acknowledge that they understand by the term 'begotten,' that which has been made; and because, although the Son of God existed before all ages, they attribute to Him, who exists not in time but before all time, a beginning and an end [17].

"Valens and Ursacius have, like two vipers brought forth by an asp, proceeded from the Arian heresy. For they boastingly declare themselves to be undoubted Christians, and yet affirm that the Word and the Holy Ghost were both crucified and slain, and that they died and rose again; and they pertinaciously maintain, like the heretics, that the Father, the Son, and the Holy Ghost are of diverse and distinct essences [18]. We have been taught, and we hold the catholic and apostolic tradition and faith and confession which teach, that the Father, the Son, and the Holy Ghost have one essence, which is termed substance [19] by the heretics. If it is asked, 'What is the essence of the Son?' we confess, that it is that which is acknowledged to be that of the Father alone; for the Father has never been, nor could ever be, without the Son, nor the Son without the Father. It is most absurd to affirm that the Father ever existed without the Son, for that this could never be so has been testified by the Son Himself, who said, '*I am in the Father, and the Father in Me* [20];' and '*I and My Father are one* [21].' None of us denies that He was begotten; but we say that He was begotten before all things, whether visible or invisible; and that He is the Creator of archangels and angels, and of the world, and of the human race. It is written, '*Wisdom which is the worker of all things taught me* [22],' and again, '*All things were made by Him* [23].'

"He could not have existed always if He had had a beginning, for the everlasting Word has no beginning, and God will never have an end. We do not say that the Father is Son, nor that the Son is Father; but that the Father is Father, and the Son of the Father Son. We confess that the Son is Power of the Father. We confess that the Word is Word of God the Father, and that beside Him there is no other. We believe the Word to be the true God, and Wisdom and Power. We affirm that He is truly the Son, yet not in the way in which others are said to be sons: for they are either gods by reason of their regeneration, or are called sons of God on account of their merit, and not on account of their being of one essence [24], as is the case with the Father and the Son. We confess an Only-begotten and a Firstborn; but that the Word is only-begotten, who ever was and is in the Father. We use the word firstborn with respect to His human nature. But He is superior (to man) in the new creation [25] (of the Resurrection), inasmuch as He is the Firstborn from the dead.

"We confess that God is; we confess the divinity of the Father and of the Son to be one. No one denies that the Father is greater than the Son: not on account of another essence [24], nor yet on account of their difference, but simply from the very name of the Father being greater than that of the Son. The words uttered by our Lord, '*I and My Father are one* [26],' are by those men explained as referring to the concord and harmony which prevail between the Father and the Son; but this is a blasphemous and perverse interpretation. We, as Catholics, unanimously condemned this foolish and lamentable opinion: for just as mortal men on a difference having arisen between them quarrel and afterwards are reconciled, so do such interpreters say that disputes and dissension are liable to arise between God the Father Almighty and His Son; a supposition which is altogether absurd and untenable. But we believe and maintain that those holy words, '*I and My Father are one*,' point out the oneness of essence [24] which is one and the same in the Father and in the Son.

"We also believe that the Son reigns with the Father, that His reign has neither beginning nor end, and that it is not bounded by time, nor can ever cease: for that which always exists never begins to be, and can never cease.

"We believe in and we receive the Holy

---

[16] Here, according to the Version of Athanasius (*Ap. cont. Ar.* 49), the Synodical Epistle ends. An argument against the genuineness of the addition is the introduction of a new formula of faith, while from the letter of Athanasius "ex synodo Alexandrinâ ad legatos apostolicæ sedis," it is plain that nothing was added to the Nicene Creed. (Labbe iii. 84.)

[17] This passage is very corrupt: the translation follows the Greek of Valesius, γεννητός ἐστιν ἅμα καὶ γενητός. It is not certain that the distinction between ἀγέννητος "unbegotten," and ἀγένητος, "uncreate," was in use quite as early as 344. If the passage is spurious and of later date, the distinction might be more naturally found.

[18] ὑποστάσεις.   [19] οὐσία.   [20] John xiv. 10.
[21] John x. 30.   [22] Wisdom vii. 22.   [23] John i. 3.

[24] ὑπόστασις.
[25] This translation follows the reading of the Allatian Codex, adopted by Valesius, τῇ καινῇ κτίσει. If we read κοινῇ for καινῇ, we must render "excels or differs in relation to the common creation" which He shares with man.
[26] John x. 30.

Ghost the Comforter, whom the Lord both promised and sent. We believe in It as sent.

"It was not the Holy Ghost who suffered, but the manhood with which He clothed Himself; which He took from the Virgin Mary, which being man was capable of suffering; for man is mortal, whereas God is immortal. We believe that on the third day He rose, the man in God, not God in the man; and that He brought as a gift to His Father the manhood which He had delivered from sin and corruption.

"We believe that, at a meet and fixed time, He Himself will judge all men and all their deeds.

"So great is the ignorance and mental darkness of those whom we have mentioned, that they are unable to see the light of truth. They cannot comprehend the meaning of the words: '*that they may be one in us*[27].' It is obvious why the word '*one*' was used; it was because the apostles received the Holy Spirit of God, and yet there were none amongst them who were the Spirit, neither was there any one of them who was Word, Wisdom, Power, or Only-begotten. '*As Thou*,' He said, '*and I are one, that they may be one in us.*' These holy words, '*that they may be one in us*,' are strictly accurate: for the Lord did not say, 'one in the same way that I and the Father are one,' but He said, 'that the disciples, being knit together and united, may be one in faith and in confession, and so in the grace and piety of God the Father, and by the indulgence and love of our Lord Jesus Christ, may be able to become one.'"

From this letter may be learnt the duplicity of the calumniators, and the injustice of the former judges, as well as the soundness of the decrees. These holy fathers have taught us not only truths respecting the Divine nature, but also the doctrine of the Incarnation [28].

Constans was much concerned on hearing of the easy temper of his brother, and was highly incensed against those who had contrived this plot and artfully taken advantage of it. He chose two of the bishops who had attended the council of Sardica, and sent them with letters to his brother; he also despatched Salianus, a military commander who was celebrated for his piety and integrity, on the same embassy. The letters which he forwarded by them, and which were worthy of himself, contained not only entreaties and counsels, but also menaces. In the first place, he charged his brother to attend to all that the bishops might say, and to take cognizance of the crimes of Stephanus and of his accomplices. He also required him to restore Athanasius to his flock; the calumny of the accusers and the injustice and ill-will of his former judges having become evident. He added, that if he would not accede to his request, and perform this act of justice, he would himself go to Alexandria, restore Athanasius to his flock which earnestly longed for him, and expel all opponents.

Constantius was at Antioch when he received this letter; and he agreed to carry out all that his brother commanded.

CHAPTER VII.

Account of the Bishops Euphratas and Vincentius, and of the plot formed in Antioch against them.

THE wonted opponents of the truth were so much displeased at these proceedings, that they planned a notoriously execrable and impious crime.

The two bishops resided near the foot of the mountain, while the military commander had settled in a lodging in another quarter.

At this period Stephanus held the rudder of the church of Antioch, and had well nigh sunk the ship, for he employed several tools in his despotic doings, and by their aid involved all who maintained orthodox doctrines in manifold calamities. The leader of these instruments was a young man of a rash and reckless character, who led a very infamous life. He not only dragged away men from the market-place, and treated them with blows and insult, but had the audacity to enter

---

27 John xvii. 21.

28 οἰκονομία. In classical Greek οἰκονομία is simply the management (a) of a household, (β) of the state. In the N.T. we have it in Luke xvi. for "stewardship," and in five other places; (i) 1 Cor. ix. 17, A.V. "dispensation," R.V. "stewardship;" (ii) Eph. i. 10 A.V. and R.V. "dispensation;" (iii) Eph. iii. 2, A.V. and R.V. "dispensation;" (iv) Col. i. 25, A.V. and R.V. "dispensation;" (v) 1 Tim. i. 4, where A.V. adopts the inferior reading οἰκοδομήν, and R.V. renders the οἰκονομίαν of ℵAFGKLP by "dispensation." Suicer gives as the meanings of the word (i) ministerium evangelii, (ii) providentia et numen quo Dei sapientia omnia moderatur, (iii) ipsa Christi naturæ humanæ assumptio, (iv) totius redemptionis mysterium et passionis Christi Sacramentum. Theodoret himself (Ed. Migne iv. 93) says τὴν ἐνανθρώπησιν δὲ τοῦ Θεοῦ Λόγου καλοῦμεν οἰκονομίαν, and quaintly distinguishes (Cant. Cant. p. 83) ἡ σμύρνα καὶ ὁ λίβανος τουτέστιν ἡ θεολογία τε καὶ οἰκονομία. On a phrase of St. Ignatius (Eph. xviii.), "ὁ χριστὸς ἐκυοφορήθη ὑπὸ Μαρίας κατ' οἰκονομίαν," Bp. Lightfoot (*Apostolic Fathers*, II. p. 75 note) writes: "The word οἰκονομία came to be applied more especially to the Incarnation because this was *par excellence* the system or plan which God had ordained for the government of His household and the dispensation of His stores. Hence in the province of theology, οἰκονομία was distinguished by the Fathers from θεολογία proper, the former being the teaching which was concerned with the Incar-

nation and its consequences, and the latter the teaching which related to the Eternal and Divine nature of Christ. The first step towards this special appropriation of οἰκονομία to the Incarnation is found in St. Paul; e.g. Ephes. i. 10, εἰς οἰκονομίαν τοῦ πληρώματος τῶν καιρῶν. . . . In this passage of Ignatius it is moreover connected with the 'reserve' of God (xix. ἐν ἡσυχίᾳ θεοῦ ἐπράχθη). Thus 'economy' has already reached its first stage on the way to the sense of 'dissimulation,' which was afterwards connected with it, and which led to disastrous consequences in the theology and practice of a later age." Cf. Newman's *Arians*, chap. i. sec. 3.

private houses, whence he carried off men and women of irreproachable character. But, not to be too prolix in relating his crimes, I will merely narrate his daring conduct towards the bishops; for this alone is sufficient to give an idea of the unlawful deeds of violence which he perpetrated against the citizens. He went to one of the lowest women of the town, and told her that some strangers had just arrived, who desired to pass the night with her. He took fifteen of his band, placed them in hiding among the stone walls at the bottom of the hill, and then went for the prostitute. After giving the preconcerted signal, and learning that the folk privy to the plot were on the spot, he went to the gate of the courtyard belonging to the inn where the bishops were lodging. The doors were opened by one of the household servants, who had been bribed by him. He then conducted the woman into the house, pointed out to her the door of the room where one of the bishops slept, and desired her to enter. Then he went out to call his accomplices. The door which he had pointed out happened to be that of Euphratas, the elder bishop, whose room was the outer of the two. Vincentius, the other bishop, occupied the inner room. When the woman entered the room of Euphratas, he heard the sound of her footsteps, and, as it was then dark, asked who was there. She spoke, and Euphratas was full of alarm, for he thought that it was a devil imitating the voice of a woman, and he called upon Christ the Saviour for aid. Onager, for this was the name of the leader of this wicked band (a name[1] peculiarly appropriate to him, as he not only used his hands but also his feet as weapons against the pious), had in the meantime returned with his lawless crew, denouncing as criminals those who were expecting to be judges of crime themselves. At the noise which was made all the servants came running in, and up got Vincentius. They closed the gate of the courtyard, and captured seven of the gang; but Onager and the rest made off. The woman was committed to custody with those who had been seized. At the break of day the bishops awoke the officer who had come with them, and they all three proceeded together to the palace, to complain of the audacious acts of Stephanus, whose evil deeds, they said, were too evident to need either trial or torture to prove them. The general loudly demanded of the emperor that the audacious act should not be dealt with synodically, but by ordinary legal process, and offered to give up the clergy attached to the bishops to be

first examined, and declared that the agents of Stephanus must undergo the torture too. To this Stephanus insolently objected, alleging that the clergy ought not to be scourged. The emperor and the principal authorities then decided that it would be better to judge the cause in the palace. The woman was first of all questioned, and was asked by whom she was conducted to the inn where the bishops were lodging. She replied, that a young man came to her, and told her that some strangers had arrived who were desirous of her company; that in the evening he conducted her to the inn; that he went to look for his band, and when he had found it, brought her in through the door of the court, and desired her to go into the chamber adjoining the vestibule. She added, that the bishop asked who was there; that he was alarmed; and that he began to pray; and that then others ran to the spot.

CHAPTER VIII.

Stephanus deposed.

AFTER the judges had heard these replies, they ordered the youngest of those who had been arrested to be brought before them. Before he was subjected to the examination by scourging, he confessed the whole plot, and stated that it was planned and carried into execution by Onager. On this latter being brought in he affirmed that he had only acted according to the commands of Stephanus. The guilt of Stephanus being thus demonstrated, the bishops then present were charged to depose him, and expel him from the Church. By his expulsion the Church was not, however, wholly freed from the plague of Arianism. Leontius, who succeeded him in his presidency, was a Phrygian of so subtle and artful a disposition, that he might be said to resemble the sunken rocks of the sea[1]. We shall presently narrate more concerning him[2].

CHAPTER IX.

The second return of Saint Athanasius.

THE emperor Constantius, having become acquainted with the plots formed against the bishops, wrote to the great Athanasius once, and twice, aye and thrice, exhorting him to

---

[1] Ὄναγρος = wild ass

[1] φασὶ δὲ καὶ νήεσσιν ἀλιπλανέεσσι χερείους
τὰς ὑφάλους πέτρας τῶν φανερῶν σπιλάδων.
                                        Anth. Pal. xi. 390.
[2] Leontius, Bishop of Antioch from A.D. 348 to 357, was one of the School of Lucianus. (Philost. iii. 15), cf. pp. 38 and 41, notes. Athanasius says hard things of him (de fug. § 26), but Dr. Salmon (Dict. Christ. Biog. s.v.) is of opinion that "we may charitably think that the gentleness and love of peace which all attest were not mere hypocrisy, and may impute his toleration of heretics to no worse cause than insufficient appreciation of the importance of the issues involved." Vide infra. chap. xix.

return from the West [1]. I shall here insert the second letter, because it is the shortest of the three.

Constantius Augustus the Conqueror to Athanasius.

"Although I have already apprised you by previous letters, that you can, without fear of molestation, return to our court, in order that you may, according to my ardent desire, be reinstated in your own bishopric, yet I now again despatch another letter to your gravity to exhort you to take immediately, without fear or suspicion, a public vehicle and return to us, in order that you may receive all that you desire."

When Athanasius returned, Constantius received him with kindness, and bade him go back to the Church of Alexandria [2]. But there were some attached to the court, infected with the errors of Arianism, who maintained that Athanasius ought to cede one church to those who were unwilling to hold communion with him. On this being mentioned to the emperor, and by the emperor to Athanasius, he remarked, that the imperial command appeared to be just; but that he also wished to make a request. The emperor readily promising to grant him whatever he might ask, he said that those in Antioch [3] who objected to hold communion with the party now in possession of the churches wanted temples to pray in, and that it was only fair that one House of God also be assigned to them. This request was deemed just and reasonable by the emperor; but the leaders of the Arian faction resisted its being carried into execution, maintaining that neither party ought to have the churches assigned to them. Constantius on this was struck with high admiration for Athanasius, and sent him back to Alexandria [4]. Gregorius was dead, having met his end at the hands of the Alexandrians themselves [5]. The people kept high holiday in honour of their pastor; feasting marked their joy at seeing him again, and praise was given to God [6]. Not long after Constans departed this life [7].

CHAPTER X.

Third exile and flight of Athanasius.

THOSE who had obtained entire ascendency over the mind of Constantius, and influenced him as they pleased, reminded him that Athanasius had been the cause of the differences between his brother and himself, which had nearly led to the rupture of the bonds of nature, and the kindling of a civil war. Constantius was induced by these representations not only to banish, but also to condemn the holy Athanasius to death; and he accordingly despatched Sebastianus [1], a military commander, with a very large body of soldiery to slay him, as if he had been a criminal. How the one led the attack and the other escaped will be best told in the words of him who so suffered and was so wonderfully saved.

Thus Athanasius writes in his Apology for his Flight:—" Let the circumstances of my retreat be investigated, and the testimony of the opposite faction be collected; for Arians accompanied the soldiers, as well for the purpose of spurring them on, as of pointing me out to those who did not know me. If they are not touched with sympathy at the tale I tell, at least let them listen in the silence of shame. It was night, and some of the people were keeping vigil, for a communion [2] was expected. A body of soldiers suddenly advanced upon them, consisting of a general [3] and five thousand armed men with naked swords, bows and arrows, and clubs, as I have already stated. The general surrounded the church, posting his men in close order, that those within might be prevented from going out. I deemed that I ought not in such a time of confusion to leave the people, but that I ought rather to be the first to meet the danger; so I sat down on my throne and desired the deacon to read a psalm, and the people to respond, ' For His mercy endureth for ever.' Then I bade them all return to their own houses. But now the general with the soldiery forced his way into the church, and surrounded the sanctuary in order to arrest me. The clergy and the laity who had remained clamorously besought me to withdraw. This I firmly refused to do until all the others had retreated. I rose, had a prayer offered, and directed all the people to retire. ' It is better,' said I, ' for me to meet the danger alone, than for any of you

---

[1] Athanasius had gone from Sardica to Naissus (in upper Dacia), and thence to Aquileia, where he was received by Constans. *Ap. ad Const.* §4, §3.

[2] Athanasius went from Aquileia to Rome, where he saw Julius again, thence to Treves to the Court of Constans, and back to the East to Antioch, where the conversation about the "one church" took place. Soc. ii. 23; Soz. iii. 20.

[3] i.e. the friends of Eustathius.

[4] The more significant from the fact that Constantius affected a more than human impassibility. Cf. the graphic account of his entry into Rome "velut collo munito rectam aciem luminum tendens, nec dextra vultum nec læva flectebat, tanquam figmentum hominis: non cum rota concutere nutans nec spuens aut os aut nasum tergens vel fricans manumve agitans visus est unquam." Amm. Marc. xvi. 10. [5] About Feb. A.D. 345.

[6] Oct. A.D. 346. Fest. Ind. The return is described by Gregory of Nazianzus (Orat. 21). Authorities, however, differ as to which return he paints.

[7] i.e. was murdered by the troops of the usurper Magnentius

at Illiberis (re-named Helena by Constantine, and now Elne, in Roussillon), A.D. 350.

[1] Probably *Syrianus*, who is described by Athanasius himself as sent to get him removed from Alexandria, but as denying that he had the written authority of Constantius. This was in Jan. A.D. 356. [2] σύναξις. Cf. p. 52 note.

[3] Syrianus. Ath. *Ap. ad Const.* § 25.

to be hurt.' When the greater number of the people had left the church, and just as the rest were following, the monks and some of the clergy who had remained came up and drew me out. And so, may the truth be my witness, the Lord leading and protecting me, we passed through the midst of the soldiers, some of whom were stationed around the sanctuary, and others marching about the church. Thus I went out unperceived, and fervently thanked God that I had not abandoned the people, but that after they had been sent away in safety, I had been enabled to escape from the hands of those who sought my life [4]."

CHAPTER XI.

The evil and daring deeds done by Georgius [1] in Alexandria.

ATHANASIUS having thus escaped the blood-stained hands of his adversaries, Georgius, who was truly another wolf, was entrusted with authority over the flock. He treated the sheep with more cruelty than wolf, or bear, or leopard could have shewn. He compelled young women who had vowed perpetual virginity, not only to disown the communion of Athanasius, but also to anathematize the faith of the fathers. The agent in his cruelty was Sebastianus, an officer in command of troops. He ordered a fire to be kindled in the centre of the city, and placed the virgins, who were stripped naked, close to it, commanding them to deny the faith. Although they formed a most sorrowful and pitiable spectacle for believers as well as for unbelievers, they considered that all these dishonours conferred the highest honour on them; and they joyfully received the blows inflicted on them on account of their faith. All these facts shall be more clearly narrated by their own pastor.

" About Lent, Georgius returned from Cappadocia, and added to the evils which he had been taught by our enemies. After the Easter week virgins were cast into prison, bishops were bound and dragged away by the soldiers, the homes of widows and of orphans were pillaged, robbery and violence went on from house to house, and the Christians during the darkness of night were seized and torn away from their dwellings. Seals were fixed on many houses. The brothers of the clergy were in peril for their brothers' sake. These cruelties were very atrocious, but still more so were those which were subsequently perpetrated. In the week following the holy festival of Pentecost, the people who were keeping a fast came out to the cemetery [2] to pray, because they all renounced any communion with Georgius. This vilest of men was informed of this circumstance, and he incited Sebastianus the military commander, a Manichean [3], to attack the people; and, accordingly, on the Lord's day itself he rushed upon them with a large body of armed soldiers wielding naked swords, and bows, and arrows. He found but few Christians in the act of praying, for most of them had retired on account of the lateness of the hour. Then he did such deeds as might be expected from one who had lent his ears to such teachers. He ordered a large fire to be lighted, and the virgins to be brought close to it, and then tried to compel them to declare themselves of the Arian creed. When he perceived that they were conquering, and giving no heed to the fire, he ordered them to be stripped naked, and to be beaten until their faces for a long while were scarcely recognisable. He then seized forty men, and inflicted on them a new kind of torture. He ordered them to be scourged with branches of palm-trees, retaining their thorns; and by these their flesh was so lacerated that some because of the thorns fixed fast in them had again and again to put themselves under the surgeon's hand; others were not able to bear the agony and died. All who survived, and also the virgins, were then banished to the Greater Oasis. They even refused to give up the bodies of the dead to their kinsfolk for burial, but flung them away unburied, and hid them just as they pleased, in order that it might appear that they had nothing to do with these cruel transactions, and were ignorant of them. But they were deceived in this foolish expectation: for the friends of the slain, while they rejoiced at the faithfulness of the deceased, deeply lamented the loss of the corpses, and spread abroad a full account of the cruelty that had been perpetrated.

" The following bishops were banished from Egypt and from Libya:—Ammonius, Muïus, Caius, Philo, Hermes, Plenius, Psinosiris, Nilammon, Agapius, Anagamphus, Marcus, Dracontius, Adelphius, another Ammonius, another Marcus, and Athenodorus; and also

---

[4] Ath. *Ap. de fug.* § 24.

[1] Georgius, a fraudulent contractor of Constantinople (Ath. *Hist. Ar.* 75), made Arian Bishop of Alexandria on the expulsion of Athanasius, in A.D. 356, was born in a fuller's shop at Epiphania in Cilicia. (Amm. Marc. xxii. 11, 3.) He was known as "the Cappadocian," and further illustrates the old saying of "Καππάδοκες Κρῆτες Κίλικες, τρία κάππα κάκιστα," and the kindred epigram

  Καππαδόκην ποτ' ἐχίδνα κακὴ δάκεν· ἀλλὰ καὶ αὐτή
    κάτθανε γευσαμένη αἵματος ἰοβόλου.

The crimes of the brutal "Antipope" (Prof. Bright in *Dict. Christ. Biog.*) are many, but he was a book-collector. (Jul. Ep. ix. 36, cf. Gibbon I. Chap. 23.) Gibbon says "the infamous George of Cappadocia has been transformed into the renowned St. George of England;" an identity sufficiently disproved.

[2] κοιμητήριον, or sleeping-place. Cf. Chrysost. ed. Migne. ii. 394.

[3] The earliest account of the system of Manes or Mani is to be found in Euseb. H.E. vii. 31. From the end of the century it made rapid progress.

the presbyters Hierax and Dioscorus[4]. These were all driven into exile in so cruel a manner that many died on the road, and others at the place of their banishment. The persecutors caused the death[5] of more than thirty bishops. For, like Ahab, their mind was set on rooting out the truth, had it been possible[6]."

Athanasius also, in a letter addressed to the virgins[7] who were treated with so much barbarity, uses the following words : " Let none of you be grieved although these impious heretics grudge you burial and prevent your corpses being carried forth. The impiety of the Arians has reached such a height, that they block up the gates, and sit like so many demons around the tombs, in order to hinder the dead from being interred."

These and many other similar atrocities were perpetrated by Georgius in Alexandria.

The holy Athanasius was well aware that there was no spot which could be considered a place of safety for him ; for the emperor had promised a very large reward to whoever should bring him alive, or his head as a proof of his death.

CHAPTER XII.

Council of Milan.

AFTER the death of Constans, Magnentius assumed the chief authority over the Western empire ; and, to repress his usurpation, Constantius repaired to Europe. But this war, severe as it was, did not put an end to the war against the Church. Constantius, who had embraced Arian tenets and readily yielded to the influence of others, was persuaded to convoke a council at Milan[1], a city of Italy, and first to compel all the assembled bishops to sign the deposition enacted by the iniquitous judges at Tyre ; and then, since Athanasius had been expelled from the Church, to draw up another confession of faith. The bishops assembled in council on

the receipt of the imperial letter, but they were far from acting according to its directions. On the contrary, they told the emperor to his face that what he had commanded was unjust and impious. For this act of courage they were expelled from the Church, and relegated to the furthest boundaries of the empire.

The admirable Athanasius thus mentions this circumstance in his Apology[2] :—" Who," he writes, " can narrate such atrocities as they have perpetrated ? A short time ago when the Churches were in the enjoyment of peace, and when the people were assembled for prayer, Liberius[3], bishop of Rome, Paulinus, bishop of the metropolis of Gaul[4], Dionysius, bishop of the metropolis of Italy[5], Luciferus, bishop of the metropolis of the Isles of Sardinia[6], and Eusebius, bishop of one of the cities of Italy[7], who were all exemplary bishops and preachers of the truth, were seized and driven into exile, for no other cause than because they could not assent to the Arian heresy, nor sign the false accusation which had been framed against us. It is unnecessary that I should speak of the great Hosius, that aged[8] and faithful confessor of the faith, for every one knows that he also was sent into banishment. Of all the bishops he is the most illustrious. What council can be mentioned in which he did not preside, and convince all present by the power of his reasoning ? What Church does not still retain the glorious memorials of his protection ? Did any one ever go to him sorrowing, and not leave him rejoicing ? Who ever asked his aid, and did not obtain all that he desired ? Yet they had the boldness to attack this great man, simply because, from his knowledge of the impiety of their calumnies, he refused to affix his signature to their artful accusations against us."

From the above narrative will be seen the violence of the Arians against these holy men. Athanasius also gives in the same book an account of the numerous plots formed by the

---

4 One Ammonius had been consecrated by Alexander, and was bishop of Pacnemunis (Ath. *ad Drac.* 210, and *Hist. Ar.* § 72). Another was apparently consecrated by Athanasius (*Hist. Ar.* § 72). An Ammonius was banished to the Upper Oasis (id.). Caius was the orthodox bishop of Thmuis. Philo was banished to Babylon (*Hist. Ar.* § 72, cf. Jer. *Vita Hilarionis* 30). Muïus, Psinosiris, Nilammon, Plenius, Marcus (the sees of these two Marci were Zygra and Philæ), and Athenodorus, were relegated to the parts about the Libyan Ammon, nine days' journey from Alexandria, only that they might perish on the road. One did die. (*Hist Ar.* § 72). Adelphius was bishop of Onuphis in the Delta, and was sent to the Thebaid (*Tom. ad Ant.* 615.) Dracontius, to whom Athanasius addressed a letter, went to the deserts about Clysma (25 m. s.w. of Suez), and Hierax and Dioscorus to Syene (Assouan (*Hist. Ar.* § 72), whither Trajan had banished Juvenal.
5 Some authorities read more mildly, "drove into exile."
6 *Ap. de fug.* § 7. Cf. *Hist. Ar.* § 72.
7 "Hæc Athanasii Epistola hodie quod sciam non extat." Valesius.
1 Athanasius was condemned at Arles (353) as well as at Milan in 355. At the latter place Constantius affected more than his father's infallibility, and exclaimed, "What I will, be that a Canon." Ath. *Hist. Ar.* § 33.

2 *Apol. de fug.* § 4 and § 5.
3 For the persecution and vacillation of Liberius, "one of the few Popes that can be charged with heresy" (Principal Barmby in *Dict. Christ. Biog.* s.v.), see also Ath. *Hist. Ar.* § 35 et seqq.
4 Treves. Dionysius was the successor of St. Maximinus and a firm champion of orthodoxy. Cf. Sulp. Sev. II. 52.
5 Milan. Paulinus was banished to Cappadocia.
6 Calaris (Cagliari). Luciferus, a vehement defender of Athanasius, was banished to Eleutheropolis in Palestine. Mr. Ll. Davies (*Dict. Christ. Biog.* s.v.), thinks the traditional story of the imprisonment of Luciferus at Milan, to prevent his outspoken advocacy of Athanasius, shews internal evidence of probability.
7 Eusebius, bishop of Vercellæ (Vercelli), was a staunch Athanasian. He was banished to Scythopolis, where the bishop Patrophilus (cf. Book I. chapter VI. and XX.), a leading Arian, was, he says, his "jailer." (Vide his letters.)
8 The epithet εὐγηρότατος felicitously describes the honoured old age of the bishop of Cordova—he was now a hundred years old (*Hist. Ar.* § 45)—before his pitiable lapse. He was sent to Sirmium (Mitrovitz).

chiefs of the Arian faction against many others :—"Did any one," said he, "whom they persecuted and got into their power ever escape from them without suffering what injuries they pleased to inflict? Was any one who was an object of their search found by them whom they did not subject to the most agonizing death, or else to the mutilation of all his limbs? The sentences inflicted by the judges are all attributable to these heretics; for the judges are but the agents of their will, and of their malice. Where is there a place which contains no memorial of their atrocities? If any one ever differed from them in opinion, did they not, like Jezebel, falsely accuse and oppress him? Where is there a church which has not been plunged in sorrow by their plots against its bishop? Antioch has to mourn the loss of Eustathius, the faithful and the orthodox[9]. Balaneæ weeps for Euphration[10]; Paltus[11] and Antaradus[12] for Cymatius and Carterius. Adrianople has been called to deplore the loss of the well-beloved Eutropius[13], and of Lucius his successor, who was repeatedly loaded with chains, and expired beneath their weight[14]. Ancyra, Berœa, and Gaza had to mourn the absence of Marcellus[15], Cyrus[16] and Asclepas[17], who, after having suffered much ill-treatment from this deceitful sect, were driven into exile. Messengers were sent in quest of Theodulus[18] and Olympius[19], bishops of Thrace, as well as of me and of the presbyters of my diocese; and had they found us, we should no doubt have been put to death. But at the very time that they were planning our destruction we effected our escape, although they had sent letters to Donatus, the proconsul, against Olympius, and to Philagrius[20], against me."

Such were the audacious acts of this impious faction against the most holy Christians. Hosius

---

[9] Cf. Book I. Chap. 20.
[10] Euphration is mentioned also in *Hist. Ar.* § 5. Balaneæ is now Banias on the coast of Syria.
[11] Now Boldo, a little to the N. of Banias.
[12] In Phœnicia, now Tortosa.
[13] "A good and excellent man," Ath. *Hist. Ar.* § 5.
[14] Vide p. 68.
[15] On the question of the orthodoxy of Marcellus of Ancyra (Angora), vide the conflicting opinions of Bp Lightfoot (*Dict. Christ. Biog.* ii. 342), and Mr. Ffoulkes (id. iii. 810). Ath. (*Apol. contra Ar.* ¿47) says of the Council of Sardica, "The book of our brother Marcellus was also read, by which the frauds of the Eusebians were plainly discovered . . . his faith was found to be correct," cf. p. 67, note.
[16] The successor of Eustathius at Berœa, cf. p. 41, note 65. Socrates says the statement that Cyrus accused Eustathius of Sabellianism is an Arian calumny (Soc. i. 24; ii. 9.).
[17] Asclepas or Æsculapius was at Tyre (p. 62), and was deposed on the charge of overturning an altar, ὡς θυσιαστήριον ἀνατρέψας (Soz. iii. 8).   [18] Vide p. 68.
[19] Bishop of Ænos in Thrace, now Enos. (*Hist. Ar.* ¿ 19.) Here was shown the tomb of Polydorus. Plin. 4, 11, 18. Virgil (Æn. iii. 18) makes Æneas call it Æneadæ, but see Conington's note.
[20] Philagrius was præfect of Egypt A.D. 335—340. Ath. (*Ep. Encyc.*) calls him "a persecutor of the Church and her virgins, an apostate of bad character."

---

was the bishop of Cordova, and was the most highly distinguished of all those who assembled at the council of Nicæa; he also obtained the first place among those convened at Sardica.

I now desire to insert in my history an account of the admirable arguments addressed by the far-famed Liberius, in defence of truth, to the emperor Constantius. They are recorded by some of the pious men of that period in order to stimulate others to the exercise of similar zeal in divine things. Liberius had succeeded Julius, the successor of Silvester, in the government of the church of Rome.

CHAPTER XIII.

Conference between Liberius, Pope of Rome, and the Emperor Constantius[1].

CONSTANTIUS.—"We have judged it right, as you are a Christian and the bishop of our city, to send for you in order to admonish you to abjure all connexion with the folly of the impious Athanasius. For when he was separated from the communion of the Church by the synod the whole world approved of the decision."

LIBERIUS.—"O Emperor, ecclesiastical sentences ought to be enacted with strictest justice: therefore, if it be pleasing to your piety, order the court to be assembled, and if it be seen that Athanasius deserves condemnation, then let sentence be passed upon him according to ecclesiastical forms. For it is not possible for us to condemn a man unheard and untried."

CONSTANTIUS.—"The whole world has condemned his impiety; but he, as he has done from the first, laughs at the danger."

LIBERIUS.—"Those who signed the condemnation were not eye-witnesses of anything that occurred; but were actuated by the desire of glory, and by the fear of disgrace at thy hands."

THE EMPEROR.—"What do you mean by glory and fear and disgrace?"

LIBERIUS.—"Those who love not the glory of God, but who attach greater value to thy gifts, have condemned a man whom they have neither seen nor judged; this is very contrary to the principles of Christians."

THE EMPEROR.—"Athanasius was tried in person at the council of Tyre, and all the bishops of the world at that synod condemned him."

---

[1] The interview took place at Milan, after the Eunuch Eusebius, Chamberlain of Constantius, had in vain tried to win over the bishop at Rome, and had exasperated him by making an improper offering at the shrine of St. Peter. (*Hist. Ar.* ¿ 86.)

LIBERIUS.—"No judgment has ever been passed on him in his presence. Those who there assembled condemned him after he had retired."

EUSEBIUS THE EUNUCH [2] foolishly interposed.—"It was demonstrated at the council of Nicæa that he held opinions entirely at variance with the catholic faith."

LIBERIUS.—"Of all those who sailed to Mareotis, and who were sent for the purpose of drawing up memorials against the accused, five only delivered the sentence against him. Of the five who were thus sent, two are now dead, namely, Theognis and Theodorus. The three others, Maris, Valens, and Ursacius, are still living. Sentence was passed at Sardica against all those who were sent for this purpose to Mareotis. They presented a petition to the council soliciting pardon for having drawn up at Mareotis memorials against Athanasius, consisting of false accusations and depositions of only one party. Their petition is still in our hands. Whose cause are we to espouse, O Emperor? With whom are we to agree and hold communion? With those who first condemned Athanasius, and then solicited pardon for having condemned him, or with those who have condemned these latter?"

EPICTETUS [3] THE BISHOP.—"O Emperor, it is not on behalf of the faith, nor in defence of ecclesiastical judgments that Liberius is pleading; but merely in order that he may boast before the Roman senators of having conquered the emperor in argument."

THE EMPEROR (addressing Liberius).—"What portion do you constitute of the universe, that you alone by yourself take part with an impious man, and are destroying the peace of the empire and of the whole world?"

LIBERIUS.—"My standing alone does not make the truth a whit the weaker. According to the ancient story, there are found but three men resisting a decree."

EUSEBIUS THE EUNUCH.—"You make our emperor a Nebuchadnezzar."

LIBERIUS.—"By no means. But you rashly condemn a man without any trial. What I desire is, in the first place, that a general confession of faith be signed, confirming that drawn up at the council of Nicæa. And secondly, that all our brethren be recalled from exile, and

reinstated in their own bishoprics. If, when all this has been carried into execution, it can be shown that the doctrines of all those who now fill the churches with trouble are conformable to the apostolic faith, then we will all assemble at Alexandria to meet the accused, the accusers, and their defender, and after having examined the cause, we will pass judgment upon it."

EPICTETUS THE BISHOP.—"There will not be sufficient post-carriages to convey so many bishops."

LIBERIUS.—"Ecclesiastical affairs can be transacted without post-carriages. The churches are able to provide means for the conveyance of their respective bishops to the sea coast [4]."

THE EMPEROR.—"The sentence which has once been passed ought not to be revoked The decision of the greater number of bishops ought to prevail. You alone retain friendship towards that impious man."

LIBERIUS.—"O Emperor, it is a thing hitherto unheard of, that a judge should accuse the absent of impiety, as if he were his personal enemy."

THE EMPEROR.—"All without exception have been injured by him, but none so deeply as I have been. Not content with the death of my eldest brother [5], he never ceased to excite Constans, of blessed memory, to enmity against me; but I, with much moderation, put up alike with the vehemence of both the instigator and his victim. Not one of the victories which I have gained, not even excepting those over Magnentius and Silvanus, equals the ejection of this vile man from the government of the Church."

LIBERIUS.—"Do not vindicate your own hatred and revenge, O Emperor, by the instrumentality of bishops; for their hands ought only to be raised for purposes of blessing and of sanctification. If it be consonant with your will, command the bishops to return to their own residences; and if it appear that they are of one mind with him who to-day maintains the true doctrines of the confession of faith signed at Nicæa, then let them come together and see to the peace of the world, in order that an innocent man may not serve as a mark for reproach."

---

[2] I adopt the suggestion of Valesius, that ἀλόγως refers not to the condemnation, but to the foolish remark of the imperial chamberlain. Another expedient for clearing Eusebius of the absurdity of saying that Athanasius was condemned at Nicæa, where he triumphed, has been to read *Tyre* for *Nicæa*.
[3] Bishop of Centumcellæ (Civita Vecchia); "a bold young fellow, ready for any mischief." A protégé of the Cappadocian Georgius, he was an Arian of the worst type, and had effected the substitution of Felix for Liberius in the Roman see by irregular and scandalous means. (Ath. *Hist. Ar.* § 75.)

[4] A passage of Ammianus Marcellinus (xxi. 16) on the "cursus publicus" has been made famous by Gibbon. "The Christian religion, which in itself is plain and simple, Constantius confounded by the dotage of superstition. Instead of reconciling the parties by the weight of his authority, he cherished and propagated, by verbal disputes, the differences which his vain curiosity had excited. The highways were covered with troops of bishops galloping from every side to the assemblies which they call synods; and while they laboured to reduce the whole sect to their own particular opinions, the public establishment of the posts was almost ruined by their hasty and repeated journeys." Gibbon, chap. xx.
[5] Constantine II. had befriended Athanasius, but the patriarch was neither directly nor indirectly responsible for his attack on Constans and his death.

THE EMPEROR.—" One question only requires to be made. I wish you to enter into communion with the churches, and to send you back to Rome. Consent therefore to peace, and sign your assent, and then you shall return to Rome."

LIBERIUS.—" I have already taken leave of the brethren who are in that city. The decrees of the Church are of greater importance than a residence in Rome."

THE EMPEROR.—" You have three days to consider whether you will sign the document and return to Rome ; if not, you must choose the place of your banishment."

LIBERIUS.—" Neither three days nor three months can change my sentiments. Send me wherever you please."

After the lapse of two days the emperor sent for Liberius, and finding his opinions unchanged, he commanded him to be banished to Berœa, a city of Thrace. Upon the departure of Liberius, the emperor sent him five hundred pieces of gold to defray his expenses. Liberius said to the messenger who brought them, " Go, and give them back to the emperor ; he has need of them to pay his troops." The empress[6] also sent him a sum of the same amount ; he said, " Take it to the emperor, for he may want it to pay his troops ; but if not, let it be given to Auxentius and Epictetus, for they stand in need of it." Eusebius the eunuch brought him other sums of money, and he thus addressed him : " You have turned all the churches of the world into a desert, and do you bring alms to me, as to a criminal? Begone, and become first a Christian[7]." He was sent into exile three days afterwards, without having accepted anything that was offered him.

CHAPTER XIV.

Concerning the Banishment and Return of the Holy Liberius.

THIS victorious champion of the truth was sent into Thrace, according to the imperial order. Two years after this event Constantius went to Rome. The ladies of rank urged their husbands to petition the emperor for the restoration of the shepherd to his flock : they added, that if this were not granted, they would desert them, and go themselves after their great pastor. Their husbands replied, that they were afraid of incurring the resentment of the emperor. " If we were to ask him," they

continued, " being men, he would deem it an unpardonable offence ; but if you were yourselves to present the petition, he would at any rate spare you, and would either accede to your request, or else dismiss you without injury." These noble ladies adopted this suggestion, and presented themselves before the emperor in all their customary splendour of array, that so the sovereign, judging their rank from their dress, might count them worthy of being treated with courtesy and kindness. Thus entering the presence, they besought him to take pity on the condition of so large a city, deprived of its shepherd, and made an easy prey to the attacks of wolves. The emperor replied, that the flock possessed a shepherd capable of tending it, and that no other was needed in the city. For after the banishment of the great Liberius, one of his deacons, named Felix, had been appointed bishop. He preserved inviolate the doctrines set forth in the Nicene confession of faith, yet he held communion with those who had corrupted that faith. For this reason none of the citizens of Rome would enter the House of Prayer while he was in it. The ladies mentioned these facts to the emperor. Their persuasions were successful ; and he commanded that the great Liberius should be recalled from exile, and that the two bishops should conjointly rule the Church. The edict of the emperor was read in the circus, and the multitude shouted that the imperial ordinance was just ; that the spectators were divided into two factions, each deriving its name from its own colours[1], and that each faction would now have its own bishop. After having thus ridiculed the edict of the emperor, they all exclaimed with one voice, " One God, one Christ, one bishop." I have deemed it right to set down their precise words. Some time after this Christian people had uttered these pious and righteous acclamations, the holy Liberius returned, and Felix retired to another city.

I have, for the sake of preserving order, appended this narrative to what relates to the proceedings of the bishops at Milan. I shall now return to the relation of events in their due course.

CHAPTER XV.

Council of Ariminum[1].

WHEN all who defended the faith had been removed, those who moulded the

---

6 Eusebia. Constantius II. was thrice married ; (i) A.D. 336 (Eus. *Vit. Const.* iv. 49), to his cousin Constantia, sister of Julian (vid. Pedigree in proleg.) ; (ii) A.D. 352, to Aurelia Eusebia, an Arian " of exceptional beauty of body and mind " (Amm. Marc. xxi. 6), and (iii) A.D. 360 or 361, to Faustina.

7 Liberius does not reckon the Arian eunuch as a Christian.

1 There were originally four factions in the Circus ; blue, green, white, and red. Domitian added two more, golden and purple. But the blue and the green absorbed the rest, and divided the multitude at the games. Cf. Juv. XI. 197.

　　" Totam hodie Romam circus capit, et fragor aurem
　　　Percutit, eventum viridis quo colligo panni."

Cf. Amm. Marc. xiv. 6, and Plin. Ep. ix. 6.

1 A.D. 359.

mind of the emperor according to their own will, flattering themselves that the faith which they opposed might be easily subverted, and Arianism established in its stead, persuaded Constantius to convene the Bishops of both East and West at Ariminum[2], in order to remove from the Creed the terms which had been devised by the Fathers to counteract the corrupt craft of Arius,—"substance[3]," and "of one substance[4]." For they would have it that these terms had caused dissension between church and church. On their assembling in synod the partizans of the Arian faction strove to trick the majority of the bishops, especially those of cities of the Western Empire, who were men of simple and unsophisticated ways. The body of the Church, they argued again and again, must not be torn asunder for the sake of two terms which are not to be found in the Bible; and, while they confessed the propriety of describing the Son as in all things "*like*" the Father, pressed the omission of the word "*substance*" as unscriptural. The motives, however, of the propounders of these views were seen through by the Council, and they were consequently repudiated. The orthodox bishops declared their mind to the emperor in a letter; for, said they, we are sons and heirs of the Fathers of the Council of Nicæa, and if we were to have the hardihood to take away anything from what was by them subscribed, or to add anything to what they so excellently settled, we should declare ourselves no true sons, but accusers of them that begat us. But the exact terms of their confession of faith will be more accurately given in the words of their letter to Constantius.

Letter[5] written to the Emperor Constantius by the Synod assembled at Ariminum.

"Summoned, we believe, at the bidding of God, and in obedience to your piety, we bishops of the Western Church assembled in synod at Ariminum in order that the faith of the Church Catholic might be set forth, and its opponents exposed. After long consideration we have found it to be plainly best for us to hold fast and guard, and by guarding keep safe unto the end, the faith established from the first, preached by Prophets, and Evangelists, and Apostles, through our Lord Jesus Christ, warden of thy empire, and champion of thy salvation. For it is plainly absurd and unlawful to make any change in the doctrines rightly and justly defined, and in matters examined at Nicæa with the cognisance of the right glorious Constantine, thy Father and Emperor, whereof the teaching and spirit was published and preached that mankind might hear and understand. This faith was destined to be the one rival and destroyer of the Arian heresy, and by it not only the Arian itself, but likewise all other heresies were undone. To this faith to add aught is verily perilous; from it to subtract aught is to run great risk. If it have either addition or loss, our foes will feel free to act as they please. Accordingly Ursacius and Valens, declared adherents and friends of the Arian dogma, were pronounced separate from our communion. To keep their place in it, they asked to be granted a *locus penitentiæ* and pardon for all the points wherein they had owned themselves in error; as is testified by the documents written by themselves, by means of which they obtained favour and forgiveness. These events were going on at the very time when the synod was meeting at Milan, the presbyters of the church of Rome being also present. It was known that Constantine, who, though dead, is worthy of remembrance, had, with all exactitude and care, set forth the creed drawn up: and now that, after receiving Baptism, he was dead, and had passed away to the peace which he deserved. We judged it absurd for us after him to indulge in any innovation, and throw a slur on all the holy confessors and martyrs who had devised and formulated this doctrine, in that their minds have ever remained bound by the old bond of the Church. Their faith God has handed down even to the times of thy own reign, through our Lord Jesus Christ, by Whose grace such empire is thine that thou rulest over all the world. Yet again those pitiable and wretched men, with lawless daring, have proclaimed themselves preachers of their unholy opinion, and are taking in hand the overthrow of all the force of the truth. For when at thy command the synod assembled, then they laid bare their own disingenuous desires. For they set about trying through villany and confusion to make innovation. They got hold of certain of their own follow-

---

[2] The eastern bishops were summoned to Seleucia, in Cilicia; the western to Ariminum, (Rimini). "A previous Conference was held at Sirmium, in order to determine on the creed to be presented to the bipartite Council. . . . The Eusebians struggled for the adoption of the Acacian *Homœon*, which the Emperor had already both received and abandoned, and they actually effected the adoption of the '*like in all things according to the Scriptures*,' a phrase in which the semi-Arians, indeed, included their '*like in substance*' or *Homœüsion*, but which did not necessarily refer to *substance* or *nature* at all. Under these circumstances the two Councils met in the autumn of A.D. 359, under the nominal superintendence of the semi-Arians; but, on the Eusebian side, the sharp-witted Acacius undertaking to deal with the disputatious Greeks, the overbearing and cruel Valens with the plainer Latins." (Newman, *Arians*, iv. § 4.) At Seleucia there were 150 bishops; at Ariminum 400.

[3] οὐσία. [4] ὁμοούσιον.

[5] This letter exists in Ath. *de Syn. Arim. et Seleu.*, Soc. ii. 39, Soz. iv. 10, and the Latin of Hilarius (Fr. viii.), which frequently differs considerably from the Greek.

ing,—one Germanius[6], and Auxentius[7], and Caius[8], promoters of heresy and discord, whose doctrine, though but one, transcends a very host of blasphemies. When, however, they became aware that we were not of their way of thinking, nor in sympathy with their vicious projects, they made their way into our meeting as though to make some other proposal, but a very short time was enough to convict them of their real intentions. Therefore in order to save the management of the Church from falling from time to time into the same difficulties, and to prevent them from being confounded in whirlpools of disturbance and disorder, it has seemed the safe course to keep what has been defined aforetime fixed and unchanged, and to separate the above-named from our communion. Wherefore we have sent envoys to your clemency to signify and explain the mind of the synod as expressed in this letter. These envoys before all things we have charged to guard the truth in accordance with the old and right definitions. They are to inform your holiness, not as did Ursacius and Valens, that there will be peace if the truth be upset; for how can the destroyers of peace be agents of peace? but rather that these changes will bring strife and disturbance, as well on the rest of the cities, as on the Roman church. Wherefore we beseech your clemency to receive our envoys with kindly ears and gentle mien, and not to suffer any new thing to flout the dead. Suffer us to abide in the definition and settlement of our Fathers, whom we would unhesitatingly declare to have done all they did with intelligence and wisdom, and with the Holy Ghost. The innovation now sought to be introduced is filling the faithful with unbelief, and unbelievers with credulity[9].

"We beg you to order bishops in distant parts, who are afflicted alike by advanced age and poverty, to be provided with facilities for travelling home, that the churches be not left long deprived of their bishops.

"And yet again this one thing we supplicate, that nothing be taken from or added to the established doctrines, but that all remain unbroken, as they have been preserved by your father's piety, and to our own day. Let us toil no longer nor be kept away from our own dioceses, but let the bishops with their own people spend their days in peace, in prayer, and in worship, offering supplication for thy empire, and health, and peace, which God shall grant thee for ever and ever. Our envoys, who will also instruct your holiness out of the sacred Scriptures, convey the signatures and salutations of the bishops."

The letter was written, and the envoys sent, but the high officers of the Imperial Court, though they took the despatch and delivered it to their master, refused to introduce the envoys, on the ground that the sovereign was occupied with state affairs. They took this course in the hope that the bishops, annoyed at delay, and eager to return to the cities entrusted to their care, would at length be compelled themselves to break up and disperse the bulwark erected against heresy. But their ingenuity was frustrated, for the noble champions of the Faith despatched a second letter to the emperor, exhorting him to admit the envoys to audience and dissolve the synod. This letter I subjoin.

The Second Letter of the Synod to Constantius.

"To Constantius the Victorious, the pious emperor, the bishops assembled at Ariminum send greeting.

"Most illustrious lord and autocrat, we have received the letter of your clemency, informing us that, in consequence of occupations of state, you have hitherto been unable to see our envoys. You bid us await their return, that your piety may come to a decision on the object we have in view, and on the decrees of our predecessors. But we venture in this letter to repeat to your clemency the point which we urged before, for we have in no way withdrawn from our position. We entreat you to receive with benign countenance the letter of our humility, wherein now we make answer to your piety, and the points which we have ordered to be submitted to your benignity by our envoys. Your clemency is no less aware than we are ourselves how serious and unfitting a state of things it is, that in the time of your most happy reign so many churches should seem to be without bishops. Wherefore once again, most glorious autocrat, we beseech you that, if it be pleasing to your humanity, you will command us to return to our churches before the rigour of winter, that we may be able, with our people, as we have done and ever do, to offer most earnest prayers for the health and wealth of

---

6 Germanus (Ath. and Soz.), Germinius (according to Hilarius), bishop of Cyzicus, was translated to Sirmium, A.D. 356. The creed composed by Marcus of Arethusa with the aid of Germinius, Valens and others, is known as "the dated creed," from the minuteness, satirized by Athanasius, with which it specifies the day (May 22, A.D. XI. Kal. Jun.), in the consulate of Eusebius and Hypatius (Ath. de Syn. § 8).

7 Auxentius, the elder, bishop of Milan, succeeded Dionysius in 355, and occupied the see till his death in 374, when Ambrose was chosen to fill his place. Auxentius, the younger, known also as Mercurinus, was afterwards set up by the Arian Court party as a rival bishop to Ambrose. A third Auxentius, a supporter of the heretic Jovinianus, is mentioned in the Epistle of Siricius. Vide reff. in Baronius and Tillemont. An Auxentius, Arian bishop of Mopsuestia, is mentioned by Philostorgius, v. 1. 2.

8 A Pannonian bishop. Ath. ad Epict.

9 The word in the text is ὡμότητα, which is supposed to have stood for *crudelitatem*, a clerical error for *credulitatem* in the Latin original.

your empire to Almighty God, and to Christ His Son, our Lord and Saviour."

CHAPTER XVI.

Concerning the Synod held at Nica[1] in Thrace, and the Confession of Faith drawn up there.

AFTER this letter they[2] irritated the emperor, and got the majority of the bishops, against their will, to a certain town of Thrace, of the name of Nica. Some simple men they deluded, and others they terrified, into carrying out their old contrivance for injuring the true religion, by erasing the words "Substance" and "of one Substance" from the Creed, and inserting instead of them the word "like." I insert their formula in this history, not as being couched in proper terms, but because it convicts the faction of Arius, for it is not even accepted by the disaffected of the present time. Now, instead of "the like" they preach "the unlike[3]."

Unsound Creed put forth at Nica in Thrace.

"We believe in one only true God, Father Almighty, of Whom are all things. And in the only-begotten Son of God, Who before all ages and before every beginning was begotten of God, through Whom all things were made, both visible and invisible : alone begotten, only-begotten of the Father alone, God of God : like the Father that begat Him, according to the Scriptures, Whose generation no one knoweth except only the Father that begat Him. This Only-begotten Son of God, sent by His Father, we know to have come down from heaven, as it is written, for the destruction of sin and death ; begotten of the Holy Ghost and the Virgin Mary, as it is written, according to the flesh. Who companied with His disciples, and when the dispensation was fulfilled, according to the Father's will, was crucified, dead, and buried, and descended to the world below, at Whom Hell himself trembled. On

the third day He rose from the dead and companied with His disciples forty days. He was taken up into Heaven, and sitteth on the right hand of His Father, and is coming at the last day of the Resurrection, in His Father's Glory, to render to every one according to his works. And we believe in the Holy Ghost, which the Only-begotten Son of God, Jesus Christ, both God and Lord, promised to send to man, the Comforter, as it is written, the Spirit of Truth. This Spirit He Himself sent after He had ascended into Heaven and sat at the right hand of the Father, from thence to come to judge both quick and dead. But the word 'the Substance,' which was too simply inserted by the Fathers, and, not being understood by the people, was a cause of scandal through its not being found in Scriptures, it hath seemed good to us to remove, and that for the future no mention whatever be permitted of 'Substance,' on account of the sacred Scriptures nowhere making any mention of the 'Substance' of the Father and the Son. Nor must one 'essence[4]' be named in relation to the person[5] of Father, Son, and Holy Ghost. And we call the Son like the Father, as the Holy Scriptures call Him and teach ; but all the heresies, both those already condemned, and any, if such there be, which have risen against the document thus put forth, let them be Anathema."

This Creed was subscribed by the bishops, some being frightened and some cajoled, but those who refused to give in their adhesion were banished to the most remote regions of the world.

CHAPTER XVII.

Synodical Act of Damasus, Bishop of Rome, and of the Western Bishops, about the Council at Ariminum.

THE condemnation of this formula by all the champions of the truth, and specially those of the West, is shewn by the letter which they wrote to the Illyrians[1]. First of the signatories was Damasus, who obtained the presidency of the church of Rome after Liberius, and was adorned with many virtues[2].

---

[1] At or near the modern Hafsa, not far to the S. of Adrianople.
[2] i.e. the Arians.
[3] "The Eusebians, little pleased with the growing dogmatism of members of their own body, fell upon the expedient of confining their confession to Scripture terms ; which, when separated from their context, were of course inadequate to concentrate and ascertain the true doctrine. Hence the formula of the *Homœon*, which was introduced by Acacius with the express purpose of deceiving or baffling the semi-Arian members of his party. This measure was the more necessary for Eusebian interests, inasmuch as a new variety of the heresy arose in the East at the same time, advocated by Aetius and Eunomius ; who, by professing boldly the pure Arian text, alarmed Constantius, and threw him back upon Basil, and the other semi-Arians. This new doctrine, called *Anomœan*, because it maintained that the *usia* or *substance* of the Son was unlike (ἀνόμοιος) the Divine *usia*, was actually adopted by one portion of the Eusebians, Valens, and his rude occidentals ; whose language and temper, not admitting the refinements of Grecian genius, led them to rush from orthodoxy into the most hard and undisguised impiety. And thus the parties stand at the date now before us (A.D. 356—361) ; Constantius being alternately swayed by Basil, Acacius, and Valens, that is by the Homousian, the Homœan, and the Anomœan, the semi-Arian, the Scripturalist, and the Arian pure" (Newman, Arians, iv. § 4).

[4] ὑπόστασις.   [5] πρόσωπον.
[1] The letter is given in Soz. vi. 23. The Latin text (Coll. Rom. ed. Holsten. p. 163) differs materially from the Greek.
[2] These were displayed after his establishment in his see. He was the nominee of the Arian party, and bloody scenes marked the struggle with his rival Ursinus. "Damasus et Ursinus, supra humanum modum ad rapiendam episcopatus sedem ardentes, scissis studiis asperrime conflictabantur, adusque mortis vulnerumque discrimina progressis. . . . Constat in basilica ubi ritus christiani conventiculum uno die centum triginta septem reperta cadavera peremptorum." Amm. Marc. xxvii. 3, 13. "But we can say that he used his success well, and that the chair of St. Peter was never more respected nor more vigorous than during his bishopric." Mr. Moberly in *Dict. Christ. Biog.* i. 782. Jerome calls him (Ep. Hier. xlviii. 230) "an illustrious man, virgin doctor of the virgin church."
But not his least claim to our regard is that in the Catacombs

With him signed ninety bishops of Italy and Galatia [3], now called Gaul, who met together at Rome. I would have inserted their names but that I thought it superfluous.

"The bishops assembled at Rome in sacred synod, Damasus and Valerianus [4] and the rest, to their beloved brethren the bishops of Illyria, send greeting in God.

"We believe that we, priests of God, by whom it is right for the rest to be instructed, are holding and teaching our people the Holy Creed which was founded on the teaching of the Apostles, and in no way departs from the definitions of the Fathers. But through a report of the brethren in Gaul and Venetia we have learnt that certain men are fallen into heresy.

"It is the duty of the bishops not only to take precautions against this mischief, but also to make a stand against whatever divergent teaching has arisen, either from incomplete instruction, or the simplicity of readers of unsound commentators. They should be minded not to slide into slippery paths, but rather whensoever divergent counsels are carried to their ears, to hold fast the doctrine of our fathers. It has, therefore, been decided that Auxentius of Milan is in this matter specially condemned. So it is right that all the teachers of the law in the Roman Empire should be well instructed in the law, and not befoul the faith with divergent doctrines.

"When first the wickedness of the heretics began to flourish, and when, as now, the blasphemy of the Arians was crawling to the front, our fathers, three hundred and eighteen bishops, the holiest prelates in the Roman Empire, deliberated at Nicæa. The wall which they set up against the weapons of the devil, and the antidote wherewith they repelled his deadly poisons, was their confession that the Father and the Son are of one substance, one godhead, one virtue, one power, one likeness [5], and that the Holy Ghost is of the same es-

sence [6] and substance. Whoever did not thus think was judged separate from our communion. Their deliberation was worthy of all respect, and their definition sound. But certain men have intended by other later discussions to corrupt and befoul it. Yet, at the very outset, error was so far set right by the bishops on whom the attempt was made at Ariminum to compel them to manipulate or innovate on the faith, that they confessed themselves seduced by opposite arguments, or owned that they had not perceived any contradiction to the opinion of the Fathers delivered at Nicæa. No prejudice could arise from the number of bishops gathered at Ariminum, since it is well known that neither the bishop of the Romans, whose opinion ought before all others to have been waited for, nor Vincentius, whose stainless episcopate had lasted so many years, nor the rest, gave in their adhesion to such doctrines. And this is the more significant, since, as has been already said, the very men who seemed to be tricked into surrender, themselves, in their wiser moments, testified their disapproval.

"Your sincerity then perceives that thisone faith, which was founded at Nicæa on the authority of the Apostles, ought to be kept secure for ever. You perceive that with us, the bishops of the East, who confess themselves Catholic, and the western bishops, together glory in it. We believe that before long those who think otherwise ought without delay to be put out from our communion, and deprived of the name of bishop, that their flocks may be freed from error and breathe freely. For they cannot be expected to correct the errors of their people when they themselves are the victims of error. May the opinion of your reverence be in harmony with that of all the priests of God. We believe you to be fixed and firm in it, and thus ought we rightly to believe with you. May your charity make us glad by your reply.

"Beloved brethren, farewell."

CHAPTER XVIII.

The Letter of Athanasius, bishop of Alexandria, concerning the same Council.

The great Athanasius also, in his letter to the Africans, writes thus about the council at Ariminum. "Under these circumstances who will tolerate any mention of the council of Ariminum or any other beside the Nicene? Who would not express detestation of the setting aside of the words of the Fathers, and the preference for those introduced at Ari-

---

it was his "labour of love to rediscover the tombs which had been blocked up for concealment under Diocletian, to remove the earth, widen the passages, adorn the sepulchral chambers with marble, and support the friable tufa walls with arches of brick and stone." "Roma Sotterranea," Northcote and Brownlow, p. 97.

3 Γαλάται = Κέλτοι, the older name, which exists in Herodotus II. 33 and IV. 49. Pausanias (I. iii. 5) says ὀψὲ δέ ποτε αὑτοὺς καλεῖσθαι Γαλάτας ἐξενίκησε, Κέλτοι γὰρ κατά τε σφᾶς τὸ ἀρχαῖον καὶ παρὰ τοῖς ἄλλοις ὠνομάζοντο. Galatia occurs on the Monumentum Ancyranum. Bp. Lightfoot (Galat. p. 3) says the first instance of Gallia (Galli) which he has found in any Greek writer is in Epictetus II. 20, 17.

4 In Sozomen, Valerius, Bishop of Aquileia. "But little is known of his life, but under his rule there grew up at Aquileia the society of remarkable persons of whom Hieronymus became the most famous." *Dict. Christ. Biog.* iv. 1102.

5 χαρακτήρ· contrast the statement in Heb. i. 3, that the Son is the χαρακτήρ of the person of the Father. χαρακτήρ in the letter of Damasus approaches more nearly our use of "character" as meaning distinctive qualities. cf. Plato Phæd. 26 B.

6 ὑπόστασις.

minum by violence and party strife? Who would wish to be associated with these men — fellows who do not, forsooth, accept their own words? In their own ten or a dozen synods they have laid down, as has been narrated already, now one thing now another; and at the present time these synods, one after another, they are themselves openly denouncing. They are now suffering the fate undergone of old by the traitors of the Jews. For as is written in the Book of the Prophet Jeremiah *" they have forsaken me the fountain of living waters and hewed them out cisterns, broken cisterns that can hold no water,"* [1] so these men, in their opposition to the Œcumenical synod, have hewed for themselves many synods which have all proved vain and like *"buds that yield no meal,"* [2] let us not therefore admit those who cite the council of Ariminum or any other but that of Nicæa, for indeed the very citers of Ariminum do not seem to know what was done there; if they had they would have held their tongues. For you, beloved, have learnt from your own representatives at that Council, and are consequently very well aware, that Ursacius, Valens, Eudoxius, and Auxentius, and with them Demophilus were asked to anathematize the Arian heresy, and made excuse, choosing rather to be its champions, and so were all deposed for making propositions contrary to the Nicene decrees. The bishops, on the contrary, who were the true servants of the Lord, and of the right faith, — about two hundred in number, — declared their adherence to the Nicene Council alone, and their refusal to entertain the thought of either subtraction from, or addition to, its decrees. This conclusion they have communicated to Constantius, by whose order the council assembled.

On the other hand the bishops who were deposed at Ariminum have been received by Constantius, and have succeeded in getting the two hundred who sentenced them grossly insulted, and threatened with not being allowed to return to their dioceses, and with having to undergo rigorous treatment in Thrace, and that in the winter, in order to force them to accept the innovators' measures.

If, then, we hear any one appealing to Ariminum, show us, let us rejoin, first the sentence of deposition, and then the document drawn up by the bishops, in which they declare that they do not seek to go beyond the terms drawn up by the Nicene Fathers, nor appeal to any other council than that of Nicæa. In reality, these are just the facts they con-

ceal, while they put prominently forward the forced confession of Thrace. They do but shew themselves friends of the Arian heresy, and strangers to the sound faith. Only let any one be willing to put side by side that great synod, and those others to which these men appeal, and he will perceive, on the one side, true religion, on the other, folly and disorder. The fathers of Nicæa met together not after being deposed, but after confessing that the Son was of the Substance of the Father. These men were deposed once, a second time, and again a third time at Ariminum, and then dared to lay down that it is wrong to attribute Substance or Essence to God. So strange and so many were the tricks and machinations concocted by the mad gang of Arius in the West against the dogmas of the Truth.

CHAPTER XIX.

Concerning the cunning of Leontius, Bishop of Antioch, and the boldness of Flavianus and Diodorus.

At Antioch Placidus was succeeded by Stephanus, who was expelled from the Church. Leontius then accepted the Primacy, but in violation of the decrees of the Nicene Council, for he had mutilated himself, and was an eunuch. The cause of his rash deed is thus narrated by the blessed Athanasius. Leontius, it seems, was the victim of slanderous statements on account of a certain young woman of the name of Eustolia.[1] Finding himself prevented from dwelling with her he mutilated himself for her sake, in order that he might feel free to live with her. But he did not clear himself of suspicion, and all the more for this reason was deposed from the presbyterate. So much Athanasius has written about the rest of his earlier life. I shall now give a summary exposure of his evil conduct. Now though he shared the Arian error, he always endeavoured to conceal his unsoundness. He observed that the clergy and the rest of the people were divided into two parts, the one, in giving glory to the Son, using the conjunction " and," the other using the preposition "through " of the Son, and applying " in " to the Holy Ghost. He himself offered all the doxology in silence, and all that those

---

[1] Jer. ii. 13.
[2] Hosea viii. 7. The text " δράγματα μὴ ἔχοντα ἰσχύν " recalls the septuagint δράγμα οὐκ ἔχον ἰσχύν.

[1] Ath. *Ap. de fug.* § 26 and *Hist. Ar.* § 28. The question of συνείσακται was one of the great scandals and difficulties of the early Church. Some suppose that the case of Leontius was the cause of the first Canon of the Nicene Council περὶ τῶν τολμώντων ἑαυτοὺς ἐκτέμνειν.

Theodoretus (iv. 12) relates an instance of what was considered conjugal chastity, and the mischiefs referred to in the text arose from the rash attempt to imitate such continence. Vide Suicer *in voc.*

standing near him could hear was the "For ever and ever." And had not the exceeding wickedness of his soul been betrayed by other means, it might have been said that he adopted this contrivance from a wish to promote concord among the people. But when he had wrought much mischief to the champions of the truth, and continued to give every support to the promoters of impiety, he was convicted of concealing his own unsoundness. He was influenced both by his fear of the people, and by the grievous threats which Constantius had uttered against any who had dared to say that the Son was unlike the Father. His real sentiments were however proved by his conduct. Followers of the Apostolic doctrines never received from him either ordination or indeed the least encouragement. Men, on the other hand, who sided with the Arian superstition, were both allowed perfect liberty in expressing their opinions, and were from time to time admitted to priestly office. At this juncture Aetius, the master of Eunomius, who promoted the Arian error by his speculations, was admitted to the diaconate. Flavianus and Diodorus, however, who had embraced an ascetic career, and were open champions of the Apostolic decrees, publicly protested against the attacks of Leontius against true religion. That a man nurtured in iniquity and scheming to win notoriety by ungodliness should be counted worthy of the diaconate, was, they urged, a disgrace to the Church. They further threatened that they would withdraw from his communion, travel to the western empire, and publish his plots to the world. Leontius was now alarmed, and suspended Aetius from his sacred office, but continued to show him marked favour.

That excellent pair Flavianus and Diodorus,[1] though not yet admitted to the priesthood and still ranked with the laity, worked night and day to stimulate men's zeal for truth. They were the first to divide choirs into two parts, and to teach them to sing the psalms of David antiphonally. Introduced first at Antioch, the practice spread in all directions, and penetrated to the ends of the earth. Its originators now collected the lovers of the Divine word and work into the Churches of the Martyrs, and with them spent the night in singing psalms to God.

When Leontius perceived this, he did not think it safe to try to prevent them, for he saw that the people were exceedingly well-disposed towards these excellent men. However, putting a colour of courtesy on his speech, he requested that they would perform this act of worship in the churches. They were perfectly well aware of his evil intent. Nevertheless they set about obeying his behest and readily summoned their choir[1] to the Church, exhorting them to sing praises to the good Lord. Nothing, however, could induce Leontius to correct his wickedness, but he put on the mask of equity,[2] and concealed the iniquity of Stephanus and Placidus. Men who had accepted the corruption of the faith of priests and deacons, although they had embraced a life of vile irregularity, he added to the roll; while others adorned with every kind of virtue and firm adherents of apostolic doctrines, he left unrecognised. Thus it came to pass that among the clergy were numbered a majority of men tainted with heresy, while the mass of the laity were champions of the Faith, and even professional teachers lacked courage to lay bare their blasphemy. In truth the deeds of impiety and iniquity done by Placidus, Stephanus, and Leontius, in Antioch are so many as to want a special history of their own, and so terrible

---

[1] Flavianus was a noble native of Antioch, and was afterwards (381-404) bishop of that see. Diodorus in later times (c. 379) became bishop of Tarsus, "one of the most deservedly venerated names in the Eastern church for learning, sanctity, courage in withstanding heresy, and zeal in the defence of the truth. Diodorus has a still greater claim on the grateful remembrances of the whole church, as, if not the founder, the chief promoter of the rational school of scriptural interpretation, of which his disciples, Chrysostom and Theodorus of Mopsuestia, and Theodoret, were such distinguished representatives." Dict. Christ. Biog. i. 836. On the renewed championship of the Antiochene church by Flavianus and Diodorus under the persecution of Valens vide iv. 22.

Socrates (vi. 8), describing the rivalry of the Homoousians and Arians in singing partizan hymns antiphonally in the streets of Antioch in the days of Arcadius, traces the mode of chanting to the great Ignatius, who once in a Vision heard angels so praising God.

But, remarks Bp. Lightfoot (Apostolic Fathers Pt. 2. I. p. 31.) "Antiphonal singing did not need to be suggested by a heavenly Vision. It existed already among the heathen in the arrangements of the Greek Chorus. It was practised with much elaboration of detail in the Psalmody of the Jews, as appears from the account which is given of the Egyptian Therapeutes. Its introduction into the Christian Church therefore was a matter of course almost from the beginning: and when we read in Pliny (Ep. x. 97) that the Christians of Bithynia sang hymns to Christ as to a god, 'alternately'(secum invicem) we may reasonably infer that the practice of antiphonal singing prevailed far beyond the limits of the church of Antioch, even in the time of Ignatius himself."

Augustine (Conf. ix. 7) states that the fashion of singing "secundum morem orientalium partium" was introduced into the Church of Milan at the time of the persecution of Ambrose by Justina, "ne populus mœroris tœdio contabesceret," and thence spread all over the globe.

Platina attributes the introduction of antiphons at Rome to Pope Damasus.

Hooker (ii. 166) quotes the older authority of "the Prophet Esay," in the vision where the seraphim cried to one another in what Bp. Mant calls "the alternate hymn."

[1] I prefer the reading of Basil Gr. and Steph. 1. ἐργάτας to the ἐραστάς of Steph. 2 and Pin.

[2] ἐπιείκειας. "The mere existence of such a word as ἐπιείκεια is itself a signal evidence of the high development of ethics among the Greeks. It expresses exactly that moderation which recognizes the impossibility, cleaving to formal law, of anticipating or providing for all cases that will emerge, and present themselves to it for decision . . . It is thus more truly just than strict justice will have been; being δίκαιον καὶ βελτίον τινὸς δικαίου, as Aristotle expresses it. Eth. Nic. V. 10. 6." Archbp. Trench's synonyms of the N. T. p. 151. The "clemency" on which Tertullus reckons in Felix is ἐπιείκεια; and in II Cor. x. St. Paul beseeches by the "gentleness" or ἐπιείκεια of Christ.

as to be worthy of the lament of David; for of them too it must be said "For lo thy enemies make a murmuring and they that hate thee lift up their head. They have imagined craftily against the people and taken counsel against thy secret ones. They have said come and let us root them out that they be no more a people: and that the name of Israel may be no more in remembrance."[1]

Let us now continue the course of our narrative.

CHAPTER XX.

Concerning the innovations of Eudoxius, of Germanicia, and the zeal of Basilius[3] of Ancyra, and of Eustathius[4] of Sebasteia against him.

GERMANICIA is a city on the coasts of Cilicia, Syria, and Cappadocia, and belongs to the province called Euphratisia. Eudoxius, the head of its church, directly he heard of the death of Leontius, betook himself to Antioch and clutched the see, where he ravaged the vineyard of the Lord like a wild boar. He did not even attempt to hide his evil ways, like Leontius, but raged in direct attack upon the apostolic decrees, and involved in various troubles all who had the hardihood to gainsay him. Now at this time Basilius had succeeded Marcellus, and held the helm of the church of Ancyra, the capital of Galatia, and Sebastia, the chief city of Armenia, was under the guidance of Eustathius. No sooner had these bishops heard of the iniquity and madness of Eudoxius, than they wrote to inform the Emperor Constantius of his audacity. Constantius was now still tarrying in the west,

and, after the death of the tyrants, was endeavouring to heal the harm they had caused. Both bishops were well known to the Emperor and had great influence with him on account of the high character they bore.

CHAPTER XXI.

Of the Second Council of Nicæa.

ON receipt of these despatches Constantius wrote to the Antiochenes denying that he had committed the see of Antioch to Eudoxius, as Eudoxius had publicly announced. He ordered that Eudoxius be banished, and be punished for the course he had taken at the Bithynian Nicæa, where he had ordered the synod to assemble. Eudoxius himself had persuaded the officers entrusted with authority in the imperial household to fix Nicæa for the Council. But the Supreme Ruler and Governor, who knows the future like the past, stopped the assembly by a mighty earthquake, whereby the greater part of the city was overthrown, and most of the inhabitants destroyed. On learning this the assembled bishops were seized with panic, and returned to their own churches. But I regard this as a contrivance of the divine wisdom, for in that city the doctrine of the faith of the apostles had been defined by the holy Fathers. In that same city the bishops who were assembling on this later occasion were intending to lay down the contrary. The sameness of name would have been sure to furnish a means of deception to the Arian crew, and trick unsophisticated souls. They meant to call the council "the Nicene," and identify it with the famous council of old. But He who has care for the churches disbanded the synod.

CHAPTER XXII.

Of the Council held at Seleucia in Isauria.

AFTER a time, at the suggestion of the accusers of Eudoxius, Constantius ordered the synod to be held at Seleucia. This town of Isauria lies on the seashore and is the chief town of the district. Hither the bishops of the East, and with them those of Pontus in Asia, were ordered to assemble.[1]

---

[1] Ps. 83.—2-3-4.

[2] Eudoxius, eighth bishop of Constantinople, and formerly of Germanicia (Γερμανικεια, now Marash, or Banicia), was one of the most violent of the Arians. He was originally refused ordination by St. Eustathius, but on the deposition of that bishop in 331 the Eusebians pushed him forward. After ruling at Germanicia for some seventeen years he intruded himself on the see of Antioch.
   Under the patronage of the Acacians he became patriarch of Constantinople in 360, and died in 370.

[3] Basilius, a learned physician, a Semiarian of Ancyra, was made bishop of that see on the deposition of Marcellus, in 336, and excommunicated at Sardica in 347. In 350 he was reinstated at the command of Constantius. He was again exiled under Acacian influence, failed to get restitution from Jovian, and probably died in exile. (Soc. ii, 20, 26, iv, 24.) Vide also Theod. ii, 23. His works are lost. Athanasius praises him as among those who were (de Synod. 603 ed. Migne) "not far from accepting the Homousion."

[4] Eustathius was bishop of Sebasteia or Sebaste (Siwas) on the Halys, from 357 to 380.
   Basil, Ep. 244, § 9, says that he was a heretic "black who could not turn white"; but he exhibited many shades of theological colour, preserving through all vicissitudes a high personal character, and a something "more than human." Basil Ep. 212, § 2. Ordained by Eulalius, he was degraded because he insisted on wearing very unclerical costume. (Soc. ii, 43.) The question of the identity of this Eustathius with the Eustathius condemned at the Council of Ancyra is discussed in the Dict. Christ. Ant. i, 709.

[1] "Now that the Semiarians were forced to treat with their late victims on equal terms, they agreed to hold a general Council. Both parties might hope for success. If the Homœan influence was strong at Court, the Semiarians were strong in the East, and could count on some help from the Western Nicenes. But the Court was resolved to secure a decision to its own mind. As a Council of the whole Empire might have been too independent, it was divided. The Westerns were to

The see of Cæsarea, the capital of Palestine, was now held by Acacius, who had succeeded Eusebius. He had been condemned by the council of Sardica, but had expressed contempt for so large an assembly of bishops, and had refused to accept their adverse decision. At Jerusalem Macarius, whom I have often mentioned, was succeeded by Maximus, a man conspicuous in his struggles on behalf of religion, for he had been deprived of his right eye and maimed in his right arm.[1]

On his translation to the life which knows no old age, Cyrillus, an earnest champion of the apostolic decrees,[2] was dignified with the Episcopal office. These men in their contentions with one another for the first place brought great calamities on the state. Acacius seized some small occasion, deposed Cyrillus, and drove him from Jerusalem. But Cyrillus passed by Antioch, which he had found without a pastor, and came to Tarsus, where he dwelt with the excellent Silvanus, then bishop of that see. No sooner did Acacius become aware of this than he wrote to Silvanus and informed him of the deposition of Cyrillus. Silvanus however, both out of regard for Cyrillus, and not without suspicion of his people, who greatly enjoyed the stranger's teaching, refused to prohibit him from taking a part in the ministrations of the church. When however they had arrived at Seleucia, Cyrillus joined with the party of Basilius and Eustathius and Silvanus and the rest in the

council. But when Acacius joined the assembled bishops, who numbered one hundred and fifty, he refused to be associated in their counsels before Cyrillus, as one stripped of his bishopric, had been put out from among them. There were some who, eager for peace, besought Cyrillus to withdraw, with a pledge that after the decision of the decrees they would enquire into his case. He would not give way, and Acacius left them and went out. Then meeting Eudoxius he removed his alarm, and encouraged him with a promise that he would stand his friend and supporter. Thus he hindered him from taking part in the council, and set out with him for Constantinople.

CHAPTER XXIII.

Of what befell the orthodox bishops at Constantinople.

CONSTANTIUS, on his return from the West, passed some time at Constantinople. There Acacius urged many accusations against the assembled bishops in presence of the emperor, called them a set of vile characters convoked for the ruin and destruction of the churches, and so fired the imperial wrath. And not least was Constantius moved by what was alleged against Cyrillus, " for," said Acacius, " the holy robe, which the illustrious Constantine the emperor, in his desire to honour the church of Jerusalem, gave to Macarius, the bishop of that city, to be worn when he performed the rite of divine baptism, all fashioned with golden threads as it was, has been sold by Cyrillus. It has been bought," he continued, " by a certain stage dancer; dancing about when he was wearing it, he fell down and perished. With a man like this Cyrillus," he went on, " they set themselves up to judge and decide for the rest of the world." The influential party at the court made this an occasion for persuading the emperor not to summon the whole synod, for they were alarmed at the concord of the majority, but only ten leading men. Of these were Eustathius of Armenia, Basilius of Galatia, Silvanus of Tarsus, and Eleusius of Cyzicus.[1]

---

meet at Ariminum in Italy, the Easterns at Seleucia in Isauria." " It was a fairly central spot, and easy of access from Egypt and Syria by sea, but otherwise most unsuitable. It was a mere fortress, lying in a rugged country, where the spurs of Mount Taurus reach the sea. Around it were the ever-restless marauders of Isauria." " The choice of such a place is as significant as if a Pan-Anglican synod were called to meet at the central and convenient port of 'Souakim.'"
Gwatkin " The Arian Controversy." pp. 93–96.
The Council met here A.D. 359.

[1] He appears to have been less conspicuous for consistency in the Arian Controversy. At Tyre he is described by Sozomen and Socrates as assenting to the deposition of Athanasius, but Rufinus (H. E. i. 17) tells the dramatic story of the success ful interposition of the aged and mutilated Paphnutius of the Thebaid, who took his vacillating brother by the hand, and led him to the little knot of Athanasians. Sozomen (iv. 203) represents him as deposed by Acacius for too zealous ortho-doxy, and replaced by Cyril, then a Semiarian. Jerome agrees with Theodoret, and makes Cyril succeed on the death of Maximus in 350 or 351. (Chron. ann. 349.)

[2] Sozomen and Socrates are less favourable to his orthodoxy. In his favour see the synodical letter written by the bishops assembled at Constantinople after the Council in 381, and addressed to Pope Damasus, which is given in the Vth book of our author, Chapter 9. He was engaged in a petty controversy with Acacius on the precedence of the sees of Cæsarea and Ælia (Jerusalem), and in 357 deposed. On appeal to the Council of Seleucia he was reinstated, but again deposed by Constantius, partly on the pretended charge of dealing im-properly with a robe given by Constantine to Macarius, which Theodoret records later (Chap. xiii.) Restored by Julian he was left in peace under Jovian and Valentinian, exiled by Valens, and restored by Theodosius. He died in 386, and left Catechetical lectures, a Homily, and an Epistle, of which the authenticity has been successfully defended, and which vindi-cate rather his orthodoxy than his ability. cf. Canon Venables. Dict. Ch. Biog. s. v.

[1] i.e., Eustathius of Sebasteia, and Basilius of Ancyra (vide note on p. 86). Silvanus of Tarsus was one of the Semiarians of high character. For his kindly entertainment of Cyril of Jerusalem vide page 87. Tillemont places his death in 363.
Eleusius of Cyzicus was also a Semiarian of the better type (cf. Hil. de Syn. p. 133). The evil genius of his life was Macedorius of Constantinople, by whose influence he was made bishop of Cyzicus in 356. Here with equal zeal he de-stroyed pagan temples and a Novatian church, and this was remembered against him when he attempted to return to his see on the accession of Julian. At Nicomedia in 366 he was moved by the threats of Valens to declare himself an Arian, and then in remorse resigned his see, but his flock refused to let him go. Socr. iv. 6.

On their arrival they urged the emperor that Eudoxius should be convicted of blasphemy and lawlessness. Constantius, however, schooled by the opposite party, replied that a decision must first be come to on matters concerning the faith, and that afterwards the case of Eudoxius should be enquired into. Basilius, relying on his former intimacy, ventured boldly to object to the emperor that he was attacking the apostolic decrees; but Constantius took this ill, and told Basilius to hold his tongue, "for to you," said he, "the disturbance of the churches is due." When Basilius was silenced, Eustathius intervened and said, "since, sir, you wish a decision to be come to on what concerns the faith, consider the blasphemies rashly uttered against the Only Begotten by Eudoxius," and as he spoke he produced the exposition of faith wherein, besides many other impieties, were found the following expressions: "Things that are spoken of in unlike terms are unlike in substance:" "There is one God the Father of whom are all things, and one Lord Jesus Christ through whom are all things." Now the term "of whom" is unlike the term "through whom;" so the Son is unlike God the Father. Constantius ordered this exposition of the faith to be read, and was displeased with the blasphemy which it involved. He therefore asked Eudoxius if he had drawn it up. Eudoxius instantly repudiated the authorship, and said that it was written by Aetius. Now Aetius was he whom Leontius, in dread of the accusations of Flavianus and Diodorus, had formerly degraded from the diaconate. He had also been the supporter of Georgius, the treacherous foe of the Alexandrians, alike in his impious words and his unholy deeds. At the present time he was associated with Eunomius and Eudoxius; for, on the death of Leontius, when Eudoxius had laid violent hands on the episcopal throne of the church at Antioch, he returned from Egypt with Eunomius, and, as he found Eudoxius to be of the same way of thinking as himself, a sybarite in luxury as well as a heretic in faith, he chose Antioch as the most congenial place of abode, and both he and Eunomius were fast fixtures at the couches of Eudoxius. His highest ambition was to be a successful parasite, and he spent his whole time in going to gorge himself at one man's table or another's. The emperor had been told all this, and now ordered Aetius to be brought before him. On his appearance Constantius showed him the document in question and proceeded to enquire if he was the author of its language. Aetius, totally ignorant of what had taken place, and unaware of the drift of the enquiry, expected that he should win praise by confession, and owned that he was the author of the phrases in question. Then the emperor perceived the greatness of his iniquity, and forthwith condemned him to exile and to be deported to a place in Phrygia. So Aetius reaped disgrace as the fruit of blasphemy, and was cast out of the palace. Eustathius then alleged that Eudoxius too held the same views, for that Aetius had shared his roof and his table, and had drawn up this blasphemous formula in submission to his judgement. In proof of his contention that Eudoxius was concerned in drawing up the document he urged the fact that no one had attributed it to Aetius except Eudoxius himself. To this the emperor enjoined that judges must not decide on conjecture, but are bound to make exact examination of the facts. Eustathius assented, and urged that Eudoxius should give proof of his dissent from the sentiments attributed to him by anathematizing the composition of Aetius. This suggestion the emperor very readily accepted, and gave his orders accordingly; but Eudoxius drew back, and employed many shifts to evade compliance. But when the emperor waxed wroth and threatened to send him off to share the exile of Aetius, on the ground that he was a partner in the blasphemy so punished, he repudiated his own doctrine, though both then and afterwards he persistently maintained it. However, he in his turn protested against the Eustathians that it was their duty to condemn the word "*Homoüsion*" as unscriptural.

Silvanus on the contrary pointed out that it was their duty to reject and expel from their holy assemblies the phrases "*out of the non-existent*" and "*creature*" and "*of another substance*," these terms being also unscriptural and found in the writings of neither prophets nor apostles. Constantius decided that this was right, and bade the Arians pronounce the condemnation. At first they persisted in refusing; but in the end, when they saw the emperor's wrath, they consented, though much against the grain, to condemn the terms Silvanus had put before them. But all the more earnestly they insisted on their demand for the condemnation of the "*Homoüsion*." But then with unanswerable logic Silvanus put both before the Arians and the emperor the truth that if God the Word is not of the non-Existent, He is not a Creature, and is not of another Substance. He is then of one Substance with God Who begat Him, as God of God and Light of Light, and has the same nature as the Begetter. This contention he urged with power and with truth, but not one of his hearers was convinced. The party of Acacius and Eudoxius raised a mighty uproar; the emperor was angered, and threatened expulsion from their churches. Thereupon Eleusius and Silvanus and the rest said that while authority to punish lay with the emperor, it was their province to decide on points of piety or impiety, and "we will not," they protested, "betray the doctrine of the Fathers."

Constantius ought to have admired both their wisdom and their courage, and their bold defence of the apostolic decrees, but he exiled them from their churches, and ordered others to be appointed in their place. Thereupon Eudoxius laid violent hands on the Church of Constantinople; and on the expulsion of Eleusius from Cyzicus, Eunomius was appointed in his place.

CHAPTER XXIV.

Synodical Epistle written against Aetius.

AFTER these transactions the emperor ordered Aetius to be condemned by a formal Letter, and, in obedience to the command, his companions in iniquity condemned their own associate. Accordingly they wrote to Georgius, bishop of Alexandria, the letter about him to which I shall give a place in my history, in order to expose their wickedness, for they treated their friends and their foes precisely in the same way.

Copy of the Letter written by the whole council to Georgius against Aetius his deacon, on account of his iniquitous blasphemy.

To the right honourable Lord Georgius, Bishop of Alexandria, the holy Synod in Constantinople assembled, GREETING.

In consequence of the condemnation of Aetius by the Synod, on account of his unlawful and most offensive writings, he has been dealt with by the bishops in accordance with the canons of the church. He has been degraded from the diaconate and expelled from the Church, and our admonitions have gone forth that none are to read his unlawful epistles, but that on account of their unprofitable and worthless character they are to be cast aside. We have further appended an anathema on him, if he abides in his opinion, and on his supporters.

It would naturally have followed that all the bishops met together in the Synod should have felt detestation of, and approved the sentence delivered against, a man who is the author of offences, disturbances and schisms, of agitation over all the world, and of rising of church against church. But in spite of our prayers, and against all our expectation, Seras, Stephanus, Heliodorus and Theophilus and their party[1] have not voted with us, and have not even consented to subscribe the sentence delivered against him, although Seras charged the aforenamed Aetius with another instance of insane arrogance, alleging that he, with still bolder impudence, had sprung forward to declare that what God had concealed from the Apostles had been now revealed to him. Even after these wild and boastful words, reported by Seras about Aetius, the aforenamed bishops were not put out of countenance, nor could they be induced to vote with us on his condemnation. We however with much long suffering bore with them[2] for a great length of time, now indignant, now beseeching, now importuning them to join with us and make the decision of the Synod unanimous; and we persevered long in the hope that they might hear and agree and give in. But when in spite of all this patience we could not shame them into acceptance of our declarations against the aforesaid offender, we counted the rule of the church more precious than the friendship of men, and pronounced against them a decree of excommunication, allowing them a period of six months for conversion, repentance, and the expression of a desire for union and harmony with the synod. If within the given time they should turn and accept agreement with their brethren and assent to the decrees about Aetius, we decided that they should be received into the church, to the recovery of their own authority in synods, and our affection. If however they obstinately persisted, and preferred human friendship to the

---

[1] Seras, or Serras, had been an Arian leader in Libya. In 356 Serras, together with Secundus, deposed bishop of Ptolemais, proposed to consecrate Aetius; he refused on the ground that they were tainted with Orthodoxy. Phil. iii. 19. In 359 he subscribed the decrees of Seleucia as bishop of Paraetonium (Al Bareton W. of Alexandria) (Epiph. Hær. lxxiii. 20). Now he is deposed (360) by the Constantinopolitan Synod. Vide Dict. Christ. Biog. s. v.

Stephanus, a Libyan bishop ordained by Secundus of Ptolemais, and concerned with him in the murder of the Presbyter Secundus, as described by Athan. in *Hist. Ar.* § 65 cf. Ath. *de Syn.* § 12.

Heliodorus was Arian bishop of Apollonia or Sozysa (Shahfah) in Libya Prima. cf. LeQuien Or. Ch. ii. 617.

Theophilus, previously bishop of Eleutheropolis in Palestine, was translated, against his vow of fidelity to that see, (Soz. iv. 24) to Castabala in Cilicia. On the place Vide Bp. Lightfoot. Ap. Fathers Pt. ii. Vol. iii. 136.

[2] συμπεριηνέχθημεν is the suggestion of Valesius for συμπεριεψηθίσθημεν, a word of no authority.

canons of the church and our affection, then we judged them deposed from the rank of the bishops. If they suffer degradation it is necessary to appoint other bishops in their place, that the lawful church may be duly ordered and at unity with herself, while all the bishops of every nation by uttering the same doctrine with one mind and one counsel preserve the bond of love.

To acquaint you with the decree of the Synod we have sent these present to your reverence, and pray that you may abide by them, and by the grace of Christ rule the churches under you aright and in peace.

CHAPTER XXV.

Of the causes which separated the Eunomians from the Arians.

EUNOMIUS in his writings praises Aetius, styles him a man of God, and honours him with many compliments. Yet he was at that time closely associated with the party by whom Aetius had been repudiated, and to them he owed his election to his bishopric.

Now the followers of Eudoxius and Acacius, who had assented to the decrees put forth at Nice in Thrace, already mentioned in this history, appointed other bishops in the churches of the adherents of Basilius and Eleusius in their stead. On other points I think it superfluous to write in detail. I purpose only to relate what concerns Eunomius.

For when Eunomius had seized on the see of Cyzicus in the lifetime of Eleusius, Eudoxius urged him to hide his opinions and not make them known to the party who were seeking a pretext to persecute him. Eudoxius was moved to offer this advice both by his knowledge that the diocese was sound in the faith and his experience of the anger manifested by Constantius against the party who asserted the only begotten Son of God to be a created being. " Let us " said he to Eunomius " bide our time ; when it comes we will preach what now we are keeping dark ; educate the ignorant ; and win over or compel or punish our opponents." Eunomius, yielding to these suggestions, propounded his impious doctrine under the shadow of obscurity. Those of his hearers who had been nurtured on the divine oracles saw clearly that his utterances concealed under their surface a foul fester of error.[1]

But however distressed they were they considered it less the part of prudence than of rashness to make any open protest, so they assumed a mask of heretical heterodoxy, and paid a visit to the bishop at his private residence with the earnest request that he would have regard to the distress of men borne hither and thither by different doctrines, and would plainly expound the truth. Eunomius thus emboldened declared the sentiments which he secretly held. The deputation then went on to remark that it was unfair and indeed quite wrong for the whole of his diocese to be prevented from having their share of the truth. By these and similar arguments he was induced to lay bare his blasphemy in the public assemblies of the church. Then his opponents hurried with angry fervour to Constantinople ; first they indicted him before Eudoxius, and when Eudoxius refused to see them, sought an audience of the emperor and made lamentation over the ruin their bishop was wreaking among them. " The sermons of Eunomius," they said, " are more impious than the blasphemies of Arius." The wrath of Constantius was roused, and he commanded Eudoxius to send for Eunomius, and, on his conviction, to strip him of his bishopric. Eudoxius, of course, though again and again importuned by the accusers, continued to delay taking action. Then once more they approached the emperor with vociferous complaints that Eudoxius had not obeyed the imperial commands in any single particular, and was perfectly indifferent to the delivery of an important city to the blasphemies of Eunomius. Then said Constantius to Eudoxius, if you do not fetch Eunomius and try him, and on conviction of the charges brought against him, punish him, I shall exile you. This threat frightened Eudoxius, so he wrote to Eunomius to escape from Cyzicus, and told him he had only himself to blame because he had not followed the hints given him. Eunomius accordingly withdrew in alarm, but he could not endure the disgrace, and endeavoured to fix the guilt of his betrayal on Eudoxius, maintaining that both he and Aetius had been cruelly treated. And from that time he set up a sect of his own for all the men who were of his way of thinking and condemned his betrayal, separated from Eudoxius and joined with Eunomius, whose name they bear up to this day. So Eunomius became the founder of a heresy, and added to the blasphemy of Arius by his own peculiar guilt. He set up a sect of his own because he was a slave to his ambition, as the facts distinctly prove. For when Aetius was condemned and exiled, Eunomius

---

[1] On the picturesque word ὕπουλος cf. Hipp: XXI, 32; Plat: Gorg. 518 E. and the well-known passage in the Œd: Tyrannus (1396) where Œdipus speaks of the promise of his youth as " a fair outside all fraught with ills below."

refused to accompany him, though he called him his master and a man of God, but remained closely associated with Eudoxius.

But when his turn came he paid the penalty of his iniquity; he did not submit to the vote of the synod, but began to ordain bishops and presbyters, though himself deprived of his episcopal rank. These then were the deeds done at Constantinople.

CHAPTER XXVI.

Of the siege of the city of Nisibis,[1] and the apostolic conversation of Bishop Jacobus.

On war being waged against the Romans by Sapor King of Persia, Constantius mustered his forces and marched to Antioch. But the enemy were driven forth, not by the Roman army, but by Him whom the pious in the Roman host worshipped as their God. How the victory was won I shall now proceed to relate.

Nisibis, sometimes called Antiochia Mygdonia, lies on the confines of the realms of Persia and of Rome. In Nisibis Jacobus whom I named just now was at once bishop, guardian,[2] and commander in chief. He was a man who shone with the grace of a truly apostolic character. His extraordinary and memorable miracles, which I have fully related in my religious history, I think it superfluous and irrelevant to enumerate again.[3]

One however I will record because of the subject before us. The city which Jacobus ruled was now in possession of the Romans, and besieged by the Persian Army. The blockade was prolonged for seventy days. "Helepoles"[1] and many other engines were advanced to the walls. The town was begirt with a palisade and entrenchment, but still held out. The river Mygdonius flowing through the middle of the town, at last the Persians dammed its stream a considerable distance up, and increased the height of its bank on both sides so as to shut the waters in. When they saw that a great mass of water was collected and already beginning to overflow the dam, they suddenly launched it like an engine against the wall. The impact was tremendous; the bulwarks could not sustain it, but gave way and fell down. Just the same fate befell the other side of the circuit, through which the Mygdonius made its exit; it could not withstand the shock, and was carried away. No sooner did Sapor see this than he expected to capture the rest of the city, and for all that day he rested for the mud to dry and the river to become passable. Next day he attacked in full force, and looked to enter the city through the breaches that had been made. But he found the wall built up on both sides, and all his labour vain. For that holy man, through prayer, filled with valour both the troops and the rest of the townsfolk, and both built the walls, withstood the engines, and beat off the advancing foe. And all this he did without approaching the walls, but by beseeching the Lord of all within the church. Sapor, moreover, was not only

[1] Now Nisibin, an important city of Mesopotamia on the Mygdonius (Hulai). Its name was changed under the Macedonian dynasty to Antiochia Mygdonica. Frequently taken and retaken it was ultimately ceded by Jovian to Sapor A.D. 363.

[2] "πολιοῦχος" is an epithet of the protecting deity of a city, as of Athens " Παλλὰς πολιοῦχος; " Ar. Eq. 581.

[3] Born in the city of which he was afterwards bishop, Jacobus early acquired fame by his ascetic austerity. While on a journey into Persia with the object at once of confirming his own faith and that of the Christian sufferers under the persecution of Sapor II, he was supposed to work wonders, of which the following, related by Theodoretus, is a specimen. Once upon a time he saw a Persian Judge delivering an unjust sentence. Now a huge stone happening to be lying close by, he ordered it to be crushed and broken into pieces, and so proved the injustice of the sentence. The stone was instantly divided into innumerable fragments, the spectators were panic-stricken, and the judge in terror revoked his sentence and delivered a righteous judgment. On the see of his native city falling vacant Jacobus was made bishop. The "Religious History" describes him as signalling his episcopate by the miracle attributed by Gregory of Nyssa to Gregory the Wonder-Worker, and by Sozomen (vii. 27) to Epiphanius. As in the "Nuremberg Chronicle," the same woodcut serves for Thales, Nehemiah, and Dante, so a popular miracle was indiscriminately assigned to saint after saint. "Once upon a time he came to a certain village, — the spot I cannot name,— and up come some beggars putting down one of their number before him as though dead, and begging him to supply some necessaries for the funeral. Jacobus granted their petition, and on behalf of the apparently dead man began to pray to God to forgive him the sins of his lifetime and grant him a place in the company of the just. Even while he was speaking, away flew the soul of the man who had up to this moment shammed death, and coverings were provided for the corpse. The holy man proceeded on his journey, and the inventors of this play told their recumbent companion to get up. But now

they saw that he did not hear, that the pretence had become a reality, and that what a moment ago was a live man's mask was now a dead man's face. So they overtake the great Jacobus, bow down before him, roll at his feet and declare that they would not have played their impudent trick but for their poverty, and implored him to forgive them and restore the dead man's soul. So Jacobus in imitation of the philanthropy of the Lord granted their prayer, exhibited his wonder working power, and through his prayer restored the life which his power had taken away."

At Nicæa Theodoret describes Jacobus as a "champion" of the orthodox "phalanx." (Relig. Hist. 1114.) At the state dinner given by Constantine to the Nicene Fathers, "James of Nisibis (so ran the Eastern tale—Biblioth. Pat. clv.) saw angels standing round the Emperor, and underneath his purple robe discovered a sackcloth garment. Constantine, in return, saw angels ministering to James, placed his seat above the other bishops, and said: 'There are three pillars of the world, Antony in Egypt, Nicolas of Myra, James in Assyria.'" Stanley, *Eastern Church*, Lect. V.

[1] Ammianus Marcellinus 23. 4. 10. thus describes the "Ἑλέπολις μηχανή." "An enormous testudo is strengthened by long planks and fitted with iron bolts. This is covered with hides and fresh wicker-work. Its upper parts are smeared with mud as a protection against fire and missiles. To its front are fastened three-pronged spear points made exceedingly sharp, and steadied by iron weights, like the thunderbolts of painters and potters. Thus whenever it was directed against anything these stings were shot out to destroy. The huge mass was moved on wheels and ropes from within by a considerable body of troops, and advanced with a mighty impulse against the weaker part of a town wall. Then unless the defenders prevailed against it the walls were beaten in and a wide breach made."

astounded at the speed of the building of
the walls but awed by another spectacle.
For he saw standing on the battlements
one of kingly mien and all ablaze with
purple robe and crown. He supposed that
this was the Roman emperor, and threatened his attendants with death for not having announced the imperial presence; but
on their stoutly maintaining that their report
had been a true one and that Constantius
was at Antioch, he perceived the meaning
of the vision and exclaimed "their God is
fighting for the Romans." Then the
wretched man in a rage flung a javelin into
the air, though he knew that he could not
hit a bodiless being, but unable to curb his
passion. Therefore the excellent Ephraim
(he is the best writer among the Syrians)
besought the divine Jacobus to mount the
wall to see the barbarians and to let fly at
them the darts of his curse. So the divine
man consented and climbed up into a tower;
but when he saw the innumerable host,
he discharged no other curse than to ask
that mosquitoes and gnats might be sent
forth upon them, so that by means of these
tiny animals they might learn the might of
the Protector of the Romans. On his prayer
followed clouds of mosquitoes and gnats;
they filled the hollow trunks of the elephants,
and the ears and nostrils of horses and other
animals. Finding the attack of these little
creatures past endurance they broke their
bridles, unseated their riders and threw the
ranks into confusion. The Persians abandoned their camp and fled head-long. So the
wretched prince learned by a slight and
kindly chastisement the power of the God
who protects the pious, and marched his
army home again, reaping for all the harvest
of the siege not triumph but disgrace.

CHAPTER XXVII.

*Of the Council of Antioch and what was done
there against the holy Meletius.*

At this time,[1] Constantius was residing
at Antioch. The Persian war was over;
there had been a time of peace, and he once
again gathered bishops together with the object of making them all deny both the formula
"of one substance" and also the formula "of
different substance." On the death of Leontius, Eudoxius had seized the see of Antioch,

but on his expulsion and illegal establishment, after many synods, at Constantinople, the church of Antioch had been left
without a shepherd. Accordingly the assembled bishops, gathered in considerable numbers from every quarter, asserted that their
primary obligation was to provide a pastor
for the flock and that then with him they
would deliberate on matters of faith. It fell
out opportunely that the divine Meletius
who was ruling a certain city of Armenia [1]
had been grieved with the insubordination of
the people under his rule and was now living
without occupation elsewhere. The Arian
faction imagined that Meletius was of the
same way of thinking as themselves, and an
upholder of their doctrines. They therefore
petitioned Constantius to commit to his
hands the reins of the Antiochene church.
Indeed in the hope of establishing their impiety there was no law that they did not
fearlessly transgress; illegality was becoming the very foundation of their blasphemy; nor was this an isolated specimen of
their irregular proceedings. On the other
hand the maintainers of apostolic doctrine,
who were perfectly well aware of the soundness of the great Meletius, and had clear
knowledge of his stainless character and
wealth of virtue, came to a common vote,
and took measures to have their resolution
written out and subscribed by all without
delay. This document both parties as a
bond of compromise entrusted to the safe
keeping of a bishop who was a noble champion of the truth, Eusebius of Samosata.
And when the great Meletius had received
the imperial summons and arrived, forth to
meet him came all the higher ranks of the
priesthood, forth came all the other orders of
the church, and the whole population of the
city. There, too, were Jews and Gentiles
all eager to see the great Meletius. Now
the emperor had charged both Meletius and
the rest who were able to speak to expound
to the multitude the text "The Lord formed
me in the beginning of his way, before his
works of old" (Prov. viii. 22. lxx), and he
ordered skilled writers to take down on the
spot what each man said, with the idea that in
this manner their instruction would be more
exact. First of all Georgius of Laodicea
gave vent to his foul heresy· After him
Acacius [2] of Cæsarea propounded a doctrine

---

[1] According to Sozomen, Sebaste; but Socrates (II.44) makes
him bishop of the Syrian Berœa Gregory of Nyssa (Orat: In
Fun Mag: Meletii) puts on record "the sweet calm look, the
radiant smile, the kind hand seconding the kind voice "
[2] On Acacius of Cæsarea vide note on page 70. At the
Synod of Seleucia in 359 he started the party of the Homœans,
and was deposed. In the reign of Jovian they inclined to

of compromise far removed indeed from the blasphemy of the enemy, but not preserving the apostolic doctrine pure and undefiled. Then up rose the great Meletius and exhibited the unbending line of the canon of the faith, for using the truth as a carpenter does his rule he avoided excess and defect. Then the multitude broke into loud applause and besought him to give them a short summary of his teaching. Accordingly after showing three fingers, he withdrew two, left one, and uttered the memorable sentence, " In thought they are three but we speak as to one." [1]

Against this teaching the men who had the plague of Arius in their hearts whetted their tongues, and started an ingenious slander, declaring that the divine Meletius was a Sabellian. Thus they persuaded the fickle sovereign who, like the well known Euripus,[2] easily shifted his current now this way and now that, and induced him to relegate Meletius to his own home.

Euzoius, an open defender of Arian tenets, was promptly promoted to his place; the very man whom, then a deacon, the great Alexander had degraded at the same time as Arius. Now the part of the people who remained sound separated from the unsound, and assembled in the apostolic church which is situated in the part of the city called the Palæa.[3]

For thirty years indeed after the attack made upon the illustrious Eustathius they had gone on enduring the abomination of Arianism, in the expectation of some favourable change. But when they saw impiety on the increase, and men faithful to the apostolic doctrines both openly attacked and menaced by secret conspiracy, the divine Meletius in exile, and Euzoius the champion of heresy established as bishop in his place, they remembered the words spoken to Lot, " Escape for thy life " ;[4] and further the law of the gospel which plainly ordains " if thy right eye offend thee pluck it out and

cast it from thee." [1] The Lord laid down the same law about both hand and foot, and added, " It is profitable for thee that one of thy members should perish and not that thy whole body should be cast into hell."

Thus came about the division of the Church.

CHAPTER XXVIII.

About Eusebius, Bishop of Samosata.

THE admirable Eusebius mentioned above, who was entrusted with the common resolution, when he beheld the violation of the covenant, returned to his own see. Then certain men who were uneasy about the written document, persuaded Constantius to dispatch a messenger to recover it. Accordingly the emperor sent one of the officers who ride post with relays of horses, and bring communications with great speed. On his arrival he reported the imperial message, but, " I cannot," said the admirable Eusebius, " surrender the deed deposited with me till I am directed so to do by the whole assembly who gave it me." This reply was reported to the emperor. Boiling with rage he sent to Eusebius again and ordered him to give it up, with the further message that he had ordered his right hand to be cut off if he refused. But he only wrote this to terrify the bishop, for the courier who conveyed the dispatch had orders not to carry out the threat. But when the divine Eusebius opened the letter and saw the punishment which the emperor had threatened, he stretched out his right hand and his left, bidding the man cut off both. " The decree," said he, " which is a clear proof of Arian wickedness, I will not give up."

When Constantius had been informed of this courageous resolution he was struck with astonishment, and did not cease to admire it; for even foes are constrained by the greatness of bold deeds to admire their adversaries' success.

At this time Constantius learned that Julian, whom he had declared Cæsar of Europe, was aiming at sovereignty, and mustering an army against his master. Therefore he set out from Syria, and died in Cilicia.[2] Nor had he the helper whom his

---

Orthodoxy; in that of Valens to Arianism (cf. Soc. iv. 2). Acacius was a benefactor to the Public Library of Cæsarea (Hieron. Ep. ad Marcellam (141). Baronius places his death in 366.

[1] Τρία τὰ νοουμένα, ὡς ἐνὶ δὲ διαλεγόμεθα " Tria sunt quæ intelliguntur, sed tanquam unum alloquimur." The narrative of Sozomen (iv. 28) enables us to supply what Theodoret infelicitously omits. It was when an Arian archdeacon rudely put his hand over the bishop's mouth that Meletius indicated the orthodox doctrine by his fingers. When the archdeacon at his wits' end uncovered the mouth and seized the hand of the confessor, " with a loud voice he the more clearly proclaimed his doctrine."

[2] The Euripus, the narrow channel between Eubœa and the mainland, changes its current during eleven days in each month, eleven to fourteen times a day. cf. Arist. Eth. N. ix.6.3. "μεταρρεῖ ὥσπερ Εὐριπος."

[3] cf. p. 34.

[4] Gen. xix. 17.

[1] Matt. v. 29.
[2] Constantius died at Mopsucrene, on the Cydnus, according to Socrates and the Chron. Alex., on *Nov.* 3, 361. Socrates (ii. 47) ascribes his illness to chagrin at the successes of Julian, and says that he died in the 46th year of his age and 39th of his reign, having for thirteen years been associated in the empire with his Father. Ammianus (xxi. 15, 2) writes, " Venit Tarsum, ubi leviore febri contactus, ratusque itinerario

Father had left him; for he had not kept intact the inheritance of his Father's

motu imminutae valetudinis excuti posse discrimen, petiit per vias difficiles Mopsucrenas, Cilliciae ultimam hinc pergentibus stationem, sub Tauri montis radicibus positam : egredique sequuto die conatus, invalenti morbi gravitate detentus est : paulatimque urente calore nimio venas, ut ne tangi quidem corpus eius posset in modum foculi fervens, cum usus deficeret medelarum, ultimum spirans deflebat exitium; mentisque sensu tum etiam integro, successorem suae potestatis statuisse dicitur Julianum. Deinde anhelitu iam pulsatus letali conticuit diuque cum anima colluctatus iam discessura, abiit e vita III. Non. Octobrium, (i.e. Oct. 5 — a different date from that given by others) imperii vitaeque anno quadragesimo et mensibus paucis." His Father having died in 337,

piety, and so bitterly bewailed his change of faith.

Constantius really reigned 24 years alone, and if we include the 13 years which Socrates reckons in the lifetime of Constantine, we only reach 37. He was born on Aug. 6, 317, and was therefore a little over 44 at his death.
"Constantius was essentially a little man, in whom his father's vices took a meaner form." "The peculiar repulsiveness of Constantius is not due to any flagrant personal vice. but to the combination of cold-blooded treachery with the utter want of any inner nobleness of character. Yet he was a pious emperor, too, in his way. He loved the ecclesiastical game, and was easily won over to the Eusebian side."
Gwatkin. "The Arian Controversy." p. 63.

BOOK III.

CHAPTER I.

Of the reign of Julianus; how from a child he was brought up in piety and lapsed into impiety; and in what manner, though at first he kept his impiety secret, he afterwards laid it bare.

CONSTANTIUS, as has been narrated, departed this life groaning and grieving that he had been turned away from the faith of his father. Julian heard the news of his end as he was crossing from Europe into Asia, and assumed the sovereignty with delight at having now no rival.

In his earlier days, while yet a lad, Julian had, as well as Gallus[1] his brother, imbibed pure and pious teaching.

In his youth and earlier manhood he continued to take in the same doctrine. Constantius, dreading lest his kinsfolk should aspire to imperial power, slew them;[2] and Julian, through fear of his cousin, was enrolled in the order of Readers,[3] and used to read aloud the sacred books to the people in the assemblies of the church.

He also built a martyr's shrine; but the martyrs, when they beheld his apostasy, refused to accept the offering; for in consequence of the foundations being, like their founder's mind, unstable, the edifice fell down[1] before it was consecrated. Such were the boyhood and youth of Julian. At the period, however, when Constantius was setting out for the West, drawn thither by the war against Magnentius, he made Gallus, who was gifted with piety which he retained to the end,[2] Cæsar of the East. Now Julian flung away the apprehension's which had previously stood him in good stead, and, moved by unrighteous confidence, set his heart on seizing the sceptre of empire. Accordingly, on his way through Greece, he sought out seers and soothsayers, with a desire of learning if he should get what his soul longed for. He met with a man who promised to predict these things, conducted him into one of the idol temples, introduced him within the shrine, and called upon the demons of deceit. On their appearing in their wonted aspect terror compelled Julian to make the sign of the cross upon his brow. They no sooner saw the sign of the Lord's victory than they were reminded of their

---

[1] On the murder of the Princes of the blood Gallus was first sent alone to Tralles or Ephesus, (Soc. iii. 1,) and afterwards spent some time with his brother Julian in Cappadocia in retirement, but with a suitable establishment. On their relationship to Constantius vide Pedigree in the prolegomena.
[2] The massacre "involved the two uncles of Constantius, seven of his cousins, of whom Dalmatius and Hannibalianus were the most illustrious, the patrician Optatus, who had married a sister of the late Emperor, and the præfect Abcavius." "If it were necessary to aggravate the horrors of this bloody scene we might add that Constantius himself had espoused the daughter of his uncle Julius, and that he had bestowed his sister in marriage on his cousin Hannibalianus." "Of so numerous a family Gallus and Julian alone, the two youngest children of Julius Constantius, were saved from the hands of the assassins, till their rage, satiated with slaughter, had in some measure subsided." Gibbon, Chap. xviii. Theodoretus follows the opinion of Athanasius and Julian in ascribing the main guilt to Constantius, but, as Gibbon points out, Eutropius and the Victors "use the very qualifying expressions;" "sinente potius quam jubente;" "incertum quo suasore;" and "v. militum." Gregory of Nazianzus (Or. iv. 21) ascribes the preservation of both Julian and his brother Gallus to the clemency and protection of Constantius.
[3] Tertullian (De Præsc. 41) is the earliest authority for the office of Anagnostes, Lector, or Reader, as a distinct order in the Church. Henceforward it appears as one of the minor orders,

and is frequently referred to by Cyprian (Epp. 29. 38, etc.). By one of Justinian's novels it was directed that no one should be ordained Reader before the age of eighteen, but previously young boys were admitted to the office, at the instance of their parents, as introductory to the higher functions of the sacred ministry. Dict. Christ. Ant. i. 80.
[1] Sozomen (v. 2) tells us that when the princes were building a chapel for the martyr Mamas, the work of Gallus stood, but that of Julian tumbled down. A more famous instance of the care of Gallus for the christian dead is the story of the translation of the remains of the martyr Babylas from Antioch to Daphne, referred to by our author (iii. 6) as well as by Sozomen v. 19, and by Rufinus x. 35. cf. Bishop Lightfoot, Ap. Fathers II. i. 42.
[2] Gallus was made Cæsar by the childless Constantius in 350, in about his 25th year. "Fuit" says Am. Marcellinus (xiv. 11. 28) "forma conspicuus bona, decente filo corporis, membrorumque recta compage, flavo capillo et molli, barba licet recens emergente lanugine tenera." His government at Antioch was not successful, and at the instigation of the Eunuch Eusebius he was executed in 354 at Pola, a town already infamous for the murder of Crispus.

own rout, and forthwith fled away. On the magician becoming acquainted with the cause of their flight he blamed him; but Julian confessed his terror, and said that he wondered at the power of the cross, for that the demons could not endure to see its sign and ran away. "Think not anything of the sort, good sir;" said the magician, "they were not afraid as you make out, but they went away because they abominated what you did." So he tricked the wretched man, initiated him in the mysteries, and filled him with their abominations.

So lust of empire stripped the wretch of all true religion. Nevertheless after attaining the supreme power he concealed his impiety for a considerable time; for he was specially apprehensive about the troops who had been instructed in the principles of true religion, first by the illustrious Constantine, who freed them from their former error and trained them in the ways of truth, and afterwards by his sons, who confirmed the instruction given by their father. For if Constantius, led astray by those under whose influence he lived, did not admit the term ὁμοούσιον, at all events he sincerely accepted the meaning underlying it, for God the Word he styled true Son, begotten of his Father before the ages, and those who dared to call Him a creature he openly renounced, absolutely prohibiting the worship of idols.

I will relate also another of his noble deeds, as satisfactory proof of his zeal for divine things. In his campaign against Magnentius he once mustered the whole of his army, and counselled them to take part all together in the divine mysteries, "for," said he, "the end of life is always uncertain, and that not least in war, when innumerable missiles are hurled from either side, and swords and battle axes and other weapons are assailing men, whereby a violent death is brought about. Wherefore it behoves each man to wear that precious robe which most of all we need in yonder life hereafter: if there be one here who would not now put on this garb let him depart hence and go home. I shall not brook to fight with men in my army who have no part nor lot in our holy rites." [1]

CHAPTER II.

Of the return of the bishops and the consecration of Paulinus.

JULIAN had clear information on these points, and did not make known the impiety

of his soul. With the object of attracting all the bishops to acquiescence in his rule he ordered even those who had been expelled from their churches by Constantius, and who were sojourning on the furthest confines of the empire, to return to their own churches. Accordingly, on the promulgation of this edict, back to Antioch came the divine Meletius, and to Alexandria the far famed Athanasius. [1]

But Eusebius, [2] and Hilarius [3] of Italy and Lucifer [4] who presided over the flock in the island of Sardinia, were living in the Thebaid on the frontier of Egypt, whither they had been relegated by Constantius. They now met with the rest whose views were the same and affirmed that the churches ought to be brought into harmony. For they not only suffered from the assaults of their opponents, but were at variance with one another. In Antioch the sound body of the church had been split in two; at one and the same time they who from the beginning, for the sake of the right worthy Eustathius, had separated from the rest, were assembling by themselves; and they who with the admirable Meletius had held aloof from the Arian faction were performing divine service in what is called the Palæa. Both parties used one confession of faith, for both parties were champions of the doctrine laid down at Nicæa. All that separated them was their mutual quarrel, and their regard for their respective leaders; and even the death of one of these did not put a stop to the strife. Eustathius died before the election of Meletius, and the orthodox party, after the exile of Meletius and the election of Euzoius, separated from the communion of the impious, and assembled by themselves; with these, the party called Eustathians could not be induced to unite. To effect an union between them the Eusebians and

---

[1] The accession of Julian was made known in Alexandria at the end of Nov. 361, and the Pagans at once rose against George, imprisoned him, and at last on Dec. 24, brutally beat and kicked him to death. The Arians appointed a successor — Lucius, but on Feb. 22 Athanasius once more appeared among his faithful flock, and lost no time in getting a Council for the settlement of several moot points of discipline and doctrine, which Theodoret proceeds to enumerate.

[2] *i.e.* of Vercellæ. Vide p. 76. From Scythopolis he had been removed to Cappadocia, and thence to the Thebaid, whence he wrote a letter, still extant, to Gregory, bp. of Elvira in Spain.

[3] Valesius supposes Hilary of Poictiers to be mentioned here, though he recognises the difficulty of the "ὁ ἐκ τῆς Ἰταλίας," and would alter the text to meet it. Possibly this is the Hilary who is said to have been bishop of Pavia from 358 to 376, and may be the "Sanctus Hilarius" of Aug. *Cont. duas Epist. Pelag* iv. 4. 7. cf. article Ambrosiaster in Dict. Christ. Biog.

[4] cf. p. 76, note. Lucifer, bishop of Cagliari, had first been relegated in 355 to Eleutheropolis, (a town of the 3d C., in Palestine, about 20 m. west of Jerusalem) whence he wrote the controversial pamphlets still extant. He vigorously abused Constantius, to whom he paid the compliment of sending a copy of his work. The emperor appears to have retorted by having him removed to the Thebaid, whence he returned in 361.

---

[1] ἀμυήτοις.

Luciferians sought to discover a means. Accordingly Eusebius besought Lucifer to repair to Alexandria and take counsel on the matter with the great Athanasius, intending himself to undertake the labour of bringing about a reconciliation.

Lucifer however did not go to Alexandria, but repaired to Antioch. There he urged many arguments in behalf of concord on both parties. The Eustathians, led by Paulinus, a presbyter, persisted in opposition. On seeing this Lucifer took the improper course of consecrating Paulinus as their bishop.

This action on the part of Lucifer prolonged the feud, which lasted for eighty-five years, until the episcopate of the most praiseworthy Alexander.[1]

No sooner was the helm of the church at Antioch put into his hands than he tried every expedient, and brought to bear great zeal and energy for the promotion of concord, and thus joined the severed limb to the rest of the body of the church. At the time in question however Lucifer made the quarrel worse and spent a considerable time in Antioch, and Eusebius when he arrived on the spot and learnt that bad doctoring had made the malady very hard to heal, sailed away to the West.

When Lucifer returned to Sardinia he made certain additions to the dogmas of the church and those who accepted them were named after him, and for a considerable time were called Luciferians. But in time the flame of this dogma too went out and it was consigned to oblivion.[2] Such were the events that followed on the return of the bishops.

CHAPTER III.

Of the number and character of the deeds done by Pagans against the Christians when they got the power from Julian.

WHEN Julian had made his impiety openly known the cities were filled with dissensions. Men enthralled by the deceits of idolatry took heart, opened the idols'

shrines, and began to perform those foul rites which ought to have died out from the memory of man. Once more they kindled the fire on the altars, befouled the ground with victims' gore, and defiled the air with the smoke of their burnt sacrifices. Maddened by the demons they served they ran in corybantic[1] frenzy round about the streets, attacked the saints with low stage jests, and with all the outrage and ribaldry of their impure processions.

On the other hand the partizans[2] of piety could not brook their blasphemies, returned insult for insult, and tried to confute the error which their opponents honoured. In their turn the workers of iniquity took it ill; the liberty allowed them by the sovereign was an encouragement to audacity and they dealt deadly blows among the Christians.

It was indeed the duty of the emperor to consult for the peace of his subjects, but he in the depth of his iniquity himself maddened his peoples with mutual rage. The deeds dared by the brutal against the peaceable he overlooked and entrusted civil and military offices of importance to savage and impious men, who though they hesitated publicly to force the lovers of true piety to offer sacrifice treated them nevertheless with all kinds of indignity. All the honours moreover conferred on the sacred ministry by the great Constantine Julian took away.

To tell all the deeds dared by the slaves of idolatrous deceit at that time would require a history of these crimes alone, but out of the vast number of them I shall select a few instances. At Askalon and at Gaza, cities of Palestine, men of priestly rank and women who had lived all their lives in virginity were disembowelled, filled with barley, and given for food to swine. At Sebaste, which belongs to the same people, the coffin of John the Baptist was opened, his bones burnt, and the ashes scattered abroad.[3]

---

[1] cf. p. 41. Eustathius died about 337, at Philippi, — probably about six years after his deposition. Alexander, an ascetic (cf. post, V. Ch. 35) did not become bishop of Antioch till 413.

[2] The raison d'être of the Luciferians as a distinct party was their unwillingness to accept communion with men who had ever lapsed into Arianism. Jerome gives 371 as the date of Lucifer's death. "To what extent he was an actual schismatic remains obscure." St. Ambrose remarks that "he had separated himself from our communion," (de excessu Satyri 1127, 47) and St. Augustine that "he fell into the darkness of schism, having lost the light of charity." (Ep. 185 n. 47.) But there is no mention of any separation other than Lucifer's own repulsion of so many ecclesiastics; and Jerome in his dialogue against the Luciferians (§ 20) calls him "*beatus* and *bonus pastor.*" J. Ll. Davies in Dict. Christ. Biog. s. v.

[1] Corybantes, the name of the priests of Cybele, whose religious service consisted in noisy music and wild, armed dances, is a word of uncertain origin. The chief seat of their rites was Pessinus in Galatia.

[2] Θιασῶται. lit. The " club-fellows," or " members of a religious brotherhood."

[3] Sebaste was a name given to Samaria by Herod the Great in honour of Augustus. cf. Rufinus H. E. xi. 28 and Theophanes, *Chronographia* i. 117. Theodoretus claims to have obtained some of the relics of the Baptist for his own church at Cyrus (Relig. Hist. 1245). On the development of the tradition of the relics, cf. Dict. Christ. Ant. i. 883. A magnificent church was built by Theodosius (Soz. vii. 21 and 24) in a suburb of Constantinople, to enshrine a head discovered by some unsound monks. The church is said by Sozomen (vii. 24) to be " at the seventh milestone," on the road out of Constantinople, and the place to be called Hebdomon or " seventh." I am indebted to the Rev. H. F. Tozer for the suggestion that Hebdomon was a promontory on the Propontis, to the west of the extreme part of the city, where the Cyclobion was, and where the Seven Towers now are; and that the Seven Towers being about six Roman miles from the Seraglio Point, which is the apex of the triangle formed by

Who too could tell without a tear the vile deed done in Phœnicia? At Heliopolis[1] by Lebanon there lived a certain deacon of the name of Cyrillus. In the reign of Constantine, fired by divine zeal, he had broken in pieces many of the idols there worshipped. Now men of infamous name, bearing this deed in mind, not only slew him, but cut open his belly and devoured his liver. Their crime was not, however, hidden from the all-seeing eye, and they suffered the just reward of their deeds; for all who had taken part in this abominable wickedness lost their teeth, which all fell out at once, and lost, too, their tongues, which rotted away and dropped from them: they were moreover deprived of sight, and by their sufferings proclaimed the power of holiness.

At the neighbouring city of Emesa[2] they dedicated to Dionysus, the woman-formed, the newly erected church, and set up in it his ridiculous androgynous image. At Dorystolum,[3] a famous city of Thrace, the victorious athlete Æmilianus was thrown upon a flaming pyre, by Capitolinus, governor of all Thrace. To relate the tragic fate of Marcus, however, bishop of Arethusa,[4] with true dramatic dignity, would require the eloquence of an Æschylus or a Sophocles. In the days of Constantius he had destroyed a certain idol-shrine and built a church in its place; and no sooner did the Arethusians learn the mind of Julian than they made an open display of their hostility. At first, according to the precept of the Gospel,[5] Marcus endeavoured to make his escape; but when he became aware that some of his own people were apprehended in his stead, he returned and gave himself up to the men of blood. After they had seized him they neither pitied his old age nor reverenced his deep regard for virtue; but, conspicuous as he was for the beauty alike of his teaching and of his life, first of all they stripped and smote him, laying strokes on every limb, then they flung him into filthy sewers, and, when they had dragged him out again, delivered him to a crowd of lads whom they charged to prick him without mercy with their pens.[1] After this they put him into a basket, smeared him with pickle[2] and honey, and hung him up in the open air in the height of summer, inviting wasps and bees to a feast. Their object in doing this was to compel him either to restore the shrine which he had destroyed, or to defray the expense of its erection. Marcus, however, endured all these grievous sufferings and affirmed that he would consent to none of their demands. His enemies, with the idea that he could not afford the money from poverty, remitted half their demand, and bade him pay the rest; but Marcus hung on high, pricked with pens, and devoured by wasps and bees, yet not only shewed no signs of pain, but derided his impious tormentors with the repeated taunt, " You are groundlings and of the earth; I, sublime and exalted." At last they begged for only a small portion of the money; but, said he, " it is as impious to give an obole as to give all." So discomfited they let him go, and could not refrain from admiring his constancy, for his words had taught them a new lesson of holiness.

CHAPTER IV.

Of the laws made by Julian against the Christians.

COUNTLESS other deeds were dared at that time by land and by sea, all over the world, by the wicked against the just, for now without disguise the enemy of God began to lay down laws against true religion. First of all he prohibited the sons of the Galileans, for so he tried to name the worshippers of the Saviour, from taking part in the study of poetry, rhetoric, and philosophy, for said he, in the words of the proverb " we are shot with shafts feathered from our own wing,"[3] for from our own books they take arms and wage war against us.

After this he made another edict ordering the Galileans to be expelled from the army.

CHAPTER V.

Of the fourth exile and flight of the holy Athanasius.

AT this time Athanasius, that victorious athlete of the truth, underwent another peril,

---

the city, the phrase at the seventh milestone is thus accounted for. Bones alleged to be parts of the scull are still shewn at Amiens. The same emperor built a church for the body on the site of the Serapeum at Alexandria.

[1] Heliopolis, the modern Baalbec, the "City of the Sun," was built at the west foot of Anti-Libanus, near the sources of the Orontes.

[2] On the Orontes; now Homs. Here Aurelian defeated Zenobia in 273.

[3] Durostorum, now Silistria, on the right bank of the Danube.

[4] Valesius (note on Soz. v. 10) would distinguish this Marcus of Arethusa from the Arian Marcus of Arethusa, author of the creed of Sirmium (Soc. H. E. ii. 30), apparently on insufficient grounds (Dict. Christ. Biog. s. v.). Arethusa was a town not far from the source of the Orontes.

[5] Matt. x. 23.

[1] The sharp iron stilus was capable of inflicting severe wounds. Cæsar, when attacked by his murderers, " caught Casca's arm and ran it through with his pen." Suetonius.

[2] γάρον, garum, was a fish-pickle. cf. the barbarous punishment of the σκάφευσις, inflicted among others on Mithridates, who wounded Cyrus at Cunaxa. (Plut. *Artaxerxes.*)

[3] cf. Aristophanes (Aves 808) " ταδ' ούχ ύπ' άλλων αλλά τοις αύτών πτεροίς."

for the devils could not brook the power of his tongue and prayers, and so armed their ministers to revile him. Many voices did they utter beseeching the champion of wickedness to exile Athanasius, and adding yet this further, that if Athanasius remained, not a heathen would remain, for that he would get them all over to his side. Moved by these supplications Julian condemned Athanasius not merely to exile,[1] but to death. His people shuddered, but it is related that he foretold the rapid dispersal of the storm, for said he "It is a cloud which soon vanishes away." He however withdrew as soon as he learnt the arrival of the bearers of the imperial message, and finding a boat on the bank of the river, started for the Thebaid. The officer who had been appointed for his execution became acquainted with his flight, and strove to pursue him at hot haste; one of his friends, however, got ahead, and told him that the officer was coming on apace. Then some of his companions besought him to take refuge in the desert, but he ordered the steersman to turn the boat's head to Alexandria. So they rowed to meet the pursuer, and on came the bearer of the sentence of execution, and, said he, "How far off is Athanasius?" "Not far," said Athanasius,[2] and so got rid of his foe, while he himself returned to Alexandria and there remained in concealment for the remainder of Julian's reign.[3]

CHAPTER VI.

Of Apollo and Daphne, and of the holy Babylas.

JULIAN, wishing to make a campaign against the Persians, dispatched the trustiest of his officers to all the oracles throughout the Roman Empire, while he himself went as a suppliant to implore the Pythian oracle of Daphne to make known to him the future. The oracle responded that the corpses lying hard by were becoming an obstacle to divination; that they must first be removed to another spot; and that then he would utter his prophecy, for, said he, "I could say nothing, if the grove be not purified." Now

at that time there were lying there the relics of the victorious martyr Babylas[1] and the lads who had gloriously suffered with him, and the lying prophet was plainly stopped from uttering his wonted lies by the holy influence of Babylas. Julian was aware of this, for his ancient piety had taught him the power of victorious martyrs, and so he removed no other body from the spot, but only ordered the worshippers of Christ to translate the relics of the victorious martyrs. They marched with joy to the grove,[2] put the coffin on a car and went before it leading a vast concourse of people, singing the psalms of David, while at every pause they shouted "Shame be to all them that worship molten images."[3] For they understood the translation of the martyr to mean defeat for the demon.

CHAPTER VII.

Of Theodorus the Confessor.

JULIAN could not endure the shame brought upon him by these doings, and on the following day ordered the leaders of the choral procession to be arrested. Sallustius was prefect at this time and a servant of iniquity, but he nevertheless was anxious to persuade the sovereign not to allow the Christians who were eager for glory to attain the object of their desires. When however he saw that the emperor was impotent to master his rage, he arrested a young man adorned with the graces of a holy enthusiasm while walking in the Forum, hung him up before the world on the stocks, lacerated his back with scourges, and scored his sides with claw-like instruments of torture. And this he did all day from dawn till the day was done; and then put chains of iron on him and ordered him to be kept in ward. Next morning he informed Julian of what had been done, and reported the young man's constancy and added that the event was for themselves a defeat and for the Christians a triumph. Persuaded of the truth of this, God's enemy suffered no more

---

[1] The crowning outrage which moved Julian to put out the edict of exile was the baptism by the bishop of some pagan ladies. The letter of Julian (Ep. p. 187) fixed Dec. 1st, 362, as the limit of Athanasius' permission to stay in Egypt, but it was on Oct. 23d (Fest. Ind.) that the order was communicated to him.

[2] The story may be compared with that of Napoleon on the return from Elba in Feb. 1815, when on being hailed by some passing craft with an enquiry as to the emperor's health, he is said to have himself taken the speaking trumpet and replied "Quite well."

[3] He concealed himself at Chœren, (? El Careon) near Alexandria, and went thence to Memphis, whence he wrote his Festal Letter for 363. Julian died June 26, 363.

[1] Babylas, bishop of Antioch from 238 to 251, was martyred in the Decian persecution either by death in prison (Euseb. H. E. vi. 39 μετὰ τὴν ὁμολογίαν ἐν δεσμωτηρίῳ μεταλλάξαντος) or by violence. (Chrys. de s. B. c. gentes) "Babylas had won for himself a name by his heroic courage as bishop of Antioch. It was related of him that on one occasion when the emperor Philip, who was a Christian, had presented himself one Easter Eve at the time of prayer, he had boldly refused admission to the sovereign, till he had gone through the proper discipline of a penitent for some offence committed. (Eus. H. E. vi. 34.) He acted like a good shepherd, says Chrysostom, who drives away the scabby sheep, lest it should infect the flock." Bp. Lightfoot, Ap. Fathers II. i. p. 40-46.

[2] "The Daphnean Sanctuary was four or five miles distant from the city." "Rufinus says six, but this appears to be an exaggeration." Bp. Lightfoot l. c.

[3] Ps. 96. 7.

to be so treated and ordered Theodorus[1] to be let out of prison, for so was named this young and glorious combatant in truth's battle. On being asked if he had had any sense of pain on undergoing those most bitter and most savage tortures he replied that at the first indeed he had felt some little pain, but that then had appeared to him one who continually wiped the sweat from his face with a cool and soft kerchief and bade him be of good courage. "Wherefore," said he, "when the executioners gave over I was not pleased but vexed, for now there went away with them he who brought me refreshment of soul." But the demon of lying divination at once increased the martyr's glory and exposed his own falsehood; for a thunderbolt sent down from heaven burnt the whole shrine[2] and turned the very statue of the Pythian into fine dust, for it was made of wood and gilded on the surface. Julianus the uncle of Julian, prefect of the East, learnt this by night, and riding at full speed came to Daphne, eager to bring succour to the deity whom he worshipped; but when he saw the so-called god turned into powder he scourged the officers in charge of the temple,[3] for he conjectured that the conflagration was due to some Christian. But they, maltreated as they were, could not endure to utter a lie, and persisted in saying that the fire had started not from below but from above. Moreover some of the neighbouring rustics came forward and asserted that they had seen the thunderbolt come rushing down from heaven.

CHAPTER VIII.

Of the confiscation of the sacred treasures and taking away of the allowances.[4]

EVEN when the wicked had become acquainted with these events they set themselves in array against the God of all; and the prince ordered the holy vessels to be handed over to the imperial treasury. Of the great church which Constantine had built he nailed up the doors and declared it closed to the worshippers wont to assemble there. At this time it was in possession of the Arians. In company with Julianus the prefect of the East, Felix the imperial treasurer, and Elpidius, who had charge of the emperor's private purse and property, an officer whom it is the Roman custom to call "Comes privatarum,"[1] made their way into the sacred edifice. Both Felix and Elpidius, it is said, were Christians, but to please the impious emperor apostatised from the true religion. Julianus committed an act of gross indecency on the Holy Table[2] and, when Euzoius endeavoured to prevent him, gave him a blow on the face, and told him, so the story goes, that it is the fate of the fortunes of Christians to have no protection from the gods. But Felix, as he gazed upon the magnificence of the sacred vessels, furnished with splendour by the munificence of Constantine and Constantius, "Behold," said he, "with what vessels Mary's son is served." But it was not long before they paid the penalty of these deeds of mad and impious daring.

CHAPTER IX.

Of what befell Julianus, the Emperor's Uncle, and Felix.

JULIANUS forthwith fell sick of a painful disease; his entrails rotted away, and he was no longer able to discharge his excrements through the normal organs of excretion,[3] but his polluted mouth, at the instant of his blasphemy, became the organ for their emission.

His wife, it is said, was a woman of conspicuous faith, and thus addressed her spouse: "Husband, you ought to bless our Saviour Christ for shewing you through your castigation his peculiar power. For

---

[1] " Gibbon seems to confuse this young man Theodorus with Theodoretus the presbyter and martyr who was put to death about this time at Antioch by the Count Julianus, the uncle of the emperor, (Soz. v. S., Ruinart's Act. Mart. Sinc. p. 605 sq.) for he speaks in his text of ' a presbyter of the name of Theodoret,' and in his notes of ' the passion of S. Theodore in the Acta Sincera of Ruinart,' " Bp. Lightfoot. p. 43.

[2] " Gibbon says, ' During the night which terminated this indiscreet procession, the temple of Daphne was in flames,' and later writers have blindly followed him. He does not give any authority, but obviously he is copying Tillemont H. E. iii. p. 407 ' en mesme temps que l'on portant dans la ville la châsse du Saint Martyr, c'est à dire la nuit suivante.' The only passage which Tillemont quotes is Ammianus, (xxii. 13) ' eodem tempore die xi. Kal. Nov.,' which does not bear him out. On the contrary the historians generally (cf. Soz. v. 20, Theod. iii. 7) place the persecutions which followed on the processions, and which must have occupied some time, before the burning of the temple." Bp. Lightfoot.

[3] νεωκόρους. νεωκόρος is the word rendered "worshipper" in Acts xix. 35 by A. V. The R. V. has correctly "templekeeper," the old derivation from κορέω = sweep, being no doubt less probable than the reference of the latter part of the word to a root √KOR=√KOL, found in colo, curo.

[4] Τῆς τῶν σιτηρεσίων ἀφαιρεσεως. This deprivation is not fur-

ther referred to in the text. Philostorgius (vii. 4) says " He distributed the allowance of the churches among the ministers of the dæmons," cf. Soz. v. 5. The restitution is recorded in Theod. iv. 4. The σιτομετριον of St. Luke xii. 42. (cf. τὴν τροφήν in Matt. xxiv. 45) is analogous to the σιτηρέσια of the text. Vide Suicer s. v.

[1] By the constitution of Constantine the two great ministers of finance were (i) the Comes sacrarum largitionum, treasurer and paymaster of the public staff of the Empire; (ii) Comes rei privatæ, who managed the privy purse and kept the liber beneficionum, an account of privileges granted by the emperor. cf. Dict. Christ. Ant. i. p.634.

[2] Τράπεζα is the word commonly employed by the Greek Fathers and in Greek Liturgies to designate the Lord's Table. Θυσιαστήριον is used by Eusebius H. E. x.4, for the Altar of the Church of Tyre, but the earlier θυσιαστήριον of Ignatius (Philad. iv.) does not appear to mean the Lord's Table. cf. Bp. Lightfoot Ap. Fathers. pt. II. ii. p. 258.

[3] ἀπόκρισις.

you would never have known who it is who is being attacked by you if with his wonted long suffering he had refrained from visiting you with these heaven-sent plagues." Then by these words and the heavy weight of his woes the wretched man perceived the cause of his disease, and besought the emperor to restore the church to those who had been deprived of it. He could not however gain his petition, and so ended his days.

Felix too was himself suddenly struck down by a heaven-sent scourge, and kept vomiting blood from his mouth, all day and all night, for all the vessels of his body poured their convergent streams to this one organ: so when all his blood was shed he died, and was delivered to eternal death.

Such were the penalties inflicted on these men for their wickedness.

CHAPTER X.

Of the Son of the Priest.

A YOUNG man who was a priest's son, and brought up in impiety, about this time went over to the true religion. For a lady remarkable for her devotion and admitted to the order of deaconesses [1] was an intimate friend of his mother. When he came to visit her with his mother, while yet a tiny lad, she used to welcome him with affection and urge him to the true religion. ·On the death of his mother the young man used to visit her and enjoyed the advantage of her wonted teaching. Deeply impressed by her counsels, he enquired of his teacher by what means he might both escape the superstition of his father and have part and lot in the truth which she preached. She replied that he must flee from his father, and honour rather the Creator both of his father and himself; that he must seek some other city wherein he might lie hid and escape the violence of the impious emperor; and she promised to manage this for him. Then, said the young man, " henceforward I shall come and commit my soul to you." Not many days afterwards Julian came to Daphne to celebrate a public feast. With him came the young man's father, both as a priest, and as accustomed to attend the emperor; and with their father came the young man and his brother, being appointed to the service of the temple and charged with the duty of ceremonially sprinkling the imperial viands. It is the custom for the festival of Daphne

to last for seven days. On the first day the young man stood by the emperor's couch, and according to the prescribed usage aspersed the meats, and thoroughly polluted them. Then at full speed he ran to Antioch,[1] and making his way to that admirable lady, " I am come," said he, " to you; and I have kept my promise. Do you look to the salvation of each and fulfil your pledge." At once she arose and conducted the young man to Meletius the man of God, who ordered him to remain for awhile upstairs in the inn. His father after wandering about all over Daphne in search of the boy, then returned to the city and explored the streets and lanes, turning his eyes in all directions and longing to light upon his lad. At length he arrived at the place where the divine Meletius had his hostelry; and looking up he saw his son peeping through the lattice. He ran up, drew him along, got him down, and carried him off home. Then he first laid on him many stripes, then applied hot spits to his feet and hands and back, then shut him up in his bedroom, bolted the door on the outside, and returned to Daphne. So I myself have heard the man himself narrate in his old age, and he added further that he was inspired and filled with Divine Grace, and broke in pieces all his father's idols, and made mockery of their helplessness. Afterwards when he bethought him of what he had done he feared his father's return and besought his Master Christ to nod approval of his deeds,[2] break the bolts, and open the doors. " For it is for thy sake," said he, " that I have thus suffered and thus acted." " Even as I thus spoke," he told me, " out fell the bolts and open flew the doors, and back I ran to my instructress. She dressed me up in women's garments and took me with her in her covered carriage back to the divine Meletius. He handed me over to the bishop of Jerusalem, at that time Cyril, and we started by night for Palestine." After the death of Julian this young man led his father also into the way of truth. This act he told me with the rest. So in this fashion these men were guided to the knowledge of God and were made partakers of Salvation.

CHAPTER XI.

Of the Holy Martyrs Juventinus and Maximinus.

Now Julian, with less restraint, or shall I say, less shame, began to arm himself against

---

[1] The earliest authorities for the order are St. Paul, Rom. xvi.1, and probably I. Tim. iii. 11; and Pliny in his letter to Trajan, if ancilla = διάκονος.

[1] Vide note on page 98.   [2] νεῦσαι.

true religion, wearing indeed a mask of moderation, but all the while preparing gins and traps which caught all who were deceived by them in the destruction of iniquity. He began by polluting with foul sacrifices the wells in the city and in Daphne, that every man who used the fountain might be partaker of abomination. Then he thoroughly polluted the things exposed in the Forum, for bread and meat and fruit and vegetables and every kind of food were aspersed. When those who were called by the Saviour's name saw what was done, they groaned and bewailed and expressed their abomination; nevertheless they partook, for they remembered the apostolic law, "Everything that is sold in the shambles eat, asking no question for conscience sake."[1] Two officers in the army, who were shield bearers in the imperial suite, at a certain banquet lamented in somewhat warm language the abomination of what was being done, and employed the admirable language of the glorious youths at Babylon, "Thou hast given us over to an impious Prince, an apostate beyond all the nations on the earth."[2] One of the guests gave information of this, and the emperor arrested these right worthy men and endeavoured to ascertain by questioning them what was the language they had used. They accepted the imperial enquiry as an opportunity for open speech, and with noble enthusiasm replied "Sir we were brought up in true religion; we were obedient to most excellent laws, the laws of Constantine and of his sons; now we see the world full of pollution, meats and drinks alike defiled with abominable sacrifices, and we lament. We bewail these things at home, and now before thy face we express our grief, for this is the one thing in thy reign which we take ill." No sooner did he whom sympathetic courtiers called most mild and most philosophic hear these words than he took off his mask of moderation, and exposed the countenance of impiety. He ordered cruel and painful scourgings to be inflicted on them and deprived them of their lives; or shall we not rather say freed them from that sorrowful time and gave them crowns of victory? He pretended indeed that punishment was inflicted upon them not for the true religion for sake of which they were really slain, but because of their insolence, for he gave out

that he had punished them for insulting the emperor, and ordered this report to be published abroad, thus grudging to these champions of the truth the name and honour of martyrs. The name of one was Juventinus; of the other Maximinus. The city of Antioch honoured them as defenders of true religion, and deposited them in a magnificent tomb, and up to this day they are honoured by a yearly festival.[1]

Other men in public office and of distinction used similar boldness of speech, and won like crowns of martyrdom.

CHAPTER XII.

Of Valentinianus the great Emperor.

VALENTINIANUS,[2] who shortly afterwards became emperor, was at that time a Tribune and commanded the Hastati quartered in the palace. He made no secret of his zeal for the true religion. On one occasion when the infatuated emperor was going in solemn procession into the sacred enclosure of the Temple of Fortune, on either side of the gates stood the temple servants purifying, as they supposed, all who were coming in, with their sprinkling whisks. As Valentinianus walked before the emperor, he noticed that a drop had fallen on his own cloak and gave the attendant a blow with his fist, "for," said he, "I am not purified but defiled." For this deed he won two empires. On seeing what had happened Julian the accursed sent him to a fortress in the desert, and ordered him there to remain, but after the lapse of a year and a few months he received the empire as a reward of his confession of the faith, for not only in the life that is to come does the just Judge honour them that care for holy things, but sometimes even here below He bestows recompense for good deeds, confirming the hope of guerdons yet to be received by what he gives in abundance now.

But the tyrant devised another contrivance against the truth, for when according to ancient custom he had taken his seat upon the imperial throne to distribute gold among the ranks of his soldiery, contrary to custom he had an altar full of hot coals introduced, and incense put upon a table, and ordered each man who was to receive the

---

[1] I. Cor. x. 25.
[2] Song of the Three Children, v. S, quoted not quite exactly from the Septuagint, which runs παρέδωκας ἡμᾶς . . . βασιλεῖ ἀδίκω καὶ πονηροτάτῳ παρὰ πᾶσαν τὴν γῆν. The text is, παρέδωκας ἡμᾶς βασιλεῖ παρανόμῳ ἀποστάτῃ παρὰ πάντα τὰ ἔθνη τὰ ὄντα ἐπὶ τῆς γῆς.

[1] cf. St. Chrysostom's homily in their honour. The Basilian menology mentions Juventinus under Oct. 9.
[2] Valentinianus, a native of Cibalis (on the Save) in Pannonia (Bosnia) was elected Feb. 26, 364, and reigned till Nov. 17, 375. Though a Christian, he was tolerant of paganism, or the peasant's religion, as in his reign heathenism began to be named (Codex Theod. xvi. ii. 18). The "shortly after" of the text means some two years.

gold first to throw incense on the altar, and then to take the gold from his own right hand. The majority were wholly unaware of the trap thus laid; but those who were forewarned feigned illness and so escaped this cruel snare. Others in their eagerness for the money made light of their salvation, while another group abandoned their faith through cowardice.

CHAPTER XIII.

Of other confessors.

AFTER this fatal distribution of money some of the recipients were feasting together at an entertainment. One of them who had taken the cup in his hand did not drink before making on it the sign of salvation.[1]

One of the guests found fault with him for this, and said that it was quite inconsistent with what had just taken place. "What," said he, "have I done that is inconsistent?" Whereupon he was reminded of the altar and the incense, and of his denial of the faith; for these things are all contrary to the Christian profession. When they heard this the greater number of the feasters moaned and bewailed themselves, and tore out handfuls of hair from their heads. They rose from the banquet, and ran through the Forum exclaiming that they were Christians, that they had been tricked by the emperor's contrivances, that they retracted their apostasy, and were ready to try to undo the defeat which had befallen them unwittingly. With these exclamations they ran to the palace loudly inveighing against the wiles of the tyrant, and imploring that they might be committed to the flames in order that, as they had been befouled by fire, by fire they might be made clean. All these utterances drove the villain out of his senses, and on the impulse of the moment he ordered them to be beheaded; but as they were being conducted without the city the mass of the people started to follow them, wondering at their fortitude and glorying in their boldness for the truth. When they had reached the spot where it was usual to execute criminals, the eldest of them besought the executioner that he would first cut off the head of the youngest, that he might not be unmanned by beholding the slaughter of the rest. No sooner had he knelt down upon the ground and the heads-

man bared his sword, than up ran a man announcing a reprieve, and while yet afar off shouting out to stop the execution. Then the youngest soldier was distressed at his release from death. "Ah," said he, "Romanus" (his name was Romanus) "was not worthy of being called Christ's martyr." What influenced the vile trickster in stopping the execution was his envy: he grudged the champions of the faith their glory. Their sentence was commuted to relegation beyond the city walls and to the remotest regions of the empire.

CHAPTER XIV.

Of Artemius the Duke.[1] Of Publia the Deaconess and her divine boldness.

Artemius[2] commanded the troops in Egypt. He had obtained this command in the time of Constantine, and had destroyed most of the idols. For this reason Julian not only confiscated his property but ordered his decapitation.

These and like these were the deeds of the man whom the impious describe as the mildest and least passionate of men.

I will now include in my history the noble story of a right excellent woman, for even women, armed with divine zeal, despised the mad fury of Julian.

In those days there was a woman named Publia, of high reputation, and illustrious for deeds of virtue. For a short time she wore the yoke of marriage, and had offered its most goodly fruit to God, for from this fair soil sprang John, who for a long time was chief presbyter at Antioch, and was often elected to the apostolic see, but from time to time declined the dignity. She maintained a company of virgins vowed to virginity for life, and spent her time in praising God who had made and saved her. One day the emperor was passing by, and as they esteemed the Destroyer an object of contempt and derision, they struck up all the louder music, chiefly chanting those psalms which mock the helplessness of idols, and saying in the words of David "The idols of the nations are of silver and gold, the work of men's hands,"[3] and after describing their insensibility, they added "like them be they that make them and all those that trust in them."[4]

---

[1] "The original mode of making the sign of the Cross was with the thumb of the right hand, generally on the forehead only, or on other objects, once or thrice. (Chrysost. *Hom. ad pop. Art. xi.*) 'Thrice he made the sign of the cross on the chalice with his finger.' (Sophron. in Prat. Spirit.)" Dict. Christ. Ant. s. v.

[1] By the Constitution of Constantine the supreme military command was given to a "Magister equitum" and a "Magister peditum." Under them were a number of "Duces" and "Comites," Dukes and Counts, with territorial titles.
[2] Ammianus Marcellinus (XXII. 11) says, "Artemius ex duce Aegypti, Alexandrinis urgentibus, atrocium criminum mole, supplicio capitali multatus est."
[3] Psalm cxv. 4.
[4] Psalm cxv. 8.

Julian heard them, and was very angry, and told them to hold their peace while he was passing by. She did not however pay the least attention to his orders, but put still greater energy into their chaunt, and when the emperor passed by again told them to strike up " Let God arise and let his enemies be scattered." [1]   On this Julian in wrath ordered the choir mistress to be brought before him; and, though he saw that respect was due to her old age, he neither compassionated her gray hairs, nor respected her high character, but told some of his escort to box both her ears, and by their violence to make her cheeks red. She however took the outrage for honour, and returned home, where, as was her wont, she kept up her attack upon him with her spiritual songs,[2] just as the composer and teacher of the song laid the wicked spirit that vexed Saul.

CHAPTER XV.

Of the Jews; of their attempt at building, and of the heaven-sent plagues that befel them.

JULIAN, who had made his soul a home of destroying demons, went his corybantic way, ever raging against true religion. He accordingly now armed the Jews too against the believers in Christ. He began by enquiring of some whom he got together why, though their law imposed on them the duty of sacrifices, they offered none. On their reply that their worship was limited to one particular spot, this enemy of God immediately gave directions for the re-erection of the destroyed temple,[3] supposing in his vanity that he could falsify the prediction of the Lord, of which, in reality, he exhibited the truth.[4] The Jews heard his words with delight and made known his orders to their countrymen throughout the world. They came with haste from all directions, contributing alike money and enthusiasm for the work; and the emperor made all the provisions he could, less from the pride of munificence than from hostility to the truth. He despatched also as governor a fit man to carry

out his impious orders. It is said that they made mattocks, shovels, and baskets of silver. When they had begun to dig and to carry out the earth a vast multitude of them went on with the work all day, but by night the earth which had been carried away shifted back from the ravine of its own accord. They destroyed moreover the remains of the former construction, with the intention of building everything up afresh; but when they had got together thousands of bushels of chalk and lime, of a sudden a violent gale blew, and storms, tempests and whirlwinds scattered everything far and wide. They still went on in their madness, nor were they brought to their senses by the divine longsuffering. Then first came a great earthquake, fit to strike terror into the hearts of men quite ignorant of God's dealings; and, when still they were not awed, fire running from the excavated foundations burnt up most of the diggers, and put the rest to flight. Moreover when a large number of men were sleeping at night in an adjacent building it suddenly fell down, roof and all, and crushed the whole of them. On that night and also on the following night the sign of the cross of salvation was seen brightly shining in the sky, and the very garments of the Jews were filled with crosses, not bright but black.[1] When God's enemies saw these things, in terror at the heaven-sent plagues they fled, and made their way home, confessing the Godhead of Him who had been crucified by their fathers. Julian heard of these events, for they were repeated by every one. But like Pharaoh he hardened his heart.[2]

---

[1] Psalm lxvii. 1.

[2] Cf. Eph. v. 19.

[3] Bp. Wordsworth (Dict. Chris. Biog. iii, 500) is in favour of the letter (Ep. 24, Ed. Didot 350) in which Julian desires the prayers of the Creator and professes a wish to rebuild and inhabit Jerusalem with them after his return from the Persian war and there give glory to the Supreme Being. It is addressed to his "brother Julus, the very venerable patriarch."

[4] This is the motive ascribed by the Arian Philostorgius (vii. 9).

[1] "The curious statement that crosses were imprinted on the bodies and clothes of persons present, is illustrated in the original edition of Newman's Essay (clxxxii.)" (i.e. on ecclesiastical miracles) "by some parallel instances quoted by Warburton from Casaubon and from Boyle. Such crosses, or cross-like impressions, are said to have followed not only a thunderstorm, but also an eruption of Vesuvius · these-crosses were seen on linen garments, as shirt sleeves, women's aprons, that had lain open to the air, and upon the exposed parts of sheets." "Chrysostom (Ed. Montfaucon, vol. v. 271, etc.) mentions 'crosses imprinted upon garments,' as a sign that had occurred in his generation, close to the mention of the Temple of Apollo that was overthrown by a thunderbolt, and separated from the wonders in Palestine that he mentions subsequently." Dr. E. A. Abbott. *Philomythus*, 189.

[2] This event " came like the vision of Constantine, at a critical epoch in the world's history. It was, as the heathen poet has it, a ' dignus vindice nodus.' All who were present or heard of the event at the time, thought, we may be sure, that it was a sign from God. As a miracle then it ranges beside those biblical miracles in which, at some critical moment, the forces of nature are seen to work strikingly for God's people or against their enemies. In the O. T. we have for example, the instances of the plagues of Egypt, the passage of the Red Sea and the drowning of Pharaoh's host, the crossing of the Jordan, the prolongation of sunlight" (? darkness. Vide " A misunderstood miracle" by the Rev. A. Smythe Palmer) " the destruction of Sennacherib's army; in the N. T. the stilling of the storm, and the earthquake and the darkness at the crucifixion." Bp. Wordsworth. Dict. Ch. Biog. ii. 513. To biblical instances may be added the defeat of Sisera and the fall of Aphek. But, too, for "the forces of nature," when the Armada was scattered, or when the siege of Leyden was raised

CHAPTER XVI.

Of the expedition against the Persians.

No sooner had the Persians heard of the death of Constantius, than they took heart, proclaimed war, and marched over the frontier of the Roman empire. Julian therefore determined to muster his forces, though they were a host without a God to guard them. First he sent to Delphi, to Delos and to Dodona, and to the other oracles[1] and enquired of the seers if he should march. They bade him march and promised him victory. One of these oracles I subjoin in proof of their falsehood. It was as follows. " Now we gods all started to get trophies of victory by the river beast and of them I Ares, bold raiser of the din of war, will be leader."[2] Let them that style the Pythian a God wise in word and prince of the muses ridicule the absurdity of the utterance. I who have found out its falsehood will rather pity him who was cheated by it. The oracle called the Tigris " beast " because the river and the animal bear the same name. Rising in the mountains of Armenia, and flowing through Assyria it discharges itself into the Persian gulf. Beguiled by these oracles the unhappy man indulged in dreams of victory, and after fighting with the Persians had visions of a campaign against the Galileans,

for so he called the Christians, thinking thus to bring discredit on them. But, man of education as he was, he ought to have bethought him that no mischief is done to reputation by change of name, for even had Socrates been called Critias and Pythagoras Phalaris they would have incurred no disgrace from the change of name — nor yet would Nireus if he had been named Thersites[1] have lost the comeliness with which nature had gifted him. Julian had learned about these things, but laid none of them to heart, and supposed that he could wrong us by using an inappropriate title. He believed the lies of the oracles and threatened to set up in our churches the statue of the goddess of lust.

CHAPTER XVII.

Of the boldness of speech of the decurion of Berœa.[2]

AFTER starting with these threats he was put down by one single Berœan. Illustrious as this man was from the fact of his holding the chief place among the magistrates, he was made yet more illustrious by his zeal. On seeing his son falling into the prevailing paganism, he drove him from his home and publicly renounced him. The youth made his way to the emperor in the near neighbourhood of the city and informed him both of his own views and of his father's sentence. The emperor bade him make his mind easy and promised to reconcile his father to him. When he reached Berœa, he invited the men of office and of high position to a banquet. Among them was the young suppliant's father, and both father and son were ordered to take their places on the imperial couch. In the middle of the entertainment Julian

---

the course of modern history would have been changed. Cressy may also be cited.

On the evidence for this event as contrasted with the so-called ecclesiastical miracles, accepted and defended by the late Cardinal Newman, vide Dr. E. A. Abbott's Philomythus pp. 1 and 5 et seq. "There is better evidence for this than for any of the preceding miracles." "The real solid testimony is that of Ammianus Marcellinus (xxiii. 1). An impartial historian, who served under Julian in the Persian campaign, and who, twenty years afterwards, recorded the interruption of the building of the Temple by terrible balls of fire." "If Ammianus had lived nearer the time of the alleged incident, or had added a statement of the evidence on which he based his stories, the details might have been defended. As it is, the circumstances, while favouring belief in his veracity, do not justify us in accepting anything more than the fact that the rebuilding of the Temple was generally believed to have been stopped by some supernatural fiery manifestation." "The rebuilding was probably stopped by a violent thunderstorm or thunderstorms."

[1] This is probably the last occasion on which the moribund oracles were consulted by any one of importance. Of Delphi, the " navel of the earth" (Strabo ix. 505) in Phocis, Cicero had written some four centuries earlier " Cur isto modo jam oracula Delphi non eduntur, non modo nostra ætate, sed jam diu, ut nihil possit esse contemptius:" Div. ii. 57. Plutarch, who died about A.D. 120, wrote already " de defectu Oraculorum."

The oracle of Apollo at Delos was consulted only in the summer months, as in the winter the god was supposed to be at Patara: so Virgil (iv. 143) writes   .

" Qualis ubi hibernam Lyciam Xanthique fluenta
   Deserit, ac Delum maternam invisit Apollo."

Dodona in Epirus was the most ancient of the oracular shrines, where the suppliant went

"————— ὄφρα θεοῖο
ἐκ δρυὸς ὑψικόμοιο Διὸς βουλὴν ἐπακούσαι."
                              Od. xiv. 327.

" The oracles " were potentially " dumb," " " Apollo . . . with hollow shriek the steep of Delphos leaving," as Milton sings, at the Nativity, but it was not till the reign of Theodosius that they were finally silenced.

[2] νῦν πάντες ὡρμήθημεν θεοὶ νίκης τρόπαια κομίσασθαι παρὰ θηρὶ ποταμῷ τῶν δ' ἐγὼ ἡγεμονεύσω θοῦρος πολεμόκλονος Ἄρης.

[1] These four illustrations, occurring in a single sentence, indicate a certain breadth of reading on the part of the writer, and bear out his character for learning. (cf. Gibbon and Jortin, remarks on Eccl. Hist. ii. 113.) Socrates, the best of the philosophers, is set against Critias, one of the worst of the politicians of Hellas; Pythagoras, the Samian sage of Magna Græcia, against Phalaris, the Sicilian tyrant who

" tauro violenti membra Perilli
   Torruit;" (Ovid. A. A. 1. 653)

but did not write the Epistles once ascribed to him. Theodoretus probably remembered his Homer when he cited Thersites as the ugliest man of the old world; —

" He was squint-eyed, and lame of either foot;
So crook-back'd that he had no breast; sharp-headed, where did shoot
Here and there spersed, thin mossy hair."
                        Il. ii. 219. Chapman's Trans.

And the juxtaposition of Pythagoras and Nireus suggests that it may possibly have been Horace who suggested Nireus as the type of beauty : —

" Nec te Pythagoræ fallant arcana renati,
   Formaque vincas Nirea," (Hor. Epod. xv.)

though Nireus appears as κάλλιστος ἀνὴρ in the same book of the Iliad as that in which Thersites is derided, and Theodoret is said to have known no Latin.

[2] Valesius points out that πολιτεύεσθαι means to hold the rank of Curiales or Decuriones. The Berœa mentioned is presumably the Syrian Berœa now Haleb or Aleppo.

said to the father, "It does not seem to me to be right to force a mind otherwise inclined and having no wish to shift its allegiance. Your son does not wish to follow your doctrines. Do not force him. Even I, though I am easily able to compel you, do not try to force you to follow mine." Then the father, moved by his faith in divine truth to sharpen the debate, exclaimed "Sir," said he "are you speaking of this wretch whom God hates[1] and who has preferred lies to truth?"

Once more Julian put on the mask of mildness and said "Cease fellow from reviling," and then, turning his face to the youth, "I," said he, "will have care for you, since I have not been able to persuade your father to do so." I mention this circumstance with a distinct wish to point out not only this worthy man's admirable boldness, but that very many persons despised Julian's sway.

CHAPTER XVIII.

Of the prediction of the pedagogue.

ANOTHER instance is that of an excellent man at Antioch, entrusted with the charge of young lads, who was better educated than is usually the case with pedagogues,[2] and was the intimate friend of the chief teacher of that period, Libanius the far-famed sophist.

Now Libanius[3] was a heathen expecting victory and bearing in mind the threats of Julian, so one day, in ridicule of our belief, he said to the pedagogue, "What is the carpenter's son about now?" Filled with divine grace, he foretold what was shortly to come to pass. "Sophist," said he, "the Creator of all things, whom you in derision call carpenter's son, is making a coffin."[4]

After a few days the death of the wretch was announced. He was carried out lying in his coffin. The vaunt of his threats was proved vain, and God was glorified.[1]

CHAPTER XIX.

Of the Prophecy of St. Julianus the monk.

A MAN who in the body imitated the lives of the bodiless, namely Julianus, surnamed in Syrian Sabbas, whose life I have written in my "Religious History," continued all the more zealously to offer his prayers to the God of all, when he heard of the impious tyrant's threats. On the very day on which Julian was slain, he heard of the event while at his prayers, although the Monastery was distant more than twenty stages from the army. It is related that while he was invoking the Lord with loud cries and supplicating his merciful Master, he suddenly checked his tears, broke into an ecstasy of delight, while his countenance was lighted up and thus signified the joy that possessed his soul. When his friends beheld this change they begged him to tell them the reason of his gladness. "The wild boar," said he, "the enemy of the vineyard of the Lord, has paid the penalty of the wrongs he has done to Him; he lies dead. His mischief is done." The whole company no sooner heard these words than they leaped with joy and struck up the song of thanksgiving to God, and from those that brought tidings of the emperor's death they learnt that it was the very day and hour when the accursed man was slain that the aged Saint knew it and announced it.[2]

---

[1] The word thus translated is either active or passive according to its accentuation. Θεομισής = hated by God; Θεομίσης = hating God.

[2] The word seems here used in its strictly Athenian sense of a slave who took charge of boys on their way between school and home (Vide Lycias 910. 2 and Plat. Rep. 373. C.) rather than in the more general sense of teacher. In Xen. Lac. 3. 1. it is coupled with διδάσκαλος: here it is contrasted with it.

[3] "One of the most noteworthy and characteristic figures of expiring heathenism." J. R. Mozley, Dict. Christ. Biog. s. v. Born in Antioch A.D. 314, he died about the close of the century. He was a voluminous author, and wrote among other things a "vain, prolix, but curious narrative of his own life." Gibbon. The most complete account of him will be found in E. R. Siever's Das Leben des Libanius.

[4] The form in the text (γλωσσόκομον) is rejected by Attic purists, but is used twice by St. John, as well as in the Septuagint. In II. Chron. xxiv. 8 (cf. II. Kings xii. 9) it means a chest. In St. John's Gospel xii. 6 and xiii. 29 it is "the bag," properly (xi. 3) "box," which Judas carried. In the Palatine anthology Nicanor the coffin maker makes these "glossokoma" or coffins. Derivatively the word means "tongue-cases," i.e. cases to keep the tongues or reeds of musical instruments. An instance of similar transfer of meaning is our word "coffin;" derivatively a wicker basket;—at one time any case or cover, and in

Shakespeare (Titus Andronicus Act V. 2, 189) pie crust. Perhaps "casket," which now still holds many things, may one day only hold a corpse.

[1] In times and circumstances totally different, it may seem that Julian's courtesy and moderation contrast favourably with the fierce zeal of the Christians. A modern illustration of the temper of the Church in Julian's reign may be found in the following account given of his dragoman by the late author of "Eothen." "Religion and the literature of the Church which he served had made him a man, and a brave man too. The lives of his honored Saints were full of heroic actions provoking imitation, and since faith in a creed involves faith in its ultimate triumph, Dthemetri was bold from a sense of true strength; his education too, though not very general in its character, had been carried quite far enough to justify him in pluming himself upon a very decided advantage over the great bulk of the Mahometan population, including the men in authority. With all this consciousness of religious and intellectual superiority, Dthemetri had lived for the most part in countries lying under Mussulman governments, and had witnessed (perhaps too had suffered from) their revolting cruelties; the result was that he abhorred and despised the Mussulman faith and all who clung to it. And this hate was not of the dull, dry, and inactive sort; Dthemetri was in his way a true crusader, and whenever there appeared a fair opening in the defence of Islam, he was ready and eager to make the assault. Such feelings, backed by a consciousness of understanding the people with whom he had to do, made Dthemetri not only firm and resolute in his constant interviews with men in authority, but sometimes also very violent and very insulting." Kinglake's "Eothen," 5th Ed., p. 270.

[2] The emperor Julian was wounded in the neighbourhood of Symbria or Hucumbra on the Tigris on the morning of June

CHAPTER XX.

Of the death of the Emperor Julian in Persia.

JULIAN's folly was yet more clearly manifested by his death. He crossed the river that separates the Roman Empire from the Persian,[1] brought over his army, and then forthwith burnt his boats, so making his men fight not in willing but in forced obedience.[2] The best generals are wont to fill their troops with enthusiasm, and, if they see them growing discouraged, to cheer them and raise their hopes; but Julian by burning the bridge of retreat cut off all good hope. A further proof of his incompetence was his failure to fulfil the duty of foraging in all directions and providing his troops with supplies. Julian had neither ordered supplies to be brought from Rome, nor did he make any bountiful provision by ravaging the enemy's country. He left the inhabited world behind him, and persisted in marching through the wilderness. His soldiers had not enough to eat and drink; they were without guides; they were marching astray in a desert land. Thus they saw the folly of their most wise emperor. In the midst of their murmuring and grumbling they suddenly found him who had struggled in mad rage against his Maker wounded to death. Ares who raises the war-din had never come to help him as he promised; Loxias had given lying divination; he who glads him in the thunderbolts had hurled no bolt on the man who dealt the fatal blow; the boasting of his threats was dashed to the ground. The name of the man who dealt that righteous stroke no one knows to this day. Some say that he was wounded by an invisible being, others by one of the Nomads who were called Ishmaelites; others by a trooper who could not endure the pains of famine in the wilderness. But whether it were man or angel who plied the steel, without doubt the doer of the deed was the minister of the will of God. It is related that when Julian had received the wound, he filled his hand with blood, flung it into the air and cried, "Thou hast won, O Galilean." Thus he gave utterance at once to a confession of the victory and to a blasphemy. So infatuated was he.[1]

CHAPTER XXI.

Of the sorcery at Carræ which was detected after his death. After he was slain the jugglery of his sorcery was detected. For Carræ is a city which still retains the relics of his false religion.

JULIAN had left Edessa on his left because it was adorned with the grace of true religion, and while in his vain folly he was journeying through Carræ, he came to the temple honoured by the impious and after going through certain rites with his companions in defilement, he locked and sealed the doors, and stationed sentinels with orders to see that none came in till his return. When news came of his death, and the reign of iniquity was succeeded by one of piety, the shrine was opened, and within was found a proof of the late emperor's manliness, wisdom, and piety.[2] For there was seen a woman hung up on high by the hairs of her head, and with her hands outstretched. The villain had cut open her belly, and so I suppose learnt from her liver his victory over the Persians.[3]

This was the abomination discovered at Carræ.

CHAPTER XXII.

Of the heads discovered in the palace at Antioch and the public rejoicings there.

IT is said that at Antioch a number of chests were discovered at the palace filled with human heads, and also many wells full of corpses. Such is the teaching of the evil deities.

26th, 363, and died at midnight. On the somewhat similar stories of Apollonius of Tyana mounting a lofty rock in Asia Minor and shouting to the crowd about him 'well done, Stephanus; excellent, Stephanus; smite the blood-stained wretch; thou hast struck, thou hast wounded, thou hast slain,' at the very moment when Domitian was being murdered at Rome (Dion Cass, 67. 18); and of Irenæus at Rome hearing a voice as of a trumpet at the exact hour when Polycarp suffered at Smyrna proclaiming 'Polycarp has been martyred' (Vid. Ep. Smyrn.). Bp. Lightfoot (Apostolic Fathers 1. 455) writes "The analogies of authenticated records of apparitions seen and voices heard at a distance at the moment of death have been too frequent in all ages to allow us to dismiss the story at once as a pure fiction." Such narratives at all events testify to a wide-spread belief.

[1] There seems to be an allusion to Cæsar's passage of the Rubicon in 49 B.C.

[2] His fleet, with the exception of a few vessels, was burned at Abuzatha, where he halted five days (Zos 3. 26).

[1] The exclamation was differently reported. Sozomen vi. 2. says that some thought he lifted his hand to chide the sun for failing to help him. It has been observed that the sound of νενικηκας Γαλιλαιε and ηπάτηκας ήλιε would not be so dissimilar in Greek as in English. Ammianus Marcellinus (xxv. 3. 9.) says that he lost all hope of recovery when he heard that the place where he lay was called Phrygia, for in Phrygia he had been told that he would die. So it befell with Cambyses at Ecbatana (Her. iii. 64), Alexander King of Epirus at the Acheron (Livy viii. 24) and Henry IV in the Jerusalem Chamber, when he asked "Doth any name particular belong unto this lodging where I first did swoon?" and on hearing that the chamber was called Jerusalem, remembered the old prediction that in Jerusalem he must die, and died.

[2] The reading εὐσέβειαν for ἀσέβειαν seems to keep up the irony.

[3] ηπατοσκοπία, or "inspection of the liver," was a recognized form of divination. cf. the Sept. of Ez. xxi. 21. "καὶ ἐπερωτῆσαι ἐν τοῖς γλυπτοῖς, καὶ ηπατοσκοπήσασθαι" and Cic. de div. ii. 13. "Caput jecoris ex omni parte diligentissime considerant; si vero id non est inventum, nihil putant accidere potuisse tristius." Vide also Æsch. Pr. V. 503, and Paley's note.

When Antioch heard of Julian's death she gave herself up to rejoicing and festivity; and not only was exultant joy exhibited in the churches, and in the shrines of martyrs, but even in the theatres the victory of the cross was proclaimed and Julian's vaticination held up to ridicule. And here I will record the admirable utterance of the men at Antioch, that it may be preserved in the memory of generations yet to come, for with one voice the shout was raised, "Maximus, thou fool, where are thy oracles? for God has conquered and his Christ." This was said because there lived at that time a man of the name of Maximus, a pretender to philosophy, but really a worker of magic, and boasting himself to be able to foretell the future. But the Antiochenes, who had received their divine teaching from the glorious yokefellows Peter and Paul, and were full of warm affection for the Master and Saviour of all, persisted in execrating Julian to the end. Their sentiments were perfectly well known to the object of them, and so he wrote a book against them and called it "Misopogon." [1]

This rejoicing at the death of the tyrant shall conclude this book of my history, for it were to my mind indecent to connect with a righteous reign the impious sovereignty of Julian.

[1] " The residence of Julian at Antioch was a disappointment to himself, and disagreeable to almost all the inhabitants." " He had anticipated much more devotion on the part of the pagans, and much less force and resistance on that of the Christians than he discovered in reality. He was disgusted at finding that both parties regretted the previous reign. ' Neither the Chi nor the Kappa' (that is neither Christ nor Constantius) ' did our city any harm' became a common saying

(Misopogon p. 357). To the heathens themselves the enthusiastic form of religion to which Julian was devoted was little more than an unpleasant and somewhat vulgar anachronism. His cynic asceticism and dislike of the theatre and the circus was unpopular in a city particularly addicted to public spectacles. His superstition was equally unpalatable. The short, untidy, long-bearded man, marching pompously in procession on the tips of his toes, and swaying his shoulders from side to side, surrounded by a crowd of abandoned characters, such as formed the regular attendants upon many heathen festivals, appeared seriously to compromise the dignity of the empire. (Ammianus xxii. 14. 3. His words 'stipatus mulierculis' etc. go far to justify Gregory's δημοσία ταῖς πορναις προὔπινε in Orat. v. 22. p. 161, and Chrysostom's more highly coloured description of the same sort of scene, for the accuracy of which he appeals to an eye witness still living, de S. Babyla in Julianum § 14. p. 667. The blood of countless victims flowed everywhere, but, to all appearance, served merely to gorge his foreign soldiery, especially the semi-barbarous Gauls, and the streets of Antioch were disturbed by their revels and by drunken parties carrying one another home to their barracks. (Amm. xxii. 12.6.)" "More secret rumours were spread of horrid nocturnal sacrifices, and of the pursuits of those arts of necromancy from which the natural heathen conscience shrank only less than the Christians." " He discharged his spleen upon the general body of the citizens of Antioch by writing one of the most remarkable satires that has ever been published which he entitled the Misopogon. ' He had been insulted,' says Gibbon, ' by satire and libels; in his turn he composed under the title of The Enemy of the Beard, an ironical confession of his own faults, and a severe satire on the licentious and effeminate manners of Antioch. The imperial reply was publicly exposed before the gates of the palace, and the Misopogon still remains a singular monument of the resentment, the wit, the inhumanity, and the indiscretion of Julian. Gibbon, Chap, xxiv.' It is of course Julian's own philosophic beard that gives the title to the pamphlet." "This pamphlet was written in the seventh month of his sojourn at Antioch, probably the latter half of January." (1. c, 364.) Bp. J. Wordsworth in Dict. Ch. Biog. iii. 507., 509.

BOOK IV.

CHAPTER I.

Of the reign and piety of Jovianus.

AFTER Julian was slain the generals and prefects met in council and deliberated who ought to succeed to the imperial power and effect both the salvation of the army in the campaign, and the recovery of the fortunes of Rome, now, by the rashness of the deceased Emperor, placed. to use the common saying, on the razor edge of peril. [1] But while the chiefs were in deliberation the troops met together and demanded Jovianus for emperor, though he was neither a general nor in the next highest rank; a man however remarkably distinguished, and for many reasons well known. His stature was great; his soul lofty. In war, and in grave struggles it was his wont to be first.

[1] The common proverbial saying, from Homer downwards; ἐπὶ ξυροῦ ἵσταται ἀκμῆς ὀλέθρος ἠὲ βιῶναι. Il. 10. 173.

Against impiety he delivered himself courageously with no fear of the tyrant's power, but with a zeal that ranked him among the martyrs of Christ. So the generals accepted the unanimous vote of the soldiers as a divine election. The brave man was led forward and placed upon a raised platform hastily constructed. The host saluted him with the imperial titles, calling him Augustus and Cæsar. With his usual bluntness, and fearless alike in the presence of the commanding officers and in view of the recent apostasy of the troops, Jovianus admirably said " I am a Christian. I cannot govern men like these. I cannot command Julian's army trained as it is in vicious discipline. Men like these, stripped of the covering of the providence of God, will fall an easy and ridiculous prey to the foe." On hearing this the troops shouted with one voice, " Hesitate not, O emperor; think it not a vile thing to command us. You shall reign over Christians

nurtured in the training of truth; our vet-
erans were taught in the school of Constantine himself; younger men among us were
taught by Constantius. This dead man's
empire lasted but a few years, all too few to
stamp its brand even on those whom it
deceived." [1]

CHAPTER II.

Of the return of Athanasius.

DELIGHTED with these words the emperor
undertook for the future to take counsel for
the safety of the state, and how to bring
home the army without loss from the campaign. He was in no need of much deliberation, but at once reaped the fruit sprung
from the seeds of true religion, for the God
of all gave proof of His own providence, and
caused all difficulty to disappear. No
sooner had the Persian sovereign been made
acquainted with Jovian's accession than he
sent envoys to treat for peace; nay more,
he despatched provisions for the troops and
gave directions for the establishment of a
market for them in the desert. A truce was
concluded for thirty years, and the army
brought home in safety from the war.[2] The
first edict of the emperor on setting foot
upon his own territory was one recalling
the bishops from their exile, and announcing the restoration of the churches to the
congregations who had held inviolate the
confession of Nicæa. He further sent a
despatch to Athanasius, the famous champion of these doctrines, beseeching that a
letter might be written to him containing
exact teaching on matters of religion.
Athanasius summoned the most learned
bishops to meet him, and wrote back exhorting the emperor to hold fast the faith
delivered at Nicæa, as being in harmony
with apostolic teaching. Anxious to benefit
all who may meet with it I here subjoin the
letter.[3]

CHAPTER III.

Synodical letter to the Emperor Jovian concern-ing the Faith.

To Jovianus Augustus most devout, most
humane, victorious, Athanasius, and the rest
of the bishops assembled, in the name of all
the bishops from Egypt to Thebaid and
Libya. The intelligent preference and pursuit of holy things is becoming to a prince
beloved of God. Thus may you keep your
heart in truth in God's hand and reign for
many years in peace.[1] Since your piety has
recently expressed a wish to learn from us
the faith of the Catholic Church, we have
given thanks to the Lord and have determined
before all to remind your reverence of the
faith confessed by the fathers at Nicæa. This
faith some have set at nought, and have devised many and various attacks on us, because of our refusal to submit to the Arian
heresy. They have become founders of
heresy and schism in the Catholic Church.
The true and pious faith in our Lord Jesus
Christ has been made plain to all as it is
known and read from the Holy Scriptures.
In this faith the martyred saints were perfected, and now departed are with the Lord.
This faith was destined everywhere to stand
unharmed, had not the wickedness of certain
heretics dared to attempt its falsification; for
Arius and his party endeavoured to corrupt
it and to bring in impiety for its destruction,
alleging the Son of God to be of the non-
existent, a creature, a Being made, and
susceptible of change. By these means they
deceived many, so that even men who
seemed to be somewhat,[2] were led away by
them. Then our holy Fathers took the initiative, met, as we said, at Nicæa, anathematized the Arian heresy, and subscribed the
faith of the Catholic Church so as to cause
the putting out of the flames of heresy by
proclamation of the truth throughout the
world. Thus this faith throughout the whole
church was known and preached. But since
some men who wished to start the Arian

---

[1] Jovianus, son of Count Varronianus of Singidunum (Belgrade), was born in 330 or 331 and reigned from June 363 to
February 364. His hasty acceptance by a part of the army
may have been due to the mistake of the sound of "Jovianus
Augustus" for that of "Julianus Augustus" and a belief
that Julian survived. "Gentilitate enim prope perciti nominis,
quod una littera discernebat, Julianum recreatum arbitrati
sunt deduci magnis favoribus, ut solebat." Amm. xxv. v. 6.
"Jovian was a brilliant colonel of the guards. In all the
army there was not a goodlier person than he. Julian's purple
was too small for his gigantic limbs. But that stately form was
animated by a spirit of cowardly selfishness. Jovian was also
a decided Christian," but "even the heathen soldiers condemned his low amours and vulgar tippling." Gwatkin,
"Arian Controversy," 119.
[2] The terms were in fact humiliating, "pacem cum Sapore
necessariam quidem sed ignobilem fecit; multatus finibus, ac
nonnulla imperii Romani parte tradita: quod ante eum annis
mille centum et duobus de viginti fere ex quo Romanum im-
perium conditum erat, nunquam accidit." Eut. brev x. 17.
[3] "Gibbon (Chap. xxv. sneers at Athanasius for assuring
Jovian 'that his orthodox faith would be rewarded with a long
and peaceful reign,' and remarks that after his death this charge

was omitted from some MSS., referring to Valesius on the
passage of Theodoret, and Jortin's *Remarks*, iv. p. 38. But
the expression is not that of a prophet who stakes his credit
on the truth of his prediction, but little more than a pious
reflection, of the nature of a wish." Bp. J. Wordsworth, Dict.
Christ. Biog. iii. 463. n. Jortin says "the good bishop's
μαντική failed him sadly; and the emperor reigned only one
year, and died in the flower of his age." The note of Valesius
will be found below.
[1] Scarcely a prophecy, even if we read ἕξεις, "you shall
keep;" a bare wish if we read ἔχοις, "may you keep." Vide
preceding note. In Athanasius we find ἔξεις. Valesius says
"The latter part of this sentence is wanting in the common
editions of Athanasius, and Baronius supposes it to have been
added by some Arian, with the object of ridiculing Athanasius
as a false prophet. As a fact the reign of Jovian was short.
But I see nothing low, spurious or factitious. Athanasius is
not in fault because Jovian did not live as long as he had
wished."
[2] Gal. vi. 3.

heresy afresh have had the hardihood to set at naught the faith confessed by the Fathers at Nicæa, and others are pretending to accept it, while in reality they deny it, distorting the meaning of the ὁμοούσιον and thus blaspheming the Holy Ghost, by alleging it to be a creature and a Being made through the Son's means, we, perforce beholding the harm accruing from blasphemy of this kind to the people, have hastened to offer to your piety the faith confessed at Nicæa, that your reverence may know with what exactitude it is drawn up, and how great is the error of them whose teaching contradicts it. Know, O holiest Augustus, that this faith is the faith preached from everlasting, this is the faith that the Fathers assembled at Nicæa confessed. With this faith all the churches throughout the world are in agreement, in Spain, in Britain,[1] in Gaul, in all Italy and Campania, in Dalmatia and Mysia, in Macedonia, in all Hellas, in all the churches throughout Africa, Sardinia, Cyprus, Crete, Pamphylia and Isauria, and Lycia, those of all Egypt and Libya, of Pontus, Cappadocia and the neighbouring districts and all the churches of the East except a few who have embraced Arianism. Of all those above mentioned we know the sentiments after trial made. We have letters and we know, most pious Augustus, that though some few gainsay this faith they cannot prejudice[2] the decision of the whole inhabited world.

After being long under the injurious influence of the Arian heresy they are the more contentiously withstanding true religion. For the information of your piety, though indeed you are already acquainted with it, we have taken pains to subjoin the faith confessed at Nicæa by the three hundred and eighteen bishops. It is as follows.

We believe in one God, Father Almighty, maker of all things visible and invisible; and in one Lord Jesus Christ, the Son of God, begotten of the Father, that is of the substance of the Father, God of God, Light of Light, very God of very God: begotten not made, being of one substance with the Father, by whom all things were made both in Heaven and in earth. Who for us men and for our salvation came down from Heaven, was incarnate and was made man.

He suffered and rose again the third day. He ascended into Heaven, and is coming to judge both quick and dead. And we believe in the Holy Ghost; the Holy Catholic and Apostolic Church anathematizes those who say there was a time when the Son of God was not; that before He was begotten He was not; that He was made out of the non-existent, or that He is of a different essence or different substance, or a creature or subject to variation or change. In this faith, most religious Augustus, all must needs abide as divine and apostolic, nor must any strive to change it by persuasive reasoning and word battles, as from the beginning did the Arian maniacs in their contention that the Son of God is of the non existent, and that there was a time when He was not, that He is created and made and subject to variation. Wherefore, as we stated, the council of Nicæa anathematized this heresy and confessed the faith of the truth. For they have not simply said that the Son is like the Father, that he may be believed not to be simply like God but very God of God. And they promulgated the term "Homoüsion" because it is peculiar to a real and true son of a true and natural father. Yet they did not separate the Holy Spirit from the Father and the Son, but rather glorified It together with the Father and the Son in the one faith of the Holy Trinity, because the Godhead of the Holy Trinity[1] is one.

CHAPTER IV.

Of the restoration of allowances to the churches; and of the Emperor's death.

WHEN the emperor had received this letter, his former knowledge of and disposition to divine things was confirmed, and he issued a second edict wherein he ordered the amount of corn which the great Constantine had appropriated to the churches to be restored.[2] For Julian, as was to be expected of one who had gone to war with our Lord and Saviour, had stopped even this mainten-

---

[1] Christianity thus appears more or less constituted in Britain more than 200 years before the mission of Augustine. But by about 208 the fame of British Christianity had reached Tertullian in Africa. The date, that of the first mention of the Church in Britain, indicates a probable connexion of its foundation with the dispersion of the victims of the persecution of the Rhone cities. The phrase of Tertullian, " places beyond the reach of the Romans, but subdued to Christ," points to a rapid spread into the remoter parts of the island. Vide Rev. C. Hole's " Early Missions," S.P.C.K.

[2] πρόκριμα ποιεῖν.

[1] " Τρίας is either the number Three, or a triplet of similar objects, as in the phrase κασιγνήτων τριάς (Rost u. Palm's Lexicon. s. v.) In this sense it is applied by Clement of Alexandria (Strom. IV. vii. 55) to the Triad of Christian graces, Faith, Hope, and Charity. As Gregory of Nazianzus says (Orat. xiii. p. 24) Τριὰς οὐ πραγμάτων ἀνίσων ἀπαριθμησις, ἀλλ' ἴσων καὶ ὁμοτίμων σύλληψις. The first instance of its application to the Three Persons in the one God is in Theophilus of Antioch (Ad Autol. ii. 15) " [† c. 185] " Similarly the word Trinitas, in its proper force, means either the number Three or a triad. It is first applied to the mystery of the Three in One by Tertullian, who says that the Church' proprie et spiritualiter ipse est spiritus, in quo est Trinitas unius divinitatis, Pater, et Filius, et Spiritus Sanctus.' De Pudicita 21." [† c. 240] Archd. Cheetham. Dict. Christ. Biog. S. V.

[2] cf. III. 8 page 99.

ance, and since the famine which visited the empire in consequence of Julian's iniquity prevented the collection of the contribution of Constantine's enactment, Jovian ordered a third part to be supplied for the present, and promised that on the cessation of the famine he would give the whole.

After distinguishing the beginning of his reign by edicts of this kind, Jovian set out from Antioch for the Bosphorus; but at Dadastanæ, a village lying on the confines of Bithynia and Galatia, he died.[1] He set out on his journey from this world with the grandest and fairest support and stay, but all who had experienced the clemency of his sway were left behind in pain. So, methinks, the Supreme Ruler, to convict us of our iniquity, both shews us good things and again deprives us of them; so by the former means He teaches us how easily He can give us what He will; by the latter He convicts us of our unworthiness of it, and points us to the better life.

CHAPTER V.

Of the reign of Valentinianus, and how he associated Valens his brother with him.

WHEN the troops had become acquainted with the emperor's sudden death, they wept for the departed prince as for a father, and made Valentinian emperor in his room. It was he who smote the officer of the temple[2] and was sent to the castle. He was distinguished not only for his courage, but also for prudence, temperance, justice, and great stature. He was of so kingly and magnanimous a character that, on an attempt being made by the army to appoint a colleague to share his throne, he uttered the well-known words which are universally repeated, "Before I was emperor, soldiers, it was yours to give me the reins of empire: now that I have taken them, it is mine, not yours, to take counsel for the state." The troops were struck with admiration at what he said, and contentedly followed the guidance of his authority. Valentinian, however, sent for his brother from Pannonia, and shared the em-

pire with him. Would that he had never done so! To Valens,[1] who had not yet accepted unsound doctrines, was committed the charge of Asia and of Egypt, while Valentinian allotted Europe to himself. He journeyed to the Western provinces, and beginning with a proclamation of true religion, instructed them in all righteousness. When the Arian Auxentius, bishop of Milan, who was condemned in several councils, departed this life,[2] the emperor summoned the bishops and addressed them as follows: "Nurtured as you have been in holy writ, you know full well what should be the character of one dignified by the episcopate, and how he should rule his subjects aright, not only with his lip, but with his life; exhibit himself as an example of every kind of virtue, and make his conversation a witness of his teaching. Seat now upon your archiepiscopal throne a man of such character that we who rule the realm may honestly bow our heads before him and welcome his reproofs, — for, in that we are men, it needs must be that we sometimes stumble, — as a physician's healing treatment."

CHAPTER VI.

Of the election of Ambrosius, the Bishop of Milan.

THUS spoke the emperor, and then the council begged him, being a wise and devout prince, to make the choice. He then replied, "The responsibility is too great for us. You who have been dignified with divine grace, and have received illumination from above, will make a better choice." So they left the imperial presence and began to deliberate apart. In the meanwhile the people of Milan were torn by factions, some eager that one, some that another, should be promoted. They who had been infected with the unsoundness of Auxentius were for choosing men of like opinions, while they of the orthodox party were in their turn anxious to have a bishop of like sentiments with themselves. When Ambrosius, who held the chief civil magistracy[3] of the district,

---

[1] At an obscure place called Dadastanæ, half way between Ancyra and Nicæa, after a hearty supper he went to bed in a room newly built. The plaster was still damp, and a brazier of charcoal was brought in to warm the air. In the morning he was found dead in his bed. (Amm. xxv. 10. 12. 13.) This was in February or March, 364.

[2] Vide page 101. "Valentinian belongs to the better class of Emperors. He was a soldier like Jovian, and held the same rank at his election. He was a decided Christian like Jovian, and, like him, free from the stain of persecution. Jovian's rough good humour was replaced in Valentinian by a violent and sometimes cruel temper, but he had a sense of duty, and was free from Jovian's vices." Gwatkin, Arian Cont. 121.

[1] "Valens was timid, suspicious, and slow, yet not ungentle in private life. He was as uncultivated as his brother, but not inferior to him in scrupulous care for his subjects. He preferred remitting taxation to fighting at the head of the legions. In both wars he is entitled to head the series of financial rather than unwarlike sovereigns whose cautious policy brought the Eastern Empire safely through the great barbarian invasions of the fifth century." Gwatkin, p. 121.

[2] Vide note on page 81.

[3] By the constitution of Constantine, beneath the governors of the twelve dioceses of the Empire were the provincial governors of 116 provinces, rectores, correctores, præsides, and consulares. Ambrosius had been appointed by Probus Consularis of Liguria and Æmilia. Probus, in giving him the appointment, was believed to have " prophesied," and said "Vade; age non ut judex, sed ut episcopus." Paulinus S.

was apprised of the contention, being afraid lest some seditious violence should be attempted he hurried to the church; at once there was a lull in the strife. The people cried with one voice "Make Ambrose our pastor," — although up to this time he was still[1] unbaptized. News of what was being done was brought to the emperor, and he at once ordered the admirable man to be baptized and ordained, for he knew that his judgment was straight and true as the rule of the carpenter and his sentence more exact than the beam of the balance. Moreover he concluded from the agreement come to by men of opposite sentiments that the selection was divine. Ambrose then received the divine gift of holy baptism, and the grace of the archiepiscopal office. The most excellent emperor was present on the occasion, and is said to have offered the following hymn of praise to his Lord and Saviour. "We thank thee, Almighty Lord and Saviour; I have committed to this man's keeping men's bodies; Thou hast entrusted to him their souls, and hast shown my choice to be righteous."

Not many days after the divine Ambrosius addressed the emperor with the utmost freedom, and found fault with certain proceedings of the magistrates as improper. Valentinian remarked that this freedom was no novelty to him, and that, well acquainted with it as he was, he had not merely offered no opposition to, but had gladly concurred in, the appointment to the bishopric. "Go on," continued the emperor, "as God's law bids you, healing the errors of our souls."

Such were the deeds and words of Valentinian at Milan.

CHAPTER VII.

Letters of the Emperors Valentinianus and Valens, written to the diocese[2] of Asia about the Homoüsion, on hearing that some men in Asia and in Phrygia were in dispute about the divine decree.

Valentinian ordered a council to be held in Illyricum[3] and sent to the disputants the decrees ratified by the bishops there assembled. They had decided to hold fast the creed put forth at Nicæa and the emperor himself wrote to them, associating his brother with him in the dispatch, urging that the decrees be kept.

The edict clearly proclaims the piety of the emperor and similarly exhibits the soundness of Valens in divine doctrines at that time. I shall therefore give it in full.

The mighty emperors, ever august, augustly victorious, Valentinianus, Valens, and Gratianus,[1] to the bishops of Asia, Phrygia, Carophrygia Pacatiana,[2] greeting in the Lord.

A great council having met in Illyricum,[3] after much discussion concerning the word of salvation, the thrice blessed bishops have declared that the Trinity of Father, Son, and Holy Ghost is of one substance.[4]

This Trinity they worship, in no wise remitting the service which has duly fallen to their lot, the worship of the great King. It is our imperial will that this Trinity be preached, so that none may say "We accept the religion of the sovereign who rules this world without regard to Him who has given us the message of salvation," for, as says the gospel of our God which contains this judgment, "we should render to Caesar the things that are Caesar's and to God the things that are God's."[5]

What say you, ye bishops, ye champions of the Word of salvation? If these be your professions, thus then continue to love one another, and cease to abuse the imperial dignity. No longer persecute those who diligently serve God, by whose prayers both wars cease upon the earth, and the assaults of apostate angels are repelled. These striving through supplication to repel all harmful demons both know how to pay tribute as the law enjoins, and do not gainsay the power of their sovereign, but with pure minds both keep the commandment of the heavenly King, and are subject to our laws. But ye have been shewn to be disobedient. We have tried every expedient but you have given yourselves up.[6] We

---

[1] Eldest son of Valentinian I. Born A.D. 359. Named Augustus 367. Succeeded his father 375; his uncle Valens 378. Murdered 383. The synod was convoked in the year of Valentinian's death.

[2] Phrygia Pacatiana was the name given in the fourth century to the province extending from Bithynia to Pamphylia. "Cum in veterum libris non nisi duæ Phrygiæ occurrant, Pacatiana et salutaris, mavult Valesius h. l. scribere, καριας φρυγίας πακατιανῆς. Sed consentientibus in vulgata lectione omnibus libris mallem servare καροφρυγίας πακατιανῆς, quam Pacatianam καροφρυγίαν dictam esse putaverim quod Cariæ proxime adhæresceret." Schulze.

[3] The date of this Council is disputed. "Pagi contending for 373, others for 375, Cave for 367." Dict. Ch. Ant. i. 813.

[4] ὁμοούσιον.

[5] Matt. 22. xxi.

[6] ἡμεις ἐχρησάμεθα τῷ ἄλφα ἕως τοῦ ὦ ὑμεῖς δὲ ἑαυτοὺς ἀπεδώκατε.

The passage is obscure and perhaps corrupt. Schulze's note is "Nisi mendosus sit locus, quod quidem suspicabatur Camerarius, sensus talis esse videtur: ' *Nos quidem primis usi sumus ad extrema,*' h. e. omnia adhibuimus et tentavimus ad pacem restituendam et cohibendas vexationes, ' *vos vero im-*

---

[1] ἀμύητος.

[2] The twelve dioceses of the Empire, as constituted under Diocletian, were (1) Oxiens; (2) Pontica; (3) Asiana; (4) Thracia; (5) Mœsia; (6) Pannonia; (7) Britanniæ; (8) Galliæ; (9) Viennensis; (10) Italiciana; (11) Hispaniæ; (12) Africa.

[3] Under Constantine Illyricum Occidentale included Dalmatia, Pannonia, Noricum, and Savia; Illyricum Orientale, Dacia, Mœsia, Macedonia and Thrace.

however wish to be pure from you, as Pilate at the trial of Christ when He lived among us, was unwilling to kill Him, and when they begged for His death, turned to the East,[1] asked water for his hands and washed his hands, saying I am innocent of the blood of this righteous man.[2]

Thus our majesty has invariably charged that those who are working in the ·field of Christ are not to be persecuted, oppressed, or ill treated; nor the stewards of the great King driven into exile; lest to-day under our Sovereign you may seem to flourish and abound, and then together with your evil counsellor trample on his covenant,[3] as in the case of the blood of Zacharias,[4] but he and his were destroyed by our Heavenly King Jesus Christ after (at) His coming, being delivered to death's judgment, they and the deadly fiend who abetted them. We have given these orders to Amegetius, to Ceronius, to Damasus, to Lampon and to Brentisius by word of mouth, and we have sent the actual decrees to you also in order that you may know what was enacted in the honourable synod.

To this letter we subjoin the decrees of the synod, which are briefly as follows.

In accordance with the great and orthodox synod we confess that the Son is of one substance with the Father. And we do not so understand the term 'of one substance' as some formerly interpreted it who signed their names with feigned adhesion; nor as some who now-a-days call the drafters of the old creed Fathers, but make the meaning of the word of no effect, following the authors of the statement that "of one substance" means "like," with the understanding that since the Son is comparable to no one of the creatures made by Him, He is like to the Father alone. For those who thus think irreverently define the Son "as a special creation of the Father," but we, with the present synods, both at Rome and in Gaul, hold that there is one and the same substance of Father, Son, and Holy Ghost, in three persons, that is in three perfect essences.[1] And we confess, according to the exposition of Nicæa, that the Son of God being of one substance, was made flesh of the Holy Virgin Mary, and hath tabernacled among men, and fulfilled all the economy [2] for our sakes in birth, in passion, in resurrection, and in ascension into Heaven; and that He shall come again to render to us according to each man's manner of life, in the day of judgment, being seen in the flesh, and showing forth His divine power, being God bearing flesh, and not man bearing Godhead.

Them that think otherwise we damn, as we do also them that do not honestly damn him that said that before the Son was begotten He was not, but wrote that even before He was actually begotten He was potentially in the Father. For this is true in the case of all creatures, who are not for ever with God in the sense in which the Son is ever with

---

potentiæ obsecuti estis.' Alias interpretationes collegit suamque addidit Valesius." The note of Valesius is as follows: hic locus valde obscurus est. Et Epiphanius quidem scholasticus ita eum vertit: et nos quidem subjicimur ei qui primus est et novissimus: vos autem vobismet arrogatis. Quæ interpretatio, meo quidem iudicio, ferri non potest. Camerarius vero sic interpretatur· nos quidem ordine a primo ad ultimum processimus tractatione nostra: ipsi vero vosmet ipsos abalienastis. At Christophersonus ita vertit: nos patientia semper a principio usque ad finem usi sumus: vos contra animi vestri impotentiæ obsecuti estis . . . mihi videtur verbum χρῆσθαι hoc loco idem significari quod communicare et commercium habere. Cujus modi est illud in Evangelio: non coïtuntur Judæi Samaritanis. (Johon IV. 9.)

[1] The turning to the East is not mentioned in the Gospel of St. Matthew or in the Apocryphal Acts of Pilate; and the Imperial Decree seems here to import a Christian practice into the pagan Procurator's tribunal. Orientation was sometimes observed in Pagan temples and the altar placed at the east end; perhaps in connexion with the ancient worship of the sun. cf. Æsch. Ag. 502; Paus. V. 23. 1; Cic. Cat. iii. §43. In. Virg. Æn. viii. 68 Æneas turns to the East when he prays to the Tiber. cf. Liv 1. 18. But praying towards the East is specially a primitive Christian custom, among the earliest authorities being Tertullian (Apol. XVI.) and Clemens Al. (Stromat. VII.7).

[2] Matthew xxvii. 24.

[3] "Locus densis," says Valesius, "tenebris obvolutus " . . . The note of Schulze is "primum ὁ παρακεκλημένος videtur malus genius esse (φθοριμαῖος δαίμων postea dicitur) qui excitaverat (παρεκάλεσε) episcopos ad dissentientes vexandos plane ut crudeles Judæi excitaverant Pilatum ut Christum interimerent; sic enim in superioribus Valentinianus dixerat. Porro Valent. non modo ad historiam Zachariæ a Judæis in templo interfecti alludit, sed, si quid video, etiam ad verba ea quibus utitur Paulus, Heb. x. 29 τὸν υἱὸν τοῦ Θεοῦ καταπατεῖν καὶ τὸ αἷμα τῆς διαθήκης κοινὸν ἡγήσασθαι, quare placet conjectura Valesii πατεῖν" (the reading adopted in the translation above), "τὰ τῆς διαθήκης αυτοῦ ὡς ἐπὶ τοῦ Ζαχαρίου τοῦ αἵματος, ut tota sententia sit: ne hodie sub nostro imperio incrementa capiatis et cum eo qui vos incitat conculcetis sanguinem fœderis, fere ut Zachariæ tempore factum est a Judæis."

[4] It is to be observed that the imperial letter does not add the probably interpolated words " son of Barachias " which are a difficulty in Matt. xxiii. 35, and do not appear in the Codex Sinaiticus.

[1] Here for the first time in our author we meet with the word Hypostasis to denote each distinct person. Compare note on page 36. "Origen had already described Father, Son and Holy Spirit as three ὑποστάσεις or Beings, in opposition to the Monarchians, who saw in them only three modes of manifestation of one and the same Being. And as Sabellius had used the words τρία πρόσωπα for these modes of manifestation, this form of expression naturally fell into disfavour with the Catholics. But when Arius insisted on (virtually) three different hypostases in the Holy Trinity, Catholics began to avoid applying the word hypostases to the Persons of the Godhead. To this was added a difficulty arising from the fact, that the Eastern Church used Greek as the official language of its theology, while the Western Church used Latin, a language at that time much less well provided with abstract theological terms. Disputes were caused, says Gregory of Nazianzus (Orat. xxi. p. 395), διὰ στενότητα τῆς παρὰ τοῖς Ἰτάλοις γλώττης καὶ ὀνομάτων πενίαν. (Compare Seneca Epist. 58.) The Latins used essentia and substantia as equivalent to the Greek οὐσία and ὑπόστασις, but interchanged them, as we have seen in the translation of the Nicene Creed with little scruple, regarding them as synonyms. They used both expressions to describe the Divine Nature common to the Three. It followed that they looked upon the expression "Three Hypostases" as implying a division of the substance of the Deity, and therefore as Arian. They preferred to speak of " tres Personæ." Athanasius also spoke of τρία πρόσωπα, and thus the words πρόσωπα and Personæ became current among the Nicene party. But about the year 360, the Neo-Nicene party, or Meletians, as they are sometimes called, became scrupulous about the use of such an expression as τρία πρόσωπα, which seemed to them to savour of Sabellianism. Thus a difference arose between the old Athanasian party and the Meletians." Archd. Cheetham in Dict. Christ. Biog. Art. " Trinity."

[2] Compare note on page 72.

the Father, being begotten by eternal generation.

Such was the short summary of the emperor. I will now subjoin the actual dispatch of the synod.

CHAPTER VIII.

Synodical Epistle of the Synod in Illyricum concerning the Faith.

"THE bishops of Illyricum to the churches of God, and bishops of the dioceses of Asia, of Phrygia, and Carophrygia Pacatiana, greeting in the Lord.

"After meeting together and making long enquiry concerning the Word of salvation, we have set forth that the Trinity of Father, Son, and Holy Ghost is of one substance. And it seemed fitting to pen a letter to you, not that we write what concerns the worship of the Trinity in vain disputation, but in humility deemed worthy of the duty.

"This letter we have sent by our beloved brother and fellow labourer Elpidius the presbyter. For not in the letters of our hands, but in the books of our Saviour Jesus Christ, is it written ' I am of Paul and I of Apollos and I of Cephas and I of Christ. Was Paul crucified for you? Or were ye baptized in the name of Paul?'[1]

"It seemed indeed fitting to our humility not to pen any letter to you, on account of the great terror which your preaching causes to all the region under your jurisdiction, separating as you do the Holy Spirit from the Father and Son. We were therefore constrained to send to you our lord and fellow labourer Elpidius to ascertain if your preaching is really of this character and to carry this dispatch from the imperial government of Rome.

"Let them who do not regard the Trinity as one substance be anathema, and if any man be detected in communion with them let him be anathema.

"But for them that preach that the Trinity is of one substance the Kingdom of Heaven is prepared.

"We exhort you therefore brethren to teach no other doctrine, nor even hold any other and vain belief, but that always and everywhere, preaching the Trinity to be of one substance, ye may be able to inherit the Kingdom of Heaven.

"While writing on this point we have also been reminded to pen this letter to you about the present or future appointment of our fellow ministers as bishops, if there be any sound men among the bishops who have already discharged a public office;[1] and, if not, from the order of presbyters: in like manner of the appointment of presbyters and deacons out of the actual priestly[2] order that they may be in every way blameless, and not from the ranks of the senate and army.

"We have been unwilling to pen you a letter at length, because of the mission of one representative of all, our lord and fellow labourer Elpidius, to make diligent enquiry about your preaching, if it really is such as we have heard from our lord and fellow labourer Eustathius.

"In conclusion, if at any time you have been in error, put off the old man and put on the new. The same brother and fellow labourer Elpidius will instruct you how to preach the true faith that the Holy Trinity, of one substance with God the Father, together with the Son and Holy Ghost, is hallowed, glorified, and made manifest, Father in Son, Son in Father, with the Holy Ghost for ever and ever. For since this has been made manifest, we shall manifestly be able to confess the Holy Trinity to be of one substance according to the faith set forth formerly at Nicæa which the Fathers confirmed. So long as this faith is preached we shall be able to avoid the snares of the deadly devil. When he is destroyed we shall be able to do homage to one another in letters of peace while we live in peace.

"We have therefore written to you in order that ye may know the deposition of the Ariomaniacs, who do not confess that the Son is of the substance of the Father nor the Holy Ghost. We subjoin their names, — Polychronius, Telemachus, Faustus, Asclepiades, Amantius, Cleopater.

"This we thus write to the glory of Father and Son and Holy Ghost for ever and ever, amen. We pray the Father and the Son our Saviour Jesus Christ with the Holy Ghost that you may fare well for many years."

---

[1] The original is here obscure, and has been altered an dinterpreted in various ways.

[2] ἐξ αὐτοῦ τοῦ ἱερατικοῦ τάγματος. It is noticeable that the word ἱερατικόν is used here of the clerical order generally, inclusive of lower ranks, such as the readers, singers, doorkeepers and orphans enumerated in the Apostolic Constitutions from whom deacons and presbyters were to be appointed. For illustrations of the phrases ἱερατικὴ τάξις and ἱερατικὸν τάγμα vide Dict. Christ. Ant. ii. 1470. The exclusively sacrificial sense sometimes given to ἱερεύς and sacerdos, with their correlatives, is modified by the fact that derivatively both only mean "the man concerned with the sacred." (ἱερός = vigorous, divine. √IS.; sacer = inviolate, holy, √SAK, fasten; of the latter the suffix adds the idea of giver.

---

[1] I. Cor. i. 12.

CHAPTER IX.

Of the heresy of the Audiani.

THE illustrious emperor thus took heed of the apostolic decrees, but Audæus, a Syrian alike in race and in speech, appeared at that time as an inventor of new decrees. He had long ago begun to incubate iniquities and now appeared in his true character. At first he understood in an absurd sense the passage "Let us make man in our image, after our likeness."[1] From want of apprehension of the meaning of the divine Scripture he understood the Divine Being to have a human form, and conjectured it to be enveloped in bodily parts; for Holy Scripture frequently describes the divine operations under the names of human parts, since by these means the providence of God is made more easily intelligible to minds incapable of perceiving any immaterial ideas. To this impiety Audæus added others of a similar kind. By an eclectic process he adopted some of the doctrines of Manes[2] and denied that the God of the universe is creator of either fire or darkness. But these and all similar errors are concealed by the adherents of his faction.

They allege that they are separated from the assemblies of the Church. But since some of them exact a cursed usury, and some live unlawfully with women without the bond of wedlock, while those who are innocent of these practices live in free fellowship with the guilty, they hide the blasphemy of their doctrines by accounting as they do for their living by themselves. The plea is however an impudent one, and the natural result of Pharisaic teaching, for the Pharisees accused the Physician of souls and bodies in their question to the holy Apostles "How is it that your Master eateth with publicans and sinners?"[3] and, through the prophet, God of such men says "Which say, 'come not near me for I am pure' this is smoke of my wrath."[4] But this is not a time to refute their unreasonable error. I therefore pass on to the remainder of my narrative.[5]

CHAPTER X.

Of the heresy of the Messaliani.

AT this time also arose the heresy of the Messaliani. Those who translate their name into Greek call them Euchitæ.[1]

They have also another designation which arose naturally from their mode of action. From their coming under the influence of a certain demon, which they supposed to be the advent of the Holy Ghost, they are called enthusiasts.[2]

Men who have become infected with this plague to its full extent shun manual labour as iniquitous; and, giving themselves over to sloth, call the imaginations of their dreams prophesyings. Of this heresy Dadoes, Sabbas, Adelphius, Hermas, and Simeones were leaders, and others besides, who did not hold aloof from the communion of the Church, alleging that neither good nor harm came of the divine food of which Christ our Master said "Whoso eateth my flesh and drinketh my blood shall live for ever."[3]

In their endeavour to hide their unsoundness they shamelessly deny it even after conviction, and abjure men whose opinions are in harmony with their own secret sentiments.

Under these circumstances Letoius, who was at the head of the church of Melitine,[4] a man full of divine zeal, saw that many monasteries, or, shall I rather say, brigands' caves, had drunk deep of this disease. He therefore burnt them, and drove out the wolves from the flock.

In like manner the illustrious Amphilochius[5] to whom was committed the charge of the metropolis of the Lycaonians and who ruled all the people, no sooner learnt that this pestilence had invaded his diocese than he made it depart from his borders and freed from its infection the flocks he fed.

Flavianus,[6] also, the far famed high-priest of the Antiochenes, on learning that these men were living at Edessa and attacking with their peculiar poison all with whom

---

[1] Gen. 1. 26.

[2] Vide note on page 75.

[3] Mark ii. 16. Observe verbal inaccuracy of quotation.

[4] Is : 65. 5. The Greek of the text is οἱ λέγοντες καθαρός εἰμι, μή μου ἅπτου οὗτος καπνὸς τοῦ θυμοῦ μου. In the Sept. the passage stand οἱ λεγοντες πόρρω ἀπ' ἐμου, μὴ ἐγγίσῃς μοι ὅτι καθαρός εἰμι, etc. The O. T. is quoted as loosely as the New.

[5] Anthropomorphism, or the attribution to God of a human form is the frequent result of an unintelligent anthropopathism, which ascribes to God human feelings. Paganism did not rise higher than the material view. Judaism, sometimes apparently anthropomorphic, taught a Spiritual God. Tertullian uses expressions which exposed him to the charge of anthropomorphism, and the Pseudo Clementines (xvii. 2) go farther. The Audæus of the text appears to be the first founder of anything like an anthropomorphic sect.

[1] The Syriac name whence comes "Messaliani" or "Massaliani" means praying people (מְצַלִּין , צְלָא Dan. vi. 1

Epiphanius rendered the name εὐχόμενοι, but they were soon generally known in Greek as εὐχῆται or εὐχῖται.

[2] The form ἐνθουσιαστὴς is ecclesiastical, and late Greek, but the verb ἐνθουσιάζειν occurs at least as early as Æschylus. (Fr. 64 a.)

[3] Compare John vi. 54 and 51; the citation as before is inexact.

[4] Melitine (Malatia). metropolis of lesser Armenia; the scene of the defeat of Chosroes Nushirvan by the Romans A.D. 577.

[5] Archbishop of Iconium, the friend of Basil and first cousin of Gregory of Nazianzus, B. probably about 344. He is not mentioned after the beginning of the 5th century.

[6] cf. ii. 19, and iv. 22. He was not consecrated bishop until 381.

they came in contact, sent a company of monks, brought them to Antioch, and in the following manner convicted them in their denial of their heresy. Their accusers, he said, were calumniating them, and the witnesses giving false evidence; and Adelphius, who was a very old man, he accosted with expressions of kindness, and ordered to take a seat at his side. Then he said " We, O venerable sir, who have lived to an advanced age, have more accurate knowledge of human nature, and of the tricks of the demons who oppose us, and have learnt by experience the character of the gift of grace. But these younger men have no clear knowledge of these matters, and cannot brook to listen to spiritual teaching. Wherefore tell me in what sense you say that the opposing spirit retreats, and the grace of the Holy Ghost supervenes." The old man was won over by these words and gave vent to all his secret venom, for he said that no benefit accrues to the recipients of Holy Baptism, and that it is only by earnest prayer that the in-dwelling demon is driven out, for that every one born into the world derives from his first father slavery to the demons just as he does his nature; but that when these are driven away, then comes the Holy Ghost giving sensible and visible signs of His presence, at once freeing the body from the impulse of the passions and wholly ridding the soul of its inclination to the worse; with the result that there is no more need for fasting that restrains the body, nor of teaching or training that bridles it and instructs it how to walk aright. And not only is the recipient of this gift liberated from the wanton motions of the body, but also clearly foresees things to come, and with the eyes beholds the Holy Trinity.

In this wise the divine Flavianus dug into the foul fountain-head and succeeded in laying bare its streams. Then he thus addressed the wretched old man. "O thou that hast grown old in evil days, thy own mouth convicts thee, not I, and thou art testified against by thy own lips." After their unsoundness had been thus exposed they were expelled from Syria, and withdrew to Pamphylia, which they filled with their pestilential doctrine.

CHAPTER XI.

In what manner Valens fell into heresy.

I WILL now pursue the course of my narrative, and will describe the beginning of the tempest which stirred up many and great billows to buffet the Church. Valens, when he first received the imperial dignity, was distinguished by his fidelity to apostolic doctrine. But when the Goths had crossed the Danube and were ravaging Thrace, he determined to assemble an army and march against them; and accordingly resolved not to take the field without the garb of divine grace, but first to protect himself with the panoply of Holy Baptism.[1] In forming this resolution he acted at once well and wisely, but his subsequent conduct betrays very great feebleness of character, resulting in the abandonment of the truth. His fate was the same as that of our first father, Adam; for he too, won over by the arguments of his wife, lost his free estate and became not merely a captive but an obedient listener to woman's wily words. His wife[2] had already been entrapped in the Arian snare, and now she caught her husband, and persuaded him to fall along with her into the pit of blasphemy. Their leader and initiator was Eudoxius, who still held the tiller of Constantinople, with the result that the ship was not steered onwards but sunk[3] to the bottom.

CHAPTER XII.

How Valens exiled the virtuous bishops.

AT the very time of the baptism of Valens Eudoxius bound the unhappy man by an oath to abide in the impiety of his doctrine, and to expel from every see the holders of contrary opinions. Thus Valens abandoned the apostolic teaching, and went over to the opposite faction; nor was it long before he fulfilled the rest of his oath; for from Antioch he expelled the great Meletius, from Samosata the divine Eusebius, and deprived Laodicea of her admirable shepherd Pelagius.[4] Pelagius had taken on him the yoke of wedlock when a very young man, and in the very bridal chamber, on the first day of his nuptials, he persuaded his bride to prefer chastity to conjugal intercourse, and taught her to accept fraternal affection in the place of marriage union. Thus he gave all honour to temperance, and possessed also within himself the sister virtues moving in tune with her, and for these reasons he was unanimously chosen for the bishopric. Nevertheless not even the bright beams of his life and conversation awed the enemy of the truth. Him, too, Valens relegated to Arabia, the divine Meletius to Armenia, and Eusebius,

---

[1] Valens was baptized in 368.   [2] Albia Dominica.
[3] The use of the word *baptized* for *submerged* is significant. Polyb. 1 : 51. 6 uses it of sinking a ship. It first appears with the technical sense of *baptized* in the Evangelists.
[4] Present at Antioch in 363; banished to Arabia in 367. Present at Constantinople in 381.

that unflagging labourer in apostolic work, to Thrace. Unflagging he was indeed, for when apprised that many churches were now deprived of their shepherds, he travelled about Syria, Phœnicia and Palestine, wearing the garb of war and covering his head with a tiara, ordaining presbyters and deacons and filling up the other ranks of the Church; and if haply he lighted on bishops with like sentiments with his own, he appointed them to empty churches.

CHAPTER XIII.

Of Eusebius, bishop of Samosata, and others.

OF the courage and prudence shewn by Eusebius after he had received the imperial edict which commanded him to depart into Thrace, I think all who have been hitherto ignorant should hear.[1]

The bearer of this edict reached his destination in the evening, and was exhorted by Eusebius to keep silent and conceal the cause of his coming. "For," said the bishop, "the multitude has been nurtured in divine zeal, and should they learn why you have come they will drown you, and I shall be held responsible for your death." After thus speaking and performing evening service, as he was wont, the old man started out alone on foot, at nightfall. He confided his intentions to one of his household servants who followed him carrying nothing but a cushion and a book. When he had reached the bank of the river (for the Euphrates runs along the very walls of the town) he embarked in a boat and told the oarsmen to row to Zeugma.[2] When it was day the bishop had reached Zeugma, and Samosata was full of weeping and wailing, for the above mentioned domestic reported the orders given him to the friends of Eusebius, and told them whom he wished to travel with him, and what books they were to convey. Then all the congregation bewailed the removal of their shepherd, and the stream of the river was crowded with voyagers.

When they came where he was, and saw their beloved pastor, with lamentations and groanings they shed floods of tears, and tried to persuade him to remain, and not abandon the sheep to the wolves. But all was of no avail, and he read them the apostolic law which clearly bids us be subjects to magistrates and authorities.[1] When they had heard him some brought him gold, some silver, some clothes, and others servants, as though he were starting for some strange and distant land. The bishop refused to take anything but some slight gifts from his more intimate friends, and then gave the whole company his instruction and his prayers, and exhorted them to stand up boldly for the apostolic decrees.

Then he set out for the Danube, while his friends returned to their own town, and encouraged one another as they waited for the assaults of the wolves.

In the belief that I should be wronging them were the warmth and sincerity of their faith to lack commemoration in my history I shall now proceed to describe it.

The Arian faction, after depriving the flock of their right excellent shepherd, set up another bishop in his place; but not an inhabitant of the city, were he herding in indigence or blazing in wealth, not a servant, not a handicraftsman, not a hind, not a gardener, nor man nor woman, whether young or old, came, as had been their wont, to gatherings in church. The new bishop lived all alone; not a soul looked at him, or exchanged a word with him. Yet the report is that he behaved with courteous moderation, of which the following instance is a proof. On one occasion he had expressed a wish to bathe, so his servants shut the doors of the bath, and kept out all who wished to come in. When he saw the crowd before the doors he ordered them to be thrown open, and directed that every one should freely use the bath. He exhibited the same conduct in the halls within; for on observing certain men standing by him while he bathed he begged them to share the hot water with him. They stood silent. Thinking their hesitation was due to a respect for him, he quickly arose and made his way out, but these persons had really been of opinion that even the water was affected with the pollution of his heresy, and so sent it all down the sinks, while they ordered a fresh supply to be provided for themselves. On being informed of this the intruder departed from the city, for he judged that it was insensate and absurd on his part to continue to reside in a city which detested him, and treated him as a common foe. On the departure of Eunomius (for this was his name) from Samosata, Lucius, an unmistakable wolf, and enemy of the sheep, was appointed in his place. But the sheep,

---

[1] Samosata, the capital of Commagene on the Euphrates, is of interest as the birthplace of Lucian (c. 120) as well as the see of this Eusebius, the valued friend of Basil and of Gregory of Nazianzus. We shall find him mentioned again v. 4.

[2] Zeugma was on the right bank of the Euphrates, nearly opposite the ancient Apamea and Seleucia and the modern Biredjik. The name is derived from the " Zeugma" or Bridge of Boats built here by Alexander. Strabo xvi. 2. 3.

[1] Titus, iii. 1.

all shepherdless as they were, shepherded themselves, and persistently preserved the apostolic doctrine in all its purity. How the new intruder was detested the following relation will set forth.

Some lads were playing ball in the market place and enjoying the game, when Lucius was passing by. It chanced that the ball was dropped and passed between the feet of the ass. The boys raised an outcry because they thought that their ball was polluted. On perceiving this Lucius told one of his suite to stop and learn what was going on. The boys lit a fire and tossed the ball through the flames with the idea that by so doing they purified it. I know indeed that this was but a boyish act, and a survival of the ancient ways; but it is none the less sufficient to prove in what hatred the town held the Arian faction.

Lucius however was no follower of the mildness of Eunomius, but persuaded the authorities to exile many others of the clergy, and despatched the most distinguished champions of the divine dogmas to the furthest confines of the Roman Empire; Evolcius, a deacon, to Oasis, to an abandoned village; Antiochus, who had the honour of being related to the great Eusebius, for he was his brother's son, and further distinguished by his own honourable character, and of priestly rank, to a distant part of Armenia. How boldly this Antiochus contended for the divine decrees will be seen from the following facts. When the divine Eusebius after his many conflicts, whereof each was a victory, had died a martyr's death, the wonted synod of the people was held, and among others came Jovinus then bishop of Perrha [1] who for some little time had held a communion with the Arians. Antiochus was unanimously chosen as successor to his uncle. When brought before the holy table and bidden there to bend the knee, he turned round and saw that Jovinus had put his right hand on his head. Plucking the hand away he bade him be gone from among the consecrators, saying that he could not endure a right hand which had received mysteries blasphemously celebrated.

These events happened somewhat later. At the time I am speaking of he was removed to the interior of Armenia.

The divine Eusebius was living by the Danube where the Goths were ravaging Thrace and besieging cities, as is described in his own works.

CHAPTER XIV.

Of the holy Barses, and of the exile of the bishop of Edessa and his companions.

BARSES, whose fame is now great not only in his own city of Edessa, and in neighbouring towns, but in Phœnicia, in Egypt, and in the Thebaid, through all which regions he had travelled with a high reputation won by his great virtue, had been relegated by Valens to the island of Aradus,[1] but when the emperor learnt that innumerable multitudes streamed thither, because Barses was full of apostolic grace, and drove out sicknesses with a word, he sent him to Oxyrynchus [2] in Egypt; but there too his fame drew all men to him, and the old man, worthy of heaven, was led off to a remote castle near the country of the barbarians of that district, by name Pheno. It is said that in Aradus his bed has been preserved to this day, where it is held in very great honour, for many sick persons lie down upon it and by means of their faith recover.

CHAPTER XV.

Of the persecution which took place at Edessa, and of Eulogius and Protogenes, presbyters of Edessa.

Now a second time Valens, after depriving the flock of their shepherd, had set over them in his stead a wolf. The whole population had abandoned the city, and were assembled in front of the town, when he arrived at Edessa. He had given orders to the prefect, Modestus by name, to assemble the troops under his orders who were accustomed to exact the tribute, to take all who were present of the armed force, and by inflicting blows with sticks and clubs, and using if need be their other weapons of war. to disperse the gathering multitude. Early in the morning, while the prefect was executing this order, on his way through the Forum he saw a woman holding an infant in her arms, and hurrying along at great speed. She had made light of the troops, and forced her way through their ranks: for a soul fired with divine zeal knows no fear of man, and looks on terrors of this kind as ridiculous sport. When the

---

[1] Jovinus was a friend of Basil (Ep. 118) as well as of Eusebius of Samosata.

Perrha, a town of Euphratensis, is more likely to have been his see than the Perga of the commoner reading.

[1] An island off the coast of Phœnicia; now Ruad. The town on the opposite mainland was Antaradus.

[2] Oxyrynchus on the Nile, at or near the modern Behnese (?) was so called because the inhabitants worshipped the "sharp-snout," or pike. Strabo xvii. 1. 40.

prefect saw her, and understood what had happened, he ordered her to be brought before him, and enquired whither she was going. " I have heard," said she, " that assaults are being planned against the servants of the Lord; I want to join my friends in the faith that I may share with them the slaughter inflicted by you." " But the baby," said the prefect, " what in the world are you carrying that for?" " That it may share with me," said she, " the death I long for."

When the prefect had heard this from the woman and through her means discovered the zeal which animated all the people, he made it known to the emperor, and pointed out the uselessness of the intended massacre. " We shall only reap," said he, " a harvest of discredit from the deed, and shall fail to quench these people's spirit." He then would not allow the multitude to undergo the tortures which they had expected, and commanded their leaders, the priests, I mean, and deacons, to be brought before him, and offered them a choice of two alternatives, either to induce the flock to communicate with the wolf, or be banished from the town to some remote region. Then he summoned the mass of the people before him, and in gentle terms endeavoured to persuade them to submit to the imperial decrees, urging that it was mere madness for a handful of men who might soon be counted to withstand the sovereign of so vast an empire. The crowd stood speechless. Then the prefect turned to their leader Eulogius, an excellent man, and said, " Why do you make no answer to what you have heard me say?" " I did not think," said Eulogius, " that I must answer, when I had been asked no question." " But," said the prefect, " I have used many arguments to urge you to a course advantageous to yourselves." Eulogius rejoined that these pleas had been urged on all the multitude and that he thought it absurd for him to push himself forward and reply; " but," he went on, " should you ask me my individual opinion I will give it you." " Well," said the prefect, " communicate with the emperor. With pleasant irony Eulogius continued, " Has he then received the priesthood as well as the empire?" The prefect then perceiving that he was not speaking seriously took it ill, and after heaping reproaches on the old man, added, " I did not say so, you fool; I exhorted you to communicate with those with whom the Emperor communicates." To this the old man replied that they had a shepherd and obeyed his direc-

tions, and so eighty of them were arrested, and exiled to Thrace. On their way thither they were everywhere received with the greatest possible distinction, cities and villages coming out to meet them and honouring them as victorious athletes. But envy armed their antagonists to report to the emperor that what had been reckoned disgrace had really brought great honour on these men; thereupon Valens ordered that they were to be separated into pairs and sent in different directions, some to Thrace, some to the furthest regions of Arabia, and others to the towns of the Thebaid; and the saying was that those whom nature had joined together savage men had put asunder, and divided brother from brother. Eulogius their leader with Protogenes the next in rank, were relegated to Antinone.[1]

Even of these men I will not suffer the virtue to fall into oblivion. They found that the bishop of the city was of like mind with themselves, and so took part in the gatherings of the Church; but when they saw very small congregations, and on enquiry learnt that the inhabitants of the city were pagans, they were grieved, as was natural, and deplored their unbelief. But they did not think it enough to grieve, but to the best of their ability devoted themselves to making these men whole. The divine Eulogius, shut up in a little chamber, spent day and night in putting up petitions to the God of the universe; and the admirable Protogenes, who had received a good education [2] and was practised in rapid writing, pitched on a suitable spot which he made into a boys' school, and, setting up for a schoolmaster, he instructed his pupils not only in the art of swift penmanship, but also in the divine oracles. He taught them the psalms of David and gave them to learn the most important articles of the apostolic doctrine. One of the lads fell sick, and Protogenes went to his home, took the sufferer by the hand and drove away the malady by prayer. When the parents of the other boys heard this they brought him to their houses and entreated him to succour the sick; but he refused to ask God for the expulsion of the malady before the sick had received the gift of baptism; urged by their longing for the children's health, the parents readily acceded, and won at last salvation both for body and soul. In every instance where he persuaded any one in health to receive the divine grace, he led him off to Eulogius, and knocking at the door besought him to open, and put the seal of the Lord on

---

[1] Antinoopolis, now Enseneh on the right bank of the Nile.
[2] The manuscripts here vary considerably.

the prey. When Eulogius was annoyed at the interruption of his prayer, Protogenes used to say that it was much more essential to rescue the wanderers. In this he was an object of admiration to all who beheld his deeds, doing such wondrous works, imparting to so many the light of divine knowledge and all the while yielding the first place to another, and bringing his prizes to Eulogius. They rightly conjectured that the virtue of Eulogius was by far the greater and higher.

On the quieting of the tempest and restoration of complete calm, they were ordered to return home, and were escorted by all the people, wailing and weeping, and specially by the bishop of the church, who was now deprived of their husbandry. When they reached home, the great Barses had been removed to the life that knows no pain, and the divine Eulogius was entrusted with the rudder of the church which he had piloted;[1] and to the excellent Protogenes was assigned the husbandry of Charræ,[2] a barren spot full of the thorns of heathendom and needing abundant labour. But these events happened after peace was restored to the churches.

CHAPTER XVI.

Of the holy Basilius, Bishop of Cæsarea, and the measures taken against him by Valens and the prefect Modestus.

VALENS, one might almost say, deprived every church of its shepherd, and set out for the Cappadocian Cæsarea,[3] at that time the see of the great Basil, a light of the world. Now he had sent the prefect before him with orders either to persuade Basil to embrace the communion of Eudoxius, or, in the event of his refusal, to punish him by exile. Previously acquainted as he was with the bishop's high reputation, he was at first unwilling to attack him, for he was apprehensive lest the bishop, by boldly meeting and withstanding his assault, should furnish an example of bravery to the rest. This artful stratagem was as ineffective as a spider's

web. For the stories told of old were quite enough for the rest of the episcopate, and they kept the wall of the faith unmoved like bastions in the circle of its walls.

The prefect, however, on his arrival at Cæsarea, sent for the great Basil. He treated him with respect, and, addressing him with moderate and courteous language, urged him to yield to the exigencies of the time, and not to forsake so many churches on account of a petty nicety of doctrine. He moreover promised him the friendship of the emperor, and pointed out that through it he might be the means of conferring great advantages upon many. "This sort of talk," said the divine man, "is fitted for little boys, for they and their like easily swallow such inducements. But they who are nurtured by divine words will not suffer so much as a syllable of the divine creeds to be let go, and for their sake are ready, should need require, to embrace every kind of death. The emperor's friendship I hold to be of great value if conjoined with true religion; otherwise I doom it for a deadly thing."

Then the prefect was moved to wrath, and declared that Basil was out of his senses. "But," said the divine man, "this madness I pray be ever mine." The bishop was then ordered to retire, to deliberate on the course to be pursued, and on the morrow to declare to what conclusion he had come. Intimidation was moreover joined with argument. The reply of the illustrious bishop is related to have been "I for my part shall come to you tomorrow the same man that I am today; do not yourself change, but carry out your threats." After these discussions the prefect met the emperor and reported the conversation, pointing out the bishop's virtue, and the undaunted manliness of his character. The emperor said nothing and passed in. In his palace he saw that plagues from heaven had fallen, for his son[1] lay sick at the very gates of death and his wife[2] was beset by many ailments. Then he recognised the cause of these sorrows, and entreated the divine man, whom he had threatened with chastisement, to come to his house. His officers performed the imperial behests and then the great Basil came to the palace.

After seeing the emperor's son on the point of death he promised him restoration to life if he should receive holy baptism at the hands of the pious, and with this pledge went his way. But the emperor, like the foolish Herod, remembered his oath, and

---

[1] Eulogius was at Rome in 369, at Antioch in 379, and Constantinople in 381.

[2] Charræ, now Harran, in Mesopotamia, on the point of divergence of the main caravan routes, is the Haran to which Terah travelled from Orfah. It was afterwards made famous by the defeat of the Romans in B.C. 53; when

　　　　"miserando funere Crassus,
"Assyrias Latio maculavit sanguine Carras."
　　　　　　　　Lucan. i. 104.

[3] Cæsarea Ad Argæum (now Kasaria) at the foot of Mount Argæus, was made a Roman province by Tiberius A.D. 18. The progress of Valens had hitherto been successful, and the Catholic cause was endangered. Bithynia had been coerced, and the mobile Galatians had given in. "The fate of Cappadocia depended on Basil." cf. Dict. Ch. Biog. i. 289.

[1] Galates. cf. Soc. iv. 26.

[2] Dominica. cf. Soc. iv. 26.

ordered some of the Arian faction who were present to baptize the boy, who immediately died. Then Valens repented; he saw how fraught with danger the keeping of his oath had been, and came to the divine temple and received the teaching of the great Basil, and offered the customary gifts at the altar. The bishop moreover ordered him to come within the divine curtains where he sat and talked much with him about the divine decrees and in turn listened to him.

Now there was present a certain man of the name of Demosthenes,[1] superintendent of the imperial kitchen, who in rudely chiding the man who instructed the world was guilty of a solecism of speech. Basil smiled and said "we see here an illiterate Demosthenes;" and on Demosthenes losing his temper and uttering threats, he continued " your business is to attend to the seasoning of soups; you cannot understand theology because your ears are stopped up." So he said, and the emperor was so delighted that he gave him some fine lands which he had there for the poor under his care, for they being in grievous bodily affliction were specially in need of care and cure.

In this manner then the great Basil avoided the emperor's first attack, but when he came a second time his better judgement was obstructed by counsellors who deceived him; he forgot what had happened on the former occasion and ordered Basil to go over to the hostile faction, and, failing to persuade him, commanded the decree of exile to be enforced. But when he tried to affix his signature to it he could not even form one tittle of a word,[2] for the pen broke, and when the same thing happened to the second and to the third pen, and he still strove to sign that wicked edict, his hand shook; he quaked, his soul was filled with fright; he tore the paper with both his hands, and so proof was given by the Ruler of the world that it was He Himself who had permitted these sufferings to be undergone by the rest, but had made Basil stronger than the snares laid against him, and, by all the incidents of Basil's case, had declared His own almighty power, while on the other hand He had proclaimed abroad the courage of good men. Thus Valens was disappointed in his attack.

CHAPTER XVII.

Of the death of the great Athanasius and the election of Petrus.

AT Alexandria, Athanasius the victorious, after all his struggles, each rewarded with a crown, received release from his labours and passed away to the life which knows no toil. Then Peter, a right excellent man, received the see. His blessed predecessor had first selected him, and every suffrage alike of the clergy and of men of rank and office concurred, and all the people strove to show their delight by their acclamations. He had shared the heavy labours of Athanasius; at home and abroad he had been ever at his side, and with him had undergone manifold perils. Wherefore the bishops of the neighbourhood hastened to meet; and those who dwelt in schools of ascetic discipline left them and joined the company, and all joined in begging that Peter might be chosen to succeed to the patriarchal chair of Athanasius.[1]

CHAPTER XVIII.

On the overthrow of Petrus and the introduction of Lucius the Arian.

No sooner had they seated him on the episcopal throne than the governor of the province assembled a mob of Greeks and Jews, surrounded the walls of the church,[2] and bade Peter come forth, threatening him with exile if he refused. He thus acted on the plea that he was fulfilling the emperor's good pleasure by bringing those of opposite sentiments into trouble, but the truth was that he was carried away by his impious passion. For he was addicted to the service of the idols, and looked upon the storms which beset the Church as a season of brilliant festivity. The admirable Peter, however, when he beheld the unforeseen conflict, secretly withdrew, and embarked in a vessel bound for Rome.

After a few days Euzoius came from Antioch with Lucius, and handed over the churches to him. This was he of whose im-

---

[1] If this Demosthenes " is the same person with the Demosthenes who four years later held the office of vicar of Pontus we have in him one of the many examples presented by the history of the Eastern empire of the manner in which base arts raised the meanest persons to the highest dignities." Dict. Chris. Biog. s. v. But the chief cook may have been a high functionary like the chief baker at the court of the Pharaohs or the Lord High Steward at that of St. James's. Of the elevation of a menial to power many parallels may be found. Demosthenes of Pontus afterwards became a partisan of the Semiarians and accused Basil's brother, Gregory of Nyssa, of dishonesty. Basil. Epist. 264, 385, 405.
[2] στοιχεῖον is a simple sound of the voice as distinguished from γράμμα, a letter.

[1] " The discussions about the year of his death may be considered as practically closed; the Festal Index, although its chronology is sometimes faulty, confirming the date of 373, given in the Maffeian fragment. The exact day, we may believe, was Thursday, May 2, on which day of the month Athanasius is venerated in the Western Church. He had sat on the Alexandrian throne forty-six complete years. He died tranquilly in his own house." Canon Bright in Dict. Christ. Biog. S. V.
[2] The church Theonas, where Syrianus nearly seized Athanasius in 356.

piety and lawlessness Samosata had already had experience. But the people nurtured in the teaching of Athanasius, when they now saw how different was the spiritual food offered them, held aloof from the assemblies of the Church.

Lucius, who employed idolators as his attendants, went on scourging some, imprisoning others; some he drove to take to flight, others' homes he rifled in rude and cruel fashion. But all this is better set forth in the letter of the admirable Peter. After recounting an instance of the impious conduct of Lucius I shall insert the letter in this work.

Certain men in Egypt, of angelic life and conversation, fled from the disquiet of the state and chose to live in solitude in the wilderness. There they made the sandy and barren soil bear fruit; for a fruit right sweet and fair to God was the virtue by whose law they lived. Among many who took the lead in this mode of life was the far-famed Antonius, most excellent master in the school of mortification, who made the desert a training place of virtue for his hermits. He after all his great and glorious labours had reached the haven where the winds of trouble blow no more, and then his followers were persecuted by the wretched and unhappy Lucius. All the leaders of those divine companies, the famous Macarius, his namesake, Isidorus, and the rest [1] were dragged out of their caves and despatched to a certain island inhabited by impious men, and never blessed with any teacher of piety. When the ship drew near to the shore of the island the demon reverenced by its inhabitants departed from the image which had been his time-old home, and filled with frenzy the daughter of the priest. She was driven in her inspired fury to the shore where the rowers were bringing the ship to land. Making the tongue of the girl his instrument, the demon shouted out through her the words uttered at Philippi by the woman possessed with the spirit of Python,[2] and was heard by all, both men and women, saying, " Alas for your power, ye servants of the Christ; everywhere we have been driven forth by you from town and hamlet, from hill and height, from wastes where no men dwell; in yon islet we had hoped to live out of the reach of your shafts, but our hope was vain; hither you have been sent by your persecutors, not to be harmed by them, but to drive us out. We are quitting the island, for we are being wounded by the piercing rays of your virtue." With these words, and words like these, they dashed the damsel to the ground, and themselves all fled together. But that divine company prayed over the girl and raised her up, and delivered her to her father made whole and in her right mind.

The spectators of the miracle flung themselves at the feet of the new comers and implored to be allowed to participate in the means of salvation. They destroyed the idol's grove, and, illuminated by the bright rays of instruction, received the grace of holy baptism. On these events becoming known in Alexandria all the people met together, reviling Lucius, and saying that wrath from God would fall upon them, were not that divine company of saints to be set free. Then Lucius, apprehensive of a tumult in the city, suffered the holy hermits to go back to their dens. Let this suffice to give a specimen of his impious iniquity. The sinful deeds he dared to do will be more clearly set forth by the letter of the admirable Peter. I hesitate to insert it at full length, and so will only quote some extracts from it.

CHAPTER XIX.

Narrative of events at Alexandria in the time of Lucius the Arian, taken from a letter of Petrus, Bishop of Alexandria.

PALLADIUS governor of the province, by sect a heathen,[1] and one who habitually prostrated himself before the idols, had frequently entertained the thought of waging war against Christ. After collecting the forces already enumerated he set out against the Church, as though he were pressing forward to the subjugation of a foreign foe. Then, as is well known, the most shocking deeds were done, and at the bare thought of telling the story, its recollection fills me with anguish. I have shed floods of tears, and I

---

[1] There are traces of some confusion about the saints and solitaries of this name at this period. " There were two hermits or monks of this name both of the 4th c., both living in Egypt, whose character and deeds are almost indistinguishable." " One of them is said to have been the disciple of Anthony, and the master of Evagrius." " The name of Macarius, like a double star, shines as a central light in the monkish history, and is enshrined alike in the Roman martyrologies, and in the legends of the Greek church. Macarius is a favourite saint in Russia." (Canon Fremantle, Dict. Christ. Biog. iii. 774.) cf. Soc. iv. 23. In iv. 24 Soc. describes both the Macari as banished to the island " which had not a single Christian inhabitant." Sozomen (vi. 20) has the same story.

There was an Isidorus, bishop of Cyrus in 378, mentioned by Theodoretus in his Religious History (1143), and an Isidorus, bishop of Athribis in Egypt. cf. Dict. Christ. Biog. s. v. But the Isidorus of the text appears to have been a monk.

[2] Acts xvi. 16, where the reading πνεῦμα πύθωνα recommended on the overwhelming authority of אABCD is adopted by the R. V., and rendered in the margin " a spirit, a python." In the text it is τὸ πνεῦμα τοῦ πύθωνος.

[1] ἐθνικός, " foreigner " a " gentile." Another common term for " heathen " in ecclesiastical Greek is Ἑλλην, but neither " Gentile " nor " Greek " expresses the required sense so well as " Heathen," which, like the cognate " Pagan," simply denotes a countryman and villager, and marks the age when Christianity was found to be mainly in towns.

should have long remained thus bitterly affected had I not assuaged my grief by divine meditation. The crowds intruded into the church called Theonas[1] and there instead of holy words were uttered the praises of idols; there where the Holy Scriptures had been read might be heard unseemly clapping of hands with unmanly and indecent utterances; there outrages were offered to the Virgins of Christ which the tongue refuses to utter, for "it is a shame even to speak of them."[2] On only hearing of these wrongs one of the well disposed stopped his ears and prayed that he might rather become deaf than have to listen to their foul language. Would that they had been content to sin in word alone, and had not surpassed the wickedness of word by deed, for insult, however bad it be, can be borne by them in whom dwells Christ's wisdom and His holy lessons. But these same villains, vessels of wrath fitted for destruction,[3] screwed up their noses and poured out, if I may so say, as from a well-head, foul noises through their nostrils, and rent the raiment from Christ's holy virgins, whose conversation gave an exact likeness of saints; they dragged them in triumph, naked as when they were born, through all the town; they made indecent sport of them at their pleasure; their deeds were barbarous and cruel. Did any one in pity interfere and urge to mercy he was dismissed with wounds. Ah! woe is me. Many a virgin underwent brutal violation; many a maid beaten on the head with clubs lay dumb, and even their bodies were not allowed to be given up for burial, and their grief-stricken parents cannot find their corpses to this day. But why recount woes which seem small when compared with greater? Why linger over these and not hurry on to events more urgent? When you hear them I know that you will wonder and will stand with us long dumb, amazed at the kindness of the Lord in not bringing all things utterly to an end. At the very altar the impious perpetrated what, as it is written,[4] neither happened nor was heard of in the days of our fathers.

A boy who had forsworn his sex and would pass for a girl, with eyes, as it is written, smeared with antimony,[5] and face reddened with rouge like their idols, in woman's dress, was set up to dance and wave his hands about and whirl round as though

he had been at the front of some disreputable stage, on the holy altar itself where we call on the coming of the Holy Ghost, while the by-standers laughed aloud and rudely raised unseemly shouts. But as this seemed to them really rather decorous than improper, they went on to proceedings which they reckoned in accordance with their indecency; they picked out a man who was very famous for utter baseness, made him strip off at once all his clothes and all his shame, and set him up as naked as he was born on the throne of the church, and dubbed him a vile advocate against Christ. Then for divine words he uttered shameless wickedness, for awful doctrines wanton lewdness, for piety impiety, for continence fornication, adultery, foul lust, theft; teaching that gluttony and drunkenness as well as all the rest were good for man's life.[1] In this state of things when even I had withdrawn from the church[2] — for how could I remain where troops were coming in — where a mob was bribed to violence—where all were striving for gain — where mobs of heathen were making mighty promises? — forth, forsooth, is sent a successor in my place. It was one named Lucius, who had bought the bishopric as he might some dignity of this world, eager to maintain the bad character and conduct of a wolf.[3] No synod of orthodox bishops had chosen him;[4] no vote of genuine clergy; no laity had demanded him; as the laws of the church enjoin.

Lucius could not make his entrance into the city without parade, and so he was appropriately escorted not by bishops, not by presbyters, not by deacons, not by multitudes of the laity; no monks preceded him chanting psalms from the Scriptures; but there was Euzoius, once a deacon of our city of Alexandria, and long since degraded along with Arius in the great and holy synod of Nicæa, and more recently raised to rule and ravage the see of Antioch, and there, too, was Magnus the treasurer,[5] notorious for every kind of impiety, leading a vast body of troops. In the reign of Julian this Magnus had burnt the church at Berytus,[6]

---

[1] Vide note on page 120.
[2] Eph. v. xii.
[3] Romans ix. 22.
[4] Joel i. 2.
[5] I adopt the reading στιβῇ for στίμμι. cf. Ez. xxiii. 40 (Sept.). ἐστίβιζον τοὺς ὀφθαλμούς σου.

[1] cf. Greg. Naz. Orat. xxv. 12. p. 464 Ed. Migne.
[2] cf. Soc. 21.
[3] Observe the pun.
[4] On the subject of episcopal election, vide Dict. Christ. Biog. iv. 335.
[5] ὁ τῶν κομητατησίων δὲ λαργιτιόνων κόμης. Valesius says,"thesauri principis, qui vulgo sacræ largitiones dicebantur, alii erant per singulas diœceses quibus prœerant comites. Alii erant in comitatu una cum principe, qui comitatenses largitiones dicebantur. His præerat comes largitionum comitatensium."
[6] Beyrout, between the ancient Byblus and Sidon. Near here St. George killed the dragon, according to the legend. Our patron saint's dragon does not seem to have been, as may possibly have been the case in some similar stories, a surviving Saurian, but simply a materialization of some picture of George vanquishing the old dragon, the Devil.

the famous city of Phœnicia; and, in the reign of Jovian of blessed memory, after barely escaping decapitation by numerous appeals to the imperial compassion, had been compelled to build it up again at his own expense.

Now I invoke your zeal to rise in our vindication. From what I write you ought to be able to calculate the character and extent of the wrongs committed against the Church of God by the starting up of this Lucius to oppose us. Often rejected by your piety and by the orthodox bishops of every region, he seized on a city which had just and righteous cause to regard and treat him as a foe. For he does not merely say like the blasphemous fool in the psalms " Christ is not true God." [1] But, corrupt himself, he corrupted others, rejoicing in the blasphemies uttered continually against the Saviour by them who worshipped the creature instead of the Creator. The scoundrel's opinions being quite on a par with those of a heathen, why should he not venture to worship a new-made God, for these were the phrases with which he was publicly greeted " Welcome, bishop, because thou deniest the Son. Serapis loves thee and has brought thee to us." So they named their native idol. Then without an interval of delay the afore-named Magnus, inseparable associate in the villainy of Lucius, cruel body-guard, savage lieutenant, collected together all the multitudes committed to his care, and arrested presbyters and deacons to the number of nineteen, some of whom were eighty years of age, on the charge of being concerned in some foul violation of Roman law. He constituted a public tribunal, and, in ignorance of the laws of Christians in defence of virtue, endeavoured to compel them to give up the faith of their fathers which had been handed down from the apostles through the fathers to us. He even went so far as to maintain that this would be gratifying to the most merciful and clement Valens Augustus. " Wretched man " he shouted " accept, accept the doctrine of the Arians; God will pardon you even though you worship with a true worship, if you do this not of your own accord but because you are compelled. There is always a defence for irresponsible compulsion, while free action is responsible and much followed by accusation. Consider well these arguments; come willingly; away with all delay; subscribe the doctrine of Arius preached now by Lucius," (so he

introduced him by name) " being well assured that if you obey you will have wealth and honour from your prince, while if you refuse you will be punished by chains, rack, torture, scourge and cruel torments; you will be deprived of your property and possessions; you will be driven into exile and condemned to dwell in savage regions."

Thus this noble character mixed intimidation with deceit and so endeavoured to persuade and compel the people to apostatise from true religion. They however knew full well how true it is that the pain of treachery to right religion is sharper than any torment; they refused to lower their virtue and noble spirit to his trickery and threats, and were thus constrained to answer him. " Cease, cease trying to frighten us with these words, utter no more vain words. We worship no God of late arrival or of new invention. Foam at us if you will in the vain tempest of your fury and dash yourselves against us like a furious wind. We abide by the doctrines of true religion even unto death; we have never regarded God as impotent, or as unwise, or untrue, as at one time a Father and at another not a Father, as this impious Arian teaches, making the Son a being of time and transitory. For if, as the Ariomaniacs say, the Son is a creature, not being naturally of one substance with the Father, the Father too will be reduced to non-existence by the non-existence of the Son, not being as they assert at one period a Father. But if He is ever a Father, his offspring being truly of Him, and not by derivation, for God is impassible, how is not he mad and foolish who says of the Son through whom all things came by grace into existence, "there was a time when he was not."

These men have truly become fatherless by falling away from our fathers throughout the world who assembled at Nicæa, and anathematized the false doctrine of Arius, now defended by this later champion. They laid down that the Son was not as you are now compelling us to say, of a different substance from the Father, but of one and the same. This their pious intelligence clearly perceived, and so from an adequate collation of divine terms they owned Him to be consubstantial.

Advancing these and other similar arguments, they were imprisoned for many days in the hope that they might be induced to fall away from their right mind, but the rather, like the noblest of the athletes in a Stadium, they crushed all fear, and from time to time as it were anointing themselves

---

[1] Ps. xiv. 1. The Sept. reads Εἶπεν ἄφρων ἐν καρδίᾳ αὐτοῦ οὐκ ἔστι Θεός, which admits of the translation " He is not God."

with the thought of the bold deeds done by their fathers, through the help of holy thoughts maintained a nobler constancy in piety, and treated the rack as a training place for virtue. While they were thus struggling, and had become, as writes the blessed Paul, a spectacle to angels and to men,[1] the whole city ran up to gaze at Christ's athletes, vanquishing by stout endurance the scourges of the judge who was torturing them, winning by patience trophies against impiety, and exhibiting triumphs against Arians. So their savage enemy thought that by threats and torments he could subdue and deliver them to the enemies of Christ. Thus therefore the savage and inhuman tyrant evilly entreated them by inflicting on them the tortures that his cruel ingenuity devised, while all the people stood wailing and shewing their sorrow in various ways. Then he once more mustered his troops, who were disciplined in disorder, and summoned the martyrs to trial, or as it might rather be called, to a foregone condemnation, by the seaport, while after their fashion hired cries were raised against them by the idolaters and the Jews. On their refusal to yield to the manifest heresy of the Ariomaniacs they were sentenced, while all the people stood in tears before the tribunal, to be deported from Alexandria to the Phœnician Heliopolis,[2] a place where none of the inhabitants, who are all given over to idols, can endure so much as to hear the name of Christ.

After giving them the order to embark, Magnus stationed himself at the port, for he had delivered his sentence against them in the neighbourhood of the public baths. He showed them his sword unsheathed, thinking that he could thus strike terror into men who had again and again smitten hostile demons to the ground with their two-edged blade. So he bade them put out to sea, though they had got no provisions on board, and were starting without one single comfort for their exile. Strange and almost incredible to relate, the sea was all afoam; grieved, I think, and unwilling, if I may so say, to receive the good men upon its surface, and so have part or lot in an unrighteous sentence. Now even to the ignorant was made manifest the savage purpose of the judge and it may truly be said "at this the heavens stood astonished."[3]

The whole city groaned, and is lamenting to this day. Some men beating on their breast with one hand after another raised a mighty noise; others lifted up at once their hands and eyes to heaven in testimony of the wrong inflicted on them, and so saying in all but words, "Hear, O heavens, and give ear, O earth,"[1] what unlawful deeds are being done. Now all was weeping and wailing; singing and sighing sounded through all the town, and from every eye flowed a river of tears which threatened to overwhelm the very sea with its tide. There was the aforesaid Magnus on the port ordering the rowers to hoist the sails, and up went a mingled cry of maids and matrons, old men and young, all sobbing and lamenting together, and the noise of the multitude overwhelmed the roar raised by the waves on the foaming sea. So the martyrs sailed off for Heliopolis, where every man is given over to superstition,[2] where flourish the devil's ways of pleasure, and where the situation of the city, surrounded on all sides by mountains that approach the sky, is fitted for the terrifying lairs of wild beasts. All the friends they left behind now alike in public in the middle of the town and each in private apart groaned and uttered words of grief, and were even forbidden to weep, at the order of Palladius, prefect of the city, who happened himself to be a man quite given over to superstition. Many of the mourners were first arrested and thrown into prison, and then scourged, torn with carding combs, tortured, and, champions as they were of the church in their holy enthusiasm, were despatched to the mines of Phennesus[3] and Proconnesus.[4]

Most of them were monks, devoted to a life of ascetic solitude, and were about twenty-three in number. Not long afterwards the deacon who had been sent by our beloved Damasus, bishop of Rome, to bring us letters of consolation and communion, was led publicly through the town by executioners, with his hands tied behind his back like some notorious criminal. After sharing the tortures inflicted on murderers, he was terribly scourged with stones and bits of lead about his very neck.[5] He went on board ship to sail, like the rest, with the

---

[1] I. Cor. iv. 9.
[2] In Cœle-Syria, near the sources of the Orontes, where the ruins of the temple of the sun built by Antoninus Pius are known by the modern equivalent of the older title — Baal-Bek. "the city of the sun."
[3] Jer. ii. 12. A V. "Be astonished, O ye heavens." But in Sept. as in text ἐξέστη ὁ οὐρανὸς ἐπὶ τούτῳ.

[1] Isaiah i. 2.
[2] Here the obvious sense of δεισιδαιμονῶν matches the "superstitious" of A. V. in Acts 17. 22.
[3] Valesius identifies Phennessus with Phynon in Arabia Petræa, now Tafileh.
[4] The island of Marmara in the sea of that name.
[5] The Roman "Flagellum" was a frightful instrument of torture, and is distinguished from the "scutica," or whip, and "virga," or rod. It was knotted with bones and bits of metal, and sometimes ended in a hook. Horace (Sat. I. iii. 119) calls it "horribile."

mark of the sacred cross upon his brow ; with none to aid and none to tempt him he was despatched to the copper mines of Phennesus. During the tortures inflicted by the magistrate on the tender bodies of little boys, some have been left lying on the spot deprived of holy rites of burial, though parents and brothers and kinsfolk, and indeed the whole city, begged that this one consolation might be given them. But alas for the inhumanity of the judge, if indeed he can be called judge who only condemns ! They who had contended nobly for the true religion were assigned a worse fate than a murderer's, their bodies lying, as they did, unburied. The glorious champions were thrown to be devoured by beasts and birds of prey.[1] Those who were anxious for conscience' sake to express sympathy with the parents were punished by decapitation, as though they had broken some law. What Roman law, nay what foreign sentiment, ever inflicted punishment for the expression of sympathy with parents? What instance is there of the perpetration of so illegal a deed by any one of the ancients? The male children of the Hebrews were indeed once ordered to be slain by Pharaoh, but his edict was suggested by envy and by fear. How far greater the inhumanity of our day than of his. How preferable, if there be a choice in unrighteousness, their wrongs to ours. How much better ; if what is illegal can be called good or bad, though in truth iniquity is always iniquity.

I am writing what is incredible, inhuman, awful, savage, barbarous, pitiless, cruel. But in all this the votaries of the Arian madness pranced, as it were, with proud exultation, while the whole city was lamenting ; for, as it is written in Exodus, " there was not a house in which there was not one dead."[2]

The men whose appetite for iniquity was never satisfied planned new agitation. Ever wreaking their evil will in evil deeds, they darted the peculiar venom of their iniquity at the bishops of the province, using the aforesaid treasurer Magnus as the instrument of their unrighteousness.

Some they delivered to the Senate, some they trapped at their good pleasure, leaving no stone unturned in their anxiety to hunt in all from every quarter to impiety, going about in all directions, and like the devil, the proper father of heresy, they sought whom they might devour.[1]

In all, after many fruitless efforts, they drove into exile to Dio-Cæsarea,[2] a city inhabited by Jews, murderers of the Lord, eleven of the bishops of Egypt, all of them men who from childhood to old age had lived an ascetic life in the desert, had subdued their inclinations to pleasure by reason and by discipline, had fearlessly preached the true faith of piety, had imbibed the pious doctrines, had again and again won victory against demons, were ever putting the adversary out of countenance by their virtue, and publicly posting the Arian heresy by wisest argument. Yet like Hell,[3] not satisfied with the death of their brethren, fools and madmen as they were, eager to win a reputation by their evil deeds, they tried to leave memorials in all the world of their own cruelty. For lo now they roused the imperial attention against certain clerics of the catholic church who were living at Antioch, together with some excellent monks who came forward to testify against their evil deeds. They got these men banished to Neocæsarea[4] in Pontus, where they were soon deprived of life in consequence of the sterility of the country. Such tragedies were enacted at this period, fit indeed to be consigned to silence and oblivion, but given a place in history for the condemnation of the men who wag their tongues against the Only begotten, and infected as they were with the raving madness of blasphemy, strive not only to aim their shafts at the Master of the universe, but further waged a truceless war against His faithful servants.

CHAPTER XX.

Of Mavia,[5] Queen of the Saracens, and the ordination[6] of Moses the monk.

At this time[7] the Ishmaelites were devastating the country in the neighbourhood of

---

[1] cf. Soph. Ant. 30, Where the corpse of Polyneikes is described as left
　　　　　" unwept unsepulchred
　　　　A prize full rich for birds." (Plumptre.)
Christian sentiment is still affected by the horror felt by the Greeks at deprivation of the rites of burial which finds striking expression in the dispute between Teucer and Menelaos about the burial of Ajax.
[2] Ex. xii. 30.

[1] I. Peter v. 8.
[2] Now Sefurieh, anciently Sepphoris ; an unimportant place till erected by Herod Antipas into the capital of Galilee.
[3] Proverbs xxvii. 20.
[4] Now Niksar, on the river Lykus, the scene of two councils ; (i.) a.d. 315, when the first canon ordered every priest to forfeit his orders on marriage (Mansi ii. 539) (ii.) a.d. 350, when Eustathius of Sebaste was condemned (Mansi, iii. 291).
[5] cf. Soz. vi. 38, and Soc. iv. 36.
[6] The word used is χειροτονία, of which it is well to trace the varying usages. These are given by the late Rev. E. Hatch (Dict. Christ. Ant. ii. 1501) as follows. " This word is used (a) in the N. T. Acts xiv, 24, χειροτονήσαντες δὲ αὐτοῖς κατ' ἐκκλησίαν πρεσβυτέρους : II. Cor. viii. 19 (of Titus) χειροτονηθεὶς ὑπὸ τῶν ἐκκλησιῶν ; (b) in sub-apostolic Greek, Ignat. ad Philad. c. 10 ; (c) in the Clementines, Clement. Ep. ad Jacob. c. 2 ; (d) in the Apostolical Constitution ; (e) in the Canon Law ; (f) in the Civil Law. Its meaning was originally " to
[7] i. e. about 375.

the Roman frontier. They were led by Mavia, a princess who regarded not the sex which nature had given her, and displayed the spirit and courage of a man. After many engagements she made a truce, and, on receiving the light of divine knowledge, begged that to the dignity of high priest of her tribe might be advanced one, Moses by name, who dwelt on the confines of Egypt and Palestine. This request Valens granted, and ordered the holy man to be conveyed to Alexandria, and there, as the most convenient place in the neighbourhood, to receive episcopal grace. When he had arrived and saw Lucius endeavouring to lay hands on him — "God forbid" said he "that I should be ordained by thine hand: the grace of the Spirit visits us not at thy calling." "Whence," said Lucius, "are you led to conjecture this?" He rejoined "I am not speaking of conjecture but of clear knowledge; for thou fightest against the apostolic decrees, and speakest words against them, and for thy blasphemous utterances thy lawless deeds are a match. For what impious man has not on thy account mocked the meetings of the Church? What excellent man has not been exiled? What barbarous savagery is not thrown into the shade by thy daily deeds?" So the brave man said, and the murderer heard him and desired to slay him, but was afraid of kindling once again the war which had come to an end. Wherefore he ordered other bishops to be produced whom Moses had requested. After receiving the episcopal grace of the right worthy faith Moses returned to the people who had asked for him, and by his apostolic teaching and miracles led them in the way that leads to truth.[1]

elect," but it came afterwards to mean even in classical Greek, simply "to appoint to office," without itself indicating the particular mode of appointment (cf. Schömann de Comitüs, p. 122). That the latter was its ordinary meaning in Hellenistic Greek, and consequently in the first ages of church history, is clear from a large number of instances; e. g. in Josephus vi. 13, 9, it is used of the appointment of David as King by God; id. xiii, 22, of the appointment of Jonathan as High Priest by Alexander; in Philo ii, 76 it is used of the appointment of Joseph as governor by Pharaoh; in Lucian, de morte Peregrini c. 41 of the appointment of ambassadors. "In Sozomen vii, 24 of the appointment of Arcadius as Augustus by Theodosius." "In later times a new connotation appears of which there is no early trace; it was used of the stretching out of the bishop's hands in the rite of imposition of hands." The writer of the above seems hardly to do justice to its early use for ordination as well as for appointment. In the Pseudo-Ig. ad. Her. c. iii, it is said of bishops ἐκεῖνοι χειροτονοῦσι, χειροθετοῦσι and Bp. Lightfoot comments "while χειροθεσία is used of laying on of hands, e. g. in confirmation, χειροτονία is said of ordination, e. g. Ap. Const. viii. 27. 'ἐπίσκοπος ὑπὸ τριῶν ἢ δύο ἐπισκόπων χειροτονείσθω.' Referring originally to the election of the Clergy χειροτονία came afterwards to be applied commonly, as here, to their ordination." Theodoretus uses the word in both senses, and sometimes either will fit in with the context.

[1] Sozomen (vi. 38) describes Lucius as remonstrating in moderate language. "Do not judge of me before you know what my creed is." Socrates (iv. 36) makes Moses charge Lucius with condemning the orthodox to exile, beasts, and burning. On Socrates Valesius annotates "Hanc narrationem

These then were the deeds done by Lucius in Alexandria under the dispensation of the providence of God.

CHAPTER XXI.

AT Constantinople the Arians filled a boat with pious presbyters and drove her without ballast out to sea, putting some of their own men on another craft with orders to set the presbyters' boat on fire. So, fighting at the same time against both sea and flames, at last they were delivered to the deep, and won the martyrs' crown.

At Antioch Valens spent a considerable time, and gave complete license to all who, under cover of the Christian name, pagans, Jews and the rest, preached doctrines contrary to those of the gospel. The slaves of this error even went so far as to perform pagan rites, and thus the deceitful fire which, after Julian, had been quenched by Jovian, was now rekindled by permission of Valens. The rites of Jews, of Dionysus, and of Demeter were now no longer performed in a corner, as they would be in a pious reign, but by revellers running wild in the forum. Valens was a foe to none but them that held the apostolic doctrine. First he drove them from their churches, the illustrious Jovian having given them also the new built church. And when they assembled close up to the mountain cliff to honour their Master in hymns, and enjoy the word of God, putting up with all the assaults of the weather, now of rain, now of snow and cold, and now of violent heat, they were not even suffered this poor protection, and troops were sent to scatter them far and wide.

CHAPTER XXII.

How Flavianus and Diodorus gathered the church of the orthodox in Antioch.

Now Flavianus and Diodorus, like breakwaters, broke the force of the advancing waves. Meletius their shepherd had been constrained to sojourn far away. But these looked after the flock, opposing their own courage and cunning to the wolves, and bestowing due care upon the sheep. Now that they were driven away from under the cliff they fed their flocks by the banks of the neighbouring river. They could not brook, like the captives at Babylon, to hang their

de episcopo Saracenis dato et de pace cum iisdem facta, desumpsit quidem Socrates, ex Rufini lib. ii. 6." Lucius was ejected from Alexandria when the reign of Valens ended with his death in 378. Theodoretus appears to confound this Lucius with an Arian Lucius who usurped the see of Samosata. Vide chap. xviii.

[1] Cf. ante, ii. 19. page 85.

harps upon the willows,[1] but they continued to hymn their maker and benefactor in all places of his dominion.[2] But not even in this spot was the meeting of the pious pastors of them that blessed the Lord suffered by the foe to be assembled. So again this pair of excellent shepherds gathered their sheep in the soldiers' training ground and there tried to show them their spiritual food in secret. Diodorus, in his wisdom and courage, like a clear and mighty river, watered his own and drowned the blasphemies of his opponents, thinking nothing of the splendour of his birth, and gladly undergoing the sufferings of the faith.

The excellent Flavianus, who was also of the highest rank, thought piety the only nobility,[3] and, like some trainer for the games, anointed the great Diodorus[4] as though he had been an athlete for five contests.[5]

At that time he did not himself preach at the services of the church, but furnished an abundant supply of arguments and scriptural thoughts to preachers, who were thus able to aim their shafts at the blasphemy of Arius, while he as it were handed them the arrows of his intelligence from a quiver. Discoursing alike at home and abroad he easily rent asunder the heretics' nets and showed their defences to be mere spiders' webs. He was aided in these contests by that Aphraates whose life I have written in my Religious History,[6] and who, preferring the welfare of the sheep to his own rest, abandoned his cell of discipline and retirement, and undertook the hard toil of a shepherd. Having written on these matters in another work I deem it now superfluous to recount the wealth of virtue which he amassed, but one specimen of his good deeds I will proceed now to relate, as specially appropriate to this history.

CHAPTER XXIII.

Of the holy monk Aphraates.

On the north of the river Orontes lies the palace. On the South a vast two storied portico is built on the city wall with lofty towers on either side. Between the palace and the river lies a public way open to passengers from the town, through the gate in this quarter, and leading to the country in the suburbs. The godly Aphraates was once passing along this thoroughfare on his way to the soldiers' training ground, in order to perform the duty of serving his flock. The emperor happened to be looking down from a gallery in the palace, and saw him going by wearing a cloak of undressed goat's skin,[1] and walking rapidly, though of advanced age. On its being remarked that this was Aphraates to whom all the town was then attached, the emperor cried out "Where are you going? Tell us." Readily and cleverly he answered "To pray for your empire." "You had better stop at home" said the emperor "and pray alone like a monk." "Yes," said the divine man, "so I was bound to do and so I always did till now, as long as the Saviour's sheep were at peace; but now that they are grievously disturbed and in great peril of being caught by beasts, I needs must leave no means untried to save the nurslings. For tell me, sir, had I been a girl sitting in my chamber, and looking after the house, and had seen a flash of flame fall and my father's house on fire, what ought I to do? Tell me; sit within and never mind the house being on fire, and wait for the flame to approach? or bid my bower good bye and run up and down and get water and try to quench the flame? Of course you will say the latter, for so a quick and spirited girl would do. And that is what I am doing now, sir. You have set fire to our Father's house and we are running about in the endeavour to put it out." So said Aphraates, and the emperor threatened him and said no more. One of the grooms of the imperial bedchamber, who threatened the godly man somewhat more violently, met with the following fate. He was entrusted with the charge of the bath, and immediately after this conversation he came down to get it ready for the emperor. On entering he lost his wits, stepped into the boiling water before it was mixed with the cold, and so met his end. The emperor sat waiting for him to announce that the bath was ready for him to enter, and after a considerable time had gone by he sent other officers to report the cause of the delay. After they had gone in and looked all about the room they discovered the chamberlain

---

[1] Psalm cxxxvii.
[2] Psalm ciii. 22.
[3] cf. "Virtus sola nobilitas."
[4] Diodorus was now a presbyter. Chrysost. (Laus Diodori § 4. tom. iii. p. 749) describes how the whole city assembled and were fed by his tongue flowing with milk and honey, themselves meanwhile supplying his necessities with their gifts. Valens retorted with redoubled violence, and anticipated the "noyades" of Carrier at Lyons. cf. Socrates iv. 17 and Dict. Christ. Biog. ii. 529.
[5] The five contests of the complete athlete are summed up in the line

ἅλμα, ποδωκείην, δίσκον, ἄκοντα, πάλην.

[6] Relig. Hist. viii.

[1] The word Sisura was used for a common upper garment, but according to the grammarian Tzetzes (Schol. Ad. Lyc. 634) its accurate meaning is the one given in the text.

slain by the heat, and lying dead in the boiling water. On this becoming known to the emperor they perceived the force of the prayers of Aphraates. Nevertheless they did not depart from the impious doctrines but hardened their heart like Pharaoh, and the infatuated emperor, though made aware of the miracle of the holy man, persisted in his mad rage against piety.

CHAPTER XXIV.

Of the holy monk Julianus.

At this time too the celebrated Julianus, whom I have already mentioned, was forced to leave the desert and come to Antioch, for when the foster children of lies, the facile framers of calumny, I mean of course the Arians, were maintaining that this great man was of their faction, those lights of the truth Flavianus, Diodorus, and Aphraates sent Acacius,[1] an athlete of virtue who afterwards very wisely ruled the church at Berœa, to the famous Julianus[2] with the entreaty that he would take pity on so many thousands of men, and at the same time convict the enemy of lies and confirm the proclamation of the truth. The miracles worked by Julianus on his way to and from Antioch and in that vast city itself are described in my Religious History, which is easily accessible to all who wish to become acquainted with them. But I am sure that no one who has enquired into human nature will doubt that he attracted all the population of the city to our assembly, for the extraordinary is generally sure to draw all men after it. The fact of his having wrought great marvels is attested even by the enemies of the truth.

Before this time in the reign of Constantius the great Antonius[3] had acted in the same way in Alexandria, for he abandoned the desert and went up and down that city, telling all men that Athanasius was the preacher of the true doctrine and that the

Arian faction were enemies of the truth. So those godly men knew how to adapt themselves to each particular opportunity, when to remain inactive, and at rest, and when to leave the deserts for towns.

CHAPTER XXV.

Of what other monks were distinguished at this period.

There were also other men at this period who emitted the bright rays of the philosophy of solitary life. In the Chalcidian[1] desert Avitus, Marcianus[2] and Abraames,[3] and more besides whom I cannot easily enumerate, strove in their bodies of sense to live a life superior to sense. In the district of Apamea,[4] Agapetus,[5] Simeon,[6] Paulus and others reaped the fruits of the highest wisdom.

In the district of the Zeugmatenses[7] were Publius[8] and Paulus. In the Cyrestian[9] the famous Acepsemas had been shut up in a cell for sixty years without being either seen or spoken to. The admirable Zeumatius, though bereft of sight, used to go about confirming the sheep, and fighting with the wolves; so they burnt his cell, but the right faithful general Trajanus got another built for him, and paid him besides other attentions. In the neighbourhood of Antioch, Marianus,[10] Eusebius,[11] Ammianus,[12] Palladius,[13] Simeon,[14] Abraames,[15] and others, preserved the divine image unimpaired; but of all these the lives have been recorded by us. But the mountain which is in the neighbourhood of the great city was decked like a meadow, for in it shone Petrus, the Galatian, his namesake the Egyptian,

---

[1] A monk of Gindarus near Antioch (Theod. Vit. Pat. ii.) afterward envoy from the Syrian churches to Rome, and Bishop of Berœa, (Aleppo) A.D. 378. He was at Constantinople in 381, (cf. v. 8.) and is famous for his opposition to Chrysostom.

[2] Julianus Sabas (i. e. Abba) an ascetic solitary of Osrhoëne, the district south of the modern Harran. He is the second of the saints of Theodoret's "Religious History," where we read that he lived on millet bread, which he ate once a week, and performed various miracles, which are recorded by Theodoret on the authority of Acacius.

[3] Antonius, St. Anthony, the illustrious and illiterate ascetic, friend and correspondent of Constantine (Soc. i. 13), the centre of many wild legends, was born in 250 A.D. in upper Egypt. Athanasius calls him the "founder of Asceticism." In 335 he revisited Alexandria to oppose the Arians, as narrated in the text. He died in his cell in 355, bequeathing his "hair shirt, his two woollen tunics, and his bed, among Amathas and Macarius who watched his last hours, Serapion, and Athanasius."

Vide Ath. Vit. S. Ant.

[1] i.e. the district round Chalcis in Syria, to be distinguished from the Macedonian Chalcidice.

[2] Native of Theodoret's see of Cyrus. He built himself a cell like the "Little Ease" of the Tower of London, and promoted orthodoxy by the influence of his austerities. † c. 385. cf. Tillemont, viii. 483.

[3] A. went on missionary journeys disguised as a pedlar, and eventually unwillingly became bishop of Carræ. Theod. Relig. Hist. 3.

[4] Presumably Apamea ad Orontem. (Famiah.)

[5] Bishop of Apamea, a comrade and disciple of Marcianus. (Relig. Hist. iii.)

[6] Also a disciple of Marcian. For fifty years he maintained a school of ascetic philosophy. cf. Chrysost. Ep. 55. and Tillemont. ix. 304. Apparently not the same as Simeones Priscus of Relig. Hist. vi.

[7] i.e. near Zeugma, on the Euphrates, opposite Apamea.

[8] vide Relig. Hist. v.

[9] i.e. round Theodoret's see of Cyrus.

[10] Uncle of Eusebius, a "faithful servant of God." Relig. Hist. iv.

[11] Relig. Hist. iv. Abbot of Mt. Coryphe, nephew of Marianus. He chained his neck to his girdle that he might be compelled to violate the prerogative of his manhood (cf. Ovid. Met i. 85) and keep his eyes on the ground.

[12] Vide Relig. Hist. iv. He had a monastery near Antioch.

[13] Relig. Hist. vii.

[14] cf. the Symeones Priscus of Relig. Hist. vi.

[15] The disciple of Ephrem Syrus. Vide Soz. iii. 16, and Eph. Syr. Act. S. Abraam.

Romanus Severus,[1] Zeno,[2] Moses, and Malchus,[3] and many others of whom the world is ignorant, but who are known to God.

CHAPTER XXVI.

Of Didymus of Alexandria and Ephraim the Syrian.

AT that period at Edessa flourished the admirable Ephraim, and at Alexandria Didymus,[4] both writers against the doctrines that are at variance with the truth. Ephraim, employing the Syrian language, shed beams of spiritual grace. Totally untainted as he was by heathen education[5] he was able to expose the niceties of heathen error, and lay bare the weakness of all heretical artifices. Harmonius[6] the son of Bardesanes[7] had once composed certain songs and by mixing sweetness of melody with his impiety beguiled the hearers, and led them to their destruction. Ephraim adopted the music of the songs, but set them to piety, and so gave the hearers at once great delight and a healing medicine. These songs are still used to enliven the festivals of our victorious martyrs.

Didymus, however, who from a child had been deprived of the sense of sight, had been educated in poetry, rhetoric, arithmetic, geometry, astronomy, the logic of Aristotle, and the eloquence of Plato. Instruction in all these subjects he received by the sense of hearing alone, — not indeed as conveying the truth, but as likely to be weapons for the truth against falsehood. Of holy scriptures he learnt not only the sound but the sense. So among livers of ascetic lives and students of virtue, these men at that time were conspicuous.

CHAPTER XXVII.

Of what bishops were at this time distinguished in Asia and Pontus.

AMONG the bishops were the two Gregorii, the one of Nazianzus[1] and the other of Nyssa,[2] the latter the brother and the former the friend and fellow worker of the great Basilius. These were foremost champions of piety in Cappadocia; and in front rank with them was Peter, born of the same parents with Basilius and Gregorius, who though not having received like them a foreign education, like them lived a life of brilliant distinction.

In Pisidia Optimus,[3] in Lycaonia Amphilochius,[4] fought in the front rank on behalf of their fathers' faith, and repelled the enemies' assaults.

In the West Damasus,[5] Bishop of Rome, and Ambrosius, entrusted with the government of Milan, smote those who attacked them from afar. In conjunction with these, bishops forced to dwell in remote regions, confirmed their friends and undid their foes by writings — thus pilots able to cope with the greatness of the storm were granted by the governor of the universe. Against the violence of the foe He set in battle array the virtue of His captains, and provided means meet to ward off the troubles of these difficult times, and not only were the churches granted this kind of protection by their loving Lord, but deemed worthy of yet another kind of guidance.

CHAPTER XXVIII.

Of the letter written by Valens to the great Valentinianus about the war, and how he replied.

THE Lord roused the Goths to war, and drew on to the Bosphorus him who knew only how to fight against the pious. Then for the first time the vain man became aware of his own weakness, and sent to his brother to ask for troops. But Valentinian replied that it were impious to help one fighting against God, and right rather to check his rashness. By this the unhappy man was filled with yet greater infatuation, yet he did not withdraw from his rash undertaking,

---

[1] Born at Rhosus. His life is given in Relig. Hist. xi.

[2] Relig. Hist. xii. He lived "without bed, lamp, fire, pitcher, pot, box, or book, or anything."

[3] Met in his old age by Jerome, to whom he told the story of his life. Born at Edessa, he ended his days at Maronia, near Antioch. Vide Jer. vita Malchi.

[4] Flourished c. 309–399. Blind from the age of four, he educated himself with marvellous patience, and was placed by Athanasius at the head of the catechetical school of Alexandria. Jerome called him his teacher and seer and translated his Treatise on the Holy Spirit. Jer. de Vir. Illust. 109.

[5] "παιδείας Ἑλληνικῆς." His ignorance of languages weakens the force of his dialectic and illustrations. Vid. Dict. Christ. Biog. s. v.

[6] Harmonius wrote about the end of the 2nd century, both in Greek and in Syriac. cf. Theod. Hæret. Fabul. Compend. i. 22, where he is said to have learned Greek at Athens.

[7] Bardesanes, or Bar Daisan, the great Syrian gnostic, was born in 155. cf. the prologue to the "Dialogues."

[1] Gregorius of Nazianzus (in Cappadocia, on the Halys) was so called not as bishop of Nazianzus. He was bishop successively of Sasima, "a detestable little village," — (Carm. xi. 439–446) — and of Constantinople, and was called "Nazianzenus" because his father and namesake was bishop of that see. On his acting as bishop at Nazianzus after his withdrawal from Constantinople, vide note on page 136.

[2] A younger brother of Basil, bishop of Cæsarea, born about 335; he was bishop of Nyssa, an obscure town of Cappadocia, from 372 to 395. Their parents were Basil, an advocate, and Emmelia. Petrus, the youngest of ten children, was bishop of Sebaste.

[3] Bishop of Antioch in Pisidia; was present at Constantinople in 381. He was a witness to the will of Gregory of Nazianzus.

[4] Vide note on p. 114.

[5] Vide note on p. 82.

and persisted in ranging himself against the truth.[1]

CHAPTER XXIX.

Of the piety of Count Terentius.

TERENTIUS, an excellent general, distinguished for his piety, had set up trophies of victory and returned from Armenia. On being ordered by Valens to choose a bóon, he mentioned one which it was becoming in a man nurtured in piety to choose, for he asked not gold nor yet silver, not land, not dignity, not a house, but that one church might be granted to them that were risking their all for the Apostolic doctrine. Valens received the petition, but on becoming acquainted with its contents he tore it up in a rage, and bade Terentius beg some other boon. The count, however, picked up the pieces of his petition, and said, " I have my reward, sir, and I will not ask another. The Judge of all things is Judge of my intention."

CHAPTER XXX.

Of the bold utterance of Trajanus the general.

AFTER Valens had crossed the Bosphorus and come into Thrace he first spent a considerable time at Constantinople, in alarm as to the issue of the war. He had sent Trajanus in command of troops against the barbarians. When the general came back beaten, the emperor reviled him sadly, and charged him with infirmity and cowardice. Boldly, as became a brave man, Trajanus replied: " I have not been beaten, sir, it is thou who hast abandoned the victory by fighting against God and transferring His support to the barbarians. Attacked by thee He is taking their side, for victory is on God's side and comes to them whom God leads. Dost thou not know," he went on, " whom thou hast expelled from their churches and to whose government these churches have been delivered by thee?" Arintheus and Victor,[2] generals like Trajanus, confirmed the truth of what he said, and implored the emperor not to be angered by reproaches which were founded upon fact.[3]

---

[1] On this Valesius remarks that Valentinian was already dead (†375) when the Goths crossed the Danube and ravaged Thrace (376). Theodoretus should have written "Gratianus" for "Valentinianus," and "nephew" for ' brother."

[2] Magister equitum.' Amm. xxxi. 7.

[3] Gibbon (chap. xxvi) records the conduct of the war by "Trajan and Profuturus, two generals who indulged themselves in a very false and favourable opinion of their own abilities." " Anhelantes altius. sed imbelles." Amm.

The battle alluded to is presumably the doubtful one of Salices. Ammianus does not, as Gibbon supposes, imply that he had himself visited this particular battlefield, but speaks generally of carrion birds as " adsuetæ illo tempore cadaveribus pasci, *ut indicant nunc usque albentes ossibus campi*," Amm. xxxi. 7. 16.

CHAPTER XXXI.

Of Isaac[1] the monk of Constantinople and Bretanio the Scythian Bishop.

IT is related that Isaac, who lived as a solitary at Constantinople, when he saw Valens marching out with his troops, cried aloud, " Whither goest thou, O emperor? To fight against God, instead of having Him as thy ally? 'Tis God himself who has roused the barbarians against thee, because thou hast stirred many tongues to blasphemy against Him and hast driven His worshippers from their sacred abodes. Cease then thy campaigning and stop the war. Give back to the flocks their excellent shepherds and thou shalt win victory without trouble, but if thou fightest without so doing thou shalt learn by experience how hard it is to kick against the pricks.[2] Thou shalt never come back and shalt destroy thy army." Then in a passion the emperor rejoined, " I shall come back; and I will kill thee, and so exact punishment for thy lying prophecy." But Isaac undismayed by the threat exclaimed, " If what I say be proved false, kill me."

Bretanio, a man distinguished by various virtues, and entrusted with the episcopal government of all the cities of Scythia, fired his soul with enthusiasm, and protested against the corruption of doctrines, and the emperor's lawless attacks upon the saints, crying in the words of the godly David, " I spoke of thy testimonies also before Kings and was not ashamed."[3]

CHAPTER XXXII.

Of the expedition of Valens against the Goths and how he paid the penalty of his impiety.

VALENS, however, spurned these excellent counsellors, and sent out his troops to join battle while he himself sat waiting in a hamlet for the victory. His troops could not stand against the barbarians' charge, turned tail and were slain one after another as they fled, the Romans fleeing at full speed and the barbarians chasing them with all their might. When Valens heard of the defeat he strove to conceal himself in the village where he lay, but when the barbarians came up they set the place on fire and together with it burnt the enemy of piety.

---

[1] Possibly the Isaac who opposed Chrysostom. Soz. viii. 9.

[2] Acts ix. 5.

[3] Psalm cxix. 46. The text quotes the Sept. ἐλάλουν ἐν τοῖς μαρτυρίοις σου ἐναντίον βασιλέων καὶ οὐκ ᾐσχυνόμην.

Thus in this present life Valens paid the penalty of his errors.[1]

CHAPTER XXXIII.

How the Goths became tainted by the Arian error.

To those ignorant of the circumstances it may be worth while to explain how the Goths got the Arian plague. After they had crossed the Danube, and made peace with Valens, the infamous Eudoxius, who was on the spot, suggested to the emperor to persuade the Goths to accept communion with him. They had indeed long since received the rays of divine knowledge and had been nurtured in the apostolic doctrines, " but now," said Eudoxius, " community of opinion will make the peace all the firmer." Valens approved of this counsel and proposed to the Gothic chieftains an agreement in doctrine, but they replied that they would not consent to forsake the teaching of their fathers. At the period in question their Bishop Ulphilas was implicitly obeyed by them and they received his words as laws which none might break. Partly by the fascination of his eloquence and partly by the bribes with which he baited his proposals Eudoxius succeeded in inducing him to persuade the barbarians to embrace communion with the emperor, so Ulphilas won them over on the plea that the quarrel between the different parties was really one of personal rivalry and involved no difference in doctrine. The result is that up to this day the Goths assert that the Father is greater than the Son, but they refuse to describe the Son as a creature, although they are in communion with those who do so. Yet they cannot be said to have altogether abandoned their Father's teaching, since Ulphilas in his efforts to persuade them to join in communion with Eudoxius and Valens denied that there was any difference in doctrine and that the difference had arisen from mere empty strife.[1]

---

[1] " On the 9th August, 378, a day long and fatally memorable in the annals of the empire, the legions of Valens moved forth from their entrenched camp under the walls of Hadrianople, and after a march of eight miles under the hot sun of August came in sight of the barbarian vanguard, behind which stretched the circling line of the waggons that guarded the Gothic host. The soldiers of the empire, hot, thirsty, wearied out with hours of waiting under the blaze of an August sun, and only half understanding that the negotiations were ended and the battle begun, fought at a terrible disadvantage but fought not ill. The infantry on the left wing seem even to have pushed back their enemies and penetrated to the Gothic waggons. But they were for some reason not covered as usual by a force of cavalry and they were jammed into a too narrow space of ground where they could not use their spears with effect, yet presented a terribly easy mark to the Gothic arrows. They fell in dense masses as they had stood. Then the whole weight of the enemy's attack was directed against the centre and right. When the evening began to close in, the utterly routed Roman soldiers were rushing in disorderly flight from the fatal field. The night, dark and moonless, may have protected some, but more met their death rushing blindly over a rugged and unknown country.

" Meanwhile Valens had sought shelter with a little knot of soldiers (the two regiments of " Lancearii and Mattiarii "), who still remained unmoved amidst the surging sea of ruin. When their ranks too were broken, and when some of his bravest officers had fallen around him, he joined the common soldiers in their headlong flight. Struck by a Gothic arrow he fell to the ground, but was carried off by some of the eunuchs and life-guardsmen who still accompanied him, to a peasant's cottage hard by. The Goths, ignorant of his rank, but eager to strip the gaily-clothed guardsmen, surrounded the cottage and attempted in vain to burst in the doors. Then mounting to the roof they tried to smoke out the imprisoned inmates, but succeeding beyond their desires, set fire to the cottage, and emperor, eunuchs, and life-guardsmen perished in the flames. Only one of the body-guard escaped, who climbed out through one of the blazing windows and fell into the hands of the barbarians. He told them when it was too late what a prize they had missed in their cruel eagerness, nothing less than the emperor of Rome.

Ecclesiastical historians for generations delighted to point the moral of the story of Valens, that he who had seduced the whole Gothic nation into the heresy of Arius, and thus caused them to suffer the punishment of everlasting fire, was himself by those very Goths burned alive on the terrible 9th of August. Thomas Hodgkin — " The Dynasty of Theodosius," page 97.

[1] Christianity is first found among the Goths and some German tribes on the Rhine about A.D. 300, the Visigoths taking the lead, and being followed by the Ostrogoths. They were converted under Arian influences, and simply accepted an Arian creed. So Salvian writes of them with singular charity, in a passage partly quoted by Milman (Lat. Christ. I. p. 349.) " Hæretici sunt sed non scientes. Denique apud nos sunt hæretici, apud se non sunt. Nam in tantum se catholicos esse judicant ut nos ipsos titulo hæreticæ appellationis infament. Quod ergo illi nobis sunt, hoc nos illis. Nos eos injuriam divinæ generationis facere certi sumus quod minorem patre filium dicant. Illi nos injuriosos patri existimant, quia æquales esse credamus. Veritas apud nos est. Sed illi apud se esse præsumunt. Honor Dei apud nos est, sed illi hoc arbitrantur honorem divinitatis esse quod credunt. Inofficiosi sunt; sed illis hoc est summum religionis officium. Impii sunt; sed hoc putant veram esse pietatem. Errant ergo, sed bono animo errant, non odio, sed affectu Dei, honorare se dominum atque amare credentes." (Salvianus de Gub. Dei V. p. 87.) The spirit of this good Presbyter of Marseilles of the 5th century might well have been more often followed in Christian controversy.

" Of the early Arian missionaries the Arian Records, if they ever existed, have almost entirely perished. The church was either ignorant of or disdained to preserve their memory. Ulphilas alone," — himself a semi-Arian, and accepter of the creed of Ariminum, —" the apostle of the Goths, has, as it were, forced his way into the Catholic records, in which, as in the fragments of his great work, his translation of the Scriptures into the Mœso-Gothic language, this admirable man has descended to posterity." " While in these two great divisions, the Ostrogoths and Visigoths, the nation gathering its descendants from all quarters, spread their more or less rapid conquests over Gaul, Italy, and Spain Ulphilas formed a peaceful and populous colony of shepherds and herdsmen on the pastures below Mt. Hæmus. He became the primate of a simple Christian nation. For them he formed an alphabet of twenty-four letters, and completed all but the fierce books of Kings "—which he omitted, as likely to whet his wild folks' warlike passions, — " his translation of the Scriptures." Milman Lat. Christ. III. Chap. ii.

The fragments of the work of Ulphilas now extant are (1) Codex Argenteus, at Upsala. (2) Codex Carolinus. (3) Ambrosian fragments published by Mai. cf. Philost. ii. 5; Soc. ii. 41 and iv. 33.

On Eudoxius, who baptized Valens, and was " the worst of the Arians," cf. note on page 86.

BOOK V.

CHAPTER I.

Of the piety of the emperor Gratianus.

How the Lord God is long suffering towards those who rage against him, and chastises those who abuse his patience, is plainly taught by the acts and by the fate of Valens. For the loving Lord uses mercy and justice like weights and scales; whenever he sees any one by the greatness of his errors over-stepping the bounds of loving kindness, by just punishment He hinders him from being carried to further extremes.

Now Gratianus, the son of Valentinianus, and nephew of Valens, acquired the whole Roman Empire. He had already assumed the sceptre of Europe on the death of his father, in whose life-time he had shared the throne. On the death of Valens without issue he acquired in addition Asia, and the portions of Libya.[1]

CHAPTER II.

Of the return of the bishops.

The emperor at once gave plain indications of his adherence to true religion, and offered the first fruits of his kingdom to the Lord of all, by publishing an edict commanding the exiled shepherds to return, and to be restored to their flocks, and ordering the sacred buildings to be delivered to congregations adopting communion with Damasus.[2]

This Damasus, the successor of Liberius in the see of Rome, was a man of most praiseworthy life and by his own choice alike in word and deed a champion of Apostolic doctrines. To put his edict in force Gratianus sent Sapor the general, a very famous character at that time, with orders to expel the preachers of the blasphemies of Arius like wild beasts from the sacred folds, and to effect the restoration of the excellent shepherds to God's flocks.

In every instance this was effected without dispute except in Antioch, the Eastern capital, where a quarrel was kindled which I shall proceed to describe.

CHAPTER III.

Of the dissension caused by Paulinus; of the innovation by Apollinarius of Laodicea, and of the philosophy of Meletius.

It has been already related how the defenders of the apostolic doctrines were divided into two parties; how immediately after the conspiracy formed against the great Eustathius, one section, in abhorrence of the Arian abomination, assembled together by themselves with Paulinus for their bishop, while, after the ordination of Euzoius, the other party separated themselves from the impious with the excellent Meletius, underwent the perils previously described, and were guided by the wise instructions which Meletius gave them. Besides these Apollinarius of Laodicea constituted himself leader of a third party, and though he assumed a mask of piety, and appeared to defend apostolic doctrines, he was soon seen to be an open foe. About the divine nature he used unsound arguments, and originated the idea of certain degrees of dignities. He also had the hardihood to render the mystery of the incarnation[1] imperfect and affirmed that the reasonable soul, which is entrusted with the guidance of the body, was deprived of the salvation effected. For according to his argument God the Word did not assume this soul, and so neither granted it His healing gift, nor gave it a portion of His dignity. Thus the earthly body is represented as worshipped by invisible powers, while the soul which is made in the image of God has remained below invested with the dishonour of sin.[2] Many more errors did he utter in his stumbling and blinded intelligence. At one time even he was ready to confess that of the Holy Virgin the flesh had been taken, at another time he represented it to have come down from heaven with God the Word, and yet again that He had been made flesh and took nothing from us. Other vain tales and trifles which I have thought it superfluous to repeat he mixed up with God's gospel promises. By arguments of this nature he not only filled his own friends with dangerous

---

[1] Gratian was proclaimed Augustus by Valentinian in 367. (Soc. iv. 11. Soz. vi. 10.) He came to the throne on the death of Valentinian at Bregetio, Nov. 17, 375. He associated his brother Valentinian II. with him, and succeeded his uncle Valens Aug. 9, 378. On Jan. 19, 379 he nominated Theodosius Augustus.
[2] Cf. note on page 82.

[1] τὸ τῆς οἰκονομίας μυστήριον. Vide note on page 72.
[2] Adopting Platonic and Pauline psychology giving body, soul and spirit (cf. I. Thess. v. 23, and Gal. v. 17) Apollinarius attributed to Christ a human body and a human soul or *anima animans* shared by man with brutes, but not the reasonable soul, spirit or *anima rationalis*. In place of this he put the Divine Logos. The Word, he said, was made Flesh not Spirit, God was manifest in the Flesh not Spirit.

doctrine but even imparted it to some among ourselves. As time went on, when they saw their own insignificance, and beheld the splendour of the Church, all except a few were gathered into the Church's communion. But they did not quite put away their former unsoundness, and with it infected many of the sound. This was the origin of the growth in the Church of the doctrine of the one nature of the Flesh and of the Godhead, of the ascription to the Godhead of the Passion of the only begotten, and of other points which have bred differences among the laity and their priests. But these belong to a later date. At the time of which I am speaking, when Sapor the General had arrived and had exhibited the imperial edict, Paulinus affirmed that he sided with Damasus, and Apollinarius, concealing his unsoundness, did the same. The divine Meletius, on the other hand, made no sign, and put up with their dispute. Flavianus, of high fame for his wisdom, who was at that time still in the ranks of the presbyterate, at first said to Paulinus in the hearing of the officer " If, my dear friend, you accept communion with Damasus, point out to us clearly how the doctrines agree, for he though he owns one substance of the Trinity openly preaches three essences.[1] You on the contrary deny the Trinity of the essences. Shew us then how these doctrines are in harmony, and receive the charge of the churches, as the edict enjoins." After so silencing Paulinus by his arguments he turned to Apollinarius and said, " I am astonished, my friend, to find you waging such violent war against the truth, when all the while you know quite clearly how the admirable Damasus maintains our nature to have been taken in its perfection by God the Word; but you persist in saying the contrary, for you deprive our intelligence of its salvation. If these our charges against you be false, deny now the novelty that you have originated ; embrace the teaching of Damasus, and receive the charge of the holy shrines."

Thus Flavianus in his great wisdom stopped their bold speech with his true reasoning.

Meletius, who ot all men was most meek, thus kindly and gently addressed Paulinus. " The Lord of the sheep has put the care of these sheep in my hands : you have received the charge of the rest : our little ones are in communion with one another in the true religion. Therefore, my dear friend, let us join our flocks ; let us have done with our dispute about the leading of them, and, feeding the sheep together, let us tend them in common. If the chief seat is the cause of strife, that strife I will endeavour to put away. On the chief seat I will put the Holy Gospel ; let us take our seats on each side of it ; should I be the first to pass away, you, my friend, will hold the leadership of the flock alone. Should this be your lot before it is mine, I in my turn, so far as I am able, will take care of the sheep." So gently and kindly spoke the divine Meletius. Paulinus did not consent. The officer passed judgment on what had been said and gave the churches to the great Meletius. Paulinus still continued at the head of the sheep who had originally seceded.

CHAPTER IV.

Of Eusebius [1] Bishop of Samosata.

APOLLINARIUS after thus failing to get the government of the churches, continued, for the future, openly to preach his new fangled doctrine, and constituted himself leader of the heresy. He resided for the most part at Laodicea ; but at Antioch he had already ordained Vitalius, a man of excellent character, brought up in the apostolic doctrines, but afterwards tainted with the heresy. Diodorus, whom I have already mentioned,[2] who in the great storm had saved the ship of the church from sinking, had been appointed by the divine Meletius, bishop of Tarsus, and had received the charge of the Cilicians. The see of Apamea[3] Meletius entrusted to John, a man of illustrious birth, more distinguished for his own high qualities than for those of his forefathers, for he was conspicuous alike for the beauty of his teaching and of his life. In the time of the tempest he piloted the assembly of his fellows in the faith supported by the worthy Stephanus. The latter was however translated by the divine Meletius to carry on another contest, for on the arrival of intelligence that Germanicia had been contaminated by the Eudoxian pest he was sent thither as a physician to ward off the disease, thoroughly trained as he had been in a complete heathen education as well as nurtured in the Divine doctrines. He did not disappoint the expectations formed of him, for by the power

---

[1] cf. page 93.
[2] Vide pages 85 and 126.
[3] Ad Orontem, now Famiah. This John was prefect at Constantinople in 381. A better known John of Apamea is an ascetic of the 5th c., fragments of whose works are among the Syriac MSS. in the British Museum.

[1] τρεῖς ὑποστάσεις.

of his spiritual instruction he turned the wolves into sheep.[1]

On the return of the great Eusebius from exile he ordained Acacius whose fame is great at Berœa,[2] and at Hierapolis Theodotus,[3] whose ascetic life is to this day in all men's mouths. Eusebius[4] was moreover appointed to the see of Chalcis, and Isidorus[5] to our own city of Cyrus; both admirable men, conspicuous for their divine zeal.

Meletius is also reported to have ordained to the pastorate of Edessa, where the godly Barses had already departed this life, Eulogius,[6] the well known champion of apostolic doctrines, who had been sent to Antinone with Protogenes. Eulogius gave Protogenes,[6] his companion in hard service, the charge of Carræ, a healing physician for a sick city.

Lastly the divine Eusebius ordained Maris, Bishop of Doliche,[7] a little city at that time infected with the Arian plague. With the intention of enthroning this Maris, a right worthy man, illustrious for various virtues, in the episcopal chair, the great Eusebius came to Doliche. As he was entering into the town a woman thoroughly infected with the Arian plague let fall a tile from the roof, which crushed in his head and so wounded him that not long after he departed to the better life. As he lay a-dying he charged the bystanders not to exact the slightest penalty from the woman who had done the deed, and bound them under oaths to obey him. Thus he imitated his own Lord, who of them that crucified Him said "Father forgive them for they know not what they do."[8]

Thus, too, he followed the example of Stephanus, his fellow slave, who, after the stones had stormed upon him, cried aloud, "Lord lay not this sin to their charge."[9] So died the great Eusebius after many and various struggles. He had escaped the barbarians in Thrace, but he did not escape the violence of impious heretics, and by their means won the martyr's crown.[1]

These events happened after the return of the bishops, and now Gratian learnt that Thrace was being laid waste by the barbarians who had burnt Valens, so he left Italy and proceeded to Pannonia.

CHAPTER V.

Of the campaign of Theodosius.

Now at this time Theodosius, on account alike of the splendour of his ancestry,[2] and of his own courage, was a man of high repute. For this reason being from time to time stricken by the envy of his rivals, he was living in Spain, where he had been born and brought up.[3] The emperor, being at a loss what measures to take, now that the barbarians, puffed up by their victory, both were and seemed well nigh invincible, formed the idea that a way out of his difficulties would be found in the appointment of Theodosius to the supreme command. He therefore lost no time in sending for him from Spain, appointing[4] him commander in chief and despatching him at the head of the assembled forces.

Defended by his faith Theodosius marched confidently forth. On entering Thrace, and beholding the barbarians advancing to meet him, he drew up his troops in order of battle. The two lines met, and the enemy could not stand the attack and broke. A rout ensued, the foe taking to flight and the conquerors pursuing at full speed. There was a great slaughter of the barbarians, for they were slain not only by Romans but even by one another. After the greater number of them had thus fallen, and a few of those who had been able to escape pursuit had crossed the Danube, the great captain dispersed the troops which he commanded among the neighbouring towns, and forthwith rode at speed to this emperor Gratianus, himself the messenger of his own triumph. Even to the emperor himself, astounded at the event, the tidings he carried seemed incredible, while others stung

---

[1] This seems to be all that is known of Stephanus of Germanicia (now Marash or Banicia in Syria) mentioned also as the see of Eudoxius. cf. Book II. p. 86.

[2] Acacius of Berœa (Aleppo) was later an opponent of Chrysostom and of Cyril, but in his old age reconciled John of Antioch with Cyril, and died at the age of more than 100 in 436.

[3] Theodotus is mentioned also in the Relig. Hist. c. iii. as paying an Easter visit to the hermit Marcian. Hierapolis, or Bambyce, is now Bumbouch in the Pachalic of Aleppo.

[4] Similarly mentioned in Relig. Hist. c. iii. Chalcis is in Cœle Syria.

[5] Also one of Marcian's Easter party. As well as these bishops there were present some men of high rank and position, who were earnest Christians. When all were seated, Marcian was asked to address them. "But he fetched a deep sigh and said ' the God of all day by day utters his voice by means of the visible world, and in the divine scriptures discourses with us, urging on us our duties, telling us what is befitting, terrifying us by threats, winning us by promises, and all the while we get no good. Marcian turns away this good like the rest of his kind, and does not care to enjoy its blessing. What could be the use of his lifting up his voice?'" Relig. Hist. iii. 3.

[6] Vide Book iv. 15. p. 118.   [7] Doliche is in Commagene.
[8] Luke xxiii. 34.   [9] Acts vii. 59.

[1] The Martyrdom of Eusebius is commemorated in the Eastern Churches on June 22; in the Roman Kalendar on June 21. We compare the fate of Abimelech at Thebez (Judges ix. 53, and II. Sam. xi. 21) and Pyrrhus, King of Epirus, at Argos, B.C. 272. "Inter confertissimos violentissime dimicans, saxo de muris ictus occiditur." Justin. xxv. 5. The story is given at greater length by Plutarch. Vit: Pyrrh:

[2] His father, a distinguished general in Britain and elsewhere, was treacherously slain in 376, probably because an oracle warned Valens of a successor with a name beginning "ΘΕΟΔ." cf. Soc. iv. 19. Soz. vi. 35. Ammian. xxix. 1. 29.

[3] At his paternal estate at Cauca in Spain; to the east of the Vaccæi in Tarraconensis.

[4] χειροτονήσας. Vide note on page 125.

with envy gave out that he had run away and lost his army. His only reply was to ask his gainsayers to send and ascertain the number of the barbarian dead, "For," said he, "even from their spoils it is easy to learn their number." At these words the emperor gave way and sent officers to investigate and report on the battle.[1]

CHAPTER VI.

Of the reign of Theodosius and of his dream.

THE great general remained, and then saw a wonderful vision clearly shewn him by the very God of the universe himself. In it he seemed to see the divine Meletius, chief of the church of the Antiochenes, investing him with an imperial robe, and covering his head with an imperial crown. The morning after the night in which he had seen the vision he told it to one of his intimate friends, who pointed out that the dream was plain and had nothing obscure or ambiguous about it.

A few days at most had gone by when the commissioners sent to investigate the battle returned and reported that vast multitudes of the barbarians had been shot down.

Then the emperor was convinced that he had done right well in selecting Theodosius for the command, and appointed him emperor and gave him the sovereignty of the share of Valens.

Upon this Gratian departed for Italy and despatched Theodosius to the countries committed to his charge. No sooner had Theodosius assumed the imperial dignity than before everything else he gave heed to the harmony of the churches, and ordered the bishops of his own realm to repair with haste to Constantinople. That division of the empire was now the only region infected with the Arian plague, for the west had escaped the taint. This was due to the

fact that Constantine the eldest of Constantine's sons, and Constans the youngest, had preserved their father's faith in its integrity, and that Valentinian, emperor of the West, had also kept the true religion undefiled.

CHAPTER VII.

Of famous leaders of the Arian faction.

THE Eastern section of the empire had received the infection from many quarters. Arius, a presbyter of Alexandria in Egypt, there begat the blasphemy. Eusebius, Patrophilus, and Aetius of Palestine, Paulinus and Gregorius of Phœnicia, Theodotus of Laodicea and his successor Georgius, and after him Athanasius and Narcissus of Cilicia, had nurtured the seeds so foully sown. Eusebius and Theognis of Bithynia; Menophantus of Ephesus; Theodorus of Perinthus and Maris of Chalcedon, and some others of Thrace famous only for their vices, had for a long time gone on watering and tending the crop of tares. These bad husbandmen were aided by the indifference of Constantius and the malignity of Valens.

For these reasons only the bishops of his own empire were summoned by the emperor to meet at Constantinople. They arrived, being in all one hundred and fifty in number, and Theodosius forbade any one to tell him which was the great Meletius, for he wished the bishop to be recognized by his dream. The whole company of the bishops entered the imperial palace, and then without any notice of all the rest, Theodosius ran up to the great Meletius, and, like a boy who loves his father, stood for a long space gazing on him with filial joy, then flung his arms around him, and covered eyes and lips and breast and head and the hand that had given him the crown, with kisses. Then he told him of his dream. All the rest of the bishops were then courteously welcomed, and all were bidden to deliberate as became fathers on the subjects laid before them.

CHAPTER VIII.

The council assembled at Constantinople.

AT this time the recent feeder of the flock at Nazianzus[1] was living at Constantino-

---

[1] Theodoret's is the sole authority for this connexion of the association of Theodosius in the Empire with a victory, and his alleged facts do not fit in with others which are better supported. Gratian, a vigorous and sensible lad of nineteen, seems to have felt that the burden was too big for his shoulders, and to have looked out for a suitable colleague. For the choice which he made, or was advised to make, he had good ground in the reputation already won by Theodosius in Britain and in the campaign of 373 against the Sarmatians and Quadi, and the elevation of the young general (born in 346, he was thirty-two when Gratian declared him Augustus at Sirmium, Jan. 19, 379) was speedily vindicated. Theodoret, with his contempt for exact chronology, may have exaggerated one of the engagements of the guerrilla warfare waged by the new emperor after his accession, when he carefully avoided the error of Valens in risking all on a pitched battle. By the end of 379 he had driven the barbarians over the Balkan range. Dr. Stokes (Dict. Christ. Biog. iv. 960) points out that between Aug. 9, 378, and Jan. 19, 379, there was not time for news to travel from Hadrianople to Mitrovitz, where Gratian was, for couriers to fetch Theodosius thither from remoter Spain, for Theodosius then in the winter months to organize and carry out a campaign.

[1] "Cave credas episcopum Nazianzi his verbis designari," says Valesius ; — because before 381 the great Gregory of Nazianzus had at the most first helped his father in looking after the church at Nazianzus, and on his father's death taken temporary and apparently informal charge of the see. But in the latter part of his note Valesius suggests that τὰ τελευταῖα may refer to the episcopate of Gregory at Nazianzus in his last days, after his abdication of the see of Constantinople,— "Atque hic sensus magis placet, magis enim convenire videtur verbis Theodoreti;" "Recent feeder," then, or "he who

ple,[1] continually withstanding the blasphemies of the Arians, watering the holy people with the teaching of the Gospel, catching wanderers outside the flock and removing them from poisonous pasture. So that flock once small he made a great one. When the divine Meletius saw him, knowing as he did full well the object which the makers of the canon [2] had before them when, with the view of preventing the possibility of ambitious efforts, they forbade the translation of bishops, he confirmed Gregory in the episcopate of Constantinople.[3] Shortly afterwards the divine Meletius passed away to the life that knows no pain, crowned by the praises of the funeral eloquence of all the great orators.

Timotheus, bishop of Alexandria, who had followed Peter, the successor of Athanasius in the patriarchate, ordained in place of the admirable Gregorius, Maximus — a cynic who had but recently suffered his cynic's hair to be shorn, and had been carried away by the flimsy rhetoric of Apollinarius. But this absurdity was beyond the endurance of the assembled bishops — admirable men, and full of divine zeal and wisdom, such as Helladius, successor of the great Basil, Gregorius and Peter, brothers of Basil, and Amphilochius from Lycaonia, Optimus from Pisidia, Diodorus from Cilicia.[4]

The council was also attended by Pelagius of Laodicæa,[1] Eulogius of Edessa,[2] Acacius,[3] our own Isidorus,[4] Cyril of Jerusalem, Gelasius of Cæsarea in Palestine,[5] who was renowned alike for lore and life and many other athletes of virtue.

All these then whom I have named separated themselves from the Egyptians and celebrated divine service with the great Gregory. But he himself implored them, assembled as they were to promote harmony, to subordinate all question of wrong to an individual to the promotion of agreement with one another. "For," said he, "I shall be released from many cares and once more lead the quiet life I hold so dear; while you, after your long and painful warfare, will obtain the longed for peace. What can be more absurd than for men who have just escaped the weapons of their enemies to waste their own strength in wounding one another; by so doing we shall be a laughing stock to our opponents. Find then some worthy man of sense, able to sustain heavy responsibilities and discharge them well, and make him bishop." The excellent pastors moved by these counsels appointed as bishop of that mighty city a man of noble birth and distinguished for every kind of virtue as well as for the splendour of his ancestry, by name Nectarius. Maximus, as having participated in the insanity of Apollinarius, they stripped of his episcopal rank and rejected. They next enacted canons concerning the good government of the church, and published a confirmation of the faith set forth at Nicæa. Then they returned each to his own country. Next summer the greater number of them assembled again in the same city, summoned once more by the needs of the church, and received a synodical letter from the bishops of the west inviting them to come to Rome, where a great synod was being assembled. They begged however to be excused from travelling thus far abroad; their doing so, they said, would be useless. They wrote however both to point out the storm which had risen against the churches, and to hint at the carelessness with which the western bishops had treated it. They also included in their letter a summary of the apostolic doctrine, but the boldness and wisdom of their expressions will be more clearly shown by the letter itself.

---

most recently fed," will mean " he who after the events at Constantinople which I am about to relate, acted as bishop of Nazianzus." Gregory left Constantinople in June 381, repaired to Nazianzus, and after finding a suitable man to occupy the see, retired to Arianzus, but was pressed to return and take a leading post in order to check Apollinarian heretics. His health broke down, and he wished to retire. He would have voted in the election of his successor, but his opponents objected on the ground that he either was bishop of Nazianzus, or not; if he was, there was no vacancy; if he was not, he had no vote. Eulalius was chosen in 383, and Gregory spent six weary years in wanderings and troubles, and at last found rest in 389.

[1] It was probably in 379 that Gregory first went to Constantinople and preached in a private house which was to him a " Shiloh, where the ark rested, an Anastasia, a place of resurrection " (Orat. 42.6). Hence the name " Anastasia " given to the famous church built on the site of the too strait house.

[2] i.e. the xvth of Nicæa, forbidding any bishop, presbyter or deacon, to pass from one city to another. Gregory himself classes it among " Νόμους πάλαι τεθνηκότας " (Carm. 1810–11).

[3] Gregory had been practically acting as bishop, when an intriguing party led by Peter of Alexandria tried to force Maximus, a cynic professor, who was one of Gregory's admiring hearers, on the Constantinopolitan Church. "At this time," i.e. probably in the middle of 380, and certainly before Nov. 24, when Theodosius entered the capital, "A priest from Thasco had come to Constantinople with a large sum of money to buy Proconnesian marble for a church. He too was beguiled by the specious hope held out to him. Maximus and his party thus gained the power of purchasing the service of a mob, which was as forward to attack Gregory as it had been to praise him. It was night, and the bishop was ill in bed, when Maximus with his followers went to the church to be consecrated by five suffragans who had been sent from Alexandria for the purpose. Day began to dawn while they were still preparing for the consecration. They had but half finished the tonsure of the cynic philosopher, who wore the flowing hair common to his sect, when a mob, excited by the sudden news, rushed in upon them, and drove them from the church. They retired into a flute player's shop to complete their work, and Maximus, compelled to flee from Constantinople, went to Thessalonica with the hope of gaining over Theodosius himself." Archdeacon Watkins. Dict. Christ. Biog. ii. 752.

[4] Helladius, successor of Basil at the Cappadocian Cæsarea,

was orthodox, but on important occasions clashed unhappily with each of the two great Gregories of Nyssa and Nazianzus. On Gregorius of Nyssa and Petrus his brother, vide page 129. Amphilochius, vide note on page 114. Optimus, vide note on page 129. Diodorus, vide note on pages 85, 126 and 133.

[1] cf. note on Chap. iv. 12, page 115.
[2] cf. note on iv. 15, page 119.
[3] Of Beroea, vide page 128. [4] I.e. of Cyrus, cf. p. 134.
[5] For fragments of his writings vide Dial. i. and iii.

CHAPTER IX.

Synodical letter from the council at Constantinople.

" To the right honourable lords our right reverend brethren and colleagues Damasus, Ambrosius, Britton, Valerianus, Ascholius, Anemius, Basilius and the rest of the holy bishops assembled in the great city of Rome, the holy synod of the orthodox bishops assembled at the great city of Constantinople, sends greeting in the Lord.

" To recount all the sufferings inflicted on us by the power of the Arians, and to attempt to give information to your reverences, as though you were not already well acquainted with them, might seem superfluous. For we do not suppose your piety to hold what is befalling us as of such secondary importance as that you stand in any need of information on matters which cannot but evoke your sympathy. Nor indeed were the storms which beset us such as to escape notice from their insignificance. Our persecutions are but of yesterday. The sound of them still rings in the ears alike of those who suffered them and of those whose love made the sufferers' pain their own. It was but a day or two ago, if I may so say, that some released from chains in foreign lands returned to their own churches through manifold afflictions; of others who had died in exile the relics were brought home; others again, even after their return from exile, found the passion of the heretics still at boiling heat, and, slain by them with stones as was the blessed Stephen, met with a sadder fate in their own than in a stranger's land. Others, worn away with various cruelties, still bear in their bodies the scars of their wounds and the marks of Christ.[1]

" Who could tell the tale of fines, of disfranchisements, of individual confiscations, of intrigues, of outrages, of prisons? In truth all kinds of tribulation were wrought out beyond number in us, perhaps because we were paying the penalty of sins, perhaps because the merciful God was trying us by means of the multitude of our sufferings. For these all thanks to God, who by means of such afflictions trained his servants and, according to the multitude of his mercies, brought us again to refreshment. We indeed needed long leisure, time, and toil to restore the church once more, that so, like physicians healing the body after long sickness and expelling its disease by gradual treatment, we might bring her back to her ancient health of true religion. It is true that on the whole we seem to have been delivered from the violence of our persecutions and to be just now recovering the churches which have for a long time been the prey of the heretics. But wolves are troublesome to us who, though they have been driven from the byre, yet harry the flocks up and down the glades, daring to hold rival assemblies, stirring seditions among the people, and shrinking from nothing which can do damage to the churches.

" So, as we have already said, we needs must labour all the longer. Since however you showed your brotherly love to us by inviting us (as though we were your own members) by the letters of our most religious emperor to the synod which you are gathering by divine permission at Rome, to the end that since we alone were then condemned to suffer persecution, you should not now, when our emperors are at one with us as to true religion, reign apart from us, but that we, to use the apostle's phrase,[1] should reign with you, our prayer was, if it were possible, all in company to leave our churches, and rather gratify our longing to see you than consult their needs. For who will give us wings as of a dove, and we will fly and be at rest?[2] But this course seemed likely to leave the churches who were just recovering quite undefended, and the undertaking was to most of us impossible, for, in accordance with the letters sent a year ago from your holiness after the synod at Aquileia to the most pious emperor Theodosius, we had journeyed to Constantinople, equipped only for travelling so far as Constantinople, and bringing the consent of the bishops remaining in the provinces for this synod alone. We had been in no expectation of any longer journey nor had heard a word about it before our arrival at Constantinople. In addition to all this, and on account of the narrow limits of the appointed time which allowed of no preparation for a longer journey, nor of communicating with the bishops of our communion in the provinces and of obtaining their consent, the journey to Rome was for the majority impossible. We have therefore adopted the next best course open to us under the circumstances, both for the better administration of the church, and for manifesting our love towards you, by strongly urging our most venerated, and honoured colleagues and brother bishops Cyriacus, Eusebius and Priscianus, to consent to travel to you.

" Through them we wish to make it plain

---

[1] Gal. vi. 17.

[1] I. Cor. iv. 8.   [2] Ps. lv. 6.

that our disposition is all for peace with unity for its sole object, and that we are full of zeal for the right faith. For we, whether we suffered persecutions, or afflictions, or the threats of emperors, or the cruelties of princes or any other trial at the hands of heretics, have undergone all for the sake of the evangelic faith, ratified by the three hundred and eighteen fathers at Nicæa in Bithynia. This is the faith which ought to be sufficient for you, for us, for all who wrest not the word of the true faith; for it is the ancient faith; it is the faith of our baptism; it is the faith that teaches us to believe in the name of the Father, of the Son, and of the Holy Ghost.

"According to this faith there is one Godhead, Power and Substance of the Father and of the Son and of the Holy Ghost; the dignity being equal, and the majesty being equal in three perfect essences[1] and three perfect persons.[2] Thus there is neither room for the heresy of Sabellius by the confusion of the essences or destruction of the individualities; thus the blasphemy of the Eunomians, of the Arians, and of the Pneumatomachi is nullified, which divides the substance, the nature and the godhead and superinduces on the uncreated consubstantial and co-eternal trinity a nature posterior, created and of a different substance. We moreover preserve unperverted the doctrine of the incarnation of the Lord, holding the tradition that the dispensation of the flesh is neither soulless nor mindless nor imperfect; and knowing full well that God's Word was perfect before the ages, and became perfect man in the last days for our salvation.

"Let this suffice for a summary of the doctrine which is fearlessly and frankly preached by us, and concerning which you will be able to be still further satisfied if you will deign to read the report of the synod of Antioch, and also that issued last year by the œcumenical council held at Constantinople, in which we have set forth our confession of the faith at greater length, and have appended an anathema against the heresies which innovators have recently inscribed.

"Now as to the particular administration of individual churches, an ancient custom, as you know, has obtained, confirmed by the enactment of the holy fathers at Nicæa, that, in every province, the bishops of the province, and, with their consent, the neighbouring bishops with them, should perform ordinations as expediency may require. In conforming with these customs note that other churches have been administered by us and the priests of the most famous churches publicly appointed. Accordingly over the new made (if the expression be allowable) church at Constantinople, which, as though from a lion's mouth, we have lately snatched by God's mercy from the blasphemy of the heretics, we have ordained bishop the right reverend and most religious Nectarius, in the presence of the œcumenical council, with common consent, before the most religious emperor Theodosius, and with the assent of all the clergy and of the whole city. And over the most ancient and truly apostolic church in Syria, where first the noble name of Christians[1] was given them, the bishops of the province and of the eastern diocese[2] have met together and canonically ordained bishop the right reverend and most religious Flavianus, with the consent of all the church, who as though with one voice joined in expressing their respect for him. This rightful ordination also received the sanction of the general council. Of the church at Jerusalem, mother of all the churches, we make known that the right reverend and most religious Cyril is bishop, who was some time ago canonically ordained by the bishops of the province, and has in several places fought a good fight against the Arians. We beseech your reverence to rejoice at what has thus been rightly and canonically settled by us, by the intervention of spiritual love and by the influence of the fear of the Lord, compelling the feelings of men, and making the edification of churches of more importance than individual grace or favour. Thus since among us there is agreement in the faith and Christian charity has been established, we shall cease to use the phrase condemned by the apostles, 'I am of Paul and I of Apollos and I of Cephas,'[3] and all appearing as Christ's, who in us is not divided, by God's grace we will keep the body of the church unrent, and will boldly stand at the judgment seat of the Lord."

These things they wrote against the madness of Arius, Aetius, and Eunomius; and moreover against Sabellius, Photinus, Marcellus, Paul of Samosata, and Macedonius. Similarly they openly condemned the innovation of Apollinarius in the phrase, "And we preserve the doctrine of the incarnation of the Lord, holding the tradition that the dispensation of the flesh is neither soulless, nor mindless, nor imperfect."

---

[1] ὑποστάσεσι.
[2] προσώποις.

[1] Acts xi. 26.
[2] Vide note on p. 53.
[3] I. Cor. i. 12.

CHAPTER X.

Synodical letter of Damasus bishop of Rome against Apollinarius and Timotheus.

WHEN the most praiseworthy Damasus had heard of the rise of this heresy, he proclaimed the condemnation not only of Apollinarius but also of Timotheus his follower. The letter in which he made this known to the bishops of the Eastern empire I have thought it well to insert in my history.

Letter of Damasus bishop of Rome.

"Most honourable sons: Inasmuch as your love renders to the apostolic see the reverence which is its due, accept the same in no niggard measure for yourselves.[1] For even though in the holy church in which the holy apostle sat, and taught us how it becomes us to manage the rudder which has been committed to us, we nevertheless confess ourselves to be unworthy of the honour, we yet on this very account strive by every means within our power if haply we may be able to achieve the glory of that blessedness. Know then that we have condemned Timotheus, the unhallowed, the disciple of Apollinarius the heretic, together with his impious doctrine, and are confident that for the future his remains will have no weight whatever. But if that old serpent, though smitten once and again, still revives to his own destruction, who though he exists without the church never ceases from the attempt by his deadly venom to overthrow certain unfaithful men, do you avoid it as you would a pest, mindful ever of the apostolic faith — that, I mean, which was set out in writing by the Fathers at Nicæa ; do you remain on steady ground, firm and unmoved in the faith, and henceforward suffer neither your clergy nor laity to listen to vain words and futile questions, for we have already given a form, that he who professes himself a Christian may keep it, the form delivered by the Apostles, as says St. Paul, 'if any one preach to you another gospel than that you have received let him be Anathema.'[2] For Christ the Son of God, our Lord, gave by his own passion abundant salvation to the race of men, that he might free from all sin the whole man involved in sin. If any one speaks of Christ as having had less of manhood or of Godhead, he is full of devils' spirits, and proclaims himself a child of hell.

"Why then do you again ask me for the condemnation of Timotheus? Here, by the judgment of the apostolic see, in the presence of Peter, bishop of Alexandria, he was condemned, together with his teacher, Apollinarius, who will also in the day of judgment undergo due punishment and torment. But if he succeeds in persuading some less stable men, as though having some hope, after by his confession changing the true hope which is in Christ, with him shall likewise perish whoever of set purpose withstands the order of the Church. May God keep you sound, most honoured sons."

The bishops assembled in great Rome also wrote other things against other heresies which I have thought it necessary to insert in my history.

CHAPTER XI.

A confession of the Catholic faith which Pope Damasus sent to Bishop Paulinus in Macedonia when he was at Thessalonica.

AFTER the Council of Nicæa there sprung up this error. Certain men ventured with profane mouths to say that the Holy Spirit is made through the Son. We therefore anathematize those who do not with all freedom preach that the Holy Spirit is of one and the same substance and power with the Father and the Son. In like manner we anathematize them that follow the error of Sabellius and say that the Father and the Son are the same. We anathematize Arius and Eunomius who with equal impiety, though with differences of phrase, maintain the Son and the Holy Spirit to be a creature. We anathematize the Macedonians who, produced from the root of Arius, have changed the name but not the impiety. We anathematize Photinus who, renewing the heresy of Ebion, confessed that our Lord Jesus Christ was only of Mary.[2] We anathematize them that main-

---

[1] This rendering seems the sense of the somewhat awkward Greek of the text, and obviates the necessity of adopting Valesius' conjecture that the "nobis" of the original Latin had been altered by a clerical error into "vobis." If we read nobis, we may translate "you shew it in no niggard measure to ourselves."
[2] Gal. i. 8.

[1] As to who this Paulinus was, and when this confession was sent to him, there has been some confusion. Theodoret has been supposed to write "bishop of Thessalonica," and then has been found fault with by Baronius for describing the Paulinus the Eustathian bishop of Antioch as of Thessalonica in order to conceal the fact of Damasus and the Antiochene Paulinus being in communion. But the patronage of this Paulinus by Damasus was notorious, and if Theodoret wanted to ignore it, he need not have inserted this document at all. But, as Valesius points out, all that Theodoret says is that Damasus sent it to bishop Paulinus, when he was at Thessalonica, and calls attention to the recognition of this by Baronius (ann. 378. 44). The letter is in the Holsteinian Collection, with the heading "Dilectissimo fratri Paulino Damasus." Paulinus was probably at Thessalonica on his way from Rome in 382.
[2] Photinus, the disciple of Marcellus of Ancyra, was condemned at the synod of Sirmium in 349. Dict. Christ. Ant. ("Sirmium, Councils of.") Sulpicius Severus writes (II. 52) "Photinus vero novam hæresim jam ante protulerat, a Sabellio quidem in unione dissentiens, sed initium Christi ex Maria prædicabat."

tain that there are two sons — one before the ages and another after the assumption of the flesh from Mary. We anathematize also all who maintain that the Word of God moved in human flesh instead of a reasonable soul. For this Word of God Himself was not in His own body instead of a reasonable and intellectual soul, but assumed and saved our soul, both reasonable and intellectual, without sin.[1] We anathematize also them that say that the Word of God is separated from the Father by extension and contraction, and blasphemously affirm that He is without essential being or is destined to die.

Them that have gone from churches to other churches we so far hold alien from our communion till they shall have returned to those cities in which they were first ordained.

If any one, when another has gone from place to place, has been ordained in his stead, let him who abandoned his own city be held deprived of his episcopal rank until such time as his successor shall rest in the Lord.

If any one denies that the Father is eternal and the Son eternal and the Holy Ghost eternal, let him be anathema.

If any one denies that the Son was begotten of the Father, that is of His divine substance, let him be anathema.

If any one denies that the Son of God is very God, omnipotent and omniscient, and equal to the Father, let him be anathema.

If any one says that the Son of God, living in the flesh when he was on the earth, was not in heaven and with the Father, let him be anathema.[2]

If any one says that in the Passion of the Cross the Son of God sustained its pain by Godhead, and not by reasonable soul and flesh which He had assumed in the form of a servant,[3] as saith the Holy Scripture, let him be anathema.

If any one denies that the Word of God suffered in the flesh and tasted death in the flesh, and was the first-born of the dead,[4] as the Son is life and giver of life, let him be anathema.

If any one deny that He sits on the right hand of the Father in the flesh which He assumed, and in which He shall come to judge quick and dead, let him be anathema.

If any one deny that the Holy Spirit is truly and absolutely of the Father, and that the Son is of the divine substance and very God of God,[1] let him be anathema.

If any one deny that the Holy Spirit is omnipotent, omniscient, and omnipresent, as also the Son of the Father, let him be anathema.

If any one say that the Holy Spirit is a created being or was made through the Son, let him be anathema.

If any one deny that the Father made all things visible and invisible, through the Son who was made Flesh, and the Holy Spirit, let him be anathema.

If any one deny one Godhead and power, one sovereignty and glory, one lordship, one kingdom, will and truth of the Father and of the Son and of the Holy Ghost, let him be anathema.

If any one deny three very persons of the Father and of the Son and of the Holy Ghost, living for ever, containing all things visible and invisible, omnipotent, judging all things, giving life to all things, creating all things and preserving all things,[2] let him be anathema.

If any one denies that the Holy Ghost is to be worshipped by all creation, as the Son, and as the Father, let him be anathema.

If any one shall think aright about the Father and the Son but does not hold aright about the Holy Ghost, anathema, because he is a heretic, for all the heretics who do not think aright about God the Son and about the Holy Ghost are convicted of being involved in the unbelief of the Jews and the heathen; and if any one shall divide Godhead, saying that the Father is God apart and the Son God, and the Holy Ghost God, and should persist that they are called Gods and not God, on account of the one Godhead and sovereignty which we believe and know there to be of the Father and of the Son and of the Holy Ghost — one God in three essences,[3] — or withdrawing the Son and the Holy Ghost so as to suggest that the Father alone is called God and believed in as one God, let him be anathema.

For the name of gods has been bestowed by God upon angels and all saints, but of the Father and of the Son and of the Holy Ghost on account of their one and equal Godhead, not the names of " gods " but the name of " our God " is predicated and proclaimed, that we may believe that we are baptized in Father and Son and Holy Ghost and not in the names of archangels or

---

[1] Vide note on Apollinarius, p. 132.
[2] John iii. 13.
[3] Phil. ii· 7.
[4] Coloss. i. 18. Rev. i. 5.

[1] Valesius supposes the Greek translator to have read *Deum verbum* for *Deum verum*, which is found in Col. Rom., and which I have followed.
[2] Latin, " Omnia quæ sunt salvanda salvantes."
[3] Θεὸν ἕνα ἐν τρισὶν ὑποστάσεσιν. The last three words are wanting in the Latin version.

angels, like the heretics or the Jews or foolish heathen.

This is the salvation of the Christians, that believing in the Trinity, that is in the Father and the Son and the Holy Ghost, and being baptized into the same one Godhead and power and divinity and substance, in Him we may trust.

These events happened during the life of Gratianus.

CHAPTER XII.

Of the death of Gratianus and the sovereignty of Maximus.

GRATIANUS in the midst of his successes in war and wise and prudent government ended his life by conspiracy.[1] He left no sons to inherit the empire, and a brother of the same name as their father, Valentinianus,[2] who was quite a youth. So Maximus,[3] in contempt of the youth of Valentinianus, seized the throne of the West.

CHAPTER XIII.

Of Justina, the wife of Valentinianus, and of her plot against Ambrosius.

AT this time Justina,[4] wife of Valentinianus the great, and mother of the young prince, made known to her son the seeds of the Arian teaching which she had long ago received. Well knowing the warmth of her consort's faith she had endeavoured to conceal her sentiments during the whole of his life, but perceiving that her son's character was gentle and docile, she took courage to bring her deceitful doctrine forward. The lad supposed his mother's counsels to be wise and beneficial, for nature so disposed the bait that he could not see the deadly hook below. He first communicated on the subject with Ambrosius, under the impression that, if he could persuade the bishop, he would be able without difficulty to prevail over the rest. Ambrosius, however, strove to remind him of his father's piety, and exhorted him to keep inviolate the heritage which he had received. He explained to him also how one doctrine differed from the other, how the one is in agreement with the teaching of the Lord and with the teaching of his apostles, while the other is totally opposed to it and at war with the code of the laws of the spirit.

The young man, as young men will, spurred on moreover by a mother herself the victim of deceit, not only did not assent to the arguments adduced, but lost his temper, and, in a passion, was for surrounding the approaches to the church with companies of legionaries and targeteers. When, however, he learnt that this illustrious champion was not in the least alarmed at his proceedings, for Ambrosius treated them all like the ghosts and hobgoblins with which some men try to frighten babies, he was exceedingly angry and publicly ordered him to depart from the church. "I shall not," said Ambrosius, "do so willingly. I will not yield the sheepfold to the wolves nor betray God's temple to blasphemers. If you wish to slay me drive your sword or your spear into me here within. I shall welcome such a death."[1]

CHAPTER XIV.

Of the information given by Maximus the tyrant to Valentinianus.

AFTER a considerable time Maximus[2] was informed of the attacks which were being made upon the loud-voiced herald of the truth, and he sent dispatches to Valentinianus charging him to put a stop to his war against true religion and exhorting him not to abandon his father's faith. In the event of his advice being disregarded he further threatened war, and confirmed what he wrote by what he did,[3] for he mustered his forces and marched for Milan where Valentinianus was then residing. When the latter heard of his approach he fled into Illyri-

---

[1] Gratianus made himself unpopular (i) by his excessive addiction to sport, playing the Commodus in the "Vivaria," when not even a Marcus Aurelius could have answered all the calls of the Empire. (Amm. xxxi. x. 19) and (ii) by affecting the society and customs of barbarians (Aur. Vict. xlvii. 6). The troops in Britain rose against him, gathered aid in the Low Countries, and defeated him near Paris. He fled to Lyons, where he was treacherously assassinated Aug. 25, 383. He was only twenty-four. (Soc. v. 11.)

[2] Valentinianus II., son of Valentinianus I. and Justina was born c. 371.

[3] Magnus Maximus reigned from 383 to 388. Like Theodosius, he was a Spaniard.

[4] Justina, left widow by Magnentius in 353, was married to Valentinian I. (we may dismiss the story of Socrates (iv. 31) that he legalized bigamy in order to marry her in the lifetime of Severa) probably in 368. Her first conflict with Ambrose was probably in 380 at Sirmium. On the murder of Gratian in 383 Maximus for four years left the young Valentinian in possession of Italy, in deference to the pleading of Ambrose. It was during this period, at Easter, 385, that Justina ungratefully attacked the bishop and demanded a church for Arian worship.

[1] This contest is described by Ambrose himself in letters to Valentinian and to his sister Marcellina, Epp. xx. xxi, and in the " Sermo de basilicis tradendis." On the apparent error of Gibbon in confusing the " vela " which were hung outside a building to mark it as claimed for the imperial property, with the state hangings of the emperor's seat inside, vide Dict. Christ. Biog. i. 95.

[2] After Easter, 387.

[3] The motives here stated seem to have had little to do with the march of Maximus over the Alps. Indeed so far from enthusiasm for Ambrose and the Ambrosian view of the faith being conspicuous in the invader, he had received the bishop at Treves as envoy from Valentinian, had refused to be diverted from his purpose, and had moreover taken offence at the objection of Ambrose to communicate with the bishops who had been concerned in the first capital punishment of a heretic — i.e. Priscillian.

cum.[1] He had learnt by experience what good he had got by following his mother's advice.

CHAPTER XV.

Of the Letter written by the Emperor Theodosius concerning the same.

WHEN the illustrious emperor Theodosius had heard of the emperor's doings and what the tyrant Maximus had written to him, he wrote to the fugitive youth to this effect: You must not be astonished if to you has come panic and to your enemy victory; for you have been fighting against piety, and he on its side. You abandoned it, and are running away naked. He in its panoply is getting the mastery of you stripped bare of it, for He who hath given us the law of true religion is ever on its side.

So wrote Theodosius when he was yet afar off, but when he had heard of Valentinian's flight, and had come to his aid, and saw him an exile, taking refuge in his own empire, his first thought was to give succour to his soul, drive out the intruding pestilence of impiety, and win him back to the true religion of his fathers. Then he bade him be of good cheer and marched against the tyrant. He gave the lad his empire again without loss of blood and slew Maximus. For he felt that he should be guilty of wrong and should violate the terms of his treaty with Gratianus were he not to take vengeance on those who had caused his ally's death.[2]

CHAPTER XVI.

Of Amphilochius, bishop of Iconium.

ON the emperor's return the admirable Amphilochius, whom I have often mentioned, came to beg that the Arian congregations might be expelled from the cities. The emperor thought the petition too severe, and refused it. The very wise Amphilochius at the moment was silent, for he had hit upon a memorable device. The next time he entered the Palace and beheld standing at the emperor's side his son Arcadius, who had lately been appointed emperor, he saluted Theodosius as was his wont, but did no honour to Arcadius. The emperor, thinking that this neglect was due to forgetfulness, commanded Amphilochius to approach and to salute his son. "Sir," said he, "the honour which I have paid you is enough." Theodosius was indignant at the discourtesy, and said, "Dishonour done to my son is a rudeness to myself." Then, and not till then, the very wise Amphilochius disclosed the object of his conduct, and said with a loud voice, "You see, sir, that you do not brook dishonour done your son, and are bitterly angry with those who are rude to him. Believe then that the God of all the world abominates them that blaspheme the Only begotten Son, and hates them as ungrateful to their Saviour and Benefactor."

Then the emperor understood the bishop's drift, and admired both what he had done and what he had said. Without further delay he put out an edict forbidding the congregations of heretics.[1]

But to escape all the snares of the common enemy of mankind is no easy task. Often it happens that one who has kept clear of lascivious passion is fixed fast in the toils of avarice; and if he prove superior to greed there on the other side is the pitfall of envy, and even if he leap safe over this he will find a net of passion waiting for him on the other side.. Other innumerable stumbling blocks the enemy sets in men's paths, trying to catch them to their ruin.[2]

Then he has at his disposal the bodily passions to help the wiles which he lays against the soul. The mind alone, if it keep awake, gets the better of him, frustrating the assault of his devices by its inclination to what is Divine. Now, since this admirable emperor had his share of human nature,[3] and was not free from its emotions, his righteous anger passed the bounds of moderation, and caused the perpetration of a savage and lawless deed. I must tell this story for the sake of those into whose hands it will fall; it does not, indeed, only involve blame of the admirable emperor, but so redounds to his credit as to deserve to be remembered.

---

[1] Valentinian and his mother fled to Thessalonica.

[2] Zosimus (iv. 44) represents Theodosius, now for two years widowed, as won over to the cause of Valentinian by the loveliness of the young princess Galla, whom he married. "He was some time in preparing for the campaign, but, when it was opened, he conducted it with vigour and decision. His troops passed up the Save Valley, defeated those of Maximus in two engagements, entered Æmona (Laybach) in triumph, and soon stood before the walls of Aquileia, behind which Maximus was sheltering himself. . . . The soldiers of Theodosius poured into the city, of which the gates had been opened to them by the mutineers, and dragged off the usurper, barefooted, with tied hands, in slave's attire, to the tribunal of Theodosius and his young brother in law at the third milestone from the city. After Theodosius had in a short harangue reproached him with the evil deeds which he had wrought against the Roman Commonwealth, he handed him over to the executioner." Hodgkin, "Dynasty of Theodosius," p. 127.

[1] Arcadius was declared Augustus early in 383 (Clinton Fast. Rome, I. p. 504). Theodosius issued his edict against the heretics in September of same year. Sozomen (7. 6) tells the story of an anonymous old man, priest of an obscure city, simple and unworldly; "this," remarks Bishop Lightfoot (Dic. Christ. Biog. i. 106), "is as unlike Amphilochius as it can possibly be."

[2] "ἀγρεύων." cf. Mark xii. 13.

[3] "Irasci sane rebus indignis, sed flecti cito." Aur. Vict. xlviii.

CHAPTER XVII.

Of the massacre of Thessalonica; the boldness of Bishop Ambrosius, and the piety of the Emperor.

THESSALONICA is a large and very populous city, belonging to Macedonia, but the capital of Thessaly and Achaia, as well as of many other provinces which are governed by the prefect of Illyricum. Here arose a great sedition, and several of the magistrates were stoned and violently treated.[1]

The emperor was fired with anger when he heard the news, and unable to endure the rush of his passion, did not even check its onset by the curb of reason, but allowed his rage to be the minister of his vengeance. When the imperial passion had received its authority, as though itself an independent prince, it broke the bonds and yoke of reason, unsheathed swords of injustice right and left without distinction, and slew innocent and guilty together. No trial preceded the sentence. No condemnation was passed on the perpetrators of the crimes. Multitudes were mowed down like ears of corn in harvest-tide. It is said that seven thousand perished.

News of this lamentable calamity reached Ambrosius. The emperor on his arrival at Milan wished according to custom to enter the church. Ambrosius met him outside the outer porch and forbade him to step over the sacred threshold. "You seem, sir, not to know," said he, "the magnitude of the bloody deed that has been done. Your rage has subsided, but your reason has not yet recognised the character of the deed. Peradventure your Imperial power prevents your recognising the sin, and power stands in the light of reason. We must however know how our nature passes away and is subject to death; we must know the ancestral dust from which we sprang, and to which we are swiftly returning. We must not because we are dazzled by the sheen of the purple fail to see the weakness of the body that it robes. You are a sovereign, Sir, of men of like nature with your own, and who are in truth your fellow slaves; for there is one Lord and Sovereign of mankind, Creator of the Universe. With what eyes then will you look on the temple of our common Lord — with what feet will you tread that holy threshold, how will you stretch forth your hands still dripping with the blood of unjust slaughter? How in such hands will you receive the all holy Body of the Lord? How will you who in your rage unrighteously poured forth so much blood lift to your lips the precious Blood? Begone. Attempt not to add another crime to that which you have committed. Submit to the restriction to which the God the Lord of all agrees that you be sentenced. He will be your physician, He will give you health."[1]

Educated as he had been in the sacred oracles, Theodosius knew clearly what belonged to priests and what to emperors. He therefore bowed to the rebuke of Ambrose, and retired sighing and weeping to the palace. After a considerable time, when eight months had passed away, the festival of our Saviour's birth came round and the emperor sat in his palace shedding a storm of tears.

Now Rufinus, at that time controller of the household,[2] and, from his familiarity with his imperial master, able to use great freedom of speech, approached and asked him why he wept. With a bitter groan and yet more abundant weeping "You are trifling, Rufinus," said the emperor, "because you do not feel my troubles. I am groaning and lamenting at the thought of my own calamity; for menials and for beggars the way into the church lies open; they can go in without fear, and put up their petitions to their own Lord. I dare not set my foot there, and besides this for me the door of heaven is shut, for I remember the voice of the Lord which plainly says, 'Whatsoever ye bind on earth shall have been bound in heaven.'"[3]

Rufinus replied "With your permission I will hasten to the bishop, and by my entreaties induce him to remit your penalty." "He will not yield" said the emperor. "I know the justice of the sentence passed by Ambrose, nor will he ever be moved by respect for my imperial power to transgress the law of God."

Rufinus urged his suit again and again, promising to win over Ambrosius; and at last the emperor commanded him to go with all despatch. Then, the victim of false

---

[1] "Botheric, the Gothic general, shut up in prison a certain scoundrel of a charioteer who had vilely insulted him. At the next races the mob of Thessalonica tumultuously demanded the charioteer's liberation and when Botheric refused rose in insurrection and slew both him and several magistrats of the City." Hodgkin 121. This was in 390.

[1] A well-known picture of Vandyke in the National Gallery, a copy with some variations of a larger picture at Vienna by Rubens, represents the famous scene of the excommunication of Theodosius.

[2] "μάγιστρος," i.e. "magister officiorum."

[3] Matt. xviii. 18. In its primary sense the binding and loosing of the Gospels is of course the binding and loosing of the great Jewish schools, i.e. prohibition and permission. The moral and spiritual binding and loosing of the scribe, to whom a key was given as a symbol of his authority to open the treasures of divine lore, has already in the time of Theodoret become the dooming or acquitting of a Janitor commanding the gate of a more material heaven.

hopes, Theodosius, in reliance on the promises of Rufinus, followed in person, himself.
No sooner did the divine Ambrose perceive
Rufinus than he exclaimed, "Rufinus, your
impudence matches a dog's, for you were
the adviser of this terrible slaughter; you
have wiped shame from your brow, and
guilty as you are of this mad outrage on the
image of God you stand here fearless, without a blush." Then Rufinus began to beg
and pray, and announced the speedy approach
of the emperor. Fired with divine zeal
the holy Ambrosius exclaimed "Rufinus,
I tell you beforehand; I shall prevent him
from crossing the sacred threshold. If he is
for changing his sovereign power into that
of a tyrant I too will gladly submit to a
violent death." On this Rufinus sent a
messenger to inform the emperor in what
mind the archbishop was, and exhorted him
to remain within the palace. Theodosius
had already reached the middle of the forum
when he received the message. "I will
go," said he, "and accept the disgrace I
deserve." He advanced to the sacred precincts but did not enter the holy building.
The archbishop was seated in the house of
salutation[1] and there the emperor approached
him and besought that his bonds might be
loosed.

"Your coming" said Ambrose "is the
coming of a tyrant. You are raging against
God; you are trampling on his laws."
"No," said Theodosius, "I do not attack
laws laid down. I do not seek wrongfully to
cross the sacred threshold; but I ask you to
loose my bond, to take into account the
mercy of our common Lord, and not to shut
against me a door which our master has
opened for all them that repent." The
archbishop replied "What repentance have
you shown since your tremendous crime?
You have inflicted wounds right hard to
heal; what salve have you applied?"
"Yours" said the emperor "is the duty
alike of pointing out and of mixing the salve.
It is for me to receive what is given me."
Then said the divine Ambrosius "You let
your passion minister justice, your passion
not your reason gives judgment. Put forth
therefore an edict which shall make the sentence of your passion null and void; let the
sentences which have been published inflicting death or confiscation be suspended for
thirty days awaiting the judgment of reason.
When the days shall have elapsed let them

that wrote the sentences exhibit their orders,
and then, and not till then, when passion has
calmed down, reason acting as sole judge
shall examine the sentences and will see
whether they be right or wrong. If it find
them wrong it will cancel the deeds; if they
be righteous it will confirm them, and the
interval of time will inflict no wrong on them
that have been rightly condemned."

This suggestion the emperor accepted and
thought it admirable. He ordered the edict
to be put out forthwith and gave it the
authority of his sign manual. On this the
divine Ambrosius loosed the bond.

Now the very faithful emperor came
boldly within the holy temple but did not
pray to his Lord standing, or even on his
knees, but lying prone upon the ground he
uttered David's cry "My soul cleaveth unto
the dust, quicken thou me according to thy
word."[1]

He plucked out his hair; he smote his
head; he besprinkled the ground with drops
of tears and prayed for pardon. When the
time came for him to bring his oblations to
the holy table, weeping all the while he
stood up and approached the sanctuary.[2]

After making his offering, as he was wont,
he remained within at the rail, but once
more the great Ambrosius kept not silence
and taught him the distinction of places.
First he asked him if he wanted anything;
and when the emperor said that he was
waiting for participation in the divine mysteries, Ambrose sent word to him by the
chief deacon and said, "The inner place,
sir, is open only to priests; to all the rest it
is inaccessible; go out and stand where
others stand; purple can make emperors, but
not priests." This instruction too the faithful
emperor most gladly received, and intimated in reply that it was not from any
audacity that he had remained within the
rails, but because he had understood that
this was the custom at Constantinople. "I
owe thanks," he added, "for being cured
too of this error."

So both the archbishop and the emperor
showed a mighty shining light of virtue.
Both to me are admirable; the former for
his brave words, the latter for his docility;

---

[1] Valesius says that this "house of salutation" according
to Scaliger was the episcopal hospitium or guest quarters. His
own opinion however is that it was the audience chamber or
chapter-house of the church where the bishop with his presbyters received the faithful who came to his church.

[1] Ps. cxix. 25.
[2] τῶν ἀνακτόρων. Ἀνάκτορον in classical Greek = temple or
shrine. e. g. Eur. And. 43 "Θέτιδος ἀνάκτορον." Archd.
Cheetham (Dict. Christ. Ant. i. 79), quoting Lobeck, says
"also the innermost recess of a temple." Eusebius (Orat.
ix) uses it of the great church built by Constantine at
Antioch. Theodoretus in the text applies it to "the innermost
recess," for Theodosius was already within the Church. The
sacrarium was in Greek commonly τὸ ἅγιον, or τὸ ἱερατεῖον.
The 31st canon of the first Council of Braga ordains "ingredi
sacrarium ad communicandum non liceat laicis nisi tantum
clericis."

the archbishop for the warmth of his zeal, and the prince for the purity of his faith.

On his return to Constantinople Theodosius kept within the bounds of piety which he had learnt from the great archbishop. For when the occasion of a feast brought him once again into the divine temple, after bringing his gifts to the holy table he straightway went out. The bishop at that time was Nectarius, and on his asking the emperor what could possibly be the reason of his not remaining within, Theodosius answered with a sigh " I have learnt after great difficulty the differences between an emperor and a priest. It is not easy to find a man capable of teaching me the truth. Ambrosius alone deserves the title of bishop."

So great is the gain of conviction when brought home by a man of bright and shining goodness.

CHAPTER XVIII.

Of the Empress Placilla.[1]

YET other opportunities of improvement lay within the emperor's reach, for his wife used constantly to put him in mind of the divine laws in which she had first carefully educated herself. In no way exalted by her imperial rank she was rather fired by it with greater longing for divine things. The greatness of the good gift given her made her love for Him who gave it all the greater, so she bestowed every kind of attention on the maimed and the mutilated, declining all aid from her household and her guards, herself visiting the houses where the sufferers lodged, and providing every one with what he required. She also went about the guest chambers of the churches and ministered to the wants of the sick, herself handling pots and pans, and tasting broth, now bringing in a dish and breaking bread and offering morsels, and washing out a cup and going through all the other duties which are supposed to be proper to servants and maids. To them who strove to restrain her from doing these things with her own hands she would say, " It befits a sovereign to distribute gold ; I, for the sovereign power that has been given me, am giving my own service to the Giver." To her husband, too, she was ever wont to say, " Husband, you ought

always to bethink you what you were once and what you have become now ; by keeping this constantly in mind you will never grow ungrateful to your benefactor, but will guide in accordance with law the empire bestowed upon you, and thus you will worship Him who gave it." By ever using language of this kind, she with fair and wholesome care, as it were, watered the seeds of virtue planted in her husband's heart.

She died before her husband, and not long after the time of her death events occurred which showed how well her husband loved her.

CHAPTER XIX.

Of the sedition of Antioch.[1]

IN consequence of his continual wars the emperor was compelled to impose heavy taxes on the cities of the empire.[2]

The city of Antioch refused to put up with the new tax, and when the people saw the victims of its exaction subjected to torture and indignity, then, in addition to the usual deeds which a mob is wont to do when it is seizing an opportunity for disorder, they pulled down the bronze statue of the illustrious Placilla, for so was the empress named, and dragged it over a great part of the town.[3] On being informed of these events the emperor, as was to be expected, was indignant. He then deprived the city of her privileges, and gave her dignity to her neighbour, with the idea that thus he could inflict on her the greatest indignity, for Antioch from the earliest times had had a rival in Laodicea.[4] He further threatened to burn and destroy the town and reduce it to the rank of a village. The magistrates however had arrested some men in the very act, and had put them to death before the tragedy came to the emperor's ears. All these orders had been given by the Emperor, but had not been carried out because of the restriction imposed by the edict which had been made by the advice of the great Ambrosius.[5] On the arrival of the commissioners who

---

[1] Valesius remarks on this " *Vera quidem sunt quæ de Flaccillæ Augustæ virtutibus hic refert Theodoretus. Sed nihil pertinent ad hunc locum ; nam Flaccilla diu ante cladem Thessalonicensium ex hac luce migraverat, et post ejus obitum Theodosius Gallam uxorem duxerat.*"

Ælia Flaccilla Augusta, Empress and Saint, is Plakilla in the Greek historians, Placidia in Philostorgius. She died at Scotumis in Thrace, Sept. 14, 385. The outbreak at Thessalonica occurred in 390.

[1] Flaccilla died, as has been said, in Sept. 385. The revolt at Thessalonica was in 390, and the disturbances at Antioch in 387. The chapters of Theodoret do not follow chronological order.

[2] More probably the money was wanted to defray the expenses of magnificent fêtes in honour of the young Arcadius, including a liberal donation to the army. On the whole incident see Chrysostom's famous *Homilies on the Statues.*

[3] The mob looted the baths, smashed the hanging lamps, attacked the prætorium, insulted the imperial portrait, and tore down the bronze statues of Theodosius and his deceased wife from their pedestals, and dragged them through the streets. A " whiff " of arrows from the guard calmed the oriental Paris of the 4th century.

[4] i.e. the Laodicea on the Syrian coast, so called after the mother of Seleucus Nicator, and now Latakia.

[5] Theodoret apparently refers to the advice given by Ambrosius after the massacre of Thessalonica, which, as we have said, took place three years *after* the insurrection at Antioch.

brought the emperor's threats, Elebichus, then a military commander, and Cæsarius prefect of the palace, styled by the Romans *magister officiorum*,[1] the whole population shuddered in consternation. But the athletes of virtue,[2] dwelling at the foot of the hill, of whom at that time there were many of the best, made many supplications and entreaties to the imperial officers. The most holy Macedonius, who was quite unversed in the things of this life, and altogether ignorant of the sacred oracles, living on the tops of the mountains, and night and day offering up pure prayers to the Saviour of all, was not in the least dismayed at the imperial violence, nor at all affected by the power of the commissioners. As they rode into the middle of the town he caught hold of one of them by the cloak and bade both of them dismount. At the sight of a little old man, clad in common rags, they were at first indignant, but some of those who were conducting them informed them of the high character of Macedonius, and then they sprang from their horses, caught hold of his knees, and asked his pardon. The old man, urged on by divine wisdom, spoke to them in the following terms: " Say, dear sirs, to the emperor ; you are not only an emperor, you are also a man. Bethink you, therefore, not only of your sovereignty, but also of your nature. You are a man, and you reign over your fellow men. Now the nature of man is formed after the image and likeness of God. Do not, therefore, thus savagely and cruelly order the massacre of God's image, for by punishing His image you will anger the Maker. Think how you are acting thus in your wrath for the sake of a brazen image. Now all who are endued with reason know how far a lifeless image is inferior to one alive and gifted with soul and sense. Take into account, too, that for one image of bronze we can easily make many more. Even you yourself cannot make one single hair of the slain."

After the good men had heard these words they reported them to the emperor, and quenched the flame of his rage. Instead of his threats he wrote a defence, and explained the cause of his anger. " It was not right," said he, " because I was in error, that indignity should be inflicted after her death on a woman so worthy of the highest praise. They that were aggrieved ought to have armed their anger against me." The emperor further added that he was grieved and distressed when he heard that some had been

executed by the magistrates. In relating these events I have had a twofold object. I did not think it right to leave in oblivion the boldness of the illustrious monk, and I wished to point out the advantage of the edict which was put out by the advice of the great Ambrosius.[1]

CHAPTER XX.

Of the destruction of the temples all over the Empire.

Now the right faithful emperor diverted his energies to resisting paganism, and published edicts in which he ordered the shrines of the idols to be destroyed. Constantine the Great, most worthy of all eulogy, was indeed the first to grace his empire with true religion ; and when he saw the world still given over to foolishness he issued a general prohibition against the offering of sacrifices to the idols. He had not, however, destroyed the temples, though he ordered them to be kept shut. His sons followed in their father's footsteps. Julian restored the false faith and rekindled the flame of the ancient fraud. On the accession of Jovian he once more placed an interdict on the worship of idols, and Valentinian the Great governed Europe with like laws. Valens, however, allowed every one else to worship any way they would and to honour their various objects of adoration. Against the champions of the Apostolic decrees alone he persisted in waging war. Accordingly during the whole period of his reign the altar fire was lit, libations and sacrifices were offered to idols, public feasts were celebrated in the forum, and votaries initiated in the orgies of Dionysus ran about in goat-skins, mangling hounds in Bacchic frenzy, and generally behaving in such a way as to show the iniquity of their master. When the right faithful Theodosius found all these evils he pulled them up by the roots, and consigned them to oblivion.[2]

CHAPTER XXI.

Of Marcellus, bishop of Apamea, and the idols' temples destroyed by him.

THE first of the bishops to put the edict in force and destroy the shrines in the city

---

[1] i.e. master of the household.
[2] i.e. the ascetic monks.

[1] cf. note on page 145.
Valesius remarks " *Longe hic fallitur Theodoretus quasi seditio Antiochena post Thessalonicensem cladem contigerit.*"
[2] " *Extat oratio Libanii ad imperatorem Theodosium pro templis in qua docet quomodo se gesserint imperatores Christiani erga paganos. Et Constantinum quidem Magnum ait duntaxat spoliasse templa, Constantium vero ejus filium prohibuisse Sacrificia : ejusque legem a secutis imperatoribus et ab ipsomet Theodosio esse observatam ; reliqua vera permissa fuisse paganis, id est turificationem et publicas epulas.*" Valesius.

committed to his care was Marcellus, trusting rather in God than in the hands of a multitude. The occurrence is remarkable, and I shall proceed to narrate it. On the death of John, bishop of Apamea, whom I have already mentioned, the divine Marcellus, fervent in spirit,[1] according to the apostolic law, was appointed in his stead.

Now there had arrived at Apamea the prefect of the East[2] with two tribunes and their troops. Fear of the troops kept the people quiet. An attempt was made to destroy the vast and magnificent shrine of Jupiter, but the building was so firm and solid that to break up its closely compacted stones seemed beyond the power of man; for they were huge and well and truly laid, and moreover clamped fast with iron and lead.[3]

When the divine Marcellus saw that the prefect was afraid to begin the attack, he sent him on to the rest of the towns, while he himself prayed to God to aid him in the work of destruction. Next morning there came uninvited to the bishop a man who was no builder, or mason, or artificer of any kind, but only a labourer who carried stones and timber on his back. "Give me," said he, "two workmen's pay; and I promise you I will easily destroy the temple." The holy bishop did as he was asked, and the following was the fellow's contrivance. Round the four sides of the temple went a portico united to it, and on which its upper story rested.[4] The columns were of great bulk, commensurate with the temple, each being sixteen cubits in circumference. The quality of the stone was exceptionally hard, and offering great resistance to the masons' tools. In each of these the man made an opening all round, propping up the superstructure with olive timber before he went on to another. After he had hollowed out three of the columns, he set fire to the timbers. But a black demon appeared and would not suffer the wood to be consumed, as it naturally would be, by the fire, and stayed the force of the flame. After the attempt had been made several times, and the plan was proved ineffectual, news of the failure was brought to the bishop, who was taking his noontide

sleep. Marcellus forthwith hurried to the church, ordered water to be poured into a pail, and placed the water upon the divine altar. Then, bending his head to the ground, he besought the loving Lord in no way to give in to the usurped power of the demon, but to lay bare its weakness and exhibit His own strength, lest unbelievers should henceforth find excuse for greater wrong. With these and other like words he made the sign of the cross over the water, and ordered Equitius, one of his deacons, who was armed with faith and enthusiasm, to take the water and sprinkle it in faith, and then apply the flame. His orders were obeyed, and the demon, unable to endure the approach of the water, fled. Then the fire, affected by its foe the water as though it had been oil, caught the wood, and consumed it in an instant. When their support had vanished the columns themselves fell down, and dragged other twelve with them. The side of the temple which was connected with the columns was dragged down by the violence of their fall, and carried away with them. The crash, which was tremendous, was heard throughout the town, and all ran to see the sight. No sooner did the multitude hear of the flight of the hostile demon than they broke out into a hymn of praise to God.

Other shrines were destroyed in like manner by this holy bishop. Though I have many other most admirable doings of this holy man to relate, — for he wrote letters to the victorious martyrs, and received replies from them, and himself won the martyr's crown, — for the present I hesitate to narrate them, lest by over prolixity I weary the patience of those into whose hands my history may fall.

I will therefore now pass to another subject.

CHAPTER XXII.

Of Theophilus, bishop of Alexandria, and what happened at the demolition of the idols in that city.

THE illustrious Athanasius was succeeded by the admirable Petrus, Petrus by Timotheus, and Timotheus by Theophilus, a man of sound wisdom and of a lofty courage.[1] By him Alexandria was set free from the error of idolatry; for, not content with razing the idols' temples to the ground, he exposed the tricks of the priests to the victims of their wiles. For they had constructed

---

[1] Romans xii. 11.

[2] Valesius points out that this was Cynegius, prefect of the East, who was sent by Theodosius to effect the closing of the idols' temples. cf. Zos: iv.

[3] καὶ σιδήρῳ καὶ μολίβδῳ προσδεδεμένοι. We are reminded of the huge cramps which must at one time have bound the stones of the Colosseum, — the ruins being pitted all over by the holes made by the middle-age pillagers who tore them away.

[4] I do not understand the description of this temple and its destruction precisely as Gibbon does. "διορύττων" does not seem to mean "undermining the foundations"; St. Matthew and St. Luke use it of the thieves who "dig through" or "break in." The word = dig through, and so into.

[1] "The perpetual enemy of peace and virtue." Gibbon. High office deteriorated his character. cf. Newman. Hist. Sketches iii.

statues of bronze and wood hollow within, and fastened the backs of them to the temple walls, leaving in these walls certain invisible openings. Then coming up from their secret chambers they got inside the statues, and through them gave any order they liked and the hearers, tricked and cheated, obeyed.[1] These tricks the wise Theophilus exposed to the people.

Moreover he went up into the temple of Serapis, which has been described by some as excelling in size and beauty all the temples in the world.[2] There he saw a huge image of which the bulk struck beholders with terror, increased by a lying report which got abroad that if any one approached it, there would be a great earthquake, and that all the people would be destroyed. The bishop looked on all these tales as the mere drivelling of tipsy old women, and in utter derision of the lifeless monster's enormous size, he told a man who had an axe to give Serapis a good blow with it.[3] No sooner had the man struck, than all the folk cried out, for they were afraid of the threatened catastrophe. Serapis however, who had received the blow, felt no pain, inasmuch as he was made of wood, and uttered never a word, since he was a lifeless block. His head was cut off, and forthwith out ran multitudes of mice, for the Egyptian god was a dwelling place for mice. Serapis was broken into small pieces of which some were committed to the flames, but his head was carried through all the town in sight of his worshippers, who mocked the weakness of him to whom they had bowed the knee.

Thus all over the world the shrines of the idols were destroyed.[4]

---

[1] In the museum at Naples is shewn part of a statue of Diana, found near the Forum at Pompeii. In the back of the head is a hole by means of a tube in connexion with which, — the image standing against a wall, — the priests were supposed to deliver the oracles of the Huntress-Maid.

It is curious to note that just at this period when the Pagan idols were destroyed, faint traces of image worship begin to appear in the Church. In another two centuries and a half it was becoming common, and in this particular point, Christianity relapsed into paganism. Littledale *Plain Reasons*, p. 47.

[2] "A great number of plates of different metals, artificially joined together, composed the majestic figure of the deity, who touched on either side the walls of the sanctuary. Serapis was distinguished from Jupiter by the basket or bushel which was placed on his head, and by the emblematic monster which he held in his right hand; the head and body of a serpent branching into three tails, which were again terminated by the triple heads of a dog, a lion, and a wolf." Gibbon, on the authority of Macrobius Sat. i. 20.

[3] Gibbon quotes the story of Augustus in Plin. Nat. Hist. xxxiii. 24. "Is it true," said the emperor to a veteran at whose home he supped, "that the man who gave the first blow to the golden statue of Anaitis was instantly deprived of his eyes and of his life?" "I was that man," replied the clear sighted veteran, "and you now sup on one of the legs of the goddess." cf. the account in Bede of the destruction by the priest Coify of the great image of the Saxon god at Goodmanham in Yorkshire.

[4] "Some twenty years before the Roman armies withdrew from Britain the triumph of Christianity was completed. Then a question occurs whether archæology casts any light on the discomfiture of Roman paganism in Britain. In proof of the affirmative a curious fact has been adduced, that the statues of pagan divinities discovered in Britain are al-

CHAPTER XXIII.

Of Flavianus bishop of Antioch and of the sedition which arose in the western Church on account of Paulinus.

AT Antioch the great Meletius had been succeeded by Flavianus who, together with Diodorus, had undergone great struggles for the salvation of the sheep. Paulinus had indeed desired to receive the bishopric, but he was withstood by the clergy on the ground that it was not right that Meletius at his death should be succeeded by one who did not share his opinions, and that to the care of the flock ought to be advanced he who was conspicuous for many toils, and had run the risk of many perils for the sheeps' sake. Thus a lasting hostility arose among the Romans and the Egyptians against the East, and the ill feeling was not even destroyed on the death of Paulinus. After him when Evagrius had occupied his see, hostility was still shewn to the great Flavianus, notwithstanding the fact that the promotion of Evagrius was a violation of the law of the Church, for he had been promoted by Paulinus alone in disregard of many canons. For a dying bishop is not permitted to ordain another to take his place, and all the bishops of a province are ordered to be convened; again no ordination of a bishop is permitted to take place without three bishops. Nevertheless they refused to take cognizance of any of these laws, embraced the communion of Evagrius, and filled the ears of the emperor with complaints against Flavianus, so that, being frequently importuned, he summoned him to Constantinople, and ordered him to repair to Rome.

Flavianus, however, urged in reply that it was now winter, and promised to obey the command in spring. He then returned home. But when the bishops of Rome, not only the admirable Damasus, but also Siricius his successor and Anastasius the successor of Siricius, importuned the emperor more vehemently and represented that, while he put down the rivals against his own authority, he suffered bold rebels against the laws of Christ to maintain their usurped authority, then he sent for him again and tried to force him to undertake the journey to Rome. On this Flavianus

---

ways or mostly broken. At Binchester, for instance, the Roman Vinovium, not far from Durham, there was found among the remains of an important Roman building a stone statue of the goddess Flora, with its legs broken, lying face downward across a drain as a support to the masonry above. It would certainly not be wise to press archæological facts too far; but the broken gods in Britain curiously tally with the edicts of Theodosius and the shattered Serapis at Alexandria." Hole *Early Missions*, p. 24.

in his great wisdom spoke very boldly, and said, " If, sir, there are some who accuse me of being unsound in the faith, or of life and conversation unworthy of the priesthood, I will accept my accusers themselves for judges, and will submit to whatever sentence they may give. But if they are contending about see and primacy I will not contest the point; I will not oppose those who wish to take them; I will give way and resign my bishopric. So, sir, give the episcopal throne of Antioch to whom you will."

The emperor admired his manliness and wisdom, and bade him go home again, and tend the church committed to his care.

After a considerable time had elapsed the emperor arrived at Rome, and once more encountered the charges advanced by the bishops on the ground that he was making no attempt to put down the tyranny of Flavianus. The emperor ordered them to set forth the nature of the tyranny, saying that he himself was Flavianus and had become his protector. The bishops rejoined that it was impossible for them to dispute with the emperor. He then exhorted them in future to join the churches in concord, put an end to the quarrel, and quench the fires of an useless controversy. Paulinus, he pointed out, had long since departed this life; Evagrius had been irregularly promoted; the eastern churches accepted Flavianus as their bishop. Not only the east but all Asia, Pontus, and Thrace were united in communion with him, and all Illyricum recognised his authority over the oriental bishops. In submission to these counsels the western bishops promised to bring their hostility to a close and to receive the envoys who should be sent them.

When Flavianus had been informed of this decision he despatched to Rome certain worthy bishops with presbyters and deacons of Antioch, giving the chief authority among them to Acacius bishop of Berœa, who was famous throughout the world. On the arrival of Acacius and his party at Rome they put an end to the protracted quarrel, and after a war of seventeen years[1] gave peace to the churches. When the Egyptians were informed of the reconciliation they too gave up their opposition, and gladly accepted the agreement which was made.

At that time Anastasius had been succeeded in the primacy of the Roman Church by Innocent, a man of prudence and ready wit. Theophilus, whom I have previously mentioned, held the see of Alexandria.[2]

[1] i.e. from 381, when Flavianus was appointed to the see of Antioch, to 398, the date of the mission of Acacius.
[2] vide Chap. xxii. He succeeded in July, 385.

CHAPTER XXIV.

Of the tyranny of Eugenius and the victory won through faith by the emperor Theodosius.

In this manner the peace of the churches was secured by the most religious emperor. Before the establishment of peace he had heard of the death of Valentinianus and of the usurpation of Eugenius and had marched for Europe.[1]

At this time there lived in Egypt[2] a man of the name of John, who had embraced the ascetic life. Being full of spiritual grace, he foretold many future events to persons who from time to time came to consult him. To him the Christ-loving emperor sent, in his anxiety to know whether he ought to make war against the tyrants. In the case of the former war he foretold a bloodless victory. In that of the second he predicted that the emperor would only win after a great slaughter. With this expectation the emperor set out, and, while drawing up his forces, shot down many of his opponents, but lost many of his barbarian allies.[3]

When his generals represented that the forces on their side were few and recommended him to allow some pause in the campaign, so as to muster an army at the beginning of spring and out-number the enemy, Theodosius refused to listen to their advice. " For it is wrong," said he, " to charge the Cross of Salvation with such infirmity, for it is the cross which leads our troops, and attribute such power to the image of Hercules which is at the head of the forces of our foe." Thus in right faith he spoke, though the men left him were few in number and much discouraged. Then when he had found a little oratory, on the top of the hill where his camp was pitched, he spent the whole night in prayer to the God of all.

About cock-crow sleep overcame him, and as he lay upon the ground he thought he saw

[1] Valentinian II. was strangled while bathing in the Rhone at Vienne, May 15, 392. Philost. xi. 1. cf. Soc. v. 25; Soz. vii. 22. Arbogastes, his Frankish Master of the Horse, who had instigated his murder, set up the pagan professor Eugenius to succeed him. Theodosius did not march to meet the murderer of his young brother-in-law till June, 394, and meanwhile his Empress Galla died, leaving a little daughter, Galla Placidia.
[2] i.e. at Lycopolis, the modern Siut, in the Thebaid. The envoy was the Eunuch Eutropius. Soz. vii. 22. Claud. i. 312.
[3] " Theodosius marched north-westwards, as before, up the valley of the Save, and to the city of Æmona." (Laybach.) " Not there did he meet his foes, but at a place about thirty miles off, half-way between Æmona and Aquileia, where the Julian Alps are crossed, and where a little stream called the Frigidus, (now the Wipbach, or Vipao) bursts suddenly from a limestone hill. Here the battle was joined between Eugenius and his Frankish patron and Theodosius with his 20,000 Gothic fœderati and the rest of the army of the East. Gainas, Saul, Bacurius, Alaric, were the chief leaders of the Teutonic troops. The first day of battle fell heavily on the fœderati of Theodosius, half of whom were left dead upon the field." Hodgkin *Dynasty of Theodosius*, p. 131. This was Sept. 5, 394.

two men in white raiment riding upon white horses, who bade him be of good cheer, drive away his fear, and at dawn arm and marshal his men for battle. "For," said they, "we have been sent to fight for you," and one said, "I am John the evangelist," and the other, "I am Philip the apostle."

After he had seen this vision the emperor ceased not his supplication, but pursued it with still greater eagerness. The vision was also seen by a soldier in the ranks who reported it to his centurion. The centurion brought him to the tribune, and the tribune to the general. The general supposed that he was relating something new, and reported the story to the emperor. Then said Theodosius, "Not for my sake has this vision been seen by this man, for I have put my trust in them that promised me the victory. But that none may have supposed me to have invented this vision, because of my eagerness for the battle, the protector of my empire has given the information to this man too, that he may bear witness to the truth of what I say when I tell you that first to me did our Lord vouchsafe this vision. Let us then fling aside our fear. Let us follow our front rank and our generals. Let none weigh the chance of victory by the number of the men engaged, but let every man bethink him of the power of the leaders."

He spoke in similar terms to his men, and after thus inspiring all his host with high hope, led them down from the crest of the hill. The tyrant saw the army coming to attack him from a distance, and then armed his forces and drew them up for battle. He himself remained on some elevated ground, and said that the emperor was desirous of death, and was coming into battle because he wished to be released from this present life : so he ordered his generals to bring him alive and in chains. When the forces were drawn up in battle array those of the enemy appeared by far the more numerous, and the tale of the emperor's troops might be easily told. But when both sides had begun to discharge their weapons the front rank proved their promises true. A violent wind blew right in the faces of the foe, and diverted their arrows and javelins and spears, so that no missile was of any use to them, and neither trooper nor archer nor spearman was able to inflict any damage upon the emperor's army. Vast clouds of dust, too, were carried into their faces, compelling them to shut their eyes and protect them from attack.

The imperial forces on the other hand did not receive the slightest injury from the storm, and vigorously attacked and slew the foe. The vanquished then recognised the divine help given to their conquerors, flung away their arms, and begged the emperor for quarter. Theodosius then yielded to their entreaty and had compassion on them, and ordered them to bring the tyrant immediately before him. Eugenius was ignorant of how the day had gone, and when he saw his men running up the hillock where he sat, all out of breath, and shewing their eagerness by their panting, he took them for messengers of victory, and asked if they had brought Theodosius in chains, as he had ordered. "No," said they, "we are not bringing him to you, but we are come to carry you off to him, for so the great Ruler has ordained." Even as they spoke they lifted him from his chariot, put chains upon him, and carried him off thus fettered, and led away the vain boaster of a short hour ago, now a prisoner of war.

The emperor reminded him of the wrongs he had done Valentinianus, of his usurped authority, and of the wars which he had waged against the rightful emperor. He ridiculed also the figure of Hercules and the foolish confidence it had inspired and at last pronounced the sentence of right and lawful punishment.

Such was Theodosius in peace and in war, ever asking and never refused the help of God.[1]

[1] Here was a crucial contest between paganism and Christianity, which might seem a "*nodus dignus vindice Deo.*" On the part played by storms in history vide note on page 103. Claudian, a pagan, was content to acknowledge the finger of providence in the rout of Eugenius, and, apostrophizing Honorius, exclaims

"*Te propter gelidis Aquilo de monte procellis*
Obruit adversas acies, revolutaque tela
Vertit in auctores, et turbine repulit hastas.
O nimium dilecte Deo, cui fundit ab antris
Æolus armatas hyemes; cui militat æther
Et conjurati veniunt ad classica venti." vii. 93.

Augustine says he heard of the "*revoluta tela*" from a soldier engaged in the battle. The appearance of St. John and St. Philip finds a pagan parallel in that of the "great twin brethren" at Lake Regillus.

"So like they were, no mortal
Might one from other know :
White as snow their armour was,
Their steeds were white as snow."

According to Spanish story St. James the Great fought on a milk-white charger, waving a white flag, at the battle of Clavijo, in 939. cf. Mrs. Jameson *Sacred and Legendary Art,* i. 234.

Sozomen (vii. 24) relates how at the very hour of the fight, at the church which Theodosius had built near Constantinople to enshrine the head of John the Baptist (cf. note on p. 96), a demoniac insulted the saint, taunting him with having had his head cut off, and said "you conquer me and ensnare my army." On this Jortin remarks "either the devil and Sozomen, or else Theodoret, seem to have made a mistake, for the two first ascribe the victory to John the Baptist and the third to John the Evangelist." *Remarks* ii. 165.

CHAPTER XXV.

Of the death of the Emperor Theodosius.[1]

AFTER this victory Theodosius fell sick and divided his empire between his sons, assigning to the elder the sovereignty which he had wielded himself and to the younger the throne of Europe.[2]

He charged both to hold fast to the true religion, " for by its means," said he, " peace is preserved, war is stopped, foes are routed, trophies are set up and victory is proclaimed." After giving this charge to his sons he died, leaving behind him imperishable fame.

His successors in the empire were also inheritors of his piety.

CHAPTER XXVI.

Of Honorius the emperor and Telemachus the monk.

HONORIUS, who inherited the empire of Europe, put a stop to the gladiatorial combats which had long been held at Rome. The occasion of his doing so arose from the following circumstance. A certain man of the name of Telemachus had embraced the ascetic life. He had set out from the East and for this reason had repaired to Rome. There, when the abominable spectacle was being exhibited, he went himself into the stadium, and, stepping down into the arena, endeavoured to stop the men who were wielding their weapons against one another. The spectators of the slaughter were indignant, and inspired by the mad fury of the demon who delights in those bloody deeds, stoned the peacemaker to death.

When the admirable emperor was informed of this he numbered Telemachus in the army of victorious martyrs, and put an end to that impious spectacle.

---

[1] Theodosius died of dropsy at Milan, Jan. 17, 395. " The character of Theodosius is one of the most perplexing in history. The church historians have hardly a word of blame for him except in the matter of the massacre of Thessalonica, and that seems to be almost atoned for in their eyes by its perpetrator's penitent submission to ecclesiastical censure. On the other hand the heathen historians, represented by Zosimus, condemn in the most unmeasured terms his insolence, his love of pleasure, his pride, and hint at the scandalous immorality of his life." " It is the fashion to call him the Great, and we may admit that he has as good a right to that title as Lewis XIV., a monarch whom in some respects he pretty closely resembles. But it seems to me that it would be safer to withhold this title from both sovereigns, and to call them not the Great, but the Magnificent." Hodgkin, *Dynasty of Theodosius.* 133.

The great champion of orthodoxy, he was no violent persecutor, and received at his death from a grateful paganism the official honours of apotheosis.

[2] Arcadius was now eighteen, and Honorius eleven. Arcadius reigned at Constantinople, the puppet of Rufinus, the Eunuch Eutropius, and his Empress, Eudoxia.

Honorius was established at Milan, till the approach of Alaric drove him to Ravenna. (402.)

CHAPTER XXVII.

Of the piety of the emperor Arcadius and the ordination of John Chrysostom.

ON the death at Constantinople of Nectarius, bishop of that see, Arcadius, who had succeeded to the Eastern empire, summoned John, the great luminary of the world. He had heard that he was numbered in the ranks of the presbyterate, and now issued orders to the assembled bishops to confer on him divine grace, and appoint him shepherd of that mighty city.[1]

This fact is alone sufficient to show the emperor's care for divine things. At the same time the see of Antioch was held by Flavianus, and that of Laodicea by Elpidius, who had formerly been the comrade of the great Meletius, and had received the impress of his life and conversation more plainly than wax takes the impression of a seal ring.[2]

He succeeded the great Pelagius;[3] and the divine Marcellus[4] was followed by the illustrious Agapetus[5] whom I have already described as conspicuous for high ascetic virtue. In the time of the tempest of heresy, of Seleucia ad Taurum, Maximus,[6] the companion of the great John, was bishop, and of Mopsuestia Theodorus,[7] both illustrious teachers. Conspicuous, too, in wisdom and character was the holy Acacius,[8] bishop of Berœa.

Leontius,[9] a shining example of many virtues, tended the flock of the Galatians.

---

[1] Nectarius died in Sept. 397, and John Chrysostom was appointed in Feb. 398. cf. Soc. vi. 2 and Soz. viii. 2.

" The only difficulty lay with Chrysostom himself and the people of Antioch. The double danger of a decided ' *nolo episcopari* ' on Chrysostom's part, and of a public commotion when the Antiocheans heard of the intention of robbing them of their favourite preacher was overcome by stratagem. Asterius, the *Comes Orientis*, in accordance with instructions received from Eutropius, induced Chrysostom to accompany him to a martyr's chapel outside the city walls. There he was apprehended by the officers of the government, and conveyed to Papae, the first post station on the road to Constantinople. His remonstrances were unheeded; his enquiries met with obstinate silence. Placed in a public chariot, and hurried on under a military escort from stage to stage, the 800 miles traversed with the utmost dispatch, the future bishop reached his imperial see a closely guarded prisoner. However unwelcome the dignity thrust on him was, Chrysostom, knowing that resistance was useless, felt it more dignified to submit without further struggle."

. . . .

" Chrysostom was consecrated February 26th A.D. 398, in the presence of a vast multitude assembled not only to witness the ceremony but also to listen to the inaugural sermon of one of whose eloquence they had heard so much. This ' *sermo enthronisticus* ' is lost." Dict. Christ. Biog. s. v. " Chrysostom."

[2] Elpidius, possibly a kind of domestic chaplain (συσκηνος) to Meletius, was afterwards a warm friend and advocate of Chrysostom. In 406 he was deposed and imprisoned for three years, and not restored till 414.

[3] Vide note on p. 115.

[4] Marcellus was bishop of Apamea.

[5] Succeeded his brother Marcellus in 398. cf. note on p. 128 and Relig. Hist. 3.

[6] Soc. vi. 3; Soz. viii, 2.   [7] Vide p. 159.   [8] Vide p. 128.

[9] Of Ancyra cf. Soz. vi, 18; and viii, 30.

CHAPTER XXVIII.

Of John's boldness for God.

WHEN the great John had received the tiller of the Church, he boldly convicted certain wrong doers, made seasonable exhortations to the emperor and empress, and admonished the clergy to live according to the laws laid down. Transgressors against these laws he forbade to approach the churches, urging that they who shewed no desire to live the life of true priests ought not to enjoy priestly honour. He acted with this care for the church not only in Constantinople, but throughout the whole of Thrace, which is divided into six provinces, and likewise of Asia, which is governed by eleven governors. Pontica too, which has a like number of rulers with Asia, was happily brought by him under the same discipline.[1]

CHAPTER XXIX.

Of the idol temples which were destroyed by John in Phœnicia.

ON receiving information that Phœnicia was still suffering from the madness of the demons' rites, John got together certain monks who were fired with divine zeal, armed them with imperial edicts and despatched them against the idols' shrines. The money which was required to pay the craftsmen and their assistants who were engaged in the work of destruction was not taken by John from imperial resources, but he persuaded certain wealthy and faithful women to make liberal contributions, pointing out to them how great would be the blessing their generosity would win.

Thus the remaining shrines of the demons were utterly destroyed.[2]

CHAPTER XXX.

Of the church of the Goths.

IT was perceived by John that the Scythians were involved in the Arian net; he therefore devised counter contrivances and discovered a means of winning them

over. Appointing presbyters and deacons and readers of the divine oracles who spoke the Scythian tongue, he assigned a church to them,[1] and by their means won many from their error. He used frequently himself to visit it and preach there, using an interpreter who was skilled in both languages, and he got other good speakers to do the same. This was his constant practice in the city, and many of those who had been deceived he rescued by pointing out to them the truth of the apostolic preaching.

CHAPTER XXXI.

Of his care for the Scythians and his zeal against the Marcionists.

ON learning that some of the Nomads encamped along the Danube were thirsty for salvation, but had none to bring them the stream, John sought out men who were filled with a love of labour like that which had distinguished the apostles, and gave them charge of the work. I have myself seen a letter written by him to Leontius, bishop of Ancyra, in which he described the conversion of the Scythians, and begged that fit men for their instruction might be sent.

On hearing that in our district[2] some men were infected with the plague of Marcion he wrote to the then bishop charging him to drive out the plague, and proffering him the aid of the imperial edicts. I have said enough to show how, to use the words of the divine apostle, he carried in his heart " the care of all the churches." [3]

His boldness may also be learnt from other sources.

CHAPTER XXXII.

Of the demand made by Gainas and of John Chrysostom's reply.

ONE Gainas, a Scythian, but still more barbarous in character, and of cruel and violent disposition, was at that time a military commander. He had under him many of his own fellow-countrymen, and with them commanded the Roman cavalry and infantry. He was an object of terror not only to all the rest but even to the emperor himself, who suspected him of aiming at usurpation.

He was a participator in the Arian pest, and requested the emperor to grant him the use of one of the churches. Arcadius replied that he would see to it and have it done. He then sent for the divine John, told him

---

[1] Valesius points out that those commentators have been in error who have supposed Theodoretus to be referring here to *ecclesiastical* divisions and officers.

Chrysostom is here distinctly described as asserting and exercising a jurisdiction over the civil " diœceses " of Pontica, Asia, and Thrace. But the quasi patriarchate was at this time only honorary. Only so late as at the recent council at Constantinople (381) had its bishop, previously under the metropolitan of Perinthus, been declared to rank next after the bishop of Rome, the metropolitans of Alexandria and Antioch standing next, but it was not till the Council of Chalcedon that the " diœceses " of Pontus, Asia, and Thrace were formally subjected to the see of Constantinople.

[2] The imperial edict for the destruction of the Phœnician Temples was obtained in 399.

[1] The Church of St. Paul. Hom. xii. pp. 512-526.
[2] *i.e.* at Cyrus.
[3] II. Cor. xi. 28.

of the request that had been made, reminded him of the power of Gainas, hinted at the usurpation which was being aimed at, and besought him to bridle the anger of the barbarian by this concession.[1] "But," said that noble man, "attempt, sir, no such promise, nor order what is holy to be given to the dogs.[2] I will never suffer the worshippers and praisers of the Divine Word to be expelled and their church to be given to them that blaspheme Him. Have no fear, sir, of that barbarian; call us both, me and him, before you; listen in silence to what is said, and I will both curb his tongue and persuade him not to ask what it is wrong to grant."

The emperor was delighted with what Chrysostom said, and on the next day summoned both the bishop and the general before him. Gainas began to request the fulfilment of the promise, but the great John said in reply that the emperor, who professed the true religion, had no right to venture on any act against it. Gainas rejoined that he also must have a place to pray in. "Why," said the great John, "every church is open to you, and nobody prevents you from praying there when you are so disposed." "But I," said Gainas, "belong to another sect, and I ask to have one church with them, and surely I who undergo so many toils in war for Romans may fairly make such a request." "But," said the bishop, "you have greater rewards for your labours, you are a general; you are vested in the consular robe, and you must consider what you were formerly and what you are now — your indigence in the past and your present prosperity; what kind of raiment you wore before you crossed the Ister, and what you are robed in now. Consider, I say, the littleness of your labours and the greatness of your rewards, and be not unthankful to them who have shewn you honour." With these words the teacher of the world silenced Gainas, and compelled him to stand dumb. In process of time, however, he made known the rebellion which he had long had at heart, gathered his forces in Thrace, and went out ravaging and plundering in very many directions. At news of this there arose an universal panic among both princes and subjects, and no one was found willing to march against him; no one thought it safe to approach him with an ambassage, for every one suspected his barbarous character.

CHAPTER XXXIII.

Of the ambassage of Chrysostom to Gainas.

THEN when every one else was passed over because of the universal panic, this great chief was persuaded to undertake the ambassage. He took no heed of the dispute which has been related, nor of the ill feeling which it had engendered, and readily set out for Thrace. No sooner did Gainas hear of the arrival of the envoy than he bethought him of the bold utterance which he had made on behalf of true religion. He came eagerly from a great distance to meet him, placed his right hand upon his eyes, and brought his children to his saintly knees. So is it the nature of goodness to put even those who are most opposed to it to the blush and vanquish them. But envy could not endure the bright rays of his philosophy. It put in practice its wonted wiles and deprived of his eloquence and his wisdom the imperial city — aye indeed the whole world.[1]

CHAPTER XXXIV.

Of the events which happened on account of Chrysostom.

AT this part of my history I know not what sentiments to entertain; wishful as I am to relate the wrong inflicted on Chrysostom, I yet regard in other respects the high character of those who wronged him. I shall therefore do my best to conceal even their names.[2] These persons had different reasons for their hostility, and were unwilling to contemplate his brilliant virtue. They found certain wretches who accused him, and, perceiving the openness of the calumny, held a meeting at a distance from the city and pronounced their sentence.[3]

The emperor, who had confidence in the clergy, ordered him to be banished. So Chrysostom, without having heard the charges brought against him, or brought forward his

---

[1] The three great officials, Aurelianus, Saturninus, and the Count John had already surrendered themselves to the arrogant Goth, and their lives had only been spared at the entreaty of Chrysostom.

[2] Matt. vii. 6.

[1] It is not clear where the mission of Chrysostom to Gainas should be placed. Gainas attacked the capital by sea and by land, but his Goths were massacred in their own church, and he was repulsed. He was finally defeated and slain in Jan. 401.

[2] The foes of Chrysostom were

(i) The empress Eudoxia, jealous of his power;

(ii) The great ladies on whose toilettes of artifice and extravagant licentiousness he had poured his scorn; among them being Marsa, Castricia, and Eugraphia;

(iii) The baser clergy whom his simplicity of life shamed. notably Acacius of Berœa, whose hostility is traced by Palladius to the meagre hospitality of the archiepiscopal palace at Constantinople, when the hungry guest exclaimed "ἐγὼ αὐτῷ ἀρτύω χύτραν" — "I'll pepper a pot for him!" (Pall. 49.) and Theophilus of Alexandria, who had never forgiven his elevation to the see, and Gerontius of Nicomedia whom he had deposed.

[3] i.e. at the suburb of Chalcedon known as "the Oak." The charges included his calling the Empress Jezebel, and eating a lozenge after the Holy Communion. Pallad. 66.

defence, was forced as though convicted on the accusations advanced against him to quit Constantinople,[1] and departed to Hieron at the mouth of the Euxine, for so the naval station is named.

In the night there was a great earthquake and the empress[2] was struck with terror. Envoys were accordingly sent at daybreak to the banished bishop beseeching him to return without delay to Constantinople, and avert the peril from the town. After these another party was sent and yet again others after them and the Bosphorus was crowded with the couriers. When the faithful people learned what was going on they covered the mouth of the Propontis with their boats, and the whole population lighted up waxen torches and came forth to meet him. For the time indeed his banded foes were scattered.[3]

But after the interval of a few months they endeavoured to enact punishment, not for the forged indictment, but for his taking part in divine service after his deposition. The bishop represented that he had not pleaded, that he had not heard the indictment, that he had made no defence, that he had been condemned in his absence, that he had been exiled by the emperor, and by the emperor again recalled. Then another Synod met, and his opponents did not ask for a trial, but persuaded the emperor that the sentence was lawful and right. Chrysostom was then not merely banished, but relegated to a petty and lonely town in Armenia of the name of Cucusus. Even from thence he was removed and deported to Pityus, a place at the extremity of the Euxine and on the marches of the Roman Empire, in the near neighbourhood of the wildest savages. But the loving Lord did not suffer the victorious athlete to be carried off to this islet, for when he had reached Comana he was removed to the life that knows nor age nor pain.[4]

The body that had struggled so bravely was buried by the side of the coffin of the martyred Basiliscus, for so the martyr had ordained in a dream.

I think it needless to prolong my narrative by relating how many bishops were expelled from the church on Chrysostom's account, and sent to live in the ends of the earth, or how many ascetic philosophers were involved in the same calamities, and all the more because I think it needful to curtail these hideous details, and to throw a veil over the ill deeds of men of the same faith as our own. Punishment however did fall on most of the guilty, and their sufferings were a means of good to the rest. This great wrong was regarded with special detestation by the bishops of Europe, who separated themselves from communion with the guilty parties. In this action they were joined by all the bishops of Illyria. In the East most of the cities shrank from participation in the wrong, but did not make a rent in the body of the church.

On the death of the great teacher of the world, the bishops of the West refused to embrace the communion of the bishops of Egypt, of the East, of the Bosphorus, and in Thrace, until the name of that holy man had been inserted among those of deceased bishops. Arsacius his immediate successor they declined to acknowledge, but Atticus the successor of Arsacius, after he had frequently solicited the boon of peace, was after a time received when he had inserted the name in the roll.[1]

CHAPTER XXXV.

Of Alexander, bishop of Antioch.

At this time the see of Alexandria was held by Cyril,[2] brother's son to Theophilus whom he succeeded; at the same time Jeru-

---

[1] For three days the people withstood his removal. At last he slipped out by a postern, and, when a nod would have roused rebellion, submitted to exile. But he was only deported a very little way.

[2] Eudoxia was the daughter of Banto, a Frankish general. Philostorgius (xi. 6), says that she "οὐ κατὰ τὴν τοῦ ἀνδρὸς διέκειτο νωθείαν, ἀλλ᾽ ἐνῆν αὐτῇ τοῦ βαρβαρικοῦ θράσους οὐκ ὀλίγον."

[3] The proceedings of "the Oak" were declared null and void, and the bishop was formally reinstated. 403.

[4] Theodoret omits the second offence to Eudoxia — his invectives on the dedication of her silver statue in front of St. Sophia in Sept. 403. (Soc. vi. 18. Soz. viii. 20.) "Once again Herodias runs wild; once again she dances; once again she is in a hurry to get the head of John on a charger." Or does the description of Herodias, and not Salome, as dancing, indicate that the calumnious sentence was not really uttered by Chrysostom, but said to have been uttered by informers whose knowledge of the Gospels was incomplete?

The discourse "in decollationem Baptistæ Joannis" is in Migne Vol. viii. 485, but it is generally rejected as spurious.

The circumstances of the deposition will be found in Palladius, and in Chrysostom's Ep. ad Innocent. The edict

was issued June 5, 404. Cucusus (cf. p. ii. 4) is on the borders of Cilicia and Armenia Minor. Gibbon says the three years spent here were the "most glorious of his life," so great was the influence he wielded.

In the winter of 405 he was driven with other fugitives from Cucusus through fear of Isaurian banditti, and fled some 60 miles to Arabissus. Early in 406 he returned. Eudoxia was dead († Oct. 4. 404) but other enemies were impatient at the old man's resistance to hardship. An Edict was procured transferring the exile to Pityus, in the N.E. corner of the Black Sea (now Soukoum in Transcaucasia) but Chrysostom's strength was unequal to the cruel hardships of the journey. Some five miles from Comana in Pontus (Tokat), clothed in white robes, he expired in the chapel of the martyred bishop Basiliskus, Sept. 14. 407. Basiliskus was martyred in 312.

[1] Atticus (Bp. of Constantinople 405-426) was forced by fear alike of the mob and the Emperor to consent to the restitution. His letters to Peter and Ædesius, deacon of Cyril of Alexandria, and Cyril's reply, (Niceph. xiv. 26-27) are interesting. Cyril "would as soon put the name of Judas on the rolls as that of Chrysostom." Dict. Christ. Biog. i. 209.

[2] Cyril occupied the Episcopal throne of Alexandria from 412 to 444. Theodoretus could not be expected to allude to the withdrawal of the Roman legions from Britain in 401, or the release of Britoins from their allegiance by Honorius in 410. The sack of Rome by the Goths in the latter year might have however claimed a passing notice.

salem was occupied by John [1] in succession to Cyril whom we have formerly mentioned. The Antiochenes were under the care of Alexander [2] whose life and conversation were of a piece with his episcopate. Before his consecration he passed his time in ascetic training and in hard bodily exercise. He was known as a noble champion, teaching by word and confirming the word by deed. His predecessor was Porphyrius who guided that church after Flavianus, and left behind him many memorials of his loving character.[3] He was also distinguished by intellectual power. The holy Alexander was specially rich in self discipline and philosophy; his life was one of poverty and self denial; his eloquence was copious and his other gifts were innumerable; by his advice and exhortation, the following of the great Eustathius which Paulinus, and after him Evagrius, had not permitted to be restored, was united to the rest of the body, and a festival was celebrated the like of which none had ever seen before. The bishop gathered all the faithful together, both clergy and laity, and marched with them to the assembly. The procession was accompanied by musicians; one hymn was sung by all in harmony, and thus he and his company went in procession from the western postern to the great church, filling the whole forum with people, and constituting a stream of thinking living beings like the Orontes in its course.

When this was seen by the Jews, by the victims of the Arian plague, and by the insignificant remnant of Pagans, they set up a groaning and wailing, and were distressed at seeing the rest of the rivers discharging their waters into the Church. By Alexander the name of the great John was first inscribed in the records [4] of the Church.

CHAPTER XXXVI.

Of the removal of the remains of John and of the faith of Theodosius and his sisters.

At a later time the actual remains of the great doctor were conveyed to the imperial city, and once again the faithful crowd turning the sea as it were into land by their close packed boats, covered the mouth of the Bosphorus towards the Propontis with their torches. The precious possession was brought into Constantinople by the present emperor,[1] who received the name of his grandfather and preserved his piety undefiled. After first gazing upon the bier he laid his head against it, and prayed for his parents and for pardon on them who had ignorantly sinned, for his parents had long ago been dead, leaving him an orphan in extreme youth, but the God of his fathers and of his forefathers permitted him not to suffer trial from his orphanhood, but provided for his nurture in piety, protected his empire from the assaults of sedition, and bridled rebellious hearts. Ever mindful of these blessings he honours his benefactor with hymns of praise. Associated with him in this divine worship are his sisters,[2] who have maintained virginity throughout their lives, thinking the study of the divine oracles [3] the greatest delight, and reckoning that riches beyond robbers' reach are to be found in ministering to the poor. The emperor himself was adorned by many graces, and not least by his kindness and clemency, an unruffled calm of soul and a faith as undefiled as it is notorious. Of this I will give an undeniable proof.

A certain ascetic somewhat rough of temper came to the emperor with a petition. He came several times without attaining his object, and at last excommunicated the emperor and left him under his ban. The faithful emperor returned to his palace, and as it was the time for the banquet, and his

---

[1] Of the five Johns more or less well known as bishop of Jerusalem this was the second—from 386 to 417. He is chiefly known to us from the severe criticisms of Jerome.

[2] Bp. from 413 to 421.

[3] Palladius (Dial. 143 et Seqq.) describes Porphyrius as a monster of frivolity, iniquity, and bitterness. It is interesting to hear both sides.

[4] Theodoret here uses the word δίπτυχον. Other words in use were ἱεραί, δέλτοι and κατάλογοι. The names engraved on these tablets were recited during the celebration of the Holy Eucharist. e. g. at Carthage in 411 we find it said of Cæcilianus: "*In ecclesia sumus in qua episcopatum gessit et diem obiit. Ejus nomen ad altare recitamus ejus memoriæ communicamus tanquam memoriæ fratris.*" (Dict. Christ. Ant. i. 561. Labbe ii. 1490.) Names were sometimes erased from unworthy motives. A survival of the use obtains in the English Church in the Prayer for the Church Militant, and more specifically in the recitation of names in the Bidding Prayer.

[1] Theodosius II. succeeded his father May 1, 408, at the age of eight. The translation of the remains of Chrysostom took place at the beginning of 438. Theodosius died in 450, and the phrase "ὁ νῦν βασιλεύων" thus limits the composition of the History. As however Theodoret does not continue his list of bishops of Rome after Cælestinus, who died in 440, we may conclude that the History was written in 438-439. But the mention of Isdigirdes II. in Chap. xxxviii. carries us somewhat further. Possibly the portions of the work were jotted down from time to time.

[2] Theodosius II. had four sisters, Flaccilla, Pulcheria, Arcadia, and Marina. Pulcheria was practically empress-regnant for a considerable period. She was only two years older than her brother, but was declared Augusta and empress July 14, 414, at the age of 15½. On his death in 450 she married Marcianus a general. Besides the relics of Chrysostom she translated in 446 those of the martyrs of Sebaste. Soz. ix. 2.

[3] "τὰ θεῖα λόγια." This is the common phrase in our author for the Holy Scriptures. According to the interpretation given by Schleiermacher and like theologians to the title of the work of Papias, "λογίων κυριακῶν ἐξηγήσεις" and to the passage of Eusebius (Ecc. Hist. iii. 39) in which Papias is quoted as saying that Matthew "Ἑβραΐδι διαλέκτῳ τὰ λόγια συνεγράψατο." Pulcheria and her sisters did not study the Scriptures, but only "the divine discourses," to the exclusion of anything that was not a discourse. cf. Salmon *Introduction to the N. T.* 4th Ed. pp. 95, 96, and Bp. Lightfoot's Essays in reply to the anonymous author of "Supernatural Religion." cf. Rom. iii. 21, Heb. v. 12, I. Pet. iv. 11, and Clem. ad Cor. liii. "For beloved you know, aye, and well know, the sacred Scriptures, and have pored over *the oracles of God.*"

guests were assembled, he said that he could not partake of the entertainment before the interdict was taken off. On this account he sent the most intimate of his suite to the bishop, beseeching him to order the imposer of the interdict to remove it. The bishop replied that an interdict ought not to be accepted from every one, and pronounced it not binding, but the emperor refused to accept this remission until the imposer of it had after much difficulty been discovered, and had restored the communion withdrawn. So obedient was he to divine laws.

In accordance with the same principles he ordered a complete destruction of the remains of the idolatrous shrines, that our posterity might be saved from the sight of even a trace of the ancient error, this being the motive which he expressed in the edict published on the subject. Of this good seed sown he is ever reaping the fruits, for he has the Lord of all on his side. So when Rhoïlas,[1] Prince of the Scythian Nomads, had crossed the Danube with a vast host and was ravaging and plundering Thrace, and was threatening to besiege the imperial city, and summarily seize it and deliver it to destruction, God smote him from on high with thunderbolt and storm, burning up the invader and destroying all his host. A similar providence was shewn, too, in the Persian war. The Persians received information that the Romans were occupied elsewhere, and so in violation of the treaty of Peace, marched against their neighbours, who found none to aid them under the attack, because, in reliance on the Peace, the emperor had despatched his generals and his men to other wars. Then the further march of the Persians was stayed by a very violent storm of rain and hail; their horses refused to advance; in twenty days they had not succeeded in advancing as many furlongs. Meanwhile the generals returned and mustered their troops.

In the former war, too, these same Persians, when besieging the emperor's eponymous city,[2] were providentially rendered ridiculous. For after Vararanes[3] had beset the aforesaid city for more than thirty days with all his forces, and had brought up many

helepoles, and employed innumerable engines, and built up lofty towers outside the wall, resistance was offered, and the assault of the attacking engines repelled, by the bishop Eunomius alone. Our men had refused to fight against the foe, and were shrinking from bringing aid to the besieged, when the bishop, by opposing himself to them, preserved the city from being taken. When one of the barbarian chieftains ventured on his wonted blasphemy, and with words like those of Rabshakeh and Sennacherib, madly threatened to burn the temple of God, the holy bishop could not endure his furious wrath, but himself commanded a balista,[1] which went by the name of the Apostle Thomas, to be set up upon the battlements, and a mighty stone to be adjusted to it. Then, in the name of the Lord who had been blasphemed, he gave the word to let go, — down crashed the stone on that impious chief and hit him on his wicked mouth, and crushed in his face, and broke his head in pieces, and sprinkled his brains upon the ground. When the commander of the army who had hoped to take the city saw what was done, he confessed himself beaten and withdrew, and in his alarm made peace.

Thus the universal sovereign protects the faithful emperor, for he clearly acknowledges whose slave he is, and performs fitting service to his Master.[2]

CHAPTER XXXVII.

Of Theodotus bishop of Antioch.

THEODOSIUS restored the relics of the great luminary of the world to the city which deeply regretted his loss. These events however happened later.[3]

Innocent the excellent bishop of Rome

---

[1] Supposed to be identified with Rogas, Rugilas, or Roas, a prince said by Priscus in his Hist. Goth. to have preceded Attila in the sovereignty of the Huns. cf. Soc. vii, 43.

[2] i.e. Rhœsina, or Theodosiopolis in Osrhoena, now Erzeroum.

[3] Vararanes V. son of Isdigirdes I. persecuted Christians in the beginning of the 5th c. cf. Soc. vii. 18. 20.

Sapor III. 385–390

Vararanes IV.	Isdigirdes I. 399–420.
390–399.	Vararanes V. 420–440.
	Isdigirdes II. 440–457.

[1] It is interesting to find in the fifth century an instance of the sacred nomenclature with which we have familiar instances in the "San Josef" and the "Salvador del mundo" of Cape St. Vincent, and the "Santa Anna" and "Santissima Trinidad" of Trafalgar. (Southey, *Life of Nelson*, Chap iv. and ix.) On the north side of Sebastopol there was an earthwork called "The Twelve Apostles." (Kinglake, *Crimea*, Vol. iv. p. 48.) St. Thomas was the supposed founder of the church of Edessa.

[2] This might have been written before the weaker elements in the character of Theodosius II. produced their most disastrous results. But he was not a satisfactory sovereign, nor a desirable champion of Christendom. In some respects like our Edward the Confessor and Henry VI. he had, in the words of Leo, "the heart of a priest as well as of an emperor." "He had fifteen prime ministers in twenty-five years, the last of whom, the Eunuch Chrysaphius, retained his power for the longest period. A.D. 443–450. During that time the empire was rapidly hurrying to destruction. The Vandals in Africa and the Huns under Attila in Europe were ravaging some of his fairest provinces while the emperor was attending to palace intrigues. . . . Chrysaphius made him favourable to Eutyches, and thus largely contributed to the establishment of the monophysite heresy." Dr. Stokes in Dict. Christ. Biog. iv. 966.

[3] This paragraph belongs more appropriately to the preceding chapter. The relics of Chrysostom were translated in 438.

was succeeded by Bonifacius, Bonifacius by Zosimus and Zosimus by Cælestinus.[1]

At Jerusalem after the admirable John the charge of the church was committed to Praylius, a man worthy of his name.[2]

At Antioch after the divine Alexander Theodotus, the pearl of purity, succeeded to the supremacy of the church, a man of conspicuous meekness and of exact regularity of life. By him the sect of Apollinarius was admitted to fellowship with the rest of the sheep on the earnest request of its members to be united with the flock. Many of them however continued marked by their former unsoundness.[3]

CHAPTER XXXVIII.

Of the persecutions in Persia and of them that were martyred there.

AT this time Isdigirdes,[4] King of the Persians, began to wage war against the churches and the circumstances which caused him so to do were as follows. A certain bishop, Abdas by name,[5] adorned with many virtues, was stirred with undue zeal and destroyed a Pyreum, Pyreum being the name given by the Persians to the temples of the fire which they regarded as their God.[6]

On being informed of this by the Magi Isdigirdes sent for Abdas and first in moderate language complained of what had taken place and ordered him to rebuild the Pyreum.

This the bishop, in reply, positively refused to do, and thereupon the king threatened to destroy all the churches, and in the end carried out all his threats, for first he gave orders for the execution of that holy man and then commanded the destruction of the churches. Now I am of opinion that to destroy the Pyreum was wrong and inexpedient, for not even the divine Apostle, when he came to Athens and saw the city wholly given to idolatry, destroyed any one of the altars which the Athenians honoured, but convicted them of their ignorance by his arguments, and made manifest the truth. But the refusal to rebuild the fallen temple, and the determination to choose death rather than so do, I greatly praise and honour, and count to be a deed worthy of the martyr's crown; for building a shrine in honour of the fire seems to me to be equivalent to adoring it.

From this beginning arose a tempest which stirred fierce and cruel waves against the nurslings of the true faith, and when thirty years had gone by the agitation still remained kept up by the Magi, as the sea is kept in commotion by the blasts of furious winds. Magi is the name given by the Persians to the worshippers of the sun and moon[1] but I have exposed their fabulous system in another treatise and have adduced solutions of their difficulties.

On the death of Isdigirdes, Vararanes, his son, inherited at once the kingdom and the war against the faith, and dying in his turn left them both together to his son.[2] To relate the various kinds of tortures and cruelties inflicted on the saints is no easy task. In some cases the hands were flayed, in others the back; of others they stripped the heads of skin from brow to beard; others were enveloped in split reeds with the cut part turned inwards and were surrounded with tight bandages from head to foot; then each of the reeds was dragged out by force, and, tearing away the adjacent portions of the skin, caused severe agony; pits were dug and carefully greased in which quantities of mice were put; then they let down the martyrs, bound hand and foot, so as not to be able to protect themselves from the animals, to be food for the mice, and the the mice, under stress of hunger, little by little devoured the flesh of the victims, causing them long and terrible suffering. By others sufferings were endured even more terrible than these, invented by the enemy of humanity and the opponent of the truth, but the courage of the martyrs was unbroken, and they hastened unbidden in their eagerness to win that death which ushers men into indestructible life.

---

[1] The accepted order is Innocent I. 402-417; Zosimus 417-418; Boniface I. 418-422; Cælestinus 422-432.

The decision of Honorius in favour of Bonifacius as against Eulalius, both elected by their respective supporters on the death of Zosimus in 418, marks an important point in the interference of temporal princes in the appointments of bishops of Rome. cf. Robertson, i. 498.

[2] Πραΰς = meek, gentle.

[3] Apollinarians survived the condemnation of Apollinarius at Constantinople in 381.

The unsoundness, i. e. the denial of the rational soul, and so of the perfect manhood of the Saviour, is discussed in Dial. I.

[4] Yezdegerd I. son of Sapor III. Vide note on p. 156.

[5] Abdas was bishop of Susa. In Soc. vii. 8 he is "bishop of Persia."

[6] The second of the six supreme councillors of Ahuramazda in the scheme of Zarathustra Spitama (Zoroaster) is Ardebehesht, light or lightness of any kind and representing the omnipresence of the good power. Hence sun, moon and stars are symbols of deity and the believer is enjoined to face fire or light in his worship. Temples and altars must be fed with holy fire. In their reverence for fire orthodox Parsees abstained from smoking, but alike of old and today they would deny the charge of worshipping fire in any other sense than as an honoured symbol.

[1] The word in the original is στοιχεῖα; on this Valesius annotates "This does not mean the four elements, for the Persian Magi did not worship the four elements but only fire and the sun and moon." In illustration of this use of the word he quotes Chrysostom. Hom. 58 in Matth.

ὁ γὰρ δαίμων ἐπὶ διαβολῇ τοῦ στοιχείου καὶ ἐπιτίθεται τοῖς ἀλοῦσι, καὶ ἀνίησιν αὐτοὺς κατὰ τοὺς τῆς σελήνης δρόμους; and St. Jerome Ep. ad Hedyb. 4 where he speaks of the days of the week as being described by the heathen " Idolorum *et elementorum nominibus.*"

[2] i. e. Isdigirdes II. 440-457.

Of these I will cite one or two to serve as examples of the courage of the rest. Among the noblest of the Persians was one called Hormisdas, by race an Achæmenid[1] and the son of a Prefect. On receiving information that he was a Christian the king summoned him and ordered him to abjure God his Saviour. He replied that the royal orders were neither right nor reasonable, " for he," so he went on, " who is taught to find no difficulty in spurning and denying the God of all, will haply the more easily despise a king who is a man of mortal nature; and if, sir, he who denies thy sovereignty is deserving of the severest punishment, how much more terrible a chastisement is not due to him who denies the Creator of the world?" The king ought to have admired the wisdom of what was said, but, instead of this, he stripped the noble athlete of his wealth and rank, and ordered him to go clad in nothing save a loin cloth, and drive the camels of the army. After some days had gone by, as he looked out of his chamber, he saw the excellent man scorched by the rays of the sun, and covered with dust, and he bethought him of his father's illustrious rank, and sent for him, and told him to put on a tunic of linen. Then thinking the toil he had suffered, and the kindness shewn him, had softened his heart, " Now at least," said he, "give over your opposition, and deny the carpenter's son." Full of holy zeal Hormisdas tore the tunic and flung it away saying, "If you think that this will make one give up the true faith, keep your present with your false belief." When the king saw how bold he was he drove him naked from the palace.

One Suenes, who owned a thousand slaves, resisted the King, and refused to deny his master. The King therefore asked him which of his slaves was the vilest, and to this slave handed over the ownership of all the rest, and gave him Suenes to be his slave. He also gave him in marriage Suenes' wife, supposing that thus he could bend the will of the champion of the truth. But he was disappointed, for he had built his house upon the rock.[2]

The king also seized and imprisoned a deacon of the name of Benjamin. After two years there came an envoy from Rome, to treat of other matters, who, when he was informed of this imprisonment, petitioned the king to release the deacon. The king ordered Benjamin to promise that he would

not attempt to teach the Christian religion to any of the Magi, and the envoy exhorted Benjamin to obey, but Benjamin, after he heard what the envoy had to say, replied, " It is impossible for me not to impart the light which I have received; for how great a penalty is due for the hiding of our talent is taught in the history of the holy gospels." [1] Up to this time the King had not been informed of this refusal and ordered him to be set free. Benjamin continued as he was wont seeking to catch them that were held down by the darkness of ignorance, and bringing them to the light of knowledge. After a year information of his conduct was given to the king, and he was summoned and ordered to deny Him whom he worshipped. He then asked the king " What punishment should be assigned to one who should desert his allegiance and prefer another?" " Death and torture," said the king. " How then" continued the wise deacon " should he be treated who abandons his Maker and Creator, makes a God of one of his fellow slaves, and offers to him the honour due to his Lord?" Then the king was moved with wrath, and had twenty reeds pointed, and driven into the nails of his hands and feet. When he saw that Benjamin took this torture for child's play, he pointed another reed and drove it into his privy part and by working it up and down caused unspeakable agony. After this torture the impious and savage tyrant ordered him to be impaled upon a stout knotted staff, and so the noble sufferer gave up the ghost.

Innumerable other similar deeds of violence were committed by these impious men, but we must not be astonished that the Lord of all endures their savagery and impiety, for indeed before the reign of Constantine the Great all the Roman emperors wreaked their wrath on the friends of the truth, and Diocletian, on the day of the Saviour's passion, destroyed the churches throughout the Roman Empire, but after nine years had gone by they rose again in bloom and beauty many times larger and more splendid than before, and he and his iniquity perished.[2]

These wars and the victory of the church had been predicted by the Lord, and the event teaches us that war brings us more blessing than peace. Peace makes us deli-

---

[1] Achæmenes was the name of the Grandfather of Cambyses, father of Cyrus, and also of a son of Darius, son of Hystaspes. Hence the Achæmenidæ were the noblest stock of Persia.
[2] Matt. vii. 24.

[1] Matt. xxv. 25.
[2] The edict of Diocletian against the Christians was issued on the feast of the Terminalia, Feb. 23, 303. Good Friday, here ἡ τοῦ σωτηρίου πάθους ἡμέρα, was commonly known as ἡμέρα τοῦ σταυροῦ, πάσχα σταυρώσιμον, and παρασκευή.
Tertullian speaks of its early observance as a general fast, and Eusebius confirms his testimony.

cate, easy and cowardly. War whets our courage and makes us despise this present world as passing away. But these are observations which we have often made in other writings.

CHAPTER XXXIX.

Of Theodorus, bishop of Mopsuestia.

WHEN the divine Theodorus was ruling the church of Antioch, Theodorus, bishop of Mopsuestia, a doctor of the whole church and successful combatant against every heretical phalanx, ended this life. He had enjoyed the teaching of the great Diodorus, and was the friend and fellow-worker of the holy John, for they both together benefited by the spiritual draughts given by Diodorus. Six-and-thirty years he had spent in his bishopric, fighting against the forces of Arius and Eunomius, struggling against the piratical band of Apollinarius, and finding the best pasture for God's sheep.[1] His brother Polychronius [2] was the excellent bishop of Apamea, a man gifted with great eloquence and of illustrious character.

I shall now make an end of my history, and shall entreat those who meet with it to requite my labour with their prayers. The narrative now embraces a period of 105 years, beginning from the Arian madness and ending with the death of the admirable Theodorus and Theodotus.[3] I will give a list of the bishops of great cities after the persecution.

List of the bishops of great cities.

Of Rome : —

Miltiades	. .	[Melchiades. 311–314]
Silvester	. . . . . .	[314–335]
Julius .	[337–352. Mark Jan. to Oct., 336]
Liberius	. . . .	[352–366]
Damasus	. . . .	[366–384]
Siricius	. . . .	[384–398]
Anastasius	. . . . . .	[398–401]
Innocentius	. . . . . .	[402–417]
Bonifacius	. . . . . .	[4][418–422]
Zosimus	. . . .	[417–418]
Cælestinus	. . . . . .	[422–432]

Of Antioch : —

Vitalius		[312–318]
Philogonius	Orthodox	[318–323]
Eustathius	. . . . . .	[1][325–328]
Eulalius		[2][328–330]
Euphronius		[3][330–332]
Placidus	Arians.	[332–342]
Stephanus		[342–348]
Leontius	. . . . .	[348–357]
Eudoxius		[357–359]
Meletius		[360 (died) 381]
Flavianus		[381–404]
Porphyrius	Orthodox.	[404–413]
Alexander		[413–419]
Theodotus	. . . . .	[419–429]
Paulinus III.	Eustathians.	[362–388]
Evagrius		[388–]

Of Alexandria : —

Peter	[301–312]
Achillas	[312–313]
Alexander	[313–326]
Athanasius	[326–341]
Gregory (Arian)	[341–347]
Athanasius	[347–356]
George (heretic)	[356–362]
Athanasius	[363–373]
Peter (disciple of Athanasius) .	[373–373]
Lucius (Arian)	[373–377]
Peter	[377–378]
Timothy	[378–385]
Theophilus	[385–412]
Cyril	[412–444]

Of Jerusalem : —

Macarius.	[324–336]
Maximus	[336–350]
Cyril	[350–388]
John	[388–416]
Praylius	[416–425]
Juvenalius	[425–458]

Of Constantinople : —

Alexander	[326–340]
Eusebius of Nicomedia (Arian)	[340–342]
Paul the Confessor . . .	[342–342]
Macedonius the enemy of the Holy Ghost	[342–360]
The impious Eudoxius . . .	[360–370]
Demophilus of Berœa in Thrace (heretic)	[370–]
Gregory of Nazianzus . . .	[4][380–381]
Nectarius	[381–398]
John Chrysostom	[398–404]
Arsacius	[404–406]
Atticus	[406–426]
Sissinnius	[426–428]

---

[1] Theodorus was born at Antioch in 350, consecrated bishop of Mopsuestia in 392, and died in 428 in Cilicia.

[2] The evidence is in favour of distinguishing this Polychronius from the monk described in the Religious History.

[3] "The date of the death of Theodotus is fixed for A.D. 429 by a passage of Theodoret's letter to Dioscorus, where, when speaking of his having taught for six years under him at Antioch, he refers to his blessed and holy memory, combined with one in his history, stating that the death of Theodore of Mopsuestia took place in the episcopate of Theodotus." Dict. Christ. Biog. iv. 983.

The last event referred to by Theodoretus seems to be the accession of Isdigirdes II. in 440. Vide pp. 155, 156.

[4] of. note on p. 156.

---

[1] Paulinus I. intervenes, 321–325.

[2] Paulinus II., 328–329, intervenes.

[3] On the difficulty of the Paulini, cf. Dict. of Christ. Biog. iv. 232 and ii. 322.

[4] Evagrius intervenes 370.

DIALOGUES

THE "ERANISTES"[1] OR "POLYMORPHUS"[2] OF THE BLESSED THEODORETUS, BISHOP OF CYRUS

PROLOGUE.

Some men, distinguished neither by family nor education, and without any of the honourable notoriety that comes of an upright life, are ambitious of achieving fame by wicked ways. Of these was the famous Alexander, the coppersmith,[3] a man of no sort of distinction at all, — no nobility of birth, no eloquence of speech, who never led a political party nor an army in the field; who never played the man in fight, but plied from day to day his ignominious craft, and won fame for nothing but his mad violence against Saint Paul.

Shimei,[4] again, an obscure person of servile rank, has become very renowned for his audacious attack on the holy David.

It is said too that the originator of the Manichæan heresy was a mere whipping-block of a slave, and, from love of notoriety, composed his execrable and superstitious writings.

The same line of conduct is pursued by many now, who after turning their backs on the honourable glory of virtue on account of the toil to be undergone ere it be won, purchase to themselves the notoriety that comes of shame and disgrace. For through eagerness to pose as champions of new doctrines they pick up and get together the impiety of many heresies, and compile this heresy of death.

Now I will endeavour briefly to dispute with them, with the double object of curing them, if I can, of their unsoundness, and of giving a word of warning to the whole. I call my work "Eranistes, or Polymorphus," for, after getting together from many unhappy sources their baleful doctrines, they produce their patchwork and incongruous conceit. For to call our Lord Christ God only is the way of Simon, of Cerdo, of Marcion,[1] and of others who share this abominable opinion.

The acknowledgment of His birth from a Virgin, but coupled with the assertion that this birth was merely a process of transition, and that God the Word took nothing of the Virgin's nature, is stolen from Valentinus and Bardesanes and the adherents of their fables.[2]

To call the godhead and the manhood of the Lord Christ one nature is the error filched from the follies of Apollinarius.[3]

Again the attribution of capacity of suffering to the divinity of the Christ is a theft from the blasphemy of Arius and Eunomius. Thus the main principle of their teaching is like beggars' gabardines — a cento of ill-matched rags.

So I call this work Eranistes or Polymorphus. I shall write it in the form of a dialogue with questions and answers, pro-

---

[1] ἔρανος — a meal to which every one contributes a share; a club feast, or pic-nic, and ἐρανιστής is in classical Greek a contributor to such a feast. But ἐρανίζω = (a) " contribute," and (β) "beg for contributions." So ἐρανιστής is by some rendered "beggar." The idea of Theodoretus seems rather that his worse character is a picker up of various scraps of heresy from different quarters, and this explanation of the name is borne out by his use of the cognate verb ἐρανίζομαι in reference to the selection by Audæus of some of the doctrines of Manes in Hist. iv. 9.

[2] Polymorphus = Multiform.

[3] II. Tim. iv. 14.

[4] II. Kings xvi. 5.

[1] Cerdo, the gnostic teacher of the middle of the 2nd c., and placed by Theodoretus (Hær. Fab. i. 24) in the reign of Antoninus, A.D. 138-161, is described by the Ps. Tertullian as denying that Christ came in the substance of the flesh, but in appearance only. According to Marcion the greater follower of Cerdo, Christ was not born at all, but came down from heaven to Capernaum A.D. 29, his body being an appearance and his death an illusion. Simon Magus, the "father of all heretics" of Irenæus (adv. Hær. pr. in lib. iii.) is apparently quoted rather as the supposed originator of Gnosticism, than from any definite knowledge of his tenets.

[2] Valentinus (taught at Rome c. 140) the arch-gnostic is identified with the doctrine of emanation. Bardesanes (Bar Daisan), who lived some thirty years later at Edessa, was a great leader of the Syrian school of oriental dualism. For mention of his son Harmonius vide Hist. p. 129.

[3] Condemned at Constantinople in 381.

positions, solutions, and antitheses, and all else that a dialogue ought to have. I shall not insert the names of the questioners and respondents in the body of the dialogue as did the wise Greeks of old, but I shall write them at the side at the beginning of the paragraphs. They, indeed, put their writings in the hands of readers highly and variously educated, and to whom literature was life. I, on the contrary, wish the reading of what I write, and the discovery of whatever good it may give, to be an easy task, even to the illiterate. This I think will be facilitated if the characters of the interlocutors are plainly shown by their names in the margin, so the disputant who argues on behalf of the apostolical decrees is called "Orthodoxos," and his opponent "Eranistes." A man who is fed by the charity of many we commonly call "Beggar;" a man who knows how to get money together we call a "Chrematistes." So we have given our disputant this name from his character and pursuits.

I beg that all those into whose hands my book may fall will lay aside all preconceived opinion and put the truth to the test. For clearness' sake I will divide my book into three dialogues. The first will contain the contention that the Godhead of the only-begotten Son is immutable. The second will by God's help show that the union of the Godhead and the manhood of the Lord Christ is without confusion. The third will contend for the impassibility of the divinity of our saviour. After these three disputations we will subjoin several others as it were to complete them, giving formal proof under each head, and making it perfectly plain that the apostles' doctrine is preserved by us.

DIALOGUE I.

THE IMMUTABLE.

Orthodoxos and Eranistes.

Orth. — Better were it for us to agree and abide by the apostolic doctrine in its purity. But since, I know not how, you have broken the harmony, and are now offering us new doctrines, let us, if you please, with no kind of quarrel, investigate the truth.

Eran. — We need no investigation, for we exactly hold the truth.

Orth. — This is what every heretic supposes. Aye, even Jews and Pagans reckon that they are defending the doctrines of the truth; and so also do not only the followers of Plato and Pythagoras, but Epicureans too,

and they that are wholly without God or belief. It becomes us, however, not to be the slaves of a priori assumption, but to search for the knowledge of the truth.

Eran. — I admit the force of what you say and am ready to act on your suggestion.

Orth. — Since then you have made no difficulty in yielding to this my preliminary exhortation, I ask you in the next place not to suffer the investigation of the truth to depend on the reasonings of men, but to track the footprints of the apostles and prophets, and saints who followed them. For so wayfarers when they wander from the high-road are wont to consider well the pathways, if haply they shew any prints of men or horses or asses or mules going this way or that, and when they find any such they trace the tracks as dogs do and leave them not till once more they are in the right road.

Eran. — So let us do. Lead on yourself, as you began the discussion.

Orth. — Let us, therefore, first make careful and thorough investigation into the divine names, — I mean substances, and essences, and persons, and proprieties, and let us learn and define how they differ the one from the other. Then let us thus handle afterwards what follows.

Eran. — You give us a very admirable and proper introduction to our argument. When these points are clear, our discussion will go forward without let or obstacle.

Orth. — Since we have decided then that this must be our course of procedure, tell me, my friend, do we acknowledge one substance of God, alike of Father and of the only begotten Son and of the Holy Ghost, as we have been taught by Holy Scripture, both Old and New, and by the Fathers in Council in Nicæa, or do we follow the blasphemy of Arius?

Eran. — We confess one substance of the Holy Trinity.

Orth. — And do we reckon hypostasis to signify anything else than substance, or do we take it for another name of substance?

Eran. — Is there any difference between substance and hypostasis?[1]

Orth. — In extra Christian philosophy there is not, for οὐσία signifies τὸ ὄν, that which is, and ὑπόστασις that which subsists. But according to the doctrine of the Fathers there is the same difference between οὐσία and ὑπόστασις as between the common and the particular, and the species and the individual.

Eran. — Tell me more clearly what is meant by race or kind, and species and individual.

---

[1] Cf. note p. 36, *History*.

Orth. — We speak of race or kind with regard to the animal, for it means many things at once. It indicates both the rational and the irrational; and again there are many species of irrational, creatures that fly, creatures that are amphibious, creatures that go on foot, and creatures that swim. And of these species each is marked by many subdivisions; of creatures that go on foot there is the lion, the leopard, the bull, and countless others. So, too, of flying creatures and the rest there are many species; yet all of them, though the species are the aforesaid, belong to one and the same animal race. Similarly the name man is the common name of mankind; for it means the Roman, the Athenian, the Persian, the Sauromatian,[1] the Egyptian, and, in a word, all who are human, but the name Paulus or Petrus does not signify what is common to the kind but some particular man; for no one on hearing of Paul turns in thought to Adam or Abraham or Jacob, but thinks of him alone whose name he has heard. But if he hears the word man simply, he does not fix his mind on the individual, but bethinks him of the Indian,[*] the Scythian, and the Massagete, and of all the race of men together, and we learn this not only from nature, but also from Holy Scripture, for God said, we read, "I will destroy man from the face of the earth,"[2] and this he spake of countless multitudes, and when more than two thousand and two hundred years had gone by after Adam, he brought universal destruction on men through the flood, and so the blessed David says: "Man that is in honour and understandeth not,"[3] accusing not one here nor one there, but all men in common. A thousand similar examples might be found, but we must not be tedious.

Eran. — The difference between the common and the proper is shewed clearly. Now let us return to discussion about οὐσία and ὑπόστασις.

Orth. — As then the name man is common to human nature, so we understand the divine substance to indicate the Holy Trinity; but the hypostasis denotes any person, as the Father, the Son and the Holy Ghost; for, following the definitions of the Holy Fathers, we say that hypostasis and individuality mean the same thing.

Eran. — We agree that this is so.

Orth. — Whatever then is predicated of the divine nature is common both to the Father, to the Son, and to the Holy Ghost, as for instance "God," "Lord," "Creator," "Almighty," and so forth.

Eran. — Without question these words are common to the Trinity.

Orth. — But all that naturally denotes the hypostasis ceases to be common to the Holy Trinity, and denotes the hypostasis to which it is proper, as, for instance, the names "Father," "Unbegotten," are peculiar to the Father; while again the names "Son," "Only Begotten," "God the Word," do not denote the Father, nor yet the Holy Ghost, but the Son, and the words "Holy Ghost," "Paraclete," naturally denote the hypostasis of the Spirit.

Eran. — But does not Holy Scripture call both the Father and the Son "Spirit"?

Orth. — Yes, it calls both the Father and the Son "Spirit," signifying by this term the incorporeal illimitable character of the divine nature. The Holy Scripture only calls the hypostasis of the Spirit "Holy Ghost."

Eran. — This is indisputable.

Orth. — Since then we assert that some terms are common to the Holy Trinity, and some peculiar to each hypostasis, do we assert the term "immutable" to be common to the substance or peculiar to any hypostasis?

Eran. — The term "immutable" is common to the Trinity, for it is impossible for part of the substance to be mutable and part immutable.

Orth. — You have well said, for as the term mortal is common to mankind, so are "immutable" and "invariable" to the Holy Trinity. So the only-begotten Son is immutable, as are both the Father that begat Him and the Holy Ghost.

Eran. — Immutable.

Orth. — How then do you advance the statement in the gospel "the word became flesh,"[1] and predicate mutation of the immutable nature?

Eran. — We assert Him to have been made flesh not by mutation, but as He Himself knows.

Orth. — If He is not said to have become flesh by taking flesh, one of two things must be asserted, either that he underwent the mutation into flesh, or was only so seen in appearance, and in reality was God without flesh.

Eran. — This is the doctrine of the disciples of Valentinus, Marcion, and of the Manichees. but we have been taught without dispute that the divine Word was made flesh.

---

[1] "*Sauromatas gentes Scytharum Græci vocant, quos Sarmatas Romani.*" Pliny iii.
[2] Gen. vi. 7.　　[3] Ps. xlix. 20.

[1] John i. 14.

Orth. — But in what sense do you mean "was made flesh"? "Took flesh," or "was changed into flesh"?

Eran. — As we have heard the evangelist say, "the word was made flesh."

Orth. — In what sense do you understand "was made"?

Eran. — He who underwent mutation into flesh was made flesh, and, as I said just now, as He knows. But we know that with Him all things are possible,[1] for He changed the water of the Nile into blood, and day into night, and made the sea dry land, and filled the dry wilderness with water, and we hear the prophet saying "Whatsoever the Lord pleased that did He in heaven, and in earth, in the seas and all deep places."[2]

Orth. — The creature is transformed by the Creator as He will, for it is mutable and obeys the nod of Him that fashioned it. But His nature is immutable and invariable, wherefore of the creature the prophet saith "He that maketh and transformeth all things."[3] But of the divine Word the great David says "Thou art the same and thy years shall not fail."[4] And again the same God says of Himself "For I am the Lord and I change not."[5]

Eran. — What is hidden ought not to "be enquired into."

Orth. — Nor yet what is plain to be altogether ignored.

Eran. — I am not aware of the manner of the incarnation. I have heard that the Word was made flesh.

Orth. — If He was made flesh by mutation He did not remain what He was before, and this is easily intelligible from several analogies. Sand, for instance, when it is subjected to heat, first becomes fluid, then is changed and congealed into glass, and at the time of the change alters its name, for it is no longer called sand but glass.

Eran. — So it is.

Orth. — And while we call the fruit of the vine grape, when once we have pressed it, we speak of it no longer as grape, but as wine.

Eran. — Certainly.

Orth. — And the wine itself, after it has undergone a change, it is our custom to name no longer wine, but vinegar.

Eran. — True.

Orth. — And similarly stone when burnt and in solution is no longer called stone, but lime. And innumerable other similar in-

stances might be found where mutation involves a change of name.

Eran. — Agreed.

Orth. — If therefore you assert that the Divine Word underwent the change in the flesh, why do you call Him God and not flesh? for change of name fits in with the alteration of nature. For if where the things which undergo change have some relation to their former condition (for there is a certain approximation of vinegar to wine and of wine to the fruit of the vine, and of glass to sand) they receive another name after their alteration, how, where the difference between them is infinite and as wide as that which divides a gnat from the whole visible and invisible creation (for so wide, nay much wider, is the difference between the nature of flesh and of Godhead) is it possible for the same name to obtain after the change?

Eran. — I have said more than once that He was made flesh not by mutation, but continuing still to be what He was, He was made what He was not.

Orth. — But unless this word " was made" becomes quite clear it suggests mutation and alteration, for unless He was made flesh by taking flesh He was made flesh by undergoing mutation.

Eran. — But the word "take" is your own invention. The Evangelist says the Word was made flesh.[1]

Orth. — You seem either to be ignorant of the sacred Scripture, or to do it wrong knowingly. Now if you are ignorant, I will teach you ; if you are doing wrong, I will convict you. Answer then ; do you acknowledge the teaching of the divine Paul to be of the Spirit?

Eran. — Certainly.

Orth. — And do you allow that the same Spirit wrought through both Evangelists and Apostles?

Eran. — Yes, for so have I learnt from the Apostolic Scripture "There are diversities of gifts but the same spirit,"[2] and again "All these things worketh that one and the selfsame spirit, dividing to every man severally as He will,"[3] and again "Having the same Spirit of the Faith."[4]

Orth. — Your introduction of the apostolic testimony is in season. If we assert that the instruction alike of the evangelists and of the apostles is of the same spirit, listen how the apostle interprets the words of the Gospel, for in the Epistle to the Hebrews he says, " Verily he took not on him the

[1] Matt. xix. 26. [2] Ps. cxxxv. 6.
[3] The reference in Schulze's edition is to Jeremiah x. 16, but here the Septuagint ὁ πλάσας τὰ πάντα does not bear out the point. The quotation is no doubt of Amos v. 8, where the LXX is ὁ ποιῶν πάντα καὶ μετασκευάζων.
[4] Ps. iii. 27. [5] Mal. iii. 6.

[1] John i. 14. [3] I. Cor. xii. 11.
[2] I. Cor. xii. 4. [4] II. Cor. iv. 13.

nature of angels, but he took on him the seed of Abraham."[1] Now tell me what you mean by the seed of Abraham. Was not that which was naturally proper to Abraham proper also to the seed of Abraham?

Eran. — No; not without exception, for Christ did no sin.

Orth.—Sin is not of nature, but of corrupt will.[2] On this very account, therefore, I did not say indefinitely what Abraham had, but what he had according to nature, that is to say, body and reasonable soul. Now tell me plainly; will you acknowledge that the seed of Abraham was endowed with body and reasonable soul? If not, in this point you agree with the ravings of Apollinarius. But I will compel you to confess this by other means. Tell me now; had the Jews a body and a reasonable soul?

Eran. — Of course they had.

Orth. — So when we hear the prophet saying, "But thou, Israel, art my servant, Jacob whom I have chosen, the seed of Abraham my friend,"[3] are we to understand the Jews to be bodies only? Are we not to understand them to be men consisting of bodies and souls?

Eran. — True.

Orth. — And the seed of Abraham not without soul nor yet intelligence, but with everything which characterizes the seed of Abraham?

Eran.—He who so says puts forward two sons.

Orth. — But he who says that the Divine Word is changed into the flesh does not even acknowledge one Son, for mere flesh by itself is not a son; but we confess one Son who took upon Him the seed of Abraham, according to the divine apostle, and wrought the salvation of mankind. But if you do not accept the apostolic preaching, say so openly.

Eran. — But we maintain that the utterances of the apostles are inconsistent, for there appears to be a certain inconsistency between " the Word was made flesh" and " took upon Him the seed of Abraham."

Orth.—It is because you lack intelligence, or because you are arguing for arguing's sake, that the consistent seems inconsistent. It does not so appear to men who use sound reasoning; for the divine apostle teaches that the Divine Word was made Flesh, not by mutation, but by taking on Him the seed

of Abraham. At the same time, too, he recalls the promise given to Abraham. Or do you not remember the promises given to the Patriarch by the God of the Universe?

Eran. — What promises?

Orth. — When He brought him out of his father's house, and ordered him to come into Palestine, did He not say to him " I will bless them that bless thee, and curse him that curseth thee, and in thy seed[1] shall all families of the earth be blessed "?

Eran. — I remember these promises.

Orth. — Remember, too, the covenants made by God with Isaac and Jacob, for He gave them, too, the same promises, confirming the former by the second and the third.

Eran. — I remember them too.

Orth. — It is in relation to these covenants that the divine apostle writes in his Epistle to the Galatians " Now to Abraham and his seed were the promises made." He saith not " seeds " as of many, but as of one . . . which is Christ,[2] very plainly showing that the manhood of Christ sprang from the seed of Abraham, and fulfilled the promise made to Abraham.

Eran. — So the apostle says.

Orth. — Enough has been said to remove all the controversy raised on this point. But I will nevertheless remind you of another prediction. The blessing given to the Patriarch Jacob and to his father and his grand father was given by him to his son Judah alone. He said " A Prince shall not fail Judah, nor a leader from his loins, until he shall have come to whom it is in store, and he is the expectation of the Gentiles."[3] Or do you not accept this prediction as spoken of the Saviour Christ?

Eran. — Jews give erroneous interpretations of prophecies of this kind, but I am a Christian; I trust in the Divine word; and I receive the prophecies without doubt.

Orth. — Since then you confess that you believe the prophecies and acknowledge the predictions have been divinely uttered about our Saviour, consider what follows as to the intention of the words of the apostle, for while pointing out that the promises made to the patriarchs have reached their fulfilment, he uttered those remarkable words[4] " He

---

[1] Heb. ii. 16.

[2] cf. Article ix. of the English Church. Sin is not a part of man's nature, but the fault or corruption of it. If in one sense the fallen Adam is the natural man, in a higher sense Christ, the Son of man, is the natural man; *i.e.* in Him the manhood is seen incorrupt. cf. p. 183 and note.

[3] Isaiah xli. 8.

[1] Gen. xii. 3. The lxx. has ἐνευλογηθήσονται ἐν σοί. In Acts iii. 25, it is τῷ σπέρματί σου: in Gal. iii. 8, ἐν σοί.

[2] Gal. iii. 16. There is here an omission of the four words " καὶ τῷ σπέρματί σου." Of the difficulty of the passage a full discussion will be found in Bishop Lightfoot's " *Galatians* " — page 141.

[3] Gen. xlix. 10. Here the text follows the Alexandrine Septuagint substituting ἕως ἂν ἔλθῃ ᾧ ἀπόκειται for ἕως ἂν ἔλθῃ τὰ ἀποκείμενα αὐτῷ.

The Vulgate runs " *Non auferetur sceptrum de Iuda, et dux de femore eius, donec veniat qui mittendus est et ipse erit expectatio gentium.*"

[4] Hebrews ii. 16.

took not on Him the nature of angels," all but saying the promise is true; the Lord has fulfilled His pledges; the fount of blessing is open to the gentiles; God had taken on Him the seed of Abraham; through it He brings about the promised salvation; through it He confirms the promise of the gentiles.

Eran. — The words of the Prophet fit in admirably with those of the apostle.

Orth. — So again the divine apostle, reminding us of the blessing of Judah, and pointing out how it received its fulfilment, exclaims [1] "For it is evident that our Lord sprang out of Judah." So too the Prophet [2] Micah and the evangelist [3] Matthew. For the former spoke his prediction, and the latter connects the prophecy with his narrative. What is extraordinary is that he says that the open enemies of the truth plainly told Herod that the Christ is born in Bethlehem, for it is written, he says, " And thou Bethlehem in the land of Judah art not the least among the Princes of Judah for out of thee shall come a Governor who shall rule my people Israel." [4] Now let us subjoin what the Jews in their malignity omitted and so made the witness imperfect. For the prophet, after saying " Out of thee shall he come forth unto me that is to be Ruler in Israel" adds " Whose goings forth have been of old, from everlasting." [5]

Eran. — You have done well in adducing the whole evidence of the Prophet, for he points out that He who was born in Bethlehem was God.

Orth. — Not God only but also Man; Man as sprung from Judah after the flesh and born in Bethlehem; and God as existing before the ages. For the words " Out of thee shall he come forth unto me that is to be Ruler," shew his birth after the flesh which has taken place in the last days; while the words " Whose goings forth have been of old, from everlasting" plainly proclaim His existence before the ages. In like manner also the divine apostle in his Epistle to the Romans bewailing the change to the worse of the ancient felicity of the Jews, and calling to mind their divine promises and legislation, goes on to say " Whose are the fathers, and of whom concerning the flesh Christ came, who is over all God blessed for ever Amen." [6] and in this same passage he exhibits Him both as Creator of all things and Lord and Ruler as God and as sprung from the Jews as man.

Eran. — Well; you have explained these passages, what should you say to the prophecy of Jeremiah? For this proclaims him to be God only.

Orth. — Of what prophecy do you speak?

Eran. — " This is our God and there shall none other be accounted of in comparison to him — he hath found out all the way of knowledge, and hath given it unto Jacob his servant and to Israel his beloved. Afterward did he shew himself upon earth and conversed with men." [1]

In these words the Prophet speaks neither of the flesh, nor of manhood, nor of man, but of God alone.

Orth. — What then is the good of reasoning? Do we say that the Divine nature is invisible? or do we dissent from the Apostle when he says [2] " Immortal, invisible, the only God."

Eran. — Indubitably the Divine nature is invisible.

Orth. — How then was it possible for the invisible nature to be seen without a body? Or do you not remember those words of the apostle in which he distinctly teaches the invisibility of the divine nature? He says " Whom no man hath seen nor can see." [3] If therefore the Divine Nature is invisible to men, and I will add too to Angels, tell me how he who cannot be seen or beheld was seen upon earth?

Eran. — The Prophet says [4] he was seen on the earth.

Orth. — And the apostle says [5] " Immortal, invisible, the only God " and [6] " Whom no man hath seen and can see."

Eran. — What then? is the Prophet lying?

Orth. — God forbid. Both utterances are the words of the Holy Ghost.

Eran. — Let us inquire then how the invisible was seen.

Orth. — Do not, I beg you, bring in human reason. I shall yield to scripture alone.

Eran. — You shall receive no argument unconfirmed by Holy Scripture, and if you bring me any solution of the question deduced from Holy Scripture I will receive it, and will in no wise gainsay it.

Orth. — You know how a moment ago we

---

[1] Hebrews vii. 14.   [4] Matthew ii. 6.
[2] Micah v. 2.   [5] Micah v. 2.
[3] Matthew ii. 5, 6.   [6] Romans ix. 5.

[1] Baruch, iii, 35, 37.
"The ascription of the prophecy of Baruch to Jeremiah may be explained by the fact that in the lxx Baruch was placed either before or after Lamentations, and was regarded in the early church as an appendix to, and of equal authority with, Jeremiah. It is so quoted by Irenaeus, Clemens Alexandrinus, and Tertullian."
Augustine de Civ. xviii, 33. quotes Baruch iii, 16. with the remark " *Hoc testimonium quidem non Hieremiæ sed Scribæ eius attribuunt qui vocabatur Baruch, sed Hieremiæ celebratius habetur.*"
[2] I. Tim. i. 17.   [4] Baruch iii. 38.   [6] I. Tim. vi. 16.
[3] I. Tim. vi. 16.   [5] I. Tim. i. 17.

made the word of the evangelist clear by means of the testimony of the apostle; and that the divine apostle showed us how the Word became Flesh, saying plainly " for verily He took not on Him the nature of angels but He took on Him the seed of Abraham." [1] The same teacher will teach us how the divine Word was seen upon the earth and dwelt among men.

Eran. — I submit to the words both of apostles and of prophets. Shew me then in accordance with your promise the interpretation of the prophecy.

Orth. — The divine apostle, writing to Timothy, also says " without controversy great is the mystery of godliness. God was manifest in the flesh, justified in the spirit, seen of angels, preached unto the Gentiles, believed on in the world, received up into glory." [2]

It is therefore plain that the divine nature is invisible, but the flesh visible, and that through the visible the invisible was seen, by its means working wonders and unveiling its own power, for with the hand He fashioned the sense of seeing and healed him that was blind from birth. Again He gave the power of hearing to the deaf, and loosed the fettered tongue, using his fingers for a tool and applying his spittle like some healing medicine. So again when He walked upon the sea He displayed the almighty power of the Godhead. Fitly, therefore, did the apostle say " God was manifest in the flesh." For through it appeared the invisible nature beheld by its means by the angel hosts, for " He was seen," he says, " of angels."

The nature then of bodiless beings has shared with us the enjoyment of this boon.

Eran. — Then did not the angels see God before the manifestation of the Saviour?

Orth. — The apostle says that He " was made manifest in the flesh and seen of angels."

Eran. — But the Lord said, " Take heed that ye despise not one of these little ones, for I say unto you that their angels do always behold the face of my Father which is in heaven." [3]

Orth. — But the Lord said again, " Not that any man hath seen the Father save he which is of God, he hath seen the Father." [1] Wherefore the evangelist plainly exclaims, " No man hath seen God at any time," [2] and confirms the word of the Lord, for he says, " The only begotten Son which is in the bosom of the Father He hath declared Him," and the great Moses, when he desired to see the invisible nature, heard the Lord God saying, " There shall no man see me and live." [3]

Eran. — How then are we to understand the words, " Their angels do always behold the face of my Father which is in heaven"?

Orth. — Just as we commonly understand what is said about men who have been supposed to see God.

Eran. — Pray make this plainer, for I do not understand. Can God be seen of men also?

Orth. — Certainly not.

Eran. — Yet we hear the divine scripture saying God appeared unto Abraham at the oak of Mamre; [4] and Isaiah says " I saw the Lord sitting upon a throne high and lifted up," [5] and the same thing is said by Micah, by Daniel and Ezekiel. And of the lawgiver Moses it is related that " The Lord spake to Moses face to face as a man speaketh unto his friend," [6] and the God of the universe Himself said, " With him will I speak mouth to mouth, even apparently and not in dark speeches." [7] What then shall we say; did they behold the divine nature?

Orth. — By no means, for God Himself said, " There shall no man see me and live."

Eran. — Then they who say that they have seen God are liars?

Orth. — God forbid — they saw what it was possible for them to see.

Eran. — Then the loving Lord accommodates his revelation to the capacity of them that see Him?

Orth. — Yes; and this He has shewn through the Prophet, " for I," He says, " have multiplied visions and by the hands of the Prophets was made like." [8] He does not say " was seen " but " was made like." And making like does not shew the very nature of the thing seen. For even the image of the emperor does not exhibit the emperor's nature, though it distinctly preserves his features.

Eran. — This is obscure and not suffi-

[1] Heb. ii. 16.

[2] I. Tim. iii. 16. Theodoretus shews no knowledge of the reading OC for O̅C̅ in this famous passage accepted by our revisers with the marginal comment " The word *God* in place of *He who* rests on no sufficient ancient evidence." Macedonius II, patriarch of Constantinople, is said to have been accused by his enemy the Emperor Anastasius of falsifying this particular passage. But if Theodoretus, who died c. 458, really wrote O̅C̅ copies of the Epistles containing this reading must have existed some half century before the dispute between Macedonius and Anastasius. Gregory of Nyssa also uses the passage as does Theodoretus; Greg. Nyss. cont. Eun. iv. 1. The accepted opinion now regards the Codex of Alexandrianus as reading ὅς.

[3] Matt. xviii. 10. Observe the omission of the words " In heaven," which A. V. inserts with ℵ B D, etc.

[1] John vi. 46.   [5] Isaiah vi. 1.
[2] John i. 18.   [6] Exodus xxxiii. 11.
[3] Exodus xxxiii. 20.   [7] Numbers xii. 8.
[4] Genesis xviii. 1. Sept.
[8] Hosea xii. 10. Sept. A. V. has " used similitudes."

ciently plain. Was not then the substance of God seen by them who beheld those revelations?

Orth. — No; for who is mad enough to dare to say so?

Eran. — But yet it is said that they saw.

Orth. — Yes; it is said; but we both in the exercise of reverent reason, and in reliance on the Divine utterances, which exclaim distinctly, " No man hath seen God at any time," affirm that they did not see the Divine Nature, but certain visions adapted to their capacity.

Eran. — So we say.

Orth. — So also then let us understand of the angels when we hear that they daily see the face of your Father.[1] For what they see is not the divine substance which cannot be circumscribed, comprehended, or apprehended, which embraces the universe, but some glory made commensurate with their nature.

Eran. — This is acknowledged.

Orth. — After the incarnation, however, He was seen also of angels, as the divine apostle says, not however by similitude of glory, but using the true and living covering of the flesh as a kind of screen. " God," he says, " was made manifest in the flesh, justified in the Spirit, seen of angels." [2]

Eran. — I accept this as Scripture, but I am not prepared to accept the novelties of phrase.

Orth. — What novelties of phrase have we introduced?

Eran. — That of the " screen." What Scripture calls the flesh of the Lord a screen?

Orth. — You do not seem to be a very diligent reader of your Bible; if you had been you would not have found fault with what we have said as in a figure. For first of all the fact that the divine apostle says that the invisible nature was made manifest through the flesh allows us to understand the flesh as a screen of the Godhead. Secondly, the divine apostle in his Epistle to the Hebrews, distinctly uses the phrase, for he says, " Having therefore, brethren, boldness to enter into the Holiest by the blood of Jesus by a new and living way, which he hath consecrated for us, through the veil, that is to say his flesh; and having an High Priest over the House of God. Coming with truth drawing near with a true heart in fulness of faith." [3]

Eran. — Your demonstration is unanswerable, for it is based on apostolic authority.

Orth. — Do not then charge us with innovation. We will adduce for you yet another prophetic authority, distinctly calling the Lord's flesh a robe and mantle.

Eran. — Should it not appear obscure and ambiguous we will say nothing against it, and be thankful for it.

Orth. — I will make you yourself testify to the truth of the promise. You know how the Patriarch Jacob, when he was addressing Judah, limited the sovereignty of Judah by the birth of the Lord.[1] " A prince shall not fail Judah, nor a leader from his loins until he shall have come to whom it is in store and he is the expectation of the Gentiles." You have already confessed that this prophecy was uttered about the saviour.

Eran. — I have.

Orth. — Remember then what follows; for he says " And unto him shall the gathering of the people be . . . he shall wash his robe in wine and his mantle in the blood of the grape." [2]

Eran. — The Patriarch spoke of garments, not of a body.

Orth. — Tell me, then, when or where he washed his cloak in the blood of the grape?

Eran. — Nay; tell me you when he reddened his body in it?

Orth. — Answer I beseech you more reverently.[3] Perhaps some of the uninitiated are within hearing.

Eran. — I will both hear and answer in mystic language.

Orth. — You know that the Lord called himself a vine?

Eran. — Yes I know that he said " I am the true vine." [4]

Orth. — Now what is the fruit of a vine called after it is pressed?

Eran. — It is called wine.

Orth. — When the soldiers wounded the Saviour's side with the spear, what did the evangelist say was poured out from it?

Eran. — Blood and water.[5]

Orth. — Well, then; he called the Saviour's blood blood of the grape, for if the Lord is called a vine, and the fruit of the vine wine, and from the Lord's side streams of blood and water flowed downwards over the rest of his body, fitly and appropriately the Patriarch foretells " He shall wash his robe in wine and his mantle in blood of the grape." For as we after the consecration call the mystic fruit of the vine

---

[1] Matthew xviii. 10.   [2] I. Tim. iii. 16.
[3] Hebrews x. 19-22. In iii. 607. ed. Migne this passage is quoted by Theodoret as in A. V.

[1] Gen. xlix. 10. Compare note on p. 6.
[2] Gen. xlix. 11.   [4] John xv. 1.
[3] μυστικωτερον.   [5] John xix. 34.

the Lord's blood, so he called the blood of the true vine blood of the grape.

Eran. — The point before us has been set forth in language at once mystical and clear.

Orth. — Although what has been said is enough for your faith, I will, for confirmation of the faith, give you yet another proof.

Eran. — I shall be grateful to you for so doing, for you will increase the favour done me.

Orth. — You know how God called His own body bread?

Eran. — Yes.

Orth. — And how in another place he called His flesh corn?

Eran. — Yes, I know. For I have heard Him saying " The hour is come that the Son of man should be glorified," [1] and " Except a corn of wheat fall into the ground and die, it abideth alone; but if it die it bringeth forth much fruit." [2]

Orth. — Yes; and in the giving of the mysteries He called the bread, body, and what had been mixed, blood.

Eran. — He so did.

Orth. — Yet naturally the body would properly be called body, and the blood, blood.

Eran. — Agreed.

Orth. — But our Saviour changed the names, and to His body gave the name of the symbol and to the symbol that of his body. So, after calling himself a vine, he spoke of the symbol as blood.

Eran. — True. But I am desirous of knowing the reason of the change of names.

Orth. — To them that are initiated in divine things the intention is plain. For he wished the partakers in the divine mysteries not to give heed to the nature of the visible objects, but, by means of the variation of the names, to believe the change wrought of grace. For He, we know, who spoke of his natural body as corn and bread, and, again, called Himself a vine, dignified the visible symbols by the appellation of the body and blood, not because He had changed their nature, but because to their nature He had added grace. [3]

Eran. — The mysteries are spoken of in mystic language, and there is a clear declaration of that which is not known to all.

Orth. — Since then it is agreed that the body of the Lord is called by the patriarch " robe" and " mantle " [1] and we have reached the discussion of the divine mysteries, tell me truly, of what do you understand the Holy Food to be a symbol and type? Of the godhead of the Lord Christ, or of His body and His blood?

Eran. — Plainly of those things of which they received the names.

Orth. — You mean of the body and of the blood?

Eran. — I do.

Orth. — You have spoken as a lover of truth should speak, for when the Lord had taken the symbol, He did not say " this is my godhead," but " this is my body;" and again " this is my blood" [2] and in another place " the bread that I will give is my flesh which I will give for the life of the world." [3]

Eran. — These words are true, for they are the divine oracles.

Orth. — If then they are true, I suppose the Lord had a body.

Eran. — No; for I maintain him to be bodiless.

Orth. — But you confess that He had a body?

Eran. — I say that the Word was made flesh, for so I have been taught.

Orth. — It seems, as the proverb has it, as if we are drawing water in a pail with a hole in it. [4] For after all our demonstrations and solutions of difficulties, you are bringing the same arguments round again.

Eran. — I am not giving you my arguments, but those of the gospels.

Orth. — And have I not given you the interpretation of the words of the gospels from those of prophets and apostles?

Eran. — They do not serve to clear up the point at issue.

Orth. — And yet we shewed how, being invisible, He was made manifest through flesh, and the relationship of this very flesh we have been taught by the sacred writers — " He took on Him the seed of Abraham." [5] And the Lord God said to the patriarch, " in thy seed shall all the nations of the earth be blessed," [6] and the apostle, " It is evident our Lord sprang out of Judah." [7] We adduced further several similar testimonies; but, since you are desirous of hearing yet others, listen to the apostle when he says, " For every high priest taken from among men is ordained that he may offer both gifts and sacrifices, wherefore it is of necessity that this man have somewhat also to offer." [8]

---

[1] John xii. 23.   [2] John xii. 24.

[3] This passage and a parallel passage from Dial. II. were quoted with force in the discussions of the English Reformation. Bp. Ridley on the foregoing writes (*A Brief Declaration of the Lord's Supper*, Parker Soc. Ed. p. 35.) " What can be more plainly said than this that this old writer saith? That although the Sacraments bear the name of the body and blood of Christ, yet is not their nature changed, but abideth still. And where is then the Papists' transubstantiation? "

[1] Gen. xlix. 2.   [2] Matt. xxvi. 28.   [3] John vi. 51.
[4] Aristotle (Œc : 1. 6. 1.) uses the proverb as we say in English "to draw water in a sieve."   [5] Heb. ii. 16.
[6] Gen. ii. 18.   [7] Heb. vii. 14.   [8] Heb. v. 1. viii. 3.

Eran. — Point out, then, how He offered after taking a body.

Orth. — The divine apostle himself clearly teaches in the very passage, for after a few words he says: "Wherefore, when He cometh into the world, He saith, sacrifice and offering thou wouldst not, but a body hast thou prepared me." [1] He does not say "into a body hast thou changed," but "a body hast thou prepared," and he shows plainly that the formation of the body was wrought by the Spirit in accordance with the utterance of the gospel, "Fear not to take unto thee Mary thy wife; for that which is generated in her is of the Holy Ghost." [2]

Eran. — The virgin then gave birth only to a body?

Orth. — It appears that you do not even understand the composition of words, much less their meaning, for he is teaching Joseph the manner, not of the generation, but of the conception. For he does not say that which is generated *of* her, i. e. made, or formed, is of the Holy Ghost. Joseph, ignorant of the mystery, was suspicious of adultery; he was therefore plainly taught the formation by the Spirit. It is this which He signified through the prophet when He said "A body hast thou prepared me" [3] for the divine Apostle being full of the Spirit interpreted the prediction. If then the offering of gifts is the special function of priests and Christ in His humanity was called priest and offered no other sacrifice save [4] His own body, then the Lord Christ had a body.

Eran. — This even I have repeatedly affirmed, and I do not say that the divine Word appeared without a body. What I maintain is not that He took a body but that He was made flesh.

Orth. — So far as I see our contest lies with the supporters of Valentinus, of Mar-

cion, and of Manes; but even they never had the hardihood to say that the immutable nature underwent mutation into flesh.

Eran. — Reviling is unchristian.

Orth. — We do not revile, but we are fighting for truth, and we are vexed at your arguing about the indisputable as though it could be disputed. However, I will endeavour to put an end to your ungracious contention. Answer now; do you remember the promises which God made to David?

Eran. — Which?

Orth. — Those which the prophet inserted in the 88th Psalm.

Eran. — I know that many promises were made to David. Which are you enquiring about now?

Orth. — Those which refer to the Lord Christ.

Eran. — Recall the utterances yourself, for you promised to adduce your proofs.

Orth. — Listen now how the prophet praises God at the very beginning of the Psalm. He saw with his prophetic eyes the future iniquity of his people, and the captivity that was in consequence foredoomed; yet he praised his own Lord for unfailing promises. "I will sing," he says, "of the mercies of the Lord for ever, with my mouth will I make known Thy faithfulness to all generations, for thou hast said, Mercy shall be built up for ever, Thy faithfulness shalt Thou establish in the very heavens." [1]

Through all this the prophet teaches that the promise was made by God on account of lovingkindness, and that the promise is faithful. Then he goes on to say what He promised, and to whom, introducing God Himself as the speaker. ("I have made a covenant with my chosen." [2]) It is the Patriarchs that He called chosen; then He goes on "I have sworn unto David my servant," [3] and He states concerning what He swore, "Thy seed will I establish for ever, and build up thy throne to all generations." [4]

Now whom do you suppose to be called the seed of David?

Eran. — The promise was made about Solomon.

Orth. — Then he made his covenant with the Patriarchs about Solomon, for before what was said about David he mentioned the promises made to the Patriarchs "I have made a covenant with my chosen," and He promised the Patriarchs that in their seed He would bless all nations. Kindly point out how the nations were blessed through Solomon.

---

[1] Heb. x. 5.

[2] Matt. i. 20. The rendering of γεννηθέν by "conceived" in the A. V. somewhat obscures the argument of Theodoret. The R. V. has "begotten" in the margin.

[3] Ps. xl. 7. Septuagint. The difficulty how to account for the rendering of אָזְנַ֫יִם כָּרִ֥יתָ לִּ֑י i. e. "My ear hast thou dug" by "σῶμα κατηρτίσω" is an old one. Did ΗΘΕΛΗΣΑ-ΣΩΤΙΑΔΕΚΑΤΗΡΤΙΣΩ get altered by mistake into ΗΘΕΛΗΣΑ-ΣΣΩΜΑΔΕΚΑΤΗΡΤΙΣΩ? "How the word σῶμα came into the lxx we cannot say; but being there it is now sanctioned for us by the citation here; not as the, or even a proper rendering of the Hebrew, but as a prophetic utterance." Alford ad loc.

[4] I have no hesitation in translating ἀλλὰ here by "save," in spite of the purist prejudice which has led even the revisers of 1881 to retain something of the awkward periphrasis by which the meaning of Matt. xx. 23 and Mark x. 40. is confused in A. V., and an Arian sense given to our Lord's declaration, "To sit on my right hand and my left is not mine to give save to them for whom it is prepared." i. e. It is His to give, but not to give arbitrarily or of caprice. Liddell and Scott, Ed. 1883, recognise and illustrate this use of ἀλλα (Vide s. v. I. 3.) which in classical Greek is vindicated by such a passage as Soph. O. T. 1331. ἔπαισε δ᾽ αὐτόχειρ νιν οὗτις ἀλλ᾽ ἐγώ, and in N. T. Greek, as well as by the crucial passage in question, in Mark ix. 8. οὐκέτι οὐδένα εἶδον ἀλλὰ τὸν Ἰησοῦν μόνον, "They no longer saw any one *save* Jesus only."

[1] Ps. lxxxix. 1. 2. [2] Ps. lxxxix. 3.
[2] Ps. lxxxix. 3. [4] Ps. lxxxix. 4.

Eran. — Then God fulfilled this promise, not by means of Solomon, but of our Saviour.

Orth. — So then our Lord Christ gave the fulfilment to the promises made to David.

Eran. — I hold that these promises were made by God, either about Solomon, or about Zerubbabel.

Orth. — Just now you used the arguments of Marcion and Valentinus and of Manes. Now you have gone over to the directly opposite faction, and are advocating the impudence of the Jews. This is just like all those who turn out of a straight road; they err and stray first one way and then another, wandering in a wilderness.

Eran. — Revilers are excluded by the Apostle from the kingdom.[1]

Orth. — Yes, if their revilings are vain. Sometimes the divine Apostle himself opportunely uses this mode of speech. He calls the Galatians " foolish,"[2] and of others he says " men of corrupt minds, reprobate concerning the faith,"[3] and again of another set, " Whose God is their belly, whose glory is in their shame,"[4] and so forth.

Eran. — What occasion did I give you for reviling?

Orth. — Do you really not think that the willing advocacy of the declared enemies of the truth furnishes the pious with very reasonable ground of indignation?

Eran. — And what enemies of the truth have I patronized?

Orth. — Now, Jews.

Eran. — How so?

Orth. — Jews connect prophecies of this kind with Solomon and Zerubbabel, in order to exhibit the groundlessness of the Christian position; but the mere words are quite enough to convict them of their iniquity, for it is written " I will establish my throne for ever."[5] Now not only Solomon and Zerubbabel, to whom such prophecies are applied by the Jews, have lived out their appointed time, and reached the end of life, but the whole race of David has become extinct; for who ever heard of any one at the present day descended from the root of David?

Eran. — But are not, then, those who are called Patriarchs of the Jews of the family of David?

Orth. — Certainly not.

Eran. — Whence, then, are they sprung?

Orth. — From the foreigner Herod, who, on his father's side, was an Ascalonite, and on his mother's an Idumæan;[1] but they, too, have all disappeared, and many years have gone by since their sovereignty came to an end. But our Lord God promised not only to maintain the seed of David for ever, but to establish his kingdom undestroyed; for He said, " I will build up my throne to all generations."

But we see that his race is gone, and his kingdom come to an end. Yet though we see this, we know that the God of the Universe is true.

Eran. — That God is true is plain.

Orth. — If, then, God is true, as in truth He is, and promised David that He would establish His race for ever, and keep his kingdom through all time, and if neither race nor kingdom are to be seen, for both have come to an end, how can we convince our opponents that God is true?

Eran. — I suppose, then, the prophecy really points to the Lord Christ.

Orth. — If, then, you confess this, let us investigate together a passage in the middle of the Psalm; we shall then more clearly see what the prophecy means.

Eran. — Lead on; I will religiously follow in your footsteps.

Orth. — After making many promises about this seed that it should be Lord both by sea and land[2] and higher than the kings of the earth and be called the first begotten of God,[3] and should boldly call God, Father[4] God also added this, " My mercy will I keep for him for evermore and my covenant shall stand fast with him. His seed also will I make to endure for ever and his throne as the days of heaven."[5]

Eran. — The promise goes beyond the bounds of human nature, for both the life and the honour are indestructible and eternal. But men endure but for a season; their nature is short lived and their kingdom even during its lifetime undergoes many and various vicissitudes, so that truly the greatness of the prophecy befits none but the Saviour Christ.

Orth. — Go on then to what follows and your opinion upon this point will be in every way confirmed, for again saith the God of the universe, " Once have I sworn by my

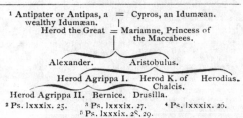

1 Antipater or Antipas, a = Cypros, an Idumæan.
  wealthy Idumæan.
  Herod the Great = Mariamne, Princess of
                     the Maccabees.

  Alexander.   Aristobulus.

  Herod Agrippa I. Herod K. of   Herodias.
                        Chalcis.
  Herod Agrippa II. Bernice. Drusilla.

2 Ps. lxxxix. 25.   3 Ps. lxxxix. 27.   4 Ps. lxxxix. 26.
                5 Ps. lxxxix. 28, 29.

1 I. Cor. vi. 10.   3 2. Tim. iii. 8.
2 Gal. iii. 1.   4 Phil. iii. 19.
           5 Ps. lxxxix. 4.

holiness, if I lie unto David, his seed shall endure for ever and his throne as the sun before me. It shall be established for ever as the moon." [1]

Then, pointing out the truth of the promise He adds, "And the witness is faithful in heaven."

Eran. — We must believe without doubt in the promises given by the faithful witness, for, if we are wont to believe men who have promised to speak the truth even if they do not confirm their words with an oath, who can be so mad as to disbelieve the Creator of the Universe, when He adds an oath to his words? For He who forbids others to swear confirmed the immutability of his counsel by an oath,[2] " that by two immutable things in which it was impossible for God to lie we might have a strong consolation who have fled for refuge to lay hold upon the hope set before us." [3]

Orth. — If then the promise is irrefragable, and among the Jews there is now neither family nor kingdom of the prophet David to be seen, let us believe that our Lord Jesus Christ is plainly called seed of David in His humanity, for of Him the life and the kingdom are both alike eternal.

Eran. — We have no doubt; and this I own to be the truth.

Orth. — These proofs then are sufficient to show clearly the manhood which our Lord and Saviour took of David's seed. But to remove all possibility of doubt by the witness of the majority, let us hear how God makes mention of the promises given to David through the voice of the prophet Isaiah. " I will make," he says, " an everlasting covenant with you," and, signifying the law-giver, he adds, " even the sure mercies of David." [4]

Since He made this promise to David, and spoke through Esaias, He will assuredly bring the promise to pass. And what follows after the prophecy is in harmony with what I say, for he saith " Behold I have given him for a witness to the people, a leader and commander to the people. Behold nations that know thee not shall call upon thee, and peoples that understand thee not shall run unto thee." [5] Now this fits in with none that are sprung from David, for who of David's descendants, as Esaias says, was made a ruler of nations? And what nations in their prayers ever called on David's descendants as God?

Eran. — About what is perfectly clear it

is unbecoming to dispute, and this plainly refers to the Lord Christ.

Orth. — Then let us pass on to another prophetic testimony and let us hear the same prophet saying " There shall come forth a rod out of the stem of Jesse and a branch shall grow out of his roots." [1]

Eran. — I think this prophecy was delivered about Zerubbabel.

Orth. — If you hear what follows, you will not remain in your opinion. The Jews have never so understood this prediction, for the prophet goes on, "and the Spirit of the Lord shall rest upon him, the spirit of wisdom and understanding, the spirit of counsel and might, the spirit of knowledge and the fear of the Lord." [2] This would never be attributed by any one to a mere man, for even to the very holy the gifts of the Spirit are given by division, as the divine apostle witnesses when he says, " To one is given by the Spirit the word of wisdom, to another the word of knowledge by the same Spirit," [3] and so on. The prophet describes Him who sprang from the root of Jesse as possessing all the powers of the spirit.

Eran. — To gainsay this were sheer folly.

Orth. — Now hear what follows. You will see some things that transcend human nature, he goes on. " He shall not judge after the sight of His eyes, neither reprove after the hearing of His ears, but with righteousness shall He judge the poor, and reprove with equity the mighty [4] of the earth, and He shall smite the earth with the word of His mouth, and with the breath of His lips shall he slay the wicked." [5] Now of these predictions some are human and some divine. Justice, truth, equity, and rectitude in giving judgment exhibit virtue in human nature.

Eran. — We have so far clearly learned that the prophet predicts the coming of our Saviour Christ.

Orth. — The sequel will shew you yet more plainly the truth of the interpretation. For he goes on, " The wolf shall dwell with the lamb," [6] and so on, whereby he teaches at once the distinction of modes of life and the harmony of faith; and experience furnishes a proof of the prediction, for they that abound in wealth, they that live in poverty, servants and masters, rulers and ruled, soldiers and citizens and they that wield the sceptre of the world are received in one font, are all taught one doctrine, are all admitted to one

---

[1] Ps. lxxxix. 35. 36. 37.   [3] Heb. vi. 18.   [5] Is. lv. 4. 5. lxx.
[2] Heb. vi. 17.   [4] Is. lv. 3.

[1] Isaiah xi. 1.   [2] Isaiah xi. 2.   [3] I. Cor. xii. 8.
[4] A. V. " reprove with equity for the meek of the earth;"
Sept. ἐλεγξει τοὺς ταπεινοὺς τῆς γῆς.
[5] Isaiah xi. 4.   [6] Is. xi. 6.

mystic table, and each of the believers enjoys an equal share.

Eran. — It is thus shewn that God is spoken of.

Orth. — Not only God but man. So at the very beginning of this prediction he says that a rod shall grow out of the root of Jesse. Then at the conclusion of the prediction he takes up once more the strain with which he began, for he says " There shall be a root of Jesse which shall stand for an ensign of the people, to it shall the Gentiles seek and his rest shall be glorious." [1] Now Jesse was the father of David, and the promise with an oath was made to David. The prophet would not have spoken of the Lord Christ as a rod growing out of Jesse if he had only known Him as God. The prediction also foretold the change of the world, for " the earth " he says " shall be full of the knowledge of the Lord as the waters cover the sea." [2]

Eran. — I have heard the prophetic utterances. But I was anxious to know clearly if the divine company of the apostles also says that the Lord Christ sprang from the seed of David according to the flesh.

Orth. — You have asked for information which so far from being hard is exceedingly easy to give you. Only listen to the first of the apostles exclaiming " David being a prophet and knowing that God had sworn an oath to him that of the fruit of his loins, according to the flesh, He would raise up Christ to sit upon His throne ; he seeing this before spake of the resurrection of Christ, that His soul was not left in hell neither His flesh did see corruption." [3]

Hence you may perceive that of the seed of David according to the flesh sprang the Lord Christ, and had not flesh only but also a soul.

Eran. — What other apostle preached this?

Orth. — The great Peter alone was sufficient to testify to the truth, for the Lord after receiving the confession of the truth given by Peter alone confirmed it by a memorable approval. But since you are anxious to hear others proclaiming this same thing, hear Paul and Barnabas preaching in Antioch in Pisidia ; for they, when they had made mention of David, continued " Of this man's seed hath God according to his promise raised unto Israel a Saviour, Jesus," [4] and so on. And in a letter to Timothy the divine Paul says " Remember that Jesus Christ of the seed of David was raised from the dead according to my gospel." [5] And, when

writing to the Romans, at the very outset he calls attention to the Davidic kin, for he says " Paul a servant of Jesus Christ, called to be an apostle, separated unto the gospel of God which He had promised before by his prophets in the holy scriptures concerning His Son which was made of the seed of David according to the flesh," [1] and so on.

Eran. — Your proofs are numerous and convincing ; but tell me why you have omitted what follows?

Orth. — Because it is not about the Godhead, but about the manhood, that you are in difficulties. Had you been in doubt about the Godhead, I would have given you proof of it. It is enough to say " according to the Flesh" to declare the Godhead which is not expressed in terms. When speaking of a relationship of man in general I do not say the son of such an one " according to the flesh," but simply "son," so the divine Evangelist writing his genealogy says " Abraham begat Isaac" [2] and does not add according to the flesh, for Isaac was merely man, and he mentions the rest in like manner, for they were men and had no qualities transcending their nature. But when the heralds of the truth are discoursing of our Lord Christ, and are pointing out to the ignorant His lower relation, they add the words " according to the flesh," thus indicating His Godhead and teaching that the Lord Christ was not only man but also Eternal God.

Eran. — You have adduced many proofs from the apostles and prophets, but I follow the words of the Evangelist " The Word was made Flesh." [3]

Orth. — I also follow this divine teaching, but I understand it in a pious sense, as meaning that He was made Flesh by taking flesh and a reasonable soul. But if the divine Word took nothing of our nature, then the covenants made with the patriarchs by the God of all with oaths were not true, and the blessing of Judah was vain, and the promise to David was false, and the Virgin was superfluous, because she did not contribute anything of our nature to the Incarnate God. Then the predictions of the prophets have no fulfilment. Then vain is our preaching, vain our faith and vain the hope of the resurrection [4] for the Apostle, it appears, lies when he says " and hath raised us up together and made us sit together in heavenly places in Christ Jesus." [5] For if the Lord Christ had nothing

---

[1] Isaiah xi. 10.   [3] Acts ii. 30-31.   [5] 2 Tim. ii. 8.
[2] Isaiah xi. 9.   [4] Acts xiii. 23.

[1] Romans i. 1-3.   [2] Matt. i. 2.   [3] John i. 14.
[4] A κενὴ ἐλπίσο πίστις would be a faith which could not possibly be realized; and ματαία ἐλπίς a hope of not impossible but very improbable fulfilment. But the distinction between κενός and ματαίος is hardly borne out by their use in the text.
[5] Ephes. ii. 6.

of our nature then He is falsely described as our first fruits, and His bodily nature has not risen from the dead and has not taken the seat in Heaven on the right hand ; and if He has obtained none of these things, how hath God raised us up together and made us sit together with Christ, when we in no wise belong to Him in Nature? But it is impious to say this, for the divine apostle, though the general resurrection has not yet taken place, though the kingdom of heaven has not yet been bestowed upon the faithful, exclaims, " He hath raised us up together and made us sit together in heavenly places in Christ Jesus," in order to teach that since the resurrection of our first fruits, and His sitting on the right hand has come to pass, we too in general shall attain the resurrection, and that all they who share in His nature and have adopted His faith, share too in the first fruits of His glory.

Eran. — We have gone through many and sound arguments, but I was anxious to know the force of the Gospel saying.

Orth. — You stand in need of no interpretation from without. The evangelist himself interprets himself. For after saying " the Word was made flesh," he goes on " and dwelt among us." [1] That is to say by dwelling in us, and using the flesh taken from us as a kind of temple, He is said to have been made flesh, and, teaching that He remained unchanged, the evangelist adds " and we beheld His glory — the glory as of the only begotten of the Father, full of grace and truth." [2] For though clad with flesh He exhibited His Father's nobility, shot forth the beams of the Godhead, and emitted the radiance of the power of the Lord, revealing by His works of wonder His hidden nature. A similar illustration is afforded by the words of the divine apostle to the Philippians : " Let this mind be in you which was also in Christ Jesus, who being in the form of God thought it not robbery to be equal with God, but made Himself of no reputation and took upon Him the form of a servant and was made in the likeness of men, and being found in fashion as a man he humbled Himself and became obedient unto death even the death of the cross." [3]

Look at the relation of the utterances. The evangelist says " the Word was made flesh and dwelt among us," the apostle, " took upon him the form of a servant ; " the evangelist " We beheld His glory, the glory as of the only begotten of the Father " — the apostle, " who being in the form of God

thought it not robbery to be equal with God." To put the matter briefly, both teach that being God and son of God, and clad with His Father's glory, and having the same nature and power with Him that begat Him, He that was in the beginning and was with God, and was God, and was Creator of the world, took upon Him the form of a servant, and it seemed that this was all which was seen ; but it was God clad in human nature, and working out the salvation of men. This is what was meant by " The word was made flesh " and " was made in the likeness of men and being found in fashion as a man." This is all that was looked at by the Jews, and therefore they said to him " For a good work we stone Thee not but for blasphemy and because that Thou being a man makest Thyself God," [1] and again " This man is not of God because He keepeth not the Sabbath Day." [2]

Eran. — The Jews were blind on account of their unbelief, and therefore used these words.

Orth. — If you find even the apostles before the resurrection thus saying, will you receive the interpretation? I hear them in the boat, after the mighty miracle of the calm, saying " what manner of man is this, that even the winds and the sea obey Him? " [3]

Eran. — This is made plain. But now tell me this ; — the divine apostle says that He " was made in the likeness of man."

Orth. — What was taken of him was not man's likeness, but man's nature. For " form of a servant " is understood just as " the form of God " is understood to mean God's nature. He took this, and so was made in the likeness of man, and was found in fashion as a man. For, being God, He seemed to be man, on account of the nature which He took. The evangelist, however, speaks of His being made in the likeness of man as His being made flesh. But that you may know that they who deny the flesh of the Saviour are of the opposite spirit, hear the great John in his Catholic Epistle saying " Every spirit that confesses that Jesus Christ is come in the flesh is of God, and every spirit that confesses not that Jesus Christ is come in the flesh is not of God, and this is that spirit of Anti-Christ." [4]

Eran. — You have given a plausible interpretation, but I was anxious to know how the old teachers of the Church have understood the passage " the word was made flesh."

Orth. —You ought to have been persuaded

---

[1] John i. 14. [2] John i. 14. [3] Phil. ii. 5. S.

[1] John x. 33. [3] Matt. viii. 27.
[2] John ix. 16. [4] 1. John iv. 2, 3.

by the apostolic and prophetic proofs; but since you require further the interpretations of the holy Fathers I will also furnish you, God helping me, this medicine.

Eran. — Do not bring me men of obscure position or doubtful doctrine. I shall not receive the interpretation of such as these.

Orth. — Does the far famed Athanasius, brightest light of the church of Alexandria, seem to you to be worthy of credit?

Eran. — Certainly, for he ratified his teaching by the suffering he underwent for the Truth's sake.

Orth. — Hear then how he wrote to Epictetus.[1] " The expression of John ' the Word was made flesh' has this interpretation, so far as can be discovered from the similar passage which we find in St. Paul ' Christ was made a curse for us.'[2] It is not because He was made a curse but because He received the curse on our behalf that He is said to have been made a curse, and so it is not because He was turned into flesh, but because He took flesh on our behalf, that He is said to have been made flesh." So far the divine Athanasius. Gregory, too, whose glory among all men is great, who formerly ruled the Imperial city at the mouth of the Bosphorus and afterwards dwelt at Nazianzus, thus wrote to Cledonius against the specious fallacies of Apollinarius.

Eran. — He was an illustrious man and a foremost fighter in the cause of piety.

Orth. — Hear him then. He says[3] " the expression ' He was made Flesh' seems to be parallel to His being said to have been made sin and a curse,[4] not because the Lord was transmuted into these, — for how could He? — but because He accepted these when He took on Him our iniquities and bore our infirmities."[5]

Eran. — The two interpretations agree.

Orth. — We have shown you the pastors of the south and north in harmony; now then let us introduce too the illustrious teachers of the west, who have written their interpretation, if with another tongue, yet with one and the same mind.

Eran. — I am told that Ambrosius, who adorned the episcopal throne at Milan, fought in the first ranks against all heresy, and wrote works of great beauty and in agreement with the teaching of the apostles.

Orth. — I will give you his interpretation. Ambrosius says in his work concerning the faith " It is written that the Word was made flesh. I do not deny that it is written, but

look at the terms used; for there follows ' and dwelt among us,' that is to say dwelt in human flesh. You are therefore astonished at the terms in which it is written that the Word was made flesh, on the assumption of flesh, by the divine Word, when also concerning sin which He had not, it is said that He was made sin, that is to say not that He was made the nature and operation of sin, but that he might crucify our sin in the flesh; let them then give over asserting that the nature of the Word has undergone change and alteration, for He who took is one and that which was taken other." [1]

It is now fitting that you should hear the teachers of the east, this being the only quarter of the world which we have hitherto left unnoticed, though they indeed might well have first witnessed to the truth, for to them was first imparted the teaching of the apostles. But since you have sharpened your tongues against the first-born sons of piety by whetting them on the hone of falsehood, we have reserved for them the last place, that after first hearing the rest, you might lay witness by the side of witness, and so at once admire their harmony, and cease from your own interminable talk. Listen then to Flavianus who for a long time right wisely moved the tiller of the church of Antioch, and made the churches which he guided ride safe over the Arian storm, by expounding to them the word of the gospel. " The Word was made flesh and dwelt among us; He is not turned into flesh, nor yet did he cease from being God, for this he was from all eternity and became flesh in the dispensation of the incarnation[2] after himself building his own temple, and taking up his abode in the passible creature." And if you desire to hear the ancients of Palestine, lend your ears to the admirable Gelasius, who did diligent husbandry in the church of Cæsarea. Now these are his words in his homily on the festival of the Lord's epiphany.[3]

---

[1] de Incar. Dom. Sac. vi. II. Ed. Ben. p. 716. The Latin of Ambrose, which is not exactly rendered by Theodoret, is as follows : — "*Sic scriptum est, inquiunt, quia Verbum caro factum est (Ioan 1, 14). Scriptum est, non nego: sed considera quid sequatur; sequitur enim : Et habitavit in nobis, hoc est, illud Verbum quod carnem suscepit, hoc habitavit in nobis, hoc est, in carne habitavit humana.*

"*Miraris ergo quia scriptum est: Verbum caro factum est, cum caro assumpta sit a Dei Verbo: quando in peccato quod non habuit, scriptum est quia peccatum factus est, hoc est, non natura operationeque peccati, utpote in similitudinem carnis peccati factus: sed ut peccatum nostrum in sua carne crucifigeret, susceptionem pro nobis infirmitatum obnoxii jam corporis peccati carnalis assumpsit.*

Desinant ergo dicere naturam Verbi in corporis naturam esse mutatam; ne pari interpretatione videatur natura Verbi in contagium mutata peccati Aliud est enim quod assumpsit, et aliud quod assumpium est."

[2] Compare note on page 72.

[3] " In the Eastern church till nearly the end of the fourth century we find, as has been said, the divine celebration of Christ's nativity and baptism on January 6th. The date of the severance of the two can be approximately fixed, for Chrysos-

---

[1] Ed. Ben. I. 2. 207.　　　[4] II. Cor. v. 21. Gal. iii. 13.
[2] Gal. iii. 13.　　　　　　　[5] Isaiah liii. 4.
[3] I Ep. ad Cled. i. Ed. Paris. p. 744.

" Learn the truth from the words of John the Fisherman, 'And the word was made flesh,' not having himself undergone change, but having taken up his abode with us. The dwelling is one thing; the Word is another; the temple is one thing, and God who dwells in it, another."

Eran. — I am much struck by the agreement.

Orth. — Now do you not suppose that the rule of the apostolic faith was kept by John, who first nobly watered the field of the church of the Antiochenes, and then was a wise husbandman of that of the imperial city?

Eran. — I hold this teacher to be in all respects an admirable one.

Orth. — Well, this most excellent man has interpreted this passage of the Gospel. He writes,[1] " When you hear that the Word was made flesh, be not startled or cast down, for the substance did not deteriorate into flesh — an idea of the uttermost impiety — but continuing to be just what it is, so took the form of a servant. For just as when the apostle says ' Christ hath redeemed us from the curse of the law, being made a curse for us,'[2] he does not say that the substance of Christ departed from His own glory, and took the substance of a curse, a position which not even devils would imagine, nor the utterly senseless, and the naturally idiotic — so remarkable being the connection between impiety and insanity. But what he does assert is that after receiving the curse due to us, He does not suffer us to be cursed for the future. It is in this sense that He is stated to have been made flesh, not because he had changed the substance into flesh, but because he had assumed the flesh, the substance remaining all the while unimpaired."[3]

You may like to hear also Severianus, Bishop of Gabala.[4] If so, I will adduce his testimony and do you lend your ears.

" The text 'the Word was made flesh ' does not indicate a deterioration of nature

but the assumption of our nature. Suppose you take the word ' was made' to indicate a change; then when you hear Paul saying ' Christ hath redeemed us from the curse of the law, being made a curse for us,' do you understand him to mean a change into the nature of a curse? Just as being made a curse had no other meaning than that He took our curse upon Himself, so the words was made flesh and dwelt among us mean nothing other than the assumption of flesh."

Eran. — I admire the exact agreement[1] of these men. For they are as unanimous in giving the same interpretations of evangelical writings as if they had met in the same place and written down their opinion together.

Orth. — Mountains and seas separate them very far from one another, yet distance does not damage their harmony, for they were all inspired by the same gift of the spirit. I would also have offered you the interpretations of the victorious champions of piety Diodorus and Theodorus, had I not seen that you were ill disposed towards them, and had inherited the hostility of Apollinarius; you would have seen that they have expressed similar experiences, drawing water from the divine Fount, and becoming themselves too, streams of the spirit. But I will pass them by, for you have declared a truceless war against them. I will, however, shew you the famous teacher of the Church, and his mind about the divine incarnation, that you may know what opinion he held concerning the assumed nature. You have no doubt heard of the illustrious Ignatius, who received episcopal grace by the hand of the great Peter,[2] and after ruling the church of Antioch, wore the crown of martyrdom. You have heard too of Irenæus, who enjoyed the teaching of Polycarp, and became a light of the western Gauls ; — of Hippolytus and Methodius, bishops and martyrs, and the rest, whose names I will append to their expressions of opinion.

Eran. — I am exceedingly desirous of hearing their testimony too.

Orth. — Hear them now bringing forward the apostolic teaching. *Testimony of Saint Ignatius, bishop of Antioch, and martyr.*

From the letter to the Smyrnæans (I.) : —

" Having a full conviction with respect to our Lord as being truly descended from David

---

tom refers to it as a matter of merely a few years' standing, in a sermon probably delivered on the Christmas day of 386 A.D. How far back we are to refer the origin of this two-fold festival it is not easy to determine, the earliest mention of any kind being the allusion by Clement of Alexandria to the annual commemoration of Christ's baptism by the Basilidians (Stromata, lib. i. c. 21). At any rate by the latter part of the fourth century the Epiphany had become one of the most important and venerable festivals in the Eastern church."
Dict. Christ. Ant. i. 617.

[1] Chrys. Ed. Sav. II. p. 598.
[2] Gal. iii. 13.
[3] The modern reader will not omit to note the bearing of these patristic interpretations of the scriptural statements that the word was " made " flesh and that Christ was " made " a curse on later controversies concerning Transubstantiation.
[4] On the northern seaboard of Syria. Severianus was at one time Chrysostom's commissary and afterwards his determined opponent.

[1] The value of Chrysostom and Severianus as independent witnesses is somewhat weakened by the fact, pointed out by Schulze, that among the writings of the former some are attributed to the latter.
[2] The Apost. Const. vii. 46. represent Ignatius as ordained by St. Paul. Malalas describes St. Peter as ordaining Ignatius on the death of Euodius. Vide article " Euodius " in Dict. Christ. Biog.

according to the flesh, son of God according to Godhead[1] and power, born really of a virgin, baptized by John that all righteousness might be fulfilled[2] by Him, really in the time of Pontius Pilate and of Herod the tetrarch crucified for our sake in the flesh."[3]

Of the same in the same epistle : —

"For what advantageth it me if a man praises me but blasphemes my Lord, in not confessing him to be a bearer of flesh? but he who does not make this confession really denies Him and is himself bearer of a corpse."[4]

Of the same from the same epistle : —

"For if these things were done by our Lord in appearance only, then it is in appearance only that I am a prisoner in chains ; and why have I delivered myself to death, to fire, to sword, to the beasts? But he who is near to the sword is near to God.[5] Only in the name of Jesus Christ that I may share his sufferings I endure all things while He, Perfect Man whom some in their ignorance deny, gives me strength."[6]

From the same in the letter to the Ephesians : —

"For our God Jesus Christ was born in Mary's womb by dispensation of God of the seed of David[7] and of the Holy Ghost who was born and was baptized that our mortality might be purified."[8]

From the same epistle : —

"If ye all individually come together by grace name by name in one faith, and in one Jesus Christ according to the flesh of David's race Son of God and Son of man."[9]

Of the same from the same epistle : —

"There is one Physician of flesh and of spirit generate and ingenerate, God in man, true life in death, Son of Mary and of God, first passible and then impassible, Jesus Christ our Lord."[10]

Lastly of the same in his epistle to the Trallians : —

"Be ye made deaf therefore when any man speaks to you apart from Jesus Christ,

who was of David's race and of Mary, who was really born and really ate and drank and was persecuted in the time of Pontius Pilate, was crucified and died, while beings on earth and beings in heaven and beings under the earth were looking on."[1]

Testimony of Irenæus bishop of Lyons, from his third book Against the heresies : —

"Why then did they add the words 'In the city of David,[2] save to proclaim the good news that the promise made by God to David, that of the fruit of his loins should come an everlasting king, was fulfilled ; a promise which indeed the Creator of the world had made."[3]

Of the same from the same book : —

"And when he says 'Hear ye now, Oh House of David'[4] he means that the everlasting King whom God promised to David that he would raise up from his body is He who was born of David's Virgin."

Of the same from the same book : —

"If then the first Adam had had a human father and had been begotten of seed, it would have been reasonable to say that the second Adam had been begotten of Joseph. But if the former was taken from earth, and his creator was God, it was necessary also that He who renews in himself the man created by God should have the same likeness of generation with that former. Why then did not God again take dust? Why did he on the other hand ordain that the formation should be made of Mary? That there might be no other creation ; that that which was being saved might be no other thing ; but that the former might himself be renewed without loss of the likeness. For then do they too fall away who allege that He took nothing from the Virgin, that they may repudiate the inheritance of the flesh and cast off the likeness."[5]

Of the same from the same book : —

"Since his going down into Mary is useless ; for why went He down into her if He was designed to take nothing from her? And further, if He had taken nothing from Mary He would not have accepted the food taken from earth whereby is nourished the body taken from earth, nor would He like Moses and Elias, after fasting forty days, have hungered, on account of His body demanding its own food, nor yet would John his disciple when writing about him have said — 'Jesus being wearied from his journey sat,'[6] nor would David have uttered the prediction about him 'And they added to

---

[1] Bp. Lightfoot (*Ap. Fathers pt. II. ii. 290*.) adopts the reading κατὰ θέλημα καὶ δύναμιν for κατὰ θεότητα, and notes "Theodoret strangely substitutes θεότητα for θέλημα. This reading . . . may be due to . . . ignorance of the absolute use of θέλημα. The Armenian translator likewise has substituted another word."

[2] Matt. iii. 15.

[3] Ig. ad Smyrn. I.

[4] There is a play here on the σαρκοφόρος, νεκροφόρος, and, possibly, θεοφόρος. Vide Pearson and Lightfoot ad loc. (Ignat. ad Smyrn. V.)

[5] "A saying to this effect is attributed to Our Lord by Didymus on Ps : lxxxviii 8. It is mentioned also by Origen Hom. XX. In Jerem : Sec. III." Bp. Lightfoot l. c.

[6] Ignat. ad Smyrn. IV.

[7] Compare note on page 72.

[8] Bp. Lightfoot adopts the reading of Cod. Med. "that by his passion he might cleanse the water." Ig. ad Eph. XVIII.

[9] Ig. ad Eph. XX.

[10] Ignat. ad Eph. VII.

[1] Ig. ad Trall. ix.
[2] Luke ii. 4.
[3] Ps. cxxxii. 11.
[4] Is. vii. 13.
[5] Cont. Hær. iii. 31.
[6] John iv. 6.

the pain of my wounds,'[1] nor would He have wept over Lazarus,[2] nor would He have sweated drops of blood,[3] nor would He have said, 'my soul is exceeding sorrowful,'[4] nor yet when He was pierced would blood and water have issued from His side.[5] For all these things are proofs of the flesh taken from earth, which He had renewed in Himself in the salvation of his own creature."[6]

Of the same from the same book :—

"For as by the disobedience of the one man who was first formed from rude earth the many were made sinners[7] and lost their life, so also was it fitting that through obedience of one man, the firstborn of a virgin, many should be made righteous and receive their salvation."[8]

Of the same from the same work :—

"'I have said ye are gods and all of you children of the Most High but ye shall die like man.'[9] This He says to them that did not accept the gift of adoption, but dishonour the incarnation of the pure generation of the word of God, deprive man of his ascent to God, and are ungrateful to the Word of God who for their sakes was made flesh. For this cause was the word made man that man receiving the word and accepting the adoption should be made God's son."[10]

Of the same from the same book :—

"Since then on account of the fore-ordained dispensation[11] the spirit came down, and the only begotten Son of God, who also is Word of the Father, when the fulness of time was come, was made flesh in man and our Lord Jesus Christ—being one and the same—fulfilled all the human dispensation as the Lord himself testifies, and the apostles confess, all the teachings of men who invented the ogdoads and tetrads and similitudes are proved plainly false."[12]

Testimony of the Holy Hippolytus, Bishop

---

[1] Ps. lxix. 26. A. V. They talk to the grief of those whom thou hast wounded. lxx. R. V. They tell of the sorrow of those whom thou hast wounded.
[2] John xi. 35.   [7] Rom. v. 19.
[3] Luke xxii. 44.   [8] Cont. Hær. iii. 20.
[4] Mat. xxvi. 28.   [9] Ps. lxxxii. 67.
[5] John xix. 34.   [10] Cont. Hær. iii. 21.
[6] Cont. Hær. iii. 32.   [11] Vide note on page 72.
[12] Adv. Hær. iii. 26. The allusion is to the gnostics and mainly to Valentinus and his school who imagined seven heavens, and a supercelestial space termed "Ogdoad." "The doctrine of an Ogdoad of the commencement of finite existence having been established by Valentinus, those of his followers who had been imbued with the Pythagorean philosophy introduced a modification. In that philosophy the tetrad was regarded with peculiar veneration, and held to be the foundation of the sensible world." Cf. Hippolytus Ref. vi. 23, p. 179 "We read there (Iren. i. xi.) of Secundus as a Valentinian who divided the Ogdoad into a right hand and a left hand tetrad, and in the case of Marcus who largely uses Pythagorean speculations about numbers the tetrad holds the highest place in the system." Dr. Salmon, Dict. Christ. Biog. iv. 72. Irenæus wrote a work, no longer extant, "on the Ogdoad." Euseb. H. E. v. 20.

and Martyr, from his discourse on "The Lord is my shepherd" :—

"And an ark of incorruptible wood was the Saviour Himself, for the incorruptibility and indestructibility of His Tabernacle signified its producing no corruption of sin. For the sinner who confesses his sin says 'My wounds stink and are corrupt because of my foolishness.'[2] But the Lord was without sin, made in His human nature of incorruptible wood, that is to say, of the Virgin and the Holy Ghost, overlaid within and without, as it were, by purest gold of the word of God."

Of the same from his discourse on El-kanah and Hannah :—

"Bring me then, O Samuel, the Heifer drawn to Bethlehem, that you may shew the King begotten of David, and anointed King and Priest by the Father."

From the same discourse :—

"Tell me, O Blessed Mary, what it was that was conceived by thee in the womb; what it was that was borne by thee in a Virgin's womb. It was the Word of God, firstborn from Heaven, on thee descending, and man firstborn being formed in a womb, that the first born Word of God might be shewn united to a firstborn man."

From the same discourse :—

"The second, which was through the prophets as through Samuel, he revokes, and turns his people from the slavery of strangers. The third, in which He took the manhood of the Virgin and was present in the flesh; who, when He saw the city wept over it."

Of the same from his discourse on the beginning of Isaiah :[3]—

"He likens the world to Egypt; its idolatry, to images; its removal and destruction to an earthquake. The Word he calls the 'Lord' and by a 'swift cloud' he means the right pure tabernacle enthroned on which our Lord Jesus Christ entered into life to undo the fall."

Testimony of the Holy Methodius,[4] bishop and martyr, from his discourse on the martyrs :—

"So wonderful and precious is martyrdom that our Lord Jesus Christ Himself, the Son of God, testified in its honour that He thought it not robbery to be equal with God, that He might crown with this grace the Manhood into whom He had come down."

Testimony of the holy Eustathius, bishop

---

[1] Ps. xxiii. 1.   [2] Ps. xxxviii. 5.   [3] Vide Isaiah xix. 1.
[4] Bishop first of Olympus and then of Patara at the beginning of the 4th c. This is the only fragment preserved by Theodoret.

of Antioch, confessor. From his interpretation of the xvith Psalm :—

"The soul of Jesus experienced both. For it was in the place of the souls of men and being made without the flesh, lives and survives. So it is reasonable and of the same substance as the souls of men, just as the flesh is of the same substance as the flesh of men, coming forth from Mary."

Of the same from his work about the soul :—

"On looking at the education of the child, or at the increase of his stature, or at the extension of time, or at the growth of the body, what would they say? But, to omit the miracles wrought upon earth, let them behold the raisings of the dead to life, the signs of the Passion, the marks of the scourges, the bruises and the blows, the wounded side, the prints of the nails, the shedding of the blood, the evidences of the death, and in a word the actual resurrection of the very body."

From the same work :—

"Indeed if any one looks to the generation of the body, he would clearly discover that after being born at Bethlehem He was wrapped in swaddling clothes, and was brought up for some time in Egypt, because of the evil counsel of the cruel Herod, and grew to man's estate at Nazareth."

From the same work :—

"For the tabernacle of the Word and of God is not the same, whereby the blessed Stephen beheld the divine glory."[1]

Of the same from his sermon on " the Lord created me in the beginning of His way ":[2]

"If the Word received a beginning of His generation from the time when passing through His mother's womb He wore the human frame, it is clear that He was made of a woman; but if He was from the first Word and God with the Father, and if we assert that the universe was made by Him, then He who is and is the cause of all created things was not made of a woman, but is by nature God, self existent, infinite, incomprehensible; and of a woman was made man, formed in the Virgin's womb by the Holy Ghost."

From the same work :—

"For a temple absolutely holy and undefiled is the tabernacle of the word according to the flesh, wherein God visibly made his habitation and dwelt, and we assert this not of conjecture, for He who is by nature the Son of this God when predicting the destruction and resurrection of the temple distinctly instructs us by His teaching when He says to the murderous Jews, 'Destroy this temple and in three days I will raise it up.'"[1]

From the same work :—

"When then the Word built a temple and carried the manhood, companying in a body with men, He invisibly displayed various miracles, and sent forth the apostles as heralds of His everlasting kingdom."

Of the same from his intrepretation of Psalm xcii :—

"It is plain then if 'He that anointeth' means God whose throne He calls 'everlasting,' the anointer is plainly by nature God, begotten of God. But the anointed took an acquired virtue, being adorned with a chosen temple of the Godhead dwelling in it."

The testimony of the holy Athanasius, Bishop of Alexandria and Confessor. From the defence of Dionysius Bishop of Alexandria :—

"'I am the vine, ye are the branches My Father is the husbandman.'[2] For we according to the body are of kin to the Lord, and for this reason He himself said 'I will declare thy name unto my brethren.'[3] And just as the branches are of one substance with the vine, and of it, so too we, since we have bodies akin to the body of the Lord, receive them of His fulness, and have it as a root for our resurrection and salvation. And the Father is called a husbandman, for He Himself through the Word tilled the vine which is the Lord's body."

Of the same from the same treatise :—

"The Lord was called a vine on account of His bodily relationship to the branches which are ourselves."

Of the same from his greater oration concerning the faith :—

"The scripture ' in the beginning was the Word '[4] clearly indicates the Godhead. The passage 'the Word was made flesh '[5] shews the human nature of the Lord."

From the same discourse :—

"' He shall wash His garments in wine '[6] that is His body, which is the vestment of the Godhead in His own blood."

Of the same from the same discourse :—

"The Word ' was '[7] is referred to His divinity, the words ' was made flesh '[8] to His body, the Word was made flesh not by being reduced to flesh, but by bearing flesh, just as any one might say such an one became or was made an old man, though not so born

---

[1] Acts vii. 57.   [2] Prov. viii. 22. Sept.

[1] John ii. 19.   [5] John i. 14.
[2] John xv. 5 and 1.   [6] Gen. xlix. 11. lxx.
[3] Ps. xii. 22.   [7] John i. 1.
[4] John i. 1.   [8] John i. 14.

from the beginning, or the soldier became a veteran, not being previously such as he became. John says, ' I became,' or ' was in the island of Patmos on the Lord's day.'[1] Not that he was made or born there, but he says ' I became or was in Patmos ' instead of saying ' I arrived;' so the Word ' arrived' at flesh, as it is said ' the Word was made flesh.' Hear the words ' I became like a broken vessel,'[2] and ' I became like a man that hath no strength, free among the dead.' "[3]

Of the same from his letter to Epictetus: —

"Whoever heard such things? Who taught them? Who learnt them? ' Out of Zion shall go forth the law and the Word of the Lord from Jerusalem.'[4] But whence did these things come forth? What hell vomited them out? To say that the body taken of Mary was of the same substance as the Godhead of the Word, or that the Word was changed into flesh and bones and hairs and a whole body; whoever heard in a church or at all among Christians that God bore a body by adoption and not by birth?"[5]

Of the same from the same Epistle: —

"But who, hearing that the Word made for Himself a passible body, not of Mary, but of His own substance, would call the sayer of these things a Christian? Who has invented so unfounded an impiety, as even to think and to say that they who affirm the Lord's body to be of Mary, conceive no longer of a Trinity, but of a quaternity in the godhead? As though they that are of this opinion described the flesh which the Saviour clothed himself with of Mary as of the substance of the Trinity.

"Whence further have some men vomited forth an impiety as bad as the foregoing, and alleged that the body is not of later time than the godhead of the Word, but has always been co-eternal with it, since it is formed of the substance of wisdom."

Of the same from the same letter: —

"So the body taken of Mary was human according to the scriptures, and real in that it was the same as our own. For Mary was our sister, since we are all of Adam, a fact which no one could doubt who remembers the words of Luke."[6]

Testimony of the holy Basil, bishop of Cæsarea: —

From the interpretation of Psalm LX.

"All strangers have stooped and been put under the yoke of Christ, wherefore also ' over Edom' does he ' cast out' his ' shoe.'[1] Now the shoe of the Godhead is the flesh which bore God whereby he came among men."

Of the same from his writings about the Holy Ghost to Amphilochius: —

"He uses the phrase ' of whom' instead of ' through whom;' as when Paul says ' made of a woman.'[2] He clearly made this distinction for us in another place where he says that the being made of the man is proper to a woman, but to a man the being made by the woman, in the words ' For as the woman is of the man so is the man by the woman.'[3] But with the object at once of pointing out the different use of these expressions, and of correcting *obiter* an error of certain men who supposed the body of the Lord to be spiritual, that he may shew how the God-bearing flesh was composed of human matter, he gives prominence to the more emphatic expression, for the expression ' by a woman ' was in danger of suggesting that the sense of the word generation was merely in passing through, while the phrase ' of the woman' makes the common nature of the child and of the mother plain enough."

Testimony of the holy Gregory bishop of Nazianus. From the former exposition to Cledonius: —

"If any one says that the flesh came down from heaven, and not from this earth, and from us, let him be Anathema. For the words ' The second man is from heaven,'[4] and ' as is the heavenly such are they also that are heavenly'[5] and ' no man hath ascended up to heaven but the son of man that came down from heaven,'[6] and any other similar passage, must be understood to be spoken on account of the union with man, as also the statement that ' all things were made by Christ,'[7] and that ' Christ dwells in our hearts,'[8] must be understood not according to the sensible, but according to the intellectual conception of the Godhead, the terms being commingled together just as are the natures."

Of the same from the same work: —

"Let us see from their own words what reason they give for the being made man, that is for the incarnation. If indeed it was that God otherwise not contained in space, might be contained in space and, as it were under a veil, might converse with men in the flesh, then their mask and their stage play are exquisite: not to say that it was possible for Him otherwise to converse

---

[1] Rev. 1. 9.
[2] Ps. xxi. 12.
[3] Ps. lxxxviii. 4. 5.
[4] Isaiah ii. 13.
[5] The antithesis is between the Greek words θέσις and φύσις. cf. "Κρινοτέλην Πινδάρου, θέσει δὲ Φιλοξένου." Corp. Ins. (add.) 2480. d.
[6] Luke iii. 3S.

[1] Ps. lx. 8.
[2] Gal. iv. 4.
[3] I. Cor. xi. 12.
[4] I. Cor. xv. 47.
[5] I. Cor. xv. 48.
[6] John iii. 13.
[7] John i. 3.
[8] Ephes. iii. 17.

with us, as of yore, in a burning bush and in human form, but if that He might undo the damnation of sin by taking like to like [1] then just as He required flesh on account of the condemned flesh, and a soul on account of the soul, so too he required a mind on account of the mind, which in Adam not only fell but, — to employ a term which physicians are accustomed to use about diseases — was affected with original malady.[2] For that which did not keep the commandment was what had received the commandment; and that which dared transgression was what had not kept the commandment; and that which specially needed salvation was what had transgressed, and that which was assumed was what needed salvation; so the mind was assumed. Now this point has been demonstrated, whether they will or no, by proofs which are so to say mathematical and necessary. But you are doing just as though, if a man were to have a diseased eye and a limping foot you were to cure the foot but leave the eye uncured; or, if a painter had painted a picture badly, were to alter the picture, but leave the painter alone, as though he were doing his work well. But if they are so constrained by these arguments as to take refuge in the statement that it is possible for God to save man, even without a mind, why then clearly He might have done so even without flesh, by the mere expression of His will, just as He works and has worked in the universe without a body. Away then with the flesh as well as with the mind! Let there be no inconsistency in your absurdity."

Testimony of the Holy Gregory, bishop of Nyssa. From his sermon on Abraham : —

" So the Word came down not naked, but after having been made flesh, not in the form of God, but in the form of a servant.[3] This then is He who said that He could do nothing of Himself.[4] For the not being able is the part of powerlessness. For as darkness is opposed to light, and death to life, so is weakness to power. But yet Christ is Power of God. Power is wholly inconsistent with not being able. For if power were powerless what is powerful? When then the Word declares that He can do nothing it is plain that He does not attribute his powerlessness to the Godhead of the Only-begotten, but connects his not being able with the powerlessness of our nature.

The flesh is weak, as it is written, 'The spirit is willing, but the flesh is weak.' " [1]

Of the same from his Book " on the Perfection of Life " : —

"Again the true lawgiver, of whom Moses was a type, hewed for Himself out of our earth the slabs of nature. No wedlock fashioned for Him the flesh that was to receive the godhead, but He Himself is made the hewer of His own flesh, graven as it is by the finger of God. For the Holy Ghost came upon the Virgin, and the power of the Highest overshadowed her.[2] And when this had come to pass, nature once again took its indestructible character, being made immortal by the marks of the divine finger."

Of the same from his Book against Eunomius : —

"We assert therefore that when He said above that wisdom built for herself a house,[3] he intimates by the phrase the formation of the flesh of the Lord, for the very wisdom made its home in no strange dwelling, but built itself its dwelling of the Virgin's body."

Of the same from the same treatise : —

"The Word was before the ages, but the flesh was made in the last times, and no one would say on the contrary either that the flesh was before the ages, or the Word made in the last times."

Of the same from the same treatise : —

" The expression ' created me ' [4] is not to be understood of the divine and the undefiled, but, as has been said, of our created nature, according to the dispensation of the incarnation." [5]

Of the same from the first discourse on the Beatitudes : —

" ' Who being in the form of God, thought it not robbery to be equal with God, but emptied himself, and took the form of a servant.' [6] What poorer, in respect of God, than the form of a servant? What more lowly, in respect of the King of all, than approach to fellowship in our poor nature? The King of Kings and Lord of Lords [7] voluntarily dons the form of servitude."

Testimony of the Holy Flavianus, bishop of Antioch. From his sermon on John the Baptist : —

" Do not think of connexion in any physical sense, nor entertain the idea of conjugal intercourse. For thy Creator is creating His own bodily temple now being born of thee."

Of the same from his book on " The Spirit of the Lord is upon me " : —

---

[1] The original for ἁρπάσας, "seizing" has ἁγιάσας i. e. hallowing.
[2] The word used is πρωτοπαθεῖν, a late and rare one. Galen uses the correlative πρωτοπάθεια to express a condition distinguished from συμπάθεια.
[3] Phil. ii. 7. [4] John v. 19.

[1] Matt. xxvi. 41.   [5] οἰκονομία. cf. note on p. 72.
[2] Luke i. 35.   [6] Phil. ii. 6. 7.
[3] Prov. ix. 1.   [7] Deut. x. 17; Rev. xvii. 14. and xix. 16.
[4] Prov. viii. 22; lxx. "ἔκτισε."

"Hear Him saying, 'The Spirit is upon me because He hath anointed me.'[1] You do not know, He says, what you read, for I, the anointed with the Spirit, am come to you. Now what is akin to us, and not the invisible nature, is anointed with the Spirit."[2]

Testimony of Amphilochius, bishop of Iconium. From his Discourse on " My Father is greater than I:"[3] —

"Distinguish me now the natures, the Divine and the human. For man was not made from God by falling away, nor was God made of man by advancement. I am speaking of God and man. When, however, you attribute the passions to the flesh and the miracles to God, you of necessity and involuntarily assign the lowly titles to the man born of Mary, and the exalted and divine to the Word Who in the beginning was God. Wherefore in some cases I utter exalted words, in others lowly, to the end that by means of the lofty I may shew the nature of the indwelling Word, and by the lowly, own the weakness of the lowly flesh. Whence sometimes I call myself equal to the Father and sometimes greater than the Father, not contradicting myself, but shewing that I am God and man, for God is of the lofty, man of the lowly; but if you wish to know how my Father is greater than I, I spoke of the flesh and not of the person of the Godhead."

Of the same from his discourse on " The Son can do nothing of Himself:"[4] —

"How was Adam disobedient in Heaven, and how of heavenly body was he formed first-formed beside the first formation? But it was the Adam of the earth who was formed at the beginning; the Adam of the earth disobeyed; the Adam of the earth was assumed. Wherefore also the Adam of the earth was saved that thus the reason of the incarnation[5] may be proved necessary and true."[6]

Testimony of the Holy John Bishop of Constantinople. From the speech which he made when the Gothic envoy had spoken before him: —

"See from the beginning what He does. He clothes Himself in our nature, powerless and vanquished, that by its means He may fight and struggle and from the beginning He uproots the nature of rebellion."

Of the same from his discourse on[1] The Festival of the Nativity: —

"For is it not of the very last stupidity for them to bring down their own gods into stones and cheap wooden images, shutting them up as it were in a kind of prison, and to fancy that there is nothing disgraceful in what they either say or do, and then to find fault with us for saying that God made a living temple for Himself of the Holy Ghost, by means of which he brought succour to the world? For if it is disgraceful for God to dwell in a human body, then in proportion as the stone and the wood are more worthless than man is it much more disgraceful for him to dwell in stone and wood. But perhaps mankind seems to them to be of less value than these senseless objects. They bring down the substance of God into stones and into dogs;[2] but many heretics into fouler things than these. But we could never endure even to hear of these things.[3] But what we say is that of a virgin's womb the Christ took pure flesh, holy and without spot, and made impervious to all sin, and restored the body[4] that was His own."

A little further on: "And we assert that when the divine Word had fashioned for Himself a holy temple by its means he brought the heavenly state into our life."

Of the same from the oration: That the lowly words and deeds of Christ were not spoken and done through lack of power, but through distinctions of dispensation.

"What then are the causes of many humble things having been said about Him both by Himself and by His apostles? The first and greatest cause is the fact of His having clothed Himself with flesh, and wishing all his contemporaries and all who have lived since, to believe that He was not a shadow, nor what was seen merely a form, but reality of nature. For if when He Himself and His apostles had spoken about Him so often in humble and in human sense, the devil yet had power to persuade some wretched and miserable men to deny the reason of the incarnation, and dare to say that He did not take flesh and so to destroy all the ground of His love for man, how many would not have fallen into this abyss if He had never said anything of the kind?"

I have now produced for you a few out of many authorities of the heralds of the truth,

---

[1] Is. lxi. 1.
[2] Of these two works no fragments exist but these two preserved by Theodoretus.
[3] John xiv. 28.
[4] John v. 19.
[5] οἰκονομία. cf. note on p. 72.
[6] cf. I. Cor. xv. 47.

[1] Migne II. 356.
[2] e.g. Anubis, the barker Anubis — cf. Virg. Æn. viii. 698, and the common oath " by the dog," unless indeed the common adjuration of Socrates νὴ τὸν κύνα may have been only a vernacular substitute for νὴ τὸν Δια, like the vulgar " law " for " Lord." The Benedictine Ed. adds " cats."
[3] cf. Ephes. v. 12.
[4] σκεῦος. cf. 2 Cor. iv. 7. 1 Thess. iv. 4. 1 Peter iii. 7. Cicero. Tusc. 1. 22 calls the body " vas animi."

not to stun you with too many. They are quite enough to show the bent of the mind of the excellent writers. It is now for you to say what force their writings seem to have.

Eran. — They have all spoken in harmony with one another, and the workers in the vineyard of the West agree with them whose husbandry is done in the region of the rising sun. Yet I perceived a considerable difference in their sayings.

Orth. — They are successors of the divine apostles; some even of those apostles were privileged to hear the holy voice and see the goodly sight. The majority of them too were adorned with the crown of martyrdom. Does it seem right for you to wag the tongue of blasphemy against them?

Eran. — I shrink from doing this; at the same time I do not approve of their great divergence.

Orth. — But now I will bring you an unexpected remedy. I will adduce one of your own beautiful heresy — your teacher Apollinarius,[1] and I will shew you that he understood the text " The Word was made flesh " just as the holy Fathers did. Hear now what he wrote about it in his " Summary."

The testimony of Apollinarius from his " Summary " : —

" If no one is turned into that which he assumes, and Christ assumed flesh, then He was not turned into flesh."

And immediately afterward he continues : —

" For also He gave himself to us in relationship by means of the body to save us. Now that which saves is far more excellent than that which is being saved. Far more excellent then than we are, is He in the assumption of a body ! But He would not have been more excellent had He been turned into flesh."

A little further on he says : —

" The simple is one, but the complex cannot be one ; he then that alleges that He was made flesh affirms the mutation of the one Word. But if the complex is also one, as man, then he who on account of the union with the flesh says the Word was made flesh means the one in complexity."

And again a little further on he says — " To be made flesh is to be made empty,[2] but the being made empty declares not man, but the Son of man, who ' emptied Himself' not by undergoing change, but by investiture."

There ; you see the teacher of your own

doctrines has introduced the word ' investiture ' and indeed in his little work upon the faith he says — " We then believe that he was made flesh, while His Godhead remained unchanged for the renewal of the manhood. For in the holy power of God there has been neither alteration nor change of place, nor inclusion " — and then shortly again — " We worship God who took flesh of the blessed virgin, and on this account in the flesh is man, but in the spirit God." And in another exposition he says — " We confess the Son of God to have been made the Son of man, not nominally but verily, on taking flesh of the Virgin Mary."

Eran. — I did not suppose that Apollinarius held these sentiments. I had other ideas about him.

Orth. — Well ; now you have learnt that not only the prophets and apostles, and they who after them were ordained teachers of the world, but even Apollinarius, the writer of heretical babbling, confesses the divine Word to be immutable, states that He was not turned into flesh but assumed flesh, and this over and over again, as you have heard. Do not then struggle to throw your master's blasphemy into the shade by your own. For, says the Lord " the disciple is not above his master." [1]

Eran. — Yes, I confess that the divine Word of God is immutable and took flesh. It were the uttermost foolishness to withstand authorities so many and so great.

Orth. — Do you wish to have a solution of the rest of the difficulties?

Eran. — Let us put off their investigation until to-morrow.

Orth. — Very well ; our synod is dismissed. Let us depart, and bear in mind what we have agreed upon.

DIALOGUE II.

THE UNCONFOUNDED.

Eranistes and Orthodoxus.

Eran. — I am come as I promised. 'Tis yours to adopt one of two alternatives, and either furnish a solution of my difficulties, or assent to what I and my friends lay down.

Orth. — I accept your challenge, for I think it right and fair. But we must first recall to mind at what point we left off our discourse yesterday, and what was the conclusion of our argument.

---

[1] cf. p. 132.   [2] σαρκωσις κένωσις. cf. Phil. ii. 7.   [1] Matt. x. 24.

Eran. — I will remind you of the end. I remember our agreeing that the divine Word remained immutable, and took flesh, and was not himself changed into flesh.

Orth. — You seem to be content with the points agreed on, for you have faithfully called them to mind.

Eran. — Yes, and I have already said that the man that withstands teachers so many and so great is indubitably out of his mind. I was moreover put to not a little shame to find that Apollinarius used the same terms as the orthodox, although in his books about the incarnation his drift has distinctly been in another direction.

Orth. — Then we affirm that the Divine Word took flesh?

Eran. — We do.

Orth. — And what do we mean by the flesh? A body only, as is the view of Arius and Eunomius, or body and soul?

Eran. — Body and soul.

Orth. — What kind of soul? The reasonable soul, or that which is by some termed the *phytic*, vegetable,[1] that is, vital? for the fable-mongering quackery of the Apollinarians compels us to ask unseemly questions.

Eran. — Does then Apollinarius make a distinction of souls? [2]

Orth. — He says that man is composed of three parts, of a body, a vital soul, and further of a reasonable soul, which he terms mind. Holy Scripture on the contrary knows only one, not two souls; and this is plainly taught us by the formation of the first man. For it is written God took dust from the earth and " formed man," and " breathed into his nostrils the breath of life, and man became a living soul." [3] And in the gospels the Lord said to the holy disciples " Fear not them which kill the body, but are not able to kill the soul; but rather fear him which is able to destroy both soul and body in hell." [4]

And the very divine Moses when he told the tale of them that came down into Egypt and stated with whom each tribal chief had come in, added, " All the souls that came out of Egypt were seventy-five," [5] reckoning one soul for each immigrant. And the divine apostle at Troas, when all supposed

Eutychus to be dead, said " Trouble not yourselves for his soul is in him." [1]

Eran. — It is shewn clearly that each man has one soul.

Orth. — But Apollinarius says two; and that the Divine Word took the unreasonable, and that instead of the reasonable, he was made in the flesh. It was on this account that I asked what kind of soul you assert to have been assumed with the body.

Eran. — I say the reasonable. For I follow the Divine Scripture.

Orth. — We agree then that the " form of a servant" assumed by the Divine Word was complete.

Eran. — Yes; complete.

Orth. — And rightly; for since the whole first man became subject to sin, and lost the impression of the Divine Image,[2] and the race followed, it results that the Creator, with the intention of renewing the blurred image, assumed the nature in its entirety, and stamped an imprint far better than the first.

Eran. — True. But now I beg you in the first place that the meaning of the terms employed may be made quite clear, that thus our discussion may advance without hindrance, and no investigation of doubtful points intervene to interrupt our conversation.

Orth. — What you say is admirable. Ask now concerning whatever point you like.

Eran. — What must we call Jesus the Christ? Man?

Orth. — By neither name alone, but by both. For the Divine Man after being made man was named Jesus Christ. " For," it is written, " Thou shalt call His name Jesus for he shall save His people from their sins," [3] and unto you is born this day in the city of David Christ the Lord.[4] Now these are angels' voices. But before the Incarnation he was named God, son of God, only begotten, Lord, Divine Word, and Creator. For it is written " In the beginning was the Word, and the word was with God, and the word was God," [5] and " all things were made by Him," [6] and " He was life," [7] and " He

---

[1] φυτικός, of or belonging to φυτόν, or plant; but though φυτὸν is opposed to ζῷον, it is also used of any creature, and here seems to mean no more than the soul of physical life, and nothing beyond.
[2] cf. p. 132.
[3] Gen. ii. 7.
[4] Matt. x. 28. of. Luke xii. 4. 5.
[5] Gen. xlvi. 20. lxx. In the Hebrew the number is but seventy, including Jacob himself. St. Stephen, as was natural in a Hellenized Jew follows the lxx. (Acts vii. 14.) For the number 75 there were doubtless important traditional authorities known to the lxx.

[1] Acts xx. 10.
[2] This " lost" must be qualified. The Scriptural doctrine is that the " image of God " though defaced and marred, is not lost or destroyed. After the flood the " image of God " is still quoted as against murder Gen. ix. 6. St. James urges it as a reason against cursing (iv. 9). cf. I. Cor. xi. 7. So the IXth Article declares original sin to be, not the nature, which is good, but the " fault and corruption of the nature of every man;" in short the " image of God," like the gifts of God, as David in Browning's " Saul" has it, " a man may waste, desecrate, *never quite lose.*" cf. p. 164 and note.
[3] Matt. i. 21.
[4] Luke ii. 11. τίκτεται is substituted for ἐτέχθη, in addition to the omission of " a Saviour which is." In this verse the MSS. do not vary.
[5] John i. 1. [6] John i. 3. [7] John i. 4.

was the true light which lighteth every man that cometh into the world." There are also other similar passages, declaring the divine nature. But after the Incarnation He was named Jesus and Christ.

Eran. — Therefore the Lord Jesus is God only.

Orth. — You hear that the divine Word was made man, and do you call him God only?

Eran. — Since He became man without being changed, but remained just what He was before, we must call Him just what He was.

Orth. — The divine Word was and is and will be immutable. But when He had taken man's nature He became man. It behoves us therefore to confess both natures, both that which took, and that which was taken.

Eran. — We must name Him by the nobler.

Orth — Man, — I mean man the animal, — is he a simple or a composite being?

Eran. — Composite.

Orth. — Composed of what component parts?

Eran. — Of a body and a soul.

Orth. — And of these natures whether is nobler?

Eran. — Clearly the soul, for it is reasonable and immortal, and has been entrusted with the sovereignty of the animal. But the body is mortal and perishable, and without the soul is unreasonable, and a corpse.

Orth. — Then the divine Scripture ought to have called the animal after its more excellent part.

Eran. — It does so call it, for it calls them that came out of Egypt souls. For with seventy-five souls, it says, Israel came down into Egypt.

Orth. — But does the divine Scripture never call any one after the body?

Eran. — It calls them that are the slaves of flesh, flesh. For " God," it is written, " said my spirit shall not always remain in these men, for they are flesh." [1]

Orth. — But without blame no one is called flesh?

Eran. — I do not remember.

Orth. — Then I will remind you, and point out to you that even the very saints are called " flesh." Answer now. What would you call the apostles? Spiritual, or fleshly?

Eran. — Spiritual; — and leaders and teachers of the spiritual.

Orth. — Hear now the holy Paul when he says " But when it pleased God who separated me from my mother's womb, and called me by his grace, to reveal his son in me that I might preach him among the heathen, immediately I conferred not with flesh and blood neither went I up to them that were apostles before me." [1] Does he so style the apostles because he blames them?

Eran. — Certainly not.

Orth. — Is it not that he names them after their visible nature, and comparing the calling which is of men with that which is of heaven?

Eran. — True.

Orth. — Then hear too the psalmist David — " Unto thee shall all flesh come." [2] Hear too, the prophet Isaiah foretelling " All flesh shall see the salvation of our God." [3]

Eran. — It is made perfectly plain that Holy Scripture names human nature from the flesh without the least blame.

Orth. — I will proceed to give you the yet further proof.

Eran. — What further?

Orth. — The fact that sometimes when giving blame the divine Scripture uses only the name of soul.

Eran. — And where will you find this in holy Scripture?

Orth. — Hear the Lord God speaking through the prophet Ezekiel " The soul that sinneth it shall die." [4] Moreover through the great Moses He saith " If a soul sin — " [5] And again " It shall come to pass that every soul that will not hear that prophet shall be cut off." [6] And many other passages of the same kind may be found.

Eran. — This is plainly proved.

Orth. — In cases, then, where there is a certain natural union, and a combination of created things, and of beings connected by service and by time, it is not the custom of holy Scripture to use a name for this being derived only from the nobler nature; it names it indiscriminately both by the meaner and by the nobler. If so, how can you find fault with us for calling Christ the Lord, man, after confessing Him to be God, when many things combine to compel us to do so?

Eran. — What is there to compel us to call the Saviour Christ, " man "?

Orth. — The diverse and mutually inconsistent opinions of the heretics.

Eran. — What opinions, and contrary to what?

---

[1] Gal. i. 15-17.
[2] Ps. lxv. 2.
[3] Is. xl. 5.
[4] Ez. xviii. 4 and 20.
[5] Lev. v. 1.
[6] The reference seems to be a loose combination of Numbers ix. 13. with Deut. xviii. 19.

---

[1] Gen. vi. 3. lxx. and Marg. in R. V.

Orth. — That of Arius to that of Sabellius. The one divides the substances: the other confounds the hypostases. Arius introduces three substances, and Sabellius makes one hypostasis instead of three.[1] Tell me now, how ought we to heal both maladies? Must we apply the same drug for both ailments, or for each the proper one?

Eran. — For each the proper one.

Orth. — We shall therefore endeavour to persuade Arius to acknowledge the substance of the Holy Trinity, and we shall adduce proofs of this position from Holy Scripture.

Eran. — Yes: this ought to be done.

Orth. — But in arguing with Sabellius we shall adopt the opposite course. Concerning the substance we shall advance no argument, for even he acknowledges but one.

Eran. — Plainly.

Orth. — But we shall do our best to cure the unsound part of his doctrine.

Eran. — We say that where he halts is about the hypostases.

Orth. — Since then he asserts there to be one hypostasis of the Trinity, we shall point out to him that the divine Scripture proclaims three hypostases.

Eran. — This is the course to take. But we have wandered from the subject.

Orth. — Not at all. We are collecting proofs of it, as you will learn in a moment. But tell me, do you understand that all the heresies which derive their name from Christ, acknowledge both the Godhead of Christ and His manhood?

Eran. — By no means.

Orth. — Do not some acknowledge the godhead alone, and some the manhood alone?

Eran. — Yes.

Orth. — And some but a part of the manhood?

Eran. — I think so. But it will be well for us to lay down the names of the holders of these different opinions, that the point under discussion may be made plainer.

Orth. — I will tell you the names. Simon, Menander, Marcion, Valentinus, Basilides, Bardesanes, Cerdo, and Manes, openly denied the humanity of Christ. On the other hand Artemon, Theodotus, Sabellius, Paul of Samosata, Marcellus, and Photinus, fell into the diametrically opposite blasphemy; for they preach Christ to be man only, and deny the Godhead which existed before the ages. Arius and Eunomius make the Godhead of the only begotten a created God-

head, and maintain that He assumed only a body. Apollinarius confesses that the assumed body was a living[1] body, but in his work deprives the reasonable soul alike of its honour and of its salvation. This is the contrariety of these corrupt opinions. But do you, with all due love of truth, tell us, must we institute a discussion with these men, or shall we let them go dashed down headlong and howling to their doom?

Eran. — It is inhuman to neglect the sick.

Orth. — Very well; then we must compassionate them, and do our best to heal them.

Eran. — By all means.

Orth. — If then you had scientifically learned how to cure the body, and round you stood many men asking you to cure them, and shewing you their various ailments, such as arise from running at the eyes, injury to the ears, tooth-ache, contraction of the joints, palsy, bile, or phlegm, what would you have done? Tell me; would you have applied the same treatment to all, or to each that which was appropriate?

Eran. — I should certainly have given to each the appropriate remedy.

Orth. — So by applying cold treatment to the hot, and heating the cold, and loosing the strained, and giving tension to the loose, and drying the moist, and moistening the dry, you would have driven out the diseases and restored the health which they had expelled.

Eran. — This is the treatment prescribed by medical science, for contraries, it is said, are the remedies of contraries.

Orth. — If you were a gardener, would you give the same treatment to all plants? or their own to the mulberry and the fig, and so to the pear, to the apple, and to the vine what is fitting to each, and in a word to each plant its own proper culture?

Eran. — It is obvious that each plant requires its own treatment.

Orth. — And if you undertook to be a ship builder, and saw that the mast wanted repair, would you try to mend it in the same way as you would the tiller? or would you give it the proper treatment of a mast?

Eran. — There is no question about these things: everything demands its own treatment, be it plant or limb or gear or tackle.

Orth. — Then is it not monstrous to apply to the body and to things without life to each its own appropriate treatment, and not to keep this rule of treatment in the case of the soul?

---

[1] Vide note on page 36.

[1] ἔμψυχον.

Eran. — Most unjust; nay, rather stupid than unrighteous. They who adopt any other method are quite unskilled in the healing art.

Orth. — Then in disputing against each heresy we shall use the appropriate remedy?

Eran. — By all means.

Orth. — And it is fitting treatment to add what is wanting and to remove what is superfluous?

Eran. — Yes.

Orth. — In endeavouring then to cure Photinus and Marcellus and their adherents, in order to carry out the rule of treatment, what should we add?

Eran. — The acknowledgment of the Godhead of Christ, for it is this that they lack.

Orth. — But about the manhood we will say nothing to them, for they acknowledge the Lord Christ to be man.

Eran. — You are right.

Orth. — And in arguing with Arius and Eunomius about the incarnation of the only begotten, what should we persuade them to add to their own confession?

Eran. — The assumption of the soul; for they say that the divine Word took only a body.

Orth. — And what does Apollinarius lack to make his teaching accurate about the incarnation?

Eran. — Not to separate the mind from the soul, but to confess that, with the body, was assumed a reasonable soul.

Orth. — Then shall we dispute with him on this point?

Eran. — Certainly.

Orth. — But under this head what did we assert to be confessed, and what altogether denied, by Marcion, Valentinus, Manes and their adherents?

Eran. — That they admitted their belief in the Godhead of Christ, but do not accept the doctrine of His manhood.

Orth. — We shall therefore do our best to persuade them to accept also the doctrine of the manhood, and not to call the divine incarnation [1] a mere appearance.

Eran. — It will be well so to do.

Orth. — We will therefore tell them that it is right to style the Christ not only God, but also man.

Eran. — By all means.

Orth. — And how is it possible for us to induce others to style the Christ ' man' while we excuse ourselves from doing so? They will not yield to our persuasion, but on the contrary will convict us of agreeing with them.

Eran. — And how can we, confessing as we do that the divine Word took flesh and a reasonable soul, agree with them?

Orth. — If we confess the fact, why then shun the word?

Eran. — It is right to name the Christ from His nobler qualities.

Orth. — Keep this rule then. Do not speak of Him as crucified, nor yet as risen from the dead, and so on.

Eran. — But these are the names of the sufferings of salvation. Denial of the sufferings implies denial of the salvation.

Orth. — And the name Man is the name of a nature. Not to pronounce the name is to deny the nature: denial of the nature is denial of the sufferings, and denial of the sufferings does away with the salvation.

Eran. — I hold it profitable to acknowledge the assumed nature; but to style the Saviour of the world man is to belittle the glory of the Lord.

Orth. — Do you then deem yourself wiser than Peter and Paul; aye, and than the Saviour Himself? For the Lord said to the Jews "Why do ye seek to kill me, a man that hath told you the truth, which I heard of my Father?"[1] And He frequently called Himself Son of Man.

And the meritorious Peter, in his sermon to the Jewish people, says, — "Ye men of Israel, hear these words. Jesus of Nazareth, a man approved of God among you."[2] And the blessed Paul, when bringing the message of salvation to the chiefs of the Areopagus, among many other things said this, —

"And the times of this ignorance God winked at; but now commandeth all men everywhere to repent: Because he hath appointed a day in the which he will judge the world in righteousness by that man whom he hath ordained, whereof he hath given assurance unto all men, in that he hath raised him from the dead."[3] He then who excuses himself from using the name appointed and preached by the Lord and his Apostles deems himself wiser than even these great instructors, aye, even than the very wellspring of the wisest.

Eran. — They gave this instruction to the unbelievers. Now the greater part of the world [4] has professed the faith.

Orth. — But we have still among us Jews

---

[1] *John* viii. 40. Note the looseness of citation.
[2] *Acts* ii. 22.   [3] *Acts* xvii. 30, 31.
[4] ἡ οἰκουμένη means of course the Empire and the adjacent countries, the "*orbis veteribus notus.*"

---

[1] οἰκονομίαν. cf. p. 72, note.

and pagans and of heretics systems innumerable, and to each of these we must give fit and appropriate teaching. But, supposing we were all of one mind, tell me now, what harm is there in calling the Christ both God and man? Do we not behold in Him perfect Godhead, and manhood likewise lacking in nothing?

Eran. — This we have owned again and again.

Orth. — Why then deny what we have again and again owned?

Eran. — I hold it unnecessary to call the Christ ' man,' — especially when believer is conversing with believer.

Orth. — Do you consider the divine Apostle a believer?

Eran. — Yes: a teacher of all believers.

Orth. — And do you deem Timothy worthy of being so styled?

Eran. — Yes: both as a disciple of the Apostle, and as a teacher of the rest.

Orth. — Very well: then hear the teacher of teachers writing to his very perfect disciple. " There is one God, and one mediator between God and man, the man Christ Jesus, who gave himself a ransom for all." [1] Do stop your idle prating, and laying down the law about divine names. Moreover in this passage that very name ' mediator' stands indicative both of Godhead and of manhood. He is called a mediator because He does not exist as God alone ; for how, if He had had nothing of our nature could He have mediated between us and God? But since as God He is joined with God as having the same substance, and as man with us, because from us He took the form of a servant, He is properly termed a mediator, uniting in Himself distinct qualities by the unity of natures of Godhead, I mean, and of manhood. [2]

Eran. — But was not Moses called a mediator, though only a man? [3]

Orth. — He was a type of the reality: but the type has not all the qualities of the reality. Wherefore though Moses was not by nature God, yet, to fulfil the type, he was called a god. For He says " See, I have made thee a god to Pharaoh." [4] And then directly afterwards he assigns him also a Prophet as though to God, for " Aaron thy brother," He says, " shall be thy Prophet." [5] But the reality is by nature God, and by nature man.

Eran. — But who would call one not

having the distinct characteristics of the archetype, a type?

Orth. — The imperial images, it seems, you do not call images of the emperor

Eran. — Yes, I do.

Orth. — Yet they have not all the characteristics which their archetype has. For in the first place they have neither life nor reason ; secondly they have no inner organs, heart, I mean, and belly and liver and the adjacent parts. Further they present the appearance of the organs of sense, but perform none of their functions, for they neither hear, nor speak, nor see ; they cannot write ; they cannot walk, nor perform any other human action ; and yet they are called imperial statues. In this sense Moses was a mediator and Christ was a mediator ; but the former as an image and type and the latter as reality. But that I may make this point clearer to you from yet another authority, call to mind the words used of Melchisedec in the Epistle to the Hebrews.

Eran. — What words?

Orth. — Those in which the divine Apostle comparing the Levitical priesthood with that of the Christ likens Melchisedec in other respects to the Lord Christ, and says that the Lord had the priesthood after the order of Melchisedec. [1]

Eran. — I think the words of the divine Apostle are as follows ; — " For this Melchisedec, king of Salem, priest of the most high God who met Abraham returning from the slaughter of the kings, and blessed him ; to whom also Abraham gave a tenth part of all ; first being by interpretation king of righteousness, and after that also king of Salem, which is king of peace ; without father, without mother, without descent, having neither beginning of days, nor end of life ; but made like unto the son of God ; abideth a priest continually." [2] I presume you spoke of this passage.

Orth. — Yes, I spoke of this ; and I must praise you for not mutilating it, but for quoting the whole. Tell me now, does each one of these points fit Melchisedec in nature and reality?

Eran. — Who has the audacity to deny a fitness where the divine apostle has asserted it?

Orth. — Then you say that all this fits Melchisedec by nature?

Eran. — Yes.

Orth. — Do you say that he was a man, or assumed some other nature?

Eran. — A man.

---

[1] I. Tim. ii. 5, 6.
[2] cf. Job ix. 33. " daysman betwixt us that might lay his hand upon us both."
[3] Gal. iii. 19. cf. Deut. v. 5.
[4] Exodus vii. 1.   [5] Ex. vii. 1.

Hebrews vi. 20.   [2] Hebrews vii. 1, 2, 3.

Orth. — Begotten or unbegotten?

Eran. — You are asking very absurd questions.

Orth. — The fault lies with you for openly opposing the truth. Answer then.

Eran. — There is one only unbegotten, who is God and Father.

Orth. — Then we assert that Melchisedec was begotten?

Eran. — Yes.

Orth. — But the passage about him teaches the opposite. Remember the words which you quoted a moment ago, " Without father, without mother, without descent, having neither beginning of days nor end of life." How then do the words " Without father and without mother " fit him ; and how the statement that he neither received beginning of existence nor end, since all this transcends humanity?

Eran. — These things do in fact overstep the limits of human nature.

Orth. — Then shall we say that the Apostle told lies?

Eran. — God forbid.

Orth. — How then is it possible both to testify to the truth of the Apostle, and apply the supernatural to Melchisedec?

Eran. — The passage is a very difficult one, and requires much explanation.

Orth. — For any one willing to consider it with attention it will not be hard to attain perception of the meaning of the words. After saying " without father, without mother, without descent, having neither beginning of days nor end of life," the divine Apostle adds " made like unto the Son of God, abideth a priest continually." [1] Here he plainly teaches us that the Lord Christ is archetype of Melchisedec in things concerning the human nature. And he speaks of Melchisedec as " made like unto the Son of God." Now let us examine the point in this manner ; — do you say that the Lord had a father according to the flesh?

Eran. — Certainly not.

Orth. — Why?

Eran. — He was born of the holy Virgin alone.

Orth. — He is therefore properly styled " without father " ?

Eran. — True.

Orth. — Do you say that according to the divine Nature He had a mother? [2]

Eran. — Certainly not.

Orth. — For He was begotten of the Father alone before the ages?

Eran. — Agreed.

Orth. — And yet, as the generation He has of the Father is ineffable, He is spoken of as " without descent." " Who " says the prophet " shall declare His generation? " [1]

Eran. — You are right.

Orth. — Thus it becomes Him to have neither beginning of days nor end of life ; for He is without beginning, indestructible, and, in a word, eternal, and coeternal with the Father.

Eran. — This is my view too. But we must now consider how this fits the admirable Melchisedec.

Orth. — As an image and type. The image, as we have just observed, has not all the properties of the archetype. Thus to the Saviour these qualities are proper both by nature and in reality ; but the story of the origin of the race has attributed them to Melchisedec. For after telling us of the father of the patriarch Abraham, and of the father and mother of Isaac, and in like manner of Jacob and of his sons, and exhibiting the pedigree of our first forefathers, of Melchisedec it records neither the father nor the mother, nor does it teach that he traced his descent from any one of Noah's sons, to the end that he may be a type of Him who is in reality without father, and without mother. And this is what the divine Apostle would have us understand, for in this very passage he says further, " But he whose descent is not counted from them received tithes of Abraham, and blessed him that had the promises." [2]

Eran. — Then, since Holy Scripture has not mentioned his parents, can he be called without father and without mother?

Orth. — If he had really been without father and without mother, he would not have been an image, but a reality. But since these are his qualities not by nature, but according to the dispensation of the Divine Scripture, he exhibits the type of the reality.

Eran. — The type must have the character of the archetype.

Orth. — Is man called an image of God?

Eran. — Man is not an image of God, but was made in the image of God. [3]

Orth. — Listen then to the Apostle. He says : " For a man indeed ought not to cover his head, forasmuch as he is the image and glory of God." [4]

Eran. — Granted, then, that he is an image of God.

Orth. — According to your argument then he must needs have plainly preserved the

---

[1] Heb. vii. 3.
[2] The bearing of this on Theodoret's relation to Nestorianism will be observed.

[1] Is. liii. 8.
[2] Heb. vii. 6.
[3] Gen. i. 27.
[4] I. Cor. xi. 7.

characters of the archetype, and have been uncreate, uncompounded, and infinite. He ought in like manner to have been able to create out of the non existent, he ought to have fashioned all things by his word and without labour, in addition to this to have been free from sickness, sorrow, anger, and sin, to have been immortal and incorruptible and to possess all the qualities of the archetype.

Eran. — Man is not an image of God in every respect.

Orth. — Though truly an image in the qualities in which you would grant him to be so, you will find that he is separated by a wide interval from the reality.

Eran. — Agreed.

Orth. — Consider now too this point. The divine Apostle calls the Son the image of the Father; for he says " Who is the image of the invisible God?" [1]

Eran. — What then; has not the Son all the qualities of the Father?

Orth. — He is not Father. He is not un-caused. He is not unbegotten.

Eran. — If He were He would not be Son.

Orth. — Then does not what I said hold good; the image has not all the qualities of the archetype?

Eran. — True.

Orth. — Thus too the divine Apostle said that Melchisedec is made like unto the Son of God.[2]

Eran. — Suppose we grant that he is without Father and without Mother and without descent, as you have said. But how are we to understand his having neither beginning of days nor end of life?

Orth. — The holy Moses when writing the ancient genealogy tells us how Adam being so many years old begat Seth,[3] and when he had lived so many years he ended his life.[4] So too he writes of Seth, of Enoch, and of the rest, but of Melchisedec he mentions neither beginning of existence nor end of life. Thus as far as the story goes he has neither beginning of days nor end of life, but in truth and reality the only begotten Son of God never began to exist and shall never have an end.

Eran. — Agreed.

Orth. — Then, so far as what belongs to God and is really divine is concerned, Melchisedec is a type of the Lord Christ; but as far as the priesthood is concerned, which belongs rather to man than to God, the Lord Christ was made a priest after the order of Melchisedec.[5] For Melchisedec was a high priest of the people, and the Lord Christ for all men has made the right holy offering of salvation.

Eran. — We have spent many words on this matter.

Orth. — Yet more were needed, as you know, for you said the point was a difficult one.

Eran. — Let us return to the question before us.

Orth. — What was the question?

Eran. — On my remarking that Christ must not be called man, but only God, you yourself besides many other testimonies adduced also the well known words of the Apostle which he has used in his epistle to Timothy — " One God, one mediator between God and men, the man, Christ Jesus, who gave himself a ransom for all to be testified in due time." [1]

Orth. — I remember from what point we diverged into this digression. It was when I had said that the name of mediator exhibits the two natures of the Saviour, and you said that Moses was called a mediator though he was only a man and not God and man. I was therefore under the necessity of following up these points to show that the type has not all the qualities of the archetype. Tell me, then, whether you allow that the Saviour ought also to be called man.

Eran. — I call Him God, for He is God's Son.

Orth. — If you call him God, because you have learnt that he is God's Son, call him also man, for he often called Himself " Son of Man."

Eran. — The name man does not apply to Him in the same way as the name God.

Orth. — As not really belonging to Him or for some other reason?

Eran. — God is his name by nature; man is the designation of the Incarnation.[2]

Orth. — But are we to look on the Incarnation as real, or as something imaginary and false?

Eran. — As real.

Orth. — If then the grace of the Incarnation is real, and what we call Incarnation is the divine Word's being made man, then the name man is real; for after taking man's nature He is called man.

Eran. — Before His passion He was styled man, but afterward He was no longer so styled.

Orth. — But it was after the Passion and the Resurrection that the divine Apostle wrote the Epistle to Timothy wherein he speaks of

---

[1] Coloss. I. 15.   [3] Gen. iv. 25.   [5] Heb. vi. 20.
[2] Hebrews vii. 3.   [4] Gen. v. 5.

[1] Tim. ii. 5, 6.   [2] οἰκονομία. Vide p. 72 n.

the Saviour Christ as man,[1] and writing after the Passion and the Resurrection to the Corinthians he exclaims "For since by man came death, by man came also the resurrection of the dead." [2] And in order to make his meaning clear he adds, "For as in Adam all die, even so in Christ shall all be made alive." [3] And after the Passion and the Resurrection the divine Peter, in his address to the Jews, called Him man.[4] And after His being taken up into heaven, Stephen the victorious, amid the storm of stones, said to the Jews, "Behold, I see the heavens opened, and the Son of man standing on the right hand of God." [5] Are we to suppose ourselves wiser than the illustrious heralds of the truth?

Eran. — I do not suppose myself wiser than the holy doctors, but I fail to find the use of the name.

Orth. — How then could you persuade them that deny the incarnation of the Lord, Marcionists, I mean, and Manichees, and all the rest who are thus unsound, to accept the teaching of the truth, unless you adduce these and similar proofs with the object of shewing that the Lord Christ is not God only but also man?

Eran. — Perhaps it is necessary to adduce them.

Orth. — Why not then teach the faithful the reality of the doctrine? Are you forgetful of the apostolic precept enjoining us to be " ready to give an answer." [6] Now let us look at the matter in this light. Does the best general engage the enemy, attack with arrows and javelins, and endeavour to break their column all alone, or does he also arm his men, and marshal them, and rouse their hearts to play the man?

Eran. — He ought rather to do this latter.

Orth. — Yes; for it is not the part of a general to expose his own life, and take his place in the ranks, and let his men go fast asleep, but rather to keep them awake for their work at their post.

Eran. — True.

Orth. — This is what the divine Paul did, for in writing to them who had made profession of their faith he said, " Take unto you the whole armour of God that ye be able to stand against the wiles of the Devil.' And again, " Stand therefore with your loins girt about with truth," [2] and so on. Bear in mind too what we have already said, that a physician supplies what nature lacks. Does

he find the cold redundant? He supplies the hot, and so on with the rest; and this is what the Lord does.

Eran. — And where will you show that the Lord has done this?

Orth. — In the holy gospels.

Eran. — Show me then and fulfil your promise.

Orth. — What did the Jews consider our Saviour Christ?

Eran. — A man.

Orth. — And that He was also God they were wholly ignorant.

Eran. — Yes.

Orth. — Was it not then necessary for the ignorant to learn?

Eran. — Agreed.

Orth. — Listen to Him then saying to them: " Many good works have I shewed you from my Father; for which of these works do ye stone me?"[1] And when they replied: " For a good work we stone thee not, but for blasphemy, and because that thou being a man makest thyself God," [2] He added " It is written in your law I said ye are gods. If he called them gods unto whom the word of God came and the scripture cannot be broken, say ye of Him whom the Father hath sanctified and sent into the world thou blasphemest, because I said I am the Son of God? If I do not the works of my father believe me not . . . that I am in the Father and the Father is in me." [3]

Eran. — In the passages you have just read you have shewn that the Lord shewed Himself to the Jews to be God and not man.

Orth. — Yes, for they did not need to learn what they knew; that He was a man they knew, but they did not know that He was from the beginning God. He adopted this same course in the case of the Pharisees; for when He saw them accosting Him as a mere man He asked them " What think ye of Christ? Whose son is He?" [4] And when they said " Of David" He went on " How then doth David calling him Lord say ' The Lord said unto my Lord sit thou on my right hand.' " [5] Then He goes on to argue, " If then He is His Lord how is He His Son?"

Eran. — You have brought testimony against yourself, for the Lord plainly taught the Pharisees to call Him not "Son of David," but " Lord of David." Wherefore He is distinctly shown wishing to be called God and not man.

Orth. — I am afraid you have not attended

---

[1] 1 Tim ii. 5.　　　　[4] Acts ii. 22.
[2] Cor. xv. 21.　　　　[5] Acts vii. 56
[3] 1 Cor. xv. 22.　　　[6] 1 Peter iii. 15.
[7] Eph. vi. 11 and 13, and observe looseness of quotation.
[8] Eph. vi. 14.

[1] John x. 32.　　　　　　　[2] John x. 33.
[3] John x. 34, 35, 36, 37, 38. Observe the variation in 34, and the omission in 38.
[4] Matt. xxii. 42.　　　　　[5] Matt. xxii. 43 and 44.

to the divine teaching. He did not repudiate the name of "Son of David," but He added that He ought also to be believed to be Lord of David. This He clearly shews in the words "If He is his Lord how is He then his Son?" He did not say "if He is Lord He is not Son," but "how is He his Son?" instead of saying in one respect He is Lord and in another Son. These passages both distinctly show the Godhead and the manhood.

Eran. — There is no need of argument. The Lord distinctly teaches that He does not wish to be called Son of David.

Orth. — Then He ought to have told the blind men and the woman of Canaan and the multitude not to call Him Son of David, and yet the blind men cried out "Thou Son of David have mercy on us." [1] And the woman of Canaan "Have mercy on me O Son of David; my daughter is grievously vexed with a Devil." [2] And the multitude : " Hosanna to the Son of David! Blessed is He that cometh in the name of the Lord." [3] And not only did He not take it ill, but even praised their faith; for the blind He freed from their long weary night and granted them the power of sight; the maddened and distraught daughter of the woman of Canaan He healed and drove out the wicked demon ; and when the chief priests and Pharisees were offended at them that shouted "Hosanna to the Son of David" He did not merely not prevent them from shouting, but even sanctioned their acclamation, for, said He, " I tell you that if these should hold their peace the stones would immediately cry out." [4]

Eran. — He put up with this style of address before the resurrection in condescension to the weakness of them that had not yet properly believed. But after the resurrection these names are needless.

Orth. — Where shall we rank the blessed Paul? among the perfect or the imperfect?

Eran. — It is wrong to joke about serious things.

Orth. — It is wrong to make light of the reading of the divine oracles.

Eran. — And who is such a wretch as to despise his own salvation?

Orth. — Answer my question, and then you will learn your ignorance.

Eran. — What question?

Orth. — Where are we to rank the divine Apostle?

Eran. — Plainly among the most perfect, and one of the perfect teachers.

Orth. — And when did he begin his teaching?

Eran. — After the ascension of the Saviour, the coming of the Spirit, and the stoning of the victorious Stephen.

Orth. — Paul, at the very end of his life, when writing his last letter to his disciple Timothy, and in giving him, as it were, his paternal inheritance by will, added " Remember that Jesus Christ of the seed of David was raised from the dead according to my gospel." [1] Then he went on to mention his sufferings on behalf of the gospel, and thus showed its truth saying, " Wherein I suffer trouble as an evil doer even unto bonds." [2]

It were easy for me to adduce many similar testimonies, but I have judged it needless to do so.

Eran. — You promised to prove that the Lord supplied the lacking instruction to them that needed, and you have shown that He discoursed about His own Godhead to the Pharisees, and to the rest of the Jews. But that He gave also His instruction about the flesh you have not shewn.

Orth. — It would have been quite superfluous to have discoursed about the flesh which was before their eyes, for He was plainly seen eating and drinking and toiling and sleeping. Furthermore, to omit the many and various events before the passion, after His resurrection He proved to His disbelieving disciples not His Godhead but His manhood; for He said, " Behold my hands and my feet that it is I myself. Handle me and see for a spirit hath not flesh and bones as ye see me have." [3]

Now I have fulfilled my promise, for we have proved the giving of instruction about the Godhead to them that were ignorant of the Godhead, and about the resurrection of the flesh to them that denied this latter. Cease therefore from contending, and confess the two natures of the Saviour.

Eran. — There were two before the union, but, after combining, they made one nature.

Orth. — When do you say that the union was effected?

Eran. — I say at the exact moment of the conception.

Orth. — And do you deny that the divine Word existed before the conception?

Eran. — I say that He was before the ages.

Orth. — And that the flesh was co-existent with Him?

---

[1] Matt. xx. 31.　　[3] Matt. xxi. 9.
[2] Matt. xv. 22.　　[4] Luke xix. 40.

[1] II. Tim. ii. 8.　　[2] Luke xxiv. 39.
[2] II. Tim. ii. 9.

Eran. — By no means.

Orth. — But was formed, after the salutation of the angel, of the Holy Ghost?

Eran. — So I say.

Orth. — Therefore before the union there were not two natures but only one. For if the Godhead pre-existed, but the manhood was not co-existent, being formed after the angelic salutation, and the union being co-incident with the formation, then before the union there was one nature, that which exists always and existed before the ages. Now let us again consider this point. Do you understand the making of flesh or becoming man to be anything other than the union?

Eran. — No.

Orth. — For when He took flesh He was made flesh.

Eran. — Plainly.

Orth. — And the union coincides with the taking flesh.

Eran. — So I say.

Orth. — So before the making man there was one nature. For if both union and making man are identical, and He was, made man by taking man's nature, and the form of God took the form of a servant, then before the union the divine nature was one.

Eran. — And how are the union and the making man identical?

Orth. — A moment ago you confessed that there is no distinction between these terms.

Eran. — You led me astray by your arguments.

Orth. — Then, if you like, let us go over the same ground again.

Eran. — We had better so do.

Orth. — Is there a distinction between the incarnation and the union, according to the nature of the transaction?

Eran. — Certainly; a very great distinction.

Orth. — Explain fully the character of this distinction.

Eran. — Even the sense of the terms shows the distinction, for the word "incarnation" shows the taking of the flesh, while the word "union" indicates the combination of distinct things.

Orth. — Do you represent the incarnation to be anterior to the union?

Eran. — By no means.

Orth. — You say that the union took place in the conception?

Eran. — I do.

Orth. — Therefore if not even the least moment of time intervened between the taking of flesh and the union, and the assumed nature did not precede the assumption and the union, then incarnation and union signify one and the same thing, and so before the union and incarnation there was one nature, while after the incarnation we speak properly of two, of that which took and of that which was taken.

Eran. — I say that Christ was of two natures, but I deny two natures.

Orth. — Explain to us then in what sense you understand the expression "of two natures;" like gilded silver? like the composition of electron?[1] like the solder made of lead and tin?

Eran. — I deny that the union is like any of these; it is ineffable, and passes all understanding.

Orth. — I too confess that the manner of the union cannot be comprehended. But I have at all events been instructed by the divine Scripture that each nature remains unimpaired after the union.

Eran. — And where is this taught in the divine Scripture?

Orth. — It is all full of this teaching.

Eran. — Give proof of what you assert.

Orth. — Do you not acknowledge the properties of each nature?

Eran. — No: not, that is, after the union.

Orth. — Let us then learn this very point from the divine Scripture.

Eran. — I am ready to obey the divine Scripture.

Orth. — When, then, you hear the divine John exclaiming "In the beginning was the word, and the word was with God, and the word was God"[2] and "By Him all things were made"[3] and the rest of the parallel passages, do you affirm that the flesh, or the divine Word, begotten before the ages of the Father, was in the beginning with God, and was by nature God, and made all things?

Eran. — I say that these things belong to God the Word. But I do not separate Him from the flesh made one with Him.

Orth. — Neither do we separate the flesh from God the Word, nor do we make the union a confusion.

Eran. — I recognise one nature after the union.

Orth. — When did the Evangelists write the gospel? Was it before the union, or a very long time after the union?

---

[1] The metallic compound called electron is described by Strabo p. 146 as the mixed residuum, or scouring, (κάθαρμα) left after the first smelting of gold ore. Pliny (H. N. xxxiii. 23) describes it as containing 1 part silver to 4 gold. cf. Soph. Antig. 1038, and Herod. i. 50.

[2] John i. 1.   [3] John i. 3.

Eran. — Plainly after the union, the nativity, the miracles, the passion, the resurrection, the taking up into heaven, and the coming of the Holy Ghost.

Orth. — Hear then John saying " In the beginning was the word, and the word was with God, and the word was God. He was in the beginning with God. All things were made by Him, and without Him was not anything made " [1] and so on. Hear too Matthew, " The book of the generation of Jesus Christ, Son of David, — Son of Abraham," — and so on.[2] Luke too traced His genealogy to Abraham and David.[3] Now make the former and the latter quotation fit one nature. You will find it impossible, for existence in the beginning, and descent from Abraham, — the making of all things, and derivation from a created forefather, are inconsistent.

Eran. — By thus arguing you divide the only begotten son into two Persons.

Orth. — One Son of God I both know and adore, the Lord Jesus Christ; but I have been taught the difference between His Godhead and his manhood. You, however, who say that there is only one nature after the union, do you make this agree with the introductions of the Evangelists.

Eran. — You appear to assume the proposition to be hard, nay impossible. Be it, I beg, short and easy; — only solve our question.

Orth. — Both qualities are proper to the Lord Christ, — existence from the beginning, and generation, according to the flesh, from Abraham and David.

Eran. — You laid down the law that after the union it is not right to speak of one nature. Take heed lest in mentioning the flesh you transgress your own law.

Orth. — Even without mentioning the flesh it is quite easy to explain the point in question, for I am applying both to the Saviour Christ.

Eran. — I too assert that both these qualities belong to the Lord Christ.

Orth. — Yes; but you do so in contemplation of two natures in Him, and applying to each its own properties. But if the Christ is one nature, how is it possible to attribute to it properties which are inconsistent with one another? For to have derived origin from Abraham and David, and still more to have been born many generations after David, is inconsistent with existence in the beginning. Again to have sprung from created beings is inconsistent with being Creator of all things; to have had human fathers with existence derived from

God. In short the new is inconsistent with the eternal.

Let us also look at the matter in this way. Do we say that the divine Word is Creator of the Universe?

Eran. — So we have learnt to believe from the divine Scriptures.

Orth. — And how many days after the creation of heaven and earth are we told that Adam was formed?

Eran. — On the sixth day.

Orth. — And from Adam to Abraham how many generations went by?

Eran. — I think twenty.

Orth. — And from Abraham to Christ our Saviour how many generations are reckoned by the Evangelist Matthew.

Eran. — Forty-two.[1]

Orth. — If then the Lord Christ is one nature how can He be Creator of all things visible and invisible and, at the same time, after so many generations, have been formed by the Holy Ghost in a virgin's womb? And how could He be at one and the same time Creator of Adam and Son of Adam's descendants?

Eran. — I have already said that both these properties are appropriate to Him as God made flesh, for I recognise one nature made flesh of the Word.

Orth. — Nor yet, my good sir, do we say that two natures of the divine Word were made flesh, for we know that the nature of the divine Word is one, but we have been taught that the flesh of which He availed Himself when He was incarnate is of another nature, and here I think that you too agree with me. Tell me now; after what manner do you say that the making flesh took place?

Eran. — I know not the manner, but I believe that He was made flesh.

Orth. — You make a pretext of your ignorance unfairly, and after the fashion of the Pharisees. For they when they beheld the force of the Lord's enquiry, and suspecting that they were on the point of conviction, uttered their reply " We do not know." [2] But I proclaim quite openly that the divine incarnation is without change. For if by any variation or change He was made flesh, then after the change all that is divine in His names and in His deeds is quite inappropriate to Him.

Eran. — We have agreed again and again that God the Word is immutable.

Orth. — He was made flesh by taking flesh.

---

[1] John i. 1-3.   [2] Matt. i. 1.   [3] Luke iii. 23.

[1] Matt. i. 17.
[2] Matt. xxi. 27. A. V. " We cannot tell."

Eran. — Yes.

Orth. — The nature of God the Word made flesh is different from that of the flesh, by assumption of which the nature of the divine Word was made flesh and became man.

Eran. — Agreed.

Orth. — Was He then changed into flesh?

Eran. — Certainly not.

Orth. — If then He was made flesh, not by mutation, but by taking flesh, and both the former and the latter qualities are appropriate to Him as to God made flesh, as you said a moment ago, then the natures were not confounded, but remained unimpaired. And as long as we hold thus we shall perceive too the harmony of the Evangelists, for while the one proclaims the divine attributes of the one only begotten — the Lord Christ — the other sets forth His human qualities. So too Christ our Lord Himself teaches us, at one time calling Himself Son of God and at another Son of man: at one time He gives honour to His Mother as to her that gave Him birth;[1] at another He rebukes her as her Lord.[2] At one time He finds no fault with them that style Him Son of David; at another He teaches the ignorant that He is not only David's Son but also David's Lord.[3] He calls Nazareth and Capernaum His country,[4] and again He exclaims "Before Abraham was I am."[5] You will find the divine Scripture full of similar passages, and they all point not to one nature but to two.

Eran. — He who contemplates two natures in the Christ divides the one only begotten into two sons.

Orth. — Yes; and he who says Paul is made up of soul and body makes two Pauls out of one.

Eran. — The analogy does not hold good.

Orth. — I know it does not,[6] for here the union is a natural union of parts that are coæval, created, and fellow slaves, but in the case of the Lord Christ all is of good will, of love to man, and of grace. Here too, though the union is natural, the proper qualities of the natures remain unimpaired.

Eran. — If the proper qualities of the natures remain distinct, how does the soul together with the body crave for food?

Orth. — The soul does not crave for food. How could it when it is immortal? But the body, which derives its vital force from the soul, feels its need, and desires to receive what is lacking. So after toil it longs for rest, after waking for sleep, and so with the rest of its desires. So forthwith after its dissolution, since it has no longer its vital energy, it does not even crave for what is lacking, and, ceasing to receive it, it undergoes corruption.

Eran. — You see that to thirst and to hunger and similar appetites belong to the soul.

Orth. — Did these belong to the soul it would suffer hunger and thirst, and the similar wants, even after its release from the body.

Eran. — What then do you say to be proper to the soul?[1]

Orth. — The reasonable, the absolute, the immortal, the invisible.

Eran. — And what of the body?

Orth. — The complex, the visible, the mortal.

Eran. — And we say that man is composed of these?

Orth. — Yes.

Eran. — Then we define[2] man as a mortal reasonable being.

Orth. — Agreed.

Eran. — And we give names to him from both these attributes.

Orth. — Yes.

Eran. — As then in this case we make no distinction, but call the same man both reasonable and mortal, so also should we do in the case of the Christ, and apply to Him both the divine and the human.

Orth. — This is our argument, although you do not accurately express it. For look you. When we are pursuing the argument about the human soul, do we only mention what is appropriate to its energy and nature?

Eran. — This only.

Orth. — And when our discussion is about the body, do we not only recall what is appropriate to it?

Eran. — Quite so.

Orth. — But, when our discourse touches the whole being, then we have no difficulty in adducing both sets of qualities, for the

---

[1] All through the argument there seems to be some confusion between the two senses of ψυχή as denoting the immortal and the animal part of man, and so between the ψυχικόν and the πνευματικόν. According to the Pauline psychology, (cf. in I. Cor. 15) the immortal and invisible could not be said to be proper to the σῶμα ψυχικόν. This "natural body" is a body of death (Rom. vii. 24) and requires to be redeemed (Rom. viii. 23) and changed into the "house which is from heaven." (II. Cor. v. 2.) Something of the same confusion attaches to the common use of the word "soul" to which we find the language of Holy Scripture frequently accommodated. On the popular language of the dichotomy and the more exact trichotomy of I. Thess. v. 23 a note of Bp. Ellicott on that passage may well be consulted.

[2] "ζῶον λογικὸν θνητόν." The definition may be compared with those of —

PLATO. — ζῶον ἄπτερον, δίπουν, πλατυώνυχον· ὃ μόνον τῶν ὄντων ἐπιστήμης τῆς κατὰ λόγους δεκτικόν ἐστι. Deff.

ARISTOTLE. — πολιτικὸν ζῶον. Pol. I. ii. 9.

---

[1] Luke ii. 51.   [3] Matt. xxii. 42.   [5] John viii. 58.
[2] John ii. 4.   [4] Mark vi. 1.
[6] This, it will be remembered is the analogy employed in the "*Quicunque vult.*"

properties both of the body and of the soul are applicable to man.

Eran. — Unquestionably.

Orth. — Well; just in this way should we speak of the Christ, and, when arguing about His natures, give to each its own, and recognise some as belonging to the Godhead, and some as to the manhood. But when we are discussing the Person we must then make what is proper to the natures common, and apply both sets of qualities to the Saviour, and call the same Being both God and Man, both Son of God and Son of Man — both David's Son and David's Lord, both Seed of Abraham and Creator of Abraham, and so on.

Eran. — That the person of the Christ is one, and that both the divine and the human are attributable to Him, you have quite rightly said, and I accept this definition of the Faith; but your real position, that in discussing the natures we must give to each its own properties, seems to me to dissolve the union. It is for this reason that I object to accept these and similar arguments.

Orth. — Yet when we were enquiring about soul and body you thought the distinction of these terms admirable, and forthwith gave it your approbation. Why then do you refuse to receive the same rule in the case of the Godhead and manhood of the Lord Christ? Do you go so far as to object to comparing the Godhead and the manhood of the Christ to soul and body? So, while you grant an unconfounded union to soul and body, do you venture to say that the Godhead and manhood of the Christ have undergone commixture and confusion?

Eran. — I hold the Godhead of the Christ aye, and His flesh too, to be infinitely higher in honour than soul and body; but after the union I do assert one nature.

Orth. — But now is it not impious and shocking, while maintaining that a soul united to a body is in no way subject to confusion, to deny to the Godhead of the Lord of the universe the power to maintain its own nature unconfounded or to keep within its proper bounds the humanity which He assumed? Is it not, I say, impious to mix the distinct, and to commingle the separate? The idea of one nature gives ground for suspicion of this confusion.

Eran. — I am equally anxious to avoid the term confusion, but I shrink from asserting two natures lest I fall into a dualism of sons.

Orth. — I am equally anxious to escape either horn of the dilemma, both the impious confusion and the impious distinction; for to me it is alike an unhallowed thought to split

the one Son in two and to gainsay the duality of the natures. But now in truth's name tell me. Were one of the faction of Arius or Eunomius to endeavour, while disputing with you, to belittle the Son, and to describe Him as less than and inferior to the Father, by the help of all their familiar arguments and citations from the divine Scripture of the text " Father, if it be possible, let this cup pass from me "[1] and that other, " Now is my soul troubled "[2] and other like passages, how would you dispose of his objections? How could you show that the Son is in no way diminished in dignity by these expressions and is not of another substance, but begotten of the substance of the Father?

Eran. — I should say that the divine Scripture uses some terms according to the theology and some according to the œconomy, and that it is wrong to apply what belongs to the œconomy to what belongs to the theology.[3]

Orth. — But your opponent would retort that even in the Old Testament the divine Scripture says many things œconomically, as for instance, " Adam heard the voice of the Lord God walking,"[4] and " I will go down now and see whether they have done altogether according to the cry of it which has come to me; and if not I will know,"[5] and again," Now I know that thou fearest God "[6] and the like.

Eran. — I might answer to this that there is a great distinction between the œconomies. In the Old Testament there is an œconomy of words; in the New Testament of deeds.

Orth. — Then your opponent would ask of what deeds?

Eran. — He shall straightway hear of the deeds of the making flesh. For the Son of God on being made man both in word and deed at one time exhibits the flesh, at another the Godhead: as of course, in the passage quoted, He shews the weakness of the flesh and of the soul, the sense namely of fear.

Orth. — But if he were to go on to say, " But he did not take a soul but only a body; for the Godhead instead of a soul being united to the body performed all the functions of the soul," with what arguments could you meet his objections?

Eran. — I could bring proofs from the divine Scripture shewing how God the Word took not only flesh but also soul.

Orth. — And what proofs of this shall we find in Scripture?

---

[1] Matt. xxvi. 39.
[2] John xii. 27.
[3] Consult note on page 72.
[4] Gen. iii. 8.
[5] Gen. xviii. 21.
[6] Gen. xxii. 12.

Eran. — Have you not heard the Lord saying " I have power to lay it down, and I have power to take it again. . . . I lay it down of myself that I might take it again." [1] And again, " Now is my soul troubled." [2] And again, " My soul is exceeding sorrowful even unto death," [3] and again David's words as interpreted by Peter " His soul was not left in hell neither did His flesh see corruption." [4] These and similar passages clearly point out that God the Word assumed not only a body but also a soul.

Orth. — You have quoted this testimony most appositely and properly, but your opponent might reply that even before the incarnation God said to the Jews, " Fasting and holy day and feasts my soul hateth." [5] Then he might go on to argue that as in the Old Testament He mentioned a soul, though He had not a soul, so He does in the New.

Eran. — But he shall be told again how the divine Scripture, when speaking of God, mentions even parts of the body as " Incline thine ear and hear " [6] and " Open thine eyes and see " [7] and " The mouth of the Lord hath spoken it " [8] and " Thy hands have made me and fashioned me " [9] and countless other passages.

If then after the incarnation we are forbidden to understand soul to mean soul, it is equally forbidden to hold body to mean body. Thus the great mystery of the œconomy will be found to be mere imagination ; and we shall in no way differ from Marcion, Valentinus and Manes, the inventors of all these figments.

Orth. — But if a follower of Apollinarius were suddenly to intervene in our discussion and were to ask " Most excellent Sir ; what kind of soul do you say that Christ assumed? " what would you answer ?

Eran. — I should first of all say that I know only one soul of man ; then I should answer, " But if you reckon two souls, the one reasonable and the other without reason, I say that the soul assumed was the reasonable. Yours it seems is the unreasonable, inasmuch as you think that our salvation was incomplete."

Orth. — But suppose he were to ask for proof of what you say ?

Eran. — I could very easily give it. I shall quote the oracles of the Evangelists " The Child Jesus grew and waxed strong in spirit and the grace of God was upon him " [10] and again " Jesus increased in wisdom and in stature and in favour with God and men." [1] I should say that these have nothing to do with Godhead for the body increased in stature, and in wisdom the soul — not that which is without reason, but the reasonable. God the Word then took on Him a reasonable soul.

Orth. — Good Sir, you have bravely broken through the three fold phalanx of your foes ; but that union, and the famous commixture and confusion, not in two ways only but in three, you have scattered and undone ; and not only have you pointed out the distinction between Godhead and manhood, but you have in two ways distinguished the manhood by pointing out that the soul is one thing and the body another, so that no longer two, according to our argument, but three natures of our Saviour Jesus Christ may be understood.

Eran. — Yes ; for did not you say that there is another substance of the soul besides the nature of the body ?

Orth. — Yes.

Eran. — How then does the argument seem absurd to you ?

Orth. — Because while you object to two, you have admitted three natures.

Eran. — The contest with our antagonists compels us to this, for how could any one in any other way argue against those who deny the assumption of the flesh, or of the soul, or of the mind, but by adducing proofs on these points from the divine Scripture ? And how could any one confute them who in their madness strive to belittle the Godhead of the only Begotten but by pointing out that the divine Scripture speaks sometimes theologically and sometimes œconomically.

Orth. — What you now say is true. It is what I, nay what all say, who keep whole the apostolic rule. You yourself have become a supporter of our doctrines.

Eran. — How do I support yours, while I refuse to acknowledge two sons ?

Orth. — When did you ever hear of our affirming two sons ?

Eran. — He who asserts two natures asserts two sons.

Orth. — Then you assert three sons, for you have spoken of three natures.

Eran. — In no other way was it possible to meet the argument of my opponents.

Orth. — Hear this same thing from us too ; for both you and I confront the same antagonists.

Eran. — But I do not assert two natures after the union.

Orth. — And yet after many generations

---

1 John x. 18, 17.
2 John xii. 27.
3 Matt. xxvi. 38.
4 Psalm xvi. 10 and Acts ii. 31.
5 Isaiah i. 13, 14. Sept.
6 Daniel ix. 18.
7 Ibid.
8 Isaiah lviii. 14.
9 Ps. cxix. 73.
10 Luke ii. 40.
1 Luke ii. 52.

of the union a moment ago you used the same words. Explain to us however in what sense you assert one nature after the union. Do you mean one nature derived from both or that one nature remains after the destruction of the other?

Eran. — I maintain that the Godhead remains and that the manhood was swallowed up by it.[1]

Orth. — Fables of the Gentiles, all this, and follies of the Manichees. I am ashamed so much as to mention such things. The Greeks had their gods' swallowings[2] and the Manichees wrote of the daughter of light. But we reject such teaching as being as absurd as it is impious, for how could a nature absolute and uncompounded, comprehending the universe, unapproachable and infinite, have absorbed the nature which it assumed?

Eran. — Like the sea receiving a drop of honey, for straightway the drop, as it mingles with the ocean's water, disappears.

Orth. — The sea and the drop are different in quantity, though alike in quality; the one is greatest, the other is least; the one is sweet and the other is bitter; but in all other respects you will find a very close relationship. The nature of both is moist, liquid, and fluid. Both are created. Both are lifeless yet each alike is called a body. There is nothing then absurd in these cognate natures undergoing commixture, and in the one being made to disappear by the other. In the case before us on the contrary the difference is infinite, and so great that no figure of the reality can be found. I will however endeavour to point out to you several instances of substances which are mixed without being confounded, and remain unimpaired.

Eran. — Who in the world ever heard of an unmixed mixture?

Orth. — I shall endeavour to make you admit this.

Eran. — Should what you are about to advance prove true we will not oppose the truth.

Orth. — Answer then, dissenting or assenting as the argument may seem good to you.

Eran. — I will answer.

Orth. — Does the light at its rising seem to you to fill all the atmosphere except where men shut up in caverns might remain bereft of it?

Eran. — Yes.

Orth. — And does all the light seem to you to be diffused through all the atmosphere?

Eran. — I am with you so far.

Orth. — And is not the mixture diffused through all that is subject to it?

Eran. — Certainly.

Orth. — But, now, this illuminated atmosphere, do we not see it as light and call it light?

Eran. — Quite so.

Orth. — And yet when the light is present we sometimes are aware of moisture and aridity; frequently of heat and cold.

Eran. — Yes.

Orth. — And after the departure of the light the atmosphere afterwards remains alone by itself.

Eran. — True.

Orth. — Consider this example too. When iron is brought in contact with fire it is fired.

Eran. — Certainly.

Orth. — And the fire is diffused through its whole substance?

Eran. — Well?

Orth. — How, then, does not the complete union, and the mixture universally diffused, change the iron's nature?

Eran. — But it changes it altogether. It is now reckoned no longer as iron, but as fire, and indeed it has the active properties of fire.

Orth. — But does not the smith call it iron, and put it on the anvil and smite it with his hammer?

Eran. — Unquestionably.

Orth. — Then the nature of the iron was not damaged by contact with the fire. If then, in natural bodies, instances may be found of an unconfounded mixture, it is sheer folly in the case of the nature which knows neither corruption nor change to entertain the idea of confusion and destruction of the assumed nature, and all the more so when this nature was assumed to bring blessing on the race.

Eran. — What I assert is not the destruction of the assumed nature, but its change into the substance of Godhead.

Orth. — Then the human race is no longer limited as heretofore?

Eran. — No.

Orth. — When did it undergo this change?

Eran. — After the complete union.

Orth. — And what date do you assign to this?

Eran. — I have said again and again, that of the conception.

---

[1] καταποθῆναι i.e., was absorbed and made to disappear. Contrast the *adsumptione Humanitatis in Deum* (or " *in Deo*,' as the older MSS. read) of the Athanasian Creed.

[2] The allusion is to the fable of Saturn devouring his children at their birth.

Orth. — Yet after the conception He was an unborn babe in the womb; after His birth, He was a babe [1] and was called a babe, and was worshipped by shepherds, and in like manner became a boy, and was so called by the angel.[2] Do you acknowledge all this? or do you think I am inventing fables?

Eran. — This is taught in the history of the divine gospels, and cannot be gainsaid.

Orth. — Now let us investigate what follows. We acknowledge, do we not, that the Lord was circumcised?

Eran. — Yes.

Orth. — Of what was there a circumcision? Of flesh or Godhead?

Eran. — Of the flesh.

Orth. — Of what was then the growth and increase in wisdom and stature?

Eran. — This, of course, is not applicable to Godhead.

Orth. — Nor hunger and thirst?

Eran. — No.

Orth. — Nor walking about, and being weary, and falling asleep?

Eran. — No.

Orth. — If then the union took place at the conception, and all these things came to pass after the conception and the birth, then, after the union, the manhood did not lose its own nature.

Eran. — I have not stated my meaning exactly. It was after the resurrection from the dead that the flesh underwent the change into Godhead.

Orth. — Then, after the resurrection, nothing of all that indicates its nature remained in it?

Eran. — If it remained, the divine change did not take place.

Orth. — How then was it that He shewed His hands and His feet to the disciples who disbelieved?

Eran. — Just as He came in when the doors were shut.

Orth. — But He came in when the doors were shut just as He came out from the womb, though the virgin's bolts and bars were undrawn, and just as He walked upon the sea. Then according to your argument not even yet had the change of nature taken place?

Eran. — The Lord shewed His hands to the Apostles in the same way as He wrestled with Jacob.

Orth. — No; the Lord does not allow us to understand it in this sense. The disciples thought they saw a spirit, but the Lord dispelled this idea, and shewed the nature of the flesh, for He said "Why are ye troubled? and why do thoughts arise in your hearts? Behold my hands and my feet, that it is I myself: handle me, and see; for a spirit hath not flesh and bones, as ye see me have." [1] And observe the exactness of the language. He does not say " is not flesh and bones," but " has not flesh and bones," in order to point out that the nature of the possessor and the nature of that which is possessed are distinct and separate. Just in the same way that which took and that which was taken are separate and distinct, and the Christ is beheld made one of both. Thus the part possessing is entirely different from the part possessed, and yet does not divide into two persons Him who is an object of thought in them. The Lord, indeed, while the disciples were still in doubt, asked for food and took and ate it, not consuming the food only in appearance, nor satisfying to the need of the body.

Eran. — But one of these alternatives must be accepted; either He partook because He needed, or else, needing not, He seemed to eat, and did not really partake of food.

Orth. — His body now become immortal required no food. Of them that rise the Lord says: " they neither marry nor are given in marriage but are as Angels." [2] The apostles however bear witness that He partook of the food, for the blessed Luke in the preface to the Acts says " being assembled together with the apostles the Lord commanded them that they should not depart from Jerusalem " [3] and the very divine Peter says more distinctly: " Who did eat and drink with Him after He rose from the dead." [4] For since eating is proper to them that live this present life, of necessity the Lord by means of eating and drinking proved the resurrection of the flesh to them that did not acknowledge it to be real. This same course He pursued in the case of Lazarus and of Jairus' daughter. For when He had raised up the latter He ordered that something should be given her to eat [5] and He made Lazarus sit with Him at the table [6] and so shewed the reality of the rising again.

Eran. — If we grant that the Lord really ate, let us grant that after the resurrection all men partake of food.

Orth. — What was done by the Saviour through a certain œconomy is not a rule and law of nature. This follows from the fact that He did other things by œconomy which shall by no means be the lot of them that live again.

---

[1] Luke ii. 12 and 16.   [2] Matt. ii. 13.

[1] Luke xxiv. 38, 39.   [3] Acts i. 4.   [5] Mark v. 43.
[2] Mark xii. 25.   [4] Acts x. 41.   [6] John xii. 21.

Eran. — What do you mean?

Orth. — Will not the bodies of them that rise become incorruptible and immortal?

Eran. — So the divine Paul has taught us. "It is sown" he says "in corruption; it is raised in incorruption; it is sown in dishonour; it is raised in glory; it is sown in weakness; it is raised in power; it is sown a natural body; it is raised a spiritual body."[1]

Orth. — But the Lord, who raises the bodies of all men, unmaimed and unmarred (for lameness of limb and blindness of eye are unknown among them that are risen),[2] left in His own body the prints of the nails, and the wound in His side, whereof are witnesses both the Lord Himself and the hand of Thomas.

Eran. — True.

Orth. — If then after the resurrection the Lord both partook of food, and shewed His hands and His feet to His disciples, and in them the prints of the nails, and His side with the mark of the wound in it, and said to them, "Handle me and see for a spirit hath not flesh and bones as ye see me have"[3] it follows that after His resurrection the nature of His body was preserved and was not changed into another substance.

Eran. — Then after the resurrection it is mortal and subject to suffering?

Orth. — By no means; it is incorruptible, impassible, and immortal.

Eran. — If it is incorruptible, impassible, and immortal, it has been changed into another nature.

Orth. — Therefore the bodies of all men will be changed into another substance, for all will be incorruptible and immortal. Or have you not heard the words of the Apostle, "For this corruptible must put on incorruption, and this mortal must put on immortality"?[4]

Eran. — I have heard.

Orth. — Therefore the nature remains, but its corruption is changed into incorruption, and its mortal into immortality. But let us look at the matter in this way; we call a body that is sick and a body that is whole, in the same way, a body.

Eran. — Unquestionably.

Orth. — Wherefore?

Eran. — Since both partake of the same substance.

Orth. — Yet we see in them a very great difference, for the one is whole, perfect, and unhurt; the other has either lost an eye, or

has a broken leg, or has undergone some other suffering.

Eran. — But to the same nature belong both health and sickness.

Orth. — So the body is called substance; disease and health are called accident.

Eran. — Of course. For these things are accidents of the body, and again cease to be so.

Orth. — In the same way corruption and death must be called accidents, and not substances, for they too are accidents and cease to be so.

Eran. — True.

Orth. — So the body of the Lord rose incorruptible, impassible, and immortal, and is worshipped by the powers of heaven, and is yet a body having its former limitation.

Eran. — In these points you seem to say sooth, but after its assumption into heaven I do not think that you will deny that it was changed into the nature of Godhead.

Orth. — I would not so say persuaded only by human arguments, for I am not so rash as to say anything concerning which divine Scripture is silent. But I have heard the divine Paul exclaiming "God hath appointed a day in the which He will judge the world in righteousness by that man whom He hath ordained whereof He hath given assurance unto all men in that He hath raised Him from the dead,"[1] and I have learnt from the holy Angels that He will come in like manner as the disciples saw Him going into heaven.[2] Now they saw His nature not unlimited. For I have heard the words of the Lord, "Ye shall see the Son of Man coming in the clouds of heaven,"[3] and I acknowledge that what is seen of men is limited, for the unlimited nature is invisible. Furthermore to sit upon a throne of glory and to set the lambs upon the right and the kids upon the left[4] indicates limitation.

Eran. — Then He was not unlimited even before the incarnation, for the prophet saw Him surrounded by the Seraphim.[5]

Orth. — The prophet did not see the substance of God, but a certain appearance accommodated to his capacity. After the resurrection, however, all the world will see the very visible nature of the judge.

Eran. — You promised that you would adduce no argument without evidence, but you are introducing arguments adapted to us.

Orth. — I have learnt these things from the divine Scripture. I have heard the words of the prophet Zechariah "They shall look on Him whom they pierced,"[6]

---

[1] I. Cor. xv. 42, 43, 44.
[2] Contrast Plato Gorgias § 169 κατεαγότα τε εἰ τοῦ ἦν μέλη ἢ διεστραμμένα ζῶντος καὶ τεθνεῶτος ταῦτα ἔνδηλα, and Virgil Æn. vi. 494.
  " *Atque hic Priamiden laniatum corpore toto*
    Deiphobum vidit lacerum crudeliter ora."
[3] Luke xxiv. 39.   [4] I. Cor. xv. 53.

[1] Acts xvii. 31.   [3] Matt. xxvi. 64.   [5] Isaiah vi. 2.
[2] Acts i. 11.   [4] Matt. xxv. 31-33.   [6] Zech. xii. 10.

and how shall the event follow the prophecy unless the crucifiers recognise the nature which they crucified? And I have heard the cry of the victorious martyr Stephen, "Behold I see the heavens opened and the Son of Man standing on the right hand of God,"[1] and he saw the visible, not the invisible nature.

Eran. — These things are thus written, but I do not think that you will be able to show that the body, after the ascension into heaven, is called body by the inspired writers.

Orth. — What has been already said indicates the body perfectly plainly; for what is seen is a body; but I will nevertheless point out to you that even after the assumption the body of the Lord is called a body. Hear the teaching of the Apostle, "For our conversation is in Heaven from whence also we look for the Saviour, the Lord Jesus, who shall change our vile body that it may be fashioned like unto his glorious body."[2] It was not changed into another nature, but remained a body, full however of divine glory, and sending forth beams of light. The bodies of the saints shall be fashioned like unto it. But if it was changed into another nature, their bodies will be likewise changed, for they shall be fashioned like unto it. But if the bodies of the saints preserve the character of their nature, then also the body of the Lord in like manner keeps its own nature unchanged.

Eran. — Then will the bodies of the saints be equal with the body of the Lord?

Orth. — In its incorruption and its immortality they too will share. Moreover in its glory they will participate, as says the Apostle, "If so be that we suffer with Him, that we may be also glorified together."[3] It is in quantity that the vast difference may be found, a difference as great as between sun and stars, or rather between master and slaves, and that which gives and that which receives light. Yet has He given a share of His own name to His servants and as He is Light, calls His saints light, for "Ye," He says, "are the Light of the world,"[4] and being named servants and being named "Sun of Righteousness"[5] He says of his servants "Then shall the righteous shine forth as the Sun."[6] It is therefore according to quality, not according to quantity, that the bodies of the saints shall be fashioned like unto the body of the Lord. Now I have shewn you plainly what you bade me.

Further, if you please, let us look at the matter in yet another way.

Eran. — One ought "to stir every stone," as the proverb says,[1] to get at the truth; above all when it is a question of divine doctrines.

Orth. — Tell me now; the mystic symbols which are offered to God by them who perform priestly rites, of what are they symbols?

Eran. — Of the body and blood of the Lord.

Orth. — Of the real body or not?

Eran. — The real.

Orth. — Good. For there must be the archetype of the image. So painters imitate nature and paint the images of visible objects.

Eran. — True.

Orth. — If, then, the divine mysteries are antitypes of the real body,[2] therefore even now the body of the Lord is a body, not changed into nature of Godhead, but filled with divine glory.

Eran. — You have opportunely introduced the subject of the divine mysteries for from it I shall be able to show you the change of the Lord's body into another nature. Answer now to my questions.

Orth. — I will answer.

Eran. — What do you call the gift which is offered before the priestly invocation?

Orth. — It were wrong to say openly; perhaps some uninitiated are present.

Eran. — Let your answer be put enigmatically.

Orth. — Food of grain of such a sort.

Eran. — And how name we the other symbol?

Orth. — This name too is common, signifying species of drink.

Eran. — And after the consecration how do you name these?

Orth. — Christ's body and Christ's blood.

Eran. — And do you believe that you partake of Christ's body and blood?

Orth. — I do.

Eran. — As, then, the symbols of the Lord's body and blood are one thing before the priestly invocation, and after the invocation are changed and become another thing; so the Lord's body after the assumption is changed into the divine substance.

Orth. — You are caught in the net you have woven yourself. For even after the consecration the mystic symbols are not de-

---

1 Acts vii. 56.
2 Phil. iii. 20, 21. Observe omission of "Christ."
3 Rom. viii. 17.   5 Malachi iv. 2.
1 Matt. v. 14.   6 Matt. xiii. 43.

1 Probably the λίθος in the stone on the Draught Board. So πάντα κινεῖν λίθον is to make every effort in the game.
2 τοῦ ὄντως σώματος ἀντίτυπά ἐστι τὰ θεῖα μυστήρια. The view of Orthodoxus, it will be seen, is not that of the Roman confession. cf. note on p. 206.

prived of their own nature; they remain in their former substance figure and form; they are visible and tangible as they were before. But they are regarded as what they are become, and believed so to be, and are worshipped [1] as being what they are believed to be. Compare then the image with the archetype, and you will see the likeness, for the type must be like the reality. For that body preserves its former form, figure, and limitation and in a word the substance of the body; but after the resurrection it has become immortal and superior to corruption; it has become worthy of a seat on the right hand; it is adored by every creature as being called the natural body of the Lord.

Eran. — Yes; and the mystic symbol changes its former appellation; it is no longer called by the name it went by before, but is styled body. So must the reality be called God, and not body.

Orth. — You seem to me to be ignorant — for He is called not only body but even bread of life. So the Lord Himself used this name' and that very body we call divine body, and giver of life, and of the Master and of the Lord, teaching that it is not common to every man but belongs to our Lord Jesus Christ Who is God and Man. "For Jesus Christ" is "the same yesterday, to-day, and forever." [3]

Eran. — You have said a great deal about this, but I follow the saints who have shone of old in the Church; show me then, if you can, these in their writings dividing the natures after the union.

Orth. — I will read you their works, and I am sure you will be astonished at the countless mentions of the distinction which in their struggle against impious heretics they have inserted in their writings. Hear now those whose testimony I have already adduced speaking openly and distinctly on these points.

Testimony of the holy Ignatius, bishop of Antioch, and martyr: —

From the Epistle to the Smyrnæans: [4] " I acknowledge and believe Him after His resurrection to be existent in the flesh: and when He came to hem that were with Peter He said to them ' Take; handle me and see, for I am not a bodiless dæmon.' [5] And straightway they took hold of him and believed."

Of the same from the same epistle : —

" And after His Resurrection He ate with them, and drank with them, as being of the flesh, although He was spiritually one with the Father."

Testimony of Irenæus, the ancient bishop of Lyons: —

From the third Book of his work "Against Heresies." (Chap. XX.)

"As we have said before, He united man to God. For had not a man vanquished man's adversary, the enemy would not have been vanquished aright; and again, had not God granted the boon of salvation we should not have possessed it in security. And had not man been united to God, he could not have shared in the incorruption. For it behoved the mediator of God and men, by means of His close kinship to either, to bring them both into friendship and unanimity, and to set man close to God and to make God known to men."

Of the same from the third book of the same treatise (Chapter XVIII) : —

" So again in his Epistle he says 'Whosoever believeth that Jesus is the Christ is born of God,' [1] recognising one and the same Jesus Christ to whom the gates of heaven were opened, on account of His assumption in the flesh. Who in the same flesh in which He also suffered shall come revealing the glory of the Father."

Of the same from the fourth book (Chapter VII) : —

"As Isaiah saith ' He shall cause them that come of Jacob to take root. Israel shall blossom and bud and fill the face of the world with fruit.' [2] So his fruit being scattered through the whole world, they who erst brought forth good fruit (for of them was produced the Christ in the flesh and the apostles) were abandoned and removed. And now they are no longer fit for bringing forth fruit."

Of the same from the same book (Chapter LIX) : —

"And he judges also them of Ebion. [3] How can they be saved unless it was God who wrought their salvation on earth, or how shall man come to God unless God came to man?"

Of the same from the same book (Chapter LXIV) : —

---

[1] προσκυνεῖται.   [3] Heb. xiii. 8.
[2] John vi. 51.   [4] Ad Smyr. III.
[5] The quotation is not from the canonical gospels. Eusebius (iii. 36) says he does not know from what source it comes. Jerome states it to be derived from the gospel lately translated by him, the gospel according to the Hebrews (Vir. Ill. 2) Origen ascribes the words to the " *Doctrina Petri*." (de Princ. Præf. 8) Bp. Lightfoot, by whom the matter is fully discussed, (Ap. Fath. pt. II. Vol. ii. p. 295) thinks that either Jerome, *more suo*, was forgetful, or had a different recension of the gospel

to the Hebrews from that used by Origen and Eusebius. Ignatius may be quoting a verbal tradition. Bp. Lightfoot further points out that Origen (l. c.) supposes the author of the *Doctrina Petri* to use this epithet ασωματον not in its philosophical sense (= incorporeal) but as meaning composed of some subtle substance and without a gross body like man. Further Origen (c. Cels. V. 5) warns us that to Christians the word dæmon has a special connotation, in reference to the powers that deceive and distract men.

[1] I. John v. 1.   [2] Isaiah xxvii. 6.   [3] Vide note on page 38.

" They who preach that Emmanuel was of the Virgin set forth the union of God the Word with His creature."

Of the same from the same treatise (Book V. Chap. I.) : —

" Now these things came to pass not in seeming but in essential truth, for if He appeared to be man though He was not man then the Spirit of God did not continue to be what in truth It is ; for the Spirit is invisible ; nor was there any truth in Him, for He was not what He appeared to be. And we have said before that Abraham and the rest of the prophets beheld Him in prophecy prophesying what was destined to come to pass in actual sight. If then now too He appeared to be of such a character, though in reality He was not what He appeared, then a kind of prophetic vision would have been given to men, and we must still look for yet another advent in which He will really be what He is now seen to be in prophecy. Now we have demonstrated that there is no difference between the statements that He only appeared in seeming and that He took nothing from Mary, for He did not really even possess flesh and blood whereby He redeemed us, unless He renewed in Himself the old creation of Adam. The sect of Valentinus are therefore vain in teaching thus that they may cast out the life of the flesh."

Testimony of the holy Hippolytus, bishop and martyr, from his work on the distribution of the talents : [1] —

" Any one might say that these and those who uphold otherwise are neighbours, erring as they do in the same manner, for even they either confess that the Christ appeared in life as mere man, denying the talent of His Godhead, or else acknowledging Him as God, on the other hand they deny the man, representing that He deluded the sight of them that beheld Him by unreal appearances ; and that He wore manhood not as a Man but was rather a mere imaginary semblance, as Marcion and Valentinus and the Gnostics teach, wrenching away the Word from the flesh, and rejecting the one talent, the incarnation."

Of the same from his letter to a certain Queen : [2] —

" He calls Him ' the first fruits of them that sleep,' as being ' the first born from the dead,' [3] and He, after His resurrection, wishing to show that that which was risen was the same as that which had undergone death.

when the disciples were doubting, called Thomas to Him, and said, ' Come hither handle me and see for a spirit hath not flesh and blood as ye see me have.' " [1]

Of the same from his discourse on Elkanah and Hannah : —

" Wherefore three seasons of the year typified the Saviour Himself that He might fulfil the mysteries predicted about Him. In the Passover, that He might shew Himself as the sheep doomed to be sacrificed and shew a true Passover as says the Apostle, ' Christ, God,[2] our Passover was sacrificed for us.' At Pentecost that He might announce the kingdom of heaven ascending Himself first into heaven and offering to God man as a gift."

Of the same from his work on the great Psalm : [3] —

" He who drew from the nethermost hell man first formed of the earth when lost and held fast in bonds of death ; He who came down from above and lifted up him that was down ; He who became Evangelist of the dead, ransomer of souls and resurrection of them that were entombed ; this was He who became succourer of vanquished man in Himself, like man firstborn Word ; visiting the first formed Adam in the Virgin ; the spiritual seeking the earthy in the womb ; the ever-living him who by disobedience died ; the heavenly calling the earthly to the world above, the highborn meaning to make the slave free by His own obedience ; He who turned to adamant man crumbled into dust and made serpents' meat ; He who made man hanging on a tree of wood Lord over him who had conquered Him and so by a tree of wood is proved victorious."

Of the same from the same book : —

" They who do not now recognise the Son of God in the flesh will one day recognise Him when He comes as judge in glory, though now in an inglorious body suffering wrong."

Of the same from the same book : —

" Moreover the apostles when they had come to the sepulchre on the third day did not find the body of Jesus, just as the children of Israel went up on the mountain, and could not find the tomb of Moses."

Of the same from his interpretation of Psalm II. : —

" When He had come into the world He

---

[1] The only fragment of this work.
[2] Several fragments of this letter will be found in Dialogue III.
[4] Coloss. i. 18.

[1] Vide John xx. 27 and Luke xxiv. 39. The quotation confuses the words of the resurrection day and of the week after.
[2] I. Cor. v. 7. The addition of ὁ Θεός has no authority.
[3] Probably the cxixth Ps. It is doubtful whether the work forms part of a Commentary on the Pss. or is quoted from a homily on this special Psalm.

was manifested as God and Man. His manhood is easy of perception because He is ahungered and aweary, in toil He is athirst, in fear He flees,[1] in prayer He grieves; He falls asleep upon a pillow, He prays that the cup of suffering may pass from Him, being in an agony He sweats, He is strengthened by an angel, betrayed by Judas, dishonoured by Caiaphas, set at nought by Herod, scourged by Pilate, mocked by soldiers, nailed to a cross by Jews, He commends His spirit to the Father with a cry, He leans His head as He breathes His last, He is pierced in the side with a spear and rolled in fine linen, is laid in a tomb, and on the third day He is raised by the Father. No less plainly may His divinity be seen when He is worshipped by angels, gazed on by shepherds, waited for by Simeon, testified to by Anna, sought out by Magi, pointed out by a Star, at the wedding feast makes water wine, rebukes the sea astir by force of winds, and on the same sea walks, makes a man blind from birth see, raises Lazarus who had been four days dead, works many and various wonders, remits sins and gives power to His disciples."

Of the same from his work on Psalm XXIV.: —

" He comes to the heavenly gates, angels travel with Him and the gates of the heavens are shut. For He hath not yet ascended into heaven. Now first to the heavenly powers flesh appears ascending. The Word then goes forth to the powers from the angels that speed before the Lord and Saviour, ' Lift the Gates ye princes and be ye lift up ye everlasting doors and the King of glory shall come in.' "[2]

Testimony of the holy Eustathius, bishop of Antioch and confessor.

From his work on The Titles of the Psalms: —

" He predicted that He would sit upon a holy throne, shewing that He has been set forth on the same throne as the divine Spirit on account of the God that dwells in Him continually."

Of the same from his work upon the Soul: —

" Before His passion in each case He predicted His bodily death, saying that He would be betrayed to the father of the High Priest, and announcing the trophy of the Cross. And after the passion, when He had risen on the third day from the dead, His disciples being in doubt as to His resurrec-

tion, He appeared to them in His very body and confessed that He had complete flesh and bones, submitting to their sight His wounded side and shewing them the prints of the nails."

Of the same from his discourse on " The Lord formed me in the beginning of His ways ":[1] —

" Paul did not say ' conformed to the Son of God' but ' conformed to the image of His Son '[2] in order to point out a distinction between the Son and His image, for the Son, wearing the divine tokens of His Father's Excellence, is an image of His Father; for since like are generated of like, offspring appear as very images of their parents, but the manhood which He wore is an image of the Son, as images even of different colours are painted on wax,[3] some being wrought by hand and some by nature and likeness. Moreover the very law of truth announces this, for the bodiless spirit of wisdom is not conformed to bodily men, but the express image[4] made man by the spirit bearing the same number of members with all the rest, and clad in similar form."

Of the same from the same work: —

" That he speaks of the body as conformed to those of men he teaches more clearly in his Epistle to the Philippians, ' our conversation ' he says ' is in Heaven from whence also we look for the Saviour, the Lord Jesus Christ, who shall change our vile body that it may be fashioned like unto His glorious body.'[5] And if by changing the form of the vile body of men He fashions it like unto His own body, then the false teaching of our opponents is shewn to be in every way worthless."

Of the same from the same work: —

" But as being born of the Virgin He is said to have been made man of the woman,[6] so He is described as being made under the law because of His sometimes walking by the precepts of the law, as for instance when His parents zealously urged His circumcision, when He was a child eight days old, as relates the evangelist Luke, afterwards ' they brought Him to present Him to the Lord,' ' bringing the offerings of purification ' ' to offer a sacrifice according to that which is said in the law of the Lord a pair of turtle doves or two young pigeons.'[7] As then the gifts of purification were offered on

---

[1] The word φεύγειν is not used of the Saviour in the Gospel. Joseph was bidden φεῦγε εἰς Αἴγυπτον. When our Lord was brought to the cliff overhanging Nazareth διελθὼν διὰ μέσου αὐτῶν ἐπορεύετο.
[2] Ps. xxiv. Sept.

[1] Proverbs viii. 22. Sept.   [2] Romans viii. 29.
[3] The original here is corrupt.
[4] χαρακτήρ cf. Heb. i. 3. I have used the equivalent given in A. V. for the Greek word of the text meaning literally stamp or impression, as on coin or seal, and so exact representation.
[5] Phil. iii. 20, 21.   [6] Gal. iv. 4.   [7] Luke ii. 22, 24.

His behalf according to the law, and He underwent circumcision on the eighth day, the Apostle very properly writes that He was thus brought under the law. Not indeed that the Word was subject to the law, (as our calumnious opponents suppose) being Himself the law, nor did God, who by one breath can cleanse and hallow all things, need sacrifices of purification. But He took from the Virgin the members of a man and became subject to the law and was purified according to the rite of the firstborn, not because He submitted to this treatment from any need on His part of such observance, but in order that He might redeem from the slavery of the law them that were sold to the doom of the curse."

Testimony of the holy Athanasius, bishop of Alexandria.

From his Second Discourse against heresies :[1] —

" We should not have been redeemed from sin and the curse had not the flesh which the Word wore been by nature that of man, for we should have had nothing in common with that which was not our own; just so man would not have been made God, had not the Word which was made flesh been by nature of the Father and verily and properly His. And the combination is of this character that to the natural God may be joined the natural man, and so his salvation and deification be secure. Therefore let them that deny Him to be naturally of the Father, and own Son of His substance, deny too that He took very flesh of man from the Virgin Mary."

Of the same from his Epistle to Epictetus : —

" If on account of the Saviour's Body being, and being described in the Scriptures as being, derived from Mary, and a human Body, they fancy that a quaternity is substituted for a Trinity, as though some addition were made by the body, they are quite wrong; they put the creature on a par with the Creator, and suppose that the Godhead is capable of being added to. They fail to see that the Word was not made flesh on account of any addition to Godhead, but that the flesh may rise. Not for the aggrandisement of the Word did He come forth from Mary, but that the human race may be redeemed. How can they think that the body ransomed and quickened by the Word can add anything in the way of Godhead to the Word that quickened it?"

Of the same from the same Epistle : —

" Let them be told that if the Word had been a creature, the creature would not have assumed a body to quicken it. For what help can creatures get from a creature standing itself in need of salvation? But the Word, Himself Creator, was made maker of created things, and therefore in the fulness of the ages He attached the creature to Himself, that once more as a Creator He might renew it, and might be able to create it afresh."

From the longer Discourse " De Fide " : —

" This also we add concerning the words ' Sit thou on my right hand,'[1] that they are said of the Lord's body. For if ' the Lord saith, do not I fill heaven and earth,'[2] as says Jeremiah, and God contains all things, and is contained of none, on what kind of throne does He sit? It is therefore the body to which He says ' Sit thou on my right hand,' of which too the devil with his wicked powers was foe, and Jews and Gentiles too. Through this body too He was made and was called High Priest and Apostle through the mystery whereof He gave to us, saying ' This is my Body for you'[3] and ' my Blood of the New Testament' (not of the Old), shed for you.'[4] Now Godhead hath neither body nor blood ; but the manhood which He bore of Mary was the cause of them, of whom the Apostles said ' Jesus of Nazareth, a man approved of God among you.' "[5]

Of the same from his book against the Arians : —

" And when he says ' Wherefore God hath also highly exalted Him and given Him a name which is above every name'[6] he speaks of the temple of the body, not of the Godhead, for the Most High is not exalted, but the flesh of the Most High is exalted, and to the flesh of the Most High He gave a name which is above every name. Nor did the Word of God receive the designation of God as a favour, but His flesh was held divine as well as Himself."

Of the same from the same work : —

" And when he says ' the Holy Ghost was not yet because that Jesus was not yet glorified,'[7] he says that His flesh was not yet glorified, for the Lord of glory is not glorified, but the flesh itself receives glory of the glory of the Lord as it mounts with Him into Heaven ; whence he says the spirit of adoption was not yet among men, because the first fruits taken from men had not yet ascended into heaven. Wherever

---

Oratio Secunda contra Arianos. Ben. Ed. I. 1. 538.

[1] Ps. cx. 1.
[2] Jerem. xxiii. 24.
[3] I. Cor. xi. 24.
[4] Matt. xxvi. 28; Mark xiv. 24.
[5] Acts ii. 22.
[6] Phil. ii. 9.
[7] John vii. 39.

then the Scripture says that the Son received, and was glorified, it speaks because of His manhood, not His Godhead."

Of the same from the same work : —

" So that He is very God both before His being made man and after His being made mediator of God and men, Jesus Christ united to the Father in spirit, and to us in flesh, who mediated between God and men, and who is not only man but also God."

Testimony of the Holy Ambrosius, bishop of Milan.

In his Exposition of the Faith : —

" We confess that our Lord Jesus Christ, the Only Begotten Son of God, was begotten before all ages, without beginning, of the Father, and that in these last days the same was made flesh of the holy Virgin Mary, assumed the manhood, in its perfection, of a reasonable soul and body, of one substance with the Father as touching His Godhead and of one substance with us as touching His manhood. For union of two perfect natures hath been after an ineffable manner. Wherefore we acknowledge one Christ, one Son, our Lord Jesus Christ; knowing that being coeternal with His own Father as touching His Godhead, by virtue of which also He is creator of all, He deigned, after the assent of the Holy Virgin, when she said to the angel ' Behold the handmaid of the Lord, be it unto me according to thy word '[1] to build after an ineffable fashion a temple out of her for Himself, and to unite this temple to Himself by her conception, not taking and uniting with Himself a body co-eternal with His own substance, and brought from heaven, but of the matter of our substance, that is of the Virgin. God the Word was not turned into flesh; His appearance was not unreal; keeping ever His own substance immutably and invariably He took the first fruits of our nature, and united them to Himself. God the Word did not take His beginning from the Virgin, but being coeternal with His own Father He of infinite kindness deigned to unite to Himself the first fruits of our nature, undergoing no mixture but in either substance appearing one and the same, as it is written ' Destroy this temple and in three days I will raise it up.'[2] For the divine Christ, as touching my substance which he took is destroyed, and the same Christ raises the destroyed temple as touching the divine substance in which also He is Creator of all things. Never at any time after the Union which He deigned to make with Himself from the moment of

the conception did He depart from His own temple, nor indeed through His ineffable love for mankind could depart.

" The same Christ is both passible and impassible ; as touching His manhood passible and as touching His Godhead impassible. ' Behold behold me, it is I, I have undergone no change ' — and when God the Word had raised His own temple and in it had wrought out the resurrection and renewal of our nature, He shewed this nature to His disciples and said ' Handle me and see for a spirit hath not flesh and ·bones as ye see me,' not ' be ' but ' have.'[1] So He says, referring to both the possessor and the possessed in order that you may perceive that what had taken place was not mixture, not change, not variation, but union. On this account too He shewed the prints of the nails and the wound of the spear and ate before His disciples to convince them by every means that the resurrection of our nature had been renewed in Him ; and further because in accordance with the blessed substance of His Godhead unchanged, impassible, immortal, He lived in need of nought, He by concession permitted all that can be felt to be brought to His own temple, and by His own power raised it up, and by means of His own temple made perfect the renewal of our nature.

" Them therefore that assert that the Christ was mere man, that God the Word was passible, or changed into flesh, or that the body which He had was consubstantial, or that He brought it from Heaven, or that it was an unreality ; or assert that God the Word being mortal needed to receive His resurrection from the Father, or that the body which He assumed was without a soul, or manhood without a mind, or that the two natures of the Christ became one nature by confusion and commixture ; them that deny that our Lord Jesus Christ was two natures unconfounded, but one person, as He is one Christ and one Son, all these the catholic and apostolic Church condemns."

Of the same :[2] —

" If then the flesh of all was in Christ or hath been in Christ subject to wrongs, how can it be held to be of one essence with the Godhead? For if the Word and the flesh which derives its nature from earth are of one essence, then the Word and the soul which He took in its perfection are of one essence, for the Word is of one nature with God both according to the Word of the Father, and the confession of the Son Himself in the words, ' I and my Father are one.' [3]

---

[1] Luke i. 38.

[2] John ii. 19.

[1] Luke xxiv. 39.
[2] De incarnat. sacram. Chap. 6.

[3] John x. 30.

Thus the Father must be held to be of the same substance with the body. Why any longer are ye wroth with the Arians, who say that the Son is a creature of God, while you assert yourselves that the Father is of one substance with His creatures?"

Of the same from his letter to the Emperor Gratianus:[1] —

"Let us preserve a distinction between Godhead and flesh. One Son of God speaks in both, since in Him both natures exist. The same Christ speaks, yet not always in the same but sometimes in a different manner. Observe how at one time He expresses divine glory and at another human feeling. As God He utters the things of God, since He is the Word; as man He speaks with humility because He converses in my essence."

On the same from the same book:[2] —

"As to the passage where we read that the Lord of glory was crucified,[3] let us not suppose that He was crucified in His own glory. But since He is both God and man, as touching His Godhead God, and as touching the assumption of the flesh, a man, Jesus Christ, the Lord of Glory, is said to have been crucified. For He partakes of either nature — that is the human and the divine. In the nature of manhood He underwent the passion in order that He who suffered might be said to be without distinction both Lord of Glory and Son of Man. As it is written 'He that came down from Heaven.'"[4]

Similarly of the same:[5] —

"Let then vain questions about words be silent, as it is written, the kingdom of God is not in 'enticing words' but in 'demonstration of the spirit.'[6] For there is one Son of God who speaks in both ways, since both natures exist in Him; but although He Himself speaks He does not speak always in the same way; for you see in Him at one time God's glory, at another time man's feeling. As God He utters divine things, being the Word; as man He utters human things, since in this nature He spoke."

Of the same from his work on the Incarnation of the Lord against the Apollinarians:[7] —

"But while we are confuting these, another set spring up who assert the body of the Christ and His godhead to be of one nature. What hell hath vomited forth so terrible a blasphemy? Really Arians are more tolerable, whose infidelity, on account of these men, is strengthened, so that with greater opposition they deny Father, Son and Holy Ghost

to be of one substance, for they did at least endeavour to maintain the Godhead of the Lord and His flesh to be of one nature."

Of the same (from the same chapter) : —

"He has frequently told me that he maintains the exposition of the Nicene Council, but in that examination our Fathers laid down that the Word of God, not the flesh, was of one substance with the Father, and they confessed that the Word came from the substance of the Father but that the flesh is of the Virgin. Why then do they hold out to us the name of the Nicene Council, while in reality they are introducing innovations of which our forefathers never entertained the thought?"

Of the same against Apollinarius:[1] —

"Refuse thou to allow that the body is by nature on a par with the Godhead. Even though thou believe the body of the Christ to be real and bring it to the altar for transformation,[2] and fail to distinguish the nature of the body and of the Godhead we shall say to thee, 'If thou offer rightly and fail to distinguish rightly, thou sinnest; hold thy peace.'[3] Distinguish what belongs naturally to us, and what is peculiar to the Word. For I had not what was naturally His, and He had not what was naturally mine, but He took what was naturally mine in order to make us partakers of what was His. And He received this not for confusion but for completion."

Of the same, a little further on :[4]—

"Let them who say that the nature of the Word has been changed into nature of the body say so no more, lest by the same interpretation the nature of the Word seem to have been changed into the corruption of sin. For there is a distinction between what took, and what was taken. Power came over the Virgin, as in the words of the angel to her, 'The power of the highest shall overshadow thee.'[5] But what was born was of the body of the Virgin, and on this account the de·

---

[1] De incarn. sacram. Chap. 4.

[2] "Offeras transfigurandum altaribus." The Benedictine Editors, by a curious anachronism, see here a reference to transubstantiation. But μεταποίησις, the word translated "transformation" implies no more than the being made to undergo a change, which may be a change in dignity without involving a change of substance. cf. pp. 200 and 201, where Orthodoxus distinctly asserts that the substance remains unchanged. Transubstantiation, definitely declared an article of faith in 1215, seems to have been first taught early in the 9th c. Vide Bp. Harold Browne on Art. xxviii.

[3] Gen. iv. 7. Sept.   [4] Id. Chap. 6.

[5] Luke i. 35. The Latin of the Benedictine edition of Ambrose is : —

Desinant ergo dicere naturam Verbi in Corporis naturam esse mutatam; ne pari interpretatione videatur natura Verbi in contagium mutata peccati. Aliud est enim quod assumpsit, et aliud quod assumptum est. Virtus venit in Virginem, sicut et Angelus ad eam dixit "quia Virtus Altissimi obumbrabit te." Sed natum est corpus ex Virgine; et ideo coelestis quidem descensio, sed humana conceptio est. Non ergo eadem carnis potuit esse divinitatisque natura.

---

[1] De Fide ii. Chap. 9.   [5] Id. Chap. 9.
[2] Chap. 7.   [6] I. Cor. ii. 4.
[3] I. Cor. ii. S.   [7] De Incarn. Sac. 6.
[4] John iii. 13.

scent was divine but the conception human. Therefore the nature of the flesh and of the godhead could not be the same." [1]

The testimony of St. Basil, Bishop of Cæsarea.

From his homily on Thanksgiving : —

"Wherefore when He wept over His friend He shewed His participation in human nature and set us free from two extremes, suffering us neither to grow over soft in suffering nor to be insensible to pain. As then the Lord suffered hunger after solid food had been digested, and thirst when the moisture in His body was exhausted; and was aweary when His nerves and sinews were strained by His journeying, it was not that His divinity was weighed down with toil, but that His body showed the wonted symptoms of its nature. Thus too when He allowed Himself to weep He permitted the flesh to take its natural course."

From the same against Eunomius : —

"I say that being in the form of God has the same force as being in God's substance, for as to have taken the form of a servant shews our Lord to have been of the substance of the manhood, so the statement that He was in the form of God attributes to Him the peculiar qualities of the divine substance." [2]

The testimony of the holy Gregorius, bishop of Nazianzus.

From his discourse De nova dominica : [3] —

"Believe that He will come again at His glorious advent judging quick and dead,[4] no longer flesh but not without a body."

"In order that He may be seen by them that pierced Him [5] and remain God without grossness."

Of the same from his Epistle to Cledonius : —

"God and man are two natures, as soul and body are two; but there are not two sons, nor yet are there here two men although Paul thus speaks of the outward man and the inward man.[6] In a word the sources of the Saviour's being are of two kinds, since the visible is distinct from the invisible and the timeless from that which is

of time, but He is not two beings. God forbid."

Of the same from the same Exposition to Cledonius : —

"If any one says that the flesh has now been laid aside, and that the Godhead is bare of body, and that it is not and will not come with that which was assumed, let him be deprived of the vision of the glory of the advent! For where is the body now, save with Him that assumed it? For it assuredly has not been, as the Manichees fable, swallowed up by the Son, that it may be honoured through dishonour; it has not been poured out and dissolved in the air like a voice and stream of perfume or flash of unsubstantial lightning. And where is the capacity of being handled after the resurrection, wherein one day it shall be seen by them that pierced Him? For Godhead of itself is invisible."

Of the same from the second discourse about the Son : —

"As the Word He was neither obedient nor disobedient, for these qualities belong to them that are in subjection and to inferiors; the former of the more tractable and the latter of them that deserve condemnation. But in the form of a servant He accommodates Himself to his fellowservants and puts on a form that was not His own, bearing in Himself all of me with all that is mine, that in Himself He may waste and destroy the baser parts as wax is wasted by fire or the mist of the earth by the sun."

Of the same from his discourse on the Theophany : —

"Since He came forth from the Virgin with the assumption of two things mutually opposed to one another, flesh and spirit, whereof the one was taken into God and the other exhibited the grace of the Godhead."

Of the same a little further on : —

"He was sent, but as Man. For His nature was twofold, for without doubt He thenceforth was aweary and hungered and thirsted and suffered agony and shed tears after the custom of a human body."

Of the same from his second discourse about the Son : —

"He would be called God not of the Word, but of the visible creation, for how could He be God of Him that is absolutely God? Just so He is called Father, not of the visible creation, but of the Word. For He was of two-fold nature. Wherefore the one belongs absolutely to both, but the other not absolutely.[1] For He is absolutely

---

[1] In the Greek text the last sentence is unintelligible and apparently corrupt. The translation follows the Latin text from which the version in the citation of Theodoret varies in important particulars. The Greek text of the quotation runs : —

Παυσάσθωσαν τοίνον οἱ λεγοντες ὡς ἡ τοῦ Λόγου φύσις εἰς σαρκὸς μεταβέβληται φύσιν· ἵνα μὴ δόξῃ μεταβληθεῖσα κατὰ τὴν αὐτὴν ἑρμηνείαν γεγενῆσθαι καὶ ἡ τοῦ Λόγου φύσις τοῖς τοῦ σώματος παθήμασι σύμφθορος. Ἕτερον γάρ ἐστι τὸ προσλαβὸν καὶ ἕτερόν ἐστι τὸ προσληφθέν. Δύναμις ἦλθεν ἐπὶ τὴν παρθένον, ὡς ὁ ἄγγελος πρὸς αὐτὴν λέγει ὅτι Δύναμις ὑψίστου ἐπισκιάσει σοι: ἀλλ᾽ ἐκ τοῦ σώματος ἦν τῆς Παρθένου τὸ τεχθέν· καὶ διὰ τοῦτο Θεία μὲν ἡ κατάβασις ἡ δὲ σύλληψις ἀνθρωπίνη· οὐκ αὐτὴ οὖν ἠδύνατο τοῦ τε σώματος πνεῦμα καὶ τῆς θεότητος φύσις.

[2] Cf. Phil. ii. 6.
[3] The passage quoted is not in the 43rd discourse *de nova dominica* but in the 40th on Holy Baptism.
[4] Acts i. 11.   [5] Zechariah xii. 10.   [6] II. Cor. iv. 16.

[1] Here the text is corrupt.

our God, but not absolutely our Father. And it is this conjunction of names which gives rise to the error of heretics. A proof of this lies in the fact that when natures are distinguished in thought, there is a distinction in names. Listen to the words of Paul. 'The God of our Lord Jesus Christ, The Father of Glory,'[1] — of Christ He is God, of glory Father, and if both are one this is so not by nature but by conjunction. What can be plainer than this? Fifthly let it be said that He receives life, authority, inheritance of nations, power over all flesh, glory, disciples or what you will; all these belong to the manhood."

Of the same from the same work : —

" ' For there is one God and one Mediator between God and men the man Christ Jesus.'[2] As man He still pleads for my salvation, because He keeps with Him the body which He took, till he made me God by the power of the incarnation — though He be no longer known according to the flesh that is by affections of the flesh and though He be without sin."

Of the same from the same work : —

" Is it not plain to all that as God He knows, and is ignorant, He says, as man? If, that is, any one distinguish the apparent from that which is an object of intellectual perception. For what gives rise to this opinion is the fact that the appellation of the Son is absolute without relation, it not being added of whom He is the Son; so to give the most pious sense to this ignorance we hold it to belong to the human, and not to the divine."

Testimony of the Holy Gregorius, bishop of Nyssa.

From his catechetical discourse : —

" And who says this that the infinity of the Godhead is comprehended by the limitation of the flesh, as by some vessel?"

Of the same from the same work : —

" But if man's soul by necessity of its nature commingled with the body, is everywhere in authority, what need is there of asserting that the Godhead is limited by the nature of the flesh?"

Of the same from the same work : —

" What hinders us then, while recognising a certain unity and approximation of a divine nature in relation to the human, from retaining the divine intelligence even in this approximation, believing that the divine even when it exists in men is beyond all limitation?"

Of the same from his work against Eunomius : —

" The Son of Mary converses with brothers, but the only begotten has no brothers, for how could the name of only begotten be preserved among brothers? And the same Christ that said ' God is a spirit'[1] says to His disciples ' Handle me,'[2] to shew that the human nature only can be handled and that the divine is intangible; and He that said ' I go'[3] indicates removal from place to place, while He that comprehends all things and ' by Whom,' as says the Apostle, ' all things were created and by Whom all things consist,'[4] had among all existing things nothing without and beyond Himself which can stand to Him in the relation of motion or removal."

Of the same from the same work : —

" ' Being by the right hand of God exalted.'[5] Who then was exalted? The lowly or the most high? And what is the lowly if it be not the human? And what is the most high save the divine? But God being most high needs no exaltation, and so the Apostle says that the human is exalted, exalted that is in being ' made both Lord and Christ.'[6] Therefore the Apostle does not mean by this term ' He made' the everlasting existence of the Lord, but the change of the lowly to the exalted which took place on the right hand of God. By this word he declares the mystery of piety, for when he says ' by the right hand of God exalted' he plainly reveals the ineffable œconomy of the mystery that the right hand of God which created all things, which is the Lord by whom all things were made and without whom nothing consists of things that were made,[7] through the union lifted up to Its own exaltation the manhood united to It."

Testimony of St. Amphilochius, bishop of Iconium.

From his discourse on " My Father is greater than I " : [8] —

" Henceforth distinguish the natures; that of God and that of man. For He was not made man by falling away from God, nor God by increase and advance from man."

Of the same from his discourse on " the Son can do nothing of Himself" : [9]—

" For after the resurrection the Lord shews both — both that the body is not of this nature, and that the body rises, for remember the history. After the passion and the resurrection the disciples were gathered together, and when the doors were shut the Lord stood in the midst of them. Never at

---

[1] Ephes. i 17.   [2] I. Tim. ii. 5.

[1] John iv. 24.   [4] Coloss. i. 16, 17.   [7] Cf. John i. 2.
[2] Luke xxiv. 39.   [5] Acts ii. 33.   [8] John xiv. 28.
[3] John xiv. 28.   [6] Acts ii. 36.   [9] John v. 19.

any time before the passion did He do this. Could not then the Christ have done this even long before? For all things are possible to God.[1] But before the passion He did not do so lest you should suppose the incarnation an unreality or appearance, and think of the flesh of the Christ as spiritual, or that it came down from heaven and is of another substance than our flesh. Some have invented all these theories with the idea that thereby they reverence the Lord, forgetful that through their thanksgiving they blaspheme themselves, and accuse the truth of a lie: for I say nothing of the lie being altogether absurd. For if He took another body how does that affect mine, which stands in need of salvation? If He brought down flesh from heaven, how does this affect my flesh which was derived from earth?"

Of the same from the same work : —

"Wherefore not before the passion, but after the passion, the Lord stood in the midst of the disciples when the doors were shut, that thou mayest know that thy natural body after being sown is 'raised a spiritual body,'[2] and that thou mayest not suppose the body that is raised to be a different body. When Thomas after the resurrection doubted, He shews him the prints of the nails, He shews him the marks of the spears. But had He not power to heal Himself after the resurrection too, when even before the resurrection He had healed all men? But by shewing the prints of the nails He shews that it is this very body; by coming in when the doors were shut He shews that it has not the same qualities; the same body to fulfil the work of the incarnation by raising that which had become a corpse, but a changed body that it fall not again under corruption nor be subject again to death."

Testimony of the blessed Theophilus, bishop of Alexandria.

From his work against Origen : —

"Our likeness which He assumed is not changed into the nature of Godhead nor is His Godhead turned into our likeness. For He remains what He was from the beginning God, and He so remains preserving our subsistence in Himself."

Of the same from the same treatise : —

"But you persist continually in your blasphemies attacking the Son of God, and using these words 'as the Son and the Father are one, so also are the soul which the Son took and the Son Himself one.' You are ignorant that the Son and the Father are one on account of their one substance and the same Godhead; but the soul and the Son are each of a different substance and different nature. For if the soul of the Son and the Son Himself are one in the same sense in which the Father and the Son are one, then the Father and the Son will be one and the soul of the Son shall one day say 'He that hath Me hath seen the Father;'[1] but this is not so; God forbid. For the Son and the Father are one because there is no distinction between their qualities, but the soul and the Son are distinguished alike in nature and substance, in that the soul which is naturally of one substance with us was made by Him. For if the soul and the Son are one in the same manner in which the Father and the Son are one, as Origen would have it, then the soul equally with the Son will be 'the brightness of God's glory and express image of His person.'[2] But this is impossible; impossible that the Son and the soul should be one as He and the Father are one. And what will Origen do when again he attacks himself? For he writes, never could the soul distressed and 'exceeding sorrowful'[3] be the 'firstborn of every creature.'[4] For God the Word, as being stronger than the soul, the Son Himself, says 'I have power to lay it down and I have power to take it again.'[5] If then the Son is stronger than His own soul, as is agreed, how can His soul be equal to God and in the form of God? For we say that 'He emptied Himself and took upon Him the form of a servant.'[6] In the extravagance of his impieties Origen surpasses all other heretics, as we have shewn, for if the Word exists in the form of God and is equal to God and if he supposes thus daring to write the soul of the Saviour to be in the form of God and equal with God, how can the equal be greater, when the inferior in nature testifies to the superiority of what is beyond it?"

Testimony of the Holy John Chrysostom, bishop of Constantinople.

From the Discourse held in the Great Church : —

"Thy Lord exalted man to heaven, and thou wilt not even give him a share of the agora. But why do I say 'to heaven'? He seated man on a kingly throne. Thou expellest him from the city."

Of the same, on the beginning of Ps. xlii. : —

"Up to this day Paul does not cease to say 'We are ambassadors for Christ as though God did beseech you by us; we pray you in

---

[1] Matt. xix 26. Mark x. 27.   [2] I. Cor. xv.

[1] John xiv. 9.   [3] Matt. xxvi. 38.   [5] John x. 18.
[2] Hebrews i. 3.   [4] Coloss. i. 15.   [6] Phil. ii. 7.

Christ's stead, be ye reconciled to God.'[1] Nor did He stand here, but taking the first fruits of thy nature He sat down ' above all principality and power and might, and every name that is named not only in this world but in the world to come.'[2] What could be equal to this honour? The first fruits of our race which has so much offended and is so dishonoured sits so high and enjoys honour so vast."

Of the same about the division of tongues : —

'' For bethink thee what it is to see our nature riding on the Cherubim and all the power of heaven mustered round about it. Consider too Paul's wisdom and how many terms he searches for that he may set forth the love of Christ to men, for he does not say simply the grace, nor yet simply the riches, but the ' exceeding great riches of His grace in His kindness.'"[3]

Of the same from his Dogmatic Oration, on the theme that the word spoken and deeds done in humility by Christ were not so spoken and done on account of infirmity, but on account of differences of dispensation : —

" And after His resurrection, when He saw His disciple disbelieving, He did not shrink from shewing him both wound and print of nails, and letting him lay his hand upon the scars, and said ' Examine and see, for a spirit hath not flesh and bones.'[4] The reason of His not assuming the manhood of full age from the beginning, and of His deigning to be conceived, to be born, to be suckled, and to live so long upon the earth, was that by the long period of the time and all the other circumstances, He might give a warranty for this very thing."

Of the same against those who assert that demons rule human affairs : —

" Nothing was more worthless than man and than man nothing has become more precious. He was the last part of the reasonable creation, but the feet have been made the head, and through the firstfruits have been borne up to the kingly throne. Just as some man noble and bountiful, on seeing a wretch escaped from shipwreck who has saved nothing but his bare body from the waves, welcomes him with open hands, clothes him in a radiant robe, and exalts him to the highest honour, so too hath God done towards our nature. Man had lost all that he had, his freedom, his intercourse with God, his abode in Paradise,

his painless life, whence he came forth like a man all naked from a wreck, but God received him and straightway clothed him, and, taking him by the hand, led him onward step by step and brought him up to heaven."

Of the same from the same work : —

" But God made the gain greater than the loss, and exalted our nature to the royal throne. So Paul exclaims ' And have raised us up together and made us sit together in heavenly places'[1] at His right hand."

Of the same from his IIIrd oration against the Jews : —

" He opened the heavens ; of foes he made friends ; He introduced them into heaven ; He seated our nature on the right hand of the throne ; He gave us countless other good things."

Of the same from his discourse on the Ascension : —

" To this distance and height did He exalt our nature. Look where low it lay, and where it mounted up. Lower it was impossible to descend than where man descended ; higher it was impossible to rise than where He exalted him."

Of the same from his interpretation of the Epistle to the Ephesians : —

" According to His good pleasure, which He had proposed in himself, that is which He earnestly desired, He was as it were in labour to tell us the mystery. And what is this mystery? That He wishes to seat man on high ; as in truth came to pass."

Of the same from the same interpretation : —

" God of our Lord Jesus Christ speaks of this and not of God the Word."

Of the same from the same interpretation : —

" ' And when we were dead in sins He quickened us together in Christ ; '[2] again Christ stands in the midst, and the work is wonderful. If the first fruits live we live also. He quickened both Him and us. Seest thou that all these things are spoken according to the flesh?"

Of the same from the gospel according to St. John : —

" Why does he add ' and dwelt among us'?[3] It is as though he said : Imagine nothing absurd from the phrase ' was made.' For I have not mentioned any change in that unchangeable nature, but of tabernacling[4] and of inhabiting. Now that which tabernacles is not identical with the tabernacle,

---

[1] II. Cor. v. 20.   [2] Ephes. i. 21.   [3] Ephes. ii. 7.
[4] Cf. Luke xxiv. 39. and John xx. 27. and cf. note on page 235.

[1] Ephes. ii. 6.   [3] John i. 14. εσκήνωσεν.
[2] Ephes. ii. 5.   [4] σκήνωσις.

but one thing tabernacles in another; otherwise there would be no tabernacling. Nothing inhabits itself. I spoke of a distinction of substance. For by the union and the conjunction God the Word and the flesh are one without confusion or destruction of the substances, but by ineffable and indescribable union."

Of the same from the gospel according to St. Matthew : —

" Just as one standing in the space between two that are separated from one another, stretches out both his hands and joins them, so too did He, joining the old and the new, the divine nature and the human, His own with ours."

Of the same from the Ascension of Christ : —

" For so when two champions stand ready for the fight, some other intervening between them, at once stops the struggle, and puts an end to their ill will, so too did Christ. As God He was wroth, but we made light of His wrath, and turned away our faces from our loving Lord. Then Christ flung Himself in the midst, and restored both natures to mutual love, and Himself took on Him the weight of the punishment laid by the Father on us."

Of the same from the same work : —

" Lo He brought the first fruits of our nature to the Father and the Father Himself approved the gift, alike on account of the high dignity of Him that bought it and of the faultlessness of the offering. He received it in His own hands, He made a chair of His own throne; nay more He seated it on His own right hand, let us then recognise who it was to whom it was said ' Sit thou on my right hand '[1] and what was that nature to which God said ' Dust thou art and to dust thou shalt return.' "[2]

Of the same a little further on : —

" What arguments to use, what words to utter I cannot tell; the nature which was rotten, worthless, declared lowest of all, vanquished everything and overcame the world. To-day it hath been thought worthy to be made higher than all, to-day it hath received what from old time angels have desired; to-day it is possible for archangels to be made spectators of what has been for ages longed for, and they contemplate our nature, shining on the throne of the King in the glory of His immortality."

Testimony of St. Flavianus, bishop of Antioch.

From the Gospel according to St. Luke : —
" In all of us the Lord writes the express

image of His holiness, and in various ways shows our nature the way of salvation. Many and clear proofs does He give us both of His bodily advent and of His Godhead working by a body's means. For He wished to give us assurance of both His natures."

Of the same on the Theophany : —

" ' Who can express the noble acts of the Lord, or shew forth all His praise?'[1] who could express in words the greatness of His goodness toward us? Human nature is joined to Godhead, while both natures remain independent."

Testimony of Cyril, bishop of Jerusalem. From his fourth catechetical oration concerning the ten dogmas.

Of the birth from a virgin : —

" Believe thou that this only begotten Son of God, on account of our sins, came down from heaven to earth, having taken on Him this manhood of like passions with us, and being born of holy Virgin and of Holy Ghost. This incarnation was effected, not in seeming and unreality, but in reality. He did not only pass through the Virgin, as through a channel, but was verily made flesh of her. Like us He really ate, and of the Virgin was really suckled. For if the incarnation was an unreality, then our salvation is a delusion. The Christ was twofold — the visible man, the invisible God. He ate as man, verily like ourselves, for the flesh that He wore was of like passions with us; He fed the five thousand with five loaves[2] as God. As man He really died. As God He raised the dead on the fourth day.[3] As man He slept in the boat. As God He walked upon the waters."[4]

Testimony of Antiochus, bishop of Ptolemais :[5] —

" Do not confound the natures and you will have a lively apprehension of the incarnation."

Testimony of the holy Hilarius, bishop and confessor,[6] in his ninth book, " de Fide":

[1] Ps. cvi. 2.
[2] Matt. xiv. 15, etc., Mark vi. 35, etc., Luke ix. 9, etc., John vi. 5, etc.
[3] John xi. 43.   [4] Matt. vii. 24; John vi. 19.
[5] This and another fragment in the Catena on St. John xix. 443, is all that survives of the works of Antiochus of Ptolemais, an eloquent opponent of Chrysostom at Constantinople, and like him, said to have a " mouth of gold."
[6] Hilary of Poictiers, † A.D. 368. The treatise quoted is known as " *de Trinitate*," and " *contra Arianos*," as well as " *de Fide*." The Greek of Theodoret differs considerably from the Latin. Of the first extract the original is *nescit plane vitam suam nescit qui Christum Jesum ut verum Deum ita et verum hominem ignorat. Et ejusdem periculi res est, Christum Jesum vel Spiritum Deum, vel carnem nostri corporis denegare. Omnis ergo qui confitebitur me coram hominibus, confitebor et ego eum coram patre meo qui est in coelis. Qui autem negaverit me coram hominibus, negabo et ego eum coram patre meo, qui est in coelis. Haec Verbum caro factum loquebatur, et homo Jesus Christus dominus majestatis docebat; Mediator ipse in se ad salutem Ecclesiae constitutus et illo ipso inter Deum et homines mediatoris sacramento utrumque unus existens, dum ipse ex unitis in idipsum naturis naturae utriusque res eadem est ; ita tamen, ut neutro careret in utroque, ne forte Deus esse homo nascendo desineret, et homo rursus Deus manendo non esset. Haec itaque humanae beati-*

" He who knoweth not Jesus the Christ
as very God and as very man, knoweth not
in reality his own life, for we incur the same
peril if we deny Christ Jesus or God the
spirit, or the flesh of our own body. 'Whosoever therefore shall confess me before men
him will I confess also before my Father
which is in Heaven, but whosoever shall
deny me before men him will I also deny
before my Father which is in Heaven.'[1]
These things spoke the Word made flesh;
these things the man Christ Jesus, Lord of
Glory, taught, being made Mediator for the
salvation of the Church in the very mystery
whereby He mediated between God and men.
Both being made one out of the natures united
for this very purpose, He was one and the
same through either nature, but so that in
both He fell short in neither, lest haply by
being born as man He should cease to be
God, or by remaining God should not be
man. Therefore this is the blessedness of the
true faith among men to preach both God
and man, to confess both word and flesh, to
recognise that God was also man, and not
to be ignorant that the flesh is also Word."

Of the same from the same book :[2] —

" So the only begotten God being born
man of a Virgin and in the fulness of the
time, being Himself ordained to work out
the advance of man to God, observed this

tudinis fides vera est, Deum et hominem praedicare, Verbum
et carnem confiteri: neque Deum nescire quod homo sit, neque
carnem ignorare quod Verbum sit.
[1] Matt. x. 32, 33.
[2] Natus igitur unigenitus Deus ex Virgine homo, et secundum plenitudinem temporum in semetipso provecturus in
Deum hominem hunc per omnia evangelici sermonis modum
tenuit, ut se filium Dei credi doceret, et hominis filium prae-
dicari admoneret: locutus et gerens homo universa quae Dei
sunt, loquens deinde et gerens Deus universa quae hominis
sunt; ita tamen, ut ipso illo utriusque generis sermone num-
quam nisi cum significatione et hominis locutus et Dei sit;
uno tamen Deo patre semper ostenso, et se in natura unius Dei
per nativitatis veritatem professo: nec tamen se Deo patri non
et filii honore et hominis conditione subdente: cum et nativitas
omnis se referat ad auctorem, et caro se universa secundum
Deum profiteatur infirmam. Hinc itaque fallendi simplices
atque ignorantes haereticis occasio est, ut quae ab eo secundum hominem dicta sunt, dicta esse secundum naturae divinae
infirmitatem mentiantur : et quia unus atque idem est loquens
omnia quae loquitur de se ipso omnia eum locutum esse con-
tendant.
Nec sane negamus, totum illum qui ejus manet, naturae
suae esse sermonem. Sed si Jesus Christus et homo et Deus
est ; et neque cum homo, tum primum Deus ; neque cum homo,
tum non etiam et Deus; neque post hominem in Deo non totus
homo totus Deus ; unum atque idem necesse est dictorum ejus
sacramentum esse, quod generis. Et cum in eo secundum
tempus discernis hominem a Deo, Dei tamen atque hominis
discerne sermonem. Et cum Deum atque hominem in tempore
confiteberis, Dei atque hominis in tempore dicta dijudica.
Cum vero ex homine et Deo rursus totius hominis, totius
etiam Dei tempus intelligis, si quid illud ad demonstra-
tionem ejus temporis dictum est, tempori coaptato quae dicta
sunt: ut cum aliud sit ante hominem Deus, aliud sit homo et
Deus, aliud sit post hominem et Deum totus homo totus Deus ;
non confundas temporibus; et generibus dispensationis sacramentum, cum pro qualitate generum ac naturarum, alium ei in
sacramento hominis necesse est sermonem fuisse non nato,
alium adhuc morituro, alium jam aeterno. Nostri igitur
causa haec omnia Jesus Christus manens et corporis nostri
homo natus secundum consuetudinem naturae nostrae locutus
est, non tamen omittens naturae suae esse quod Deus est. Nam
tametsi in partu ac passione ac morte naturae nostrae rem
peregit, res tamen ipsas omnes virtute naturae suae gessit.

order of things, through all the words of the
gospels, that He might teach belief in Himself, as Son of God, and keep us in mind to
preach Him as Son of Man. As being man
He always spoke and acted as is proper to
man, but in such a manner as never to speak
in this same mode of speech as touching both
save with the intention of signifying both
God and Man. But hence the heretics
derive a pretext for catching in their traps
simple and ignorant men : what was spoken
by our Lord in accordance with His manhood they falsely assert to have been uttered
in the weakness of His divine nature, and
since one and the same person spake all the
words He used they urged that all He uttered
He uttered about Himself. Now even we
do not deny that all His extant words are
of His own nature. But granted that the
one Christ is man and God; granted that
when man He was not then first God;
granted that when man He was then also
God, granted that after the assumption of
the manhood in the Lord, the Word was
man and the Word was God, it follows of
necessity that there is one and the same
mystery of His words as there is of His generation. Whenever in Him, as occasion may
require, you distinguish the manhood from
the Godhead, then also endeavour to separate
the words of God from the words of man.
And whenever you confess God and man,
then discern the words of God and man.
And when the words are spoken of God and
man, and again of man wholly and wholly of
God, consider carefully the occasion. If anything was spoken to signify what was appropriate to a particular occasion, apply the
words to the occasion. A distinction must
be observed between God before the manhood, man and God, man wholly and God
wholly after the union of the manhood and
Godhead. Take heed therefore not to confuse the mystery of the incarnation in the
words and acts. For it must needs be that
according to the quality of the kinds of
natures a distinction lies in the manner of
speech, before the manhood was born, in accordance with the mystery when it was still
approaching death, and again when it was
everlasting. ' For if in His birth and in His
passion and in His death He acted in accordance with our nature He nevertheless
effected all this by the power of His own
nature.' "

Of the same in the same book : —

" Do you then see that thus God and man
are confessed, so that death is predicated of
man, and the resurrection of the flesh, of
God ; for consider the nature of God and the

power of the resurrection, and recognise in the death the œconomy as touching man. And since both death and resurrection have been brought about in their own natures, bear in mind, I beg you, the one Christ Jesus, who was of both. I have shortly demonstrated these points to you to the end that we may remember both natures to have been in our Lord Jesus Christ 'for being in the form of God He took the form of a servant.'"[1]

Testimony of the very holy bishop Augustinus.

From his letter to Volusianus. Epistle III: "But now He appeared as Mediator between God and man, so as in the unity of His person to conjoin both natures, by combining the wonted with the unwonted, and the unwonted with the wonted."

Of the same from his exposition of the Gospel according to John:[2]— "What then, O heretic? Since Christ is also man, He speaks as man; and dost thou slander God? He in Himself lifts man's nature on high, and thou hast the hardihood to cheapen His divine nature."

Of the same from his book on the Exposition of the Faith:— "It is ours to believe, but His to know, and so let God the Word Himself, after receiving all that is proper to man, be man, and let man after His assumption and reception of all that is God, be no other than God. It must not be supposed because He is said to have been incarnate and mixed, that therefore His substance was diminished. God knows that He mixes Himself without the natural corruption, and He is mixed in reality. He knows also that He so received in Himself as that no addition of increment accrues to Himself, as also He knows He infused His whole self so as to incur no diminution. Let us not then, in accordance with our weak intelligence, and forming conjectures on the teaching of experience and the senses, suppose that God and man are mixed after the manner of things created and equal mixed together, and that from such a confusion as this of the Word and of the flesh a body as it were was made. God forbid that this should be our belief, lest we should suppose that after the manner of things which are confounded together two natures were brought into one hypostasis.[3] For a mention of this kind implies destruction of both parts; but Christ Himself, containing but not contained, who examines us but is Him-

self beyond examination, making full but not made full, everywhere at one and the same time being Himself whole and pervading the universe, through His pouring out His own power, as being moved with mercy. was mingled with the nature of man, though the nature of man was not mingled with the divine."

Testimony of Severianus, bishop of Gabala.[1]

From "the Nativity of Christ":— "O mystery truly heavenly and yet on earth — mystery seen and not apparent for so was the Christ after His birth; heavenly and yet on earth; holding and not held; seen and invisible; of Heaven as touching the nature of the Godhead, on earth as touching the nature of the manhood; seen in the flesh, invisible in the spirit; held as to the body not to be holden as to the Word."

Testimony of Atticus,[2] bishop of Constantinople.

From his letter to Eupsychius:— "How then did it behove the Most Wise to act? By mediation of the flesh assumed, and by union of God the Word with man born of Mary, He is made of either nature, so that the Christ made one of both, as constituted in Godhead, abides in the proper dignity of His impassible nature, but in flesh. being brought near to death, at one and the same time shews the kindred nature of the flesh how through death to despise death, and by His death confirms the righteousness of the new covenant."

Testimony of Cyril, bishop of Alexandria.
From his letter to Nestorius:[3]— "The natures which have been brought together in the true unity are distinct, and of both there is one God and Son, but the difference of the natures has not been removed in consequence of the union."

Of the same from his letter against the Orientals:[4]— "There is an union of two natures, wherefore we acknowledge one Christ, one Son, one Lord. In accordance with this perception of the unconfounded union we acknowledge the Holy Virgin as Mother of God[5]

---

[1] Phil. ii. 7.　　[2] Tract 78.
[3] cf. p. 36. Here ὑπόστασις = person.

[1] Severianus, like Antiochus of Ptolemais, was moved to leave his remote diocese (Gabala is now Gibili, not far south of Latakia) to try his fortunes as a popular preacher at Constantinople: There he met with success, and was kindly treated by Chrysostom, but he turned against his friend, and was a prime agent in the plots against him. The date of his death is unknown.
[2] Cf. p. 154, note. Atticus was a determined opponent of heresy as well as of Chrysostom.
[3] Ep. iv. Ed. Aub. V. ii. 23.　　[4] id. vi. 157.
[5] The word in the text is the famous θεοτόκος, the watchword of the Nestorian controversy. It may be doubtful whether either the English "Mother of God" or the Latin "Deipara" exactly represents the idea intended to be expressed by the subtler Greek. Even Nestorius did not object to the Θεοτόκος when rightly understood. The explanation of

because the Word of God was made flesh and was made man, and from the very conception united to Himself the temper taken from her." [1]

Of the same : —

" There is one Lord Jesus Christ, even if the difference be recognised of the natures of which we assert the ineffable union to have been made."

Of the same : —

" Therefore, as I said, while praising the manner of the incarnation, we see that two natures came together in inseparable union without confusion and without division,[2] for the flesh is flesh and no kind of Godhead, although it was made flesh of God; in like manner the Word is God, and not flesh, although He made the flesh His own according to the œconomy."

Of the same from his interpretation of the Epistle to the Hebrews : —

" For although the natures which came together in unity are regarded as different and unequal with one another, I mean of flesh and of God, nevertheless the Son, Who was made of both, is one."

Of the same from his interpretation of the same Epistle : —

" Yet though the only begotten Word of God is said to be united in hypostasis to flesh, we deny there was any confusion of the natures with one another, and declare each to remain what it is."

Of the same from his commentaries : —

" The Father's Word, born of the Virgin, is named man, though being by nature God as partaking of flesh and blood like us[1] for thus He was seen by men upon earth, without getting rid of His own nature, but assuming our Manhood perfect according to its own reason."

Of the same concerning the Incarnation (Schol. c. 13) : —

" Then before the incarnation there is one Very God, and in manhood He remains what He was and is and will be ; the one Lord Jesus Christ then must not be separated into man apart and into God apart, but recognising the difference of the natures and preserving them unconfounded with one another, we assert that there is one and the same Christ Jesus."

Of the same after other commentaries : —

" There is plain perception of one thing dwelling in another, namely the divine nature in manhood, without undergoing commixture or any confusion, or any change into what it was not. For what is said to dwell in another does not become the same as that in which it dwells, but is rather regarded as one thing in another. But in the nature of the Word and of the manhood the difference points out to us a difference of natures alone, for of both is perceived one Christ. Therefore he says that the Word ' Tabernacled among us,'[2] carefully observing the freedom from confusion, for he recognises one only begotten Son who was made flesh and became man."

Now, my dear sir, you have heard the great lights of the world ; you have seen the beams of their teaching, and you have received exact instruction how, not only after the nativity, but after the passion which wrought salvation, and the resurrection, and the ascension, they have shewn the union of the Godhead and of the manhood to be without confusion.

Eran. — I did not suppose that they distinguished the natures after the union, but I have found an infinite amount of distinction.

Orth. — It is mad and rash against those noble champions of the faith so much as to wag your tongue. But I will adduce for you the words of Apollinarius, in order that you may know that he too asserts the union to be without confusion. Now hear his words.

Testimony of Apollinarius.

From his summary : —

" There is an union between what is of God and what is of the body. On the one side is the adorable Creator Who is wisdom and power eternal ; these are of the God-

---

the symbolum drawn up by Theodoret himself at Ephesus for presentation to the Emperor is "Ἑνα χριστὸν, ἕνα υἰὸν, ἕνα κύριον ὁμολογοῦμεν. κατὰ ταύτην τῆς ἀσυγχύτου ἐνώσεως ἔννοιαν ὁμολογοῦμεν τὴν ἁγίαν, παρθένον θεοτόκον, διὰ τὸ τὸν θεὸν λόγον σαρκωθῆναι καὶ ἐνανθρωπῆσαι καὶ ἐξ αὐτῆς τῆς συλλήψεως ἐνῶσαι ἑαυτῷ τὸν ἐξ αὐτῆς ληφθέντα ναόν." The great point sought to be asserted was, the union of the two Natures. Gregory of Nazianzus (li. 738) says Ἐι τις οὐ θεοτόκον τὴν Μαρίαν ὑπολαμβάνει χωρίς ἐστι τῆς Θεότητος.

[1] Here Cyril adopts the terms of the document given in the preceding note.

[2] ἀσυγχύτως καὶ ἀδιαιρέτως. These adverbs recall the famous words of Hooker. Ecc. Pol. v. 54. 10.

" There are but four things which concur to make complete the whole state of our Lord Jesus Christ: his Deity, his manhood, the conjunction of both, and the distinction of the one from the other being joined in one. Four principal heresies there are which have in those things withstood the truth : Arians, by bending themselves against the Deity of Christ; Apollinarians, by maiming and misinterpreting that which belongeth to his human nature; Nestorians, by rending Christ asunder, and dividing him into two persons; the followers of Eutyches, by confounding in his person those natures which they should distinguish. Against these there have been four most famous ancient general councils : the council of Nice to define against Arians; against Apollinarians the Council of Constantinople; the council of Ephesus against Nestorians; against Eutychians the Chalcedon Council. In four words, ἀληθῶς, τελέως, ἀδιαιρέτως, ἀσυγχύτως, truly, perfectly, indivisibly, distinctly; the first applied to his being God, and the second to his being Man, the third to his being of both One, and the fourth to his continuing in that one Rest : we may fully by way of Abridgement comprise whatsoever antiquity hath at large handled either in declaration of Christian belief, or in refutation of the foresaid heresies. Within the compass of which four heads, I may truly affirm, that all heresies which touch but the person of Jesus Christ, whether they have risen in these later days, or in any age heretofore, may be with great facility brought to confine themselves."

---

head. On the other hand is the Son of Mary, born at the last time, worshipping God, advancing in wisdom, strengthened in power; these are of the body. The suffering on behalf of sin and the curse came and will not pass away nor yet be changed into the incorporeal."

And again a little further on : —

"Men are consubstantial with the unreasoning animals as far as the unreasoning body is concerned; they are of another substance in so far forth as they are reasonable. Just so God who is consubstantial with men according to the flesh is of another substance in so far forth as He is Word and Man."

And in another place he says : —

"Of things which are mingled together the qualities are mixed and not destroyed. Thus it comes to pass that some are separate from the mixed parts as wine from water, nor yet is there mingling with a body, nor yet as of bodies with bodies, but the mingling preserves also the unmixed, so that, as each occasion may require, the energy of the Godhead either acts independently or in conjunction, as was the case when the Lord fasted, for the Godhead being in conjunction in proportion to its being above need, hunger was hindered, but when it no longer opposed to the craving its superiority to need, then hunger arose, to the undoing of the devil. But if the mixture of the bodies suffered no change, how much more that of the Godhead?"

And in another place he says : —

"If the mixture with iron which makes the iron itself fire does not change its nature, so too the union of God with the body implies no change of the body, even though the body extend its divine energies to what is within its reach."

To this he immediately adds : —

"If a man has both soul and body, and these remain in unity, much more does the Christ, who has Godhead and body, keep both secure and unconfounded."

And again a little further on : —

"For human nature is partaker of the divine energy, as far as it is capable, but it is as distinct as the least from the greatest. Man is a servant of God, but God is not servant of man, nor even of Himself. Man is a creature of God, but God is not a creature of man, nor even of Himself."

And again : —

"If any one takes in reference to Godhead and not in reference to flesh the passage the 'Son doeth what He seeth the Father do,'[1] wherein He Who was made flesh is distinct from the Father Who was not made flesh, divides two divine energies. But there is no division. So He does not speak in reference to Godhead."

Again he says : —

"As man is not an unreasoning being, on account of the contact of the reasoning and the unreasoning, just so the Saviour is not a creature on account of the contact of the creature with God uncreate."

To this he also adds : —

"The invisible which is united to a visible body and thereby is beheld, remains invisible, and it remains without composition because it is not circumscribed with the body, and the body, remaining in its own measure, accepts the union with God in accordance with its being quickened, nor is it that which is quickened which quickens."

And a little further on he says : —

"If the mixture with soul and body, although from the beginning they coalesce, does not make the soul visible on account of the body, nor change it into the other properties of the body, so as to allow of its being cut or lessened, how much rather God, who is not of the same nature as the body, is united to the body without undergoing change, if the body of man remains in its own nature, and this when it is animated by a soul, then in the case of Christ the commingling does not so change the body as that it is not a body."

And further on he says again : —

"He who confesses that soul and body are constituted one by the Scripture, is inconsistent with himself when he asserts that this union of the Word with the body is a change, such change being not even beheld in the case of a soul."

Listen to him again exclaiming clearly : —

"If they are impious who deny that the flesh of the Lord abides, much more are they who refuse wholly to accept His incarnation."

And in his little book about the Incarnation he has written : —

"The words 'Sit thou on my right hand'[1] He speaks as to man, for they are not spoken to Him that sits ever on the throne of glory, as God the Word after His ascension from earth, but they are said to Him who hath now been exalted to the heavenly glory as man, as the Apostles say 'for David is not ascended into the heavens, but he saith himself the Lord said unto my Lord sit thou on my right hand.'[2] The order is human, giving a beginning to the sitting; but it is a divine dignity to sit together with God 'to whom thousand thousands minister and

[1] John v. 19.
[1] Ps. cx. 1. [2] Acts ii. 34.

before whom ten thousand times ten thousand stand.'"[1]

And again a little further on:—

"He does not put His enemies under Him as God but as man, but so that the God who is seen and man are the same. Paul too teaches us that the words 'until I make thy foes thy footstool'[2] are spoken to men, describing the success as His own of course in accordance with His divinity 'According to the working whereby He is able even to subdue all things unto Himself.'[3] Behold Godhead and manhood existing inseparably in one Person."

And again:—

"'Glorify me with thine own self with the glory which I had with thee before the world was.'[4] The word 'glorify' He uses as man, but His having this glory before the ages He reveals as God."

And again:—

"But let us not be humiliated as thinking the worship of the Son of God humiliation, even in His human likeness, but as though honouring some king appearing in poor raiment with his royal glory, and above all seeing that the very garb in which He is clad is glorified, as became the body of God and of the world's Saviour which is seed of eternal life, instrument of divine deeds, destroyer of all wickedness, slayer of death, and prince of resurrection; for though it had its nature from man it derived its life from God, and its power and divine virtue from heaven."

And again:—

"Whence we worship the body as the Word; we partake of the body as of the spirit."

Now it has been plainly shewn you that the author who was first to introduce the mixture of the natures openly uses the argument of a distinction between them; thus he has called the body garb, creature and instrument; he even went so far as to call it slave, which none of us has ever ventured to do. He also says that it was deemed worthy of the seat on the right hand, and uses many other expressions which are rejected by your vain heresy.

Eran. — But why then did he who was the first to introduce the mixture insert so great a distinction in his arguments?

Orth. — The power of truth forces even them that vehemently fight against her to agree with what she says, but, if you will, let us now begin a discussion about the impassibility of the Lord.

Eran. — You know that musicians are accustomed to give their strings rest, and they slacken them by turning the pegs; if then things altogether void of reason and soul stand in need of some recreation, we who partake of both shall do nothing absurd if we mete out our labour in proportion to our power. Let us then put it off till to-morrow.

Orth. — The divine David charges us to give heed to the divine oracles by night and by day; but let it be as you say, and let us keep the investigation of the remainder of our subject till to-morrow.

DIALOGUE III.

THE IMPASSIBLE.

Orthodoxus and Eranistes.

Orth. — In our former discussions we have proved that God the Word is immutable, and became incarnate not by being changed into flesh, but by taking perfect human nature. The divine Scripture, and the teachers of the churches and luminaries of the world have clearly taught us that, after the union, He remained as He was, unmixed, impassible, unchanged, uncircumscribed; and that He preserved unimpaired the nature which He had taken. For the future then the subject before us is that of His passion, and it will be a very profitable one, for thence have been brought to us the waters of salvation.

Eran. — I am also of opinion that this discourse will be beneficial. I shall not however consent to our former method, but I propose myself to ask questions.

Orth. — And I will answer, without making any objection to the change of method. He who has truth on his side, not only when he questions but also when he is questioned, is supported by the might of the truth. Ask then what you will.

Eran. — Who, according to your view, suffered the passion?

Orth. — Our Lord Jesus Christ.

Eran. — Then a man gave us our salvation.

Orth. — No; for have we confessed that our Lord Jesus Christ was only man?

Eran. — Now define what you believe Christ to be.

Orth. — Incarnate Son of the living God.

Eran. — And is the Son of God God?

Orth. — God, having the same substance as the God Who begat Him.

---

[1] Dan. vii. 10.   [3] Phil. iii. 21.
[2] Acts ii. 35.   [4] John xvii. 5.

Eran. — Then God underwent the passion.

Orth. — If He was nailed to the cross without a body, apply the passion to the Godhead; but if he was made man by taking flesh, why then do you exempt the passible from the passion and subject the impassible to it?

Eran. — But the reason why He took flesh was that the impassible might undergo the passion by means of the passible.

Orth. — You say impassible and apply passion to Him.

Eran. — I said that He took flesh to suffer.

Orth. — If He had had a nature capable of the Passion He would have suffered without flesh; so the flesh becomes superfluous.

Eran. — The divine nature is immortal, and the nature of the flesh mortal, so the immortal was united with the mortal, that through it He might taste of death.

Orth. — That which is by nature immortal does not undergo death, even when conjoined with the mortal; this is easy to see.

Eran. — Prove it; and remove the difficulty.

Orth. — Do you assert· that the human soul was immortal, or mortal?

Eran. — Immortal.

Orth. — And is the body mortal or immortal?

Eran. — Indubitably mortal.

Orth. — And do we say that man consists of these natures?

Eran. — Yes.

Orth. — So the immortal is conjoined with the mortal?

Eran. — True.

Orth. — But when the connexion or union is at an end, the mortal submits to the law of death, while the soul remains immortal, though sin has introduced death, or do you not hold death to be a penalty?

Eran. — So divine Scripture teaches. For we learn that when God forbade Adam to partake of the tree of knowledge He added " on the day that ye eat thereof ye shall surely die." [1]

Orth. — Then death is the punishment of them that have sinned?

Eran. — Agreed.

Orth. — Why then, when soul and body have both sinned together, does the body alone undergo the punishment of death?

Eran. — It was the body that cast its evil eye upon the tree, and stretched forth its hands, and plucked the forbidden fruit. It was the mouth that bit it with the teeth, and

ground it small, and then the gullet committed it to the belly, and the belly digested it, and delivered it to the liver; and the liver turned what it had received into blood and passed it on to the hollow vein [1] and the vein to the adjacent parts and they through the rest, and so the theft of the forbidden food pervaded the whole body. Very properly then the body alone underwent the punishment of sin.

Orth. — You have given us a physiological disquisition on the nature of food, on all the parts that it goes through and on the modifications to which it is subject before it is assimilated with the body. But there is one point that you have refused to observe, and that is that the body goes through none of these processes which you have mentioned without the soul. When bereft of the soul which is its yoke mate the body lies breathless, voiceless, motionless; the eye sees neither wrong nor aright; no sound of voices reaches the ears, the hands cannot stir; the feet cannot walk; the body is like an instrument without music. How then can you say that only the body sinned when the body without the soul cannot even take a breath?

Eran. — The body does indeed receive life from the soul, and it furnishes the soul with the penal possession of sin.

Orth. — How, and in what manner?

Eran. — Through the eyes it makes it see amiss; through the ears it makes it hear unprofitable sounds; and through the tongue utter injurious words, and through all the other parts act ill.

Orth. — Then I suppose we may say Blessed are the deaf; blessed are they that have lost their sight and have been deprived of their other faculties, for the souls of men so incapacitated have neither part nor lot in the wickedness of the body. And why, O most sagacious sir, have you mentioned those functions of the body which are culpable, and said nothing about the laudable? It is possible to look with eyes of love and of kindliness; it is possible to wipe away a tear of compunction, to hear oracles of God, to bend the ear to the poor, to praise the Creator with the tongue, to give good lessons to our neighbour, to move the hand in mercy, and in a word to use the parts of the body for complete acquisition of goodness.

Eran. — This is all true.

Orth. — Therefore the observance and

---

[1] Gen. ii. 17.

[1] The *vena cava*, by which the blood returns to the heart. The physiology of Eranistes would be held in the main " orthodox " even now, and shews that Theodoret was well abreast of the science accepted before the discovery of the circulation of the blood.

transgression of law is common to both soul and body.

Eran. — Yes.

Orth. — It seems to me that the soul takes the leading part in both, since it uses reasoning before the body acts.

Eran. — In what sense do you say this?

Orth. — First of all the mind makes, as it were, a sketch of virtue or of vice, and then gives to one or the other form with appropriate material and colour, using for its instruments the parts of the body.

Eran. — So it seems.

Orth. — If then the soul sins with the body; nay rather takes the lead in the sin, for to it is entrusted the bridling and direction of the animal part, why, as it shares the sin, does it not also share the punishment?

Eran. — But how were it possible for the immortal soul to share death?

Orth. — Yet it were just that after sharing the transgression, it should share the chastisement.

Eran. — Yes, just.

Orth. — But it did not do so.

Eran. — Certainly not.

Orth. — At least in the life to come it will be sent with the body to Gehenna.

Eran. — So He said "Fear not them which kill the body, but are not able to kill the soul; but rather fear him which is able to destroy both soul and body in hell." [1]

Orth. — Therefore in this life it escapes death, as being immortal; in the life to come, it will be punished, not by undergoing death, but by suffering chastisement in life.

Eran. — That is what the divine Scripture says.

Orth. — It is then impossible for the immortal nature to undergo death.

Eran. — So it appears.

Orth. — How then do you say, God the Word tasted death? For if that which was created immortal is seen to be incapable of becoming mortal, how is it possible for him that is without creation and eternally immortal, Creator of mortal and immortal natures alike, to partake of death?

Eran. — We too know that His nature is immortal, but we say that He shared death in the flesh.

Orth. — But we have plainly shewn that it is in no wise possible for that which is by nature immortal to share death, for even the soul created together with, and conjoined with, the body and sharing in its sin, does not share death with it, on account of the immor-

tality of its nature alone. But let us look at this same position from another point of view.

Eran. — There is every reason why we should leave no means untried to arrive at the truth.

Orth. — Let us then examine the matter thus. Do we assert that of virtue and vice some are teachers and some are followers?

Eran. — Yes.

Orth. — And do we say that the teacher of virtue deserves greater recompense?

Eran. — Certainly.

Orth. — And similarly the teacher of vice deserves twofold and threefold punishment?

Eran. — True.

Orth. — And what part shall we assign to the devil, that of teacher or disciple?

Eran. — Teacher of teachers, for he himself is father and teacher of all iniquity.

Orth. — And who of men became his first disciples?

Eran. — Adam and Eve.

Orth. — And who received the sentence of death?

Eran. — Adam and all his race.

Orth. — Then the disciples were punished for the bad lessons they had learnt, but the teacher, whom we have just declared to deserve two-fold and three-fold chastisement, got off the punishment?

Eran. — Apparently.

Orth. — And though this so came about we both acknowledge and declare that the Judge is just.

Eran. — Certainly.

Orth. — But, being just, why did He not exact an account from him of his evil teaching?

Eran. — He prepared for him the unquenchable flame of Gehenna, for, He says, " Depart from me ye cursed into everlasting fire prepared for the devil and his angels." [1] And the reason why he did not here share death with his disciples is because he has an immortal nature.

Orth. — Then even the greatest transgressors cannot incur death if they have an immortal nature.

Eran. — Agreed.

Orth. — If then even the very inventor and teacher of iniquity did not incur death on account of the immortality of his nature, do you not shudder at the thought of saying that the fount of immortality and righteousness shared death?

Eran. — Had we said that he underwent

---

[1] Matt. x. 28.

[1] Matt. xxv. 41.

the passion involuntarily, there would have been some just ground for the accusation which you bring against us. But if the passion which is preached by us was spontaneous and the death voluntary, it becomes you, instead of accusing us, to praise the immensity of His love to man. For He suffered because He willed to suffer, and shared death because He wished it.

Orth. — You seem to me to be quite ignorant of the divine nature, for the Lord God wishes nothing inconsistent with His nature, and is able to do all that He wishes, and what He wishes is appropriate and agreeable to His own nature.

Eran. — We have learnt that all things are possible with God.[1]

Orth. — In expressing yourself thus indefinitely you include even what belongs to the Devil, for to say absolutely all things is to name together not only good, but its opposite.

Eran. — But did not the noble Job speak absolutely when he said " I know that thou canst do all things and with thee nothing is impossible "?[2]

Orth. — If you read what the just man said before, you will see the meaning of the one passage from the other, for he says " Remember, I beseech thee, that thou hast made me as the clay and wilt thou bring me into dust again? Hast thou not poured me out as milk and curdled me like cheese? Thou hast clothed me with skin and flesh and hast fenced me with bones and sinews, thou hast granted me life and favour." [3] And then he adds : —

" Having this in myself I know that thou canst do all things and that with thee nothing is impossible." [4] Is it not therefore all that belongs to these things that he alleges to belong to the incorruptible nature, to the God of the universe?

Eran. — Nothing is impossible to Almighty God.

Orth. — Then according to your definition sin is possible to Almighty God?

Eran. — By no means.

Orth. — Wherefore?

Eran. — Because He does not wish it.

Orth. — Wherefore does He not wish it?

Eran. — Because sin is foreign to His nature.

Orth. — Then there are many things which He cannot do, for there are many kinds of transgression.

Eran. — Nothing of this kind can be wished or done by God.

Orth. — Nor can those things which are contrary to the divine nature.

Eran. — What are they?

Orth. — As, for instance, we have learnt that God is intelligent and true Light.

Eran. — True.

Orth. — And we could not call Him darkness or say that He wished to become, or could become, darkness.

Eran. — By no means.

Orth. — Again, the Divine Scripture calls His nature invisible.

Eran. — It does.

Orth. — And we could never say that It is capable of being made visible.

Eran. — No, surely.

Orth. — Nor comprehensible.

Eran. — No ; for He is not so.

Orth. — No ; for He is incomprehensible, and altogether unapproachable.

Eran. — You are right.

Orth. — And He that is could never become non-existent.

Eran. — Away with the thought !

Orth. — Nor yet could the Father become Son.

Eran. — Impossible.

Orth. — Nor yet could the unbegotten become begotten.

Eran. — How could He.

Orth. — And the Father could never become Son?

Eran. — By no means.

Orth. — Nor could the Holy Ghost ever become Son or Father.

Eran. — All this is impossible.

Orth. — And we shall find many other things of the same kind, which are similarly impossible, for the Eternal will not become of time, nor the Uncreate created and made, nor the infinite finite, and the like.

Eran. — None of these is possible.

Orth. — So we have found many things which are impossible to Almighty God.

Eran. — True.

Orth. — But not to be able in any of these respects is proof not of weakness, but of infinite power, and to be able would certainly be proof not of power but of impotence.

Eran. — How do you say this?

Orth. — Because each one of these proclaims the unchangeable and invariable character of God. For the impossibility of good becoming evil signifies the immensity of the goodness ; and that He that is just should never become unjust, nor He that is true a liar, exhibits the stability and the strength that there is in truth and righteousness. Thus the true light could never become darkness ; He that is could never become non-

---

existent, for the existence is perpetual and the light is naturally invariable. And so, after examining all other examples, you will find that the not being able is declaratory of the highest power. That things of this kind are impossible in the case of God, the divine Apostle also both perceived and laid down, for in his Epistle to the Hebrews [1] he says, " that by two immutable things, in which it was impossible for God to lie we might have a strong consolation." [2] He shews that this incapacity is not weakness, but very power, for he asserts Him to be so true that it is impossible for there to be even a lie in Him. So the power of truth is signified through its want of power. And writing to the blessed Timothy, the Apostle adds " It is a faithful saying, for if we be dead with Him we shall also live with Him, if we suffer we shall also reign with Him ; if we deny Him He will also deny us, if we believe not yet He abideth faithful, He cannot deny Himself." [3] Again then the phrase " He cannot" is indicative of infinite power, for even though all men deny Him He says God is Himself, and cannot exist otherwise than in His own nature, for His being is indestructible. This is what is meant by the words " He cannot deny Himself." Therefore the impossibility of change for the worse proves infinity of power.

Eran. — This is quite true and in harmony with the divine words.

Orth. — Granted then that with God many things are impossible, — everything, that is, which is repugnant to the divine nature, — how comes it that while you omit all the other qualities which belong to the divine nature, goodness, righteousness, truth, invisibility, incomprehensibility, infinity, and eternity, and the rest of the attributes which we assert to be proper to God, you maintain that His immortality and impassibility alone are subject to change, and in them concede the possibility of variation and give to God a capacity indicative of weakness?

Eran. — We have learnt this from the divine Scripture. The divine John exclaims " God so loved the world that He gave His only begotten Son," [4] and the divine Paul, " For if when we were enemies we were reconciled to God by the death of His Son, much more being reconciled we shall be saved by His life." [5]

Orth. — Of course all this is true, for these are divine oracles,[1] but remember what we have often confessed.

Eran. — What?

Orth. — We have confessed that God the Word the Son of God did not appear without a body, but assumed perfect human nature.

Eran. — Yes ; this we have confessed.

Orth. — And He was called Son of Man because He took a body and human soul.

Eran. — True.

Orth. — Therefore the Lord Jesus Christ is verily our God ; for of these two natures the one was His from everlasting and the other He assumed.

Eran. — Indubitably.

Orth. — While, then, as man He underwent the passion, as God He remained incapable of suffering.

Eran. — How then does the divine Scripture say that the Son of God suffered?

Orth. — Because the body which suffered was His body. But let us look at the matter thus ; when we hear the divine Scripture saying " And it came to pass when Isaac was old his eyes were dim so that he could not see," [2] whither is our mind carried and on what does it rest, on Isaac's soul or on his body?

Eran. — Of course on his body.

Orth. — Do we then conjecture that his soul also shared in the affection of blindness?

Eran. — Certainly not.

Orth. — We assert that only his body was deprived of the sense of sight?

Eran. — Yes.

Orth. — And again when we hear Amaziah saying to the prophet Amos, " Oh thou seer go flee away into the land of Judah," [3] and Saul enquiring : " Tell me I pray thee where the seer's house is," [4] we understand nothing bodily.

Eran. — Certainly not.

Orth. — And yet the words used are significant of the health of the organ of sight.

Eran. — True.

Orth. — Yet we know that the power of the Spirit when given to purer souls inspires prophetic grace and causes them to see even hidden things, and, in consequence of their thus seeing, they are called seers and beholders.

Eran. — What you say is true.

Orth. — And let us consider this too.

Eran. — What?

Orth. — When we hear the story of the divine evangelists narrating how they brought to God a man sick of the palsy, laid upon a

---

[1] C. f. note on Page 37. From the middle of the IIIrd century onward we find acceptation of the Pauline authorship Among writers who quote the Ep. as St. Paul's are Cyril of Jerusalem, the two Gregories, Basil, and Chrysostom, as well as Theodoret.
[2] Heb. vi. 18.   [4] John iii. 16.
[3] II. I. Tim. ii. 11–13.   [5] Romans v. 10.

[1] cf. note on page 155.   [3] Amos vii. 12.
[2] Gen. xxvii. 1.   [4] I. Sam. ix. 18.

bed, do we say that this was paralysis of the parts of the soul or of the body?

Eran. — Plainly of the body.

Orth. —And when while reading the Epistle to the Hebrews we light upon the passage where the Apostle says "Wherefore lift up the hands which hang down and the feeble knees and make straight paths for your feet lest that which is lame be turned out of the way, but let it rather be healed," [1] do we say that the divine Apostle said these things about the parts of the body?

Eran. — No.

Orth. — Shall we say that he was for removing the feebleness and infirmity of the soul and stimulating the disciples to manliness?

Eran. — Obviously.

Orth. — But we do not find these things distinguished in the divine Scripture, for in describing the blindness of Isaac he made no reference to the body, but spoke of Isaac as absolutely blind, nor in describing the prophets as seers and beholders did he say that their souls saw and beheld what was hidden, but mentioned the persons themselves.

Eran. — Yes; this is so.

Orth. — And he did not point out that the body of the paralytic was palsied, but called the man a paralytic.

Eran. —True.

Orth. —And even the divine Apostle made no special mention of the souls, though it was these that he purposed to strengthen and to rouse.

Eran. — No; he did not.

Orth. — But when we examine the meaning of the words, we understand which belongs to the soul and which to the body.

Eran. — And very naturally; for God made us reasonable beings.

Orth. — Then let us make use of this reasoning faculty in the case of our Maker and Saviour, and let us recognise what belongs to His Godhead and what to His manhood.

Eran. — But by doing this we shall destroy the supreme union.

Orth. — In the case of Isaac, of the prophets, of the man sick of the palsy, and of the rest, we did so without destroying the natural union of the soul and of the body; we did not even separate the souls from their proper bodies, but by reason alone distinguished what belonged to the soul and what to the body. Is it not then monstrous that while we take this course in the case of souls and bodies, we should refuse to do so in the case of our Saviour, and confound natures which differ not in the same proportion as soul from

body, but in as vast a degree as the temporal from the eternal and the Creator from the created?

Eran. —The divine Scripture says that the Son of God underwent the passion.

Orth. — We deny that it was suffered by any other, but none the less, taught by the divine Scripture, we know that the nature of the Godhead is impassible. We are told of impassibility and of passion, of manhood and of Godhead, and we therefore attribute the passion to the passible body, and confess that no passion was undergone by the nature that was impassible.

Eran. — Then a body won our salvation for us.

Orth. — Yes; but not a mere man's body, but that of our Lord Jesus Christ, the only begotten Son of God. If you regard this body as insignificant and of small account, how can you hold its type to be an object of worship and a means of salvation? and how can the archetype be contemptible and insignificant of that of which the type is adorable and honourable?

Eran. — I do not look on the body as of small account, but I object to dividing it from the Godhead.

Orth. — We, my good sir, do not divide the union but we regard the peculiar properties of the natures, and I am sure that in a moment you will take the same view.

Eran. — You talk like a prophet.

Orth. — No; not like a prophet, but as knowing the power of truth. But now answer me this. When you hear the Lord saying "I and my Father are one," and "He that hath seen me hath seen the Father," [2] do you say that this refers to the flesh or to the Godhead?

Eran. — How can the flesh and the Father possibly be of one substance?

Orth. — Then these passages indicate the Godhead?

Eran. — True.

Orth. — And so with the text, "In the beginning was the Word and the Word was God," [3] and the like.

Eran. — Agreed.

Orth. — Again when the divine Scripture says, "Jesus therefore being wearied with his journey sat thus on the well," [4] of what is the weariness to be understood, of the Godhead or of the body?

Eran. —I cannot bear to divide what is united.

Orth. — Then it seems you attribute the weariness to the divine nature?

---

[1] Heb. xii. 12, 13.

[1] John x. 30.
[2] John xiv. 9.
[3] John i. 1.
[4] John iv. 6.

Eran. — I think so.

Orth. — But then you directly contradict the exclamation of the prophet " He fainteth not neither is weary; there is no searching of His understanding. He giveth power to the faint and to them that have no might he increaseth strength." [1] And a little further on " But they that wait upon the Lord shall renew their strength, they shall mount up with wings as eagles, they shall run and not be weary and they shall walk and not faint." [2] Now how can He who bestows upon others the boon of freedom from weariness and want, possibly be himself subject to hunger and thirst?

Eran. — I have said over and over again that God is impassible, and free from all want, but after the incarnation He became capable of suffering.

Orth. — But did He do this by admitting the sufferings in His Godhead, or by permitting the passible nature to undergo its natural sufferings and by suffering proclaim that what was seen was no unreality, but was really assumed of human nature? But now let us look at the matter thus: we say that the divine nature was uncircumscribed.

Eran. — Aye.

Orth. — And uncircumscribed nature is circumscribed by none.

Eran. — Of course not.

Orth. — It therefore needs no transition for it is everywhere.

Eran. — True.

Orth. — And that which needs no transition needs not to travel.

Eran. — That is clear.

Orth. — And that which does not travel does not grow weary.

Eran. — No.

Orth. — It follows then that the divine nature, which is uncircumscribed, and needs not to travel, was not weary.

Eran. — But the divine Scripture says that Jesus was weary, and Jesus is God; " And our Lord Jesus Christ, by whom are all things." [3]

Orth. — But the exact expression of the divine Scripture is that Jesus " was wearied " not " is wearied." [4] We must consider how one and the other can be applied to the same person.

Eran. — Well; try to point this out, for you

are always for forcing on us the distinction of terms.

Orth. — I think that even a barbarian might easily make this distinction. The union of unlike natures being conceded, the person of Christ on account of the union receives both; to each nature its own properties are attributed; to the uncircumscribed immunity from weariness, to that which is capable of transition and travel weariness. For travelling is the function of the feet; of the muscles to be strained by over exercise.

Eran. — There is no controversy about these being bodily affections.

Orth. — Well then; the prediction which I made, and you scoffed at, has come true; for look; you have shewn us what belongs to manhood, and what belongs to Godhead.

Eran. — But I have not divided one son into two.

Orth. — Nor do we, my friend; but giving heed to the difference of the natures, we consider what befits godhead, and what is proper to a body.

Eran. — This distinction is not the teaching of the divine Scripture; it says that the Son of God died. So the Apostle; — " For if when we were enemies we were reconciled to God by the death of His Son." [1] And he says that the Lord was raised from the dead for " God " he says " raised the Lord from the dead." [2]

Orth. — And when the divine Scripture says " And devout men carried Stephen to his burial and made great lamentation over him " [3] would any one say that his soul was committed to the grave as well as his body?

Eran. — Of course not.

Orth. — And when you hear the Patriarch Jacob saying " Bury me with my Fathers " [4] do you suppose this refers to the body or to the soul?

Eran. — To the body; without question.

Orth. — Now read what follows.

Eran. — " There they buried Abraham and Sarah his wife. There they buried Isaac and Rebekah his wife and there I buried Leah." [5]

Orth. — Now, in the passages which you have just read, the divine Scripture makes no mention of the body, but as far as the words used go, signifies soul as well as body. We however make the proper distinction and say that the souls of the patriarchs were immortal, and that only their bodies were buried in the double cave. [6]

---

[1] Isaiah xl. 2S, 29. cf. Sept.
[2] Isaiah xl. 31.   [3] I. Cor. viii. 6.
[4] The text of John iv. 6 is κεκοπιακὼς ἐκαθέζετο, i.e., after being weary sate down. κοπιῶν ἐκαθέζετο would = "while being weary sate down." The force of the passage seems to be that Scripture states our Lord to have been wearied once, — not to be wearied now; though of course in classical Greek λέγει (historicè) αὐτὸν κοπιᾶν might mean " said that he was in a state of weariness."

[1] Rom. v. 10.   [3] Acts viii. 2.   [5] Gen. xlix. 31.
[2] Acts xiii. 30.   [4] Gen. xlix. 29.
[6] "The Machpelah," always in Hebrew with the article הטכפלה = " the double (cave)."

It is interesting to contrast the heathen idea, that the shadow goes to Hades while the self is identified with the body, with

Eran. — True.

Orth. — And when we read in the Acts how Herod slew James the brother of John with a sword,[1] we are not likely to hold that his soul died.

Eran. — No; how could we? We remember the Lord's warning "Fear not them which kill the body but are not able to kill the soul." [2]

Orth. — But does it not seem to you impious and monstrous in the case of mere men to avoid the invariable connexion of soul and body, and in the case of scriptural references to death and burial, to distinguish in thought the soul from the body and connect them only with the body, while in trust in the teaching of the Lord you hold the soul to be immortal, and then when you hear of the passion of the Son of God to follow quite a different course? Are you justified in making no mention of the body to which the passion belongs, and in representing the divine nature which is impassible, immutable and immortal as mortal and passible? While all the while you know that if the nature of God the Word is capable of suffering, the assumption of the body was superfluous.

Eran. — We have learnt from the Divine Scriptures that the Son of God suffered.

Orth. — But the divine apostle interprets the Passion, and shews what nature suffered.

Eran. — Show me this at once and clear the matter up.

Orth. — Are you not acquainted with the passage in the Epistle to the Hebrews in which the divine Paul[3] says "For which cause He is not ashamed to call them brethren saying 'I will declare thy name unto my brethren, in the midst of the Church will I sing praise unto Thee.' And again, 'Behold I and the children which God hath given me.'" [4]

Eran. — Yes, I know this, but this does not give us what you promised.

Orth. — Yes: even these suggest what I promised to shew. The word brotherhood signifies kinship, and the kinship is due to the assumption of the nature, and the assumption openly proclaims the impassibility of the Godhead. But to understand this the more plainly read what follows.

Eran. — "Forasmuch then as the children are partakers of flesh and blood, He also Himself likewise took part of the same that through death He might destroy him that hath

the power of death . . . and deliver them who through fear of death were all their life subject to bondage." [1]

Orth. — This, I think, needs no explanation; it teaches clearly the mystery of the œconomy.

Eran. — I see nothing here of what you promised to prove.

Orth. — Yet the divine Apostle teaches plainly that the Creator, pitying this nature not only seized cruelly by death, but throughout all life made death's slave, effected the resurrection through a body for our bodies, and, by means of a mortal body, undid the dominion of death; for since His own nature was immortal He righteously wished to stay the sovereignty of death by taking the first fruits of them that were subject to death, and while He kept these firstfruits (i.e. the body) blameless and free from sin, on the one hand He gave death license to lay hands on it and so satisfy its insatiability, while on the other, for the sake of the wrong done to this body, he put a stop to the unrighteous sovereignty usurped over all the rest of men. These firstfruits unrighteously engulfed He raised again and will make the race to follow them.

Set this explanation side by side with the words of the Apostle, and you will understand the impassibility of the Godhead.

Eran. — In what has been read there is no proof of the divine impassibility.

Orth. — Nay: does not the statement of the divine Apostle, that the reason of His making the children partakers of the flesh and blood was that through death He might destroy him that hath the power of death, distinctly signify the impassibility of the Godhead, and the possibility of the flesh, and that because the divine nature could not suffer He assumed the nature that could and through it destroyed the power of the devil?

Eran. — How did He destroy the power of the devil and the dominion of death through the flesh?

Orth. — What arms did the devil use at the beginning when he enslaved the nature of men?

Eran. — The means by which he took captive him who had been constituted citizen of Paradise, was sin.

Orth. — And what punishment did God assign for the transgression of the commandment?

Eran. — Death.

Orth. — Then sin is the mother of death, and the devil its father.

---

the Christian belief, that the self lives while the body is buried e.g. Homer (Il. i. 4) says that while the famous "wrath" sent many heroes' souls to Hades, it made "*them*" a prey to dogs and birds. cf. xxiii. 72. "ψυχαὶ εἰδωλα καμόντων."

[1] Acts xii. 2.
[2] Matt. x. 28.
[3] Vide note on Pages 37 and 220.
[4] Heb. ii. 11, 12, 13.

[1] Heb. ii. 14, 15.

Eran. — True.

Orth. — War then was waged against human nature by sin. Sin seduced them that obeyed it to slavery, brought them to its vile father, and delivered them to its very bitter offspring.

Eran. — That is plain.

Orth. — So with reason the Creator, with the intention of destroying either power, assumed the nature against which war was being waged, and, by keeping it clear of all sin, both set it free from the sovereignty of the devil, and, by its means, destroyed the devil's dominion. For since death is the punishment of sinners, and death unrighteously and against the divine law seized the sinless body of the Lord, He first raised up that which was unlawfully detained, and then promised release to them that were with justice imprisoned.

Eran. — But how do you think it just that the resurrection of Him who was unlawfully detained should be shared by the bodies which had been righteously delivered to death?

Orth. — And how do you think it just that, when it was Adam who transgressed the commandment, his race should follow their forefather?

Eran. — Although the race had not participated in the famous transgression, yet it committed other sins, and for this cause incurred death.

Orth. — Yet not sinners only but just men, patriarchs, prophets, apostles, and men who have shone bright in many kinds of virtue, have come into death's meshes.

Eran. — Yes; for how could a family sprung of mortal parents remain immortal? Adam after the transgression and the divine sentence, and after coming under the power of death, knew his wife, and was called father; having himself become mortal he was made father of mortals; reasonably then all who have received mortal nature follow their forefather.

Orth. — You have shewn very well the reason of our being partakers of death. The same however must be granted about the resurrection, for the remedy must be meet for the disease. When the head of the race was doomed, all the race was doomed with him, and so when the Saviour destroyed the curse, human nature won freedom; and just as they that shared Adam's nature followed him in his going down into Hades, so all the nature of men will share in newness of life with the Lord Christ in His resurrection.

Eran. — The decrees of the Church must be given not only declaratorily but demon-

stratively. Tell me then how these doctrines are taught in the divine Scripture.

Orth. — Listen to the Apostle writing to the Romans, and through them teaching all mankind: " For if through the offence of one many be dead, much more the grace of God, and the gift by grace, which is by one man, Jesus Christ, hath abounded unto many. And not as it was by one that sinned, so is the gift; for the judgment was by one to condemnation, but the free gift is of many offences unto justification. For if by one man's offence death reigned by one; much more they which receive abundance of grace and of the gift of righteousness shall reign in life by one, Jesus Christ " [1] and again: " Therefore as by the offence of one judgment came upon all men to condemnation; even so by the righteousness of one the free gift came upon all men unto justification of life. For as by one man's disobedience many were made sinners so by the obedience of one shall many be made righteous." [2] And when introducing to the Corinthians his argument about the resurrection he shortly reveals to them the mystery of the œconomy, and says: " But now is Christ risen from the dead and become the first fruits of them which slept. For since by man came death by man came also the resurrection of the dead. For as in Adam all die, even so in Christ shall all be made alive." [3] So I have brought you proofs from the divine oracles. Now look at what belongs to Adam compared with what belongs to Christ, the disease with the remedy, the wound with the salve, the sin with the wealth of righteousness, the ban with the blessing, the doom with the delivery, the transgression with the observance, the death with the life, hell with the kingdom, Adam with Christ, the man with the Man. And yet the Lord Christ is not only man but eternal God, but the divine Apostle names Him from the nature which He assumed, because it is in this nature that he compares Him with Adam. The justification, the struggle, the victory, the death, the resurrection, are all of this human nature; it is this nature which we share with Him; in this nature they who have exercised themselves beforehand in the citizenship of the kingdom shall reign with Him. Of this nature I spoke, not dividing the Godhead, but referring to what is proper to the manhood.

Eran. — You have gone through long discussions on this point, and have strengthened your argument by scriptural testimony, but if the passion was really of the flesh, how is it

---

[1] Rom. v. 15, 16, 17. [3] I. Cor. xv. 20, 21, 22.
[2] Rom. v. 18, 19.

that when he praises the divine love to men, the Apostle exclaims, " He that spared not His own Son but delivered Him up for us all," [1] what son does he say was delivered up?

Orth. — Watch well your words. There is one Son of God, wherefore He is called only begotten.

Eran. — If then there is one Son of God, the divine Apostle called him own Son.

Orth. — True.

Eran. — Then he says that He was delivered up.

Orth. — Yes, but not without a body, as we have agreed again and again.

Eran. — It has been agreed again and again that He took body and soul.

Orth. — Therefore the Apostle spoke of what relates to the body.

Eran. — The divine Apostle says distinctly " Who spared not his own Son."

Orth. — When then you hear God saying to Abraham " Because thou hast not withheld thy son thy only son," [2] do you allege that Isaac was slain?

Eran. — Of course not.

Orth. — And yet God said " Thou hast not withheld," and the God of all is true.

Eran. — The expression " thou hast not withheld " refers to the readiness of Abraham, for he was ready to sacrifice the lad, but God prevented it.

Orth. — Well; in the story of Abraham you were not content with the letter, but unfolded it and made the meaning clear. In precisely the same manner examine the meaning of the words of the Apostle. You will then see that it was by no means the divine nature which was not withheld, but the flesh nailed to the Cross. And it is easy to perceive the truth even in the type. Do you regard Abraham's sacrifice as a type of the oblation offered on behalf of the world?

Eran. — Not at all, nor yet can I make words spoken rhetorically in the churches a rule of faith.

Orth. — You ought by all means to follow teachers of the Church, but, since you improperly oppose yourself to these, hear the Saviour Himself when addressing the Jews ; " Your Father Abraham rejoiced to see my day and he saw it and was glad." [3] Note that the Lord calls His passion " a day."

Eran. — I accept the Lord's testimony and do not doubt the type.

Orth. — Now compare the type with the reality and you will see the impassibility of the Godhead even in the type. Both in the

former and in the latter there is a Father ; both in the former and the latter a well beloved Son, each bearing the material for the sacrifice. The one bore the wood, the other the cross upon his shoulders. It is said that the top of the hill was dignified by the sacrifice of both. There is a correspondence moreover between the number of days and nights and the resurrection which followed, for after Isaac had been slain by his father's willing heart, on the third day after the bountiful God had ordered the deed to be done, he rose to new life at the voice of Him who loves mankind.[1] A lamb was seen caught in a thicket, furnishing an image of the cross, and slain instead of the lad. Now if this is a type of the reality, and in the type the only begotten Son did not undergo sacrifice, but a lamb was substituted and laid upon the altar and completed the mystery of the oblation, why then in the reality do you hesitate to assign the passion to the flesh, and to proclaim the impassibility of the Godhead?

Eran. — In your observations upon this type you represent Isaac as living again at the divine command. There is nothing therefore unseemly if, fitting the reality to the type, we declare that God the Word suffered and came to life again.

Orth. — I have said again and again that it is quite impossible for the type to match the archetypal reality in every respect, and this may also be easily understood in the present instance. Isaac and the lamb, as touching the difference of their natures, suit the image, but as touching the separation of their divided persons[2] they do so no longer. We preach so close an union of Godhead and of manhood as to understand one person [3] undivided, and to acknowledge the same to be both God and man, visible and invisible, circumscribed and uncircumscribed, and we apply to one of the persons all the attributes which are indicative alike of Godhead and of manhood. Now since the lamb, an unreasoning being, and not gifted with the divine image,[4] could not possibly prefigure the restoration to life, the two divide between them the type of the mystery of the œconomy, and while one furnishes the image of death, the other supplies that of the resurrection. We find precisely the same thing in the Mosaic sacrifices, for in them too may. be seen a

---

[1] Rom. xiii. 32.
[2] Gen. xxii. 16.
[3] John viii. 56.

[1] The sacrifice of Isaac so far as his father's part in it is concerned is regarded as having actually taken place at the moment of his felt willingness to obey. In the interval of the journey to Mount Moriah Isaac is dead to his father.
[2] ὑπόστασις.　　　　[3] πρόσωπον.
[4] It is to be noted that Theodoret thus apparently regards the divine image as consisting in the intelligence or λόγος. And in the implication that Isaac had the divine image he expresses the Scriptural view that this was marred, not lost, by the fall.

type outlined in anticipation of the passion of salvation.

Eran. — What Mosaic sacrifice foreshadows the reality?

Orth. — All the Old Testament, so to say, is a type of the New. It is for this reason that the divine Apostle plainly says — " the Law having a shadow of good things to come "[1] and again "now all these things happened unto them for ensamples."[2] The image of the archetype is very distinctly exhibited by the lamb slain in Egypt, and by the red heifer burned without the camp, and moreover referred to by the Apostle in the Epistle to the Hebrews, where he writes " Wherefore Jesus also that he might sanctify the people with his own blood, suffered without the gate."[3]

But of this no more for the present. I will however mention the sacrifice in which two goats were offered, the one being slain, and the other let go.[4] In these two goats there is an anticipative image of the two natures of the Saviour ; — in the one let go, of the impassible Godhead, in the one slain, of the passible manhood.

Eran. — Do you not think it irreverent to liken the Lord to goats?

Orth. — Which do you think is a fitter object of avoidance and hate, a serpent or a goat?

Eran. — A serpent is plainly hateful, for it injures those who come within its reach, and often hurts people who do it no harm. A goat on the other hand comes, according to the Law, in the list of animals that are clean and may be eaten.

Orth. — Now hear the Lord likening the passion of salvation to the brazen serpent. He says : " As Moses lifted up the serpent in the wilderness even so must the Son of man be lifted up : that whosoever believeth in Him should not perish, but have eternal life."[5] If a brazen serpent was a type of the crucified Saviour, of what impropriety are we guilty in comparing the passion of salvation with the sacrifice of the goats?

Eran. — Because John called the Lord " a lamb,"[6] and Isaiah called Him " lamb" and " sheep."[7]

Orth. — But the blessed Paul calls Him " sin "[8] and " curse."[9] As curse therefore He satisfies the type of the accursed serpent ; as sin He explains the figure of the sacrifice of the goats, for on behalf of sin, in the Law, a goat, and not a lamb, was offered. So the Lord in the Gospels likened the just to lambs, but

sinners to kids ;[1] and since He was ordained to undergo the passion not only on behalf of just men, but also of sinners, He appropriately foreshadows His own offering through lambs and goats.

Eran. — But the type of the two goats leads us to think of two persons.

Orth. — The passibility of the manhood and the impassibility of the Godhead could not possibly be prefigured both at once by one goat. The one which was slain could not have shewn the living nature. So two were taken in order to explain the two natures. The same lesson may well be learnt from another sacrifice.

Eran. — From which?

Orth. — From that in which the lawgiver bids two pure birds be offered — one to be slain, and the other, after having been dipped in the blood of the slain, to be let go. Here also we see a type of the Godhead and of the manhood — of the manhood slain and of the godhead appropriating the passion.

Eran. — You have given us many types, but I object to enigmas.

Orth. — Yet the divine Apostle says that the narratives are types.[2] Hagar is called a type of the old covenant ; Sarah is likened to the heavenly Jerusalem ; Ishmael is a type of Israel, and Isaac of the new people. So you must accuse the loud trumpet of the Spirit for giving its enigmas for us all.

Eran. — Though you urge any number of arguments, you will never induce me to divide the passion. I have heard the voice of the angel saying to Mary and her companions, " Come, see the place where the Lord lay."[3]

Orth. — This is quite in accordance with our common customs ; we speak of the part by the name which belongs to all the parts. When we go into the churches where are buried the holy apostles or prophets or martyrs, we ask from time to time, " Who is it who lies in the shrine ? " and those who are able to give information say in reply, Thomas, it may be, the Apostle,[4] or John the Baptist,[5] or Stephen the protomartyr,[6] or any other of the saints, mentioning them by name, though perhaps only a few scanty relics of them lie here. But no one who hears these names which are common to both body and soul will imagine that the souls also are shut up in the chests ; everybody knows that the chests contain only the bodies or even small portions of the bodies.

---

[1] Matt. xxv. 32. [2] Gal. iv. 24 et seqq. [3] Matt. xxviii. 6.
[4] St. Thomas was buried at Edessa. Soc. iv. 18, Chrys. Hom. in Heb. 26.
[5] Vide p. 96.
[6] St. Stephen's remains were said to have been found at Jerusalem, and widely dispersed. cf. Dict. Christ. Ant. II. 1929.

[1] Heb. x. 1. [4] Lev. xvi. [7] Is. liii. 7.
[2] I Cor. x. 11. [5] John iii. 14, 15. [8] II. Cor. v. 21.
[3] Heb. xiii. 12. [6] John i. 29, 36. [9] Gal. iii. 13.

The holy angel spoke in precisely the same manner when he described the body by the name of the person.

Eran. — But how can you prove that the angel spoke to the women about the Lord's body?

Orth. — In the first place, the tomb itself suffices to settle the question, for to a tomb is committed neither soul nor Godhead whose nature is uncircumscribed; tombs are made for bodies. Furthermore this is plainly taught by the divine Scripture, for so the holy Matthew narrates the event, " When the even was come there came a rich man of Arimathæa named Joseph who also himself was Jesus' disciple: he went to Pilate and begged the body of Jesus. Then Pilate commanded the body to be delivered, and when Joseph had taken the body, he wrapped it in a clean linen cloth, and laid it in his own new tomb, which he had hewn out in the rock: and he rolled a great stone to the door of the sepulchre and departed." [1] See how often he mentions the body in order to stop the mouths of them who blaspheme the Godhead. The same course is pursued by the thrice blessed Mark, whose narrative I will also quote. " And now when the even was come, because it was the preparation, that is, the day before the Sabbath, Joseph of Arimathæa, an honourable counsellor, which also waited for the kingdom of God, came, and went in boldly unto Pilate, and craved the body of Jesus. And Pilate marvelled if He were already dead; and calling unto him the centurion, he asked him whether He had been any while dead. And when he knew it of the centurion, he gave the body to Joseph, and he brought fine linen, and took him down, and wrapped Him in the linen, and laid Him in a sepulchre," [2] and so on. Observe with admiration, the harmony of terms, and how consistently and continuously the word body is introduced. The illustrious Luke, too, relates just in the same way how Joseph begged the body and after he had received it treated it with due rites. [3] By the divine John we are told yet more. " Joseph of Arimathæa being a disciple of Jesus, but secretly for fear of the Jews, besought Pilate that he might take away the body of Jesus; and Pilate gave him leave. He came therefore and took the body of Jesus. And there came also Nicodemus, which at the first came to Jesus by night, and brought a mixture of myrrh and aloes about a hundred pound weight. Then took they the body of Jesus and wound it in linen clothes with the spices, as the manner of the Jews is to bury. Now in the place where He was crucified there was a garden; and in the garden a new sepulchre, wherein was never man yet laid. There laid they Jesus therefore because of the Jews' preparation day, for the sepulchre was nigh at hand." [1] Observe how often mention is made of the body; how the Evangelist shows that it was the body which was nailed to the cross, the body begged by Joseph of Pilate, the body taken down from the tree, the body wrapped in linen clothes with the myrrh and aloes, and then the name of the person given to it; and Jesus said to have been laid in a tomb. Thus the angel said, " Come see the place where the Lord lay," [2] naming the part by the name of the whole; and we constantly do just the same. In this place, we say, such an one was buried; not the body of such an one. Every one in his senses knows that we are speaking of the body, and such a mode of speech is customary in divine Scripture. Aaron, we read, died and they buried him on Mount Hor. [3] Samuel died and they buried him at Ramah, [4] and there are many similar instances. The same use is followed by the divine Apostle when speaking of the death of the Lord. " I delivered unto you first of all," he writes, " that which I also received how that Christ died for our sins according to the Scriptures; and that He was buried, and that He rose again the third day according to the Scriptures," [5] and so on.

Eran. — In the passages we have just now read the Apostle does not mention a body, but Christ the Saviour of us all. You have brought evidence against your own side, and wounded yourself with your own weapon.

Orth. — You seem to have very quickly forgotten the long discourse in which I proved to you over and over again that the body is spoken of by the name of the person. This is what is now done by the divine Apostle, and it can easily be proved from this very passage. Now let us look at it. Why did the divine writer write thus to the Corinthians?

Eran. — They had been deceived by some into believing that there is no resurrection. When the teacher of the world learnt this he furnished them with his arguments about the resurrection of the bodies.

Orth. — Why then does he introduce the resurrection of the Lord, when he wishes to prove the resurrection of the bodies?

---

[1] Matt. xxvii. 57-60.   [3] Luke xxiii. 50 et Seqq.
[2] Mark xv. 42-46.

[1] John xix. 38-42.   [4] I. Sam. xxv. 1.
[2] Matt. xxviii. 6.   [5] I. Cor. xv. 3, 4.
[3] Deut. x. 6.

Eran. — As sufficient to prove the resurrection of us all.

Orth. — In what is His death like the death of the rest, that by His resurrection may be proved the resurrection of all?

Eran. — The reason of the incarnation, suffering, and death of the only begotten Son of God, was that He might destroy death. Thus, after rising, by His own resurrection He preaches the resurrection of all.

Orth. — But who, hearing of a resurrection of God, would ever believe that the resurrection of all men would be exactly like it? The difference of the natures does not allow of our believing in the argument of the resurrection. He is God and they are men, and the difference between God and men is incalculable. They are mortal, and subject to death, like to the grass and to the flower. He is almighty.

Eran. — But after His incarnation God the Word had a body, and through this He proved His likeness to men.

Orth. — Yes; and for this reason the suffering and the death and the resurrection are all of the body, and in proof of this the divine Apostle in another place promises renewal of life to all, and to them that believe in the resurrection of their Saviour, yet look upon the general resurrection of all as a fable, he exclaims, " Now if Christ be preached that He rose from the dead, how say some among you that there is no resurrection of the dead? But if there is no resurrection of the dead, then is Christ not risen, and if Christ be not risen . . . your faith is vain, you are yet in your sins." [1] And from the past he confirms the future, and from what is disbelieved he disproves what is believed, for he says, If the one seems impossible to you, then the other will be false ; if the one seems real and true, then let the other in like manner seem true, for here too a resurrection of the body is preached, and this body is called the first fruits of those. The resurrection of this body after many arguments he affirms directly, " But now is Christ risen from the dead and become the firstfruits of them that slept, for since by man came death, by man came also the resurrection of the dead, for as in Adam all die, even so in Christ shall all be made alive," [2] and he does not only confirm the argument of the resurrection, but also reveals the mystery of the œconomy. He calls Christ man that he may prove the remedy to be appropriate to the disease.

Eran. — Then the Christ is only a man.

Orth. — God forbid. On the contrary, we have again and again confessed that He is not only man but eternal God. But He suffered as man, not as God. And this the divine Apostle clearly teaches us when he says " For since by man came death, by man came also the resurrection of the dead." [1] And in his letter to the Thessalonians, he strengthens his argument concerning the general resurrection by that of our Saviour in the passage " For if we believe that Jesus died and rose again, even them also which sleep in Jesus will God bring with him." [2]

Eran. — The Apostle proves the general resurrection by means of the Lord's resurrection, and it is clear that in this case also what died and rose was a body. For he would never have attempted to prove the general resurrection by its means unless there had been some relation between the substance of the one and the other. I shall never consent to apply the passion to the human nature alone. It seems agreeable to my view to say that God the Word died in the flesh.

Orth. — We have frequently shewn that what is naturally immortal can in no way die. If then He died He was not immortal ; and what perils lie in the blasphemy of the words.

Eran. — He is by nature immortal, but He became man and suffered.

Orth. — Therefore He underwent change, for how otherwise could He being immortal submit to death? But we have agreed that the substance of the Trinity is immutable. Having therefore a nature superior to change, He by no means shared death.

Eran. — The divine Peter says " Christ hath suffered for us in the flesh." [3]

Orth. — This agrees with what we have said, for we have learnt the rule of dogmas from the divine Scripture.

Eran. — How then can you deny that God the Word suffered in the flesh?

Orth. — Because we have not found this expression in the divine Scripture.

Eran. — But I have just quoted you the utterance of the great Peter.

Orth. — You seem to ignore the distinction of the terms.

Eran. — What terms? Do you not regard the Lord Christ as God the Word?

Orth. — The term Christ in the case of our Lord and Saviour signifies the incarnate Word, the Immanuel, God with us, [4] both God and man, but the term " God the

---

[1] I. Cor. xv. 12, 13, 17.   [2] I. Cor. xv. 21, 22.

[1] I. Cor. xv. 21.   [3] I. Peter iv. 1.
[2] I. Thess. iv. 14.   [4] Matt. i. 23.

Word" so said signifies the simple nature, before the world, superior to time, and incorporeal. Wherefore the Holy Ghost that spake through the holy Apostles nowhere attributes passion or death to this name.

Eran. — If the passion is attributed to the Christ, and God the Word after being made man was called Christ, I hold that he who states God the Word to have suffered in the flesh is in no way unreasonable.

Orth. — Hazardous and rash in the extreme is such an attempt. But let us look at the question in this way. Does the divine Scripture state God the Word to be of God and of the Father?

Eran. — True.

Orth. — And it describes the Holy Ghost as being in like manner of God?

Eran. — Agreed.

Orth. — But it calls God the Word only begotten Son.

Eran. — It does.

Orth. — It nowhere so names the Holy Ghost.

Eran. — No.

Orth. — Yet the Holy Ghost also has Its subsistence of the Father and God.

Eran. — True.

Orth. — We grant then that both the Son and the Holy Ghost are both of God the Father; but would you dare to call the Holy Ghost Son?

Eran. — Certainly not.

Orth. — Why?

Eran. — Because I do not find this term in the divine Scripture.

Orth. — Or begotten?

Eran. — No.

Orth. — Wherefore?

Eran. — Because I no more learn this in the divine Scripture.

Orth. — But what name can properly be given to that which is neither begotten nor created?

Eran. — We style it uncreated and unbegotten.

Orth. — And we say that the Holy Ghost is neither created nor begotten.

Eran. — By no means.

Orth. — Would you then dare to call the Holy Ghost unbegotten?

Eran. — No.

Orth. — But why refuse to call that which is naturally uncreate, but not begotten, unbegotten?

Eran. — Because I have not learnt so from the divine Scripture, and I am greatly afraid of saying or using language which Scripture does not use.

Orth. — Then, my good sir, I maintain the same caution in the case of the passion of salvation; do you too avoid all the divine names which Scripture has avoided in the case of the passion, and do not attribute the passion to them.

Eran. — What names?

Orth. — The passion is never connected with the name "God."

Eran. — But even I do not affirm that God the Word suffered apart from a body, but say that He suffered in flesh.

Orth. — You affirm then a mode of passion, not impassibility. No one would ever say this even in the case of a human body. For who not altogether out of his senses would say that the soul of Paul died in flesh? This could never be said even in the case of a great villain; for the souls even of the wicked are immortal. We say that such or such a murderer has been slain, but no one would ever say that his soul had been killed in the flesh. But if we describe the souls of murderers and violators of sepulchres as free from death, far more right is it to acknowledge as immortal the soul of our Saviour, in that it never tasted sin. If the souls of them who have most greatly erred have escaped death on account of their nature, how could that soul, whose nature was immortal and who never received the least taint of sin, have taken death's hook?

Eran. — It is quite useless for you to give me all these long arguments. We are agreed that the soul of the Saviour is immortal.

Orth. — But of what punishment are you not deserving, you who say that the soul, which is by nature created, is immortal, and are for making the divine substance mortal for the Word; you who deny that the soul of the Saviour tasted death in the flesh, and dare to maintain that God the Word, Creator of all things, underwent the passion?

Eran. — We say that He underwent the passion impassibly.

Orth. — And what man in his senses would ever put up with such ridiculous riddles? Who ever heard of an impassible passion, or of an immortal mortality? The impassible has never undergone passion, and what has undergone passion could not possibly be impassible. But we hear the exclamation of the divine Paul: "Who only hath immortality dwelling in the light which no man can approach unto." [1]

Eran. — Why then do we say that the invisible powers too and the souls of men, aye and the very devils, are immortal?

---

[1] I. Tim. vi. 16.

Orth. — We do say so; that God is absolutely immortal. He is immortal not by partaking of substance, but in substance; He does not possess an immortality which He has received of another. It is He Himself who has bestowed their immortality on the angels and on them that thou hast just now mentioned. How, moreover, when the divine Paul styles Him immortal and says that He only hath immortality, can you attribute to Him the passion of death?

Eran. — We say that He tasted death after the incarnation.

Orth. — But over and over again we have confessed Him immutable. If being previously immortal He afterwards underwent death through the flesh, a change having preceded His undergoing death; if His life left Him for three days and three nights, how do such statements fall short of the most extreme impiety? For I think that not even they that are struggling against impiety can venture to let such words fall from their lips without peril.

Eran. — Cease from charging us with impiety. Even we say that not the divine nature suffered but the human; but we do say that the divine shared with the body in suffering.

Orth. — What can you mean by sharing in suffering? Do you mean that when the nails were driven into the body the divine nature felt the sense of pain?

Eran. — I do.

Orth. — Both now and in our former investigations we have shewn that the soul does not share all the faculties of the body; but that the body while it receives vital force has the sense of suffering through the soul. And even supposing us to grant that the soul shares in pain with the body we shall none the less find the divine nature to be impassible, for it was not united to the body instead of a soul. Or do you not acknowledge that He assumed a soul?

Eran. — I have often acknowledged it.

Orth. — And that He assumed a reasonable Soul?

Eran. — Yes.

Orth. — If then together with the body He assumed the soul, and we grant that the soul shared in suffering with the body, then the soul, not the Godhead, shared the passion with the body; it shared the passion, receiving pangs by means of the body. But possibly somebody might agree to the soul sharing suffering with the body, but might deny its sharing death, because of its having an immortal nature. On this account the Lord said " Fear not them which kill the

body but are not able to kill the soul." [1] If then we deny that the soul of the Saviour shared death with the body, how could any one accept the blasphemy you and your friends presumptuously promulgate when you dare to say that the divine nature participated in death? This is the more inexcusable when the Lord points out at one time that the body [2] was being offered, at another that the soul was being troubled. [3]

Eran. — And where doth the Lord shew that the body was being offered? Or are you going to bring me once more that well worn passage " Destroy this temple and in three days I will raise it up "? [4] Or with your conceited self-sufficiency are you going to quote me the words of the Evangelist? " But He spake of the temple of his body. When therefore He was risen from the dead His disciples remembered that He had said this unto them and they believed the Scripture and the words which He had said." [5]

Orth. — If you have such a detestation of the divine words which preach the mystery of the incarnation, why, like Marcion and Valentinus and Manes, do you not destroy texts of this kind? For this is what they have done. But if this seems to you rash and impious, do not turn the Lord's words into ridicule, but rather follow the Apostles in their belief after the resurrection that the Godhead raised again the temple which the Jews had destroyed.

Eran. — If you have any good evidence to adduce, give over gibing and fulfil your promise.

Orth. — Remember specially those words of the gospels in which the Lord made a comparison between manna and the true bread.

Eran. — I remember.

Orth. — In that passage after speaking at some length about the bread of life, he added, " The bread that I will give is my flesh which I will give for the life of the world." [6] In these words may be understood alike the bounty of the Godhead and the boon of the flesh.

Eran. — One quotation is not enough to settle the question.

Orth. — The Ethiopian eunuch had not read much of the Bible, but when he had found one witness from the prophets he was guided by it to salvation. But not all Apostles and prophets and all the preachers of the truth who have lived since then are

---

[1] Matt. x. 28.
[2] Heb. x. 10.
[3] John xii. 27.
[4] John ii. 19.
[5] John ii. 21. 22.
[6] John vi. 21.

enough to convince you. Nevertheless I will bring you some further testimony about the Lord's body. You cannot but know that passage in the Gospel history where, after eating the passover with His disciples, our Lord pointed to the death of the typical lamb and taught what body corresponded with that shadow.[1]

Eran. — Yes I know it.

Orth. — Remember then what it was which our Lord took and broke, and what H: called it when He had taken it.

Eran. — I will answer in mystic language for the sake of the uninitiated. After taking and breaking it and giving it to His disciples He said, " This is my body which was given for you "[2] or according to the apostle " broken "[3] and again, " This is my blood of the New Testament which is shed for many." [4]

Orth. — Then when exhibiting the type of the passion He did not mention the Godhead?

Eran. — No.

Orth. — But He did mention the body and blood.

Eran. — Yes.

Orth. — And the body was nailed to the Cross?

Eran. — Even so.

Orth. — Come, then; look at this. When after the resurrection the doors were shut and the Lord came to the holy disciples and beheld them affrighted, what means did He use to destroy their fear and instead of fear to infuse faith?

Eran. — He said to them " Behold my hands and my feet that it is I myself; handle me and see; for a spirit hath not flesh and bones as ye see me have." [5]

Orth. — So when they disbelieved He shewed them the body?

Eran. — He did.

Orth. — Therefore the body rose?

Eran. — Clearly.

Orth. — And I suppose what rose was what had died?

Eran. — Even so.

Orth. — And what had died was what was nailed to the cross?

Eran. — Of necessity.

Orth. — Then according to your own argument the body suffered?

Eran. — Your series of arguments forces us to this conclusion.

Orth. — Consider this too. Now I will be questioner, and do you answer as becomes a lover of the truth.

Eran. — I will answer.

Orth. — When the Holy Ghost came down upon the Apostles, and that wonderful sight and sound collected thousands to the house, what did the chief of the apostles in the speech he then made say concerning the Lord's resurrection?

Eran. — He quoted the divine David, and said that he had received promises from God that the Lord Christ should be born of the fruit of his loins and that in trust in these promises he prophetically foresaw His resurrection, and plainly said that His soul was not left in Hades and that His flesh did not see corruption.[1]

Orth. — His resurrection therefore is of these.

Eran. — How can any one in his senses say that there is a resurrection of the soul which never died?

Orth. — How comes it that you who attribute the passion, the death and the resurrection to the immutable and uncircumscribed Godhead have suddenly appeared before us in your right mind and now object to connecting the word resurrection with the soul?

Eran. — Because the word resurrection is applicable to what has fallen.

Orth. — But the body does not obtain resurrection apart from a soul, but being renewed by the divine will, and conjoined with its yokefellow, it receives life. Was it not thus that the Lord raised Lazarus?

Eran. — It is plain that not the body alone rises.

Orth. — This is more distinctly taught by the divine Ezekiel,[2] for he points out how the Lord commanded the bones to come together, and how all of them were duly fitted together, and how He made sinews and veins and arteries grow with all the flesh pertaining to them and the skin that clothes them all, and then ordered the souls to come back to their own bodies.

Eran. — This is true.

Orth. — But the Lord's body did not undergo this corruption, but remained unimpaired, and on the third day recovered its own soul.

Eran. — Agreed.

Orth. — Then the death was of what had suffered?

Eran. — Without question.

Orth. — And when the great Peter mentioned the resurrection, and the divine David too, they said that His soul was not left in

---

[1] Matt. xvii. 26. Mark xiv. 22. Luke xxii. 19. I. Cor. xi. 24.
[2] Luke xxii. 19. [3] I. Cor. xi. 24.
[4] Matt. xxvi. 2S and Mark xiv. 24.
[5] Luke xxiv. 39.

[1] Acts ii. 29 et seqq. and Ps. xvi. 10.
[2] Ez. xxxvii. 7 et seqq.

Hell, but that His body did not undergo corruption?

Eran. — They did.

Orth. — Then it was not the Godhead which underwent death, but the body by severance from the soul?

Eran. — I cannot brook these absurdities.

Orth. — But you are fighting against your own arguments; it is your own words which you are calling absurd.

Eran. — You slander me; not one of these words is mine.

Orth. — Suppose any one to ask what is the animal which is at once reasonable and mortal, and suppose some one else to answer, — man; which of the two would you call interpreter of the saying? The questioner or the answerer?

Eran. — The answerer.

Orth. — Then I was quite right in calling the arguments yours? For you, I ween, in your answers, by rejecting some points and accepting others, confirmed them.

Eran. — Then I will not answer any longer; do you answer.

Orth. — I will answer.

Eran. — What do you say to those words of the Apostle " Had they known it they would not have crucified the Lord of glory "? [1] in this passage he mentions neither body nor soul.

Orth. — Therefore you must not put the words " in the flesh " in it, — for this is your ingenious invention for decrying the Godhead of the Word — but must attribute the passion to the bare Godhead of the Word.

Eran. — No; no. He suffered in the flesh, but His incorporeal nature was not capable of suffering by itself.

Orth. — Ah! but nothing must be added to the Apostle's words.

Eran. — When we know the Apostle's meaning there is nothing absurd in adding what is left out.

Orth. — But to add anything to the divine words is wild and rash. To explain what is written and reveal the hidden meaning is holy and pious.

Eran. — Quite right.

Orth. — We two then shall do nothing unreasonable and unholy in examining the mind of the Scriptures.

Eran. — No.

Orth. — Let us then look together into what seems to be hidden.

Eran. — By all means.

Orth. — Did the great Paul call the divine James the Lord's brother? [2]

Eran. — He did.

Orth. — But in what sense are we to regard him as brother? By relationship of His godhead or of His manhood?

Eran. — I will not consent to divide the united natures.

Orth. — But you have often divided them in our previous investigations, and you shall do the same thing now. Tell me; do you say that God the Word was only begotten Son?

Eran. — I do.

Orth. — And only begotten means only Son.

Eran. — Certainly.

Orth. — And the only begotten cannot have a brother?

Eran. — Of course not, for if He had had a brother He would not be called the only begotten.

Orth. — Then they were wrong in calling James the brother of the Lord. For the Lord was only begotten, and the only begotten cannot have a brother.

Eran. — No, but the Lord is not incorporeal and the proclaimers of the truth are referring only to what touches the godhead.

Orth. — How then would you prove the word of the apostle true?

Eran. — By saying that James was of kin with the Lord according to the flesh.

Orth. — See how you have brought in again that division which you object to.

Eran. — It was not possible to explain the kinship in any other way.

Orth. — Then do not find fault with those who cannot explain similar difficulties in any other way.

Eran. — Now you are getting the argument off the track because you want to shirk the question.

Orth. — Not at all, my friend. That will be settled too by the points we have investigated. Now look; when you were reminded of James the brother of the Lord, you said that the relationship referred not to the Godhead but to the flesh.

Eran. — I did.

Orth. — Well, now that you are told of the passion of the cross, refer this too to the flesh.

Eran. — The Apostle called the crucified " Lord of Glory," [1] and the same Apostle called the Lord " brother of James."

Orth. — And it is the same Lord in both cases. If then you are right in referring the relationship to the flesh you must also refer the passion to the flesh, for it is perfectly ridiculous to regard the relationship without

---

[1] I. Cor. ii. 8.   [2] Gal. i. 19.   [1] I. Cor. ii. 8.

distinction and to refer the passion to Christ without distinction.

Eran. — I follow the Apostle who calls the crucified " Lord of glory."

Orth. — I follow too, and believe that He was " Lord of glory." For the body which was nailed to the wood was not that of any common man but of the Lord of glory. But we must acknowledge that the union makes the names common. Once more : do you say that the flesh of the Lord came down from heaven?

Eran. — Of course not.

Orth. — But was formed in the Virgin's womb?

Eran. — Yes.

Orth. — How, then, does the Lord say " If ye shall see the Son of man ascend up where He was before," [1] and again " No man hath ascended up to heaven but He that came down from heaven, even the Son of man which is in heaven? " [2]

Eran. — He is speaking not of the flesh, but of the Godhead.

Orth. — Yes ; but the Godhead is of the God and Father. How then does He call him Son of man?

Eran. — The peculiar properties of the natures are shared by the person, for on account of the union the same being is both Son of man and Son of God, everlasting and of time, Son of David and Lord of David, and so on with the rest.

Orth. — Very right. But it is also important to recognise the fact that no confusion of natures results from both having one name. Wherefore we are endeavouring to distinguish how the same being is Son of God and also Son of man, and how He is " the same yesterday, to-day, and for ever," [3] and by the reverent distinction of terms we find that the contradictions are in agreement.

Eran. — You are right.

Orth. — You say that the divine nature came down from heaven and that in consequence of the union it was called the Son of man. Thus it behoves us to say that the flesh was nailed to the tree, but to hold that the divine nature even on the cross and in the tomb was inseparable from this flesh, though from it it derived no sense of suffering, since the divine nature is naturally incapable of undergoing both suffering and death and its substance is immortal and impassible. It is in this sense that the crucified is styled Lord of Glory, by attribution of the title of the impassible nature to the passible,

since, as we know, a body is described as belonging to this latter.

Now let us examine the matter thus. The words of the divine Apostle are " Had they known it they would not have crucified the Lord of Glory." [1] They crucified the nature which they knew, not that of which they were wholly ignorant : had they known that of which they were ignorant they would not have crucified that which they knew : they crucified the human because they were ignorant of the divine. Have you forgotten their own words. " For a good work we stone thee not but for blasphemy, and because that thou, being a man, makest thyself God." [2] These words are a plain proof that they recognised the nature they saw, while of the invisible they were wholly ignorant : had they known that nature they would not have crucified the Lord of glory.

Eran. — That is very probable, but the exposition of the faith laid down by the Fathers in council at Nicæa says that the only begotten Himself, very God, of one substance with the Father, suffered and was crucified.

Orth. — You seem to forget what we have agreed on again and again.

Eran. — What do you mean?

Orth. — I mean that after the union the holy Scripture applies to one person terms both of exaltation and of humiliation. But possibly you are also ignorant that the illustrious Fathers first mentioned His taking flesh and being made man, and then afterwards added that He suffered and was crucified, and thus spoke of the passion after they had set forth the nature capable of passion.

Eran. — The Fathers said that the Son of God, Light of Light, of the substance of the Father, suffered and was crucified.

Orth. — I have observed more than once that both the Divine and the human are ascribed to the one Person. It is in accordance with this position that the thrice blessed Fathers, after teaching how we should believe in the Father, and then passing on to the person of the Son, did not immediately add " and in the Son of God," although it would have very naturally followed that after defining what touches God the Father they should straightway have introduced the name of Son. But their object was to give us at one and the same time instruction on the theology and on the œconomy, [3] lest there should be supposed to be any distinction between the Person of the Godhead and the Person of the Manhood. On this account

[1] John vi. 62.   [2] John iii. 13.   [3] Heb. xiii. 8.   [1] I. Cor. ii. 8.   [3] Vide note on page 72.
[2] John x. 33.

they added to their statement concerning the Father that we must believe also in our Lord Jesus Christ, the Son of God. Now after the incarnation God the Word is called Christ, for this name includes alike all that is proper to the Godhead and to the manhood. We recognise nevertheless that some properties belong to the one nature and some to the other, and this may at once be understood from the actual terms of the Creed. For tell me: to what do you apply the phrase " of the substance of the Father"? to the Godhead, or to the nature that was fashioned of the seed of David?

Eran. — To the Godhead, as is plain.

Orth. — And the clause " Very God of very God"; to which do you hold this belongs, to the Godhead or to the manhood?

Eran. — To the Godhead.

Orth. — Therefore neither the flesh nor the soul is of one substance with the Father, for they are created, but the Godhead which formed all things.

Eran. — True.

Orth. — Very well, then. And when we are told of passion and of the cross we must recognise the nature which submitted to the passion; we must avoid attributing it to the impassible, and must attribute it to that nature which was assumed for the distinct purpose of suffering. The acknowledgment on the part of the most excellent Fathers that the divine nature was impassible; and their attribution of the passion to the flesh is proved by the conclusion of the creed, which runs " But they who state there was a time when He was not, and before He was begotten He was not, and He was made out of the non-existent, or who allege that the Son of God was of another essence or substance mutable or variable, these the holy catholic and apostolic Church anathematizes." See then what penalties are denounced against them that attribute the passion to the divine nature.[1]

Eran. — They are speaking in this place of mutation and variation.

Orth. — But what is the passion but mutation and variation? For if, being impassible before His incarnation, He suffered after His incarnation, He assuredly suffered by undergoing mutation ; and if being immortal before He became man, He tasted death, as you say, after being made man, He underwent a complete alteration by being made mortal after being immortal. But expressions of this kind, and their authors with them, have all been expelled by the illustrious Fathers from the

bounds of the Church, and cut off like rotten limbs from the sound body. We therefore exhort you to fear the punishment and abhor the blasphemy.

Now I will show you that in their own writings the holy Fathers have held the opinions we have expressed. Of the witnesses I shall bring forward some took part in that great Council ; some flourished in the Church after their time ; some illuminated the world long before. But their harmony is broken neither by difference of periods nor by diversity of language ; like the harp their strings are several and separate but like the harp they make one harmonious music.

Eran. — I was anxious for and shall be delighted at such citations. Instruction of this kind cannot be gainsaid, and is most useful.

Orth. — Now ; open your ears and receive the streams that flow from the spiritual springs.

Testimony of the holy Ignatius, bishop of Antioch, and martyr.

From his Epistle to the Smyrnæans : —

" They do not admit Eucharists and oblations, because they do not confess the Eucharist to be flesh of our Saviour Jesus Christ which suffered for our sins and which of His goodness the Father raised." [1]

Testimony of Irenæus, bishop of Lyons.

From his third book against heresies (Chap. xx.) : —

" It is clear then that Paul knew no other Christ save Him that suffered and was buried and rose and was born, whom he calls man, for after saying, ' If Christ be preached that He rose from the dead,' [2] he adds, giving the reason of His incarnation, ' For since by man came death by man came also the resurrection of the dead,' [3] and on all occasions in reference to the passion, the manhood and the dissolution of the Lord, he uses the name of Christ as in the text, ' Destroy not him with thy meat for whom Christ died,' [4] and again, ' But now in Christ ye who sometimes were far off are made nigh in the blood of Christ,' [5] and again, ' Christ hath redeemed us from the curse of the law, being made a

---

[1] See the Creed as published by the Council. p. 50.

[1] The quotation is not quite exact, " Εὐχαριστίας καὶ προσφορὰς οὐκ ἀποδέχονται " being substituted for εὐχαριστίας καὶ προσευχῆς ἀπεχονται. Bp. Lightfoot (Ap. Fath. II. ii. 307) notes, " the argument is much the same as Tertullian's against the Docetism of Marcion (adv. Marc. iv. 40), 'Acceptum panem et distributum discipulis corpus suum illum fecit, Hoc est corpus meum dicendo, id est figura mei corporis. Figura autem non fuisset, nisi veritatis esset corpus, ceterum vacua res quod est phantasma, figuram capere non posset.' The Eucharist implies the reality of Christ's flesh. To those who deny this reality it has no meaning at all ; to them Christ's words of institution are false; it is in no sense the flesh of Christ." Cf. Iren. iv. 18, 5.

[2] I. Cor. xv. 12.   [3] I. Cor. xv. 21.

[4] Rom. xiv. 15.

[5] Ephes. ii. 13. Observe slight differences.

curse for us: for it is written, Cursed is every one that hangeth on a tree.'" [1]

Of the same from the same work. (Chapter xxi.) : —

"For as He was Man that He might be tempted, so was He Word that He might be glorified. In His temptation, His crucifixion and His dying, the Word was inoperative; but in His victory, His patience, His goodness, His resurrection and His assumption it was co-operative with the manhood."

Of the same from the fifth book of the same work : —

"When with His own blood the Lord had ransomed us, and given His soul on behalf of our souls, and His flesh instead of our flesh."

The testimony of the holy Hippolytus, bishop and martyr.

From his letter to a certain Queen : —

"So he calls Him 'The firstfruits of them that slept,' [2] and 'The first born of the dead.' [3] When He had risen and was wishful to show that what had risen was the same body which died, when the Apostles doubted, He called to Him Thomas and said 'Handle me and see; for a spirit hath not flesh and bones as ye see me have.' " [4]

Of the same from the same letter : —

"By calling Him firstfruits He bore witness to what we have said, that the Saviour, after taking the flesh of the same material, raised it, making it firstfruits of the flesh of the just, in order that all we that believe might have expectation of our resurrection through trust in Him that is risen."

Of the same from his discourse on the two thieves : —

"The body of the Lord gave both to the world,—the holy blood and the sacred water."

Of the same from the same discourse : —

"And the body being, humanly speaking, a corpse, has in itself great power of life, for there flowed from it what does not flow from dead bodies — blood and water, — that we might know what vital force lies in the indwelling power in the body, so that it is a corpse evidently unlike others, and is able to pour forth for us causes of life." [5]

Of the same from the same discourse : —

"Not a bone of the holy Lamb is broken. The type shews that the passion cannot

touch the power, for the bones are the power of the body."

Testimony of the holy Eustathius, bishop of Antioch, and confessor.

From his book on the soul : —

"Their impious calumny can be refuted in a few words; they may be right, unless He voluntarily gave up His own body to the destruction of death for the sake of the salvation of men. First of all they attribute to Him extraordinary infirmity in not being able to repel His enemies' assault."

Of the same from the same book : —

"Why do they, in the concoction of their earth-born deceits, make much of proving that the Christ assumed a body without a soul? In order that if they could seduce any to lay down that this is the case, then, by attributing to the divine Spirit variations of affection, they might easily persuade them that the mutable is not begotten of the immutable nature."

Of the same from his discourse on "the Lord created me in the beginning of His ways" : [1] —

"The man Who died rose on the third day, and, when Mary was eager to lay hold of His holy limbs, He objected, and cried 'Touch me not.[2] For I am not yet ascended to my Father; but go to my brethren and say unto them, I ascend unto my Father and your Father and to my God and your God.' [3] Now the words 'I am not yet ascended to my Father,' were not spoken by the Word and God, who came down from heaven, and was in the bosom of the Father, nor by the Wisdom which contains all created things, but were uttered by the man who was compacted of various limbs, who had risen from the dead, who had not yet after His death gone back to the Father, and was reserving for Himself the first fruits of His progress."

Of the same from the same work : —

"As he writes he expressly describes the man who was crucified as Lord of Glory, declaring Him to be Lord and Christ, just as the Apostles with one voice when speaking to Israel in the flesh say 'Therefore let all the house of Israel know assuredly that God hath made that same Jesus, Whom ye have crucified, both Lord and Christ.' [4] He so made Jesus Christ who suffered. He did not so make the Wisdom nor yet the Word who has the might of dominion from the beginning, but Him who was lifted up on high and stretched out His hands upon the Cross."

Of the same from the same work : —

---

[1] Gal. iii. 13 and Deut. xxi. 23.
[2] I. Cor. xv. 20.   [3] Coloss. i. 18.
[4] cf. Luke xxiv. 39. And for the application of these words to St. Thomas cf. page 210.
[5] The effusion of water and blood is now well known to have been a natural consequence of the "broken heart." On the rupture of the heart the blood fills the pericardium, and then coagulates. The wound of the lance gave passage to the collected blood and serum. cf. Dr. Stroud's "*Physical Cause of the Death of Christ,*" first published in 1847.

---

[1] Prov. viii. 22. lxx.
[2] i.e. literally, try not to lay hold of me.
[3] John xx. 17.   [4] Acts ii. 36.

" For if He is incorporeal and not subject to manual contact, nor apprehended by eyes of flesh, He undergoes no wound, He is not nailed by nails, He has no part in death, He is not hidden in the ground, He is not shut in a grave, He does not rise from a tomb."

Of the same from the same book : —

" ' No man taketh it from me. . . . I have power to lay it down and I have power to take it again.' [1] If as God He had the double power, He yet yielded to them who were striving of evil counsel to destroy the temple, but by His resurrection He restored it in greater splendour. It is proved by incontrovertible evidence that He of Himself rose and renewed His own house, and the great work of the Son is to be ascribed to the divine Father; for the Son does not work without the Father, as is declared in the unimpeachable utterances of the holy Scriptures. Wherefore at one time the divine Parent is described as having raised the Christ from the dead, at another time the Son promises to raise His own temple. If then from what has previously been laid down the divine spirit of the Christ is proved to be impassible, in vain do the accursed assail the apostolic definitions. If Paul says that the Lord of Glory was crucified, clearly referring to the manhood, we must not on this account refer suffering to the divine. Why then do they put these two things together, saying that the Christ was crucified from infirmity ? "

Of the same from the same work : —

" But had it been becoming to attribute to Him any kind of infirmity, any one might have said that it was natural to attach these qualities to the manhood, though not to the fulness of the Godhead, or to the dignity of the highest wisdom, or to Him who according to Paul is described as God over all." [2]

Of the same from the same book : —

" This then is the manner of the infirmity according to which He is described by Paul as coming to death, for the man lives by God's power when plainly associated with God's spirit, since from the preceding statements He who is believed to be in Him is proved to be also the power of the Most High."

Of the same from the same : —

"As by entering the Virgin's womb He did not lessen His power, so neither by the fastening of His body to the wood of the cross is His spirit defiled. For when the body was crucified on high the divine Spirit of wisdom dwelt even within the body, trod in heavenly places, filled all the earth, reigned over the depths, visited and judged the soul

of every man, and continued to do all that God continually does, for the wisdom that is on high is not prisoned and contained within bodily matter, just as moist and dry material are contained within their vessels and are contained by but do not contain them. But this wisdom, being a divine and ineffable power, embraces and confirms alike all that is within and all that is without the temple, and thence proceeding beyond comprehends and sways at once all matter."

Of the same from the same work : —

" But if the sun being a visible body, apprehended by the senses, endures everywhere such adverse influences without changing its order, or feeling any blow, be it small or great; can we suppose the incorporeal Wisdom to be defiled and to change its nature because its temple is nailed to the cross or destroyed or wounded or corrupted? The temple suffers, but the substance abides without spot, and preserves its entire dignity without defilement."

Of the same from his work on the titles of the Psalms of Degrees : —

" The Father who is perfect, infinite, incomprehensible, and is incapable alike of adornment or disfigurement, receives no acquired glory; nor yet does His Word, who is God begotten of Him, through whom are angels and heaven and earth's boundless bulk and all the form and matter of created things; but the man Christ raised from the dead is exalted and glorified to the open discomfiture of His foes."

Of the same from the same work : —

" They however who have lifted up hatred against Him, though they be fenced round with the forces of His foes, are scattered abroad, while the God and Word gloriously raised His own temple."

Of the same from his interpretation of the 92nd Psalm : —

" Moreover the prophet Isaiah following the tracks of His sufferings, among other utterances exclaims with a mighty voice 'And we saw Him and He had no form nor beauty. His form was dishonoured and rejected among the sons of men,' [1] thus distinctly showing that the marks of indignity and the sufferings must be applied to the human but not to the divine. And immediately afterwards he adds ' Being a man under stroke, and able to bear infirmity.' [2] He it is who after suffering outrage was seen to have no form or comeliness, then again was changed and clothed with beauty, for the God dwelling in Him was not led like a lamb to death

---

[1] John x. 18. [2] Rom. ix. 5. [1] Isaiah liii. 2, 3. Sept. [2] Isaiah liii. 3. Sept.

and slaughtered like a sheep, for His nature is invisible."

Testimony of the Holy Athanasius, bishop of Alexandria, and confessor.

From his letter to Epictetus : —

"Whoever reached such a pitch of impiety as to think and say that the Godhead itself of one substance with the Father was circumcised, and from perfect became imperfect; and to deny that what was crucified on the tree was the body, asserting it on the contrary to be the very creative substance of wisdom?"

Of the same from the same treatise : —

"The Word associated with Himself and brought upon Himself what the humanity of the Word suffered, that we might be able to share in the Godhead of the Word. And marvellous it was that the sufferer and He who did not suffer were the same; sufferer in that His own body suffered and He was in it while suffering, but not suffering because the Word, being by nature God, was impassible. And He Himself the incorporeal was in the passible body, and the body contained in itself the impassible Word, destroying the infirmities of His body."

Of the same from the same letter : —

"For being God and Lord of Glory, He was in the body ingloriously crucified; but the body suffered when smitten on the tree, and water and blood flowed from its side; but being temple of the Word, it was full of the Godhead. Wherefore when the sun saw its Creator suffering in His outraged body, it drew in its rays, and darkened the earth. And that very body with a mortal nature rose superior to its own nature, on account of the Word within it, and is no longer touched by its natural corruption, but clothed with the superhuman Word, became incorruptible."

Of the same from his greater discourse on the Faith : —

"Was what rose from the dead, man or God? Peter, the Apostle, who knows better than we, interprets and says, 'and when they had fulfilled all that was written of Him they took Him down from the tree and laid Him in a sepulchre, but God raised Him from the dead.'[1] Now the dead body of Jesus which was taken down from the tree, which had been laid in a sepulchre, and entombed by Joseph of Arimathæa, is the very body which the Word raised, saying, 'Destroy this temple, and in three days I will raise it up.'[2] It is He who quickens

all the dead, and quickened the man Christ Jesus, born of Mary, whom He assumed. For if while on the cross[1] He raised corpses of the saints that had previously undergone dissolution, much more can God the everliving Word raise the body, which He wore, as says Paul, 'For the word of God is quick and powerful.'"[2]

Of the same from the same work : —

"Life then does not die, but quickens the dead; for as the light is not injured in a dark place, so life cannot suffer when it has visited a mortal nature, for the Godhead of the Word is immutable and invariable as the Lord says in the prophecy about Himself 'I am the Lord I change not.'"[3]

Of the same from the same work : —

"Living He cannot die but on the contrary quickens the dead. He is therefore, by the Godhead derived from the Father, a fount of light; but He that died, or rather rose from the dead, our intercessor, who was born of the Virgin Mary, whom the Godhead of the Word assumed for our sake, is man."

Of the same from the same work : —

"It came to pass that Lazarus fell sick and died; but the divine Man did not fall sick nor against His own will did He die, but of His own accord came to the dispensation of death, being strengthened by God the Word who dwelt within Him, and who said 'No man taketh it from me but I lay it down of myself. I have power to lay it down and I have power to take it again.'[4] The Godhead then which lays down and takes the life of man which He wore is of the Son, for in its completeness He assumed the manhood, in order that in its completeness He might quicken it, and, with it, the dead."

Of the same from his discourse against the Arians : —

"When therefore the blessed Paul says the Father 'raised' the Son 'from the dead'[5] John tells us that Jesus said 'Destroy this temple and in three days I will raise it up . . . but He spake' of His own 'body.'[6] So it is clear to them that take heed that at the raising of the body the Son is said by Paul to have been raised from the dead, for he refers what concerns the body to the Son's person, and just so when he says 'the Father gave life to the Son'[7] it must be understood that the life was given to the Flesh. For if He Himself is life how can the life receive life?"

---

[1] The quotation seems to be a confusion between Acts ii. 24, and Acts xiii. 29. Sic in Athan. Ed. Migne. II. 1030.
[2] John iii. 19.

[1] But "after his resurrection" appears to qualify the statement "arose" as well as "appeared" in Matt. xxviii. 53.
[2] Hebrews iv. 12.
[3] Malachi iii. 6.
[4] John x. 18.
[5] Acts xiii. 30.
[6] John ii. 19 and 21.
[7] John v. 26.

Of the same from his work on the Incarnation : —

"For when the Word was conscious that in no other way could the ruin of men be undone save by death to the uttermost, and it was impossible that the Word who is immortal and Son of the Father should die, to effect His end He assumes a body capable of death, that this body, being united to the Word, who is over all, might, in the stead of all, become subject to death, and because of the indwelling Word might remain incorruptible, and so by the grace of the resurrection corruption for the future might lose its power over men. Thus offering to death, as a sacrifice and victim free from every spot, the body which He had assumed, by His corresponding offering He straightway destroyed death's power over all His kind; for being the Word of God, above and beyond all men, He rightly offered and paid His own temple and bodily instrument, as a ransom for all souls due to death. And thus by means of the like (body) being associated with all men, the incorruptible Son of God rightly clothed all men with incorruption by the promise of the resurrection, for the corruption inherent in death no longer has any place with men, for the sake of the Word who dwelt in them by the means of the one body."

Of the same from the same work : —

"Wherefore, after His divine manifestations in His works, now also on behalf of all He offered sacrifice, yielding to death His own temple instead of all, that He might make all men irresponsible and free from the ancient transgression, and, exhibiting His own body as incorruptible firstfruits of the resurrection of mankind, might shew Himself stronger than death. For the body, as having a common substance — for it was a human body, although by a new miracle its constitution was of the Virgin alone — being mortal, died after the example of its like; but by the descent of the Word into it no longer suffered corruption, according to its own nature, but, on account of God the Word who dwelt within it, was delivered from corruption."

Of the same from the same work : —

"Whence, as I have said, since it was not possible for the Word being immortal to die, He took upon Himself a body capable of death, in order that He might offer this same body for all, and He Himself in His suffering on behalf of all through His descent into this body might ' destroy Him that hath the power of death.' " [1]

Of the same from the same work : [1] —

"For the body in its passion, as is the nature of bodies, died, but it had the promise of incorruption through the Word that dwelt within it. For when the body died the Word was not injured; but He was Himself impassible, incorruptible, and immortal, as being God's Word, and being associated with the body He kept from it the natural corruption of bodies, as says the Spirit to Him ' thou wilt not suffer thy Holy One to see corruption.' " [2]

The testimony of the holy Damasus, bishop of Rome : [3] —

"If any one say that, in the passion of the Cross, God the Son of God suffered pain, and not the flesh with the soul, which the form of the servant put on and assumed, as the Scripture saith, Let him be anathema."

Testimony of the holy Ambrosius, bishop of Milan.

From his book on the Catholic faith : —

"There are some men who have reached such a pitch of impiety as to think that the Godhead of the Lord was circumcised, and from perfect was made imperfect; and that the divine substance, Creator of all things, and not the flesh, was on the tree."

Of the same from the same work : —

"The flesh suffered; but the Godhead is free from death. He yielded His body to suffer according to the law of human nature. For how can God die, when the soul cannot die? ' Fear not,' He says, ' them which kill the body but are not able to kill the soul.' [4] If then the soul cannot be slain how can the Godhead be made subject to death?"

Testimony of the holy Basilius, bishop of Cæsarea : —

"It is perfectly well known to every one who has the least acquaintance with the meaning of the words of the Apostle that he is not delivering to us a mode of theology but is explaining the reasons of the œconomy,[5] for he says ' God hath made that same Jesus whom ye have crucified both Lord and Christ.' [6] Thus he is plainly directing his argument to His human and visible nature."

Testimony of the holy Gregorius, bishop of Nazianzus.

From his letter to the blessed Nectarius, bishop of Constantinople : —

"The saddest thing in what has befallen the churches is the boldness of the utterances of Apollinarius and his party. I cannot understand how your Holiness has allowed them to

---

[1] Heb. ii. 14.

[1] This passage is not found in the discourse on the Incarnation, but a similar passage occurs in the third oration against the Arians. Ed. Ben. p. 606.
[2] Ps. xvi. 10.
[3] Epist. iii. Ad Paulinum.
[4] Matt. x. 28.
[5] cf. note on p. 72.
[6] Acts ii. 36.

arrogate to themselves the power of assembling on the same terms with us."

And a little further on : —

" I will no longer call this serious ; it is indeed saddest of all that the only begotten God Himself, Judge of all who exist, the Prince of Life, the Destroyer of Death, is made by him mortal and alleged to receive suffering in His own Godhead. He represents the Godhead to have shared with the body in the dissolution of that three days' death of the body, and so after the death to have been again raised by the Father."

Of the same from his former exposition to Cledonius : —

" It is the contention of the Arians that the manhood was without a soul, that they may refer the passion to the Godhead and represent the same power as both moving the body and suffering."

Of the same from his discourse about the Son : —

" It remained for us to treat of what was commanded Him and of His keeping the commandments and doing all things pleasing to Him ; and further of His perfection, exaltation, and learning obedience by all that He suffered,[1] His priesthood, His offering, His betrayal, His entreaty to Him that hath power to save Him from death, His agony, His bloody sweat, His prayer and similar manifestations, were it not clear to all that all these expressions in connexion with His Passion in no way signify the nature which was immutable and above suffering."

Of the same from his Easter Discourse (Or. ii.) : —

" ' Who is this that cometh from Edom ? '[2] and from the earth, and how can the garments of the bloodless and bodiless be red as of one that treadeth in the wine-fat ? Urge in reply the beauty of the garment of the body which suffered and was made beautiful in suffering, and was made splendid by the Godhead, than which nothing is lovelier nor more fair."

Testimony of Gregory, bishop of Nyssa.

From his catechetical oration : —

" And this is the mystery of the dispensation of God concerning the manhood and of the resurrection from the dead, not to prevent the soul from being separated from the body by death according to the necessary law of human nature, and to bring them together again through the resurrection."

Of the same from the same work : —

" The flesh which received the Godhead, and which through the resurrection was ex-

alted with the Godhead, is not formed of another material, but of ours ; so, just as in the case of our own body, the operation of one of the senses moves to general sensation the whole man united to that part, in like manner just as though all nature were one single animal, the resurrection of the part pervades the whole, being conveyed from the part to the whole by what is continuous and united in nature. What then do we find extraordinary in the mystery that the upright stoops to the fallen to raise up him that lies low ? "

Of the same from the same work : —

" It would be natural also in this part not to heed the one and neglect the other ; but in the immortal to behold the human, and to be curiously exact about the diviner quality in the manhood."

Of the same from his work against Eunomius : —

" 'Tis not the human nature which raises Lazarus to life. 'Tis not the impassible power which sheds tears over the dead. The tear belongs to the man ; the life comes from the very life. The thousands are not fed by human poverty ; omnipotence does not hasten to the fig tree. Who was weary in the way, and who by His word sustains all the world without being weary ? What is the brightness of His glory, what was pierced by the nails ? What form is smitten in the passion, what is glorified for everlasting ? The answer is plain and needs no interpretation."

Of the same from the same treatise : —

" He blames them that refer the passion to the human nature. He wishes himself wholly to subject the Godhead itself to the passion, for the proposition being twofold and doubtful, whether the divinity or the humanity was concerned in the passion, the denial of the one becomes the positive condemnation of the other. While therefore they blame them who see the passion in the humanity, they will bestow unqualified praise on them that maintain the Divinity of the Son of God to be passible. But the point established by these means becomes a confirmation of their own absurdity of doctrine ; for if, as they allege, the Godhead of the Son suffers while that of the Father in accordance with its substance is conserved in complete impassibility, it follows that the impassible nature is at variance with the nature which sustains suffering."

The testimony of the holy Amphilochius, bishop of Iconium.

From his discourse on the text " Verily, verily I say unto you, he that heareth my

---

[1] cf. Heb. v. 8.   [2] Isaiah lxiii. 1.

word and believeth on Him that sent me hath everlasting life ": [1] —

"Whose then are the sufferings? Of the flesh. Therefore if you give to the flesh the suffering, give it also the lowly words; and ascribe the exalted words to Him to Whom you assign the miracles. For the God when He is in the act of working wonders naturally speaks in high and lofty language worthy of His works and the man when He is suffering fitly utters lowly words corresponding with His sufferings."

Of the same from his discourse on "My Father is greater than I": [2] —

"But when you give the sufferings to the flesh and the miracles to God, you must of necessity, though unwillingly, give the lowly words to the man born of Mary, and the high and lofty words becoming God, to the Word who existed in the beginning. The reason why I utter sometimes lofty words and sometimes lowly is that by the lofty I may show the nobility of the indwelling Word, and by the lowly make known the infirmity of the lowly flesh. So at one time I call myself equal to the Father and at another I call the Father greater; and in this I am not inconsistent with myself, but I shew that I am God and man; God by the lofty and man by the lowly. And if you wish to know in what sense my Father is greater than I, I spoke in the flesh and not in the person of the Godhead."

Of the same from his discourse on "If it be possible let this cup pass from me": [3] —

"Ascribe not then the sufferings of the flesh to the impassible God, for I, O heretic, am God, and man; God, as the miracles prove; man as is shewn by the sufferings. Since then I am God and man, tell me, who was it who suffered? If God suffered, you have spoken blasphemy; but if the flesh suffered, why do you not attribute the passion to Him to whom you ascribe the dread? For while one is suffering another feels no dread; while man is being crucified God is not troubled."

Of the same from his discourse against the Arians: —

"And not to prolong what I am saying, I will shortly ask you, O heretic, did He who was begotten of God before the ages suffer, or Jesus who was born of David in the last days? If the Godhead suffered, thou hast spoken blasphemy; if, as the truth is, the manhood suffered, for what reason do you hesitate to attribute the passion to man?"

Of the same from his discourse concerning the Son: —

"Peter said, 'God hath made this Jesus both Lord and Christ' [1] and said too, 'this Jesus whom ye crucified God hath raised up.' [2] Now it was the manhood, not the Godhead, which became a corpse, and He who raised it was the Word, the power of God, who said in the Gospel, 'Destroy this temple and in three days I will raise it up.' [3] So when it is said that God hath made Him who became a corpse and rose from the dead both Lord and Christ, what is meant is the flesh, and not the Godhead of the Son."

Of the same from his discourse on "The Son can do nothing of Himself": [4] —

"For He had not such a nature as that His life could be held by corruption, since His Godhead was not forcibly reduced to suffering. For how could it? But the manhood was renewed in incorruption. So he says 'For this mortal must put on immortality and this corruptible must put on incorruption.' [5] You observe the accuracy; he points distinctly to 'this mortal' that you may not entertain the idea of the resurrection of any other flesh."

Testimony of the holy Flavianus, bishop of Antioch.

On Easter Day: —

"Wherefore also the cross is boldly preached by us, and the Lord's death confessed among us, though in nothing did the Godhead suffer, for the divine is impassible, but the dispensation was fulfilled by the body."

Of the same on Judas the traitor: —

"When therefore you hear of the Lord being betrayed, do not degrade the divine dignity to insignificance, nor attribute to divine power the sufferings of the body. For the divine is impassible and invariable. For if through His love to mankind He took on Him the form of a servant, He underwent no change in nature. But being what He ever was, he yielded the divine [6] body to experience death."

Testimony of Theophilus, bishop of Alexandria.

From his Heortastic Volume: —

"Of unreasoning beings the souls are not taken and replaced; they share in the corruption of the bodies, and are dissolved into dust. But after the Saviour at the time of the cross had taken the soul from His own body, He restored it to the body again when He rose from the dead. To assure us of this He uttered the words of the psalmist, the predictive exclamation, 'Thou wilt not

---

[1] John v. 24.   [3] Matt. xxvi. 39.
[2] John xiv. 28.

[1] Acts ii. 36.   [3] John ii. 19.
[2] Acts ii. 24. The citation is loose. [4] John v. 19.
[5] I. Cor. xv. 53. Observe the inaccuracy of the quotation.
[6] The Latin translator, as though observing the apparent impropriety of the epithet, here renders θεῖον by "*sanctissimum*."

leave my soul in Hell nor suffer thine Holy One to see corruption.'" [1]

Testimony of the blessed Gelasius, bishop of Cæsarea in Palestine: —

"He was bound, He was wounded, He was crucified, He was handled, He was marked with scars, He received a lance's wound, and all these indignities were undergone by the body born of Mary, while that which was begotten from the Father before the ages none was able to harm, for the Word had no such nature. For how can any one constrain Godhead? How wound it? How make red with blood the incorporeal nature? How surround it with grave bands? Grant now what you cannot contravene and, constrained by invincible reason, honour Godhead."

Testimony of the holy John, bishop of Constantinople.

From his discourse on the words "My Father worketh hitherto and I work": [2] —

"'What sign shewest Thou unto us seeing that Thou doest these things?' [3] What then does He reply Himself? 'Destroy this temple,' He says, 'and in three days I will raise it up,' [4] speaking of His own body, but they did not understand Him."

And a little further on: —

"Why does not the evangelist pass this by? Why did he add the correction, 'But He spake of the temple of his body'? [5] for He did not say destroy this 'body,' but 'temple' that He might shew the indwelling God. Destroy this temple which is far more excellent than that of the Jews. The Jewish temple contained the Law; this temple contains the Lawgiver; the former the letter that killeth; the latter the spirit that giveth life." [6]

Of the same from the discourse "That what was spoken and done in humility was not so done and spoken on account of infirmity of power but different dispensations": —

"How then does He say 'If it be possible'? [7] He is pointing out to us the infirmity of the human nature, which did not choose to be torn away from this present life, but stepped back and shrank on account of the love implanted in it by God in the beginning for the present life. If then when the Lord Himself so often spoke in such terms, some have dared to say that He did not take flesh, what would they have said if none of these words had been spoken by Him?"

Of the same from the same work: —

"Observe how they spoke of His former age. Ask the heretic the question Does God dread? Does He draw back? Does He shrink? Does He sorrow? and if he says yes, stand off from him for the future, rank him down below with the devil, aye lower even than the devil, for even the devil will not dare to say this. But, should he say that each of these things is unworthy of God, reply — neither does God pray; for apart from these it will be yet another absurdity should the words be the words of God, for the words indicate not only an agony, but also two wills; one of the Son and another of the Father, opposed to one another. For the words 'Not as I will, but as Thou wilt,' are the words of one indicating this."

Of the same from the same work: —

"For if this be spoken of the Godhead there arises a certain contradiction, and many absurdities are thereby produced. If on the contrary it be spoken of the flesh, the expressions are reasonable, and no fault can be found with them. For the unwillingness of the flesh to die incurs no condemnation; such is the nature of the flesh and He exhibits all the properties of the flesh except sin, and indeed in full abundance, so as to stop the mouths of the heretics. When therefore He says 'If it be possible let this cup pass from me' and 'not as I will but as Thou wilt,' He only shews that He is really clothed with the flesh which fears death, for it is the nature of the flesh to fear death, to draw back and to suffer agony. Now He leaves it abandoned and stripped of its own activity, that by shewing its weakness He may convince us also of its nature. Sometimes however He conceals it, because He was not mere man."

Testimony of Severianus, bishop of Gabala.

From his discourse on the seals: —

"The Jews withstand the apparent, ignorant of the non-apparent; they crucify the flesh; they do not destroy the Godhead. For if my words are not destroyed together with the letter which is the clothing of speech, how could God the Word, the fount of life, die together with the flesh? The passion belongs to the body, but impassibility to the dignity."

See then how they whose husbandry is in the East and in the West, as well as in the South and in the North, have all been shewn by us to condemn your vain heresy, and all openly to proclaim the impassibility of the divine Nature. See how both tongues, I mean both Greek and Latin, make one harmonious confession about the things of God.

---

[1] Ps. xvi. 10. [4] John ii. 19. [6] cf. II. Cor. iii. 6.
[2] John v. 17. [5] John ii. 21. [7] Matt. xxvi. 39.
[3] John ii. 18.

Eran. — I am myself astonished at their harmony, but I observe a considerable difference in the terms they use.

Orth. — Do not be angry. The very force of their fight against their adversaries is the cause of their seeming immoderate. The same thing is to be observed in the case of planters; when they see a plant bent one way or another, they are not satisfied with bringing it to a straight line, but bend it still further in the opposite direction, that by its being bent still further from the straight it may attain its upright stature. But that you may know that the very promoters and supporters of this manifold heresy strive to surpass even the heretics of old by the greatness of their blasphemies, listen once more to the writings of Apollinarius which proclaim the impassibility of the divine nature, and confess the passion to be of the body.

Testimony of Apollinarius.

From his summary : —

" John spoke of the temple which was destroyed, namely the body of Him that raised it, and the body is entirely united to Him and He is not another among them. And if the body of the Lord was one with the Lord, the properties of the body were constituted His properties on account of the body."

And again : —

" And the truth is that His conjunction with the body does not take place by circumscription of the Word, so that He has nothing beyond His incorporation. Wherefore even in death immortality abides with Him; for if He transcends this composition, so does He also the dissolution. Now death is dissolution. But He was not comprehended in the composition; had He been so, the universe would have been made void; nor in the dissolution did He, like the soul, suffer the deprivation which succeeds dissolution."

And again : —

" As the Saviour says that the dead bodies go forth from their tombs, though their souls do not go forth thence, just so He says that He Himself will rise from the dead, although it is only His body that rises."

In another similar work he writes : —

" Of man is the rising from the dead; of God is the raising. Now Christ both rose and raised, for He was God and man. Had the Christ been only man He would not have quickened the dead, and if He had been only God, He would not on His own account apart from the Father have quickened any of the dead. But Christ did both; the same being is both God and man. If the Christ had been only man He would not

have saved the world; if He had been only God He would not have saved it through suffering, but Christ did both, so He is God and man. If the Christ had been only man or if only God He could not have been a Mediator between men and God."

And a little further on : —

" Now flesh is an instrument of life fitted to the capacity for suffering in accordance with the divine will. Words are not proper to the Flesh, nor are deeds. Being made subject to the capacity for suffering, as is natural to the flesh, it prevails over the suffering because it is the flesh of God."

And again a little further on : —

" The Son took flesh of the Virgin and travelled to the world. This flesh He filled with the Holy Ghost to the sanctification of us all. So He delivered death to death and destroyed death through the resurrection to the raising of us all."

From his tract concerning the faith : —

" Since the passions are concerned with the flesh His power possessed its own impassibility, so to refer the passion to the power is an impious error."

And in his tract about the incarnation he further writes : —

" Here then He shews that it was the same man who rose from the dead and God who reigns over all creation."

You see now that one of the professors of vain heresy plainly preaches the impassibility of the Godhead, calls the body a temple, and persists in maintaining that this body was raised by God the Word.

Eran. — I have heard and I am astonished; and I am really ashamed that our doctrines should appear less tenable than the innovation of Apollinarius.

Orth. — But I will bring you a witness from yet another heretical herd distinctly preaching the impassibility of the Godhead of the only begotten.

Eran. — Whom do you mean?

Orth. — You have probably heard of Eusebius the Phœnician, who was bishop of Emesa by Lebanon.[1]

Eran. — I have met with some of his writings, and found him to be a supporter of the doctrines of Arius.

Orth. — Yes; he did belong to that sect, but in his endeavour to prove that the Father was greater than the only begotten he declares the Godhead of the depreciated Son to be im-

---

[1] Eusebius, bishop of Emesa (now Hems, where Heliogabalus received the purple, and Aurelian defeated Zenobia) c. 341–359 is called by Jerome " *Signifer Arianæ factionis.*" Chron. sub ann. x Constantii. Theodoret also mentions writings of his against Apelles (Hær. fab. i. 25.)

passible and for this opinion he contended with long and extraordinary perseverance.

Eran. — I should be very much obliged if you would quote his words too.

Orth. — To comply with your wish I will adduce somewhat longer evidence. Now listen to what he says, and fancy that the man himself is addressing us.

Testimony of Eusebius of Emesa: —

" Wherefore does he fear death? Lest he suffer anything from death? For what was death to Him? Was it not the severance of the power from the flesh? Did the power receive a nail that it should fear? If our soul suffers not the body's infirmities when united with it, but the eye grows blind and yet the mind retains its force; and a foot is cut off and yet the reasoning power does not halt — and this nature evidences, and the Lord sets His seal on, in the words ' Fear not them which kill the body but are not able to kill the soul ' (and if they cannot kill the soul, it is not because they do not wish, but because they are not able, though they would like to make the soul share the suffering of the body yoked with it) — shall He who created the soul and formed the body suffer as the body suffers, although He does take upon Himself the body's sufferings? But Christ suffered for us, and we lie not. ' And the bread that I will give is my flesh.' [1] This He gave for us.

" That which can be mastered was mastered ; that which can be crucified was crucified, but He that had power alike to dwell in it and to leave it said ' Father into thy hands I commend my Spirit,' [2] not into the hands of them who were trying to hasten His death. I am not fond of controversy ; I rather avoid it ; with all gentleness I wish to enquire into the points at issue between us as between brothers. Do not I say truly that the power could not be subject to the sufferings of the flesh? I say nothing ; let him who will say what the power suffered. Did it fail? See the danger. Was it extinct? See the blasphemy. Did it no longer exist? This is the death of power. Tell me what can so master it that it suffered and I withdraw. But, if you cannot tell me. why do you object to my not telling you? What you cannot tell me, that it did not receive. Drive a nail into a soul and I will admit that it can be driven into power. But it was in sympathy. Tell me what you mean by ' in sympathy.' As a nail went into the flesh, so pain into the power. Let us understand ' was in sympathy ' in this

sense. Then pain was felt by the power which was not smitten. For pain always follows on suffering. But if a body often despises pain while the mind is sound, on account of the vigour of its thought, then in this case let some one explain impartially what suffered and what suffered with or was in sympathy. What then? Did not Christ die for us? How did He die? ' Father, into thy hands I commend my Spirit.' [1] The Spirit departed ; the body remained ; the body remained without breath. Did He not die then? He died for us. The Shepherd offered the sheep, the Priest offered the sacrifice, He gave Himself for us. ' He that spared not His own Son but delivered Him up for us all.' [2] I do not reject the words, but I want the meaning of the words. The Lord says that the bread of God came down from Heaven,[3] and though I cannot express it more clearly on account of the mysteries, He says in explanation ' It is my flesh.' Did the flesh of the Son come down from heaven? No. How then does He say, and that in explanation, the bread of God lives and came down from Heaven? He refers the properties of the power to the flesh, because the power which assumed the flesh came down from heaven. Change the terms then ; He refers to the power what the flesh suffers. How did Christ suffer for us? He was spat upon, He was smitten on the cheek, they put a crown about His brow, His hands and feet were pierced. All these sufferings were of the body, but they are referred to Him that dwelt therein. Throw a stone at the Emperor's statue. What is the cry? ' You have insulted the Emperor.' Tear the Emperor's robe. What is the cry? ' You have rebelled against the Emperor.' Crucify Christ's body. What is the cry? ' Christ died for us.' But what need of me and thee? Let us go to the Evangelists. How have you received from the Lord how the Lord died? They read ' Father into thy hands I commend my Spirit.' [4] The Spirit on high, the body on the Cross for us. So far as His body is attributed to Himself He offered the sheep."

Of the same from the same book : —

" He came to save our nature ; not to destroy His own. If I consent to say that a camel flies, you directly count it strange, because it does not fit in with its nature ; and you are quite right. And if I say that men live in the sea you will not accept it ; you are quite right. It is contrary to nature. As then if I say strange things about these

---

[1] John vi. 51.   [2] Luke xxiii. 46.

[1] Luke xxiii. 46.   [3] John vi. 51.
[2] Romans viii. 32.   [4] Luke xxiii. 46.

natures you count it strange; if I say that the Power which was before the ages, by nature incorporeal, in dignity impassible, which exists with the Father and by the Father's side, on His right hand and in glory, if I say that this incorporeal nature suffers, will you not stop your ears? If you will not stop your ears when you hear this, I shall stop my heart. Can we do anything to an angel? Smite him with a sword? Or cut him in pieces? Why do I say to an angel? Can we to a soul? Does a soul receive a nail? A soul is neither cut nor burnt. Do you ask why? Because it was so created. Are His works impassible and He Himself passible? I do not reject the œconomy; on the contrary, I welcome the ill-treatment. Christ died for us and was crucified. So it is written; so the nature admitted. I do not blot out the words nor do I blaspheme the nature. But this is not true. Very well, then let something truer be said. The teacher is a benefactor, never harsh, never an enemy, unless the pupil be headstrong. Have you anything good to say? My ears are gratefully open. Does any one want to quarrel? Let him quarrel at his leisure. Could the Jews crucify the Son of God and make the power itself a dead body? Can the living die? The death of this power is its failure. Even when we die, our body is left. But if we make that power a dead body we reduce it to non-existence. I am afraid you cannot hear. If the body die, the soul is separated from it and remains; but if the soul die, since it has no body, it altogether ceases to exist. A soul by dying altogether ceases to be. For the death of the immortals is a contradiction of their existence. Consider the alternative; for I do not dare even to mention it. We say these things as we understand them, but if any one is contentious, we lay down no law. But I know one thing, that every man must reap the fruit of his opinions. Each man comes to God and brings before Him what he has said and thought about Him. Do not suppose that God reads books, or is troubled by having to recollect what you said or who heard you: all is made manifest. The judge is on the throne. Paulus [1] is brought before Him. 'Thou saidst I was a man; thou hast no life with Me. Thou knewest not Me; I know not thee.' Up comes another. 'Thou saidst I was one of the things that are created.[2] Thou knewest not My dignity; I know not thee.' Up comes another. 'Thou saidst that I did not assume a body. Thou madest light of My grace. Thou shalt not share My immortality.' Up comes another. 'Thou saidst that I was not born of a Virgin to save the body of the Virgin; thou shalt not be saved.' Each one reaps the fruit of his opinions about the faith."

You see the other sect of your teachers, in which you supposed that you had learnt the suffering of the Godhead of the only Begotten, abhors this blasphemy, preaches the impassibility of the Godhead, and quits the ranks of them who dare to attribute the passion to it.

Eran. — Yes; I am astonished at the conflict, and I admire the man's sense and opinions.

Orth. — Then, my good Sir, imitate the bees. As you flit in mental flight about the meads of the divine Scripture, among the fair flowers of these illustrious Fathers, build us in your heart the honey-comb of the faith. If haply you find anywhere herbage bitter and not fit to eat, like these fellows Apollinarius and Eusebius, but still not quite without something that may be meet for making honey, it is reasonable that you should sip the sweet and leave the poisonous behind, like bees who lighting often on baneful bushes leave all the deadly bane behind and gather all the good. We give you this advice, dear friend, in brotherly kindness. Receive it and you will do well. And if you hearken not we will say to you in the word of the apostle "We are pure." [3] We have spoken, as the prophet says, what we have been commanded.

---

[1] i.e. Paul of Samosata.
[2] τῶν ὄντων in the original; lit: of the things that are, which might have an orthodox interpretation, tho' strictly speaking there is no such thing as "τὸ ὄν;" there is only "ὁ ὤν," i.e. God. But Schulze is no doubt right in explaining τῶν ὄντων here to refer to created things.
[3] Acts xx. 26.

DEMONSTRATIONS BY SYLLOGISMS

THAT GOD THE WORD IS IMMUTABLE

1. We have confessed one substance of the Father, of the Son, and of the Holy Ghost, and have agreed that it is immutable. If then there is one substance of the Trinity, and it is immutable, then the only begotten Son, who is one person of the Trinity, is immutable. And, if He is immutable, He was not made flesh by mutation, but is said to have been made flesh after taking flesh.

2. If God the Word was made flesh by undergoing mutation into flesh, then He is not immutable. For no one in his senses would call that which undergoes alteration immutable. And if He is mutable He is not of one substance with Him that begat Him. How indeed is it possible for one part of an uncompounded substance to be mutable and the other immutable? If we grant this we shall fall headlong into the blasphemy of Arius and Eunomius, who assert that the Son is of another substance.

3. If the Lord is consubstantial with the Father, and the Son was made flesh by undergoing change into flesh, then the substance is at once mutable and immutable, which blasphemy if any one has the hardihood to maintain, he will no doubt make it worse by his blasphemy against the Father, for inasmuch as the Father shares the same substance, he will assuredly call Him mutable.

4. It is written in the divine Scriptures that God the Word took flesh, and also a soul. And the most divine Evangelist says the Word was made flesh.[1] We must therefore perforce do one of two things : either we must admit the mutation of the Word into flesh, and reject all divine Scripture, both Old and New, as teaching lies, or in obedience to the divine Scripture, we must confess the assumption of the flesh, banishing mutation from our thoughts, and piously regarding the word of the Evangelist. This latter we must do inasmuch as we confess the nature of God the Word to be immutable, and have countless testimonies to the assumption of the flesh.

5. That which inhabits a tabernacle is distinct from the tabernacle which is inhabited.[2] The Evangelist calls the flesh a tabernacle, and says that God the Word taber-

nacled therein. "The Word," he says, "was made flesh and dwelt among us."[1] Now if He was made flesh by mutation, He did not dwell in flesh. But we have been taught that He dwelt in flesh; for the same Evangelist in another place calls His body a temple.[2] We must therefore believe the Evangelist's explanation and interpretation of what to some seemed ambiguous.

6. If when the Evangelist wrote " the Word was made flesh " he had added nothing which could remove the ambiguity, perhaps the controversy about the passage might have had some reasonable excuse, from the obscurity of the terms used. But since he immediately went on to say " and dwelt in us," the combatants contend to no purpose. The former clause is explained by the latter.

7. The immutability of God the Word is plainly proclaimed by the most wise Evangelist, for after saying " the Word was made flesh and dwelt among us," he immediately adds, " And we beheld His glory, the glory as of the only-begotten of the Father, full of grace and truth."[3] But if, according to the foolish, He had undergone mutation into flesh, He would not have remained what He was, but if even when enveloped in the flesh He emitted the rays of His Father's nobility, it follows that the nature which He has is immutable, and it shines even in the body and sends abroad the brightness of the nature which is unseen. For that light nothing can dim. " For the light shineth in the darkness, and the darkness comprehendeth it not,"[4] as saith the very divine John.

8. The illustrious Evangelist was desirous of explaining the glory of the only-begotten, but was unable to carry out his purpose. He therefore shews it by His fellowship with the Father. For he says He is of that nature ; just as though any one to persons beholding Joseph sunk in a slavery inconsistent with his rank, and unaware of the splendour of his descent, were to point out that Jacob was his father, and his forefather Abraham. So in this sense the Evangelist said that when He dwelt among us He did not dim the glory of His nature, "For we beheld His glory, the

---

[1] John i. 14.   [2] σκηνοῦν and σκηνούμενον.

[1] John i. 14. The argument rather requires the rendering " dwelt *in* us," which is that of the Rheims Version. "*In nobis qui caro sumus.*" Bengel. But see Alford *in loc.*
[2] John ii. 19.   [3] John i. 14.   [4] John i. 5.

glory as of the only-begotten of the Father." So if even when He was made flesh it was plain who He was, then He remained who he was, and did not undergo the mutation into flesh.

9. We have confessed that God the Word took not a body only but also a soul. Why then did the divine Evangelist omit in this place mention of the soul and mention the flesh alone? Is it not plain that he exhibited the visible nature and by its means signified the nature united to it? For the mention of the soul is understood of course in that of the flesh. For when we hear the prophet saying "Let all flesh bless His holy name," [1] we do not understand the prophet to be exhorting bodies of flesh without souls, but believe the whole to be summoned to give praise in the summoning of a part.

10. The words "the Word was made flesh" are plainly indicative not of mutation, but of His unspeakable loving-kindness. For after the illustrious Evangelist had said "in the beginning was the Word, and the Word was with God and the Word was God," and had declared Him to be Creator of the visible and invisible, and had called Him life and true light, adding other similar expressions, and had spoken concerning the Godhead in such terms as human reason can take in and the language at its command can express, he went on "And the Word was made flesh," as though smitten with amazement and astounded at the boundless loving-kindness. His existence is eternal; He is God; He made all things; He is source of eternal life and of true light; and on account of the salvation of men He put about Him the tabernacle of flesh. And He was supposed to be only that which He appeared. So for this reason he did not even mention a soul but only the perishable and mortal flesh. Of the soul as being immortal he said nothing in order to exhibit the boundlessness of the kindness.

11. The divine Apostle calls [2] the Lord Christ seed of Abraham. But if this is true, as true it is, then God the Word was not changed into flesh, but took on Him the seed of Abraham, according to the teaching of the Apostle himself.

12. God swore to David that of the fruit of his loins, according to the flesh, He would raise up the Christ, as the prophet [3] said and as the great Peter interpreted. [4] But if God the Word was called Christ after mutation into flesh, we shall nowhere find the truth in the oaths. Yet we have been taught that God cannot lie; nay rather is Himself the truth. Therefore God the Word did not undergo change into flesh, but in accordance with the promise, took firstfruits of David's seed.

PROOFS THAT THE UNION WAS WITHOUT CONFUSION.

1. Those who believe that after the union there was one nature both of Godhead and of manhood, destroy by this reasoning the peculiarities of the natures; and their destruction involves denial of either nature. For the confusion of the united natures prevents us from recognising either that flesh is flesh or that God is God. But if even after the union the difference of the united natures is clear, it follows that there is no confusion and that the union is without confusion. And if this is confessed then the Master Christ is not one nature, but one Son shewing either nature unimpaired.

2. We too assert the union, and ourselves confess that it took place at the conception; if then by the union the natures were mixed and confounded, how was the flesh after the birth not seen to possess any new quality, but exhibited the human character, preserved the dimensions of the babe, was wrapped in swaddling clothes, and sucked a mother's breast? And if all this did not come to pass in mere phantasy and seeming, then they admit of neither phantasy nor seeming; then what was seen was truly a body. And if this be granted then the natures were not confounded by the union, but each remained unimpaired.

3. The authors of this patchwork and incongruous heresy at one time assert that God the Word was made flesh, and at another declare that the flesh underwent a change into nature of Godhead. Either statement is futile and vain and full of falsehood, for if God the Word, as they argue, was made flesh, why then do they call Him God, and this alone, and refuse to name Him man as well, and find great fault with us who in addition to confessing Him as God also call Him man? But if the flesh was changed into the nature of Godhead, wherefore do they substitute the antitypes of the body? For the type is superfluous when the reality is destroyed.

4. An incorporeal nature is not corporeally circumcised, but the word corporeally is added on account of the spiritual circumcision of the heart; so then the circumcision is of a body; but the Master Christ is circumcised after the union. And if this is granted then the argument of the confusion is confuted.

---

[1] Ps. cxlv. 21.
[2] Hebrews ii. 16.
[3] Psalm cxxxii. 11.
[4] Acts ii. 30.

5. We have learnt that the Saviour Christ hungered and thirsted, and we have believed that this was so really and not in seeming, but such conditions belong not to a bodiless nature but to a body. The Master Christ then had a body which before the resurrection was affected according to its nature. And to this the divine Apostle bears testimony when he says "For we have not an High Priest which cannot be touched with the feeling of our infirmities but was in all points tempted like as we are yet without sin." [1] For the sin is not of the nature but of the evil will.[2]

6. Of the divine nature the prophet David says, "Behold He that keepeth Israel shall neither slumber nor sleep." [3] But the narrative of the Evangelist describes the Master Christ as sleeping in the boat. Now not sleeping and being asleep are two contrary ideas, so the prophet contradicts the Gospels if, as they argue, the Master Christ was God alone. There is no contradiction, for both prophecies and gospels flow from one and the same spirit. The Master Christ therefore had a body, akin to all other bodies, affected by the need of sleep. So the argument for the confusion is proved a fable.

7. Of the divine nature the prophet Isaiah said, "He shall neither be hungry nor weary" [4] and so on. But the Evangelist says "Jesus being weary with his journey sat thus on the well;" [5] and "shall not be weary" is contrary to "being weary." Therefore the prophecy is contrary to the narrative of the gospels. But they are not contrary, for both are of one God. Not being weary is of the uncircumscribed nature which fills all things. But moving from place to place is of the circumscribed nature; and when that which moves is constrained to travel it is subject to the weariness of the wayfarer. Therefore what walked and was weary was a body, for the union did not confound the natures.

8. To the divine Paul when shut up in prison the Master Christ said "Be not afraid Paul" [6] and so on. But the same Christ, who drove away Paul's fear, Himself so feared, as testifies the blessed Luke that He sweated from all His body drops of blood, and with them sprinkled all the ground about His body, and was strengthened by angelic succour,[7] and these statements are opposed to one another, for

how can fearing be other than contrary to driving away fear? Yet they are not contrary. For the same Christ is by nature God and man; as God He strengthens them that need consolation; as man He receives consolation through an angel. And although the Godhead and the Spirit were present as an anointing, the body and the soul were not then supported either by the Godhead united to them or by the Holy Ghost, but this service was entrusted to an angel in order to exhibit the infirmity both of the soul and of the body and that through the infirmity might be seen the natures of the infirm. Now these things plainly happened by the permission of the divine nature, that, among them that were to live in future times, believers in the assumption of the soul and of the body might be vindicated by these demonstrations, and their opponents by plain proof convicted. If then the union was effected by the conception, and, as they argue, made both natures one, how could the properties of the natures continue unimpaired, the soul agonize, and the body sweat so as to sweat bloody drops from excess of fear? But if the one is natural to the body and the other to the soul, then the union did not effect one nature of flesh and Godhead, but one Son appeared shewing forth in Himself both the human and the divine.

9. Should they say that after the resurrection the body underwent mutation into Godhead they may properly be answered thus. Even after the resurrection the body was seen circumscribed with hands and feet and all the body's parts; it was tangible and visible; it had wounds and scars, as it had before the resurrection. One then of two alternatives must be maintained. Either these parts must be attributed to the divine nature, if the body when changed into the divine nature had these parts; or on the other hand it must be confessed that the body remained within the bounds of its own nature. Now the divine nature is simple and incomposite, but the body is composite and divided into many parts; therefore it was not changed into the nature of Godhead, but even after the resurrection though immortal, incorruptible and full of divine glory, it remains a body with its own circumscription.

10. To the unbelieving apostles the Lord after His resurrection shewed His hands, His feet, and the prints of the nails; then further to teach them that what they saw was not a vision He added "a spirit hath not flesh and bones as ye see me have." [1]

---

[1] Hebrews iv. 15. [2] cf. note on page 164. [3] Psalm cxxi. 4.
[4] Isaiah xl. 28. lxx.   [5] John iv. 6.
[6] When Paul was brought into the castle the Lord stood by him and said, "Be of good cheer Paul" (Acts xxiii. 11.) "Fear not Paul" was said when he was being exceedingly tossed in the tempest (Acts xxvii. 24).
[7] Luke xxii. 44.

[1] Luke xxiv. 39.

Therefore the body was not changed into spirit it was flesh and bones and hands and feet. Consequently even after the resurrection the body remained a body.

11. The divine nature is invisible, but the thrice blessed Stephen said that he saw the Lord,[1] so even after the resurrection the Lord's body is a body, and it was seen by the victorious Stephen, since the divine nature cannot be seen.

12. If all mankind shall see the Son of man coming on the clouds of heaven, according to the Lord's own words,[2] and He said to Moses "No man shall see me and live,"[3] and both are true, then He will come with the body with which He ascended into heaven. For that body is visible, and of this the angel spoke to the Apostles "This same Jesus which is taken up from you into Heaven shall so come in like manner as ye have seen Him go into Heaven."[4] If this is true, as true it is, then there is not one nature of flesh and Godhead, but the union is without confusion.

PROOF THAT THE DIVINITY OF THE SAVIOUR IS IMPASSIBLE.

1. Alike by the divine Scripture and by the holy Fathers assembled at Nicæa we have been taught to confess that the Son is of one substance with God the Father. The impassibility of the Father is also taught by the nature and proclaimed by the divine Scripture. We shall then further confess the Son to be impassible, for this definition is enforced by the identity of substance. Whenever then we hear the divine Scripture proclaiming the cross and the death of the Master Christ we attribute the passion to the flesh, for in no wise is the Godhead, being by nature impassible, capable of suffering.

2. "All things that the Father hath are mine"[5] says the Master Christ, and one out of all is impassibility. If therefore as God He is impassible, He suffered as man. For the divine nature does not undergo suffering.

3. The Lord said "the bread which I will give is my flesh which I will give for the life of the world,"[6] and again "I am the good shepherd and know my sheep and am known of mine . . . and I lay down my life for the sheep."[7] So body and soul are both given by the good shepherd for the sheep who have soul and body.

4. The nature of men is compounded of body and soul. But it sinned and stood in need of a sacrifice free from every spot. So the Creator took a body and a soul, and keeping them clean from the stains of sin for men's bodies gave His body and for their souls His soul. If this is true, and true it is, for these are words of truth itself, then wild and blasphemous are they who ascribe passion to the divine nature.

5. The blessed Paul called the Christ "the first born of the dead;"[1] and I suppose the first born has the same nature as they of whom He is called first born. As man then He is first born of the dead, for He first destroyed the pangs of death and gave to all the sweet hope of another life. As He rose so He suffered. As man then He suffered but as awful God He remained impassible.

6. The divine Apostle calls our Saviour Christ "the firstfruits of them that slept,"[2] but the firstfruits are related to the whole whereof they are firstfruits. He is not therefore called firstfruits as God, for what relationship is there between Godhead and manhood? The former is an immortal nature, the latter mortal. Such is the nature of them that sleep, of whom Christ is called firstfruits. To this nature belong death and resurrection, and in its resurrection we have a proof of the general resurrection.

7. When the Master Christ wished to persuade the doubting Apostles that He had destroyed death and risen, He shewed them parts of His body, His side, His hands, His feet and the marks of the passion preserved therein. This body then rose, and this, I ween, was shown to the disbelievers. What rose is what was buried, and what was buried is what had died, and what had died is of course what was nailed to the cross. So the divine nature united to the body remained impassible.

8. They who describe the flesh of the Lord as giver of life make life itself mortal by their words. They ought to have seen that it was giver of life through the life united to it. But if according to their argument the life is mortal, how could the flesh being itself by nature mortal, and made life-giving through the life, remain life-giving?

9. God the Word is by nature immortal, and the flesh by nature mortal, but after the passion by union with the Word the flesh itself became immortal. How then is it not absurd to say that the giver of such immortality shared death?

[1] Acts vii. 55.   [4] Acts i. 11.   [6] John vi. 51.
[2] Matt. xxvi. 64.   [5] John xvi. 15.   [7] John x. 14. 15.
[3] Exodus xxxiii. 20.

[1] Coloss. i. 18.   [2] I. Cor. xv. 20.

10. They who maintain that God the Word suffered in the flesh should be asked the meaning of what they say, and should they have the hardihood to reply that when the body was pierced with nails the divine nature was sensible of pain, let them learn that the divine nature did not fill the part of a soul. God the Word had assumed a soul with the body. Should they reject this argument as blasphemous, and should they assert that the flesh suffered by nature, and that God the Word made the passion His own as of His own flesh, let them not propound puzzling and murky phrases, but let them clearly propound the meaning of the ill sounding phrase. They will have all those who wish to follow the divine Scripture as their supporters in this interpretation.

11. The divine Peter in his Catholic Epistle says that Christ suffered in the flesh.[1] But he who hears that Christ suffered does not understand God the Word incorporeal, but incarnate. The name of Christ indicates both natures; but the word "flesh" connected with the passion signifies not that both, but that one of the two, suffered. For he that hears that Christ suffered in the flesh thinks of Him as impassible in that He was God, and attributes the passion to the flesh alone. For just as when we hear him saying that God had sworn to David of the fruit of his loins according to the flesh to raise up the Christ, we do not say that God the Word derived His origin from David, but that the flesh which God the Word took was akin to David, so must he who hears that Christ suffered in the flesh, recognise that the passion belongs to the flesh, and confess the impassibility of the Godhead.

12. When on the cross the Lord Christ said, "Father into Thy hands I commend my spirit,"[2] this spirit is said by the Arians and the Eunomians to be the Godhead of the only-begotten, for they hold that the body which He took was without a soul, but the heralds of the truth say that the soul was so called and they base their opinion on the following passages. The right wise Evangelist immediately adds "And having said thus He gave up the ghost."[3] So says Luke, and the blessed Mark similarly adds "He gave up the ghost."[4] The divine Matthew writes, "yielded up the Ghost,"[5] and the divine John, "gave up the Ghost."[1] All speak according to the usage of men, for we are accustomed to use all these expressions about those who die; none of them conveys any meaning of Godhead, but they all signify the soul, and if any one were to receive the Arian sense of the passage none the less even thus will it shew the immortality of the divine nature. For Christ commended it to the Father. He did not yield it to death. If then they that deny the assumption of the soul, and maintain God the Word to be a creature, and assert that He was in the body in place of a soul, deny that He was delivered to death, how can they obtain pardon who while they confess one substance of the Trinity, and leave the soul in its own immortality, impudently dare to say that God the Word of one substance with the Father tasted death?

13. If Christ is both God and man, as the divine Scripture teaches, and the illustrious Fathers persistently preached, then He suffered as man, but as God remained impassible.

14. If they acknowledge the assumption of the flesh, and declare it to be passible before the resurrection, and preach that the nature of the Godhead is impassible, why, leaving the passible nature, do they attribute the passion to the impassible?

15. If our Lord and Saviour nailed the handwriting to the cross, as says the divine Apostle,[2] He then nailed the body, for on his body every man like letters marks the prints of his sins, wherefore on behalf of sinners He gave up the body that was free from all sin.

16. When we say that the body or the flesh or the manhood suffered, we do not separate the divine nature, for as it was united to one hungering, thirsting, aweary, even asleep, and undergoing the passion, itself affected by none of these but permitting the human nature to be affected in its own way, so it was conjoined to it even when crucified, and permitted the completion of the passion, that by the passion it might destroy death; not indeed receiving pain from the passion, but making the passion its own, as of its own temple, and of the flesh united to it, on account of which flesh also the faithful are called members of Christ, and He Himself is styled the head of them that believed.

---

[1] I. Pet. i. 1.   [3] Luke xxiii. 46.   [5] Matt. xxvii. 50.
[2] Luke xxiii. 46.   [4] Mark xv. 39.

[1] John xix. 30.   [2] Col. ii. 14.

LETTERS OF THE BLESSED THEODORET,
BISHOP OF CYRUS

I. *To an unknown correspondent.*

In the words of the prophet we find the wise hearer mentioned with the excellent councillor.[1] I, however, send the book I have written on the divine Apostle, not as much to a wise hearer as to a just and clever judge. When goldsmiths wish to find out if their gold is refined and unalloyed, they apply it to the touchstone; and just·so I sent my book to your reverence, for I wish to know whether it is what it should be, or needs some fining down. You have read it and returned it, but have said nothing to me on this point. Your silence leads me to conjecture that the judge has given sentence of condemnation, but is unwilling to hurt my feelings by telling me so. Pray dismiss any such idea, and do not hesitate to tell me your opinion about the book.

II. *To the same.*

When men love warmly, I doubt whether in the case of the children of those whom they love, they can be impartial judges. Justice is carried away by affection. Fathers fancy that their ugly boys are beautiful, and sons do not see the uncomeliness of their fathers. Brother looks at brother in the light of affection rather than of nature. It is thus that I am afraid your holiness has judged what I have written, and that the sentence has been delivered by warmth of feeling. For truly the power of love is very great, and not seldom it keeps out of sight considerable errors in our friends. It is because you have so much of it, my dear friend, that you have wreathed what I have written with your kindly praises. All I can do is to ask your piety to beseech the good Lord to ratify your eulogy, and make the man you have praised something like the picture painted in the words of his admirers.

III. *To Bishop Irenæus.*[2]

Comparisons of this kind are forbidden by the divine Apostle. In his Epistle to the Romans he writes "Therefore judge no-

thing before the time until the Lord come who both will bring to light the hidden things of darkness and will make manifest the counsels of the heart: and then shall every man have praise of God."[1] And he is quite right; for we can see only·outward deeds, but the God of all knows also the intention of the doers, and when He delivers his sentence judges not so much the work as the will. So He will crown the divine Apostle who became to the Jews as a Jew, to them that were under the law as under the law, and to them that were without law as without law,[2] for his object in thus assuming an actor's mask was that he might do good to mankind. His was no time-server's career. The gain he got was loss, but he secured the good of them whom he taught. As I said, then, the divine Paul bids us wait for the judgment of God. But we are venturing on high themes; we are handling a theology passing understanding and words; not, like the unholy heretics, seeking blasphemous positions, but endeavouring to confute their impiety, and as far as in us lies to give praise to the Creator; we shall therefore do nothing unreasonable in attempting to reply to your enquiry.

You have suggested the case of an impious judge giving to two athletes of piety the alternative of sacrificing to demons, or flinging themselves into the sea. You describe the one as choosing the latter and plunging without hesitation into the deep, while the other, refusing both, shews quite as much abhorrence of the worship of idols as his companion, but declines to commit himself to the waves, and waits for this fate to be violently forced upon him. You have suggested these circumstances, and you ask which of these two took the better course. I think that you will agree with me that the latter was the more praiseworthy. No one ought to withdraw himself from life unbidden, but should await either a natural or a violent death. Our Lord gave us this lesson when He bade those that are persecuted in one city flee to another and again commanded them to quit even this and depart to another.[3] In obedience to this teaching the divine Apostle escaped the violence

[1] Isaiah iii. 3. Sept.
[2] Irenæus, Count of the Empire and afterwards bishop of Tyre, was a friend and frequent correspondent of Theodoret. He was deposed at the Latrocinium in 449. cf. Epp. XII, XVI, XXXV.

[1] I. Cor. iv. 5.   [2] I. Cor. ix. 20, 21.   [3] Matt. x. 23.

of the governor of the city, and had no hesitation in speaking of the manner of his flight, but spoke of the basket, the wall, and the window, and boasted and glorified in the act.[1] For what looks discreditable is made honourable by the divine command. In the same manner the Apostle called himself at one time a Pharisee[2] and at another a Roman,[3] not because he was afraid of death, but acting quite fairly in fight.[4] In the same way when he had learnt the Jews' plot against him he appealed to Cæsar[5] and sent his sister's son to the chief captain to report the designs hatched against him, not because he clung to this present life, but in obedience to the divine law. For assuredly our Lord does not wish us to throw ourselves into obvious peril; and this is taught us by deed as well as by word, for more than once He avoided the murderous violence of the Jews. And the great Peter, first of the Apostles, when he was loosed from his chains and had escaped from the hands of Herod, came to the house of John, who was surnamed Mark, and after removing the anxiety of his friends by his visit and bidding them maintain silence, betook himself to another house in the endeavour to conceal himself more effectually by the removal.[6] And we shall find just the same kind of wisdom in the old Testament, for the famous Moses, after playing the man in his struggle with the Egyptian and finding out the next day that the homicide had become known, ran away, travelled a long journey, and arrived at the land of Midian.[7] In like manner the great Elias when he had learnt Jezebel's threats did not give himself up to them which wished to kill him, but left the world and hurried to the desert.[8] And if it is right and agreeable to God to escape the violence of our enemies, surely it is much more right to refuse to obey them when they order a man to become his own murderer. Our Lord did not give in to the devil when he bade Him throw Himself down,[9] and when he had armed against Him the hands of the Jews by means of the scourge and the thorns and the nails, and the creature was urging Him to bring wholesale destruction on His wicked foes, the Lord Himself forbade, because He knew that His

Passion was bringing salvation to the world, and it was for this reason that just before His Passion He said to His Apostles " Pray that ye enter not into temptation,"[1] and taught us to pray " Lead us not into temptation."[2] Now let us shift our ground a little, and we shall see our way more clearly. Let us eliminate the sea from the argument, and suppose the judge to have given each of the martyrs a sword, and ordered the one who refused to sacrifice to cut off his own head; who in his senses would have endured to redden his hand with his own blood, become his own headsman, lift his hand against himself, in obedience to the judge's order?

Clearly your second martyr deserves the higher praise. The former indeed deserves credit for his zeal, but the latter is adorned by right judgment as well.

I have answered you according to the measure of the wisdom given me; He who knows thoughts as well as acts, will shew which of the two was right in the day of His appearing.

IV. Festal.

The Creator of our souls and bodies has given His bounty to both, and at one and the same time has overwhelmed us with good things that both heart and senses can feel. At the time of the sacred feast He has given us the rain we so much longed for, that our celebration might be clear of sadness. We have praised our bountiful Lord, and now as we are wont write a festal letter and address your piety with the request that you will aid us with your prayers.

V. Festal.

The God who made us gives us care and sorrow after our sin. But He has furnished us with divine occasions of consolation by appointing divine feasts. The thoughts they suggest both remind us of God's gifts to us, and promise complete freedom from all our troubles. Enjoying these good things and filled with cheerfulness, we address your magnificence, and, according to the custom of the festival, pay friendship's debt.

VI. Festal.

Our loving Lord has allowed us, with the zeal of folks who love the Christ, to celebrate the divine feast of salvation and enjoy the fruit of the spiritual blessing that flows from it. Since we know the disposition of your Piety toward us, we write to tell you this.

---

[1] The word in the text for basket is σαργάνη, a basket of twisted work (שֶׂרֶג) commonly rope — the word used by St. Paul himself in II. Cor. xi. 33. In Acts ix. 25 St. Luke writes ἐν σπυρίδι, σπυρίς (? σπείρω) being the large rope basket of Matt. xv. 37, and distinguished from the κόφινος of Matt. xiv. 20 and of Juvenal III. 14, " *Judæis quorum cophinus fænumque supellex*," and VI. 542.
[2] Acts xxiii. 6. [3] Acts xxii. 25.
[4] " *Dolus an virtus quis in hoste requirat?* " Virg Æn. ii. 390.
[5] Acts xxv. 11. [6] Acts xii. 12, etc. [7] Exod. ii. 11 etc.
[8] I. Kings xix. 1 etc. [9] Matt. iv. 6.

[1] Matt. xxvi. 41. [2] Luke xi. 4.

For they who have friendly thoughts to others are always pleased to hear cheering intelligence of them.

VII.　To Theonilla.

Had I heard of the death of your dignity's most honourable husband I should have written long ago, and now my object in writing is not to lull your great sorrow to sleep by consolatory words. They are unnecessary. They who have learnt the wisdom of philosophers and consider what this life is, find reason strong enough to meet and break grief's rising surge. And even while you are remembering your long companionship, reason recognises the divine decrees, and to meet the forces of the tears of sorrow marshals at once the course of nature, the law of God, and the hope of the resurrection. Knowing this as I do, there is no necessity to use many words. I only beseech you to avail yourself of good sense in the hour of need. Think of the death of him who is gone as no more than a long journey, and wait for the promise of our God and Saviour. For He who promised the resurrection cannot lie, and is the fount of truth.

VIII.　To Eugraphia.

It is needless for me to bring once more to bear upon your grief the spells of the spirit. The mere mention of the sufferings that wrought our salvation is enough to quench distress, even at its worst. Those sufferings were all undergone for humanity. Our Lord did not destroy death to make one body victorious over death, but through that one body to effect our common resurrection, and make our hope of it a sure and certain hope. And if even while our holy celebrations are bringing you manifold refreshment of soul, you cannot overcome your sense of sorrow, let me beg you, my honoured friend, to read the very words of the marriage contract which follow on the mention of the dowry, and to see how the wedding is preceded by the reminder of death. Knowing as we do that men are mortal, and bethinking us of the peace of survivors, it is customary to lay down what are called conditions, and for no hesitation to be shewn at the mention of death before the joining together in marriage. These are the plain words " If the husband should die first it is agreed that so and so be done ; if this lot should first fall to the wife, so and so." We knew all this before the wedding ; we are waiting for it so to say every

day. Why then take it amiss? The union must needs be broken either by the death of the husband or the departure of the wife. Such is the course of life. You know, my excellent friend, alike God's will and human nature; dispel then your despondency and wait for the fulfilment of the common hope of the just.

IX.　To an anonymous correspondent.

Your piety is annoyed and distressed at the sentence passed on me unjustly and without a trial. I am comforted that you are so feeling. Had I been justly condemned I should have been sorry at having given my judges reasonable grounds for what they have done, but, as it is, my conscience is quite clear, and I feel joyful and exultant and look forward to the remission of other sins on account of this injustice. Naboth lives in men's memories only because he suffered that unjust death. Only pray that we be not abandoned of God and let the enemy continue to do his worst. God's good will is enough to make me very cheerful and if He is on my side I despise all my troubles as trifles.[1]

X.　To the learned Elias.

Legislators have made laws in aid of the oppressed, and advocates have practised the orator's arts to help them that stand in need of fair defence. You, my friend, have studied eloquence and the law. Now put your art in practice, and by it put down the oppressors, help them that are put down by them, and defend them with the law as with a shield. Let no guilty client enjoy the benefit of your advocacy, even though he be your friend.

Now one of these guilty men is that villain Abraham. After being settled for a considerable time on an estate belonging to the church, he then took several partners in his rascality, and has had no hesitation in owning his proceedings. I have sent him to you with an account of his doings, the parties he has wronged, and the reverend sub-deacon Gerontius. I do not want you to deliver the guilty man to the authorities, but in the hope that when his victims have told you all they have had to put up with, and have made you, my learned friend, feel sympathy for their case, you may be induced to compel the wicked fellow to restore what he has stolen.

---

[1] Probably the condemnation referred to is the imperial Edict of March 449 relegating Theodoret to the limits of his own diocese. cf. Epp. 79. 80.

XI. To Flavianus bishop of Constantinople.

The Creator and Guide of the Universe has made you a luminary of the world, and changed the deep moonless night into clear noon. Just as by the haven's side, the beacon light shews sailors in the night time the harbour mouth, so shines the bright ray of your holiness to give great comfort to all that are attacked for true religion's sake, and shews them the safe port of the Apostles' faith. They that know it already are filled with comfort, and they that knew it not are saved from being dashed upon the rocks. I indeed am especially bound to praise the giver of all good, because I have found a noble champion who drives away fear of men by the power of the fear of God, fights heartily in the front rank for the doctrines of the Gospel, and gladly bears the brunt of the apostolic war. So to-day every tongue is moved in eulogy of your holiness, for it is not only the nurslings of true religion who admire the purity of your faith, but the praises of your courage are sung even by the enemies of the truth. Falsehood vanishes at truth's lightning flash.

I write thus knowing that the very reverend and pious Hypatius the reader, both readily obeys the bidding of your holiness, and constantly, my Lord, mentions your laudable deeds. I salute you as holy and right dear to God. I exhort you to support us with your prayers that we may lead the rest of our lives according to God's laws.

XII. To the bishop Irenæus.[1]

Job, that famous tower of adamant and noble champion of goodness, was not shaken even by blows of continuous troubles of every sort and kind, but stood impregnable and firm. At the end however of all his trials the righteous Law-giver explained the reason of them in the words, " Dost thou think that I answered thee for any other reason than that thou mightest appear just?"[2] I think that these words are known to your piety which is able to support the many and various attacks of troubles and anxieties, and so far from shrinking from them, exhibits the strength and stability of your administration. So the bountiful Lord, seeing the bravery and holiness of your soul, has refused to keep a worthy champion in concealment, and has brought him forth to the contest to adorn your venerable head with a crown of victory, and give your struggles as a high example of good service to the rest. So, my dear friend, conquer in this battle too, and bear bravely the death of your son-in-law, my own dear friend. Conquer in your wisdom the claims of kinsmanship and the memory of a noble and generous character, a memory which must always recall something beyond painter's art or rhetorician's skill. Repel the assault of sorrow by the thought of Him who wisely administers all the affairs of men, with perfect knowledge of the future and right guidance of it for our good. Let us join in the joy of him who has been delivered from this life's storms. Let us rather give thanks because, wafted by kindly winds, he has cast anchor in the windless haven and has escaped the grievous shipwrecks whereof this life is full. But need I say all this to one who is a tried gladiator of goodness? Need I, as it were, anoint for endurance one who is a trainer of other athletes? Still I write. It is a comfort to myself to write as I do. I am really and truly grieved when I remember an intimacy that I esteemed so highly. Once more I praise the great Guide of all, Who both knows what would be good for us and guides our life accordingly. I have dictated this after writing my former communication, on one of my friends in Antioch telling me that the end had come.

XIII. To Cyrus.

I had heard of the island of Lesbos, and its cities Mitylene, Methymna, and the rest; but I was ignorant of the fruit of the vine cultivated in it.[1] Now, thanks to your diligence, I have become acquainted with it, and I admire both its whiteness and the delicacy of its flavour. Perhaps time may even improve it, unless it turns it sour ; for wine, like the body, and plants, and buildings, and other things made by hand, is damaged by time. If, as you say, it makes the drinker longlived, I am afraid it will be of little use to me, for I have no desire to live a long life, when life's storms are so many and so hard.

I was however much pleased to hear of the health of the monk. Really my anxiety about him was quite distressing, and I wrongly blamed the doctors, for his complaint required the treatment they gave. I have sent you a little pot of honey which the Cilician bees make from storax flowers.

---

[1] Vide note on Letter III.   [2] Job xl. 3. lxx.

[1] On the wine of Lesbos cf. Hor. Car. i. 17, " innocentis pocula Lesbii ; " Aulus Gellius tells the story how Aristotle, when asked to nominate his successor, and wishing to point out the superiority of Theophrastus to Menedemus, called first for a cup of Rhodian, and then of Lesbian, and after sipping both, exclaimed ἡδίων ὁ Λέσβιος. Nact. Att. xiii. 5.

XIV. To Alexandra.

Had I only considered the character of the loss which you have sustained, I should have wanted consolation myself, not only because I count that what concerns you concerns me, be it agreeable or otherwise, but because I did so dearly love that admirable and truly excellent man. But the divine decree has removed him from us and translated him to the better life. I therefore scatter the cloud of sorrow from my soul, and urge you, my worthy friend, to vanquish the pain of your sorrow by the power of reason, and to bring your soul in this hour of need under the spell of God's word. Why from our very cradles do we suck the instruction of the divine Scriptures, like milk from the breast, but that, when trouble falls upon us, we may be able to apply the teaching of the Spirit as a salve for our pain? I know how sad, how very grievous it is, when one has experienced the worth of some loved object, suddenly to be deprived of it, and to fall in a moment from happiness to misery. But to them that are gifted with good sense, and use their powers of right reason, no human contingency comes quite unforeseen ; nothing human is stable ; nothing lasting ; nor beauty, nor wealth, nor health, nor dignity ; nor any of all those things that most men rank so high. Some men fall from a summit of opulence to lowest poverty ; some lose their health and struggle with various forms of disease ; some who are proud of the splendour of their lineage drag the crushing yoke of slavery. Beauty is spoilt by sickness and marred by old age, and very wisely has the supreme Ruler suffered none of these things to continue nor abide, with the intent that their possessors, in fear of change, may lower their proud looks, and, knowing how all such possessions ebb and flow, may cease to put their confidence in what is short lived and fleeting, and may fix their hopes upon the Giver of all good. I am aware, my excellent friend, that you know all this, and I beg you to reflect on human nature ; you will find that it is mortal, and received the doom of death from the beginning. It was to Adam that God said " Dust thou art and to dust thou shalt return." [1] The giver of the law is He that never lies, and experience witnesses to His truth. Divine Scripture tells us " all men have one entrance into life and the like going out," [2] and every one that is born awaits the grave. And all do not live a like length of time ; some men come to an end all too soon ;

some in the vigour of manhood, and some after they have experienced the trials of old age. Thus, too, they who have taken on them the marriage yoke are loosed from it, and it must needs be that either husband first depart or wife reach this life's end before him. Some have but just entered the bridal chamber when their lot is weeping and lamentation ; some live together a little while. Enough to remember that the grief is common to give reason ground for overcoming grief. Besides all this, even they who are mastered by bitterest sorrow may be comforted by the thought that the departed was the father of sons ; that he left them grown up ; that he had attained a very high position, and in it, so far from giving any cause for envy, made men love him the more, and left behind him a reputation for liberality, for hatred of all that is bad, for gentleness and indeed for every kind of moral virtue. [1]

But what excuse for despondency will be left us if we take to heart God's own promises and the hopes of Christians ; the resurrection, I mean, eternal life, continuance in the kingdom, and all that " eye hath not seen, nor ear heard, neither have entered into the heart of man, the things which God hath prepared for them that love Him " ? [2] Does not the Apostle say emphatically, " I would not have you to be ignorant brethren concerning them which are asleep, that ye sorrow not even as others which have no hope " ? [3] I have known many men who even without hope have got the better of their grief by the force of reason alone, and it would indeed be extraordinary if they who are supported by such a hope should prove weaker than they who have no hope at all. Let us then, I implore you, look at the end as a long journey. When he went on a journey we used indeed to be sorry, but we waited his return. Now let the separation sadden us indeed in some degree, for I am not exhorting what is contrary to human nature, but do not let us wail as over a corpse ; let us rather congratulate him on his setting forth and his departure hence, because he is now free from a world of uncertainties, and fears no further change of soul or body or of corporeal conditions. The strife now ended, he waits for his reward. Grieve not overmuch for orphanhood and widowhood. We have a greater Guardian

---

[1] The virtues specified are (i) ἐλευθερία; (ii) μισοπονηρία; and (iii) πραότης.
  The more classical Greek for ἐλευθερία, the character of the ἐλεύθερος, was ἐλευθεριότης. — ἐλευθερία being used for freedom, or license ; Vide Arist. Eth. Nic. iv. 1.
  The μισοπόνηρος is a hater of knavery, as in Dem. 584, 12.
  On the high character of the πρᾶος cf. Aristotle. Eth. Nic. iv. 5. and Archbp. Trench, synonyms of the N. T. p. 148.
[2] I. Cor. ii. 9.   [3] I. Thess. iv. 13.

whose law it is that all should take good care of orphans and widows and about whom the divine David says " The Lord relieveth the fatherless and widow, but the way of the wicked He turneth upside down.[1] Only let us put the rudders of our lives in His hands, and we shall meet with an unfailing Providence. His guardianship will be surer than can be that of any man, for His are the words " Can a woman forget her sucking child that she should not have compassion on the son of her womb? Yet will I not forget thee."[2] He is nearer to us than father and mother for He is our Maker and Creator. It is not marriage that makes fathers, but fathers are made fathers at His will.

I am now compelled thus to write because my bonds[3] do not suffer me to hasten to you, but your most God-loving and most holy bishop is able unaided to give all consolation to your very faithful soul by word and by deed, by sight and by communication of thought and by that spiritual and God-given wisdom of his whereby I trust the tempest of your grief will be lulled to sleep.

XV. To Silvanus the Primate.[4]

I know that in my words of consolation I am somewhat late, but it is not without reason that I have delayed to send them, for I have thought it worth while to let the violence of your grief take its course. The cleverest physicians will never apply their remedies when a fever is at its height, but wait for a favourable opportunity for using the appliances of their skill. So after reckoning how sharp your anguish must be, I have let these few days go by, for if I myself was so distressed and filled with such sorrow by the news, what must not have been the sufferings of a husband and yokefellow, made, as the Scripture says, one flesh,[5] at the violent sundering of the union cemented both by time and love? Such pangs are only natural; but let reason devise consolation by reminding you that humanity is frail and sorrow universal, and also of the hope of the resurrection and the will of Him who orders our lives wisely. We must needs accept the decrees of inestimable wisdom, and own them to be for our good; for they who reflect thus piously shall reap piety's rewards, and so delivered from immoderate lamentations shall pass their lives in peace. On the other hand they

whom sorrow makes its slaves will gain nothing by their wailing, but will at once live weary lives and grieve the Guardian of us all. Receive then, my most honoured friend, a fatherly exhortation " The Lord gave and the Lord hath taken away. He hath done whatsoever pleased Him. Blessed be the name of the Lord."[1]

XVI. To Bishop Irenæus.[2]

There is nothing good, it seems, in prospect for us, so, far from calming down, the tempest troubling the Church seems to rise higher every day. The conveners of the Council have arrived and delivered the letters of summons to several of the Metropolitans including our own, and I have sent a copy of the letter to your Holiness to acquaint you how, as the poet has it, " Woe has been welded by woe."[3] And we need only the Lord's goodness to stay the storm. Easy it is for Him to stay it, but we are unworthy of the calm, yet the grace of His patience is enough for us, so that haply by it we may get the better of our foes. So the divine apostle has taught us to pray "for He will with the temptation also make a way to escape that ye may be able to bear it."[4] But I beseech your godliness to stop the mouths of the objectors and make them understand that it is not for them who stand, as the phrase goes, out of range, to scoff at men fighting in the ranks and giving and receiving blows; for what matters it what weapon the soldier uses to strike down his antagonists? Even the great David did not use a panoply when he slew the aliens' champion,[5] and Samson slew thousands on one day with the jawbone of an ass.[6] Nobody grumbles at the victory, nor accuses the conqueror of cowardice, because he wins it without brandishing a spear or covering himself with his shield or throwing darts or shooting arrows. The defenders of true religion must be criticized in the same way, nor must we try to find language which will stir strife, but rather arguments which plainly proclaim the truth and make those who venture to oppose it ashamed of themselves.

What does it matter whether we style the holy Virgin at the same time mother of Man and mother of God, or call her mother and servant of her offspring, with the addition that she is mother of our Lord Jesus Christ as man, but His servant as God, and so at once avoid the term which is the pretext of

---

[1] Ps. cxlvi. 9.   [2] Isaiah xlix. 15.
[3] i.e. confinement to the limits of his own diocese by the decree of March, 449.
[4] cf. note on p. 261. Nothing is known of this Silvanus.
[5] Gen. ii. 24.

[1] Job i. 21.   [2] cf. Epp. iii, xii, and xxxv.
[3] Homer II. xvi. iii. κακὸν κακῷ ἐστήρικτο. For Theodoret's knowledge of Homer cf. pp. 104 and 258.
[4] I. Cor. x. 13.   [5] I. Sam. xvii.   [6] Judges xv. 16.

calumny, and express the same opinion by another phrase? And besides this it must also be borne in mind that the former of these titles is of general use, and the latter peculiar to the Virgin; and that it is about this that all the controversy has arisen, which would God had never been. The majority of the old Fathers have applied the more honourable title to the Virgin, as your Holiness yourself has done in two or three discourses; several of these, which your godliness sent to me, I have in my own possession, and in these you have not coupled the title mother of Man with mother of God, but have explained its meaning by the use of other words. But since you find fault with me for having left out the holy and blessed Fathers Diodorus and Theodorus in my list of authorities, I have thought it necessary to add a few words on this point.

In the first place, my dear friend, I have omitted many others both famous and illustrious. Secondly this fact must be borne in mind, that the accused party is bound to produce unimpeachable witnesses, whose testimony even his accusers cannot impugn. But if the defendant were to call into court authorities accused by the prosecutors, even the judge himself would not consent to receive them. If I had omitted these holy men in compiling an eulogy of the Fathers, I should, I own, have been wrong, and should have proved myself ungrateful to my teachers. But if when under accusation I have brought forward a defence, and have produced unimpeachable witnesses, why do men who are unwilling to see any of these testimonies lay me under unreasonable blame? How I reverence these writers is sufficiently shewn by my own book in their behalf, in which I have refuted the indictment laid against them, without fear of the influence of their accusers or even of the secret attack made upon myself. These people who are so fond of foolish talk had better get some other excuse for their sleight of words. My object is not to make my words and deeds fit the pleasure of this man or that man, but to edify the church of God, and please her bridegroom and Lord. I call my conscience to witness that I am not acting as I do through care of material things, nor because I cling to the honour with all its cares, which I shrink from calling an unhappy one. I would long ago have withdrawn of my own accord, did I not fear the judgment of God. And now know well that I await my fate. And I think that it is drawing near, for so the plots against me indicate.[1]

---

[1] This letter appears to be written shortly before the meeting of the Robber Synod in 449.

XVII.   To the Deaconess Casiana.

Had I only considered the greatness of your sorrow, I should have put off writing a little while, that I might make time my ally in my attempt to cure it, but I know the good sense of your piety, and so I make bold to offer you some words of consolation suggested partly by human nature, and partly by divine Scripture. For our nature is frail, and all life is full of such calamities, and the universal Governor and Ruler of the World, — the Lord who wisely orders our concerns, — gives us by means of His divine oracles consolation of various kinds, of which the writings of the holy Evangelists and the divine utterances of the blessed prophets are full. But I am sure it is needless to cull these passages, and suggest them to your piety, nurtured as you have been from the beginning in the inspired word, ruling your life in accordance with them, and needing no other teaching. But I do implore you to remember those words that charge us to master our feelings, and promise us eternal life, proclaim the destruction of death, and announce the common resurrection of us all. Besides all this, nay, before all this, I ask you to reflect that He who has bidden these things so be is the Lord, that He, is a Lord all wise and all good, Who knows exactly what is best for us, and to this end guides all our life. Sometimes death is better than life, and what seems distressing is really pleasanter than fancied joys. I beg your piety to accept the consolation offered by my humility, that you may serve the Lord of all by nobly bearing your pain, and affording to men as well as women an example of true wisdom. For all will admire the strength of mind which has bravely borne the attack of grief and broken the force of its violent assault by the magnanimity of its resolution. And we are not without great comfort in the living likenesses of your departed son; for he has left behind him offspring worthy of deep affection, who may be able to stay the excess of our sorrow.

Lastly I implore you to remember in your grief what your bodily infirmity can endure, and to avoid increasing your sufferings by mourning overmuch; and I implore our Lord of His infinite resources to give you ground of consolation.

XVIII.   To Neoptolemus.

Whenever I cast my eyes on the divine law which calls those who are joined together in marriage "one flesh,"[1] I am at a

---

[1] Gen. ii. 24.

loss how to comfort the limb that has been sundered, because I take account of the greatness of the pang. But when I consider the course of nature, and the law which the Creator has laid down in the words " Dust thou art and to dust thou shalt return," [1] and all that goes on daily in all the world on land and sea — for either husbands first approach the end of life or this lot first befalls the wives — I find from these reflections many grounds of consolation ; and above all the hopes that have been given us by our Lord and Saviour. For the reason of the accomplishment of the mystery of the incarnation was that we, being taught the defeat of death, should no more grieve beyond measure at the loss by death of those we love, but await the longed-for fulfilment of the hope of the resurrection. I entreat your Excellency to reflect on these things, and to overcome the pain of your grief ; and all the more because the children of your common love are with you, and give you every ground of comfort. Let us then praise Him who governs our lives wisely, nor rouse His anger by immoderate lamentation, for in His wisdom He knows what is good for us, and in His mercy He gives it.

XIX. *To the Presbyter Basilius.*

I have found the right eloquent orator Athanasius to be just what your letter described him. His tongue is adorned by his speech, and his speech by his character, and all about him is brightened by his abundant faith. Ever, most God-beloved friend, send us such gifts. You have given me, be assured, very great pleasure through my intercourse with him.

XX. *To the Presbyter Martyrius.*

Natural disposition appears in us before resolution of character, and, in this sense, takes the lead ; but disposition is overcome by resolution, as is plainly proved by the right eloquent orator Athanasius. Though an Egyptian by birth, he has none of the Egyptian want of selfcontrol, but shews a character tempered by gentleness. [2] He is moreover a warm lover of divine things. On this account he has spent many days with me, expecting to reap some benefit from his stay. But I, as you know, most God-beloved friend, shrink from trying so to derive good from others, and am far from being able to impart it to those who seek it, and this not because I grudge, but because I have not the wherewithal, to give. Where-

fore let your holiness pray that what is said of me may be confirmed by fact, and that not only may good things be reported of me by word, but proved in deed.

XXI. *To the learned Eusebius.*

The disseminators of this great news, with the idea that it would be very distasteful to me, fancied that they might in this way annoy me. But I by God's grace welcomed the news, and await the event with pleasure. Indeed very grateful to me is any kind of trouble which is brought on me for the sake of the divine doctrines. For, if we really trust in the Lord's promises, " The sufferings of this present time are not worthy to be compared with the glory that shall be revealed in us." [1]

And why do I speak of the enjoyment of the good things which are hoped for? For even if no prize had been offered to them that struggle for the sake of true religion, Truth alone by her own unaided force would herself have been sufficient to persuade them that love her to welcome gladly all perils in her cause. And the divine Apostle is witness of what I say, exclaiming as he does, " Who shall separate us from the love of Christ? Shall tribulation, or distress, or persecution, or famine, or nakedness, or peril or sword? As it is written, ' For thy sake we are killed all the day long ; we are accounted as sheep for the slaughter.' " [2]

And then to teach us that he looks for no reward, but only loves his Saviour, he adds straightway " Nay in all these things we are more than conquerors through him that loved us." [3]

And he goes on further to exhibit his own love more clearly. " For I am persuaded, that neither death, nor life, nor angels, nor principalities, nor powers, nor things present, nor things to come, nor height, nor depth, nor any other creature, shall be able to separate us from the love of God, which is in Christ Jesus our Lord." [4]

Behold, my friend, the flame of apostolic affection ; see the torch of love. [5]

I covet not, he says, what is His. I only long for Him ; and this love of mine is an unquenchable love and I would gladly forego all present and future felicity, aye, suffer and endure again all kinds of pain so as to keep with me this flame in all its force. This was exemplified by the divine writer in deed

---

[1] Gen. iii. 19.   [2] On πραότης vide note on p. 254.

[1] Rom. viii. 18.   [3] Rom. viii. 37.
[2] Rom. viii. 35. 36.   [4] Rom. viii. 38. 39.
[5] ἔρωτος. The use of this word in this connexion is in contrast with the spirit of the writers of the N. T., in which ἔρως and its correlatives never appear.

as well as in word and everywhere by land and sea he has left behind him memorials of his sufferings. So when I turn my eyes on him and on the rest of the patriarchs, prophets, apostles, martyrs, priests, what is commonly reckoned miserable I cannot but hold to be delightful. I confess to a feeling of shame when I remember how even they who never learnt the lessons we have learnt, but followed no other guide but human nature alone, have won conspicuous places in the race of virtue. The famous Socrates, son of Sophroniscus, when under the calumnious indictment, not only treated the lies of his accusers with contempt, but expressed his cheerfulness in the midst of his troubles in the words, " Anytus and Meletus [1] can kill me, but they cannot harm me." And the orator of Pæania,[2] who was as wise as he was eloquent, enriched both the men of his own day and them that should come after him with the saying : " to all the race of men the end of life is death, even though one shut himself up for safety in a cell ; so good men are bound ever to put their hand to every honourable work, ever defending themselves with good hope as with a shield, and bravely to bear whatever lot may be given them by God." [3]

Moreover a writer of earlier date than Demosthenes, I mean the son of Olorus, wrote many noble sentiments, and among them this " We must bear what the gods send us of necessity and the fortune of war with courage." [4] Why need I quote philosophers, historians, and orators ? For even the men who gave higher honour to their mythology than to the truth have inserted many useful exhortations in their stories ; as Homer in his poems introduces the wisest of the Hellenes preparing himself for deeds of valour, where he says

" He chid his angry spirit and beat his breast,
And said ' Forbear my mind, and think on this :
There hath been time when bitterer agonies
Have tried thy patience.' " [5]

Similar passages might easily be collected

from poets. orators, and philosophers, but for us the divine writings are sufficient.

I have quoted what I have to prove how disgraceful it were for the mere disciples of nature to get the better of us who have had the teaching of the prophets and the apostles, trusting in the Saviour's sufferings and looking for the resurrection of the body, freedom from corruption, the gift of immortality and the kingdom of heaven.

So, my dear friend, comfort those who are discouraged at the stories bruited abroad, and if anybody is pleased at them, tell them that we are happy too, that we are exulting and dancing with joy, and that what they call punishment we are looking for as the kingdom of heaven itself.

To inform those who do not know in what mind we are, be assured, most excellent friend, that we believe, as we have been taught, in the Father, the Son, and the Holy Ghost. There is no truth in the slander of some that we have been taught to believe, or have been baptized, or do believe, or teach others to believe, in two Sons. As we know one Father and one Holy Ghost so we know one Son, our Lord Jesus Christ, the only begotten Son of God, God the Word who was made man. We do not however deny the properties of the natures. We hold them to be in error who divide the one Lord Jesus Christ into two Sons, and we also call them enemies of the truth who endeavour to confound the natures. We believe an union to have been made without confusion, and we reckon some qualities to be proper to the manhood and others to the Godhead ; for just as the man — I mean man in general — reasonable and mortal being, has a soul and has a body, and is reckoned to be one being, just so the distinction between the two natures does not divide the one man into two persons, but we recognise in the one man both the immortality of the soul and the mortality of the body, and acknowledge the invisible soul and the visible body, but, as I said, one being at once reasonable and mortal ; so do we recognise our Lord and God, I mean the Son of God our Lord Christ, even after His incarnation, to be one Son ; for the union is indivisible, as we know it is without confusion. We acknowledge too that the Godhead is without beginning, and that the manhood is of recent origin ; for the one nature is of the seed of Abraham and David, from whom descended the holy Virgin, but the divine nature was begotten of the God and Father before the ages without time, without passions, without severance. But suppose the distinction between flesh

---

[1] Apol. Soc. xviii. ἐμὲ μὲν γὰρ οὐδὲν ἂν βλάψειεν οὔτε Μέλητος οὔτε Ἄνυτος, οὐδὲ γὰρ ἂν δύναιτο.
[2] I.e. Demosthenes who belonged to Pæania a demus of Attica on the eastern slope of Hymettus, and so was called ὁ Παιανεύς.
[3] Demosth. de Cor. 258.
The sentiment finds various expression in ancient writers e.g. Euripides, in a fragment of the lost " Ægeus,"
Κατθανεῖν δ' ὀφείλεται
καὶ τῷ κατ'οἴκους ἐκτὸς ἡμένῳ πόνων.
and Propertius El. III. 10.
" Ille licet ferro cautus se condat et ære,
Mors tamen inclusum protrahit inde caput."
[4] Thucydides II. lxiv. 3. φέρειν τε χρὴ τά τε δαιμόνια ἀναγκαίως, τά τε ἀπὸ τῶν πολεμίων ἀνδρείως.
The quotation is from the speech of Pericles to the Athenians in B.C. 430 in which he encourages and soothes them under adversity.
[5] Homer Od. xx. 17. (Chapman's Translation.) cf. notes on pp. 104, 255, 258, 259, and 260.

and Godhead to be destroyed, what weapons shall we use in our war with Arius and Eunomius? How shall we undo their blasphemy against the only begotten? As it is, we apply the words of humiliation as to man, the words of exaltation and divinity as to God, and the setting forth of the truth is very easy to us.

But this disquisition on the faith is exceeding the limits of a letter. Still even these few words are enough to show the character of the apostolic faith.[1]

XXII. To Count Ulpianus.

It is said that what is faulty in men's ways may be brought to order and improved by words. But I think that characters made beautiful by nature, themselves make words fair, though they stand in need of none, just as bodies naturally beautiful need no artificial colouring. These qualities are conspicuous in the right eloquent orator Athanasius, and I have been the more pleased with him because he is an ardent lover of your Excellency, and is constantly sounding your praises. Here, however, I have striven with him, and in enumerating your high qualities, have outdone him, for I know more about good deeds of yours than he. I am however vexed at not being able to praise them all, and to see that my summary of your virtues falls short of what might be said in your praise, but if God grant it even to approach the truth you will hold the pre-eminence in every kind of virtue among all your contemporaries.[2]

XXIII. To the Patrician Areobindas.[3]

In distributing wealth and poverty among men the Creator and Governor of all gives no unjust judgment, but gives the poverty of the poor to the rich as a means of usefulness. So He brings chastisement upon men not merely in the infliction of punishment for their faults, but to provide the wealthy with opportunities for shewing kindness to mankind. This year the Lord has sent us scourges, far less than our sins, but enough to distress the husbandmen, of whose sufferings I lately made your magnificence acquainted through your own hinds. Pity, I beseech you, the tillers of the ground, who have spent their toil with but very little result. Be this bad year a suggestion of spiritual abundance, and do ye through the exercise of compassion gather in the harvest

of the compassion of God. On this account the excellent Dionysius has hurried to your greatness to tell you of the trouble, that he may receive the remedy. He carries this letter, like a suppliant's branch of olive, in the hope that by its means he may receive greater kindness.

XXIV. To Andreas Bishop of Samosata.

Your piety, nursling of God's love, longs, I am sure, for my society. But I am all the more eager for yours in proportion as I know that from it more advantage will accrue to me. Want somehow naturally makes our wishes the stronger, but the Lord of all is able to give us what we long for. He rules all things Himself; knows what is sure to do us good, and never ceases to give every man this boon. I really cannot tell you how much delighted I was with your letter, and the very honourable and devout deacon Thalassius increased my pleasure by telling me what I was very anxious to know, for what can be more welcome to me than news that all goes well with you? And what is it that so increases your welfare as the moderation of the great men among us? You have acted like a wise and active physician who does not wait to be sent for, but comes of his own accord to them that need his care. This has given me great pleasure, and I have learnt by my own experience what the poet means when he says " laughing through her tears."[1] May the bountiful Giver of all good things grant your holiness to excel in them, and to make us emulous of what is praiseworthy in all good men. Help us then my dear friend, and persuade him who can to grant our petition.[2]

XXV. Festal.

When the only begotten God had been made Man, and had wrought out our salvation, they who in those days saw Him from whom these bounties flowed kept no feast. But in our time, land and sea, town and hamlet, though they cannot see their benefactor with eyes of sense, keep a feast in memory of all He has done for them ; and so great is the joy flowing from these celebrations that the streams of spiritual gladness run in all directions. Wherefore we now salute your piety, at once to signify the cheerfulness which the feast has caused in us, and to ask your prayers that we may keep it to the end.

---

[1] Garnerius dates this letter in Sept. or Oct., 449.

[2] Nothing more seems to be known either of Ulpianus or of this Athanasius.

[3] Areobindas was consul in 434, and died, according to Marcellinus, in 449.

[1] Hom. II. VI. 484, cf. quotations from Homer pp. 104, 255, 258, 259, 260.

[2] It is to Andreas of Samosata that Theodoret addressed the famous letter on the errors of Cyril numbered 162. He is mentioned by Athanasius Sinaita.

XXVI. Festal.

The fountains of the Lord's kindness are ever gushing forth with good things for them that believe; but some further good is conveyed by the celebrations which preserve the memory of the greatest of benefits to them that keep the feasts with more good will. We have just now celebrated the rites and enjoyed their blessing, and thus salute your piety, for so the custom of the feast and law of love enjoins.

XXVII. To Aquilinus, deacon and Archimandrite.

No one who has won the divine adoption weeps for orphanhood, for what guardian care can be more powerful than that of our Father which is on high, because of Him fathers of earth are fathers. By His will some are made fathers by nature, some by grace. To Him then let us hold fast and keep alive the memory of them that are dead. For we shall be the better for the recollection of them that have lived well, rousing us to imitation of them.

XXVIII. To Jacobus, presbyter and monk.

They who have made the vigour of their manhood bright by virtuous industry hasten happily towards old age, gladdened by the recollection of their former victories, and for old age's sake rid of further struggle. This joy I think your own piety possesses, and that you bear your old age the more easily for the recollection of the labours of your youth.

XXIX. To Apellion.

The sufferings of the Carthaginians would demand, and, in their greatness, perhaps out-task, the power of the tragic language of an Æschylus or a Sophocles. Carthage of old was with difficulty taken by the Romans. Again and again she contended with Rome for the mastery of the world, and brought Rome within danger of destruction. Now the ruin has been the mere byplay of barbarians. Now dignified members of her far-famed senate wander all over the world, getting means of existence from the bounty of kindly strangers, moving the tears of beholders, and teaching the uncertainty and instability of the lot of man.

I have seen many who have come thence, and I have felt afraid, for I know not, as the Scripture says, "what the morrow will bring forth."[1] Not least do I admire the

admirable and most honourable Celestinianus, so bravely does he bear his misfortune, and makes the loss of his happiness an occasion for philosophy, praising the governor of all, and holding that to be good which God either ordains or suffers to be. For the wisdom of divine Providence is unspeakable. He is travelling with his wife and children, and I beg your excellency to treat him with an hospitality like that of Abraham. With perfect confidence in your benevolence I have undertaken to introduce him to you, and I am telling him how generous is your right hand.[1]

XXX. To Aerius the Sophist.[2]

Now is the time for your Academy to prove the use of your discussions. I am told that a brilliant assemblage collects at your house, of which the members are both illustrious by birth and polished of speech, and that you debate about virtue and the immortality of the soul, and other kindred subjects. Show now opportunely your nobility of soul and wealth of virtue, and receive the most admirable and honourable Celestinianus in the spirit of men who have learnt the rapid changes of human prosperity. He was formerly an ornament of the city of Carthage, where he flung open the doors of his house to many priests, and never thought to need a stranger's kindness. Be his spokesman, my friend, and aid him in his need of your voice, for he cannot suffer the advice of the poet which bids him that needeth speak though he be ashamed.[3]

Persuade I beg you any of your society who are capable of so doing to emulate the hospitality of Alcinous,[4] to remove the poverty which has unexpectedly befallen him, and to change his evil fortune into good. Let them praise our kindly Lord for making us wise by other men's calamities, not having sent us to strangers' houses and having brought strangers to our doors. To men that shew kindness He promises to give what words cannot express and no intelligence can understand.

XXXI. To Domnus bishop of Antioch.[5]

The most admirable and honourable Celestinianus is a native of the famous Carthage, and of an illustrious family in that city.

---

[1] The name Celestinianus varies in the MSS. with Celesticacus. Theodoret's letter in his behalf may be placed shortly after the sack of Carthage by Genseric in 439.
[2] A Christian Sophist of Cyrus. cf. Letter LXVI.
[3] This passage is corrupt, and I cannot discover the quotation. There may not impossibly be a reference to Hom. Od. xvii. 345.
[4] Hom. Od. vii.   [5] cf. Epp. So – 110 – 112.

Now he has been exiled from it. He is wandering in foreign parts, and has to look to the benevolence of them that love God. He carries with him a burden from which he cannot escape and which increases his care — I mean his wife, his children and his servants, for whom he is at great expense. I wonder at his spirit. For he praises the great Pilot as though he were being borne by favourable breezes, and cares nothing for the terrible storm. From his calamity he has reaped the fruit of piety, and this thrice blessed gain has been brought him by his misfortune; for while he was in prosperity he never accepted this teaching, but when the evil day left him bare, among the rest of his losses he lost his impiety too, and now possesses the wealth of the faith, and for its sake thinks little of his ruin.

I therefore beseech your holiness to let him find a fatherland in these foreign parts, and to charge them that abound in riches to comfort one who once was endowed like themselves, and to scatter the dark cloud of his calamity. It is only right and proper that among men of like nature, where all have erred, they that have escaped chastisement should bring comfort to them that have fallen on evil days, and by their sympathy for these latter propitiate the mercy of God.

XXXII. To the Bishop Theoctistus.[1]

If the God of all had forthwith inflicted punishment on all that err he would utterly have destroyed all men. But He spares; He is a merciful Judge; and therefore some He chastises, and to others He gives the lesson of the punishment of the chastised. An instance of this merciful dealing has been shewn in our times. Exiles from what was once known as Libya, but is now called Africa, have been brought by Him to our doors, and by shewing us their sufferings He moves us to fear, and by fear rouses us to sympathy; thus He accomplishes two ends at once, for He both benefits us by their chastisement, and to them by our means brings comfort. This comfort I now beg you to give to the very admirable and honourable Celestinianus, a man who once was an ornament of the Africans' chief city, but now has neither city nor home, nor any of the necessaries of life. Now it is proper that those who in the jurisdiction of your holiness have been entrusted with the pastoral care of souls should bring before their fellow citizens what is for their good, for indeed they need such

teaching. For this reason, as we know, the divine Apostle in his Epistle to Titus writes "Let ours also learn to maintain good works for necessary uses,"[1] for if our city, solitary as it is, and with only a small population, and that a poor one, succours the strangers, much rather may Berœa,[2] which has been nurtured in true religion, be expected to do so, especially under the leadership of your holiness.

XXXIII. To Stasimus, Count and Primate.[3]

To narrate the sufferings of the most honourable and dignified Celestinianus would require tragic eloquence. Tragic writers set forth fully the ills of humanity, but I can only in a word inform your excellency that his country is Libya, so long on all men's tongues, his city the far famed Carthage, his hereditary rank a seat in her famous council, his circumstances affluent. But all this is now a tale, mere words stripped bare of realities. The barbarian war has deprived him of all this. But such is fortune; she refuses to remain always with the same men and hastens to change her abode to dwell with others.[4] I beg to introduce this guest to your excellency, and beseech you that he may enjoy your far famed beneficence. I beg also that through your excellency he may become known to all those who are in office and opulence, in order that you may both become a means of advantage to them and win the higher reward from our merciful God.

XXXIV. To the Count Patricius.

All kinds of goodness are praiseworthy, but all are made more beautiful by loving kindness. For it we earnestly pray the God of all; through it alone we obtain forgiveness when we err; it makes wealth stoop to the poor, and because I know that your Excellency is richly endowed with it I confidently commend to you the admirable and excellent Celestinianus, once lord of vast wealth and possessions and suddenly stripped of all, but bearing his poverty as easily as few men bear their riches. The subject of the tragedy involving the fall of his fortunes is the barbarian invasion of Libya and Carthage. I have introduced him to your greatness; pray suggest his case to others, and move them to pity. You will win

---

1 Bp. of the Syrian Berœa. He succeeded Acacius in 437. cf. Ep. 134.

1 Titus 3. 14.
2 i.e. The Syrian Berœa, Aleppo or Haleb.
3 The title Primas was applied in civil Law to (a) the Decuriones of a municipality, and (b) to the chiefs of provincial governments. Cod. Theod. vii. 18. 13, ix. 40. 16 etc.
4 cf. Horace I. xxxiv. 14 and III. xxix. 52 " nunc mihi nunc alii benigna."

greater gain by giving many a lesson in loving kindness.

XXXV.   To the Bishop Irenæus.[1]

You are conspicuous, my Lord, for many forms of goodness, and your holiness is beautified in an especial degree by loving-kindness, by contempt of riches, and by a generosity that gushes forth for the help of them that need. I know too that you deem worthy of more than ordinary attention those who have been brought up in prosperity and have fallen from it into trouble. Knowing this as well as I do I venture to make known to you the very admirable and excellent Celestinianus. He was once well known in Carthage for wealth and position, now stripped of these he is favourably known by his piety and philosophy, for he bears what men call misfortune with resignation because it has brought him to the salvation of his soul. He came to me with a letter which described his former prosperity, and after he had passed several days with me I proved the truth of what was said of him by experience. I have therefore no hesitation in commending him to your Holiness, and begging you to make him known to the well-to-do men of the city. It is probable that when they have learnt what has befallen him, in fear of a like fate befalling themselves, they will endeavour to escape judgment by shewing mercy. He has no resource but to go about begging, as he is put to the greater expense because he has with him his wife and children, and the domestics who with him escaped the violence of the barbarians.

XXXVI.   To Pompianus, Bishop of Emesa.

I know very well that your means are small and your heart is great, and that in your case generosity is not prevented by limited resources. I therefore introduce to your holiness the admirable and excellent Celestinianus, once enjoying much wealth and prosperity, but now escaped from the hands of the barbarians with nothing but freedom, and having no means of livelihood except the mercy of men like your piety. And cares crowd round him, for travelling with him are his wife, children and servants, whom he has brought with him from no motives but those of humanity, for he cannot think it right to dismiss them when they refuse to abandon him. I beg you of your goodness to make him known to our wealthy citizens, for I think that, after being informed by your holiness and seeing how soon pros-

perity may fall away, they will bethink them of our common humanity, and, in imitation of your magnanimity, will give him such help as they can.

XXXVII.   To Salustius the Governor.[1]

When rulers keep the scales of justice true, and let them hang in even balance, they confer all kinds of benefits upon their subjects; if they are also gifted with prudence and further show loving-kindness to him that needs it, manifold advantages accrue from their rule to them that live under it. Having enjoyed these good things through your excellency, and having experienced them in your former administration, they have now been moved with joy at the information that to your munificence the helm of government has been entrusted. I pray that they may gain yet greater good, that your excellency may win still higher praise, and that the encomiums of your eulogists may be vindicated by the addition to all your other honourable titles to fame of that colophon[2] of good things — true religion. As I was compelled to pass several days in Hierapolis I hoped to have the pleasure of meeting your excellency, and persistently enquired of new comers if the insignia of office had been conveyed to you. But I was compelled by the divine feast of salvation to return in haste to the city entrusted to me. Now however that I have received your excellency's letter, with very great pleasure I return your salutation, and without delay have sent, as you requested, the honourable and pious deacon who is by God's grace a water-finder. May the Lord in His loving kindness grant him both to do good service to the city and increase your excellency's glory.

XXXVIII.   Festal.

The divine feast of salvation has brought us the founts of God's good gifts, the blessing of the Cross, and the immortality which sprang from our Lord's death, the resurrection of our Lord Jesus Christ which gives promise of the resurrection of us all. These being the gifts of the feast, such its exhibition of the bounty of divine grace, it has filled us with spiritual gladness. But encompassed as we are on every side by many and

---

[1] i.e. of Tyre.

[1] i.e. of the Euphratensis.

[2] Colophon was one of the twelve Ionian cities founded by Mopsus on the coast of Asia Minor and was one of the claimants for being the birthplace of Homer. To put a colophon to anything became a proverbial expression for to put the crowning touch, to complete — from the fact according to Strabo (C. 643) that the Colophonian cavalry was so excellent as at once to decide and finish a battle in which it appeared. So the place and date of the edition of a book, with the device of the printer, appended to old editions is called a colophon.

great calamities, the brightness of the feast is dimmed, and lamentation and wailing are mingled with our psalmody. Such sorrows does sin bring forth. It is sin which has filled our life with pangs; it is on account of sin that death is lovelier to us than life; it is on account of sin that when we think in imagination of that incorruptible tribunal we shudder even at the life to come. So may your piety pray that God's loving-kindness may light on us, and that this gloomy and terrible cloud may be dispersed and sunshine again quickly give us joy.

XXXIX. Festal.

My wish was to write in cheerful terms and sound the note of the spiritual joy of the feast, but I am prevented by the multitude of our sins, which are bringing on us the judgment of God. For who indeed can be so insensible as not to perceive the divine wrath? May your piety then pray that affairs may undergo a change for the better; that so we too may change the style of our letter, and write words of cheerfulness instead of those of wailing.

XL. To Theodorus the Vicar.[1]

The custom of the feast bids me write a festal letter, but the cloud of our calamities suffers me not to gather the usual happy fruit from it. Who is so stony-hearted as not to be shocked and affrighted at the anger and grief of the Lord? Who is not stirred to the memory of faults? Who does not look for the righteous sentence? All this dims the brightness of the feast, but the Lord is full of loving-kindness, and we trust He will not actually fulfil His threats, but will look mercifully on us, scatter our sadness, open the springs of mercy, and shew His wonted long suffering. I salute your greatness, and beseech you to send me news of the health I sincerely trust you are enjoying.

XLI. To Claudianus.[2]

The divine Celebration has as usual conferred on us its spiritual boons; but the sour fruits of sin have not suffered us to enjoy them with gladness. They have had their usual results; in the beginning they caused thorns, caltrops, sweats, toil and pain to sprout; at the present moment sin sets the earth quaking against us, and makes nations rise against us on every side. And we lament

because we force the good Lord, who is wishful to do us good, to do us ill, and compel Him to inflict punishment.

Yet when we bethink us of the unfathomable depths of His pity we are comforted, and trust that the Lord will not cast off His people, neither will He forsake His inheritance.[1] While saluting your magnificence I beseech you to give me news of your much-wished for health.

XLII. To Constantius the prefect.[2]

Did no necessity compel me to address a letter to your greatness, I might haply be found guilty of presumption, for neither taking due measure of myself nor recognising the greatness of your power. But now that all that is left of the city and district which God has committed to my charge is in peril of utterly perishing, and certain men have dared to bring calumnious charges against the recent visitation, I am sure your magnificence will pardon the boldness of my letter when you enquire into the necessity of the case, and my own object in writing. I groan and lament at being compelled to write against a man over whose errors one ought to throw a veil, because he is of the clerical order. Nevertheless I write to defend the cause of the poor whom he is wronging. After being charged with many crimes and excluded from the Communion, pending the assembly of the sacred Synod, in alarm at the decision of the episcopal council he has made his escape from this place, thereby trampling, as he supposed, on the laws of the Church, and, by his contempt of the sentence of excommunication has laid bare his motive. He has undertaken an accusation not even fit for men of mean crafts, and in consequence of his ill-feeling towards the illustrious Philip has proceeded against the wretched tax-payers. I feel that it is quite needless for me to mention his character, his course of life from the beginning and the greatness of his wrong-doings, but this one thing I do beseech your Excellency, not to believe his lies, but to ratify the visitation, and spare the wretched tax-payers. Aye, spare the thrice wretched decurions who cannot exact the moneys demanded of them. Who indeed is ignorant of the severity of the taxation of the acres among us? On this account most of our landowners have fled, our hinds have run away, and the greater part of our lands are deserted. In discussing the land there will be no impropriety in our using geometrical terms. Of our coun-

---

[1] τοποτηρητής, vicarius, or lieutenant, is used of "Vicars" both civil and ecclesiastical.

[2] In Vatican MS. to Salustianus. The mention of the earthquake fixes the date of this letter in 447, a year when the Huns were ravaging the eastern empire.

[1] Psalm xciv. 14.

[2] This and the five following letters may be placed in 446, after the promulgation of the law of Theodosius "de relevatis, aderatis, vel donatis possessionibus" late in 445.

try the length is forty milestones, and the breadth the same. It includes many high mountains, some wholly bare, and some covered with unproductive vegetation. Within this district there are fifty thousand free jugers,[1] and besides that ten thousand which belong to the imperial treasury. Now only let your wisdom consider how great is the wrong. For if none of the country had been uncultivated, and it had all furnished easy husbandry for the hinds, they would nevertheless have sunk under the tribute, unable to endure the severity of the taxation. And here is a proof of what I say. In the time of Isidorus[2] of glorious memory, fifteen thousand acres were taxed in gold, but the exactors of the Comitian assessment, unable to bear the loss, frequently complained, and by offerings besought your high dignity to let them off two thousand five hundred for the unproductive acres, and your excellency's predecessors in this office ordered the unproductive acreage to be taken off the unfortunate decurions, and an equivalent number to be substituted for the Comitian; and not even thus are they able to complete the tale.

So with many words I ask your favour, and beseech your magnificence to put aside the false accusations that are made against the wretched tax-payers, to stem the tide of distress in this unhappy district, and let it once more lift its head. Thus you will leave an imperishable memory of honour to future generations. I am joined in my supplication to you by all the saints of our district, and especially by that right holy and pious man of God, the Lord Jacobus,[3] who holds silence in such great esteem that he cannot be induced to write, but he prays that our city, which is made illustrious by having him as neighbour and is protected by his prayers, may receive the boon which I ask.

XLIII.　To the Augusta Pulcheria.[4]

Since you adorn the empire by your piety and render the purple brighter by your faith, we make bold to write to you, no longer conscious of our insignificance in that you always pay all due honour to the clergy. With these sentiments I beseech your majesty to deign to show clemency to our unhappy country, to order the ratification of the visitation which has been several times made, and not to accept the false accusations which some men have brought against it.

I beseech you to give no credit to him who bears indeed the name of bishop, but whose mode of action is unworthy even of respectable slaves.[1] He has been himself under serious charges and subject to the bann of excommunication under the most holy and God-beloved archbishop of Antioch, the Lord Domnus, pending the summoning of the episcopal council for the investigation of the charges against him. He has now made his escape, and betaken himself to the imperial city, where he plies the trade of an informer, attacking the country which is his mother country with its thousands of poor, and, for the sake of his hatred to one, wags his tongue against all. Out of regard to what is becoming to me I will say nothing as to his character and education, and indeed he shows only too plainly what he has at present in hand. But of the district I will say this, that when the whole province had its burdens lightened, this portion, although it bore a very heavy share of the burden, never enjoyed the benefit of relaxation. The result is that many estates are deprived of husbandmen; nay, many are altogether abandoned by their owners, while the wretched decurions have demands made on them for these very properties, and, being quite unable to bear the exaction, betake themselves some to begging, and some to flight. The city seems to be reduced to one man, and he will not be able to hold out unless your piety supplies a remedy. But I am in hopes that your serenity will heal the wounds in the city and add yet this one more to your many good deeds.

XLIV.　To the patrician[2] Senator.

Thanks be to the Saviour of the world because to your greatness He is ever adding dignity and honour. The reason of my not writing up to this time to exhibit the delight which I have felt at the colophon[3] of your honour, has been my wish not to trouble your magnificence. At the moment of my now writing, the district which Providence has committed to my care stands as the proverb has it on a razor's edge.[4] You will remember the visitation which was made at the time when we first were benefited by your presence among us; how it was

---

[1] i.e., 28,800 sq. ft. "*jugum vocant quod juncti boves uno die exarare possint.*" Varro R. R. i. 10.
[2] For many years Prefect of the East.
[3] Presumably the Jacobus of Relig. Hist. XXI, an ascetic disciple of Maro.
[4] *Vide* p. 155 n.

[1] The delator referred to in these letters is presumably Athanasius of Perrha, who was deposed by Domnus II bishop of Antioch, in the middle of the fifth century. As Tillemont points out (Vol. XV. pp. 261-3 ed. 1740) we cannot make the identification with certainty, but the circumstances correspond with what is known of this Athanasius. There was a Perrha, now Perrin, about twenty miles north of Samosata (Samisat).
[2] From the time of the Emperor Constantine the title patrician designated a high court functionary.
[3] Cf. note on page 262.　　[4] Cf. note page 107.

with difficulty established in the time of the most excellent prefect the Lord Florentius ;[1] and how it was confirmed by the present holder of the office. An individual who bears the name of bishop, but of ways unworthy even of stage players, has fled from the episcopal synod at a time when he was lying under sentence of excommunication and is endeavouring to calumniate and discredit the visitation, while through his hatred to the illustrious Philip he assails the truth. I therefore beseech your excellency to make his lies of none effect, and that the visitation lawfully confirmed may remain undisturbed. It is indeed becoming to your greatness to reap the fruit of this good deed among the rest, to receive the acclamations of those whom you are benefiting, and so to do honour at once to the God of all and to his true servant the very man of God the Lord Jacob,[2] who joins with me in sending you this supplication. Had it been his wont to write he would have written himself.

XLV. To the Patrician Anatolius.[3]

Your greatness knows full well how all the inhabitants of the East feel towards your magnificence, as sons feel towards an affectionate father. Why then have you shewn hate to them that love you, deprived them of your kindly care, and driven them all to weeping and lamentation by putting your own advantage before the service of others? In truth I think there is not one of them that fear the Lord who is not much grieved at losing your official sway, and I think that even all the rest, although they have not right knowledge about divine things, when they reflect on the kindnesses you have conferred, share in these sentiments of distress. I for my part am specially sorry when I bethink me of your dignity and your unaffected character, and I pray the God of all ever to bestow on you the bulwark of His invincible right hand, and supply you with abundance of all kinds of blessings. We beseech your excellency no less when absent than when present to extend to us your accustomed protection, and to undo the rage of that unworthy bishop of ours whose purposes are perfectly well known to your greatness. He is endeavouring, as I am informed, to work the entire ruin of our district, and has accepted

the part of an informer to culumniate the recent visitation, and this when all in a word know that the taxation of our district is very heavy, and that in consequence many estates have been abandoned by the husbandmen. But this man, in contempt of his excommunication, and in flight from the holy synod, has thrust out his tongue against the unhappy poor. May your magnificence then consent to look to it that the truth be not vanquished by a lie. And I bring the same supplication about the Cilicians. For we cease not to wail till the iniquity be undone. The Lord, who promises to reward even a drop of water, will requite you for this trouble.

XLVI. To the learned Petrus.

Nothing is able to stay the praiseworthy purpose of them that highly esteem what is right. That this is the case is confirmed by the grief shown by your magnificence at the news you have lately received, and your refusal to overlook the attack that right has suffered. You have opportunely put away your distress, and righteously stopped the mouth of the enemy of the truth. No sooner did we hear of this, and found true philosophy so coupled with rhetorical skill, than we felt the more warmly disposed towards your excellence. Now we beseech you the more earnestly to counteract this fine fellow's lies and confirm the comfort given to the unhappy poor.

XLVII. To Proclus,[1] Bishop of Constantinople.

A year ago, thanks to your holiness, the illustrious Philip governor of our city was delivered from serious danger. After entering into the enjoyment of the security which he owed to your kindness, he filled our ears with your praises. But all your labour a certain most pious personage was endeavouring to make null and void. The visitation made several times twelve years ago he calumniates, and has adopted a style of slander which would be unbecoming even in a respectable slave. Now I beseech your sanctity to put a stop to his lies, and to induce the illustrious præfects to ratify the decision which they duly and mercifully gave. As a matter of fact our city was taxed more severely than all the cities of the provinces, and after every city had been relieved ours continued to this day assessed at over sixty-two thousand acres. At last the occupants of that seat of honour were with difficulty in-

---

[1] To the same Florentius is addressed the important letter LXXXIX wherein Theodoret defends himself from charges of heterodoxy. Before 449 he had six times attained the high position of Prefect of the East.

[2] i.e. the ascetic mentioned in letter XLI.

[3] Anatolius, consul in 440, was Magister militum in the East. He was a true friend to Theodoret. This letter may be placed in 444.

[1] Proclus was enthroned at Constantinople in 434, on the death of Maximianus.

duced to send inspectors of the district; their report was first received by Isidorus of famous memory and confirmed by the glorious and Christ-loving lord Florentius, and the whole matter was very carefully enquired into by our present ruler, whose equity adorns the throne, and he confirmed the assessment by an imperial decree. But this truth-loving person, all for his hatred of one single individual, the excellent Philip, has declared war against the poor. Under these circumstances I implore your holiness to array the forces of your righteous eloquence against his eloquence of wrong, to throw your shield over the truth which is attacked and at once prove her strength and the futility of lies.

XLVIII. To Eustathius, bishop of Berytus.[1]

I have gladly received the accusation, although I have no difficulty in disproving the indictment. I have written not three letters only but four; and I suspect one of two things; either those who promised to convey the letters did me wrong in the matter of their delivery, or else your piety, though in receipt of them, is yet anxious for more, and so gets up a charge of idleness against me. I, as I said before, am not distressed at the accusation, for it is plain proof to me of the warmth of your affection. Continue then to ply your craft, cease not to prefer your complaint and so to cause pleasure to myself.

XLIX. To Damianus,[2] bishop of Sidon.

It is the nature of mirrors to reflect the faces of them that gaze into them, and so whoever looks at them sees his own form. This is the same too with the pupils of the eyes, for they shew in them the likeness of other people's features. Of this your holiness furnishes an instance, for you have not seen my ugliness, but have beheld with admiration your own beauty. I really have none of the qualities which you have mentioned. It is nevertheless my prayer that your words may be vindicated by actual fact, and I beseech your piety by your prayers to cause it to come to pass that your praises may not fall to the ground through having no reality to correspond with them.

L. To the Archimandrite Gerontius.[1]

The characters of souls are often depicted in words and their unseen forms revealed; so now your reverence's letter exhibits the piety of your holy soul. Your waiting for that sentence, your anxiety, your search for advocates and preparation for a defence, clearly indicate your soul's zeal about divine things. We on the contrary are in a manner inactive and sleepy; we are nurtured in idleness, and stand in need of much assistance from prayers. Give them to us, O man beloved of God, that now at all events we may wake up and give some care to the soul.

LI. To the presbyter Agapius.[2]

The works of virtue are admirable in themselves, but yet more admirable do they appear if they find an eloquence able to report them well. Neither of these advantages has been lacking in the case of the bishop beloved of God, the lord Thomas, for he himself has contributed his own labours on behalf of piety, and has found in your holiness a tongue to bestow meet praise on those labours. Coming as he did with such testimony in his favour we have been all the more delighted to see him, and, after enjoying his society for a short space, have dismissed him to his charge.

LII. To Ibas, bishop of Edessa.[3]

It is, I think, of His providential care for our common salvation that the God of all brings on some men certain calamities, that chastisement may prove to be to them that have erred a healing remedy; to virtue's athletes an encouragement to constancy; and to all who look on a beneficial exemplar. For it is natural that when we see others punished we should be filled with fear ourselves. In view of these considerations I look on the trouble of Africa as a general advantage. In the first place when I bear in mind their former prosperity and now look on their sudden overthrow, I see how variable are all human affairs, and learn a twofold lesson; — not to rejoice in felicity as though it would never come to an end, nor be distressed at calamities as hard to bear. Then I recall the memory of past errors, and tremble lest I fall into like sufferings. My main motive in now writing to you is to introduce to your holiness the very God-

[1] Eustathius of Berytus (Beyrout) was a bad specimen of the time-serving ecclesiastic. Fierce in his attacks on Ibas, and a prominent member of the Latrocinium in 449, he narrowly escaped deposition himself at Chalcedon in 451.

[2] At Chalcedon Damianus of Sidon voted for the deposition of Dioscorus. (Labbe Conc. IV. 443.) In this and in the preceding letter we find Theodoret in friendly communication with representatives of the two antagonistic parties. The date of the correspondence can only be conjectured.

[1] All that is known of Gerontius is his being the recipient of the letter. "Archimandrite" = ἄρχων τῆς μάνδρας, i.e. ruler of the fold or byre.

[2] Neither Agapius nor the bishop mentioned in this letter can be identified.

[3] C. 435-457.

beloved bishop Cyprianus,[1] who starting from the famous Africa is now compelled, by the savagery of the barbarians, to travel in foreign lands.

He has brought a letter to us from the very holy bishop the lord Eusebius,[2] who wisely rules the Galatians. When your piety has received him with your wonted kindness I beg you to send him with a letter to whatever pious bishops you may think fit so that while he enjoys their kindly consolation he may be the means of their receiving heavenly and lasting benefits.

LIII. To Sophronius, bishop of Constantina.[3]

Since I know, O God-beloved, how generous and bountiful is your right hand, I put a coveted boon within your reach; for just as men hungry for this world's gain are annoyed at the sight of them that stand in need of pecuniary aid, so the liberal are delighted, because the riches they reach after are heavenly. A man who furnishes this excellent opportunity is the God-beloved bishop Cyprianus, formerly known among them that minister to others, but now, while he gives a deplorable account of the African calamities, he has to look to the benevolence of others, and depends on the bounty of pious souls. I hope that he too will enjoy your brotherly kindness, and will be forwarded with letters to other havens of refuge.

LIV. Festal.

By our divine and saving celebrations both the down-hearted are cheered, and the joyous made yet more joyful. This I have learnt by experience, for, when whelmed in the waves of despair, I have risen superior to the surge at sight of the haven of the feast. May your piety pray that I may be wholly rescued from this storm, and that our loving Lord may grant me forgetfulness of my sorrow.

LV. Festal.

We are much distressed, for we are gifted with the nature not of rocks but of men, but the recollection of the Lord's Epiphany has been to me a very potent medicine; so at once I write, according to the custom of the feast, and salute your magnificence with a prayer that you may live in prosperity and repute.

LVI. Festal.

My grief is now at its height and my mind is seriously affected by it, but I have thought it right to fulfil the custom of the feast, so now I take my pen to salute your reverence and pay the debt of affection.

LVII. To the præfect Eutrechius.[1]

Besides other boons the Ruler of the universe has granted to us that of hearing of your excellency's honour, and of congratulating at once yourself on your elevation and your subjects on so gentle a rule. I have thought it wrong to give no expression to my satisfaction and to refrain from manifesting it by letter. Your magnificence knows quite well how warm is our affection towards you — an affection most warmly reciprocated. And being so filled with love we beseech the Giver of all good things ever to pour on you His manifold gifts.

LVIII. To the consul Nomus.[2]

I am divided in mind at the idea of sending a letter to your greatness. On the one hand I know how everything depends on your judgment; I see you under the weight of public anxieties, and so think it better to be silent. On the other hand, being well aware of the breadth and capacity of your intelligence, I cannot bear to say nothing, and am afraid of being charged with negligence. I am moreover stimulated by the longing regret left with me by the short taste I had of your society. My full enjoyment of it was prevented by the disease and death of that most blessed man, so now I think writing will be a comfort. I pray the Master of all to guide your life that it be ever borne on favourable breezes and so we may reap the benefit of your kindly care.

LIX. To Claudianus.[3]

Sincere friendships are neither dissolved by distance of place nor weakened by time. Time indeed inflicts indignities on our bodies, spoils them of the bloom of their beauty, and brings on old age; but of friendship he makes the beauty yet more blooming, ever kindling its fire to greater warmth and brightness. So separated as I am from your magnificence by many a day's march, pricked by the goad of friendship I indite you this letter of salutation. It is conveyed by the standard-bearer Patroinus, a man

[1] Nothing seems known of this Cyprian beyond this mention of his expulsion by the Vandals. The letter is thus dated after 439.
[2] Eusebius of Ancyra. The name also appears as Eulalius. Baron. Ann. 440.
[3] Tella or Constantina in Osrhoene. Sophronius was cousin of Ibas of Edessa.

[1] Prefect of the East in 447. Theodoret writes to him again when in 448 or 449 Theodosius II had been induced to relegate him to his own diocese. Vide Letters LXXX and LXXXI.
[2] Nomus was consul in 445.
[3] cf. Epp. XLI and XCIX, but there are no notes of identity.

who on account of his high character is worthy of all respect, for he endeavours with much zeal to observe the laws of God. Deign, most excellent sir, to give us by him information of your excellency's precious health, and of the desired fulfilment of your promise.

LX.   To Dioscorus, bishop of Alexandria.[1]

Among many forms of virtue by which we hear that your holiness is adorned (for all men's ears are filled by the flying fame of your glory, which speeds in all directions) special praise is unanimously given to your modesty, a characteristic of which our Lord in His law has given Himself as an ensample, saying, "Learn of me; for I am meek and lowly in heart;"[2] for though God is high, or rather most high He honoured at His incarnation the meek and lowly spirit. Looking then to Him, sir, you do not behold the multitude of your subjects nor the exaltation of your throne, but you see rather human nature, and life's rapid changes, and follow the divine laws whose observance gives us the kingdom of heaven. Hearing of this modesty on the part of your holiness, I take courage in a letter to salute a person sacred and dear to God, and I offer prayers whereof the fruit is salvation. Occasion is given me to write by the very pious presbyter Eusebius, for when I heard of his journey thither I immediately indited this letter to call upon your holiness to support us by your prayers, and by your reply to give us a spiritual feast, sending to us who are hungry the blessed banquet of your words.

LXI.   To the presbyter Archibius.

I did not let the two letters which I had just received from you go unheeded, but wrote without delay, and gave my letter to the very devout presbyter Eusebius.[3] In consequence of some delay, it was for the time postponed, for the weather kept the vessels within the harbour, inasmuch as it indicated a coming storm at sea and bade sailors and pilots wait awhile. So I discharged this debt for the time, not that I may cease to be a debtor but that I may increase the debt. For this obligation becomes many times greater by being discharged, inasmuch as they who try to observe the laws of friendship increase the potency of its love, and, blowing sparks into a flame, kindle a greater warmth of affection, while all who are fired thereby strive to surpass one another in love. Receive

then my defence, my venerable friend; forgive me; and send me a letter to tell me how you are.

LXII.   To the presbyter John.

A saying of one of the men who used to be called wise was, "Live unseen." I applaud the sentiment, and have determined to confirm the word by deed, for I see no impropriety in gathering what is good from others, just as bees, it is said, gather their honey and draw forth the sweet dew from bitter herbs as well as from them that are good to eat, and I myself have seen them settling on a barren rock and sucking up its scanty moisture. Far more reasonable is it for them that are credited with reason to harvest what is good from every source; so, as I said, I try to live unseen, and above all men am I a lover of peace and quiet. On his recent return from your part of the world the very pious presbyter Eusebius announced that you had held a certain meeting, and that in the course of conversation mention had been made of me, and that your piety spoke with praise of my insignificant self. I have therefore deemed it ungrateful, and indeed unfair, that he who spoke thus well and kindly of me should fail to be paid in like coin; for although we have done nothing worthy of praise still we admire the intention of them that thus praise us, for such praise is the off-spring of affection. Wherefore I salute your reverence, using as a means of conveyance of my letter him who has brought to me the unwritten words which you have spoken about me. When, most pious sir, you have received my letter, write in reply. You were first in speech; I in writing; and I answer speech by letter. It remains now to you to answer letter for letter.

LXIII.   Festal.[1]

We have enjoyed the wonted blessings of the Feast. We have kept the memorial Feast of the Passion of Salvation; by means of the resurrection of the Lord we have received the glad tidings of the resurrection of all, and have hymned the ineffable loving kindness of our God and Saviour. But the storm tossing the churches has not suffered us to take our share of unalloyed gladness. If, when one member is in pain the whole body is partaker of the pang,[2] how can we forbear from lamentation when all the body is distressed? And it intensifies our dis-

---

1 Dioscorus succeeded Cyril in 444, and this letter is probably dated soon after.
2 Matt. xi. 29.
3 This name suggests correspondence of date with the preceding.

1 Garnerius gives the conjectural date 447.
2 Cf. I. Cor. xii. 26.

couragement to think that these things are the prelude of the general apostasy. May your piety pray that since we are in this plight we may get the divine succour, that, as the divine Apostle phrases it, we may " be able to withstand the evil day." [1] But if any time remain for this life's business, pray that the tempest may pass away, and the churches recover their former calm, that the enemies of the truth may no more exult at our misfortunes.

LXIV. Festal.

When the Master underwent the Passion of salvation for the sake of mankind, the company of the sacred Apostles was much disheartened, for they knew not clearly what was to be the Passion's fruit. But when they knew the salvation that grew therefrom, they called the proclamation of the Passion glad tidings, and eagerly offered it to all mankind. And they that believed, as being enlightened in mind, cheerfully received it, and keep the Feast in memory of the Passion, and make the moment of death an opportunity for entertainment and festivity. For the close connexion with it of the resurrection does away with the sadness of death, and becomes a pledge for the resurrection of all. After just now taking part in this celebration, we send you these tidings of the feast as though they were some fragrant perfume, and salute your piety.

LXV. To the general Zeno. [2]

To be smitten by human ills is the common lot of all men; to endure them bravely and rise superior to their attack is no longer common. The former is of human nature; the latter depends upon resolution. It is on this account that we wonder how the philosophers resolved on the noblest course of life and conquered their calamities by wisdom. And philosophy is produced by our reason's power, which rules our passions and is not led to and fro by them. Now one of human ills is grief, and it is this which we exhort your excellency to overcome, and it will not be difficult for you to rise victorious over this feeling, if you consider human nature, and take to heart the uselessness of sorrow. For what gain will it be to the departed that we should wail and lament? When, however, we reflect upon the common birth, the long years of intercourse, the splendid service in the field, and the far-famed achievements, let us reflect that he who was adorned by them was a man subject to the law of death; that

moreover all things are ordained by God, who guides the affairs of men in accordance with His sacred knowledge of what will be for their good. Thus have I written so far as the limits of a letter would allow me, beseeching your eminence for all our sakes to preserve your health, which is wont to be maintained by cheerfulness and ruined by despondency. Wherefore in my care for the advantage of us all I have penned this letter.

LXVI. To Aerius the Sophist. [1]

She that gave you birth and nurtured you invites you to the longed-for feast. The holy shrine is crowned by a roof; it is fitly adorned; it is eager for the inhabitants for whom it was erected. These are Apostles and Prophets, loud-voiced heralds of the old and new covenant. Adorn, therefore, the feast with your presence; receive the blessing which swells forth from it, and make the feast more joyous to us.

LXVII. To Maranas.

It was thy work, my good Sir, to call the rest also to the feast of the dedication. Through thy zeal and energy the holy temple has been built, and the loud-voiced heralds of the truth have come to dwell therein, and guard them that approach thither in faith. Nevertheless I write and signify the season of the feast.

LXVIII. To Epiphanius.

It was my wish to summon you to the feast of holy Apostles and Prophets, not only as a citizen, but as one who shares both my faith and my home. But I am prevented by the state of your opinions. Therefore I put forward no other claims than those of our country, and I invite you to participate in the precious blessing of the holy Apostles and Prophets. This participation no difference of sentiment hinders.

LXIX. To Eugraphia. [2]

Had I not been unavoidably prevented, I should no sooner have heard that your great and glorious husband had fallen asleep than I should straightway have hurried to your side. I have enjoyed at your hands many and various kinds of honour, and I owe you full many thanks. When hindered, much against my will, from paying my debt, I deemed it ill-advised to send you a letter at

---

[1] Eph. vi. 13.
[2] cf. Ep. LXXI. Zeno was consul in 448. Nothing is known of his brother.

[1] cf. Ep. XXX. This letter, conveying an invitation to a church which Aerius had built at Cyrus, his native city, was probably written early in the episcopate of Theodoret.
[2] cf. Ep. VIII.

the very moment, when your grief was at its height; when it was impossible for my messenger to approach your excellency, and when grief prevented you from reading what I wrote. But now that your reason has had time to wake from the intoxication of grief, to repress your emotion, and to discipline the license of sorrow, I have made bold to write and to beseech your excellency to bethink you of human nature, to reflect how common is the loss you deplore, and, above all, to accept the divine teaching, and not let your distress go beyond the bounds of your faith. For your most excellent husband, as the Lord Himself said, "is not dead but sleepeth"[1] — a sleep a little longer than he was wont. This hope has been given us by the Lord; this promise we have received from the divine oracles. I know indeed how distressing is the separation, how most distressing; and especially so when affection is made stronger by sympathy of character and length of time. But let your grief be for a journey into a far country, not for a life ended. This kind of philosophy is particularly becoming to them that be brought up in piety, and it is of this philosophy that I beseech you, my respected friend, to seek the adornment. And I do not offer you this advice as a man labouring himself under insensibility; in truth my heart was grieved when I learnt of the departure of one I loved so well. But I call to mind the Ruler of the world and His unspeakable wisdom, which ordains everything for our good. I implore your holiness to take these reflections to heart, to rise superior to your sorrow, and praise God who is the Master of us all. It is with ineffable providence that He guides the lives of men.

LXX. *To Eustathius, bishop of Ægæ.*[2]

The story of the noble Mary is one fit for a tragic play. As she says herself, and as is attested by several others, she is a daughter of the right honourable Eudæmon. In the catastrophe which has overtaken Libya she has fallen from her father's free estate, and has become a slave. Some merchants bought her from the barbarians, and have sold her to some of our countrymen. With her was sold a maiden who was once one of her own domestic servants; so at one and the same time the galling yoke of slavery fell on the servant and the mistress. But the servant refused to ignore the difference between them, nor could she forget the old superiority: in their calamity she preserved her kindly feeling, and, after

waiting upon their common masters, waited upon her who was reckoned her fellow slave, washed her feet, made her bed, and was mindful of other like offices. This became known to the purchasers. Then through all the town was noised abroad the free estate of the mistress and the servant's goodness. On these circumstances becoming known to the faithful soldiers who are quartered in our city (I was absent at the time) they paid the purchasers their price, and rescued the woman from slavery. After my return, on being informed of the deplorable circumstances, and the admirable intention of the soldiers, I invoked blessings on their heads, committed the noble damsel to the care of one of respectable deacons, and ordered a sufficient provision to be made for her. Ten months had gone by when she heard that her father was still alive, and holding high office in the West, and she very naturally expressed a desire to return to him. It was reported that many messengers from the West are on the way to the fair which is now being held in your parts. She requested to be allowed to set out with a letter from me. Under these circumstances I have written this letter, begging your piety to take care of a noble girl, and charge some respectable person to communicate with mariners, pilots, and merchants, and commit her to the care of trusty men who may be able to restore her to her father. There is no doubt that those who, when all hope of recovery has been lost, bring the daughter to the father, will be abundantly rewarded.

LXXI. *To Zeno,*[1] *General and Consul.*

Your fortitude rouses universal admiration, tempered as it is by gentleness and meekness, and exhibited to your household in kindliness, to your foes in boldness. These qualities indicate an admirable general. In a soldier's character the main ornament is bravery, but in a commander prudence takes precedence of bravery; after these come self-control and fairness, whereby a wealth of virtue is gathered. Such wealth is the reward of the soul which reaches after good, and with its eyes fixed on the sweetness of the fruit, deems the toil right pleasant. For to virtue's athletes the God of all, like some great giver of games, has offered prizes, some in this life, and some in that life beyond which has no end. Those in this present life your excellency has already enjoyed, and you have achieved the highest honour. Be it also the lot of your greatness to obtain too those abiding and perpetual blessings, and to re-

---

[1] Luke viii. 52.
[2] On the seaboard of Cilicia, now Ayas. The date may be 443 or 444.

[1] Zeno was Consul in 448. cf. Ep. LXV.

ceive not only the consul's robe, but also the garment that is indescribable and divine. Of all them that understand the greatness of that gift this is the common petition.

LXXII. To Hermesigenes the Assessor.[1]

At the time when men were whelmed in the darkness of ignorance, all did not keep the same feasts, but celebrated distinct ceremonies in different cities. In Ælis were the Olympian games, at Delphi the Pythian, at Sparta the Hyacinthian, at Athens the Panathenaic, the Thesmophoria, and the Dionysian. These were the most remarkable, and further some men celebrated the revel feast of some dæmons and some of others. But now that those mists have been scattered by intellectual light, in every land and sea mainlanders and islanders together keep the feast of our God and Saviour, and whithersoever any one may wish to travel abroad, journey he either towards rising or towards setting sun, everywhere he will find the same celebration observed at the same time. There is no longer necessity, in obedience to the law of Moses which was adapted to the infirmity of the Jews, to come together into one city and keep the feast in memory of our blessings, but every town, every village, the country and the farthest frontiers, are filled with the grace of God, and in every spot divine shrines and precincts are consecrated to the God of all. So through every town we observe our several festivals and communicate with one another in the feast. It is the same God and Lord who is honoured in our hymns and to whom our mystic sacrifices are offered. On this account, as is well known, we neighbours address one another by letter and signify the joy that comes to us in the feast. So now do I to you and offer the festal salutation to your excellency. You will without doubt reply and honour the custom of the feast.

LXXIII. To Apollonius.[2]

Themistocles the son of Neocles, the farfamed and admirable general, is described by the admiring historian as endowed with natural virtue alone. Of Pericles, however, the son of Xanthippus, it is said that he also derived ability from his education to charm his hearers by his persuasive eloquence, and was gifted with the power alike of knowing what measures should be taken and of enforcing them by word of mouth. In writing about him there is no impropriety in my using his own words. These things illustrate your magnificence, for God, our Crea-

tor, hath given you natural capacity, and your education makes its brilliance the more conspicuous. Nothing then is wanting to the full complement of your high qualities save only knowledge of their Author; be but this added, and the tale of virtues which we shall have will be complete. Thus I write to you on receiving news of your arrival, beseeching the Giver of all good to grant a beam of light to your soul's eye, to show you the greatness of His boon, to kindle your love of that possession, and to grant the longed for favour to him that longs for it.[1]

LXXIV. To Urbanus.

It has been granted to us by our generous Lord once again to enjoy the feast and to send to your excellency the festal salutation. We pray that you may be well and prosperous, and share the ineffable and divine boon which to them that approach supplies the seeds of the blessings hoped for, and gives the symbols of the life and kingdom that have no end. These things we beseech the loving Lord to impart to you, for it is natural for friends to ask that their friends may be blessed.

LXXV. To the Clergy of Berœa.

I perceive that it is with reason that I am well disposed to your reverences, for I have been assured by your kindly letter that my affection was returned. For this affection of mine towards you I have many reasons. First of all there is the fact that your father, that great and apostolic man, was my father too. Secondly I look upon that truly religious bishop,[2] who now rules your church, as I might on a brother both in blood and in sympathy. Thirdly there is the near neighbourhood of our cities, and fourthly our frequent intercourse with one another, which naturally begets friendship and increases it when it is begotten. If you like, I will name yet a fifth, and that is that we have the same close connexion with you as the tongue has with the ears, the former uttering speech, and the latter receiving it; for you most gladly listen to my words, and I am delighted to let fall my little drop upon you.

---

[1] Thucydides, (I. 138,) writes of Themistocles that "to a greater degree than any other man he was to be admired for the natural ability which he displayed; for by his inborn capacity, he was an unrivalled judge of what the emergency of the moment required, and unsurpassed in his forecast of the future, and this without the aid of previous or additional instruction."

The same historian (II. 60) records the speech of Pericles in his own vindication in which he says "I think myself inferior to none in knowing what measures should be taken and in enforcing them by word of mouth."

[2] Theoctistus; who, we learn from Letter CXXXIV, did not prove himself a friend in need, succeeded Acacius in 438. Garnerius, apparently on insufficient grounds, would therefore date the letter before this year.

---

[1] "*Nullus est sive temporis sive personæ index.*" Garnerius.
[2] cf. Ep. CIII. Apollonius was Comes Sacrarum Largitionum in 436.

But the colophon[1] of our union is our harmony in faith; our refusal to accept any spurious doctrines; our preservation of the ancient and apostolic teaching, which has been brought to you by hoary wisdom and nurtured by virtue's hardy toil. I beseech you therefore to take greater care of the flock, to preserve it unharmed for the Shepherd, and boldly to utter the famous words of the patriarch " that which was born of beasts I offered not unto Thee." [2]

LXXVI. To Uranius, Governor of Cyprus.

True friendship is strengthened by intercourse, but separation cannot sunder it, for its bonds are strong. This truth might easily be shewn by many other examples, but it is enough for us to verify what I say by our own case. Between me and you are indeed many things, mountains, cities, and the sea, yet nothing has destroyed my recollection of your excellency. No sooner do we behold any one arriving from those towns which lie on the coast, than the conversation is turned on Cyprus and on its right worthy governor, and we are delighted to have tidings of your high repute. And lately we have been gratified to an unusual degree at learning the most delightful news of all: for what, most excellent sir, can be more pleasing to us than to see your noble soul illuminated by the light of knowledge? For we think it right that he who is adorned with many kinds of virtue should add to them also its colophon, and we believe that we shall behold what we desire. For your nobility will doubtless eagerly seize the God-given boon, moved thereto by true friends who clearly understand its value, and guided to the bountiful God " Who wills all men to be saved and to come to the knowledge of the truth," [3] netting men by men's means to salvation, and bringing them that He captures to the ageless life. The fisherman indeed deprives his prey of life, but our Fisher frees all that He takes alive from death's painful bonds, and therefore " did he shew himself upon earth, and conversed with men," [4] bringing men His life, conveying teaching by means of the visible manhood, and giving to reasonable beings the law of a suitable life and conversation. This law He has confirmed by miracles, and by the death of the flesh has destroyed death. By raising the flesh He has given the promise of resurrection to us all, after giving the resurrection of His own precious body as a worthy pledge of ours. So loved He men even when they hated Him that the mystery of the œconomy fails to

obtain credence with some on account of the very bitterness of His sufferings, and it is enough to show the depths of His loving kindness that He is even yet day by day calling to men who do not believe. And He does so not as though He were in need of the service of men, — for of what is the Creator of the universe in want? — but because He thirsts for the salvation of every man. Grasp then, my excellent friend, His gift; sing praises to the Giver, and procure for us a very great and right goodly feast.

LXXVII. To Eulalius, bishop of Persian Armenia.[1]

I know that Satan has sought to sift you as wheat,[2] and that the Lord has allowed him so to do that He may shew the wheat, and prove the gold, crown the athletes, and proclaim the victors' names. Nevertheless I fear and tremble, not indeed distressed for the sake of you who are noble champions of the truth, but because I know that it comes to pass that some men are of feebler heart. If among twelve apostles one was found a traitor, there is no doubt that among a number many times as great any one might easily discover many falling short of perfection. Thus reflecting I have been confounded and filled with much discouragement, for, as says the divine Apostle, " whether one member suffer all the members suffer with it." [3] " We are members one of another," [4] and form one body, having the Lord Christ for head.[5] Yet one consolation I have in my anxiety, when I bethink me of your holiness. For brought up as you have been in the divine oracles, and taught by the arch-shepherd what are the good shepherd's marks, there is no doubt that you will lay down your life for the sheep. For, as the Lord says, " he that is an hireling " when he sees " the wolf coming," " fleeth because he is an hireling, and careth not for the sheep," but " the good shepherd giveth his life for the sheep." [6] Just so it is not in peace that the best general shews his inborn valour, but in time of war, by at once stimulating others and himself exposing himself to peril for his men. For it would be preposterous that he should enjoy the dignity of his command, and, in the hour of need, run out of danger's way. Thus the thrice blessed prophets ever acted, making light of the safety of their bodies, and, for the sake of the Jews who hated and rejected them, underwent all kinds of peril and toil. Of them the divine apostle

---

[1] cf. p. 262 n. [2] Gen. xxxi. 39. [3] I. Tim. ii. 4. [4] Baruch iii. 38.

[1] On the persecution in Persia see page 157.
[2] Luke xxii. 31. [4] Eph. iv. 25. [6] John x. 12, 13, 11.
[3] I. Cor. xii. 26. [5] Col. i. 18.

says "they were stoned, they were sawn asunder, were tempted, were slain by the sword; they wandered about in sheepskins and goatskins, being destitute, afflicted, tormented, of whom the world was not worthy; they wandered in deserts and mountains, and in dens and caves of the earth."[1] Thus the divine apostles travelled preaching over all the world, without home, bed, bedding, board, or any of the necessaries of life, but scourged, racked, imprisoned, and undergoing countless kinds of death. And all this they underwent, not for the sake of their friends, but voluntarily facing these perils for the sake of the men who were persecuting them. A far stronger claim is made on you now to accept the peril at present assailing you, for the sake of fellow-believers and brothers and children. This affection is shown even by unreasoning animals, for sparrows may be seen fighting with all their force in behalf of their brood, and putting out in their defence all the strength they have; other kinds of birds moreover undergo danger for their young. But why do I speak of birds? Bears too, and leopards, wolves, and lions, voluntarily suffer any pain for the safety of their offspring, for instead of fleeing from the hunter they will await his attack and do battle for their young.

I have adduced these instances not as though anointing your piety for endurance and courage by the example of brute beasts, but to console myself in my despondency, and to be assured that you will not leave Christ's flock without a shepherd when wolves make their attack, but will invoke the Lord of the flock to help you and will heartily do battle in its behalf. A crisis like this proves who is a shepherd and who a hireling; who diligently feeds the flock and who on the other hand feeds on the milk and thinks little of the safety of the sheep. "But God is faithful, who will not suffer you to be tempted above that ye are able; but will with the temptation also make a way to escape that ye may be able to bear it."[2] But one thing I do beseech your reverence, and that is to have greater heed of the unsound; and not only to strengthen the unstable but also to raise the fallen, for shepherds by no means neglect those of their flock who have fallen sick, but keep them apart from the rest, and try in every possible way to restore them, and so must we do. We must make them that are slipping stand up, and give them a helping hand and a word of encouragement. When they are bitten we must heal them; we must not give up the attempt

to save them nor leave them in the devil's maw. Thus ever acted the divine Apostle Paul; and when the Galatians, after receiving the baptism of salvation, and the gift of the divine Spirit, fell away into the sickness of Judaism, and received circumcision, he wailed and lamented more exceedingly than the most affectionate mother, and tended them and freed them from that infirmity. We can hear him exclaiming, "My little children, of whom I travail in birth again until Christ be formed in you."[1] So too the teacher of the Corinthians, who had committed that abominable fornication, he both chastised as might a father, and very skilfully treated, and after cutting him off in the first Epistle, readmitted him in the second and says, "So that contrariwise ye ought rather to forgive him and comfort him lest perhaps such a one should be swallowed up with overmuch sorrow."[2] And again, "Lest Satan should get an advantage of us for we are not ignorant of his devices."[3] In the same manner too those who partook of things offered to idols he properly rebuked, suitably exhorted, and freed from their grievous error.

Wherefore our Lord Jesus Christ permitted the first of the apostles, whose confession He had fixed as a kind of groundwork and foundation of the Church, to waver to and fro, and to deny Him, and then raised Him up again. And thus He gave us two lessons: not to be confident in our own strength, and to strengthen the unstable. Reach out, therefore, I beseech you, a hand to them that are fallen, "draw them out of the horrible pit, out of the miry clay, and set their feet upon a rock," and "put a new song into their mouth, even praise unto our God,"[4] that their example of life may become an example of salvation, that "many shall see it and fear and shall trust in the Lord."[5] Let them be prevented from participating in the holy mysteries, but let them not be kept from the prayer of the catechumens, nor from hearing the divine Scriptures and the exhortation of teachers,[6] and let them be prohibited from partaking of the sacred mysteries, not till death, but during a given

---

[1] Heb. xi. 37, 38. [2] I. Cor. x. 13.

[1] Gal. iv. 19.   [3] II. Cor. ii. 11.   [5] Ps. xl. 3.
[2] II. Cor. ii. 7.   [4] Psalm xl. 2 and 3.
[6] "It is noticeable that with systematic discipline as to the persons taught, there was no order of teachers. It was part of the pastoral office to watch over the souls of those who were seeking admission to the Church, as well as those who were in it, and thus bishops, priests, deacons, or readers might all of them be found, when occasion required, doing the work of a Catechist. The Doctor Audientium of whom Cyprian speaks, was a Lector in the Church of Carthage. Augustine's Treatise *de Catechizandis Rudibus*, was addressed to Deogratias as a deacon; the *Catecheses* of Cyril of Jerusalem were delivered by him partly as a deacon, partly as a presbyter. The word *catechist* implies accordingly a function, not a class." Dean Plumptre in Dict. Christ. Ant. i. 319.

time, till they recognise their ailment, covet health, and are properly contrite for having abandoned their true Prince and deserted to a tyrant, and for having left their benefactor and gone over to their foe.

The same lessons are given us by the precepts of the holy and blessed Fathers. I write as I do, not to teach you piety, but to remind you as a brother might, knowing well that even the best of pilots in the moment of the storm needs monition even from his men. So the great and famous Moses, renowned throughout the world, who did those mighty works of wonder, did not refuse the counsel of Jethro, a man still sunk in idolatrous error; for he did not regard his impiety, but acknowledged the soundness of his advice. Moreover I implore your piety to offer earnest prayer to God in my behalf that for the remaining days of my life I may live in accordance with His laws.

Thus have I written by the most honourable and religious presbyter Stephanus, whom on account of the goodness of his character I have seen with great pleasure.

LXXVIII. To Eusebius, bishop of Persian Armenia.

Whenever anything happens to the helmsman, either the officer in command at the bows, or the seaman of highest rank, takes his place, not because he becomes a self-appointed helmsman, but because he looks out for the safety of the ship. So again in war, when the commander falls, the chief tribune assumes the command, not in the attempt to lay violent hands on the place of power, but because he cares for his men. So too the thrice blessed Timothy when sent by the divine Paul took his place.[1] It is therefore becoming to your piety to accept the responsibilities of helmsman, of captain, of shepherd, gladly to run all risk for the sake of the sheep of Christ, and not to leave His creatures abandoned and alone. It is rather yours to bind up the broken, to raise up the fallen, to turn the wanderer from his error, and keep the whole in health, and to follow the good shepherds who stand before the folds and wage war against the wolves. Let us remember too the words of the patriarch Jacob; "In the day the drought consumed me and the frost by night and my sleep departed from my eyes. The rams of thy flock I have not eaten. That which was born of beasts I brought not unto thee. I bare the loss of

it. Of my hand didst thou require it, whether stolen by day or stolen by night."[1] These are the marks of the shepherd; these are the laws of the tending of the sheep. And if of brute cattle the illustrious patriarch had such care, and offered this defence to him who trusted them to his charge, what ought not we to do who are entrusted with the charge of reasonable sheep, and who have received this trust from the God of all, when we remember that the Lord for them gave up His life? Who does not fear and tremble when he hears the word of God spoken through Ezekiel? "I judge between shepherd and sheep because ye eat the fat and clothe yourselves with the wool and ye feed not the flocks."[2] And again, "I have made thee a watchman unto the house of Israel; when thou speakest not to warn the wicked from his wicked way, the same wicked man shall die in his iniquity but his blood shall I require at thine hand."[3] With this agree the words spoken in parables by the Lord. "Thou wicked and slothful servant . . . Thou oughtest to have put my money to the exchangers, and then at my coming I should have received the same with usury."[4] Up then, I beseech you, let us fight for the Lord's sheep. Their Lord is near. He will certainly appear and scatter the wolves and glorify the shepherds. "The Lord is good unto them that wait for Him, to the soul that seeketh Him."[5] Let us not murmur at the storm that has arisen for the Lord of all knoweth what is good for us. Wherefore also when the Apostle asked for release from his trials He would not grant his supplication but said, "My grace is sufficient for thee, for my strength is made perfect in weakness."[6] Let us then bravely bear the evils that befall us; it is in war that heroes are discerned; in conflicts that athletes are crowned; in the surge of the sea that the art of the helmsman is shewn; in the fire that the gold is tried. And let us not, I beseech you, heed only ourselves, let us rather have forethought for the rest, and that much more for the sick than for the whole, for it is an apostolic precept which exclaims "Comfort the feeble minded, support the weak."[7] Let us then stretch out our hands to them that lie low, let us tend their wounds and set them at their post to fight the devil. Nothing will so vex him as to see them fighting and smiting again. Our Lord is full of loving-kindness. He re-

---

1 Cf. I. Cor. iv. 17 and I. Thess. iii. 2.

1 Gen. xxxi. 40. 38. 39. 2 Ezekiel xxxiv. 2, and cf. 17.
3 Cf. Ezekiel iii. 17, 18. Quotations are apparently from memory.
4 Matt. xxv. 26, 27. 6 II. Cor. xii. 9.
5 Lamentations iii. 25. 7 I. Thess. v. 14.

ceives the repentance of sinners. Let us hear His own words: " As I live saith the Lord I have no pleasure in the death of the wicked, but that the wicked turn from his way and live." [1] So He prefaced His words with an oath, and He who forbids oaths to others swore Himself to convince us how He desires our repentance and salvation. Of this teaching the divine books, both the old and the new, are full, and the precepts of the holy Fathers teach the same.

But not as though you were ignorant have I written to you; rather have I reminded you of what you know, like those who standing safe upon the shore succour them that are tossed by the storm, and shew them a rock, or give warning of a hidden shallow, or catch and haul in a rope that has been thrown. " And the God of peace shall bring Satan under your feet shortly " [2] and shall gladden our ears with news that you have passed from storm to calm, at His word to the waves " Peace be still." [3]

And do you too offer prayers for us, for you who have undergone peril for His sake can speak with greater boldness. [4]

LXXIX. *To Anatolius the Patrician.* [5]

The Lord God has given your excellency to us to be at the present time a source of very great comfort, and has afforded us a meet haven for the storm. We have therefore confidence in informing your lordship of our distress. Not long ago we acquainted your excellency that the right honourable Count Rufus had shewn us an order written in the imperial handwriting commanding the gallant general to provide with prudence and diligence for our residence at Cyrus, and not to suffer us to depart to another city, on the ground that we are endeavouring to summon synods to Antioch, and are disturbing the orthodox. [6] Now I make known to you that in obedience to the imperial letter I have come to Cyrus. After an interval of six or seven days they sent the devoted Euphronius, the commander, with a letter begging me to acknowledge in writing that the imperial order had been shown me. I therefore promised to remain in Cyrus and its adjacent district, and to tend the sheep entrusted to my care. I therefore beseech your excellency to make exact enquiry, both

whether these orders had really been issued, and for what reason. I am indeed conscious of many other sins, but I do not know that I have erred either against the Church of God, or against public order. And I write as I do, not because I take it ill to have to live at Cyrus, for in truth she is dearer to me than any of the most famous cities, because my office in her has been given me by God. But the fact of my being bound to her not by preference but by compulsion does seem somewhat grievous, and besides it does give a handle to the wicked to grow bold and to refuse to obey our exhortations.

Under these circumstances I beseech your lordship, if no order of the kind has really been issued, to let me know; but if the letter really comes from the victorious emperor, tell his pious majesty not readily to believe calumnies, nor give ear to accusers alone, but to demand an account from the accused. Though really the evidence of the facts alone was quite enough to persuade his piety that the charges against me were false. For when did I ever make myself offensive about anything to his serene majesty or his chief officers? Or when was I ever obnoxious to the many and illustrious owners here? It is on the contrary well known to your excellency that I have spent a considerable portion of my ecclesiastical revenues in erecting porticoes and baths, building bridges, and making further provision for public objects. But if any persons take it ill that I mourn over the ruin of the churches of Phœnicia, be it known to your lordship that it is impossible for me not to grieve when I see the horn of the Jews exalted on high and the Christians in tears and sorrow, though they send them to the very ends of the earth. [1] We cannot fight against the apostolic decrees, for we remember the word of the Apostle which says, " We ought to obey God rather than men," [2] and more terrible to us than any of the pains of this life is the " judgment seat of Christ " [3] the Lord, before whom we shall all stand to render an account of our words and of our deeds. On account of that judgment seat the hardships of this present life must be endured. For them that suffer wrong the hope of what is to come is consolation enough, but to us the loving Lord has given further comfort in you, most excellent sir, whose life is bright with piety and faith.

---

[1] Ezekiel 33. 1.   [2] Rom. xvi. 20.   [3] Mark iv. 39.
[4] These letters on the Persian persecution might be placed anywhere while it lasted c. 420–450. Garnerius suggests 443. Eulalius and Eusebius are unknown.
[5] cf. Epp. XLV. XCII. CXI. CXIX. CXXI. CXXXVIII.
[6] This edict of Theodosius is dated by Tillemont March 30, 449. Theodoret received the order for his relegation to Cyrus while he was at Antioch, and at once submitted.

[1] The allusion appears to be to the edict of Feb. 448, ordering the deposition of Theodoret's friend Irenæus bishop of Tyre, on the ground of his being a digamus and a heretic. Irenæus was degraded from the priesthood and forbidden to appear in Tyre. cf. Epp. III. XII. XVI. XXXV.
[2] Acts v. 29.   [3] Romans xiv. 10.

LXXX. To the prefect Eutrechius.[1]

I have been much astonished that no information has been sent me by your lordship of the plots against me. To counteract them would very likely have been a difficult matter to any one not having the means of convicting their promoters of lies; but to give information of what was going on needed not so much power as friendliness, and we had hoped that when your excellency had been summoned to the imperial city, and had been chosen to adorn the prefect's exalted seat, every tempest of the Church would be calmed down. But we suffer from such disturbances as we did not see even in the beginning of the dispute. The churches of Phœnicia are in trouble; in trouble are those of Palestine, as all unanimously report; and the distress is proved by the letters of the most pious bishops. All the saints among us groan and every pious congregation is lamenting. While looking for a cessation of our former troubles we have been afflicted with new ones. I myself have been forbidden to quit the coasts of Cyrus, if the dispatch is true which has been shewn me, and which is said to be an autograph of our victorious emperor. It runs as follows "Since so and so the bishop of this city is continually assembling synods and this is a cause of trouble to the orthodox, take heed with proper diligence and wisdom that he resides at Cyrus, and does not depart from it to another city." I have accepted the sentence, and remain still. Your lordship can bear witness to my sentiments, for you know how on my arrival at Antioch I departed in a hurry, on account of those who wished to detain me there. And those were unquestionably wrong who gave both their ears to my calumniators and would not keep one for me. Even to murderers, and to them that despoil other men's beds, an opportunity is given of defending themselves, and they do not receive sentence till they have been convicted in their own presence, or have made confession of the truth of the charges on which they are indicted. But a high priest who has held the office of bishop for five and twenty years[2] after passing his previous life in a monastery, who has never troubled a tribunal, nor yet on any single occasion been prosecuted by any man, is treated as a mere plaything of calumny, without being allowed even the common privilege of grave-robbers of being questioned as to the truth of the accusations brought against them. Yet they have done wrong; I have done no wrong. But I am ready for even more serious troubles. Though they be ever so much annoyed at my bewailing the calamities of Phœnicia I shall not cease so to do so long as I behold them. The only judgment that is awful to me is the judgment of God. For them, nevertheless, I pray that from the God of all they may obtain forgiveness; for your excellency, that you may ever live in honour, excel in all good things, speak boldly against lies, and fight on the side of the truth. And let the contrivers of this plot know that, though I depart to the uttermost ends of the earth, God will not suffer the confirmation of impious doctrines, but will nod His head and destroy them that bow down to doctrines of abomination.

LXXXI. To the Consul Nomus.[1]

For but a brief portion of a day I enjoyed the society of your lordship, for I was deprived by unavoidable circumstances of what I so earnestly desired. I had hoped that our short interview would have kindled good will and friendly intercourse, but I was disappointed. I have now written you two letters, without receiving any reply; and by the imperial decree I am forbidden to travel beyond the boundaries of Cyrus. For this apparent punishment cause there is none, except the fact of my convening an episcopal synod. No indictment was published; no prosecutor appeared; the defendant was not convicted; but the sentence was given. We submit, for we know the reward of the wronged. I am aware however that Festus the Procurator who was entrusted with the government of the Jews when they demanded the death of the divine Paul, publicly replied, "It is not lawful to us Romans to deliver any man before that he which is accused have the accusers face to face, and have license to answer for himself concerning the crime laid against him."[2] Now these words were spoken by one who was no believer in our Master, Christ, but was a slave to the errors of polytheism. I was never asked whether I was assembling synods or not, or for what reason I was assembling them, or what umbrage this could give, either to the Church or to the government; yet just as though I had been a very guilty

---

[1] Vide Letter LVII.

[2] This brings us to about the year 423, when Theodoret was consecrated bishop at the approximate age of 30, after passing seven years in the monastery of Nicerte, three miles from Apamea, and one hundred and twenty from Cyrus. Cf. Ep. CXIX.

[1] Cf. Letter LVIII. Nomus was an influential officer of Theodosius II., being "*Magister Officiorum*" in 443, consul in 445 and patrician in 449. A friend of Dioscorus, he opposed Theodoret and was instrumental in procuring the decree which confined the bishop to his diocese in 449.

[2] Acts xxv. 16. Observe the variations in the citation.

criminal I am prohibited from visiting other cities; while to every one else every city lies open, and that not only to Arians and Eunomians, but to Manichees and Marcionists, to them that are sick with the unsoundness of Valentinus and Montanus, aye to pagans and Jews, while I, a foremost champion of the teaching of the Gospels, am from every city excluded. Some however maintain that I do not adhere to it. Then let there be a council: let there be assembled there the godly bishops who are capable of judging: then let there be assembled those in office and in rank who have been instructed in divine lore. Let me state what I hold, and let the judges declare what opinion is agreeable to the teaching of the Apostles. I have not thus written from any desire to see the great city, nor from trying to travel to any other. In fact I rather love the quiet of them whose wish is to administer the churches in a monastic state. I should like your excellency to know that neither in the time of the blessed and sainted Theodotus, nor in that of John of blessed memory, nor in that of the very holy lord bishop Domnus, did I of my own accord enter Antioch; five or six times I was invited but I with difficulty assented, and when I did assent it was in obedience to the canon of the Church which orders him who is summoned to a synod and refuses to be present to be held guilty. And when I appeared, what thing unpleasing to God did I do? Was it that I removed from the sacred lists the names of such and such a man guilty of unspeakable wickedness? Was it that I ordained to the priesthood men of character and of honourable life? Was it that I preached the gospel to the people? If these things are worthy of indictment and punishment, I gladly welcome yet severer punishments for their sake. My accusers compel me to speak. Even before my conception my parents promised to devote me to God; from my swaddling-bands they devoted me according to their promise and educated me accordingly; the time before my episcopate I spent in a monastery and then was unwillingly consecrated[1] bishop. Five and twenty years I so lived that I was never summoned to trial by any one nor ever brought accusation against any. Not one of the pious clergy who were under me ever frequented a court. In so many years I never took an obol nor a garment from any one. Not one of my domestics ever received a loaf or an egg. I could not endure the thought of possessing anything save the rags I wore. From the

revenues of my see I erected public porticoes; I built two large bridges; I looked after the public baths. On finding that the city was not watered by the river running by it, I built the conduit, and supplied the dry town with water. But not to mention these matters I led eight villages of Marcionists with their neighbourhood into the way of truth; another full of Eunomians and another of Arians I brought to the light of divine knowledge, and, by God's grace, not a tare of heresy was left among us. All this I did not effect with impunity; many a time I shed my blood; many a time was I stoned by them and brought to the very gates of death. But I am a fool in my boasting, yet my words are spoken of necessity, not of consent. Once the thrice blessed Paul was compelled to act in the same way to stop the mouths of his accusers. Yet I put up with seeming ignominy and count it high honour, for I hear the voice of the Apostle crying, "All that will live godly in Christ Jesus shall suffer persecution."[1]

But I beseech your excellency to give heed to the affairs of the Church, and calm the storm that has arisen, for in fact not even at the beginning of the dispute was the Church beset by such confusion. No one informs you of the greatness of the peril, of the lamentations of the Christians in Phœnicia and of the wails of our holiest monks. Wherefore I have written to you at some length, that on learning the agitation of the Church your excellency might stay it, and reap the fruits of the benefit which such action will produce.

LXXXII. To Eusebius, bishop of Ancyra.[2]

I had hoped at this time to hear frequently from your holiness. Suffering as I do under charges which are plain calumny I stand in need of brotherly consolation. For they who are now renewing the heresy of Marcion, Valentinus, Manes, and of the other Docetæ, annoyed at my publicly pillorying their heresy, have endeavoured to deceive the imperial ears, by calling me a heretic and falsely accusing me of dividing into two sons our one Lord Jesus Christ, the divine Word made man. Their utterances did not meet with the success that they expected. A despatch was therefore written to the right honourable and glorious commander and consul, containing indeed no accusation of heresy, but certain other charges no less

---

[1] Cf. note on page 276.

[1] II. Tim. iii. 12.
[2] Eusebius was present at the Council of Chalcedon in 451 Mansi vi. 565 c. See also Letter CIX. A Latin translation of this letter is in Baronius ann. 443.

unfounded. They alleged that I was endeavouring to assemble frequent synods at Antioch; that certain persons thereupon took umbrage; that for this reason I ought to desist from these proceedings and manage the churches entrusted to my charge. When this communication was shewn me I caught at the sentence as an opportunity of good. For in the first place I gained the rest I so much longed for; furthermore I trust in the wiping out of the stains of the many errors I have committed, on account of the wrong devised against me by the enemies of truth. Even in this present life our supreme Ruler very plainly shews us what care He takes of them that suffer wrong. While I have been remaining at rest, prisoned within the boundaries of my own country; while throughout the East all men have been distressed and have been bitterly lamenting though compelled to silence by the terror that has fallen on them (for what has befallen me has stricken terror into the hearts of all) the Lord has stooped from heaven, has convicted my calumniators of their falsehood, and laid bare their impious intent. They armed even Alexandria against me and by means of their worthy instruments are dinning into all men's ears that I am preaching two sons instead of one.

I, on the contrary, am so far from holding this abominable opinion, that, on finding some of the holy fathers of the Nicene Council opposing in their treatises the madness of Arius and forced in their struggle against their opponents to make too marked a distinction, I have objected, and refused to admit such distinction, for I know how the exigencies of the distinction result in exaggeration.

And lest any one should suppose that I am speaking as I do through fear, let any one who likes get hold of my ancient writings written before the Council of Ephesus, and those written after it twelve years ago. For by God's grace I interpreted all the Prophets and the Psalms and the Apostles: I wrote long ago against the Arians, the Macedonians, the sophistry of Apollinarius and the madness of Marcion: and in every one of my books by God's grace the mind of the Church shines clear. Moreover I have written a book on the Mysteries, another on Providence, another on the Questions of the Magi, a life of the Saints, and besides these, not to name every one in detail, many more.[1]

I have enumerated them not for ambition's sake, but to challenge my accusers and my judges to put any of my writings they may choose to the test. They will find that by God's grace I hold no other opinion than just that which I have received from holy Scripture.

When, then, your holiness has heard this from me, I beg you to inform the ignorant and to persuade the unbridled tongues that revile me and all who are deceived by them, not to believe what they have heard of me from my calumniators. Beg them to believe rather the Lawgiver when he exclaims "Men shall not receive a false report."[1] Ask them to wait till the facts are proved.

My prayer is that the churches may enjoy a calm and that this long and painful storm may vanish away. But if the multitude of our sins suffer not this to come to pass; if for their sakes we are delivered to the sifter; we pray that we may share the perils undergone for the faith, in order that since we have not the confidence that comes from this life, at least for guarding the faith in its integrity we may meet with pity and pardon in the day of the appearance of the Lord. And for this we beseech your holiness to join us in our prayers.

LXXXIII. Of Theodoretus, bishop of Cyrus, to Dioscorus, Archbishop of Alexandria.

To them that suffer under false accusation the greatest comfort is given by the words of Scripture. When such a sufferer is wounded by the lying words of an unbridled tongue, and feels the sharp stings of distress, he remembers the story of the admirable Joseph, and as he beholds that model of chastity, an exemplar of every kind of virtue, suffering, under a calumnious charge, imprisoned and fettered for invading another man's bed, and spending a long time in a dungeon, his pain is lightened by the remedy that the story furnishes. So again when he finds the gentle David, hunted as a tyrant by Saul, and then catching his enemy and letting him go unharmed, an anodyne is given him in his distress. But when he sees the Lord Christ Himself, Maker of the ages, Creator of all things, very God, and Son of the very God, called a gluttonous man and a wine bibber by the wicked Jews, it is not only consolation but rather great joy that is given him in that he is deemed worthy of sharing the sufferings of the Lord.

---

[1] The works mentioned are (a) those on the Octateuch, the Books of Samuel, Kings, and Chronicles, the Psalms, Canticles, and the Prophets; (β) on the xiv Epp. of St. Paul, including the Hebrews; the *Dialogues*, and the *Hæreticarum*

Fabularum Compendium; (γ) XII Books on the mysteries of the Faith; (ε) the "*de Providentia;*" (ζ) on the *Questions of the Magi*, and (η) the *Religious History*. Of these (γ) and (ζ) are lost.
[1] Ex. xxiii. 1. lxx. and marg.

Thus I was compelled to write when I read the letters of your holiness to the most pious and sacred archbishop Domnus, for there was contained in them the statement that certain men have come to the illustrious city administered by your holiness, and have accused me of dividing the one Lord Jesus Christ into two sons, and this when preaching at Antioch, where innumerable hearers swell the congregation. I wept for the men who had the hardihood to contrive the vain calumny against me. But I grieved, and, my Lord, forgive me, forced as I am by pain to speak, that your pious excellency did not reserve one ear unbiassed for me instead of believing the lies of my accusers. Yet they were but three or four or about a dozen, while I have countless hearers to testify to the orthodoxy of my teaching. Six years I continued teaching in the time of Theodotus, bishop of Antioch, of blessed and sacred memory, who was famous alike for his distinguished career and for his knowledge of the divine doctrines. Thirteen years I taught in the time of bishop John of sacred and blessed memory, who was so delighted at my discourses as to raise both his hands and again and again to start up: your holiness in your own letters has borne witness how, brought up as he was from boyhood with the divine oracles, the knowledge which he had of the divine doctrines was most exact. Besides these this is the seventh year of the most pious lord archbishop Domnus.[1] Up to this present day, after the lapse of so long a time, not one of the pious bishops, not one of the devout clergy has ever at any time found any fault with my utterances. And with how much gratification Christian people hear our discourses your godly excellency can easily learn, alike from those who have travelled thence hither, and from those who reached your city from us.

All this I say not for the sake of boasting, but because I am forced to defend myself. It is not the fame of my sermons to which I am calling attention; it is their orthodoxy alone. Even the great teacher of the world who is wont to style himself last of saints and first of sinners, that he might stop the mouths of liars was compelled to set forth a list of his own labours; and in shewing that this account of his sufferings was of necessity, not of free will, he added "I am become a fool in glorying; ye have compelled me."[2] I own myself wretched — aye thrice wretched. I am guilty of many errors. Through faith alone I look for finding some mercy in the

day of the Lord's appearing. I wish and I pray that I may follow the footprints of the holy Fathers, and I earnestly desire to keep undefiled the evangelic teaching which was in sum delivered to us by the holy Fathers assembled in council at the Bithynian Nicæa. I believe that there is one God the Father and one Holy Ghost proceeding from the Father:[1] so also that there is one Lord Jesus Christ, only begotten Son of God, begotten of the Father before all ages, brightness of His glory and express image of the Father's person,[2] on account of man's salvation, incarnate and made man and born of Mary the Virgin in the flesh. For so are we taught by the wise Paul "Whose are the Fathers and of whom as concerning the flesh Christ came, who is over all, God blessed for ever. Amen,"[3] and again "Concerning His Son Jesus Christ our Lord which was made of the seed of David according to the flesh and declared to be the Son of God with power according to the spirit of holiness."[4] On this account we also call the holy Virgin "Theotokos,"[5] and deem those who object to this appellation to be alienated from true religion.

In the same manner we call those men corrupt and exclude them from the assembly of the Christians, who divide our one Lord Jesus Christ into two persons or two sons or two Lords, for we have heard the very divine Paul saying "One Lord, one faith, one baptism"[6] and again "One Lord Jesus Christ by Whom are all things"[7] and again "Jesus Christ the same yesterday and to-day and for ever"[8] and in another place — "He that descended is the same also that ascended up far above all heavens."[9] And countless other passages of this kind may be found in the Apostle's writings, proclaiming the one Lord.

So too the divine Evangelist exclaims, "And the Word was made flesh and dwelt among us and we beheld His glory, the glory as of the only begotten of the Father, full of grace and truth."[10]

And his namesake exclaimed, "After me cometh one who is preferred before me for He was before me."[11] And when he had shewn one person, he expressed both the divine and the human, for the words "man" and "comes" are human, but the phrase "He was before me" expresses the divine. But

1 Domnus succeeded his Uncle John at Antioch in 441.
2 II. Cor. xii. 11.

1 The first formal insertion of the addition *filioque* is said to be in a Creed put forth at a council of Toledo about A.D. 400. At the third council of Toledo A.D. 589, the Nicæno-Constantinopolitan Creed was promulgated with the addition — "*ex Patre et Filio procedentem.*"
2 Heb. i. 3.   6 Eph. iv. 5.   10 John i. 14.
3 Rom. ix. 5.   7 I. Cor. viii. 6. 11 John i. 15.
4 Rom. i. 3, 4.   8 Heb. xiii. 8.
5 cf. note on page 213.   9 Ephes. iv. 10.

nevertheless he did not recognise a distinction between Him who came after and Him who was before, but owned the same being to be eternal as God, but born man, after himself, of the Virgin.

Thus too, the thrice blessed Thomas, when he had put his hand on the flesh of the Lord, called Him Lord and God, saying "My Lord and my God." [1] For through the visible nature he discerned the invisible.

So do we know no difference between the same flesh and the Godhead but we own God the Word made man to be one Son.

These lessons we have learnt alike from the holy Scripture and from the holy Fathers who have expounded it, Alexander and Athanasius, loud voiced heralds of the truth, who have been ornaments of your apostolic see; from Basil and from Gregory and the rest of the lights of the world; and that, in our endeavour to shut the mouths of them that dare to oppose the blessed Theophilus and Cyril, we use their works, our own writings testify. For we are most anxious by the medicines supplied by very holy men to heal them that deny the distinction between the Lord's flesh and the Godhead, and who maintain at one moment that the divine nature was changed into flesh, and at another that the flesh was transmuted into nature of Godhead.

For they clearly instruct us in the distinction between the two natures, and proclaim the immutability of the divine nature, calling the flesh of the Lord divine as being made flesh of God the Word; but the doctrine that it was transmuted into nature of Godhead they repudiate as impious.

I think that your excellency is well aware that Cyril of blessed memory often wrote to me, and when he sent his books against Julian to Antioch, and in like manner his book on the scapegoat, he asked the blessed John, bishop of Antioch, to shew them to the great teachers of the East; and in compliance with this request the blessed John sent us the books. I read them with admiration, and I wrote to Cyril of blessed memory; and he wrote back to me praising my exactitude and kindness. This letter I have preserved.

That I twice subscribed the writings of John of blessed memory concerning Nestorius my own hand bears witness, but this is the kind of thing whispered about me by men who try to conceal their own unsoundness by calumniating me.

Therefore I implore your holiness to turn your back on the liars; to give heed to the Church's quiet and either to heal by salutary medicines them that are trying to destroy the doctrines of the truth, or, if they refuse to accept your treatment, to expel them from the fold, to the end that the sheep may be spared from contagion. I beg you to give me your customary salutation. That I have written you my true sentiments is proved by my works on the holy Scriptures and against the Arians and Eunomians.

I will in addition write yet a brief word. If any one refuses to confess the holy Virgin to be "Theotokos," or calls our Lord Jesus Christ bare man, or divides into two sons Him who is one only begotten and first born of every creature, I pray that he may fall from hope in Christ, and let all the people say amen, amen.

Now that I have thus spoken, deign, my lord, to give me your sacred prayers, and to cheer me by a letter in reply telling me that your holiness has turned your back on my accusers.

I and my household salute all thy brotherhood in piety in Christ.

LXXXIV.   To the bishops of Cilicia.[1]

Your piety has heard of the calumnies directed against me. The opponents of the truth allege that I divide our one Lord Jesus Christ, the only begotten Son of God, into two sons, and it is said by some that a ground for their calumny is derived from a handful of men among you who hold these opinions, and who divide God the Word made man into two sons. They ought to listen to those words of the Apostle which openly declare "one Lord Jesus Christ by whom are all things," [2] and again "one Lord, one faith, one baptism." [3] They ought to have followed the Master's teaching, for the Lord Himself says "And no man hath ascended up to heaven, but he that came down from heaven, even the Son of man which is in Heaven." [4] And again "If ye shall see the Son of Man ascend up where He was before." [5] And the tradition of holy baptism teaches us that there is one Son, just as there is one Father and one Holy Ghost. I hope then that your piety will deign, if there really are any, though I cannot believe it, who disobey the apostolic doctrines to close their mouths, to rebuke them as the laws of the Church require, and teach them to follow the footsteps of the holy Fathers and preserve undefiled the faith laid down at Nicæa in Bithynia by the holy and blessed Fathers, as summing

---

[1] John xx. 28.

[1] This encyclical is probably of the same date as the preceding.
[2] I. Cor. viii. 6.   [4] John iii. 13.
[3] Ephes. iv. 5.   [5] John vi. 62.

up the teaching of Evangelists and Apostles. For it becomes you who love God to give heed both to God's glory and our common credit, and not to overlook the attacks which are made upon us all through the ignorance or contentiousness of these few men — if they really are guilty, and if they are not, like ourselves, suffering from the whetted tongues of false accusers.

Deign to remember us in your prayers to God, for so the law of love ordains.

LXXXV. To the bishop Basil.[1]

The chief good is said by the divine Paul to be love,[2] and by love he ordered the nurslings of the faith to be fed. Of this love your piety possesses great wealth, and so has told me what was befitting and given me pleasant news. For to them that fear the Lord what can be pleasanter than the health and harmony of the doctrines of the truth? Be well assured, most godly sir, that we were much delighted to hear the intelligence of our common friend; and in proportion to our previous distress at hearing that he described the nature of flesh and of Godhead as one, and openly attributed the passion of salvation to the impassible Godhead, so were all rejoiced to read the letters of your holiness, and to learn that he maintains in their integrity the properties of the natures, and denies both the change of God the Word into flesh, and the mutation of the flesh into the nature of Godhead, maintaining on the contrary that in the one Son, our Lord Jesus Christ, God the Word made man, the properties of either nature abide unconfounded. We praise the God of all for the harmony of divine faith. We have however written to either Cilicia,[3] although our intelligence is imperfect, as to whether there are really any opponents of the truth, and have charged the godly bishops to search and examine if there are any who divide the one Lord Jesus Christ into two sons, and either to bring them to their senses by admonition, or cut them off from the roll of the brethren. For in fact we equally repudiate both those who dare to assert one nature of flesh and Godhead, and those who divide the one Lord Jesus Christ into two sons and strive to go beyond the definitions of the Apostles.

But let your holiness be well assured that we are disposed to peace. For if the prophet says, "With them that hate peace I was

peaceful," [1] much more readily do we welcome the peace of God.

Some of those men who have been fed on lies have hurried to Alexandria and patched up calumnies against me, with the result that the godly bishop of that city, led away by their statements, although he had been fully informed by my letters, has sent a pious bishop to the imperial city. I beg you therefore to shew your accustomed kindness to him, and to confront falsehood with the truth.

LXXXVI.[2] To Flavianus, bishop of Constantinople.

At the present time, most God-beloved lord, I have received many buffetings of billows, but I called upon the great Pilot, and have been able to stand firm against the storm; the attacks, however, now made upon me transcend every story in tragedy. In relation to the attacks which are being plotted against the apostolic faith, I thought that I should find an ally and fellow-worker in the most godly bishop of Alexandria, the lord Dioscorus,[3] and so sent him one of our pious presbyters, a man of remarkable prudence, with a synodical letter informing his piety that we abide in the agreement made in the time of Cyril of blessed memory, and accept the letter written by him as well as that written by the very blessed and sainted Athanasius to the blessed Epictetus, and, before these, the exposition of the faith laid down at Nicæa in Bithynia by the holy and blessed Fathers. We exhorted him to induce those who are unwilling to abide by these documents at once to abide by them. But one of the opposite party, who keep up these disturbances, by tricking some of those who are on the spot and contriving countless calumnies against myself has stirred an iniquitous agitation against me.

But the very godly bishop Dioscorus has written us a letter such as never ought to have been written by one who has learnt from the God of all not to listen to vain words. He has believed the charges brought against me as though he had made personal enquiry into every one of them, and had arrived at the truth after questioning, and has thus condemned me. I however have bravely borne the calumnious charge, and have written him back a courteous letter, representing to his piety that the whole charge is

---

[1] There appears to be nothing in this letter or in Letter CII. also addressed to bishop Basil to identify the recipient. Basil bishop of Seleucia in Isauria was at the Latrocinium and at Chalcedon. Basil, bishop of Trajanopolis was also present at the same councils. Garnerius is in favour of the former, and notes the date as 448.
[2] I. Cor. xiii. 13.   [3] Vide note on p. 44.

[1] Ps. cxx. 6 and 7. lxx.
[2] This important letter may be placed between the sentence of deposition issued by Dioscorus in Feb. 448 and the imperial edict of March 449; probably before November 448, when Eutyches was arraigned before the Synod of Constantinople presided over by Flavian.
[3] cf. Letter LX, written probably not long after the consecration of Dioscorus in 444.

false, and that not one of the godly bishops of the East holds opinions contrary to the apostolic decrees. Moreover the pious clergy whom he sent as messengers have been convinced by the actual evidence of the facts. These however he has dismissed unheeded, and, lending his ears to my calumniators, has acted in a manner quite incredible, were it not that the whole church bears witness to it. He put up with them that were crying Anathema against me; nay he stood up in his place and confirmed their words by adding his voice to theirs. Besides all this he sent certain godly bishops to the imperial city, as we learnt, in the hope of increasing the agitation against me. I in the first place have for champion Him who seeth all things, for it is on behalf of the divine decrees that I am wrestling — next after Him I invoke your holiness to fight in defence of the faith that is attacked, and do battle on behalf of the canons that are being trodden under foot. When the blessed Fathers were assembled in that imperial city [1] in harmony with them that had sat in council at Nicæa, they distinguished the dioceses, and assigned to each diocese the management of its own affairs, expressly enjoining that none should intrude from one diocese into another. They ordered that the bishop of Alexandria should administer the government of Egypt alone, and every diocese its own affairs.[2]

Dioscorus, however, refuses to abide by these decisions; he is turning the see of the blessed Mark upside down; and these things he does though he perfectly well knows that the Antiochene metropolis possesses the throne of the great Peter, who was teacher of the blessed Mark, and first and coryphæus of the chorus of the apostles.[3]

But I know the majesty of the see, and I know and take measure of myself. I have learnt from the first the humility of the Apostles. I beseech your holiness not to overlook the trampling underfoot of the holy canons, and to stand forward zealously as champion of the divine faith, for in that faith we have hope of our salvation and on its ac-

count are confident that we shall meet with mercy.

But that your holiness may not be ignorant of this, know, my lord, that he shewed his ill-will towards me from the time of my assenting, in obedience to the canons of the holy Fathers, to the synodical letters issued in your see in the time of Proclus of blessed memory; on this point he has chidden me once and again on the ground of my violating the rights of the church of Antioch and, as he says, of that of Alexandria. Remembering this, and finding, as he thinks, an opportunity, he has exhibited his hostility. But nothing is stronger than the truth. Truth is wont to conquer even with few words. I beseech your holiness to remember me in your prayers to the Lord that I may have power to prevail against the waves that are beating me hither and thither.

LXXXVII. To Domnus, bishop of Apamea.[1]

The law of brotherly love demanded that I should receive many letters from your godliness at this time. For the divine Apostle charges us to weep with them that weep and rejoice with them that do rejoice.[2] I have not received a single one, although just lately I was visited by some of the pious monks of your monastery with the pious presbyter Elias. Nevertheless I have written, and I salute your holiness; and I make you acquainted with the fact that the consolation of the Master has stood me in stead of all other, for in truth not even had I as many mouths as I have hairs on my head, could I worthily praise Him for my being deemed worthy of suffering on account of my confession of Him, and for the apparent disgrace which I hold more august than any honour. And if I be banished to the uttermost parts of the earth all the more will I praise Him as being counted worthy of greater blessings. Nevertheless I hope your holiness will put up prayers for the quiet of the holy churches. It is because of the storm that is assailing them that I wail and groan and lament. That quiet, as I know, was driven away by the Osrhoene clergy,[3] who poured out countless words against me, although I had no share in their condemnation, nor in the sentence passed upon them; on the contrary, as your holiness knows, I besought

---

[1] i.e. in Constantinople in 381. The second Canon of the Council is referred to,—confining each bishop to his own "diocese," i.e. a tract comprising more than one province. So the bishop of Alexandria was restricted to Egypt.

[2] The immediate cause of this enactment by the Constantinopolitan Fathers was the interference of Peter of Alexandria in the appointment to the see of Constantinople, when the orthodox party nominated Gregory of Nazianzus. cf. p. 136.

[3] The third Canon of Constantinople had enacted that henceforth the see of the new capital should rank next after Rome. In the text the precedence of Antioch before Alexandria is based on association with St. Peter. "The so-called Cathedra Petri, which is kept in a repository of the wall of the apse of the Vatican Basilica," and was "exhibited in 1866" "is probably a throne made for or presented to Charles the Bold in 875." Dict. Christ. Ant. ii. 1960. For the connexion of St. Peter with Antioch see Routh Rell. Sac. i. 179.

[1] Domnus of Apamea is to be distinguished from Domnus II, bishop of Antioch the recipient of Letters XXXI, CX, CXII and CLXXX. He was present at Chalcedon in 451. This letter may be placed in 448-9.

[2] Romans xii. 15. Observe the inversion.

[3] The action of the Osrhoene clergy here referred to is their accusation of Theodoret's friend Ibas of Edessa. The "sentence" was that of excommunication delivered by Ibas. The leaders of the cabal against him were instigated by Uranius, bishop of Himeria, one of Ibas's suffragans. cf. note on p. 291.

that the communion might be given to them at Easter. But slanderers find no difficulty in saying what they like. My consolation lies in the blessing of the Master who said, " Blessed are ye when men shall revile you and persecute you and shall say all manner of evil against you falsely for my sake; rejoice and be exceeding glad: for great is your reward in heaven: for so persecuted they the prophets which were before you." [1]

LXXXVIII.   To Taurus the Patrician. [2]

Slanderers have forced me to go beyond the bounds of moderation, and compel me to write to you who have adorned the highest offices, and obtained the most distinguished honours. I therefore implore you to pardon me, for I do not write in self sufficiency, but because I am thrust forward by necessity. It is not because I expect to fall unjustly into trouble and distress, for this is the common fate of all who have sincerely served God, but because I desire to persuade your excellency that those who accuse my opinions are producing false charges against me. From my mother's breast I have been nurtured on apostolic teaching, and the creed laid down at Nicæa by the holy and blessed Fathers I have both learnt and teach. All who hold any other opinion I charge with impiety, and if any one persists in asserting that I teach the contrary, let him not bring a charge which I cannot defend, but convict me to my face. For this is agreeable to the laws alike of God and of man, but to whom is it so becoming to champion the wronged as to you, O friend of Christ, to whom boldness of utterance is given by the splendour of your lineage, the greatness of your rank and your foremost place in the law?

LXXXIX.   To Florentius the patrician. [3]

In sending a letter to your greatness I am daring what is beyond me, but the cause of my daring is not self-confidence, but the slanders of my calumniators. I have thought it well worth while to instruct your righteous ears how openly the impugners of my opinions are calumniating me. I have been guilty, I own, of many errors, but up to now I have ever kept the faith of the apostles undefiled, and on this account alone I have cherished the hope that I shall meet with mercy on the day of the Lord's appearing. On behalf of this faith I continue to

contend against every kind of heresy; this faith I am ever giving to the nurslings of piety; by means of this faith I have metamorphosed countless wolves into sheep, and have brought them to the Saviour who is the Arch-shepherd of us all. So have I learnt not only from the apostles and prophets but also from the interpreters of their writings, Ignatius, Eustathius, Athanasius, Basil, Gregory, John, and the rest of the lights of the world; and before these from the holy Fathers in council at Nicæa, whose confession of the faith I preserve in its integrity, like an ancestral inheritance, styling corrupt and enemies of the truth all who dare to transgress its decrees. I invoke your greatness, now that you have heard from me in these terms, to shut the mouths of my calumniators. It is in my opinion wholly unreasonable to accept as true what is charged against men in their absence; rather is it lawful and right that those who wish to appear as prosecutors should accuse the defendants in their presence, and endeavour to convict them face to face. Under these conditions the judges will without difficulty be able to arrive at the truth.

XC.   To Lupicinus the Master. [1]

I have passed through the contests of my prime. I see before me the confines of old age, and have expected as an old man to have more honour given me. But I am a mark for the shafts of slander, and am driven to meet by defence accusations levelled against me. Under these circumstances, I beseech your excellency not to believe the lies of my accusers. Had I been living a life of silence, there might have been room for the suspicion of unorthodoxy. But I am continually discoursing in the churches, and therefore have, by God's grace, innumerable witnesses to the soundness of what I teach. I follow the laws and rules of the apostles. I test my teaching by applying to it, like a rule and measure, the faith laid down by the holy and blessed Fathers at Nicæa. If any one maintain that I hold any contrary opinion, let him accuse me face to face; let him not slander me in my absence. It is fair that even the defendant should have an opportunity of speech, and meet with his defence the charges brought against him, and that then and not till then should the judges lawfully pronounce their sentence. This favour I beg

---

[1] Matt. v. 11, 12.

[2] Garnerius dates Letters LXXXVIII–CIX in 447. They belong rather to 448-449.

[3] Florentius, Præfect of the Imperial Guard, and already six times Præfect of the East, was present as a lay commissioner at the trial of Eutyches in 449 and at Chalcedon in 451.

[1] i.e., *magister officiorum*, one of the great state officers under the Constantinian constitution. He had control over posts, police, arsenals, and the imperial correspondence, and, from his authority in the palace, was a kind of " comptroller," or " master of the household." cf. Rufinus, p. 123.

through your excellency's assistance. If any men wish to condemn me unheard, I accept with willingness even their unjust sentence. For I wait for the judgment of the Master, where we need neither witnesses nor accusers. Before Him, as says the divine Apostle, "all things are naked and opened."[1]

XCI. To the prefect Eutrechius.[2]

I well know, and need no words to tell me, how your excellency regards me. Actions speak more clearly than words, but I have been anxious for you to know the cause of the accusation that is brought against me. For I am suffering under a most extraordinary charge, being at one and the same time attacked as unmarried, and as having been married twice.[3] If my present calumniators assert that I am falsifying the apostolic doctrine, why in the world, instead of accusing me in my absence, do they not attempt to convict me face to face? This fact alone is enough to give utter refutation to their lies, for it is because they know that I have innumerable witnesses to the apostolic character of my doctrines that they have urged an undefended indictment against me. Lawful judges must on the contrary keep one ear unbiassed for the accused. If they give both to the pleadings of the opponents, and deliver a sentence acceptable to them, I shall put up with the injustice as bringing me nearer to the kingdom of heaven, and shall await that impartial tribunal, where there is neither prosecutor, nor counsel, nor witness, nor distinction in rank, but judgment of deeds and words and righteous retribution. "For," it is said, "we must all appear before the judgment seat of Christ that every one may receive the things done in his body according to that he hath done whether it be good or bad."[4]

XCII. To Anatolius the Patrician.[5]

The very holy lord archbishop Domnus has arranged for the most pious bishops to repair to the imperial city, with a view to the complete refutation of the false accusation made against us all. At this time we stand in especial need of the aid of your magnificence, since the Lord of all has endowed you with the gifts of pure faith, of warm zeal in its behalf, of intelligence and capacity, and power withal to carry out your prudent counsels. I beg you therefore to defend the cause of the wronged, to contend against lies, and champion the apostolic teaching now assailed. Without doubt the master and guide of the churches will bless your endeavour, will scatter the lowering cloud, and bless the nurslings of the faith with clear sky. Even should He permit the tempest to prevail, your greatness will reap your perfect reward, and we shall bow our heads before the storm, ready to live with cheerfulness wheresoever it may drive us, and waiting the judgment of God and his true and righteous sentence.

XCIII. To Senator the Patrician.

I cherish an indelible memory of your magnificence, and now by very religious and holy bishops I salute you. The very holy lord bishop Domnus has arranged for them to journey to the imperial city in order to put an end to the false charges raised against him. For certain men have contrived manifest calumnies against me, and have grievously disturbed the churches for whose sake the Lord Christ "endured the Cross despising the shame";[2] in whose behalf the band of the divine apostles and companies of victorious martyrs were delivered to many kinds of death. On behalf of their peace I call on your magnificence to contend. It had been easy for the God of all to have nodded His head and scattered the lowering clouds; but He bides His time, and thereby at once shews the endurance of them that are assailed, and gives us opportunities of doing good.

XCIV. To Protogenes[3] the Præfect.

The loving-kindness of the Lord has already given you an opportunity of carrying out your good intentions. He has given you a greater opportunity now, that your excellency may the more easily champion the cause of the truth that is assailed, bring lies to nought, and give the churches the calm for which they so intensely long. Your excellency has already learned from many other sources how great is the surge by which the churches in the East are overwhelmed, but you will acquire more accurate information concerning it from the very religious bishops who, on account of it, have undertaken their long journey in

---

[1] Heb. iv. 13.
[2] vide p. 267.
[3] This appears to be merely a figurative description of the inconsistency of the charges, for there was no question of Theodoret's being a " digamos."
[4] II. Cor. v. 10.
[5] Seven Letters are addressed to Anatolius; viz., XLV, LXXIX, XCII, CXI, CXIX, CXXI, and CXXXVIII.

[1] Senator was consul in 436, three years after the probable date of Theodoret's earlier letter to him (cf. Letter XLIV. p. 264.) He was present at Chalcedon.
[2] Heb. xii. 2.
[3] Protogenes was Præfect of the East and Consul in 449 and was present at the Council of Chalcedon.

the winter, relying, next after the Grace of God, on the providence of your authority. Disperse for us, then, O Christian man, the storm, change the moonless night into clear sunshine, and bridle the tongues set wagging against us. We by God's grace are ever fighting for the apostolic decrees, and we preserve undefiled the faith laid down at Nicæa, and style impious all who dare to violate its dogmas. In evidence of the truth of what I say may be cited my catechumens, those who are from time to time baptized by me, and the hearers of my discourses in the churches. If they mean to accuse me in accordance with the law, they must convict me in my presence, not slander me in my absence. In this manner your excellency, when giving judgment in other cases, is wont to deliver your sentences, perceiving on which side lies the right from the pleadings both of the prosecution and of the defence.

XCV. To the præfect Antiochus.[1]

You have laid aside the cares of your very important government, but your fame flourishes among all; for they that have reaped the fruit of your benevolence, and they are many and everywhere, persistently extol it, proclaiming your good report in all directions, and stirring their hearers' tongues to join in the chorus of acclamation. When I behold the worthy fruit which adorns with its beauty its far-famed stem, I am delighted. For this reason I call your excellency to greater and higher deeds, and beseech you to give heed to the tranquillity of the churches. They have been overwhelmed with a great storm by the contrivers of calumnies against me, and under these circumstances the very religious bishops, making light of a long journey, of infirmity, and of old age, have left their own flocks unshepherded, and undertaken to travel this great distance, in their eagerness to confute the lies told against us all. I beseech your greatness to give them your protection, to shew care for the calumniated East, and your forethought for the welfare of the apostolic faith. It is only fitting that you should add this further glory to the rest of your good deeds.

XCVI. To Nomus the Patrician.[2]

I have written to you two letters, indeed I think three, but without getting any answer.

I had wished to say no more, but to know my own place and the greatness of dignities, and to beg you to inform me of the cause of your silence. Really I do not know what offence I can have given to your excellency. We err unwillingly as well as willingly, and sometimes are quite ignorant in what way we are transgressing. I therefore beg your greatness, remembering the divine laws which plainly charge us "If thy brother shall trespass against thee go and tell him his fault between him and thee alone"[1] to deign to make plain to me the origin of the annoyance, that I may either prove myself innocent, or, made aware of where I was wrong, may beg your pardon. In my confidence in the evidence of my conscience I hope for the former. All men are adorned by magnanimity, and not least those who, following the example of your excellency, trained in outside education as well as instructed in divine principles, both hear the apostolic laws loudly exclaiming "Let not the sun go down upon your wrath"[2] and remember the words of Homer[3]

"In fit bounds contain thy mighty mind;
Benignity is best."

I have thus written not as though giving you information, but to remind one who is much occupied, and I do so in remembrance of the law of the Lord, who says "Therefore if thou bring thy gift to the altar, and there rememberest that thy brother hath ought against thee; leave there thy gift before the altar, and go thy way; first be reconciled to thy brother and then come and offer thy gift."[4] In obedience to these words I have thought it right to salute your excellency by the most pious bishops, and to exhort you to give heed to the tranquillity of the churches. They are indeed overwhelmed by a great storm.

XCVII. To the Count Sporacius.[5]

I am delighted with your excellency's letter. My pleasure has been increased by the very religious presbyter and monk Iamblichus, who has told me of your warm zeal, your earnestness in religion, and your real goodwill to me. On hearing of this as well as of the efforts of the glorious and pious lord

---

[1] Antiochus was Consul in 431.

[2] cf. Letters LVIII and LXXXI. Nomus the consul and Nomus the patrician are distinguished in Schulze's Index to the Letters, but there seems no reason to doubt their identity. Nomus the powerful minister of Theodosius II. was consul in 445 and patrician in 449, to which year this third letter may be referred.

[1] Matt. xviii. 15.   [3] Il. ix. 256. cf. pp. 104 and 255.
[2] Ephes. iv. 26.   [4] Matt. v. 23, 24.
[5] Sporacius or Asporacius was present at Chalcedon in 451, as *comes domesticorum*, or one of the two commanders of the body guard. It was at his request that Theodoret wrote his *Hæreticarum fabularum compendium* which he dedicates "To the most magnificent and glorious lord Sporacius my Christ-loving son." To Sporacius was also addressed the short treatise "*adversus Nestorium*" of which some editors have doubted the genuineness. The present letter may be dated in 449.

Patricius[1] on my behalf I give you the apostolic blessing which the blessed Onesiphorus obtained from that holy tongue ; " The Lord give mercy to your house, for he oft refreshed me and was not ashamed of my chain ; " " The Lord grant unto him that he may find mercy of the Lord in that day." [2] This I pray for you, even though the enemies of the truth inflict on me yet greater miseries as they suppose ; for we have been taught to regard men's purpose ; but be sure of this, that with true religion death to me is very pleasant, and exile to the ends of the earth. Still we are distressed at the storm of the churches, which the Lord of all is mighty to disperse.

XCVIII. To Pancharius.

We are distressed to see the tempest of the churches, but their Master and Ruler ever through mighty billows shows to men His own wisdom and power. He rebukes the winds and brings about a calm as He did when He was in the apostles' boat.[3] So, though I am distressed, nevertheless because I know this power of our Saviour and am aware of what He arranges for us, even though adversity befall me, I give thanks, and accept it as a gift of God. I have learned the lesson to care little for the present, and to wait for the expected blessings. But it behoves your excellency zealously to defend the apostolic faith, that you may receive from the God of all the recompense of such conduct.

XCIX. To Claudianus the Antigrapharius.[4]

Although you have not yet met me, I think that your excellency is aware of the open calumnies that have been published against me, for you have often heard me preaching in church, when I have proclaimed the Lord Jesus, and have pointed out the properties alike of the Godhead and of the manhood ; for we do not divide one Son into two, but, worshipping the Only-begotten, point out the distinction between flesh and Godhead. This, indeed, is I think confessed even by the Arians, who do not call the flesh Godhead, nor address the Godhead as flesh. Holy Scripture clearly teaches us both natures. Nevertheless, though I have ever thus spoken, certain men are uttering lying words against me. But I rely on my conscience and have as witness to my teaching Him who looks into the hearts. So, as the prophet says, I regard the contrivances of

calumny as " a spider's web." [1] I await the great judgment which needs no words, but makes manifest what in the meanwhile is unknown.

I send this by the very religious bishops, thinking it worth while to salute your excellency by them and to remind you of your promise. For attacked as I am I do not cease to go a-hunting, for I know that even the sacred apostles in the midst of the assaults made upon them did not cease to ply the net of the spirit.

C. To Alexandra.[2]

I have recently received your excellency's letter. For the zeal you have shewn on my behalf I thank you, and pray the God of all to guard the goods you have, to increase them with further boons, and to grant you the enjoyment of future and everlasting blessings. I think that He hears the prayer even of them that are sentenced to relegation, and all the more when it is for the sake of His divine doctrine that they are undergoing apparent disgrace. I am writing by the very religious bishops, and I beg that they may meet with your kindly care. It is for the sake of the faith of the gospel and the peace of the churches that they have undertaken this long journey.

CI. To the Deaconess Celarina.

The flames of the war against us have been lit up again. After yielding awhile, the enemy of men has once more armed against us men nurtured in lies, who utter open slander against me, and say that I divide our one Lord Jesus Christ into two sons. I however know the distinction between Godhead and manhood, and confess one Son, God the Word made man. I assert that He is God eternal, who was made man at the end of days, not by the change of the Godhead, but by the assumption of the manhood. It is however needless for me to inform your piety of my sentiments, for you have exact knowledge of what I preach, and how I instruct the ignorant. I beseech you therefore since the workers of lies have poured their insults upon all the godly bishops of the East at once, and overwhelmed the churches with a storm, that your piety will show all possible zeal on behalf of the doctrines of the gospel and the peace of the churches. On this account the very godly bishops have left the churches shepherded by them, have disregarded the inclemency

---

[1] Cf. Letter XXXIV.   [2] II. Tim. i. 16 and 18.   [3] Matt. viii. 26.
[4] " Fuit vero ἀντιγραφεὺς apud Græcos quem Galli vocant Contrôleur général des finances." Garnerius.

[1] Isaiah lix. 5.   [2] cf. Letter XIV.

of winter, and endured the labours of their long journey, that they may calm the tempest which has arisen. I am sure that your godly excellency will regard them as champions of piety and governors of the churches.

CII. To Bishop Basilius.[1]

There is nothing remarkable in the reproaches that are directed against me being heard in silence by men who do not know me; but that your holiness should not refute the lies of my revilers, or at least should do so only to a certain extent, and with no great heartiness, passes the belief of any one who knows your character and conduct. And I say this not because friendship ought to be preferred to truth, but because the witness of truth is on the side of friendship. Your reverence has very often heard me preaching in church, and, in other assemblies where I have spoken on doctrinal questions; you have listened to what I have said, and I do not know of any occasion on which you have found fault with me for expressing unorthodox opinions. But what is the case at the present moment? Why in the world, my dear friend, do you not utter a word against falsehood, while you allow a friend to be calumniated and the truth to be assailed? If this is because you disregard the helpless and insignificant, remember the plain proclamation of the commandment of the Lord " Take heed that ye despise not one of these little ones which believe in me, for I say unto you that in heaven their angels do always behold the face of my Father which is in heaven." [2] If however it is the influence of my calumniators which imposes silence upon you, you must listen to the other law which says " Thou shalt not honour the person of the mighty " [3] and " Judge righteous judgment " [4] and " Thou shalt not follow a multitude to do evil " [5] and " He that shutteth his eyes from seeing evil and stoppeth his ears from hearing of blood." [6] You may find innumerable similar passages in holy Scripture, which I have thought it needless to collect when writing to a man brought up in the divine oracles, and watering Christian people with his teaching. But this I will say, that we shall all stand before the judgment seat of Christ, and shall give account of our words and deeds. I, who for every other reason dread this tribunal, now that I

am encompassed with calumny, find my chief consolation in the thought of it.

CIII. To the Count Apollonius.[1]

The very godly bishops have been led to travel to the imperial city by the calumnies uttered against me, and I by their holinesses send your excellency my salutation, and pay the debt of friendship, not indeed to wipe out the cherished obligation, but to make it greater. For in truth the obligations of friendship are increased by their discharge. That I should now be reaping the fruits of calumny is not extraordinary, for, in that I am human, there is nothing that I must not expect. All troubles of this kind must be borne by them that have learned wisdom; one thing only is distressing — that harm should accrue to the soul.

CIV. To Flavianus,[2] Bishop of Constantinople.

I have already in another letter informed your holiness how openly the calumniators of our teaching are slandering us.[3] Now in like manner by means of the very godly bishops I do the same, having not only these as witnesses of the orthodoxy of my teaching but also countless other men who are my hearers in the churches of the East. Above and beyond all these I have my conscience, and Him who sees my conscience. And I know too how the divine Apostle often appealed to the testimony of his conscience, for " our rejoicing is this, the testimony of our conscience " [4] and again " I say the truth in Christ I lie not, my conscience also bearing me witness in the Holy Ghost." [5] Know then, O holy and godly sir, that no one has ever at any time heard us preaching two sons; in fact this doctrine seems to me abominable and impious, for there is one Lord Jesus Christ through whom are all things. Him I acknowledge both as everlasting God and as man in the end of days, and I give Him one worship as only begotten. I have learned however the distinction between flesh and Godhead, for the union is unconfounded. Thus drawn up as it were in battle array to oppose the madness of Arius and Eunomius, we very easily refute the blasphemy hazarded by them against the only begotten, by applying what was spoken in humility about the Lord, and suitably to

---

[1] Cf. Letter LXXXV. There seems nothing to indicate whether this Basil is Basil of Seleucia or Basil of Trajanopolis, both of whom were present at the Latrocinium and took part against Theodoret. Garnerius refers it to the former, a timeserver of the court.
[2] Matt. xviii. 10 and 6.　　[4] John vii. 24.
[3] Leviticus xix. 15.　　[5] Ex. xxiii. 2.
[6] Isaiah xxxiii. 15. Observe the inversion.

[1] Cf. Letter LXXIII. Apollonius was "comes sacrarum largitionum" in 436.
[2] Cf. Letters XI. and LXXXVI. This letter may probably be placed between the sentence of internement and the assembling of the Latrocinium.
[3] Compare Letter LXXXVI.
[4] II. Cor. i. 12.　　[5] Rom. ix. 1.

His assumed nature, to man, and, on the other hand, what becomes the divine and signifies the divine nature, to God; not dividing Him into two persons, but teaching that both the former and latter attributes belong to the only begotten, the latter to Him as God the Creator and Lord of all, and the former as made man on our account. For divine Scripture says that He was made man, not by mutation of the Godhead, but by assumption of human nature, of the seed of Abraham. This the divine Apostle openly says in the words "For verily He took not on Him the nature of angels, but He took on Him the seed of Abraham, wherefore in all things it behoved Him to be made like unto His brethren."[1] And again "Now to Abraham and his seed were the promises made: he saith not and to seeds, as of many; but as of one, and to thy seed, which is Christ."[2]

These and similar passages have been cut out of divine Scripture by Simon, Basilides, Valentinus, Bardesanes, Marcion, and the man who is named after his maniacal heresy.[3] So they style the Master Christ God only, and describe Him as having nothing human about Him, but appearing in imagination and appearance as man to men. On the other hand the Arians and Eunomians say that God the Word assumed only a body, and that He Himself supplied the place of a soul in the body. And Apollinarius describes the Master's body as endued with a soul;[4] but, deriving, I know not whence, the idea of a distinction between soul and intelligence,[5] deprives intelligence of its share in the achieved salvation.[6] The teaching of the divine Apostles lays down on the contrary that a soul both reasonable and intelligent was assumed together with flesh, and the salvation of which the hope is held out to them that believe is complete.

There is yet another gang of heretics who hold differently. Photinus,[7] Marcellus,[8] and Paul of Samosata,[9] assert that our Lord and God was only man. When arguing with these we are under the necessity of advancing proofs of the Godhead, and of shewing that the Master Christ is everlasting God. When, on the other hand, we are contending with the former faction, which calls our Lord Jesus Christ God only, we are obliged to marshal against them the forces of the divine Scripture, and collect from it evidence of the assumption of the manhood. For a physician must use remedies appropriate to the disease, and suit the medicine to the case.

Now, therefore, I beseech your holiness to scatter the slander raised against me, and bridle the tongues now vainly reviling me. For, after the incarnation, I worship one Son of God, one Lord Jesus Christ, and denounce as impious all who hold otherwise. Deign, sir, to give me too your holy prayers, that, by God's grace, I may reach the other side of the ocean of danger, and drop my anchor in the windless haven of the Lord.

CV. To Eulogius the Œconomus.[1]

We have heard from many sources of your piety's efforts on behalf of true religion. It is therefore right that you should readily succour one who is calumniated for the same cause, and should refute the revilers' lies. You, O godly Sir, know what I hold, and what I teach, and that no one has ever heard of my preaching two sons. Exert, I implore you, in this case too your divine energy, and stop the mouths of the evil speakers. In conflicts of this kind one must help not only one's friends but even those who have caused us pain.

CVI. To Abraham the Œconomus.

By the godly bishops I salute you. I beseech you to give heed to the churches' calm, and to disperse the waves of calumny. "Whatsoever a man soweth that shall he also reap,"[2] as says the divine Apostle. Without doubt then he who fights for the apostolic doctrines shall reap the fruit of the apostolic blessing and enjoy the Apostles' devotion.

CVII. To the presbyter Theodotus.

The struggles which your piety has undergone on behalf of the apostolic doctrines are not unknown, but are frequently mentioned alike by those who have known them by experience, and by others who have heard of them from these. Continue, my dear sir, your efforts, and fight for the doctrines of the Fathers. For these I too am

---

[1] Heb. ii. 16. 17.   [3] i.e. Manes.   [5] ψυχή and νοῦς.
[2] Gal. iii. 16.   [4] ἔμψυχον.   [6] cf. pp. 132 and 140.
[7] Disciple of Marcellus. cf. Soc. ii. 30. Theodoret, in his interpretation of the Ep. to the Hebrews, links him with Sabellius. (Ed. Migne. iii. 547.)
[8] cf. p. 139.
[9] Patriarch of Antioch 260-270. Bp. Wordsworth calls him "the Socinus of the 3rd c." Samosata (Samsat) was capital of the Commagene in Syria.

[1] In an ecclesiastical sense the title œconomus was used of
(i) the treasurer of a particular church: e.g. Cyriacus of Constantinople (Chron. Pasch. p. 378).
(ii) a diocesan official. The Council of Chalcedon ordered that every diocese should have its œconomus.
(iii) the custos monasterii, who had charge of the secular affairs of the monastery, as the diocesan œconomus of those of the diocese.
[2] Gal. vi. 7.

buffeted in all directions and, while I receive the shock of the great waves, I beseech our Governor either to nod his head and scatter the tempest, or enable the victims of the storm by His grace to play the man.

CVIII. To Acacius the Presbyter.

True indeed is the promise of David's Psalm, for through him the Spirit of truth gave this promise to them that believe, " Commit thy way unto the Lord, trust also to him ; and he shall bring it to pass ; and he shall bring forth thy righteousness as the light and thy judgment as the noonday." [1] This we find too has come to pass in the case of your piety. For the great care you bestow upon them that are weeping for their orphanhood, and your struggles on behalf of the apostolic doctrines, are in every one's mouth, and so, as the prophets say, " Hidden things are made manifest." Since I too have heard of your piety's admirable exertions I write to salute you, most godly sir, and beseech you to increase your glory by adding to your labours, and to fight on behalf of the doctrine of the Gospels, that we may both keep the inheritance of our fathers unimpaired, and bring our Master His talent with good usury. [2]

CIX. To Eusebius, Bishop of Ancyra. [3]

Many are the devices secretly plotted against me, and through me patched up against the faith of apostles. I am however comforted by the sufferings of the Saints, Prophets, Apostles, Martyrs, and men famous in the churches in the word of Grace ; and besides these by the promises of our God and Saviour, for in this present life He has promised us nothing pleasant or delightful, but rather trouble, toil, and peril, and attacks of enemies. " In the world," He says, " ye shall have tribulation," [4] and " if they have persecuted me they will also persecute you," [5] and " If they have called the master of the house Beelzebub how much more shall they call them of his household," [6] and " The time cometh when whosoever killeth you will think he doeth God service," [7] and " Straight is the gate and narrow the way which leadeth unto life," [8] and " When they persecute you in this city flee you into another," [9] and I might quote all similar passages. The divine

Apostle too speaks in the same strain. " Yea and all that will live godly in Christ Jesus shall suffer persecution, but evil men and seducers shall wax worse and worse, deceiving and being deceived." [1] These words give me the greatest comfort in this distress. As the calumnies uttered against me have probably reached your holiness's ears, I beseech your holiness to give no credence to the lies of my slanderers. I am not aware of ever having taught anyone up to the present time to believe in two sons. I have been taught to believe in one only begotten, our Lord Jesus Christ, God the Word made man. But I know the distinction between flesh and Godhead, and regard as impious all who divide our one Lord Jesus Christ into two sons, as well as those who, travelling in an opposite direction, call the Godhead and manhood of the master Christ one nature. For these exaggerations stand opposed to one another, while between them lies the way of the doctrines of the Gospel, beautified by the footprints of prophets and apostles, and of all who after them have been conspicuous for the gift of teaching. I was anxious to adduce their opinions, and to point out how they bear witness in favour of my own, but I want more words than a letter allows room for, wherefore I have written summarily what I have been taught about the incarnation of the only begotten ; I send my statement to your godly excellency. [2] I have written not with the object of teaching others, but of making my defence against the accusations brought against me, and of explaining my sentiments to those who are ignorant of them. After your holiness has read what I have written, if you find it in conformity with the apostolic doctrines, I hope you will confirm my opinion by what you reply — if, on the contrary, anything that I have said jars with the divine teaching, I request to be told of it by your holiness. For, though I have spent much time in teaching, I still need one to teach me. " We know," says the divine Apostle " in part," [3] and again he says, " If any man think that he knoweth anything he knoweth nothing yet as he ought to know." [4] So I hope that I may hear the truth from your holiness, and that you may also give heed to the calm of the Church, and fight for the divine doctrines. It is for their sakes that the very godly bishops, making light of the difficulties of the journey, and of the winter, have set out for the imperial city, in the

---

[1] Psalm xxxvii. 5. 6.
[2] On the care of orphans in the early church vide Ig. Ep. Smyrn. VI. and Bp. Lightfoot's note. At Constantinople the Orphanotrophus was a priest of high rank.
[3] Cf. Letter LXXXII.   [5] John xv. 20.   [7] John xvi. 2.
[4] John xv. 33.   [6] Matt. 25.   [8] Math. vii. 14.
[9] Math. x. 23.

[1] II. Tim. iii. 12. 13.
[2] Garnerius supposes this to refer to Dial. II.
[3] I. Cor. xiii. 9.   [4] I. Cor. viii. 2.

endeavour to bring about some end to the storm. Send them I pray you, on their way with your prayers and with your prayers too strengthen me.[1]

CX. To Domnus, bishop of Antioch.[2]

When I read your letter I remembered the very blessed Susannah, who when she saw the famous villains, and believed that the God of all was present, uttered that remarkable cry, " I am straitened on every side ; "[3] but nevertheless preferred to fall into the snares of slander rather than to despise the just God. And I, sir, have two alternatives, as I have often said, to offend God and wound my conscience, or to fall by man's unjust sentence. The most pious emperor, I think, knows nothing of this. For what hindered him from writing, and ordering the ordination to take place, if in truth it so pleased him? Why in the world do they utter threats without and cause alarm, and yet do not send letters openly ordering it? One of two things must be true ; either the very pious emperor is not induced to write, or they are trying to make us break the law and afterwards be indicted by them for illegality. I have before me the example of the blessed Principius,[4] for in that case, when they had given orders by writing, they punished him for obedience. Moreover the letters which I read on the very day of the letter-bearer's arrival are of a contrary tenour. For one of the holy monks has written to some one that he has received letters both from the very illustrious guardsman and the very glorious ex-magister stating that the case of the very godly lord bishop Irenæus will stand more favourably, and in return for this good will they ask prayers on their behalf. I think therefore that a reply ought to be written to the clergy who have written from the imperial city to the effect that[5] " in

obedience to the sentence of the very godly bishops of Phœnicia, and knowing both the zeal and the magnanimity and love for the poor and all the other virtues of the very godly bishop Irenæus, and in addition to this the orthodoxy of his opinions, I have ordained him. I am not aware that he has ever objected to apply to the holy Virgin the title ' Theotokos,' or has ever held any other opinions contrary to the doctrines of the Gospel. As to the question of digamy, I have followed my predecessors ; for Alexander of blessed and sacred memory, the ornament of this apostolic see, as well as the very blessed Acacius, bishop of Berœa, ordained Diogenes of blessed memory who was a ' digamus ; '[1] and similarly the blessed Praylius ordained Domninus of Cæsarea who was a ' digamus.'[2] We have therefore followed precedent, and the example of men well known and illustrious both for learning and character. Proclus, bishop of Constantinople, of blessed memory well aware of this and many other instances, both himself accepted the ordination, and wrote in praise and admiration of it. So too did the leading godly bishops of the Pontic Diocese,[3] and all the Palestinians.

" No doubt has been raised about the matter, and we hold it wrong to condemn a man illustrious for many and various noble actions." In my opinion it is becoming to write in these terms. If your holiness holds any other view, let what seems good to you be done. I, as they suppose, have undergone one punishment, and am ready by God's help to undergo yet another. Even a third and fourth, if they like, by the stay of God's grace I will endure, praising the Lord. If your holiness thinks right, let us see what answer comes from Palestine, and, after considering more exactly what course is to be taken, let us so write to Constantinople.

CXI. To Anatolius the patrician.[4]

Your excellency will be recompensed for the kindness you have shewn me by the God

---

[1] The route of the bishops would be by land, in consequence of the dangers of the sea voyage in winter time. From Ancyra (Angora) they would follow the course of the Sangarius into Bithynia, and would cross thence via Chalcedon to Constantinople.

[2] This letter is placed by Garnerius in the end of 447 on account of its allusion to Proclus, who died in October 447, and to the deposition of Irenæus of Tyre, for which the formal edict was issued in Feb. 448, but which was perhaps rumoured earlier. But by some the death of Proclus is placed a year earlier.

[3] Hist. of Susannah 22.

[4] Of the blessed Principius nothing is known. cf. Tillemont, XV. 267.

[5] " The phraseology of this letter has given rise to much misapprehension. The use of the first person has led some to suppose that Theodoret, who belonged to another province, was the consecrator of Irenæus, or that he took part in his consecration, or even with the Abbé Martin (le Pseudo-Synode d'Éphèse, pp. 84, 85) that it is erroneously ascribed to Theodoret, and was really written by Domnus. It is clear from the tenor of the epistle that it was written by Theodoret, and that the first person is employed by him as writing in Domnus' name. (Tillemont xv. pp. 871, 872.) " Dict. Christ. Biog. iii. 281 n.

It is in consonance with this theory that Alexander of An-

tioch is described as bishop of *this* apostolic see, a phrase natural for Domnus to use, but not for Theodoret.

[1] It is uncertain who this Diogenes was ; he cannot have been Diogenes of Cyzicus, for he was alive and present at Chalcedon in 451.

[2] No more is known of. Domninus or Praylius. cf. p. 157. " It is clear from the Philosophumena of Hippolytus (ix, 12.) that by the beginning of the third century the rule of monogamy for the clergy was well established, since he complains that in the days of Callistus ' digamist and trigamist bishops, priests, and deacons *began* to be admitted.' " Dict. Christ. Ant. i. 552.

[3] The Pontic Diocese is one of the twelve civil divisions of the Constantinian empire.

[4] This letter is in reply to that written by Anatolius on the receipt of Letter XCII. Garnerius, who places the decree of relegation earlier than Tillemont, dates it about the end of April 448.

of all, for all that is done for His sake has its reward. I laugh at all my slanderers. The bodies of them who are most severely scourged do not feel the pain, because the scourged flesh is deadened. Still I lament over them whose unrestrained mouths utter such lies. In what way have the accusers of the godly bishop Ibas [1] been wronged by me that they should utter such calumnies against me? To begin with, I was not even one of the judges, for in obedience to the imperial decree I was living at Cyrus. Moreover, as I have heard from many, they all along treated my absence as a grievance, for I had arranged for their partaking of the Holy Communion at the Easter feast of salvation,[2] and as they often expressed a wish to meet me, I received them with kindness and advised them as to the proper course to take. But that I may also speak in the defence of the very godly bishop the lord Domnus, what was the proper course for him to take? He was openly attacked; he saw men deposed by a synodical sentence sent into another diocese, and resuming their priestly functions in violation of the laws of the Church; he saw things holy and divine laughed at and turned into ridicule by the enemies of the Church; what was he to do? When he knew this he handed over the case to others, and not only to the very godly lord Ibas, but also to the holy lord bishop Symeon of Amida, that the metropolitans of the two provinces might hear the charges. What fairness is there in charging the same persons with cruelty and kindness? If we excommunicate, we run into danger; if we do not excommunicate, we do not escape it. We alone of all the world are objects of attack. Other dioceses are at peace. We alone are exposed to calumniators, — specially I myself, though I took no part in the trial, and am absolutely without responsibility in the matter.

Thus have I been forced to write on reading your lordship's letter, and on learning from it how for these reasons a great commotion has been made against me, a man confined to my diocese; a man of peace; one not even deliberating with the godly bishops of the province. As a matter of fact, although there have been already two episcopal ordinations in our province, I took part in neither.

Were I not restrained by the imperial decree I would have gone away, and spent the remainder of my days in some remote spot. I am faint for the plots hatched against me. I am sure those Edessenes never put together their slander against me of their own accord. They were prompted to these attacks on me by their truly truthful neighbours. I thank our Saviour that he has deemed me worthy of the beatitudes of the Gospel, all unworthy though I be. For this reason I have gladly accepted the sentence of relegation. 'I am ready for exile, and, for the sake of the "hope laid up for me," [1] welcome whatever fate they may inflict. I pray without ceasing for your excellency, and beseech all the saints to share in my petitions.

CXII. To Domnus, bishop of Antioch.[2]

When news was brought to me that the pettiness of the victorious emperor had been put an end to, a reconciliation effected between him and the very godly bishop,[3] the summons to the council cancelled, and the peace of the churches restored, I hoped that our troubles were a thing of the past. But I am deeply distressed at what I hear from your holiness. It is impossible to hope for any good from this notorious council, unless the merciful Master with His wonted providence shall undo the riotous demons' devices. Even in the great synod, I mean that of Nicæa, the Arian party voted with the orthodox and set their hands to the apostolic exposition. But they did not cease to war against the truth till they had torn asunder the body of the Church. For thirty years the supporters of the apostolic doctrines and they who were infected with the Arian blasphemy continued in communion with one another. But at Antioch,[4] when the latest council was finished, when they had seated the man of God, the great Meletius, on the apostolic throne, and then after a few days ejected him by the imperial authority, Euzoius who was affected with the undoubted plague of Arius was put forward, and straightway the champions of apostolic doctrines seceded and thereafter the division continued.

As I look back on what happened then,

---

[1] The leaders of the attack on Ibas, (bishop of Edessa and metropolitan, in 436) were four presbyters, Samuel, Cyrus, Eulogius, and Maras. The cabal chose the moment for action when Domnus visited Hierapolis for the enthronization of Stephen, and in 445 Ibas was summoned by Domnus to Antioch, but did not come. In 448 the eighteen charges — some frivolous, some of gross heresy — were formally heard, and Domnus decided in favor of Ibas. cf. p. 283, note.

[2] i.e. recommended Ibas not to excommunicate his accusers.

[1] Col. i. 5.

[2] Garnerius points out that the indications of the date of this letter are clear. It mentions the imperial summons to the Latrocinium, and contains Theodoret's advice to Domnus as to what companions he should take with him. It must therefore be placed between the arrival of the summons at Antioch and the departure of Domnus for Ephesus. The summons is dated the 30th of March, and appointed the 1st of August for the meeting. Antioch is a clear thirty days' journey from Ephesus and Domnus had not yet chosen his companions. We may therefore date the letter in the May of 449.

[3] Presumably Irenæus of Tyre.

[4] i.e., in 361. For Theodoret's account of the circumstances vide pp. 92, 93.

and look forward to similar events in the future, my wretched spirit sighs and wails, for I see no prospect of good. The men of the other dioceses do not know the poison which lies in the Twelve Chapters ; [1] having regard to the celebrity of the writer of them, they suspect no mischief, and his successor in the see[2] is I think adopting every means to confirm them in a second synod. For supposing he who lately wrote them at command, and anathematized all who did not wish to abide by them, were presiding over an œcumenical council, what could he not effect? And be well assured, my lord, that no one who knows the heresy they contain will brook to accept them, though twice as many men of this sort decree them. Before now, though a larger number have rashly confirmed them, I resisted at Ephesus, and refused to communicate with the writer of them till he had agreed to the points laid down by me, and had harmonized his teaching with them, without making any mention of the Chapters. This your holiness can ascertain without any difficulty if you order the acts of the synod to be investigated ; for they are preserved as is customary with the synodical signatures, and there are extant more than fifty synodic acts shewing the accusation of the Twelve Chapters. For before the journey to Ephesus the blessed John [3] had written to the very godly bishops Eutherius of Tyana, Firmus of Cæsarea, and Theodotus of Ancyra, denouncing these Chapters as Apollinarian.[4] And at Ephesus the exposition and confirmation of these Chapters was the cause of our deposition of the Alexandrian and of the Ephesian.[5] Moreover at Ephesus many synodic letters were written both to the victorious emperor, and to the great officers, about these Chapters ; and in like manner to the laity at Constantinople and to the reverend clergy. Moreover when we were summoned to Constantinople we had five discussions in the imperial presence, and afterwards sent the emperor three protestations. And to the very godly bishops of the West, of Milan I mean, of Aquileia, and of Ravenna, we wrote on the same subject, protesting that the Chapters were full of the Apollinarian novelty. Furthermore their writer received a letter from the blessed John by the hands of the blessed Paul,[1] openly blaming them ; and in like manner from Acacius of blessed memory. And to give your holiness concise information on the subject I have sent you both the letter of the blessed Acacius, as well as that of the blessed John to the blessed Cyril, in órder that you may perceive that though they were writing to him on the subject of agreement they blamed these Chapters. And the blessed Cyril himself, in his letter to the blessed Acacius plainly indicated the drift of these Chapters in the words " I have written this against his innovations and when peace is made they will be made manifest." The very defence proves the accusation. I have sent you the copy of what he wrote at the time of the agreement, that you may see, my lord, that he made no mention of them, and that those who attend the Council are under an obligation to bring forward what was written at the time of the agreement, and to state plainly what had caused the difference and on what terms the sundered parts were atoned. For they who are summoned to fight for the truth must flinch from no toil, and must invoke the divine aid, that we may preserve unimpaired the heritage bequeathed us by our forefathers.

Your holiness must look out for men of like mind among the godly bishops and make them companions of your journey ; and likewise of the reverend clergy those who are zealous for the truth, lest betrayed even by them of our own side we are either driven to do something displeasing to the God of all, or, in our abandonment, fall an easy prey to our foes.

It is faith in which we have our hopes of salvation, and we must leave no means untried to prevent aught spurious being brought into it, and the apostolic teaching from being corrupted.

I write you these words from far away, with sighs and with groans, and I beseech our common Master to scatter this dark cloud and bestow on us once more the boon of the bright sunshine.

---

[1] Cyril wrote his IIIrd letter to Nestorius probably on Nov. 3, 430. " To the end of the letter were appended twelve 'articles' or 'chapters,' couched in the form of anathematisms against the various points of the Nestorian theory." " These propositions were not well calculated to reclaim Nestorius; nor were they indeed so worded throughout as to approve themselves to all who essentially agreed with Cyril as to the personal Deity of Christ. On the contrary the abruptness of their tone, and a certain one-sidedness . . . made some of them open, *prima facie*, to serious criticism from persons who, without being Nestorians, felt that in the attack on Nestorianism the truth of Christ's real and permanent manhood might be in danger of losing its due prominence." Canon Bright, Dict. Christ. Biog. i. 766.

[2] Dioscorus succeeded Cyril at Midsummer, 444.

[3] i.e. John of Antioch. He reached Ephesus June 27, 431.

[4] Eutherius of Tyana (Kiliss Hissar in Karamania) was a strong Nestorian, and signed the appeal of Nestorius after his deposition in 431. On July 17th John and his adherents were deposed. Firmus of the Cappadocian Cæsarea (still " Kasaria ") himself a graceful letter writer, was an anti-Nestorian. Theodotus of Ancyra also sided with Cyril.

[5] i.e. Cyril and Memnon. " No sooner had John reached Ephesus, than before he had washed and dressed after his journey, in the inn itself, late at night, in secret session, by the connivance of the Count Candidianus, a sentence was passed on Cyril and Memnon — on Cyril, on the accusation of Theodoret." Cf. Garnerius Hist. Theod., and Cyril. Ep. ad Cœlest. Labbe iii. 663.

[1] John of Antioch sent Paul of Emesa to confer with Cyril on terms of peace in 432.

CXIII. To Leo, bishop of Rome.

If Paul, the herald of the truth, the trumpet of the Holy Ghost, hastened to the great Peter[2] in order that he might carry from him the desired solution of difficulties to those at Antioch who were in doubt about living in conformity with the law, much more do we, men insignificant and small, hasten to your apostolic see[3] in order to receive from you a cure for the wounds of the churches. For every reason it is fitting for you to hold the first place, inasmuch as your see is adorned with many privileges. Other cities are indeed adorned by their size, their beauty, and their population; and some which in these respects are lacking are made bright by certain spiritual boons. But on your city the great Provider has bestowed an abundance of good gifts. She is the largest, the most splendid, the most illustrious of the world, and overflows with the multitude of her inhabitants. Besides all this, she has achieved her present sovereignty, and has given her name to her subjects. She is moreover specially adorned by her faith, in due testimony whereof the divine Apostle exclaims "your faith is spoken of throughout the whole world."[4] And if even after receiving the seeds of the message of salvation her boughs were straightway heavy with these admirable fruits, what words can fitly praise the piety now practised in her? In her keeping too are the tombs that give light to the souls of the faithful, those of our common fathers and teachers of the truth, Peter and Paul.[5] This

thrice blessed and divine pair arose in the region of sunrise, and spread their rays in all directions. Now from the region of sunset, where they willingly welcomed the setting of this life, they illuminate the world. They have rendered your see most glorious; this is the crown and completion[1] of your good things; but in these days their God has adorned their throne[2] by setting on it your holiness, emitting, as you do, the rays of orthodoxy. Of this I might give many proofs, but it is enough to mention the zeal which your holiness lately shewed against the ill-famed Manichees, proving thereby your piety's earnest regard for divine things. Your recent writings, too, are enough to indicate your apostolic character. For we have met with what your holiness has written concerning the incarnation[3] of our God and Saviour, and we have marvelled at the exactness of your expressions.

For both writings agreed in setting forth both the everlasting Godhead of the Only-begotten derived from the everlasting Father, and the manhood derived from the seed of Abraham and David; and that the nature assumed was in all things like unto us, being unlike to us in this respect alone, that it remained free from all sin; since it springs not of nature but of free will.

The letters moreover contain this, that the Only-begotten Son of God is one, and his Godhead impassible, immutable, and invariable, like the Father who begat Him and the Holy Spirit; and that on this account He took the passible nature, divine nature being incapable of suffering, that by the suffering of His own flesh He might bestow freedom from suffering on them that have believed in Him. These statements and others of like nature were contained in your letters. We, in admiration of your spiritual wisdom, have lauded the grace of the Holy Ghost uttered through you, and we invoke and beseech and beg and implore your highness to protect the churches of God that are now assailed by the storm.

We had expected that through the instrumentality of the representatives[4] sent by your holiness to Ephesus, the tempest

---

[1] This celebrated letter may be dated towards the end of 449, allowing time for news to reach Theodoret of his deposition at the Latrocinium on August 11. In 445 Leo had procured the well known decree from Valentinian III, addressed to the famous Aetius in connexion with the dispute with Hilary of Arles, constituting the bishop of Rome the chief authority in the Western Church, basing his demands not so much on the recognised precedence of the imperial see as on the supposed primacy of St. Peter. But in 451, only two years after the date of Theodoret's letter the council of Chalcedon (Can. xxviii), after recording the canon (iii) of Constantinople that "the bishop of Constantinople shall have the primacy of honour after the bishop of Rome, because that Constantinople is new Rome," added "we decree the same things concerning the privileges of Constantinople, which is new Rome. The Fathers formerly gave the primacy to the see of old Rome, because she was the imperial city, and gave like privileges to new Rome, rightly judging that the city which enjoyed like imperial privileges should also be honoured in matters ecclesiastical, being next in rank." We are yet very far from later claims. Indeed even Gregory the Great when he protested against the title of œcumenical bishop, assumed by John the Faster, did not claim it for himself.

[2] Paul and Barnabas went up to Jerusalem, not to Peter, but "unto the Apostles and elders." Acts xv. 2. Peter took a leading part in the discussion, but the "sentence" was pronounced not by Peter, but by James, and the decree was that of "the Apostles and elders with the whole Church." The slight "wresting" of the scriptures of which Theodoret is guilty is due rather to a desire to compliment an important personage than in anticipation of later controversies.

[3] Rome was the only apostolic see in the West.

[4] Rom. i. 8.

[5] The traditional places of sepulture are, of half of each of the holy bodies, the shrine of SS. Peter and Paul in the crypt of St. Peter's; of the remaining moiety of St. Peter the Lateran; of St. Paul, St. Paolo fuori le Mura.

[1] Κολοφών. cf. note on page 262.

[2] St. Paul is treated as in a sense bishop of Rome. The idea may have some bearing on the hypothesis sometimes adopted, to avoid the difficulties in the early Roman succession, that there was a Gentile line derived from St. Paul, who ordained Linus, and after him Cletus; and that for the Jewish brethren St. Peter ordained Clement.

[3] His dogmatic epistles and his sermons. He is not known to have written any large treatise.

[4] Dioscorus presided, and next him sat Julius of Puteoli, who in company with the presbyter Renatus, and the deacon Hilarius (successor to Leo in the papacy) had carried to Flavian the famous "tome" of Leo in June 449. Leo (Epp. XXXII. and XXXIV.) describes his legates as sent "de latere meo." According to one version of the story Renatus died at Delos on the way out. Labbe IV: 1079.

would have been done away, but we have fallen under severer attacks of the storm. For the very righteous bishop of Alexandria was not content with the illegal and very unrighteous deposition of the most holy and godly bishop of Constantinople, the lord Flavianus, nor was his soul satisfied with a similar slaughter of the rest of the bishops, but me too in my absence he stabbed with a pen, without summoning me to the bar, without trying me in my presence, without questioning me as to my opinions about the incarnation of our God and Saviour. Even murderers, tomb-breakers, and adulterers, are not condemned by their judges until they have themselves confirmed by confession the charges brought against them, or have been clearly convicted by the testimony of others. Yet I, nurtured as I have been in the divine laws, have been condemned by him at his pleasure, when all the while I was five and thirty days' march away.

Nor is this all that he has done. Only last year when two fellows tainted with the unsoundness of Apollinarius had gone thither and patched up slanders against me, he stood up in church and anathematized me, and that after I had written to him and explained my opinions to him.

I lament the disturbance of the church, and long for peace. Six and twenty years have I ruled the church entrusted to me by the God of all, aided by your prayers. Never in the time of the blessed Theodotus,[1] the chief bishop of the East; never in the time of his successors in the see of Antioch, did I incur the slightest blame. By the help of God's grace working with me more than a thousand souls did I rescue from the plague of Marcion; many others from the Arian and Eunomian factions did I bring over to our Master Christ. I have done pastoral duty in eight hundred churches, for so many parishes does Cyrus contain; and in them, through your prayers, not even one tare is left, and our flock is delivered from all heresy and error. He who sees all things knows how many stones have been cast at me by evil heretics, how many conflicts in most of the cities of the East I have waged against pagans, against Jews, against every heresy. After all this trial and all this danger I have been condemned without a trial.

But I await the sentence of your apostolic see. I beseech and implore your holiness to succour me in my appeal to your fair and righteous tribunal. Bid me hasten to you, and prove to you that my teaching follows the footprints of the apostles. I have in my

possession what I wrote twenty years ago; what I wrote eighteen, fifteen, twelve, years ago; against Arians and Eunomians, against Jews and pagans; against the magi in Persia; on divine Providence; on theology; and on the divine incarnation. By God's grace I have interpreted the writings of the apostles and the oracles of the prophets. From these it is not difficult to ascertain whether I have adhered to the right rule of faith, or have swerved from its straight course. Do not, I implore you, spurn my prayer; regard, I implore you, the insults piled after all my labours on my poor grey head.

Above all, I implore you to tell me whether I ought to put up with this unrighteous deposition or not; for I await your decision. If you bid me abide by the sentence of condemnation, I abide; and henceforth I will trouble no man, and will wait for the righteous tribunal of our God and Saviour. God is my witness, my lord, that I care not for honour and glory. I care only for the scandal that has been caused, in that many of the simpler folk, and especially those whom I have rescued from various heresies, cleaving to the authority of my judges and quite unable to understand the exact truth of the doctrine, will perhaps suppose me guilty of heresy.

All the people of the East know that during all the time of my episcopate I have not acquired a house, not a piece of ground, not an obol, not a tomb, but of my own accord have embraced poverty, after distributing, at the death of my parents, the whole of the property which I inherited from them.

Above all I implore you, O holy sir, beloved of God, to grant me the help of your prayers. I have told you this by the reverend and godly presbyters Hypatius and Abramius chorepiscopi[1] and by Alypius exarch[2] of our monks. I would hasten to you myself were I not kept back by the chains of the imperial order, which imprison me as they do others. Treat my messengers, I beseech you, as a father might his sons; give them kindly and unbiassed audience; deign to grant your protection to my old age,[3] slandered as it is and attacked in vain. Above all, regard, to the utmost of your power, the faith conspired against; preserve for the churches the inheritance of their fathers un-

---

[1] Patriarch at Antioch 420-429.

[1] No word exactly renders the title of these ministers, discharging functions of an episcopal kind, though without high responsibility. They are first mentioned in the Councils of Ancyra and of Neo-Cæsarea and fifteen of them subscribed the decrees of Nicæa.

[2] Exarch, in its most ordinary ecclesiastical sense nearly equivalent to patriarch, came also to be used of officers charged with the visitation of monasteries.

[3] If born in 386 (Garnerius), Theodoret would now be 63. Tillemont says 393.

impaired. So will your holiness receive the recompense due for such deeds from the great Giver of all good gifts.[1]

CXIII. (a).[2] From Pope Leo to Theodoret.

To our much beloved brother Theodoretus, bishop, Leo, bishop.

CXIV.[3] To Andiberis.

The reverend presbyter Peter is distinguished not only by his priestly rank, but also by his wise practice in medicine. During his long residence with us he has won all hearts by his conciliatory manners. On learning of my departure he has now determined to leave Cyrus; I therefore commend him to your excellency, and hope that, fully capable as he is of doing good service to the city, — for when he lived at Alexandria he practised the same profession, — he will meet with kindness at your hands.

CXV. To Apella.

When I undertook the direction of the see of Cyrus, I procured for it from all directions men who practised necessary arts, and besides this induced skilful physicians to live there. Of these one is the reverend presbyter Peter, who practises his profession with wisdom, and adorns it by his character. On my departure, several have left the city and Peter also has determined to leave. Under these circumstances I beseech your excellency to give him your kind care. He is well able to attend the sick and to wage war against their ailments.

CXVI.[4] To the presbyter Renatus.

We have heard of the warm and right-eous zeal of your holiness, and the just and lawful boldness of speech which you employed in condemning the audacious proceedings at Ephesus. Nor is this known to us alone, but the fame of your orthodoxy has gone out into all lands, and all men are celebrating your righteousness, your zeal, your boldness, and your denunciation of my unfair treatment. And your holiness took this course after seeing one massacre. If you had seen the others which took place after your departure you would perhaps have emulated the fervour of the famous Phinehas.[1] I am one of those who was subsequently condemned, being forbidden by the imperial order to attend the council, and sentenced in my absence.[2]

Six and twenty years have I been a bishop; innumerable labours have I undergone; I have struggled hard for the truth; I have freed tens of thousands of heretics from their errors and brought them to the Saviour; and now they have stripped me of my priesthood; they are exiling me from the city. For my old age, for my hairs grown gray in the truth, they have no respect. Wherefore, I beseech your sanctity, persuade the very sacred and holy archbishop[3] to bid me hasten to your council. For that holy see has precedence over all churches in the world, for many reasons; and above all for this, that it is free from all taint of heresy, and that no bishop of heterodox opinion has ever sat upon its throne, but it has kept the grace of the apostles undefiled.[4] Confident in your justice I shall accept your decisions, whatever they may be, and shall claim to be judged by my writings. More than thirty books have I written against Arius and Eunomius, against Marcion, against Macedonius, against the heathen and against Jews; I have interpreted the holy Scriptures, and any one who likes may easily learn that I have followed in the steps of the apostles, proclaiming the one Son, one Father, and one Holy Ghost; one Godhead of the Trinity, one sovereignty, one power, eternity, immutability, impassibility, one will;[5] that the Godhead of the Lord Jesus Christ was perfect, perfect the

---

[1] The tone of this letter, it need hardly be said, is quite inconsistent with the later idea of an "appeal to Rome." It is "an appeal," but the appeal of a wronged man for the support, succour, and advice, of a brother bishop of the highest position and character. It does not on the face of it suggest that Leo has any authority to review or alter the sentence of the council. Tillemont (Mém. Ecc. xv. 294) observes that though addressed to Leo in person the appeal is really made to the bishops of the West in council. Leo remonstrated, but Theodosius and his court maintained that the decrees of the Latrocinium must stand.

[2] In Migne's edition here follows the reply of Leo to Theodoret, which appears as Letter CXX. in the works of Leo.

[3] Written after the deposition at Ephesus, and when Theodoret is either on the point of departing, or has departed, from Cyrus to the Apamean monastery. The simultaneous exercise of the clerical and medical professions points perhaps to the continuance of the class of "Silverless martyrs," i.e. physicians who took no fee but healed on condition that their patients should turn to Christ. The legendary Saints of the unfeed faculty are Cosmo and Damian, the brothers whose church occupies the site of the Temple of Remus, or of the Penates, in the Roman Forum.

[4] This letter will be of the same date as CXIII. Theodoret was aware that Leo was to be represented at the Latrocinium by Renatus as well as by Julius of Puteoli and the archdeacon Hilarius, but had not heard that he had never reached Ephesus. We are told on the authority of Felix, the author of the "Breviarium Hæresis Eutychianæ" that Renatus died at Delos on the way out. This death is however discredited by Quesnel and some other authorities.

[1] Numbers xxv. 7.

[2] Hilarius did leave Ephesus before the second session of the council (Cf. Leo Ep. XLVI) and before the deposition of Theodoret, when Heraclius was trying to bring about the "massacre" may refer to the brutal treatment of Flavian by the adherents and bullies of Dioscorus.

[3] i.e. Leo.

[4] This is more or less true up to the time of Leo the great, but Leo the great was the first pope who was an eminent theologian. Liberius is a doubtful case. Cf. page 76.

[5] The Monothelite Controversy dates from two centuries after Theodoret, when Heraclius was trying to bring about religious union in his empire. Pope Honorius asserted two energies, but one will. Monothelitism was definitely condemned at Constantinople in 681, and Honorius anathematized.

manhood taken for our salvation and for our sakes delivered unto death. I do not know one Son of man and another Son of God, but one and the same, Son of God and God begotten of God, and Son of man, through the form of the servant, of the seed of Abraham and David. These and like doctrines I continue to teach; these also I have found in the writings of the most holy and sacred lord archbishop Leo, and I praise the Lord of all that I agree with his apostolic doctrines. Receive, I beseech you, my supplication, and do not overlook the wrongs under which I suffer. On this account I have sent to your holiness the godly presbyters Hypatius and Abramius, chorepiscopi, and Alypius exarch of our monks, adorned as they are by good lives, and able by word of mouth to give you exact information as to the affairs of my insignificant self.

CXVII.   To the bishop Florentius.[1]

Truly the grace of our God and Saviour has not yet abandoned the human race, but has left us a seed in your holiness " lest we should become as Sodom, and be made like unto Gomorrah." [2] This seed suffers us not altogether to faint, but charges us to wait for the passing away of the dire storm; this renders us hopeful.

We have therefore sent to your holiness the very godly presbyters Hypatius and Abramius, chorepiscopi, and Alypius, exarch of our monks, that you may put an end to the disaster which has befallen the churches of the East; that in the first place you may confirm the faith handed down to us from the first by the holy Apostles, may proscribe the heresy that has started up, and openly convict the men who have the hardihood to debase the preaching of the Œconomy; [3] and secondly may fight as champion of them who are being attacked for the truth's sake. For it is in the cause of the apostolic Faith, most holy, that we have undergone that unrighteous massacre, because we refused to abandon the truth of the Gospel doctrines. Now it behoves your holiness not to overlook the unjust persecution of men of like mind with yourself, but by your just help to put a stop to injustice, and

teach the assailants of the truth that men who strive to act unscrupulously at their own good pleasure cannot be allowed to work out their ends.

CXVIII.   To the Archdeacon of Rome.[1]

A terrible storm has attacked our churches, but the adherents of the apostolic faith have in your holiness a safe and quiet haven. Not only do you champion the cause of the doctrines of the Gospel, but you utterly detest the wrong done to me. I was living far away at a distance of thirty-five days' journey, when I was condemned at their good pleasure by those most righteous judges. Teaching which has obtained in the churches from the coming of God our Saviour till this day they have abandoned. They have introduced a novel and bastard doctrine, diametrically contrary to the tradition of the apostles, and are openly at war with them that hold to the ancient instruction. Deign, then, most godly sir, to kindle the zeal of the very sacred and holy archbishop, that the churches of the East too may enjoy your kindly care. Above all fight in behalf of the faith delivered from the beginning by the holy apostles; preserve the heritage of our fathers unimpaired, and scatter the mist that oppresses us. Give us instead of moonless night clear sunshine, and condemn the wickedness of the massacre unrighteously wrought against us. It is becoming to your holiness to add yet this act of zeal to your other good deeds.

CXIX.   To Anatolius the patrician.[2]

Your excellency has been fully informed as to the acts of the most righteous judges at Ephesus, for their sound has gone out into all lands and their most just judgment to the ends of the world. [3] What church has not felt the storm that has been raised by it? The one side wronged, the other were wronged, but they who neither suffered nor did the wrong share the distress of the wronged, and lament over them that so savagely and against all laws human and divine massacred their own members. Even house breakers caught in the very act are first tried and then punished by their judges; even murderers, violators of sepulchres, and adulterers, are first haled before the bench, and their accusers ordered to make their

---

[1] There were at this time two well known personages of the name of Florentius to whom this letter may possibly have been addressed. Florentius the patrician, recipient of Letter LXXXIX., and Florentius bishop of Sardis. Against the former hypothesis are the terms of the letter; against the latter the character and sympathies of the metropolitan of Lydia, if, as Garnerius thinks, he was an Eutychian. Canon Venables (Dict. Christ Biog. II. 540) supposes a Florentius bishop of a nameless western see. Garnerius and others think the letter was probably really addressed to the clergy or bishops assembled in synod at Rome.

[2] Romans ix. 25.   [3] Vide page 72.

[1] Cf. note on page 293. Garnerius however is doubtful whether the archdeacon is Hilarius or another. The evidence seems in favour of the identity.
[2] This letter is of the same date as the rest of the present series. Theodoret has heard of his deposition and is expecting the sentence of banishment.
[3] Cf. Psalm xix. 4.

indictment, and the motive of the witnesses is tested to see that they are not giving evidence to curry favour with the prosecutors, or are prejudiced against the defendants; and after this they are bidden to make their defence to the charges brought against them. This is done twice, thrice; sometimes even four times; and then, and not till then, after the truth has been sought in the words of both accuser and accused, the sentence is given. As to how these men judged in the case of the rest I will say nothing, lest I may seem a meddler in what does not concern me. I am forced to speak on behalf of myself alone, for the unrighteous deed of violence compels me. The imperial order kept me at home, and prevented me from travelling beyond the bounds of the city placed under my pastoral care. The decision of the synod went against me, and a man was condemned who was five and thirty days' journey away.

Now the God of all said to the patriarch Abraham about Sodom and Gomorrah: "Because the cry of Sodom and Gomorrah is very great and because their sin is very grievous; I will go down now and see whether they have done altogether according to the cry of it which is come unto me; and if not, I will know."[1] He knew quite well the wickedness of those men, and nevertheless He said, "I will go down and see," so teaching us to wait for the proof of facts. But these men never summoned me to trial, they never heard the sound of my voice, they refused to hear from me a statement of my opinions, and handed me over, as a victim to be slaughtered, to the rage of the enemies of the truth.

I, however, welcome my rest, and especially so at the present time, when the apostolic decrees have been by many destroyed, and the new heresy strengthened. But lest any one who does not know me should believe that the slanders uttered against me are true, and should be scandalized at the idea of my holding opinions other than those of the gospel, I implore your excellency to ask as a favour from the victorious sovereign that I may go to the West, and there plead my cause before the very godly and holy bishops; and if I be found transgressing in the least degree the rule of the faith, that I may be plunged into the midst of the deep sea. If he will not grant you this request, let him at least command me to inhabit my monastery,[2] which is a hundred and twenty miles away from Cyrus, seventy-five from Antioch, and lies three miles away from Apamea.

Of these petitions, if possible, I ask the former; if not at least I implore that, through your excellency's interposition, the second may be granted me. I shall ever carry the memory of your kindness in my heart and on my lips, supplicating the Lord of hosts to requite your excellency as well with present as with future blessings. I am compelled to write to you in these terms because I have heard that certain persons are endeavouring to compass my removal from this place.

CXX. To Lupicius.[1]

Even the enemies of the truth must, I think, be indignant at the injustice and illegality of the violence done us. It is only reasonable that the nurslings of the truth, at whose head stands your excellency, should be still more distressed at this new and surprising tragedy. It is only right that those who are the more grieved should show the more earnestness and zeal to counteract the deeds impiously and illegally done; and restore to its previous concord the Church's body now in peril of being torn asunder. Wherefore I beseech your excellency to reckon the present crisis an opportunity for spiritual reciprocity; to give on your side earnestness on behalf of the truth, and to receive from our generous Master alike His kindly care in this present life and in the life to come the kingdom of heaven.

CXXI. To Anatolius the patrician.[2]

The Lord who overlooks and governs all things has shewn both the apostolic truth of my doctrines, and the falsehood of the slander laid at my door. For the writings sent from the right godly and holy lord Leo, archbishop of Great Rome, to Flavianus of holy memory and to the rest assembled at Ephesus, are entirely in harmony with what I myself have written and have always preached in church. So soon therefore as I had read them, I praised the loving-kindness of the Lord, in that He had not wholly forsaken the churches, but had protected the spark of orthodoxy; or — shall I not rather say? — not a spark, but a very great torch, such as might enkindle and enlighten the world; for he has truly, in his writings, observed the apostolic stamp, and in them we have found at once what has

---

[1] Gen. xviii. 20. 21.　　[2] i.e. Nicerte.

[1] Garnerius reads Lupicinus and identifies him with the recipient of Letter XC. Letter CXX is of the same date as the preceding.
[2] This letter may be dated shortly after Letter CXIX. Garnerius points out that it contains a short summary of the orthodox tradition, but makes no mention of the council of Ephesus in 431.

been delivered by the holy and blessed prophets and apostles, and their successors in the preaching of the Gospel, and moreover the holy Fathers assembled at Nicæa. By these I confess that I abide, and indict all who hold other doctrines as guilty of impiety. Side by side with these writings of mine I have set one of the letters sent by him to Ephesus, to the end that when your excellency reads them you may remember the words which I have often spoken in church, may recognise the harmony of the doctrines, and may hate the utterers of the lie, as well as those who have set up their new heresy in opposition to the doctrines of the Apostle.

CXXII.[1] To Uranius[2] bishop of Emesa.

I have been greatly delighted that we who correspond in character should have corresponded by letter. But I do not quite see what you mean by saying "Are not these my words?" If it were said only for the sake of salutation, I am not annoyed at it; but if it is intended to remind me of the advice which recommended silence, and of the so-called œconomy,[3] I am very much obliged, but I do not accept the suggestion. For the divine Apostle charges us to take quite the opposite course. "Be instant in season and out of season."[4] And the Lord says to this very spokesman, "Be not afraid, but speak"[5] and to Isaiah, "Cry aloud, spare not"[6] and to Moses "Go down, charge the people"[7] and to Ezekiel "I have made thee a watchman unto the house of Israel," and it shall be "if thou warn not the wicked,"[8] and the like: for I think it needless to write at length to one who knows. Not only therefore are we not distressed at having spoken freely, but we even rejoice and are glad, and laud Him who has thought us worthy of these sufferings; aye and call on my friends to encounter the same perils. If they know that we do not keep the apostolic rule of the faith, but swerve to the right hand or the left, let them hate us; let them join the opposite side; let them be ranked with them that are at war with us. But if they bear witness to our holding the right teaching of the gospel message, we hail them with the cry, "Do you too 'stand having your loins girt about with truth, . . . and your feet shod with the preparation of the gospel of peace,'"[1] and so on, for it is said that virtue comprises not only temperance, righteousness, and prudence, but also courage, and that by means of courage the rest of its component parts are preserved. For righteousness needs the alliance of courage in its war against wrong; temperance vanquishes intemperance by the aid of courage. And for this reason the God of all said to the prophet "The just shall live by his faith, and if any man draw back, my soul shall have no pleasure in him."[2] Shrinking he calls cowardice. Hold fast then, my dear friend, to the apostolic doctrines, for "He that shall come will come, and will not tarry,"[3] and "He shall render to every man according to his deeds,"[4] for "the fashion of this world passeth away,"[5] and the truth shall be made manifest.

CXXIII. To the same.

Your letter was a long one, and a pleasant one, and it shews how warm and genuine is your affection. So delighted am I with it that I am not at all sorry for having erroneously conjectured the meaning of the beginning of your former one. For my misapprehension of the intention of your letter has disclosed your brotherly love, made plain the sincerity of your faith, and shewn your zeal for the true religion. We have indeed shared between us the words and the trials of the prophet; your holiness has used the words; I am buffeted by the hurricane and billows, and against the rowers of the ship I exclaim in his words "They that observe lying vanities forsake their own mercy."[6] Perhaps He who is Jonah's Lord and mine will grant that I too may rise and be released from the monster. But if the surge continue to boil I trust that even thus I shall enjoy the divine protection, and learn by my own experience how His strength is "made perfect in weakness,"[7] for He has measured the peril by my infirmity. The divine prophet whom I have mentioned was flung into the sea by his shipmates one and all, but I am granted the consolation of your holiness, and of other godly men. For them

---

[1] The two following letters are written from the monastery at Nicerte where Theodoret found a retreat after his banishment from Cyrus. Garnerius would place the former late in 449, and the latter early in 450.

[2] Uranius, bishop of Emesa in Phœnicia, was present at the two trials of Ibas, at Tyre in February and at Berytus in September 448. At the Latrocinium he was accused of immorality and of episcopal usurpation. It was during his episcopate that the head of the Baptist was supposed to be found at Emesa. Cf. notes on pp. 96 and 242.

[3] Cf. note on p. 72. Here οἰκονομία is used for *discreet silence* like the German "*Zurückhaltung*," and the French "*ménagement*." Cf. the Socratic ἐρωνεία and the Latin *dissimulatio*.

[4] II. Tim. iv. 2.
[5] Acts xviii. 9.
[6] Isaiah lviii. 1.
[7] Exodus xix. 21.
[8] Ezekiel iii. 17. 19. inexact quotation.

[1] Ephes. vi. 14.
[2] Heb. x. 38. Cf. Hab. ii. 4. Sept. Note inverted quotation of Habakkuk.
[3] Heb. x. 37.
[4] Rom. ii. 6.
[5] I. Cor. vii. 31.
[6] Jonah ii. 8.
[7] II. Cor. xii. 9.

and for your godliness I pray that the blessing bestowed upon the excellent Onesiphorus may be yours, for you have not blushed at my gibes ; nay rather you have shared in my afflictions for the faith's sake.

And one thing which I wish you to know is that, though other godly bishops have sent me their bounty, I have declined to receive it ; — not from any want of respect to the senders, God forbid ; — but because hitherto food convenient for me has been provided by Him Who gives it even to the ravens without stint. In the case of your reverence I have acted differently, for really the warmth of your affection has overcome what has hitherto been my fixed principle. For be well assured, my godly friend, that ever since friendship grew up between us the fire of our love has been kindled to greater heat.

CXXIV. To the learned Maranas.[1]

I too am distressed at the calamities of the Church, and wail over the storm that is raging ; for myself I am glad to be quit of agitation, and to be enjoying a calm which is delightful to me. As to the men whom your learning states to be still carrying on their iniquities, the day is not far distant when they will pay the penalty of their present rash lawlessness. All things are governed by the Lord of all with weight and rule, and whenever any fall away into unbounded iniquity His long suffering comes to an end, and He then acts as Judge and appoints punishment. Foreseeing this I pray that they may cease from their license that I may not be compelled to weep once more for them as I behold them undergoing chastisement.

Your excellency I can never forget, and I beg our common Master to fill your house with blessing.

CXXV. To Aphthonius, Theodoritus, Nonnus, Scylacius, Aphthonius, Joannes, Magistrates of the Zeugmatensis.

I know the strength and stability of your faith, and have been filled with the greatest possible delight, for, since we worshippers of the eternal Trinity constitute one body, it is only natural that together with the members that are sound the rest of the members should rejoice. So says the divine Apostle ; " Whether one member be honoured all the members rejoice with it." [2] I therefore rejoice with you in your struggles on behalf of the apostolic doctrines and your following

of the famous Naboth in more excellent things. Naboth for his vineyard's sake suffered most unrighteous slaughter, because he would not give up the heritage of his fathers. You are fighting not for vineyards, but for divine doctrines, and reject this new-fangled and spurious heresy as blackening the brightness of the teaching of the gospel ; you do not suffer the number of the blessed Trinity to be diminished or increased. For it is diminished by those who ascribe the passion of the only begotten to the Godhead ; it is increased by those who have the audacity to introduce a second son. You believe in one only begotten, as you do in one Father and in one Holy Ghost. In the only begotten made flesh you behold the assumed nature which He took from us and offered on our behalf. The denial of this nature puts our salvation far from us ; for if the Godhead of the only begotten is impassible, as the nature of the Trinity is impassible, and we refuse to acknowledge that which is by nature adapted to suffer, then the preaching of a passion which never happened is idle and vain. For if that which suffers has no existence how could there be a passion? We declare that the divine nature is impassible ; — a doctrine confessed by our opponents as well as by ourselves. How then could there be a passion when there is no subject capable of suffering? The great mystery of the œconomy will appear an appearance, a mere seeming instead of the reality. This is the fable started by Valentinus, Bardesanes, Marcion and Manes. But the teaching handed down to the churches from the beginning recognises, even after the incarnation, one Son, our Lord Jesus Christ, and confesses the same to be everlasting God, and man made at the end of days ; made man not by the mutation of the Godhead but by the assumption of the manhood. For suppose the divine nature to have undergone mutation into the human nature, then it did not remain what it was ; and if it is not what it was, they who have these objects of worship are false in calling Him God. We, on the contrary, recognise the only begotten Son of God to be immutable as God, and Son of the very God. For we have learnt from the divine Scripture that being in the form of God He took the form of the servant ; [1] and took on Him the seed of Abraham, not was changed into Abraham's seed ; and shared just as we do both in flesh and blood and in a soul immortal and immaculate. Preserving these for our sinful bodies He offered His

---

[1] Cf. Letter LXVII. This letter may be dated during Theodoret's banishment to Nicerte in 449, and is evidently in reply to a letter of condolence from the advocate.

[2] I. Cor. xii. 26.

[1] Phil. ii. 6 and 7.

sinless body and for our souls His soul free from all stain. It is for this reason that we have the hope of the common resurrection, for the race will assuredly share with its first fruits, and as we have shared with Adam in his death, so too with Christ our Saviour shall we be sharers in His life. This the divine Apostle has plainly taught us, for " now " he says " is Christ risen from the dead and become the first fruits of them that slept. For since by man came death, by man came also the resurrection of the dead, for as in Adam all die, even so in Christ shall all be made alive." [1]

I write thus not to inform you but to re-mind you. I have tried to be brief, but I fear I have transgressed the limits of a letter. I was however urged to write by the very reverend and godly presbyter and archi-mandrite Mecimas, who, in obedience to the law of love, has undertaken so long a jour-ney, told us of your excellency's zeal, and begged us to inflame it by a letter. I have therefore granted his supplication, and writ-ten my letter, and I implore the Lord of all to keep you safe in the faith and make stronger than him who sifts us. [2]

CXXVI. To the Bishop Sabinianus. [3]

I praised your holiness on your quitting the envied see. Once it was venerable ; now it is ridiculous, for we have made it a thing to be bought and sold. I was as-tounded to hear of your having appealed to the men who ejected you. You ought to have done just the contrary, and, on being in-vited to grasp the tiller, to have declined to do so, on the ground that your shipmates had become your foes. Are you not aware, most godly sir, what our Saviour, through His sacred apostles, taught us to preach? Do you not know what the heirs of the apostolic doctrines have just now laid down as objects of worship? For who of the old teachers from the time when the message was first preached down to the period of the darkness that now obtains, ever listened to any one preaching one nature of flesh and Godhead or dared at any time to call the nature of the only begotten passible? These doctrines in our day are by some men openly and boldly uttered, while among others their utterance is overlooked, and by silence men become participators in the blasphemy. What then,

may well be asked, is the proper course to be taken by those who abominate such doc-trines? They have, I should reply, two alternatives before them ; they may either come to close quarters, and prove the spuri-ousness of the doctrines, or they may decline communion with their opponents as openly impious.

I, indeed, have received the wrong done me as a divine blessing. I do not mean that I have thanked them that have wronged me ; how could I thank fratricides, and men who have become followers of Cain?

But I praise my Master for thinking me worthy of the lot of them that suffer wrong, for separating me from wrong-doers and blasphemers, and for giving me my most delightful rest.

CXXVII. To Jobius, presbyter and archi-mandrite. [1]

The patriarch Abraham won a victory in his old age. [2] The great Moses was now an old man when, so long as he stretched out his hands in prayer, he vanquished Amalek. [3] The divine Samuel [4] was an old man when he put the aliens to flight. These are em-ulated by your venerable old age. In our wars for true religion's sake you are play-ing the man, and championing the cause of the gospel doctrines, and putting young men in the shade by the vigour of your spirit.

I rejoice to hear it, and am glad, and long to embrace your right venerable gray hairs. This I cannot do, for your reverence is kept at home by your years, and I am kept in durance here by the imperial decree. But I cheat my love by this letter, and give your piety this most loving embrace. I call upon you in your prayers to help the churches now whelmed in the storm, and to win for me the divine support, assailed as I am for the sake of the doctrines of the gospel, and standing sorely in need of help from above.

CXXVIII. To Candidus, presbyter and archi-mandrite. [5]

I am afraid that the vigour of your godly soul has been overcome by old age, and that you do not keep your hands stretched out as usual. So Amalek is trying to win. May there be some to succour your weakness, as once of old Ur and Aaron supported the

---

[1] I. Cor. xv. 20. 21. 22.   [2] cf. Luke xxii. 31.
[3] Sabinianus succeeded Athanasius bishop of Perrha on the deposition of the latter at Antioch in 445. He was deposed at the Latrocinium and Athanasius restored. Both bishops signed at Chalcedon as bishops of Perrha (Labbe iv, 602, 590. Dict: Christ: Biog: iv, 574. The letter may be dated 450. Theodoret chides Sabinianus for appealing to the dominant wrong doers against his expulsion.

[1] Jobius was an orthodox archimandrite of Constantinople, and subscribed the deposition of Eutyches by the hand of his deacon Andreas at Constantinople in 448. (Labbe iv, 232) In 450 Leo addresses him with other archimandrites (Ep. LXXI page 1012). This letter seems to have been written about the time of the Latrocinium.
[2] Gen. xiii. 15.   [3] Ex. xvii. 13.   [4] I. Sam. vii. 12.
[5] Garnerius would date this letter at the time of the council of Chalcedon.

hands of the law-giver, that you may over-throw Amalek and save Israel. These are days when we specially need more earnest prayers, when Gentiles and Jews and every heresy are at peace, and the Church alone is beaten by the storm and surrounded by the boisterous billows.

We indeed specially need the aid of your prayers, for those whom we reckoned to be fighting on our side are fighting on that of our foes.

CXXIX. To Magnus Antoninus the presbyter.[1]

Sailors at night are cheered by the sight of the harbour lights, and so are they who are in peril for the sake of the apostolic faith by the zeal of them that share the faith. We have great comfort in what we hear of your godliness's efforts on behalf of the divine doctrines, for this mind has been given you by the Giver of all good gifts and for the safe keeping of these doctrines you undergo every toil. Now I, comforted by your zeal, make an insignificant return, calling on you to persevere in your divine labours, to de-spise your adversaries as an easy prey, (for what is weaker than they who are destitute of the truth?) and to trust in Him who said "I will not fail thee nor forsake thee,"[2] and "Lo I am with you alway even unto the end of the world."[3] Help me too with your prayers that I may confidently say "The Lord is on my side; I will not fear: what can man do unto me?"[4]

CXXX. To Bishop Timotheus.[5]

Not without purpose does the supreme Ruler allow the spirits that are against us to agitate the waves of impiety. He does so that He may try the courage of the sailors, and, while He exhibits some men's manliness, convicts others of cowardice, stripping the mask from the faces of some who put on an appearance of piety, and proclaiming others as foremost fighters in the ranks of the truth. We have seen an instance of this in the present time. The storm rose high; some shewed their secret impiety; some aban-doned the truth which they were holding, went over to the phalanx of our foes, and now, with them, are smiting the very men

whom they used to call their chiefs. The witnesses of these things detest the enemy and pity the deserters, but are afraid to give aid to the victims of the attack upon the apostolic doctrines. Nay, suppose the traitors to urge them with greater insistency, they will perhaps themselves pass over to the side of the assailants, will give no quarter to their fellow-believers, but will drive against them their barbs side by side with the very men whom they accuse. They will act thus though they have been taught by the divine Scripture that a wrong done to one's neighbour incurs punishment, while the suffering of injustice entails great and lasting rewards.

Your own piety, your zeal for the faith, and your good will to myself, have been proved by this agitation. Twice you have written me a letter in contempt of all that might deter you, and have thus shewn your brotherly affection. You have also indicated the conflict you are sustaining on behalf of the apostolic doctrines. You ask me to tell you by letter what we ought to think and preach concerning the passion of salvation. I have received your request with delight, and, not indeed to give you information but only to remind one who is beloved of God, will proceed to tell you what I have learnt from the divine Scripture and from the Fathers who have inter-preted it.

Know then, most godly sir, that before all things it is necessary to observe the dis-tinction of terms, and, in addition to this, the cause of the divine incarnation. Once let these be made clear, and there will be no ambiguity left about the passion. We will therefore first, to those who endeavour to contradict us, put this enquiry. Which of the names given to the only begotten Son of God are anterior to the incarnation, and which posterior, or rather, connected with the operation of the œconomy? They will reply that the terms anterior are, "God the Word," "only begotten Son," "Almighty," and "Lord of all creation"; and that the names "Jesus Christ" belong to the incar-nation. For, after the incarnation, God the Word, the only begotten Son of God is called Jesus Christ; for "Behold" He says "unto you is born this day Christ the Lord"[1] and because others had been called christs, priests, kings, and prophets, lest any one should suppose Him to be like unto them, the angels conjoined the title Lord with that of Christ, in order to prove the supreme

[1] Garnerius supposes that this Antoninus is the same as the Antoninus mentioned as living in Theodoret's Religious History and thinks that the Solitary may have become an Archimandrite after 445 when the Religious History was written, but the mss. vary as to the superscription of the letter, which may be addressed to Magnus, Antonius and others.
[2] Joshua i. 5.   [3] Matthew xxviii. 20.   [4] Psalm cxviii. 6.
[5] Timotheus was Bishop of Doliche, a town of the Euphra-tensis. He was present at Antioch when Athanasius of Perrha was deposed, and also at Chalcedon. The letter may be dated from Nicerte in 450.

[1] Luke ii. 11.

dignity of Him that was born. And, again, Gabriel says to the blessed Virgin, "Behold thou shalt conceive in thy womb, and bring forth a son and shalt call His name Jesus" [1] "for He shall save His people from their sins." [2] Before the incarnation, however, He was never called either Christ or Jesus. For truly the divine Prophets, in their predictions of things to come, used the words, just as they prophesied about the birth, the cross, and the passion, when the events had not yet come to pass. Nevertheless, even after the incarnation He is called God the Word, Lord, Almighty, only begotten Son, Maker, and Creator. For He was not made man by mutation, but, remaining just what He was, assumed what we are, for "Being in the form of God," to use the words of the divine Apostle "He took the form of a servant." [3] On this account, therefore, even after the incarnation, He is called also by the titles which are anterior to the incarnation, since His nature is invariable and immutable. But when relating the passion the divine Scripture nowhere uses the term God, since that is the name of the absolute nature. No one on hearing the words "In the beginning was the Word and the Word was with God, and the Word was God" [4] and similar expressions, would suppose that the flesh existed before the ages, or is of one substance with the God of the universe, or was Creator of the world. Every one knows that these terms are proper to the Godhead. Nor would any one on reading the genealogy of St. Matthew suppose that David and Abraham according to nature were forefathers of God, for it is the assumed nature which is derived from them.

Since then these points are plain and indubitable even among extreme heretics, and we acknowledge both the nature which is before the ages, and that which is of recent time, so are we bound to recognise at once the passibility of the flesh, and the impassibility of the Godhead, not dividing the union nor separating the only begotten into two persons, but contemplating the properties of the natures in the one Son. In the case of soul and body, which are of natures contemporary and naturally united, we are accustomed to make this distinction, describing the soul as simple, reasonable, and immortal, but the body as complex, passible, and mortal. We do not divide the union, nor cut one man in two. Far rather, then, in the case of the Godhead, begotten of the Father before the ages, and of the manhood assumed of David's seed, is it becoming to adopt a similar course, and distinctly to recognise the everlasting, eternal, simple, uncircumscribed, immortal, and invariable character of the one nature, and the recent, complex, circumscribed, and fluctuating nature of the other. We acknowledge the flesh to be now immortal and incorruptible, although before the resurrection it was susceptible of death and of passion; for how otherwise was it nailed to the tree, and committed to the tomb? And though we recognise the distinction of the natures, we are bound to worship one Son, and to acknowledge the same as Son of God and Son of man, form of God, and form of a servant, Son of David, and Lord of David, seed of Abraham, and creator of Abraham. The union causes the names to be common, but the community of names does not confound the natures. With them that are right-minded some names are plainly appropriate as to God, and others as to man; and in this way both the passible and the impassible are properly used of the Lord Christ, for in His humanity He suffered, while as God He remained impassible. If, according to the argument of the impious, it was in the Godhead that He suffered, then, I apprehend, the assumption of the flesh, was supererogatory; for suppose the divine nature to have been capable of undergoing passion, then He did not need the passible manhood. But grant that, as even their own argument contends, the Godhead was impassible, and the passion was real, let them beware of denying that which suffered, lest they deny with it the reality of the passion; for if that which suffers does not exist, then the passion is unreal. Now for any one who likes to open the quaternion [1] of the sacred evangelists, it is easy to perceive that the divine Scripture distinctly proclaims the passion of the body, and to learn from them how Joseph of Arimathæa came to Pilate, and begged the body of Jesus; how Pilate ordered the body of Jesus to be delivered, how Joseph took down the body of Jesus from the tree and wrapped the body of Jesus in the linen cloth, and laid it in the new tomb. All this is described by the four evangelists with frequent mention of the body. But if our opponents adduce the words of the angel to Mary and her companions, "Come

---

[1] Luke i. 31.
[2] Matt. i. 21. Observe the confusion of quotation.
[3] Phil. ii. 6.   [4] John i. 1.

[1] The word τετρακτύς commonly expresses the sum of the first four numbers in the Pythagorean system, i.e. 10, the root of creation; (1+2+3+4=10.) Cf. the Pythagorean oath " Ναὶ μα τὸν ἁμετέρᾳ ψυχᾳ παραδόντα τετρακτύν." Its use for τετραδεῖον or τετράδιον (cf. Acts xii. 4) may indicate acceptance of the theory of the mystic and necessary number of the gospels of which early and remarkable expression is found in Irenæus (cont. Hær. iii. 11.)

where the Lord lay," [1] let them be referred to the passage in the Acts which states that devout men " carried Stephen to his burial " [2] and observe that it was not the soul, but the body, of the victorious Stephen, to which the customary rites were paid. And to this very day, when we approach the shrines of the victorious martyrs, we commonly enquire what is the name of him who is buried in the grave, and those who are acquainted with the facts reply peradventure " Julian the martyr," or " Romanus," or, " Timotheus." [3]

Very often it is not entire bodies that are buried, but only very small remains, yet nevertheless we speak of the body by the name that belongs to the whole man. It was in this sense that the angel called the body of the Lord, " Lord," because it was the body of the Lord of the universe. Moreover the Lord Himself promised to give on behalf of the life of the world, not His invisible nature, but His body. " For," He says, " the bread that I will give is my flesh which I will give for the life of the world," [4] and when He took the symbol of divine mysteries, He said, " This is my body which is given for you." [5] Or according to the version of the Apostle, " broken." [6] In no place where He spoke of the passion did He mention the impassible Godhead.

It is therefore before all things necessary that the question should be put to those who are endeavouring to contradict us whether they confess that the perfect manhood was assumed by God the Word, and assert the union to have been made without confusion. Once let these points be admitted, and the rest will follow in due course, and the passion will be attributed to the passible nature. I have now summed up these heads and have exceeded the limits of my letter. I have sent also what I lately wrote at the suggestion of a very godly and holy man of God, the lord ——[7] in the form of a concise instruction designed to teach the truth of the apostolic doctrines. Should I find a good copyist, I will also send your holiness what I have written in the form of a dialogue,[8] extending the argument, and strengthening my positions, by the teaching of the Fathers. I have moreover now sent a few statements of the ancient teachers, sufficient to shew the drift of their instruction. Give me in return, most godly sir, the succour of your prayers, that I may pass through the terrible tempest and reach the quiet haven of the Saviour.

CXXXI. To Longinus, Archimandrite of Doliche.[1]

You have shewn alike your zeal for the true religion, and your love for your neighbour, both of which are at the present time clearly connected, for it is for the sake of the apostolic decrees that I am being attacked, because I refuse to give up the heritage of my fathers, and prefer to undergo any suffering to looking lightly on the robbery of one tittle from the faith of the Gospel. You have accepted fellowship in my sufferings, not only by comforting me by means of your letter, but further by sending to me the very honourable and pious Matthew and Isaac. You shall hear, I am well assured, from the lips of the righteous Lord, " I was in prison, and ye visited me." [2] We are small and of no account, and burdened by a great load of sins, but the Lord is bountiful and generous. He remembers the small rather than the great, and says, " Inasmuch as ye have done it unto one of the least of these " [3] " which believe in me " [4] " ye have done it unto me." [5] I pray you in that you are conspicuous for right doctrine, and shine by worthiness of life, and therefore have great boldness before God, help me in your prayers, that I may be able " to stand," to use the words of the Apostle,[6] " against the wiles of error," escape the sins of the destroyer, and stand, though with little boldness, in the day of the appearing before the righteous Judge.

CXXXII. To Ibas, bishop of Edessa.[7]

The Lord has taught them that suffer wrong not to be cast down, but to rejoice,

---

[1] Matt. xxviii. 6.   [2] Acts viii. 2.
[3] There were many martyrs of the name of Julianus. Theodoret might have visited a shrine of Julianus martyred at Emesa in the reign of Numerian. A Romanus was one of the seven martyrs at Samosata in the persecution of Diocletian. Among martyred Timothei was one who suffered at Gaza in 304.
[4] John vi. 51.   [6] I. Cor. xi. 24.
[5] Luke xxii. 19.   [7] The name is omitted.
[8] Garnerius identifies the " short instruction " with the composition mentioned in letter CIX. and sent to Eusebius of Ancyra; and the bishop whose name is omitted with the same Eusebius. But in his note on CIX. he thinks this composition is a part of Dial. II. It would seem from this letter that the composition in question was distinct from the Dialogues.

[1] Sent presumably at the same time as the preceding. Nothing is recorded of Longinus. It will be remembered that the name, recorded also in the Acts of Linus as that of an officer commanding the executioners of St. Paul, is assigned by tradition to the soldier who wounded the Saviour's side.
[2] Matt. xxv. 36.   [4] Matt. xviii. 6.
[3] Matt. xxv. 40.   [5] Matt. xxv. 40.
[6] Eph. iv. 14, and vi. 11. As in the case of the former citation Theodoret seems to be quoting from memory, and coupling the two passages in which the word μεθοδεία occurs. " Wiles " fits in better with the evident allusion to Eph. vi. 11, than the periphrasis by which A. V. renders iv. 14, and for which the revisers substitute " the wiles of error." " μεθοδεία " may be exactly described as " ἡ ἀποστολικὴ φωνή," for it occurs nowhere but in these two passages.
[7] To console him under the unjust sentence of the Latrocinium.

and to derive consolation from the examples of old. For from the period of the first men down to our own days we find instances of men who have been zealous in the worship of the God of all, and yet have been wronged by those with whom their lot was cast, and have fallen into many and grievous troubles. Of these I would have gone through the entire list, had I not been writing to one of accurate knowledge of the divine Scriptures. But since you, O beloved of God, have been nurtured from your boyhood in the divine oracles, I have thought it needless so to do. I only ask you to cast your eyes on them, and to look on all the kind-hearted clergy that have done wrong, with sorrow; on all that look lightly on wrong doing, with pity; and to be sorrowful for the disquiet of the Church. I ask you to rejoice and be glad that I am a sharer in suffering for the sake of true religion, and to praise without ceasing Him who has imposed this lot on me. As for honour and comfort and the dignity of sees and wretched reputation, let us yield them to the murderers.[1]

Let us cleave only to the doctrines of the gospel, and with them, if need be, endure any extremity of pain, and choose honourable penury rather than wealth with its many cares.

I am not writing in these terms in order to give you exhortation, for I know the courage of your holiness in trouble. My object is to make my own mind known to your piety, and to inform you that you have on your side comrades who are gladly incurring peril for the truth's sake. I have been anxious for some time to write thus to you, but I have been unable to find anyone to convey my letter. Now I have met with the very honourable and pious presbyter Ozeas, a man who is at once engaged in the battle for truth and attached to your piety. So I write and salute your holiness, and beg you to give me both the prop of your prayers and the comfort of a letter from you.

CXXXIII. To John, bishop of Germanicia.[2]

I have always known, sir, that you are not unmindful of our friendship. And it has ever been my wish and prayer that your piety should give heed to exact truth, and shun the communion of traitors to true religion, ascribing to the Supreme Ruler His care on our behalf. For indeed, while I have been silent and inactive, He has put an end to our very keen and terrible sufferings, and has replaced the dire tempest by this bright calm. And now that the loving-kindness of the Lord has granted us this blessing, I find the quiet of my retreat indeed delightful, for I feel the necessity of persuading those who have been led away by the slanders launched against me, and of both convincing them of the truth of the teaching of the gospels, and refuting the attack of falsehood. When once this refutation is finished, and the victory of the truth is secured, it is my purpose to quit public life, and withdraw to the rest that I so greatly long for. As to the foes of the truth I cry with the prophet, "Their memorial is perished with a noise, but the Lord shall endure for ever."[1] As to ourselves, I sing with the Psalmist, "He sent from above, He took me, He drew me out of many waters, He delivered me from my strong enemy."[2]

This letter is in reply to two received from your holiness, one conveyed by Anastasius, the presbyter of Berœa, and one by the standard-bearer Theodotus. In your last letter you mention another, but this has not been delivered. As to my journey thither I can say nothing till I know what orders are given concerning me by the most pious emperor. His letter has not yet arrived.

CXXXIV. To Theoctistus, Bishop of Berœa.[3]

Our Saviour, Lawgiver, and Lord, was once asked, "What is the first commandment?" His reply was "Thou shalt love the Lord thy God with all thy heart, and with all thy soul, and with all thy mind." And He added "This is the first commandment: and the second is like unto it, Thou shalt love thy neighbour as thyself." Then He said further "On these two commandments hang all the law and the prophets."[4]

He then who keeps these, according to the definition of the Lord, plainly fulfils the Law; and he who transgresses them is guilty of

[1] It will be remembered that Flavianus had actually died from the brutal treatment he had received at the hands — and the feet — of Dioscorus with his partisans and bullies, and "*migravit ad Dominum dolore plagarum*," Aug. 11, 449, three days after he was carried from St. Mary's at Ephesus to his dungeon. (Liberatus Brev. xix. Dict. Christ. Biog. i. 858.)

[2] John of Germanicia (vide p. 86 n.) was on the Nestorian side at Ephesus in 431, and so naturally associated with Theodoret. At Chalcedon he was compelled to pronounce a special anathema against Nestorius. (Mansi vii. 193, Dict. Christ. Biog. iii. 374.) The letter is written after the deposition and before the banishment to Nicerte. Cf. Ep. 147.

[1] Ps. ix, 6, 7, lxx.   [2] Ps. xviii. 16, 17.

[3] This letter marks the change in the condition of affairs which followed on the death of Theodosius on July 29, 450, and the accession of Pulcheria and Marcian. Eutyches was exiled, the eunuch Chrysaphius banished and executed, of 450 or early in 451. The earlier letter (xxxii) to Theoctistus claims on behalf of Celestinianus a kindness which Theodoret in his then hour of need had failed to receive. It may be placed in the autumn of

[4] Matt. xxii. 36-40.

transgressing the whole Law. Let us then examine, before the exact and righteous tribunal of our conscience, whether we have fulfilled the divine commandments. Now the first is kept by him who guards the faith given by God in its integrity, who abominates its assailants as enemies of the truth and hates heartily all those who hate the beloved; and the second by him who most highly esteems the care of his neighbour and who, not only in prosperity but also in apparent misfortunes, observes the laws of friendship. They, on the other hand, who look after their own safety, as they suppose, who on its account make little of the laws of friendship and take no heed of their friends when assaulted and attacked, are reckoned to belong to the number of the wicked and of them that are without. The Lord of all requires better things at the hands of His disciples. "Love" He says " your enemies, for if ye love them which love you, what reward have ye? for the sinners and the publicans do this." [1] I, however, have not received even such kindness as publicans receive. Publicans, do I say? I have not even received the consolation given to murderers and wizards in their dungeons. If every one had imitated this cruelty, nothing else would have been left then for me in my life time but to be wasted by want, and, at my death, instead of being committed to a tomb, to be made meat [2] for dogs and wild beasts. But I have found support in those who care nought for this present life, but await the enjoyment of everlasting blessings, and these furnish me with manifold consolation. But the loving Lord " caused judgment to be heard from heaven; the earth feared and was still, when God arose to judgment." [3] But the wicked shall perish. [4] The falsehood of the new heresy has been proscribed, and the truth of the divine Gospels is publicly proclaimed. I for my part exclaim with the blessed David, " Blessed be the Lord God who only doeth wondrous things, and blessed be His glorious name: and let the whole earth be filled with His glory; amen and amen." [5]

CXXXV. To Bishop Romulus. [6]

You have reminded me of the ancient

story, and remarked how the King of the Syrians, bethinking him of the loving kindness of the kings of Israel, assumed the form of a suppliant and failed not to obtain his petition. Remember therefore, sir, the divine wrath. God delivered Ahab to utter destruction for using mercy, and delivered his sentence through the mouth of the prophet, saying " Thy life shall go for his life and thy people for his people." [1] We are thus commanded to temper mercy with justice, since not every kind of mercy is pleasing to the God of all. The present state of affairs specially requires prudent council; for we are contending on behalf of the divine doctrines, wherein we have the hope of our salvation. But herein, too, may be seen the great difference between man and man. Some men are verily infected with the common impiety; while others, without distinction, advance at one time one doctrine, and at another its opposite. Some who know the truth conceal it in the secret chambers of their soul, while they preach impiety with the rest; others again who are filled with envy have made their private ill-will an occasion of waging war against the truth, and wreak all kinds of mischief against the prophets of the truth. Again, there are who embrace the truth of the apostolic doctrines, and yet because they are afraid of the power of the dominant party are too cowed to proclaim it, and though they lament at the abundance of our misfortunes, nevertheless side with them that set the mighty surge a-rolling. It is in this last category that we place your reverence. We have believed you to be sound in the divine doctrines, and think that you keep your affection for me, and are borne along with the time for no other reason than your cowardice. Under these circumstances though I am not writing to any of the rest, I write to your holiness, and receive your reply. I see your drift and to some extent I pardon your pusillanimity. But the loving Lord has now removed all occasions of cowardice, by exhibiting the new-fangled impiety, and shewing the plain truth of the gospels. I, even though my mouths were as many as my hairs, cannot praise as I ought the loving-kindness of the Lord for compelling my strongest opponents openly to preach what has been preached by me. For I have heard that he who shares your holiness's roof, when he heard that anathemas

---

[1] cf. Matt. v. 44. 46 instead of τίνα μισθὸν ἔχετε; the text has τί πλέον ποιεῖτε.
[2] The use of the somewhat rare and poetical word Βορά suggests a possible allusion to several well known passages in the dramatists; e.g. Æsch. Pr. 583, Soph. Ant. 30 and Eur. Phœn. 1603.
[3] Psalm lxxv. 8 and 9.   [4] Psalm xxxvii. 20.
[5] Psalm lxxii. 18, 19.
[6] Romulus, bishop of Chalcis in Cœle Syria, sided with the dominant hæretical party through pusillanimity. He was

at Chalcedon in 451. Who may have been his crab-gaited friend can only be conjectured.
It would appear that edicts anathematizing Eutyches were published soon after the accession of Marcian.
[1] I. Kings xx. 42.

had been published in the great cities, ceased to imitate the crooked gait of crabs, and, after disputing in a certain assembly about doctrines, walked in the straight road. Never must we suit our words to the season, but ever preserve the unbending rule of truth.

CXXXVI. To Cyrus Magistrianus.[1]

I was very much distressed to hear of the trouble which had befallen you. How indeed could I fail to suffer, making as I do your interest mine, and remembering the apostolic law which bids us not only " rejoice with them that do rejoice, but also weep with them that weep "?[2] Suffering itself is able to draw even those that are at enmity with one another into sympathy.

What is so grievous as to lose a wife; one who bore blamelessly the yoke of wedlock, one who made her husband's life pleasant, one who shared the care of the family; one who managed the household and shared in the direction of everything; one who was ready to suggest whatever might be likely to be of service, and to comply with the wishes of her husband? But what sorrow could surpass the committal to the tomb of the mother at the same moment as the son whom she bore; a son who had been carefully trained and had received a learned education; one who, you hoped, would be the stay of your old age; buried in the very spring of his manhood, when the down was just beginning to grow upon his cheeks? Did we only look at the character of the calamity, it admits of no consolation. But when we bethink us how our race is doomed to die; that against that race the divine fiat has gone forth; that suffering is common, for life is full of such woes; we shall bravely bear what has happened, shall repel the assaults of despair, and shall raise that wonderful song of praise " The Lord gave and the Lord hath taken away; the Lord hath done what seemed to him good; blessed be the name of the Lord." [3] But we have many more reasons for consolation. We have been distinctly taught the hopes of the resurrection, and we look for the time when the dead shall live again. We know how the Lord many times called death sleep. If we trust, as in truth we do, the Saviour's words, we are bound not to mourn those that have fallen asleep, even though their sleep lasts

somewhat longer than it is wont. We must await the resurrection. We must remember that the Ruler of the world in His wisdom, and clearly knowing as He does not the present only but the future also, guides events for our good. A wise man who knew all this full well reasons about deaths of this kind and says, " Yea; speedily was he taken away, lest that wickedness should alter his understanding." [1]

Let us submit I beg you to the wise Ruler of all; let us submit to His decrees. Whether they be pleasant or whether they be grievous, they are good and profitable, they make men wise; for them that endure they ordain crowns.

CXXXVII. To the Archimandrite John.[2]

The blessed David fell into several errors, which God, who wisely orders all things, has caused to be recorded for the good of them that were to come after. But it was not on their account that Absalom, parricide, murderer, impious, and altogether vile, started his wild war against his father. The reason of his beginning that most unrighteous struggle was because he coveted the sovereignty. The divine David, however, when these events were coming to pass, began to remember the wrong that he had done. I too am conscious within myself of the guilt of many errors, but I have kept undefiled the dogmatic teaching of the Apostles. And they who have trampled upon all laws human and divine, and condemned me in my absence, have not sentenced me for what I have done wrong, for my secret deeds are not made manifest to them; but they have contrived false witness and calumny against me, or rather in their open attack upon the doctrines of the Apostles have proscribed me for my obedience to them. " So the Lord awaked as one out of sleep; He smote His enemies in the hinderparts and put them to a perpetual shame." [3] Counterfeit and spurious doctrines He has scattered to the winds, and has provided for the free preaching of those which He has handed down to us in the holy Gospels. To me this suffices for complete delight. I do not even long for a city in which I have passed all my time in hard work; all I long for is to see the establishment of the truth of the Gospels. And now the Lord has satisfied this longing. I am therefore very glad

---

[1] There is here neither note of time, nor certainty whether this Cyrus is the Cyrus who is thanked in Ep. XIII. for the Lesbian wine. The superscriptions of both letters are unfavourable to theories identifying him with any possible bishop of the name.

[2] Romans xii. 15.   [3] Job i. 21. lxx.

[1] Wisdom iv. ii.

[2] A Johannes was an Archimandrite of Constantinople and was present at Chalcedon in 451, (Labbe iv. 512 d) but there is no evidence to identify the recipient of the present letter, which may be dated from Nicerte not long after the death of Theodosius.

[3] Psalm lxxviii. 65 and 66.

and happy, and I sing praises to our generous Lord, and I invite your reverence to rejoice with me, and, with our praises, to put up the earnest prayer that the men who say now one thing and now another and change about to suit the hour, like the chameleons who assume the colour of the leaves, may be strengthened by the loving-kindness of the Lord, established upon the rock, and, of His mercy, made to pay the highest honour to the truth.

CXXXVIII. *To Anatolius the patrician.*[1]

I have cordially welcomed the rest which has fallen to my lot, and am harvesting its beneficial and pleasant results. Our Christ-loving Emperor,[2] after reaping the empire as fruit of his true piety, has offered as first-fruits of his sovereignty to Him that bestowed it, the calm of the storm-tossed churches, the triumph of the invaded faith, the victory of the doctrines of the Gospel. To these he has added the righting of the wrong done to me. Of a wrong so great and of such a kind who ever heard? What murderer was ever doomed in his absence? What violator of wedlock was ever condemned without a hearing? What burglar, grave-breaker, wizard, church-robber, or doer of any other unlawful deed, was ever prevented, when eager to appeal to the law, and slain when far away by the sentence of his judge? In their cases nothing of the kind was ever known. For, by our law, plaintiff and defendant are bidden to stand face to face before the judge, while the judge has to wait for the production of plain truth, and then, and not till then, either dismiss the accused as innocent, or punish him as being reached by the indictment. In my case the course pursued has been just the opposite. The emperor's letter forbade me to approach the far-famed synod, and the most righteous judges condemned me in my absence, not after fair trial, but after extravagant laudation of the documents which were produced to incriminate me. Neither the law of God nor shame of man stayed the deed of blood. Orders were given by the president,[3] fling-

ing the truth to the winds, and courting the power of the hour. He was obeyed by men who think as I do, whose doctrines are my doctrines, and who had expressed admiration of me and mine. None the less did that day convict some men of treachery; some of cowardice; while to me a ground of confidence was given by my sufferings for the truth's sake. And to me our master Christ hath granted the boon " not only of believing on Him but also of suffering for His sake." [1] For the greatest of all gifts of grace are sufferings for the Master's sake, and the divine Apostle puts them even before great marvels.

In these boons I too glory, humble and insignificant as I am, and having no other ground of boasting. And I beseech your excellency to offer on behalf of my poor self expressions of thanksgiving to the emperor, lover of Christ, and to the most pious Augusta,[2] dear to God, instructress of the good, for she has requited our generous Lord with such gifts, and has made her zeal for true religion the foundation and groundwork of her sway. Besides this, beg their godly majesties to complete the work that has been so well marked out, and to summon a council, not, like the last, composed of a turbulent rabble, but — kept quite clear of all of these — of men who decide on and highly value divine things, and esteem all human affairs as of less account than the truth. If their majesties wish to bring about the ancient peace for the churches, and I am sure that they do, beg their pious graces to take part in the proceedings, that their presence may overawe those of a contrary mind and the truth may have none to gainsay her, but may herself by her own unaided powers examine into the position of affairs, and the character of the apostolic doctrines.

I make this request to your excellency, not because I long to see Cyrus again, for your lordship knows what a solitary town it is, and how I have somehow or other managed to conceal its ugliness by my great expenditure on all kinds of buildings, but to the end that what I preach may be shewn to be in agreement with apostolic doctrines

---

[1] This is the last of the series of Theodoret's letters to his illustrious friend. It expresses his gratitude for his restitution by Marcian and begs Anatolius to use his best endeavours to get a council called to settle the difficulties of the Church. The letter thus dates itself in the year 451 and indicates that the calling of the council of Chalcedon was to some extent due to Theodoret's initiative. At the earlier sessions at Chalcedon Marcian was represented by Anatolius, and it was partly the authority of Anatolius which overbore the protests of Dioscorus and his party against the admission of Theodoret.

[2] Marcian was crowned Emperor on August the 24th 450. Theodosius II. had died on the preceding 28th of July.

[3] " Dioscorus presided, and next to him Julian, or Julius, the representative of the ' most holy bishop of the Roman Church' then Juvenal of Jerusalem, Domnus of Antioch, and, his lowered position indicating what was to come, Flavian of

Constantinople." Canon Bright in Dict. Christ. Biog. i. 856; Mansi. vi. 607.

[1] Phil. i. 29.

[2] cf. p. 155 n. " A sudden and total revolution at once took place. The change was wrought, — not by the commanding voice of ecclesiastical authority, — not by the argumentative eloquence of any great writer, who by his surpassing abilities awed the world into peace, — not by the reaction of pure Christian charity, drawing the conflicting parties together by evangelic love. It was a new dynasty on the throne of Constantinople. The feeble Theodosius dies; the masculine Pulcheria, the champion and the pride of orthodoxy, the friend of Flavianus and Leo ascends the throne, and gives her hand, with a share of the empire, to a brave soldier Marcianus." Milman, Lat. Christ. 1. 264.

while the inventions of my opponents are counterfeit and base. Once let this come to pass, by God's help be it spoken, and I shall pass the remainder of my days in cheerful contentment, wherever the Master may bid me dwell. To you who have been brought up in the true religion, and are dowered with the wealth of goodness it is becoming to make this effort, and by your urgent counsel to render yet more zealous our most pious emperor and the Christ-loving Augusta, zealous already as they are to strengthen their glorious empire by laudable and rightful energy.

CXXXIX. To Aspar, Consular and Patrician.[1]

To the other good deeds of your excellency must be added your having acquainted our pious and most christian emperor, whom God's grace has appointed for the blessing of his subjects, of the enormous wrong done against me, and your having by a righteous edict annulled an edict which was nothing of the kind. Supported by divine Providence I have made what they reckoned a punishment a means of good, and I have welcomed my rest with delight; but none the less I have been wrongly and illegally treated, though in no single point guilty of the errors which the enemies of the truth slanderously laid at my door, but yet made to suffer the penalty of the greatest criminals. Nay, my fate has been yet harder than theirs. I was judged without a trial; I was doomed in my absence; when forbidden by the emperor's orders to go to Ephesus I received the most righteous sentence of my holy judges. All this has now been undone by his most serene majesty, through the active interposition of your excellency. I, for my part, feeling that I should be wrong to keep silent and not offer you my thanks, have availed myself of this letter, whereby I beseech your excellency to speak in warm terms in my behalf both to the victorious and Christian emperor and to the very godly and pious Augusta. On their behalf I implore our good Lord as earnestly as lies in my power to guard their empire in security, and to grant that it may be at once a source of loving protection for their subjects, and of terror to their foes, and establish honourable peace for all. May your excellency be induced to petition them completely to put an end to the agitation of the Church, and order the assembling of the

council; not, like the last, of men who from their habits of unruliness throw the synod into confusion, but, in peace and quiet, of members instructed in divine things, and in the habit of confirming the apostolic decrees and rejecting what is spurious and at variance with the truth. And I express this hope to the end that your excellency may reap the good which such a course of conduct is likely to produce.

CXL. To the Master Vincomalus.[1]

I have been much astonished to learn that your magnificence, though quite unacquainted with me and mine, and knowing only the wrong that had been done me, stood up as my advocate, and left no means untried to undo the results of the conspiracy against me. But your excellency will assuredly receive recompense from our bountiful Lord, for He who promised to give a reward for a little water will doubtless give greater recompense to the givers of greater gifts.

I have indeed endured such sufferings as none, or at least very few, of the ancients have undergone, and this not only from my open foes, but, as I apprehend, from my real friends. The former attacked me, the latter betrayed me.

Who in the world ever heard of such a trial? Who ever commanded a criminal to be tried in his absence after chaining him up at a distance of more than five and thirty stages? What judge has ever been so savage and inhuman as not only to try men, aye but to condemn men the sound of whose voice he has never heard, and this in most savage and inhuman fashion? The Lord has ordered the erring brother, who spurns advice, after a first, second and third admonition, to be treated as " an heathen man and a publican."[2] Now these most equitable and righteous judges have not even given to them of the same faith with themselves the treatment which they give to heathen men and publicans. These indeed they do see and occasionally converse with, and that with all honour and deference where they appear to be of rank and dignity. But they have ordered me to be cut off from home, from water, from everything. This is the way in which they have wished to become imitators of our Father in heaven " Who maketh His sun to rise on the evil and on the good

---

[1] Garnerius has substituted for *Aspar* the name Abienus who was Consul in 450. Schulze would retain the ordinary reading of *Aspar*. The recipient of the letter, whoever he be, is thanked for his part in the rescinding of the acts of the late Latrocinium.

[1] The internal evidence of the letter makes it synchronize with the preceding. The advocacy of the cause of Theodoretus by Vincomalus is the more striking in that it does not appear to have been suggested by personal friendship. Vincomalus was Consul Designate in 452. (Dict. Christ. Biog. iv. 1159. Labbe iv. 843.) *Magister* = " *Magister Officiorum*," cf. note on p. 283.

[2] Matt. xviii. 17.

and sendeth rain on the just and on the unjust."[1] But of these men I will say no more. The tribunal of the Lord is at hand where is required not stage pretence but the reality of life. Now I beseech your excellency to express my thanks to the emperor, the lover of Christ and victorious, and to the very pious and godly Augusta, for having made true religion the firm root of their pious empire, and to implore their majesties to make the peace of the churches firm by commanding the assembling of a council, not of men of violence who throw the discussion into confusion, but of the lovers of the truth who confirm the apostolic teaching, and repudiate this new fangled and spurious heresy. And I pray that of these honourable endeavours you may reap the fruit at the hands of our loving Lord.

CXLI. To Marcellus, Archimandrite of the Acoemetæ.[2]

Bright is made your holiness by your goodly life, exhibiting on earth the image of the conversation of the angels, but it is made still brighter by your zeal for the apostolic faith. As keel to boat, as corner-stone to house, so to them that choose to live in piety is the truth of the doctrines of the Gospel. For this truth when assailed you have bravely fought, not striving to protect it as though it were weak, but shewing your godly disposition; for the teaching of our Master Christ is gifted with stability and strength, in accordance with the promise of the same Saviour, "that the gates of hell shall not prevail against it."[3] It is the loving and bountiful Lord who has thought right that I too should be dishonoured and slain on behalf of this doctrine. For truly we have reckoned dishonour honour, and death life. We have heard the words of the apostle "For unto us it is given by God not only to believe on Him, but also to suffer for His sake."[4] But the Lord arose like the sleeper, and stopped the mouths of them that uttered blasphemy against God

[1] Matt. v. 45.
[2] The Acoemetæ, "sleepless," or "unresting," were an order of monks established in the 5th century by Alexander, an officer of the imperial household. Marcellus, the third Abbot, was a second founder, and was warmly supported by the patriarch Gennadius of Constantinople. (458–71.) Before Chalcedon he joined with other orthodox abbots to petition Marcian against Eutyches. (Labbe iv. 531 Dict. Christ. Biog. iii. 813). Alexander's foundation was of 300 monks of various nations, divided into six choirs, and so arranged that the work of praise and prayer should "never rest." This has been copied elsewhere and since,
"where tapers day and night
On the dim altar burned continually,
In token that the house was evermore
Watching to God."
Wordsworth, Exc. viii.
[3] Matt. xvi. 18. [4] Phil. i. 29.

and injustice against me. But He has made the tongues of the pious pour forth their fountains in their wonted message. I, however, am gathering the delightful fruits of rest; as I look at the agitation of the churches I am grieved, but I rejoice and am glad at being freed from cares. I have ever been gratified at your admirable piety, but heretofore I have not written, not from any lack of regard for the dictates of charity, but because I have waited for some suitable occasion. Just now, having fallen in with the most pious and prudent monks who have been sent by your holiness on other business, I have lost no time in carrying out my wish. I salute your godliness. I beg you in the first place to support me with your prayers, and further to cheer me by a letter, for by God's grace I have been attacked for the Gospel's sake.

CXLII. To the same.

I have already addressed your reverence in another letter, and have delivered it to your much respected brethren. Now again I address your holiness. I am induced to do so both by your admirable life, and by the praiseworthy zeal which you have shewn on behalf of the apostolic faith, fearless alike of imperial power and of episcopal combination. For granted that the majority of the council consented under coercion, still they did confirm the new fangled heresy by their signatures. Your holiness, however, was shaken by none of these things, but abided by the ancient doctrines which the Lord, by means of both the prophets and the apostles, has taught the churches to hold. These decrees I pray that I may preserve, and keep to the end my faith and confession in one Father, one Son and one Holy Ghost. For the incarnation of the only begotten made no addition to the number of the Trinity. Even after the incarnation the Trinity is still a Trinity. This is the teaching I have received from the beginning; this has been my faith; in this was I baptized; this have I preached; in this have I baptized, this I continue to hold. Of them that utter a lie about the Father the Lord has said "When he speaketh a lie he speaketh of his own,"[1] for what is said of the teacher is appropriate to the disciples. So these men who employ lies against me speak of their own, and do not describe what is mine. I am comforted by my Master's words "Blessed are ye when men shall revile you and persecute you and shall say all manner

[1] John viii. 44.

of evil against you falsely for my sake. Rejoice and be exceeding glad for great is your reward in heaven." [1]

I entreat your piety to pray that I may not have my part among the wrong doers, but among them that suffer wrong on account of the truth of the Gospels.

CXLIII. To Andrew, Monk of Constantinople. [2]

I have never seen your piety nor have we ever communicated by letter, but I have become warmly attached to you. What has wrought the charm and continues to inflame it is the report unanimously brought by the tasters of your honey. All express admiration of the orthodoxy of your faith, the brightness of your life, the constancy of your soul, the harmoniousness of your character, the attractiveness and sweetness of your society and all the other characteristics of the true foster child of philosophy. For all these reasons I am attached to your godliness, and my longing has made me even begin a correspondence; but, my dear sir, grant me as soon as possible what I desire and let me have written communication from you. For when friends are at a distance considerable comfort is given them by epistolary communication. You will write to no man of heterodox opinions, but to one nurtured in the teaching of the apostles and preacher not of a quaternity but of a Trinity, for in reality I see little difference in the impiety of those who have the hardihood to endeavour to contract into one the two natures of the Only-begotten and those who endeavour to divide our Lord Jesus Christ, the Son of the living God, God the Word made man, into two sons; if such indeed there be; I cannot think so; but Arians, Eunomians, and Apollinarians too have ever shamelessly fabricated this slander against the Church, and indeed laborious students may easily perceive that our far famed Fathers, [3] lights of the churches, laboured at the hands of the foes of the truth under this accusation which is now levelled against me by the most excellent champions of the new fangled heresy. Our wise Lord has laid bare their impiety, for He could not endure to confirm the unholy heresy by His long suffering.

Be sure then, sir, that you will be writing

to one of like sentiments with your own; and of this you can easily assure yourself from my copious writings.

Write then to me in return, and again your letter, by God's leave, shall serve to kindle affection. And before you write, give me the help of your prayers, and beseech our good Lord to guide my feet into the right road, that I may travel the rest of my journey in accordance with His laws. You who have won right of access from your unstained life will easily persuade Him Who is eager to give us His good gifts.

CXLIV. To the soldiers. [1]

Human nature is everywhere the same, but pursuits in life are many and various. Some men prefer a sailor's career, some a soldier's; some men become athletes, some husbandmen; some ply one craft and some another. To pass by all other differences, some men are zealous and diligent about divine things, and get themselves instructed in the exact teaching of the apostolic doctrines; while others, on the contrary, become slaves of the belly, and suppose that the enjoyment of base pleasures is happiness. Others again are there, lying in a mean between these two extremes, who do not exhibit this praiseworthy enthusiasm, nor embrace a life of incontinence, but still honour the simplicity of the faith. Men who attack the statement that some things are altogether impossible with God must not, I apprehend, be classed with the zealous and the well instructed in divine things, but rather either with those who have no exact knowledge of the apostolic doctrines, or those who have been enslaved by pleasures and shift hither and thither at the caprice of a moment, setting forth now one thing and now another.

You have asked me to write on these points. I should prefer at the present time to keep silence. But in obedience to the commandment of the Lord, "Give to every man that asketh of thee," [2] I am constrained briefly to reply.

I say then that the God of the universe can do all things, but that in the word "all" is comprehended only what is right and good, for He who is naturally both wise and good admits of nothing that is of a contrary nature, but only what becomes his nature. If any objectors gainsay this statement, ask them if the God of the universe, the lawgiver of

---

[1] Matt. v. 11, 12.

[2] Garnerius identifies this Andrew with an archimandrite who was in favour of the deposition of Eutyches at Flavian's Constantinopolitan Council in 448.

[3] "No one," says Garnerius "will have any doubt as to the reference being to Diodorus of Tarsus and Theodorus of Mopsuestia who compares the words used with Letter XVI, with the end of Dialogue I, and with expressions in both the ecclesiastical and religious history." Cf. pp. 256, 175, 133, and 136.

[1] From the mention at the end of the letter of the epistle of Leo to Flavianus, Garnerius argues that it must be dated at the end of 449 or somewhat later. The epistle of Leo is dated on the 13th of June and could not have reached Theodoret in his detention at Cyrus till the autumn.

[2] Luke vi. 30.

truth, can lie. If they say that lying is possible to God, expel them from your company as impious and blasphemous. Should they agree that lying is not possible to the God of the universe, ask them in the second place, if He who is the fount of justice can become unjust. Should they allow that this too is impossible to the God of all, you must yet again enquire if the unfathomable depth of wisdom can become unwise, God cease to be God, the Lord cease to be the Lord, the Creator be no Creator, the Good not good but evil and the true Light not light but its opposite. If they admit that all these things and the like are impossible to God, you must say to them therefore many things are impossible with God; and that their being impossible so far from being a proof of want of power, indicates on the contrary the greatest power.

Even in the case of our own soul, when we say that it cannot die, we do not predicate weakness of it, but we proclaim its capacity of immortality. And similarly when we confess the immutability, impassibility, and immortality of God, we cannot attribute to the divine nature change, passion, or death. Suppose them to urge that God can do whatever He will, you must reply to them that He wishes to do nothing which it is not His nature to do; He is by nature good, therefore He does not wish anything evil; He is by nature just, therefore He does not wish anything unjust; He is by nature true, therefore He abominates falsehood; He is by nature immutable, therefore He does not admit of change; and if He does not admit of change He is always in the same state and condition. This He Himself asserts through the prophet. "I am the Lord I change not." [1] And the blessed David says "Thou art the same and Thy years shall have no end." [2] If He is the same He undergoes no change. If He is naturally superior to change and mutation He has not become from immortal, mortal nor from impassible, passible, for had this been possible He would not have taken on Him our nature. But since He has an immortal nature, He took a body capable of suffering, and with the body a human soul. Both of these He kept unstained from the defilements of sin, and gave His soul for the sake of the souls that had sinned, and His body for the sake of the bodies that had died. And since the body that was assumed is described as body of the very only begotten Son of God, He refers the passion of the body to Himself. But the four evangelists testify that it was not the divine nature but the body which was

nailed to the cross, all teaching with one voice that Joseph of Arimathea came to Pilate and begged the body of Jesus; that he took down the body of Jesus from the tree and wrapped in fine linen, and laid in his own new tomb the body of Jesus; that Mary the Magdalene came to the tomb seeking the body of Jesus and ran to His disciples, and reported these things when she could not find the body of Jesus.

This is the unanimous teaching of the evangelists. But if your opponents urge that the angels said "Come see the place where the Lord lay" [1] let the foolish folk learn that the divine Scripture says also about the victorious Stephen "And devout men carried Stephen to his burial." [2] And yet it was the body only which was deemed proper for burial, while the soul was not buried together with the body; nevertheless the body alone was spoken of by the common name. Similarly the blessed Jacob said to his sons "Bury me with my fathers." [3] He did not say "Bury my body." Then he went on "There they buried Abraham and Sarah his wife; there they buried Isaac and Rebekah his wife; and there I buried Leah." [4] He did not say "their bodies." The names are common to bodies or souls, but nevertheless it is only the bodies which he called by the common names. In this manner too we constantly describe the shrines of the holy apostles, prophets and martyrs, one it may be of Dionysius, another of Julianus another of Cosmas. [5] And yet we know that only fragmentary remains of bodies lie there, while the souls in diviner regions are at rest. Precisely the same custom is to be found in common use, for such an one, we say, died; and such an one lies in this place; although we know that the soul is immortal and does not share the tomb with the body. In this sense the angel said "Come see the place where the Lord lay" [6] not because he shut the Godhead in the tomb, but because he spoke of the Lord's body by the Lord's name.

In proof of this being the view of the holy Fathers let them mark the words of Athanasius, illustrious archbishop of Alexandria, who adorned his episcopate with confession. He exclaims "Life cannot die, but rather quickens the dead."

Let them hear too the words of the far-

---

[1] Matt. xxviii. 6.   [3] Gen. xlix. 29.
[2] Acts viii. 2.   [4] Gen. xlix. 31.
[5] Cf. note onp. 30 3. Among martyred Dionysii were (i) one of the Seven Sleepers of Ephesus, (ii) one at Tripoli (iii) another at Corinth, (iv and v) and two at Cæsarea, in the persecution of Diocletian. Cosmas and Damianus are the famous semi-mythical physicians, the Silverless Martyrs. Vide p. 295.
[6] Matthew xxviii. 6.

---

[1] Malachi iii. 6.   [2] Ps. cii. 27.

famed Damasus bishop of Rome, " If any-one allege that on the cross pain was under-gone by the Godhead and not by the body with the soul, the form of the servant which He had taken in its completeness, let him be anathema." [1]

Let them hear too the very sacred and holy bishop of the Church of the Romans, the lord Leo, who has now written " The Son of God suffered as He was capable of suffering, not according to the nature which assumed but that which was assumed. For the impassible nature assumed the passible body, and gave it for us, to the end that He might work out our salvation and at the same time preserve His own nature impassible."

And again " For He did not come to de-stroy His own nature but to save ours." [2]

If therefore they accuse us for saying that God can do what He wishes, but that He wishes what is becoming to His own nature, and what is unbecoming He neither wishes nor is capable of; let them accuse too these saints and all the rest who maintain this position. Let them accuse even the Apostle who says 'That by two immutable things in which it was impossible for God to lie." [3] And again " If we believe not, yet He abideth faithful : He cannot deny Himself." [4]

Repeat these passages to your opponents, and if they are convinced, praise the good Lord for that, by means of your zeal, He has benefited them. If they remain uncon-vinced, enter into no discussion with them about doctrines, for it is forbidden by the divine apostle to " strive about words to no profit but to the subverting of the hearers." [5] But do you keep inviolate the teaching of the Gospels, that in the day of His appear-ing you may bring to the righteous Judge what has been entrusted to you with its due interest, and may hear the longed for words " Well done good and faithful servant; thou hast been faithful over a few things I will make thee ruler over many things. Enter thou into the joy of thy Lord." [6]

CXLV. To the Monks of Constantinople. [7]

There is nothing new or surprising in the fact that the men who have made their tongues weapons against our God and Sa-

viour should also aim their shafts of false-hood against His right minded servants. It must needs be that the servants who grieve sorely at the outrage inflicted on their Master should share it. That so it should be they have been forewarned by their Lord Himself, Who consoles His holy disciples with the words " If they have persecuted me they will also persecute you." [1] " If they have called the Master of the house Beelzebub, how much more shall they call them of His household." [2] Then He cheered them by pointing out that calumny is easily detected, for He went on " There is nothing covered that shall not be revealed and hid that shall not be known." [3] I have often seen the truth of the divine prediction, but I see it with special clearness now. The authors of the calumny against me, who have bought my destruction for large sums of money, have been distinctly seen to be involved in the unsoundness of Valentinus and Bardesanes. They had hoped to cloke their own iniquity if only they could whet their tongues on the hone of falsehood in order to wound me. For ever since I saw that the heresy long ago extinguished had been renewed by these men I never ceased to cry aloud, bearing my testimony in private and in public, as well in social gatherings as in the temples of God, and strive to confute their conspiracy against the faith. They have consequently poured out their insults on my head, and allege that I preach two sons. But they ought to have convicted me to my face, not slandered me behind my back. They have done just the contrary. They tied me hand and foot at Cyrus by the imperial decree; they com-pelled the very righteous judges to condemn me without a trial, and delivered their most equitable sentence against a man who was five and thirty stages away. Such treatment was never suffered by any criminal charged with witchcraft or robbery of the dead, by murderer or by adulterer. But for the present I will leave the judges alone, for the Lord is at hand " Who judges the world with righte-ousness and the people with his truth ; " [4] Who exacts an account not only of words and deeds, but even of evil thoughts. But I think it right to refute the false charge which has been made. What proof have they of my asserting two sons? Had I been one of the silent kind there might have been some ground for the suspicion, but my task has been to contend on behalf of the apostolic decrees, to bring the pasture of instruction to the Lord's flocks, and to this end I have

---

1 Damas. Epist. ad Paulinum.   4 II. Tim. ii. 13.
2 Leo Epist. ad Flavianum.   5 II. Tim. ii. 14.
3 Hebrews vi. 18.   6 Matt. xxv. 23.
7 This, remarks Garnerius, is less a letter than a prolix exposition of Theodoret's view of the Incarnation. Theodoret mentions his condemnation at the Latrocinium and the exile of Eutyches, but says nothing of the favourable action towards himself of Marcianus. Theodosius died on the 29th of July, and Marcian began his reign on the 25th of August, 450. Theodoret could not possibly hear of the exile of Eutyches before the end of September. The document may therefore be dated in the late autumn of 450 before Theodoret had received the imperial permission to return to Cyrus.

---

1 John xv. 20.   3 Matt. x. 26.
2 Matt. x. 25.   4 Ps. xcvi. 13.

written five and thirty books interpreting the divine Scripture, and proving the falsehood of the heresies. The falsehoods these men have concocted are therefore easy of refutation. Tens on tens of thousands of hearers testify that I have taught the truth of the doctrines of the Gospel, and for any one who likes to bring them to the test my writings lie before the world. Not on behalf of a duality of sons, but of the only begotten Son of God, against the heathen, against Jews, against the recipients of the plague of Arius and Eunomius, against the supporters of the madness of Apollinarius, against the victims of the corruption of Marcion, I have never ceased to struggle; trying to convince the heathen that the Eternal Son of the ever living God is Himself Creator of the Universe; the Jews that about Him the prophets uttered their predictions, the Arians and Eunomians that He is of one substance, of one dignity and of equal power with the Father; Marcion's mad adherents that He is not only good but just; and Saviour not, as they fable, of another's works, but of His own. Once for all, fighting against each heresy, I charge men to fall down and worship the one Son.

And what need is there of many words, when it is possible to refute falsehood in few? We provide that those who year by year come up for holy baptism should carefully learn the faith set forth at Nicæa by the holy ,and blessed Fathers; and initiating them as we have been bidden,[1] we baptize them in the name of the Father and of the Son and of the Holy Ghost, pronouncing each name singly. Furthermore when performing divine service in the churches, both at the beginning and the decline of day and when dividing the day itself into three parts, we glorify the Father the Son and the Holy Ghost.[2] If, as our slanderers allege, we preach two sons, which do we glorify and which do we leave unworshipped? It were the wildest folly to believe that there are two sons, and to give the doxology to one alone. And who is so distraught as, while hearing the words of the divine Paul " one Lord, one faith, one baptism,"[3] and again " there is one Lord Jesus Christ by Whom are all things,"[4] to lay down the law at variance with the teaching of the Spirit, and cut the one in two. But I am prating unnecessarily, for these

men, nurtured in falsehood as they are, do not even dare to assert that they have ever heard me say anything of the kind; but they affirm that I preach two sons because I confess the two natures of our Master Christ. And they refuse to perceive that every human being has both an immortal soul and a mortal body; yet no one has hitherto been found to call Paul two Pauls because he has both soul and body, any more than Peter two Peters or Abraham or Adam. Everyone recognises the distinction of the natures, and does not call one man two Pauls. Precisely in the same way, when styling our Lord Jesus Christ the only begotten Son of God, God the Word incarnate, both Son of God and Son of Man, as we have been taught by the divine Scripture, we do not assert two sons, but we do confess the peculiar properties of the Godhead and of the manhood. The party however who deny the nature assumed of us men cannot hear these arguments without irritation.

It is only right that I should point out from what sources they have derived this impiety. Simon, Menander, Cerdo, and Marcion absolutely deny the incarnation, and call the birth from a Virgin fable. Valentinus, however, Basilides, Bardesanes, and Harmonius and their following, accept the conception of the Virgin and the birth; but they deny that God the Word took anything from the Virgin, but made as it were a transit through her as through a conduit, and appeared to mankind in semblance only, and seeming to be a man, in like manner as He was seen by Abraham and certain others of the ancients: Arius and Eunomius on the contrary held that He assumed a body, but that the Godhead played the part of the soul, in order that they may attribute to it what was lowly in His words and deeds. Apollinarius did indeed assert that He assumed a soul with the body, not the reasonable soul, but the soul which is called animal or phytic.[1] Their contention is that the Godhead took the part of the mind. He had learnt the distinction of soul and of mind from the philosophers that are without while divine Scripture says that man consists of soul and body. For we read " And the Lord God formed man of the dust of the ground and breathed into his nostrils the breath of life and man became a living soul."[2] And the Lord in the sacred Gospels said to His apostles " Fear not them which kill the body but are not able to kill the soul."[3]

---

[1] μυσταγωγοῦντες. μυσταγωγέω came ultimately to equal "baptize." The word and its correlatives had long passed out of special mystic use. In Cicero a μυσταγωγός is a "Cicerone" (Verr. iv. 59) and Strabo uses μυσταγωγεῖν for to be a guide. (812.)

[2] Reference appears to be made here to offices at the 3d, 6th, and 9th hours, and to morning and evening services, without specification of their number.

[3] Ephes. iv. 5.   [4] I. Cor. viii. 6.

[1] i.e. the life common to man with animals and plants. cf. p. 194 n.

[2] Gen. ii. 7.   [3] Matt. x. 28.

So great is the divergence between the doctrines. These men have now done their best to outdo Apollinarius, Arius and Eunomius, in their impiety and have now endeavoured to plant anew the heresy sown of old by Valentinus and Bardesanes, and afterwards uprooted by most excellent husbandmen. Like Valentinus and Bardesanes they have denied that the body of our Lord was assumed of our nature. But the Church, following the footprints of the Apostles, contemplates in the Lord Christ both perfect Godhead and perfect manhood. For just as He took a body, not that He needed a body, but by its means to give immortality to all bodies; so too He took a soul, the guide of the body, that every soul by its means might share His immutability. For even if souls are immortal, they are not however immutable; for they undergo many and frequent changes, as they experience pleasure, now from one object, and now from another. Whence it cometh about that we err when we are changed and are inclined to what is worse. But after the resurrection our bodies enjoy immortality and incorruptibility, and our souls impassibility and immutability. For this reason the only begotten Son of God took both a body and a soul, preserved them free from all blame, and offered the sacrifice for the race. And this is why He is called our high priest; and He is named high priest not as God but as man. He makes the offering as man, and accepts the sacrifice with the Father and the Holy Spirit as God. If only Adam's body had sinned, it alone should have benefited by the cure. But since the soul not only shared in the sin but was first in the sin, for first the thought forms an image of the sin and then carries it out by means of the body, it was just, I ween, that the soul too should be healed. But it is perhaps superfluous to demonstrate these points by reasoning, when the divine Scripture clearly proclaims them. This doctrine is distinctly taught by the holy David and the very divine Peter, the one foretelling from distant ages, and the other interpreting his prediction. The words of the first of the apostles are "David therefore being a prophet, and knowing that God had sworn with an oath to him, that of the fruit of his loins, according to the flesh, He would raise up Christ to sit on his throne; he seeing this before spake of the resurrection of Christ that His soul was not left in hell neither His flesh did see corruption." [1]

Now he has given us much instruction on the same point in these few words. First he states that the assumed nature derives its descent from the loins of David; secondly that He took not a body only, but also an immortal soul, and thirdly that He delivered body and soul to death, and, after taking them again, raised them as He would. His own words are "Destroy this temple and in three days I will raise it up." [1] But we have learnt that the divine nature is immortal. What suffered was the passible, and the impassible remained impassible. For God the Word was made man, not to render the impassible nature passible, but on the passible nature, by means of the Passion, to bestow the boon of impassibility. And the Lord Himself in the holy Gospels at one time says " I have power to lay down my life and I have power to take it again, no man taketh it from me but I lay it down of myself;" " That I may take it again." [2] And again " Therefore doth my Father love me because I lay down my life for the sheep," [3] and again " Now is my soul troubled " [4] " my soul is exceeding sorrowful even unto death" [5] and of His body He says " The bread that I will give is my flesh which I will give for the life of the world," [6] and when He delivered the divine mysteries and broke the symbol and distributed it, He added " This is my body which is being *broken* for you for the remission of sins," [7] and again " This is my blood which is shed for many for the remission of sins," [8] and again " Except ye eat the flesh of the Son of Man and drink His blood ye have no life in you" [9] and " Whosoever eateth my flesh and drinketh my blood hath eternal life " " in himself " he adds. [10] Innumerable passages of the same character may be quoted, both in the old Testament and the new, pointing out the assumption both of the body and of the soul, and that they are descended from Abraham and David. Joseph of Arimathea when he came to Pilate begged the body of Jesus, and the fourfold authority [11] of the holy Gospels tells us how he received the body, wrapped it in the linen cloth, and committed it to the tomb. I do, indeed, sorrow and lament that I am compelled by the attacks of error to adduce against men supposed to be of one and the same faith with myself the

---

1 Acts ii. 30 and 31. Ps. xvi. 10.

1 John ii. 19.
2 John x. 18. 17.   Observe the inversion and inexactitude.
3 John x. 17 and 15.   5 Matt. xxvi. 38.
4 John xii. 27.   6 John vi. 51.
7 I. Cor. xi. 24. Matt. xxvi. 28. But it is to be noticed that for St. Paul's word κλώμενον, i.e. " being broken," Theodoret substitutes θρυπτόμενον, i.e. "being crushed," or "broken small," a verb not used by the evangelists. And the clause " for the remission of sins " is misplaced.
8 Matt. xxvi. 28.   10 John vi. 54.
9 John vi. 53.   11 Cf. note on page 302.

arguments which I have already urged against the victims of the plague of Marcion, — of whom, by God's grace, I have converted more than ten thousand, and brought them to Holy Baptism. What child of the church ever had any doubts on these points? Who has not cited this teaching of the holy Fathers? The works of the great Basil are full of it; as well as those of his fellow soldiers Gregory and Amphilochius, and of those who in the West have been illustrious teachers of grace, Damasus, bishop of great Rome, and Ambrose of Milan; and Cyprian of Carthage who for the sake of these doctrines won the martyr's crown. Five times was the famous Athanasius driven from his flock and compelled to dwell in exile; and in the cause of these doctrines strove too his master Alexander. Eustathius, Meletius, and Flavianus, luminaries of the East, and Ephraim, harp of the Spirit, who daily waters the people of Syria with the streams of grace; John and Atticus, loud heralds of the truth; and men of an earlier age than they, Ignatius, Polycarp, Irenæus, Justin, and Hippolytus, of whom the more part not only shine at the head of the company of bishops, but also adorn the martyr's band.

He, too, who now rules great Rome and diffuses in all directions from the West the rays of right teaching, the most holy Leo, has expressed to me this distinctive mark of the faith in his own letters. All these have clearly taught that the only begotten Son of God and everlasting God, ineffably begotten of the Father, is one Son; and that after the incarnation He was called both Son of man and man, not because He was changed into manhood, for His nature is immutable, but because He took what was ours. They teach too that He was both impassible and immortal as God, and mortal and passible as man; but after the resurrection even in relation to His humanity He received impassibility and immortality, for, though the body remained a body, still it is impassible and immortal, verily a divine body and glorified with divine glory. This is distinctly told us by the blessed Paul in the words " For our conversation is in heaven from whence also we look for the Saviour, our Lord Jesus Christ, who shall change our vile body that it may be fashioned like unto the body of His glory."[1] He does not say to "His glory" but to "the body of His glory," and the Lord Himself, when He had said to His apostles "There be some standing here which shall not taste of death till they see the Son

of man coming in His Father's glory,"[1] took them after six days into an exceeding high mountain, and was transfigured before them, and His face became as the sun, and His raiment was bright like the light.[2] By these means He shewed the manner of the second advent. He taught that the assumed nature is not uncircumscribed (for this is characteristic of the Godhead alone) but that it shall send forth flashes of the divine glory, and emit rays of light transcending the powers of the sense of sight. With this glory He was taken up; with this the angels said that He should come; for their words were "He who was taken from you into heaven shall so come in like manner as ye have seen him go into heaven."[3] When moreover He was seen by the divine apostles after the resurrection, He shewed them both hands and feet; and to Thomas He shewed also His side and the wounds of the nails and of the spear. For on account of those men who positively deny the assumption of the flesh, and further of those others who assert that after the resurrection the nature of the body was changed into the nature of Godhead, He preserved unaltered the prints of the nails and of the spear. And while raising all other bodies free from every disfigurement,[4] in His own body He left the marks of His sufferings, to the end that deniers of the assumption of the body may be convicted of their error by means of His sufferings; and holders of the notion that His body was changed into another nature may be taught by the print of the nails that it abides in its own proper qualities. Suppose any one to imagine that he has a proof that the body of the Lord did not remain a body after the resurrection in the fact that He came in to the disciples when the doors were shut, let such an one remember how He walked upon the sea while His body was still mortal, how He was born after keeping the seals of virginity intact, and how again when encircled by them that were plotting against Him He frequently escaped from their hands. But why need I mention the Lord, who was not only man, but God before the ages, and to whom it was easy to do whatsoever He would? Let them tell how Habakkuk was translated from Judæa into Babylon in a moment of time and passed through the covering of the den, and brought the food to Daniel, and returned again, without destroying the seals of the den.[5] It is sheer foolishness to enquire into the manner of the miracles of the Lord,

---

[1] Phil. iii. 20 and 21.

[1] Matt. xvi. 28. Observe variation. The MSS. agree.
[2] Cf. Matt. xxxvii. 1. 2.   [4] Cf. p. 199. n.
[3] Acts i. 11.   [5] Bel and the Dragon. 36.

but in addition to what has been said it ought also to be known that after the resurrection our bodies also will be incorruptible and immortal, and being released from what is earthly will become light and æthereal. This moreover is distinctly taught us by the divine Paul in the words " It is sown in corruption, it is raised in incorruption, it is sown in weakness it is raised in power; it is sown in dishonour it is raised in glory ; it is sown a natural body it is raised a spiritual body " [1] and in another place " We shall be caught up in the clouds to meet the Lord in the air." [2] If then the bodies of the saints become light and æthereal and easily travel through the air, we cannot wonder that the Lord's body united to the Godhead of the only begotten, when, after the resurrection, it had become immortal, entered in when the doors were shut.

Countless other proofs might be quoted without difficulty from apostles and prophets. But what has been already said is enough to show the drift of my teaching. I believe in one Father, one Son and one Holy Ghost ; and I confess one Godhead, one Lordship, one substance and three hypostases. For the incarnation of the only begotten did not add to the number of the Trinity, and make the Trinity a quaternity, but, even after the incarnation the Trinity was still a Trinity. And while confessing that the only begotten Son of God was made man I do not deny the nature which He took, but confess, as I have said, both the nature which took and the nature which was taken. The union did not confound the properties of the natures. For if the air by receiving the light through all its parts does not cease to be air, nor yet at the same time destroy the nature of the light, for with our eyes we behold the light and by our feeling we recognise the air, as it meets us cold or hot, or moist or dry, so it were sheer folly to call the union of the Godhead and the manhood confusion. If created natures which share at once subordinate and temporal existence, when united and in some sense mingled, yet remain unimpaired, and, when the light withdraws, the nature of the air is left alone, much more proper is it, I apprehend, for the nature which fashioned all things, when conjoined with and united to the nature which it assumed from us, to be acknowledged to continue itself in its purity, and in like manner to preserve unimpaired that which it had assumed. Gold, too, when brought in contact with the fire, participates both in the

colour and power of fire, but it does not lose its own nature, but at the same time remains gold and has the active qualities of fire. In this manner also the Lord's body is a body, but impassible, incorruptible, immortal, of the Lord, divine and glorified with the divine glory. It is not separated from the Godhead, nor yet is of any one else, save of the only begotten Son of God Himself. For it does not show to us another person, but the only-begotten Himself clad in our nature.

This is the doctrine which I am continually preaching. They on the other hand who deny the incarnation wrought on our behalf have called me a heretic, adopting a course something like that of unchaste females, who, while they sell their own charms, assail honest women with the insults of their profession, and apply language proper to their own wantonness to women who hold such wantonness in abhorrence. This is how Egypt has acted. She has herself fallen willingly into the thraldom of base desire. She has lavished her servile adulation on a man of chaste character. Then, failing to entice him by her wiles, or to trap him in the snares of her voluptuous passion, she describes one who is faithful to purity as an adulterer.

But these men will be called to account by God, as well for their devices against the faith as for the snares they have laid against me. I only charge those who have been influenced by the false accusations uttered against me to keep one ear for the accused, and not to give both to the accusers. In this manner they will fulfil the divine law which lays down " Thou shalt not raise a false report," [1] and " Judge righteously between every man and his brother." [2] In these words the divine law charges us not to believe the calumnies uttered against the absent but to judge the accused face to face.

CXLVI. To John the Œconomus. [3]

Rest and a life free from care are very grateful to me. I have therefore blocked the door of the monastery, and decline intercourse with my friends.

But I have received information that fresh attacks are being made against the Faith of the Gospels, and therefore conclude that there may be danger in my silence. When wrong has been done some mortal prince, not only

---

[1] Ex. xxiii. 1.   [2] Deut. i. 16.
[3] Cf. note on page 288. This letter, or rather doctrinal statement is incomplete. Garnerius supposes it to have been written during Theodoret's retirement after the Council of Chalcedon. There he cut himself off from society and wished to devote himself to study and contemplation.

---

[1] I. Cor. xv. 42. 43.   [2] I. Thess. iv. 17.

the guilty authors of the outrage but they also who have been standing by and made no effort to drive off the assailants, are in peril of punishment: What penalty then ought not to be undergone by men who can venture to look lightly on the utterance of blasphemy against our God and Saviour? This is the fear which has impelled me now to write and expose the innovations of which I have been informed.

It is said that a common report in the city represents that after certain presbyters had offered prayer, and concluded it in the wonted manner, while some said "For to Thee belongs glory and to thy Christ and to the Holy Ghost;" and others "Through grace and loving kindness of thy Christ, with whom belongs glory to Thee with thy holy Spirit," the very wise archdeacon prohibited the use of the expression, "the Christ" and said that the "only begotten" ought to be glorified. If this is true it were impossible to exceed the impiety. For he either divides the one Lord Jesus Christ into two sons and regards the only begotten Son as lawful and natural, but the Christ as adopted and spurious, and consequently unmeet for being honoured in doxology; or else he is endeavouring to support the heresy which has now burst in on us with the riot of wild revelry. Had a grievous tempest been now oppressing us, any one might have supposed that the blasphemer suited his blasphemy to the necessity of the moment, through fear of the power of the originators of the heresy. But now that He who is blasphemed has rebuked the winds and the sea, and blessed the storm-tossed churches with a calm, while everywhere by land and sea the proclamation of the apostles is preached, what room is there for the blasphemy? While not even they who have lately basely inserted among the doctrines of the Church that flesh and godhead are of one and the same nature have ever forbidden the offering of praise to the Lord Christ. This fact may be easily ascertained from those who have returned thence. A man holding the foremost place in the ecclesiastical rank ought to have known the divine Scripture, and to have learnt from it that just as the heralds of the truth rank the only begotten Son with the Father, so accordingly using the title of "the Christ" instead of that of "Son" they number Him sometimes with the Father and sometimes with the Holy Ghost; for the Christ is none other than the only begotten Son of God. So we may quote the divine Paul writing to the Corinthians, but teaching the world, that "There is

one God the Father of whom are all things . . . and one Lord Jesus Christ by whom are all things."[1] Thus he calls the same person, Christ, Jesus, Lord, and Creator of all things. And writing to the Thessalonians he says "Now God Himself and our Father and our Lord Jesus Christ direct our way unto you."[2] And in his second epistle to the same he puts the Christ before the Father, not to invert the order, but to teach that the order of the names does not indicate a distinction of dignity and nature. His words are "Now our Lord Jesus Christ Himself, and God, even our Father, which hath loved us, and hath given us everlasting consolation and good hope through grace, comfort your hearts, and stablish you in every good word and work."[3] And at the end of his Epistle to the Romans after certain exhortations he adds "I beseech you brethren for the Lord Jesus Christ's sake and for the love of the spirit."[4] Now if he had known the Christ as being any other than the Son he would not have put Him before the Holy Ghost. Writing to the Corinthians, at the very beginning of his letter, he mentions the name of Christ as alone sufficient to influence the faithful. "Now I beseech you brethren by the name of our Lord Jesus Christ that ye all speak the same thing"[5] and when writing to them a second time he thus concludes "The peace of our Lord Jesus Christ and the love of God the Father and the communion of the Holy Ghost be with you all."[6] Here he puts the name of Christ not only before the Spirit, but also before the Father and this in all the churches is the beginning of the Liturgy of the Mystery.

According, then, to this extraordinary regulation the august name of our God and Saviour, Jesus Christ, ought to be omitted from the mystic writings. But it is unnecessary to say more on this point. The opening of every one of his letters is distinguished by the divine Apostle with this address. At one time it is "Paul a servant of Jesus Christ called to be an apostle."[7] At another "Paul called to be an apostle of Jesus Christ."[8] At another "Paul a servant of God and an apostle of Jesus Christ."[9] And suiting his benediction to his exordium he deduces it from the same source and links the title of the Son with God the Father, saying "Grace to you and peace from God our Father and the Lord Jesus Christ."[10] And he graces the conclusion of his letters

---

1 I. Cor. viii. 6.
2 I. Thess. iii. 11.
3 II. Thess. ii. 16, 17.
4 Romans xv. 30.
5 I. Cor. i. 10.
6 II. Cor. 13. 14.
7 Romans i. 1.
8 I. Cor. i. 1.
9 Titus i. 1.
10 Romans i. 7.

with the blessing "The grace of our Lord Jesus Christ be with you all, amen."[1]

Copious additional evidence may be found whereby it may be learnt without difficulty that our Lord Jesus Christ is no other person than the Son which completes the Trinity. For the same before the ages was only begotten Son and God the Word, and after the resurrection He was called Jesus and Christ, receiving the names from the facts. Jesus means Saviour; "Thou shalt call His name Jesus for He shall save His people from their sins."[2]

He is named Christ from being as man anointed with the Holy Ghost, and called our High Priest, Apostle, Prophet and King. Long ago the divine Moses exclaimed "The Lord thy God will raise up unto thee a prophet, from the midst of thee, of thy brethren, like unto me."[3] And the divine David cries "The Lord hath sworn and will not repent, Thou art a priest forever after the order of Melchisedek."[4] This prophecy is confirmed by the divine Apostle.[5] And again "seeing then that we have a great High Priest that has passed into the heavens, Jesus the Son of God, let us hold fast our profession."[6]

That as God, He is king before the ages that prophetic minstrelsy teaches us in the words "Thy throne, O God, is for ever and ever; the sceptre of Thy kingdom is a right sceptre."[7]

His majesty as man is also shown us. For having the sovereignty of all things as God and Creator, He assumes this majesty as man, wherefore it is added "Thou lovest righteousness and hatest wickedness, therefore God thy God hath anointed thee with the oil of gladness above thy fellows."[8] And in the second psalm the anointed one himself says "Yet was I set as king by Him upon the holy hill of Sion, I will declare the decree of the Lord. The Lord hath said unto me 'Thou art my Son this day have I begotten Thee; ask of me and I shall give Thee the heathen for thine inheritance and the uttermost parts of the earth for thy possession.'"[9] This He said as man, for as man He receives what as God He possesses. And at the very beginning of the psalm the gift of prophecy ranks Him with God the Father in the words "Why do the heathen rage and the people imagine a vain thing. The kings of the earth set themselves and the rulers take counsel together against the Lord and against His anointed."[10]

Let no one then foolishly suppose that the Christ is any other than the only begotten Son. Let us not imagine ourselves wiser than the gift of the Spirit. Let us hear the words of the great Peter, "Thou art the Christ, the Son of the living God."[1] Let us hear the Lord Christ confirming this confession, for "On this rock," He says, "I will build my church and the gates of Hell shall not prevail against it."[2] Wherefore too the wise Paul, most excellent master builder of the churches, fixed no other foundation than this. "I," he says, "as a wise master builder have laid the foundation, and another buildeth thereon. But let every man take heed how he buildeth thereon. For other foundation can no man lay than that is laid, which is Jesus Christ."[3] How then can they think of any other foundation, when they are bidden not to fix a foundation, but to build on that which is laid? The divine writer recognises Christ as the foundation, and glories in this title, as when he says, "I am crucified with Christ: nevertheless I live; yet not I but Christ liveth in me."[4] And again "To me to live is Christ and to die is gain,"[5] and again "For I determined not to know anything among you save Jesus Christ and Him crucified."[6] And a little before he says, "But we preach Christ crucified to the Jews a stumblingblock and to the Greeks foolishness, but unto them which are called both Jews and Greeks, Christ the power of God and the wisdom of God."[7] And in his Epistle to the Galatians he writes, "But when it pleased God who separated me from my mother's womb and called me by His grace to reveal His Son in me that I might preach Him among the heathen."[8] But when writing to the Corinthians he does not say we preach "the Son" but "Christ crucified," herein doing no violence to his commission, but recognising the same to be Jesus, Christ, Lord, only begotten, and God the Word. For the same reason too at the beginning of his letter to the Romans he calls himself "servant of Jesus Christ" and describes himself as "separated unto the gospel of God, which He had promised afore by His prophets in the Holy Scriptures, concerning His Son Jesus Christ our Lord, which was made of the seed of David according to the flesh; and declared to be the Son of God

---

1 Romans xvi. 4. 5 Hebrews vii. 21. 8 Psalm xlv. 7.
2 Matt. i. 21. 6 Hebrews iv. 14. 9 Psalm ii. 6, 7, 8. lxx.
3 Deut. viii. 15. 7 Psalm xlv. 6. 10 Psalm ii. 1, 2.
4 Psalm cxii. 4.

1 Matt. xvi. 16.
2 It will be observed that our author omits the verse containing the famous paronomasia, and that what he regards the Saviour as confirming is not any supposed authority on the part of the speaker but the identification of Himself with the Christ and of the Christ with the Son of the living God.
3 I. Cor. iii. 10, 11. 5 Phil. i. 21. 7 I. Cor. i. 23, 24.
4 Gal. ii. 19. 6 I. Cor. ii. 2. 8 Gal. i. 15, 16.

with power," [1] and so on. He calls the same both Jesus Christ, and Son of David, and Son of God, as God and Lord of all, and yet in the middle of his epistle, after making mention of the Jews, he adds, " whose are the fathers, and of whom as concerning the flesh Christ came, who is over all God blessed for ever, amen." [2] Here he says that He who according to the flesh derived His descent from the Jews is eternal God and is praised by the right minded as Lord of all created things. The same teaching is given us in the Apostle's words to the excellent Titus " Looking for that blessed hope, and the glorious appearing of the great God and our Saviour Jesus Christ." [3] Here he calls the same both Saviour, and great God, and Jesus Christ. And in another place he writes, " In the kingdom of Christ and of God." [4] Moreover the chorus of the angels announced to the shepherds " Unto you is born this day in the city of David . . . Christ the Lord." [5]

But to men who meditate on God's law day and night, it is indeed needless to write all the proofs of this kind; the above are sufficient to persuade even the most obstinate opponents not to divide the divine titles. One point, however, I cannot endure to omit. He is alleged to have said that there are many Christs but one Son. Into this error I suppose he fell through ignorance. For if he had read the divine Scripture, he would have known that the title of the Son has also been bestowed by our bountiful Lord on many. The lawgiver Moses, the writer of the ancient history, says " And the sons of God saw the daughters of men that they were fair and they took them wives of them," [6] and the God of all Himself said to this Prophet " Thou shalt say unto Pharaoh, Israel is my son even my first-born." [7] In the great song he says " Rejoice O ye nations with His people and let all the sons of God be strong in Him ; " [8] and by the mouth of the prophet Isaiah He says " I have nourished and brought up sons (children) and they have rebelled against me ; " [9] and through the thrice blessed David " I have said ye are gods and all of you are children of the Most High," [10] and to the Romans the wise Paul wrote in

this manner, " For as many as are led by the Spirit of God, they are the sons of God. For ye have not received the spirit of bondage again to fear ; but ye have received the spirit of adoption, whereby we cry, Abba, Father. For the Spirit itself beareth witness with our spirit, that we are the children of God. And if children, then heirs ; heirs of God and joint-heirs with Christ : if so be that we suffer with Him that we may be also glorified together ; " [1] and to the Galatians he writes " And because ye are sons God hath sent forth the spirit of His Son into your hearts, crying, Abba, Father. Wherefore thou art no more a servant but a son ; and if a son then an heir of God through Jesus Christ." [2] The lesson he gives to the Ephesians is " in love having predestinated us into the adoption of children by Jesus Christ to Himself." [3]

If then, because the name of the Christ is common, we ought not to glorify the Christ as God, we shall equally shrink from worshipping Him as Son, since this also is a name which has been bestowed upon many. And why do I say the Son? The very name of God itself has been given by God to many. " The Lord the God of gods hath spoken and called the earth." [4] And " I have said Ye are gods," [5] and " Thou shalt not revile the gods." [6] Many too have appropriated this name to themselves. The dæmons who have deceived mankind have given this title to idols ; whence Jeremiah exclaims, " The gods that have not made the heavens and the earth even they shall perish from the earth and from under these heavens ; " [7] and again " They made to themselves gods of silver and gods of gold ; " [8] and the prophet Isaiah when he had mocked the making of the idols, and said " He burneth part thereof in the fire with part thereof he eateth flesh he warmeth himself and saith Aha I am warm I have seen the fire," [9] went on " and the residue thereof he maketh a god and falleth down unto it and saith ' Deliver me for thou art my god ' " [10] and so the prophet laments over them and says " Know that their heart is ashes." [11] And the Psalmist David has taught us to sing " For all the gods of the nations are idols, but the Lord made the heavens." [12]

But this common use of titles gives no offence to men who are instructed in true religion. We are aware that the dæmons have falsely bestowed upon themselves and

---

[1] Romans i. 1-4.   [2] Romans ix. 5.   [3] Titus ii. 13.
[4] Ephes. v. 5. Here the A. V. rather obscures the force of the original. The R. V. alters to " in the kingdom of Christ and God," but even this hardly brings out Theodoret's views of ἐν τῇ βασιλείᾳ τοῦ Χριστοῦ καὶ Θεοῦ, " in the kingdom of the Christ and God." The MSS. do not vary. At the same time it will be borne in mind that the anarthrous use of " Θεός " is not infrequent, and that some commentators (cf. Alford ad loc.) would hesitate to ground on this passage the argument of the text. The reading of א and B in John i. 18 "ὁ μονογενὴς Θεός " is significant.
[5] Luke ii. 11.   [7] Exodus iv. 22.   [9] Is. i. 2.
[6] Gen. vi. 2.   [8] Deut. xxxii. 43. lxx.   [10] Psalm lxxxii. 6.

[1] Romans viii. 14-17.   [2] Gal. iv. 6. 7.
[3] Ephes. i. 4. 5. Observe the position of " in love " which agrees with the margin of R. V.
[4] Psalm l. 1. lxx.   [6] Exodus ii. 28.
[5] Psalm lxxxii. 6.   [7] Jeremiah x. 11.
[8] This seems to be an inaccurate quotation of Baruch vi. 11. cf. p. 165 n.   [9] Isaiah xliv. 16.   [10] Isaiah xliv. 17.
[11] Isaiah xliv. 20. lxx.   [12] Psalm xcvi. 5.

on idols the divine name, while the saints have received this honour of free grace.

In reality and by nature it is the God of all, and His only-begotten Son and the Holy Spirit which are God. This is distinctly taught us by the admirable Paul in the words "For though there be that are called gods whether in heaven or in earth, as there are gods many and lords many, but to us there is but one God, the Father, of whom are all things, and we in Him; and one Lord by whom are all things and we by Him."[1] And the Holy Spirit is called the Spirit of God and so also is the soul of man, for, it is written, "His breath goeth forth,"[2] and "O ye spirits and souls of the righteous bless ye the Lord,"[3] and the Psalmist David called the angels spirits. "Who maketh His angels spirits and His ministers a flame of fire."[4] Why indeed do I mention the angels and the souls of men? Even the dæmons are so called by the Lord "He shall take unto him seven other spirits more wicked than himself and they shall enter in, and the last state of that man shall be worse than the first."[5] But even this application of the name does not offend the pious reader, for the Father and His only begotten Son and His Holy Spirit are one God by nature; and the divine Word made man, our Lord Jesus Christ, is by nature one Son, only begotten of the Father; and the Comforter who completes the number of the Trinity is one Holy Ghost. Thus though many are named fathers, we worship one Father, the Father before the ages, who Himself gave this title to men, as the Apostle says, "For this cause I bow my knees unto the Father of our Lord Jesus Christ, of whom every fatherhood in heaven and earth is named."[6] Let us not then, because others are called christs, rob ourselves of the worship of our Lord Jesus Christ. For just as though many are called gods and fathers, there is one God and Father over all and before the ages; and though many are called sons, there is one real and natural Son; and though many are styled spirits there is one Holy Ghost; just so though many are called christs there is one Lord Jesus Christ by Whom are all things. And very properly does the Church cling to this name; for she has heard Paul, escorter of the Bride, exclaiming "I have espoused you to one husband that I may present you as a chaste virgin to Christ,"[7] and

again "Husbands love your wives as Christ also loved the Church,"[1] and again "For this cause shall a man leave his father and mother, and shall be joined unto his wife, and they two shall be one flesh. This is a great mystery; but I speak concerning Christ and the Church."[2] Listen to him as he says "Christ hath redeemed us from the curse of the law, being made a curse for us,"[3] and elsewhere "Know ye not that so many of us as were baptized unto Jesus Christ were baptized into His death,"[4] and in another place, "For as many of you as have been baptized into Christ have put on Christ,"[5] and again "Put ye on the Lord Jesus Christ, and make not provision for the flesh, to fulfil the lust thereof."[6]

They who are blessed by the boons of God and have learnt to know these passages and others like them, kindled with warm love for their bountiful Master, constantly carry on their lips this His dearest name and cry in the words of the Song of Songs "My beloved is mine and I am his;" "I sat down under his shadow with great delight, and his fruit was sweet to my taste."[7] And besides all this that name of ours which we love so well we have derived from the name of Christ. We are called Christians.[8]

Of this name the Lord of all says, "The Lord God shall call His servants by another name which shall be blessed on the earth"[9] and the following is the reason why the Church specially clings to this name. When the only-begotten Son of God was made man,

---

[1] Ephes. v. 25.
[2] Ephes. v. 31. 32.
[3] Gal. iii. 13.
[4] Rom. vi. 3.
[5] Gal. iii. 27.
[6] Rom. xiii. 14.
[7] Canticles ii. 16. 3.
[8] Acts xi. 26. "The word seems to have been in the first instance a nickname fastened by the heathen populace of Antioch on the followers of Christ, who still continued to style themselves the 'disciples' or the 'saints' or the 'brethren' or the 'believers,' and the like. The biting gibes of the Antiochene populace which stung to the quick successive emperors — Hadrian, M. Aurelius, Severus, Julian — would be little disposed to spare the helpless adherents of this new 'superstition.' Objection indeed has been taken to the Antiochene origin of the name on the ground that the termination is Roman, like Pompeianus, Caesarianus, and the like. But this termination, if it was Latin, was certainly Asiatic likewise, as appears from such words as Ἀσιανός, βακτριανός, Σαρδιανός, Τραλλιανός, Ἀρειανός, Μενανδριανός, Σαβελλιανός. The next occurrence of the word in a Christian document is on the occasion of St. Paul's apearance before Festus (A. D. 60). It is not however put in the mouth of a believer, but occurs in the scornful jest of Agrippa, 'With but little persuasion thou wouldest fain make me a Christian' (Acts xxvi. 28). The third and last example occurs a few years later. In the first Epistle of St. Peter, presumably about A. D. 66 or 67, the Apostle writes 'Let not any of you suffer as a murderer or a thief . . . but if (he suffers) as a Christian, let him not be ashamed but glorify God' (iv. 15). Here again the term is not the Apostle's own, but represents the charge brought against the believers by their heathen accusers. In the New Testament there is no indication that the name was yet adopted by the disciples of Christ as their own. Thus Christian documents again confirm the statement of Tacitus that as early as the Neronian persecution this name prevailed, and the same origin also is indirectly suggested by those notices, which he directly states — not 'qui sese appellabant Christianos' but 'quos vulgus appellabat Christianos.' It was a gibe of the common people against 'the brethren.'" Bp. Lightfoot Ap. Fathers, II. i. 417.
[9] Isaiah lxv. 15. 16. lxx.

---

[1] I. Cor. viii. 5. 6.
[2] Psalm cxlvi. 4.
[3] Song of the three holy children 63.
[4] Psalm civ. 4.
[5] Matt. xii. 43. Luke xi. 26. Observe difference of tense and variation.
[6] Ephes. iii. 14. R. V. marg. It will be seen that the argument of Theodoret does not admit of the translation "whole family" as in A. V.
[7] II. Cor. xi. 2.

then He was named Christ, then human nature received the beams of intellectual light; then the heralds of the truth shed their beams upon the world. Teachers of the Church, however, constantly used the names of the only begotten without distinction; at one time they glorify the Father, the Son and the Holy Ghost; at another the Father with Christ and the Holy Ghost; yet as far as the sense is concerned there is here no difference. Wherefore after the Lord had commanded to baptize in the name of the Father and of the Son and of the Holy Ghost the blessed Peter said to them who received his preaching and asked what they must do, "Believe and be baptized every one of you in the name of our Lord Jesus Christ,"[1] as though this name contained in itself all the potency of the divine command. The same teaching is clearly given us by the great Basil, luminary of the Cappadocians,[2] or rather of the world. His words are "the name of Christ is the confession of the whole." It indicates at once the Father, who anointed, the Son, who was anointed, and the Holy Ghost whereby He was anointed. Furthermore the thrice blessed Fathers assembled in council at Nicæa, after saying that we must believe in one God, the Father, added "and in one Lord Jesus Christ, the only begotten Son of God." Thereby they teach that the Lord Jesus Christ is Himself the only begotten Son of God.

To what has been said it must also be added that we must not affirm that after the ascension the Lord Christ is not Christ but only begotten Son. The divine Gospels and the history of the Acts and the Epistles of the Apostle himself were, as we know, written after the ascension. It is after the ascension that the divine Paul exclaims "Seeing then that we have a great High Priest that is passed into the heavens, Jesus the Son of God, let us hold fast our profession."[3] And again, "For Christ is not entered into the holy places made with hands, which are the figures of the true; but into Heaven itself, now to appear in the presence of God for us."[4] And again after speaking of our hope in God he adds "which hope we have as an anchor both sure and stedfast, and which entereth into that within the veil; whither the forerunner is for us entered, even Jesus made an High Priest for ever after the order of Mel-

chisedec."[1] And when writing to the blessed Titus about the second advent he says, "Looking for that blessed hope, and the glorious appearing of the great God and our Saviour Jesus Christ."[2] And to the Thessalonians he wrote in similar terms "For they themselves show of us what manner of entering in we had unto you, and how we turned to God from idols to serve the living and true God; and to wait for His Son from heaven, whom He raised from the dead, even Jesus, which delivered us from the wrath to come."[3] And again "And the Lord make you to increase and abound in love one toward another, and toward all men, even as we do toward you: to the end he may stablish your hearts unblamable in holiness before God, even our Father, at the coming of our Lord Jesus Christ with all his saints."[4] And again when writing to the same a second time he says, "Now we beseech you, brethren, by the coming of our Lord Jesus Christ, and by our gathering together unto him."[5] And a little further on when predicting the destruction of antichrist he adds, "Whom the Lord shall consume with the spirit of his mouth, and shall destroy with the brightness of his coming."[6] And when exhorting the Romans to concord he says, "But why dost thou judge thy brother? or why dost thou set at naught thy brother? for we shall all stand before the judgment seat of Christ. For it is written, as I live, saith the Lord, every knee shall bow to me, and every tongue shall confess to God."[7] And the Lord Himself when announcing His second advent besides other things says too this "Then if any man shall say unto you, Lo, here is Christ, or there; believe it not. For as the lightning cometh out of the east, and shineth even unto the west, so shall also the coming of the Son of Man be."[8]

And after the immortality and incorruptibility of His body He called Himself Son of Man, naming Himself from the nature which was seen, inasmuch as the divine nature is indeed invisible to angels, as the Lord Himself had said "No one hath seen God at any time."[9] And to the great Moses He said "There shall no man see me and live."[10]

---

[1] Acts ii. 38. "Believe" substituted for "repent."
[2] i.e. of Cæsarea. The Cappadocian Cæsarea originally called Mazaca is still Kasaria.
[3] Heb. iv. 14. On the opinion of the Pauline authorship of the Epistle to the Hebrews cf. note on page 37. The Alexandrian view is shewn to have affected the Eastern Church. For the reading "Jesus Christ" instead of Jesus the Son of God on which Theodoret's argument depends there is no manuscript authority. [4] Heb. ix, 24.

[1] Heb. vi, 19, 20.
[2] Titus ii, 13. Cf. note on page 319 on the passage Ephes. v, 5. Here, however, the position of the article is in favour of the interpretation "Jesus Christ, the great God and our Saviour" which was generally adopted by the Greek orthodox Fathers in their controversy with the Arians and by the majority of ancient and modern commentators. But see Alford *ad loc.* for such arguments as may be adduced in favour of taking σωτήρ as anarthrous like Θεός.
[3] I Thess. i. 9, 10.   [6] II Thess. ii. 8.
[4] I Thess. iii. 12, 13. [7] Romans xiv. 10. 16.
[5] II Thess. ii. 1.   [8] Matt. xxiv. 23 and 27.
[9] John i. 18. The "no *man*" of A. V. does not admit of Theodoret's argument.
[10] Ex. xxxiii 20. lxx. οὐδεὶς ὄψεται.

The words "Henceforth know we no man after the flesh; yea, though we have known Christ after the flesh; yet now henceforth know we Him no more,"[1] were not written by the divine Apostle in order to annul the assumed nature, but for the confirmation of our own future incorruption, immortality, and spiritual life.

The Apostle therefore continues "Therefore if any man be in Christ he is a new creature; old things are passed away; behold all things are become new."[2] He speaks of what is to be in the future as though it had already come to pass. We have not yet been gifted with immortality, but we shall be; and when so gifted we shall not become bodiless, but we shall put on immortality. "For" says the divine Apostle, "we would not be unclothed, but clothed upon, that mortality might be swallowed up of life."[3] And again "For this corruptible must put on incorruption, and this mortal must put on immortality."[4] Thus he did not speak of the Lord as bodiless, but taught us to believe that even the visible nature is incorruptible, and glorified with the divine glory. This instruction he has given us yet more clearly in the Epistle to the Philippians; "For our conversation" he writes "is in heaven; from whence also we look for the Saviour, the Lord Jesus Christ; who shall change our vile body, that it may be fashioned like unto his glorious body."[5] By these words he teaches us distinctly that the body of the Lord is a body, but a divine body, and glorified with the divine glory.

Let us, then, not shun the name whereby we enjoy salvation, and whereby all things are made new, as says our teacher himself in his Epistle to the Ephesians, — "According to His good pleasure which He hath purposed in Himself; that in the dispensation of the fulness of time He might gather together in one all things in Christ, both which are in heaven, and which are on earth, even in Him."[6] Let us rather learn from this blessed language how we are bound to glorify our benefactor, by connecting the name of Christ with our God and Father. In his Epistle to the Romans the Apostle says "my gospel, and the preaching of Jesus Christ, according to the revelation of the mystery, which was kept secret since the world began, but now is made manifest, and by the scriptures of the prophets, according to the commandment of the everlasting God,

made known to all nations for the obedience of faith; to God only will be glory through Jesus Christ forever. Amen."[1] Writing to the Ephesians he thus gives praise — "Now unto Him that is able to do exceeding abundantly above all that we ask or think, according to the power that worketh in us, unto Him be glory in the Church by Christ Jesus throughout all ages, world without end. Amen."[2] And a little before he says, "For this cause I bow my knee unto the Father of our Lord Jesus Christ of whom the whole family in heaven and earth is named."[3] And considerably farther on he says "Giving thanks always for all things unto God and the Father in the name of our Lord Jesus Christ."[4] And when he requites with benediction the liberality of the Philippians he says "But my God shall supply all your need according to His riches in glory by Christ Jesus."[5] And for the Hebrews he prayed, "Now the God of peace, that brought again from the dead our Lord Jesus Christ, that great shepherd of the sheep, through the blood of the everlasting covenant, make you perfect in every good work, to do His will, working in you that which is well pleasing in His sight, through Jesus Christ; to whom be glory for ever and ever. Amen."[6] And not only when glorifying, but also when exhorting and protesting, the Apostle conjoins the Christ with God the Father. To the blessed Timothy he exclaims "I charge thee therefore before God and the Lord Jesus Christ."[7] And again "I give thee charge in the sight of God who quickeneth all things, and before Jesus Christ, who before Pontius Pilate witnessed a good confession; that thou keep this commandment without spot, unrebukable, until the appearing of our Lord Jesus Christ; which in His times He shall shew, who is the blessed and only Potentate, the King of kings and Lord of lords; who only hath immortality, dwelling in the light which no man can approach unto; whom no man hath seen, nor can see; to whom be honour and power everlasting. Amen."[8]

These are the lessons we have learnt from the divine Apostles; this is the teaching given us by John and Matthew, those mighty rivers of the gospel message. The latter says "The book of the generation of Jesus Christ the son of David, the son of Abraham;"[9] and the former when he shewed the things which were before the ages wrote, "In the

---

[1] II. Cor. v. 16
[2] II. Cor. v. 17.
[3] II. Cor. v. 4.
[4] I. Cor. xv. 53.
[5] Phil iii. 20, 21.
[6] Eph. i. 9, 10.

[1] Rom. xvi. 25, 26, 27.
[2] Eph. iii. 20, 21.
[3] Eph. iii. 14. A. V.
[4] Eph. v. 20.
[5] Phil. iv. 19.

[6] Heb. xiii. 20, 21.
[7] II. Tim. iv. 1.
[8] I. Tim. vi. 13. 14. 15. 16.
[9] Matt. i. 1.

beginning was the Word and the Word was with God and the Word was God. The same was in the beginning with God. All things were made by Him."

CXLVII.[2] To John, Bishop of Germanicia.

Immediately on receipt of your holiness's former letter I replied. About the present state of affairs, it is impossible to entertain any good hope. I apprehend that this is the beginning of the general apostasy. For when we see that those who lament what was done as they say, by violence, at Ephesus, show no signs of repentance, but abide by their unlawful deeds and are building up a superstructure at once of injustice and of impiety; when we see that the rest take no concerted action to deny their deeds and do not refuse to hold communion with men who abide by their unlawful action, what hope of good is it possible for us to entertain? Had they been expressing their admiration of what has happened as though all had been well and rightly done, it would only have been proper for them to abide by what they themselves commend. But if, as they say, they are lamenting what has been done and stating it to have been done by force and violence, why in the world do they not repudiate what has been unlawfully done? Why is the present, which lasts for such a little time, preferred before what is sure to come to pass? Why in the world do they openly lie and deny that any innovation has been introduced into doctrine? On account of what murders and witchcrafts have I been expelled? What adulteries did the man commit? What tombs did the man violate? It is perfectly clear even to outsiders that it was for doctrine that I and the rest were expelled. Why the Lord Domnus too, because he would not accept "the Chapters"[3] was deposed by these excellent persons who called them admirable and confessed that they abided by them. I had read their propositions, and they rejected me as the head and front of the heresy and expelled others for the same reason.[4]

What has happened proves plainly enough that they supposed the Saviour to have laid down the law of practical virtue rather for Hamaxobians[1] than for them. When some men had given in charges against Candidianus, the Pisidian,[2] accusing him of several acts of adultery and other iniquities, it is said that the president of the council remarked, "If you are bringing accusation on points of doctrine, we receive your charges; we have not come here to decide about adulteries." Accordingly Athenius and Athanasius[3] who had been expelled by the Eastern Synod were bidden to return to their own churches; just as though our Saviour had laid down no laws about conduct, and had only ordered us to observe doctrines — which those most sapient persons have been foremost in corrupting. Let them then cease to mock; let them no longer attempt to conceal the impiety which they have confirmed by blows as well as by words. If this is not the case, let them tell us the reasons of the massacres; let them own in writing the distinction between the natures of our Saviour, and that the union is without confusion; let them declare that after the union both Godhead and manhood remained unimpaired. "God is not mocked."[4] Let the chapters be denied which they have often repudiated, and now at Ephesus have sanctioned. Do not let them trick your holiness by their lies. They used to praise my utterances at Antioch, being brethren, and when made readers, and ordained deacons, presbyters and bishops; and at the end of my discourse they used to embrace me and kiss me, on head, on breast, on hands; and some of them would cling to my knees, calling my doctrine apostolic, — the very doctrine that they have now condemned, and anath-

---

[1] John i. 1. 2. 3. Here this document abruptly terminates.

[2] The following letters omitted in the volume of Sirmondus have been published in the Auctarium of Garnerius and elsewhere. The following letter number CXLVII is the CXXVth in all the manuscripts. Schulze remarks that he would have replaced it in its own rank but for the confusion which would thus have been introduced in quotation. John, bishop of Germanicia is also the recipient of Letter CXXXIII. This is written a few days after the former, late in 449 or at the beginning of 450.

[3] i.e. the twelve articles or chapters couched in the form of anathema against the heads of Nestorian doctrine, appended to Cyril's third letter to Nestorius.

[4] It has been pointed out before (Page 293) that at the Latrocinium Domnus was compelled to yield his presidential seat as Patriarch of Antioch, Dioscorus presiding, the Roman legate sitting second, and Juvenal of Jerusalem third. "Cowed by the dictatorial spirit of Dioscorus and unnerved by

the outrageous violence of Barsumas and his band of brutal monks he consented to revoke his former condemnation of Eutyches." "This cowardly act of submission was followed by a still baser proof of weakness, the condemnation of the venerable Flavian. Dioscorus having thus by sheer intimidation obtained his ends revenged himself for their former opposition to his wishes upon those whose cowardice had made them the instruments of his nefarious designs, and proceeded to mete out to them the same measure they had dealt to Flavian. Domnus was the last to be deposed. The charges alleged against him were his reported approval of a Nestorian sermon preached before him at Antioch by Theodoret, on the death of Cyril, and some expressions in letters written by him to Dioscorus condemning the obscure character of Cyril's anathematisms."

Canon Venables in Dic. Chris. biog. vol I. p. 879.

[1] i.e. wild nomad tribes who live in waggons (ἁμαξόβιοι). These Horace (Car. iii. 24, 10) takes as a better type of character than wealthy villa-builders;—

"*Campestres melius Scythæ*
 Quorum plaustra vagas rite trahunt domos
 Vivunt."

[2] Bishop of Antioch in Pisidia. He was of the orthodox party and stated himself to have been bred from childhood in the Catholic faith. (Conc. iv. 304.) His name is also written Calendio (Tillem. xv. 579, Dic. Chris. Biog. I, 395).

[3] Athanasius of Perrha, the delator of earlier letters (vide note on page 264) had been deposed from his bishopric at a synod of uncertain date held between 444 and 449 at Antioch under Domnus, and replaced by Sabinianus.

[4] Gal. vi. 7.

ematized. They used to call me luminary, not only of the East, but of the whole world, and now I forsooth have been proscribed and, so far as lies in their power, I have not even bread to eat. They have anathematized even all who converse with me. But the man whom but a little while ago they deposed and called Valentinian and Apollinarian they have honoured as a martyr of the faith, rolling at his feet, asking his pardon and calling him spiritual father. Do even woodlice change their colour to match the stones or chameleons their skin to suit the leaves, as these men do their mind to match the times? I give up to them see, dignity, rank, and all the luxury of this life. On the side of the apostolic doctrines I await the evils which they deem terrible, finding sufficient consolation in the thought of the judgment of the Lord. For I hope that for the sake of this injustice the Lord will remit me many of my sins.

Now I implore your holiness to beware of the fellowship of iniquity and to insist on their repudiation of what has been done. If they refuse shun them as traitors to the faith. That your reverence should wait awhile to see if the tempest will pass, we have not thought subject for blame. But after the ordination of the primate of the East [1] every man's mind will be made manifest. Deign, Sir, to pray for me. At this time I am sorely in want of that help that I may hold out against all that is being devised against me.

CXLVIII *in the Edition of Garnerius*

is " the minute of the most holy bishop Cyril, delivered to Posidonius, when sent by him to Rome, in the matter of Nestorius." (Cyrill. Ep. XI. tom. lxxvii. 85.)

CXLIX is " *Copy of the Letter written by John, bishop of Antioch, to Nestorius."*

This letter has sometimes been supposed to have been really composed by Theodoret.[2]

CL. *Letter of Theodoretus, bishop of Cyrus, to Joannes, bishop of Antioch.*[3]

I have been much distressed at reading the anathematisms which you have sent to request me to refute in writing, and to make plain to all their heretical sense. I have been distressed at the thought that one appointed to the shepherd's office, entrusted with the charge of so great a flock and appointed to heal the sick among his sheep, is both himself unsound, and that to a terrible degree, and is endeavouring to infect his lambs with his disease and treats the sheep of his folds with greater cruelty than that of wild beasts. They, indeed, tear and rend the sheep that are dispersed and separated from the flock; but he in its very midst, and while thought to be its saviour and its guardian introduces secret error among the victims of their confidence in him. Against an open assault it is possible to take precautions, but when an attack is made in the guise of friendship, its victim is found off his guard and hurt is easily done him. Hence foes who make war from within are far more dangerous than those who attack from without.

I am yet more grieved that it should be in the name of true religion and with the dignity of a shepherd that he should give utterance to his heretical and blasphemous words, and renew that vain and impious teaching of Apollinarius which was long ago stamped out. Besides all this there is the fact that he not only supports these views but even dares to anathematize those who decline to participate in his blasphemies; — if he is really the author of these productions and they have not proceeded from some enemy of the truth who has composed them in his name and, as the old story has it, flung the apple of discord [1] in the midst, and so fanned the flame on high.

But whether this composition comes from himself or from some other in his name, I, for my part, by the aid of the light of the Holy Ghost, in the investigation of this heretical and corrupt opinion, according to the measure of the power given me, have refuted them as best I could. I have confronted them with the teaching of evangelists and apostles. I have exposed the monstrosity of the doctrine, and proved how vast is its divergence from divine truth. This I have done by comparing it with the words of the Holy Spirit, and pointing out what strange and jarring discord there is between it and the divine.

Against the hardihood of this anathema-

---

[1] i.e. Maximus, who was appointed by the Latrocinium to succeed Domnus in the see of Antioch, and consecrated by Anatolius in defiance of right and usage. Or possibly the irregularity of the nomination of Maximus may lead Theodoret to regard the see as vacant. Garnerius understands the reference to be to an interval between the appointment and consecration of Maximus.

[2] Vide Migne Pat. lxxvii. 1449.
" A letter so admirable in tone and feeling, so happy in its expression, that it has been attributed to the practised pen of Theodoret." (Canon Venables, Dict. Christ. Biog. iii. 350.) Tillemont describes it as " *très belle, très bien faite et très digne de la réputation qu'avait ce prélat."*

[3] This letter may be dated in February 431. Celestine and Cyril had written to John of Antioch in relation to the condemnation of Nestorius by the western bishops at Rome in August 430. Theodoret was at Antioch on the arrival of these letters

and hence additional probability is given to the theory that he wrote the reply referred to in the preceding note. Then came the publication of Cyril's chapter or anathemas which Theodoret undertook to refute. Letter CL. is prefixed to his remarks on them.

[1] The " old story " is a comparatively late addition to the myth of the marriage of Peleus.

tizing, thus much I will say, that Paul, the clear-voiced herald of truth, anathematized those who had corrupted the evangelic and apostolic teaching and boldly did so against the angels, not against those who abided by the laws laid down by theologians; these he strengthened with blessings, saying, "And as many as walk according to this rule, peace be on them and mercy and on the Israel of God."[1] Let then the author of these writings reap from the Apostle's curse the due rewards of his labours and the harvest of his seeds of heresy. We will abide in the teaching of the holy Fathers.

To this letter I have appended my counter arguments, that on reading them you may judge whether I have effectively destroyed the heretical propositions. Setting down each of the anathematisms by itself, I have annexed the counter statement that readers may easily understand, and that the refutation of the dogmas may be clear.[2]

CLI. Letter or address of Theodoret to the monks of the Euphratensian, the Osrhoene, Syria, Phœnicia, and Cilicia.[3]

When I contemplate the condition of the Church at the present crisis of affairs, — the tempest which has recently beset the holy ship, the furious blasts, the beating of the waves, the deep darkness of the night, and, besides all this, the strife of the mariners, the struggle going on between oarsmen, the drunkenness of the pilots, and, lastly, the untimely action of the bad, — I bethink me of the laments of Jeremiah and cry with him, " my bowels, my bowels! I am pained at my very heart, my heart maketh a noise in me,"[4] and to put away despondency's great cloud by the drops from my eyes, I have recourse to founts of tears. Amid a storm so wild it is fitting that the pilots be awake, to battle with the tempest, and take heed for the safety of the ship: the sailors ought to cease from their strife, and strive to undo the danger alike by prayer and skill: the mariners ought to keep the peace, and quarrel neither with one another nor with the pilots, but implore the Lord of the sea to banish the darkness by His rod. No one now is willing to do anything of the kind; and, just as

happens in a night-engagement, we cannot recognise one another, we leave our enemies alone, and waste our weapons against our own side; we wound our comrades for foes, while all the while the bystanders laugh at our drunken folly, enjoy our disasters, and are delighted to see us engaged in mutual destruction. The responsibility for all this lies with those who have striven to corrupt the apostolic faith, and have dared to add a monstrous doctrine to the teaching of the Gospels; with them that have accepted the impious " Chapters " which they have sent forth with anathematisms to the imperial city, and have confirmed them, as they have imagined, by their own signatures. But these " Chapters " have sprouted without doubt from the sour root of Apollinarius; they are tainted with Arian and Eunomian error; look into them carefully, and you will find that they are not clear of the impiety of Manes and Valentinus.[1]

In his very first chapter he rejects the dispensation[2] which has been made on our behalf, teaching that God the Word did not assume human nature, but was Himself changed into flesh, thus laying down that the incarnation took place not in reality but in semblance and seeming. This is the outcome of the impiety of Marcion, Manes, and Valentinus.

In his second and third chapters, as though quite oblivious of what he had stated in his preface, he brings in the hypostatic union, and a meeting by natural union, and by these terms he represents that a kind of mixture and confusion was effected of the divine nature and of the form of the servant. This comes of the innovation of the Apollinarian heresy.

In his fourth chapter he denies the distinction of the terms of evangelists and apostles, and refuses to allow, as the teaching of the orthodox Fathers has allowed, the terms of divine dignity to be understood of the divine nature, while the terms of humility, spoken in human sense, are applied to the nature assumed; whence the rightminded can easily detect the kinship with impiety. For Arius and Eunomius, asserting the only begotten Son of God to be a creature, and made out of the non-existent, and a servant, have ventured to apply to His godhead what is said in lowly and human sense; establishing by such means the difference of substance and the unlike-

---

[1] Gal. vi. 16.
[2] The Refutation of the anathematisms of Cyril is to be found in Migne Pat. lxxvi. Col 393. Vide also the prolegomena.
[3] This document did not appear in the original edition of the Letters. A fragment in Latin was published in the Auctarium of Garnerius. The complete composition is given by Schulze from a MS. in the Imperial Library at Vienna. The date may be assigned as early in 431. As Cyril had weaned the monks of Egypt and even of Constantinople from the cause of Nestorius, so Theodoret attempts to win over the solitaries of the East from Cyril.
[4] Jer. iv. 19.

[1] " *Nihil contumeliosius*," remarks Garnerius, " *in Cyrilli personam et doctrinam dici potest.*" Some have even thought the expressions too bitter for Theodoret. But the mild man could hit hard sometimes. He felt warmly for Nestorius and against Cyril, and (accepting Tillemont's date) he was now about 38.
[2] οἰκονομία. Vide p. 72.

ness. Besides this, to be brief, he argues that the very impassible and immutable Godhead of the Christ suffered, and was crucified, dead, and buried. This goes beyond even the madness of Arius and Eunomius, for this pitch of impiety has not been reached even by them that dare to call the maker and creator of the universe a creature. Furthermore he blasphemes against the Holy Ghost, denying that It proceeds from the Father, in accordance with the word of the Lord, but maintaining that It has Its origin of the Son. Here we have the fruit of the Apollinarian seed; here we come near the evil husbandry of Macedonius. Such are the offspring of the Egyptian, viler children of a vile father. This growth, which men, entrusted with the healing of souls, ought to make abortive while yet in the womb, or destroy as soon as it is born, as dangerous and deadly to mankind, is cherished by these excellent persons, and promoted with great energy, alike to their own ruin and to that of all who will listen to them. We, on the contrary, earnestly desire to keep our heritage untouched; and the faith which we have received, and in which we have been ourselves baptized, and baptize others, we strive to preserve uninjured and undefiled. We confess that our Lord Jesus Christ, perfect God and perfect man, of a reasonable soul and body, was begotten of the Father before the ages, as touching the Godhead; and in the last days for us men and our salvation (was born) of the Virgin Mary; that the same Lord is of one substance with the Father as touching the Godhead, and of one substance with us as touching the manhood. For there was an union of two natures. Wherefore we acknowledge one Christ, one Son, one Lord; but we do not destroy the union; we believe it to have been made without confusion, in obedience to the word of the Lord to the Jews, "Destroy this temple and in three days I will raise it up."[1] If on the contrary there had been mixture and confusion, and one nature was made out of both, He ought to have said "Destroy me and in three days I shall be raised." But now, to show that there is a distinction between God according to His nature, and the temple, and that both are one Christ, His words are "Destroy this temple and in three days I will raise it up," clearly teaching that it was not God who was undergoing destruction, but the temple. The nature of this latter was susceptible of destruction, while the power of the former

raised what was being destroyed. Furthermore it is in obedience to the divine Scriptures that we acknowledge the Christ to be God and man. That our Lord Jesus Christ is God is asserted by the blessed evangelist John " In the beginning was the Word and the Word was with God and the Word was God. He was in the beginning with God. All things were made by Him and without Him was not anything made that was made."[1] And again, " That was the true light which lighteth every man that cometh into the world."[2] And the Lord Himself distinctly teaches us, " He that hath seen me hath seen the Father."[3] And "I and my Father are one"[4] and "I am in the Father and the Father in me,"[5] and the blessed Paul in his epistle to the Hebrews says " Who being the brightness of His glory and the express image of His person, and upholding all things by the word of His power "[6] and in the epistle to the Philippians " Let this mind be in you, which was also in Christ Jesus; who being in the form of God thought it not robbery to be equal with God but made Himself of no reputation and took upon Him the form of a servant."[7] And in the Epistle to the Romans, " Whose are the fathers and of whom as concerning the flesh Christ came who is over all God blessed for ever. Amen."[8] And in the epistle to Titus " Looking for that blessed hope and the glorious appearing of the great God and our Saviour Jesus Christ."[9] And Isaiah exclaims " Unto us a child is born, unto us a son is given: and the government shall be upon His shoulder; and His name shall be called, Angel of great counsel, Wonderful, Counsellor, The mighty God, powerful, the Prince of Peace, the Father of the Age to come."[10] And again " In chains they shall come over and they shall fall unto thee. They shall make supplication unto thee saying, surely God is in thee and there is none else, there is no God. Verily thou art a God that hidest thyself, O God of Israel, the Saviour."[11] The name Emmanuel, however, indicates both God and man, for it is interpreted in the Gospel to mean " God with us,"[12] that is to say "God in man," God in our nature. And the divine Jeremiah too utters the prediction " This is our God and there shall none other be accounted of in comparison with him. He hath found out all

---

[1] John ii. 19.

[1] John i. 1.
[2] John i. 9.
[3] John xiv. 9.
[4] John x. 30.
[5] John x. 38 transposed.
[6] Hebrews i. 3.
[7] Phil. ii. 5, 6, 7.
[8] Romans ix. 5.
[9] Tit. ii. 13.
[10] Is. ix. 6. (LXX. Alex.)
[11] Isaiah xlv. 14, 15.
[12] Matt. i. 23.

the way of knowledge and hath given it unto Jacob His servant and to Israel His beloved and afterward did He show Himself upon earth and conversed with men." [1] And countless other passages might be found as well in the holy gospels and in the writings of the apostles as in the predictions of the prophets, setting forth that our Lord Jesus Christ is very God.

That after the Incarnation He is spoken of as Man our Lord Himself teaches in His words to the Jews " Why go ye about to kill me ? " " A man that hath told you the truth." [2] And in the first Epistle to the Corinthians the blessed Paul writes " For since by man came death, by man came also the resurrection of the dead," [3] and to show of whom he is speaking he explains his words and says, " For as in Adam all die even so in Christ shall all be made alive." [4] And writing to Timothy he says, " For there is one God and one mediator between God and men, the man Christ Jesus." [5] In the Acts in his speech at Athens " The times of this ignorance God winked at; but now commandeth all men everywhere to repent; because He hath appointed a day in the which He will judge the world in righteousness by that man whom He hath ordained, whereof He hath given assurance unto all men, in that He hath raised him from the dead." [6] And the blessed Peter preaching to the Jews says, " Ye men of Israel, hear these words; Jesus of Nazareth, a man approved of God among you by miracles and wonders and signs which God did by Him in the midst of you," [7] and the prophet Isaiah when predicting the sufferings of the Lord Christ, whom but just before he had called God, calls man in the passage " A man of sorrows and acquainted with grief." " Surely he hath borne our griefs and carried our sorrows." [8] I might have collected other consentient passages of holy Scripture and inserted them in my letter had I not known you to be practised in the divine oracles as befits the man called blessed in the Psalms. [9] I now leave the collection of evidence to your own diligence and proceed with my subject.

We confess then that our Lord Jesus Christ is very God and very man. We do not divide the one Christ into two persons, but we believe two natures to be united without confusion. We shall thus be able without diffi-

culty to refute even the manifold blasphemy of the heretics : for many and various are the errors of those who have rebelled against the truth, as we shall proceed to point out. Marcion and Manes deny that God the Word assumed human nature and do not believe that our Lord Jesus Christ was born of a Virgin. They say that God the Word Himself was fashioned in human form and appeared as man rather in semblance than in reality.

Valentinus and Bardesanes admit the birth, but they deny the assumption of our nature and affirm that the Son of God employed the Virgin as it were as a mere conduit.

Sabellius the Libyan, Photinus, Marcellus the Galatian, and Paul of Samosata say that a mere man was born of the Virgin, but openly deny that the eternal Christ was God.

Arius and Eunomius maintain that God the Word assumed only a body of the Virgin.

Apollinarius adds to the body an unreasonable soul, as though the incarnation of God the Word had taken place not for the sake of reasonable beings but of unreasonable, while the teaching of the Apostles is that perfect man was assumed by perfect God, as is proved by the words " Who being in the form of God took the form of a servant ; " [1] for " form " is put instead of " nature " and " substance " and indicates that having the nature of God He took the nature of a servant.

When therefore we are disputing with Marcion, Manes and Valentinus, the earliest inventors of impiety, we endeavour to prove from the divine Scriptures that the Lord Christ is not only God but also man.

When, however, we are proving to the ignorant that the doctrine of Arius, Eunomius and Apollinarius about the œconomy is incomplete, we show from the divine oracles of the Spirit that the assumed nature was perfect.

The impiety of Sabellius, Photinus, Marcellus, and Paulus, we refute by proving by the evidence of divine Scripture that the Lord Christ was not only man but also eternal God, of one substance with the Father. That He assumed a reasonable soul is stated by our Lord Himself in the words " Now is my soul troubled ; and what shall I say ? Father save me from this hour ; but for this cause came I unto this hour." [2] And again " My soul is exceeding sorrowful even unto death." [3] And in another place " I

---

[1] Baruch iii. 35, 36, 37. From the time of Irenæus the book of Baruch, friend and companion of Jeremiah, was commonly quoted as the work of the great prophet. e.g. Iren. adv. Hær. v. 35, 1. cf. note on p. 165.
[2] John vii. 19 and viii. 40.
[3] I. Cor. xv. 21.
[4] I. Cor. xv. 22.
[5] I. Tim. ii. v.
[6] Acts xvii. 30, 31.
[7] Acts ii. 22.
[8] Isaiah liii. 3 and 4.
[9] Psalm i. 2.

[1] Phil. ii. 6 and 7.
[2] John xii. 27.
[3] Matt. xxvi. 38.

have power to lay down my soul (life A. V.) and I have power to take it again. No man taketh it from me." [1] And the angel said to Joseph, "Take the young child and His mother and go into the land of Israel; for they are dead which sought the young child's soul (life A. V.)" [2] And the Evangelist says "Jesus increased in wisdom and stature and in favour with God and man." Now what increases in stature and wisdom is not the Godhead which is ever perfect, but the human nature which comes into being in time, grows, and is made perfect.

Wherefore all the human qualities of the Lord Christ, hunger, I mean, and thirst and weariness, sleep, fear, sweat, prayer, and ignorance, and the like, we affirm to belong to our nature which God the Word assumed and united to Himself in effecting our salvation. But the restitution of motion to the maimed, the resurrection of the dead, the supply of loaves, and all the other miracles we believe to be works of the divine power. In this sense I say that the same Lord Christ both suffers and destroys suffering; suffers, that is, as touching the visible, and destroys suffering as touching the ineffably indwelling Godhead. This is proved beyond question by the narrative of the holy evangelists, from whom we learn that when lying in a manger and wrapped in swaddling clothes, He was announced by a star, worshipped by magi and hymned by angels. Thus we reverently discern that the swaddling bands and the want of a bed and all the poverty belonged to the manhood; while the journey of the magi and the guiding of the star and the company of the angels proclaim the Godhead of the unseen. In like manner He makes His escape into Egypt and avoids the fury of Herod by flight, [3] for He was man; but as the Prophet says "He shakes the idols of Egypt," [4] for He was by nature God. He is circumcised; He keeps the law; and offers offerings of purification, because He sprang from the root of Jesse. And, as man, He was under the law; and afterwards did away with the law and gave the new covenant, because He was a lawgiver and had promised by the prophets that He Himself would give it. He was baptized by John; and this shews His sharing what is ours. He is testified to by the Father from on high and is pointed out by the Spirit; this proclaims Him eternal. He hungered; but He fed many thousands with five loaves; the latter is divine, the former human. He thirsted and He asked for water; but He was the well of life; the former of His human weakness, the latter of His divine power. He fell asleep in the boat, but he put the tempest of the sea to sleep; the former of His human nature, the latter of His efficient and creative power which has gifted all things with their being. He was weary as he walked; but He healed the halt and raised dead men from their tombs; the former of human weakness, the latter of a power passing that of this world. He feared death and He destroyed death; the former shows that He was mortal, the latter that He was immortal or rather giver of life. "He was crucified," as the blessed Paul says "through weakness." [1] But as the same Paul says "Yet He liveth by the power of God." [2] Let that word "weakness" teach us that He was not nailed to the tree as the Almighty, the Uncircumscribed, the Immutable and Invariable, but that the nature quickened by the power of God, was according to the Apostle's teaching dead and buried, both death and burial being proper to the form of the servant. "He broke the gates of brass and cut the bars of iron in sunder" [3] and destroyed the power of death and in three days raised His own temple. These are proofs of the form of God in accordance with the Lord's words "Destroy this temple and in three days I will raise it up." [4] Thus in the one Christ through the sufferings we contemplate the manhood and through the miracles we apprehend the Godhead. We do not divide the two natures into two Christs, and we know that of the Father God the Word was begotten and that of the seed of Abraham and David our nature was assumed. Wherefore also the blessed Paul says when discoursing of Abraham "He saith not and to seeds as of many; but as of one, and to thy seed which is Christ," [5] and writing to Timothy he says "Remember that Jesus Christ of the seed of David was raised from the dead according to my gospel." [6] And to the Romans he writes "Concerning His son Jesus Christ . . . which was made of the seed of David according to the flesh." [7] And again "Whose are the fathers and of whom as concerning the flesh Christ came." [8] And the Evangelist writes "The book of the generation of Jesus Christ, the Son of David, the Son of Abraham," [9] and the blessed Peter in the Acts says David "being a prophet and knowing that God had sworn with an oath to him that of the fruit of his loins, He would raise up Christ to sit on his throne, he

---

[1] John x. 18 varied.   [3] Vide note on Page 203.
[2] Matt. ii. 20.   [4] Isaiah xix. 1.

[1] II. Cor. xiii. 4.   [4] John ii. 19.   [7] Romans i. 3.
[2] II. Cor. xiii. 4.   [5] Gal. iii. 16.   [8] Romans ix. 5.
[3] Psalm cvii. 16.   [6] II. Tim. ii. 8.   [9] Matt. i. 1.

seeing this before spake of his resurrection," [1] and God says to Abraham " In thy seed shall all the nations of the earth be blessed," [2] and Isaiah " There shall come forth a rod out of the stem of Jesse and a branch shall grow out of His roots; and there shall rest upon Him [3] the spirit of wisdom and understanding the spirit of counsel and might, the spirit of knowledge and of piety and the spirit of the fear of the Lord shall fill Him." [4] And a little further on " And in that day there shall be a root of Jesse which shall stand for an ensign of the people; to it shall the Gentiles seek; and His rest shall be glorious." [5]

From these quotations it is made plain that according to the flesh, the Christ was descended from Abraham and David and was of the same nature as theirs; while according to the Godhead He is Everlasting Son and Word of God, ineffably and in superhuman manner begotten of the Father, and co-eternal with Him as brightness and express image and Word. For as the word in relation to intelligence and brightness in relation to light are inseparably connected, so is the only begotten Son in relation to His own Father. We assert therefore that our Lord Jesus Christ is only begotten, and first born Son of God; only begotten both before the incarnation and after the incarnation, but first-born after being born of the Virgin. For the name first-born seems to be in a sense contrary to that of only begotten, because the only Son begotten of any one is called only begotten, while the eldest of several brothers is called first-born. The divine Scriptures state God the Word alone to have been begotten of the Father; but the only begotten becomes also first-born, by taking our nature of the Virgin, and deigning to call brothers those who have trusted in Him; so that the same is only begotten in that He is God, first born in that He is Man. Thus acknowledging the two natures we adore the one Christ and offer Him one adoration, for we believe that the union took place from the moment of the conception in the Virgin's holy womb. Wherefore also we call the holy Virgin both Mother of God [6] and Mother of man, since the Lord Christ Himself is called God and man in the divine Scripture. The

name Emmanuel proclaims the union of the two natures. If we acknowledge the Christ to be both God and Man and so call Him, who is so insensate as to shrink from using the term " Mother of man " with that of " Mother of God"? For we use both terms of the Lord Christ. For this reason the Virgin is honoured and called "full of grace." [1] What sensible man then would object to name the Virgin in accordance with the titles of the Saviour, when on His account she is honoured by the faithful? For He who was born of her is not worshipped on her account, but she is honoured with the highest titles on account of Him Who was born from her.

Suppose the Christ to be God only, and to have taken the origin of His existence from the Virgin, then let the Virgin be styled and named only " Mother of God " as having given birth to a being divine by nature. But if the Christ is both God and man and was God from everlasting (inasmuch as He did not begin to exist, being co-eternal with the Father that begat Him) and in these last days was born man of His human nature, then let him who wishes to define doctrine in both directions devise appellations for the Virgin with the explanation which of them befits the nature and which the union. But if any one should wish to deliver a panegyric and to compose hymns, and to repeat praises, and is naturally anxious to use the most august names; then, not laying down doctrine as in the former case, but with rhetorical laudation, and expressing all possible admiration at the mightiness of the mystery, let him gratify his heart's desire, let him employ high names, let him praise and let him wonder. Many instances of this kind are found in the writings of orthodox teachers. But on all occasions let moderation be respected. All praise to him who said that " moderation is best," although he is not of our herd. [2]

This is the confession of the faith of the Church; this is the doctrine taught by evangelists and apostles. For this faith, by God's grace I will not refuse to undergo many deaths. This faith we have striven to convey to them that now err and stray, again and again challenging them to discussion, and eager to show them the truth, but with-

---

[1] Acts. ii. 30. [2] Gen. xxii. 18.
[3] Here in the LXX comes in "The spirit of God." It is unlikely that Theodoret should have intended to omit this, and the omission is probably due as in similar cases to the carelessness of a copyist in the case of a repetition of a word.
[4] Isaiah xi. 1. 2. 3. 7. [5] Isaiah xi. 10.
[6] On the word Θεοτόκος cf. note on Page 213.
Jeremy Taylor (ix. 637 ed. 1861) defends it on the bare ground of logic which no doubt originally recommended it. "Though the blessed virgin Mary be not in Scripture called Θεοτόκος ' the mother of God.' yet that she was the mother of Jesus and that Jesus Christ is God, that we can prove from Scripture, and that is sufficient for the appellation."

[1] Luke i. 28.
[2] Cleobulus of Lindos is credited with the maxim ἄριστον μέτρον. Theognis, (335) transmits the famous μηδὲν ἄγαν attributed by Aristotle (Rhet. ii. 12, 14) to Chilon of Sparta. Ovid makes Phoebus say to Phaethon " Medio tutissimus ibis" (Met. ii. 137); and quotations from many other writers may be found all

"Turning to scorn with lips divine
The falsehood of extremes!"

out success. With a suspicion of their probably plain confutation, they have shirked the encounter; for verily falsehood is rotten and yokefellow of obscurity. "Every one," it is written "that doeth evil cometh not to the light lest his deeds should be reproved"[1] by the light.

Since, therefore, after many efforts, I have failed in persuading them to recognise the truth, I have returned to my own churches, filled at once with sorrow and with joy; with joy on account of my own freedom from error; and with sorrow at the unsoundness of my members. I therefore implore you to pray with all your might to our loving Lord, and to cry unto Him, "'Spare Thy people, O Lord and give not Thy heritage to reproach.'[2] Feed us O Lord that we become not as we were in the beginning when Thou didst not rule over us nor was Thy name invoked to help us. 'We are become a reproach to our neighbours, a scorn and derision to them that are round about us,'[3] because wicked doctrines have come into Thy inheritance. They have polluted Thy holy temple in that the daughters of strangers have rejoiced over our troubles. A little while ago we were of one mind and one tongue and now are divided into many tongues. But, O Lord our God, give us Thy peace which we have lost by setting Thy commandments at naught. O Lord we know none other than Thee. We call Thee by Thy name. 'Make both one and break down the middle wall of the partition,'[4] namely the iniquity that has sprung up. Gather us one by one, Thy new Israel, building up Jerusalem and gathering together the outcasts of Israel.[5] Let us be made once more one flock[6] and all be fed by Thee; for Thou art the good Shepherd 'Who giveth His life for the sheep.'[7] 'Awake, why sleepest Thou O Lord, arise cast us not off forever.'[8] Rebuke the winds and the sea; give Thy Church calm and safety from the waves."

These words and words like these I implore you to utter to the God of all; for He is good and full of loving-kindness and ever fulfils the will of them that fear Him. He will therefore listen to your prayer, and will scatter this darkness deeper than the plague of Egypt. He will give you His own calm of love, and will gather them that are scattered abroad and welcome them that have been cast out. Then shall be heard "the voice of rejoicing and salvation in the tabernacles of the righteous."[1] Then shall we cry unto Him we have been "glad according to the days wherein Thou hast afflicted us and the years wherein we have seen evil,"[2] and you when you have been granted your prayer shall praise Him in the words "Blessed be God which hath not turned away my prayer nor His mercy from me."[3]

Proof that after the Incarnation our Lord Jesus Christ, was one Son.

The authors of slanders against me allege that I divide the one Lord Jesus Christ into two sons. But so far am I from holding this opinion that I charge with impiety all who dare to say so. For I have been taught by the divine Scripture to worship one Son, our Lord Jesus Christ, the only begotten Son of God, God the Word incarnate. For we confess the same to be both God eternal, and made man in the last days for the sake of man's salvation; but made man not by the change of the Godhead but by the assumption of the manhood. For the nature of this godhead is immutable and invariable, as is that of the Father who begat Him before the ages. And whatever would be understood of the substance of the Father will also be wholly found in the substance of the only begotten; for of that substance He is begotten. This our Lord taught when He said to Philip "He that hath seen me hath seen the Father"[4] and again in another place "All things that the Father hath are mine,"[5] and elsewhere "I and the Father are one,"[6] and very many other passages may be quoted setting forth the identity of substance.

It follows that He did not become God: He was God. "In the beginning was the Word, and the Word was with God; and the Word was God."[7] He was not man: He became man, and He so became by taking on Him our nature: So says the blessed Paul; — "Who being in the form of God thought it not robbery to be equal with God, but made Himself of no reputation, and took upon Him the form of a servant."[8] And again; "For verily He took not on Him the nature of angels; but He took on Him the seed of Abraham."[9] And again; Forasmuch then as the children are partakers of flesh and blood, He also Himself likewise took part of the same."[10] Thus

---

1 John iii. 20.
2 Joel ii. 17.
3 Psalm lxxix. 4.
4 Cf. Ephes. ii. 14.
5 Psalm cxlvii. 2.
6 John x. 10.
7 John x. 11.
8 Psalm xliv. 23.

1 Psalm cxviii. 15.
2 Psalm xc. 15.
3 Psalm lxvi. 20.
4 John xiv. 9.
5 John xvi. 15.
6 John x. 30.
7 John i. 1.
8 Phil. ii. 6. 7.
9 Heb. ii. 16.
10 Heb. ii. 14.

He was both passible and impassible; mortal and immortal; passible, on the one hand, and mortal, as man; impassible, on the other, and immortal, as God. As God He raised His own flesh, which was dead; — as His own words declare: "Destroy this temple, and in three days I will raise it up."[1] And as man, He was passible and mortal up to the time of the passion. For, after the resurrection, even as man He is impassible, immortal, and incorruptible; and He discharges divine lightnings; not that according to the flesh He has been changed into the nature of Godhead, but still preserving the distinctive marks of humanity. Nor yet is His body uncircumscribed, for this is peculiar to the divine nature alone, but it abides in its former circumscription. This He teaches in the words He spake to the disciples even after His resurrection " Behold my hands and feet that it is I myself; handle me and see; for a spirit hath not flesh and bones as ye see me have."[2] While He was thus beheld He went up into heaven; thus has He promised to come again, thus shall He be seen both by them that have believed and them that have crucified, for it is written " They shall look on Him whom they pierced."[3] We therefore worship the Son, but we contemplate in Him either nature in its perfection, both that which took, and that which was taken; the one of God and the other of David. For this reason also He is styled both Son of the living God and Son of David; either nature receiving its proper title. Accordingly the divine scripture calls him both God and man, and the blessed Paul exclaims " There is one God, and one mediator between God and men, the man Christ Jesus; who gave Himself a ransom for all."[4] But Him whom here he calls man in another place he describes as God for he says " Looking for that blessed hope and the glorious appearing of the great God and our Saviour Jesus Christ."[5] And yet in another place he uses both names at once saying " Of whom as concerning the flesh Christ came who is over all God blessed for ever. Amen."[6]

Thus he has stated the same Christ to be of the Jews according to the flesh, and God over all as God. Similarly the prophet Isaiah writes " A man of sorrows and ac-quainted with grief. . . . Surely He hath borne our griefs and carried our sorrows,"[1] and shortly afterwards he says " Who shall declare His generation?"[2] This is spoken not of man but of God. Thus through Micah God says " Thou Bethlehem in the land of Judah art not the least among the princes of Judah, for out of thee shall come a governor that shall rule my people Israel, whose goings forth have been as of old from everlasting."[3] Now by saying " From thee shall come forth a ruler " he exhibits the œconomy of the incarnation; and by adding " whose goings forth have been as of old from everlasting" he declares the Godhead begotten of the Father before the ages.

Since we have been thus taught by the divine scripture, and have further found that the teachers who have been at different periods illustrious in the Church, are of the same opinion, we do our best to keep our heritage inviolate; worshipping one Son of God, one God the Father, and one Holy Ghost; but at the same time recognising the distinction between flesh and Godhead. And as we assert them that divide our one Lord Jesus Christ into two sons to transgress from the road trodden by the holy apostles, so do we declare the maintainers of the doctrine that the Godhead of the only begotten and the manhood have been made one nature to fall headlong into the opposite ravine. These doctrines we hold; these we preach; for these we do battle.

The slander of the libellers that represent me as worshipping two sons is refuted by the plain facts of the case. I teach all persons who come to holy Baptism the faith put forth at Nicæa; and, when I celebrate the sacrament of regeneration I baptize them that make profession of their faith in the name of the Father, and of the Son, and of the Holy Ghost, pronouncing each name by itself. And when I am performing divine service in the churches it is my wont to give glory to the Father and to the Son and to the Holy Ghost; not sons, but Son. If then I uphold two sons, whether of the two is glorified by me, and whether remains unhonoured? For I have not quite come to such a pitch of stupidity as to acknowledge two sons and leave one of them without any tribute of respect. It follows then even from this fact that the slander is proved slander, — for I worship one only begotten Son, God the Word incarnate. And I call the holy Virgin " Mother of God "[4] because she has given birth to the Emmanuel, which means " God

---

[1] John ii. 29.
[2] Luke xxiv. 39.
[3] John xix. 37. Cf. Zec. xii. 10.
[4] I. Tim. ii. 5. 6.
[5] Tit. ii. 13.
[6] Rom. ix. 5. The first implicit denial of the sense here given by Theodoret to this remarkable passage is said to be found in an assertion of the Emperor Julian that neither Paul nor Matthew nor Mark ever ventured to call Jesus God. In the early church it was commonly rendered in its plain and grammatical sense, as by Irenæus, Tertullian, Athanasius, and Chrysostom. Cf. Alford *in loc.*

---

[1] Is. liii. 3. 4.
[2] Isaiah liii. 8.
[3] Matt. ii. 6 and Mic. v. 2.
[4] Θεοτόκος. cf. p. 213.

with us." [1]   But the prophet who predicted the Emmanuel a little further on has written of him that " Unto us a child is born, unto us a son is given ; and the government shall be upon his shoulders ; and his name is called Angel of great counsel, wonderful, counsellor, mighty God, powerful, Prince of peace, Father of the age to come." [2]   Now if the babe born of the Virgin is styled " Mighty God," then it is only with reason that the mother is called " Mother of God." For the mother shares the honour of her offspring, and the Virgin is both mother of the Lord Christ as man, and again is His servant as Lord and Creator and God.

On account of this difference of term He is said by the divine Paul to be " without father, without mother, without descent, having neither beginning of days nor end of life." [3]   He is without father as touching His humanity ; for as man He was born of a mother alone.   And He is without mother as God, for He was begotten from everlasting of the Father alone.   And again He is without descent as God while as man He has descent.   For it is written " The book of the generation of Jesus Christ the son of David, the son of Abraham." [4]   His descent is also given by the divine Luke. [5]   So again, as God, He has no beginning of days for He was begotten before the ages ; neither has He an end of life, fo· His nature is immortal and impassible.   But as man He had both a beginning of days, for He was born in the reign of Augustus Cæsar, and an end of life, for He was crucified in the reign of Tiberius Cæsar.   But now, as I have already said, even His human nature is immortal ; and, as He ascended, so again shall He come according to the words of the Angel — " This same Jesus which is taken up from you into Heaven shall so come in like manner as ye have seen Him go into Heaven." [6]

This is the doctrine delivered to us by the divine prophets ; this is the doctrine of the company of the holy apostles ; this is the doctrine of the great saints of the East and of the West ; of the far-famed Ignatius, who received his archpriesthood by the right hand of the great Peter, and for the sake of his confession of Christ was devoured by savage beasts ; [7]   and of the great Eustathius, who presided over the assembled council, and on account of his fiery zeal for true religion was

driven into exile. [1]   This doctrine was preached by the illustrious Meletius, at the cost of no less pains, for thrice was he driven from his flock in the cause of the apostles' doctrines ; [2]   by Flavianus, [3]   glory of the imperial see ; and by the admirable Ephraim, instrument of divine grace, who has left us in the Syriac tongue a written heritage of good things ; [4]   by Cyprian, the illustrious ruler of Carthage and of all Libya, who for Christ's sake found a death in the fire ; [5]   by Damasus, bishop of great Rome, [6]   and by Ambrose, glory of Milan, who preached and wrote it in the language of Rome. [7]

The same was taught by the great luminaries of Alexandria, Alexander and Athanasius, men of one mind, who underwent sufferings celebrated throughout the world. This was the pasture given to their flocks by the great teachers of the imperial city, by Gregory, shining friend and supporter of the truth ; by John, teacher of the world, by Atticus, their successor alike in see and in sentiment. [8]   By these doctrines Basil, great light of the truth, and Gregory sprung from the same parents, [9]   and Amphilochius, [10]   who from him received the gift of the high-priesthood, taught their contemporaries, and have left the same to us in their writings for a goodly heritage.   Time would fail me to tell of Polycarp, [11]   and Irenæus, [12]   of Methodius [13]   and Hippolytus, [14]   and the rest of the teachers of the Church.   In a word I assert that I follow the divine oracles and at the same time all these saints.   By the grace of the spirit they dived into the depths of God-inspired scripture and both themselves perceived its mind, and made it plain to all that are willing to learn.   Difference in tongue has wrought no difference in doctrine, for they were channels of the grace of the divine spirit, using the stream from one and the same fount.

[1] i.e. Eustathius of Bercœa and Antioch, who, according to Theodoret (H. E. i. 6, p. 43.), sat at Nicæa on Constantine's right hand. (Contra. I. Soz. i. 19.) He was exiled on account of the accusation got up against, him by Eusebius of Nicomedia.
[2] Meletius of Antioch. cf. pp. 92, 93. He presided at Constantinople in 381, and died while the Council was sitting,
[3] Of Constantinople, murdered at the Latrocinium.
[4] Vide p. 129.
[5] cf. Ep. LII. St. Cyprian was beheaded at Carthage, Aug. 13, 258, his last recorded utterance being his reply to the reading of the sentence " That Thascius Cyprianus be beheaded with the sword," " Thanks be to God." Theodoret's " fire " is either an error, or means the fiery trial of martyrdom.
[6] Vide p. 82.   [7] cf. pp. 110, 174.
[8] i.e. Gregory of Nazianzus, put in possession of St. Sophia by Theodosius I. Nov. 24, 380, Chrysostom, consecrated by Theophilus of Alexandria, Feb. 26, 398, and Atticus, who succeeded Arsacius the usurper in 406.
[9] Gregory of Nyssa. cf. p. 129.   [11] † 155.
[10] Of Iconium. cf. p. 114.   [12] † c. 202.
[13] Commonly known as bishop of Patara, though Jerome speaks of him as of Tyre. The place and time of his death are doubtful. Eusebius calls him a contemporary. (cf. Jer. Cat. 83, and Socr. vi. 13.)
[14] According to Döllinger the first anti-pope. cf. reff. p. 177.

---

[1] Matt. i. 23.   [4] Matt. i. 1.
[2] Is. ix. 6. LXX. Alex.   [5] Luke iii. 23.
[3] Heb. vii. 3.   [6] Acts i. 11.
[7] The martyrdom of Ignatius may be placed within a few years of 110, — before or after. In the 4th c. Oct. 17 was named as the day both of his birth and death. Bp. Lightfoot. Ap. Fathers II. i. 30 and 46.

CLII. Report of the (bishops) of the East to the Emperor, giving information of their proceedings, and explaining the cause of the delay in the arrival of the bishop of Antioch.[1]

In obedience to the order of your pious letter we have journeyed to the Ephesian metropolis. There we have found the affairs of the Church in confusion, and disturbed by internecine war. The cause of this is that Cyril of Alexandria and Memnon of Ephesus have banded together and mustered a great mob of rustics, and have forbidden both the celebration of the great feast of Pentecost, and the evening and morning offices.[2]

They have shut the sacred churches and martyrs' shrines; they have assembled apart with the victims of their deceit; they have wrought innumerable iniquities, trampling under foot alike the canons of the holy Fathers, and your own decrees. And the action has been taken in face of the order given both in writing and by word of mouth by the most excellent count Candidianus,[3] envoy of your Christ-loving majesty, that the council must await the arrival of the very holy bishops, coming from all quarters of the Empire, and then and not till then formally assemble in obedience to your piety's commands. Moreover Cyril of Alexandria had written to me, the bishop of Antioch, two days before the meeting of their synod, that the whole council was awaiting my arrival. We have therefore deposed both the aforenamed, Cyril and Memnon, and have excluded them from all the services of the church. The rest, who have participated in their iniquity, we have excommunicated, until they shall reject and anathematize the Chapters[4] issued by Cyril, which are full of the Eunomian and Arian heresies, and shall, in obedience to your piety's command, assemble together with us, and shall in an orderly manner and with all exactitude, together with ourselves, examine into the questions at issue, and confirm the pious doctrine of the holy Fathers.

As to the delay in my own arrival be it known to your piety that, in consideration of the distance of the way by land, — and this was our route, — I have come very quickly, I have travelled forty stages without pausing to rest on the way; so your Christian majesty may learn from the inhabitants of the towns on the route. Besides this I was detained many days in Antioch by the famine there; by the daily tumults of the people; and by the unusual severity of the rainy season, which caused the torrents to swell, and threatened danger to the town.

CLIII. Report of the same to the empresses Pulcheria and Eudoxia.

We had expected to be able to report to your pious majesties in different terms, but we are now compelled to make known to you the following facts, forced as we are by the irregular exercise of despotic power by Cyril of Alexandria and Memnon of Ephesus. The proper course to have been pursued, in accordance with the laws of the Church, and the command of your pious majesties, would have been to wait for the arrival of the godly bishops on the road, and in common with them to examine into the questions at issue concerning the true faith, and investigate the point offered for discussion, and, after exact enquiry, to confirm the doctrines of the apostles. They had written to me that they would wait for our arrival. They heard that we were only three stages off. Then they assembled an unconstitutional council by themselves, and have ventured on proceedings iniquitous, irregular, and bristling with absurdities. And this they have done though the most honourable count Candidianus, sent by your pious and Christian majesties for good order's sake, expressly charged them, alike in writing and by word of mouth, to wait for the arrival of the godly bishops who had been convened, and to attempt no innovation on the true faith, but to take their stand on the directions of our godly-minded sovereigns. Now in spite of their having heard the imperial letter and the advice of the most honourable count Candidianus, they have nevertheless made naught of due order. As the prophet says "They hatch cockatrice' eggs, and weave the spider's web; and he that would eat of their eggs when he breaks them findeth rottenness, and therein is a viper,"[1] Wherefore we confidently cry "Their webs shall not become garments, neither shall they cover themselves with their works."[2]

They have shut the churches and the martyrs' shrines; they have forbidden the celebration of the holy feast of Pentecost; besides this

---

[1] Cyril's party met on June 22, 431, — numbering 198, in the Church of the Virgin. John of Antioch with his fourteen supporters did not arrive till the 27th. Unable to start from their diocese before April 26, the octave of Easter, they did not assemble at Antioch till May 10, and then were delayed by a famine. Immediately on their arrival the "Conciliabulum" of the 43 anti-Cyrillians met with indecent precipitancy.

[2] Both parties, regarding their opponents as excommunicate, forbade them to perform their sacred functions.

[3] "*Comes domesticorum*" commander of the guards, was representative of Theodosius II. and Valentinian III. at Ephesus. Candidianus was at first disposed to demur to the condemnation of Nestorius as disorderly and irregular, and to side with the Orientals.

[4] cf. p. 292.

[1] Is. lix. 5, lxx.   [2] Is. lix. 6.

they have sent the minions of their disorderly despotism into bishops' private houses, uttering shocking threats, and forcing them to affix their signatures to illegal acts. We therefore considering all their preposterous conduct, have deposed the aforenamed Cyril and Memnon, and deprived them of their episcopate. Their associates in irregularity, whether influenced by sycophancy or by fear, we have excommunicated, until, coming to a knowledge of their own wounds, they shall heartily repent, shall anathematize the heretical Chapters of Cyril, which are tainted with the heresy of Apollinarius, Arius, and Eunomius, shall recover the faith of the Fathers in Council at Nicæa, and, in obedience to the pious commands of our Christian sovereigns, shall, peacefully and without any tumult, assemble in synod, be willing to examine with care the questions submitted to them, and honestly protect the purity of the faith of the Gospel..

CLIV.   *Report of the same to the Senate of Constantinople.*[1]

CLV.   *Letter of John, bishop of Antioch and his supporters, to the clergy of Constantinople.*[2]

CLVI.   *Letter of the same to the people of Constantinople.*[3]

CLVII.   *Report of the Council of (the bishops of) the East to the victorious Emperor, announcing a second time the deposition of Cyril and of Memnon.*[4]

Your piety, which shines forth for the good of the empire and of the churches of God, has commanded us to assemble at Ephesus, in order to bring about peace and gain for the Church, rather than to confuse and disturb it. And the commands of your majesty plainly and distinctly indicate your pious and peaceful intentions for the churches of Christ. But Cyril of Alexandria, a man, it would seem, born and bred for the bane of the churches, after taking into partnership the audacity of Memnon of Ephesus, has first of all transgressed against your quieting and pious decree, and has so shewed his general depravity. Your majesty had

ordered an investigation and careful testing to be made concerning the faith, and that with the consent and concord of all. Cyril, challenged, or rather himself convicting himself, on the count of the Apollinarian doctrines, by means of the letter which he lately sent to the imperial city, with anathematisms, whereby he is convicted of sharing the views of the impious and heretic Apollinarius, pays no heed to this condition of things, and, as though we were living with no emperor to govern us, is proceeding to every kind of lawlessness. He ought himself to be called to account for his unsound opinion about our Lord Jesus Christ; but, usurping an authority given him neither by the canons, nor by your edicts, he is hurrying headlong into every kind of disorder and illegality.

Moved by these things the holy Synod, which has refused to accept his devices for the damage of the faith, for the aforesaid reasons deposes him. It deposes Memnon also, who has been his counsellor and abettor through all, who has kept up constant agitation against the very holy bishops for refusing to assent to his pernicious heterodoxy; who has shut the churches and every place of prayer, as if we were living among the heathen and the enemies of God; who has brought in the Ephesian mob, so that every day we are in supreme danger, while we look not to defence, but heed the right doctrines of true religion. For the destruction of these men is identical with the establishment of orthodoxy.

From his own Chapters your majesty can have no difficulty in perceiving his impious mind. He is convicted of trying, so to say, to raise from Hades the impious Apollinarius, who died in his heresy, and of attacking the churches and the orthodox faith. He is shewn in his publications to anathematize at once evangelists and apostles and them that succeeded them as forefathers of the Church, who, moved not by their own imaginations, but by the holy Spirit, have preached the true faith, and proclaimed the gospel; a faith and gospel indeed opposed to what this man holds and teaches and by inculcating which he wishes to give his own private iniquity the mastery of the world. Since this is intolerable to us we have followed the proper course, relying at once on the divine grace and on your majesty's good will.

We know that you give to nothing higher honour than to the sacred faith in which both you and your thrice blessed forefathers have been brought up. From them you have received the perpetual sceptre of empire, ever

---

[1] This Report, couched in almost identical terms with the preceding, I omit, although commonly accepted as the composition of Theodoret.

[2] This is also merely a short summary of CLII. and CLIII.

[3] Omitted as being a repetition of the preceding.

[4] The Latin version of the title begins "*Relatio orientalis conciliabuli.*" So the rival and hurried gathering of the Easterns was styled. The following letter is a further justification of their action, and illustrates the readiness and ability, if not the temper and prudence, of the bishop of Cyrus, its probable author.

putting down the opponents of the apostolic doctrines. Such an opponent is the aforesaid Cyril, who, with the aid of Memnon, has captured Ephesus as he might some fortress, and justly shares with his ally the sentence of deposition. Justly: for, besides all that has been said, they have boldly tried every means of assault and every violence against us, who, to come together in council in ratification of your edict, have disregarded every claim of home and country and self.

We are now the prey of tyranny, unless your piety intervene and order us to assemble in some other place, near at hand, where we shall be able, from the scriptures, and from the writings of the Fathers, to refute beyond contradiction both Cyril and the victims of his ingenuity. We have mercifully expelled these men from communion with the suggested hope of salvation in case they should repent; although, as if on some campaign of uncivilized soldiery, they have up to this moment furnished him with the means of his illegality. Some were deposed long ago, and have been restored by Cyril. Some have been excommunicated by their own metropolitans, and admitted by him again into communion. Others have been impaled on various accusations, and have been promoted by him to honour. All through, the main motive of his action has been the endeavour to achieve his heretical purpose by the force of numbers, for he does not reckon as he ought that in what relates to true religion, it is not numbers that are required, but rather correctness of doctrine, and the truth of the doctrine of the apostles. Men are needed who are competent to establish these points not by audacity and masterful self-assertion but by pious use of apostolic testimony and example.

For all these reasons we beseech and implore your majesty to bear prompt aid to assaulted truth, and to remedy without delay these men's masterful madness; for, like a hurricane, it is sweeping the less moderate among us into pernicious heresy. Your piety has had care for the churches in Persia and among the barbarians; it is only right that you should not neglect those which are tossed by the storm within the boundaries of the Roman empire.

CLVIII. Report of (the bishops of) the East to the very pious emperor, which they delivered with the preceding Report to the right honourable count Irenæus.

On receiving the letter of your piety we entertained hopes that the Egyptian storm which has lately struck the churches of

God would be driven away. But we have been disappointed. Those men have been made even yet more daring by their madness; they have given no heed to the sentence of deposition justly and in due form passed upon them, nor have become any more moderate in consequence of the rebuke of your majesty. They have trampled down alike the laws of your piety, and the canons of the holy Fathers, and, some of them being deposed and some excommunicated, keep festivals, and celebrate communion, in Houses of Prayer. And we, as we have already informed your Christ-loving majesty, on the receipt of your clemency's kindly letter, though our only desire was to pray in the church of the Apostles, have not only been prevented, but actually stoned, and chased for a considerable distance, so that we were compelled to effect our safety by flight at full speed. Our opponents on the contrary think that they may act just as they please. They have declined to make investigation of the questions at issue, and to undertake the defence of Cyril's heretical Chapters, rejecting the plain proofs of the impiety which they contain. They are impudent from mere impudence, while the examination of the questions before us requires not impudence, but calmness, knowledge, and skill in matters of doctrine.

Under these circumstances we have been under the necessity of sending forward the most honourable Count Irenæus, to approach your piety, and to explain the position of affairs. He has accurate information concerning all that has occurred, and has learned from us many modes of cure, whereby it may be possible to bring about the restoration of tranquillity to the holy churches of God. We beseech your clemency to grant him patient audience, and to give orders for the prompt carrying out of whatever measures may seem good to your piety, that we be not here crushed beyond all endurance.

CLIX. Letter of the same to the Præfect and to the Master.[1]

CLX. Letter of the same to the Governor and Scholasticus.[2]

CLXI. Report presented to the Emperor by John, archbishop of Antioch and his supporters through Palladius Magistrianus.[3]

---

[1] Written at the same time and under the same circumstances as the former, of which it is an abbreviation, and is consequently omitted.

[2] Omitted as merely repeating the representation of CLVII.

[3] This document defends the action of the conciliabulum, speaking of Cyril, in consequence of their deposition, as

CLXII. Letter of Theodoretus to Andreas, bishop of Samosata, written from Ephesus.[1]

Writing from Ephesus I salute your holiness, I congratulate you on your infirmity, and deem you dear to God, in that you have known what evil deeds have been going on here by report, and not by personal experience. Evil indeed! They transcend all imagination and all incidents of history; they compel a continual downpour of tears. The body of the Church is in peril of dismemberment; — nay, rather I may say it has received the first incision; — unless the wise Healer restore and re-connect the unsound and severed limbs. Once again the Egyptian is raging against God, and warring with Moses and Aaron His servants, and the more part of Israel are on the side of the foe; for all too few are the sound who willingly suffer for true religion's sake. Ancient principles are trodden under foot. Deposed men perform priestly functions, and they who have deposed them sit sighing at home. Men excommunicated by the same sentence as the deposed have relieved the deposed of their deposition of their own free will. Such is the mockery of a synod held by Egyptians, by Palestinians, by men from the Pontic and Asian dioceses, and by the West in their company.[2]

What players in a pantomime, in the days of paganism, even in any farce so held up religion to ridicule? Indeed what farce-writer ever performed such a play? What dramatist ever wrote so sad a tragedy? Such and so great are the troubles that have beset God's Church, whereof I have narrated but a very small part.

CLXIII. First Letter of the Commissioners of the East, sent to Chalcedon, among whom was Theodoretus.[3]

On our arrival at Chalcedon, for neither we ourselves nor our opponents were permitted to enter Constantinople, on account of the seditions of the excellent monks, we heard that eight days before we had appeared (behold the glory of the most pious prince) the lord Nestorius was dismissed from Ephesus, free to go where he would; whereat we are much distressed, since verily deeds done illegally and informally now seem to have some force. Let your holiness however be assured that we shall eagerly join the battle for the Faith, and are willing to fight even unto death. To-day, the 11th of the month Gorpiæum,[1] we are expecting our very pious Emperor to cross over to the Rufinianum,[2] and there to hear the trial.

We therefore beg your holiness to pray the Lord Christ to help us to be able to confirm the faith of the holy Fathers, and to pluck up by the roots these Chapters which have sprouted to the damage of the Church. We implore your holiness to think and act with us, and to abide in your ready devotion to the orthodox faith. When this letter was written the lord Himerius[3] had not yet met us, being peradventure hindered on the road. But do not let this trouble you. Only let your piety strenuously support us, and we trust that gloom will disappear, and the truth shine forth.

CLXIV. Second Epistle of the same to the same, expressing premature triumph in victory.[4]

Through the prayers of your holiness our most pious prince has granted us an audience, and by God's grace we have got the better of our opponents, as all our views have been accepted by the most Christ-loving emperor. The reports of others were read, and what seemed unfit to be received, and had no further importance, he rejected. They were full of Cyril, and petitioned that he might be summoned to give an account of himself. So far they have not prevailed, but have heard discourses on true religion, that is on the system of the Faith, and that the faith of the blessed Fathers was confirmed. We further refuted Acacius[5] who had laid down in his Commentaries that the Godhead was possible. At this our pious emperor was so shocked at the enormity of the blasphemy that he flung off his mantle, and stepped

---

"lately" bishop of Alexandria, and demanding the exile of Memnon.

[1] This letter may be dated "towards the end of July or in the beginning of August 431, after the restitution of Cyril and Memnon on July 16, and before the departure of Theodoret from Ephesus on August 20." Garnerius. Andrew of Samosata wrote objections to Cyril's Chapters in the name of the bishops of the East. He was prevented by illness from being present at Ephesus in 431, as he was also from the synod assembled at Antioch in 444 to hear the cause of Athanasius of Perrha. He was a warm supporter of Nestorius.

This letter exists only in the Latin Version, and is to be found also in Mansi Collect. Conc. ix. 293.

[2] In Ep. CLXI. the numbers are specified; — " Of Egyptians fifty; of Asiani under Memnon, leader of the tyranny, forty; of the heretics in Pamphylia called Messalianitæ, twelve; besides those attached to the same metropolitan " (i.e. Amphilochius of Side) " and others deposed and excommunicated in divers places by synods or bishops, who constitute nothing but a mere turbulent and disorderly mob, entirely ignorant of the divine decrees."

[3] Another version of the title runs " To the very holy and wise synod assembled at Ephesus, Joannes, Paulus, Aprin-

gius, Theodoretus, greeting." The letter may be dated in Sept. 431. Paul, bishop of Emesa, was ultimately an active peacemaker in the dispute. Apringius was bishop of Chalcis. It only exists in the Latin.

[1] The Macedonian name for September.
[2] A villa in the vicinity of Chalcedon.
[3] Metropolitan of Nicomedia; one of the "Conciliabulum."
[4] Also only in Latin.
[5] Bishop of Melitene in Armenia Secunda, an ardent anti-Nestorian, who remonstrated with Cyril for consenting to make peace with the Orientals.

back. We know that the whole assembly welcomed us as champions of true religion.

It has seemed good to our most pious emperor that anyone should explain his own views, and report them to his piety. We have replied that it is impossible for us to make any other exposition than that made by the blessed Fathers at Nicæa, and so it has pleased his majesty. We therefore offered the form subscribed by your holiness. Moreover, the whole population of Constantinople is continually coming out to us to implore us to fight manfully for the Faith. We do our best to restrain them, to avoid giving offence to our opponents. We have sent a copy of the expositing, that two copies may be made, and you may subscribe them both.

CLXV. *Letter of the same to the same.*[1]

To the very pious bishops now in Ephesus: Johannes, Himerius, Paulus, Apringius, Theodoretus, greeting. For the fifth time an audience has been granted us. We entered largely into the question of the heretical Chapters, and swore again and again to the very pious emperor that it was impossible for us to hold communion with our opponents unless they rejected the Chapters. We pointed out moreover that even if Cyril did abjure his Chapters he could not be received by us, because he had become the heresiarch of so impious a heresy. Nevertheless we gained no ground, because our adversaries were urgent, and their hearers could neither restrain them in their insolent endeavour, nor compel them to come to enquiry and argument. They thus evade the investigation of the Chapters, and allow no discussion concerning them. We, however, as you entreat, are ready to insist to the death. We refuse to receive Cyril and his Chapters; we will not admit these men to Communion till the improper additions to the Faith be rejected. We therefore implore your holiness to continue to show at once our mind and our efforts. The battle is for true religion; for the only hope we have, — on account of which we look forward to enjoying, in the world to come, the loving-kindness of our Saviour. As to the very pious and holy bishop Nestorius, be it known to your piety that we have tried to introduce a word about him, but have hitherto failed, because all are ill-affected toward him. We will notwithstanding do our best, though this is so, to take advantage of any opportunity that

may offer, and of the goodwill of the audience, to carry out this purpose, God helping us. But that your holiness may not be ignorant of this too, know that we, seeing that the partisans of Cyril have deceived everyone by domineering, cheating, flattering, and bribing, have more than once besought the very pious emperor and most noble princes both to send us back to the East, and let your holiness go home. For we are beginning to learn that we are wasting time in vain, without nearing our end, because Cyril everywhere shirks discussion, in his conviction that the blasphemies published in his Twelve Chapters can be openly refuted. The very pious emperor has determined, after many exhortations, that we all go every one to his own home, and that, further, both the Egyptian and Memnon of Ephesus are to remain in their own places. So the Egyptian will be able to go on blindfolding by bribery. The one, after crimes too many to tell, is to return to his diocese. The other, an innocent man, is barely permitted to go home. We and all here salute you and all the brotherhood with you.

CLXVI. *First petition of the commissioners, addressed from Chalcedon, to the Emperor.*

It had been much to be desired that the word of true religion should not be adulterated by ridiculous explanations, and least of all by men who have obtained the priesthood and high office in the churches, and who have been induced, we know not how, by ambition, by lust of authority, and by certain poor promises, to despise all the commandments of Christ. Their only motive has been the desire to pay court to a man who has the presumption to hope that he and his abettors will be able to manage the whole business with success; I mean Cyril of Alexandria. Of his own frivolity he has intruded into the holy churches of God heretical doctrines which he believes himself able to support by argument. He expects to escape the chastisement of sinners by the sole help of Memnon and the bishops of the aforesaid conspiracy.

We are lovers of silence; in general we advise a philosophic course of action. Now, however, sensible that to be silent and to cultivate philosophy would be to throw away the Faith, we turn in supplication to you who, next to the Goodness on high, are the sole preserver of the world. We know that it specially belongs to you to be anxious for

---

[1] Only in Latin.

true religion, as having, up to this present day, continually protected it, and being in turn protected by it.

We beg you therefore to receive this treatise, as though our defence were to be pleaded in the presence of the most holy God; not because we are less active in the sacred cause, but because we are devoted to true religion, and are speaking in its behalf. For in Christian times the clergy have no more bounden duty than to bear testimony before so faithful a prince, however ready we might have been to yield our bodies and to lay down our lives a thousand times in the battle for the faith. We therefore beseech you by God who seeth all things, by our Lord Jesus Christ who will judge all men in righteousness, by the Holy Ghost by whose grace you hold your empire, and by the elect angels who are your guardians and whom one day you shall see standing by the awful throne, and ceaselessly offering unto God that dread doxology which it is now sought to corrupt; we beseech your piety, besieged as you now are by the craftiness of certain men who are forbidding access to you, and are supporting the introduction into the faith of heretical Chapters, utterly at variance with sound doctrine, and tainted with heresy, to order all who subscribe them, or assent to them, and wish, after your promised pardon, to dispute further, to come forth and submit to the discipline of the Church. Nothing, sir, is more worthy of an emperor than to fight for the truth, for which you hurried to join battle with Persians and other barbarians, when Christ granted you to win fair victories in acknowledgment of your zeal towards Him. We beseech you that the questions at issue may be put before your piety in writing, for thus their purport will be more easily perceived, and the transgressors will be convicted for all future time. If however anyone, heedless of the utterances for which he shall be at fault, shall wish by his teaching to prevail over the right faith, it will be the part of your justice and judgment to consider whether the very name of teachers has not been thrown away by men who are reluctant to run any risks concerning the doctrines which they introduce, refusing to be obedient to your orders, that they may escape conviction for having done wrong; nor reckoning them worth refutation, that their mutual conspiracy be not proved fruitless. For now it is clear, from those that have been ordained by them that some of them, in return for this impiety, have bethought them of obliging certain persons by the concession of dignities and

have devised certain other means. This will become still more clear; and your piety will soon see that they will distribute the rewards of their treachery, as though they were the spoils of the faith of Christ.

But we, of whom some were long ago ordained by the very pious Juvenal, bishop of Jerusalem, have kept silence, although it was our duty to contend for the canon, that we might not seem to be troubled for our own reputation's sake. We are now perfectly well aware of his active trickery through Phœnicia Secunda and Arabia. We really have not time to attend to such things. We are men who have preferred rather to be deprived of the very places of which the ministry has been entrusted to us, and so of our life, than of our ready zeal for the faith. To the attempts of those men we will oppose the sentence of God and of your piety.

Now also we beg that true religion may be your one and primary care, and that the brightness of orthodoxy, which at length with difficulty blazed forth in the days of Constantine of holy name, was maintained by your blessed grandfather and father, and was extended by your majesty among the Persians and other barbarians, be not allowed to grow dim in the very innermost courts of your imperial palace, or, in your serenity's days, to be dispersed.

You will not send, sir, a divided Christianity into Persia; nor here at home will there be anything great, while we are distressed by disputes, and while there is no one existing on their side to settle them; no one will take part in a divided Word and Sacraments; no one without loss of faith will cut himself off from such famous fathers and saints who have never been condemned. No imperial successes will be permitted to a people at variance among themselves; a burst of derision will be roused from the enemies of true religion; and all the other noxious consequences of their malignant controversy are too numerous to reckon.

If there is anyone who thinks little of the science of theology, let that one be any one in the world rather than he to whom the Lord has given the supreme government of the world. Our petition is that your piety will give judgment, for God will guide your intelligence into exact comprehension. Finally, should this be impracticable (and all the engagements of your piety we cannot know) we beseech your serenity to give us leave to travel safely home. We are aware that to the dioceses entrusted to us cause of offence is given by so protracted a delay, on account of those men who even in sacred matters look out for opportunities of dissension whence no advantage can be derived.

CLXVII. Second petition of the same, sent from Chalcedon to Theodosius Augustus.

Your piety has been informed on several occasions, both by ourselves in person and by our emissaries, that the doctrine of the true faith seems to stand in danger of being corrupted, and that the body of the Church is apparently being rent asunder by men who are turning everything upside down, trampling upon all church order, and all imperial law, and throwing everything into confusion, that they may confirm the heresy propounded by Cyril of Alexandria. For when we were first summoned by your piety to Ephesus, to enquire into the question which had arisen, and to confirm the evangelic and apostolic faith laid down by the holy Fathers, before the arrival of all the bishops who had been convened, the holders of their own private Council confirmed in writing the heretical Chapters, which are at one with the impiety of Arius, Eunomius and Apollinarius. Some they deceived; some they terrified; others already charged with heresy, they received into communion; and others who had not communicated with them were bribed into so doing; others again were fired with the hope of dignities for which they were unfit; so these men gathered round them a great crowd of adherents, as though they had no idea that true religion is shewn not by numbers, but by truth.

The dispatch of your piety was read a second time by the most honourable Count Candidianus, ordering that the questions recently raised be examined in a quiet and brotherly manner. When however all the pious bishops were assembling, the reading had no effect.

Then came the noble Palladius Magistrianus, bringing another dispatch from your majesty, to the effect that all enactments passed privately and apart must be rescinded; that the Council must be assembled afresh, and the true doctrine ratified; but, as usual, this your pious mandate was treated with contempt by these unscrupulous persons.

Then again arrived the right honourable Master John, at that time "Comes Largitionum," bringing another pious letter to the effect that the depositions of the three had been decreed, that the offences which had sprung up were to be removed, and the faith laid down at Nicæa by the holy and blessed Fathers was to be ratified by all. As usual these universal mockers transgressed this law too.

For after hearing the letter they did not change their mode of action; they held communion with the deposed; spoke of them as bishops, and refused to allow the Chapters, which had been propounded to the loss and corruption of the pious faith to be rejected; notwithstanding their having been frequently summoned by us to discussion. For we had ready to hand a plain refutation of the heretical Chapters.

In evidence of these statements we have the right honourable Master, who when both sides had been summoned a third and a fourth time, not venturing to make this conduct an excuse on account of their disobedience, thought it worth while to summon us hither.

We came at once; on our arrival we allowed ourselves no rest making our petition, both before your piety and before the illustrious assembly, that they would take up the quarrel for the Chapters and enter into discussion concerning them, or on the other hand reject them as contrary to the right faith, abiding by the faith as laid down by the blessed fathers in council at Nicæa.

They refused to do anything of the kind; they persisted in their heretical procedure; yet they were allowed to attend the churches, and to perform their priestly functions. We, however, alike at Ephesus and here, have been for a long time deprived of communion; alike there and here we have undergone innumerable perils; and while we were being stoned and all but slain by slaves dressed up as monks, we took it all for the best, as willingly enduring such treatment in the cause of the truth.

Afterwards it seemed good to your majesty that we and the opposite party should assemble once again, that the recalcitrant might be compelled to examine the doctrines. While we were waiting for this to come to pass your piety set out for the city, and ordered the very men who were being accused of heresy and had been therefore some of them deposed by us, and others excommunicated and thereafter to be subjected to the discipline of the Church, to come to the city and perform priestly functions, and ordain.[1] We however who in the cause of true religion have undertaken a struggle so tremendous; we who have shrunk from no peril in our battle for right doctrine, have neither been bidden to enter the city to serve the cause of the imperilled Faith and strive for orthodoxy; nor have we been permitted to return home;[2]

---

[1] i.e. Maximianus, in succession to Nestorius, Oct. 25, 431.

[2] Nestorius was permitted to return to his old monastery at Antioch.

but here we are in Chalcedon distressed and groaning for the Church oppressed by schism.

Wherefore since we are in receipt of no reply we have thought it necessary to inform your piety by this present letter, before God and Christ and the Holy Ghost, that if any one shall have been ordained (before the settlement of right doctrines) by these men of heretical opinions, he must necessarily be cut off from the whole church, as well from the clergy as the dissentient laity. For none of the pious will endure that communion be granted to heretics, and their own salvation be nullified.

And when this shall have come to pass, then your piety shall be compelled to act against your will. For the schism will grow beyond all expectation, and thereby the champions of true religion will be saddened, unable to endure the loss of their own souls, and the establishment of those impious doctrines of Cyril which the contentious are desirous of defending.

Many indeed of the supporters of true religion will never allow the acceptance of Cyril's doctrines; we shall never allow it, who all are of the diocese of the East of your province, of the diocese of Pontus, of Asia, of Thrace, of Illyricum and of the Italies, and who also sent to your piety the treatise of the most blessed Ambrose, written against this nascent superstition.

To avoid all this, and the further troubling of your piety, we beg, beseech, and implore you to issue an edict that no ordination take place before the settlement of the orthodox faith, on account of which we have been convened by your Christ-loving highness.

CLXVIII. Third demand of the same, addressed from Chalcedon to the sovereigns.

We never expected the summons of your piety to meet with this result. We were honourably convoked, as priests by prince; we were convoked to ratify the faith of the holy Fathers; and therefore, in due obedience to a pious prince, we came. On our arrival we were no less faithful to the Church, nor less respectful to your edict. From the day of our arrival at Ephesus till the present moment we have without intermission followed your behests.

As it seems, however, our moderation, in these times, has not been of the slightest use to us; nay, rather, so far as we can see, it has stood very much in our way. We indeed who have thus behaved have been up to the present time detained in Chalcedon;

and now we are told that we may go home. They however who have thrown everything into confusion, who have filled the world with tumult, who are striving to rend churches in twain, and who are the open assailants of true religion, perform priestly functions, crowd the churches, and as they imagine have authority to ordain, though in truth it is illegally claimed by them, stir up seditions in the church, and what ought to be spent upon the poor they throw away upon their bullies.

But you are not only their emperor; you are ours too. For no small portion of your empire is the East, wherein the right faith has ever shone, and, besides, the other provinces and dioceses from which we have been convened.

Let not your majesty despise the faith which is being corrupted, in which you and your forefathers have been baptized; on which the Church's foundations are laid; for which most holy martyrs have rejoiced to suffer countless kinds of death; by aid of which you have vanquished barbarians and destroyed tyrants; which you are needing now in your war for the subjugation of Africa. For on your side will fight the God of all if you struggle on behalf of His holy doctrines and forbid the dismemberment of the body of the church: for dismembered it will be if the opinion prevail which Cyril has introduced into the Church and other heretics have confirmed.

To these truths we have often already borne testimony before God both in Ephesus and in this place. I have furnished information to your holiness, giving an account as before the God of all. For this is required of us, as is taught in the divine Scripture both by prophets and apostles; as says the blessed Paul "I give thee charge in the sight of God, who quickeneth the dead, and of Lord Jesus Christ, who before Pontius Pilate witnessed a good confession;"[1] and as God charged Ezekiel to announce to the people, adding threats and saying, "when thou givest him not warning, . . . his blood will I require at thine hand."[2]

In awe of this sentence, once again we inform your majesty that they who have been permitted to hold churches, and who teach the doctrines of Apollinarius, Arius, and Eunomius, perform all sacred functions irregularly and in violation of the canons, and destroy the souls of all who approach them; if, indeed, any shall be found willing to listen to them. For by the grace of God

---

[1] I. Tim. vi. 13. [2] Ez. iii. 18.

whose Providence is over all, and who wishes all men to be saved, the more part of the people is sound, and warmly attached to pious doctrines. It is on their account that we grieve.

And in our anguish and alarm lest the plague creeping on by little and little should attack more, and the evil become general, we thus instruct your serenity, and continue to give you exhortation; we implore your majesty to yield to our prayers and to prohibit any addition to be made to the Faith of the holy Fathers assembled in council at Nicæa.

And if after this our entreaty your piety reject this doctrine, which was given in the presence of God, we will shake off the dust of our feet against you, and cry with the blessed Paul, "We are pure from your blood." [1] For we cease not night and day from the moment of our arrival at this distinguished council to bear witness to prince, nobles, soldiers, priests and people, that we hold fast the Faith delivered to us by the Fathers.

CLXIX. Letter written by Theodoretus, bishop of Cyrus, from Chalcedon to Alexander of Hierapolis. [2]

We have left no means untried, of courtesy, of sternness, of entreaty, of eloquence before the most pious emperor, and the illustrious assembly, testifying before God who sees all things and our Lord Jesus Christ who shall judge the world in justice, [3] and the Holy Spirit and his elect angels, lest the Faith be despised which is now being corrupted by the maintainers and bold subscribers of heretical doctrines; and that charge be given for it to be laid down in the same terms as at Nicæa and for the rejection of the heresy introduced to the loss and ruin of true religion. Up to this time however we have produced not the slightest effect, our hearers being carried now in one direction and now in another.

Nevertheless all these difficulties have not been able to deter me from urging my point, but by God's grace I have pressed on. I have even stated to our pious emperor with an oath that it is perfectly impossible for Cyril and Memnon to be reconciled with me, and that we can never communicate with any one who has not previously repudiated the heretical Chapters. This then is our mind.

The object of men who "seek their own not the things which are Jesus Christ's" [1] is to be reconciled with them against our will. But this is no business of mine, for God weighs our motives and tries our character, nor does He inflict chastisement for what is done against our will. Be it known to your holiness that if ever I said a word about our friend [2] either before the very pious emperor or the illustrious assembly, I was at once branded as a rebel. So intensely is he hated by the court party. This is most annoying. The most pious emperor, especially, cannot bear to hear his name mentioned and says publicly "Let no one speak to me of this man." On one occasion he gave an instance of this to me. Nevertheless as long as I am here I shall not cease to serve the interests of this our father, knowing that the impious have done him wrong.

My desire is that both your piety and I myself get quit of this. No good is to be hoped from it, in as much as all the judges trust in gold, and contend that the nature of the Godhead and manhood is one.

All the people however by God's grace are in good case, and constantly come out to us. I have begun to discourse to them and have celebrated very large communions.

On the fourth occasion I spoke at length about the faith and they listened with such delight that they did not go away till the seventh hour but held out even till the midday heat. An enormous crowd was gathered in a great court, with four verandahs, and I preached from above from a platform near the roof.

All the clergy with the excellent monks are on the contrary utterly opposed to me, so that when we came back from the Rufinianum, after the visit of the very pious emperor, stone throwing began and many of my companions were wounded, by the people and false monks.

The very pious emperor knew that the mob was gathered against me and coming up to me alone he said, "I know that you are assembling improperly." Then, said I, "As you have allowed me to speak hear me with favour. Is it fair for excommunicated heretics to be doing duty in churches, while I, who am fighting for the Faith and am therefore excluded by others from communion, am not allowed to enter a church?" He replied "What am I to do?" I said, "What your *comes largitionum* did at Ephesus. When he found that some were

---

[1] Acts. xx. 26.
[2] Dated by Garnerius at the end of September or beginning of October 431, before the order had been given for the withdrawal of the Easterns and the entry of the other party to consecrate a bishop.
[3] cf. II. Tim. iv. 1.

[1] Phil. ii. 21.   [2] i.e. Nestorius.

assembling, but that we were not assembling, he stopped them saying, 'If you are not peaceful I will allow neither party to assemble.' It would have become your piety also to have given directions to the bishop here to forbid both the opposite party and ourselves to assemble before our meeting together to make known your righteous sentence to all." To this he replied "It is not for me to order the bishop;" and I answered "Neither shall you command us, and we will take a church, and assemble. Your piety will find that there are many more on our side than on theirs." In addition to this I pointed out that we had neither reading of the holy Scripture, nor oblation; but only "prayer for the Faith and for your majesty, and pious conversation." So he approved, and made no further prohibition. The result is that increased crowds flock to us, and gladly listen to our teaching. I therefore beg your piety to pray that our case may have an issue pleasing to God. I am in daily danger, suspecting the wiles of both monks and clergy, as I witness alike their influence and their negligence.

CLXX. Letter of certain Easterns, who had been sent to Constantinople, to Bishop Rufus.

To our most godly and holy fellow-minister Rufus, Joannes, Himerius, Theodoretus, and the rest, send greeting in the Lord.[1]

True religion and the peace of the Church suffer, we think, in no small degree, from the absence of your holiness. Had you been on the spot you might have put a stop to the disturbances which have arisen, and the violence that has been ventured on, and might have fought on our side for the subjection of the heresies introduced into the orthodox Faith, and that doctrine of apostles and evangelists which, handed down from time to time from father to son, has at length been transmitted to ourselves.

And we do not assert this without ground, for we have learnt the mind of your holiness from the letter written to the very godly and holy Julianus, bishop of Sardica,

for that letter as is right charged the above named very godly bishop to fight for the Faith laid down by the blessed fathers assembled in council at Nicæa, and not to allow any corruption to be introduced into those invincible definitions which are sufficient at once to exhibit the truth and to refute falsehood. So your holiness rightly, justly, and piously advised, and the recipient of the letter followed your counsel. But many of the members of the council, to use the word of the prophet, "have gone aside," and have "altogether become filthy,"[1] for they have abandoned the Faith which they received from the holy Fathers, and have subscribed the twelve Chapters of Cyril of Alexandria, which teem with Apollinarian error, are in agreement with the impiety of Arius and Eunomius, and anathematize all who do not accept their unconcealed unorthodoxy. To this plague smiting the Church vigorous resistance has been offered by us who have assembled from the East, and others from different dioceses, with the object of securing the ratification of the Faith delivered by the blessed Fathers at Nicæa. For in it, as your holiness knows, there is nothing lacking whether for the teaching of evangelic doctrines, or for the refutation of every heresy.

For the sake of this Faith we continue to struggle, despising alike all the joys and sorrows of mortal life, if only we may preserve untouched this heritage of our fathers. For this reason we have deposed Cyril and Memnon; the former as prime mover in the heresy, and the latter as his aider and abettor in all that has been done to ratify and uphold the Chapters published to the destruction of the Church. We have also excommunicated all that have dared to subscribe and support these impious doctrines till they shall have anathematized them, and returned to the Faith of the Fathers at Nicæa.

But our long-suffering has done them no good. To this day they continue to do battle for those pernicious doctrines and have impaled themselves on the law of the canon which distinctly enacts "If any bishop deposed by a synod, or presbyter or deacon deposed by his own bishop, shall perform his sacred office, without waiting for the judgment of a synod, he is to have no opportunity for defending himself, not even in another synod: but also all who communicate with him are to be expelled from the church." Now this law has been broken

---

[1] After pointing out that superscription, style, expression, sentiments, and circumstances all indicate Theodoret as the writer of this letter, Garnerius proceeds "The objection of Baronius that mention is made of Martinus, bishop of Milan, when there never was a Martinus bishop of Milan, is not of great importance. Theodoret at a distance might easily write Martinus for Martinianus, or a copyist might abbreviate the name to this form." The date of the letter is marked as after the order to the bishops to remain at Constantinople, and before permission was given them to return home. The Letters were also written to Martinianus of Milan, to John of Ravenna, and to John of Aquileia, but only that to Rufus is extant. Rufus is probably the bishop of Thessalonica.

[1] Ps. xiv. 3.

both by the deposed and the excommunicate. For immediately after the deposition and the excommunication becoming known to them, they performed sacred functions, and they continue to do so, in plain disbelief of Him who said " Whatsoever ye shall bind on earth shall be bound in heaven." [1]

With this we have thought well to acquaint your holiness at once, but in expectation of some favourable change, we have waited up to the present time. But we have been disappointed. They have continued to fight for this impious heresy, and pay no attention to the counsels of the very pious emperor. On five separate occasions he has met us, and ordered them either to reject the Chapters of Cyril as contrary to the Faith, or to be willing to do battle in their behalf, and to shew in what way they are in agreement with the confession of the Fathers. We have our proofs at hand, whereby we should have shewn that they are totally opposed to the teaching of orthodoxy, and for the most part in agreement with heresy.

For in these very Chapters the author of the noxious productions teaches that the Godhead of the only begotten Son suffered, instead of the manhood which He assumed for the sake of our salvation, the indwelling Godhead manifestly appropriating the sufferings as of Its own body, though suffering nothing in Its own nature; and further that there is made one nature of both Godhead and manhood, — for so he explains " The Word was made flesh," [2] as though the Godhead had undergone some change, and been turned into flesh.

And, further, he anathematizes those who make a distinction between the terms used by apostles and evangelists about the Lord Christ, referring those of humiliation to the manhood, and those of divine glory to the Godhead, of the Lord Christ. It is with these views that Arians and Eunomians, attributing the terms of humiliation to the Godhead, have not shrunk from declaring God the Word to be made and created, of another substance, and unlike the Father.

What blasphemy follows on these statements it is not difficult to perceive. There is introduced a confusion of the natures, and to God the Word are applied the words " My God, my God, why hast thou forsaken me;" [3] and " Father, if it be possible let this cup pass from me," [4] the hunger, the thirst, and the strengthening by an angel; His saying " Now is my soul troubled," [5] and " my soul is exceeding sorrowful, even unto

death," [1] and all similar passages belonging to the manhood of the Christ. Any one may perceive how these statements correspond with the impiety of Arius and Eunomius; for they, finding themselves unable to establish the difference of substance, connect, as has been said, the sufferings, and the terms of humiliation, with the Godhead of the Christ.

And be your reverence well assured that now in their churches the Arian teachers preach no other doctrine than that the supporters of the " homousion " at present hold the same views as Arius, and that, after long time, the truth has now at last been brought to light.

We on the contrary abide in the teaching, and follow in the pious footprints, of the blessed Fathers assembled at Nicæa, and of their illustrious successors, Eustathius of Antioch, Basil of Cæsarea, Gregory, John, Athanasius, Theophilus, Damasus of Rome, and Ambrose of Milan. For all these, following the words of the apostles, have left us an exact rule of orthodoxy, which all we of the East earnestly desire to preserve unmoved. The same is the wish of the Bithynians, the Paphlagonians, of Cappadocia Secunda, Pisidia, Mysia, Thessaly, and Rhodope, and very many more of the different provinces. The Italians too, it is evident, will not endure this new-fangled doctrine; for the very godly and holy Martinus, [2] bishop of Milan, has written a letter to us, and has sent to the very pious emperor a work by the blessed Ambrose on the incarnation of the Lord, of which the teaching is opposed to these heretical Chapters.

And be it known to your holiness that Cyril and Memnon have not been satisfied with corrupting the orthodox Faith, but have trampled all the canons under foot. For they have received into communion men excommunicated in various provinces and dioceses. Others lying under charges of heresy, and of the same mind as Celestius and Pelagius, (for they are Euchitæ, or Enthusiasts[3]) and therefore excommunicated by their diocesans and metropolitans, they have, in defiance of all ecclesiastical discipline received into communion, so swelling their following from all possible quarters, and shewing their eagerness to enforce their teaching less by piety than by violence. For when they had been stripped bare of piety they devised, in their

---

1 Matt. xviii. 18. 3 Ps. xxii. 1. 5 John xii. 27.
2 John i. 14. 4 Matt. xxvi. 39.

1 Matt. xxvi. 38. 2 Vide note on superscription.
3 cf. note on p. 114. Celestius, an Irishman of good family, was associated with Pelagius at Rome. Both were condemned at Ephesus in 431. The connexion of Pelagius with the Euchitæ may be suggested by the denial of the former of original sin and the depreciation by the latter of baptism as producing no results.

extremity, another sort of force, — walls of flesh, with the idea that by their showers of bribery they might vanquish the faith of the Fathers. But so long as your holiness puts forth your strength, and you continue to fight, as you are wont, in defence of true religion, none of these devices will be of the least avail. We exhort you therefore, most holy sir, to beware of the communion of the unscrupulous introducers of this heresy; and to make known to all, both far and near, that these are the points for which the thrice blessed Damasus deposed the heretics Apollinarius, Vitalius, and Timotheus; and that the Epistle in which the writer has concealed his heresy and coloured it with a coating of truth, must not in simplicity be received. For in the Chapters he has boldly laid bare his impiety, and dared to anathematize all who disagree with him, while in the letter he has vilely endeavoured to harm the simpler readers.

Your holiness must therefore beware of neglecting this matter, lest when, too late, you see this heresy confirmed, you grieve in vain, and suffer affliction at being no longer able to defend the cause of truth.

We have also sent you a copy of the memorial which we have given to the most pious and Christ-loving emperor, containing the faith of the holy Fathers at Nicæa, wherein we have rejected the newly-invented heresies of Cyril, and adjudged them to be opposed to the orthodox faith.

Since in accordance with the orders of the very pious emperor only eight of us travelled to Constantinople, we have subjoined the copy of the order given us by the holy synod, that you may be acquainted with the provinces contained in it. Your holiness will learn them from the signatures of the metropolitans. We salute the brotherhood which is with you.

CLXXI. *Letter of Theodoret to John, bishop of Antioch, after the reconciliation.*[1]

God, who governs all things in wisdom, who provides for our unanimity, and cares for the salvation of His people, has caused us to be assembled together, and has shewn us that the views of all of us are in agreement with one another. We have assembled together, and read the Egyptian Letter;[2] we

have carefully examined its purport, and we have discovered that its contents are quite in accordance with our own statements, and entirely opposed to the Twelve Chapters, against which up to the present time we have continued to wage war, as being contrary to true religion. Their teaching was that God the Word was carnally made flesh; that there was an union of hypostasis, and that the combination in union was of nature, and that God the Word was the first-born from the dead. They forbade all distinction in the terms used of our Lord, and further contained other doctrines at variance with the seeds sown by the apostles, and outcome of heretical tares. The present script, however, is beautified by apostolic nobility of origin. For in it our Lord Jesus Christ is exhibited as perfect God and perfect man; it shews two natures, and the distinction between them; an unconfounded union, made not by mixture and compounding, but in a manner ineffable and divine, and distinctly preserving the properties of the natures; the impassibility and immortality of God the Word; the passibility and temporary surrender to death of the temple, and its resurrection by the power of the united God; that the holy Spirit is not of the Son, nor derives existence from the Son, but proceeds from the Father, and is properly stated to be of the Son, as being of one substance.[1] Beholding this orthodoxy in the letter, we have hymned Him who heals our stammering tongues, and changes our discordant noises into the harmony of sweet music.[2]

CLXXII. *Letter of Theodoretus to Nestorius.*[3]

To the very reverend and religious lord and very holy Father, Nestorius, the bishop Theodoretus sends greeting in the Lord. Your holiness is, I think, well aware that I take no pleasure in cultivated society, nor in the interests of this life, nor in reputation, nor am I attracted by other sees. Had I learnt this lesson from no other source, the very solitude of the city[4] over which I am called to preside would suffice to teach me this philosophy. It is not indeed dis-

---

[1] This Letter appears to be that of the Euphratensian synod. ("*probat primum hæc vox ἐν κοινῶ, in conventu: deinde pluralis numerus ubique positus.*" Garnerius.)

Garnerius would date it during the negotiations for reconciliation, when John of Antioch visited Acacius at Berœa, after the Orientals had accepted Cyril's formula of faith. Schulze would rather place it after the negotiations were over.

[2] Presumably the letter written by Cyril to Acacius, setting forth his own view, and representing that peace might be

attained if the Orientals would give up Nestorius. It exists in Latin. Synod. Mansi, V. 831.

[1] Vide p. 279. Note.

[2] The following paragraph, found only in the Vatican MS., and described by Schulze as "inept," is omitted. It has no significance.

[3] Of this letter the Greek copies have perished. Three Latin versions exist.

(i) In Synod c. 120. Mans. v 898.

(ii) *In synodi quintæ collatione.* Mans. IX. 204.

(iii) A version of Marius Mercator from the Recension of Garnerius. The two latter are both given in Migne, Theod. IV. 486. The translation given follows the former of these two. The date appears to be not long after the receipt by Theodoret of the Chapters of Cyril.

[4] cf. p. 307.

tinguished only for solitude, but also by very many disturbances which may check the activity even of those who most delight in them.

Let no one therefore persuade your holiness that I have accepted the Egyptian writings as orthodox, with my eyes shut, because I covet any see. For really, to speak the truth, after frequently reading and carefully examining them, I have discovered that they are free from all heretical taint, and I have hesitated to put any stress upon them, though I certainly have no love for their author, who was the originator of the disturbances which have agitated the world. For this I hope to escape punishment in the day of Judgment, since the just Judge examines motives. But to what has been done unjustly and illegally against your holiness, not even if one were to cut off both my hands would I ever assent, God's grace helping me and supporting my infirmity. This I have stated in writing to those who require it. I have sent to your holiness my reply to what you wrote to me, that you may know that, by God's grace, no time has changed me like the centipedes and chameleons who imitate by their colour the stones and leaves among which they live. I and all with me salute all the Brotherhood who are with you in the Lord.

CLXXIII. Letter to Andreas, Monk of Constantinople.[1]

" God is faithful who will not suffer you to be tempted above that ye are able; but will with the temptation also make a way to escape that ye may be able to bear it," [2] and convicts falsehood, — although now refuted assertion of the falsehood is approved, — and the power of truth has been shewn. For, lo, they, who by their impious reasoning had confused the natures of our Saviour Christ, and dared to preach one nature, and therefore insulted the most holy and venerable Nestorius, high priest of God, their mouths held, as the prophet says, with bit and bridle [3] and turned from wrong to right, have once again learnt the truth, adopting the statement of him who in the cause of truth has borne the brunt of the battle. For instead of one nature they now confess two, anathematizing all who preach mixture and confusion. They adore the impassible Godhead of Christ; they attribute passion to the flesh; they distinguish between the terms of the Gospels, ascribing the lofty and divine

to the Godhead, and the lowly to the manhood. Such are the writings now brought from Egypt.

CLXXIV. To Himerius, bishop of Nicomedia.[1]

We wish to acquaint your holiness that on reading and frequently discussing the letter brought from Egypt we find it in harmony with the doctrine of the Church. Of the twelve Chapters we have proved the contrary, and up to the present time we continue to oppose them. We have therefore determined, if your holiness has recovered the churches divinely entrusted to you, that you ought to communicate with the Egyptians and Constantinopolitans and others who have fought with them against us, because they have professed to hold our faith, or I should rather say the faith of the apostles; but not to give your consent to the alleged condemnation of the very holy and venerable Nestorius. For we hold it impious and unjust in the case of charges in which both appeared as defendants to lavish favour on the one and shut the door of repentance on the other. Far more unjust and impious is it to condemn an innocent man to death. Your holiness should be assured that you ought not to communicate with them before you have recovered your churches. For this not only I but all the holy bishops of our district decreed in the recent Council.

CLXXV. To Alexander of Hierapolis.[2]

I have already informed your holiness that if the doctrine of the very holy and venerable bishop, my lord Nestorius, is condemned, I will not communicate with those who do so. If it shall please your holiness to insert this in the letter which is being sent to Antioch so be it. Let there then, I beseech you, be no delay!

CLXXVI. Letter to the same Alexander after he had learnt that John, bishop of Antioch, had anathematized the doctrine of Nestorius.[3]

Be it known to your holiness that when I read the letter addressed to the emperor I was much distressed, because I know perfectly well that the writer of the letter, being of the same opinions, has unwisely and

[1] cf. Epp. CXLIII and CLXXVII.
[2] I Cor. x. 13.
[3] Ps. xxxi. 9.

[1] Himerius was of the "Conciliabulum," and a staunch Nestorian. LeQuien points out that he, as well as Theodoret, became ultimately reconciled to the victorious party.
[2] This according to Marius Mercator is the conclusion of a letter to Alexander of Hierapolis. Garnerius had edited it as the conclusion of the preceding letter to Himerius. Vide Mans. V. 880.
[3] This letter was also edited by Garnerius as addressed to Himerius but is inscribed by Schulze to Alexander of Hierapolis. It is to be found complete in Mans. 927.

impiously condemned one who has never held or taught anything contrary to sound doctrine. But the form of anathema, though it be more likely than his assent to the condemnation, to grieve a reader, nevertheless has given me some ground of comfort, in that it is laid down not in wide general terms, but with some qualification. For he has not said " We anathematize his doctrine " but '' whatever he has either said or held other than is warranted by the doctrine of the apostles."

CLXXVII. Letter to Andreas, bishop of Samosata.[1]

The illustrious Aristolaus has sent Magisterianus from Egypt with a letter of Cyril in which he anathematizes Arius, Eunomius, Apollinarius and all who assert Christ's Godhead to be passible and maintain the confusion and commixture of the two natures. Hereat we rejoice, although he did withhold his consent from our statement. He requires further subscription to the condemnation which has been passed, and that the doctrine of the holy bishop Nestorius be anathematized. Your holiness well knows that if any one anathematizes, without distinction, the doctrine of that most holy and venerable bishop, it is just the same as though he seemed to anathematize true religion.

We must then if we are compelled anathematize those who call Christ mere man, or who divide our one Lord Jesus Christ into two sons and deny His divinity, etc.

CLXXVIII. Letter to Alexander of Hierapolis.[2]

I think that more than all the very holy and venerable bishop, my lord John, must have been gratified at my refusing either to give my consent to the condemnation of the very holy and venerable bishop Nestorius or to violate the pledges made at Tarsus, Chalcedon and Ephesus.[3]

He remembers also what was frequently received from us at Antioch after our departure.

Let no one therefore deceive your holiness into the belief that I should ever do this,

for God is without doubt on my side and strengthening me.

CLXXIX. Letter of Cyril to John, bishop of Antioch, against Theodoret.[1]

CLXXX. Letter of Theodoretus, as some suppose, to Domnus, bishop of Antioch, written on the death of Cyril, bishop of Alexandria.[2]

At last and with difficulty the villain has gone. The good and the gentle pass away all too soon; the bad prolong their life for years.

The Giver of all good, methinks, removes the former before their time from the troubles of humanity; He frees them like victors from their contests and transports them to the better life, that life which, free from death, sorrow and care, is the prize of them that contend for virtue. They, on the other hand, who love and practise wickedness are allowed

---

[1] Vide Migne LXXVII. 327. Cyril. Ep. lxiii.

[2] This letter is inserted in the Act. Synod. (vide Mans. ix. 295) as addressed to John, but Garnerius, with general acceptance, has substituted Domnus. Its genuineness was contested by Baronius (an. vi. 23) not only on the ground of its ascription to John who predeceased Cyril four years; but also because its expressions are at once too Nestorian in doctrine and too extreme in bitterness to have been penned by Theodoret. Garnerius is of opinion that the extreme Nestorianism and bitterness of feeling are no arguments against the authorship of Theodoret; and, as we have already had occasion to notice, our author can on occasion use very strong language, as for instance in Letter CL. p. 324, where he alludes to Cyril as a shepherd not only plague smitten himself but doing his best to inflict more damage on his flock than that caused by beast of prey, by infecting his charge with his disease.

"It must be needless to add that Cyril's character is not to be estimated aright by ascribing any serious value to a coarse and ferocious invective against his memory, which was quoted as Theodoret's in the fifth General Council (Theodor. Ep. 180; see Tillemont, xiv. 784). If it were indeed the production of the pen of Theodoret, the reputation which would suffer from it would assuredly be his own." Canon Bright. Dict. Christ. Biog. I.

"The long and bitter controversy in which both parties did and said many things they must have had cause deeply to regret, was closed by the death of Cyril, June 9, or 27, 444. With Baronius, 'the cautious' Tillemont, Cardinal Newman and Dr. Bright, we should be glad to 'utterly scout' the idea, that the 'atrocious letter' on Cyril's death ascribed to Theodoret by the Fifth Œcumenical Council (Theod. ed Schulze, Ep. 180; Labbe, v. 507) which he was said to have delivered by way of pæan (Bright u. s. 176) and 'the scarcely less scandalous' sermon (ib.) can have been written by him. 'To treat it as genuine would be to vilify Theodoret.' 'The Fathers of the Council' writes Dr. Newman 'are no authority on such a matter' (Hist. Sketches p. 359). A painful suspicion of their genuineness, however, still lingers and troubles our conception of Theodoret. The documents may have been garbled, but the general tone too much resembles that of undisputed polemical writings of Theodoret's to allow us entirely to repudiate them. We wish we could. Neander (vol. iv. p. 13, note, Clark's tr.) is inclined to accept the genuineness of the letter, the arguments against which he does not regard as carrying conviction, and to a large extent deriving their weight from Tillemont's 'Catholic standpoint.' That Theodoret should speak in this manner of Cyril's character and death cannot, he thinks, appear surprising to those who, without prejudice, contemplate Cyril and his relations to Theodoret. The playful description, after the manner of Lucian, of a voyage to the Shades below, is not to be reckoned a very sharp thing even in Theodoret. The advice to put a heavy stone over his grave to keep Cyril down is sufficient proof that the whole is a bitter jest. The world felt freer now Cyril was gone; and he does not shrink from telling a friend that he could well spare him. 'The exaggeration of rhetorical polemics requires many grains of allowance.'" Canon Venables. Dict. Christ. Biog. iv.

---

[1] This letter is to be found complete in Latin in Mans. Synod. 840, Schulze's Index inscribing it to Andreas the Constantinopolitan monk. cf. Ep. CLXII. and note.

[2] The complete letter is given in another Latin version Baluz. Synod. LXVI. Garnerius makes it the conclusion of the letter to Andrew of Samosata.

[3] The order of events is reversed. John and his friends went from Ephesus to Chalcedon, from Chalcedon via Ancyra to Tarsus, where he was in his own patriarchate, and held a council, confirming Cyril's deposition, and pledging its members never to abandon Nestorius. Again at Antioch the same course was repeated.

a little longer to enjoy this present life, either that sated with evil they may afterwards learn virtue's lessons, or else even in this life may pay the penalty for the wickedness of their own ways by being tossed to and fro through many years of this life's sad and wicked waves.

This wretch, however, has not been dismissed by the ruler of our souls like other men, that he may possess for longer time the things which seem to be full of joy. Knowing that the fellow's malice has been daily growing and doing harm to the body of the Church, the Lord has lopped him off like a plague and " taken away the reproach from Israel." [1] His survivors are indeed delighted at his departure. The dead, maybe, are sorry. There is some ground of alarm lest they should be so much annoyed at his company as to send him back to us, or that he should run away from his conductors like the tyrant of Cyniscus in Lucian.[2]

Great care must then be taken, and it is especially your holiness's business to undertake this duty, to tell the guild of undertakers to lay a very big and heavy stone upon his grave, for fear he should come back again, and show his changeable mind once more. Let him take his new doctrines to the shades below, and preach to them all day and all night. We are not at all afraid of his dividing them by making public addresses against true religion and by investing an immortal nature with death. He will be stoned not only by ghosts learned in divine law, but also by Nimrod, Pharaoh and Sennacherib, or any other of God's enemies.

But I am wasting words. The poor fellow is silent whether he will or no, " his breath goeth forth, he returneth to his earth, in that very day his thoughts perish." [3] He is doomed too to silence of another kind. His deeds, detected, tie his tongue, gag his mouth, curb his passion, strike him dumb and make him bow down to the ground.

I really am sorry for the poor fellow. Truly the news of his death has not caused me unmixed delight, but it is tempered by sadness. On seeing the Church freed from a plague of this kind I am glad and rejoice; but I am sorry and do mourn when I think that the wretch knew no rest from his crimes, but went on attempting greater and

more grievous ones till he died. His idea was, so it is said, to throw the imperial city into confusion by attacking true doctrines a second time, and to charge your holiness with supporting them. But God saw and did not overlook it. " He put his hook into his nose and his bridle into his lips," [1] and turned him to the earth whence he was taken. Be it then granted to your holiness's prayers that he may obtain mercy and pity and that God's boundless clemency may surpass his wickedness. I beg your holiness to drive away the agitations of my soul. Many different reports are being bruited abroad to my alarm announcing general misfortunes. It is even said by some that your reverence is setting out against your will for the court, but so far I have despised these reports as untrue. But finding every one repeating one and the same story I have thought it right to try and learn the truth from your holiness that I may laugh at these tales if false, or sorrow not without reason if they are true.

CLXXXI. Letter to Abundius, bishop of Como.[2]

To my dear lord and very holy brother Abundius Theodoretus sends greeting in the Lord. I have discovered that your piety religiously preserves the true and apostolic faith; and I have thanked Almighty God that the truth which was in peril has been renewed and brought to light by your holiness.

Of old, after the flood, it came to pass that Noah and his sons were left for seed of the human race. Just so in our own day are reserved the fathers of the West, that by them the holy churches of the East may be able to preserve that true religion which has been threatened with devastation and destruction by a new and impious heresy. Well may we quote those words of the prophet " Except the Lord of hosts had left unto us a very small remnant we should have been as Sodom and we should have been like unto Gomorrah. " [3] So upon us from this impious heresy the wrath of God has fallen like a flood and invasion.

Now we acknowledge the presence of our

---

[1] I. Sam. xvii. 26.
[2] Lucian. " Cataplus sive Tyrannus."
Cyniscus and Megapenthes come to the shore of Styx in the same batch of ghosts.
Megapenthes begs hard of Clotho to let him go back again, but Cyniscus the philosopher, who professes great delight at having died at last, refuses to get into the boat. " No; by Zeus, not till we have bound this fellow here, and set him on board, for I am afraid he will get over you by his entreaties."
[3] Ps. cxlvi. 4.

[1] Isaiah xxxvii. 29.
[2] This letter may be dated from Nicerte in the autumn of 450 when Abundius was at Constantinople on a mission from Leo, after the failure to get Theodosius to agree to the summary of the Council in the West. Theodosius died a few days after the arrival of the envoys at Constantinople. Theodoret is anxious to encourage the Roman Legates to support the orthodox cause in the Imperial city, to repair the mischief caused by the Latrocinium, and to show the court that he and his friends Ibas and Aquilinus had the support of Leo. Abundius, fourth bishop of Como (450–469) represented Leo at Chalcedon. Manzoni, in the Promessi Sposi, reminds us of the local survival of the name.
[3] Isaiah i. 9.

Saviour in a human body, and one Son of God, His perfect Godhead and His perfect manhood. We do not divide our one Lord Jesus Christ into two sons for He is one; but we recognise the distinction between God and man; we know that one is of the Father, the other of the seed of David and Abraham, according to the divine Scriptures, and that the divine nature is free from passion, the body which was before subject to passion being now itself too free from passion; for after the resurrection it is plainly delivered from all passion.

This we have learnt from the letter of the very holy and religious Archbishop our lord Leo. For we have read what he wrote to Flavianus, of holy and blessed memory, and have thanked the loving-kindness of the Lord because we have found an advocate and defender of the truth. To this letter I have given my adhesion, and have subjoined a copy of it to my present epistle, which I have also subscribed and have thereby proved that I obey the apostolic rules, that is true doctrines; that I abide in them to this day, and am suffering in their cause.

Assent has also been given by my lord Ibas and my lord Aquilinus against whom the inventors of the new heresy have armed the imperial power.

It remains for you with your very holy colleagues to bring aid to the sacred Church, and to drive away the war that threatens it. Banish the impious party which has been roused against the truth; give back the churches their ancient peace; so will you receive from the Lord, Who has promised to grant this boon, the fruits of your apostolic labours.

All the very religious and godly presbyters and reverend deacons and brethren by your holiness I greet; and I and all who are with me salute your reverence.[1]

---

[1] After all the storms of controversy and quarrel which we have followed in the course of the dialogues and letters of the Blessed Bishop of Cyrus; after the lurid leap of grim pleasantry which, if not actually penned by Theodoret, indicates a temper that must have often shewn itself in these troubled times; there is something pathetic and encouraging in the concilatory conclusion of this last letter. Cyril has been dead for years, and his weaknesses are forgotten in a confession which his more moderate opponents could accept. The subscription of Theodoret to the tome of Leo is an earnest of harmony and concord. The calmer wisdom of the West asserts the truth which underlay the furious disputes of the subtler East. The last word of the drama is Peace.

JEROME AND GENNADIUS

LIVES OF ILLUSTRIOUS MEN

Translated, with Introduction and Notes, by

ERNEST CUSHING RICHARDSON, Ph.D.,

LIBRARIAN OF PRINCETON COLLEGE

CONTENTS

JEROME AND GENNADIUS

LIVES OF ILLUSTRIOUS MEN

I. INTRODUCTION

THIS combined work of Jerome and Gennadius is unique and indispensable in the history of early Christian literature, giving as it does a chronological history in biographies of ecclesiastical literature to about the end of the fifth century.

For the period after the end of Eusebius' Church History it is of prime value.

1. TIME AND PLACE OF COMPOSITION, AND CHARACTER.

1. *The work of Jerome* was written at Bethlehem in 492. It contains 135 writers from Peter up to that date. In his preface Jerome limits the scope of his work to those who have written on Holy Scriptures, but in carrying out his plans he includes all who have written on theological topics; whether Orthodox or Heretic, Greek, Latin, Syriac, and even Jews and Heathen (Josephus, Philo, Seneca). The Syriac writers mentioned are however few. Gennadius apologizes for the scanty representation which they have in Jerome on the ground that the latter did not understand Syriac, and only knew of such as had been translated.

The motive of the work was, as the preface declares, to show the heretics how many and how excellent writers there were among the Christians. The direct occasion of the undertaking was the urgency of his friend Dexter, and his models were, first of all Suetonius, and then various Greek and Latin biographical works including the *Brutus* of Cicero.

Jerome expressly states in his preface that he had no predecessor in his work, but very properly acknowledges his indebtedness to the Church History of Eusebius, from whom he takes much verbatim. The first part of the work is taken almost entirely from Eusebius.

The whole work gives evidence of hasty construction (e.g., in failure to enumerate the works of well-known writers or in giving only selections from the list of their writings) but too much has been made of this, for in such work absolute exhaustiveness is all but impossible, and in the circumstances of those days, such a list of writers and their works is really remarkable. He apologizes in the preface for omitting such as are not known to him in his " out of the way corner of the earth." He has been accused of too great credulity, in accepting e.g., the letters of Paul to Seneca as genuine, but on the other hand he often shows himself both cautious (Hilary, *Song of S.*) and critical (Minutius Felix *De Fato*).

The work was composed with a practical purpose rather than a scientific one and kept in general well within that purpose — giving brief information about writers not generally known. This is perhaps why in writing of the better known writers like Cyprian he does not enumerate their works.

2. *The work of Gennadius* was written about 480 according to some, or 492 to 495 according to others. Ebert with the Benedictins and others before him, makes an almost conclusive argument in favor of the earlier date on the ground that Gennadius speaks of

Timotheus Aelurus who died in 477 as still living. This compels the rejection of the paragraph on Gennadius himself as by a later hand, but this should probably be done at any rate, on other grounds. The mss. suggest that Gennadius ended with John of Antioch, although an hypothesis of three editions before the year 500, of which perhaps two were by Gennadius, has grounds. The bulk of the work at least was composed about 480 (probably chapters 1–90) and the remainder added perhaps within a few years by Gennadius or more probably two other hands.

Gennadius' style is as bare and more irregular than Jerome's but he more frequently expresses a critical judgment and gives more interesting glimpses of his own — the semi-Pelagian — point of view. The work appears more original than Jerome's and as a whole hardly less valuable, though the period he covers is so much shorter.

2. LITERATURE.

1. *The literature on Jerome* is immense. The oftenest quoted general works are Zöckler, *Hieronymus*. Gotha, 1865 and Thierry, *St. Jérome* Par. 1867. On Jerome in general the article by Freemantle in Smith and Wace *Dict. of Christian Biography* is the first for the English reader to turn to. Ceillier and other patrologies, while sufficiently full for their purpose, give very little special treatment to this work, Ebert (*Gesch. chr.-Lat.-Lit.* Lpz. 1874) being a partial exception to this statement. The best literary sources are the prolegomena and notes to the various editions of the work itself. Much the same may be said of *Gennadius* though the relative importance of his catalogue among his writings gives that a larger proportionate attention. In English the article by Cazenove in Smith and Wace and in French the account in the Histoire litteraire de la France are the best generally accessible references.

2. *Literature on the writers mentioned by Jerome and Gennadius.* Any one who cares to follow up in English the study of any of the writers mentioned in the Lives of illustrious men will find tools therefor: 1. For the earlier writers to the time of Eusebius, Eusebius Church History tr. M'Giffert (N. Y. Chr. Lit. Co.) *notes*. 2. For the whole period: Smith and Wace Dict. of Christian Biography, 4 vols. and more accessible to most (though a cheap reprint of Smith and Wace is now threatened) Schaff. Church Hist. (N. Y. Scribners) where at the end of each volume an account is given of the chief writers of the period including admirable bibliographical reference.

Of course the best source is the works themselves: *The Ante-Nicene Fathers*, ed. Coxe, *The Nicene and Post-Nicene Fathers* ed. Schaff and Wace. (N. Y. Christian Literature Co.) For further research the student is referred to the list of Patrologies and Bibliographies in the supplementary volume of the Ante-Nicene Fathers, to the bibliography of Ante-Nicene Fathers in the same volume, to Chevalier. Dict. des sources hist. and the memoranda by Sittl, in the Jahresberichte ü. d. fortschr. d. class. Alterthwiss. 1887 sq.

3. MANUSCRIPTS.

The manuscripts of Jerome and Gennadius are numerous. The translator has seen 84 mss. of Jerome and 57 of Gennadius and has certain memoranda of at least 25 more and hints of still another score. It is certainly within bounds to say that there are more than 150 mss. of Jerome extant and not less than 100 of Gennadius.

The oldest of those examined (and all the oldest of which he could learn were seen) are at Rome, Verona, Vercelli, Montpellier, Paris, Munich and Vienna.

4. EDITIONS.

The editions of Jerome are relatively as numerous as the mss. The *Illustrious men* is included in almost all the editions of his collected works, in his collected " minor writings" and in many of the editions of his epistles (most of the editions in fact from 1468 to about 1530.)

It is several times printed separately or with Gennadius or other catalogues. The editions of Gennadius are less numerous but he is often united with Jerome in the editions of Jerome's collected works, and generally in the separate editions.

The following list of editions is printed as illustrative. It does not pretend to be complete, but is simply a list of such as have been personally examined by the translator up to date; s. l. et a (6) + 390 ff, 62, 11.; s. l. et a (1468?) 223ff, 2 col. 50 11.; Rome 1468. *P. de Max;* (Compluti?) 1470; Rome 1470; Mogunt 1470; s. l. et a. (Augsb. Zainer 1470) ; s. l. et a. 1470, 4° 23 11: s. a. "JA. RV" 1471?; Rome 1479; Parma 1480; Ven. 1488; Basil 1489; Ven. 1490; Basil 1492 Norimb. 1495; s. l. 1496?; Basil 1497; Lyons, 1508; Paris 1512; Lyons 1513; Lyons 1518 Basil 1525 Lyons 1526 (Erasmus) ; Basil 1526 (Erasm) Basil 1529 Lyons 1530 Paris 1534; Frankfort 1549; Bas. 1553; Bas. 1565; Rome 1565-; Rome 1576 Colon 1580; Paris 1609; Helmst 1611-12 Cologne 1616; Frf. [1622]; Antw. 1639 Frf. 1684; Paris 1706 (Martianay & Pouget); Helmst. 1700; Hamb. 1718; Veron. 1734-42 (Vallarsi) ; repr. 1766-72 ; Florence 1791 ; Paris 1865 (Migne) ; Lpz. 1879 (Herding) Turin 1875, 1877, 1885 (Jerome only).

Andreas, Erasmus, Victorinus, Graevius, Martianay, Miraeus, Fabricius, Cyprian are among the earlier editors but Erasmus is *facile princeps* in popularity of reprint. The edition of Vallarsi in 1734-42 was a decided advance toward a critical text. Various editors before him had made use of various mss. especially the " Corbeiensis " or " Sangermanensis" but secondarily mss. at Wulfenbüttel, Munich, the Bodleian, Nürnberg, " Sigbergensis," " Gemblacensis," " Marcianus " and others. Vallarsi founded his edition largely on a Verona ms. (still there) on the " Corbeiensis " so much used and praised before (now Paris Lat. 12161) " St Crucis " one at Lucca of the 9th century and more or less on mss. employed by previous editors. This edition has remained the standard and is the one adopted for the Migne edition.

The most recent edition which pretends to a critical character is that of Herding (Lpz. 1879). The editions by Tamietti are simply school editions of Jerome only, and make no pretensions to a critical text. The edition of Herding is founded on a transcript of Vat. Reg. 2077, 7th century; Bamberg 677, 11th century; Bern, 11 cent. and a much mutilated Nürnberg ms. of the 14th century. But it appears that the transcript of Vaticanus only covered the Jerome and a few scanty readings from Gennadius and the same is true of the collation made for this editor later from the Paris ms. (Corbeiensis).

Sittl, (Jahresber; u. class. Alterthumsw. 1888. 2 p. 243) says that the edition " without the preface which contains a collation of Codex Corbeiensis would be worthless." This is a little strong, for the readings he gives from Vaticanus have a decided value in default of other sources for its readings and his strict following of this often produces a correct reading against Vallarsi who was naturally inclined to follow Veronensis and Corbeiensis both of which were probably a good deal manipulated after they left the hand of Gennadius. The collation of Corbeiensis besides excluding Gennadius is not over exact and some of the most effaced pages seem to have been given up entirely by the collator.

5. TRANSLATIONS.

An early translation of Jerome's work into Greek was made by Sophronius and used by Photius. A translation purporting to be his is given by Erasmus. There has been a good deal of controversy over this, some even accusing Erasmus of having forged it entire. It is an open question with a general tendency to give Erasmus the benefit of the doubt. The present translator while holding his judgment ready to be corrected by the finding of a ms. or other evidence, inclines to reject *in toto*, regarding it as for the most part translated by Erasmus from some South German or Swiss ms., or, if that be not certain, at least that the translation is too little established to be of any use for textual purposes. There is a modern translation of select works of Jerome in French by Matougues. The chief sources for comparison used by the translator have been Sophronius (or Erasmus) Matougues, M'Giffert's Eusebius for the first part of Jerome where he takes so liberally from Eusebius, and scattered selections here and there in Ceillier, Smith and Wace, *Dict.* and other literary-historical works.

6. THE PRESENT TRANSLATION.

1. *Text.* It was proposed at first to make the translation from the text of Herding. This, and all editions, gave so little basis for scientific certainty in regard to various readings that a cursory examination of mss. was made. At the suggestion of Professor O. von Gebhardt of Berlin the examination was made as thorough and systematic as possible with definite reference to a new edition. The translator hoped to finish and publish the new text before the translation was needed for this series, but classification of the mss. proved unexpectedly intricate and the question of the Greek translation so difficult that publication has been delayed. The material has however been gathered, analyzed, sifted and arranged sufficiently to give reasonable certainty as to the body of the work and a tolerably reliable judgment on most of the important variations.

While anxious not to claim too much for his material and unwilling to give a final expression of judgment on disputed readings, until his table of mss. is perfected, he ventures to think that for substantial purposes of translation, if not for the nicer ones of a new text, the material and method which he has made use of will be substantially conclusive.

The following translation has been made first from the text of Herding and then corrected from the manuscripts in all places where the evidence was clearly against the edition. In places where the evidence is fairly conclusive the change has been made and a brief statement of evidence given in the notes. When the evidence is really doubtful the reading has been allowed to stand with evidence generally given.

The materials of evidence used are 1. eight mss. collated entire by the translator A. Parisinus (Corbeiensis or Sangermanensis, 7 cent.) T. Vaticanus Reg., 7 cent.; 25 Veronensis, 8 cent.; 30 Vercellensis 8 cent.; 31 Monspessalanensis, 8 or 9 cent.; a Monacensis 8 cent.; e Vindobonensis 8 or 9; H. Parisinus 10 or 9.

2. Occasional support from readings gathered by him from other mss., chiefly 10 Cassenatensis 9 cent.; 21 Florentinus, 11 cent.; 32 Toletanus 13 cent.; 40 Guelferbyrtinus, 10? cent.

3. Readings from mss. mentioned by other editors.

4. The various editions, but mainly confined to Vallarsi and Herding in Jerome, Fabricius and Herding in Gennadius.

The translator has examined nearly 90 mss. and secured more or less readings from nearly all with reference to an exact table. The readings of several are extensive enough to have pretty nearly the value of full collations. Quotations are occasionally made from these (e.g. from 10, 21, 29, 32, 40, etc.) but practically quotations from the eight mentioned mss. cover the evidence and without a table more would rather obscure than otherwise.

There is no opportunity here to discuss the relative value of these used. It may be said however that they are the oldest mss., and include pretty much all the oldest. Though age itself is by no means conclusive, the fact that they certainly represent several independent groups makes it safe to say that a consensus of seven against one or even six against any two (with certain reservations) or in the case of Gennadius of 5 against 2 is conclusive for a reading. As a matter of fact against many readings of Herding and even of Vallarsi, are arranged all these mss., and against some nearly all or even every ms. seen, e.g. Her. p. 73 d. 12 reads morti dari with Migne-Fabricius but all these mss. have mutandam and so 91. 22 " seven " for " eight." On p. 161. 7. Her. omits Asyncritus against mss. and all modern eds., so 44. 3. " Ponti," 51. 7 " ut quidem putant ; " 77. 25. " firmare " and a score of other places.

Of course this is not enough evidence or discussion for a critical scholastic text but for the practical illustrative purpose in hand will serve. Any evidence which does not give a well digested genealogy of mss. and the evidence for their classification must be reckoned as incomplete, —all that the above evidence can claim to do, is to give the translator's judgment respecting the readings and *illustrative* evidence, but it is not probable that the completed table will alter many (if any) of these readings which are given in view of a tentative table which will likely prove final.

2. *The Translation itself.* The plan of this work includes (a) a translation, in which the translator has tried to give a fair representation of the text in a not too ragged form but has failed to improve on the original. The works were written as science rather than literature and have many facts but no style. The translator has therefore aimed rather at representing these facts than at producing a piece of polite literature. (b) Notes are subjoined including, first the brief biographical data which every one wants first to orient himself by, secondly textual notes, and thirdly, occasional explanatory notes.

II. JEROME

LIVES OF ILLUSTRIOUS MEN

PREFACE

You have urged me, Dexter,[1] to follow the example of Tranquillus[2] in giving a systematic account of ecclesiastical writers, and to do for our writers what he did for the illustrious men of letters among the Gentiles, namely, to briefly set before you all those who have published[3] any memorable writing on the Holy Scriptures, from the time of our Lord's passion until the fourteenth year of the Emperor Theodosius.[4] A similar work has been done by Hermippus[5] the peripatetic, Antigonus Carystius,[6] the learned Satyrus,[7] and most learned of all, Aristoxenus the Musician,[8] among the Greeks, and among the Latins by Varro,[9] Santra,[10] Nepos,[11] Hyginus,[12] and by him through whose example you seek to stimulate[13] us, — Tranquillus.

But their situation and mine is not the same, for they, opening the old histories and chronicles could as if gathering from some great meadow, weave some[14] small crown at least for their work. As for me, what shall I do, who, having no predecessor, have, as the saying is, the worst possible master, namely myself, and yet I must acknowledge that Eusebius Pamphilus in the ten books of his Church History has been of the utmost assistance, and the works of various among those of whom we are to write, often testify to the dates of their authors. And so I pray the Lord Jesus,[15] that what your Cicero, who stood at the summit of Roman eloquence, did not scorn to do, compiling in his *Brutus*, a catalogue of Latin orators, this I too may accomplish in the enumeration of ecclesiastical writers, and accomplish in a fashion worthy of the exhortation which you made. But if, perchance any of those who are yet writing have been overlooked by me in this volume, they ought to ascribe it to themselves, rather than to me, for among those whom I have not read, I could not, in the first place, know those who concealed their own writings, and, in the second place, what is perhaps well known to others, would be quite unknown to me in this out of the way corner of the earth.[16] But surely when they are distinguished by their writings, they will not very greatly grieve over any loss in our non-mention of them. Let Celsus, Porphyry, and Julian learn, rabid as they are against Christ, let their followers, they who think the church has had no philosophers or orators or men of learning, learn how many and what sort of men founded, built and adorned it, and cease to accuse our faith of such rustic simplicity, and recognize rather their own ignorance.

In the name of the Lord Jesus Christ, farewell.[17]

---

1 *Dexter.* Compare chapters 132 and 106.

2 *Tranquillus.* C. Suetonius Tranquillus (about A. D. 100). *De illustribus grammaticis ; De claris rhetoribus.*

3 *Published* or handed down "*Prodiderunt.*" Some mss. read "*tradiderunt,*" and Jerome usually employs "*Edo*" for publish.

4 *Fourteenth year of the Emperor Theodosius.* A. D. 492.

5 *Hermippus* of Smyrna. (3rd century B. C.) *Lives of distinguished men.*

6 *Antigonus.* Antigonus of Carystus (Reign of Ptolemy Philadelphus?).

7 *Satyrus.* A Peripatetic (Reign of Ptolemy Philopator) "wrote a collection of biographies."

8 *Aristoxenus the musician.* A Peripatetic, pupil of Aristotle, wrote lives of various Philosophers.

9 *Varro.* M. Terentius Varro the "most learned of the Romans" (died B.C. 28) published among other things a series of "portraits of seven hundred remarkable personages" (Ramsay in Smith's *Dictionary*).

10 *Santra.* Santra the Grammarian?

11 *Nepos.* Cornelius Nepos friend of Cicero wrote *Lives of Illustrious men.*

12 *Hyginus.* Caius Julius Hyginus, freedman of Augustus and friend of Ovid.

13 *Seek to stimulate* 30 31 a [H e 21] and the mass of mss. also Fabricius; *stimulate.* A.T. Migne. Her.

14 *Some* A H 25 31 e 21. Fabricius; *No* T a? Migne Her.

15 *The Lord Jesus* A H T 25 31 e; *The Lord Jesus Christ* a; *Our Lord Jesus Christ* Bamb. Bern; *My Lord Jesus Christ* Norimb.

16 *Out of the way corner of the earth* i.e., Bethlehem.

17 *In the name of the Lord Jesus Christ farewell* T 25 31 a 21; do. omitting *Christ* A; omit all H e.

LIST OF WRITERS.

1. Simon Peter.
2. James, the brother of our Lord.
3. Matthew, surnamed Levi.
4. Jude, the brother of James.
5. Paul, formerly called Saul.
6. Barnabas, surnamed Joseph.
7. Luke, the evangelist.
8. Mark, the evangelist.
9. John, the apostle and evangelist.
10. Hermas.
11. Philo Judæus.
12. Lucius Annæus Seneca.
13. Josephus, son of Matthias.
14. Justus of Tiberias.
15. Clemens the bishop.
16. Ignatius the bishop.
17. Polycarp the bishop.
18. Papias the bishop.
19. Quadratus the bishop.
20. Aristides the philosopher.
21. Agrippa Castor.
22. Hegesippus the historian.
23. Justin the philosopher.
24. Melito the bishop.
25. Theophilus the bishop.
26. Apollinaris the bishop.
27. Dionysius the bishop.
28. Pinytus the bishop.
29. Tatian the heresiarch.
30. Phillip the bishop.
31. Musanus.
32. Modestus.
33. Bardesanes the heresiarch.
34. Victor the bishop.
35. Iranæus the bishop.
36. Pantænus the philosopher.
37. Rhodo, the disciple of Tatian.
38. Clemens the presbyter.
39. Miltiades.
40. Apollonius.
41. Serapion the bishop.
42. Apollonius the senator.
43. Theophilus another bishop.
44. Baccylus the bishop.
45. Polycrates the bishop.
46. Heraclitus.
47. Maximus.
48. Candidus.
49. Appion.
50. Sextus.
51. Arabianus.
52. Judas.
53. Tertullian the presbyter.
54. Origen, surnamed Adamantius.
55. Ammonius.
56. Ambrose the deacon.
57. Trypho the pupil of Origen.
58. Minucius Felix.
59. Gaius.
60. Berillus the bishop.
61. Hippolytus the bishop.
62. Alexander the bishop.
63. Julius the African.
64. Gemimus the presbyter.
65. Theodorus, surnamed Gregory the bishop.
66. Cornelius the bishop.
67. Cyprian the bishop.
68. Pontius the deacon.
69. Dionysius the bishop.
70. Novatianus the heresiarch.
71. Malchion the presbyter.
72. Archelaus the bishop.
73. Anatolius the bishop.
74. Victorinus the bishop.
75. Pamphilus the presbyter.
76. Pierius the presbyter.
77. Lucianus the presbyter.
78. Phileas the bishop.
79. Arnobius the rhetorician.
80. Firmianus the rhetorician, surnamed Lactantius.
81. Eusebius the bishop.
82. Reticius the bishop.
83. Methodius the bishop.
84. Juvencus the presbyter.
85. Eustathius the bishop.
86. Marcellus the bishop.
87. Athanasius the bishop.
88. Antonius the monk.
89. Basilius the bishop.
90. Theodorus the bishop.
91. Eusebius another bishop.
92. Triphylius the bishop.
93. Donatus the heresiarch.
94. Asterius the philosopher.
95. Lucifer the bishop.
96. Eusebius another bishop.
97. Fortunatianus the bishop.
98. Acacius the bishop.
99. Serapion the bishop.
100. Hilary the bishop.
101. Victorinus the rhetorician.
102. Titus the bishop.
103. Damasus the bishop.
104. Apollinarius the bishop.
105. Gregory the bishop.
106. Pacianus the bishop.
107. Photinus the heresiarch.
108. Phœbadius the bishop.
109. Didymus the Blind.
110. Optatus the bishop.
111. Acilius Severus the senator.
112. Cyril the bishop.
113. Euzoius the bishop.
114. Epiphanius the bishop.
115. Ephrem the deacon.
116. Basil another bishop.

117. Gregory another bishop.
118. Lucius the bishop.
119. Diodorus the bishop.
120. Eunomius the heresiarch.
121. Priscillianus the bishop.
122. Latronianus.
123. Tiberianus.
124. Ambrose the bishop.
125. Evagrius the bishop.
126. Ambrose the disciple of Didymus.
127. Maximus, first philosopher, then bishop.
128. Another Gregory, also a bishop.
129. John the presbyter.
130. Gelasius the bishop.
131. Theotimus the bishop.
132. Dexter, son of Pacianus, now prætorian prefect.
133. Amphilochius the bishop.
134. Sophronius.
135. Jerome the presbyter.

CHAPTER I.

SIMON PETER [1] the son of John, from the village of Bethsaida in the province of Galilee, brother of Andrew the apostle, and himself chief of the apostles, after having been bishop of the church of Antioch and having preached to the Dispersion[2] — the believers in circumcision,[3] in Pontus, Galatia, Cappadocia, Asia and Bithynia — pushed on to Rome in the second year of Claudius to overthrow Simon Magus,[4] and held the sacerdotal chair there for twenty-five years until the last, that is the fourteenth, year of Nero. At his hands he received the crown of martyrdom being nailed to the cross with his head towards the ground and his feet raised on high, asserting that he was unworthy to be crucified in the same manner as his Lord. He wrote two epistles which are called Catholic, the second of which, on account of its difference from the first in style, is considered by many not to be by him. Then too the Gospel according to Mark, who was his disciple and interpreter, is ascribed to him. On the other hand, the books, of which one is entitled his Acts, another his Gospel, a third his Preaching, a fourth his Revelation, a fifth his " Judgment " are rejected as apocryphal.[5]

Buried at Rome in the Vatican near the triumphal way he is venerated by the whole world.[1]

CHAPTER II.

JAMES,[2] who is called the brother of the Lord,[3] surnamed the Just, the son of Joseph by another wife, as some think, but, as appears to me, the son of Mary sister of the mother of our Lord of whom John makes mention in his book,[4] after our Lord's passion at once ordained by the apostles bishop of Jerusalem, wrote a single epistle, which is reckoned among the seven Catholic Epistles and even this is claimed by some to have been published by some one else under his name, and gradually, as time went on, to have gained authority. Hegesippus who lived near the apostolic age, in the fifth book of his Commentaries, writing of James, says " After the apostles, James the brother of the Lord surnamed the Just was made head of the Church at Jerusalem. Many indeed are called James. This one was holy from his mother's womb. He drank neither wine nor strong drink, ate no flesh, never shaved or anointed himself with ointment or bathed. He alone had the privilege of entering the Holy of Holies, since indeed he did not use woolen vestments but linen and went alone into the temple and prayed in behalf of the people, insomuch that his knees were reputed to have acquired the hardness of camels' knees." He says also many other things, too numerous to mention. Josephus also in the 20th book of his Antiquities, and Clement in the 7th of his Outlines mention that on the death of Festus who reigned over Judea, Albinus was sent by Nero as his successor. Before he had reached his province, Ananias the high priest, the youthful son of Ananus of the priestly class taking advantage of the state of anarchy, assembled a council and publicly tried to force James to deny that Christ is the son of God. When he refused Ananius ordered him to be stoned. Cast down from a pinnacle of the temple, his legs broken, but still half alive,

---

1 Died 65-6 or 67.
2 *Dispersion.* The technical " Dispersion " — the Jews out of Judea. Cf. Peter 1. 1. See Westcott in Smith's *Dict. of Bible.*
3 *Circumcision* a paraphrase for " *Hebrews* " in Eusebius and Rufinus.
4 *Simon Magus.* That Peter met Simon Magus in Rome is a post-apostolic legend. Compare the Clementine literature.
5 *Apocryphal.* For literature on apocryphal works see *Ante-Nic. Fath.* ed. Coxe (N. Y. Chr. Lit. Co.,) vol. 9 pp. 95 sq. The *Acts, Gospel, Preaching* and *Revelation* are mentioned by Eusebius. The *Judgment* was added by Jerome.

This last has been much discussed of late in connection with the recently discovered *Teaching of the Twelve.* The identification of the Teaching with the Judgment is credited to Dr. von Gebhardt (Salmon in Smith and Wace *Dict.* v. 4 (1887) pp. 810-11). The recent literature of it is immense. Compare Schaff, *Oldest Church Manual,* and literature in *Ante-Nic. Fath.* vol. 9 pp. 83-86.
1 The textual variations on the chapter are numerous enough but none of them are sustained by the better mss. e.g. " *First Simon Peter*" " *Simon Peter the Apostle* " " *Peter the Apostle* " . . . " *Called canonical* " . . . " *are considered apocryphal* " . . . " *the whole city.*"
2 Died 62 or 63 (according to Josephus and Jerome) or 69 (Hegesippus).
3 *Brother of the Lord.* Gal. 1. 19.
4 *in his book* Joh. 19, 25.

raising his hands to heaven he said, "Lord forgive them for they know not what they do." Then struck on the head by the club of a fuller such a club as fullers are accustomed to wring out garments [1] with — he died. This same Josephus records the tradition that this James was of so great sanctity and reputation among the people that the downfall of Jerusalem was believed to be on account of his death. He it is of whom the apostle Paul writes to the Galatians that "No one else of the apostles did I see except James the brother of the Lord," and shortly after the event the Acts of the apostles bear witness to the matter. The Gospel also which is called the Gospel according to the Hebrews,[2] and which I have recently translated into Greek and Latin and which also Origen[3] often makes use of, after the account of the resurrection of the Saviour says, "but the Lord, after he had given his grave clothes to the servant of the priest, appeared to James (for James had sworn that he would not eat bread from that hour in which he drank the cup of the Lord until he should see him rising again from among those that sleep)" and again, a little later, it says "'Bring a table and bread,' said the Lord." And immediately it is added, "He brought bread and blessed and brake and gave to James the Just and said to him, ' my brother eat thy bread, for the son of man is risen from among those that sleep.'" And so he ruled the church of Jerusalem thirty years, that is until the seventh year of Nero, and was buried near the temple from which he had been cast down. His tombstone with its inscription was well known until the siege of Titus and the end of Hadrian's reign. Some of our writers think he was buried in Mount Olivet, but they are mistaken.

CHAPTER III.

MATTHEW,[4] also called Levi, apostle and aforetimes publican, composed a gospel of Christ at first published in Judea in Hebrew [5] for the sake of those of the circumcision who believed, but this was afterwards translated into Greek though by what author is uncertain. The Hebrew itself has been preserved until the present day in the library at Caesarea which Pamphilus so diligently gathered. I have also had the opportunity

of having the volume described to me by the Nazarenes[1] of Beroea,[2] a city of Syria, who use it. In this it is to be noted that wherever the Evangelist, whether on his own account or in the person of our Lord the Saviour quotes the testimony of the Old Testament he does not follow the authority of the translators of the Septuagint but the Hebrew. Wherefore these two forms exist "Out of Egypt have I called my son," and " for he shall be called a Nazarene."

CHAPTER IV.

JUDE[3] the brother of James, left a short epistle which is reckoned among the seven catholic epistles, and because in it[4] he quotes from the apocryphal book of Enoch it is rejected by many. Nevertheless by age and use it has gained authority and is reckoned among the Holy Scriptures.

CHAPTER V.

PAUL,[5] formerly called Saul, an apostle outside the number of the twelve apostles, was of the tribe of Benjamin and the town of Giscalis[6] in Judea. When this was taken by the Romans he removed with his parents to Tarsus in Cilicia. Sent by them to Jerusalem to study law he was educated by Gamaliel a most learned man whom Luke mentions. But after he had been present at the death of the martyr Stephen and had received letters from the high priest of the temple for the persecution of those who believed in Christ, he proceeded to Damascus, where constrained to faith by a revelation, as it is written in the Acts of the apostles, he was transformed from a persecutor into an elect vessel. As Sergius Paulus Proconsul of Cyprus was the first to believe on his preaching, he took his name from him because he had subdued him to faith in Christ, and having been joined by Barnabas, after traversing many cities, he returned to Jerusalem and was ordained apostle to the Gentiles by Peter, James and John. And because a full account of his life is given in the Acts of the Apostles, I only say this, that the twenty-fifth year after our Lord's passion, that is the second of Nero, at the time when Festus Procurator of Judea succeeded Felix, he was sent bound to Rome, and remaining for two years in free custody, disputed daily with the Jews

---

[1] garments A H 25 30 e 21; wct garments T e 29.
[2] Gospel according to the Hebrews. Compare Lipsius Gospels apocr, in Smith and Wace, Dict. v. 2 pp. 709–12.
[3] Origen. H 31 a e 1021; Adamantius A T 25.
[4] Died after 62.
[5] Gospel . . . in Hebrew. Jerome seems to regard the Gospel according to the Hebrews mentioned by him above as the original Hebrew Text of Matthew. cf. Lightfoot, Ignatius v. 2. p. 295.

[1] Nazarenes=Nasaraei. See Smith and Wace s.v.
[2] Beroea some mss. read Veria and so Herding. The modern Aleppo.
[3] Died after 62.
[4] in it H 31 a e 10 21; omit A T 25 30.
[5] Died 67?, probably after 64 at least.
[6] Giscalis, supposed thus to have originated at Giscalis and to have gone from there to Tarsus, but this is not generally accepted.

concerning the advent of Christ. It ought to be said that at the first defence, the power of Nero having not yet been confirmed, nor his wickedness broken forth to such a degree as the histories relate concerning him, Paul was dismissed by Nero, that the gospel of Christ might be preached also in the West. As he himself writes in the second epistle to Timothy, at the time when he was about to be put to death dictating his epistle as he did while in chains; "At my first defence no one took my part, but all forsook me: may it not be laid to their account. But the Lord stood by[1] me and strengthened me; that through me the message might be fully proclaimed and that all the Gentiles might hear, and I was delivered out of the mouth of the lion"[2] — clearly indicating Nero as lion on account of his cruelty. And directly following he says "The Lord delivered me from the mouth of the lion" and again shortly "The Lord delivered me[3] from every evil work and saved me unto his heavenly kingdom,"[4] for indeed he felt within himself that his martyrdom was near at hand, for in the same epistle he announced "For I am already being offered and the time of my departure is at hand."[5] He then, in the fourteenth year of Nero on the same day with Peter, was beheaded at Rome for Christ's sake and was buried in the Ostian way, the twenty-seventh year after our Lord's passion. He wrote nine epistles to seven churches: *To the Romans* one, *To the Corinthians* two, *To the Galatians* one, *To the Ephesians* one, *To the Philippians* one, *To the Colossians* one, *To the Thessalonians* two; and besides these to his disciples, *To Timothy* two, *To Titus* one, *To Philemon* one. The epistle which is called the *Epistle to the Hebrews* is not considered his, on account of its difference from the others in style and language, but it is reckoned, either according to Tertullian to be the work of Barnabas, or according to others, to be by Luke the Evangelist or Clement afterwards bishop of the church at Rome, who, they say, arranged and adorned the ideas of Paul in his own language, though to be sure, since Paul was writing to Hebrews and was in disrepute among them he may have omitted his name from the salutation on this account. He being a Hebrew wrote Hebrew, that is his own tongue and most fluently while the

things which were eloquently written in Hebrew were more eloquently turned into Greek[1] and this is the reason why it seems to differ from other epistles of Paul. Some read one also to[2] the Laodiceans but it is rejected by everyone.

CHAPTER VI.

BARNABAS[3] the Cyprian, also called Joseph the Levite, ordained apostle to the Gentiles with Paul, wrote one *Epistle*, valuable for the edification of the church, which is reckoned among the apocryphal writings. He afterwards separated from Paul on account of John, a disciple also called Mark,[4] none the less exercised the work laid upon him of preaching the Gospel.

CHAPTER VII.

LUKE[5] a physician of Antioch, as his writings indicate, was not unskilled in the Greek language. An adherent of the apostle Paul, and companion of all his journeying, he wrote a *Gospel*, concerning which the same Paul says, "We send with him a brother whose praise in the gospel is among all the churches"[6] and to the Colossians "Luke the beloved physician salutes you,"[7] and to Timothy "Luke only is with me."[8] He also wrote another excellent volume to which he prefixed the title *Acts of the Apostles*, a history which extends to the second year of Paul's sojourn at Rome, that is to the fourth[9] year of Nero, from which we learn that the book was composed in that same city. Therefore the *Acts of Paul and Thecla*[10] and all the fable about the lion baptized by him we reckon among the apocryphal writings,[11] for how is it possible that the inseparable companion of the apostle in his other affairs, alone should have been ignorant of this thing. Moreover Tertullian who lived near those times, mentions a certain presbyter in Asia, an adherent of the apostle Paul,[12] who was convicted by John of having been the author of the book,

---

1 *The Lord stood by* all mss. and eds; *God.* Her.
2 *lion.* 2 Tim. 4. 16–17.
3 *from the mouth of the lion, and again shortly* "*The Lord delivered me*" (substantially) A H 25 30 31 a e etc.; omit T. Her. There are slight variations; *God* H 21 Bamb Bern. Norimb.; *I was delivered* Val. Cypr. Tam. Par 1512 etc.
4 *The Lord . . . kingdom* 2 Tim. 4. 18.
5 *for I . . . at hand* 2 Tim. 4. 6.

1 *into* H 31 a e. and many others; *in* A T 25 30.
2 *also to* A H T 25 30 a e Norimb, Bamb.; *also* 31; omit, Her. who seems to have omitted on some evidence possibly Bern.
3 Died in Salamis 53 (Ceillier Papebroch), 56 (Braunsberger), 61 (Breviarum romanum), 76 (Nirschl). The discussion of the date of his death is a good deal mixed up with the question of the authenticity of the work.
4 *Mark* Acts 15, 37. 5 Died 83–4?.
6 *we send . . . churches* 2 Cor. 8. 18.
7 *Luke . . . salutes you* Col. 4. 14.
8 *Luke . . . with me* 2 Tim. 4. 11.
9 *fourth* A T H 25 30 31 Val. etc.; *fourteenth.* Her. Sigbert. S. Crucis.
10 *Acts of Paul and Thecla* (Acts = Journeyings) Cf. Acts of Paul and Thecla, tr. in Ante Nic. Fath. v. 8 pp. 487–92.
11 *apocryphal writings* A H 31 e a Bamb Norimb. Val. etc.; *apocrypha* Her. T 25 30.
12 *apostle Paul* A H e a etc. Val; omit *Paul* T 25 30 31 Her.

and who, confessing that he did this for love of Paul, resigned his office of presbyter. Some suppose that whenever Paul in his epistle says " according to my gospel " he means the book of Luke and that Luke not only was taught the gospel history by the apostle Paul who was not with the Lord in the flesh, but also by other apostles. This he too at the beginning of his work declares, saying " Even as they delivered unto us, which from the beginning were eyewitnesses and ministers of the word." So he wrote the gospel as he had heard it, but composed the Acts of the apostles as he himself had seen. He was buried at Constantinople to which city, in the twentieth year of Constantius, his bones together with the remains of Andrew the apostle were transferred.

CHAPTER VIII.

MARK[1] the disciple and interpreter of Peter wrote a short gospel at the request of the brethren at Rome embodying what he had heard Peter tell. When Peter had heard this, he approved it and published it to the churches to be read by his authority as Clemens in the sixth book of his Hypotyposes and Papias, bishop of Hierapolis, record. Peter also mentions this Mark in his first epistle, figuratively indicating Rome under the name of Babylon " She who[2] is in Babylon elect together with you saluteth you[3] and so doth Mark my son." So, taking the gospel which he himself composed, he went to Egypt and first preaching Christ at Alexandria he formed a church so admirable in doctrine and continence of living that he constrained all followers of Christ to his example. Philo most learned of the Jews seeing the first church at Alexandria still Jewish in a degree, wrote a book[4] on their manner of life as something creditable to his nation telling how, as Luke says, the believers had all things in common[5] at Jerusalem, so he recorded that he saw[6] was done at Alexandria, under the learned Mark. He died in the eighth year of Nero and was buried at Alexandria, Annianus succeeding him.[7]

CHAPTER IX.

JOHN,[1] the apostle whom Jesus most loved, the son of Zebedee and brother of James, the apostle whom Herod, after our Lord's passion, beheaded, most recently of all the evangelists wrote a *Gospel*, at the request of the bishops of Asia, against Cerinthus and other heretics and especially against the then growing dogma of the Ebionites, who assert that Christ did not exist before Mary. On this account he was compelled to maintain His divine nativity. But there is said to be yet another reason for this work, in that when he had read Matthew, Mark, and Luke, he approved indeed the substance of the history and declared that the things they said were true, but that they had given the history of only one year, the one, that is, which follows the imprisonment of John and in which he was put to death. So passing by this year the events of which had been set forth by these, he related the events of the earlier period before John was shut up in prison, so that it might be manifest to those who should diligently read the volumes of the four Evangelists. This also takes away the discrepancy which there seems to be between John and the others. He wrote also one *Epistle* which begins as follows " That which was from the beginning, that which we have heard, that which we have seen with our eyes and our hands handled concerning the word of life" which is esteemed by all men who are interested in the church or in learning. The other two of which the first is " The elder to the elect lady and her children " and the other " The elder unto Gaius[2] the beloved whom I love in truth," are said to be the work of John the presbyter to the memory of whom another sepulchre is shown at Ephesus to the present day, though some think that there are two memorials of this same John the evangelist. We shall treat of this matter in its turn[3] when we come to Papias his disciple. In the fourteenth year then after Nero,[4] Domitian having raised a second persecution he was banished to the island of Patmos, and wrote the *Apocalypse*, on which Justin Martyr and Irenæus afterwards wrote commentaries. But Domitian having been put to death and his acts, on account of his excessive cruelty, having been annulled by the senate, he returned to Ephesus under

---

[1] Flourished 45 to 55?.
[2] *She who* A H T 25 30 31 a e Val etc; *the church which.* Her. and one mentioned by Vallarsi, also in Munich mss. 14370.
[3] *She who . . . saluteth you* 1. Pet. 5. 13.
[4] *a book* A H 31 a e etc; *and* Her.; omit T 25 30. This work entitled *On a contemplative life* is still extant but is generally regarded as not by Philo.
[5] *had all things in common* Acts 2. 44.
[6] *so . . . saw* A H a e 31? Val.; *so he saw and recorded.* T 25 30 Her.
[7] *Annianus succeeding him* A H T 25 30 a e Val etc.; omit Her. 31.

---

[1] Exiled to Patmos 94-95.
[2] *Gaius* A H 25 30 31 a e; *Caius* Her. T.
[3] *in its turn* A H T 31 a e Val. etc; omit T. 25 30.
[4] *after Nero* A H 30 31 a e. Bamb. Norimb. Cypr. Val.; omit T 25

Pertinax[1] and continuing there until the time of the emperor Trajan, founded and built churches throughout all Asia, and, worn out by old age, died in the sixty-eighth year after our Lord's passion and was buried near the same city.

CHAPTER X.

HERMAS[2][3] whom the apostle Paul mentions in writing to the Romans "Salute[4] Phlegon, Hermes, Patrobas, Hermas[5] and the brethren that are with them"[6] is reputed to be the author of the book which is called *Pastor* and which is also read publicly in some churches of Greece. It is in fact a useful book and many of the ancient writers quote from it as authority, but among the Latins it is almost unknown.

CHAPTER XI.

PHILO[7] the Jew, an Alexandrian of the priestly class, is placed by us among the ecclesiastical writers on the ground that, writing a book concerning the first church of Mark the evangelist at Alexandria, he writes to our praise, declaring not only that they were there, but also that they were in many provinces and calling their habitations monasteries. From this[8] it appears that the church of those that believed in Christ at first, was such as now the monks desire to imitate,[9] that is, such that nothing is the peculiar property of any one of them, none of them rich, none poor, that patrimonies are divided among the needy, that they have leisure for prayer and psalms, for doctrine also and ascetic practice, that they were in fact as Luke declares believers were at first at Jerusalem. They say that under Caius[10] Caligula he ventured to Rome, whither he had been sent as legate of his nation, and that when a second time he had come to

Claudius, he spoke in the same city with the apostle Peter and enjoyed his friendship, and for this reason also adorned the adherents of Mark, Peter's disciple at Alexandria, with his praises. There are distinguished and innumerable works by this man: *On the five books of Moses*, one book *Concerning the confusion of tongues*, one book *On nature and invention*, one book *On the things which our senses desire and we detest*, one book *On learning*, one book *On the heir of divine things*, one book *On the division of equals and contraries*, one book *On the three virtues*, one book *On why in Scripture the names of many persons are changed*, two books *On covenants*, one book *On the life of a wise man*, one book *Concerning giants*, five books *That dreams are sent by God*, five books of *Questions and answers on Exodus*, four books *On the tabernacle and the Decalogue*, as well as books *On victims and promises or curses*, *On Providence*, *On the Jews*, *On the manner of one's life*, *On Alexander*, and *That dumb beasts have right reason*, and *That every fool should be a slave*, and *On the lives of the Christians*, of which we spoke above, that is, lives of apostolic men, which also he entitled, *On those who practice the divine life*, because in truth they contemplate divine things and ever pray to God, also under other categories, two *On agriculture*, two *On drunkenness*. There are other monuments of his genius which have not come to our hands. Concerning him there is a proverb among the Greeks " Either Plato philonized, or Philo platonized," that is, either Plato followed Philo, or Philo, Plato, so great is the similarity of ideas and language.

CHAPTER XII.

LUCIUS ANNÆUS SENECA[1] of Cordova, disciple of the Stoic Sotion[2] and uncle of Lucan the Poet, was a man of most continent life, whom I should not place in the category of saints were it not that those *Epistles of Paul to Seneca and Seneca[3] to Paul*, which are read by many, provoke me. In these, written when he was tutor of Nero and the most powerful man of that time, he says that he would like to hold such a place among his countrymen as Paul held among Christians. He was put to death by Nero two years before Peter and Paul were crowned with martyrdom.

---

[1] *Pertinax* A H T 25 30 31 a e Norimb. Cypr. etc; *Nerva Pertinax* Bamb. Ambros. Her.; *Nerva principe.* Val.

[2] The date of Hermas depends on what Hermas is supposed to be the author. ●He is supposed to be 1 the Hermas of the New Testament, or 2 the brother of Pius I (139–54) or 3 a still later Hermas. All these views have distinguished advocates, but this view of Jerome taken from Origen through Eusebius is not much accepted.

[3] *Hermas* A T 25 30 e; *Herman* Her. Val. a 31; *Hermam* H Cypr.

[4] *Salute* (omitting Asyncritus) A H T 25 30 31 a e etc. Cypr.; add *Asyncritus* Val. Her. Greek from the New Testament.

[5] *Hermes Patrobas Hermas* A H T 25 30 a e Val. Gr. etc.; omit Hermes. A Her.

[6] *Salute . . . them* Rom. 15, 14.

[7] Visited Rome A. D. 40, and must have lived (Edersheim) ten or fifteen years after his return.

[8] *From this* etc. Acts 2, 4; 4, 32.

[9] *desire to imitate* the mss.; *strive to be* Cypr. Fabr. Val., on account of the difficult construction with *imitate*.

[10] *Caius* Cypr. Fabr. Val.; *Gaius* all the mss.; omit Her.

[1] Died 65.

[2] *Sotion* Cypr. Val. Her.; *Phothion fotion, fotinus Socion* or *Sozonis*, the mss.

[3] *and Seneca* A H e a 21 10 Fabr. Val. etc.; *or Seneca* T 25 30 31 Her.

CHAPTER XIII.

JOSEPHUS,[1] the son of Matthias, priest of Jerusalem, taken prisoner by Vespasian and his son Titus, was banished. Coming to Rome he presented to the emperors, father and son, seven books *On the captivity of the Jews*, which were deposited in the public library and, on account of his genius, was found worthy of a statue at Rome. He wrote also twenty books of *Antiquities*, from the beginning of the world until the fourteenth year of Domitian Cæsar, and two of *Antiquities against Appion*, the grammarian of Alexandria who, under Caligula, sent as legate on the part of the Gentiles against Philo, wrote also a book containing a vituperation of the Jewish nation. Another book of his entitled, *On allruling wisdom*, in which the martyr deaths of the Maccabeans are related is highly esteemed. In the eighth book of his *Antiquities* he most openly acknowledges that Christ was slain by the Pharisees on account of the greatness of his miracles, that John the Baptist was truly a prophet, and that Jerusalem was destroyed because of the murder of James the apostle. He wrote also concerning the Lord after this fashion : " In this same time was Jesus, a wise man, if indeed it be lawful to call him man. For he was a worker of wonderful miracles, and a teacher of those who freely receive the truth. He had very many adherents also, both of the Jews and of the Gentiles, and was believed to be Christ, and when through the envy of our chief men Pilate had crucified him, nevertheless those who had loved him at first continued to the end, for he appeared to them the third day alive. Many things, both these and other wonderful things are in the songs of the prophets who prophesied concerning him and the sect of Christians, so named from Him, exists to the present day."

CHAPTER XIV.

JUSTUS,[2][3] of Tiberias of the province of Galilee, also attempted to write a *History of Jewish affairs* and certain brief *Commentaries* on the Scriptures but Josephus convicts him of falsehood. It is known that he wrote at the same time as Josephus himself.

CHAPTER XV.

CLEMENT,[4] of whom the apostle Paul writing to the Philippians says " With Clem-

---

1 Born A. D. 37, died after 97. 2 Flourished 100.
3 *Justus* a 21 10 Fabr. Val.; *Justinus* others.
4 Bishop 91 or 2-101. Died 110 (Euseb. Ch. Hist.) It is by no means certain that Clemens Romanus is the Clemens mentioned in the New Testament. Compare discussions by

ent and others of my fellow-workers whose names are written in the book of life," [1] the fourth bishop of Rome after Peter, if indeed the second was Linus and the third Anacletus,[2] although most of the Latins think that Clement was second after the apostle.[3] He wrote, on the part of the church of Rome, an especially valuable *Letter to the church of the Corinthians*, which in some places is publicly read, and which seems to me to agree in style with the epistle to the Hebrews which passes under the name of Paul but it differs from this same epistle, not only in many of its ideas, but also in respect of the order of words, and its likeness in either respect is not very great. There is also a second *Epistle* under his name which is rejected by earlier writers, and a *Disputation between Peter and Appion* written out at length, which Eusebius in the third book of his Church history rejects. He died in the third year of Trajan and a church built at Rome preserves the memory of his name unto this day.

CHAPTER XVI.

IGNATIUS,[4] third bishop of the church of Antioch after Peter the apostle, condemned to the wild beasts during the persecution of Trajan, was sent bound to Rome, and when he had come on his voyage as far as Smyrna, where Polycarp the pupil of John was bishop, he wrote one epistle *To the Ephesians*, another *To the Magnesians* a third *To the Trallians* a fourth *To the Romans*, and going thence, he wrote *To the Philadelphians* and *To the Smyrneans* and especially *To Polycarp*, commending to him the church at Antioch. In this last [5] he bore witness to the Gospel which I have recently translated, in respect of the person of Christ saying, " I indeed saw him in the flesh after the resurrection and I believe that he is," and when he came to Peter and those who were with Peter, he said to them " Behold ! touch me and see me how that I am not an incorporeal spirit " and straightway they touched him and believed. Moreover it seems worth while inasmuch as we have made mention of such a man and of the *Epistle* which he wrote *to the Romans*, to give a few " quotations " [6]: " From Syria even unto Rome I

Salmon in Smith and Wace, and M'Giffert in his translation of Eusebius.
[1] *With Clement . . . life* Phil. 4, 3.
[2] *Anacletus* Val. Fabr. Her.; *Anencletus, Anincletus, Anenclitus*, H 25 31 e; *Cletus* (or Elitus). T 30 31; *Anicletus*, 10; *Anecletus*, A; *Aneclitus*, a.
[3] *apostle* A H 25 30 31 a e; *apostle Peter* T Fabr. Val. Her.
[4] Bishop about 70, died about 107.
[5] *In this last* etc. Eusebius from whom he quotes says *Smyrneans*. Lightfoot maintains that Jerome had never seen the Epistles of Ignatius.
[6] *quotations* etc. This is taken bodily from Eusebius. The translation is M'Giffert's adapted to the Latin of Jerome.

fight with wild beasts, by land and by sea, by night and by day, being bound amidst ten leopards, that is to say soldiers who guard me and who only become worse when they are well treated. Their wrong doing, however, is my schoolmaster, but I am not thereby justified. May I have joy of the beasts that are prepared for me; and I pray that I may find them ready; I will even coax them to devour me quickly that they may not treat me as they have some whom they have refused to touch through fear. And if they are unwilling, I will compel them to devour me. Forgive me my children, I know what is expedient for me. Now do I begin to be a disciple, and desire none of the things visible that I may attain unto Jesus Christ. Let fire and cross and attacks of wild beasts, let wrenching of bones, cutting apart of limbs, crushing of the whole body, tortures[1] of the devil, — let all these come upon me if only I may attain unto the joy which is in Christ."

When he had been condemned to the wild beasts and with zeal for martyrdom heard the lions roaring, he said " I am the grain of Christ. I am ground by the teeth of the wild beasts that I may be found the bread of the world." He was put to death the eleventh year of Trajan and the remains of his body lie in Antioch outside the Daphnitic gate in the cemetery.

CHAPTER XVII.

POLYCARP[2] disciple of the apostle John and by him ordained bishop of Smyrna was chief of all Asia, where he saw and had as teachers some of the apostles and of those who had seen the Lord. He, on account of certain questions concerning the day of the Passover, went to Rome in the time of the emperor Antoninus Pius while Anicetus ruled the church in that city. There he led back to the faith many of the believers who had been deceived through the persuasion of Marcion and Valentinus, and when. Marcion met him by chance and said " Do you know us " he replied, " I know the firstborn of the devil." Afterwards during the reign of Marcus Antoninus and Lucius Aurelius Commodus in the fourth persecution after Nero, in the presence of the proconsul holding court at Smyrna and all the people crying out against him in the Amphitheater, he was burned. He wrote a very valuable *Epistle to the Philippians*

which is read to the present day in the meetings in Asia.

CHAPTER XVIII.

PAPIAS,[1] the pupil of John, bishop of Hierapolis in Asia, wrote only five volumes, which he entitled *Exposition of the words of our Lord*, in which, when he had asserted in his preface that he did not follow various opinions but had the apostles for authority, he said " I considered what Andrew and Peter said, what Philip, what Thomas, what James, what John,[2] what Matthew or any one else among the disciples of our Lord, what also Aristion and the elder John, disciples of the Lord had said, not so much that I have their books to read, as that their living voice is heard until the present day in the authors themselves." It appears through this catalogue of names that the John who is placed among the disciples is not the same as the elder John whom he places after Aristion in his enumeration. This we say moreover because of the opinion mentioned above, where we record that it is declared by many that the last two epistles of John are the work not of the apostle but of the presbyter.

He is said to have published a *Second coming of Our Lord or Millennium*. Irenæus and Apollinaris and others who say that after the resurrection the Lord will reign in the flesh with the saints, follow him. Tertullian also in his work *On the hope of the faithful*, Victorinus of Petau and Lactantius follow this view.

CHAPTER XIX.

QUADRATUS[3] disciple of the apostles, after Publius bishop of Athens had been crowned with martyrdom on account of his faith in Christ, was substituted in his place, and by his faith and industry gathered the church scattered by reason of its great fear. And when Hadrian passed the winter at Athens to witness the Eleusinian mysteries and was initiated into almost all the sacred mysteries of Greece, those who hated the Christians took opportunity without instructions from the Emperor to harass the believers. At this time he presented to Hadrian a work composed in behalf of our religion, indispensable, full of sound argument and faith and worthy of the apostolic teaching. In which, illustrating the antiquity of his period, he says that he has seen

---

[1] *tortures* A H T 25 30 31 e; *all the tortures* a. Fabr. Val. Her.
[2] Bishop 106 or 7 —157-168 (?); 154 sq (Lipsius) Authorities differ as to dates of his death from 147-175. Bishop certainly (Salmon) 110.

[1] 130 (Salmon).
[2] *what John* A H 25 30 31 a e; omit T Her.
[3] Flourished 126 (125)? Not the Athenian bishop (Salmon). Work not extant.

many who, oppressed by various ills, were healed by the Lord in Judea as well as some who had been raised from the dead.

CHAPTER XX.

ARISTIDES[1] a most eloquent Athenian philosopher, and a disciple of Christ while yet retaining his philosopher's garb, presented a work to Hadrian at the same time that Quadratus presented his. The work contained a systematic statement of our doctrine, that is, an *Apology* for the Christians, which is still extant and is regarded by philologians as a monument to his genius.

CHAPTER XXI.

AGRIPPA[2] surnamed Castor, a man of great learning, wrote a strong refutation of the twenty-four volumes which Basilides the heretic had written against the Gospel, disclosing all his mysteries and enumerating the prophets Barcabbas and Barchob[3] and all the other barbarous names which terrify the hearers, and his most high God Abraxas, whose name was supposed to contain the year according to the reckoning[4] of the Greeks. Basilides died at Alexandria in the reign of Hadrian, and from him the Gnostic sects arose. In this tempestuous time also, Cochebas leader of the Jewish faction put Christians to death with various tortures.

CHAPTER XXII.

HEGESIPPUS[5] who lived at a period not far from the Apostolic age, writing a *History* of all ecclesiastical events from the passion of our Lord, down to his own period, and gathering many things useful to the reader, composed five volumes in simple style, trying to represent the style of speaking of those whose lives he treated. He says that he went to Rome in the time of Anicetus, the tenth bishop after Peter, and continued there till the time of Eleutherius, bishop of the same city, who had been formerly deacon under Anicetus. Moreover, arguing against idols, he wrote a history, showing from what error they had first arisen, and this work indicates in what age he flourished.[6] He says, " They built monuments and temples to their dead as we see

up to the present day,[1] such as the one to Antinous, servant to the Emperor Hadrian, in whose honour also games were celebrated, and a city founded bearing his name, and a temple with priests established." The Emperor Hadrian is said to have been enamoured of Antinous.

CHAPTER XXIII.

JUSTIN,[2] a philosopher, and wearing the garb of philosopher, a citizen of Neapolis, a city of Palestine, and the son of Priscus Bacchius, laboured strenuously in behalf of the religion of Christ, insomuch that he delivered to Antoninus Pius and his sons and the senate, a work written *Against the nations*, and did not shun the ignominy of the cross. He addressed another book also to the successors of this Antoninus, Marcus Antoninus Verus and Lucius Aurelius Commodus. Another volume of his *Against the nations*, is also extant, where he discusses the nature of demons, and a fourth against the nations which he entitled, *Refutation* and yet another *On the sovereignty of God*, and another book which he entitled, *Psaltes*, and another *On the Soul*, the *Dialogue against the Jews*, which he held against Trypho, the leader of the Jews, and also notable volumes *Against Marcion*, which Irenæus also mentions in the fourth book[3] *Against heresies*, also another book *Against all heresies* which he mentions in the *Apology* which is addressed to Antoninus Pius. He, when he had held διατριβάς in the city of Rome, and had convicted Crescens the cynic, who said many blasphemous things against the Christians, of gluttony and fear of death, and had proved him devoted to luxury and lusts, at last, accused of being a Christian, through the efforts and wiles of Crescens, he shed his blood for Christ.

CHAPTER XXIV.

MELITO[4] of Asia, bishop of Sardis, addressed a book to the emperor Marcus Antoninus Verus, a disciple of Fronto the orator, in behalf of the Christian doctrine. He wrote other things also, among which are the following: *On the passover*, two books, one book *On the lives of the prophets*, one book *On the church*,[5] one book *On the*

---

[1] Flourished 125, apology presented about 133.
[2] Flourished about 130 or 135.
[3] Various readings are *Barcobus, Barcobeth, Barcho et, Bascobus et*.
[4] *reckoning* all but T and Her. which have *nomenclature*.
[5] Died 180. Wrote his history in part before 167, and published after 175.
[6] *He flourished* T H a e 25 30 Val. Fabr.; *They flourished* Her.

[1] *up to the present day* A H 31 e a; *to day* T 25 30.
[2] Born about 104 (100?), Christian 133 (before 132 *Holland*) wrote apology about 150, died 167.
[3] *fourth book* A T 25 30 Val. Her.; *fifth* H 31 a e Fabr. and early editions; The right reference is probably Bk. 4 ch. 10 but he himself is mentioned in book 5 and it is likely Jerome wrote 5.
[4] Bishop about 150, died between 171 and 180.
[5] *On the church* A 25 30 e a; omit T 31 e a [H].

Lord's day, one book *On faith*, one book *On the psalms* (?) one *On the senses*, one *On the soul and body*, one *On baptism*, one *On truth*, one *On the generation of Christ*, *On His prophecy*[1] one *On hospitality* and another which is called the *Key* — one *On the devil*, one *On the Apocalypse of John*, one *On the corporeality of God*, and six books of *Eclogues*. Of his fine oratorical genius, Tertullian, in the seven books which he wrote against the church on behalf of Montanus, satirically says that he was considered a prophet by many of us.

CHAPTER XXV.

THEOPHILUS,[2] sixth bishop of the church of Antioch, in the reign of the emperor Marcus Antoninus Verus composed a book *Against Marcion*, which is still extant, also three volumes *To Autolycus* and one *Against the heresy of Hermogenes* and other short and elegant treatises, well fitted for the edification of the church. I have read, under his name, commentaries *On the Gospel* and *On the proverbs of Solomon* which do not appear to me to correspond in style and language with the elegance and expressiveness of the above works.

CHAPTER XXVI.

APOLLINARIS,[3] bishop of Hierapolis in Asia, flourished in the reign of Marcus Antoninus Verus, to whom he addressed a notable volume in behalf of the faith of the Christians. There are extant also five other books of his *Against the Nations*, two *On truth* and *Against the Cataphrygians* written at the time when Montanus was making a beginning with Prisca and Maximilla.

CHAPTER XXVII.

DIONYSIUS,[4] bishop of the church of Corinth, was of so great eloquence and industry that he taught not only the people of his own city and province but also those of other provinces and cities by his letters. Of these one is *To the Lacedæmonians*, another *To the Athenians*, a third *To the Nicomedians*, a fourth *To the Cretans*, a fifth *To the church at Amastrina and to the other churches of Pontus*, a sixth *To the Gnosians and to Pinytus bishop of the same city*, a seventh *To the Romans*, addressed to Soter their bishop, an eighth *To Chrysophora* a holy woman. He flourished in the reign of Marcus Antoninus Verus and Lucius Aurelius Commodus.

CHAPTER XXVIII.

PINYTUS[1] of Crete, bishop of the city of Gnosus, wrote to Dionysius bishop of the Corinthians, an exceedingly elegant letter in which he teaches that the people are not to be forever fed on milk, lest by chance they be overtaken by the last day while yet infants, but that they ought to be fed also on solid food, that they may go on to a spiritual old age. He flourished under Marcus Antoninus Verus and Lucius Aurelius Commodus.[2]

CHAPTER XXIX.

TATIAN[3] who, while teaching oratory, won not a little glory in the rhetorical art, was a follower of Justin Martyr and was distinguished so long as he did not leave his master's side. But afterwards, inflated[4] by a swelling of eloquence, he founded a new heresy which is called that of the Encratites, the heresy which Severus afterwards augmented in such wise that heretics of this party are called Severians to the present day. Tatian wrote besides innumerable volumes, one of which, a most successful book *Against the nations*, is extant, and this is considered the most significant of all his works. He flourished in the reign of Marcus Antoninus Verus and Lucius Aurelius Commodus.

CHAPTER XXX.

PHILIP[5] bishop of Crete, that is of the city of Gortina, whom Dionysius mentions in the epistle which he wrote to the church of the same city, published a remarkable book *Against Marcion* and flourished in the time of Marcus Antoninus Verus and Lucius Aurelius Commodus.

CHAPTER XXXI.

MUSANUS,[6] not inconsiderable among those who have written on ecclesiastical doctrine, in the reign of Marcus Antoninus Verus wrote a book to certain brethren who had turned aside from the church to the heresy of the Encratites.

---

[1] *On truth . . . prophecy* A H 25 30 31 e a Val. etc; omit T Her.
[2] Bishop in 168, died after 181 (some 176-86).
[3] Claudius Apollinaris died before 180.
[4] Bishop about 170, died about 180.

[1] Died about 180.
[2] *That they may go on . . . Commodus* A 25 30 31 e a Fabr. Val; omit T H ? Her.
[3] Born about 130, died after 172.
[4] *inflated* A H 30 31 a e Val etc.; *elated* T 25 Her.
[5] Bishop about 160, died about 180.
[6] Flourished 204?.

CHAPTER XXXII.

MODESTUS [1] also in the reign of Marcus Antoninus and Lucius Aurelius Commodus wrote a book *Against Marcion* which is still extant. Some other compositions pass under his name but are regarded by scholars as spurious.

CHAPTER XXXIII.

BARDESANES [2] of Mesopotamia is reckoned among the distinguished men. He was at first a follower of Valentinus and afterwards his opponent and himself founded a new heresy. He has the reputation among the Syrians of having been a brilliant genius and vehement in argument. He wrote a multitude of works against almost all heresies which had come into existence in his time. Among these a most remarkable and strong work is the one which he addressed to Marcus Antoninus *On fate*, and many other volumes *On persecution* which his followers translated from the Syriac language into Greek. If indeed so much force and brilliancy appears in the translation, how great it must have been in the original.

CHAPTER XXXIV.

VICTOR, [3] thirteenth bishop of Rome, wrote, *On the Paschal Controversy* and some other small works. He ruled the church for ten years in the reign of the Emperor Severus.

CHAPTER XXXV.

IRENAEUS, [4] a presbyter under Pothinus the bishop who ruled the church of Lyons in Gaul, being sent to Rome as legate by the martyrs of this place, on account of certain ecclesiastical questions, presented to Bishop Eleutherius certain letters under his own name which are worthy of honour. Afterwards when Pothinus, nearly ninety years of age, received the crown of martyrdom for Christ, he was put in his place. It is certain too that he was a disciple of Polycarp, the priest and martyr, whom we mentioned above. He wrote five books *Against heresies* and a short volume, *Against the nations* and another *On discipline*, a letter to Marcianus his brother *On apostolical preaching*, a book of *Various treatises; also to Blastus, On schism*, [5] to Florinus *On monarchy* or

That God is not the author of evil, also an excellent *Commentary on the Ogdoad* at the end of which indicating that he was near the apostolic period he wrote "I adjure thee whosoever shall transcribe this book, by our Lord Jesus Christ and by his glorious advent at which He shall judge the quick and the dead, that you diligently compare, after you have transcribed, and amend it according to the copy from which you have transcribed it and also that you shall similarly transcribe this adjuration as you find it in your pattern." Other works of his are in circulation to wit: to Victor the Roman bishop *On the Paschal controversy* in which he warns him not lightly to break the unity of the fraternity, if indeed Victor believed that the many bishops of Asia and the East, who with the Jews celebrated the passover, on the fourteenth day of the new moon, were to be condemned. But even those who differed from them did not support Victor in his opinion. He flourished chiefly in the reign of the Emperor Commodus, who succeeded Marcus Antoninus Verus in power.

CHAPTER XXXVI.

PANTAENUS, [2] a philosopher of the stoic school, according to some old Alexandrian custom, where, from the time of [3] Mark the evangelist the ecclesiastics were always doctors, was of so great prudence and erudition both in scripture and secular literature that, on the request of the legates of that nation, he was sent to India by Demetrius bishop of Alexandria, where he found that Bartholomew, one of the twelve apostles, had preached the advent of the Lord Jesus according to the gospel of Matthew, and on his return to Alexandria he brought this with him written in Hebrew characters. Many of his commentaries on Holy Scripture are indeed extant, but his living voice was of still greater benefit to the churches. He taught in the reigns of the emperor Severus and Antoninus surnamed Caracalla.

CHAPTER XXXVII.

RHODO, [4] a native of Asia, instructed in the Scriptures at Rome by Tatian whom we mentioned above, published many things especially a work *Against Marcion* in which he tells how the Marcionites differ from one another as well as from the church and says

---

[1] Flourished 180–190.   [2] Flourished about 172.
[3] Bishop about 190 (or 185 according to others) died 202 or 197.
[4] Born between 140 and 145, died 202 or later.
[5] *schism* H A 31 a e Val. Eusebius etc : *chrism* A T 25 30.

[1] *Ogdoad* "Octava" is translation for "Ogdoad" used by Eusebius and explained to refer to the Valentinian Ogdoads. (M'Giffert.)
[2] At Alexandria about 179, died about 216.
[3] T reads *following the example of* and makes a more manageable text.
[4] Flourished 186.

that the aged Apelles, another heretic, was once engaged in a discussion with him, and that he, Rhodo, held Apelles up to ridicule because he declared that he did not know the God whom he worshipped. He mentioned in the same book, which he wrote to Callistion, that he had been a pupil of Tatian at Rome. He also composed elegant treatises *On the six days of creation* and a notable work *against the Phrygians.*[1] He flourished in the reigns of Commodus and Severus.

CHAPTER XXXVIII.

CLEMENS,[2] presbyter of the Alexandrian church, and a pupil of the Pantaenus mentioned above, led the theological school at Alexandria after the death of his master and was teacher of the Catechetes. He is the author of notable volumes, full of eloquence and learning, both in sacred Scripture and in secular literature; among these are the *Stromata*, eight books, *Hypotyposes* eight books, *Against the nations* one book, *On pedagogy,*[3] three books, *On the Passover, Disquisition on fasting* and another book entitled, *What rich man is saved?* one book *On Calumny, On ecclesiastical canons and against those who follow the error of the Jews* one book which he addressed to Alexander bishop of Jerusalem. He also mentions in his volumes of *Stromata* the work of Tatian *Against the nations* which we mentioned above and a *Chronography* of one Cassianus, a work which I have not been able to find. He also mentioned certain Jewish writers against the nations, one Aristobulus and Demetrius and Eupolemus who after the example of Josephus asserted the primacy of Moses and the Jewish people. There is a letter of Alexander the bishop of Jerusalem who afterwards ruled the church with Narcissus, on the ordination of Asclepiades the confessor, addressed to the Antiochians congratulating them, at the end of which he says " these writings honoured[4] brethren I have sent to you by the blessed presbyter Clement, a man illustrious and approved, whom you also know and with whom now you will become better acquainted a man who, when he had come hither by the special providence of God, strengthened and enlarged the church of God." Origen is known to have been his disciple. He flourished more-

over during the reigns of Severus and his son Antoninus.

CHAPTER XXXIX.

MILTIADES[1] of whom Rhodo gives an account in the work which he wrote against Montanus, Prisca and Maximilla, wrote a considerable volume against these same persons, and other books *Against the nations and the Jews* and addressed an *Apology* to the then ruling emperors. He flourished in the reign of Marcus Antoninus and Commodus.

CHAPTER XL.

APOLLONIUS,[2] an exceedingly talented man, wrote against Montanus, Prisca and Maximilla a notable and lengthy volume, in which he asserts that Montanus and his mad prophetesses died by hanging, and many other things, among which are the following concerning Prisca and Maximilla, " if they denied that they have accepted gifts, let them confess that those who do accept are not prophets and I will prove by a thousand witnesses that they have received gifts, for it is by other fruits that prophets are shown to be prophets indeed. Tell me, does a prophet dye his hair? Does a prophet stain her eyelids with antimony? Is a prophet adorned with fine garments and precious stones? Does a prophet play with dice and tables? Does he accept usury? Let them respond whether this ought to be permitted or not, it will be my task to prove that they do these things." He says in the same book, that the time when he wrote the work was the fortieth year after the beginning of the heresy of the Cataphrygians. Tertullian added to the six volumes which he wrote *On ecstasy* against the church a seventh, directed especially against Apollonius, in which he attempts to defend all which Apollonius refuted. Apollonius flourished in the reigns of Commodus and Severus.

CHAPTER XLI.

SERAPION,[3] ordained bishop of Antioch in the eleventh year of the emperor Commodus, wrote a letter to Caricus and Pontius[4] on the heresy of Montanus, in which he said " that you may know moreover that the madness of this false doctrine, that is the

---

[1] *Phrygians* A 31 a e with Eusebius; *Cataphrygians* T 25 30 " according to the usage of the Latins " (cf. M'Giffert).
[2] Born about 160, died about 217.
[3] *On pedagogy* = " The Instructor."
[4] *honoured* literally " lordly " perhaps like the conventional formula " Lords and brethren."

[1] Flourished 180–190.
[2] Bishop about 106, flourished 210.
[3] Bishop 199, died 211.
[4] *Caricus and Pontius.* So Valesius and others with Eusebius but mss. except " a " have Carinus and it is interesting to note that the same ms. reads Ponticus with most mss. of Eusebius.

doctrine of a new prophecy, is reprobated by all the world, I have sent to you the letters of the most holy Apollinaris bishop of Hierapolis in Asia." He wrote a volume also to Domnus, who in time of persecution went over to the Jews, and another work on the gospel which passes under the name of Peter, a work to the church of the Rhosenses in Cilicia who by the reading of this book had turned aside to heresy. There are here and there short letters of his, harmonious in character with the ascetic life of their author.

CHAPTER XLII.

APOLLONIUS,[1] a Roman senator under the emperor Commodus, having been denounced by a slave as a Christian, gained permission to give a reason for his faith and wrote a remarkable volume which he read in the senate, yet none the less, by the will of the senate, he was beheaded for Christ by virtue of an ancient law among them, that Christians who had once been brought before their judgment seat should not be dismissed unless they recanted.

CHAPTER XLIII.

THEOPHILUS,[2] bishop of Caesarea in Palestine, the city formerly called Turris Stratonis, in the reign of the emperor Severus wrote, in conjunction with other bishops, a synodical letter of great utility against those who celebrated the passover with the Jews on the fourteenth day of the month.

CHAPTER XLIV.

BACCHYLUS,[3] bishop of Corinth, was held in renown under the same emperor Severus, and wrote, as representative of all the bishops who were in Achaia, an elegant work *On the passover*.

CHAPTER XLV.

POLYCRATES[4] bishop of the Ephesians with other bishops of Asia who in accordance with some ancient custom celebrated the passover with the Jews on the fourteenth of the month, wrote a synodical letter against Victor bishop of Rome in which he says that he follows the authority of the apostle John and of the ancients. From this we make the following brief quotations, " We therefore celebrate the day according to usage, inviolably, neither adding anything to nor taking anything from it, for in Asia lie the remains of the greatest saints of those who shall rise again on the day of the Lord, when he shall come in majesty from heaven and shall quicken all the saints, I mean Philip one of the twelve apostles who sleeps at Hierapolis and his two daughters who were virgins until their death and another daughter of his who died at Ephesus full of the Holy Spirit. And John too, who lay on Our Lord's breast and was his high priest carrying the golden frontlet on his forehead, both martyr and doctor, fell asleep at Ephesus and Polycarp bishop and martyr died at Smyrna. Thraseas of Eumenia also, bishop and martyr, rests in the same Smyrna. What need is there of mentioning Sagaris, bishop and martyr, who sleeps in Laodicea and the blessed Papyrus and Melito, eunuch in the Holy Spirit, who, ever serving the Lord, was laid to rest in Sardis and there awaits his resurrection at Christ's advent. These all observed the day of the passover on the fourteenth of the month, in nowise departing from the evangelical tradition and following the ecclesiastical canon. I also, Polycrates, the least of all your servants, according to the doctrine of my relatives which I also have followed (for there were seven of my relatives bishops indeed and I the eighth) have always celebrated the passover when the Jewish people celebrated the putting away of the leaven. And so brethren being sixty-five years old in the Lord and instructed by many brethren from all parts of the world, and having searched all the Scriptures, I will not fear those who threaten us, for my predecessors said " It is fitting to obey God rather than men." I quote this to show through a small example the genius and authority of the man. He flourished in the reign of the emperor Severus in the same period as Narcissus of Jerusalem.

CHAPTER XLVI.

HERACLITUS[1] in the reign of Commodus and Severus wrote commentaries on the Acts and Epistles.

CHAPTER XLVII.

MAXIMUS,[2] under the same emperors propounded in a remarkable volume the famous questions, *What is the origin of evil?* and *Whether matter is made by God.*

CHAPTER XLVIII.

CANDIDUS[3] under the above mentioned emperors published most admirable treatises *On the six days of creation.*

---

[1] Died about 185. [3] Bishop about 190–200.
[2] Died about 190. [4] Bishop about 196.

[1] Flourished about 193. [3] Flourished about 196.
[2] Bishop of Jerusalem 185.

CHAPTER XLIX.

APPION[1] under the emperor Severus likewise wrote treatises *On the six days of creation.*

CHAPTER L.

SEXTUS[2] in the reign of the emperor Severus wrote a book *On the resurrection.*

CHAPTER LI.

ARABIANUS[3] under the same emperor published certain small works relating to christian doctrine.

CHAPTER LII.

JUDAS,[4] discussed at length the seventy weeks mentioned in Daniel and wrote a *Chronography* of former times which he brought up to the tenth year of Severus. He is convicted of error in respect of this work in that he prophesied that the advent of Anti-Christ would be about his period, but this was because the greatness of the persecutions seemed to forebode the end of the world.

CHAPTER LIII.

TERTULLIAN[5] the presbyter, now regarded as chief of the Latin writers after Victor and Apollonius, was from the city of Carthage in the province of Africa, and was the son of a proconsul or Centurion, a man of keen and vigorous character, he flourished chiefly in the reign of the emperor Severus and Antoninus Caracalla and wrote many volumes which we pass by because they are well known to most. I myself have seen a certain Paul an old man of Concordia, a town of Italy, who, while he himself was a very young man had been secretary to the blessed Cyprian who was already advanced in age. He said that he himself had seen how Cyprian was accustomed never to pass a day without reading Tertullian, and that he frequently said to him, " Give me the master," meaning by this, Tertullian. He was presbyter of the church until middle life, afterwards driven by the envy and abuse of the clergy of the Roman church, he lapsed to the doctrine of Montanus, and mentions the new prophecy in many of his books.

He composed, moreover, directly against the church, volumes: *On modesty, On persecution, On fasts, On monogamy,* six books *On ecstasy,* and a seventh which he

wrote *Against Apollonius.* He is said to have lived to a decrepit old age, and to have composed many small works, which are not extant.

CHAPTER LIV.

ORIGEN,[1] surnamed Adamantius, a persecution having been raised against the Christians in the tenth year of Severus Pertinax, and his father Leonidas having received the crown of martyrdom for Christ, was left at the age of about seventeen, with his six brothers and widowed mother, in poverty, for their property had been confiscated because of confessing Christ. When only eighteen years old, he undertook the work of instructing the Catechetes in the scattered churches of Alexandria. Afterwards appointed by Demetrius, bishop of this city, successor to the presbyter Clement, he flourished many years. When he had already reached middle life, on account of the churches of Achaia, which were torn with many heresies, he was journeying to Athens, by way of Palestine, under the authority of an ecclesiastical letter, and having been ordained presbyter by Theoctistus and Alexander, bishops of Caesarea and Jerusalem, he offended Demetrius, who was so wildly enraged at him that he wrote everywhere to injure his reputation. It is known that before he went to Caesarea, he had been at Rome, under bishop Zephyrinus. Immediately on his return to Alexandria he made Heraclas the presbyter, who continued to wear his philosopher's garb, his assistant in the school for catechetes. Heraclas became bishop of the church of Alexandria, after Demetrius. How great the glory of Origen was, appears from the fact that Firmilianus, bishop of Caesarea, with all the Cappadocian bishops, sought a visit from him, and entertained him for a long while. Sometime afterwards, going to Palestine to visit the holy places, he came to Caesarea[2] and was instructed at length by Origen in the Holy Scriptures. It appears also from the fact that he went to Antioch, on the request of Mammaea, mother of the Emperor Alexander, and a woman religiously disposed, and was there held in great honour, and sent letters to the Emperor Philip, who was the first among the Roman rulers, to become a christian, and to his mother, letters which are still extant. Who is there, who does not also know that he was so assiduous in the study of Holy Scriptures, that contrary to the spirit of his time, and

---

[1] Flourished about 196.   [3] Flourished about 196.
[2] Flourished about 196.   [4] 202.
[5] Born about 160, christian 195, apology 198, died about 245.

---

[1] Born at Alexandria 185, died at Tyre 253.
[2] *Caesarea.* Caesarea in Palestine.

of his people, he learned the Hebrew language, and taking the Septuagint translation, he gathered the other translations also in a single work, namely, that of Aquila, of Ponticus the Proselyte, and Theodotian the Ebonite, and Symmachus an adherent of the same sect who wrote commentaries also on the gospel according to Matthew, from which he tried to establish his doctrine. And besides these, a fifth, sixth, and seventh translation, which we also have from his library, he sought out with great diligence, and compared with other editions. And since I have given a list of his works, in the volumes of letters which I have written to Paula, in a letter which I wrote against the works of Varro, I pass this by now, not failing however, to make mention of his immortal genius, how that he understood dialectics, as well as geometry, arithmetic, music, grammar, and rhetoric, and taught all the schools of philosophers, in such wise that he had also diligent students in secular literature, and lectured to them daily, and the crowds which flocked to him were marvellous. These, he received in the hope that through the instrumentality of this secular literature, he might establish them in the faith of Christ.

It is unnecessary to speak of the cruelty of that persecution which was raised against the Christians and under Decius, who was mad against the religion of Philip, whom he had slain, — the persecution in which Fabianus, bishop of the Roman church, perished at Rome, and Alexander and Babylas, Pontifs of the churches of Jerusalem and Antioch, were imprisoned for their confession of Christ. If any one wishes to know what was done in regard to the position of Origen, he can clearly learn, first indeed from his own epistles, which after the persecution, were sent to different ones, and secondly, from the sixth book of the church history of Eusebius of Caesarea, and from his six volumes in behalf of the same Origen.

He lived until the time of Gallus and Volusianus, that is, until his sixty-ninth year, and died at Tyre, in which city he also was buried.

CHAPTER LV.

AMMONIUS,[1] a talented man of great philosophical learning, was distinguished at Alexandria, at the same time. Among many and distinguished monuments of his genius, is the elaborate work which he composed *On the harmony of Moses and Jesus,* and the

Gospel canons, which he worked out, and which Eusebius of Caesarea, afterwards followed. Porphyry falsely accused him of having become a heathen again, after being a Christian, but it is certain that he continued a Christian until the very end of his life.

CHAPTER LVI.

AMBROSIUS,[1] at first a Marcionite but afterwards set right by Origen, was deacon in the church, and gloriously distinguished as confessor of the Lord. To him, together with Protoctetus the presbyter, the book of Origen, *On martyrdom* was written. Aided[2] by his industry, funds, and perseverance, Origen dictated a great number of volumes. He himself, as befits a man of noble nature, was of no mean literary talent, as his letters to Origen indicate. He died moreover, before the death of Origen, and is condemned by many, in that being a man of wealth, he did not at death, remember in his will, his old and needy friend.

CHAPTER LVII.

TRYPHO,[3] pupil of Origen, to whom some of his extant letters are addressed, was very learned in the Scriptures, and this many of his works show here and there, but especially the book which he composed *On the red heifer*[4] in Deuteronomy, and *On the halves,* which with the pigeon and the turtledoves were offered by Abraham as recorded in Genesis.[5]

CHAPTER LVIII.

MINUCIUS[6] FELIX, a distinguished advocate of Rome, wrote a dialogue representing a discussion between a Christian and a Gentile, which is entitled *Octavius,* and still another work passes current in his name, *On fate,* or *Against the mathematicians,* but this although it is the work of a talented man, does not seem to me to correspond in style with the above mentioned work. Lactantius also mentions this Minucius in his works.

CHAPTER LIX.

GAIUS,[7] bishop of Rome, in the time of Zephyrinus, that is, in the reign of Antoninus, the son of Severus, delivered a very notable disputation *Against Proculus,* the follower of Montanus, convicting him of

---

[1] Died about 250.
[2] aided a T e Val. Her.; " *and to him* " A H 25 30; " *and to this time* " a 31.
[3] Flourished about 240.
[4] red heifer Numb. 19, 2. (?) or Deut. Ch. 21.
[5] *Genesis* 15, 9-10.
[6] Flourished 196?   [7] Died about 217.

---

[1] Flourished 220.

temerity in his defence of the new prophecy, and in the same volume also enumerating only thirteen epistles of Paul, says that the fourteenth, which is now called, *To the Hebrews*, is not by him, and is not considered among the Romans to the present day as being by the apostle Paul.

CHAPTER LX.

BERYLLUS,[1] bishop of Bostra in Arabia, after he had ruled the church gloriously[2] for a little while, finally lapsed into the heresy which denies that Christ existed before the incarnation. Set right by Origen, he wrote various short works, especially letters, in which he thanks Origen. The letters of Origen to him, are also extant, and a dialogue between Origen and Beryllus as well, in which heresies are discussed. He was distinguished during the reign of Alexander, son of Mammaea, and Maximinus and Gordianus, who succeeded him in power.

CHAPTER LXI.

HIPPOLYTUS,[3] bishop of some church (the name of the city I have not been able to learn) wrote *A reckoning of the Paschal feast* and *chronological tables* which he worked out up to the first year of the Emperor Alexander. He also discussed the *cycle* of sixteen years, which the Greeks called ἐκκαιδεκαετηρίδα and gave the cue to Eusebius, who composed on the same Paschal feast a cycle of nineteen years, that is ἐννεακαιδεκαετηρίδα. He wrote some commentaries on the Scriptures, among which are the following: *On the six days of creation, On Exodus, On the Song of Songs, On Genesis, On Zechariah, On the Psalms, On Isaiah, On Daniel, On the Apocalypse, On the Proverbs, On Ecclesiastes, On Saul, On the Pythonissa, On the Antichrist, On the resurrection, Against Marcion, On the Passover, Against all heresies*, and an exhortation *On the praise of our Lord and Saviour*, in which he indicates that he is speaking in the church in the presence of Origen. Ambrosius, who we have said was converted by Origen from the heresy of Marcion, to the true faith, urged Origen to write, in emulation of Hyppolytus, commentaries on the Scriptures, offering him seven, and even more secretaries, and their expenses, and an equal number of copyists, and what is still more, with incredible zeal, daily exacting work

from him, on which account Origen, in one of his epistles, calls him his "Taskmaster."

CHAPTER LXII.

ALEXANDER,[1] bishop of Cappadocia, desiring to visit the Holy Land, came to Jerusalem, at the time when Narcissus, bishop of this city, already an old man, ruled the church. It was revealed to Narcissus and many of his clergy, that on the morning of the next day, a bishop would enter the city, who should be assistant on the sacerdotal throne. And so it came to pass, as it was predicted, and all the bishops of Palestine being gathered together, Narcissus himself being especially urgent, Alexander took with him the helm of the church of Jerusalem. At the end of one of his epistles, written to the Antinoites *On the peace of the church*. He says "Narcissus, who held the bishopric here before me, and now with me exercises his office by his prayers, being about a hundred and sixteen years old, salutes you, and with me begs you to become of one mind." He wrote another also *To the Antiocheans*, by the hand of Clement, the presbyter of Alexandria, of whom we spoke above, another also *To Origen*, and *In behalf of Origen against Demetrius*, called forth by the fact that, according to the testimony of Demetrius, he had made Origen presbyter. There are other epistles of his to different persons. In the seventh persecution under Decius, at the time when Babylas of Antioch was put to death, brought to Caesarea and shut up in prison, he received the crown of martyrdom for confessing Christ.

CHAPTER LXIII.

JULIUS AFRICANUS,[2] whose five volumes *On Chronology*, are yet extant, in the reign of Marcus Aurelius Antoninus, who succeeded Macrinus, received a commission to restore the city of Emmaus, which afterwards was called Nicopolis. There is an epistle of his to Origen, *On the question of Susanna*, where it is contended that this story is not contained in the Hebrew, and is not consistent with the Hebrew etymology in respect of the play on "prinos and prisai," "schinos and schisai." In reply to this, Origen wrote a learned epistle. There is extant another letter of his, *To Aristides*, in which he discusses at length the discrepancies, which appear in the genealogy of our Saviour, as recorded by Matthew and Luke.

---

[1] Flourished about 230.
[2] *gloriously* A 31 e a 10 21 Bamb. Norimb. Val.; omit T 25 30 H Her.
[3] Bishop 217-8, died 229-38.

---

[1] Bishop at Jerusalem 212, died 250.
[2] . . . 221.

CHAPTER LXIV.

GEMINUS,[1] presbyter of the church at Antioch, composed a few monuments of his genius, flourishing in the time of the Emperor Alexander and Zebennus, bishop of his city, especially at the time at which Heraclas was ordained Pontiff of the church at Alexandria.

CHAPTER LXV.

THEODORUS,[2] afterwards called Gregory, bishop of Neocaesarea in Pontus, while yet a very young man, in company with his brother Athenodorus, went from Cappadocia to Berytus, and thence to Caesarea in Palestine, to study Greek and Latin literature. When Origen had seen the remarkable natural ability of these men, he urged them to study philosophy, in the teaching of which he gradually introduced the matter of faith in Christ, and made them also his followers. So, instructed by him for five years, they were sent back by him to their mother. Theodorus, on his departure, wrote a panegyric of thanks to Origen, and delivered it before a large assembly, Origen himself being present. This panegyric is extant at the present day.

He wrote also a short, but very valuable, paraphrase *On Ecclesiastes*, and current report speaks of other epistles of his, but more especially of the signs and wonders, which as bishop, he performed to the great glory of the churches.

CHAPTER LXVI.

CORNELIUS,[3] bishop of Rome, to whom eight letters of Cyprian are extant, wrote a letter to Fabius,[4] bishop of the church at Antioch, *On the Roman, Italian, and African councils*, and another *On Novatian, and those who had fallen from the faith*, a third *On the acts of the council*, and a fourth very prolix one to the same Fabius, containing the causes of the Novatian heresy and an anathema of it. He ruled the church for two years under Gallus and Volusianus. He received the crown of martyrdom for Christ, and was succeeded by Lucius.

CHAPTER LXVII.

CYPRIAN[5] of Africa, at first was famous as a teacher of rhetoric, and afterwards on the persuasion of the presbyter Caecilius,

from whom he received his surname, he became a Christian, and gave all his substance to the poor. Not long after he was inducted into the presbytery, and was also made bishop of Carthage. It is unnecessary to make a catalogue of the works of his genius, since they are more conspicuous than the sun.

He was put to death under the Emperors Valerian and Gallienus, in the eighth persecution, on the same day that Cornelius was put to death at Rome, but not in the same year.

CHAPTER LXVIII.

PONTIUS,[1] deacon of Cyprian, sharing his exile until the day of his death, left a notable volume *On the life and death of Cyprian*.

CHAPTER LXIX.

DIONYSIUS,[2] bishop of Alexandria, as presbyter had charge of the catechetical school under Heraclas, and was the most distinguished pupil of Origen. Consenting to the doctrine of Cyprian and the African synod, on the rebaptizing[3] of heretics, he sent many letters to different people, which are yet extant; He wrote one to Fabius, bishop of the church at Antioch, *On penitence*, another *To the Romans*, by the hand of Hippolytus, two letters *To Xystus*, who had succeeded Stephen, two also *To Philemon and Dionysius*, presbyters of the church at Rome, and another *To* the same *Dionysius*, afterwards bishop of Rome, and *To Novatian*, treating of their claim that Novatian had been ordained bishop of Rome, against his will. The beginning of this epistle is as follows: "Dionysius to Novatian, his brother greeting. If you have been ordained unwillingly, as you say, you will prove it, when you shall willingly retire."

There is another epistle of his also *To Dionysius and Didymus*, and many *Festal epistles on the passover*, written in a declamatory style, also one to the church of Alexandria *On exile*, one *To Hierax*,[4] bishop in Egypt, and yet others *On mortality*, *On the Sabbath*, and *On the gymnasium*, also one *To Hermammon* and others *On the persecution of Decius*, and two books *Against Nepos the bishop*, who asserted in his writings a thousand years reign in the body. Among other things he diligently discussed the *Apocalypse of John*, and wrote *Against Sabellius* and *To Ammon*, bishop of Ber-

[1] Presbyter at Antioch about 232.
[2] Gregory of Neocaesarea, born 210-15, bishop 240, died about 270.
[3] Bishop 251, died 252.
[4] *Fabius*. Some mss. Fabianus.
[5] Born about 200, bishop 248, died at Carthage 258.

[1] Died about 260.
[2] Presbyter 232, exiled 250 and 257, died 265.
[3] *rebaptizing* a e Val. Her.; *baptizing* A? H T 25 30 31.
[4] *Hierax* e Euseb. Val. Her. *Heraclas* A H T 25 30 31.

nice, and *To Telesphorus*, also *To Euphranor*, also four books *To Dionysius*, bishop of Rome, to the Laodiceans *On penitence*, to Origen *On martyrdom*, to the Armenians *On penitence*,[1] also *On the order of transgression*, to Timothy *On nature*, to Euphranor *On temptation*, many letters also *To Basilides*, in one of which he asserts that he also began to write commentaries on Ecclesiastes. The notable epistle which he wrote against Paul of Samosta, a few days before his death is also current. He died in the twelfth year of Gallienus.

CHAPTER LXX.

NOVATIANUS,[2] presbyter of Rome, attempted to usurp the sacerdotal chair occupied by Cornelius, and established the dogma of the Novatians, or as they are called in Greek, the Cathari, by refusing to receive penitent apostates. Novatus, author of this doctrine, was a presbyter of Cyprian. He wrote, *On the passover*, *On the Sabbath*, *On circumcision*, *On the priesthood*, *On prayer*,[3] *On the food of the Jews*, *On zeal*, *On Attalus*, and many others, especially, a great volume *On the Trinity*, a sort of epitome of the work of Tertullian, which many mistakenly ascribe to Cyprian.

CHAPTER LXXI.

MALCHION,[4] the highly gifted presbyter of the church at Antioch, who had most successfully taught rhetoric in the same city, held a discussion with Paul of Samosata, who as bishop of the church at Antioch, had introduced the doctrine of Artemon, and this was taken down by short hand writers. This dialogue is still extant, and yet another extended epistle written by him, in behalf of the council, is addressed to *Dionysius and Maximus*, bishops of Rome and Alexandria.

He flourished under Claudius and Aurelianus.

CHAPTER LXXII.

ARCHELAUS,[5] bishop of Mesopotamia, composed in the Syriac language, a book of the discussion which he held with Manichaeus, when he came from Persia. This book, which is translated into Greek, is possessed by many.

He flourished under the Emperor Probus, who succeeded Aurelianus and Tacitus.

CHAPTER LXXIII.

ANATOLIUS[1] of Alexandria, bishop of Laodicea in Syria, who flourished under the emperors Probus and Carus, was a man of wonderful learning in arithmetic, geometry, astronomy, grammar, rhetoric, and dialectic. We can get an idea of the greatness of his genius from the volume which he wrote *On the passover* and his ten books *On the institutes of arithmetic*.

CHAPTER LXXIV.

VICTORINUS,[2] bishop of Pettau, was not equally familiar with Latin and Greek. On this account his works though noble in thought, are inferior in style. They are the following: Commentaries *On Genesis*, *On Exodus*, *On Leviticus*, *On Isaiah*, *On Ezekiel*, *On Habakkuk*, *On Ecclesiastes*, *On the Song of Songs*, *On the Apocalypse of John*, *Against all heresies* and many others. At the last he received the crown of martyrdom.

CHAPTER LXXV.

PAMPHILUS[3] the presbyter, patron of Eusebius bishop of Caesarea, was so inflamed with love of sacred literature, that he transcribed the greater part of the works of Origen with his own hand and these are still preserved in the library at Caesarea. I have twenty-five volumes[4] of Commentaries of Origen, written in his hand, *On the twelve prophets* which I hug and guard with such joy, that I deem myself to have the wealth of Croesus. And if it is such joy to have one epistle of a martyr how much more to have so many thousand lines which seem to me to be traced in his blood. He wrote an *Apology for Origen* before Eusebius had written his and was put to death at Caesarea in Palestine in the persecution of Maximinus.

CHAPTER LXXVI.

PIERIUS,[5] presbyter of the church at Alexandria in the reign of Carus and Diocletian, at the time when Theonas ruled as bishop in the same church, taught the people with great success and attained such elegance of language and published so many treatises on all sorts of subjects (which are still extant) that he was called Origen Junior. He was remarkable for his self-discipline, devoted to voluntary poverty, and thoroughly acquainted with the dialectic art. After the

---

[1] *penitence* A T 25 30 a Her.; *penitence likewise Canon on penitence* H 31 e 10 21 Val.
[2] Flourished about 250 sq.
[3] *Prayer* A H 25 30 31 21; *Ordination* e T Her.
[4] Flourished 272. [5] Flourished about 278.

---

[1] Born about 230, bishop 270, died about 283.
[2] Bishop of Pettau 303, died 304. [3] Died 309.
[4] *volumes* A H 31 a e 10 21 Val.; omit T 25 30 Her.
[5] Flourished before 299.

persecution, he passed the rest of his life at Rome. There is extant a long treatise of his *On the prophet Hosea* which from internal evidence appears to have been delivered on the vigil of Passover.

CHAPTER LXXVII.

LUCIANUS,[1] a man of great talent, presbyter of the church at Antioch, was so diligent in the study of the Scriptures, that even now certain copies of the Scriptures bear the name of Lucian. Works of his, *On faith*, and short *Epistles* to various people are extant. He was put to death at Nicomedia for his confession of Christ in the persecution of Maximinus, and was buried at Helenopolis in Bithynia.

CHAPTER LXXVIII.

PHILEAS[2] a resident of that Egyptian city which is called Thmuis, of noble family, and no small wealth, having become bishop, composed a finely written work in praise of martyrs and arguing against the judge who tried to compel him to offer sacrifices, was beheaded for Christ during the same persecution in which Lucianus was put to death at Nicomedia.

CHAPTER LXXIX.

ARNOBIUS[3] was a most successful teacher of rhetoric at Sicca in Africa during the reign of Diocletian, and wrote volumes *Against the nations* which may be found everywhere.

CHAPTER LXXX.

FIRMIANUS,[4] known also as Lactantius, a disciple of Arnobius, during the reign of Diocletian summoned to Nicomedia with Flavius the Grammarian whose poem *On medicine* is still extant, taught rhetoric there and on account of his lack of pupils (since it was a Greek city) he betook himself to writing. We have a *Banquet* of his which he wrote as a young man in Africa and an *Itinerary* of a journey from Africa to Nicomedia written in hexameters, and another book which is called *The Grammarian* and a most beautiful one *On the wrath of God*, and *Divine institutes against the nations*, seven books, and an *Epitome* of the same work in one volume, without a title,[5] also two books *To Asclepiades*, one book *On persecution*, four books of *Epistles to Probus*, two

books of *Epistles to Severus*, two books of *Epistles to his pupil Demetrius*[1] and one book to the same *On the work of God or the creation of man*. In his extreme old age he was tutor to Crispus Caesar a son of Constantine in Gaul, the same one who was afterwards put to death by his father.

CHAPTER LXXXI.

EUSEBIUS[2] bishop of Caesarea in Palestine was diligent in the study of Divine Scriptures and with Pamphilus the martyr a most diligent investigator of the Holy Bible. He published a great number of volumes among which are the following: *Demonstrations of the Gospel* twenty books *Preparations for the Gospel* fifteen books, *Theophany*[3] five books, *Church history* ten books, *Chronicle of Universal history* and an *Epitome* of this last. Also *On discrepancies between the Gospels*, *On Isaiah*, ten books, also *Against Porphyry*, who was writing at that same time in Sicily as some think, twenty-five books, also one book of *Topics*, six books of *Apology for Origen*, three books *On the life of Pamphilus*, other brief works *On the martyrs*, exceedingly learned *Commentaries on one hundred and fifty Psalms*, and many others. He flourished chiefly in the reigns of Constantine the Great and Constantius. His surname Pamphilus arose from his friendship for Pamphilus the martyr.

CHAPTER LXXXII.

RETICIUS[4] bishop of Autun, among the Aedui, had a great reputation in Gaul in the reign of Constantine. I have read his commentaries *On the Song of Songs* and another great volume *Against Novatian* but besides these, I have found no works of his.

CHAPTER LXXXIII.

METHODIUS,[5] bishop of Olympus in Lycia and afterwards of Tyre, composed books *Against Porphyry* written in polished and logical style also a *Banquet of the ten virgins*, an excellent work *On the resurrection*, against Origen and *On the Pythonissa* and *On free will*, also against Origen. He also wrote commentaries *On Genesis* and *On the Song of Songs* and many others which are widely read. At the end of the recent

---

[1] Died 312.
[2] Died after 306.
[3] Flourished 295.
[4] Died 325.
[5] *without a title* "that is a compendium of the last three books only" as Cave explains it. Ffoulkes in Smith and W. But no.

[1] *two books . . . Severus . . - Demetrius* e a H 10 21 Val.; omit T 25 30 31 Her.
[2] Born 267, bishop about 315, died about 338.
[3] *Theophany* T 31 Val. Her.; omit A H 25 30 a? e.
[4] Bishop 313, died 334.　[5] Died 311 or 312.

persecution or, as others affirm, in the reign of Decius and Valerianus, he was crowned with martyrdom at Chalcis in Greece.

CHAPTER LXXXIV.

JUVENCUS,[1] a Spaniard of noble family and presbyter, translating the four gospels almost verbally in hexameter verses, composed four books. He wrote some other things in the same metre relating to the order of the sacraments. He flourished in the reign of Constantinus.

CHAPTER LXXXV.

EUSTATHIUS,[2] a Pamphilian from Side, bishop[3] first of Beroea in Syria and then of Antioch, ruled the church and, composing many things against the doctrine of the Arians, was driven into exile under the emperor Constantius[4] into Trajanopolis in Thrace where he is until this day. Works of his are extant *On the soul, On ventriloquism Against Origen* and *Letters* too numerous to mention.

CHAPTER LXXXVI.

MARCELLUS,[5] bishop of Ancyra, flourished in the reign of Constantinus and Constantius and wrote many volumes of various *Propositions* and especially against the Arians. Works of Asterius and Apollinarius against him are current, which accuse him of Sabellianism. Hilary too, in the seventh book of his work *Against the Arians*, mentions him as a heretic, but he defends himself against the charge through the fact that Julius and Athanasius bishops of Rome and Alexandria communed with him.

CHAPTER LXXXVII.

ATHANASIUS[6] bishop of Alexandria, hard pressed by the wiles of the Arians, fled to Constans emperor of Gaul. Returning thence with letters and, after the death of the emperor, again taking refuge in flight, he kept in hiding until the accession of Jovian, when he returned to the church and died in the reign of Valens. Various works by him are in circulation; two books *Against the nations* one *Against Valens* and *Ursacius, On virginity*, very many *On the persecutions of the Arians*, also *On the titles of the Psalms* and *Life of Anthony the monk*, also *Festal epistles* and other works too numerous to mention.

CHAPTER LXXXVIII.

ANTHONY[1] the monk, whose life Athanasius bishop of Alexandria wrote a long work upon, sent seven letters in Coptic to various monasteries, letters truly apostolic in idea and language, and which have been translated into Greek. The chief of these is *To the Arsenoites*. He flourished during the reign of Constantinus and his sons.

CHAPTER LXXXIX.

BASIL[2] bishop of Ancyra, [a doctor of][3] medicine, wrote a book *Against Marcellus and on virginity* and some other things — and in the reign of Constantius was, with Eustathius of Sebaste, primate of Macedonia.

CHAPTER XC.

THEODORUS,[4] bishop of Heraclea in Thrace, published in the reign of the emperor Constantius commentaries *On Matthew and John, On the Epistles* and *On the Psalter*. These are written in a polished and clear style and show an excellent historical sense.

CHAPTER XCI.

EUSEBIUS[5] of Emesa, who had fine rhetorical talent, composed innumerable works suited to win popular applause and writing historically he is most diligently read by those who practise public speaking. Among these the chief are, *Against Jews, Gentiles and Novatians* and *Homilies on the Gospels*, brief but numerous. He flourished in the reign of the emperor Constantius in whose reign he died, and was buried at Antioch.

CHAPTER XCII.

TRIPHYLIUS, bishop of Ledra or Leucotheon,[7] in Cyprus, was the most eloquent man of his age, and was distinguished during the reign of Constantius. I have read his *Commentary on the Song of Songs.* He is said to have written many other works, none of which have come to our hand.

---

[1] Flourished 330.
[2] Died 337, (or according to others 370-82.) Jerome in this chapter seems, unless the usual modern view is confused, to have mixed up Eustathius of Antioch with Eusebius of Sebaste.
[3] *Bishop* A H T 25 30 Her; omit 31 32 a e Val.
[4] *Constantius* this is supposed to be an evident slip for *Constantinus* (Compare Venables in Smith and Wace *Dict.* v. 2, p. 383) but if there is confusion with Eustathius of Sebaste as suggested above possibly the latter's deposition by Constantius is referred to. But the difficulty remains almost as great.
[5] Died 372, or 374 (Ffoulkes.)
[6] Born about 206. died 272.

[1] Born 251, died 356.
[2] Bishop of Ancyra 336-344, 353-60, 361-3.
[3] *A doctor of* So T? and some editions. Most mss. omit (gnarus) but it needs to be supplied in translation.
[4] Bishop 335, died 355?   [6] Bishop 344, died about 370.
[5] Died before 359.   [7] *Leucotheon* = Leuteon.

CHAPTER XCIII.

DONATUS,[1] from whom the Donatians arose in Africa in the reigns of the emperors Constantinus and Constantius, asserted that the scriptures were given up to the heathen by the orthodox during the persecution, and deceived almost all Africa, and especially Numidia by his persuasiveness. Many of his works, which relate to his heresy, are extant, including *On the Holy Spirit*, a work which is Arian in doctrine.

CHAPTER XCIV.

ASTERIUS,[2] a philosopher of the Arian party, wrote, during the reign of Constantius, commentaries *On the Epistle to the Romans*, *On the Gospels* and *On the Psalms*, also many other works which are diligently read by those of his party.

CHAPTER XCV.

LUCIFER,[3] bishop of Cagliari, was sent by Liberius the bishop, with Pancratius and Hilary, clergy of the Roman church, to the emperor Constantius, as legates for the faith. When he would not condemn the Nicene faith as represented by Athanasius, sent again to Palestine, with wonderful constancy and willingness to meet martyrdom, he wrote a book against the emperor Constantius and sent it to be read by him, and not long after he returned to Cagliari in the reign of the emperor Julian and died in the reign of Valentinian.

CHAPTER XCVI.

EUSEBIUS,[4] a native of Sardinia, at first a lector at Rome and afterwards bishop of Vercelli, sent by the emperor Constantius to Scythopolis, and afterwards to Cappadocia, on account of his confession of the faith, returned to the church under the emperor Julian and published the *Commentaries of Eusebius of Caesarea on the Psalms*, which he had translated from Greek into Latin, and died during the reign of Valentian and Valens.

CHAPTER XCVII.

FORTUNATIANUS,[5] an African by birth, bishop of Aquilia during the reign of Constantius, composed brief *Commentaries on the gospels* arranged by chapters, written in a rustic style, and is held in detestation because, when Liberius bishop of Rome was driven into exile for the faith, he was induced by the urgency of Fortunatianus to subscribe to heresy.

CHAPTER XCVIII.

ACACIUS,[1] who, because he was blind in one eye, they nicknamed "the one-eyed," bishop of the church of Caesarea in Palestine, wrote seventeen volumes *On Ecclesiastes* and six of *Miscellaneous questions*, and many treatises besides on various subjects. He was so influential in the reign of the emperor Constantius that he made Felix bishop of Rome in the place of Liberius.

CHAPTER XCIX.

SERAPION,[2] bishop of Thmuis, who on account of his cultivated genius was found worthy of the surname of Scholasticus, was the intimate friend of Anthony the monk, and published an excellent book *Against the Manichaeans*, also another *On the titles of the Psalms*, and valuable *Epistles* to different people. In the reign of the emperor Constantius he was renowned as a confessor.

CHAPTER C.

HILARY,[3] bishop of Poitiers in Aquitania, was a member of the party of Saturninus bishop of Arles. Banished into Phrygia by the Synod of Beziérs he composed twelve books *Against the Arians* and another book *On Councils* written to the Gallican bishops, and *Commentaries on the Psalms* that is on the first and second, from the fifty-first to the sixty-second, and from the one hundred and eighteenth to the end of the book. In this work he imitated Origen, but added also some original matter. There is a little book of his *To Constantius* which he presented to the emperor while he was living in Constantinople, and another *On Constantius* which he wrote after his death and a book *Against Valens and Ursacius*, containing a history of the Ariminian and Selucian Councils and *To Sallust the prefect* or *Against Dioscurus*, also a book of *Hymns and mysteries*, a commentary *On Matthew* and treatises *On Job*, which he translated freely from the Greek of Origen, and another elegant little work *Against Auxentius* and *Epistles* to different persons. They say he has written *On the Song of Songs* but this work is not known to us. He died at Poictiers during the reign of Valentinianus and Valens.

[1] Bishop 313,—355.
[2] Asterius of Cappadocia, died about 330.
[3] Bishop 353, died 370.
[4] Born about 315, Bishop about 340, exiled 355–62, died 371–5.
[5] Flourished 343–355.

[1] Bishop about 338, died 365–6.
[2] Serapion the scholastic, died about 358.
[3] Bishop 350–5, exiled 356–60, died at Poitiers 367–8.

CHAPTER CI.

VICTORINUS,[1] an African by birth, taught rhetoric at Rome under the emperor Constantius and in extreme old age, yielding himself to faith in Christ wrote books against Arius, written in dialectic style and very obscure language, books which can only be understood by the learned. He also wrote *Commentaries on the Epistles.*

CHAPTER CII.

TITUS[2] bishop of Bostra, in the reign of the emperors Julian and Jovinian wrote vigorous works against the Manichaeans, and some other things. He died under Valens.

CHAPTER CIII.

DAMASUS,[3] bishop of Rome, had a fine talent for making verses and published many brief works in heroic metre. He died in the reign of the Emperor Theodosius at the age of almost eighty.

CHAPTER CIV.

APOLLINARIUS,[4] bishop of Laodicea, in Syria, the son of a presbyter, applied himself in his youth to the diligent study of grammar, and afterwards, writing innumerable volumes on the Holy Scriptures, died in the reign of the Emperor Theodosius. There are extant thirty books by him *Against Porphyry*, which are generally considered as among the best of his works.[5]

CHAPTER CV.

GREGORY,[6] bishop of Elvira,[7] in Baetica, writing even to extreme old age, composed various treatises in mediocre language, and an elegant work *On Faith.* He is said to be still living.

CHAPTER CVI.

PACIANUS,[8] bishop of Barcelona, in the Pyrenees Mountains, a man of chaste eloquence, and as distinguished by his life as by his speech, wrote various short works, among which are *The Deer,*[9] and *Against*

the Novatians, and died in the reign of Emperor Theodosian, in extreme old age.

CHAPTER CVII.

PHOTINUS,[1] of Gallograecia, a disciple of Marcellus, and ordained bishop of Sirmium, attempted to introduce the Ebionite heresy, and afterwards having been expelled from the church by the Emperor Valentinianus, wrote many volumes, among which the most distinguished are *Against the nations*, and *To Valentinianus.*

CHAPTER CVIII.

PHOEBADIUS,[2] bishop of Agen, in Gaul, published a book *Against the Arians.* There are said to be other works by him, which I have not yet read. He is still living, infirm with age.

CHAPTER CIX.

DIDYMUS,[3] of Alexandria, becoming blind while very young, and therefore ignorant of the rudiments of learning, displayed such a miracle of intelligence as to learn perfectly dialectics and even geometry, sciences which especially require sight. He wrote many admirable works: *Commentaries on all the Psalms, Commentaries on the Gospels of Matthew and John, On the doctrines*, also two books *Against the Arians*, and one book *On the Holy Spirit*, which I translated in Latin, eighteen volumes *On Isaiah*, three books of commentaries *On Hosea*, addressed to me, and five books *On Zechariah*, written at my request, also commentaries *On Job*, and many other things, to give an account of which would be a work of itself.[4] He is still living, and has already passed his eighty-third year.

CHAPTER CX.

OPTATUS[5] the African, bishop of Milevis,[6] during the reign of the Emperors Valentinianus and Valens, wrote in behalf of the Catholic party six books against the calumny of the Donatian party, in which he asserts that the crime of the Donatists is falsely charged upon the catholic party.

---

1 Caius or Fabius Marius Victorinus, died about 370.
2 Ordained 361, died 371.
3 Pope Damasus, died 380.
4 Apollinaris the younger, Bishop 362, died about 390.
5 *Works* " generally recognized as authentic " Matougues.
6 Gregory Baeticus Bishop of Elvira 359-392.
7 *Elvira*, Eliberi or Grenada.
8 Bishop about 360, died about 390.
9 *Deer*, This title has given rise to a good deal of conjecture. Fabricius's conjecture that it referred to certain games held on the Kalends of January is doubted by Vallarsi, but appears to have been really acute, from the fact that two mss. read " The deer [Cervulus] on the Kalends of January and against other pagan games."

---

1 Bishop about 347, deposed 351, died about 376.
2 Bishop 358, died about 392.
3 Born about 311, flourished about 315, died 396.
4 *itself* " The titles of which are well known." Matougues.
5 Flourished about 370.
6 *Milevis* or Mileum = Milah " a town of Numidia 25 miles north-west of Cirta." *Phillott.*

CHAPTER CXI.

ACILIUS SEVERUS[1] of Spain, of the family of that Severus to whom Lactantius' two books of *Epistles* are addressed, composed a volume of mingled poetry and prose which is a sort of guide book to his whole life. This he called *Calamity* or *Trial*.[2] He died in the reign of Valentinianus.

CHAPTER CXII.

CYRIL,[3] bishop of Jerusalem often expelled by the church, and at last received, held the episcopate for eight consecutive years, in the reign of Theodosius. Certain *Catechetical lectures* of his, composed while he was a young man, are extant.

CHAPTER CXIII.

EUZOIUS,[4] as a young man, together with Gregory, bishop of Nazianzan, was educated by Thespesius the rhetorician at Caesarea, and afterwards when bishop of the same city, with great pains attempted to restore the library, collected by Origen and Pamphilus, which had already suffered injury. At last, in the reign of the Emperor Theodosian, he was expelled from the church. Many and various treatises of his are in circulation, and one may easily become acquainted with them.

CHAPTER CXIV.

EPIPHANIUS,[5] bishop of Salamina in Cyprus, wrote books *Against all heresies*, and many others which are eagerly read by the learned, on account of their subject matter, and also by the plain people, on account of their language. He is still living, and in his extreme old age composes various brief works.

CHAPTER CXV.

EPHRAIM,[6] deacon of the church at Edessa, composed many works in the Syriac language, and became so distinguished that his writings are repeated publicly in some churches, after the reading of the Scriptures. I once read in Greek a volume by him *On the Holy Spirit*, which some one had translated from the Syriac, and recognized even in translation, the incisive power of lofty genius.
He died in the reign of Valens.

CHAPTER CXVI.

BASIL,[1] bishop of Caesarea in Cappadocia, the city formerly called Mazaca, composed admirable carefully written books *Against Eunomius*, a volume *On the Holy Spirit*, and nine homilies *On the six days of creation*, also a work *On asceticism* and short treatises on various subjects. He died in the reign of Gratianus.

CHAPTER CXVII.

GREGORY,[2] bishop of Nazianzen, a most eloquent man, and my instructor in the Scriptures, composed works, amounting in all to thirty thousand lines, among which are *On the death of his brother Caesarius, On charity, In praise of the Maccabees, In praise of Cyprian, In praise of Athanasius, In praise of Maximus the philosopher* after he had returned from exile. This latter however, some superscribe with the pseudonym of Herona, since there is another work by Gregory, upbraiding this same Maximus, as if one might not praise and upbraid the same person at one time or another as the occasion may demand. Other works of his are a book in hexameter, containing, *A discussion between virginity and marriage*, two books *Against Eunomius*, one book *On the Holy Spirit*, and one *Against the Emperor Julian*. He was a follower of Polemon in his style of speaking. Having ordained his successor in the bishopric, during his own life time, he retired to the country where he lived the life of a monk and died, three years or more ago, in the reign of Theodosius.

CHAPTER CXVIII.

LUCIUS,[3] bishop of the Arian party after Athanasius, held the bishopric of the church at Alexandria, until the time of the Emperor Theodosius, by whom he was deposed.
Certain festal epistles of his, *On the passover* are extant, and a few short works of *Miscellaneous propositions*.

CHAPTER CXIX.

DIODORUS,[4] bishop of Tarsus enjoyed a great reputation while he was still presbyter of Antioch. Commentaries of his *On the epistles* are extant, as well as many other works in the manner of Eusebius the great of Emesa, whose meaning he has followed,

[1] Died before 376. Fabricius and Migne read Aquilus, Honorius has Achilius but the mss. read as above. This is the only source of information and the work is lost.
[2] *Trial* "Vicissitudes or proofs." Matougues.
[3] Cyril of Jerusalem, born about 315, Bishop 350-7, 359-60, 362-7, 378 to his death in 386.
[4] Deposed about 379.
[5] Born about 310, bishop about 368-9, died 403.
[6] Ephrem of Nisibis = Ephrem Syrus died 378.

[1] Basil the Great, born 329, bishop 370 died 379.
[2] Gregory Nazianzan born about 325, Bishop 373, died 389.
[3] Lucius bishop of Samosata, at Alexandria 373, deposed 378.
[4] Died before 394.

but whose eloquence he could not imitate on account of his ignorance of secular literature.

CHAPTER CXX.

Eunomius,[1] bishop of Cyzicus and member of the Arian party, fell into such open blasphemy in his heresy, as to proclaim publicly what the others concealed. He is said to be still living in Cappadocia, and to write much against the church. Replies to him have been made by Apollinarius, Didymus, Basil of Caesarea, Gregory Nazianzen, and Gregory of Nyssa.

CHAPTER CXXI.

Priscillianus,[2] bishop of Abila, belonged to the party of Hydatius and Ithacius, and was put to death at Tréves by the tyrant Maximus. He published many short writings, some of which have reached us. He is still accused by some, of being tainted with Gnosticism, that is, with the heresy of Basilides or Mark, of whom Irenaeus writes, while his defenders maintain that he was not at all of this way of thinking.

CHAPTER CXXII.

Latronianus[3] of Spain, a man of great learning, and in the matter of versification worthy to be compared with the poets of ancient time, was also put to death at Tréves with Priscillianus, Felicissimus, Julianus, and Euchrotia, coöriginators with him of schism. Various fruits of his genius written in different metres are extant.

CHAPTER CXXIII.

Tiberianus,[4] the Baetican, in answer to an insinuation that he shared the heresy of Priscillian, wrote an apology in pompous and mongrel language. But after the death of his friends, overcome by the tediousness of exile, he changed his mind, as it is written in Holy Scripture " the dog returned to his vomit," and married a nun, a virgin dedicated to Christ.

CHAPTER CXXIV.

Ambrose[5] bishop of Milan, at the present time is still writing. I withhold my judgment of him, because he is still alive, fearing either to praise or blame lest in the one event, I should be blamed for adulation, and in the other for speaking the truth.

CHAPTER CXXV.

Evagrius,[1] bishop of Antioch, a man of remarkably keen mind, while he was yet presbyter read me various treatises on various topics, which he had not yet published. He translated also the *Life of the blessed Anthony* from the Greek of Athanasius into our language.

CHAPTER CXXVI.

Ambrose[2] of Alexandria, pupil of Didymus, wrote a long work *On doctrines* against Apollinaris, and as some one has lately informed me, *Commentaries on Job*. He is still living.

CHAPTER CXXVII.

Maximus[3] the philosopher, born at Alexandria, ordained bishop at Constantinople and deposed, wrote a remarkable work *On faith* against the Arians and gave it to the Emperor Gratianus, at Milan.

CHAPTER CXXVIII.

Gregory[4] bishop of Nyssa, the brother of Basil of Caesarea, a few years since read to Gregory Nazianzan and myself a work against Eunomius. He is said to have also written many other works, and to be still writing.

CHAPTER CXXIX.

John,[5] presbyter of the church at Antioch, a follower of Eusebius of Emesa and Diodorus, is said to have composed many books, but of these I have only read his *On the priesthood*.

CHAPTER CXXX.

Gelasius,[6] bishop of Caesarea in Palestine after Euzoius, is said to write more or less in carefully polished style, but not to publish his works.

CHAPTER CXXXI.

Theotimus,[7] bishop of Tomi, in Scythia, has published brief and epigrammatical treatises, in the form of dialogues, and in olden style. I hear that he is now writing other works.

---

1 Bishop 360, died before 396.
2 Flourished 379, condemned 380, died 385.
3 Died 385.
4 End of 4th Century.
5 Born about 340, baptized 374, died 397.

1 Bishop of Antioch, 388, died 393.
2 Died after 392.
3 A Cynic. Bishop 379.
4 Born 339-2, bishop 372, deposed 376, restored 378, died after 394.
5 John Chrysostom born at Antioch about 347, at Constantinople 398, deposed 403, died 407.
6 Bishop 379, died 394-5.
7 Bishop of Tomes? 392-403.

CHAPTER CXXXII.

DEXTER,[1] son of Pacianus whom I mentioned above, distinguished in his generation and devoted to the Christian faith, has, I am told, written a *Universal History*, which I have not yet read.

CHAPTER CXXXIII.

AMPHILOCHIUS,[2] bishop of Iconium, recently read to me a book *On the Holy Spirit*, arguing that He is God, that He is to be worshipped, and that He is omnipotent.

CHAPTER CXXXIV.

SOPHRONIUS,[3] a man of superlative learning, wrote while yet a lad, *In praise of Bethlehem*, and recently a notable volume, *On the overthrow of Serapis*, and also to Eustachius, *On virginity*, and a *Life of Hilarion the monk*. He rendered short works of mine into Greek in a very finished style, the *Psalter* also, and the *Prophets*, which I translated from Hebrew into Latin.

CHAPTER CXXXV.

I, JEROME,[4] son of Eusebius, of the city of Strido, which is on the border of Dalmatia and Pannonia and was overthrown by the Goths, up to the present year, that is, the fourteenth of the Emperor Theodosius, have written the following: *Life of Paul the monk*, one book of *Letters to different persons*, an *Exhortation to Heliodorus*, *Controversy of Luciferianus and Orthodoxus*, *Chronicle of universal history*, *28 homilies*

of *Origen on Jeremiah and Ezekiel*, which I translated from Greek into Latin, *On the Seraphim*, *On Osanna*, *On the prudent and the prodigal sons*, *On three questions of the ancient law*, *Homilies on the Song of Songs* two, *Against Helvidius*, *On the perpetual virginity of Mary*, To Eustochius, *On maintaining virginity*, one book of *Epistles to Marcella*, a consolatory letter to Paula *On the death of a daughter*, three books of *Commentaries on the epistle of Paul to the Galatians*, likewise three books of *Commentaries on the epistle to the Ephesians*, *On the epistle to Titus* one book, *On the epistle to Philemon* one, *Commentaries on Ecclesiastes*, one book of *Hebrew questions on Genesis*, one book *On places in Judea*, one book of *Hebrew names*, *Didymus on the Holy Spirit*, which I translated into Latin one book, *39 homilies on Luke*,[1] *On Psalms 10 to 16*, seven books, *On the captive Monk*, *The Life of the blessed Hilarion*. I translated the *New Testament* from the Greek, and the *Old Testament* from the Hebrew,[2] and how many *Letters* I have written *To Paula and Eustochius* I do not know, for I write daily. I wrote moreover, two books of *Explanations on Micah*, one book *On Nahum*, two books *On Habakkuk*, one *On Zephaniah*, one *On Haggai*, and many others *On the prophets*, which are not yet finished, and which I am still at work upon.[3]

---

[1] Flavius Lucius Dexter flourished 395.
[2] Amphilochius of Cappadocia, bishop 375, died about 400.
[3] Flourished 392. Author also of Greek translation of Jerome's Illustrious **Men**?
[4] Born 331, died 420.

[1] *39 homilies*, T 25 30 Her.; *39 homilies of Origen* A H 31 e a etc.
[2] *The Old Testament from the Hebrew* A H 30 31 a e; omit T 25 Her.
[3] There are many brief additions to the chapter on Jerome himself, the most common one (B C D I S V W X Y Z 1 2 4 5 6 7 9 11 12 14 15 17 19 20 21 26 27 28 33 42 m o p r t u v y z) being " Two books *Against Jovinian* and an *Apology* addressed to Pammachus." Some add also " and an *Epitaphium*." A and k give a long additional account of Jerome.

III. GENNADIUS

LIST OF THE AUTHORS WHOM GENNADIUS ADDED, AFTER THE DEATH OF THE BLESSED JEROME [1]

1. James; surnamed the Wise.
2. Julius, bishop of Rome.
3. Paulonas the presbyter.
4. Vitellius the African.
5. Macrobius the presbyter.
6. Heliodorus the presbyter.
7. Pachomius the presbyter-monk.
8. Theodorus, his successor.
9. Oresiesis the monk.
10. Macarius the monk.
11. Evagrius the monk.
12. Theodorus the presbyter.
13. Prudentius.
14. Audentius the bishop.
15. Commodianus.
16. Faustinus the presbyter.
17. Rufinus the presbyter.
18. Tichonius the African.
19. Severus the presbyter.
20. Antiochus the bishop.
21. Severianus the bishop.
22. Nicaeas the bishop.
23. Olympius the bishop.
24. Bachiarius.
25. Sabbatius the bishop.
26. Isaac.
27. Ursinus.
28. Another Macarius.
29. Heliodorus the presbyter.
30. John, bishop of Constantinople.
31. John, another bishop.
32. Paulus the bishop.
33. Helvidius.
34. Theophilus the bishop.
35. Eusebius the bishop.
36. Vigilantius the presbyter.
37. Simplicianus the bishop.
38. Vigilius the bishop.
39. Augustine the bishop.
40. Orosius the presbyter.
41. Maximus the bishop.
42. Petronius the bishop.
43. Pelagius the heresiarch.
44. Innocentius the bishop.
45. Caelestius, follower of Pelagius.
46. Julianus the bishop.
47. Lucianus the presbyter.
48. Avitus the presbyter.
49. Paulinus the bishop.
50. Eutropius the presbyter.
51. Another Evagrius.
52. Vigilius the deacon.
53. Atticus the holy bishop.
54. Nestorius the heresiarch.
55. Caelestinus the bishop.
56. Theodorus the bishop.
57. Fastidius the bishop.
58. Cyrillus the bishop.
59. Timotheus the bishop.
60. Leporius the presbyter.
61. Victorinus the rhetorician.
62. Cassianus the deacon.
63. Philippus the presbyter.
64. Eucherius the bishop.
65. Vincentius the Gaul.
66. Syagrius.
67. Isaac the presbyter.
68. Salvianus the presbyter.
69. Paulinus the bishop.
70. Hilarius the bishop.
71. Leo the bishop.
72. Mochimus the presbyter.
73. Timotheus the bishop.
74. Asclepius the bishop.
75. Peter the presbyter.
76. Paul the presbyter.
77. Pastor the bishop.
78. Victor the bishop.
79. Voconius the bishop.
80. Musaeus the presbyter.
81. Vincentius the presbyter.
82. Cyrus the monk.
83. Samuel the presbyter.
84. Claudianus the presbyter.
85. Prosper.
86. Faustus the bishop.
87. Servus Dei the bishop.
88. Victorius.
89. Theodoritus the bishop.
90. Gennadius the bishop.
91. Theodulus the presbyter.
92. John the presbyter.
93. Sidonius the bishop.
94. Gelasius the bishop.
95. Honoratus the bishop.
96. Cerealis the bishop.
97. Eugenius the bishop.
98. Pomerius the bishop.
99. Gennadius.

---

[1] *List . . . Jerome.* This is in a few mss. only.

CHAPTER I.

JAMES,[1] surnamed the Wise, was bishop of Nisibis the famous city of the Persians and one of the confessors under Maximinus the persecutor. He was also one of those who, in the Nicean council, by their opposition overthrew the Arian perversity of the Homoousia. That the blessed Jerome mentions this man in his *Chronicle* as a man of great virtues and yet does not place him in his catalogue of writers, will be easily explained if we note that of the three or four Syrians whom he mentions he says that he read them translated into the Greek. From this it is evident that, at that period, he did not know the Syriac language or literature, and therefore he did not know a writer who had not yet been translated into another language. All his writings are contained in twenty-six books namely *On faith, Against all heresies, On charity towards all, On fasting, On prayer, On particular affection towards our neighbor, On the resurrection, On the life after death, On humility, On penitence,[2] On satisfaction, On virginity, On the worth[3] of the soul, On circumcision, On the blessed grapes, On the saying in Isaiah,* "the grape cluster shall not be destroyed," *That Christ is the son of God and consubstantial with the Father, On chastity, Against the Nations, On the construction of the tabernacle, On the conversation of the nations, On the Persian kingdom, On the persecution of the Christians.* He composed also a *Chronicle* of little interest indeed to the Greeks, but of great reliability in that it is constructed only on the authority of the Divine Scriptures. It shuts the mouths of those who, on some daring guess, idly philosophize concerning the advent of Antichrist, or of our Lord. This man died in the time of Constantius and according to the direction of his father Constantine was buried within the walls of Nisibis, for the protection evidently of the city, and it turned out as Constantine had expected. For many years after, Julian having entered Nisibis and grudging either the glory of him who was buried there or the faith of Constantine, whose family he persecuted on account of this envy, ordered the remains of the saint to be carried out of the city, and a few months later, as a matter of public policy, the Emperor Jovian who succeeded Julian, gave over to the barbarians the city which, with the adjoining territory, is subject unto the Persian rule until this day.

CHAPTER II.

JULIUS,[1] bishop of Rome, wrote to one Dionysius a single epistle *On the incarnation of Our Lord*, which at that time was regarded as useful against those who asserted that, as by incarnation there were two persons in Christ, so also there were two natures, but now this too is regarded as injurious for it nourishes the Eutychian and Timothean heresies.

CHAPTER III.

PAULONAS,[2] the Presbyter, disciple of the blessed deacon Ephraim a man of very energetic character and learned in the holy scriptures was distinguished among the doctors of the church while his master was still living and especially as an extemporaneous orator. After the death of his master, overcome by love of reputation, separating himself from the church, he wrote many things opposed to the faith. The blessed Ephraim when on the point of death is reported to have said to him as he stood by his side — See to it, Paulonas that you do not yield yourself to your own ideas, but when you shall think that you understand God wholly, believe that you have not known, — for he felt beforehand from the studies or the words of Paulonus, that he was investigating new things, and was stretching out his mind to the illimitable, whence also he frequently called him the new Bardesanes.

CHAPTER IV.

VITELLIUS[3] the African, defending the Donatist schism wrote *Why the servants of God are hated by the world*, in which, except in speaking of us as persecutors, he published excellent doctrine. He wrote also *Against the nations* and against us as traditors of the Holy Scriptures in times of persecution, and wrote much *On ecclesiastical procedure.* He was distinguished during the reign of Constans son of the emperor Constantinus.

CHAPTER V.

MACROBIUS[4] the Presbyter was likewise as I learned from the writings of Optatus, afterwards secretly bishop of the Donatians in Rome. He wrote, having been up to this

---

1 Became bishop before 325, died after 350.
2 *On penitence.* A few mss. read " patience " for " penitence " but the only one which the translator has been able to find which gives both is one at Wolfenbüttel dated 1460, nor is it in the earliest editions (e.g.) Nürn. Koburger 1495, Paris 1512). But the later editions (Fabricius, Herding) have both.
3 *worth*, mss. generally; *feeling*, editions generally.

1 Bishop (Pope) 337, died 352.   3 Fourth century.
2 Flourished 370.   4 Bishop about 370.

time a presbyter in the church of God, a work *To confessors and virgins*, a work of ethics indeed, but of very necessary doctrine as well and fortified with sentiments well fitted for the preservation of chastity. He was distinguished first in our party in Africa and afterwards in his own, that is among the Donatians or Montanists at Rome.

CHAPTER VI.

HELIODORUS[1] the Presbyter wrote a book entitled *An introductory treatise on the nature of things*, in which he showed that the beginning of things was one, that nothing was coaeval with God, that God was not the creator of evil, but in such wise the creator of all good, that matter, which is used for[2] evil, was created by God after evil was discovered, and that nothing material whatever can be regarded as established in any other way than by God, and that there was no other creator than God, who, when by His foreknowledge He knew that nature was to be changed,[3] warned of punishment.

CHAPTER VII.

PACHOMIUS[4] the monk, a man endowed with apostolic grace both in teaching and in performing miracles, and founder of the Egyptian monasteries, wrote an *Order of discipline* suited to both classes of monks, which he received by angelic dictation. He wrote letters also to the associated bishops of his district, in an alphabet concealed by mystic sacraments so as to surpass customary human knowledge and only manifest to those of special grace or desert, that is *To the Abbot Cornelius* one, *To the Abbot Syrus* one, and one *To the heads of all monasteries* exhorting that, gathered together to one very ancient monastery which is called in the Egyptian language Bau, they should celebrate the day of the Passover together as by everlasting law. He urged likewise in another letter that on the day of remission, which is celebrated in the month of August, the chief bishops should be gathered together to one place, and wrote one other letter to the brethren who had been sent to work outside the monasteries.

CHAPTER VIII.

THEODORUS,[5] successor to the grace and the headship of the above mentioned Abbot Pachomius, addressed to other monasteries letters written in the language of Holy Scripture, in which nevertheless he frequently mentions his master and teacher Pachomius and sets forth his doctrine and life as examples. This he had been taught he said by an Angel that he himself might teach again. He likewise exhorts them to remain by the purpose of their heart and desire, and to restore to harmony and unity those who, a dissension having arisen after the death of the Abbot, had broken the unity by separating themselves from the community. Three hortatory epistles of his are extant.

CHAPTER IX.

ORESIESIS[1] the monk, the colleague of both Pachomius and Theodorus, a man learned to perfection in Scripture,[2] composed a book seasoned with divine salt and formed of the essentials of all monastic discipline and to speak moderately, in which almost the whole Old and New Testament is found set forth in compact dissertations — all, at least, which relates to the special needs of monks. This he gave to his brethren almost on the very day of his death leaving, as it were, a legacy.

CHAPTER X.

MACARIUS,[3] the Egyptian monk, distinguished for his miracles and virtues, wrote one letter which was addressed to the younger men of his profession. In this he taught them that he could serve God perfectly who, knowing the condition of his creation, should devote himself to all labours, and by wrestling against every thing which is agreeable in this life, and at the same time imploring the aid of God would attain also to natural purity and obtain continence, as a well merited gift of nature.

CHAPTER XI.

EVAGRIUS[4] the monk, the intimate disciple of the above mentioned Macarius, educated in[5] sacred and profane literature and distinguished, whom the book which is called the *Lives of the fathers* mentions as a most continent and erudite man, wrote many things of use to monks among which are these: *Suggestions against the eight principal sins*. He was first to mention or among the first at least to teach these setting against them eight books taken from the testimony of the Holy Scriptures only, after the example of our Lord, who always met

---

[1] About 360.
[2] *Used for* T 35 31 a e 21; *inclined to* 30? ? Fabr. Her.
[3] *changed* A T 25 30 31 a e 21 10 Bamb. Bern. Gemblac. Sigberg. Guelfenb.; *given over to death* Fabr. Her. etc.
[4] Born about 292, died 348.   [5] Born about 314, died 367.

[1] Died about 380.
[2] *Scripture* 25 30 a e 10 : *Holy Scriptures* A T 31 21.
[3] Born about 300, died 390 (391).
[4] Born 345, died 399.
[5] *educated in* T 31 e Her.; omit A 25 30 a.

his tempter with quotations from Scripture, so that every suggestion, whether of the devil or of depraved nature had a testimony against it. This work I have, under instructions, translated into Latin translating with the same simplicity which I found in the Greek. He composed also a book of *One hundred sentiments* for those living simply as anchorites, arranged by chapters, and one of *Fifty sentiments* for the erudite and studious, which I first translated into Latin. The former one, translated before, I restored, partly by retranslating and partly by emendation, so as to represent the true meaning of the author, because I saw that the translation was vitiated and confused by time. He composed also a doctrine of the common-life suited to Cenobites and Synodites,[1] and to the virgin consecrated to God, a little book suitable to her religion and sex. He published also a few collections of opinions very obscure and, as he himself says of them, only to be understood by the hearts of monks, and these likewise I published in Latin. He lived to old age, mighty in signs and miracles.

CHAPTER XII.

THEODORUS,[2] presbyter of the church at Antioch, a cautious investigator and clever of tongue, wrote against the Apollinarians and Anomians *On the incarnation of the Lord*, fifteen books containing as many as fifteen thousand verses, in which he showed by the clearest reasoning and by the testimony of Scripture that just as the Lord Jesus had a plenitude of deity, so he had a plenitude of humanity. He taught also that man consists only of two substances, soul and body and that sense and spirit are not different substances, but inherent inborn faculties of the soul through which it is inspired and has rationality and through which it makes the body capable of feeling. Moreover the fourteenth book of this work treats wholly of the uncreated and alone incorporeal and ruling nature of the holy Trinity and of the rationality of animals which he explains in a devotional spirit, on the authority of Holy Scriptures. In the fifteenth volume he confirms and fortifies the whole body of his work by citing the traditions of the fathers.

CHAPTER XIII.

PRUDENTIUS,[3] a man well versed in secular literature, composed a *Trocheum*[1] of selected persons from the whole Old and New Testament. He wrote a commentary also, after the fashion of the Greeks, *On the six days of creation* from creation of the world until the creation of the first man and his fall. He wrote also short books which are entitled in the Greek, *Apotheosis, Psychomachia* and *Hamartigenia*, that is *On divinity, On spiritual conflict, On the origin of sin.* He wrote also *In praise of martyrs*, an invitation to martyrdom in one book citing several as examples and another of *Hymns*, but specially directed *Against Symmachus*[2] who defended idolatry, from which we learn that Palatinus was a soldier.

CHAPTER XIV.

AUDENTIUS,[3] bishop of Spain, wrote a book against the Manicheans, Sabellians and Arians and very particularly against the Photinians who are now called Bonosiacians. This book he entitled *On faith against heretics*, and in it he showed the Son to have been cöeternal with the Father and that He did not receive the beginning of his deity from God the Father, at the time when conceived by the act of God, he was born of the Virgin Mary his mother in true humanity.

CHAPTER XV.

COMMODIANUS,[4] while he was engaged in secular literature read also our writings and, finding opportunity, accepted the faith. Having become a Christian thus and wishing to offer the fruit of his studies to Christ the author of his salvation, he wrote, in barely tolerable semi-versified language, *Against the pagans*, and because he was very little acquainted with our literature he was better able to overthrow their [doctrine] than to establish ours. Whence also, contending against them concerning the divine counterpromises, he discoursed in a sufficiently wretched and so to speak, gross fashion, to their stupefaction and our despair. Following Tertullian, Lactantius and Papias as authorities he adopted and incul-

---

1 *Synodites* a kind of monks.
2 Theodore of Mopsuesta (?), born at Antioch (?) about 350, died 428.
3 Born at Saragossa 348, was at Rome in 405, died in Spain 408?

1 *Trocheum.* There is much controversy over the word, some maintaining that it should be Dittochaeon= "the double food or double testament" (Lock in Smith and Wace) or Diptychon. It is a description of a series of pictures from the Bible. The mss. read Trocheum a. e.; Troceum T 25; Trocetum 30; Trocleum A; Tropeum 31. A recent monograph on the subject has not yet come to hand.
2 *Symmachus.* Two works are here confused, the work against Symmachus, and the Cathemerinon hymns, in the preface to which the quotation occurs.
3 Bishop of Toledo about 390. (Chevalier) or in the reign of Constantius (Ceillier), 370 (Hoefer).
4 Flourished about 270. There is wide variety of opinion respecting this date, some placing as early as 250 and some nearly one hundred years later.

cated in his students good ethical principles and especially a voluntary love of poverty.

CHAPTER XVI.

FAUSTINUS[1] the presbyter wrote to Queen Flaccilla seven books *Against the Arians and Macedonians*, arguing and convicting them by the testimonies of the very Scriptures which they used, in perverted meaning, for blasphemy. He wrote also a book which, together with a certain presbyter named Marcellinus, he addressed to the emperors Valentinianus, Theodosius and Arcadius, in defence of their fellow Christians. From this it appears that he acquiesced in the Luciferian schism, in that in this same book he blames Hilary of Poitiers and Damasus, bishop of Rome, for giving ill-advised counsel to the church, advising that the apostate[2] bishops should be received into communion for the sake of restoring the peace. For it was as displeasing to the Luciferians to receive the bishops who in the Ariminian council had communed with Arius, as it was to the Novatians to receive the penitent apostates.

CHAPTER XVII.

RUFINUS,[3] presbyter of the church at Aquileia, was not the least among the doctors of the church and had a fine talent for elegant translation from Greek into Latin. In this way he opened to the Latin speaking church the greater part of the Greek literature; translating the works of Basil of Caesarea in Cappadocia, Gregory Nazianzan, that most eloquent man, the *Recognitions* of Clement of Rome, the *Church history* of Eusebius of Caesarea in Palestine, the *Sentences* of Xystus,[4] the *Sentences* of Evagrius and the work of Pamphilus Martyr *Against the mathematicians*. Whatever among all these which are read by the Latins have prefatory matter, have been translated by Rufinus, but those which are without Prologue have been translated by some one else who did not choose to write a prologue. Not all of Origen, however, is his work, for Jerome translated some which are identified by his prologue. On his own account, the same Rufinus, ever through the grace of God published an *Exposition of the Apostles' creed* so excellent that other expositions are regarded as of no account in comparison. He also wrote in a threefold sense, that is, the historical, moral and mystical sense, on Jacob's blessing on

the patriarchs. He wrote also many epistles exhorting to fear of God, among which those which he addressed to Proba are preeminent. He added also a tenth and eleventh book to the ecclesiastical history which we have said was written by Eusebius and translated by him. Moreover he responded to a detractor of his works, in two volumes, arguing and proving that he exercised his talent with the aid of the Lord and in the sight of God, for the good of the church, while he, on the other hand, incited by jealousy had taken to polemics.

CHAPTER XVIII.

TICHONIUS,[1] an African by nationality was, it is said, sufficiently learned in sacred literature, not wholly unacquainted with secular literature and zealous in ecclesiastical affairs. He wrote books *On internal war* and *Expositions of various causes* in which for the defence of his friends, he cites the ancient councils and from all of which[2] he is recognized to have been a Donatist. He composed also eight *Rules for investigating and ascertaining the meaning of the Scriptures*, compressing them into one volume. He also expounded the Apocalypse of John entire, regarding nothing in it in a carnal sense, but all in a spiritual sense. In this exposition he maintained the angelical nature[3] to be corporeal, moreover he doubts that there will be a reign of the righteous on earth for a thousand years after the resurrection, or that there will be two resurrections of the dead in the flesh, one of the righteous and the other of the unrighteous, but maintains that there will be one simultaneous resurrection of all, at which shall arise even the aborted and the deformed lest any living human being, however deformed, should be lost. He makes such distinction to be sure, between the two resurrections as to make the first, which he calls the apocalypse of the righteous, only to take place in the growth of the church where, justified by faith, they are raised from the dead bodies of their sins through baptism to the service of eternal life, but the second, the general resurrection of all men in the flesh. This man flourished at the same period with the above mentioned Rufinus during the reign of Theodosius and his sons.

CHAPTER XIX.

SEVERUS[4] the presbyter, surnamed Sul-

---

[1] Flourished about 384.
[2] *Apostate* = prevaricatores.
[3] Born 345, at Jerusalem about 390, died 410.
[4] *Xystus* T 25 30 e; Sextus A 31 a Xystus of Rome T Her.

[1] 399.
[2] *from all of which* A 25 30 31 a; *from which* e T Her.
[3] *angelical nature* etc., "that the human body is an abode of angels" (angelicam stationem corpus esse) Phillott, in Smith and Wace.
[4] Sulpicius Severus born after 353, died about 410.

pitius, of the province of Aquitania, a man distinguished by his birth, by his excellent literary work, by his devotion to poverty and by his humility, beloved also of the sainted men Martin bishop of Tours and Paulinus Nolanus, wrote small books which are far from despicable. He wrote to his sister many *Letters* exhorting to love of God and contempt of the world. These are well known. He wrote two to the above mentioned Paulinus Nolanus and others to others, but because, in some, family matters are included, they have not been collected for publication. He composed also a *Chronicle*, and wrote also to the profit of many, a *Life of the holy Martin*, monk and bishop, a man famous for signs and wonders and virtues.[1] He also wrote a *Conference between Postumianus and Gallus*, in which he himself acted as mediator and judge of the debate. The subject matter was the manner of life of the oriental monks and of St. Martin—a sort of dialogue in two divisions. In the first of these he mentions a decree of the bishops at the synod of Alexandria in his own time to the effect that Origen is to be read, though cautiously, by those who are wise, for the good that is in him, and is to be rejected by the less able on account of the evil. In his old age, he was led astray by the Pelagians, and recognizing the guilt of much speaking, kept silent until his death, in order that by penitent silence he might atone for the sin which he had contracted by speaking.

CHAPTER XX.

ANTIOCHUS[2] the bishop, wrote one long[3] volume *Against avarice* and he composed a homily, full of[4] godly penitence and humility *On the healing of the blind man* whose sight was restored by the Saviour. He died during the reign of the emperor Arcadius.

CHAPTER XXI.

SEVERIANUS,[5] bishop of the church of Gabala, was learned in the Holy Scriptures and a wonderful preacher of homilies. On this account he was frequently summoned by the bishop John and the emperor Arcadius to preach a sermon at Constantinople. I have read his *Exposition of the epistle to the Galatians* and a most attractive little work *On baptism and the feast of Epiphany.* He died in the reign of Theodosius, his son by baptism.

CHAPTER XXII.

NICEAS,[1][2] bishop of the city of Romatia, composed, in simple and clear language, six books of *Instruction for neophites.* The first of these contains, How candidates who seek to obtain grace of baptism ought to act, the second, On the errors of relationship, in which he relates that not far from his own time a certain Melodius, father of a family, on account of his liberality and Garadius[3] a peasant, on account of his bravery, were placed, by the heathen, among the gods. A third book *On faith in one sovereign*, a fourth *Against genealogy*,[4] a fifth *On the creed*, a sixth *On the sacrifice of the paschal lamb.* He addressed a work also *To the fallen virgin*, an incentive to amendment for all who have fallen.

CHAPTER XXIII.

OLYMPIUS[5] the bishop, a Spaniard by nationality, wrote a book of faith against those who blame nature and not the will, showing that evil was introduced into nature not by creation but by disobedience.

CHAPTER XXIV.

BACHIARIUS,[6] a Christian philosopher, prompt and ready and minded to devote his time to God, chose travel as a means of preserving the integrity of his purpose. He is said to have published acceptable small works but I have only read one of them, a work *On faith*, in which he justified himself to the chief priest of the city, defending himself against those who complained and misrepresented his travel, and asserting that he undertook his travel not through fear of men but for the sake of God, that going forth from his land and kindred he might become a cö-heir with Abraham the patriarch.

CHAPTER XXV.

SABBATIUS,[7] bishop of the Gallican province, at the request of a certain virgin, chaste and devoted to Christ, Secunda by name, composed a book *On faith* against Marcion and Valentinus his teacher, also

---

[1] *Virtues* or miracles.
[2] Bishop of Ptolemais (Acre) about 400, died about 408.
[3] *long.* a 25 30 31; *great* A T e.
[4] *full of* A 25 30 31 a e; *on* T 21 Her.
[5] Severianus of Emesa. Bishop 400-3, died after 408.

[1] Nicetas Bishop of "Remessianen" or Romaciana or Remetiana in Dacia before 392, died after 414.
[2] T and 31 read *Niceta* or *Nicetas*, but other mss. *Niceas* and so Fabricius and Her.
[3] *Garadius* A T 31 a e; *Gadarius* 25 30 Her.
[4] *Genealogy* T 25 30 21; *genethlogiam* 31 a e.
[5] Bishop of Barcelona about 316.
[6] A Spanish bishop. Flourished about 400.
[7] St. Servais, Bishop of Tongres 338, died at Maestricht 384. The patron saint of Maestricht. Supposed by some to be the same as Phebadius (Faegadius, Phaebadius, Segatius, Sabadius Phitadius (called in Gascony Fiari)? bishop of Agen. Flourished 440 (Cave).

against Eunomius and his Master Aëtius, showing, both by reason and by testimony of the Scriptures, that the origin of the deity is one, that the Author of his eternity and the Creator of the earth out of nothing, are one and the same, and likewise concerning Christ, that he did not appear as man in a phantasm but had real flesh through which eating, drinking, weary and weeping, suffering, dying, rising again he was demonstrated to be man indeed. For Marcion and Valentinus had been opposed to these opinions asserting that the origin of Deity is twofold and that Christ came in a phantasm. To Aëtius indeed and Eunomius his disciple, he showed that the Father and Son are not of two natures and equal in divinity but of one essence and the one from the other, that is the Son from the Father, the one cöeternal with the other, which belief Aëtius and Eunomius opposed.

CHAPTER XXVI.

ISAAC[1] wrote *On the Holy Trinity* and a book *On the incarnation of the Lord*, writing in a very obscure style of argument and involved language, maintaining that three persons exist in one Deity, in such wise that any thing may be peculiar to each which another does not have, that is to say, that the Father has this peculiarity that He, himself without source, is the source of others, that the Son has this peculiarity, that, begotten, He is not posterior to the begetter, that the Holy Spirit has this peculiarity, that He is neither made nor begotten but nevertheless is from another. Of the incarnation of the Lord indeed, he writes that the person of the Son of God is believed to be one, while yet there are two natures existing in him.

CHAPTER XXVII.

URSINUS[2] the monk wrote against those who say that heretics should be rebaptized, teaching[3] that it is not legitimate nor honouring God, that those should be rebaptized who have been baptized either in the name of Christ alone or in the name of the Father and of the Son and of the Holy Spirit, though the formula has been used in a vitiated sense. He considers that after the simple confession of the Holy Trinity and of Christ, the imposition of the hands of the catholic priest is sufficient for salvation.

CHAPTER XXVIII.

MACARIUS[1] another monk, wrote at Rome books *Against the mathematicians*, in which labour he sought the comfort of oriental writings.

CHAPTER XXIX.

HELIODORUS,[2] presbyter of Antioch, published an excellent volume gathered from Holy Scriptures *On Virginity*.

CHAPTER XXX.

[JOHN[3][4] bishop of Constantinople, a man of marvelous knowledge and in sanctity of life, in every respect worthy of imitation, wrote many and very useful works for all who are hastening to divine things. Among them are the following *On compunction of soul* one book, *That no one is injured except by himself*, an excellent volume *In praise of the blessed Paul the apostle*, *On the excesses and ill reputation* of Eutropius a praetorian prefect and many others, as I have said, which may be found by the industrious.]

CHAPTER XXXI.

ANOTHER John,[5][6] bishop of Jerusalem, wrote a book against those who disparaged his studies, in which he shows that he follows the genius of Origen not his creed.

CHAPTER XXXII.

PAUL the bishop wrote a short work *On penitence* in which he lays down this law for penitents; that they ought to repent for their sins in such manner that they be not beyond measure overwhelmed with despairing sadness.

CHAPTER XXXIII.

HELVIDIUS,[7] a disciple of Auxentius and imitator of Symmachus, wrote, indeed, with zeal for religion but not according to knowledge, a book, polished neither in language nor in reasoning, a work in which he so attempted to twist the meaning of the Holy Scriptures to his own perversity, as to venture to assert on their testimony that Joseph and Mary, after the nativity of our Lord, had children who were called brothers of the

---

[1] Converted Jew, flourished about 385.
[2] Flourished above 440.
[3] Omit "*teaching*" e T 31.

[1] Flourished fifth century. [2] Flourished about 440.
[3] John Chrysostom born at Antioch about 347, bishop of Constantinople 398, deposed 403, died 407.
[4] This whole paragraph is omitted by most mss., though T and 21 have it.
[5] Bishop 386, died 417.
[6] *John* A 25 30 31 a e; *another John* [T ?] 21.
[7] Fourth century.

Lord. In reply to his perverseness Jerome, published a book against him, well filled with scripture proofs.[1]

CHAPTER XXXIV.

THEOPHILUS,[2] bishop of the church[3] of Alexandria, wrote one great volume *Against Origen* in which he condemns pretty nearly all his sayings and himself likewise, at the same time saying that he was not original in his views but derived them from the ancient fathers especially from Heraclas, that he was deposed from[4] the office of presbyter driven from the church and compelled to fly from the city. He also wrote *Against the Anthropomorphites*, heretics who say that God has the human form and members, confuting in a long discussion and arguing by testimonies of Divine Scripture and convincing. He shows that, according to the belief of the Fathers, God is to be thought of as incorporal, not formed with any suggestion of members at all, and therefore there is nothing like Him among created things in substance, nor has the incorruptibility nor unchangeableness nor incorporeality of his nature been given to any one but that all intellectual natures are corporeal, all corruptible, all mutable, that He alone should not be subject to corruptibility or changeableness, who alone has immortality and life. Likewise the return of the paschal feast which the great council at Nicea had found would take place after ninety years at the same time, the same month and day adding some observations on the festival and explanations he gave to the emperor Theodosius. I have read also three books *On faith*, which bear his name but, as their language is not like his, I do not very much think they are by him.

CHAPTER XXXV.

EUSEBIUS[5] wrote *On the mystery of our Lord's cross* and the faithfulness of the apostles, and especially of Peter, gained by virtue of the cross.

CHAPTER XXXVI.

VIGILANTIUS,[6] a citizen of Gaul, had the church of Barcelona. He wrote also with some zeal for religion but, overcome by the desire for human praise and presuming above his strength, being a man of polished language but not practised in the meaning of

Scriptures, he expounded the vision of Daniel in a perverted sense and said other frivolous things which are necessarily mentioned in a catalogue of heretics. [To him also the blessed Jerome the presbyter responded.][1]

CHAPTER XXXVII.

SIMPLICIANUS,[2] the bishop, exhorted Augustine then presbyter, in many letters, that he should exercise his genius and take time for exposition of the Scriptures that, as it were, a new Ambrosius, the task master of Origen might appear. Wherefore also he sent to him many examinations of scriptures. There is also an epistle of his of *Questions* in which he teaches by asking questions as if wishing to learn.

CHAPTER XXXVIII.

VIGILIUS[3] the bishop wrote to one Simplicianus a small book *In praise of martyrs* and an epistle containing the acts of the martyrs in his time among the barbarians.

CHAPTER XXXIX.

AUGUSTINE,[4] of Africa, bishop of Hipporegensis, a man renowned throughout the world for learning both sacred and secular, unblemished in the faith, pure in life, wrote works so many that they cannot all be gathered. For who is there that can boast himself of having all his works, or who reads with such diligence as to read all he has written?[5] As an old man even, he published fifteen books *On the Trinity* which he had begun as a young man. In which, as scripture says, brought into the chamber of the king and adorned with the manifold garment of the wisdom of God, he exhibited a church not having spot or wrinkle or any such thing. In his work *On the incarnation of the Lord* also he manifested a peculiar piety. On the resurrection of the dead he wrote with equal sincerity, and left it to the less able to raise doubts respecting abortions.[6][7]

[1] *In reply* . . . *proofs* A T 25 30 21; omit e 31 a.
[2] Bishop 385, died 412.   [3] *Church* T 21; *city* A 25 30 31 a.
[4] *deposed* 25 31 a e ?; *elect* A 30; *stripped of* T.
[5] Bishop of Milan 451, died 462.
[6] At Jerusalem 394, heretic about 404.

[1] *to him* . . . *responded* A Her.; omit T 25 30 31 a e.
[2] Bishop of Milan 397, died 400.
[3] Bishop of Trent 388, died 405.
[4] Born at Tagaste 354, baptized at Milan 387, bishop of Hippo 395, died 430.
[5] *all he has written* e T A 30 31 a Her.; 25 Fabr. add "wherefore on account of his much speaking Solomon's saying came true that '*In the multitude of words there wanteth not sin.*'" This expression in the editions has been the ground of much comment on Gennadius' Semi-pelagian bias, but it almost certainly does not represent the original form of the text.
[6] *Abortions* "That abortions . . . shall rise again I make bold neither to affirm nor to deny" Augustine De civ. Dei. 22, 13.
[7] T 31 end thus; A omits *and left* . . . *abortions* but adds a few lines of other matter; e adds differing matter; a adds *remained a catholic; 30* adds *remained a catholic and died in the same city — the city which is still called Hypporegensis*; while 25 adds a vast amount.

CHAPTER XL.

OROSIUS,[1] a Spanish presbyter, a man most eloquent and learned in history, wrote eight books against those enemies of the Christians who say that the decay of the Roman State was caused by the Christian religion. In these rehearsing the calamities and miseries and disturbances of wars, of pretty much the whole world from the creation[2] he shows that the Roman Empire owed to the Christian religion its undeserved continuance and the state of peace which it enjoyed for the worship of God.

In the first book he described the world situated within the ever flowing stream of Oceanus and intersected by the Tanais, giving the situations of places, the names, number and customs of nations, the characteristics of various regions, the wars begun and the formation of empires sealed with the blood of kinsmen.

This is the Orosius who, sent by Augustine to Hieronymus to teach the nature of the soul, returning, was the first to bring to the West relics of the blessed Stephen the first martyr then recently found. He flourished almost[3] at the end of the reign of the emperor Honorius.

CHAPTER XLI.

MAXIMUS,[4] bishop of the church at Turin, a man fairly industrious in the study of the Holy Scripture, and good at teaching the people extemporaneously, composed treatises *In praise of the apostles and John the Baptist*, and a *Homily on all the martyrs*. Moreover he wrote many acute comments on passages from the Gospels and the Acts of the Apostles. He wrote also two treatises, *On the life[5] of Saint Eusebius*, bishop of Vercelli, and confessor, and *On Saint Cyprian*, and published a monograph *On the grace of baptism*. I have read his *On avarice, On hospitality, On the eclipse of the moon, On almsgiving, On the saying in Isaiah, Your winedealers mix wine with water, On Our Lord's Passion*, A general treatise *On fasting by the servants of God, On the quadragesimal fast* in particular, and *That there should be no jesting on fast day, On Judas*, the betrayer, *On Our Lord's cross, On His sepulchre, On His resurrection, On the accusation and trial*

of Our Lord before Pontius Pilate, On the Kalends of January, a homily *On the day of Our Lord's Nativity*, also homilies *On Epiphany, On the Passover, On Pentecost*, many also, *On having no fear of carnal foes, On giving thanks after meat, On the repentance of the Ninivites*, and other homilies of his, published[1] on various occasions, whose names I do not remember. He died in the reign of Honorius and Theodosius the younger.

CHAPTER XLII.

PETRONIUS,[2] bishop of Bologna in Italy[3] a man of holy life and from his youth practised in monastic studies, is reputed to have written the *Lives of the Fathers*, to wit of the Egyptian monks, a work which the monks accept as the mirror and pattern of their profession. I have read a treatise which bears his name *On the ordination of bishops*, a work full of good reasoning and notable for its humility, but whose polished style shows it not to have been his, but perhaps, as some say, the work of his father Petronius,[4] a man of great eloquence and learned in secular literature. This I think is to be accepted, for the author of the work describes himself as a praetorian prefect. He died in the reign of Theodosius and Valentinianus.

CHAPTER XLIII.

PELAGIUS[5] the heresiarch, before he was proclaimed a heretic wrote works of practical value for students: three books *On belief in the Trinity*, and one book of *Selections from Holy Scriptures bearing on the Christian life*. This latter was preceded by tables of contents, after the model of Saint Cyprian the martyr. After he was proclaimed heretic, however, he wrote works bearing on his heresy.

CHAPTER XLIV.

INNOCENTIUS,[6] bishop of Rome, wrote the decree which the Western churches passed against the Pelagians and which his successor, Pope Zosimus, afterwards widely promulgated.

CHAPTER XLV.

CAELESTIUS,[7] before he joined Pelagius, while yet a very young man, wrote to his

---

1 Paulus Orosius of Tarragon, the historian, flourished about 413 or 417. His history was begun after 416 and finished in 417.
2 *from the creation* (" from the whole period of the earth ") A 25 30 31 a e; omit T 21 Her.
3 *almost* 25 30 31 a e; omit T A Her.
4 Maximus of Vercelli, bishop of Turin about 415, died 466–470.
5 omit *life* A 30 a.

---

1 *published* T 30 21 Her.; *delivered* A 25 31 a e.
2 Bishop of Bologna 430, died before 350.
3 *in Italy* A 30 31 a e; omit T 25 21 Her.
4 *Petronius* A 25 30 31; omit T a?.
5 At Rome about 400, at Carthage 411, heretic 417.
6 Bishop or " Pope " 402, died 417.
7 Heretic 412–417.

parents three epistles *On monastic life*, written as short books, and containing moral maxims suited to every one who is seeking God, containing no trace of the fault which afterwards appeared but wholly devoted to the encouragement of virtue.

CHAPTER XLVI.

JULIANUS[1] the bishop, a man of vigorous character, learned in the Divine Scriptures, and proficient both in Greek and Latin, was, before he disclosed his participation in the ungodliness of Pelagius, distinguished among the doctors of the church. But afterwards, trying to defend the Pelagian heresy, he wrote four books, *Against Augustine*, the opponent of Pelagius, and then again, eight books more. There is also a book containing a discussion, where each defends his side.

This Julianus, in time of famine and want, attracting many through the alms which he gave, and the glamour of virtue, which they cast around him, associated them with him in his heresy. He died during the reign of Valentinianus, the son of Constantius.

CHAPTER XLVII.

LUCIANUS[2] the presbyter, a holy man to whom, at the time when Honorius and Theodosius were Emperors, God revealed the place of the sepulchre and the remains of Saint Stephen the Protomartyr, wrote out that revelation in Greek, addressing it to all the churches.

CHAPTER XLVIII.

AVITUS[3] the presbyter, a Spaniard by race, translated the above mentioned work of the presbyter Lucianus into Latin, and sent it with his letter annexed, by the hand of Orosius the presbyter, to the Western churches.

CHAPTER XLIX.

PAULINUS,[4] bishop of Nola in Campania, composed many brief works in verse, also a consolatory work to Celsus *On the death of a christian and baptized child*, a sort of epitaph, well fortified with christian hope, also many *Letters to Severus*. and *A panegyric* in prose written before he became bishop, *On victory over tyrants* which was addressed to Theodosius and maintained that victory lay rather in faith and prayer, than in arms. He wrote also a *Sacramentary* and *Hymnal*.

He also addressed many letters to his sister, *On contempt of the world*, and published treatises of different sorts, on various occasions.[1]

The most notable of all his minor works. are the works *On repentance*, and *A general panegyric of all the martyrs*. He lived in the reign of Honorius and Valentinianus, and was distinguished, not only for erudition[2] and holiness of life, but also for his ability to cast out demons.

CHAPTER L.

EUTROPIUS,[3] the presbyter, wrote to two sisters, handmaids of Christ, who had been disinherited by their parents on account of their devotion to chastity and their love for religion, two *Consolatory letters* in the form of small books, written in polished and clear language and fortified not only by argument, but also by testimonies from the Scriptures.

CHAPTER LI.

ANOTHER Evagrius[4] wrote a *Discussion between Simon the Jew and Theophilus the Christian*, a work which is very well known.

CHAPTER LII.

VIGILIUS[5] the deacon, composed out of the traditions of the fathers a *Rule for monks*, which is accustomed to be read in the monastery for the profit of the assembled monks. It is written in condensed and clear language and covers the whole range of monastic duties.

CHAPTER LIII.

ATTICUS[6] bishop of Constantinople, wrote to the princess daughters[7] of the Emperor Arcadius, *On faith and virginity*, a most excellent work, in which he attacks by anticipation the Nestorian doctrine.

CHAPTER LIV.

NESTORIUS[8][9] the heresiarch, was regarded, while presbyter of the church at Antioch, as a remarkable extemporaneous teacher,[10] and

---

[1] Bishop of Eclanum about 416.
[2] Lucianus of Caphargamala, flourished 415.
[3] Avitus of Braga, died 440.
[4] Pontius Meropius (Anicius?) Paulinus, Born at Bordeaux 353 (354?), pupil of Ausonius, baptized before 389, bishop before 410, died 431.

[1] *on various occasions* is omitted by T 31 e.
[2] *erudition* A T 31 a e 21; *observation* 25 30 Her.
[3] Pupil of Augustine about 430.
[4] Pupil of St. Martin of Tours 405.
[5] Flourished about 430.
[6] Bishop of Constantinople 406, died 425.
[7] *Daughters* Pulcheria and her sisters.
[8] Bishop of Constantinople 428, deposed 431, died in the Thebaid about 439.
[9] *Nestorius* 25 30 Her; *Nestor* A T 31 a e 21.
[10] *teacher* A T 30 31 a e; omit 25 Her.

composed a great many treatises on various *Questions*, into which already at that time [1] he infused that subtle evil, which afterwards became the poison of acknowledged impiety, veiled meanwhile by moral exhortation. But afterwards, when commended by his eloquence and abstemiousness he had been made pontiff of the church at Constantinople, showing openly what he had for a long while concealed, he became a declared enemy of the church, and wrote a book *On the incarnation of the Lord*, formed of sixty-two passages from Divine Scripture, used in a perverted meaning. What he maintained in this book may be found in the catalogue of heretics.

CHAPTER LV.

CAELESTINUS,[2] bishop of Rome, addressed a volume to the churches of the East and West, giving an account of the decree of the synod against the above mentioned Nestorius and maintaining that while there are two complete natures in Christ, the person of the Son of God is to be regarded as single. The above mentioned Nestorius was shown to be opposed to this view. Xystus likewise, the successor of Caelestinus, wrote on the same subject and to the same Nestorius and the Eastern bishops, giving the views of the Western bishops against his error.

CHAPTER LVI.

THEODOTUS,[3][4] bishop of Ancyra in Galatia, while at [5] Ephesus, wrote against Nestorius a work of defence and refutation,[6] written, to be sure, in dialectic style, but interwoven with passages from the Holy Scriptures. His method was to make statements and then quote proof texts from the Scriptures.

CHAPTER LVII.

FASTIDIUS,[7] bishop in Britain, wrote to one Fatalis, a book *On the Christian life*, and another *On preserving the estate of virginity*,[8] a work full of sound doctrine, and doing honour to God.

CHAPTER LVIII.

CYRIL,[9] bishop of the church at Alexandria, published various treatises on various *Questions*, and also composed many homilies, which are recommended for preaching by the Greek bishops. Other books of his are ; *On the downfall of the synagogue*, *On faith against the heretics*, and a work directed especially against Nestorius and entitled, *A Refutation*, in which all the secrets of Nestorius are exposed and his published opinions are refuted.

CHAPTER LIX.

TIMOTHEUS,[1] the bishop composed a book *On the nativity of Our Lord according to the flesh*, which is supposed to have been written at Epiphany.

CHAPTER LX.

LEPORIUS,[2] formerly monk afterwards presbyter, relying on purity,[3] through his own free will and unaided effort, instead of depending on the help of God, began to follow the Pelagian doctrine. But having been admonished by the Gallican doctors, and corrected by Augustine in Africa, he wrote a book containing his retraction, in which he both acknowledges his error and returns thanks for his correction. At the same time in correction of his false view of the incarnation of Christ, he presented the Catholic view, acknowledging the single person of the Son of God, and the two natures existing in Christ in his substance.[4]

CHAPTER LXI.

VICTORINUS,[5] a rhetorician of Marseilles, wrote to his son Etherius, a commentary *On Genesis*, commenting, that is, from the beginning of the book to the death of the patriarch Abraham, and published four [6] books in verse, words which have a savour of piety indeed, but, in that he was a man busied with secular literature and quite untrained in the Divine Scriptures, they are of slight weight, so far as ideas are concerned.

He died in the reign of Theodosius and Valentinianus.

CHAPTER LXII.

CASSIANUS,[7] a Scythian by race, ordained deacon by bishop John the Great, at Constantinople, and a presbyter at Marseilles, founded two monasteries, that is to say one for men and one for women, which are still

---

[1] *at that time* A T a e; omit 25 30 31.
[2] Bishop (Pope) of Rome 422, died 432.
[3] Theodotus Bishop of Ancyra 431-8.
[4] *Theodotus* T ? a e; *Theodorus* a 25 30 31 Fabr. Her.
[5] *while at* T 31 e 21; *while formerly at* 25 30 a A?.
[6] *and refutation* A 25 30 a; omit T 31 e 21.
[7] Flourished 420.
[8] *virginity* T 31 e 21; *widowhood* A 25 30 a Fabr. Her.
[9] Born about 376, bishop of Alexandria 412, died 444.

[1] From position evidently flourished before 450.
[2] Flourished 418-430.
[3] *purity* T 31 a e 21; *purity of life* A 25 30.
[4] *in his substance* A T 30 31 a e 21; omit 25 Her.
[5] Claudius Marius Victor (Victorius or Victorinus) of Marseilles died 445.
[6] *four* A T 31 a e; *three* 25 30.
[7] Johannes Cassianus died 450.

standing. He wrote from experience, and in forcible language, or to speak more clearly, with meaning back of his words, and action back of his talk. He covered the whole field of practical directions, for monks of all sorts, in the following works : *On dress,* also *On the canon of prayers,* and the *Usage in the saying of Psalms,* (for these in the Egyptian monasteries, are said day and night), three books. One of *Institutes,* eight books *On the origin, nature and remedies for the eight principal sins,* a book on each sin. He also compiled *Conferences* with the Egyptian fathers, as follows : *On the aim of a monk and his creed, On discretion, On three vocations to the service of God, On the warfare of the flesh against the spirit and the spirit against the flesh, On the nature of all sins, On the slaughter of the saints, On fickleness of mind, On principalities, On the nature of prayer, On the duration of prayer, On perfection, On chastity, On the protection of God, On the knowledge of spiritual things, On the Divine graces, On friendship, On whether to define or not to define, On three ancient kinds of monks and a fourth recently arisen, On the object of cenobites and hermits, On true satisfaction in repentance, On the remission of the Quinquagesimal fast, On nocturnal illusions, On the saying of the apostles, " For the good which I would do, I do not, but the evil which I would not, that I do," On mortification,* and finally at the request of Leo the archdeacon, afterwards bishop of Rome, he wrote seven books against Nestorius, *On the incarnation of the Lord,* and writing this, made an end, both of writing and living, at Marseilles, in the reign of Theodosius and Valentinianus.

CHAPTER LXIII.

PHILIP,[1] the presbyter Jerome's best pupil, published a *Commentary on Job,* written in an unaffected style. I have read his *Familiar letters,* exceedingly witty, exhorting the endurance of poverty and sufferings. He died in the reign of Martianus and Avitus.

CHAPTER LXIV.

EUCHERIUS,[2] bishop of the church at Lyons, wrote to his relative Valerianus, *On contempt for the world and worldly philosophy,* a single letter, written in a style which shows sound learning and reasoning. He wrote also to his sons, Salonius and Veranius, afterward bishops, a discussion *On cer-*

tain obscure passages of Holy Scriptures, and besides, revising and condensing certain works of Saint Cassianus, he compressed them into one volume, and wrote other works suited to ecclesiastical or monastic pursuits. He died in the reign of Valentinianus and Martianus.

CHAPTER LXV.

VINCENTIUS,[1] the Gaul, presbyter in the Monastery on the Island of Lerins, a man learned in the Holy Scriptures and very well informed in matters of ecclesiastical doctrine, composed a powerful disputation, written in tolerably finished and clear language, which, suppressing his name, he entitled *Peregrinus against heretics.* The greater part of the second book of this work having been stolen, he composed a brief reproduction of the substance of the original work, and published in one [book]. He died in the reign of Theodosius and Valentinianus.

CHAPTER LXVI.

SYAGRIUS[2] wrote *On faith,* against the presumptuous words, which heretics assume for the purpose of destroying or superseding the names of the Holy Trinity, for they say that the Father ought not to be called Father, lest the name, Son should harmonize with that of Father, but that he should be called the Unbegotten or the Imperishable and the Absolute, in order that whatever may be distinct from Him in person, may also be separate in nature, showing that the Father, who is unchangeable in nature may be called the Unbegotten, though the Scripture may not call Him so, that the person of the Son is begotten from Him, not made, and that the person of the Holy Spirit proceeds from Him not begotten, and not made. Under the name of this Syagrius I found seven books, entitled *On Faith and the rules of Faith,* but as they did not agree in style, I did not believe they were written by him.

CHAPTER LXVII.

ISAAC,[3] presbyter of the church at Antioch, whose many works cover a long period, wrote in Syriac especially against the Nestorians and Eutychians. He lamented the downfall of Antioch in an elegiac poem, taking up the same strain that Ephraim, the deacon, sounded on the downfall of Nicomedia. He died during the reign of Leo and Majorianus.

---

[1] Died about 455.   [2] Bishop about 435, died 450.

[1] Presbyter 434, died before 450.
[2] Syagrius of Lyons, died 486.
[3] Isaac of Amida (Diarbekir) presbyter died about 460.

CHAPTER LXVIII.

SALVIANUS,[1] presbyter of Marseilles, well informed both in secular and in sacred literature, and to speak without invidiousness, a master among bishops, wrote many things in a scholastic and clear style, of which I have read the following: four books *On the Excellence of virginity*, to Marcellus the presbyter, three books *Against avarice*, five books *On the present judgment*,[2] and one book *On punishment according to desert*, addressed to Salonius the bishop, also one book of *Commentary on* the latter part of the book of *Ecclesiastes*, addressed to Claudius bishop of Vienne, one book of *Epistles*.[3] He also composed one book in verse after the Greek fashion, a sort of *Hexaemeron*, covering the period from the beginning of Genesis to the creation of man, also many *Homilies* delivered to the bishops, and I am sure I do not know how many *On the sacraments*. He is still living at a good old age.

CHAPTER LXIX.

PAULINUS[4] composed treatises *On the beginning of the Quadragesimal*, of which I have read two, *On the Passover Sabbath*, *On obedience*, *On penitence*, *On neophytes*.

CHAPTER LXX.

HILARY,[5] bishop of the church at Arles, a man learned in Holy Scriptures, was devoted to poverty, and earnestly anxious to live in narrow circumstances, not only in religiousness of mind, but also in labour of body. To secure this estate of poverty, this man of noble race and very differently brought up, engaged in farming, though it was beyond his strength, and yet did not neglect spiritual matters. He was an acceptable teacher also, and without regard to persons administered correction to all.[6] He published some few things, brief, but showing immortal genius, and indicating an erudite mind, as well as capacity for vigorous speech; among these that work which is of so great practical value to many, his *Life of Saint Honoratus*, his predecessor. He died during the reign of Valentinianus and Martianus.

CHAPTER LXXI.

LEO,[1] bishop[2] of Rome, wrote a letter *to Flavianus*, bishop of the church at Constantinople, against Eutyches the presbyter, who at that time, on account of his ambition for the episcopate was trying to introduce novelties into the church. In this he advises Flavianus, if Eutyches confesses his error and promises amendment, to receive him, but if he should persist in the course he had entered on, that he should be condemned together with his heresy. He likewise teaches in this epistle and confirms by divine testimony that as the Lord Jesus Christ is to be considered the true son of the Divine Father, so likewise he is to be considered true man with human nature, that is, that he derived a body of flesh from the flesh of the virgin and not as Eutyches asserted, that he showed a body from heaven.[3] He died in the reign of Leo and Majorianus.

CHAPTER LXXII.

MOCHIMUS,[4] the Mesopotamian, a presbyter at Antioch, wrote an excellent book *Against Eutyches*, and is said to be writing others, which I have not yet read.

CHAPTER LXXIII.

TIMOTHEUS,[5][6] when Proterius[7] had been put to death by the Alexandrians, in response to popular clamour, willingly or unwillingly allowed himself to be made bishop by a single bishop in the place of him who had been put to death. And lest he, having been illegally appointed, should be deservedly deposed at the will of the people who had hated Proterius, he pronounced all the bishops of his vicinity to be Nestorians, and boldly presuming to wash out the stain on his conscience by hardihood, wrote a very persuasive book to the Emperor Leo, which he attempted to fortify by testimonies of the Fathers, used in a perverted sense, so far as to show, for the sake of deceiving the emperor and establishing his heresy, that Leo of Rome, pontiff of the city, and the synod of Chalcedon, and all the Western bishops were fundamentally Nestorians. But by the grace of God, the enemy of the church was refuted and overthrown at the Council of Chalcedon. He is said to be living in exile, still an heresiarch,

---

[1] Born about 390, Presbyter about 428, died about 484.
[2] *present judgment* more generally known as *Divine Providence* (De gubernatione Dei.)
[3] *one book of epistles* a 25 30; omit A T 31 e 21.
[4] From position evidently flourished about 450.
[5] Born about 401, bishop 429, died 449.
[6] *correction to all;* Her. adds *work of preaching* but has the support of no good mss.

[1] Leo the Great, Bishop (Pope) 440, died 461.
[2] *bishop:* A 30 31 e have *pontiff*.
[3] T and 21 add after *heaven* " and he addressed another letter on this same subject to the Emperor Leo in whose reign also he died."
[4] Presbyter 457.
[5] Bishop of Alexandria 380, died 385.
[6] *Timotheus* 31 e add Bishop of Alexandria.
[7] Proterius; 25 30 Fabr. Her. add *the bishop*.

and it is most likely so. This book of his for learning's sake, I translated by request of the brethren into Latin and prefixed a caveat.[1]

CHAPTER LXXIV.

ASCLEPIUS,[2] the African, bishop of a large see[3] within the borders of Bagais, wrote against the Arians, and is said to be now writing against the Donatists. He is famous for his extemporaneous teaching.

CHAPTER LXXV.

PETER,[4] presbyter of the church at Edessa, a famous preacher, wrote *Treatises* on various subjects, and *Hymns* after the manner of Saint Ephrem, the deacon.

CHAPTER LXXVI.

PAUL[5] the presbyter, a Pannonian by nationality, as I learned from his own mouth, wrote *On preserving virginity, and contempt for the world*, and the *Ordering of life or the correction of morals*, written in a mediocre style, but flavoured with divine salt. The two books were addressed to a certain noble virgin devoted to Christ, Constantia by name, and in them he mentions Jovinian the heretic and preacher of voluptuousness and lusts, who was so far removed from leading a continent and chaste life, that he belched forth his life in the midst of luxurious banquets.[6]

CHAPTER LXXVII.

PASTOR[7] the bishop composed a short work, written in the form of a creed, and containing pretty much the whole round of Ecclesiastical doctrine in sentences. In this, among other heresies which he anathematizes without giving the names of their authors, he condemns the Priscillians and their author.

CHAPTER LXXVIII.

VICTOR,[8] bishop of Cartenna in Mauritania, wrote one long book against the Arians, which he sent to king Genseric by his followers, as I learned from the preface to the work,[9] and a work *On the repentance of the publican*,[10] in which he drew up a rule of life for the penitent, according to the authority of Scriptures. He also wrote a consolatory work to one Basilius, *On the death of a son*, filled with resurrection hope and good counsel. He also composed many *Homilies*, which have been arranged as continuous works and are as I know, made use of by brethren anxious for their own salvation.

CHAPTER LXXIX.

VOCONIUS,[1] bishop of Castellanum in Mauritania, wrote *Against the enemies of the church, Jews, Arians, and other heretics*. He composed also an excellent work *On the Sacraments*.[2]

CHAPTER LXXX.

MUSAEUS,[3] presbyter of the church at Marseilles, a man learned in Divine Scriptures and most accurate in their interpretation, as well as master of an excellent scholastic style, on the request of Saint Venerius the bishop, selected from Holy Scriptures passages suited to the various feast days of the year, also passages from the Psalms for responses suited to the season, and the passages for reading. The readers in the church found this work of the greatest value, in that it saved them trouble and anxiety in the selection of passages, and was useful for the instruction of the people as well as for the dignity of the service. He also addressed to Saint Eustathius[4] the bishop, successor to the above mentioned man of God, an excellent and sizable volume, a *Sacramentary*,[5] divided into various sections, according to the various offices and seasons, Readings and Psalms, both for reading and chanting, but also filled throughout with petitions to the Lord,[6] and thanksgiving for his benefits. By this work we know him to have been a man of strong intelligence and chaste eloquence. He is said to have also delivered homilies, which are, as I know, valued by pious men, but which I have not read. He died in the reign of Leo and Majorianus.

CHAPTER LXXXI.

VINCENTIUS[7] the presbyter, a native of Gaul, practised in Divine Scripture and possessed of a style polished by speaking

---

[1] *This book . . . caveat* A T 25 30 31 a e 21 Fabr.; omit Migne. Her.
[2] Bishop of Bagais (Vagen) about 485.
[3] *large see* A T 25 30 31 a? e earliest eds.; *small village.* Fabr. Migne. Her.
[4] Flourished 450.   [6] T adds several lines.
[5] Flourished 430?.   [7] Bishop in Spain? about 400.
[8] Victor of Cartenna (Tenez Afr.) bishop about 450.
[9] *which he sent . . . work* A T 30 31 e 21 Fabr. ; omit 25 a Her.
[10] *publican* Fabr. Migne, Her.: *On public penance*, A T 30 31 a? e?: omit *publican* 25 Bamb Bern. the oldest editions.

[1] Bishop of Castellan in Mauritania about 450.
[2] *Sacraments* or *of Sacraments* i.e. a Sacrementary.
[3] Died before 461.
[4] *Eustathius* 31 e; *Eustasius* A T a. ed. 1512; *Eusebius* 25, 30; *Eustachius* Fabr. Migne, Her.
[5] *Sacramentary* or *On the Sacraments*.
[6] *the Lord* T 25 30 31 a e *God* Fabr. Her.
[7] Apparently about 450.

and by wide reading, wrote a Commentary *On the Psalms.* A part of this work, he read in my hearing, to a man of God, at Cannatae, promising at the same time, that if the Lord should spare his life and strength, he would treat the whole Psalter in the same way.

CHAPTER LXXXII.

CYRUS,[1] an Alexandrian by race, and a physician by profession, at first a philosopher then a monk, an expert speaker, at first wrote elegantly and powerfully against Nestorius, but afterwards, since he began to inveigh against him too intemperately[2] and dealt in syllogism rather than Scripture, he began to foster the Timothean doctrine. Finally he declined to accept the decree of the council of Chalcedon, and did not think the doctrine that after the incarnation the Son of God comprehended two natures, was to be acquiesced in.

CHAPTER LXXXIII.

SAMUEL,[3] presbyter of the church at Edessa, is said to have written many things in Syriac against the enemies of the church, especially against the Nestorians, the Euty-chians and the Timotheans, new heresies all, but differing from one another. On this account he frequently speaks of the triple beast, while he briefly refutes by the opinion of the church, and the authority of Holy Scriptures, showing to the Nestorians, that the Son was God in man, not simply man born of a Virgin, to the Eutychians, that he had true human flesh, taken on by God, and not merely a body made of thick air, or shown from Heaven; to the Timotheans, that the Word was made flesh in such wise, that the Word remains Word in substance, and, human nature remaining human nature, one person of the Son of God is produced by union, not by mingling. He is said to be still living at Constantinople, for at the beginning of the reign of Anthemius, I knew his writings, and knew that he was in the land of the living.

CHAPTER LXXXIV.

CLAUDIANUS,[1] presbyter of the church at Vienne, a master speaker, and shrewd in argument, composed three books, *On the con-dition and substance of the soul,* in which he discusses how far anything is incorporeal excepting God.

[He wrote also some other things, among which are, *A Hymn on Our Lord's Passion,* which begins " Pange lingua gloriosi." He was moreover brother of Mamertus, bishop of Vienne.][2] (*See note.*)

CHAPTER LXXXV.

PROSPER[3] of Aquitania, a man scholastic in style and vigorous in statement, is said to have composed many works, of which I have read a *Chronicle,* which bears his name, and which extends from the creation of the first man, according to Divine Script-ure, until the death of the Emperor Valenti-nianus and the taking of Rome by Genseric king of the Vandals. I regard as his also an anonymous book against certain works of Cassianus, which the church of God finds salutary, but which he brands as injurious, and in fact, some of the opinions of Cassian and Prosper on the grace of God and on free will are at variance with one another. Epistles of Pope Leo against Eutyches, *On the true incarnation of Christ,* sent to various persons, are also thought[4] to have been dictated by him.

CHAPTER LXXXVI.

FAUSTUS,[5] first abbot of the monastery at Lerins, and then made bishop[6] of Riez in Gaul, a man studious of the Divine Script-ures, taking his text from the historic creed of the church, composed a book *On the Holy Spirit,* in which he shows from the belief of the fathers, that the Holy Spirit is consubstantial and cöeternal with the Father and the Son, the fulness of the Trinity and therefore God.[7] He published also an ex-cellent work, *On the grace of God, through which we are saved,*[8] in which he teaches that the grace of God always invites, pre-

---

[1] Flourished 460.
[2] *since he began to inveigh against him too intemperately* Norimb. and the eds., but the other mss. read "*nevertheless*" *inveigh* or "*inveighs less*" or "*more*" and "*is found*" for "*inveigh.*" T 21 25 a Wolfenb. agree in reading *in illo minus invenitur* instead of *in illum nimius invenitur.* Norimb has same with nimius instead of minus. The reading of T 21 25 a Wolfenb. thus reinforced and in view of the fact of the easy confusion of *minus* and *nimius* in transcribing, is the most probable reading, but it is hard to decide and harder still to make sense of it.
[3] Presbyter 467.

[1] Claudianus Ecdicius Mamertus died 473-4.
[2] *wrote . . . Vienne* is said to be in a certain manuscript of the Monastery of " St. Michaelis de Tumba " but is omitted by A T 25 30 31 a e 21 Bamb. Bern. etc etc. and certainly does not belong in text. It is left in brackets above because given in the editions.
[3] Born 403, wrote chronicle 445? died 463.
[4] *thought* A 25 30 31 a e 21; *said* T Fabr. Her.
[5] Abbot of Lerins 433-4, bishop of Riez 462, exiled 477-84, died 490.
[6] *Made bishop* A T 31 e 21; *bishop* a 25 30.
[7] *and therefore God* T 25 31 a e 21 [31 A?;] *obtaining* Fabr. Her.; Bamb and ed. 1512 read *and therefore* but join to next sentence.
[8] *saved* A T 25; add *and the free will of the human mind in which we are saved* 30 31 a e.

cedes and helps our will, and whatever gain that freedom of will may attain for its pious effect, is not its own desert, but the gift of grace. I have read also a little book of his *Against the Arians and Macedonians*, in which he posits a coëssential Trinity, and another against those who say that there is anything incorporeal in created things, in which he maintains from the testimony of Scriptures, and by quotations from the fathers, that nothing is to be regarded as incorporeal but God. There is also a letter of his, written in the form of a little book, and addressed to a certain deacon, named Graecus, who, leaving the Catholic faith, had gone over to the Nestorian impiety.

In this epistle he admonishes him to believe that the holy Virgin Mary did not bring forth a mere human being, who afterwards should receive divinity, but true God in true man. There are still other works by him, but as I have not read, I do not care to mention them. This excellent doctor is enthusiastically believed in and admired. He wrote afterwards also to Felix, the Praetonian prefect, and a man of Patrician rank, son of Magnus the consul, a very pious letter, exhorting to the fear of God, a work well fitted to induce one to repent with his whole heart.

CHAPTER LXXXVII.

SERVUS DEI [1] the bishop, wrote against those who say that Christ while living in this world did not see the Father with his eyes of flesh — But after his resurrection from the dead and his ascension into heaven when he had been translated into the glory of God the Father as in reward so to speak to him for his abnegation and a compensation for his martyrdom. In this work he showed both from his own argument and from the testimony of Sacred Scriptures that the Lord Jesus from his conception by the Holy Spirit and his birth of the Virgin through which true God in true man himself also man made God was born, always beheld with his eyes of flesh both the Father and the Holy Spirit through the special and complete union of God and man.

CHAPTER LXXXVIII.

VICTORIUS [2] the Aquitanian, a careful [3] reckoner, on invitation of St. Hilary bishop of Rome, composed a *Paschal cycle* with the most careful investigation following his four predecessors, that is Hippolytus, Eu-

sebius, Theophilus and Prosper, and extended the series of years to the year five hundred and thirty-two, reckoning in such wise that in the year 533 the paschal festival should take place again on the same month and day and the same moon as on that first year when the Passion and resurrection of our Lord took place.

CHAPTER LXXXIX.

THEODORETUS,[1] [2] bishop of Cyrus (for the city founded by Cyrus king of the Persians preserves until the present day in Syria the name of its founder) is said to have written many works. Such as have come to my knowledge are the following: *On the incarnation of the Lord, Against Eutyches the presbyter and Dioscorus* bishop of Alexandria who deny that Christ had human flesh; strong works by which he confirmed through reason and the testimony of Scripture that He had real flesh from the maternal substance which he derived from His Virgin mother just as he had true deity which he received at birth by eternal generation from God the Father. There are ten books of the ecclesiastical history which he wrote in imitation of Eusebius of Caesarea beginning where Eusebius ends and extending to his own time, that is from the Vicennalia of Constantine until the accession of the elder Leo in whose reign he died.

CHAPTER XC.

GENNADIUS [3] Patriarch [4] of the church of Constantinople, a man brilliant in speech and of strong genius, was so richly equipped by his reading of the ancients that he was able to expound the prophet Daniel entire commenting on every word.

He composed also many Homilies. He died while the elder Leo was Emperor.

CHAPTER XCI.

THEODULUS,[5] [6] a presbyter in Coelesyria is said to have written many works, but the only one which has come to my hand, is the one which he composed *On the harmony of divine Scripture*, that is, the Scriptures of the Old and New Testaments, against the ancient heretics who on account of discrepancies in the injunctions of the ritual, say that the God of the Old Testament is different

---

[1] Bishop of "Tiburcisen" about 406-11.
[2] Wrote 457. 30 a read Victorinus.
[3] *careful* T 25 30 31 a Fabr.; *most diligent* A Norimb?; Bern Norimb. et alt add *of the Scriptures: of measures* Her.

[1] Theodoret born about 393, bishop of Cyrrhaus 423, wrote 450, died 457.
[2] *Theodoretus* A a e; *Theodoritus* 31; *Theodorus* T 25 30.
[3] Bishop (or "Pontiff") 458, died 471.
[4] Patriarch (Pontiff) A T 30 31 e 21; bishop 25 a Fabr. Her.
[5] Died 492 (C) — rather before 491.
[6] *Theodulus* A T 31 a e; *Theodorus* 25 30 21.

from the God of the New. In this work he shows it to have been by the dispensation of one and the same God, the author of both Scriptures, that one law should be given by Moses to those of old in a ritual of sacrifices and in judicial laws, and another to us through the presence of Christ in the holy mysteries and future promises, that they should not be considered different, but as dictated by one spirit and one author, since these things which if observed only according to the letter, would slay, if observed according to the spirit, would give life to the mind. This writer died three years since [1] in the reign of Zeno.

CHAPTER XCII.

[Sidonius [2] bishop of the Arverni wrote several acceptable works and being a man sound in doctrine as well as thoroughly imbued with divine and human learning and a man of commanding genius wrote a considerable volume of *Letters* to different persons written in various metres or in prose and this showed his ability in literature. Strong in Christian vigour even in the midst of that barbaric ferocity which at that time oppressed the Gauls he was regarded as a catholic father and a distinguished doctor. He flourished during the tempest which marked the rule of Leo and Zenos.][3]

CHAPTER XCIII.

John [4] of Antioch first grammarian, and then Presbyter, wrote against those who assert that Christ is to be adored in one substance only and do not admit that two natures are to be recognized in Christ. He taught according to the Scriptural account that in Him God and man exist in one person, and not the flesh and the Word in one nature.

He likewise attacked certain sentiments of Cyril, bishop of Alexandria, unwisely [5] delivered by Cyril against Nestorius, which now are an encouragement and give strength to the Timotheans.[6] He is said to be still living and preaching.

---

[1] *three years since* A T 30? 31 21; omit 25 a.
[2] Caius Sollius Apollinaris Sidonius born about 430, bishop 472, died about 488.
[3] This chapter is in Norimb. and three only of the mss. seen by the translator N. British Museum Harl. 3155, xv cent.; 43 Wolfenbüttel 838 xv cent.; k Paris B. N. Lat. 896. It is omitted by A T 25 30 31 a e 21 etc. etc. etc. and really has no place in the text, but as it was early introduced and is in the editions (not however the earliest ones) it is given here.
[4] Flourished 477-495.
[5] *unwisely* T 25 30 31 e; *unwisely saying* A? a?
[6] *Timotheans* A T 25 30 31 a e 21 etc; add *which is absurd* Fabr. Migne, Her.

CHAPTER XCIV.

[Gelasius,[12] bishop of Rome wrote *Against Eutyches and Nestorius* a great and notable volume, also *Treatises* on various parts of the scripture and the sacraments written in a polished style. He also wrote *Epistles against Peter and Acacius* which are still preserved in the catholic church. He wrote also *Hymns* after the fashion of bishop Ambrosius. He died during the reign of the emperor Anastasius.

CHAPTER XCV.

Honoratus,[3] bishop of Constantina in Africa wrote a letter to one Arcadius who on account of his confession of the catholic faith had been exiled to Africa by King Genseric.[4] This letter was an exhortation to endure hardness for Christ and fortified by modern examples and scripture illustrations showing that perseverance in the confession of the faith not only purges past sins but also procures the blessing of martyrdom.

CHAPTER XCVI.

Cerealis [5] the bishop, an African by birth, was asked by Maximus bishop of the Arians whether he could establish the catholic faith by a few testimonies of Divine Scripture and without any controversial assertions. This he did in the name of the Lord, truth itself helping him, not with a few testimonies as Maximus had derisively asked, but proving by copious proof texts from both Old and New Testaments and published in a little book.

CHAPTER XCVII.

Eugenius,[6] bishop of Carthage in Africa and public confessor, commanded by Huneric [7] King of the Vandals to write an exposition of the catholic faith and especially to discuss the meaning of the word Homoousian, with the consent of all the bishops and confessors of Mauritania in Africa and Sardinia and Corsica, who had remained in the catholic faith, composed a book of faith, fortified not only by quotations from the Holy Scriptures but by testimonies of the Fathers, and sent it by his companions in confession. But now, exiled as a reward for his faithful tongue, like an anxious shep-

---

[1] Bishop 492, died 496.
[2] From this point to the end is bracketed, as a large part of the mss. end with John of Antioch. Of our mss. Gelasius and Gennadius are contained in 25 30 e [2], Honoratus to Pomerius in A 30 31 e [2] 40.
[3] Bishop of Constantina (Cirta) 437.
[4] *exiled by King Genseric;* omit e [2] 30 31 40.
[5] Bishop of " Castelli Ripensis " in Africa 484.
[6] Bishop 479, died 505.   [7] *Huneric* A; omit e [2] 30 31 40.

herd over his sheep he has left behind works urging them to remember the faith and the one sacred baptism to be preserved at all hazards. He also wrote out the *Discussions* which he held through messengers with the leaders of the Arians and sent them to be given to Huneric by his major domo. Likewise also he presented to the same, petitions for the peace of the Christians which were of the nature of an *Apology*, and he is said to be still living for the strengthening of the church.

CHAPTER XCVIII.

POMERIUS[1] the Mauritanian was ordained presbyter in Gaul. He composed a dialectical treatise in eight books *On the nature of the soul and its properties*, also one *On the resurrection* and its particular bearing for the faithful in this life and in general for all men, written in clear language and style, in the form of a dialogue between Julian the bishop, and Verus the presbyter. The first book contains discourses on what the soul is and in what sense it is thought to be created in the image of God, the second, whether the soul should be thought of as corporeal or incorporeal, the third, how the soul of the first man[2] was made, fourth, whether the soul which is put in the body at birth is newly created and without sin, or produced from the substance of the first man like a shoot from a root it brings also with it the original sin of the first man,

fifth, a review of the fourth book of the discussion,[1] and an inquiry as to what is the capability of the soul, that is its possibilities, and that it gains its capability from a single and pure will, the sixth, whence arises the conflict between flesh and the spirit, spoken of by the apostle, seventh, on the difference between the flesh and the spirit in respect of life, of death and of resurrection, the eighth, answers to questions concerning the things which it is predicted will happen at the end of the world, to such questions, that is, as are usually propounded concerning the resurrection. I remember to have once read a hortatory work of his, addressed to some one named Principius, *On contempt of the world, and of transitory things*, and another entitled, *On vices and virtues*. He is said to have written yet other works, which have not come to my knowledge, and to be still writing. He is still living, and his life is worthy of Christian profession, and his rank in the church.

CHAPTER XCIX.

I GENNADIUS,[2] a presbyter of Marseilles, have written eight books *Against all heresies*, five[3] books *Against Nestorius*, ten[4] books *Against Eutyches*, three books *Against Pelagius*, also treatises *On the Millennium* and *On the Apocalypse of Saint John*, also an epistle *On my creed*, sent to the blessed Gelasius, bishop of Rome.]

---

[1] Died 498.
[2] *the first man* A; *the first man's soul* e[2] 30 31 40.

[1] *discussion* 30 40 e[2]; *discussion and definition* A 31.
[2] Died 496.   [3] *five* e 25 30; *six* Fabr. Her.
[4] *ten* e 25 30; *six* Norimb Her.; *eleven* Guelefenb.

LIFE AND WORKS OF RUFINUS

WITH

JEROME'S APOLOGY AGAINST RUFINUS,

Translated with Prolegomena and Notes,

BY

THE HON. AND REV. WILLIAM HENRY FREMANTLE, M.A.,

Canon of Canterbury, Fellow and Tutor of Baliol College, Oxford.

PROLEGOMENA

ON THE

LIFE AND WORKS OF RUFINUS

NOTE. — The References (where a simple number is given) are to the pages in this Volume.

TYRANNIUS RUFINUS is chiefly known from his relation to Jerome, first as an intimate friend and afterwards as a bitter enemy. The immense influence of Jerome. through all the ages in which criticism was asleep, has unduly lowered his adversary. But he has some solid claims of his own on our recognition. His work on the Creed, besides its intrinsic merits, must always be an authority as a witness to the state of the creed as held in the Italian churches in the beginning of the 5th century, as also to the state of the Canon and the Apocrypha at that time. And it is to his translations that we are indebted for our knowledge of many of the works of Origen, including the greatest of them all, the Περὶ Ἀρχῶν. We are the more grateful for his services because they were so opportune. The works of Origen, which had been neglected in the West for a century and to such an extent that the Pope Anastasius says (433) that he neither knows who he was nor what he wrote, came suddenly into notice in the last quarter of a century before Alaric's sack of Rome A.D. 385–410: and it was at this moment that Rufinus appeared, according to his friend Macarius' dream (439) like a ship laden with the merchandize of the East, an Italian who had lived some 25 years in Greek lands, and sufficiently equipped for the work of a translator. Through his labours during the last 13 years of that eventful time a considerable part of the works of the great Alexandrian have floated down across the ocean of the Dark Ages, and, while lost in their native Greek, have in their Latin garb come to enrich the later civilization of the West.

Rufinus was born at Concordia (Jer. Ep. v. 2. comp. with Ep. x. and De Vir. Ill.
A.D. 344-5. § 53) between Aquileia and Altinum, a place of some importance, which was destroyed by the Huns in 452 but afterwards rebuilt. His birth was about the year 344 or 345, he being slightly older than Jerome. Nothing is known of his education or the events of his youth; but that he was early acquainted with Jerome and was interested in sacred literature is seen from the fact that in 368 when Jerome went with Bonosus to Gaul, Rufinus begged him to copy for him the works of Hilary on the Psalms and on the Councils of the Church (Jer. Ep. v. 2). His mother did not die till the year 397, as is seen from Jerome's mention of her (Letter LXXXI, 1), and it would
A.D. 372-3. appear that both his parents were Christians. But he was not baptized till about his 28th year. He was at that time living at Aquileia, where he had embraced the monastic state, and was a member of the company of young ascetics to which Jerome and Bonosus belonged. The presence among them of Hylas (Jerome Letter III, 3) the freedman of Melania, the wealthy and ascetic Roman matron, shows that that relation had already begun which was afterwards of such importance in the life of Rufinus. It must have been just before the breaking up of that company that he was baptized, for Jerome, writing of him (Ep. iv. 2) in 374 from Antioch says " He has but lately been washed and is as white as snow." He himself gives a full account of his baptism in his Apology (436).

When this company of friends was scattered, Rufinus joined the noble Roman lady, Melania, in her pilgrimage to the East (Jer. Letter iv. 2). He visited the monasteries of Egypt, and apparently desired to remain there; but a persecution arose against
A.D. 373. the orthodox monks from Lucius the Arian bishop of Alexandria, seconded by the governor, both being prompted by the Arian Emperor Valens: the monasteries were in many cases broken up (Sozomen, vi, 19, Socrates iv, 21-3, Rufinus Eccl.

Hist. ii, 3), and Rufinus himself for a while suffered imprisonment and was then banished from Egypt (430 Eccl. Hist. ii, 4). Rufinus probably on coming out of prison joined Melania who had then settled at Dio Cæsarea (Pallad. Hist. Laus. § 117) on the coast of Palestine for the purpose of making a home for the Egyptian exiles on their way to their various destinations. He states in his Apology (466) that he was 6 years in Egypt, and that he returned there again, after an interval, for two years more. He was a pupil both of Didymus, then head of the catechetical school, who wrote for him a treatise on the death of infants (534), and of Theophilus, afterward Bishop of Alexandria (528), and that he saw many of the well-known hermits (466), such as Serapion and Macarius, whom he describes in his History of the Monks. Whether Melania returned with him to Egypt, or whether she went to Jerusalem, we do not know : it is also uncertain whether a journey which he made (Eccl. Hist. ii. 8) to Edessa was undertaken at this time. The date of the settlement of Melania on the Mount of Olives according to Jerome's Chronicle is 379, or, according to our present reckoning of dates, 377. We may suppose that Rufinus joined her in 379. This was his home for eighteen years, till the year 397.

Rufinus was ordained at Jerusalem, probably about the time when John, with whom he was closely connected, succeeded Cyril in the Bishopric (A.D. 386). The great resources of Melania were added to his own which seem to have been not inconsiderable. He built habitations for monks on the Mount of Olives, and employed them in learned pursuits, and in copying manuscripts. On the arrival of Jerome at Bethlehem, the old friendship was renewed, though not apparently with all its former warmth. Jerome certainly at times visited Rufinus and once at least stayed with him (465), and he and his friends brought MSS. to be copied by the monks of the Mount of Olives (465). He gave lectures on Christian writers and doctrine, of which a satirical account is given at a later period by Jerome[1] in his letter to Rusticus (cxxv, § 18). The nick-name Grunnius which he there gives him was probably caused by some trick of the voice. But we may gather from Jerome that he read the Greek church writers diligently and lectured upon them, a study which enabled him to do much good work at a later time. It is probable that he lectured in Greek, since he says in 397 that his Latin was weak through disuse (439). We may set against Jerome's depreciatory description the account given by Palladius (Hist. Laus. § 118). " Rufinus, who lived with Melania, was a man of congenial spirit, and of great nobility and strength of character. No man has ever been known of greater learning or of gentler disposition." Palladius also speaks of the princely hospitality of Melania and Rufinus : " They received," he says, " bishops and monks, virgins and matrons and helped them out of their own funds : They passed their life offending none and being helpers of the whole world." It is said by Palladius that he had heard from Melania that she had been present at the death of Pambas in Egypt which took place in the year 385, and it is probable that Rufinus accompanied her on this occasion. He himself records[2] a journey which he made to Edessa and Charrhoe, when he saw settlements of the monks like those which he had previously seen in Egypt. But the date of this journey does not appear. It may have been undertaken in order to visit some of the exiles from Egypt before his establishment on the Mt. of Olives. He records also the visits of the remarkable men who were entertained by him; Bacurius, who had been king of the Ubii, and afterwards count of the Domestics under Theodosius, and was governor or duke of Palestine when Rufinus settled there ; and Ædesius the companion of Frumentius the Missionary to the tribes in the N. W. of India. But his chief interest and occupation throughout seems to have been with his monks at Mt. Olivet with perhaps some connection with the diocesan work of his friend John, the Bp. of Jerusalem. Palladius records that Rufinus and Melania were the means of restoring to the communion of the church 400 monks. What was this schism, which Palladius describes as being "on account of Paulinus" ? It is probable that the words relate to the monks of Bethlehem whose alienation from the Church of Jerusalem had been due to the ordination of Paulinian, Jerome's brother, by Epiphanius. We know that Rufinus before leaving Palestine was reconciled to Jerome (Jer. Ap. iii. 26, 33) ; and we know also that Jerome's book against John, Bishop of Jerusalem, which describes the schism was suddenly broken off ;[3]

---

[1] " He came in with a slow and stately step; he spoke with a broken utterance, sometimes with a kind of disjointed sobs rather than words. He had a pile of tomes upon the table; and then, with a frown and a contraction of the nostrils, and his forehead wrinkled up, he snapped his fingers to call the attention of his audience. What he said had no depth in it; but he criticized others, and pointed out their defects, as though he would exclude them from the Senate of Christian teachers. He was rich, and entertained freely, and many flocked round him in his public appearances. He was as luxurious as Nero at home, as stern as Cato abroad; as full of contradictions as the Chimæra."

[2] Hist. Eccl. ii. 8.

[3] For the date of this work, see the Note prefixed to it in the translation of Jerome's works, Vol. vi. of this series.

and that he remained from that time forward at one with his Bishop. We may be allowed to believe that the influence of Melania as well as Rufinus had been exerted for some time previously to bring about this happy result.

Rufinus' part in the controversy thus terminated is partly known and partly the subject of inference. The original source of discord is not known. It is possible that Rufinus, who had been mentioned by Jerome in his Chronicle (A.D. 378) as being, together with Florentius and Bonosus, a specially distinguished monk, did not find himself included in his
382.   friend's Catalogue of Church writers (De Vir. Ill.) published at Bethlehem.

When Aterbius began the Origenist troubles at Jerusalem, Rufinus, who treated him with merited scorn (Jer. Ap. iii, 33) probably felt some resentment at Jerome who, by "giving satisfaction" to the heresy hunter, had countenanced his proceedings. Rufinus appears as Bishop John's adviser during the visit of Epiphanius (Jer. Letter li, 2,
392.   6), as the chief of a chorus of presbyters who applauded their own bishop and derided Epiphanius as a " silly old man;"[1] and as present when Epiphanius remonstrated with his brother-bishop. He is also mentioned by Epiphanius in his letter to John (Jer. Letter li. 6) as holding an important place in the Church, " May God free you and all about you, especially the presbyter Rufinus, from the heresy of Origen, and all others." This sentence will suggest to all who are familiar with church-controversies a whole series of scenes in the schism which continued between Bethlehem and Jerusalem during the next five years. Jerome believed Rufinus to have injured him at every turn, to have procured the abstraction of a Manuscript of his from the house occupied by Fabiola on her visit to Bethlehem (Apol. iii, 4) perhaps to have been in league with Vigilantius (Comp. Jer. Ep. lxi, 3 with Apol. iii, 4, 19). But such insinuations have the appearance rather of the suspicions prompted by anger than of actual fact. In any case they were condoned when
397. •   the two old companions who had been so long parted by ecclesiastical strife met together at the Church of the Resurrection at a solemn eucharistic feast, and joined hands in token of reconciliation, and when Jerome accompanied his friend some way on his journey before their final parting (Jer. Vol. iii, 24).

He arrived in Italy, in company with Melania, early in the spring of 397. They were there received by Paulinus of Nola with great honour.[2] Melania went on at once to Rome; but Rufinus stopped at the monastery of Pinetum near Terracina. His welcome by the Abbot Urseius and the philosopher Macarius, and their request to him to translate various Greek books, amongst others the Περὶ Ἀρχῶν of Origen, are described in his Prefaces to the Benedictions of the Patriarchs, the Apology of Pamphilus and the translations of Origen (417, 418, 420, 439). The preface to Origen's chief work (427) had the worst and most lasting results. He says that, being aware of the odium attaching to the name of Origen, he had feared to translate the work: but that the example of Jerome (whom he does not name but whose great ability he extols) in translating Origen encourages him to follow in his steps. This Preface, with this translation of the Περὶ Ἀρχῶν, was published in Rome early in the year 398, Rufinus having moved there to stay with Melania. At Rome he lived in the circle of Melania, her son Publicola and his wife Albina, with their daughter the younger Melania and her husband Pinianus, to whom we may probably add the Pope
A.D.   Siricius, and certainly Apronianus, a young noble whom he speaks of as his son in
400-403.   the faith (435, 564). Jerome's friend Eusebius of Cremona was also in Rome, and on friendly terms with him (445). But on the appearance of the work of Origen with Rufinus' Preface, a great ferment arose leading to the violent controversy between Rufinus and Jerome which is described in the Preface to their Apologies (434, 482).

Meanwhile, Rufinus had left Rome probably in 398, having obtained the usual Literæ Formatæ from the Pope Siricius, who died that year, to introduce him to other
A.D. 398.   churches.[3] We hear of him at Milan, where in the presence of the Bishop, Simplicianus,[4] he met Eusebius of Cremona, and heard him read out a letter of Theophilus containing some passages from the Περὶ Ἀρχῶν, against which he vehemently protested (490). He then, having probably visited his native city of Concordia, where his mother,[5] possibly his father also (430, 502) was still living, took up his abode at Aquileia. There he was welcomed by the bishop, Chromatius, by whom he had been baptized some 26 or 27 years before. Rufinus probably arrived at Aquileia in the beginning of 399, and remained

---

[1] See Jerome's expressions in his book "Against John of Jerusalem" c. 11, which evidently refer to Rufinus: " grinning like a dog and turning up his nose."
[2] Paulinus Ep. xxix, 12.   [3] Jer. Ep. cxxvii, 9 Ap. iii. 21.
[4] Successor of Ambrose, and Bishop A.D. 397-400. See the Letter of Anastasius to him. Jer. Ep. xcv.
[5] She died soon after. See Jerome Ep. lxxxi, 1.

399-408. there 9 or 10 years. It was during this period that all his principal works except the Commentary on the Benedictions of the patriarchs, the translation of the Περὶ
• 'Αρχῶν and Pamphilus' Apology, and the book on the Adulterations of Origen were composed. It was soon after his settlement at Aquileia that he heard from Apronianus of the letter of Jerome to Pammachius and Oceanus[1] expressing his anger against him for the mention he had made of Jerome in the Preface to the Περὶ 'Αρχῶν. The conciliatory letter to Rufinus which accompanied this and which was an answer to a friendly one from Rufinus[2] was not sent on by Jerome's friends (489) ; and Rufinus, thinking that his old friend had completely turned against him, composed his Apology (434-482) which drew forth Jerome's reply (482-541). This controversy is placed in full before the reader of this volume in an English translation, with prefatory notes. It may therefore be treated very shortly here.

Rufinus' Apology is an answer to Jerome's letter to Pammachius and Oceanus. It is addressed to Apronianus of Rome. He makes a profession of his Christian standing and faith, especially on the points raised by the Origenistic controversy; he describes the circumstances which had led him to translate the books of Origen, and defends his method of translation, which, he says, has been misrepresented by men sent from the East to lay snares for him. His method, he declares, was the same which had been used by Jerome, who boasted that through him the Latins knew all that was good in Origen and nothing of the bad. Where he found passages in Origen's writings, in flagrant contradiction to the orthodox opinion he had maintained elsewhere, he concluded that the passage had been falsified by heretics, and restored the more orthodox statement which he believed to have been originally there. He then turns round upon Jerome and points out that, in his Commentaries on the Ephesians, written some 10 years before, to which he specially referred in his Letter as showing his freedom from heresy, he had practically adopted the opinions now imputed to Origen as heretical, such as the fall of souls from a previous state into the prison house of earthly bodies, and the universal restoration of spiritual beings.

In the second book he clears himself from the imputation of following Origen and Plato in believing in the lawfulness of using occasional falsehood in the government and training of men. But he imputes to his adversary a systematic use of falsehood in reference to his reading heathen authors, while he professed in his letter to Eustochium (Jer. Ep. xxii) to have solemnly promised never even to possess them. He then takes a wider view of Jerome's writings, showing how, in this Letter to Eustochium, his books against Jovinian, etc., he had by his satirical pictures held up to ridicule the various classes of Christians, clergy, monks, virgins : how he had praised Origen indiscriminately as a teacher second only to the Apostles : how he had defamed men like Ambrose, and therefore his present accusations were little worth : how he boasted of having taken as his teachers not only Origenists like Didymus or heretics like Apollinarius, but heathen like Porphyry, and had made his translation of the Old Testament under the influence of the Jew Baranina (whose name Rufinus perverts into Barabbas). He concludes by summarizing his accusations and calling upon the reader to choose between him and his opponent.

This Apology was only sent to a few friends of Rufinus (530) ; but portions of it became known to Jerome's friends and his brother Paulinian (493) carried them to Bethlehem, together with Rufinus' Apology addressed to Pope Anastasius. Jerome had also before him the letter of Anastasius to John Bishop of Jerusalem (509) showing his dislike of Rufinus' proceedings. On these he grounds his own Apology, which was originally in two books and was addressed to Pammachius and Marcella A.D. 402.

In the first book he blames Rufinus' breach of friendship after the reconciliation which had taken place at Jerusalem ; he then shows that he was compelled to translate the Περὶ 'Αρχῶν in order to show what it really was. He declares that the Apology of Origen translated by Rufinus as the work of Pamphilus was really written by Eusebius ; that Origen had been condemned by Theophilus and Anastasius, by East and West alike, and by the decree of the Emperors. He defends himself for having used heathen and heretical teachers, and help of a Jewish scholar in translating the Old Testament. As to his Commentaries on the Ephesians he declares that he merely put side by side the opinions of various commentators, indicating at times his knowledge that some were heretical : and as to his anti-Ciceronian dream, he ridicules the idea that a man can be bound by his night visions.

In the second book he criticizes Rufinus' Apology addressed to Anastasius as to both its style and its matter, and blames him for his treatment of Epiphanius, and endeavours to implicate him in the imputation of heresy. He then defends his translation of the Old Testament, showing by copious quotations from the Prefaces to the Books that he had done nothing condemnatory of the Septuagint, whose version he had himself translated into Latin and constantly used in familiar expositions.

This Apology was brought to Rufinus at Aquileia by a merchant who was leaving again in two days (522). Chromatius no doubt urged him, as he urged Jerome (520) not to continue the controversy and he yielded. He wrote, however, a private letter to Jerome, which has been lost, sending him an accurate copy of his Apology, and while declining public controversy, yet declaring that he could have said even more than before, and divulged things which would have been worse to Jerome than death. Jerome in his answer written A.D. 403, which forms B. iii of his Apology, declares that the controversy is Rufinus' fault, and defends his friends for their conduct towards him, even in holding back the conciliatory letter written in 399 ; but shows how a way might still be open for friendship. He touches again upon most of the points dwelt on in the previous books, defending himself and accusing Rufinus, and ends by declaring that his bitter reply was necessitated first by Rufinus' threats, and secondly by his abhorrence of heresy, from all complicity with which he must at any price clear himself.

This book closed the controversy. Rufinus did not reply, Jerome did not relent. Nothing in Rufinus' subsequent writings reflects on Jerome; but Jerome is never weary of expressing his hatred of Rufinus, speaking of him after his death as "the Scorpion"[1] and writing malignant satirical descriptions of him like that in his letter to Rusticus.[2]

It may be observed, however, that notwithstanding the violent words used on both sides, it was possible for eminent churchmen to esteem and befriend both parties. Augustine, on receiving Jerome's Apology, laments, in words which must have been felt by Jerome as a severe reproach, that two such men, so loved by the churches, should thus tear each other to pieces. Chromatius, while he kept up communications with Jerome, and supplied him with funds for his literary work, was also the friend and adviser of Rufinus.

Rufinus' friends at Aquileia, like those at the Pinetum and at Rome, were anxious to gain from him a knowledge of the great church-writers of the East, and especially of Origen. No one at Aquileia seems to have known Greek. He makes excuses in his Prefaces (430, 563, 565, etc.) for the difficulty of the task and his own short-comings which seem to be partly conventional, partly genuine. But he did a work which he alone or almost alone at that period was qualified to do. His translations of Origen and Pamphilus were already known. We learn from Jerome (536) that Rufinus had translated parts of the LXX. He now translated Eusebius' Church History, and added to it two books of his own; he translated the so-called Recognitions of Clement, which till then were almost unknown in Italy. He wrote a History of the Monks of the East, partly from personal knowledge, partly from what he had heard or read of them. And he translated the Commentaries of Origen upon the Heptateuch or 1st seven books of Scripture, except Numbers and Deuteronomy; and those on the Epistle to the Romans. He also wrote his exposition of the Creed (541–563), and probably some other works which have not come down to us.

The first part of his stay at Aquileia was troubled by the controversy with Jerome. He also received from his friends at Rome the intelligence that his Preface and
400–402. translation of the Περὶ Ἀρχῶν had been brought to the notice of the Pope Anastasius, by Pammachius and Marcella (430); and probably the letter of the Pope to Venerius Bishop of Milan, which is quoted in Anastasius' letter to John of Jerusalem (433) was also brought to his knowledge. Though there is no reason to suppose, as has been often done, that the Pope passed sentence upon him, still less that he
400. summoned him to Rome. Rufinus was so far affected by what he heard of the adverse feeling excited in the Pope's mind toward him that he thought it desirable to write an explanation or apology (430–2) vindicating his action in the translation of Origen, and giving an exposition of his own belief on some of the principal points dealt with in the Περὶ Ἀρχῶν. From the letter of Anastasius to John of Jerusalem we gather that John had written to him in the interest of Rufinus, and had blamed Jerome's friends at Rome, perhaps also Jerome himself, for the part they had taken in reference to him. It is a curious fact that this letter was known to Jerome but not to Rufinus during the controversy (509); but it can hardly be inferred with any certainty from this that John had changed sides and favoured Jerome at Rufinus' expense.

After 8 or 9 years at Aquileia Rufinus returned to Rome. His friend Chromatius of Aquileia had died in 405. Anastasius of Rome had also passed away (A.D. 402),
408. and his successor Innocentius was without prejudice against Rufinus. Melania was either there or with Paulinus at Nola. Her son Publicola had died in 406, but his widow Albina was with her, and her granddaughter the younger Melania with her husband Pinianus. The siege of Rome by Alaric was impending, and the whole party were starting by way of Sicily and Africa, in both of which Melania had property, intending eventually to reach Palestine. He joined their "religious company" as he tells us in the Preface to Origen on Numbers (568) which, according to Palladius (Hist. Laus. 119) formed a vast caravan with slaves, virgins and eunuchs; and he was with them in Sicily when Alaric burned Rhegium (568) the flames of which they saw across the straits.

This translation of Numbers was his last work. He was at that time suffering in his eyes; and he died soon afterwards in Sicily, as we learn from Jerome's malicious words "The Scorpion now lies underground between Enceladus and Porphyrion."[3] The undying hatred of Jerome towards him has unduly lowered him in the estimation of the Church. He was far below Jerome in literary ability, but in their great controversy he displayed more magnanimity than his rival, being willing to forego a public answer to his provoking

¹ Jer. Ep. cxxvii. 10.   ² Jer. Ep. cxxv.   ³ Jer. Pref. to Comm. on Ezek. B. I.

apology. He was highly esteemed by the eminent churchmen of his time and the Bishops near whom he lived. Chromatius of Aquileia was his friend; for Petronius of Bologna he wrote his monastic history, for Gaudentius of Brixia he translated the Clementine Recognitions, for Laurentius (perhaps of his native Concordia) he composed his work on the Creed. Paulinus of Nola continued his friendship for him to the end. Above all Augustine speaks of him as the object of love and of honour; and, in his reply to Jerome[1] who had sent him his Apology, says: "I grieved, when I had read your book, that such discord should have arisen between persons so dear and so intimate, bound to all the churches by a bond of affection and of renown."

We may conclude this notice by two quotations from writers who lived shortly after the death of Rufinus; the first of which shows how unfairly the fame of Jerome has pressed on the memory of his antagonist, while the second may be taken as the verdict of unprejudiced history. Pope Gelasius, at a Council at Rome in 494, drew up a list of books to be received in the church, in which he says of Rufinus: "He was a religious man, and wrote many books of use to the Church, and many commentaries on the Scripture; but, since the most blessed Jerome infamed him on certain points, we take part with him (Jerome) in this and in all cases in which he has pronounced a condemnation." (Migne's Patrologia vol. lix. col. 175). On the other hand Gennadius, in his list of Ecclesiastical writers (c. 17) says: "Rufinus, the presbyter, of Aquileia, was not the least of the church-teachers, and showed an elegant genius in his translations from Greek into Latin;" and, after giving a list of his writings, he continues: "He also replied in two volumes to him who decried his works, showing convincingly that he had exercised his powers through the might which God had given him, and for the good of the church, and that it was through a spirit of rivalry that his adversary had employed his pen in defaming him."

WORKS OF RUFINUS.

I. Original Works which still Survive.

1. *A Commentary on the Benedictions of the 12 Patriarchs.* This short work was composed at the monastery of Pinetum near Terracina during Lent in the year 398, at the request of Paulinus of Nola. Rufinus had stayed with Paulinus on his first arrival with Melania in Italy (Paulinus. Ep. xxix, 12.) and Paulinus wrote to him (417) after he had gone to Pinetum begging him to give an explanation of the blessing of Jacob in Judah. Rufinus, though not replying for a time, sent his exposition, and afterwards, on a second request from Paulinus, added the exposition of the rest of the blessings in the Patriarchs, like the son in the parable (as he explains in a graceful letter prefixed to the work) who said "I go not," but afterwards repented and went.

The exposition is well written and clear; but it is not in itself of much value. The text on which he comments is very faulty: for instance, in the Blessing of Reuben, instead of the words "the excellency of dignity and the excellency of power," it has "*durus conversatione, et durus, temerarius.*" When Rufinus adheres to the plain interpretation of the passage his comments are sensible and clear; but he soon passes to the mystic sense: Reuben is God's first-born people, the Jews, and the couch which he defiles is the law of the Old Testament; and the moral interpretation is grounded on the supposed meaning of Reuben, "the Son who is seen," that is the visible, carnal man, who breaks through the law. So, in Judah's "binding his foal to the vine," the explanation given, as he says, by the Jews, that the vines will be so plentiful that they are used even for tying up the young colts, is dismissed. The foal is the Christian Church the offspring of Israel which is God's ass, and is bound to Christ the true vine.

2. *A dissertation on the adulteration of the works of Origen by heretics,* subjoined to his translation of Pamphilus' Apology for Origen. This will be found in the present volume pp. 421–427.

3. *An apology addressed to the Pope Anastasius.* See the introductory note prefixed to the translation of this work (429) now first translated into English.

4. *The Apology for himself against the attacks of Jerome.* See the introductory statement prefixed to the translation (434–5).

5. *Ecclesiastical History in Two Books,* being a continuation of the History of Eusebius translated by Rufinus into Latin. This work was composed at Aquileia at the

---

[1] Aug. Letter 73 (In Jerome's Letters No. 110).

request of the Bishop, Chromatius. The date is probably 401, since in the Preface Rufinus says that he had been requested to translate Eusebius at the time when Alaric was invading Italy. This must allude to the first of Alaric's invasions, in 400, since the second invasion (402) would have been marked by some word such as " Iterum," and at the 3d in 408 Chromatius had already died. The history does not attempt to give more than the chief events, and these are told with little sense of proportion, the Council of Ariminum occupying about 20 lines, while the story of the right arm of Arsenius which Athanasius was accused of cutting off takes up five times that space. Some documents of great importance, however, are given, such as the canons of Nicæa, and the Creed as it issued from the council. But there is much credulity, as shown in the account of the Discovery of the True Cross by Helena mother of Constantine, and the stories of the death of Arius and the attempted rebuilding of the Jewish Temple under Julian. Rufinus has none of the critical power needed for a true historian. We may add that all that is valuable in his history is incorporated into the works of Socrates (translated in Vol. iii. of this Series). See especially B. ii, c. 1.

6. *The History of the Monks* which is a description of the Egyptian Solitaries appears to have no mark of its date : But it was, no doubt, composed at Aquileia between 398 and 409, probably in the later part of that period. It was written in the name of Petronius Bishop of Bologna, and records his experiences, which he says he had been often requested by the monks of Mt. Olivet to commit to writing. It is full of strange stories like those in Jerome's Lives of the Hermits Hilarion and Malchus.[1] There is often a verbal resemblance between this book and the Lausiac History of Palladius; indeed, they at times record the same adventures (compare the story of the crocodiles, Ruf. Hist. Mon. xxxiii. 6 with Pall. Hist. Laus. cl., where even the same prayers and texts are put into the mouths of the two narrators.) But it is probable that in these cases Palladius is indebted to Rufinus.

7. *The Exposition of the Creed* is described in the note prefixed to the Translation (541).

8. *The Prefaces to the Books of Origen,* translated by Rufinus, and to the *Apology of Pamphilus for Origen,* together with the *Book on the Adulteration of Origen's Writings* are given in this volume (420–427). That to the Περὶ Ἀρχῶν (427) is the document on which the great controversy between Jerome and Rufinus turns. That to Numbers gives personal details of importance, while the Peroration to the Ep. to the Romans exhibits the method used in translating. The Preface and Epilogue to the work of Pamphilus are of great importance in connexion with the controversy between Jerome and Rufinus.

II. TRANSLATIONS FROM GREEK WRITERS.

1. *The Rule of St. Basil,* translated at Pinetum for the Abbat Urseius in 397 or 398. This was the first work written by Rufinus of which we have any knowledge.

2. *The Apology of Pamphilus for Origen.* This formed the 1st book of an Apology for Origen's teaching in 6 books, which were composed by Eusebius and Pamphilus during the latter's imprisonment at Cæsarea previous to his martyrdom. Eusebius speaks of this work in a general way (H. E. vi. 33) as written by himself and Pamphilus. The last book, however, was written by Eusebius alone after the death of Pamphilus. The part translated by Rufinus is only the 1st book, and this he believed to be by Pamphilus alone. Jerome in his Apology (487, 514) asserted that the whole was by Eusebius alone. But his bitter feeling led him astray in this. The Apology for Origen has perished with the exception of this 1st book which survives in Rufinus' Translation. The Preface which he prefixed to the work, and the Epilogue which he subjoined to it under the name of " The book concerning the adulteration of the works of Origen " are given in our translation (420–427). This work was written at Pinetum near Terracina at the request of Macarius, to whom the Preface is addressed, in the end of 397 or the beginning of 398. For the questions relating to the authorship of the Apology the reader is referred to the Apologies of Jerome and Rufinus (esp. pp. 487, 514), to Lightfoot's Article on Eusebius in the Dict. of Eccl. Biography, and the Prolegomena to the Translation of Eusebius in this Series, p. 36.

3. *Origen's* Περὶ Ἀρχῶν. This translation was also made at the request of Macarius, and was finished as the Preface to B. iii. shows in the Lent of 398. The questions raised by this Translation are discussed in the Introductions to the Works of Jerome (Vol. vi of

---

[1] See those Lives translated in Vol. vi of this Series.

this Series), and of Rufinus in this Volume ; and the controversy itself is developed in their Apologies (434–540). The greater part of the Περὶ ’Αρχῶν is known to us only through this translation.

4. *Origen's Homilies.* Those on *the Books of Moses and of Joshua* were translated at various times during the last 10 years of Rufinus' life. He had intended, as he states in his Preface to the Book of Numbers, to translate all that had been written by Origen on the Pentateuch : he accomplished this as regards the first three books, and also as to the book of Joshua, at the request of Chromatius; the book of Numbers he only finished in Sicily, just before his death ; and the Commentaries on Deuteronomy he did not live to translate. In these translations, as he tells us (567), he did not scruple to supply what he found to be omitted in the Greek, the Homilies being of a hortatory kind, whereas Rufinus' object was an exposition of the text.

The Translation of the *Homilies on Judges*, though there is no Preface to it, is ascribed to Rufinus by Fontanini, who maintains that in this case, the name of Rufinus being discredited on account of Jerome's diatribe against him, the editors have suppressed the Preface, while in some other cases they have substituted the name of Jerome for that of Rufinus.

The Translation of Origen's *Commentary on the 36th, 37th and 38th Psalms* is unquestionably by Rufinus; it is dedicated to Apronianus, and may have been written in Rome (Fontanini col. 188, beginning of ch. viii). The Preface is given by us in this volume. Fontanini also gives to Rufinus a Translation of Origen's Homilies on 1 Kings and on Canticles. The books on Joshua and Judges he translated as he found them (567), but in the next he adopted a different method.

The works of Origen on the Ep. to the Romans were very long, and Rufinus did not scruple to condense them (reducing the 25 books of Origen to 10), as he clearly states in his Peroration (567). This work he addressed to Heraclius, and it was composed during his stay at Aquileia.

Rufinus had hoped, as we learn from the same Peroration (567), to translate some at least of the Commentaries of Origen upon the other Epistles of St. Paul; but he first determined to finish those upon the Pentateuch, a task in which, as we have seen, he was overtaken by death.

5. *The Translation of 10 Tracts of St. Basil and 8 of Gregory Nazianzen.* These are to be found in the works of Basil and Gregory, but without Prefaces; they are, however, mentioned by Rufinus himself in his Eccl. Hist. ii. 9, and in a letter to Apronianus quoted by Fontanini Vit. Ruf. II., viii, I. col. 189.

6. *The Sentences of Xystus,* which have been variously attributed to a philosopher who flourished in the reign of Augustus, and is quoted by Seneca, and to Xystus, or Sixtus, Bp. of Rome, who suffered martyrdom in 258. They are called the Annulus (’εγχειρίδιον) as inseparable from the hand. Rufinus speaks of them in his Preface, translated in this volume, as being traditionally ascribed to the Bishop; he does not pledge himself to this opinion, but does not deny it; and recent research has shown that, though they may have a basis in heathen philosophy, they are in their present form the writings of a Christian. Jerome, however, scoffs at Rufinus again and again, as either through ignorance or heterodoxy ascribing to a Christian Bishop and martyr the work of a Pythagorean (See Jerome ad Ctesiphontem (Ep. cxxxiii. c. 3), Comm. on Ezek. B. vi. ch. 8, on Jerem. B. iv. ch. 22. The whole matter is fully discussed in Dict. of Christian Biog. Art. Xystus.)

7. *The Sentences of Evagrius Ponticus (or Iberita or Galatus)* in three treatises, (1) *to Virgins,* (2) *To Monks,* (3) *On the Passionless State.* These are described with bitter depreciation as heretical works by Jerome (Ad Ctes. Ep. 133 c. 3. Pref. to Anti-Pelagian Dialogue and to B. iv. of Comm. on Jerem.) but approved by Gennadius (c. 9.) who issued an amended version of Rufinus' translation. Rufinus' translation is said to be in the Vatican library by Fontanini (Vita Rufini Lib. II. c. iv. in Migne's Patrologia Vol. 21 col. 205.)

8. *The Recognitions of Clement* supposed to have been written by Clement Bishop of Rome, but now known to be a work of 50 or 60 years later. The translation of it was asked for by Silvia sister of Rufinus the Prætorian Prefect, and was unsuccessfully attempted by Paulinus of Nola (see his letter to Rufinus in Fontanini as above, col. 208.) After the death of Silvia, Gaudentius Bp. of Brixia where she died as a saint, urged Rufinus to make the translation (Peror. to Ep. to Rom. 567) Preface of Rufinus.)

9. The translation of *Eusebius' Eccl. History* in 9 books, a work much valued in

Gaul, and often reprinted in later times. The Preface (Migne's Rufinus col. 461) is addressed to Chromatius, and says that it was demanded by him at the time of Alaric's invasion of Italy (A.D. 400) as an antidote to the unsettlement of men's minds. Rufinus speaks humbly of himself as having little practice in Latin writing. He says that he has compressed the 10th book which contained little of real history, and added what remained of it to Book 9. See Prolegomena to Eusebius in this Series Vol. i p. 54.

It is a curious and important fact that all the translations known to have been made by Rufinus have survived. This is due no doubt to their being the only translations extant in the Middle Ages of great writers like Origen and Basil, and to the impossibility of procuring others. The uncritical spirit of the time may have been favourable to them. Had they been recognized as the works of Rufinus, they might have been destroyed; but it was possible, even after the revival of learning, to attribute many of them to Jerome.

Gennadius mentions a series of Rufinus' letters, which have not survived, amongst which were several of special importance addressed to Proba, a lady who is highly commended by Jerome in his letter to Demetrias.[1] Jerome also mentions (537) some translations of Rufinus from Latin into Greek, but his allusion is somewhat vague; and some translations from the LXX (536). A translation of Josephus, and a Commentary on the first 75 Psalms, and on Hosea, Joel and Amos, a Life of St. Eugenia and a Book on the Faith have been attributed to Rufinus but are believed not to be his. These, with the exception of the translation of Josephus, are given by Vallarsi in his edition of Rufinus. Besides these, translations of Origen's Seven Homilies on Matthew and one on John, and of his treatises on Mary Magdalen and on Christ's Epiphany have at times been attributed to Rufinus.

We do not propose to go minutely into the Bibliography of Rufinus' Works. Some of them were among the earliest printed books. The Editio Princeps of the *Commentary on the Creed* bears date *Oxford, 1468*, but is commonly believed to be really of 1478; that of the *Ecclesiastical History, Paris, 1474;* that of the *History of the Monks*, undated, is believed to be of 1471; that of the *Commentaries of Origen* is of 1503 (Aldus Minutius); that of the *Sayings of Xystus* of 1507, and of the Περὶ Ἀρχῶν is of 1514 (Venice). They continued to be reprinted up to 1580; but, with the exception of the *Sayings of Xystus*, no further editions were published till the edition of Vallarsi (Verona, 1745), and the Life by Fontanini (Rome, 1742). Since that date, though various editions and translations of the *Expositions of the Creed* have appeared, no attempt has been made to give the whole of Rufinus' writings. Migne (Patrologia, Vol. xxi., Paris, 1849) is contented to reprint Vallarsi without alteration.

No complete edition of Rufinus' Works, therefore, exists. The volume of Migne's Patrologia (21) contains the Life by Fontanini (Rome, 1742), the Notice by Schœnemann (Leipzig, 1792), and Vallarsi's edition (Verona, 1745) of Rufinus' chief works, viz. The Benedictions of the Patriarchs, the Commentary on the Creed, the Monastic History, the Ecclesiastical History, the Apology against Jerome, and the Apology addressed to Anastasius. Vallarsi had intended to edit the Translations from Greek writers, but did not accomplish this. The Prefaces to these translations, some of which are of great importance, have therefore to be sought by the student in the editions of the writers to whose works they are prefixed. They are collected and translated in this Volume for the first time.

We have in the present work not attempted to translate all the original works of Rufinus. We have omitted the Exposition of the Benedictions of the Twelve patriarchs, the Ecclesiastical History and the History of the Monks. The rest we have given. They include his Apologies, together with the Letter of Pope Anastasius about him to John of Jerusalem, the Prefaces to the Περὶ Ἀρχῶν and the Apology of Pamphilus, and the Epilogue to the latter work, called the Dissertation on the adulteration of the Works of Origen, together with the Prefaces which are still extant to his Translations of Origen's Commentaries and his Peroration to Origen on Romans. We have also included his best-known work, his Commentary on the Creed, a translation of which has kindly been placed at our service by Dr. Heurtley, Lady Margaret Professor of Theology at Oxford.

---

[1] Letter cxxx, 7.

WORKS OF RUFINUS TRANSLATED IN THIS VOLUME

WRITINGS OF RUFINUS

PREFACE TO THE COMMENTARY ON THE BENEDICTIONS OF THE TWELVE PATRIARCHS

Rufinus had arrived with Melania, in Italy, in the spring of 397, after a stay in the East of some 25 years. They had visited Paulinus at Nola, and had been entertained by him with the highest honours. Melania probably remained in Campania, where she had property, engaged in family affairs; but Rufinus set out for Rome. He stopped, however, for some months at the monastery of Pinetum near Terracina, with his friend Urseius the Abbot.

His work on Jacob's Benedictions on his sons in Gen. xlix was occasioned by the following letter from Paulinus, who alludes to it in writing to Sulpicius Severus (Ep. xxviii). "I have written a short note to the Presbyter Rufinus, the companion of the saintly Melania in her spiritual journey, a truly holy and truly learned man, and one united with me on this account in the closest affection." The work itself, being an Exposition of Scripture, is not given, but only the Preface.

Paulinus to his brother Rufinus, all best wishes.[1]

1. Even a short letter from one so like-minded as yourself is a great refreshment, like the dew which revives a thirsty field when the rivers are low. But while I confess that I have been refreshed by this letter which, though short, is still from you, and is sent by the servant of our common children, yet I have been troubled at hearing that all at once through the disquiet of your anxiety and the uncertainty caused by delay, you have determined that you must go to Rome. May the Lord grant you to receive joy in the Lord from what we are doing: so that, as now we share in your anxiety, so we may rejoice in your joy, and that we may still have some beginnings of hope that we may enjoy your presence, when you begin to see clearly your way and the will of the Lord concerning you.

2. You are kind enough, with that affection which makes you love me as yourself, to desire that I should take up more seriously the study of Greek literature. I acknowledge the kindness which dictates this wish; but I am unable to give it effect, unless, through God's blessing on my earnest desires, I should have the happiness of your company for a longer time. How can I gain any proficiency in a foreign tongue in the absence of him who might teach me what I do not know? I think that, in the matter of the translation of St. Clement,[1] besides the other defects of my abilities, you noticed this especially as showing the weakness caused by my want of practice, that where I had been unable to understand the words or to express them accurately, I have translated them according to my idea of their drift, or, to speak more truly, set down what I thought ought to be there. All the more therefore do I need that, through God's mercy, I may have your company in fuller measure; for that will be like wealth to the poor or like gathering the crumbs which fall from the rich man's table with the eager appetite of the bondman's heart.

3. At the moment when I was writing these words my eye fell upon a passage of Scripture, occurring in a portion which I had set down for reading, namely that in which Judah is blessed by Jacob; and I determined after a time to knock at the door of your mind, for which the Lord had given me this most timely occasion. I beg you, if you love me, or rather because you love me so greatly, to write and say how you understand this blessing of the Patriarchs; and, if there are some things in it which are worth knowing but hard to understand, impart to me also the knowledge of them; especially of that passage which says: "Binding his

---

[1] *Salutem*, a word implying well-being generally as well as health.

[1] That is, the Recognitions. See the Preface to Rufinus' Translation in this volume, with the explanatory note prefixed to it.

colt to the vine and his ass's[1] colt to the hair-cloth."[2] Tell me what is the colt and the ass's colt, and why his colt is to be bound to the vine, but the ass's colt to the hair cloth.

The answer of Rufinus forms the Preface to his Exposition of the Benedictions.

1. The more I excuse myself to you, and the more I assert that I am unable to respond to your inquiries, the more instant you become in your requests, and the harder become your demands: you treat me as you would an ox whose laziness you have discovered, and prick his flanks and back as he stops and turns back with goads of ever increasing sharpness. I must point out to you, therefore, that, even if I am able to bow my neck low so as just to drag the heavy yoke which you lay upon me, yet I have no chance of bursting at a rapid pace into the open and wide-spreading plains through a form of speech which flows at large and pours itself forth over far-extending space. Bear with me therefore if my resolution has been but tardily fulfilled, and if I come up only at a feeble pace to the point to which you call me.

2. You ask me how the passage in Genesis is to be understood in which Israel the father of the patriarchs is represented as predicting what he saw would happen to each of his sons, and says of Judah, amongst other things: "Binding his colt to the vine, and his ass's colt to the tendril of the vine." You write it " and his ass's colt to the hair-cloth " (cilicium) ; but in the Greek it stands : καὶ τῇ ἕλικι τὸν πῶλον τῆς ὄνου αὐτοῦ. The Greeks call by the name ἕλικα (twist) not the sprigs of the vine (as our copies have it) but

those sickle-like shoots[1] by which it supports itself on branches of trees or poles or the supports of the kind which I think the farmers call goatikins ;[2] so that the vine is made safe by these clinging shoots from all danger of falling, and the tendril can either become loaded with grapes or grow out in unfettered length. I think therefore that this very word (helici), like some others, must have been set down a long time ago in the Latin versions, and that it was afterwards supposed by unintelligent copyists that by helici, hair-cloth (cilicium) must be meant.

3. It is easy in this way to emend the mistakes of the translation ; but it is not so easy to find out the meaning of the expression itself unless we take into consideration the whole passage. But the treatment of this passage would be placed in a fuller and clearer light if we could go back to the beginning of the whole of these Benedictions. But this implies no small amount of leisure and of time ; or, to speak in a more Christian sense, it demands a mind illuminated by the Holy Spirit. My talent is but slight, and there are many demands on my time ; and my friends are urging me to comply with their requests about Origen.[3] But, so far as these circumstances admit, and so great a matter can be treated with brevity, I will state at once what appears to me the true meaning of this passage, for the love with which you bid me trust you in everything, and without prejudice to the judgment of others, who may have something better to say about it.

---

[1] Gen. xlix. ii.
[2] This is a mistaken reading (though said by Vallarsi to be accepted by both Ambrose and Augustin), Cilicium for ἕλικι. Rufinus adopts the latter. " Binding his ass's colt to the tendril of the vine."

[1] The word in the text *rucinnulos* is unknown in Latin. The most likely conjecture as to the right reading is *ruscarias quibus* (that is *ruscarias falculas*—sickles for weeding out butcher's broom, as mentioned by Cato and Varro).
[2] Capreolos. Properly little goats, thus used for the props, the fork of which resembled the horns of the goat. The word is also used for the tendrils of the vine, and is by some derived from *capio*.
[3] That is about the translation of the Περὶ Ἀρχῶν. See the Preface to this further on.

PREFACE TO BOOK II.

Rufinus, as we see by his Preface to the former book, considered it unsatisfactory to expound the Blessing upon Judah apart from those on his brethren. Paulinus therefore, taking the occasion of their common friend Cerealis' journey to Rome, sends the following letter to induce Rufinus to expound the remaining Benedictions.

Paulinus to his brother Rufinus, all good wishes.

1. Although our son Cerealis declared to me that it was uncertain whether, in returning as he now does to St. Peter,[1] he would be able to visit you, yet it appears to me that it

---

[1] That is to Rome.

would be blamable in me and vexatious to you were I not to write to you by him in whom you have a part as well as I. It seems to me preferable to lose some letter paper by his not visiting you rather than to lose credit with you as I think I should do by his visiting you without it : and therefore I have entrusted this letter, I will not say to chance, but to faith: for I believe that the Lord will direct to you the way both of our son and of my letter; since to those who long for good all will turn to good; and indeed he longs for you as you ought to be longed for by one who understands the good he may gain from your society. I believe that this longing of his in a good matter will not be lost, according to his faith and piety: and therefore I have confidence that he will reach you and abide with you, and that I shall see the saving help of the Lord doubled towards you, since in him you will have the accession of a good son and pupil and assistant, and he will find in you a father and teacher of all good things given to him from the Lord, who will add to the efficacy and power of his prayers the strength of spiritual grace. As to myself, though I have the assurance that when you return to the East you will be unwilling to depart without visiting me, yet my sins make me fear that the daughter of Baby- lon, may turn you away from me. I pray therefore with earnest longings to the Lord that he would give me not according to my deserts but according to my desire and may direct your course to me in the way of peace; for such as do not walk in that way are reprobate and condemned and incapable of truly longing for your presence.

2. But now for the business part of my letter. I charge you, with the importunity, with which I am in the habit of knocking at your door even in the middle of the night, being driven by fear of a refusal to the modest attitude of a supplicant, to show me kindness once more, and to expound the Benedictions on the twelve Patriarchs. You have already made a beginning with the prophecy relating to Judah, and have given, according to the precept, a threefold inter- pretation of it. I now beg you to expound the prophecy as it relates to each of the sons of Judah: so that I may myself become possessed of the truth by your means, and may also gain through your help the favor and the praise which will accrue to me; for I shall thus be able to make answer to those who have thought well to consult me on the difficulties of this passage of Scripture not with foolish words drawn from my own un- derstanding but with divine truth flowing from your inspiration.

Rufinus, though at this time busy with his larger works, the translations of Pamphilus' de- fence of Origen, and Origen's Περὶ Αρχῶν, and, though about to set out for Rome, lost no time in composing the work which Paulinus demanded, and sent it him with the following letter.

Rufinus to his brother Paulinus, the Man of God, with all good wishes.

1. Though our common son Cerealis did not visit me, he felt what pain he would cause me if he delayed my reception of your letter, and forwarded it to me. In reading it I felt, as usual, a continual increase in my yearning towards you: but I found towards its close a request from which I have frequently begged you to excuse me — I mean the request which you make that I should write some- thing in answer to your questions as to the interpretation of passages of Scripture. I thought that I should lead you to desist from these questions by the writings I have once and again sent you, which have given evi- dence of my ignorance and of the roughness of my speech.

2. But since you still are not weary of commanding me, I have at once, to the best of my powers, added to what I had written at your desire on the Benediction of Judah the comments on the remaining eleven patri- archs. I acted like the man in the parable of the two sons. I thought that I should thus best fulfil the father's will: and though when he ordered me to go into the vineyard I had said I will not go, yet after a while I went. If, as I grant, there is some rashness in the fact that with so little capacity we attempt such a great task, I would say, with sub- mission to you, that this must be most justly imputed to you, since, through your excessive love for me you do not see that my measure of knowledge, as of other virtues, is but slight. I wrote this work in the days of Lent, while I was staying in the monastery of Pinetum, and I wrote it for you. But I found it impossible to conceal this poor work from the brethren who were there: and they, considering that a thing which had been honoured by your approval must be of great importance, extorted from me the permis- sion to copy it for themselves. Thus, while you demand from me food for yourself you give refreshment to others also. Farewell, and be in peace, my most loving brother, most true worshipper of God, and an Israel- ite in whom there is no guile. I entreat you who are so full of the grace of God to hold me still in remembrance.

TRANSLATION OF PAMPHILUS' DEFENCE OF ORIGEN.

Written at Pinetum A.D. 397.

While Rufinus was staying at Pinetum, a Christian named Macarius[1] sought his advice and assistance. He was engaged in a controversy with the Mathematici, a class of men who had deserted the scientific studies from which they took their name, and had turned to astrology and a belief in Fatalism. Macarius, having heard of Origen's greatness in the region of Christian speculation, earnestly desired some knowledge of his writings: but was unable to attain it through ignorance of Greek. He declared to Rufinus that he had had a dream in which he saw a ship laden with Eastern merchandize arriving in Italy, and that it was declared to him that this ship would contain the means of attaining the knowledge he desired. The coming of Rufinus seemed to him the fulfilment of his dream, and he earnestly besought him to impart to him some of the treasures of his Greek learning, and especially to translate for him Origen's great speculative work, the Περὶ Ἀρχῶν, that is On First Principles.[2] Rufinus hesitated, knowing that there was a strong prejudice against Origen, and that he was looked on, especially in the West, as a heretic, though his writings were little known there. He yielded, however, to the solicitations of Macarius: but to guard against the imputation of heresy, he undertook three preliminary works. First, he translated the Apology of the Martyr Pamphilus for Origen; secondly, he wrote a short treatise on the Adulteration by heretics of the works of Origen; and, thirdly, in translating the Περὶ Ἀρχῶν he prefixed to it an elaborate Preface in justification of his course in translating the work. All these documents became the subject of vehement controversy which found its expression in the letter of Jerome to his friends at Rome, and the Apologies of Rufinus and Jerome translated in this volume.

The Apology of Pamphilus for Origen forms the sixth book of a work undertaken by him in connexion with Eusebius of Cæsarea, the Church Historian. Pamphilus was a great collector of books, and a learned man, but Eusebius was the chief writer. Pamphilus was put to death in the last persecution, that under Galerius; and Eusebius having at a later time fallen under suspicion of Arianism, it was attempted by those who disliked Origen, to dissociate Pamphilus from all connexion with the work. There seems however no reason to doubt, notwithstanding Jerome's violent protestations, that Pamphilus was associated with Eusebius throughout the work, and that he actually wrote the sixth book. The translation of this Apology was made first, and sent out with a Preface which runs as follows:

You have been moved by your desire to know the truth, Macarius, who are "a man greatly beloved,"[3] to make a request of me, which will bring you the blessing attached to the knowledge of the truth; but it will win for me the greatest indignation on the part of those who consider themselves aggrieved whenever any one does not think evil of Origen. It is true that it is not my opinion about him that you have asked for, but that of the holy martyr Pamphilus; and you have requested to have the book which he is said to have written in his defence in Greek translated for you into Latin: nevertheless I do not doubt that there will be some who will think themselves aggrieved if I say anything in his defence even in the words of another man. I beg them to do nothing in the spirit of presumption and of prejudice; and, since we must all stand before the judgment seat of Christ, not to refuse to hear the truth spoken, lest haply they should do wrong through ignorance. Let them consider that to wound the consciences of their weaker brethren by false accusations is to sin against Christ; and therefore let them not lend their ears to the accusers, nor seek an account of another man's faith from a third party, especially when an opportunity is given them for gaining personal and direct knowledge, and the substance and quality of each man's faith is to be known by his own confession. For so the Scripture says: [4] "With the heart man believeth unto righteousness, and with the mouth confession is made unto salvation": and: [5] "By his words shall each man be justified, and by his word shall he be condemned." The opinions of Origen in the various parts of Scripture are clearly set forth in the present work: as to the cause of our finding certain places in which he contradicts himself, an explanation will be offered in the short document subjoined.[6] But as for myself, I hold that which has been handed down to us from the holy fathers, namely, that the Holy Trinity is coeternal, and of a single nature, virtue and substance; that the Son of God in these last times has been made man, has suffered for

---

[1] See the account in Rufinus' Apology I. 11.
[2] The word may also mean On beginnings, or the speculation of the Alexandrian theology.
[4] Rom. x, 10.   [5] Matt. xii, 37.
On Principalities and Powers: these ideas being connected together in
[3] Daniel x. 11, ix. 23. The name Macarius means Blessed.
[6] See the Epilogue, infra.

our transgressions and rose again from the dead in the very flesh in which he suffered, and thereby imparted the hope of the resurrection to the whole race of mankind. When we speak of the resurrection of the flesh, we do so, not with any subterfuges, as is slanderously reported by certain persons; we believe that it is this very flesh in which we are now living which will rise again, not one kind of flesh instead of another, nor another body than the body of this flesh. When we speak of the body rising we do so in the words of the apostle; for he himself made use of this word: and when we speak of the flesh, our confession is that of the Creed. It is an absurd invention of maliciousness to think that the human body is different from the flesh. However, whether we speak of that which is to rise, according to the common faith, as the flesh, or, according to the Apostle, as the body, this we must believe, that according to the clear statement of the Apostle, that which shall rise shall rise in power and in glory; it will rise an incorruptible and a spiritual body: for "corruption cannot inherit incor-ruption." We must maintain this preëminence of the body, or flesh, which is to be: but, with this proviso, we must hold that the resurrection of the flesh is perfect and entire; we must on the one hand maintain the identity of the flesh, while on the other we must not detract from the dignity and glory of the incorruptible and spiritual body. For so the Scripture speaks. This is what is preached by the reverend Bishop John at Jerusalem; this we with him both confess and hold. If any one either believes or teaches otherwise, or insinuates that we believe differently from the exposition of our faith, let him be anathema. Let this then be taken as a record of our belief by any who desire to know it. Whatever we read and whatever we do is in accordance with this account of our faith; we follow the words of the Apostle, [1] " proving all things, holding fast that which is good, avoiding every form of evil." [2] " And as many as walk by this rule, peace be upon them and upon the Israel of God."

---

[1] Thess. v, 21, 22.   [2] Gal. vi, 16.

RUFINUS'S EPILOGUE TO PAMPHILUS THE MARTYR'S APOLOGY FOR ORIGEN,

OTHERWISE

The Book Concerning the Adulteration of the Works of Origen.

Addressed to Macarius at Pinetum A.D. 397.

The next work was sent out at the same time with Pamphilus' Apology. Rufinus believed that Origen's works had been adulterated by heretics so as to turn his assertions into support of their own opinions. He thererore, in his translation of the Περὶ Ἀρχῶν, altered many things which had a heterodox meaning as found in the ordinary MSS. of Origen, so as to make the work consistent with itself and with the orthodox views expressed in other parts of Origen's writings. How far this process was legitimate or honest must be judged from a perusal of the controversy which followed; but it should be borne in mind, first, that the standard of literary exactness and conscientiousness was not the same in those days as in ours; secondly, that when everything depended on copyists, there was room for infinite variations in the copies, whether through negligence, ignorance or fraud; thirdly, that the principles adopted by Rufinus were precisely those acknowledged by his great opponent Jerome, in his Treatise De Optimo Genere Interpretandi, and his Letter to Vigilantius (Letters lxvi and lxi).

My object in the translation from Greek into Latin of the holy martyr Pamphilus' Apology for Origen, which I have given in the preceding volume according to my abil-ity and the requirements of the matter, is this: I wish you to know through full information that the rule of faith which has been set forth above in his writings is that which we must embrace and hold; for it is clearly shown that the Catholic opinion is contained in them all. Nevertheless you have to allow that there are found in his books certain things not only different from this but in certain cases even repugnant to it; things which our canons of truth do not sanction, and which we can neither receive nor approve. As to the cause of this an opinion has reached me which has been widely entertained, and which I wish to be fully known by you and by those who desire to know what is true, since it is possible also that some who have before been actuated by the love of fault-finding may acquiesce in the truth and reason of the matter when they have it set before them; for some seem determined to believe anything in the world to be true rather than that which withdraws from them the occasions of fault-finding. It must, I think, be felt to be wholly impossible that a man so learned and so wise, a man whom even his accusers may well admit to have been neither foolish nor insane, should have written what is contrary and repugnant to himself and his own opinions. But even suppose that this could in some way have happened; suppose, as some perhaps have said, that in the decline of life he might have forgotten what he had written in his early days, and have made assertions at variance with his former opinions; how are we to deal with the fact that we sometimes find in the very same passages, and, as I may say, almost in successive sentences, clauses inserted expressive of contrary opinions? Can we believe that in the same work and in the same book, and even sometimes, as I have said, in the following paragraph,.a man could have forgotten his own views? For example that, when he had said just before that no passage in all the Scripture could be found in which the Holy Spirit was spoken of as made or created, he could have immediately added that the Holy Spirit had been made along with the rest of the creatures? or again, that the same man who clearly states that the Father and the Son are of one substance, or as it is called in Greek Homoousion, could in the next sentence say that He was of another substance, and was a created being, when he had but a little before described him as born of the very nature of God the Father? Or again in the matter of the resurrection of the flesh, could he who so clearly declared that it was the nature of the flesh which ascended with the Word of God into heaven, and there appeared to the celestial Powers, presenting a new image of himself for them to worship, could he, I ask you, possibly turn round and say that this flesh

was not to be saved? Such things could not happen even in the case of a man who had taken leave of his senses and was not sound in the brain. How, therefore, this came to pass, I will point out with all possible brevity. The heretics are capable of any violence, they have no remorse and no scruples: this we are forced to recognize by the audacities of which they have been frequently convicted. And, just as their father the devil has from the beginning made it his object to falsify the words of God and twist them from their true meaning, and subtilely to interpolate among them his own poisonous ideas, so he has left these successors of his the same art as their inheritance. Accordingly, when God had said to Adam, "You shall eat of all the trees of the garden;" he, when he wished to deceive Eve interpolated a single syllable, by which he reduced within the narrowest bounds God's liberality in permitting all the fruits to be eaten. He said: "Yea, hath God said, Ye shall not eat of *any* tree of the garden?" and thus, by suggesting the complaint that God's command was severe, he more easily persuaded her to transgress the precept. The heretics have followed the example of their father, the craft of their teacher. Whenever they found in any of the renowned writers of old days a discussion of those things which pertain to the glory of God so full and faithful that every believer could gain profit and instruction from it, they have not scrupled to infuse into their writings the poisonous taint of their own false doctrines; this they have done, either by inserting things which the writers had not said or by changing by interpolation what they had said, so that their own poisonous heresy might more easily be asserted and authorized by passing under the name of all the church writers of the greatest learning and renown; they meant it to appear that well-known and orthodox men had held as they did. We hold the clearest proofs of this in the case of the Greek writers; and this adulteration of books is to be found in the case of many of the ancients; but it will suffice to adduce the testimony of a few, so that it may be more easily understood what has befallen the writings of Origen.

Clement, the disciple of the Apostles, who was bishop of the Roman church next to the Apostles, was a martyr, wrote the work which is called in the Greek Ἀναγνωρισμός, or in Latin, The Recognition.[1] In these books

---

[1] Rufinus was deceived as was the whole world until the revival of learning, in believing this fabrication to be the work of Clement. It is really a romance in the form of an autobiography of Clement, supposed to be addressed to James of Jerusalem; and was written probably in Asia Minor or Syria

he sets forth again and again in the name of the Apostle Peter a doctrine which appears to be truly apostolical: yet in certain passages the heresy of Eunomius is so brought in that you would imagine that you were listening to an argument of Eunomius himself, asserting that the Son of God was created out of no existing elements. Then again that other method of falsification is introduced, by which it is made to appear that the nature of the devil and of other demons has not resulted from the wickedness of their will and purpose, but from an exceptional and separate quality of their creation, although he in all other places had taught that every reasonable creature was endowed with the faculty of free will. There are also some other things inserted into his books which the church's creed does not admit. I ask, then, what we are to think of these things? Are we to believe that an apostolic man, nay, almost an apostle (since he writes the things which the apostles speak), one to whom the apostle Paul bore his testimony in the words, " With Clement and others, my fellow labourers, whose names are in the book of life " was the writer of words which contradict the book of life? or are we to say, as we have said before, that perverse men, in order to gain authority for their own heresies by the use of the names of holy men, and so procure their readier acceptance, interpolated these things which it is impossible to believe that the true authors either thought or wrote?

Again, the other Clement, the presbyter of Alexandria, and the teacher of that church, in almost all his books describes the three Persons as having one and the same glory and eternity: and yet we sometimes find in his books passages in which he speaks of the Son as a creature of God. Is it credible that so great a man as he, so orthodox in all points, and so learned, either held opinions mutually contradictory, or left in writing views concerning God which it is an impiety, I will not say to believe, but even to listen to?

Once more, Dionysius the Bishop of Alexandria, was a most learned maintainer of the church's faith, and in passages without end defended the unity and eternity of the Trinity, so earnestly that some persons of less insight imagine that he held the views of Sabellius; yet in the books which he wrote against the heresy of Sabellius, there are things inserted of such a character that the Arians endeavour to shield themselves

under his authority, and on this account the holy Bishop Athanasius felt himself compelled to write an apology for his work, because he was assured that he could not have held strange opinions or have written things in which he contradicted himself, but felt sure that these things had been interpreted by ill disposed men.

This opinion we have been led to form by the force of the facts themselves, in the case of these very reverend men and doctors of the church; we have found it impossible, I say, to believe that those reverend men who again and again have supported the church's belief should in particular points have held opinions contradictory to themselves. As to Origen, however, in whom, as I have said above, are to be found, as in those others, certain diversities of statement, it will not be sufficient to think precisely as we think or feel about those who enjoy an established reputation for orthodoxy; nor could a similar charge be met by a similar excuse, were it not that its validity is shown by words and writings of his own in which he makes this fact the subject of earnest complaint. What he had to suffer while still living in the flesh, while still having feeling and sight, from the corruption of his books and treatises, or from counterfeit versions of them, we may learn clearly from his own letter which he wrote to certain intimate friends at Alexandria; and by this you will see how it comes to pass that some things which are self-contradictory are found in his writings.[1]

" Some of those persons who take a pleasure in accusing their neighbours, bring against us and our teaching the charge of blasphemy, though from us they have never heard anything of the kind. Let them take heed to themselves how they refuse to mark that solemn injunction which says that [2] ' Revilers shall not inherit the kingdom of God,' when they declare that I hold that the father of wickedness and perdition, and of those who are cast forth from the kingdom of God, that is the devil, is to be saved, a thing which no man can say even if he has taken leave of his senses and is manifestly insane. Yet it is no wonder, I think, if my teaching is falsified by my adversaries, and is corrupted and adulterated in the same manner as the epistle of Paul the Apostle. Certain men, as we know, compiled a false epistle under the name of Paul, so that they might trouble the Thessalonians as if the day of the Lord were nigh at hand, and thus

---

about A.D. 200. See Article " Clementine Literature " in Dict. of Ch. Biog.

[1] The letter is headed " On the adulteration and corruption of his books; from the 4th book of the letters of Origen: a letter written to certain familiar friends at Alexandria."
[2] 1 Cor. vi, 10.

beguile them. It is on account of that false epistle that he wrote these words in the second epistle to the Thessalonians : ¹ ' We beseech you, brethren, by the coming of our Lord Jesus Christ and our gathering together unto him ; to the end that ye be not quickly shaken from your mind, nor yet be troubled, either by spirit or by word or by letter as sent from us, as that the day of the Lord is at hand. Let no man beguile you in any wise.' It is something of the same kind, I perceive, which is happening to us also. A certain promoter of heresy, after a discussion which had been held between us in the presence of many persons, and notes of it had been taken, procured the document from those who had written out the notes, and added or struck out whatever he chose, and changed things as he thought right, and published it abroad as if it were my work, but pointing in triumphant scorn at the expressions which he had himself inserted. The brethren in Palestine, indignant at this, sent a man to me at Athens to obtain from me an authentic copy of the work. Up to that time I had never even read it over again or revised it : it had been so completely neglected and thrown aside that it could hardly be found. Nevertheless, I sent it : and, — God is witness that I am speaking the truth, — when I met the man himself who had adulterated the work, and took him to task for having done so, he answered, as if he were giving me satisfaction : ' I did it because I wished to improve that treatise and to purge away its faults.' What kind of a purging was this that he applied to my dissertation ? such a purging as Marcion or his successor Apelles after him gave to the Gospels and to the writings of the Apostle. They subverted the true text of Scripture ; and this man similarly first took away the true statements which I had made, and then inserted what was false to furnish grounds for accusation against me. But, though those who have dared to do this are impious and heretical men, yet those who give credence to such accusations against us shall not escape the judgment of God. There are others also, not a few, who have done this through a wish to throw confusion into the churches. Lately, a certain heretic who had seen me at Ephesus and had refused to meet me, and had not opened his mouth in my presence, but for some reason or other had avoided doing so, afterwards composed a dissertation according to his own fancy, partly mine, partly his own, and sent it to his disciples in various places : I know

that it reached those who were in Rome, and I doubt not that it reached others also. He was behaving in the same reckless way at Antioch also before I came there : and the dissertation which he brought with him came into the hands of many of our friends. But when I arrived, I took him to task in the presence of many persons, and, when he persisted, with a complete absence of shame, in the impudent defence of his forgery, I demanded that the book should be brought in amongst us, so that my mode of speech might be recognized by the brethren, who of course knew the points on which I am accustomed to insist and the method of teaching which I employ. He did not, however, venture to bring in the book, and his assertions were refuted by them all and he himself was convicted of forgery, and thus the brethren were taught a lesson not to give ear to such accusations. If then any one is willing to trust me at all — I speak as in the sight of God — let him believe what I say about the things which are falsely inserted in my letter. But if any man refuses to believe me, and chooses to speak evil of me, it is not to me that he does the injury : he will himself be arraigned as a false witness before God, since he is either bearing false witness against his neighbour, or giving credit to those who bear it."

Such are the complaints which he made while still living, and while he was still able to detect the corruptions and falsifications which had been made in his books. There is another letter of his, in which I remember to have read a complaint of the falsifying of his writings ; but I have not a copy of it at hand, otherwise I could add to those which I have quoted a second testimony in favour of his good faith and veracity direct from himself. But I think that I have said enough to satisfy those who listen to what is said, not in the interest of strife and detraction, but in that of a love of truth. I have shown and proved in the case of the saintly men of whom I have made mention, and of whose orthodoxy there is no question, that, where the tenor of a book is presumably right, anything which is found in it contrary to the faith of the church is more properly believed to have been inserted by heretics than to have been written by the author : and I cannot think it an absurd demand that the same thing should be believed in the case of Origen, not only because the argument is similar but because of the witness given by himself in the complaints which I have brought out from his writings : otherwise we must believe that, like a silly or insane per-

---

¹ 2 Thess. ii, 1-3.

son, he has written in contradiction to himself.

As to the possibility that the heretics may have acted in the violent manner supposed, such wickedness may easily be believed of them. They have given a specimen of it, which makes it credible in the present case, in the fact that they have been unable to keep off their impious hands even from the sacred words of the Gospel. Any one who has a mind to see how they have acted in the case of the Acts of the Apostles or their Epistles, how they have befouled them and gnawed them away, how they have defiled them in every kind of way, sometimes adding words which expressed their impious doctrine, sometimes taking out the opposing truths, will understand it most fully if he will read the books of Tertullian written against Marcion. It is no great thing that they should have corrupted the writings of Origen when they have dared to corrupt the sayings of God our Saviour. It is true that some persons may withhold their assent from what I am saying on the ground of the difference of the heresies; since it was one kind of heresy the partisans of which corrupted the Gospels, but it is another which is aimed at in these passages which, as we assert, have been inserted in the works of Origen. Let those who have such doubts consider that, as in all the saints dwells the one spirit of God (for the Apostle says, [1] "The spirits of the prophets are subject to the prophets," and again, [2] "We all have been made to drink of that one spirit"); so also in all the heretics dwells the one spirit of the devil, who teaches them all and at all times the same or similar wickedness.

There may, however, be some to whom the instances we have given have less persuasive force because they have to do with Greek writers; and therefore, although it is a Greek writer for whom I am pleading, yet, since it is the Latin tongue which is, so to speak, entrusted with the argument, and they are Latin people before whom you have earnestly begged me to plead the cause of these men, and to show what wounds they suffer by the calumnious renderings of their works, it will be satisfactory to show that things of the same kind have happened to Latin as well as Greek writers, and that men approved for their saintly character have had a storm of calumny raised against them by the falsification of their works. I will recount things of still recent memory, so that nothing may be lacking to the manifest credibility of my contention, and its truth may lie open for all to see.

Hilary Bishop of Pictavium [1] was a believer in the Catholic doctrine, and wrote a very complete work of instruction with the view of bringing back from their error those who had subscribed the faithless creed of Ariminum.[2] This book fell into the hands of his adversaries and ill wishers, whether, as some said, by bribing his secretary, or by no matter what other cause. He knew nothing of this: but the book was so falsified by them, the saintly man being all the while entirely unconscious of it, that, when his enemies began to accuse him of heresy in the episcopal assembly, as holding what they knew they had corruptly inserted in his manuscript, he himself demanded the production of his book as evidence of his faith. It was brought from his house, and was found to be full of matter which he repudiated: but it caused him to be excommunicated and to be excluded from the meeting of the synod. In this case, however, though the crime was one of unexampled wickedness, the man who was the victim of it was alive, and present in the flesh; and the hostile faction could be convicted and brought to punishment, when their tricks became known and their machinations were exposed. A remedy was applied through statements, explanations, and similar things: for living men can take action on their own behalf, the dead can refute no accusations under which they labour.

Take another case. The whole collection of the letters of the martyr Cyprian is usually found in a single manuscript. Into this collection certain heretics who held a blasphemous doctrine about the Holy Spirit inserted a treatise of Tertullian on the Trinity, which was faultily expressed though he is himself an upholder of our faith: and from the copies thus made they wrote out a number of others; these they distributed through the whole of the vast city of Constantinople at a very low price: men were attracted by this cheapness and readily bought up the documents full of hidden snares of which they knew nothing; and thus the heretics found means of gaining credit for their impious doctrines through the authority of a great name. It happened,

---

[1] 1 Cor. xiv, 32.   [2] 1 Cor. xii, 13.

[1] Poictiers.
[2] There seem to be no means of throwing light upon this story. Hilary was not at the council of Ariminum, but at that of Seleucia, held the same year (359). On his return to Gaul in 361 he endeavoured, in various meetings of bishops to reunite with the Homoousians those who had subscribed the creed of Ariminum. (See Art. on Hilary Pictav. in Dict. of Christ. Biography.) It may have been in one of these meetings that this scene occurred.

however, that, shortly after the publication, there were found there some of our catholic brothers who were able to expose this wicked fabrication, and recalled as many as they could reach from the entanglements of error. In this they partly succeeded. But there were a great many in those parts who remained convinced that the saintly martyr Cyprian held the belief which had been erroneously expressed by Tertullian.

I will add one other instance of the falsification of a document. It is one of recent memory, though it is an example of the primeval subtlety, and it surpasses all the stories of the ancients.

Bishop Damasus, at the time when a consultation was held in the matter of the reconciling of the followers of Apollinarius to the church,[1] desired to have a document setting forth the faith of the church, which should be subscribed by those who wished to be reconciled. The compiling of this document he entrusted to a certain friend of his, a presbyter and a highly accomplished man,[2] who usually acted for him in matters of this kind. When he came to compose the document, he found it necessary, in speaking of the Incarnation of our Lord, to apply to him the expression "Homo Dominicus." The Apollinarists[3] took offence at this expression, and began to impugn it as a novelty. The writer of the document thereupon undertook to defend himself, and to confute the objectors by the authority of ancient Catholic writers; and he happened to show to one of those who complained of the novelty of the expression a book of the bishop Athanasius in which the word which was under discussion occurred. The man to whom this evidence was offered appeared to be convinced, and asked that the manuscript should be lent to him so that he might convince the rest who from their ignorance were still maintaining their objections. When he had got the manuscript into his hands he devised a perfectly new method of falsification. He first erased the passage in which the expression occurred, and then wrote in again the same words which he had erased. He returned the paper, and it was accepted without question. The controversy about this expression again arose; the manuscript

was brought forward: the expression in question was found in it, but in a position where there had been an erasure: and the man who had brought forward such a manuscript lost all authority, since the erasure seemed to be the proof of malpractice and falsification.. However, in this case as in one which I mentioned before, it was a living man who was thus treated by a living man, and he at once did all in his power to lay bare the iniquitous fraud which had been committed, and to remove the stain of this nefarious act from the man who was innocent and had done no evil of the kind, and to attach it to the real author of the deed, so that it should completely overwhelm him with infamy.

Since, then, Origen in his letter complains with his own voice that he has suffered such things at the hands of the heretics who wished him ill, and similar things have happened in the case of many other orthodox men among both the dead and the living, and since in the cases adduced, men's writings are proved to have been tampered with in a similar way: what determined obstinacy is this, which refuses to admit the same excuse when the case is the same, and, when the circumstances are parallel, assigns to one party the allowance due to respect, but to another infamy due to a criminal. The truth must be told, and must not lie hid at this point; for it is impossible for any man really to judge so unjustly as to form different opinions on cases which are similar. The fact is that the prompters of Origen's accusers are men who make long controversial discourses in the churches,[1] and even write books the whole matter of which is borrowed from him, and who wish to deter men of simple mind from reading him, for fear that their plagiarisms should become widely known, though, indeed, their appropriations would be no reproach to them if they were not ungrateful to their master.

For instance, one of these men,[2] who thinks that a necessity is laid upon him,[3] like that of preaching the Gospel, to speak evil of Origen among all nations and tongues, declared in a vast assembly of Christian hearers that he had read six thousand of his works. Surely, if his object in reading these were, as he is in the habit of asserting, only to acquaint himself with Origen's faults, ten or twenty or at most thirty of these works would have sufficed for the purpose.

---

[1] This was in 382, the year after the Council of Constantinople. Jerome had come from Constantinople to Rome with the Eastern Bishops Epiphanius of Salamis in Cyprus and Paulinus of Antioch. His position at Rome is described in the words of his letter (cxxiii) to Ageruchia, c. 10. " I was assisting Damasus in matters of ecclesiastical literature, and answering the questions discussed in the Councils of the East and the West."

[2] Jerome.

[3] Apollinaris, in his reaction from Arianism, held that the Godhead supplied the place of the human soul in Christ. Hence their objection to this expression.

[1] This is believed to refer to Epiphanius, whose anti-Origenistic sermon at Jerusalem in the year 394 greatly irritated the Bishops John and Rufinus. See Jerome Ep. li, and "Against John of Jerusalem," c. 14.

[2] Epiphanius.

[3] 1 Cor. ix, 16.

But to read six thousand books is no longer wishing to know the man, but giving up almost one's whole life to his teaching and researches. On what ground then can his words be worthy of credit when he blames men who have only read quite a few of these books while their rule of faith is kept sacred and their piety unimpaired.

What has been said may suffice to show what opinion we ought to form of the books of Origen. I think that every one who has at heart the interests of truth, not of controversy, may easily assent to the well-proved statements I have made. But if any man perseveres in his contentiousness, we have no such custom.[1] It is a settled custom among us, when we read him, to hold fast that which is good, according to the apostolic in-

junction. If we find in these books anything discrepant to the Catholic faith, we suspect that it has been inserted by the heretics, and consider it as alien from his opinion as it is from our faith. If, however, this is a mistake of ours, we run, as I think, no danger from such an error; for we ourselves, through God's help, continue unharmed by avoiding what we hold in suspicion and condemn: and further we shall not be accounted accusers of our brethren before God (you will remember that the accusing of the brethren is the special work of the devil, and that he received the name of devil[1] from his being a slanderer). Moreover, we thus escape the sentence pronounced on evil speakers, which separates those who are such from the kingdom of God.

---

[1] Adapted from 1 Cor. xi, 16.

[1] Διάβολος (diabolus) from διαζάλλω to slander.

PREFACE TO THE TRANSLATIONS OF ORIGEN'S BOOKS

Περὶ Ἀρχῶν.

Addressed to Macarius, at Pinetum, A.D. 397.

The Translation of the two first Books of the Περὶ Ἀρχῶν was issued soon after, or contemporaneously with the Apology of Pamphilus. The Preface to them was intended to remove prejudices by showing that Jerome (who though not named is clearly described) had been Rufinus' precursor in translating Origen. The compliments paid to Jerome were no doubt sincere: but the use made of his previous action can hardly be justified. Rufinus knew well that Jerome's view of Origen had to some extent altered, that a disagreeable controversy had sprung up at Jerusalem about him, in which he and Jerome had taken opposite sides: and that the animosity aroused by this had with the greatest difficulty been allayed, and a reconciliation effected at the moment when he had quitted Palestine. This Preface with the Translation of the Περὶ Ἀρχῶν was the most immediate cause of the violent controversy and the final estrangement between Rufinus and Jerome.

I am aware that a great many of our brethren were incited by their longing for Scriptural knowledge to demand from various men who were versed in Greek literature that they would give the works of Origen to men who used the Latin tongue, and thus make him a Roman. Among these was that brother and associate of mine to whom this request was made by bishop Damasus, and who when he translated the two homilies on the Song of Songs from Greek into Latin prefixed to the work a preface[1] so full of beauty and so magnificent that he awoke in every one the desire of reading Origen and eagerly investigating his works. He said that to the soul of that great man the words might well be applied:
[2] "The King has brought me into his cham-

---

[1] Translated among Jerome's works in this Series.
[2] Cant. i, 4.

ber": and he declared that Origen in his other books had surpassed all other men, but in this had surpassed himself. What he promises in this Preface is, indeed, that he will give to Roman ears not only these books but many others of Origen. But I find that he is so enamoured of his own style that he pursues a still more ambitious object, namely, that he should be the creator of the book, not merely its translator. I am then following out a task begun by him and commended by his example; but it is out of my power to set forth the words of this great man with a force and an eloquence like his: and I have therefore to fear that it may happen through my fault that the man whom he justly commends as a teacher of the church both in knowledge and in wisdom second only to the Apostles may be thought to have a far lower rank through my poverty of language. When I reflected on this I was inclined to keep silence, and not to assent to the brethren who were constantly adjuring me to make the translation. But your influence is such, my most faithful brother Macarius, that even the consciousness of my unfitness is not sufficient to make me resist. I have therefore yielded to your importunity though it was against my resolution, so that I might no longer be exposed to the demands of a severe taskmaster; but I have done so on this condition and on this understanding, that in making the translation I should follow as far as possible the method of my predecessors, and especially of him of whom I have already made mention. He, after translating into Latin above seventy of the books of Origen which he called Homiletics, and also a certain number of the "Tomes," proceeded to purge and pare away in his translation all the causes of stumbling which are to be found in the Greek works; and this he did in such a way that the Latin reader will find nothing in them which jars with our faith. In his steps, therefore, I follow, not, indeed, with the power of eloquence which is his, but, as far as may be, in his rules and method, that is, taking care not to promulgate those things which are found in the books of Origen to be discrepant and contradictory to one another. The cause of these variations I have set forth very fully for your information in the Apology which Pamphilus wrote for the books of Origen, to which I have appended a very short treatise [1] showing by proofs which seem to me quite clear that his books have been in very many cases falsified by heretical and ill-disposed persons. This is especially the case with the books which you now require me to translate, namely, the Περὶ Ἀρχῶν, which may be rendered either Concerning First Principles or Concerning Principalities. These books are in truth, apart from these questions, exceedingly obscure and difficult; for in them he discusses matters over which the philosophers have spent their whole lives without any result. But our Christian thinker has done all that lay in his power to turn to purposes of sound religion the belief in a creator and the order of the created world which they had made subservient to their false religion. Wherever therefore I

---

[1] See the Translation in this Volume.

have found in his books anything contrary to the truth concerning the Trinity which he has in other places spoken of in a strictly orthodox sense, I have either omitted it as a foreign and not genuine expression or set it down in terms agreeing with the rule of faith which we find him constantly assenting to. There are things, no doubt, which he has developed in somewhat obscure language, wishing to pass rapidly over them, and as addressing those who have experience and knowledge of such matters; in these cases I have made the passage plain by adding words which I had read in other books of his where the matter was more fully treated. I have done this in the interest of clearness: but I have put in nothing of my own; I have only given him back his own words, though taken from other passages. I have explained this in the Preface, so that those who calumniate us should not think that they had found in this fresh material for their charges. But let them take heed what they are about in their perversity and contentiousness. As for me, I have not undertaken this laborious task (in which I trust that God will be my helper in answer to your prayers) for the sake of shutting the mouths of calumnious men, but with the view of supplying material for the increase of real knowledge to those who desired it. This only I require of every man who undertakes to copy out these books or to read them, in the sight of God the Father, the Son, and the Holy Ghost, and adjure him by our faith in the coming kingdom, by the assurance of the resurrection of the dead, by the eternal fire which is prepared for the devil and his angels (even as he trusts that he shall not possess as his eternal inheritance that place where there is weeping and gnashing of teeth, and where their fire will not be quenched and their worm will not die) that he should neither add nor take away, that he should neither insert nor change, anything in that which is written but that he should compare his copy with that from which it is copied and correct it critically letter for letter, and that he should not keep by him a copy which has not received correction or criticism, lest, if his copy is not thus distinct, the difficulty of the meaning may beget a still greater obscurity in the mind of the readers.

PREFACE TO BOOK III. OF THE Περὶ Ἀρχῶν.

Rufinus had now come to Rome. The translation of B. III. and IV. had been made probably at Pinetum early in 398. He was already aware of the strong feelings aroused by his Translation of B. I. and II., and he complains that parts of his work were obtained by Jerome's friends while still uncorrected, and used to his discredit (Apol. i, 18-21, ii, 44); but he continued the work, prefixing to it the following Preface as his justification.

Reader, remember me in your sacred moments of prayer, that I may be a worthy follower of the Spirit. It was you, Macarius, by whose instigation, I might say by whose compulsion, I translated the two first books of the Περὶ Ἀρχῶν. I did it during Lent; and at that time your near presence, my Christian brother, and your fuller leisure, forced me also into fuller diligence. But now that you are living at the opposite end of Rome from me, and my taskmaster pays his visits more seldom, I have taken longer in unfolding the sense of the two last books. You will remember that in my former preface I gave you warning that some people would be full of indignation when they found that I had no harm to say of Origen: and this, as I think you have found, has not been long in coming to pass. But if those demons who excite men's tongues to evil speaking, have been already set on fire by that first part of the work, though in it the author had not yet fully laid bare their devices, what will be the effect of this second part, in which he is going to disclose all the secret labyrinths through which they creep into the hearts of men and deceive the hearts of the weak and the frail? You will see disorder springing up on all sides, and party spirit will be raised, and an outcry will spread all through the town, and Origen will be summoned to the bar and condemned for his attempt to dispel the darkness of ignorance by the light of the Gospel's lamp. But all this will matter very little to those who are endeavouring to hold fast the sound form of the catholic faith while exercising their minds in the study of divine things.

I think it necessary, however, to remind you of the principle which I acted upon in reference to the former books, and which I have observed in the present case also, namely, not to set down in my translation things evidently contradictory to our belief and to the author's opinions as elsewhere expressed, but to pass them over as not genuine but inserted by others. On the other hand I have not, either in the former books or in these, omitted the novel opinions which he has expressed about the formation of the reasonable creation, considering that it is not in such things that the faith mainly consists, but that what he is aiming at is merely knowledge and the exercise of the faculties, and that possibly there may be certain heresies which may have to be answered in this way. Only, in cases where he may have chosen to repeat in these later books what he had said before in the earlier, I have thought it expedient to cut out certain portions for the sake of brevity.

Those whose object in reading these books is to gain knowledge, not to disparage their author, would do well to seek the aid of men more skilled than themselves in interpreting them. For it is an absurd thing to get grammarians to explain to us the fictions of the poets' writings and the laughable stories of the comedians, and yet to think that books which speak of God and the celestial powers, and the whole universe, and which discuss all the errors of pagan philosophy and of heretical pravity are things which any one can understand without a teacher to explain them. In this way it comes to pass that men prefer to remain in ignorance and to pronounce rash judgments on things which are difficult and obscure rather than to gain an understanding of them by diligent study.

RUFINUS' APOLOGY IN DEFENCE OF HIMSELF

Sent to Anastasius, Bishop of the City of Rome

This document was called forth by accusations against Rufinus made, soon after his accession, to Anastasius, who held the Roman see from 498 to 503. The authority of the Roman Popes at this time was not what it afterwards became, and it is improbable that Anastasius should have summoned Rufinus, as some suppose him to have done, from Aquileia, where he was living on confidential terms with the Bishop Chromatius, to come to Rome to answer a formal accusation or to be judged by him. But since Rome was the centre of information, a Christian would not wish to be ill-thought of by its Bishop. Those who accused Rufinus were the friends of Jerome at Rome, especially the noble widow Marcella and the Senator Pammachius. They had endeavoured to gain some condemnation of Rufinus from Siricius before his death in November 398; but Siricius befriended Rufinus ("his simplicity was imposed on," according to Jerome).[1] On the election of Anastasius, however, in 399, they accused Rufinus of having, by his translation of Origen's Περὶ Ἀρχῶν introduced heresy into the Roman church. Jerome thus speaks of Marcella, Ep. cxxvii. 10. " She was the cause of the condemnation of the heretics: she brought witnesses who had been at a former time under their instruction, and thus imbued with error and heresy; she showed how many there were who had been deceived; she had the volumes of the Περὶ Ἀρχῶν brought in, and pointed out the alterations which the Scorpion[2] had made in them: till at last letters were written, and that more than once, summoning the heretics to come and defend themselves; but they did not dare to come. So great was the force of conviction brought to bear on them that, to prevent their heresy being exposed in their presence, they chose to stay away and be condemned." From the letter of Anastasius to John of Jerusalem about Rufinus we gather that, while he strongly disapproved the translation of Origen, he left Rufinus himself to his own conscience, and did not care to know what had become of him. The letter of Rufinus, though called an Apology, bears no trace of being an answer to a summons or judgment of the Pontiff, but merely a reply to statements which were likely to prejudice him in the Pontiff's opinion. The year in which the Apology was written was 400 A.D.

1. It has been brought to my knowledge that certain persons, in the course of a controversy which they have been raising in your Holiness' jurisdiction on matters of faith or on other points, have made mention of my name. I venture to believe that your Holiness, who have been trained from your infancy in the strict principles of the Church, has refused to listen to any calumnies which may have been directed against an absent person, and one who has been favourably known to you as united with you in the faith and love of God. Nevertheless, since I hear it reported that my reputation has been attacked, I have thought it right to make my position clear to your Holiness in writing. It was impossible for me to do this in person. I have just returned to my family[3] after an absence of nearly 30 years; and it would have been harsh and almost inhuman to come away again so soon from those whom I had been so late in revisiting. The labour also of my long journey has left me too weak to begin the journey again. My object in this letter is not to remove some stain of suspicion from your mind, which I regard as a holy place, as a kind of divine sanctuary which does not admit any evil thing. Rather, I desire that the confession I am about to make to you may be like a stick placed in your hands to drive away any envious persons who may be barking like dogs against me.

2. My faith, indeed, was sufficiently proved when the heretics persecuted me. I was at that time sojourning in the church of Alexandria, and underwent imprisonment and exile which was then the penalty of faithfulness; yet for the sake of any who may wish to put my faith to the test, or to hear and learn what it is I will declare it. I believe that the Trinity is of one nature and godhead, of one and the same power and substance; so that between the Father, the Son and the Holy Ghost there is no diversity at all, except that the one is the Father, the second the Son, and the third the Holy Ghost. There is a Trinity of real and living Persons, a unity of nature and substance.

3. I also confess that the Son of God has in these last days been born of the Virgin

---

[1] Jerome Letter cxxvii, 9.

[2] The Scorpion is Jerome's name for Rufinus, especially after his death. He means that Rufinus had altered the too palpable expressions of heresy, so that the more subtle expressions of it might gain acceptance.

[3] Rufinus uses the word "*parentes*." Jerome in his Apology (ii, 2) scoffs at the notion that a man of Rufinus' age (about 55) could have parents living, and supposes that he is making a false suggestion by using the word in the sense in which it was vulgarly used — that of relations generally, as it is now used in French.

and the Holy Spirit: that he has taken upon him our natural human flesh and soul; that in this he suffered and was buried and rose again from the dead; that the flesh in which he rose was that same flesh which had been laid in the sepulchre; and that in this same flesh, together with the soul, he ascended into heaven after his resurrection: from whence we look for his coming to judge the quick and the dead.

4. But, further, as to the resurrection of our own flesh, I believe that it will be in its integrity and perfection; it will be this very flesh in which we now live. We do not hold, as is slanderously reported by some men, that another flesh will rise instead of this; but this very flesh, without the loss of a single member, without the cutting off of any single part of the body; none whatever of all its properties will be absent except its corruptibility. It is this which is promised by the holy Apostle concerning the body: It is sown in corruption, it is raised in incorruption; it is sown in weakness, it is raised in power; it is sown in dishonour, it is raised in glory; it is sown a natural body, it is raised a spiritual body. This is the doctrine which has been handed down to me by those from whom I received holy baptism in the Church of Aquileia; and I think that it is the same which the Apostolic See has by long usage handed down and taught.

5. I affirm, moreover, a judgment to come, in which judgment every man is to receive the due meed of his bodily life, according to that which he has done, whether good or evil. And, if in the case of men the reward is to be according to their works, how much more will this be so in the case of the devil, who is the universal cause of sin? Of the devil himself our belief is that which is written in the Gospel, namely, that both he and all his angels, will receive as their portion the eternal fire, and with him those who do his works, that is, who become the accusers of their brethren. If then any one denies that the devil is to be subjected to the eternal fires, may he have his part with him in the eternal fire, so that he may know by experience the fact which he now denies.

6. I am next informed that some stir has been made on the question of the nature of the soul. Whether complaints on a matter of this kind ought to be entertained instead of being put aside, you must yourself decide. If, however, you desire to know my opinion on the subject, I will state it frankly. I have read a great many writers on this question, and I find that they express divers opinions. Some of those whom I have read hold that the soul is infused together with the material body through the channel[1] of the human seed; and of this they give such proofs as they can. I think that this was the opinion of Tertullian or Lactantius among the Latins, perhaps also of a few others. Others assert that God is every day making new souls, and infusing them into the bodies which have been framed in the womb; while others again believe that the souls were all made long ago, when God made all things of nothing, and that all that he now does is to plant out each soul in its body as it seems good to him. This is the opinion of Origen, and of some others of the Greeks. For myself, I declare in the presence of God that, after reading each of these opinions, I am up to the present moment unable to hold any of them as certain and absolute; the determination of the truth in this question I leave to God and to any to whom it shall please him to reveal it. My profession on this point is therefore, first, that these several opinions are those which I have found in books, but, secondly, that I as yet remain in ignorance on the subject, except so far as this, that the Church delivers it as an article of faith that God is the creator of souls as well as of bodies.

7. Now as to another matter. I am told that objections have been raised against me because, forsooth, at the request of some of my brethren, I translated certain works of Origen from Greek into Latin. I suppose that every one sees that it is only through ill will that this is made a matter of blame. For, if there is any offensive statement in the author, why is this to be twisted into a fault of the translator? I was asked to exhibit in Latin what stands written in the Greek text; and I did nothing more than fit the Latin words to the Greek ideas. If, therefore, there is anything to praise in these ideas, the praise does not belong to me; and similarly as to anything to which blame may attach. I admit that I put something of my own into the work; as I stated in my Preface, I used my own discretion in cutting out not a few passages; but only those as to which I had come to suspect that the thing had not been so stated by Origen himself; and the statement appeared to me in these cases to have been inserted by others, because in other places I

---

[1] Traducem, properly, the layer, by which the vine is propagated, and hence the medium through which life is communicated. This is the theory of the "traducianists" who thus made the soul to be derived from the parent by procreation. It is contrasted with that of the "creationists" who held that each soul was separately created, and infused into the child at the moment when life began.

had found the author state the matter in a catholic sense. I entreat you therefore, holy, venerable and saintly father, not to permit a storm of ill will to be raised against me because of this, nor to sanction the employment of partisanship and of calumny — weapons which ought never to be used in the Church of God. Where can simple faith and innocence be safe if they are not protected in the Church? I am not a defender or a champion of Origen; nor am I the first who has translated his works. Others before me had done the very same thing, and I did it, the last of many, at the request of my brethren. If an order is to be given that such translations are not to be made, such an order holds good for the future, not the past; but if those are to be blamed who have made these translations before any such order was given, the blame must begin with those who took the first step.

8. As for me, I declare in Christ's name that I never held, nor ever will hold, any other faith but that which I have set forth above, that is, the faith which is held by the Church of Rome, by that of Alexandria, and by my own church of Aquileia; and which is also preached at Jerusalem; and if there is any one who believes otherwise, whoever he may be, let him be Anathema. But those who through mere ill will and malice engender dissensions and offences among their brethren, and cause them to stumble, shall give account of it in the day of judgment.

THE LETTER OF ANASTASIUS,

BISHOP OF THE CHURCH OF ROME TO JOHN BISHOP OF JERUSALEM CONCERNING THE CHARACTER OF RUFINUS

The letter of Anastasius to John of Jerusalem was written in the year 401; it is spoken of in Jerome's Apol. iii., c. 21, which was written in the first half of 402, as "the letter of last year." Jerome intimates in the same passage that it was only one of several letters of the same character which Anastasius wrote to the East. Rufinus had not seen it, and refused to believe its genuineness. But there seems to be no reason for doubting this. Anastasius had, at the earnest request of Theophilus of Alexandria, formally condemned Origenism. And Rufinus' translations of Origen's Περὶ Ἀρχῶν and of Pamphilus' Vindication of Origen, and his own book on the Falsification of Origen's works were taken at Rome as a defence of Origenism generally. Rufinus, however, appealed continually, and especially in his Apology to Anastasius, to the church of Jerusalem, where he had been ordained. "My faith," he says, "is that which is preached at Jerusalem." Anastasius, therefore, in condemning Origen would be understood as condemning Rufinus, and might also seem to condemn his Bishop John of Jerusalem. This will account for the fulsome praises with which the letter opens. John, moreover, had written "to consult" Anastasius about Rufinus, which probably implies some action in Rufinus' interest; but the fact that Jerome knew the contents of the letter and Rufinus did not seems to show that Bishop John had become more friendly with Jerome and less so with Rufinus.

1. The kind words of approval that you have addressed, my dear Bishop, to your brother Bishop, is a fresh mark of your long tried affection. It is a high commendation which you confer upon me, a most lavish recognition of my services. I thank you for this proof of your love; and, following you at a distance in my littleness, I bring the tribute of my words to honour the splendour of your holiness and those virtues which the Lord has conferred upon you. You excel all others so far, the splendour of your praise shines forth so conspicuously, that no words which I can use can equal your deserts. Yet your glory excites in me such admiration that I cannot turn away from the attempt to describe it, even though I can never do so adequately. And, first, the praise which you have bestowed on me out of the serene heaven of your great spirit forms part of your own glory: for it is the majesty of your episcopate, shining forth like the sun upon the opposite quarter of the world, which has reflected its own brightness upon us. And you give me your friendship unreservedly; you do not weigh me in the balance of criticism. If it is right for you to praise me, must not your praise be echoed back to you? I beg you therefore, for your own sake no less than mine, that you will not praise me any more to my face. I ask this for two reasons: if the praise is undeserved it must excite in your brother-bishop a sense of pain; if it is true, it must make him blush.

2. Let me come to the subject of your letter. Rufinus, about whom you have done me the honour to ask my advice, must bring his conscience to the bar of the divine majesty.

It is for him to see how he can approve himself to God as maintaining his true allegiance to him.

3. As for Origen, whose writings he has translated into our language, I have neither formerly known, nor do I now seek to know either who he was or what expression he may have given to his thought. But as to the feeling left by this matter on my own mind I should be glad to speak with your holiness for a moment. The impression which I have received is this, — and it has been brought out clearly by the reading of parts of Origen's works by the people of our City, and by the sort of mist of blindness which it threw over them, — that his object was to disintegrate our faith, which is that of the Apostles, and has been confirmed by the traditions of the fathers, by leading us into tortuous paths.

4. I want to know what is the meaning of the translation of this work into the Roman tongue. If the translator intends by it to put the author in the wrong, and to denounce to the world his execrable deeds, well and good. In that case he will expose to well-merited hatred one who has long laboured under the adverse weight of public opinion. But if by translating all these evil things he means to give his assent to them, and in that sense gives them to the world to read, then the edifice which he has reared at the expense of so much labour serves for nothing else than to make the guilt the act of his own will, and to give the sanction of his unlooked for support to the overthrow of all that is of prime importance in the true faith as held by Catholic Christians from the time of the Apostles till now.

5. Far be such teaching from the catholic system of the Church of Rome. It can never by any possibility come to pass that we should accept as reasonable things which we condemn as matters of law and right. We have, therefore, the assurance that Christ our God, whose providence reaches over the whole world, bestows his approval on us when we say that it is wholly impossible for us to admit doctrines which defile the church, which subvert its well-tried moral system, which offend the ears of all who are witnesses of our doings and lay the ground for strife and anger and dissensions. This was the motive which led me to write my letter to Venerius [1] our brother in the Episcopate, the character of which, written as it was in my weakness but with great care and diligence, you will realize by what I now subjoin : " Whence, then, he who translated the work has gained and preserves this assurance of innocence I am not greatly troubled to know : it fills me with no vain alarm. I certainly shall omit nothing which may enable me to guard the faith of the Gospel amongst my own people, and to warn, as far as in me lies, those who form part of my body, in whatever part of the world they live, not to allow any translation of profane authors to creep in and spring up amongst them, which will seek to unsettle the mind of devout men by spreading its own darkness among them. Moreover, I cannot pass over in silence an event which has given me great pleasure, the decree issued by our Emperors, [2] by which every one who serves God is warned against the reading of Origen, and all who are convicted of reading his impious works are condemned by the imperial judgment." In these words my formal sentence was pronounced.

6. You are troubled by the complaint which people make as to our treatment of Rufinus, so that you pursue certain persons [3] with vague suspicions. But I will meet this feeling of yours with an instance taken from holy writ, namely, where it is said : " Man seeth not as God seeth ; for God looketh upon the heart, but man upon the countenance." Therefore, my dearly beloved brother, put away all your prejudice. Weigh the conduct of Rufinus in your own unbiassed judgment ; ask yourself whether he has not translated Origen's words into Latin and approved them, and whether a man who gives his encouragement to vicious acts committed by another differs at all from the guilty party. In any case I beg you to be assured of this, that he is so completely separate from all part or lot with us, that I neither know nor wish to know either what he is doing or where he is living. I have only to add that it is for him to consider where he may obtain absolution.

---

[1] Appointed bishop of Milan in 400, in succession to Simplicianus.
[2] Arcadius and Honorius.
[3] Probably the friends of Jerome at Rome, Pammachius and Marcella.

THE APOLOGY OF RUFINUS

Addressed to Apronianus, in Reply to Jerome's Letter to Pammachius,[1] written at Aquileia A.D. 400

IN TWO BOOKS

In order to understand the controversy between Jerome and Rufinus it is necessary to look back over their earlier relations. They had been close friends in early youth (Jerome, Ep. iii, 3, v, 2.) and had together formed part of a society of young Christian ascetics at Aquileia in the years 370–3. Jerome's letter (3) to Rufinus in 374 is full of affection; in 381 he was placed in Jerome's Chronicle (year 378) as "a monk of great renown," and when, after some years, they were neighbours in Palestine, Rufinus with Melania on the Mt. of Olives, Jerome with Paula at Bethlehem, they remained friends. (Ruf. Apol. ii. 8 (2) .) In the disputes about Origenism which arose from the visits of Aterbius (Jer. Apol. iii, 33) and Epiphanius (Jerome Against John of Jerusalem, 11), they became estranged, Jerome siding with Epiphanius and Rufinus with John (Jer. Letter li, 6. Against John of Jerusalem 11). They were reconciled before Rufinus left Palestine in 397 (Jer. Apol. i, 1, iii, 33). But when Rufinus came to Italy and at the request of Macarius[2] translated Origen's Περὶ Ἀρχῶν, the Preface which he prefixed to this work was the occasion for a fresh and final outbreak of dissension. The friends of Jerome of whom Pammachius, Oceanus and Marcella were the most prominent, were scandalized at some of the statements of the book, and still more at the assumption made by Rufinus that Jerome, by his previous translations of some of Origen's works, had proved himself his admirer. They also suspected that Rufinus' translation had made Origen speak in an orthodox sense which was not genuine and that heterodox statements had been suppressed. They therefore wrote to Jerome at Bethlehem a letter (translated among Jerome's letters in this Series No. lxxxiii) begging for information on all these points. Jerome in reply made a literal translation of the Περὶ Ἀρχῶν, and sent it accompanied by a letter (lxxxiv) in which he declared that he had never been a partisan of Origen's dogmatic system, though he admired him as a commentator. He fastened on some of the most questionable of Origen's speculations, his doctrine of the resurrection, of the previous existence of souls and their fall into human bodies, and the ultimate restoration of all spiritual beings; his permission, in agreement with Plato, of the use of falsehood in certain cases; and some expressions about the relation of the Persons of the Godhead which, at least to Western ears, seemed a denial of their equality. He appealed to his own commentaries on Ecclesiastes and on the Ephesians to show that he rejected these doctrines; and he urged that, even if he had once had too indiscriminate an admiration of Origen, he had in later years judged more clearly.

In the main Jerome's defence was valid. But it demanded considerateness in his judges; and this quality was absent in himself. He judged Origen's opinions harshly, and spoke of his views as poisonous (Letter lxxxiv, 3); and, when we contrast the lenity of his former judgments on the same points with his present violence, it becomes evident that he was more concerned for his own reputation than for truth. Rufinus charges him (Apol. i. c. 23 to 44) with maintaining, in his Commentaries on the Ephesians (written twelve years earlier in 388) to which Jerome had appealed (Ep. lxxxiv, 2) the views which he now denounced; and the charge, though urged too far, is substantially made out. The opinions of Origen which he introduced into this Commentary about the fall of souls out of a previous state of bliss into human bodies are set down with hardly a word of objection (comm. on ch. i, v. 4), and his speculations on the Powers and Principalities of the world to come (ib. v. 21) and on the rise of Lucifer and his angels to be subjects of Christ's Kingdom (id. ii, 7) and their part in the final restoration of all things (id. iv, 16) are adopted as his own, thus giving some justification for Rufinus' attack (Apol. i, 34–36. &c.). His defence of himself therefore is hardly candid. And his allusions to his opponent are exasperating, e.g. when he speaks (Letter lxxxiv, 1) of some persons " who love me so well that they cannot be heretics without me. " " I wonder that, while they speak in detraction of the flesh, they live carnally and thus cherish and nourish delicately their enemy " (Id. 8). He hardly argues fairly as to Rufinus' assertion that Origen's works had suffered from falsification; and he is carried so far by his animosity that he denies the Apology of Pamphilus for Origen to be by Pamphilus, though he had himself attributed it to him (De Vir. Ill. c. 7. 5) and no one can doubt that it is his. (See Dict. of Christ. Biog. Art. Pamphilus.)

But though writing thus for his friends generally, Jerome wrote at the same time a friendly letter to Rufinus himself in answer, it would seem, to one from him, (Letter lxxxi.) in which he speaks of their common friends, and of the death of Rufinus' mother, and says that he has charged a friend whom he is sending to Italy to visit Rufinus and assure him of his high esteem; and, while remonstrating with him for his Preface to the Περὶ Ἀρχῶν, merely says " I have begged my other friends to avoid a quarrel. I count on your sense of equity not to give occasion to impatient persons; for you will not find every one, like me, able to take pleasure in praises framed to suit a purpose." [3]

Had this letter reached Rufinus, the ensuing controversy would have been avoided. But it never reached him. It was sent through Pammachius, and he and Jerome's other friends kept it back, while they published the letter sent them with Jerome's translation of the Περὶ Ἀρχῶν. Rufinus, who was now at Aquileia, having left Rome probably early in 399, wrote the Apology, addressing it to his friend and convert Apronianus at Rome.

---

[1] Ep. 84.   [2] See the Translation of Rufinus' Prefaces given above, and the notes prefixed to them.
[3] Or Feigned praises — figuratis laudibus.

BOOK I.

The following is an epitome of the argument:

I have read the document sent from the East by our friend and good brother to a distinguished member of the Senate, Pammachius, which you have copied and forwarded to me. It brought to my mind the words of the Prophet: [1] "The sons of men whose teeth are spears and arrows and their tongue a sharp sword." But for these wounds which men inflict on one another with the tongue we can hardly find a physician; so I have betaken myself to Jesus, the heavenly physician, and he has brought out for me from the medicine chest of the Gospel an antidote of sovereign power; he has assuaged the violence of my grief with the assurance of the righteous judgment which I shall have at his hands. The potion which our Lord dispensed to me was nothing else than these words: [2] "Blessed are ye when men persecute you and say all manner of evil against you falsely. Rejoice and leap for joy, for great is your reward in heaven, for so persecuted they the Prophets which were before you." With this medicine I was content, and, as far as the matter concerned me, I had determined for the future to keep silence; for I said within myself, [1] "If they have called the Master of the house Beelzebub, how much more them of his household?" (that is, you and me, unworthy though we are). And, if it was said of him, [2] "He is a deceiver, he deceiveth the people," I must not be indignant if I hear that I am called a heretic, and that the name of mole is applied to me because of the slowness of my mind, or indeed my blindness. Christ who is my Lord, aye, and who is God over all, was called [3] "a gluttonous man and a wine bibber, a friend of publicans and sinners." How can I, then, be angry when I am called a carnal man [4] who lives in luxury?

2. Nevertheless, a necessity, as it were, is laid upon me to reply, as a simple matter of justice: I mean, because many, as I hear, are likely to be upset by what he has written

---

[1] Ps. lvii, 4.
[2] Matt. v, 11, 12.
[1] Matt. x, 25.
[2] John vii, 12.
[3] Matt. xi, 19.
[4] Jerome Ep. lxxxiv, 8.

unless the true state of the case is laid before them. I am compelled, against my resolution and even my vows, to make reply, lest by keeping silence I should seem to acknowledge the accusation to be true. It is, indeed, in most cases, a Christian's glory to follow our Lord's example of silence, and thereby to repel the accusation; but to follow this course in matters of faith causes stumbling blocks to spring up in vast numbers. It is true that, in the beginning of his invective he promises that he will avoid personalities, and reply only about the things in question and the charges made against him; but his profession in both cases is false; for how can he answer a charge when no charge has been made? and how can a man be said to avoid personalities when he never ceases to attack and tear to pieces the translator of the books in question from the first line to the last of his invective? I shall avoid all pretence of saying less than I mean, and similar subterfuges of hypocrisy which are hateful in God's sight; and, though my words may be uncouth and my style unadorned, I will make my reply. I trust, and I shall not trust in vain, that my readers will pardon my lack of skill, since my object is not to amuse others but to endeavour to clear myself from the reproaches directed against me. My wish is that what may shine forth in me may not be style but truth.

3. But, before I begin to clear up these points, there is one in which I confess that he has spoken the truth in an eminent degree; namely, when he says that he is not rendering evil speaking for evil speaking. This, I say, is quite true; for it is not for evil speaking but for speaking well of him and praising him that he has rendered reproach and evil speaking. But it is not true, as he says, that he turns the left cheek to one who smites him on the right. It is on one who is stroking him and caressing him on the cheek that he suddenly turns and bites him. I praised his eloquence and his industry in the work of translating from the Greek. I said nothing in derogation of his faith; but he condemns me on both these points. He must therefore pardon me if I say some things rather roughly and rudely; for he has challenged to a reply a man who has no great rhetorical skill, and who has not, as he knows, the power to make one whom he wishes to injure and to wound appear to have received neither wounds nor injuries. Those who love this kind of eloquence must seek it in a man whom every light report stirs up to fault-finding and vituperation, and who thinks himself bound, as if he were

the censor, to be always coming up to set things to rights. A man who desires to clear himself from the stains which have been cast upon him, does not trouble himself, in the answer which he is compelled to make, about the elegance and neat turns of his reply, but only about its truth.

4. At the very beginning of his work he says, "As if they could not be heretics by themselves, without me." I must first show that, whether with him or without him, we are no heretics: then, when our status is made clear, we shall be safe from having the infamous imputation hurled at us from other men's reports. I was already living in a monastery, where, as both he and all others know, about 30 years ago, I was made regenerate by Baptism, and received the seal of the faith at the hands of those saintly men, Chromatius,[1] Jovinus[2] and Eusebius,[3] all of them now bishops, well-tried and highly esteemed in the church of God, one of whom was then a presbyter of the church under Valerian of blessed memory, the second was archdeacon, the third Deacon, and to me a spiritual father, my teacher in the creed and the articles of belief. These men so taught me, and so I believe, namely, that the Father, the Son and the Holy Spirit are of one Godhead, of one Substance: a Trinity coeternal, inseparable, incorporeal, invisible, incomprehensible, known to itself alone as it truly is in its perfection: For "No man[4] knoweth the Son but the Father, neither knoweth any man the Father but the Son": and the Holy Spirit is he who "searcheth[5] the deep things of God": that this Trinity, therefore, is without all bodily visibility, but that it is with the eye of the understanding that the Son and the Holy Spirit see the Father even as the Father sees the Son and the Holy Spirit; and further, that in this Trinity there is no diversity except that one is Father, another Son and a third Holy Spirit. There is a Trinity as touching the distinction of persons, a unity in the reality of the Substance. We received, further, that the only begotten Son of God, through whom in the beginning all existing things were made, whether visible or invisible, in these last days took upon him a human body and Soul, and was made man, and suffered for our salvation; and the third day he rose again from

---

[1] Bp. of Aquileia at the time of this Apology, and maintaining friendly relations with both Jerome and Rufinus. (Ruf. Pref. to Eusebius in this Volume. Jer. Ep. vii, lx. 19, Pref. to Bks. of Solomon &c. &c.)
[2] See Jerome Ep. vii. It is not known of what church he was Bp.
[3] Brother of Chromatius. See an allusion to him in Jerome, Ep. viii, and lx, 19. His see is unknown.
[4] Matt. xi, 27. [5] 1 Cor. ii, 10.

the dead in that very flesh which had been laid in the sepulchre; and in that very same flesh made glorious he ascended into the heavens, whence we look for his coming to judge the quick and the dead. But further we confess that he gave us hope that we too should rise in a similar manner, so that we believe that our resurrection will be in the same manner and process, and in the same form, as the resurrection of our Lord himself from the dead: that the bodies which we shall receive will not be phantoms or thin vapours, as some slanderously affirm that we say, but these very bodies of ours in which we live and in which we die. For how can we truly believe in the resurrection of the flesh, unless the very nature of flesh remains in it truly and substantially? It is then without any equivocation, that we confess the resurrection of this real and substantial flesh of ours in which we live.

5. Moreover, to give a fuller demonstration of this point, I will add one thing more. It is the compulsion of those who calumniate me which forces me to exhibit a singular and special mystery of my own church. It is this, that, while all the churches thus hand down the Sacrament of the Creed in the form which, after the words "the remission of sins" adds "the resurrection of the flesh," the holy church of Aquileia (as though the Spirit of God had foreseen the calumnies which would be spoken against us) puts in a particular pronoun at the place where it delivers the resurrection of the dead; instead of saying as others do, "the resurrection of the flesh," we say "the resurrection of *this* flesh." At this point, as the custom is at the close of the Creed, we touch the forehead of this flesh with the sign of the cross, and with the mouth of this flesh, which we have so touched, we confess the resurrection; that so we may stop up every entrance through which the poisoned tongue might bring in its calumnies against us. Can any confession be fuller than this? Can any exposition of the truth be more perfect? Yet I see that this remarkable provision of the Holy Spirit has been of no profit to us. Evil and busy tongues still find room for cavilling. Unless, says he, you name the members one by one, and expressly designate the head with its hair, the hands, the feet, the belly, and that which is below the belly, you have denied the resurrection of the flesh.

6. Behold the discovery of this man of the new learning! a thing which escaped the notice of the Apostles when they delivered the faith to the Church; a thing which none of the saints knew till it was revealed to this man by the spirit of the flesh. He indeed cannot expound it without bringing in an indecency. Nevertheless, I will set it forth in his hearing both more worthily and more truly. Christ is the first fruits of those that sleep;[1] he is also called [2] the first begotten from the dead; as also the Apostle says, [3] "Christ is the beginning, afterward they that are Christ's." Since then we have Christ as the undoubted first fruits of our resurrection, how can any question arise about the rest of us? It must be evident that, whatever the members, the hair, the flesh, the bones, were in which Christ rose, in the same shall we also rise. For this purpose he offered himself to the disciples to touch after his resurrection, so that no hesitation as to his resurrection should remain. Since then Christ has given his own resurrection as a typical instance, one that is quite evident, and (as I may say) capable of being felt and handled by the hand, who can be so mad as to think that he himself will rise otherwise than as He rose who opened the door of the resurrection? This also confirms the truth of this confession of ours that, while it is the actual natural flesh and no other which will rise, yet it will rise purged from its faults and having laid aside its corruption; so that the saying of the Apostle is true: [4] "It is sown in corruption, it will be raised in incorruption; it is sown in dishonour, it will be raised in glory; it is sown a natural[5] body, it will be raised a spiritual body." Inasmuch then as it is a spiritual body, and glorious, and incorruptible, it will be furnished and adorned with its own proper members, not with members taken from elsewhere, according to that glorious image of which Christ is set forth as the perpetual type, as it is said by the Apostle: [6] "Who shall change the body of our humiliation, that it may be conformed to the body of his glory."

7. Since then, in reference to our hope of the resurrection, Christ is set forth all through as the archetype, since he is the first born of those who rise, and since he is the head of every creature, as it is written, [7] "Who is the head of all, the first born from the dead, that in all things he might have the preëminence;" how is it that we stir up these vain strifes of words, and conflicts of evil surmises? Does not the faith of the church consist in the confession which I have set forth above? And is it not evident that men are moved to accuse others not by difference of belief, but by perversity of disposition?

---

[1] 1 Cor. xv, 20. [4] 1 Cor. xv, 42–4. [6] Phil. iii, 21.
[2] Rev. i, 5. [5] animale. [7] Col. i, 18.
[3] 1 Cor. xv, 23.

At this point, however, in arguing about the resurrection of the flesh, our friend, as his habit is, mixes up what is ridiculous and farcical with what is serious. He says:

"Some poor creatures of the female sex among us are fond of asking what good the resurrection will be to them? They touch their breasts, and stroke their beardless faces, and strike their thighs and their bellies, and ask whether this poor weak body is to rise again. No, they say, if we are to be like angels we shall have the nature of angels."

Who the poor women are whom he thus takes to task, and whether they are deserving of his attacks, he knows best. And if he considers himself to be one of those who are bound to preach that it is not our part to attack another out of revenge, but that in this instance he is right in attacking others when they have given him no cause for revenge; or if, again, he considers that it is no business of his to take care that weak women of his company should be subjected to attacks only for real causes, and not for such false and fictitious reasons as these — of all this, I say, he is himself the best judge. For us it is sufficient to act as he said that he would act: we shall not render evil for evil. But it is evident that the man who is angry with a woman because she says that she hopes not to have a frail body in the resurrection is of the opinion that the frailties of the body will remain. Only, what then, we ask, are we to make of the words of the Apostle: "It is sown in weakness, it will be raised in power; it is sown a natural body, it will be raised a spiritual body"? What frailty can you suppose to exist in a spiritual body? It is to rise in power; how then is it again to be frail? If it is frail, how can it be in power? Are not those poor women after all more right than you, when they say that their bodily frailty cannot have dominion over them in the world beyond? Why should you mock at them, when they are only following the Apostle's words: "This corruptible must put on incorruption, and this mortal must put on immortality"? The Apostles never taught that the body which would rise from the dead would be frail, but, on the contrary, that it would rise in power and in glory. Whence comes this opinion which you now produce? Perhaps it is one obtained from some of your Jews,[1] which is now to be promulgated as a new law for the church, so that we may learn their ways: for in truth the Jews have such an opinion as this about the resurrection ; they believe that

they will rise, but in such sort as that they will enjoy all carnal delights and luxuries, and other pleasures of the body. What else, indeed, can this "bodily frailty" of yours mean except members given over to corruption, appetites stimulated and lusts inflamed?

8. But suffer it to be so, I beg you, as you are lovers of Christ, that the body is to be in incorruption and without these conditions when it rises from the dead : then let such things henceforward cease to be mentioned. Let us believe that in the resurrection even lawful intercourse will no longer exist between the sexes, since there would be danger that unlawful intercourse would creep in if such things remained present and unforgotten. What is the use of carefully and minutely going over and discussing "the belly and what is below it"? You tell us that we live amidst carnal delights : but I perceive that it is your belief that we are not to give up such things even in the resurrection. Let us not deny that this very flesh in which we now live is to rise again : but neither let us make men think that the imperfections of the flesh are wrapped up in it and will come again with it. The flesh, indeed, will rise, this very flesh and not another : it will not change its nature, but it will lose its frailties and imperfections. Otherwise, if its frailties remain, it cannot even be immortal. And thus, as I said, we avoid heresy, whether with you or without you. For the faith of the Church, of which we are the disciples, takes a middle path between two dangers : it does not deny the reality of the natural flesh and body when it rises from the dead, but neither does it assert, in contradiction to the Apostle's words,[1] that in the kingdom which is to come corruption will inherit incorruption. We therefore do not assert that the flesh or body will rise, as you put it, with some of its members lost or amputated, but that the body will be whole and complete, having laid aside nothing but its corruption and dishonour and frailty and also having amputated all the imperfections of mortality : nothing of its own nature will be lacking to that spiritual body which shall rise from the dead except this corruption.

9. I have made answer more at length than I had intended on this single article of the resurrection, through fear lest by brevity I should lay myself open to fresh aspersions. Consequently, I have made mention again and again not only of the body, as to which cavils are raised, but of the flesh : and not only of the flesh ; I have added "this flesh;" and further I have spoken not only of "this

---

[1] Rufinus frequently taunts Jerome with having paid too much heed to the Jewish teachers from whom he learned Hebrew.

[1] Cor. xv, 50.

flesh " but of " this natural flesh ; " I have not even stopped here, but have asserted that not even the completeness of the several members would be lacking. I have only demanded that it should be held as part of the faith that, according to the words of the Apostle, it should rise incorruptible instead of corruptible, glorious instead of dishonoured, immortal instead of frail, spiritual instead of natural ; and that we should think of the members of the spiritual body as being without taint of corruption or of frailty. I have set forth my faith in reference to the Trinity, the Incarnation of the Lord our Saviour, to his Passion and Resurrection, his second coming and the judgment to come. I have also set it forth in the matter of the resurrection of our flesh, and have left nothing, I think, in ambiguity. Nothing in my opinion remains to be said, so far as the faith is concerned.

10. But in this, he says, I convict you, that you have translated the work of Origen, in which he says that there is to be a restitution of all things, in which we must believe that not only sinners but the devil himself and his angels will at last be relieved from their punishment, if we are to set before our minds in a consistent manner what is meant by the restitution of all things. And Origen, he says, teaches further that souls have been made before their bodies, and have been brought down from heaven and inserted into their bodies. I am not now acting on Origen's behalf, nor writing an apology for him. Whether he stands accepted before God or has been cast away is not mine to judge : to his own lord he stands or falls.[1] But I am compelled to make mention of him in a few words, since our great rhetorician, though seeming to be arguing against him is really striking at me ; and this he does no longer indirectly, but ends by openly attacking me with his sword drawn and turns his whole fury against me. I say too little in saying that he attacks me ; for indeed, in order to vent his rage against me, he does not even spare his old teacher :[2] he thinks that in the books which I have translated he can find something which may enable him to hurl his calumnies against me. In addition to other things which he finds to blame in me he adds this invidious remark, that I have chosen for translation a work which neither he nor any of the older translators had chosen. I will begin, therefore, since it is here that I am chiefly attacked, by stating

how it came to pass that I attempted the translation of this work in preference to any other, and I will do so in the fewest and truest words. This is, no doubt, superfluous for you, my well-beloved son, since you know the whole affair as it occurred ; yet it is desirable that those who are ignorant of it should know the truth : besides, both he and all his followers make this a triumphant accusation against me, that I promised in my Preface to adopt one method of translation but adopted a different one in the work itself. Hence, I will make an answer which will serve not only for them, but for many besides whose judgment is perverted either by their own malice or by the accusations which others make against me.

11. Some time ago, Macarius, a man of distinction from his faith, his learning, his noble birth and his personal life, had in hand a work against fatalism or, as it is called, Mathesis,[1] and was spending much necessary and fruitful toil on its composition ; but he could not decide many points, especially how to speak of the dispensations of divine Providence. He found the matter to be one of great difficulty. But in the visions of the night the Lord, he said, had shown him the appearance of a ship far off upon the sea coming towards him, which ship, when it entered the port, was to solve all the knotty points which had perplexed him. When he arose, he began anxiously to ponder the vision, and he found, as he said, that that was the very moment of my arrival ; so that he forthwith made known to me the scope of his work, and his difficulties, and also the vision which he had seen. He proceeded to inquire what were the opinions of Origen, whom he understood to be the most renowned among the Greeks on the points in question, and begged that I would shortly explain his views on each of them in order. I at first could only say that the task was one of much difficulty : but I told him that that saintly man the Martyr Pamphilus had to some extent dealt with the question in a work of the kind he wished, that is, in his Apology for Origen. Immediately he begged me to translate this work into Latin. I told him several times that I had no practice in this style of composition, and that my power of writing Latin had grown dull through the neglect of nearly thirty years. He, however, persevered in his request, begging earnestly that by any kind of words that might be possible, the things which he

---

[1] Rom. xiv, 4.
[2] That is, Origen. Rufinus insinuates that Jerome owed and cared more for Origen than he chose to avow.

[1] This word originally meant simply learning. It was then applied in a special sense to mathematics. But the mathematici under the later Roman Empire became identified with astrologers.

longed to know should be placed within his reach. I did what he wished in the best language in my power; but this only inflamed him with greater desire for the full knowledge of the work itself from which, as he saw, the few translations which I had made had been taken. I tried to excuse myself; but he urged me with vehemence, taking God to witness of his earnest request to me not to refuse him the means which might assist him in doing a good work. It was only because he insisted so earnestly, and it seemed clear that his desire was according to the will of God, that I at length acquiesced, and made the translation.

12. But I wrote a Preface [1] to each of these works, and in both, but especially in the Preface to the work of Pamphilus, which was translated first, I set in the forefront an exposition of my faith, affirming that my belief is in accordance with the catholic faith; and I stated that whatever men might find in the original or in my translation, my share in it in no way implicated my own faith, and further, in reference to the Περὶ Ἀρχῶν I gave this warning. I had found that in these books some things relating to the faith were set forth in a catholic sense, just as the Church proclaims them, while in other places, when the very same thing is in question, expressions of a contrary kind are used. I had thought it right to set forth these points in the way in which the author had set them forth when he had propounded the catholic view of them: on the other hand, when I found things which were contrary to the author's real opinion, I looked on them as things inserted by others, (for he witnesses by the complaints contained in his letter that this has been done), and therefore rejected them, or at all events considered that I might omit them as having none of the " godly edifying in the faith." It will not, I think, be considered superfluous to insert these passages from my Prefaces, so that proof may be at hand for each statement. And further, to prevent the reader from falling into any mistake as to the passages which I insert from other documents, I have, where the quotation is from my own works, placed a single mark against the passage, but, where the words are those of my opponent, a double mark.[2]

13. In the Preface to the Apology of Pamphilus, after a few other remarks, I said :

'What the opinions of Origen are may be gathered from the tenor of this treatise. But as for those things in which he is found to contradict himself, I will point out how this has come to pass in a few words which I have added at the close of this Preface. As for us, we believe what has been delivered to us by the holy Prophets, namely : that the holy Trinity is coeternal, and is of one power and substance : and that the Son of God in these last days was made man and suffered for our sins, and, in that very flesh in which he suffered, rose from the dead; and thereby imparted the hope of a resurrection to the whole race of men. When we speak of the resurrection of the flesh, we do so not with any subterfuges, as some slanderously affirm : we believe that the flesh which is to rise is this very flesh in which we now live : we do not put one thing for another, nor when we say body, mean something different from this flesh. If, therefore, we say that the body is to rise again, we speak as the Apostle spoke; for this word body was the word which he employed : Or if, again, we speak of the flesh, our confession coincides with the words of the creed. It is a foolish and calumnious invention to imagine that the human body can be anything but flesh. Whether, then, we say that it is flesh according to the common faith, or body according to the Apostle, which is to rise again, our belief must be held, according to the definition given by the Apostle, with the understanding that that which is to rise again is to be raised in power and in glory, an incorruptible and a spiritual body. While, therefore, we maintain the superior excellence of the body or flesh which is to be, we must hold that the flesh which rises again will be real and perfect; the actual nature of the flesh will be preserved, while the glorious condition of the uncorrupted and spiritual body will not be impaired. For so it is written : [1]" Corruption shall not inherit incorruption." This is what is preached at Jerusalem in the church of God, by its reverend bishop John : this is what we with him confess and hold. If any one believes or teaches anything besides this, or thinks that we believe otherwise than as we have stated, let him be anathema.'

If then any one wishes to have a statement of our faith, he has it in these words. And whatever we read or affirm, or whatever translations we make, we do it without prejudice to this faith of ours, according to the words of the apostle : [2]" Prove all things, hold fast that which is good. Abstain from every form of evil." " And as many as follow this rule, peace be upon them; and upon the Israel of God."

14. I wrote these words beforehand as a statement of my faith, when as yet none of these calumniators had arisen, so that it should be in no man's power to say that it was merely because of their admonition or their compulsion that I said things which I had not believed before. Moreover, I promised that, whatever the requirements of translation might be, I would, while complying with them, maintain the principles of my faith inviolate. How then can any room be left

---

[1] See these Prefaces translated in the earlier part of this Volume.
[2] Corresponding to the single and double inverted commas used in this translation.

[1] 1 Cor. xv, 50.   [2] 1 Thess. v, 21, 22; Gal. vi, 16.

for evil, when the very first word of my confession preserves and defends me from the suspicion of holding any doctrine inconsistent with it? Besides, as I have said above, I have learned from the words of the Lord that every one shall be justified or condemned from his own words and not from those of others.

But I will show how, in the Preface [1] which I prefixed to the books Περὶ Ἀρχῶν, I declared what was to be the regulative principle of my translation, and will prove it, as in the former case, by quoting the words themselves: for it is right to quote from this document also whatever is pertinent to the matter in hand. I had made honourable mention of the man who now turns my praise of him into an accusation against me, for his services in having led the way and having translated a great many works of Origen before I had begun: I had praised both his eloquence as an expositor and his diligence as a translator, and had said that I took him as my model in doing a similar work. And then, after a few more sentences, I continued thus:

' Him therefore we take as our model so far as in us lies, not indeed in the power of his eloquence, but in his method of doing his work, taking care not to reproduce things which are found in the books of Origen discrepant and contrary to his own true opinion.'

I beg the reader to observe what I have said, and not to let this sentence escape him because of its brevity. What I said was that ' I would not reproduce the things which are found in the books of Origen discrepant and contrary to his own true opinion.' I did not make a general promise that I would not reproduce what was contrary to the faith, nor yet what was contrary to me or to some one else, but what was contrary to or discrepant from Origen himself. My opponents must not be allowed to propagate a false statement against me by snatching at a part of this sentence and saying that I had promised not to reproduce anything which was contrary to or discrepant from my own belief. If I had been capable of such conduct, I certainly should not have dared to make a public profession of it. If you find that this has been done in my work, you will know how to judge of it. But if you find that it has not been done, you will not think that I am to blame, since I never gave you any pledge which would bind me to do it.

15. But let me add what comes after. My Preface continued as follows:

'The causes of these discrepancies I have more fully set forth in the Apology which Pamphilus expressly wrote for the works of Origen, to which I added a very short paper in which I shewed by proofs which appear to me quite clear, that his books have been in very many places tampered with by heretics and ill disposed men, and especially the very books which you ask me to translate, namely, the Περὶ Αρχῶν, which may be rendered "Concerning Beginnings" [1] or "Concerning Principalities," which are in any case most obscure and most difficult. For in these books Origen discusses matters on which the philosophers have spent their whole lives without finding out the truth. In these matters, man's belief in a creator and his reasoning about the created world which had been made use of by the philosophers for the purposes of their own profanity, the Christian writer turns to the support of the true faith.'

Here also I beg you to mark my words carefully, and to observe that I said ' belief in a Creator,' but ' reasoning about the created world;' since what is said about God belongs to the domain of faith, but our discussions about created things to the domain of reason. I continued:

' Wherever, therefore, in his works we find erroneous definitions of the Trinity as to which he has in other places expressed his views in accordance with the true faith, we have either left them out as passages which had been falsified or inserted, or else have changed the expression in accordance with the rule of faith which the writer again and again lays down.'

Have I here, I ask, written incautiously? Have I said that I expressed the matter according to the rule of our faith, which would have been evidently going far beyond the scope of a translator whose duty was merely to turn Greek into Latin? On the contrary I said that I expressed these passages according to the rule of faith which I found again and again laid down by Origen himself. Moreover I added:

'I grant that, when he has expressed a thing obscurely, as a man does when he is writing for those who have technical knowledge of the subject and wishes to go over it rapidly, I have made the sentence plainer by adding the fuller expression which he had given of the same thing in some of his other works which I had read. I did this simply in the interests of clearness. But I have expressed nothing in my own words; I have only restored to Origen what was really Origen's though found in other parts of his works.'

16. I should have thought that this statement, I mean the words, 'I have expressed nothing in my own words; I have only re-

---

stored to Origen what was really Origen's, though found in other part of his works,' would of itself have been sufficient for my defence even before the most hostile judges. Have I thrust myself forward in any way? Have I ever led men to expect that I should put in anything of my own? Where can they find the words which they pretend that I have said, and on which they ground their calumnious accusations, namely, that I have removed what was bad and put good words instead, while I had translated literally all that is good? It is time, I think, that they should show some sense of shame, and should cease from false charges and from taking upon themselves the office of the devil who is the accuser of the brethen. Let them listen to the words 'I have put in no words of my own.' Let them listen to them again and hear them constantly reiterated, 'I have put in no words of my own; I have only restored to Origen what was really Origen's, though found in other parts of his works.' And let them see how God's mercy watched over me when I put my hand to this work; let them mark how I was led to forebode the very acts which they are doing. For my Preface continues thus:

'I have given this statement in my Preface for fear that my detractors should think that they had found a fresh reason for accusing me.'

When I said a *fresh* charge I alluded to the charge which they had previously made against the reverend Bishop John for the letter written by him to the reverend Bishop Theophilus[1] on the articles of faith: they pretended that when he spoke of the human body he meant something — I know not what — different from flesh. Therefore I spoke of a *fresh* charge. Take notice, then, I say, of the conduct of these perverse and contentious men.

'I have undertaken this great labour, (which I have only done at your entreaty) not with a view of shutting the mouths of my calumniators, which indeed is impossible unless God himself should do it, but in order to give solid information to those who are seeking to advance in knowledge.'

But, to show you that I foresaw and foretold that they would falsify what I was writing, observe what I said in the following passage:

'Of this I solemnly warn every one who may read or copy out these books, in the sight of God the Father, the Son and the Holy Ghost, and

[1] Of Alexandria. He was at first friendly to Origenism, afterwards bitterly opposed to it. John wrote to him complaining of the conduct of Epiphanius, and explaining his own views. See Jerome's letter (lxxxii) to Theophilus, and his Treatise Against John of Jerusalem. In the latter of these charges occur like those here noticed by Rufinus.

adjure him by our belief in the kingdom which is to come, by the assurance of the resurrection from the dead, and *by that eternal fire which is prepared for the devil and his angels*, — I adjure him, as he would not have for his eternal portion that place where there is weeping and gnashing of teeth, where their worm dieth not and their fire is not quenched, that he should add nothing to this writing, take away nothing, insert nothing, and change nothing.'

Nevertheless, after I had warned them by all these dread and terrible forms of adjuration, these men have not been afraid to become falsifiers and corrupters of my work, though they profess to believe that the resurrection of the flesh is a reality of the future. Why, if they even believed the simple fact of the existence of God, they would never set their hands to acts so injurious and so impious. I ask, further, what line of my Preface can be pointed to in which I have, as my accuser says, praised Origen up to the skies, or in which I have called him, as he once did, an Apostle or a Prophet, or anything of the kind. I may ask indeed in what other matter they find any ground of accusation. I made at the outset a confession of my faith in terms which I think agree in all respects with the confession of the Church. I made a clear statement of my canons of translation, which indeed in most respects were taken from the model furnished by the very man who now comes forward as my accuser. I declared what was the purpose I set before me in making the translation. Whether I have proved capable of fulfilling the task more or less completely is, no doubt, a matter for the judgment of those who read the work, and who may be expected to praise it or to ridicule it, but not to make it a ground for accusation when it is a question of turning words from one language into another with more or less propriety.

17. But I have said that these men would have been unable to find grounds for accusation on the points I have mentioned, however they may take them, unless they had first falsified them. It appears to me therefore desirable that the chief matter on which they have laid their forgers' hands should be inserted in this Apology, lest they should think that I am intentionally withdrawing it from notice because they after making their own additions to it allege it as a ground of false accusation. In the book which I translated there is a passage in which I examine the tenets of those who believe that God has a bodily shape and who describe him as clothed with human members and dress. This is openly asserted

by the heretical sects of the Valentinians and Anthropomorphites, and I see that those who are now our accusers have been far too ready to hold out the hand to them. Origen in this passage has defended the faith of the church against them, affirming that God is wholly without bodily form, and therefore also invisible; and then, following out his scrutiny in a logical manner, he says a few words in answer to the heretics, which I thus translated into Latin.[1]

"But these assertions will perhaps be held to have little authority by those whose desire is to be instructed out of the Holy Scriptures in the things of God, and who require that from that source should be drawn the proof of the preëminence of the nature of God over that of the human body. Consider whether the Apostle does not say the same thing when he speaks thus of Christ:[2] "Who is the image of the invisible God, the first born of every creature." The nature of God is not, as some think, visible to some and not to others, for the Apostle does not say The image of God who is invisible to men, or to sinners; but he speaks quite distinctly of the nature of God in itself, where he says "The image of the invisible God." John also says in his Gospel,[3] "No man hath seen God at any time," by which he distinctly declares to all who can understand, that there is no being to whom God is visible; not as if he were naturally visible and, like a being of attenuated substance, escaped and eluded our glance; but that, in his own nature it is impossible for him to be seen. But perhaps you will ask me my opinion as to the Only begotten himself. Well, if I should say that even to him the nature of God is invisible, since it is its very nature to be invisible, do not dismiss my answer as if it were impious or absurd, for I will at once give you my reason for it. Observe that seeing is a different thing from knowing. Seeing and being seen belong to bodies; to know and to be known belong to the intellectual nature. Whatever then is merely a property of bodies, this we must not attribute to the Father or the Son; but that which belongs to the nature of Deity governs the relations of the Father and the Son. Moreover, Christ himself in the Gospel[4] did not say "No man seeth the Son but the Father nor the Father but the Son," but " No man knoweth the Son but the Father, neither doth any one know the Father but the Son." By this it is clearly shown that what is called seeing and being seen in the case of bodily existence is called knowledge in the case of the Father and the Son: their intercourse is maintained through the power of knowledge not through the weakness of visibility. Since, therefore, an incorporeal nature cannot properly be said to see or to be seen, therefore in the Gospel it is not said either that the Father is seen by the Son or the Son by the Father but that each is known by the other. And if any one should ask how it is that it is said[5] "Blessed are the pure in heart for they shall see God," I think that this text will confirm my assertion still more. For what else is it to see God with the heart than, according to the explanation I have given above, to understand Him with the mind and to know Him?"

18. This is the chief passage which those who were sent from the East to lay snares for me tried to brand as heretical, not only by perversely misunderstanding it, but by falsifying the words. But I could see nothing to suspect in it, as also in several similar passages of the writer I was translating, nor did I think that there was any reason to leave it out, since there was nothing said in it as to a comparison of the Son with the Father, but the question related to the nature of the Deity itself, whether in any sense the word visibility could be applied to it. Origen was answering, as I have said before, the heretics who assert that God is visible because they say that he is corporeal, the faculty of sight being a property of the body; for which reason the Valentinian heretics, of whom I spoke above, declare that the Father begat and the Son was begotten in a bodily and visible sense. He therefore shrank, I presume, from the word Seeing as a suspicious term, and says that it is better, when the question turns upon the nature of the Deity, that is, upon the relation of the Father and the Son, to use the word which the Lord himself definitely chose, when he said: "No man knoweth the Son save the Father, neither doth any know the Father save the Son." He thought that all occasion which might be given to the aforesaid heresies would be shut out if, in speaking of the nature of the Deity he used the word Knowledge rather than Vision. 'Vision' might seem to afford the heretics some support. The word Knowledge on the other hand preserves the true relation of Father and Son in one nature never to be set apart; and this is specially confirmed by the authoritative language of the Gospel. Origen thought also that this mode of speaking would ensure that the Anthropomorphites should never in any way hear God spoken of as visible. It did not seem to me right that this reasoning, since it made no difference between the persons of the Trinity, should be completely thrown on one side, though indeed there were some words in the Greek, which perhaps were somewhat incautiously used, and which I thought it well to avoid using. I will suppose that readers may hesitate in their judgment whether or not even so, it is an argument which can be employed with effect against the aforesaid heresies. I will even grant that those who are practised in judging of words and their sense in matters of this kind and who, besides being experts, are God-fearing men, men who do nothing through strife or vain glory, whose mind is equally free from envy and favour and prejudice may say that the point

---

1 Περὶ Ἀρχῶν Book I. c. 1.   2 Col. i, 15.
3 John i, 18.   4 Matt. xi, 27.   5 Matt. v, 8.

is of little value either for edification or for the combating of heresy; even so, is it not competent for them to pass it over and to leave it aside as not valid for the repulse of our adversaries? Suppose it to be superfluous, does that make it criminous? How can we count as a criminal passage one which asserts the equality of the Father the Son and the Holy Spirit in this point of invisibility? I do not think that any one can really think so. I say any one: for there is no evidence that anything contained in my writings is offensive in the eyes of my accusers; for, if they had thought so, they would have set down my words as they stood in my translation.

19. But what did they actually do? Consider what it was and ask yourself whether the crime is not unexampled? Recall the passage which says: " But perhaps you will ask me my opinion as to the Only-begotten himself. Well, if I should say that even to him the nature of God is invisible, since it is its very nature to be invisible, do not dismiss my answer as if it were impious or absurd, for I will at once give you my reason for it." Well, in the place of the words which I had written, " I will at once give you my reason for it" they put the following words: " Do not dismiss my answer as if it were impious or absurd, for, as the Son does not see the Father, so the Holy Spirit also does not see the Son." If the man who did this, the man who was sent from their monastery[1] to Rome as the greatest expert in calumny, had been employed in the forum and had committed this forgery in some secular business every one knows what would be the consequence to him according to the public laws, when he was convicted of the crime. But now, since he has left the secular life, and has turned his back upon business and entered a monastery, and has connected himself with a renowned master, he has learned from him to leave his former self-restraint and to become a furious madman: he was quiet before, now he is a mover of sedition: he was peaceable, now he provokes war: instead of concord, he is the promoter of strife. For faith he has learnt perfidiousness, for truth forgery. He would, you may well think, have been the complete exemplar of wickedness and criminality of this kind, if you had not had before you the image of that woman Jezebel.[2] She is the same who made up the accusation against Naboth the Zezreelite for the sake of the vineyard, and sent word to the wicked elders to urge against him a false indictment, saying that he had blessed, that is cursed, God and the king. I know not whether of the two is to be accounted the happier, she who sends the command or they who obey it in all its iniquity. These matters are serious; such a crime, as far as I know, is hitherto all but unheard of in the Church. Yet there is something more to be said. What is that you ask. It is this, that those who are guilty should become the judges, that those who plotted the accusation should also pronounce the sentence. It is, indeed, no new thing for a writer to make a mistake or a slip in his words, and in my opinion it is a venial fault, for the Scripture also says, [1] " In many things we all stumble: if any stumbleth not in word the same is a perfect man." Is it thought that some word is wrong? Then let it be corrected or amended, or, if expediency so require, let it be taken out. But to insert in what another man has written things he never wrote, to put in false words for no other purpose than to defame your brother, to corrupt his writings in order to attach a mark of infamy to the author, and to insinuate your ideas into the ears of the multitude so as to throw confusion into the minds of the simple; and all this with the object of staining a man's reputation among his fellows; I ask you whose work this can be except that of him who was a liar from the beginning, and who, from accusing the brethren, received the name of Diabolus, which means accuser. For when he to whom I have alluded[2] recited at Milan one of these sentences which had been tampered with, and I cried out that what he was reading was falsified, he, being asked from whom he had received the copy of the work said that a certain woman named Marcella had given it him. As to her, I say nothing, whosoever she may be. I leave her to her own conscience and to God. I am content with God's own witness and with yours. When I say yours, I mean your own and that of Macarius himself, the saintly man for whom I was doing that work: for both of you read my papers themselves at the first, even before they had been completed, and you have by you the completely corrected copies. You can bear witness to what I say. The words " as the Son does not see the Father, so also the Holy Spirit

---

[1] Jerome's friend Eusebius of Cremona, of whom Rufinus complains as having taken occasion from this old friendship to purloin and falsify his MSS. See below c. 20, 21.
[2] Marcella. See below in this chapter. Also, Jerome Letter cxxvii, c. 9, 10.

[1] James iii, 2.
[2] Eusebius of Cremona, Jerome's friend and emissary, alluded to above in this chapter.

does not see the Son" not only were never written by me, but on the contrary I can point out the forger by whom they were written. If any man says that as the Father does not see the Son, so the Son does not see the Father or that the Holy Spirit does not see the Father and the Son as the Father sees the Son and the Son and the Holy Spirit, let him be anathema. For he sees, and sees most truly; only, as God sees God and the Light sees the Light; not as flesh sees flesh, but as the Holy Spirit sees, not with the bodily senses, but by the powers of the Deity. I say, if any one denies this, let him be anathema for all eternity. But, as the Apostle says, [1] " He that troubles you shall bear his judgment, whosoever he be."

20. I remember indeed that one of these people, when he was convicted of having falsified this passage, answered me that it was so in the Greek, but that I had, of purpose, changed it in the Latin. I do not, indeed, treat this as a serious accusation, because, though what they say is untrue, yet, even supposing that the words did stand so in the Greek, and I had changed them in the Latin, this is nothing more than I had said in my Preface that I should do. If I had done this with the view of making an expression which in the Greek was calculated to make men stumble run more suitably in the Latin, I should have been acting only according to my expressed purpose and plan. But I say to my accusers: You certainly did not find these words in the Latin copies of my work. Whence then did it come into the papers from which he was reading? I, the translator, did not so write it. Whence then came the words which you who have got no such words of mine turn into a ground of accusation? Am I to be accused on the ground of your forgeries? I put the matter in the plainest possible way. There are four books of the work which I translated; and in these books discussions about the Trinity occur in a scattered way, almost as much as one in each page. Let any man read the whole of these and say whether in any passage of my translation such an opinion concerning the Trinity can be found as that which they calumniously represent as occurring in this chapter. If such an opinion can be found, then men may believe that this chapter also is composed in the sense which they pretend. But if in the whole body of these books no such difference of the persons of the Trinity exists anywhere, would not a critic be mad or fat-

uous if he decided, on the strength of a single paragraph, that a writer had given his adherence to a heresy which in the thousand or so other paragraphs of his work he had combated? But the circumstances of the case are by themselves sufficient to shew the truth to any one who has his wits about him. For if this man had really found the passage in question in my papers, and had felt a difficulty in what he read, he would of course have brought the documents to me and have at once asked for explanations, since, as you well know, we were living as neighbours in Rome. Up to that time we often saw one another, greeted one another as friends, and joined together in prayer; and therefore he would certainly have conferred with me about the points which appeared to him objectionable; he would have asked me how I had translated them, and how they stood in the Greek.

21. I am sure that he would have felt that he had enjoyed a triumph if he could have shown that through his representations I had been induced to correct anything that I had said or written. Or, if he had been driven by his mental excitement to expose the error publicly instead of correcting it, he certainly would not have waited till I had left Rome to attack me, when he might have faced me there and put me to silence. But he was deterred by the consciousness that he was acting falsely; and therefore he did not bring to me as their author the documents which he was determined to incriminate, but carried them round to private houses, to ladies, to monasteries, to Christian men one by one, wherever he might make trouble by his ex parte statements. And he did this just when he was about to leave Rome, so that he might not be arraigned and made to give an account of his actions. Afterwards, by the directions, as I am told, of his master, he went about all through Italy, accusing me, stirring up the people, throwing confusion into the churches, poisoning even the minds of the bishops, and everywhere representing my forbearance as an acknowledgment that I was in the wrong. Such are the arts of the disciple. Meanwhile the master, out in the East, who had said in his letter to Vigilantius [1] " Through my labour the Latins know all that is good in Origen and are ignorant of all that is bad," set to work upon the very books which I had translated, and in his new translation inserted all that I had left out as untrustworthy, so that

[1] Gal. v, 10.

[1] Jerome, Letter lxi, c. 2; a passage which shows that Jerome had adopted much the same method as Rufinus in translating Origen.

now, the contrary of what he had boasted has come to pass. The Romans by his labour know all that is bad in Origen and are ignorant of all that is good. By this means he endeavours to draw not Origen only but me also under the suspicion of heresy : and he goes on unceasingly sending out these dogs of his to bark against me in every city and village, and to attack me with their calumnies when I am quietly passing on a journey, and to attempt every speakable and unspeakable mischief against me. What crime, I ask you, have I committed in doing exactly what you have done? If you call me wicked for following your example, what judgment must you pronounce upon yourself?

22. But now I will turn the tables and put my accuser to the question. Tell me, O great master, if there is anything to blame in a writer, is the blame to be laid on one who reads or translates his works? Heaven forbid, he will say; certainly not; why do you try to circumvent me by your enigmatical questions? Am not I myself both a reader and a translator of Origen? Read my translations and see if you can find any one of his peculiar doctrines in them ; especially any of those which I now mark for condemnation. When driven to the point he says :

" If you wish thoroughly to see how abhorent the very suggestion of such doctrines has always been to me, read my Commentaries on the Epistle of Paul to the Ephesians, and you will see from what I have written there what an opinion I formed of him from reading and translating his works." [1]

I ask, can we accept this man as a great and grave teacher, who in one of his works praises Origen and in another condemns him? who in his Introductions calls him a master second only to the Apostles, but now calls him a heretic? What heretic, I ask, was ever called a master of the churches? " It is true, he replies, I was wrong about this ; but why do you go on bringing up this unfortunate Preface [2] against me? Read my Commentaries, and especially those which I have designated." Is there any one who will think this satisfactory? He has composed a great many books, in almost all of which he trumpets forth the praises of Origen to the skies : these books through all these years have been read and are being read by all men : many of these readers after

accepting his opinions have left this world and gone into the presence of the Lord. They hold the opinion about Origen which they had learnt from the statements of this man, and they departed in hope that, according to this man's assurance, they would find him there as a master second only to the Apostles ; but if we are to trust his present writings, they have found him in a state of condemnation, among the impious heretics and the heathen. Is this man now to turn round from his former contention, and to say, " For some thirty years I have been, in my studies and in my writings, praising Origen as equal to the Apostles, but now I pronounce him a heretic?" How is this? Has he come upon some new books of his which he had never read before? Not at all. It is from these same sayings of Origen that he formerly called him an Apostle and now calls him a heretic. But it is impossible that this should really have been so. For either he was right in his former praises, and his judgment has since been perverted by some kind of extreme ill feeling, and in that case no attention is to be paid to him ; or else his former praises were mistaken, and he is now condemning himself, and in that case what judgment does he think others will pass upon him, when, according to the words of the Apostle,[1] he passes condemnation on himself.

22 (a). But, " Surely," he says, "this judgment is done away with since I have repented." Not so fast! We all err, it is true, and especially in word; and we all may repent of our errors. But can a man do penance, and accuse others, and judge and condemn them, all in the same moment? That would be as if a harlot who had abstained from her harlotry for a night or two, should feel called upon to begin writing laws in favour of chastity, and not only to enact these laws, but to proceed to throw down the monuments of all the women who have died, because she suspected that they had led lives like her own. You do penance for having formerly been a heretic, and you do right. But what has that to do with me who never was a heretic at all? You are right in doing penance for your error : but the true way of doing penance is, not by accusing others but by crying for mercy, not by condemning but by weeping. For what sincerity can there be in penitence when the penitent makes a decree of indulgence for himself? He who repents of what he has spoken ill does not cure his

---

[1] The words are not quoted literally from Jerome's letter to Pammachius and Oceanus (Ep. lxxxiv. c. 2) the passage referred to ; but they give the sense fairly well. See also the letter to Vigilantius (lxi. c. 2).

[2] *Præfati unculam.* That is, the Preface to Origen's Song of Songs, in which he says that Origen has not only surpassed every one else, but also in this work has surpassed himself.

[1] Perhaps from 1 Cor. xi, 29, or Rom. xiv, 23.

wound by speaking ill again, but by keeping silence. For thus it is written: [1] "Thou hast sinned, be at peace." But now you first bring yourself in a criminal, then you absolve yourself from your crime, and forthwith change yourself from a criminal into a judge. This may be no trouble to you who thus mock at us, but it is a trouble to us if we suffer ourselves to be mocked by you.

23. But let us come to these two Commentaries which he alone excepts from the general condemnation and renunciation which he pronounces upon all the rest of his works; we shall see with what modesty and self-restraint he conducts himself in these: Remember that it is by these alone that he has chosen to prove that he is sound in the faith, and that he is altogether opposed to Origen. Let us examine then as witnesses these two books which alone of all his writings are satisfactory to him, namely, the three books of his commentary on the Epistle of Paul to the Ephesians, and the single book (I think) on Ecclesiastes. Let us for a moment look into the one which comes forward first, the Commentary on the Epistle to the Ephesians. Even here I recognize in his arguments the influence of him who is as his fellow, his partner and his brother mystic, to use his own expression.[2] And first of all, as to these poor weak women about whom he makes himself merry, because they say that after the resurrection they will not have their frail bodies, since they will be like the angels. Let us hear what he has to say about them. In the third book of his Commentaries on the Epistle of Paul to the Ephesians, on the passage in which it is said, [3] "He who loveth his own wife loveth himself, for no man ever hated his own flesh;" after a few other remarks, he says:

"Let us men then cherish our wives and let our souls cherish our bodies in such a way as that the wives may be turned into men and the bodies into spirits, and that there may be no difference of sex, but that, as among the angels there is neither male nor female, so we who are to be like the angels may begin here to be what it is promised that we shall be in heaven."

24. How, I ask, can you, seeing that your Commentaries contain such doctrines, put them forward to prove your soundness in the faith, and to confute those ideas which you reprove? How do your words tend to reprove those women whom we have spoken of? Besides, has any woman gone so far as to say what you write, namely, that women are to be turned into men and bodies into souls? If bodies are to be turned into spirits, then, according to you, there will be no resurrection not only of the flesh but even of the body, which you admit to be the doctrine even of those whom you have set down as heretics. Where are we to look any more for the body, if it is reduced to a spirit? In that case everything will be spirit, the body will be nowhere. And again, if the wives are to be turned into men, according to this suggestion of yours, that there is to be no difference of sex whatever, by which I suppose you mean that the female sex will entirely cease, being converted into the male, and the male sex will alone remain; I am not sure that you would have the permission of the women to speak here on behalf of their sex. But, even suppose that they grant you this, then with what consistency can you argue that the male sex is any longer necessary, when the female is shown not to be necessary? for there is a natural bond which unites the sexes in mutual dependence, so that, if one does not exist, there is no need of the other. And further, if it is man alone who is to receive at the resurrection the form of clay which was originally given in paradise, what becomes of that which is written, [1] "He made them male and female, and blessed them"? And then, if, as both you yourself say, and also these poor women whom you arraign, there is neither man nor woman, how can bodies be turned into souls, or women into men, since Paradise does not allow the existence of either sex, nor does the likeness of angels, as you say, admit it? And I marvel how you can demand from others a strict opinion upon the continuance of the diversity of sex when you yourself, as soon as you begin to discuss it, find yourself involved in so many knotty questions that to evolve yourself out of them becomes impossible. How much more right would your action be if you were to imitate us whom you blame in such matters as these and allow God to be the only judge of them, as is indeed the truth. It would be far better for you to confess your ignorance of them than to write things which in a little while you have to condemn. I should like to ask my accuser whether he can conscientiously say that he would ever have found, I do not say in any, even the least, work of mine, but even in any familiar letter which I might have written carelessly to a friend, such

---

[1] Possibly a kind of paraphrase of our Lord's words to the woman taken in adultery. John viii, 11.

[2] συμμύστην, that is one who partakes with us in the mysteries; hence, initiated into the same secret, or special opinions.

[3] Ephes. v, 28.

[1] Gen. i, 27.

things as that bodies were to be turned into spirits and wives into men, were it not that he had put them forward as if he wished them to be inserted in brazen letters on the gates of cities, and recited in the forum, in the Senate house and in front of the rostra. If he had found any such thing in my writings, imagine how many heads of accusation he would have set down, how many volumes he would have compiled, how he would be assailing me with all the arms and shafts of that teeming breast of his; how he would have said: "I tell you that he is deceiving you by speaking of the resurrection of the body, for he denies the resurrection of the flesh; or even if he confesses the resurrection of the flesh he denies that of the members and the sex: but, if you do not believe me, behold and see the very words of his letter, in which he says that bodies are to be turned into souls and wives into men." Yet, when you write this, we are not to call you a heretic, but are to give satisfaction to you as though you were our master. And as for those women whom you have attacked with your indecent reproaches, they will, when they stand before the judgment seat of Christ, bring forward what you have taught them in these Commentaries as well as the things which you have since written, with insults which show that you had forgotten yourself; and both the one and the other will be read out there, where the favour of men will have ceased, and the applause for which you pay by flattery will be silent, and they will be judged together with their author for these words and deeds of yours before Christ the righteous judge.

25. But now let us go on to discuss what he writes further as to God's judgment,[1] for this too is a matter of the faith. We shall find that as he alters the faith about the resurrection of the flesh in other points, so he does in reference to God's judgment. In the first book of the Commentaries on the Ep. of Paul to the Ephesians, he deals with that passage in which the Apostle says: "Even as he chose us in him before the foundation of the world that we should be holy and without blemish before him." On this he says:

"For the foundation of the world the Greek has καταβολῆς κόσμου. The word καταβολή does not mean the same which we understand by foundation. We, therefore, shall not attempt to render a word for a word, which is here impossible on account of the poverty of our language and

also the novelty of the sense, and because, as some one has said, the Greeks have a larger discourse and a happier tongue than ours. We must explain the force of the word by some sort of periphrasis. καταβολή is properly used when something is thrown down and is cast from a higher into a lower place, or else when anything is taking its beginning. Hence those who lay the first foundations of future houses are said καταβεβληκέναι, that is to have thrown down the first foundations. Paul thus used the word to show that God framed all things out of nothing: he assigned to Him not a creation nor a building up, nor a making but a καταβολή, that is, a beginning of a foundation. He wishes to show that there was not some other thing antecedent to creatures, and out of which creatures were formed, as is held by the Manichæans and other heretics, who begin with a maker and a material, but that all things were made out of nothing. But, as to our election to be holy and without blemish before him, that is, before God, previously to the making of the world, of which the Apostle speaks, this belongs to the foreknowledge of God, to whom all future things are as if they were already done, and all things are known before they come into being: as Paul is predestinated in the womb of his mother, and Jeremiah before his birth is sanctified, chosen, and confirmed, and, as a type of Christ, is sent to be a prophet of the nations."

26. So far he has set forth a single exposition of the passage; but on whose authority he wishes us to receive this interpretation he has not made clear. What he has done is to make void this first interpretation by what comes after: for he goes on: "But there is another, who tries to shew that God is just." He therefore points out that by that first exposition the justice of God is not vindicated, which of course is contrary to the faith: and he goes on through the mouth of this 'other,' whose assertions he evidently wishes to exhibit as being what is everywhere held for catholic and indubitable, to give a testimony by which he will, as he asserts, seek to show that God is just. Let us see then what this 'other man' says, who proclaims the justice of God.

"Another man," he says, "who seeks to vindicate the justice of God, argues that it is not according to his own pre-judgment and knowledge, but according to the merit of the elect that God's choice of men is determined; and he says that, before the creation of the visible world, of sky and earth and seas and all that they contain, there existed other invisible creatures, among which also were souls; and that these souls, for reasons known to God alone, were *cast down*[1] into this vale of tears, this place of our mournful pilgrimage, and that this is shewn by the prayer uttered by a holy man of old who, having his habitation fixed here, yet longed to return to his original abode: "Woe is me that my sojourning is prolonged, that I have my habitation among the inhabitants of

---

[1] *Quæstiones*. Examinations or inquisitions. It seems here to mean the method which God follows in distinguishing between individuals.

[1] καταβολή "foundation," means literally "casting down."

Kedar," [1] "my soul has long been a pilgrim," and again "O wretched man that I am, who will deliver me from the body of this death?" [2] and in another place "It is better to return and be with Christ," [3] and elsewhere, "Before I was brought low, I sinned;" [4] and other words of a like character."

This relates, they say to the souls' condition before they were *cast down* into the world. The reader of this will be apt to say, Master, you seem to tell us, yet do not really tell us, who these men are who say this, that the souls of men existed before they were cast down into the world. Then he will reply, "Was I not right in saying that you were blind, and no better than a mole? Did I not say before, that they are those who assert that God is just, — by which, if you had any sense at all, you would understand that I mean myself: for I am not such a heretic as not to include myself among those who vindicate the justice of God, which indeed all must do who have the least tincture of good sense." Then they will reply, "Tell us, then, master, tell us, what it is that these men say, and you among them? We understand that you say that before the souls were cast down into the world, and before the world, which was made up of souls, had been cast down together with its inhabitants into the abyss, God chose Paul and those like him, who were holy and undefiled. But if men are chosen, they are chosen out of a great number; there must be many in a worse condition out of whom the election is made. However, just as in the Babylonian captivity, when Nebuchadnezzar carried away the people into Chaldæa, Ezekiel and Daniel and the Three Children, and Haggai and Zechariah were sent with them, not because they deserved to become captives, but that they might be a comfort to those who were carried away; so also, in that ' casting down' of the world, those who had been chosen by God before the world was, were sent to instruct and train the sinful souls, so that these, through their preaching, might return to the place from which they had fallen; and this is what is meant by the words of the eighty-ninth Psalm: [5] "Lord thou hast been our refuge in generation and in offspring, before the mountains were established, or the earth and the world were made;" that is to say, that before the world was made, and a beginning was made of the generation of all things, God was a refuge to his saints."

27. Such are the doctrines which are to be found in these works of yours which you single out from all that you have written, and which you desire men to read over again to the prejudice of all the rest. It is in these very Commentaries that these doctrines are written. There was, you say, an invisible world before this visible one came into being. You say that in this world, along with the other inhabitants, that is the angels, there were also souls. You say that these souls, for reasons known to God alone, enter into bodies at the time of birth in this visible world: those souls, you say, who in a former age had been inhabitants of heaven, now dwell here, on this earth, and that not without reference to certain acts which they had committed while they lived there. You say further that all the saints, such as Paul and others like him in each generation were predestinated by God for the purpose of recalling them by their preaching to that habitation from which they had fallen: and all this you support by very copious warranties of Scripture. But are not these statements precisely those for which you now arraign Origen, and for which alone you demand that he should be condemned? What 'other' than him who says such things as these do you condemn in your writings? And yet if these statements are to be condemned, as you now urge, you will first pronounce judgment on these statements, and then find that you have condemned yourself by anticipation. No other refuge remains for you. There is no room for any of these twists and turns for which you blame others: for it is just when you are doing penance and have been converted, when you have been corrected and put in the way of amendment, that you have stamped these books with fresh authority, to prove to us by their means what your opinion was as to the doctrines which ought to be condemned: and therefore what you have there written must be taken as if we heard you now distinctly making the statements contained in them. Yet in these very books you yourself make the statements which you say are to be condemned. But no! you will say: it is not I that make them. It is the 'other' who thus speaks, that is, of course, the man who I now declare ought to be condemned. Well, let us recall, if you please, that particular line in which you change the person of the speaker, that we may see who it is whom you represent as building up this strange theory. You say, then, that it is 'another,' who is endeavouring to show that God is just, who says these

1 Ps. cxx, 5.   4 Ps. cxix, 67.
2 Rom. vii, 24.   5 In our numbering, Ps. xc.
3 Phil. i, 23.

things which we have set down just above. If you say that this 'other' who by this assertion of his proves God to be just is separate and divers from yourself, what then, I ask, is your own opinion? Must we say that you deny that God is just? Oh, great Master, you who see so sharply, and are so hard upon the moles that have no eyes:[1] you seem to have got yourself into a most impossible position, where you are shut in on every side. Either you must deny that God is just by declaring yourself other than, and contrary to, him who says these things, or if you confess God to be just, as all the Church does, then it is you yourself who make the assertions in question; in which case the sentence which you pass upon another falls upon you, you are thrust through with your own spear. I think that this is enough for your conviction before the most righteous judges whose judgment anticipates that of God: not that they would condemn the man who sees the mote in his brother's eye but does not see the beam in his own; but they would try to bring him to a better mind and to true repentance.

28. But it is possible that this particular passage may have escaped his observation, although he thought that he had revised these books so as to make them perfectly clear, and put them forward as giving a profession of his faith, to the prejudice of all the rest. Let us see then what are his opinions in other parts. In the same book when he comes to the passage where it is written "According to the good pleasure of his will, to the praise of his glory," he makes these remarks among others:

"Here certain men seize upon the opportunity to introduce their peculiar views: they believe that before the foundation of the world, the souls of men dwelt in the heavenly Jerusalem with the angels, and with all the other celestial powers. They think that it would be impossible, in accordance with the good pleasure of God, and the praise of his glory and of his grace, to explain the fact that some men are born poor and barbarous, in slavery and weakness, while others are born as wealthy Roman citizens, free and with strong health; that some are born in a low, some in a high station, that they are born in different countries, in different parts of the world: unless there are some antecedent causes for which each individual soul had its lot assigned according to its merits. Moreover, the passage which some think that they understand, (though they do not) the passage of the Epistle to the Romans which says, [2] "Hath not the potter a right over the clay from the same lump to make one part a vessel unto honour, and another unto dishonour?" these men take as supporting this same view; for they argue that, just as the distinction between

leading a good life or a bad, one of labour or self-indulgence, would be of little account if we did not believe in the judgment of God which is to come, so also the difference of conditions under which men are born would impugn the justice of God unless they were the results of the soul's previous deserts. For, if we do not accept this view, they say, it cannot be 'the good pleasure of God' nor 'to the praise of his glory and grace' that he should have chosen some before the foundation of the world to be holy and undefiled, and to partake of the adoption through Jesus Christ, and should have appointed others to the lowest position and to everlasting punishment; he could not have loved Jacob before he came forth from the womb and hated Esau before he had done anything worthy of hatred, unless there were some antecedent causes which would, if we knew them, prove God to be just."

29. What can be more distinct than this statement? What could possibly be thought or said whether by Origen or by any of those whom you say that you condemn, which would be clearer than this, that the inequality of conditions which exists among those who are born into this world is ascribed to the justice of God? You say that the cause of the salvation or perdition of each soul is to be found in itself, that is, in the passions and dispositions which it has shown in its previous life in that new Jerusalem which is the mother of us all. "But this too," he will say no doubt, "is not said by myself. I described it as the opinion of another: moreover, I used the expression 'they seize upon the opportunity.'" Well, I do not deny that you make it appear that you are speaking of another. But you have not denied that this man about whom you are speaking is in agreement and accord with you: you have not said that he is in opposition or hostility to you. For, when you use this formula of 'another' in reference to one who is really opposed to you, you habitually, after setting down a few of his words, at once impugn and overthrow them: you do this in the case of Marcion, Valentinus, Arius and others. But when, as in this instance, you use, indeed, this formula of 'another,' but report his words fortified by the strongest assertions and by the most abundant testimonies of Scripture, is it not evident even to us who are so slow of understanding, and whom you speak of as 'moles,' that he whose words you set down and do not overthrow, is no other than yourself, and that we have here a case of the figure well known to rhetoricians, when they use another man's person to set forth their own opinions. Such figures are resorted to by rhetoricians when they are afraid of offending particular people, or when they wish to avoid exciting ill-will against themselves. But, if you think that you have avoided blame by putting for-

---

[1] *Talpas oculis captos.* Virg. Georg. i, 183.
[2] Rom. ix, 21.

ward 'another' as the author of these statements, how much more free from it is he whom you accuse. For his mode of action is much more cautious. He is not content with merely saying, "This is what others say," or "so some men think," but, "As to this or that I do not decide, I only suggest," and, "If this seems to any one more probable, let him hold to it, putting the other aside." He has been very careful in his statements, as you know; and yet you summon him to be tried and condemned. You think that you have escaped because you speak of 'another': but the points on which you condemn him are precisely those in which you follow and imitate him.

30. But let us proceed in our study of these Commentaries; otherwise, in dwelling too long upon a few special points, we may be prevented from taking notice of the greater number. In the same book and the same passage[1] are the words "To the end that we should be unto the praise of his glory, we who had before hoped in Christ." His comment is:

"If it had been simply said 'We have trusted in Christ,' and there had not been the prefix 'before,' which stands in the Greek προηλπικότες, the sense would be quite clear, namely, that those who have hoped in Christ have been chosen in due order[2] and have been predestinated according to the purpose of him who orders all things according to the counsel of his own will. But, as it stands, the addition of the preposition 'before' compels us to explain it according to the same ideas which we argued in a former place to be necessary for the explanation of the passage, "Who hath blessed us with every spiritual blessing in the heavenly places in Christ, even as he chose us in him before the foundation of the world, that we should be holy and without blemish before him:" namely, that God had blessed us before in heaven with all spiritual blessing, and had chosen us before the world was framed; and that thus we are said to have hoped in Christ 'before,' that is, in the time when we were elected and predestinated and blessed in heaven."

31. But let this pass, for what follows is of more importance. I thank God that he has relieved me from a very serious burden of suspicion. Perhaps I seemed to some people to be acting contentiously and calumniously when I insinuated that, according to a figure of rhetoric, when he spoke of 'another' he meant himself. But to prevent all further doubt from resting in the minds of his hearers, he has himself declared that it is so. Like a truly good teacher, who would not wish any ambiguity about his sayings to remain in the minds of his pupils, he has been so good as to shew quite clearly

who that 'other' was of whom he had spoken before. He therefore says, "But, as it stands, the addition of the preposition 'before' leads us to explain it according to the ideas which we argued in a former place to be necessary." You see, he means that it is we, and not some other, no one knows who, as you may have thought, who in the former place argued thus, when we were expounding the words "Who hath blessed us with every spiritual blessing in the heavenly places in Christ." It was to meet the case of the less intelligent persons, who might think that what was there said was spoken by some one else, to prevent any error on the point remaining in the minds of those whom he had begged to read these books so that they might see what his opinion of Origen was, that he now acknowledges this opinion as his own, and, no longer speaking of 'another,' says what we have quoted before; namely, that, as God had before blessed us with all spiritual blessing in Christ in the heavenly places, and had chosen us before the foundation of the world; so also we are said to have trusted in Christ at that former time in which we were elected and predestinated and blessed in heaven. He himself therefore, as it seems to me, has by his own testimony, absolved me from all suspicion of speaking a calumny when I say that that 'other' is no 'other' than himself.

30 (a). But, I undertook to shew something of more importance still in what follows. After he had said that we had hoped in Christ before, and that in the time before the foundation of the world and before we were born in our bodies, we had been blessed and chosen in heaven, he again introduces that 'other' of his, and says: "Another, who does not admit this doctrine that we had a previous existence and had hope in Christ before we lived in this body, would have us understand the matter in his own way." In this passage this 'other,' whoever he may be, has put forth all his ill savour. Let him tell us then whom he means by this 'other' who does not admit this opinion that before we lived in this body we both existed and hoped in Christ — for which he requires us to condemn Origen. Whom does he wish us to understand by this 'other'? Is it some one opposed to himself? What do you say, great master? You are pressed by that two-horned dilemma of which you are so fond of speaking to your disciples. For, if you say that by this 'other' who does not admit that souls existed before they lived in the body you mean yourself, you have betrayed

the secret which in the previous passages was concealed. It is now found out that you by your own confession are that other who have fashioned all the doctrines of which you now demand the condemnation. But if we are not to believe you to be the 'other' of the former passage, so that the doctrines which you now impugn may not be ascribed to you, we have no right to consider you in this case to be the 'other' who does not admit that our souls existed before we lived in bodies. Choose either side you like as the ground of your acquittal. This 'other,' whom you so frequently bring in, are we to understand by him yourself or some one else? Do you wish that he should be thought by us to be a catholic or a heretic? Is he to be acquitted or condemned? If that 'other' of yours is a catholic, the man who said in the former passage that before this visible world our souls had their abode among the angels and the other heavenly powers in the heavenly places in Jerusalem which is above, and that they there contracted those dispositions which caused the diversities of their birth into the world and of the other conditions to which they are now subject, then these must be esteemed to be catholic doctrines, and we know that it is an impiety to condemn what is catholic. But if you call this 'other' a heretic, you must also brand as a heretic the 'other' who will not admit that souls existed and hoped in Christ before they were born in the body. Which way can you get out of this dilemma, my master? Whither will you break forth? To what place will you escape? Whichever way you betake yourself, you will stick fast. Not only is there no avenue by which you can withdraw yourself; there is not even the least breathing space left you. Is this all the profit you have gained from Alexander's Commentaries on Aristotle, and Porphyry's Introduction? Is this the result of the training of all those great Philosophers by whom you tell us you were educated, with all their learning, Greek and Latin, and Jewish into the bargain? Have they ended by bringing you into these inextricable straits, in which you are so pitifully confined that the very Alps could give you no refuge?

31 (a). But let us spare him now. We must bend to our examination of the books; for, to use an expression of his own, a great work leaves no time for sleep; though indeed he himself spares nobody, and does not so much use reasonable speech as lash with the scourge of his tongue whomsoever he pleases; and any one who refuses to flatter him must expect to be branded at once as a

heretic both in his treatises and in hundreds of letters sent to all parts of the world. Let us not follow his example, but rather that of the patriarch David, who, when he had surprised his enemy Saul in the cave and might have slain him, refused to do so, but spared him. This man knows well how often I have done the same by him, both in word and deed; and if he does not choose to confess it, he has it fixed at least in his mind and conscience. I will pardon him then, though he never pardons others, but condemns men for their words without any consideration or charity; and for the present I will let him come out from this pit, until he falls into that other, from which all of us together will be unable to deliver him, however much we may wish and strive. He has to explain how it comes to pass that, in the first passage, where that doctrine was being asserted which sought to vindicate the justice of God, he really meant to speak of some one else, and that that person was the one whom he now wishes to have condemned; yet in the second passage, where the speaker says the opposite and does not admit what has been said before, the 'other' whom he speaks of means himself. It is possible that he may feel sure that this was what he meant, but that he was not able to make it plain in writing. Let us give him the benefit of the doubt, and assume that in this latter passage the 'other' is himself, and that it is he who does not admit the doctrine which holds that before our life in the body began our souls existed and hoped in Christ. I will quote the entire passage, and prosecute a fresh and diligent inquiry to see what it tends to. He says thus:

"Another who does not admit this doctrine that before our life in the body began our souls existed and trusted in Christ, changes the sense of the passage so as to mean that, in the advent of our Lord and Saviour, when in his name [1] every knee shall bow, of things heavenly and earthly and infernal, and every tongue shall confess that Jesus Christ is Lord, to the glory of God the Father, when all things shall be made subject to him, there will be some who are made subject willingly, but others only by necessity; and that those who before his coming in his majesty have hoped in him will be to the praise of his glory; that these therefore are called [2] Fore-hopers; but that those who are only found to believe through necessity, when even the devil and his angels will be unable to reject Christ as King are to be called simply Hopers. and that they are not for the praise of his glory. And this we see partly fulfilled even now, since we can distinguish between the reward of those who follow God willingly and those who follow Him

---

[1] Phil. ii, 10, 11.
[2] Jerome uses the Greek word προηλπικότας. It seems best to coin a new one to represent the peculiar idea.

through necessity. But,[1] whether by pretence or in truth, let Christ be proclaimed: only let each of them understand, both the Hopers and the Fore-hopers, that for the difference of their hope they will receive different rewards."

32. In this passage all room for doubt is removed. In the former passage you said that those who before hoped in Christ are those who, before they were born in bodies in this visible world, dwelt in heaven and had hope in Christ. But, to prevent this being supposed to be your own doctrine, you introduced another interpretation, namely, that at that time when every knee shall bow to Jesus as Lord, the universal creation, of things heavenly, earthly and infernal, will consist of persons subjected to him in two different ways, some willingly, some by necessity. You add that all the saints, who now believe on him through the word of preaching are subject to him willingly, and that these are called Fore-hopers, that is those who have beforehand hoped in Christ: but that those who are subject to him by necessity are those who have not believed now through the preaching of the word, but who then will no longer be able to deny him, such as the devil and his angels, and those who with them have been obliged by necessity to believe: and that all these, and amongst them the devil and his angels, who shall afterwards believe, shall not be called Fore-hopers, because that name belongs to those who believed in Christ before, and hoped in him willingly, whereas these others only did so afterward and by necessity: and you add that, consequently, they will receive different rewards. But you assign rewards, though they may be inferior ones, to all, even to those who now do not believe, that is, the devil and his angels; and, though now you hold the mere opinion, not the mature judgment, of another worthy of condemnation who thinks it possible that the devil may one day have a respite from punishment, you bring him into the kingdom of God to receive the second reward. This also you wish us to understand, that, as it matters not whether Christ is preached in truth or by necessity, so it is of no consequence whether we believe by necessity or willingly.

33. These are the things which we learn from the Commentaries to which you direct us. These are the rules for the confusion[2] of our faith which you teach us. You wish

us to condemn in others what you teach yourself in private. For, of course, if you are now that 'other' who do not admit the doctrine which holds that our souls existed in heaven before they were joined to bodies, you are undoubtedly the man who not only promise pardon to the devil and his angels and all unbelievers but also undertake that they shall be endowed with rewards of the second order. But if you deny this second doctrine, you must be the author of that which we first discussed. And I wonder that those able and learned men who read these writings of his about which he now writes in commendation, should laugh at me because he calls me a mole, and should not feel that he is all the while thinking of them much more as moles, for not seeing that the things I have pointed out are imbedded in his books. For, if he thought that they could understand as well as read, he would never have requested them to get a copy of those books with a view to the condemnation of the very things which their master there teaches; for these very things which he urges us to condemn are most plainly and manifestly contained in them. I have shewn, at all events, that he himself in these chosen Commentaries of his asserts the doctrines which he desires to have condemned in another man's books, namely, that souls existed in heaven before they were born in bodies in this world, and that all sinners and unbelievers, together with the devil and his angels, will, at the time when every knee shall bow to Jesus of things heavenly and things earthly and things infernal, not only receive pardon, but also be summoned to receive the second order of rewards.

34. It is indeed a thing so unheard of to believe that a man can pronounce condemnation on the fabric which he himself has reared, that I doubt not it will with difficulty win credit; and I feel that what you desire is that I should, if possible, produce from his writings instances of this so clear that no room whatever may be left for doubting; that is, passages in which that 'other' of which he is so fond is not named at all; and this I will do. In this same book he declares his belief that, in the end of the age,[1] Christ and his saints will have their throne above the demons in such a way that the demons themselves will act according to the will of Christ and his saints who reign over them. In commenting upon the passage where the Apostle says, [2] " That in the ages to come

---

[1] Phil. i, 18.
[2] *Regulas confusionis fidei.* Another reading is *Confessionis.* But probably Rufinus meant to give point to his expression by substituting for the well known words " Rule of faith," " Rule of confusion of faith."

[1] *Sæculi;* usually translated by 'the end of the world,' which, however, hardly gives the true meaning.
[2] Eph. ii, 7.

he might show the exceeding riches of his grace in kindness toward us in Christ Jesus," after a few other remarks, he says:

"We who formerly were held bound by the law of the infernal place, and, through our vices and sins were given over both to the works of the flesh and to punishment, shall now reign with Christ and sit together with him. But we shall sit, not in some kind of low place, but[1] above all Principalities and power and Dominion, and every name that is named not only in this age but in the age to come. For, if Christ has been raised from the dead, and sits at the right hand of God in heavenly places, far above all Principality and Power and Dominion, and above every name that is named, not only in this age but in the age to come, we also must of necessity sit and reign with Christ and sit above those things above which he sits. But the careful reader will at this point make his inquiry and say: What? is man then greater than the angels and all the powers of heaven? I make answer, though it is hazardous to do so, that the Principalities and Powers and Mights and Dominions, and all names that are named not only in this age but in that which is to come must refer (since all things are subjected to the feet of Christ) not to the good part of them but the opposite; the Apostle means by these expressions the rebellious angels, and the prince of this world, and Lucifer who once was the morning star, over whom in the end of the age the saints must sit with Christ, who communicates this privilege to them. These Powers are now infernal powers, abusing their freedom for the worst purposes, wandering everywhere and running together down the steep places of sin. But when they have Christ and the saints sitting on thrones above them, they will begin to be ruled according to the will of those who reign over them."

Surely there is no ambiguity remaining here; the passage needs no one to bring out its points. He says in the most distinct terms, without bringing in the person of any 'other,' that the rebellious angels and the prince of this world, and Lucifer who once was the morning star, will in the end, when Christ sits and reigns over them with his saints, be fellows and sharers, not only of his kingdom but also of his will; for to act according to the will of Christ and of all his saints is to have arrived at the highest blessedness, and the perfection which we are taught in the Lord's Prayer to ask of the Father is none other than this, that his will may be done in earth as it is in heaven.

35. But I beg you to listen patiently as I follow him in his continual recurrence to these same doctrines —not indeed in all that he says of them, for it is so much that I should have to write many volumes if I tried to exhaust it — but as much as will satisfy the reader that it is not by chance that he slips into these notions which he now proposes

for imitation to his disciples, but that he supports them by large and frequent assertion. Let us see what it is that he teaches us in these the most approved of his Commentaries. In this same book he teaches that there is for men the possibility of both rising and falling, not in the present age only but in that which is to come. On the passage in which the words occur: "Far above all Principality and Power and Might and Dominion, and every name that is named not only in this age but in that which is to come," he has the following among other remarks:

"If, however, there are Principalities, Virtues, Powers and Dominions, they must necessarily have subjects who fear them and serve them and gain power from their strength; and this gradation of offices will exist not only in the present age but in that which is to come; and it must be possible that one may rise through these various stages of advancement and honour, while another sinks, that there will be risings and fallings, and that our spirits may pass under each of these Powers, Virtues, Principalities, and Dominions one after the other."

36. I will address the Master in one of his own phrases.[1] Why, after nearly four hundred years, do you give such teachings as these to the Latin people with their peaceable and simple minds! Why do you inflict on unaccustomed ears new-sounding words, which no one finds in the writings of the Apostles? I beseech you, spare the ears of the Romans, spare that faith which the Apostle praised.[2] Why do you bring out in public what Peter and Paul were unwilling to publish? Did not the Christian world exist without any of these things until — not as you say I made my translations, but up to the time when you wrote what I have quoted, that is till some fifteen years ago? For what is this teaching of yours, that in the world to come there will still be risings and fallings, — that some will go forward and some go back? If that be true, then what you say, that in this world life is either acquired or lost, is not true; unless it has some occult meaning. I do not find that you repent of any of these doctrines which these commentaries contain. Again, you teach that the Church is to be understood as being one body made up not of men only but of angels and all the powers of heaven. You say in commenting on the passage of the same book, in which the words occur [3]"And gave him to be head over all the Church," a little way down: "The Church may be understood as consisting not of men alone, but also of angels, and of all the powers, and

[1] Eph. i, 21.   [1] Jerome, Letter lxxxiv, 8.   [2] Rom. 1, 8.   [3] Eph. i, 22.

reasonable creatures." Again, you say that souls, because in that former life they knew God, now know him not as one previously unknown, but as though after having forgotten him they came to recognize him again. These are the words used in a passage of the same book:

"The words which he uses "In the knowledge of him"[1] some interpret by recalling that between γνῶσις and 'επίγνωσις (Gnosis and Epignosis) that is, between knowing and recognition there is this difference, that Knowing has reference to things which we did not know before and have since begun to know, while Recognition has to do with those things which we afterwards remember. Our souls, then, they say, have a kind of apprehension of a former life, after they have been cast down into human bodies, and have forgotten God their Father; but now we know him by revelation, according to that which is written:[2] "All the ends of this world shall remember and turn to the Lord;" and there are many similar passages."

38.[3] Now, as to the expression which he uses, "Some persons say," I think it has been made clear by what I have previously said, that, when he says "some persons say" or "Another says," and does not controvert the opinions which are thus introduced, it is he himself who is this 'certain' or 'other' person. And this is proved by the numerous cases which I have pointed out in which he expresses opinions agreeing with these without the introduction of any such person. We must consider therefore in each case whether he expresses any dissent from the 'other.' For instance, an opinion is put forward that the stars and the other things that are in heaven are reasonable beings and capable of sinning. We must see, therefore, what his own opinion is on this point. Turn to his note, in this book,[4] upon the passage "He must reign till he hath put all his enemies under his feet."[5] You will find, some way down, the words:

"It may be observed that no one is without sin, that Even the stars are not clean in his sight,[6] and Every creature trembles at the coming of the Creator. Hence it is not only things on earth but also things in heaven which are said to have been cleansed by our Saviour's cross."

Again, as to the opinion that it is because of their being in this body of humiliation or body of death that men are called children of wrath, he says, in commenting on the words[7] 'We were the children of wrath, even as others.' (Comm. on Ephes. on this verse, some way down.)

"We must hold that men are by nature children of wrath because of this[1] 'body of humiliation' and[2] 'body of death,' and because[3] 'the heart of man is disposed to evil from his youth.'"

Again, on the opinion that there is first a creation of the soul and afterwards a fashioning of the body he says (at the same passage, a long way down)

"And observe carefully that he does not say, 'We are his forming and fashioning, but[4] 'We are his making.' For 'fashioning' implies the fact of man's origin from the slime of the earth: but 'making' from his origin according to the image and similitude of God. And this distinction is confirmed by the words of the 118th Psalm[5] "Thy hands have made me and fashioned me." 'Making' has the first place, 'fashioning' comes after.'

Are there any other things which he wishes us to condemn? He has only to mention them, and we can draw them out from his own books, or rather from the bottom of his own heart. For instance, We are to condemn as a pestilent assertion that the nature of human souls and of angels is the same. But let us see what his own opinion is on this point as given in the books which he specially puts before us as containing the pattern of his profession and his rule of faith. Turn to the passage,[6] "He came and preached peace to them which were afar off and to them that were nigh." His comment on this first expounds the words of Jews and Gentiles, and then goes on:

"This has been said in accordance with the Vulgate[7] translation. But, if a man reads the words of the Apostle when he says of Christ,[8] "Making peace through the blood of his cross for those that are in earth and for those that are in heaven" and the rest that is said in that place, he will not consider that it is we who are called the spiritual Israel are intended by 'those afar off,' and that the Jews, who are merely called 'Israel after the flesh' are 'those who are nigh.' He will modify the whole meaning of the passage, and apply it to the angels and the heavenly powers and to human souls, and as implying that Christ by his blood joined together things in earth and things in heaven which before were at variance, who brought back the sheep which had grown sickly upon the mountains to be with the rest, and put back the last piece of money among those which had before been safe."

39. You observe how much difference he makes between the souls of men and the angels. Merely the difference between the

---

1 Eph. i, 17.
2 Ps. xxii, 27.
3 There is no chapter numbered 37.
4 Comm. on Eph. i, 22.

5 1 Cor. xv, 25.
6 Job xxv, 5.
7 Eph. ii, 3.

1 Phil. iii, 21.
2 Rom. vii, 24.
3 Gen. viii, 21.
4 Workmanship Eng. Ver. Eph. ii, 10.
5 With us Ps. cxix, 73.
6 Eph. ii, 17.
7 That is, the old Latin Version, then *commonly used*, or Vulgata. It was superseded by Jerome's Version, which in its turn became the Vulgate.
8 Col. i, 20, slightly altered.

one sheep and the others, between one drachma and the rest. But he adds something more, a little way further; he says:

"As to what the Apostle says, " That he might create in himself of two one new man, so making peace," though it seems to be even more applicable than the former passage to the case of Jews and Gentiles, it may be adapted to our understanding of the passage in this way: We may suppose him to mean that man, who was made after the image and similitude of God, is after his reconciliation to receive the same form which the angels now have and he has lost: and he calls him a new man because he is renewed day by day, and is to dwell in the new world."

The souls of men then, differ, according to him, from the angels as sheep from sheep or as drachma from drachma; and men will have that form hereafter which the angels now have, but which men once had and had lost. If then there is no difference between them in nature, in shape or in form, I wonder that our learned man is not ashamed to condemn another person for saying what he himself has said, and especially when you observe that this is an exposition not of the Vulgate rendering but of the real meaning of the Apostle. But see what is added further in the same place. He presently says:

" And the creation of the new man will be fully and completely perfected when things in heaven and things in earth shall be joined in one, and we have access to the Father in one spirit, in one feeling and mind. There is something similar suggested by Paul to all thoughtful readers in another Epistle (though some do not receive it as his), in these words: [1] " All these, having had witness borne of their faith, received not the promise, God having provided some better thing for us, that apart from us they should not be made perfect." For this reason the whole creation [2] groans and travails with pain in sympathy with us who groan in this tabernacle, who have conceived in the womb by the fear of God,[3] and are in grief and wait for the revelation of the sons of God; and it waits to be delivered from the vanity of the bondage to which it is now subject; so that there may be one shepherd and one flock, and that the petition in the Lord's Prayer may be fulfilled, " Thy will be done in earth as it is in heaven." "

We are to understand then that things in heaven and those on earth, that is, Angels and men, formerly had one form and one sheepfold, and that so it will be in their future restoration, since Christ will come to make both into one flock, and men are to be what angels now are, and what they, that is their souls, previously were. I ask then,

with what face you can mock, as we lately saw you, so pleasantly, or rather not pleasantly at all but scurrilously, at those poor women who, striking their bellies and thighs, said that they should not after the resurrection have those frail bodies but would be like the angels and have a life like theirs. You reprove with bitter raillery these poor women for saying the very things which are now produced as passages from these selected Commentaries of yours. Do not you think this is somewhat as if a man were to accuse another of theft, while he had the very thing that had been stolen concealed in the bosom of his toga; and as if, after inveighing against the supposed thief in a long and magnificent peroration, after bringing forward witnesses and taking the oath in due form, he should have the stolen article extracted from his toga which he supposed himself to have convicted another of stealing.

There is another point. You find fault with others because, when questions are asked them about such matters, they do not answer at once, but hesitate and use gestures rather than words. Yet you say that the Apostle does much the same, at least, that he ' insinuates' something of this kind in his Epistle to thoughtful men. If Paul does not plainly declare these things, but ' insinuates' them, and this not to everybody but only to thoughtful people, why do you, whom we are bringing to see your errors, laugh at us poor creatures when we say about things which the Apostle has not plainly declared either that we do not know, or that we stand in doubt, and that, since we do not get a full understanding but a hint of his meaning, we do not declare but suggest an explanation. If the things which eye hath not seen nor ear heard, and which have not entered into the heart of man have been revealed to you; if you have attained to that which is perfect, and that which is in part is done away for you; shout aloud and proclaim the truth, and make quite plain the things which you say the Apostle ' insinuates,' since not only what he insinuates but what he asserts, as you tell us, now falls under your ban. All these things on which you now desire us to pronounce anathema are those which you had ascribed to the Apostle in your exposition of his words, and had taught as contained in the scope of his statements.

40. There are one or two more things on which he wishes condemnation to be passed. One is this: that these men say that the body is a prison, and like a chain round the soul; and that they assert that the soul does not depart, but returns to the place where it

---

[1] Heb. xi, 39, 40.   [2] Rom. viii, 22.
[3] *Qui a timore Dei in utero concepimus.* The expression is meant to carry out the metaphor of the word συνωδινει "travaileth together."

originally was. Let me give quotations to show his opinion on this point also. In the second book of these Commentaries, on the passage "For this cause, I, Paul, the prisoner of Jesus Christ," he says, a little way down;

"The Apostle in several passages calls the body the chain of the soul, because the soul is kept shut up as it were in a prison; and thus we may speak of Paul being kept close in the bonds of the body and does not return to be with Christ, so that his preaching to the Gentiles may be perfectly accomplished."

And again in the third book of these Commentaries, on the words, "for which I am an ambassador in chains,"[1] after some discussion of the passage, he speaks in the character of that 'other' which is himself:

"Another contends that he speaks thus because of the [2] body of our humiliation and the chain with which we are encompassed, so that we [3] know not yet as we ought to know, and see [4] by means of a mirror in a riddle: and that he will be able to disclose the mysteries of the Gospel only when he has cast off this chain and gone forth free from his prison. Yet perhaps even in chains that man may be considered as free who has his conversation in heaven, and of whom it may be said : [5] "You are not in the prison nor in the flesh, but in the spirit, if so be that the spirit of God dwelleth in you."

And in the Commentary on Paul's Epistle to Philemon, at the place where he says [6] "Epaphras my fellow-prisoner greeteth you," some way down he ·says:

"Possibly, however, as some think, a more recondite and mysterious view is set before us, namely, that the two companions had been captured and bound and brought down into this vale of tears."

41. You see how he represents these opinions as things which are held as a kind of esoteric mystery by certain persons, of whom, however, he is one, as we have shewn over and over again: only, he uses this figure of speech so that he may escape the imputations attached to this mystic gnosis. You see, he will tell us, how the matter stands. You would never think of attributing to me the opinion that all things are eventually to be restored to one condition, and to be made up again into one body. I beg you not to impute this to me. If I say that an opinion is another man's, let it be another's ; if you afterwards find any opinion written down without any 'other' person being thrown in, you will be right in ascribing it to me. What then? are we to lose the fruit of all the trouble we have taken

further back on this point? Such is the power of effrontery. However, let it be as he chooses; I put aside the truth of the matter and accept his own terms; but he will still be convicted. I will refer on the matter now in hand to the second book of these Commentaries, at the passage [1] "Giving diligence to keep the unity of the Spirit in the bond of peace. There is one body and one spirit, even as ye were called in one hope of your calling." After several remarks, he proceeds:

"The question arises how there can be one hope of our calling, when in the Father's house there are many mansions : to which we reply that the kingdom of heaven is the one hope of our calling, as being the one house of our Father's but that in one house there are many mansions or rooms. For there is one glory of the sun, another of the moon, another of the stars. But certainly it is possible that there is a deeper meaning, namely, that in the consummation of the world, all things are to be restored to their primitive condition, and that then we shall all be made one body, and formed anew into the perfect man, and that thus the Saviour's Prayer will be fulfilled in us, [2] 'Father, grant that, as thou and I are one, so they also may be one in us.'"

42. I have given you one instance in which he has expressed his own opinion without any ambiguity on the universal resurrection. I will give one more, and with this bring to an end the first book of my Apology. His statements, indeed, on this point are innumerable. The one I select is on the passage where it is written: [3] "From whom all the body, fitly framed and knit together through that which every joint supplieth according to the working in due measure of each several part, maketh the increase of the body unto the building up of itself in love." He begins thus:

"In the end of all things, when we shall have begun to know God face to face, and shall have come to the measure of the age [4] of the fulness of Christ, of whose fulness we all have received,[5] so that Christ will not be in us in part but wholly, and, leaving the rudiments of babes, we shall have grown into the perfect man, of whom the Prophet says, [6] "Behold the man whose name is the East," and whom John the Baptist announces in the words : [7] "After me cometh a man who has come to be [8] before me, for he was before me"; then by the concurrence in a common faith, and in a common recognition of the Son of God, whom now through the variety of men's minds we cannot know and recognize with one and the same faith, the whole body, which before had been disintegrated and torn into many parts, will be joined and fitted together, and brought into one; so that there will be but one administration, and

---

1 Eph. vi, 20. 3 1 Cor. viii, 2. 5 Rom. viii, 9.
2 Col. iii, 21. 4 1 Cor. xiii, 12. 6 Philem. 23.

1 Eph. iv, 3. 3 Eph. iv, 16.
2 John xvii, 21 slightly altered.
4 Eph. iv, 13. The Greek word means either age or stature.
5 John i, 16. 6 Zech. vi, 12. The Branch, Eng. Ver.
7 John i, 30. 8 Ante me factus est.

one and the same operation, and an absolute perfection of the one age,[1] whereby the whole body will grow equally, and all its members according to their measure will receive an increase of age. But this whole process of up-building, by which the body of the church is increased in all its members, will be completed by mutual love. We can understand the whole mass of rational creatures by the example of a single rational animal; and whatever we say of the single creature, we may be sure will be applicable to every creature. Let us imagine this creature, then, to have had all its limbs, veins and flesh so torn apart that neither bone should cleave to bone nor muscle be joined to muscle, that the eyes lie in one place apart, the nose in another, that the hands are placed here and the feet thrown out there, and the rest of the members are in a similar way dispersed and divided. Then let us suppose that a physician arrives on the spot, of such skill as to be able to imitate the acts of Æsculapius, as told in the stories of the heathen, and to raise up a new form, the new man Virbius.[2] It will be necessary for him to restore each member to its own place, to couple joint to joint, and to replace the various parts and glue them together, so as to make the body one again. So far this single comparison has carried us. But now let us take another typical case, so as, by a similar illustration to make clear that which we wish to have understood. A child is growing up; moment by moment, though the process is hidden from us, he is tending to perfect maturity. His hands enlarge, his feet undergo a proportional increase; the belly, though we cannot see it, is filled, the shoulders widen unmarked by the eyes, and all the members in each part grow according to their measure, but in such a way that they evidently increase not for themselves but for the body. So will it be in the time of the restitution of all things, when the true physician Jesus Christ, shall come to restore to health the whole body of the church which is now dispersed and torn. Every one, according to the measure of his faith and his recognition of the Son of God (it is called recognition because he first knew him and afterwards ceased from knowing him), will receive his proper place, and will begin to be what he once had been: not that, according to another opinion which is a heresy,[3] all will be placed in one condition,[4] that is, all restored to the condition of Angels, but that every member will be perfected according to its measure and office: for instance, that the apostate angel will begin to be that which he was originally made, and man who had been cast out of the garden of Eden will be brought back to cultivate the garden again. But all these things will be so constituted that they will be joined to one another by mutual love, each member rejoicing with its fellow and being gladdened by its advancement; and so the church of the first born, the body of Christ, will dwell in the heavenly Jerusalem which the Apostle in another place calls the mother of the Saints."

43. These things which you have said are read by all who know Latin, and you yourself request them to read them: such sayings, I mean as these: that all rational creatures, as can be imagined by taking a single rational animal as an example, are to be formed anew into one body, just as if the members of a single man after being torn apart should be formed anew by the art of Æsculapius into the same solid body as before: that there will be among them as amongst the members of the body various offices, which you specify, but that the body will be one, that is, of one nature: this one body made up of all things you call the original church, and to this you give the name of the body of Christ; and further you say that one member of this church will be the apostate angel, that is, of course, the devil, who is to be formed anew into that which he was first created: that man in the same way, who is another of the members, will be recalled to the culture of the garden of Eden as its original husbandman. All those things you say one after the other, without bringing in the person of that 'other' whom you usually introduce when you speak of such matters cautiously, and like one treading warily, so as to make men think that you had some hesitation in deciding matters so secret and abstruse. Origen indeed, the man whose disciple you do not deny that you are, and whose betrayer you confess yourself to be, always did this, as we see, in dealing with such matters. But you, as if you were the angel speaking by the mouth of Daniel or Christ by that of Paul, give a curt and distinct opinion on each point, and declare to the ears of mortals all the secrets of the ages to come. Then you speak thus to us: "O multitude of the faithful, place no faith in any of the ancients. If Origen had some thoughts about the more secret facts of the divine purposes, let none of you admit them. And similarly if one of the Clements said any such things, whether he who was a disciple of the apostle or he of the church of Alexandria who was the master of Origen himself; yes even if they were said by the great Gregory of Pontus, a man of apostolic virtues, or by the other Gregory, of Nazianzus, and Didymus the seeing[1] prophet, both of them my teachers, than whom the world has possessed none more deeply taught in the faith of Christ. All these have erred as Origen has erred; but let them be forgiven, for I too have erred at times, and I am now behaving myself as a penitent, and ought to be forgiven. But Origen, since he said the

---

[1] Or stature, see above.
[2] Formerly Hippolytus. See the story in Ovid, Met. xv, 544.
[3] Or, "according to another heresy" — *Juxta aliam hæresim*. See Jer. Apol. i, 27.
[4] Lit. age. The word may come either from taking the wrong meaning of the Greek word for Stature, or may be a synonym for the word Æon, which would here mean a range or order of being.

[1] Didymus, the blind teacher of Alexandria. Jerome who admired him, though he was a disciple of Origen, delights in calling him, in contrast to his blindness, the Seer.

same things which I have said, shall receive no forgiveness though he has done penance; nay, for saying the things which we all have said, he alone shall be condemned. He it is who has done all the mischief; he who betrayed to us the secret of all that we say or write, of all which makes us seem to speak learnedly, of all that was good in Greek but which we have made bad in Latin. Of all these let no man listen to a single one. Accept those things alone which you find in my Commentaries, and especially in those on the Epistle to the Ephesians, in which I have most painfully confuted the doctrines of Origen. My researches have reached this result, that you must believe and hold the resurrection of the flesh in this sense that men's bodies will be turned into spirits and their wives into men; and that before the foundation of the world souls existed in heaven, and thence, for reasons known to God alone, were brought down into this valley of tears, and were inserted into this body of death; that, in the end of the ages the whole of nature, being reasonable, will be fashioned again into one body as it was in the beginning, that man will be recalled into Paradise, and the apostate angel will be exalted above Peter and Paul, since they, being but men, must be placed in the lower position of paradise, while he will be restored to be that which he was originally created; and that all shall together make up the Church of the first born in heaven, and, while placed each in his separate office, shall be equally members of Christ: but all of them taken together will be the perfect body of Christ. Hold then to these things, my faithful and discreet disciples, and guard them as my unhesitating definitions of truth; but for the same doctrines pronounce your condemnation upon Origen; so you will do well. Fare ye well."

44. You do all this, you know well enough, laughing at us in your sleeve: and you profess penitence merely to deceive those to whom you write. Even if your penitence is sincere, as it should be, what is to become of all those souls who for so many years have been led astray by this poisonous doc-

trine as you call it which you then professed. Besides, who will ever mend his ways on account of your penitence, when that very document, in which you are at once the penitent, the accuser and the judge, sends your readers back to those same doctrines as those which they are to read and to hold. Lastly, even if these things were not so, yet you yourself, after your penitence, have stopped up every avenue of forgiveness. You say that Origen himself repented of these doctrines, and that he sent a document to that effect to Fabian who was at that time Bishop of the city of Rome; and yet after this repentance of his, and after he has been dead a hundred and fifty years, you drag him into court and call for his condemnation. How is it possible then that you should receive forgiveness, even though you repent, since he who before was penitent for emitting those doctrines gains no forgiveness? He wrote just as you have written: he repented as you have repented. You ought therefore either both of you to be absolved for your repentance, or, if you refuse forgiveness to a penitent (which I do not desire to see you insist upon), to be both of you equally condemned. There is a parable of the Gospel which illustrates this. A woman taken in adultery was brought before our Lord by the Jews, so that they might see what judgment he would pronounce according to the law. He, the merciful and pitying Lord, said: "He that is without sin among you let him first cast a stone at her." And then, it is said, they all departed. The Jews, impious and unbelieving though they were, yet blushed through their own consciousness of guilt;[1] since they were sinners, they would not appear publicly as executing vengeance on sinners. And the robber upon the cross, said to the other robber who was hanging like him on a cross, and was blaspheming, "Dost not thou fear God, seeing we are in the same condemnation?" But we condemn in others the things of which we ourselves are conscious; yet we neither blush like the Jews nor are softened like the robber.

---

[1] John viii, 9.

RUFINUS' APOLOGY.

BOOK II.

In the first book of my Apology I have dealt with the accusations of dogmatic error which he endeavours unjustly to fix upon others, and have, by producing his own testimony, turned them back against him. In the second book, I shall be able, now that I have settled and put aside the matters which have to do with controversies of faith, more confidently to reply to him on the other heads of his accusation. For there is another and a very grave accusation, which has, like the former, to be cut down by the scythe of truth. It is this. He says[1] that certain persons have joined themselves to Origen in a secret society of perjury, and that the forms of initiation are to be found in the Sixth book of his Miscellanies:[2] and that

---

[1] Letter lxxxiv. 3 (end).
[2] Stromateis, meaning collections of short essays on important subjects, disconnected, and thrown out like things scattered or strewn on the ground.

this mystery has been detected by no one but himself through all this space of time. I should only excite his ridicule were I to declare, even with an oath, that I was an entire stranger to such a secret society of perjury. The road by which I propose to reach the declaration of the truth is more direct: it is by proving, which I can do quite easily, that I have never possessed those books nor borrowed them from others to read. Not only cannot I defend myself from an accusation the meaning of which I do not know, but I do not see how a matter can be made the subject of a charge against me as to which I do not even know what it is, or whether it exists at all. I only know that my accuser declares that either Origen wrote or his disciples hold, that, when the Scripture says "He that speaketh truth with his neighbour" the words apply to a neighbour only in the sense of one of the initiated, a member of this secret society: and again that the Apostle's words "We speak wisdom among them that are perfect" and the words of Christ "Give not that which is holy unto dogs, neither cast ye your pearls before swine," imply that truth is not to be communicated to all.

2. Let us see what my adversary himself says on this point in those Commentaries which he has selected. In the second book, in commenting on the words [1]"Wherefore, putting away lying, speak every man truth to his neighbour, for we are members one of another" (after a short introduction) he speaks as follows:

" Hence Paul himself, who was one of the perfect, says in another Epistle " We speak wisdom among them that are perfect." [2] This then is what is commanded, that those mystic and secret things, which are full of divine truth, should be spoken by each man to his neighbour, so that day unto day may utter speech and night to night shew knowledge,[3] that is, that a man should show all those clear and lucid truths which he knows to those to whom the words can be worthily addressed: "Ye are the light of the world." [4] On the other hand, he should exhibit everything involved in darkness and wrapped up in the mist of symbols to others who are themselves nothing but mist and darkness, those of whom it is said "And there was darkness under his feet," [5] that is, of course, under the feet of God. For on Mount Sinai Moses enters into the whirlwind and the mist where God was; and it is written of God, " He has made darkness his secret place." [6] Let each man then thus speak truth in a mystery to his neighbour, and not give that which is holy to dogs nor cast his pearls before swine; [7] but those who are anointed with the oil of truth, them let him lead into the bridechamber of the spouse, into the inner sanctuary of the King."

Observe, I beg you, look carefully and see whether in all this passage there is any one else but himself on whom the condemnation can fall. If his adversaries were looking for an opportunity of convicting and destroying him on the ground of what he has written, what other course could they take, and what other testimonies could they wish to produce against him than these which he produces against himself as if he were pleading against another? If it were sought to pronounce a condemnation against him, his own letter would suffice. You have only to change the name; the test of the accusation suits no one but himself alone. What he calls on us on the one hand to condemn, he exhorts us on the other hand to follow: what he asserts, that he reproves: what he hates, that he does. How happy must be his disciples who obey and imitate him!

3. He has endeavoured, indeed, to brand us with the stain of this false teaching by speaking to some of our brethren, and he repeats this by various letters, according to his recognized plan of action. It is nothing to me what he may write or assert, but, since he raises this question about a doctrine of perjury, I will state my opinion upon it, and then leave him to pass judgment upon himself. It is this. Since our Lord and Saviour says in the Gospels " It was said to them of old time, Thou shalt not forswear thyself, but shalt pay to the Lord thy vows, but I say unto you, Swear not at all; " [1] I say that every one who teaches that for any cause whatever we may swear falsely, is alien from the faith of Christ and from the unity of the catholic church.

4. But I should like, now that I have satisfied you on my own account, and supported my opinion by an anathema, to make this plain to you further, that he himself declares that in certain orgies and mystical societies to which he belongs perjury is practised by the votaries and associates. That is a certain and most true saying of our God, " By their fruits ye shall know them," [2] and this also "A tree is known by its fruits." [3] Well: he says that I have accepted this doctrine of perjury. If then I have been trained to this practice, and this evil tree has indeed its roots within me, it is impossible but that corresponding fruits should have grown upon me, and also that I should have gathered some society of mystic associates around me. As regards myself whom alone he seeks to injure by all

1 Eph. iv, 25.   4 Matt. v, 14.   6 Ps. xviii, 11.
2 1 Cor. ii, 6.   5 Ps. xviii, 9.   7 Matt. vii, 6.
3 Ps. xix, 2.

1 Matt. v, 33, 34.   2 Matt. vii, 16-20.   3 Luke vi, 44.

that he writes, I will not bear witness to myself, nor will I say that there are cases of necessity in which it is right to swear: for I wish to avoid reproach through timidity if not through prudence; and, at all events, if I fail in obedience to the command, I will acknowledge my error. I will therefore make no boast of this. But, whether I have erred or acted prudently, he at all events can lay his finger on no act of mine by which he can convict me. But I can shew from his writings, that he not only holds this doctrine of perjury, but practises this foul vice as a sacred duty. I will bring nothing against him which has been trumped up by ill will, as he does against me; but I will produce him and his writings as witnesses against himself, so that it may be made clear that it is not his enemies who accuse but he who convicts himself.

5. When he was living at Rome he wrote[1] a treatise on the preservation of virginity, which all the pagans and enemies of God, all apostates and persecutors, and whoever else hate the Christian name, vied with one another in copying out, because of the infamous charges and foul reproaches which it contained against all orders and degrees among us, against all who profess and call themselves Christians, in a word, against the universal church; and also because this man declared that the crimes imputed to us by the Gentiles, which were before supposed to be false were really true, and indeed that much worse things were done by our people than those laid to their charge. First, he defames the virgins themselves of whose virtue he professed to be writing, speaking of them in these words:[2]

"Some of them change their dress and wear the costume of men, and are ashamed of the sex in which they were born; they cut their hair short, and raise their heads with the shameless stare of eunuchs. There are some who put on Cilician jackets,[3] and with hoods made up into shape, make themselves like horned owls and night birds, as if they were becoming babies again."

There are a thousand such calumnies, and worse than these, in the book. He does not even spare widows, for he says of them,[4] "They care for nothing but the belly and what is next it;" and he adds many other obscene remarks of this kind. As to the whole race of Solitaries, it would take too long to give the passages written by him in which he attacks them with the foulest abuse.

It would be a shame even to recount the indecent attacks which he makes upon the Presbyters and the deacons. I will, however, give the beginning of this violent invective, by which you may easily imagine what a point he reaches in its later stages.[1]

"There are some," he says, "of my own order, who only seek the office of Presbyter or deacon so that they may have more license to visit women. They care for nothing but to be well dressed, to be well scented, to prevent their feet from being loose and bulging. Their curly hair bears the mark of the crisping iron; their fingers sparkle with rings; and they walk on tiptoe, for fear a fleck of mud from the road should touch their feet. When you see them, you would take them for bridegrooms rather than clerics."

He then goes on to hurl his reproaches against our priests and ministers, specifying their faults, or rather their crimes; and to represent the access allowed them to married ladies not only in a disgraceful light, but so as to seem positively execrable: and after having cut to pieces with his satirical defamation the whole race of Christians, he does not even spare himself, as you shall presently hear.

6. For I will now return, after a sort of digression, to the point I had proposed, and for the sake of which it was necessary to mention this treatise. I will shew that perjury is looked upon by him as lawful, to such a point that he does not care for its being detected in his writings. In this same treatise he admonishes the reader that it is wrong to study secular literature, and says,[2] "What has Horace to do with the Psaltery, or Virgil with the Gospels, or Cicero with St. Paul? Will not your brother be offended if he sees you sitting at meat in that idol's temple?" And then, after more of the same kind, in which he declares that a Christian must have nothing to do with the study of secular literature, he gives an account of a revelation divinely made to him and filled with fearful threatenings upon the subject. He reports that, after he had renounced the world, and had turned to God, he nevertheless was held in a tight grip by his love of secular books, and found it hard to put away his longing for them.[3]

Suddenly I was caught up in the spirit and dragged before the judgment seat of the Judge; and here the light was so bright, and those who stood around were so radiant, that I cast myself upon the ground and did not dare to look up. Asked who and what I was I replied 'I am a Christian.' But He who presided said: 'Thou liest; thou art a follower of Cicero and not of Christ. For where thy treasure is there will thy heart be

---

[1] See letter xxii. to Eustochium. In it Jerome pointed out the worldliness of professing Christians, and the inconsistencies and hypocrisies of many of the clergy and monks.
[2] Letter xxii. c. 27 (end).
[3] Of goats' hair, used by soldiers and sailors.
[4] Letter xxii. c. 29 (middle).

[1] Id. c. 28.   [2] Id. 29 (end).   [3] Id. 30.

also.' Instantly I became dumb, and amid the strokes of the lash — for He had ordered me to be scourged — I was tortured more severely still by the fire of conscience, considering with myself that verse 'In the grave, who shall give thee thanks?' Yet for all that I began to cry and to bewail myself saying: 'Have mercy upon me, O Lord; have mercy upon me.' Amid the sound of the scourges this cry still made itself heard. At last the bystanders, falling down before the knees of Him who presided, prayed that He would have pity on my youth, and that He would give me space to repent of my error. He might still, they urged, inflict torture upon me, should I ever again read the works of the Gentiles. Under the stress of that awful moment I should have been ready to make even still larger promises than these. Accordingly I made oath and called upon His name, saying 'Lord, if ever again I possess worldly books, or if ever again I read such, I have denied thee.' On taking this oath, I was dismissed, and returned to the upper world.

7. You observe how new and terrible a form of oath this is which he describes. The Lord Jesus Christ sits on the tribunal as judge, the angels are assessors, and plead for him; and there, in the intervals of scourgings and tortures, he swears that he will never again have by him the works of heathen authors nor read them. Now look back over the work we are dealing with, and tell me whether there is a single page of it in which he does not again declare himself a Ciceronian, or in which he does not speak of ' our Tully,' ' our Flaccus,' ' our Maro.'[1] As to Chrysippus and Aristides, Empedocles and all the rest of the Greek writers, he scatters their names around him like a vapour or halo, so as to impress his readers with a sense of his learning and literary attainments. Amongst the rest, he boasts of having read the books of Pythagoras. Many learned men, indeed, declare these books to be non-extant: but he, in order that he may illustrate every part of his vow about heathen authors, declares that he has read even those which do not exist in writing. In almost all his works he sets out many more and longer quotations from these whom he calls ' his own' than from the Prophets and Apostles who are ours. Even in the works which he addresses to girls and weak women, who desire, as is right, only to be edified by teaching out of our Scriptures, he weaves in illustrations from ' his own' Flaccus and Tullius and Maro.

8. Take the treatise which[2] he entitles " On the best mode of translating," though there is nothing in it except the addition of the title which is of the best, for all is of the worst; and in which he proves those to be heretics with whom he is now in commun-

ion, thus incurring the condemnation of our Apostle (not his, for those whom he calls ' his ' are Flaccus and Tully) who says. " He who judges[1] is condemned if he eat." In that treatise, which tells us that no works of any kind reasonably admit of a rendering word for word (though he has come round now to think such rendering reasonable)[2] he inserts whole passages from a work of Cicero.[3] But had he not said, " What has Horace to do with the Psalter, or Maro with the Gospels, or Cicero with the Apostle? Will not your brother be offended if he sees you sitting in that idol temple?" Here of course he brings himself in guilty of idolatry; for if reading causes offence, much more does writing. But, since one who turns to idolatry does not thereby become wholly and completely a heathen unless he first denies Christ, he tells us that he said to Christ, as he sat on the judgment seat with his most exalted angel ministers around him, " If I ever hereafter read or possess any heathen books, I have denied thee," and now he not only reads them and possesses them, not only copies them and collates them, but inserts them among the words of Scripture itself, and in discourses intended for the edification of the Church. What I say is well enough known to all who read his treatises, and requires no proof. But it is just like a man who is trying to save himself from such a gulf of sacrilege and perjury, to make up some excuse for himself, and to say, as he does: " I do not now read them, I have a tenacious memory, so that I can quote various passages from different writers without a break, and I now merely quote what I learned in my youth." Well: if some one were to ask me to prove that before the sun rose this morning there was night over the earth, or that at sunset the sun had been shining all day, I should answer that, if a man doubted about what all men knew, it was his business to shew cause for his doubts, not for me to shew cause for my certainty. Still in this instance, where a man's soul is at stake, and the crime of perjury and of impious denial of Christ is alleged, a condemnation must not be thought to be a thing of course, even though the facts are known and understood by all men. We are not to imitate him who condemns the accused before they have undergone any examination; and not only without a hearing, but without summoning them to appear; and not only unsummoned, but when they are already

---

[1] Cicero, Horace and Virgil.   [2] Letter lvii.

[1] Discerns it. Vulg. Rom. xiv, 23. He that doubteth A.V.
[2] In the translation of the Περὶ Ἀρχῶν made by Jerome for Pammachius and Oceanus, he rendered word for word.
[3] Letter lvii. 5.

dead; and not only the dead, but those whom he had always praised, till then; and not only those whom he had praised, but whom he had followed and had taken as his masters. We must fear the judgment of the Lord, who says [1] "Judge not and ye shall not be judged," and again, "With what measure ye mete it shall be measured to you again." Therefore, though it is really superfluous, I will bring against him a single witness, but one who must prevail, and whom he cannot challenge, that is, once more, himself and his own writings. All can attest what I say in reference to this treatise of his; and my assertion about it seems to be superfluous; but I must make use of some special testimony, lest what I say should seem unsatisfactory to those who have not read his works.

9. When he wrote his treatises against Jovinian, and some one had raised objections to them, he was informed of these objections by Domnio, that old man whose memory we all revere; and in his answer to him [2] he said that it was impossible that a man like him should be in the wrong, since his knowledge extended to everything that could be known: and he proceeded to enumerate the various kinds of syllogisms, and the whole art of learning and of writing (of course supposing that the man who found fault with him knew nothing about such things). He then goes on thus: [3]

"It was foolish, it appears, in me to think that I could not know all these things without the philosophers, and to look upon the end of the stylus which strikes out and corrects as better than the end with which we write. It was useless for me, it seems, to have translated [4] the Commentaries of Alexander, and for my learned master to have brought me into the knowledge of Logic through the 'Introduction' of Porphyry; and, putting aside humanistic teachers, there was no reason why I should have had Gregory Nazianzen and Didymus as my teachers in the Scriptures."

This, you observe, is the man who said to Christ, I have denied thee if ever I am found to possess or to read the works of the heathen. He might, one would think, at all events have left out Porphyry, who was Christ's special enemy, who endeavoured as far as in him lay to completely subvert the Christian religion, but whom he now glories in having had as his instructor in his Introduction to Logic. He cannot put in the plea that he had learned these things at a former time: for, before his conversion, he and I equally were wholly ignorant of the

Greek language and literature. All these things came after his oath, after that solemn engagement had been made. It is of no use for us to argue in such a case. It will at once be said to us: Man, you are wrong, God is not mocked, and no syllogisms spun out of the books of Alexander will avail with him. I think, my brother, it was an ill-omened event that you submitted to the Introduction of Porphyry. Into what has that faithless man introduced you? If it is into the place where he is now, that is the place where there is weeping and gnashing of teeth; for there dwell the apostate and the enemies of God; and perhaps the perjurers will go there too.

10. You chose a bad introducer. If you will take my counsel, both you and I will by preference turn to him who introduces us to the Father and who said [1] 'No man cometh unto the Father but by me.' I lament for you, my brother, if you believe this; and if you believe it not, I still lament that you hunt through all sorts of ancient and antiquated documents for grounds for suspecting other men of perjury, while perjury, lasting and endless with all its inexplicable impiety, remains upon your own lips. Might not these words of the Apostle be rightly applied to you: [2] "Thou that art called a Jew and restest in the law, and makest thy boast in God, being instructed out of the law, and trustest that thou thyself art a leader of the blind, a light of them that sit in darkness, an instructor of the foolish, a teacher of babes, who hast a form of knowledge and of the truth in the law: Thou therefore, that teachest others, teachest thou not thyself? Thou that sayest a man should not commit adultery, dost thou commit adultery? Thou that preachest that a man should not steal, dost thou steal? Thou that abhorrest idols, dost thou commit sacrilege" — that is perjury? And, what comes last and most important, "The name of God is blasphemed among the Gentiles through you," and your love of strife.

8 (2). We will pass on to clear up another of the charges, if only he will confess under the stress of his own consciousness of wrong that he has been convicted both of perjury and of making a false defence. Otherwise, if he attempts to deny what I say, I can produce as witnesses any number of my brethren, who, while living in the cells built by me on the Mount of Olives, copied out for him most of the Dialogues of Cicero. I often, as they wrote them out,

---

[1] Matt. vii, 1, 2. [2] Ep. l. [3] Ep. l. 1.
[4] Verti. Possibly used like Versare for 'turning over the leaves,' 'making constant use of.'

[1] John xiv, 6. [2] Rom. ii, 17-24.

had in my hands quaternions[1] of these Dialogues; and I looked them over myself, in recognition of the fact that he gave them much larger pay than is usually given for writings of other sorts. He himself also came to see me at Jerusalem from Bethlehem, bringing with him a book which contained a single Dialogue of Cicero, and also one of Plato's in Greek; he will not pretend to deny having given me that book, and having stayed some time with me. But what is the use of delaying so long over a matter which is clearer than the light? To all that I have said this addition is to be made, after which all further comment is superfluous; that after he had settled in the monastery at Bethlehem, and indeed not so long ago, he took the office of a teacher in grammar, and explained 'his own' Maro and the comedians and lyrical and historical writers to young boys who had been entrusted to him that he might teach them the fear of the Lord: so that he actually became a teacher and professor in the knowledge of those heathen authors, as to whom he had sworn that if he even read them he would have denied Christ.

9 (2). But now let us look at the other points which he blames. He says that the doctrines in question are of heathen origin, but in this judgment he condemns himself. He calls these doctrines heathenish; yet he himself incorporates them into his works. He here makes a mistake. Still, we ought to stretch out the hand to him, and not to press him too far: for it is only because he soars so completely above the world on the wings of his eloquence, and is borne along by the full tide of invective and vituperation that he forgets himself and his reason loses its place. Do not be so rash, my brother, as to condemn yourself unnecessarily. Neither you nor Origen are at once to be set down among the heathen if, as you have yourself said, you have written these things to vindicate the justice of God, and to make answer to those who say that everything is moved by chance or by fate: if, I say, it is from your wish to show that God's providence which governs all things is just that you have said the, causes of inequality have been acquired by each soul through the passions and feelings of the former life which it had in heaven; or even if you said that it is in accordance with the character of the Trinity, which is good and simple and unchangeable that every creature should in the end of all things be restored to the state in which it was first

created; and that this must be after long punishment equal to the length of all the ages, which God inflicts on each creature in the spirit not of one who is angry but of one who corrects, since he is not one who is extreme to mark iniquity; and that, his design like a physician being to heal men, he will place a term upon their punishment. Whether in this you spoke truly, let God judge; anyhow such views seem to me to contain little of impiety against God, and nothing at all of heathenism, especially if they were put forward with the desire and intention of finding some means by which the justice of God might be vindicated.

10 (2). I would not, therefore, have you distress yourself overmuch about these points, nor expose yourself needlessly either to penance or to condemnation. But there is a matter of real importance, as to which I can neither excuse nor defend you; namely, a statement openly made by you which is not only heathenish but beyond all heathenism and impiety — the statement in the treatise which I have mentioned above,[1] that God has a mother-in-law. Has anything so profane as this or so impious been said even by any of the heathen poets? It would be a foolish question to ask whether you find anything of the kind in the holy Scriptures. I only ask whether 'your' Flaccus or Maro, whether Plautus or Terence, or even whether any writer of Satires among all their unclean and immodest sayings has ever uttered such an outrage against God. No doubt you were led astray by the fact that the girl to whom you addressed the treatise[2] was called the bride of Christ: and hence you thought that her mother according to the flesh might be called the mother-in-law of God. You did not recollect that such things are said not according to the order of the flesh, but according to the grace of the spirit. For a woman is called the bride of Christ because the word of God is united in a kind of mystic wedlock with the human soul. But if the mother of the girl in question is related to Christ by this spiritual connexion, she herself should be called the bride of Christ, not the mother-in-law of God. As it is, you might as well go on to call the father of the girl God's father-in-law, and her sister his sister-in-law, or to call the girl herself God's daughter-in-law. The fact is, you were so anxious to appear completely possessed of

---

[1] *Quaterniones* may mean 'sets of four.' It seems more likely to be used for a '*cahier*' of four sheets.

[1] Ep. xxii. c. 20.
[2] The word "*Dei*" has crept in, apparently, wrongly. If it stands the meaning would be, 'To whom you were teaching the word of God,' or the allusion may be to Ps. xlv, 10, with which the Letter to Eustochium begins, 'Hearken O daughter so shall the King desire thy beauty.'

the eloquence of Plautus or of Cicero, that you forgot that the Apostle speaks of the whole church, parents and children, mothers and daughters, brothers and sisters, all together, as one virgin or bride, when he says, [1] " I determined this very thing, to present you as a chaste virgin to one man, which is Christ." But you boast that you follow not Paul's but Porphyry's Introduction, and, since he wrote his impious and sacrilegious books against Christ and against God, you have fallen, through his introduction, into this abyss of blasphemy.

11. If, then, you really intend to do an act of repentance for those evil speeches of yours, if you are not merely mocking us by saying this, and if you are not in your heart such a lover of strife and contention that you are willing even to defame yourself on this sole condition that you may be able thereby to besmirch another; if it is not in pretence but in good faith that you repent of what you have said amiss, come and do penance for this great and foul blasphemy; for it is indeed blasphemy against God. For if a man oversteps the mark by speaking erroneously of mere creatures, this is not such a very execrable crime, especially if he does it, as you say, not with a set purpose of blasphemy, but in seeking to vindicate the justice of God. But to lift up your mouth against the heaven is a grave offence; to speak violence and blasphemy against the Most High is worthy of death. Let us bestow our lamentations upon that which is hard to cure; for what man is there who has the jaundice,[2] and is in danger both of looks and life, who will complain loudly because of a little hangnail on his foot or because a scratch made with his own finger which easily yields to remedies, is not yet cured?

12. I think very little, indeed, of one reproach which he levels against me, and think it hardly worthy of a reply; that, namely, in which, in recounting the various teachers whom he hired, as he says, from the Jewish synagogue, he says, in order to give me a sharp prick, " I have not been my own teacher, like some people," meaning me of course, for he brings the whole weight of his invective to bear against me from beginning to end. Indeed, I wonder that he should have chosen to make a point of this, when he had a greater and easier matter at hand by which to disparage me, namely this, that, though I stayed long among many eminent teachers, yet I have nothing to show which is worthy of their teaching or their training. He indeed, has not in his whole life stayed more than thirty days at Alexandria where Didymus lived; yet almost all through his books he boasts, at length and at large, that he was the pupil of Didymus the seer, that he had Didymus as his initiator,[1] that is, his preceptor in the holy Scriptures; and the material for all this boasting was acquired in a single month. But I, for the sake of God's work, stayed six years, and again after an interval for two more, where Didymus lived, of whom alone you boast, and where others lived who were in no way inferior to him, but whom you did not know even by sight, Serapion and Menites, men who are like brothers in life and character and learning; and Paul the old man, who had been the pupil of Peter the Martyr; and, to come to the teachers of the desert, on whom I attended frequently and earnestly, Macarius the disciple of Anthony, and the other Macarius, and Isidore and Pambas, all of them friends of God, who taught me those things which they themselves were learning from God. What material for boasting should I have from all these men, if boasting were seemly or expedient! But the truth is, I blush even while I weave together these past experiences, which I do with the intention, not of showing you, as you put it, that my masters did not do justice to my talents, but, what I grieve over far more, that my talents have not done justice to my masters.

But it is foolish in me to enumerate these holy Christian men. It is not of them that he is thinking when he says that he has not like me been his own teacher. It is of Barabbas [2] whom, unlike me, he took as his teacher from the Synagogue, and of Porphyry by whose introduction he and not I had his introduction into Logic. Pardon me for this that I have preferred to be thought of as an unskilled and unlearned man rather than to be called the disciple of Barabbas. For, when Christ and Barabbas were offered for our choice, I in my simplicity made choice of Christ. You, it appears, are willing to join your shouts with those who say, [3] " Not this man but Barabbas." And I should like to know what Porphyry, that friend of yours who wrote his blasphemous books against our religion, taught you? What good did you get from either of those masters of whom you boast so much, the one drawing his inspiration from

---

[1] 2 Cor. xi, 2.
[2] *Morbus regius ;* used variously for jaundice and leprosy. See Jer. Life of Hilarion, c. 34.

[1] The word is given in Greek, καθηγητής.
[2] The name of Jerome's Jewish teacher of Hebrew, which Rufinus here perverts, was Baranina. Letter lxxxiv. c. 3.
[3] John xviii, 40.

the idols which represent demons, the other, as you tell us, from the Synagogue of Satan. Nothing, as far as I see, but what they knew themselves. From Porphyry you gained the art of speaking evil of Christians, to strike at those who live in virginity and continence, at our deacons and presbyters, and to defame in your published writings, every order and degree of Christians. From that other friend of yours, Barabbas, whom you chose out of the synagogue rather than Christ, you learned to hope for a resurrection not in power but in frailty, to love the letter which kills and hate the spirit which gives life, and other more secret things, which, if occasion so require, shall afterwards in due time be brought to light.

13. But why should I prolong this discussion? I shall take no notice of his reproaches and railings; I shall make no answer to his violent attacks, that daily task of his, for which Porphyry sharpened his pen. For I have chosen Jesus, not Barabbas, for my master, and he has taught me to be silent when reviled. I will come to the point where I will shew how much truth there is in the excuses for himself and the accusations against me which he has heaped together. He says[1] that it is only in two short Prefaces that he ever was known to have praised Origen; and that his praise extended only to his work as an interpreter of Scripture, in which nothing is said of doctrine or of the faith, and that in those parts of his works which he has himself translated there is absolutely nothing advanced of the kind which he now reproves in the interest of the Synagogue rather than that of the edification of Christians. It ought, one would think, be enough to put him to silence, that those very things which he set forth in his own books he blames in those of others; nevertheless, let us see how far these other assertions of his are true. In the Preface[2] to the commentaries of Origen on Ezekiel, contained in fourteen homilies or short orations, he writes thus to one Vincentius:

"It is a great thing which you ask of me, my friend, that I should translate Origen into Latin, and present to the ears of Romans a man of whom we may say in the words of Didymus the seer, that he was a teacher of the churches second only to the Apostles."

And a little way on he adds:

"I will briefly state for your information that Origen's works on the whole of Scripture are of three

kinds. First come the Extracts or Notes, called in Greek *Scholia*, in which he shortly and summarily touches upon the things which seemed to him obscure or to present some difficulty. The second kind is the *Homiletics*, of which the present commentary is a specimen. The third kind is what he called Tomes, or as we say Volumes. In this part of his work he gives all the sails of his genius to the breathing winds; and, drawing off from the land, he sails away into mid ocean. I know that you wish that I should translate his writings of all kinds. I have before mentioned the reason why this is impossible; but I promise you this, that if, through your prayers, Jesus gives me back my health, I intend to translate, I will not say all, for that would be rash, but very many of them; on this condition, however, which I have often set you, that I should provide the words and you the secretary."

14. Take, again, the Preface to the Song of Songs:

"To the most holy Pope Damasus. Origen in his other books has surpassed all other men: in the Song of Songs he has surpassed himself. The work consists of eleven complete volumes, and reaches a length of nearly twenty thousand lines. In these he discusses first the version of the Septuagint; then those of Aquila, Symmachus, and Theodotion, and last of all a Fifth Version which he states that he discovered on the coast of Actium, and this he does so grandly and so freely that it seems to me as if the words were fulfilled in him which say, [1]"The king has brought me into his bedchamber." It would require a vast amount of time, of labour, and of money to translate a work so great and of so much merit into the Latin language. I therefore leave it unattempted; and have merely translated, and that without elegance, but correctly, these two Tracts which he composed in ordinary language for babes and sucklings. I give you a mere taste of his opinions, not a full meal; but enough to make you realize what is the worth of his greater works, when the smaller give you so much pleasure."

15. Also in the Preface of his Commentary on Micah, which was written to Paula and Eustochium, he says, after some few remarks:

"As to what they say, that it is not right for me to rifle the works of Origen, and thereby to defile the writings of the ancients, they think this a telling piece of abuse; but it is, in my opinion, the highest praise, since I am seeking to imitate those who are approved not only by us, but by all thoughtful men."

16. Again, in the Preface to his book on the meaning of Hebrew names, he says, some way down:

"For fear that, when the edifice has been completed, the last touch, so to speak, should be wanting, I have explained the words and names of the New Testament, partly through a wish to follow the steps of Origen, whom all but the ignorant

---

[1] Letter lxxxiv, 2.
[2] See this Preface translated among Jerome's works in this Series.

[1] Cant. i, 4.

acknowledge to have been the greatest teacher of the churches next to the Apostles. Among the rest of the illustrious monuments of his genius is the labour which he has bestowed upon this, desiring to complete as a Christian what Philo as a Jew had left undone."

17. Once more, in his letter to Marcella he says : [1]

"Ambrose, who supplied the paper, the money and the secretaries by the aid of which our Adamantius [2] and Chalcenterus [3] completed his innumerable books, in a certain letter written to the same person from Athens, declares that he never had a meal, when Origen was present, without something being read, and that he never went to bed without having some brother read aloud from the holy Scriptures. This he said he continued day and night, so that prayer waited upon reading and reading upon prayer."

18. Lastly, take the following from another letter to Marcella :

"The blessed Martyr Pamphilus, whose life Eusebius the Bishop of Cæsarea set forth in some three volumes, wished to rival Demetrius Phalereus and Pisistratus, in his zeal to establish a library of sacred books : he sought out all through the world representative works of great minds, which are their true and everlasting monuments; but most of all he acquired at great expense all the books written by Origen, and gave them to the church at Cæsarea. This library was afterwards partly destroyed; but Acatius and later on Euzoius, Bishops of that church, endeavoured to reëstablish it in parchment volumes. The last of these recovered a great many works, and left us an inventory of them, but he shews that he could not find the Commentary on the hundred and twenty-sixth Psalm and the Tract on the Hebrew letter Pe, by the fact that he does not mention it. Not that so great a man as Adamantius passed over anything, but that, through the negligence of his successors it did not remain to times within our memory."

19. But perhaps you will say to me : "Why do you fill your paper with this superfluous matter? Does even my friend say that it is a crime to name Origen, or to give him praise for his talents? If Origen is proclaimed as 'such and so great a man,' this makes us the more anxious to be told whether he is in other passages spoken of as 'an apostolic man,' or 'a teacher of the churches,' or by any similar expressions which appear to commend not only his talents but his faith." This then shall be done. It was indeed for this purpose that I produced the passage where he speaks of him as 'such and so great a man,' because it was, if I am not mistaken, in the Preface this laudatory expression is used about him that he also claims the right of Origen to be

called an Apostle or a Prophet, and to be praised even to the heavens. And in the same way, if there are passages in which I happen to have praised Origen's learning, all my praise is just of this kind. This man rouses all this alarm in you because of such expressions of mine ; but he maintains that it is unjust to bring up similar expressions against him when they occur in his own writings. But, since he does not choose to stand on equal terms with us before the tribunal of opinion, but condemns us on mere suspicion, while he himself does not hold himself bound even by his own handwriting ; since he, I say, does not think it necessary in such a matter to observe the rule of holy Scripture which demands that each man should be judged without respect of persons ; I will make answer for myself, not according to the demands of justice, but according to his wishes. He says to me : "If you have translated Origen, you are to be blamed ; but I, even if I have said the very things for which I blame him, have done well, and these ought to be read and held as true. If you have praised his talents or his knowledge, you have committed a crime; if I have praised his talents, it goes for nothing."

20. Well then ; he says, "Give me an instance in which I have so praised him as to defend his system of belief." You have no right to ask this, I reply ; yet I will follow where you lead. There is a certain writing of his [1] in which he gives a short catalogue of the works which Varro wrote for the Latins, and of those which Origen wrote in Greek for the Christians. In this he says :

Antiquity marvels at Marcus Terentius Varro because of the countless books which he wrote for Latin readers; and Greek writers are extravagant in their praise of their man of brass, because he has written more works than one of us could so much as copy. But since Latin ears would find a list of Greek writers tiresome, I shall confine myself to the Latin Varro. I shall try to shew that we of to-day are sleeping the sleep of Epimenides and devoting to the amassing of riches the energy which our predecessors gave to sound if secular learning.

Varro's writings include forty-five books of antiquities, four concerning the life of the Roman people.

But why, you ask me, have I thus mentioned Varro and the man of brass? Simply to bring to your notice our Christian man of brass, or, rather, man of adamant — Origen, I mean — whose zeal for the study of Scripture has fairly earned for him this latter name. Would you learn what monuments of his genius he has left us? The following list exhibits them. His writings comprise thirteen books on Genesis, two books of Mystical Homilies, notes on Exodus, notes on Leviticus . . . also

---

[1] Letter xliii, 1.   [2] Indomitable or made of adamant.
[3] Indefatigable; lit. Brazen-bowelled.

[1] Letter xxxiii.

single books, four books on First Principles, two books on the Resurrection, two dialogues on the same subject.

And, after enumerating all his works as if making an exact index, he added what follows:

So you see the labours of this one man have surpassed those of all previous writers both Greek and Latin. Who has ever managed to read all that he has written? Yet what reward have his exertions brought him? He stands condemned by his bishop, Demetrius, only the bishops of Palestine, Arabia, Phœnicia, and Achaia dissenting. Imperial Rome consents to his condemnation, and even convenes a senate to censure him, not — as the rabid hounds who now pursue him cry — because of the novelty or heterodoxy of his doctrines, but because men could not tolerate the incomparable eloquence and knowledge, which, when once he opened his lips, made others seem dumb.

I have written the above quickly and incautiously, by the light of a poor lantern. You will see why, if you think of those who to-day represent Epicurus and Aristippus.

21. Now suppose that while you were writing this, as you tell us you did, quickly not cautiously, by the poor glimmering light of a lantern, some Prophet had stood by you and had cried out: " O writer, suppress those words, restrain your pen; for the time is coming and is not far off when you will make a schism and separate yourself from the church; and, in order that you may find a colorable excuse for this schism, you will begin to defame these very books which you now make out to be so admirable. You will then say that the man whom you call your own Brazen-heart,[1] and whose name you are just about to write down as Adamantine because of the merit of his praise-worthy labours, did not write books for the edification of the soul but venomous heresies. This man, further, whom you rightly describe as not having been condemned by Demetrius on the ground of his belief, who you say was not accused of bringing in strange doctrines, you will then pronounce worthy of execration because of his strange doctrines; as to what you are writing about mad dogs bringing feigned charges against him, you will yourself feign the same: and the Senate of Rome as you call it, you will then stir up against him as you complain that they now do by your letters of admonition, your vehement attestations, and satellites flying in all directions. This is the return that you will make to your admirable Brazen-heart for all his labours. Therefore beware how you write now, for, if you write as you are doing and afterwards act as I have said, you will

---

with more justice be condemned by your own judgment than he by that of others." Would you, do you think, have given credit to that prophet? Would you not have thought it more likely that he was mad than that you would ever come to such a pass? The fact is that in controversies of this kind there is no thought of sparing a friend if only an enemy can be injured. But you go beyond even this point: you do not spare yourself in your attempt to ruin not your enemies but your friends.

22. In the Preface to his book on Hebrew Questions, after many other remarks, he says:

" I say nothing of Origen. His name (if I may compare small things to great) is even more than my own the object of ill will, because though following the common version in his Homilies which were spoken to common people, yet in his Tomes, that is, in his fuller discussion of Scripture, he yields to the Hebrew as the truth, and though surrounded by his own forces occasionally seeks the foreign tongue as his ally. I will only say this about him, that I should gladly have his knowledge of the Scriptures even if accompanied with all the ill-will which clings to his name, and that I do not care a straw for these shades and spectral ghosts whose nature is said to be to chatter in dark corners and be a terror to babies."

I really can no longer wonder or complain of his unfriendly dealings with me since he has not spared ' such men, such great men.' For another man whom he tears to pieces is Ambrose that Bishop of sacred memory. In what manner, and with what disparagement he attacks him, I will show in a similar way from one of his Prefaces, in which, nevertheless, he praises Origen. It is the Preface to Origen's homilies on Luke addressed to Paula and Eustochium.

A few days ago you told me that you had read some commentaries on Matthew and Luke, of which one was equally dull in perception and expression, the other frivolous in expression, sleepy in sense. Accordingly, you requested me to translate without such trifling, our Adamantius' 39 homilies on Luke, just as they are found in the original Greek: I replied that it was an irksome task and a mental torment to write, as Cicero phrases it, with another man's heart, not one's own: but yet I will undertake it as your requests reach no higher than this. The demand which the sainted Blæsia once made at Rome, that I should' translate into our language his twenty-five volumes on Matthew, five on Luke and thirty-two on John is beyond my powers, my leisure and my energy. You see what weight your influence and wishes have with me. I have laid aside for a time my books on Hebrew Questions to use my energies which your judgment holds fruitful in translating these commentaries which, good or bad, are his work, and not mine: especially as I hear on the left of me the raven — that ominous bird — croaking and mocking in an extraordinary way at the colours of

all the other birds, because of his own utter black-
ness. And so, before he change his note, I confess that these treatises are Origen's recreation no
less than dice are a boy's : very different are the serious pursuits of his manhood and of his old age. If
my proposal meet with your approbation, if I am
still able to undertake the task, and if the Lord
grant me opportunity to translate them into Latin,
so that I may complete the work I have now deferred, you will then be able to see, aye, and all who
speak Latin will learn through you, the mass of valuable knowledge of which they have hitherto been ignorant, but which they have now begun to acquire.
Besides this I have arranged to send you shortly
the commentaries on Matthew of that eloquent
man Hilarius, and of the blessed martyr Victorinus, which, different as their style may be, one
spirit has enabled them to write : these will give
you some idea of the study which our Latins also
have in former days bestowed upon the Holy
Scriptures.

23. You see by this what his opinions are
about Origen and also about Ambrose. If
he should deny that his strictures apply to
Ambrose, which every one knows, he will
be convicted in the first place by the fact
that there is a Commentary of his on Luke
which is current among the Latins, and none
by any other hand. But secondly he knows
that I possess a letter of his in which, while
he discharges others, he makes his strictures
fall upon Ambrose. But, since that letter
contains certain more secret matters, I do
not wish to see it published before the right
time ; and therefore I will corroborate what
I say by other proofs similar to it. In the
meantime let this be counted as demonstrated
by what I have said above, that he extols
Origen's writings as in every way admirable,
and declares that ' if he translates them, the
Roman tongue will then recognize what a
store of good it had hitherto been ignorant of
and now has begun to understand,' that is
the twenty six books on Matthew, the five
on Luke, and the thirty two on John. These
are the books to which he gives the highest
honour ; and in these absolutely everything
is to be found which is contained in the
books on Περὶ Ἀρχῶν, the groundwork of his
charges against me, only set forth with greater
breadth and fulness. If then he promises
that he will translate these, why does he condemn me for a similar course? But now I
have undertaken to prove how violently he
attacks a man who is worthy of all admiration, Ambrose, Bishop of Milan, who was
not to that church alone but to all the
churches like a column or an impregnable
fortress. I will therefore set forth a Preface
of his by which you may see in what foul
and unworthy terms he assails even a man of
such eminence, and also how he praises
Didymus to the sky, though he has since

cast him down even to the infernal region ;
and further how he speaks of the city of
Rome, which now through the grace of God is
reckoned by Christians as their capital, words
which were only applicable when its inhabitants were a nation who were heathens and
princes who were persecutors.

24. The Preface is that for the treatise of
Didymus on the Holy Spirit. It is addressed
to Paulinianus, and is as follows.

" While I was an inhabitant of Babylon, a settler
in the land of the purple harlot, and lived under
the law of the Quirites, I attempted to write some
poor stuff about the Holy Spirit and dedicated the
work to the Pontiff of that city. When on a sudden
that pot which Jeremiah saw after the almond rod [1]
began to seethe from the face of the North ; and
the whole senate of the Pharisees raised a clamour
and no mere imaginary scribe but the whole faction
of the ignorant as if I had declared war against
them, laid their heads together against me. I
therefore returned with all speed to Jerusalem, like
a man going back to his home, and, after having
lived in sight of the cottage of Romulus and the
Lupercal [2] with its naked games, I am now in
sight of Mary's inn and the Saviour's cave. And so,
Paulinianus my dear brother, since the aforenamed
Pontiff Damasus, who had impelled me to undertake this work, now sleeps in the Lord, it is here
in Judea that I warble the song which I could not
sing in a strange land, provoked thereto by you
and by Paula and Eustochium those handmaids of
Christ whom I revere, and aided by your prayers ;
for this land which bore the Saviour is more
august to me than that which bore the man who
slew his brother. [3] I have in the title ascribed the
work to its true authors for I preferred to be known
as the translator of another man's work than to
imitate certain people and, like the ungainly jackdaw, deck myself in another bird's plumage. I
read some time ago the treatise of a certain person
on the Holy Spirit, and I recognized then, according to the sentence of Terence, [4] bad things in Latin
taken from good things in Greek. There is nothing in it of close reasoning, nothing downright
and manly, such as draws us into assent even
against our will, but all is flaccid and soft, sleek
and pretty, picked out with the rarest colours. But
Didymus, [5] my own Didymus, who has the eyes of
the bride in the Song of Songs, those eyes which
Jesus bade us lift up upon the whitening fields,
looks afar into the depths, and has once more given
us cause to call him, as is our wont, the Seer
Prophet. Whoever reads the work will recognize
the plagiarisms of the Latins, and will despise the
derivative streams, as soon as he begins to drink at
the fountain head. He is rude in speech, yet not
in knowledge ; [6] his very style marks him as one
like the apostle as well by the grandeur of the sense
as by the simplicity of the words."

25. You observe how he treats Ambrose.

---

[1] Jer. i, 11, 13.
[2] These games took place at Rome each February in honour
of Lupercus the god of fertility. Two noble youths, after a
sacrifice of goats and dogs, ran almost naked about the city
with thongs cut from the skins, a stroke from which was believed to impart fertility to women.
[3] Romulus, the founder of Rome who slew his brother
Remus.
[4] Eun. Prol. The sentiment, not the words, are quoted
above.
[5] The blind teacher of Alexandria.   [6] 2 Cor. xi, 6.

First, he calls him a crow and says that he is black all over; then he calls him a jackdaw who decks himself in other birds' showy feathers; and then he rends him with his foul abuse, and declares that there is nothing manly in a man whom God has singled out to be the glory of the churches of Christ, who has [1] spoken of the testimonies of the Lord even in the sight of persecuting kings and has not been alarmed. The saintly Ambrose wrote his book on the Holy Spirit not in words only but with his own blood; for he offered his life-blood to his persecutors, and shed it within himself, although God preserved his life for future labours. Suppose that he did follow some of the Greek writers belonging to our Catholic body, and borrowed something from their writings, it should hardly have been the first thought in your mind, (still less the object of such zealous efforts as to make you set to work to translate the work of Didymus on the Holy Spirit,) to blaze abroad what you call his plagiarisms, which were very possibly the result of a literary necessity when he had to reply at once to some ravings of the heretics. Is this the fairness of a Christian? Is it thus that we are to observe the injunction of the Apostle, [2] " Do nothing through faction or through vain glory"? But I might turn the tables on you and ask, [3] Thou that sayest that a man should not steal, dost thou steal? I might quote a fact I have already mentioned, namely, that, a little before you wrote your commentary on Micah, you had been accused of plagiarizing from Origen. And you did not deny it, but said: " What they bring against me in violent abuse I accept as the highest praise; for I wish to imitate the man whom we and all who are wise admire." Your plagiarisms redound to your highest praise; those of others make them crows and jackdaws in your estimation. If you act rightly in imitating Origen whom you call second only to the Apostles, why do you sharply attack another for following Didymus, whom nevertheless you point to by name as a Prophet and an apostolic man? For myself I must not complain, since you abuse us all alike. First you do not spare Ambrose, great and highly esteemed as he was; then the man of whom you write that he was second only to the Apostles, and that all the wise admire him, and whom you have praised up to the skies a thousand times over, not as you say in two, but in innumerable places, this man who was before an Apostle, you now turn

round and make a heretic. Thirdly, this very Didymus whom you designate the Seer-Prophet, who has the eye of the bride in the Song of Songs, and whom you call according to the meaning of his name [1] an Apostolic man, you now on the other hand criminate as a perverse teacher, and separate him off with what you call your censor's rod, into the communion of heretics. I do not know whence you received this rod. I know that Christ once gave the keys to Peter: but what spirit it is who now dispenses these censors' rods, it is for you to say. However, if you condemn all those I have mentioned with the same mouth with which you once praised them, I who in comparison of them am but like a flea, must not complain, I repeat, if now you tear me to pieces, though once you praised me, and in your Chronicle [2] equalled me to Florentius and Bonosus for the nobleness, as you said, of my life.

26. There is also an astonishing action of his in relation to Melania, which I must not pass by in silence because of the shame which those who hear it may feel. She was the granddaughter of the Consul Marcellinus; and in these very Chronicles [3] he had narrated how she was the first lady of the Roman nobility to visit Jerusalem; how she had left her son, then a little child, behind her at Rome, and how the name of Thecla was given her on account of her signal merit and virtue. But afterwards, when he found that some of his deeds were disapproved by this lady through the stricter discipline of her life, he erased her name from all the copies of his work.

It has been necessary for me to bring together the large number of passages which I have adduced from his works, so as to put to the test the truth of his statement, [4] that it is only in two short prefaces that he has made mention of Origen with praise, and that not because of his faith but his talent; that he has praised in him the commentator not the doctrinal teacher. I have actually brought forward ten.

27. But there is danger of expanding my treatise too far and becoming burdensome to the reader; it is sufficient that in the passages I have cited he speaks of Origen as almost an Apostle and a teacher of the churches, and says that it is not because of his novel doctrines as the mad dogs pretend that the senate

---

[1] Ps. cxix, 46. [2] Phil. ii, 3. [3] Rom. ii, 21.

[1] *Sensuum nomine.* Thomas the Apostle is called Didymus. John xi, 16.
[2] See the continuation by Jerome of the Chronicle of Eusebius (not included in this translation) A.D. 381 "Florentius, Bonosus and Rufinus became known as distinguished monks."
[3] Chronicle. A.D. 377. [4] Letter lxxxiv. 2.

of Rome is excited against him; that he follows him because he himself and all the wise approve him; and all the other testimonies, adduced from his prefaces which are inserted above. But, however these matters may stand, and whatever your relations may be to these writers whether ancient or modern, and whether you call them Apostles or mere wantons,[1] Prophets or perverse teachers, what is that to me? It is for you to do penance for all your changes of opinion, your violent words and the wounds you have inflicted on good men, whether you have yet done so or not. As for myself, what is the meaning of your saying "If they have followed me when I erred, let them follow me also in my amendment?" Get thee behind me! Far be such a thing from me. I never followed you or any other man in your errors, but in the strength of Christ I will follow, not you nor any other man, but the Catholic church. But you, who have written all these things who have followed those whom you knew to be in error, you who, as I have shewn, have written so unworthily of God, go you, I say, and do penance, if at least you have any hope that your crime of blasphemy can be pardoned.

27 a. I ask whether you can produce anything which I have written, by which you may convict me of having fallen into heresy even in my youth, — anything of such a character as the heresies of which, though you will not confess it, you now stand convicted. I said that I had followed or imitated you in your system of translating, in that alone and in nothing else. Yet you say that by this I have done you all the injury which you complain of. I followed you in such things as I saw that you had done in the Homilies on the Gospel according to Luke. Take the passage: "My soul doth magnify the Lord, and my spirit hath rejoiced in God my Saviour." When you found that the Greek Commentary had something relating to the Son of God which was not right, you passed it over; whereas the words about the Spirit, which as you may remember, are expressed in the ordinary way, you not only did not pass over but added a few words of your own to make the expression more clear. And so in the note on the words, [2] "Behold, when the voice of thy salutation came into my ears, the babe leaped in my womb," you render: " Because this was not the beginning of his substance," and you add of your own the words "and nature," though both these and

a thousand other things in your translations of these homilies or those on Isaiah or Jeremiah, but more particularly in those on Ezekiel, you have now withdrawn. But, in certain places where you found things relating to the faith, that is the Trinity, expressed in a strange manner, you left out words at your discretion. This mode of translation we have both of us observed, and if any one finds fault with it, it is you who ought to make answer, since you made use of it before me. But now the practice which you blame is undoubtedly one for which you may yourself incur blame. The practice of translating word for word you formerly pronounced to be both foolish and injurious. In this I followed you. You can hardly mean that I am to repent of this because you have now changed your opinion, and say that you have translated the present work with literal exactness. In previous cases you took out what was unedifying in matters of faith, though you did so in such a way as not to excise them wholly nor in all cases. For instance, in the Homilies on Isaiah, at the Vision of God[1] Origen refers the words to the Son and the Holy Spirit; and so you have translated, adding, however, words of your own which would make the passage have a more acceptable sense. It stands thus: "Who are then these two Seraphim? My Lord Jesus Christ and the Holy Spirit:" but you add of your own, "And do not think that there is any difference in the nature of the Trinity, when the functions indicated by the several persons are preserved." The same thing I have done in a great many cases, either cutting out words or bending them into a sounder meaning. For this you bid me do penance. I do not think that you are of this opinion as regards yourself. If then on this ground no penitence is due from either of us, what other things are there of which you invite me to repent?

28. I repeat that there are no writings of mine in which there is any error to be corrected. There are many of yours which, as I have shewn, according to your present opinion, ought to be wholly condemned. You made an exception in favour of the Commentaries on the Ephesians, in which you imagined that you had written more correctly. But even you must have seen, as I have shewn, how like they are all through to Origen's views; and, indeed, how they contain something more extreme than the views of which you demand the condemnation. And, were it not that you had cut yourself off from the power of repentance

---

[1] Venerarios, belonging to Venus or love. It might mean 'beloved ones.'   [2] Luke i, 44.

[1] Is. vi.

by saying "Read over my Commentaries on the Ep. to the Ephesians, and you will acknowledge that I have opposed the doctrines of Origen;" possibly you might wish to turn round and do penance for those, and in this case, as in the rest, to condemn yourself. As far as I am concerned, I give you full leave to repent of these also; indeed, the best thing that you can do is to do penance for all that you have said and also for all that you are going to say; for it is certain that all that you have ever written is to be repented of. But if any one blame me for having translated anything at all of Origen's, then I say that I am the last of many who have done the deed, and the blame, if any, should begin with the first. But does any one ever punish a deed the doing of which he had not previously forbidden. We did what was permissible. If there is to be a new law, it holds good only for the future. But it may be said that the works themselves ought to be condemned and their author as well. If that be so, what is to happen to the other author who writes the same things, as I have shewn most fully above? He must receive a similar judgment. I do not ask for this nor press for it, although he acts a hostile part towards me. But I cannot but see that he is heaping up such a judgment for himself by his rash condemnation of others.

29. But I must deal with you once more by quoting your own words. You say of me in that invective of yours[1] that I have by my translation shewn that Origen is a heretic while I was a Catholic. The words are: "That is to say, I am a Catholic, but he whom I was translating is a heretic." Yes you say it, I have read it. Well then, if, as you tell us, the result of my whole work is to show that I am a Catholic and Origen a heretic, what more do you want? Is not your whole object gained if Origen is proved a heretic and I a Catholic? If you bear witness that I have said this and have thus given you satisfaction by the whole of my work, what cause of accusation against me remains? What purpose was served by that Invective of yours against me? If I proved Origen to be a heretic and myself a Catholic, was I right or not? If I was, then why do you subject to blame and accusation what was rightly done? But, if it was not right that Origen should be called a heretic, why do you make a charge against me on that head? What need was there for you to translate in a worse sense what I had already translated according to your principles,

[1] Namely, Ep. lxxxiv, c. 7.

though in a less elegant style? Especially what need was there for you to play your readers false, and, when they expected one thing, for you to do another? They imagine that you are acting in opposition to those who defend Origen as Catholic; but the person whom you combat and accuse is the man who you say has pronounced him a heretic. Perhaps it was for this that you invited me to do penance; and I had misunderstood you. But even of this I must say that I could not repent, if my repentance implied that I thought all things which are found in his works are catholic. Whether what is uncatholic is his own or, as I think, inserted by others, God only knows: at all events these things, when brought to the standard of the faith and of truth are wholly rejected by me. What then is it that you want me to say? That Origen is a heretic? That is what you say that I have done, and you blame it. That he is a catholic then? Again you make this a ground of accusation against me. Point out more clearly what you mean; possibly there is something which you can find out that lies between the two. This is all the wit that you have gathered from the acuteness of Alexander and Porphyry and Aristotle himself: This is the issue of all the boasting which you make of having from infancy to old age been versed and trained in the schools of rhetoric and philosophy, that you set forth with the intention of pronouncing sentence on Origen as a heretic, and in the very speech in which you are delivering judgment turn upon the man whom you are addressing and accuse him because he also has shown Origen to be a heretic. I beg all men to note that there is in all this no care for the faith or for truth, no earnest thought of religion and sound judgment; there is nothing but the practised lust of evil speaking and accusing the brethren which works in his tongue, nothing but rivalry with his fellow men in his heart, nothing but malice and envy in his mind. So much is this the case that, before any cause of ill feeling existed, and I spoke of you with praise as my brother and colleague, you nevertheless were angry at my advances. Forgive me for not knowing that you were what the Greeks call acatonomastos (ακατονόμαστος), one whom no one dares to address by name. Still, I wonder that you should call upon me to condemn what you complain of me for branding as wrong.

30. It seems needless to make any answer to that part of his indictment in which he says that the works of the Martyr Pamphilus, expressed as they are with so much faithful-

ness and piety, are either not to be considered genuine or if genuine, to be treated
with contempt. Is there any one to whose
authority he will bow? Is there any one
whom he will refrain from abusing? All
the old Greek writers of the church, according to him, have erred. As to the Latins,
how he disparages them, how he attacks
them one by one, both those of the old and
those of modern times, any one who reads his
various work knows well. Now even the
Martyrs fail to gain any respect from him.
"I do not believe," he says "that this is
really the work of the Martyr." If such an
argument were admitted in the case of the
works of any writer, how can we prove
their genuineness in any particular case? If
I were to say, It is not true that books of
Miscellanies are Origen's as you maintain,
how can they be proved to be his? His
answer is, From their likeness to the rest.
But, just as, when a man wants to forge
some one's signature, he imitates his handwriting, so he who wishes to introduce his
own thoughts under another man's name,
is sure to imitate the style of him whose
name he has assumed. But, to pass over
for brevity's sake all that might with great
justice be said on this point, if you were
determined to be so bold as to question the
works of the Martyr, you ought to have
brought out publicly the actual statements
which seemed to you liable to question, and
then every reader could have seen what was
absurd in them and what was reasonable,
what was unsuitable to or against the system
of the Apostles; and especially the great impiety, whatever it may have been, in expiation
of which you tell us that the Martyr shed
his blood. A man who read those actual
words would be able to say, not, as now, on
your judgment but on his own, either that
the martyr had gone wrong, or that a treatise
which was so full of absurdity and unbelief
..ad been composed by some one else. But,
as it is, you know well that if the writings
which you impugn are read by any one, the
blame will be turned back upon him who
has unjustly found fault; and therefore you
do not cite the passages which you impugn,
but with that 'censor's rod' of yours, and by
your own arrogant authority, you make your
decrees in this style: "Let this book be cast
out of the libraries, let that book be retained; and again, if today a book is accepted, tomorrow if any one but myself has
praised it, let it be cast out, and with it
the man who praised it. Let this one be
counted as Catholic, even though he seems
at times to have gone wrong; let that man

have no pardon for his error, even though
he has said the same things as myself, and
let no man translate him nor read him, for
fear he should recognize my plagiarisms.
This man indeed was a heretic, but he was
my master. And this other, though he is a
Jew, and of the Synagogue of Satan, and is
hired to sell words for gain, yet he is my
master who must be preferred to all others,
because it is among the Jews alone that the
truth of the Scriptures dwells." If the universal Church had with one voice conferred
on you this authority, and had demanded of
you that you should be the judge of each and
all, would it not have been your duty to
refuse to allow so heavy and perilous a burden to be laid upon you? But now we have
made such progress in the daily habit of
disparaging others that we no longer spare
even the martyrs. But let us suppose that
the work is not that of the martyr Pamphilus,
but of some other unknown member of the
church; did he, whoever he may have been,
employ his own words, I ask, so that we are
called upon to defer to the merits of the
writer? No. He sets out quotations from
the works of Origen himself, and exhibits his
opinion upon each question not in the words
of the apologist but in those of the accused himself; and, just as in the present
treatise what I have quoted from your writings carried much more force than what I
have said myself, so also the defence of Origen lies not in the authority of his apologist, but in his own words. The question of
authorship is superfluous, when the defence
is so conducted as to dispense with the
author's aid.

31. But I must come to that head of his
inculpation of me which is most injurious
and full of ill-will; nay, not of ill-will only
but of malice. He says: Which of all the
wise and holy men before us has dared to
attempt the translation of these books which
you have translated? I myself, he adds,
though asked by many to do it, have always
refused. But the fact is, the excuse to be
made for those holy men is easy enough; for
it by no means follows because a man of
Latin race is a holy and a wise man, that he
has an adequate knowledge of the Greek
language; it is no slur upon his holiness that
he is wanting in the knowledge of a foreign
tongue. And further, if he has the knowledge
of the Greek language, it does not follow that
he has the wish to make translations. Even
if he has such a wish, we are not to find fault
with him for not translating more than a few
works, and for translating some rather than
others. Every man has power to do as he

likes in such matters according to his own free will or according to the wish of any one who asks him to make the translation. But he brings forward the case of the saintly men Hilary and Victorinus, the first of whom, though well-known as a commentator, translated nothing, I believe, from the Greek; while the other himself tells us that he employed a learned presbyter named Heliodorus to draw what he needed from the Greek sources, while he himself merely gave them their Latin form because he knew little or nothing of Greek. There is therefore a very good reason why these men should not have made this translation. That you should have acted in the same way is, I admit, a matter for wonder. For what further audacity, what larger amount of rashness, would have been required to translate those books of Origen, after you had put almost the whole of their contents into your other works, and, indeed, had already published in books bearing your own name all that is said in those which you now declare worthy of blame?

32. Perhaps it was a greater piece of audacity to alter the books of the divine Scriptures which had been delivered to the Churches of Christ by the Apostles to be a complete record of their faith by making a new translation under the influence of the Jews. Which of these two things appears to you to be the less legitimate? As to the sayings of Origen, if we agree with them, we agree with them as the sayings of a man; if we disagree, we can easily disregard them as those of a mere man. But how are we to regard those translations of yours which you are now sending about everywhere, through our churches and monasteries, through all our cities and walled towns? are they to be treated as human or divine? And what are we to do when we are told that the books which bear the names of the Hebrew Prophets and lawgivers are to be had from you in a truer form than that which was approved by the Apostles? How, I ask, is this mistake to be set right, or rather, how is this crime to be expiated? We hold it a thing worthy of condemnation that a man should have put forth some strange opinions in the interpretation of the law of God; but to pervert the law itself and make it different from that which the Apostles handed down to us, — how many times over must this be pronounced worthy of condemnation? To the daring temerity of this act we may much more justly apply your words: "Which of all the wise and holy men who have gone before you has dared to put his hand to that work?" Which of them would have pre-

sumed thus to profane the book of God, and the sacred words of the Holy Spirit? Who but you would have laid hands upon the divine gift and the inheritance of the Apostles?

33. There has been from the first in the churches of God, and especially in that of Jerusalem, a plentiful supply of men who being born Jews have become Christians; and their perfect acquaintance with both languages and their sufficient knowledge of the law is shewn by their administration of the pontifical office. In all this abundance of learned men, has there been one who has dared to make havoc of the divine record handed down to the Churches by the Apostles and the deposit of the Holy Spirit? For what can we call it but havoc, when some parts of it are transformed, and this is called the correction of an error? For instance, the whole of the history of Susanna, which gave a lesson of chastity to the churches of God, has by him been cut out, thrown aside and dismissed. The hymn of the three children, which is regularly sung on festivals in the Church of God, he has wholly erased from the place where it stood. But why should I enumerate these cases one by one, when their number cannot be estimated? This, however, cannot be passed over. The seventy translators, each in their separate cells, produced a version couched in consonant and identical words, under the inspiration, as we cannot doubt, of the Holy Spirit; and this version must certainly be of more authority with us than a translation made by a single man under the inspiration of Barabbas. But, putting this aside, I beg you to listen, for example, to this as an instance of what we mean. Peter was for twenty-four years Bishop of the Church of Rome. We cannot doubt that, amongst other things necessary for the instruction of the church, he himself delivered to them the treasury of the sacred books, which, no doubt, had even then begun to be read under his presidency and teaching. What are we to say then? Did Peter the Apostle of Christ deceive the church and deliver to them books which were false and contained nothing of truth? Are we to believe that he knew that the Jews possessed what was true, and yet determined that the Christians should have what was false? But perhaps the answer will be made that Peter was illiterate, and that, though he knew that the books of the Jews were truer than those which existed in the church, yet he could not translate them into Latin because of his linguistic incapacity. What then! Was the tongue of fire given by the Holy Spirit

from heaven of no avail to him? Did not the Apostles speak in all languages?

34. But let us grant that the Apostle Peter was unable to do what our friend has lately done. Was Paul illiterate? we ask; He who was a Hebrew of the Hebrews, touching the law a Pharisee, brought up at the feet of Gamaliel? Could not he, when he was at Rome, have supplied any deficiencies of Peter? Is it conceivable that they, who prescribed to their disciples that they should give attention to reading,¹ did not give them correct and true reading? These men who bid us not attend to Jewish fables and genealogies, which minister questioning rather than edification; and who, again, bid us beware of, and specially watch, those of the circumcision; is it conceivable that they could not foresee through the Spirit that a time would come, after nearly four hundred years, when the church would find out that the Apostles had not delivered to them the truth of the old Testament, and would send an embassy to those whom the apostles spoke of as the circumcision, begging and beseeching them to dole out to them some small portion of the truth which was in their possession: and that the Church would through this embassy confess that she had been for all those four hundred years in error; that she had indeed been called by the Apostles from among the Gentiles to be the bride of Christ, but that they had not decked her with a necklace of genuine jewels; that she had fondly thought that they were precious stones, but now had found out that those were not true gems which the Apostles had put upon her, so that she felt ashamed to go forth in public decked in false instead of true jewels; and that she therefore begged that they would send her Barabbas, even him whom she had once rejected to be married to Christ, so that in conjunction with one man chosen from among her own people, he might restore to her the true ornaments with which the Apostles had failed to furnish her.

35. What wonder is there then that he should tear me to pieces, being as I am of no account; or that he should wound Ambrose, or find fault with Hilary, Lactantius and Didymus? I must not greatly grieve over any injury of my own in the fact that he has attempted to do my work of translating over again, when he is only treating me with the same contempt with which he has treated the Seventy translators. But this emendation of the Seventy, what are we to think of it? Is it not evident, how greatly the

grounds for the heathens' unbelief have been increased by this proceeding? For they take notice of what is going on amongst us. They know that our law has been amended, or at least changed; and do you suppose they do not say among themselves, "These people are wandering at random, they have no fixed truth among them, for you see how they make amendments and corrections in their laws whenever they please," and indeed it is evident that there must have been previous error where amendment has supervened, and that things which undergo change at the hand of man cannot possibly be divine. This has been the present which you have made us with your excess of wisdom, that we are all judged even by the heathen as lacking in wisdom. I reject the wisdom which Peter and Paul did not teach. I will have nothing to do with a truth which the Apostles have not approved. These are your own words:¹ "The ears of simple men among the Latins ought not after four hundred years to be molested by the sound of new doctrines." Now you are yourself saying: "Every one has been under a mistake who thought that Susanna had afforded an example of chastity to both the married and the unmarried. It is not true. And every one who thought that the boy Daniel was filled with the Holy Spirit and convicted the adulterous old men, was under a mistake. That also was not true. And every congregation throughout the universe, whether of those who are in the body or of those who have departed to be with the Lord, even though they were holy martyrs or confessors, all who have sung the Hymn of the three children have been in error, and have sung what is false. Now therefore after four hundred years the truth of the law comes forth for us; it has been bought with money from the Synagogue. When the world has grown old and all things are hastening to their end, let us change the inscriptions upon the tombs of the ancients, so that it may be known by those who had read the story otherwise, that it was not a gourd² but an ivy plant under whose shade Jonah rested; and that, when our legislator pleases, it will no longer be the shade of ivy but of some other plant.

36. But Origen also, you will tell us, in composing his work called the Hexapla, adopted the asterisks,³ taking them from the

---

¹ Tim. iv, 13.

¹ Jer. Letter lxxxiv. c. 8.
² This change of the gourd for the ivy forms the ground-work of a curious story told by Augustine, to which no doubt Rufinus here alludes See Ep. civ, 5 of the collection of Jerome's letters. Augustin Letter lxxi.
³ The asterisks denoted that the words to which they were attached were added, and the obeli (†) that something had

translation of Theodotion. How is this? You produce Origen sometimes for condemnation, sometimes for imitation, at your own caprice. But can it be admitted as right that you should bring in the same man as your advocate whom just now you were accusing? Can you take as an authority for your actions one whom you yourself have previously condemned, and to the condemnation of whom you stirred up the Roman senate? You ought to have made provision for this beforehand. No man begins by cutting the trunk of a tree when he is intending to lean against it; and no man first impugns the faith of another and then invokes his faith in his own defence. Whether Origen did as you say or not, makes no difference to you. If you wish that his case should be a precedent for yours, read over your judgment upon him, and see what you have said. You used the expression: "This is not clearing yourself but only seeking abettors of your crime." Apply this to yourself; your business is not to seek abettors of your crime, but to find means of justification for your conduct. However, let us see whether anything of the kind was done by Origen whom you make both plaintiff and defendant. I do not find a single passage which he translated from the Hebrew. How then can your action and his be said to be alike? What he did was this. He proved that apostates and Jews had translated the writings which the Jews specially read: and, since it would frequently happen in the course of discussion that they falsely asserted that some things had been taken out and others put in in our copies of the Scriptures, Origen desired to shew to our people what reading obtained among the Jews. He therefore wrote out each of their versions in separate pages or columns, and pointed out by means of certain specified marks at the head of each line what had been added or subtracted by them; and he merely put these marks of his in the work of others, not in his own; so that we might understand not what we ourselves but what the Jews believed to have been either removed or inserted. This was no more than what is done in the army when a list is made out containing the names of the soldiers. If the captain wishes to see how many of them have survived after an action, he sends a man to make inquiry; and he makes his own mark, a (θ) (theta), for instance, as is commonly done, against the name of each soldier who has fallen, and puts some other

mark of his own to designate the survivors. Do you suppose that he who makes one mark against the name of a dead man and another of his own against that of a survivor, will be thought to have done anything which causes the one to be dead and the other to be alive? He has only, as is well understood, marked the names of those who have been killed by others, so as to call attention to the fact. Just in the same way, Origen pointed out by certain marks of his own, namely, the signs of asterisks and obeli,[1] which words had been, so to speak, killed by other translators, and those which had been superfluously introduced. But he put in no single word of his own, nor did he make it appear that the certainty of our copies was in any point shaken; but those things which, as the actual words run, seemed wanting in plainness and clearness, he showed to be full of the mysteries of a spiritual meaning. What comfort then can the conduct of Origen give you in this matter, when your work is shown to be quite unlike his, and when all your labour is spent upon making one letter kill the next, whereas his endeavour, on the contrary, is to vindicate the Spirit which giveth life?

37. This action is yours, my brother, yours alone. It is clear that no one in the church has been your companion or confederate in it, but only that Barabbas whom you mention so frequently. What other spirit than that of the Jews would dare to tamper with the records of the church which have been handed down from the Apostles? It is they, my brother, you who were most dear to me before you were taken captive by the Jews, it is they who are hurrying you into this abyss of evil. It is their doing that those books of yours are put forth in which you brand your Christian brethren, not sparing even the martyrs, and heap up accusations speakable and unspeakable against Christians of every degree, and mar our peace, and cause a scandal to the church. It is they who cause you to pass sentence upon yourself and your own writings as upon words which you once spoke as a Christian. We all of us have become worthless in your eyes, while they and their evil acts are all your delight. If you had but listened to Paul where he says in his Epistle: [2] "If any brother be overtaken in a fault ye who are spiritual restore such a one in the spirit of meekness," you would never have let your passions swell up so as altogether to break through the order of our spiritual discipline.

---

been subtracted. See Jerome's Preface to the Books of Kings in this Series.

[1] Stars and spits.   [2] Gal. vi, 1.

Suppose that I had written something which was injurious to you; suppose that I had done some injustice to you a man of the highest eloquence, who were my brother and my brother presbyter, whom also I had pronounced worthy of imitation in your method of translation: even so, this was the first complaint which you had received of any injury on my part since friendship had been restored between us, and that with difficulty and much trouble. But suppose that you had reason to be offended at the fact that, in my translation of Origen, I passed over some things which appeared to me unedifying in point of doctrine — though in this I only did what you had done. Possibly I was deserving of blame and correction for this. You say that some of the brethren sent letters to you demanding that the faults of the translator should be pointed out. What then did you do, you who are a man of spiritual attainments? What a model, what an example of conduct in such matters is this which you have given! You not only blazen forth the shame of your brother's nakedness to those who are without, but you yourself tear away the covering of his nakedness. Suppose even that what I did was not done as you had done it, suppose that, through some access of drunkenness creeping unawares upon me, I had laid bare my own shame as the Patriarch did; would it have been a curse which you would have incurred if you had walked backward and made your reply like a soft cloak to cover my reproach, if the letter of the brother who was wide-awake had veiled the brother who lay exposed through his own drowsiness in writing?

38. But you will say, It was impossible for me to reply otherwise than I did. The letter which I received was such that, if I had not replied and retranslated literally the books which you had translated paraphrastically, I should myself have been thought to be a follower of Origen. I will not at present say anything as to the character of that letter, except that it bears the name of a man of high rank, Pammachius: but I ask, would there have been anything uncourteous in such a reply as this: " My brothers we ought not readily to judge of other men's works. You remember what you did when I had sent my books against Jovinian to Rome,[1] and when some persons understood them in a different sense from that in which, if my memory serves me, I had composed them. They were read by a

great many people, and almost every one was offended by them, you yourself, as was believed, amongst them. Did you not on that occasion withdraw from circulation the copies which had been exposed to sale publicly in the forum, and send them, not to some one else, but to me, at the same time pointing out the grounds on which you thought so many had been offended? And I, as you remember, wrote an Apology in new terms, so as to give a sounder meaning, as far as I could, to expressions to which a different sense had been attributed. Well, it is but fair that as we would that men should do to us so we should do to them : and therefore, as you sent me back my books for correction, so do now with these books: send them back to their author, and hint to him what you think blameable in them, so that, if in anything he has gone wrong, he may correct it. Besides, though I have exercised my talents on many subjects, and laboured out many works, this is almost the first work which he has attempted, and possibly even this he has done under compulsion, so that it is not strange if he has not gone quite straight at first. We should not seize upon opportunities for disparaging men who are Christians, but seek their advantage by correcting what they have done wrong."

39. If your reply to him had been couched in terms like these, would you not have ministered grace and edification both to him, since he has been initiated into the fear of God, and to all your other readers, whereas these invectives of yours are the cause of sadness and confusion to all who fear God, since they see you a prey to this hideous lust of detraction, and me driven to the wretched necessity of recrimination. But, as I have said, this evidence was unnecessary. You yourself in the books you published against Jovinian, at one time assert, as can be shewn, the same things which you blamed in·him, while at another you fall into the opposite extreme, and declare marriage to be so disgraceful a state that its stain cannot even be washed away by the blood of martyrdom. But, if it appeared to you an easy thing for your friend to procure what amounts to a correction of the dogma of the Manichæans as it was originally expressed in these books, and that when they were already published and placed in the hands of many persons to copy, what difficulty would there have been in my correcting a work which was not my own but a translation of that of another man, if any mistakes could be pointed out in it, I will not say by reason, but even by envy? especially when it was

1 See Jerome's letter to Pammachius (Letter xlviii) describing his friend's remonstrance, and defending himself.

still in rough sheets, which I had not read over again or corrected, and which were not published when your friends took possession of them. Was it an impossibility to get these writings corrected which were then in an uncorrected state? But the sting does not proceed from that quarter; he would have found nothing to blame there It proceeds wholly from the fact that he was afraid that it might come to light what is the source of all that he says, and whence he gains the reputation of a learned man and a great expounder of the Scriptures.

40. I explained the reasons which induced me to make the translation so that it should be seen that I acted, not in the spirit of contention and rivalry, in which he so often acts, but from the necessity which I have explained above; and I did it as an aid to a good and useful undertaking.[1] I hoped that it might impart something both of lucidity and of brightness to one who, though with little culture, was composing a serious work. Do we not know cases in which old houses have been of use in the construction of new ones? Sometimes a stone is taken from the parts of an old house which are remote and concealed, to decorate the portal of the new house and adorn its entrance. And at times an edifice of modern architecture is supported by the strength of a single ancient beam. Are we then to place ourselves in opposition to those who rightly use what is old in building up what is new? Are we to say, You are not allowed to transfer the materials of the old house to the new, unless you join each beam to its beam, each stone to its stone, unless you make a portico of what was a portico before, a chamber of what was a chamber; and this must further involve building up the most secret recesses from what were such before, and the sewers from the former sewers : for every large house must have such places. This is the process of translating word for word, which in former days you esteemed inadmissible, but which you now approve. But you claim that what is in itself unlawful is lawful for you, while for us even what is lawful you impute as a crime. You think it right that you should be praised for changing the words of the Sacred Books and Divine volumes; but if we, when we imitate you in translating a human work, pass over anything which seems to us not to be edifying, we are to have no pardon for this at your hands, though you yourself set us the example.

41. However, let him act in these mat-

1 That is, the work which Macarius was writing upon Fate, as explained in this Apology i. 11.

ters as he himself thinks lawful or expédient. Let me recapitulate in the end of this book what I have said in a scattered way in my own defence. He had said of me that it seemed as if I could not be a heretic without him; I therefore set forth my belief and, in respect of the resurrection of the dead I proved that he rather than I was in error, since he spoke of the resurrection body as frail. I shewed also that he did away with the distinction of sex in the other world, saying that bodies would become souls women men. I next revealed the causes which had led to my translation — very proper causes in my opinion; I shewed that it was not because I was stimulated by contentiousness, nor because I was desirous of glory, but because I was incited by the fear of God, that I imported a store of old Greek material to be used in the new Latin construction, that I furbished up the old armour which had become enveloped in rust, not with a view to excite a civil war but to repel a hostile attack. I then introduced the chief matter on which they have laid their forgers' hands, the adulterous blasphemy against the Son of God and the Holy Spirit, a thing quite alien from me, but brought in by these men in their wickedness as I shewed by quotations.

42. I then took up one by one the points in which he had blamed Origen, with the intention of striking at me and discrediting my work of translation. I shewed from those very Commentaries of his from which he had said that we might expect to learn and test his belief, that on three points, namely the previous state of the soul, the restitution of all things, and his views concerning the devil and apostate angels, he has himself written the same things which he blames in Origen. I convicted him of having said that the souls of men were held bound in this body as in a prison; and I proved that he had asserted in these very Commentaries that the whole rational creation of angels and of human souls formed but a single body. I next shewed that, as to an association for perjury, there was no one who had so much to do with it in its deepest mysteries as himself; and in accordance with this I proved that the doctrine that truth and the higher teaching ought not to be disclosed to all men was taught by him in these same Commentaries. I next took up the question of secular literature, as to which he had made this declaration to Christ as he sat on the judgment seat and ordered him to be beaten : " If ever I read or possess the books of the heathen, I have denied Thee ; " and I shewed

clearly that he not only reads and possesses these books now, but that he supports all the bragging of which his teaching is full on his knowledge of them; so much so that he boasts of having been introduced to the knowledge of logic through the Introduction of Porphyry the prince of unbelievers. And, while he says that it is a doctrine of the heathen, to speak in this or that manner both about the soul and about other creatures, I shewed that he had spoken of God in a more degrading manner than any of the heathen when he said that God had a mother-in-law. But further, whereas he had declared that he had only mentioned Origen in two short Prefaces, and then not as a man of apostolic rank but merely as a man of talent, I, though for brevity's sake only bringing forward ten of his Prefaces, established the fact that in each of them he had spoken of him not only as an apostolic man but as a teacher of the churches next after the apostles, and as one whose teaching was followed by himself and all wise men.

43. Moreover, I pointed out clearly that it is habitual to him to disparage all good men, and that, if he can find something to blame in one man after another of those who are highly esteemed and have gained a name in literature, he thinks that he has added to his own reputation. I shewed also how shamefully some of Christ's [1] priests have been assailed by him; and how he has spared neither the monks nor the virgins, nor those who live in continency, whom he had praised before; how he has defamed in his lampoons every order and degree of Christians; how shamefully and foully he assailed even Ambrose, that saintly man, the memory of whose illustrious life still lives in the hearts of all men: how even Didymus, whom he had formerly ranked among the seer-prophets and Apostles, now he places among those whose teaching diverges from that of the churches; how he brands with the marks of ignorance or of folly every single writer of ancient and of modern days; and finally does not spare even the martyrs. All these things I have brought to the proof of his own works and his own testimony, not to that of external witnesses. I have gone through each particular, and have brought out the evidence from those very books of his which he most commends, books which alone he excepted as containing nothing of which he needed to repent, while he says that he repents of all his other sayings and writings; not

that his repentance is sincere, but that he is driven into such straits that he must choose either to feign penitence or to forfeit the vantage ground which enables him to bite and wound any one whom he pleases. I therefore preferred not to touch his other writings, so that his conviction might come out of those alone out of which he had himself closed the door of repentance. Last of all I have shown that he has altered the sacred books which the Apostles had committed to the churches as the trustworthy deposit of the Holy Spirit, and that he who calls out about the audacity shewn in translating mere human works himself commits the greater crime of subverting the divine oracles.

44. It remains that every reader of this book should give his suffrage for one or the other of us, judging as he desires that he may himself be judged by God; and that he should not injure his own soul by favoring either party unjustly. Also, my beloved son Apronianus, go to Pammachius, that saintly man whose letter is put forward by our friend in this Invective or Bill of Indictment of his, and adjure him in Christ's name to incline in his judgment to the cause of innocence not that of party-spirit: it is the cause of truth that is at stake, and religion not party should be our guide. It is a precept of our Lord [1] to " judge not according to the appearance, but judge a righteous judgment," and, just as in each one of the least of his brethren it is Christ who is thirsty and hungry, who is clothed and fed; so in these who are unjustly judged it is He who is judged unrighteously. When some are hated without a cause, he will speak on their behalf and say: [2] " You have hated me without a cause." What judgment does he think will be formed of this cause and of his action in it before the tribunal of Christ? He remembers well no doubt how, when the men we are speaking of had written and published his books against Jovinian, and men were already reading them and finding fault with them, he withdrew them from the hands of the readers, and stopped their remarks, and blamed them for their blame of his friend; and how, further, he sent the books back to the author, with the suggestion that he should either correct those passages which had been found fault with, or in any way that he would set matters right. But when what I had written fell into his hands, — it was not then a book but merely a number of imperfect, uncorrected papers, which had been sub-

<hr>

[1] *Sacerdotes.* This is almost always applied to Bishops. Here the allusion is chiefly to Jerome's attack upon Ambrose. See Sect. 23-25.

[1] John vii, 24.   [2] John xv, 25.

tracted by fraud and theft by some scoundrel; he did not bring it to me and complain of it, though I was close at hand; he did not deign even to rebuke me or to convict me of wrong through some friend, as it might have been, or even some enemy; but sent my papers to the East, and set to work the tongue of that man who never yet knew how to control it. Would it have been against the precepts of our religion if he had met me face to face? Did he think me so utterly unworthy of holding converse with him, that it was not worth while even to argue with me? Yet for us too Christ died, for our salvation also He shed his blood. We are sinners, I grant, but we belong to his flock and are numbered among his sheep. Pammachius, however, must be held in honour for his excellent deeds wrought through faith in Christ, which should be an example to all others; for he has counted his rank as nothing worth, and has made himself equal to the humble; consequently, I was unwilling to see him carried away by human partisanship and contention, lest his faith should suffer damage in any way. At all events we shall see how far he preserves a right judgment when he sees that that great master Jerome [1] taught, in the commentaries which he selected as satisfactory even after his repentance, the very things which he condemns in others as being alien to his own teaching. We shall think that his former action was a mistake due to ignorance if he recognizes it and sets it right. As for myself, though [2] under the compulsion of necessity, I have endeavoured to make answer to him who had attacked me with such great bitterness, yet for this also I ask for forgiveness if I have handled the matter too sharply; for God is my witness how truly I can say that I have kept silence on many more points than I have brought forward. I could not wholly keep silence in the presence of accusations which I know to be undeserved, when I heard from many that my silence would bring their own faith into peril.

45. After this Apology had been written, one of the brethren who came to us from you at Rome and helped me in revising it, observed that one point in my defence had been passed over which he had heard adversely dwelt upon by my detractors there. The point turns upon a statement in my Preface, where I said of him who is now my persecutor and accuser that in the works of Origen which he translated there are found certain grounds of offence in the Greek, but that he has in his translation so cleared them away that the Latin reader will find nothing in them which is dissonant from our faith. On this sentence they remark: "You see how he has praised his method of translation and has borne his testimony that in the books he has translated no grounds of offence are to be found, and promised that he would himself follow the same method. Why then is not his own translation free from grounds of offence, as he bears witness is the case with the writings of the other?

46. I suppose it is not to be wondered at that I am always blamed for the points in which I have praised him. It is quite right, no doubt. But to come to the matter itself. I said that when grounds of offence appeared in the Greek he had cleared them away in his Latin translation; and not wrongly; but he had done this just in the same sense as I have done it. For instance, in the Homilies on Isaiah, he explains the two Seraphim as meaning the Son and the Holy Ghost, and he adds this of his own: "Let no one think that there is a difference of nature in the Trinity when the offices of the Persons are distinguished"; and by this he thinks that he has been able to remedy the grounds of offence. I in a similar way occasionally removed, altered or added a few words, in the attempt to draw the meaning of the writer into better accordance with the straight path of the faith. What did I do in this which was different or contrary to our friend's system? what which was not identical with it? But the difference lies in this, that I was judging of his writings without ill-will or detraction, and therefore saw in them not what might lend itself to depreciation, but what the translator aimed at; whereas he is seeking for occasions for calumniating others, and therefore finds fault with those things in my writings which he himself has formerly written. And indeed he is right in blaming me, since I have pronounced what he has said to be right, whereas in his judgment it is reprehensible. This holds in reference to the doctrine he has expressed about the Trinity; namely, that the two Seraphim are the Son and the Holy Ghost, from which especially the charge of blasphemy is drawn, that is, if he is to be judged according to the system which he has adopted in dealing with me. But according to the system which I have adopted in judging of his writings, apart from the matter of calumny, he is not to be held guilty because of what he has added on his own account to explain the author's meaning.

---

[1] The older editions do not contain the name.
[2] Some copies read *visi* instead of *nisi sumus:* I seemed to be compelled.

47. As regards the resurrection of the flesh, I think that my translation contains the same doctrines which are preached in the churches. As to the other points which relate to the various orders of created beings, I have already said that they have nothing to do with our faith in the Deity. But if he appeals to these for the sake of calumniating others, though they have hitherto presented no ground of offence, I do not deny his right to do so, if he thinks well to revoke my judgment by which he might have been absolved, and to enforce his own, by which he ought to be condemned. It is not my judgment on him which is blameable, but his own, which takes others to task for doing what he approves in himself. But this is a new method of judgment according to which I am defending my own accuser, and he considers that he has at last gained the victory over me when he has brought himself in guilty. But suppose that a Synod of Bishops should accept the sentences you have pronounced, and should demand that all the books which contain the impugned doctrines, together with their authors, should be condemned; then these books must be condemned first as they stand in the Greek; and then what is condemned in Greek must undoubtedly be condemned in the Latin. Then will come the turn of your own books; they will be found to contain the same things, even according to your own judgment. And as it has been of no advantage to Origen that you have praised him, so it will be of no profit to you that I have pleaded in your behalf. I shall then be bound to follow the judgment of the Catholic Church whether it is given against the books of Origen or against yours.

JEROME'S APOLOGY FOR HIMSELF AGAINST THE BOOKS OF RUFINUS.

Addressed to Pammachius and Marcella from Bethlehem, A.D. 402.

BOOK I.

The documents which Jerome had before him when he wrote his Apology were (1) Rufinus' Translation of Pamphilus' Apology with the Preface prefixed to it and the book on the Falsification of the Books of Origen, (2) the Translation of the Περὶ Ἀρχῶν and Rufinus' Preface, (3) The Apology of Rufinus addressed to Anastasius (see p. 430), and (4) Anastasius' letter to John of Jerusalem (p. 432 Apol. ii, 14, iii, 20). He had also other letters of Anastasius like that addressed to the Bishop of Milan (Jerome Letter 95. See also Apol. iii, 21). But he had not the full text of Rufinus' Apology (c. 4, 15). He received letters from Pammachius and Marcella, at the beginning of the Spring of 402, when the Apology written at Aquileia at the end of 400 had become known to Rufinus' friends for some time. They had been unable to obtain a full copy, but had sent the chief heads of it, and had strongly urged Jerome to reply. At the same time his brother Paulinianus who had been some three years in the West, returned to Palestine by way of Rome, and there heard and saw portions of Rufinus' Apology, which he committed to memory (Apol. i, 21, 28) and repeated at Bethlehem. To these documents Jerome replies.

The heads of the First Book are as follows.

1. It is hard that an old friend with whom I had been reconciled should attack me in a book secretly circulated among his disciples.

2. Others have translated Origen. Why does he single me out?

3. He gave me fictitious praise in his Preface to the Περὶ Ἀρχῶν. Now, since I defend myself, he writes 3 books against me as an enemy.

4, 5. He spoke of me as united in faith with him; but what is his faith? Why are his books kept secret? I can meet any attack.

6. I translated the Περὶ Ἀρχῶν because you demanded it, and because his translation slurred over Origen's heresies.

7. My translation put away ambiguities, and showed the real character of the book, and of the previous translation.

8. My translation of Origen's Commentaries created no excitement; his first translation, of Pamphilus' Apology, roused all Rome to indignation.

9. But the work was really Eusebius's, who tells us that Pamphilus wrote nothing.

10. After the condemnation of Origen by Theophilus and Anastasius, it would be wise in Rufinus to give up this pretended defence.

11. I had praised Eusebius as well as Origen only as writers; and was forced to condemn them as heretics. Why should this be taken amiss?

12. I wrote a friendly letter to Rufinus, which my friends kept back.

13. There is nothing to blame in my getting the help of a Jew in translating from the Hebrew.

14. There is nothing strange in my praising Origen before I knew the Περὶ Ἀρχῶν.

15. The accusations seem inconsistent, but I knew them only by report.

16. The office of a commentator.

17. We must distinguish methods of writing, and not expect a vulgar simplicity in the various compositions of cultured men.

18. My assertion was true, that Origen permitted the use of falsehood.

19. The accusation about a mistranslation of Ps. ii is easily explained.

20. In the difficulties of the translator and the commentator we must get help where we can.

21. In the Commentary on Ephesians I acted straightforwardly in giving the views of Origen and others.

22. As to the passage " He hath chosen us before the foundation of the world."

23. As to the passage " Far above all rule and authority &c."

24. As to the passage " That in the ages to come &c."

25. As to " Paul the prisoner of Jesus Christ."

26. As to " The body fitly framed &c."

27. I quoted Origen's views as, " According to another heresy."

28, 29. As to " Men loving their wives as their own bodies."

30. To the charge of reading secular books I reply that I remember what I learned in youth.

31. Also, a promise given in a dream must not be pressed. Why should such things be raked up by old friends against one another?

32. I am right in my contention that all sins are remitted in baptism.

I have learned not only from your letter but from those of many others that cavils are raised against me in the school of Tyrannus,[1] "by the tongue of my dogs from the enemies by himself"[2] because I have translated the books Περὶ Ἀρχῶν into Latin. What unprecedented shamelessness is this! They accuse the physician for detecting the poison: and this in order to protect their vendor of drugs, not in obtaining the reward of innocence but in his partnership with the criminal; as if the number of the offenders diminished the crime, or as if the accusation depended on our personal feelings not on the facts. Pamphlets are written against me; they are forced on every one's attention; and yet they are not openly published, so that the hearts of the simple are disturbed, and no opportunity is given me of answering. This is a new way of injuring a man, to make accusations which you are afraid of sending abroad, to write what you are obliged to hide. If what he writes is true, why is he afraid of the public? if it is false, why has he written it? We read when we were boys the words of Cicero: " I consider it a lack of self-control to write anything which you intend to keep hidden."[3] I ask, What is it of which they complain? Whence comes this heat, this madness of theirs? Is it because I have rejected a feigned laudation?[4] Because I refused the praise offered in insincere words? Because under the name of a friend I detected the snares of an enemy? I am called in this Preface brother and colleague, yet my supposed crimes are set forth openly, and it is proclaimed that I have written in favour of Origen, and have by my praises exalted him to the skies. The writer says that he has done this with a good intention. How then does it come to pass that he now casts in my teeth, as an open enemy, what he then praised as a friend? He declared that he had meant to follow me as his predecessor in his translation, and to borrow an authority for his work from some poor works of mine. If that was so, it would have been sufficient for him to have stated once for all that I had written. Where was the necessity for him to repeat the same things, and to force them on men's notice by iteration, and to turn over the same words again and again, as if no one would believe in his praises? A praise which is simple and genuine does not show all this anxiety about its credit with the reader. How is it that he is afraid that, unless he produces my own words as witnesses, no one will believe him when he praises me? You see that we perfectly understand his arts; he has evidently been to the theatrical school, and has learned up by constant practice the part of the mocking encomiast. It is of no use to put on a veil of simplicity, when the schemer is detected in his malicious purpose. To have made a mistake once, or, to stretch the point, even twice, may be an unlucky chance; but how is it that he makes the supposed mistake with his eyes open, and repeats it, and weaves this mistake into the whole tissue of his writings so as to make it impossible for me to deny the things for which he praises me? A true friend who knew what he was about would, after our previous misunderstanding and our reconciliation, have avoided all appearance of suspicious conduct, and would have taken care not to do through inadvertence what might seem to be done advisedly. Tully says in his book of pleadings for Galinius: " I have always felt that it was a religious duty of the highest kind to preserve every friendship that I have

---

[1] Acts xix, 9. Rufinus's prænomen was Tyrannius.

[2] Ps. lxviii, 23 Jerome's version is here, as in many cases unintelligible through a perverse literalism and an incorrect Hebrew text. In our Revised Version it stands: " That the tongue of thy dogs may have its portion from thine enemies."

[3] Cic. Quæst. Acad. Lib. i.

[4] That is, The Preface of Rufinus to his Translation of the Περὶ Ἀρχῶν (p. 427-8).

formed; but most of all those in which kindness has been restored after some disagreement. In the case of friendships which have never been shaken, if some attention has not been paid, the excuse of forgetfulness, or at the worst of neglect is readily accepted; but after a return to friendship, if anything is done to cause offence, it is imputed not to neglect but to an unfriendly intention, it is no longer a question of thoughtlessness but of breach of faith." So Horace writes in his Epistle to Florus

[1] "Kindness, ill-knit, cleaves not but flies apart."

2. What good does it do me that he declares on his oath that it was through simplicity that he went wrong? His praises are, as you know, cast in my teeth, and the laudation of this most simple friend (which however has not much either of simplicity or of sincerity in it) is imputed to me as a crime. If he was seeking a foundation of authority for what he was doing, and wishing to shew who had gone before him in this path he had at hand the Confessor Hilary, who translated the books of Origen upon Job and the Psalms consisting of forty thousand lines. He had Ambrose whose works are, almost all of them, full of what Origen has written; and the martyr Victorinus, who acts really with 'simplicity,' and without setting snares for others. As to all these he keeps silence; he does not notice those who are like pillars of the church; but me, who am but like a flea and a man of no account, he hunts out from corner to corner. Perhaps the same simplicity which made him unconscious that he was attacking his friend will make him swear that he knew nothing of these writers. But who will believe that he does not know these men whose memory is quite recent, even though they were Latins, being as he is such a very learned man, and one who has so great a knowledge of the old writers, especially the Greeks, that, in his zeal for foreign knowledge he has almost lost his own language?[2] The truth is it is not so much that I have been praised by him as that those writers have not been attacked. But whether what he has written is praise (as he tries to make simpletons believe) or an attack, (as I feel it to be from the pain which his wounds give me), he has taken care that I should have none of my contemporaries to bring me honor by a partnership in praise, nor consolation by a partnership in vituperation.

3. I have in my hands your letter,[1] in which you tell me that I have been accused, and expect me to reply to my accuser lest silence should be taken as an acknowledgment of his charges. I confess that I sent the reply; but, though I felt hurt, I observed the laws of friendship, and defended myself without accusing my accuser. I put it as if the objections which one friend had raised at Rome were being bruited about by many enemies in all parts of the world, so that every one should think that I was replying to the charges, not to the man. Will you tell me that another course was open to me, that I was bound by the law of friendship to keep silence under accusation, and, though I felt my face, so to say, covered with dirt and bespattered with the filth of heresy, not even to wash it with simple water, for fear that an act of injustice might be imputed to him. This demand is not such as any man ought to make or such as any man ought to accept. You openly assail your friend, and set out charges against him under the mask of an admirer; and he is not even to be allowed to prove himself a catholic, or to reply that the supposed heresy on which this laudation is grounded arises not from any agreement with a heresy, but from admiration of a great genius. He thought it desirable to translate this book into Latin; or, as he prefers to have it thought he was compelled, though unwilling, to do it. But what need was there for him to bring me into the question, when I was in retirement, and separated from him by vast intervals of land and sea? Why need he expose me to the ill-will of the multitude, and do more harm to me by his praise than good to himself by putting me forward as his example? Now also, since I have repudiated his praise, and, by erasing what he had written, have shewn that I am not what my friend declared, I am told that he is in a fury, and has composed three books against me full of graceful Attic raillery, making those very things the object of attack which he had praised before, and turning into a ground of accusation against me the impious doctrines of Origen; although in that Preface in which he so lauded me, he says of me: "I shall follow the rules of translation laid down by my predecessors, and particularly those acted on by the writer whom I have just mentioned. He has rendered into Latin more than seventy of Origen's homiletical treatises, and a few also of his commentaries on the Apostle; and in

---

[1] Hor. Ep. B. i, Ep. iii, 32.
[2] See Ruf. Apol. i, 11. "I had grown dull in my Latinity through the disuse of nearly 30 years."

[1] Jerome Letter lxxxiii Pammachius to Jerome: "Refute your accuser; else, if you do not speak out, you will appear to consent."

these, wherever the Greek text presents a stumbling block, he has smoothed it down in his version and has so emended the language used that a Latin writer can find no word that is at variance with our faith. In his steps, therefore, I propose to walk, if not displaying the same vigorous eloquence, at least observing the same rules."

4. These words are his own, he cannot deny them. The very elegance of the style and the laboured mode of speech, and, surpassing all these, the Christian ' simplicity' which here appears, reveal the character of their author. But there is a different phase of the matter: Eusebius, it seems, has depraved these books; and now my friend who accuses Origen, and who is so careful of my reputation, declares that both Eusebius and I have gone wrong together, and then that we have held correct opinions together, and that in one and the same work. But he cannot now be my enemy and call me a heretic, when a moment before he has said that his belief was not dissonant from mine. Then, I must ask him what is the meaning of his balanced and doubtful way of speaking: " The Latin reader," he says, " will find nothing here discordant from our faith." What faith is this which he calls his? Is it the faith by which the Roman Church is distinguished? or is it the faith which is contained in the works of Origen? If he answers " the Roman," then we are the Catholics, since we have adopted none of Origen's errors in our translations. But if Origen's blasphemy is his faith, then, though he tries to fix on me the charge of inconsistency, he proves himself to be a heretic. If the man who praises me is orthodox, he takes me, by his own confession as a sharer in his orthodoxy. If he is heterodox, he shews that he had praised me before my explanation because he thought me a sharer in his error. However, it will be time enough to reply to these books of his which whisper in corners and made their venomous attacks in secret, when they are published and come out from their dark places into the light, and when they have been able to reach me either through the zeal of my friends or the imprudence of my adversaries. We need not be much afraid of attacks which their author fears to publish and allows only his confederates to read. Then and not till then will I either acknowledge the justice of his charges, or refute them, or retort upon the accuser the accusations he has made: and will shew that my silence has been the result not of a bad conscience but of forbearance.

5. In the meantime, I desired to free myself from suspicion in the implicit judgment of the reader, and to refute the gravest of the charges in the eyes of my friends. I did not wish it to appear that I had been the first to strike, seeing that I have not, even when wounded, aimed a blow against my assailant, but have only sought to heal my own wound. I beg the reader to let the blame rest on him who struck the first blow, without respect of persons. He is not content with striking; but, as if he were dealing with a man whom he had reduced to silence and who would never speak again, he has written three elaborate books and has made out from my works a list of " Contradictions "[1] worthy of Marcion. Our minds are all on fire to know at once what his doctrine is and what is this madness of mine which we had not expected. Perhaps he has learnt (though the time for it has been short) all that is necessary to make him my teacher, and a sudden flow of eloquence will reveal what no one imagined that he knew.

[2] " Grant it, O Father; mighty Jesus, grant.
Let him begin the engagement hand to hand."

Though he may brandish the spear of his accusations and hurl them against us with all his might, we trust in the Lord our Saviour that his truth will encompass us as with a shield, and we shall be able to sing with the Psalmist : [3] " Their blows have become as the arrows of the little ones," and [4] " Though an host should encamp against me, my heart shall not fear; though war should rise against me, even then will I be confident." But of this at another time. Let us now return to the point where we began.

6. His followers object to me, (and

[5] " Weary of work
They ply the arms of Ceres,")

that I have translated into the Latin tongue the books of Origen Περὶ Ἀρχῶν, which are pernicious and repugnant to the faith of the Church. My answer to them is brief and succinct: " Your letters, my brother Pammachius, and those of your friends, have compelled me. You declared that these books had been falsely translated by another, and that not a few things had been inter-

---

1 Ἀντιθέσεις. Marcion, a Gnostic of the second century drew out a list of Contradictions between the Law (which he rejected) and the Gospel.
2 This is altered from Virg. Æn. x, 875.
  " Sic Pater ille Deum faciat, sic altus Apollo,
   Incipias conferre manum."
3 Supposed to be a version of Ps. lxiv, 8.
4 Ps. xxvii, 3, 4.
5 Æn: i, 177.
					Cerealiaque arma
				Expediunt, fessi rerum.

polated or added or altered. And, lest your letters should fail to carry conviction, you sent a copy of this translation, together with the Preface in which I was praised. As soon as I had run my eye over these documents, I at once noticed that the impious doctrine enunciated by Origen about the Father, the Son and the Holy Spirit, to which the ears of Romans could not bear to listen, had been changed by the translator so as to give a more orthodox meaning. His other doctrines, on the fall of the angels, the lapse of human souls, his prevarications about the resurrection, his ideas about the world, or rather Epicurus's middle-spaces,[1] on the restitution of all to a state of equality, and others much worse than these, which it would take too long to recount, I found that he had either translated as they stood in the Greek, or had stated them in a stronger and exaggerated manner in words taken from the books of Didymus, who is the most open champion of Origen. The effect of all this is that the reader, finding that the book expressed the catholic doctrine on the Trinity, would take in these heretical views without warning.

7. One who was not his friend would probably say to him: Either change everything which is bad, or else make known everything which you think thoroughly good. If for the sake of simple Christians you cut out everything which is pernicious, and do not choose to put into a foreign language the things that you say have been added by heretics; tell us everything which is pernicious. But, if you mean to make a veracious and faithful translation, why do you change some things and leave others untouched? You make an open profession in the prologue that you have amended what is bad and have left all that is best: and therefore, if anything in the work is proved to be heretical, you cannot enjoy the license given to a translator but must accept the authority of a writer: and you will be openly convicted of the criminal intent of besmearing with honey the poisoned cup so that the sweetness which meets the sense may hide the deadly venom. These things, and things much harder than these, an enemy would say; and he would draw you before the tribunal of the church, not as the translator of a bad work but as one who assents to its doctrines. But I am satisfied with having simply defended myself. I expressed in Latin just what I found in the Greek text of the books Περὶ Ἀρχῶν, not wishing the reader to believe what was in my translation, but wishing him not to believe what was in yours. I looked for a double advantage as the result of my work, first to unveil the heresy of the author and secondly to convict the untrustworthiness of the translator. And, that no one might think that I assented to the doctrine which I had translated, I asserted in the Preface how I had been compelled to make this version and pointed out what the reader ought not to believe. The first translation makes for the glory of the author, the second for his shame. The one summons the reader to believe its doctrines, the other moves him to disbelieve them. In that I am claimed against my will as praising the author; in this I not only do not praise him, but am compelled to accuse the man who does praise him. The same task has been accomplished by each, but with a different intention: the same journey has had two different issues. Our friend has taken away words which existed, alleging that the books had been depraved by heretics: and he has put in those which did not exist, alleging that the assertions had been made by the author in other places; but of this he will never convince us unless he can point out the actual places whence he says that he has taken them. My endeavour was to change nothing from what was actually there; for my object in translating the work was to expose the false doctrines which I translated. Do you look upon me as merely a translator? I was more. I turned informer. I informed against a heretic, to clear the church of heresy. The reasons which led me formerly to praise Origen in certain particulars are set forth in the treatise prefixed to this work. The sole cause which led to my translation is now before the reader. No one has a right to charge me with the author's impiety, for I did it with a pious intention, that of betraying the impiety which had been commended as piety to the churches.

8. I had given Latin versions, as my friend tauntingly says, of seventy books of Origen, and of some parts of his Tomes, but no question was ever raised about my work; no commotion was felt on the subject in Rome. What need was there to commit to the ears of the Latins what Greece denounces and the whole world blames? I, though translating many of Origen's work in the course of many years, never created a scandal: but you, though unknown before, have by your first and only work become notorious for your rash proceeding. Your Preface tells us that you have also translated the work of Pamphilus the martyr in defence

---

[1] *Intermundia.* Spaces between the worlds, in which, according to Epicurus, the Gods reside.

of Origen; and you strive with all your might to prevent the church from condemning a man whose faith the martyr attests. The real fact is [1]that Eusebius Bishop of Cæsarea, as I have already said before, who was in his day the standard bearer of the Arian faction, wrote a large and elaborate work in six books in defence of Origen, showing by many testimonies that Origen was in his sense a catholic, that is, in our sense, an Arian. The first of these six books you have translated and assigned it to the martyr. I must not wonder, therefore, that you wish to make me, a small man and of no account, appear as an admirer of Origen, when you bring the same calumny against the martyr. You change a few statements about the Son of God and the holy Spirit, which you knew would offend the Romans, and let the rest go unchanged from beginning to end; you did, in fact, in the case of this Apology of Pamphilus as you call it, just what you did in the translation of Origen's Περὶ Ἀρχῶν. If that book is Pamphilus's, which of the six books is Eusebius's first? In the very volume which you pretend to be Pamphilus's, mention is made of the later books. Also, in the second and following books, Eusebius says that he had said such and such things in the first book and excuses himself for repeating them. If the whole work is Pamphilus's, why do you not translate the remaining books? If it is the work of the other, why do you change the name? You cannot answer; but the facts make answer of themselves: You thought that men would believe the martyr, though they would have turned in abhorrence from the chief of the Arians.

9. Am I to say plainly what your intention was, my most simple-minded friend? Do you think that we can believe that you unwittingly gave the name of the martyr to the book of a man who was a heretic, and thus made the ignorant, through their trust in Christ's witness, become the defenders of Origen? Considering the erudition for which you are renowned, for which you[2] are praised throughout the West as an illustrious litterateur,[2] so that the men of your party all speak of you as their Coryphæus, I will not suppose that you are ignorant of Eusebius' [3] Catalogue, which states the fact that the martyr Pamphilus never wrote a single

book.[1] Eusebius himself, the lover and companion of Pamphilus, and the herald of his praises, wrote three books in elegant language containing the life of Pamphilus. In these he extols other traits of his character with extraordinary encomiums, and praises to the sky his humility; but on his literary interests he writes as follows in the third book: "What lover of books was there who did not find a friend in Pamphilus? If he knew of any of them being in want of the necessaries of life, he helped them to the full extent of his power. He would not only lend them copies of the Holy Scriptures to read, but would give them most readily, and that not only to men, but to women also if he saw that they were given to reading. He therefore kept a store of manuscripts, so that he might be able to give them to those who wished for them whenever occasion demanded. He himself however, wrote nothing whatever of his own, except private letters which he sent to his friends, so humble was his estimate of himself. But the treatises of the old writers he studied with the greatest diligence, and was constantly occupied in meditation upon them."

10. The champion of Origen, you see, the encomiast of Pamphilus, declares that Pamphilus wrote nothing whatever, that he composed no single treatise of his own. And you cannot take refuge in the hypothesis that Pamphilus wrote this book after Eusebius's publication, since Eusebius wrote after Pamphilus had attained the crown of martyrdom. What then can you now do? The consciences of a great many persons have been wounded by the book which you have published under the name of the martyr; they give no heed to the authority of the bishops who condemn Origen, since they think that a martyr has praised him. Of what use are the letters of the bishop Theophilus or of the pope Anastasius, who follow out the heretic in every part of the world, when your book passing under the name of Pamphilus is there to oppose their letters, and the testimony of the martyr can be set against the authority of the Bishops? I think you had better do with this mistitled[2] volume what you did with the books Περὶ Ἀρχῶν. Take my advice as a friend, and do not be distrustful of the power of your art; say either that you never wrote it, or else

---

[1] See this question fully argued out by Lightfoot in the Dict. of Christian Biography, Art. Eusebius of Cæsarea. He says: "The Defence of Origen was the joint work of Pamphilus and Eusebius:" and "Jerome's treatment of this matter is a painful exhibition of disingenuousness, &c." See De V. Ill. lxxv.   [2] Συγγραφεύς.
[3] Συντίχμα. No work of Eusebius appears to have borne this title. The work alluded to is either the *Life of Pamphilus* or the Book *On the Martyrs of Palestine.*

[1] "The existence of a work which consisted mainly of extracts from Origen with Comments, and of which he was only the joint author, is quite reconcilable with this statement. Indeed, the very form of the expression in the original, corresponding to '*ipse quidem*' '*proprii*' was probably chosen so as to exclude this work of compilation and partnership." Lightfoot, Art. Eusebius of Cæsarea, in Dict. of Christian Biography.
[2] Ψευδεπιγράφῳ.

that it has been depraved by the presbyter Eusebius.[1] It will be impossible to prove against you that the book was translated by you. Your handwriting is not forthcoming to shew it; your eloquence is not so great as that no one can imitate your style. Or, in the last resort, if the matter comes to the proof, and your effrontery is overborne by the multitude of testimonies, sing a palinode after the manner of Stesichnus. It is better that you should repent of what you have done than that a martyr should remain under calumny, and those who have been deceived under error. And you need not feel ashamed of changing your opinion; you are not of such fame or authority as to feel disgraced by the confession of an error. Take me for your example, whom you love so much, and without whom you can neither live nor die, and say what I said when you had praised me and I defended myself.

11. Eusebius the Bishop of Cæsarea, of whom I have made mention above, in the sixth book of his Apology for Origen makes the same complaint against Methodius the bishop and martyr, which you make against me in your praises of me. He says: How could Methodius dare to write now against Origen, after having said this thing and that of his doctrines? This is not the place in which to speak of the martyr; one cannot discuss every thing in all places alike. Let it suffice for the present to mention that one who was an Arian complains of the same things in a most eminent and eloquent man, and a martyr, which you first make a subject of praise as a friend and afterwards, when offended turn into an accusation. I have given you an opportunity of constructing a calumny against me if you choose, in the present passage. " How is it," you may ask, " that I now depreciate Eusebius, after having in other places praised him?" The name Eusebius indeed is different from Origen; but the ground of complaint is in both cases identical. I praised Eusebius for his Ecclesiastical History, for his Chronicle, for his description of the holy land; and these works[2] of his I gave to the men of the same language as myself by translating them into Latin. Am I to be called an Arian because Eusebius, the author of those books, is an Arian? If you should dare to call me a heretic, call to mind your Preface to the Περὶ Ἀρχῶν, in which you bear me witness that I am of the same faith with yourself: and I at the same time

entreat you to hear patiently the expostulation of one who was formerly your friend. You enter into a warm dispute with others, and bandy mutual reproaches with men of your own order; whether you are right or wrong in this is for you to say. But as against a brother even a true accusation is repugnant to me. I do not say this to blame others; I only say that I would not myself do it. We are separated from one another by a vast interval of space. What sin had I committed against you? What is my offence? Is it that I answered that I was not an Origenist? Are you to be held to be accused because I defend myself? If you say you are not an Origenist and have never been one, I believe your solemn affirmation of this: if you once were one, I accept your repentance. Why do you complain if I am what you say that you are? Or is my offence this that I dared to translate the Περὶ Ἀρχῶν after you had done it, and that my translation is supposed to detract from your work? But what was I to do? Your laudation of me, or accusation against me, was sent to me. Your 'praise' was so strong and so long that, if I had acquiesced in it, every one would have thought me a heretic. Look at what is said in the end of the letter which I received from Rome: [1] " Clear yourself from the suspicions which men have imbibed against you, and convict your accuser of speaking falsely; for if you leave him unnoticed, you will be held to assent to his charges." When I was pressed by such conditions, I determined to translate these books, and I ask your attention to the answer which I made. It was this: [2] " This is the position which my friends have made for me, (observe that I did not say ' my friend,' for fear of seeming to aim at you) ; if I keep silence I am to be accounted guilty: if I answer, I am accounted an enemy. Both these conditions are hard; but of the two I will choose the easier: for a quarrel can be healed, but blasphemy admits of no forgiveness." You observe that I felt this as a burden laid upon me; that I was unwilling and recalcitrating; that I could only quiet my presentiment of the quarrel which would ensue from this undertaking by the plea of necessity. If you had translated the books Περὶ Ἀρχῶν without alluding to me, you would have a right to complain that I had afterwards translated them to your prejudice. But now you have no right to complain, since my work was only an answer to the attack you had made on me under the guise

---

[1] Eusebius of Cremona, Jerome's friend, whom Rufinus accused of stealing and publishing his MSS.
[2] Jerome translated the Chronicle and the Description of the Holy Land, but not this History. This was done later by Rufinus.

---

[1] Jerome Letter lxxxiii. [2] Letter lxxxiv. 12.

of praise; for what you call praise all understand as accusation. Let it be understood between us that you accused me, and then you will not be indignant at my having replied. But now suppose that you wrote with a good intention, that you were not merely innocent but a most faithful friend, out of whose mouth no untruth ever proceeded, and that it was quite unconsciously that you wounded me. What is that to me who felt the wound? Am I not to take remedies for my wound because you inflicted it without evil intention? I am stricken down and stricken through, with a wound in the breast which will not be appeased; my limbs which were white before are stained with gore; and you say to me: "Pray leave your wound untouched, for fear that I may be thought to have wounded you." And yet the translation in question is a reproof to Origen rather than to you. You altered for the better the passages which you considered to have been put in by the heretics. I brought to light what the whole Greek world with one voice attributes to him. Which of our two views is the truer it is not for me nor for you to judge; let each of them be touched by the censor's rod of the reader. The whole of that letter in which I make answer for myself is directed against the heretics and against my accusers. How does it touch you who profess to be both an orthodox person and my admirer, if I am a little too sharp upon heretics, and expose their tricks before the public? You should rejoice in my invectives: otherwise, if you are vexed at them, you may be thought to be yourself a heretic. When anything is written against some particular vice, but without the mention of any name, if a man grows angry he accuses himself. It would have been the part of a wise man, even if he felt hurt, to dissemble his consciousness of wrong, and by the serenity of his countenance to dissipate the cloud that lay upon his heart.

12. Otherwise, if everything which goes against Origen and his followers is supposed to be said by me against you, we must suppose that the letters of the popes Theophilus and Epiphanius and the rest of the bishops which at their desire I lately translated[1] are meant to attack you and tear you to pieces; we must suppose too that the rescripts of the Emperors which order that the Origenists should be banished from Alexandria and from Egypt have been written at my dictation. The abhorrence shown by the Pontiff of the city of Rome against these men was nothing but a scheme of mine. The out-

burst of hatred which immediately after your translation blazed up through the whole world against Origen who before had been read without prejudice was the work of my pen. If I have got all this power, I wonder that you are not afraid of me. But I really acted with extreme moderation. In my public letter[1] I took every precaution to prevent your supposing that anything in it was directed against you; but I wrote at the same time a short letter[2] to you, expostulating with you on the subject of your ' praises.' This letter my friends did not think it right to send you, because you were not at Rome, and because, as they tell me, you and your companions were scattering accusations of things unworthy of the Christian profession about my manner of life. But I have subjoined a copy of it to this book, so that you may understand what pain you gave me and with what brotherly self-restraint I bore it.

13. I am told, further, that you touch with some critical sharpness upon some points of my letter, and, with the well-known wrinkles rising on your forehead and your eyebrows knitted, make sport of me with a wit worthy of Plautus, for having said that I had a Jew named Barabbas for my teacher. I do not wonder at your writing Barabbas for Barañina, the letters of the names being somewhat similar, when you allow yourself such a license in changing the names themselves, as to turn Eusebius into Pamphilus, and a heretic into a martyr. One must be cautious of such a man as you, and give you a wide berth; otherwise I may find my own name turned in a trice, and without my knowing it, from Jerome to Sardanapalus. Listen, then, O pillar of wisdom, and type of Catonian severity. I never spoke of him as my master; I merely wished to illustrate my method of studying the Holy Scriptures by saying that I had read Origen just in the same way as I had taken lessons from this Jew. Did I do you an injury because I attended the lectures of Apollinarius and Didymus rather than yours? Was there anything to prevent my naming in my letter that most eloquent man Gregory?[3] Which of all the Latins is his equal? I may well glory and exult in him. But I only mentioned those who were subject to censure, so as to show that I only read Origen as I had listened to them, that is, not on account of his soundness in the faith but on account of the excellence of his learning. Origen himself, and Clement and Eusebius, and

[1] Ep. lxxxiv to Pammachius and Oceanus.   [2] Letter lxxxi.
[3] Nazianzen, to whose instructions Jerome attached himself at Constantinople in 381.

many others, when they are discussing script-ural points, and wish to have Jewish author-ity for what they say, write : " A Hebrew stated this to me," or " I heard from a Hebrew," or, " That is the opinion of the Hebrews." Origen certainly speaks of the Patriarch Huillus who was his contemporary, and in the conclusion of his thirtieth Tome on Isaiah (that in the end of which he explains the words [1] " Woe to Ariel which David took by storm ") uses his exposition of the words, and confesses that he had adopted through his teaching a truer opinion than that which he had previously held. He also takes as written by Moses not only the eighty-ninth Psalm [2] which is entitled "A prayer of Moses the Man of God," but also the eleven following Psalms which have no title ac-cording to Huillus's opinion ; and he makes no scruple of inserting in his commentaries on the Hebrew Scriptures the views of the Hebrew teachers.

14. It is said that on a recent occasion, where the letters of Theophilus exposing the errors of Origen were read, our friend stopped his ears, and along with all present pro-nounced a distinct condemnation upon the author of so much evil ; and that he said that up to that moment he had never known that Origen had written anything so wrong. I say nothing against this : I do not make the observation which perhaps another might make, that it was impossible for him to be ignorant of that which he had himself trans-lated, and an apology for which by a heretic he had published under the name of a martyr, whose defence also he had undertaken in his own book ; as to which I shall have some ad-verse remarks to make later on if I have time to write them. I only make one ob-servation which does not admit of contradic-tion. If it is possible that he should have misunderstood what he translated, why is it not possible that I should have been ignorant of the book Περὶ Ἀρχῶν which I had not be-fore read, and that I should have only read those Homilies which I translated, and in which he himself testifies that there is noth-ing wrong ? But if, contrary to his expressed opinion, he now finds fault with me for those things for which he before had given me praise, he will be in a strait between two ; either he praised me, believing me to be a heretic but confessing that he shared my opinion ; or else, if he praised me before as orthodox, his present accusations come to nothing, and are due to sheer malice. But perhaps it was only as my friend that he for-merly was silent about my errors, and now that he is angry with me brings to light what he had concealed.

15. This abandonment of friendship gives no claim to my confidence ; and open enmity brings with it the suspicion of falsehood. Still I will be bold enough to go to meet him, and to ask what heretical doctrine I have ex-pressed, so that I may either, like him, ex-press my regret and swear that I never knew the bad doctrines of Origen, and that his in-fidelity has now for the first time been made known to me by the Pope Theophilus ; or that I may at least prove that my opinions were sound and that he, as his habit is, had not understood them. It is impossible that in my Commentaries on the Ephesians which I hear he makes the ground of his accusa-tion, I should have spoken both rightly and wrongly ; that from the same fountain should have proceeded both sweet water and bitter ; and that whereas throughout the work I con-demned those who believe that souls have been created out of angels, I should suddenly have forgotten myself and have defended the opinion which I condemned before. He can hardly raise an objection to me on the score of folly, since he has proclaimed me in his works as a man of the highest culture and eloquence ; otherwise such silly verbosity as he imputes is the part, one would think, of a pettifogger and a babbler rather than of an eloquent man. What is the point of his written accusations I do not know, for it is only report of them, not the writings, which has reached me ; and, as the Apostle tells us it is a foolish thing to beat the air. How-ever, I must answer in the uncertainty till the certainty reaches me : and I will begin by teaching my rival in my old age a lesson which I learned in youth, that there are many forms of speech, and that, according to the subject matter not only the sentences but the words also of writings vary.

16. For instance, Chrysippus and Antip-ater occupy themselves with thorny ques-tions : Demosthenes and Æschines speak with the voice of thunder against each other ; Lysias and Isocrates have an easy and pleasing style. There is a wonderful differ-ence in these writers, though each of them is perfect in his own line. Again : read the book of Tully *To Herennius;* read his *Rhetoricians;* or, since he tells us that these books fell from his hands in a merely inchoate and unfinished condition, look through his three books *On the orator,* in which he introduces a discussion between Crassus and Antony, the most eloquent orators of that day ; and a fourth book called *The Orator*

---

[1] Is. xxix, 1, " Where David encamped." Rev. Ver.
[2] Ps. xc.

which he wrote to Brutus when already an old man; and you will realize that History, Oratory, Dialogue, Epistolary writing, and Commentaries, have, each of them, their special style. We have to do now with Commentaries. In those which I wrote upon the Ephesians I only followed Origen and Didymus and Apollinarius, (whose doctrines are very different one from another) so far as was consistent with the sincerity of my faith: for what is the function of a Commentary? It is to interpret another man's words, to put into plain language what he has expressed obscurely. Consequently, it enumerates the opinions of many persons, and says, Some interpret the passage in this sense, some in that; the one try to support their opinion and understanding of it by such and such evidence or reasons: so that the wise reader, after reading these different explanations, and having many brought before his mind for acceptance or rejection, may judge which is the truest, and, like a good banker, may reject the money of spurious mintage. Is the commentator to be held responsible for all these different interpretations, and all these mutually contradicting opinions because he puts down the expositions given by many in the single work on which he is commenting? I suppose that when you were a boy you read the commentaries of Asper upon Virgil and Sallust, those of Vulcatius upon Cicero's Orations, of Victorinus upon his Dialogues and upon the Comedies of Terence, and also those of my master Donatus on Virgil, and of others on other writers such as Plautus, Lucretius, Flaccus, Persius and Lucan. Will you find fault with those who have commented on these writers because they have not held to a single explanation, but enumerate their own views and those of others on the same passage?

17. I say nothing of the Greeks, since you boast of your knowledge of them, even to the extent of saying that, in attaching yourself to foreign literature, you have forgotten your own language. I am afraid that, according to the old proverbs, I might be like the pig teaching Minerva, and the man carrying fagots into the wood. I only wonder that, being as you are the Aristarchus[1] of our time, you should have shewn ignorance of these matters which every boy knows. It is, no doubt, from your mind being fixed on the meaning of what you write, but partly also from your being so sharp-sighted for the manufacture of calumnies against me, that

you despise the precepts of Grammarians and orators, that you make no attempt to set straight words which have got transposed when the sentence has become complicated, or to avoid some harsh collocation of consonants, or to escape from a style full of gaps. It would be ridiculous to point to one or two wounds when the whole body is enfeebled and broken. I will not select portions for criticism; it is for him to select any portion which is free from faults. He must have been ignorant even of the Socratic saying: "Know thyself."

To steer the ship the untaught landsman fears;
Th' untrain'd attendant dares not give the sick
The drastic southernwood. The healing drug
The leech alone prescribes. Th' artificer
Alone the tools can wield. But poetry
Train'd or untrain'd we all at random write.[1]

Possibly he will swear that he has never learned to read and write; I can easily believe that without an oath. Or perhaps he will take refuge in what the Apostle says of himself: "Though I be rude in speech, yet not in knowledge." But his reason for saying this is plain. He had been trained in Hebrew learning and brought up at the feet of Gamaliel, whom, though he had attained apostolic rank, he was not ashamed to call his master; and he thought Greek eloquence of no account, or at all events, in his humility, he would not parade his knowledge of it. So that [2] 'his preaching should stand not in the persuasive wisdom of words but in the power of the things signified.' He despised other men's riches since he was rich in his own. Still it was not to an illiterate man who stumbled in every sentence that Festus cried, as he stood before his judgment seat: "Paul thou art beside thyself; much learning doth make thee mad." You who can hardly do more than mutter in Latin, and who rather creep like a tortoise than walk, ought either to write in Greek, so that among those who are ignorant of Greek you may pass for one who knows a foreign tongue; or else, if you attempt to write Latin, you should first have a grammar-master, and flinch from the ferule, and begin again as an old scholar among children to learn the art of speaking. Even if a man is bursting with the wealth of Crœsus and Darius, letters will not follow the money-bag. They are the companions of toil and of labour, the associates of the fasting not of the full-fed, of self-mastery not of self-indulgence.[4] It is

---

[1] A native of Samothrace who died at Cyprus B. C. 157. He was tutor to the children of Ptolemy Philometor, and was renowned as a rhetorician and a critic.

[1] Horace Ep. ii, 1, 114-7.
[2] 1 Cor. ii, 4. "Not in persuasive words of wisdom, but in demonstration of the Spirit and of power." Rev. Ver.
[3] Acts xxvi, 24.
[4] Jerome often accuses Rufinus of self-indulgence. See esp. Letter cxxv, c. 18.

told of Demosthenes that he consumed more oil than wine, and that no workman ever shortened his nights as he did. He for the sake of enunciating the single letter Rho was willing to take a dog as his teacher; and yet you make it a crime in me that I took a man to teach me the Hebrew letters. This is the sort of wisdom which makes men remain unlearned: they do not choose to learn what they do not know. They forget the words of Horace:

Why through false shame do I choose ignorance,
Rather than seek to learn?

That Book of Wisdom also which is read to us as the work of Solomon says: [1] " Into a malicious soul wisdom shall not enter, nor dwell in the body that is subject to sin. For the Holy Spirit of discipline[2] will flee deceit and remove from thoughts which are without understanding." The case is different with those who only wish to be read by the vulgar, and do not care how they may offend the ears of the learned; and they despise the utterance of the poet which brands the forwardness of noisy ignorance.

'Twas you, I think, whose ignorance in the streets
Murder'd the wretched strain with creaking reed.

If you want such things, there are plenty of curly-pated fellows in every school who will sing you snatches of doggrel from Miletus; or you may go to the exhibition of the Bessi[3] and see people shaking with laughter at the Pig's Testament, or at any jesters' entertainment where silly things of this kind are run after. There is not a day but you may see the dressed-up clown in the streets whacking the buttocks of some blockhead, or half-pulling out people's teeth with the scorpion which he twists round for them to bite. We need not wonder if the books of know-nothings find plenty of readers.

18. Our friends take it amiss that I have spoken of the Origenists as confederated together by orgies of false oaths. I named the book in which I had found it written, that is, the sixth book of Origen's Miscellanies, in which he tries to adapt our Christian doctrine to the opinions of Plato. The words of Plato in the third book of the Republic[4] are as follows: " Truth, said Socrates, is to be specially cultivated. If, however, as I was saying just now, falsehood is disgraceful and useless to God, to men it is sometimes useful, if only it is used as a stimulant[5] or a medicine; for no one can doubt that

some such latitude of statement must be allowed to physicians, though it must be taken out of the hands of those who are unskilled. That is quite true, it was replied; and if one admits that any person may do this, it must be the duty of the rulers of states at times to tell lies, either to baffle the enemy or to benefit their country and the citizens. On the other hand to those who do not know how to make a good use of falsehood, the practice should be altogether prohibited." Now take the words of Origen: " When we consider the precept[1] 'Speak truth every man with his neighbour,' we need not ask, Who is my neighbour? but we should weigh well the cautious remarks of the philosopher. He says, that to God falsehood is shameful and useless, but to men it is occasionally useful. We must not suppose that God ever lies, even in the way of economy;[2] only, if the good of the hearer requires it, he speaks in ambiguous language, and reveals what he wills in enigmas, taking care at once that the dignity of truth should be preserved and yet that what would be hurtful if produced nakedly before the crowd should be enveloped in a veil and thus disclosed. But a man on whom necessity imposes the responsibility of lying is bound to use very great care, and to use falsehood as he would a stimulant or a medicine, and strictly to preserve its measure, and not go beyond the bounds observed by Judith in her dealings with Holofernes, whom she overcame by the wisdom with which she dissembled her words. He should act like Esther who changed the purpose of Artaxerxes by having so long concealed the truth as to her race; and still more the patriarch Jacob who, as we read, obtained the blessing of his father by artifice and falsehood. From all this it is evident that if we speak falsely with any other object than that of obtaining by it some great good, we shall be judged as the enemies of him who said, I am the truth." This Origen wrote, and none of us can deny it. And he wrote it in the book which he addressed to the ' perfect,' his own disciples. His teaching is that the master may lie, but the disciple must not. The inference from this is that the man who is a good liar, and without hesitation sets before his brethren any fabrication which rises into his mouth, shows himself to be an excellent teacher.

19. I am told that he also carps at me for the translation I have given of a phrase in the Second Psalm. In the Latin it

---

[1] Wisd. of Sol. i, 4, 5.   [2] *Eruditionis.*
[3] A tribe of Thrace; probably troupes of them came to exhibit in Rome.
[4] p. 389.   [5] *Condimentum,* or seasoning.

[1] Eph. iv, 25.
[2] *Pro Dispensatione.* The word Economy is used in modern discussions on this subject in the sense of dispensing truth partially to those not wholly fit for its full disclosure.

stands: "Learn discipline," in the Hebrew it is written Nescu Bar; and I have given it in my commentary, Adore the Son; and then, when I translated the whole Psalter into the Latin language, as if I had forgotten my previous explanation, I put "Worship purely." No one can deny, of course, that these interpretations are contrary to each other; and we must pardon him for being ignorant of the Hebrew writing when he is so often at a loss even in Latin. Nescu, translated literally, is Kiss. I wished not to give a distasteful rendering, and preferring to follow the sense, gave the word Worship; for those who worship are apt to kiss their hands and to bare their heads, as is to be seen in the case of Job who declares that he has never done either of these things,[1] and says [2] "If I beheld the sun when it shined, or the moon walking in brightness, and my heart rejoiced in secret and I kissed my hand with my mouth, which is a very great iniquity, and a lie to the most high God." The Hebrews, according to the peculiarity of their language use this word Kiss for adoration; and therefore I translated according to the use of those whose language I was dealing with. The word Bar, however, in Hebrew has several meanings. It means Son, as in the words Barjona (son of a dove) Bartholomew (son of Tholomæus), Bartimæus, Barjesus, Barabbas. It also means Wheat, and A sheaf of corn, and Elect and Pure. What sin have I committed, then, when a word is thus uncertain in its meaning, if I have rendered it differently in different places? and if, after taking the sense "Worship the Son" in my Commentary, where there is more freedom of discussion, I said "Worship purely" or "electively" in my version of the Bible itself, so that I should not be thought to translate capriciously or give grounds for cavil on the part of the Jews. This last rendering, moreover, is that of Aquila and Symmachus: and I cannot see that the faith of the church is injured by the reader being shewn in how many different ways a verse is translated by the Jews.

20. Your Origen allows himself to treat of the transmigration of souls, to introduce the belief in an infinite number of worlds, to clothe rational creatures in one body after another, to say that Christ has often suffered, and will often suffer again, it being always profitable to undertake what has once been profitable. You also yourself assume such an authority as to turn a heretic into a martyr, and to invent a heretical falsification of the books of Origen. Why may not I then discuss about words, and in doing the work of a commentator teach the Latins what I learn from the Hebrews? If it were not a long process and one which savours of boasting, I should like even now to shew you how much profit there is in waiting at the doors of great teachers, and in learning an art from a real artificer. If I could do this, you would see what a tangled forest of ambiguous names and words is presented by the Hebrew. It is this which gives such a field for various renderings: for, the sense being uncertain, each man takes the translation which seems to him the most consistent. Why should I take you to any outlandish writers? Go over Aristotle once more and Alexander the commentator on Aristotle; you will recognize from reading these what a plentiful crop of uncertainties exists; and you may then cease to find fault with your friend in reference to things which you have never had brought to your mind even in your dreams.

21. My brother Paulinian tells me that our friend has impugned certain things in my commentary on the Ephesians: some of these criticisms he committed to memory, and has indicated the actual passages impugned. I must not therefore refuse to meet his statements, and I beg the reader, if I am somewhat prolix in the statement and the refutation of his charges, to allow for the necessary conditions of the discussion. I am not accusing another but endeavouring to defend myself and to refute the false accusation of heresy which is thrown in my teeth. On the Epistle to the Ephesians Origen wrote three books. Didymus and Apollinarius also composed works of their own. These I partly translated, partly adapted; my method is described in the following passage of my prologue: "This also I wish to state in my Preface. Origen, you must know, wrote three books upon this Epistle, and I have partly followed him. Apollinarius also and Didymus published certain commentaries on it, from which I have culled some things, though but few; and, as seemed to me right, I put in or took out others; but I have done this in such a way that the careful reader may from the very first see how far the work is due to me, how far to others." Whatever fault there is detected in the exposition given of this Epistle, if I am unable to shew that it exists in the Greek books from which I have stated it to have been translated into Latin, I will acknowledge that the fault is mine

---

[1] To the elements of nature, or the idols.
[2] Job xxxi, 26, 28.

and not another's. However, that I should not be thought to be raising quibbles, and by this artifice of self-excuse to be escaping from boldly meeting him, I will set out the actual passages which are adduced as evidences of my fault.

22. To begin. In the first book I take the words of Paul: [1] "As he hath chosen us before the foundation of the world, that we might be holy and unspotted before him." This I have interpreted as referring not, according to Origen's opinion, to an election of those who had existed in a previous state, but to the foreknowledge of God; and I close the discussion with these words:

"His assertion that we have been chosen before the foundation of the world that we should be holy and without blemish before him, that is, before God, belongs to the foreknowledge of God, to whom all things which are to be are already made, and are known before they come into being. Thus Paul was predestinated in the womb of his mother: and Jeremiah before his birth is sanctified, chosen, confirmed, and, as a type of Christ, sent as a prophet to the Gentiles."

There is no crime surely in this exposition of the passage. Origen explained it in a heterodox sense, but I followed that of the church. And, since it is the duty of a commentator to record the opinions expressed by many others, and I had promised in the Preface that I would do this, I set down Origen's interpretation, though without mentioning his name which excites ill will.

"Another," I said, "who wishes to vindicate the justice of God, and to shew that he does not choose men according to a prejudgment and foreknowledge of his own but according to the deserts of the elect, thinks that before the visible creation of sky, earth, sea and all that is in them, there existed the invisible creation, part of which consisted of souls, which, for certain causes known to God alone, were cast down into this valley of tears, this scene of our affliction and our pilgrimage; and that it is to this that we may apply the Psalmist's prayer, he being in this low condition and longing to return to his former dwelling place: [2] "Woe is me that my sojourn is prolonged; I have inhabited the habitations of Kedar, my soul hath had a long pilgrimage." And also the words of the Apostle: [3] "O wretched man that I am, who shall deliver me from the body of this death?" and [4] "It is better to return and to be with Christ;" and [5] "Before I was brought low, I sinned." He adds much more of the same kind."

Now observe that I said "Another who wishes to vindicate," I did not say "who succeeds in vindicating." But if you find a stumbling block in the fact that I condensed a very long discussion of Origen's into a brief statement so as to give the reader a glimpse

of his meaning; if you declare me to be a secret adherent of his because I have not left out anything which he has said, I would ask you whether it was not necessary for me to do this, so as to avoid your cavils. Would you not otherwise have declared that I had kept silence on matters on which he had spoken boldly, and that in the Greek text his assertions were much stronger than I represented? I therefore put down all that I found in the Greek text, though in a shorter form, so that his disciples should have nothing which they could force upon the ears of the Latins as a new thing; for it is easier for us to make light of things which we know well than of things which take us unprepared. But after I had shewn Origen's interpretations of the passage, I concluded this section with words to which I beg your attention:

"The Apostle does not say 'He chose us before the foundation of the world because we were then holy and without blemish;' but 'He chose us that we might be holy and without blemish,' that is, that we who before were not holy and without blemish might afterwards become such. This expression will apply even to sinners who turn to better things; and thus the words remain true, 'In thy sight shall no man living be justified,' that is, no one in his whole life, in the whole of the time that he has existed in the world. If the passage be thus understood, it makes against the opinion that before the foundation of the world certain souls were elected because of their holiness, and that they had none of the corruption of sinners. It is evident that Paul and those like him were not elected because they were holy and without blemish, but they were elected and predestinated so that in their after life, by means of their works and their virtues, they should become holy and without blemish."

Does any one dare, then, after this statement of my opinion, to accuse me of assent to the heresy of Origen? It is now almost eighteen years since I composed those books, at a time when the name of Origen was highly esteemed in the world, and when as yet his work the Περὶ Ἀρχῶν had not reached the ears of the Latins: and yet I distinctly stated my belief and pointed out what I did not agree with. Hence, even if my opponent could have pointed out anything heretical in other places, I should be held guilty only of the fault of carelessness, not of the perverse doctrines which both in this place and in my other works I have condemned.

23. I will deal shortly with the second passage which my brother tells me has been marked for blame, because the complaint is exceedingly frivolous, and bears on its face its calumnious character. The passage[1] is that in

---

[1] Eph. i, 4.   [3] Rom. vii, 24.   [5] Ps. cxix, 67.
[2] Ps. cxx, 5.   [4] Phil. i, 23.

[1] Eph. i, 20, 21.

which Paul declares that God " made him to sit at his right hand in the heavenly places, far above all rule and authority and power and dominion, and every name that is named, not only in this world but also in that which is to come." After stating various expositions which have been given, I came to the offices of the ministers of God, and spoke of the principalities and powers, the virtues and dominions : and I add :

" They must assuredly have others who are subject to them, who are under their power and serve them, and are fortified by their authority: and this distribution of offices will exist not only in the present world but in the world to come, so that each individual will rise or fall from one step of advancement and honour to another, some ascending and some descending, and will come successively under each of these powers, virtues, principalities, and dominions."

I then went on to describe the various divine offices and ministries after the similitude of the palace of an earthly king, which I fully described ; and I added :

" Can we suppose that God the Lord of lords and King of kings, is content with a single order of servants? We speak of an archangel because there are other angels of whom he is chief: and so there would be nothing said of Principalities, Powers and Dominions unless it were implied that there were others of inferior rank."

But, if he thinks that I became a follower of Origen because I mentioned in my exposition these advancements and honours, these ascents and descents, increasings and diminishings ; I must point out that to say, as Origen does, that Angels and Cherubim and Seraphim are turned into demons and men, is a very different thing from saying that the Angels themselves have various offices allotted to them, — a doctrine which is not repugnant to that of the church. Just as among men there are various degrees of dignity distinguished by the different kinds of work, as the bishop, the presbyter and the other Ecclesiastical grades have each their own order, while yet all are men ; so we may believe that, while they all retain the dignity of Angels, there are various degrees of eminence among them, without imagining that angels are changed into men, and that men are new-made into angels.

24. A third passage with which he finds fault is that in which I gave a threefold interpretation of the Apostle's words : [1] " That in the ages to come he might shew the exceeding riches of his grace in kindness towards us in Christ Jesus." The first was

my own opinion, the second the opposite opinion held by Origen, the third the simple explanation given by Apollinarius. As to the fact that I did not give their names, I must ask for pardon on the ground that it was done through modesty. I did not wish to disparage men whom I was partly following, and whose opinions I was translating into the Latin tongue. But, I said, the diligent reader will at once search into these things and form his own opinion. And I repeated at the end: Another turns to a different sense the words ' That in the ages to come he might shew the exceeding riches of his grace.' " Ah," you will say, " I see that in the character of the diligent reader you have unfolded the opinions of Origen." I confess that I was wrong. I ought to have said not The diligent but The blasphemous reader. If I had anticipated that you would adopt measures of this kind I might have done this, and so have avoided your calumnious speeches. It is, I suppose, a great crime to have called Origen a diligent reader, especially when I had translated seventy books of his and had praised him up to the sky, — for doing which I had to defend myself in a short treatise [1] two years ago in answer to your trumpeting of my praises. In those ' praises ' which you gave me you laid it to my charge that I had spoken of Origen as a teacher of the churches, and now that you speak in the character of an enemy you think that I shall be afraid because you accuse me of calling him a diligent reader. Why, even shopkeepers who are particularly frugal, and slaves who are not wasteful, and the care-takers who made our childhood a burden to us and even thieves when they are particularly clever, we speak of as diligent ; and so the conduct of the unjust steward in the Gospel is spoken of as wise. Moreover [2] " The children of this world are wiser than the children of light," and [3] " The serpent was wiser than all the beasts which the Lord had made on the earth."

25. The fourth ground of his censure is in the beginning of my Second Book, in which I expounded the statement which St. Paul makes " For this cause I Paul, the prisoner of Jesus Christ for you Gentiles." The passage in itself is perfectly plain ; and I give, therefore, only that part of the comment on it which lends itself to malevolent remark :

" The words which describe Paul as the prisoner of Jesus Christ for the Gentiles may be understood of his martyrdom, since it was when he was

---

[1] Eph. ii, 7.

[1] Jerome Letter 84.   [2] Luke xvi, 8.   [3] Gen. iii, 1.

thrown into chains at Rome that he wrote this Epistle, at the same time with those to Philemon and the Colossians and the Philippians, as we have formerly shewn. Certainly we might adopt another sense, namely, that, since we find this body in several places called the chain of the soul, in which it is held as in a close prison, Paul may speak of himself as confined in the chains of the body, and so that he could not return and be with Christ; and that thus he might perfectly fulfil his office of preaching to the Gentiles. Some commentators, however, introduce another idea, namely, that Paul, having been predestinated and consecrated from his mother's womb, and before he was born, to be a preacher to the Gentiles, afterwards took on the chains of the flesh."

Here also, as before, I gave a three fold exposition of the passage : in the first my own view, in the second the one supported by Origen, and the third the opinion of Apollinarius going contrary to his doctrine. Read over the Greek commentaries. If you do not find the fact to be as I state it, I will confess that I was wrong. What is my fault in this passage? The same, I presume, as that to which I made answer before, namely, that I did not name those whose views I quoted. But it was needless at each separate statement of the Apostle to give the names of the writers whose works I had declared in the Preface that I meant to translate. Besides, it is not an absurd way of understanding the passage, to say that the soul is bound in the body until Christ returns and, in the glory of the resurrection, changes our corruptible and mortal body for incorruption and immortality : for it is in this sense that the Apostle uses the expression, "O wretched man that I am; who shall deliver me from the body of this death?" calling it the body of death because it is subject to vices and diseases, to disorders and to death; until it rises with Christ in glory, and, having been nothing but fragile clay before, becomes baked by the heat of the holy Spirit into a jar of solid consistency, thus changing its grade of glory, though not its nature.

26. The fifth passage selected by him for blame is the most important, that in which I explain the statement of the Apostle. [1] "From whom all the body fitly framed and knit together through every juncture of ministration, according to the working in due measure of every several part, maketh the increase of the body unto the building up of itself in love." Here I summed up in a short sentence Origen's exposition which is very long and goes over the same ideas in various words; yet so as to leave

out none of his illustrations or his assertions.. And when I had come to the end, I added :

"And so in the restitution of all things, when Jesus Christ the true physician comes to restore to health the whole body of the Church, which now lies scattered and rent, every one will receive his proper place according to the measure of his faith and his recognition of the Son of God (the word 'recognize' implies that he had formerly known him and afterwards had ceased to know him), and shall then begin to be what he once had been; yet not in such a way as that, as held by another heresy, all should be placed in one rank, and, by a renovating process, all become angels; but that each member, according to its own measure and office shall become perfect : for instance, that the apostate angel shall begin to be that which he was by his creation, and that man who had been cast out of paradise shall be restored again to the cultivation of paradise;" and so on.

27. I wonder that you with your consummate wisdom have not understood my method of exposition. When I say, 'But not in such a way that, as held by another heresy, all should be placed in one rank, that is, all by a reforming process become angels, ' I clearly shew that the things which I put forward for discussion are heretical, and that one heresy differs from the other. Which (do you ask?) are the two heresies? The one is that which says that all reasonable creatures will by a reforming process become angels; the other, that which asserts that in the restitution of the world each thing will become what it was originally created; as for instance that devils will again become angels, and that the souls of men will become such as they were originally formed; that is, by the reforming process will become not angels but that which God originally made them, so that the just and the sinners will be on an equality. Finally, to shew you that it was not my own opinion which I was developing but two heresies which I was comparing with one another, both of which I had found stated in the Greek, I completed my discussion with this ending :

"These things, as I have said before, are more obscure in our tongue because they are put in a metaphorical form in Greek; and in every metaphor, when a translation is made word for word from one language into another, the budding sense of the word is choked as it were with brambles."

If you do not find in the Greek the very thought which I have expressed, I give you leave to treat all that I say as my own.

28. The sixth and last point which I am told that he brings against me (that is if my brother has not left anything unreported) is that, in the interpretation of the Apostle's

---

[1] Eph. iv, 16.

words, [1] "He that loveth his wife loveth himself, for no one ever hated his own flesh, but nourisheth and cherisheth it, even as Christ also the church," after my own simple explanation I propounded the question raised by Origen, speaking his views, though without mentioning his name, and saying:

"I may be met by the objection that the statement of the Apostle is not true when he says that no man hates his own flesh, since those who labour under the jaundice or consumption or cancer or abscesses, prefer death to life, and hate their own bodies;" and my own opinion follows immediately: "The words, therefore, may be more properly taken in a metaphorical sense."

When I say metaphorical, I mean to shew that what is said is not actually the case, but that the truth is shadowed forth through a mist of allegory. However, I will set out the actual words which are found in Origen's third book: "We may say that the soul loves that flesh which is to see the salvation of God, that it nourishes and cherishes it, and trains it by discipline and satisfies it with the bread of heaven, and gives it to drink of the blood of Christ: so that it may become well-liking through wholesome food, and may follow its husband freely, without being weighed down by any weakness. It is by a beautiful image that the soul is said to nourish and cherish the body as Christ nourishes and cherishes the church, since it was he who said to Jerusalem: [2]

"How often would I have gathered thy children together as a hen gathereth her chickens under her wings and thou wouldst not;" and that thus this corruptible may put on incorruption, and that, being poised lightly, as upon wings, may rise more easily into the air. Let us men then cherish our wives, and let our souls cherish our bodies in such a way as that wives may be turned into men and bodies into spirits, and that there may be no difference of sex, but that, as among the angels there is neither male nor female, so we, who are to be like the Angels, may begin to be here what it is promised that we shall be in heaven."

29. The simple explanation of my own opinion in reference to the passage I stated before in these words:

"Taking the simple sense of the words, we have a command, following on the precept of mutual kindness between man and wife, that we should nourish and cherish our wives: that is, that we should supply them with the food and clothing which are necessary."

This is my own understanding of the passage. Consequently, my words imply that all that follows after and might be brought up against me must be understood as spoken not as my own view but that of my opponents. But it might be thought that my resolution of the difficulty of the passage is too short and peremptory, and that it wraps the true sense, according to what has been said above, in the darkness of allegory, so as to bring it down from its true meaning to one less true. I will therefore come nearer to the matter, and ask what there is in the other interpretation with which you need disagree. It is this 'I suppose, that I said that souls should cherish their bodies as men cherish their wives, so that this corruptible may put on incorruption, and that, being lightly poised as upon wings, it may rise more easily into the air. When I say that this corruptible must put on incorruption, I do not change the nature of the body, but give it a higher rank in the scale of being. And so as regards what follows, that, being lightly poised as upon wings, it may more easily rise into the air: He who gets wings, that is, immortality, so that he may fly more lightly up to heaven, does not cease to be what he had been. But you may say, I am staggered by what follows:

"Let us men then cherish our wives, and let our souls cherish our bodies, in such a way as that wives may be turned into men and bodies into spirits, and that there may be no difference of sex, but that, as among the angels there is neither male nor female, so we, who are to be like the angels, may begin to be on earth what it is promised that we shall be in heaven."

You might justly be staggered, if I had not, after what goes before, said "We may begin to be what it is promised that we shall be in heaven." When I say, "We shall begin to be on earth," I do not take away the difference of sex; I only take away lust, and sexual intercourse, as the Apostle does when he says, "The time is short; it remaineth therefore that those who have wives be as though they had none;" and as the Lord implied when, in reply to the question of which of the seven brothers the woman would be the wife, he answered: [1] "Ye err, not knowing the Scriptures nor the power of God; for in the resurrection they shall neither marry nor be given in marriage: but they shall be as the angels of God." And, indeed, when chastity is observed between man and woman, it begins to be true that there is neither male nor female; but, though living in the body, they are being changed into angels, among whom there is neither male nor female.

[1] Eph. v, 28, 29.   [2] Matt. xxiii, 37.   [1] Matt. xxii.

The same is said by the same Apostle in another place: [1] "As many of you as were baptized into Christ did put on Christ. There can be neither Jew nor Greek, there can be neither bond nor free, there can be no male and female : for ye are all one in Christ Jesus."

30. But now, since my pleading has steered its course out of these rough and broken places, and I have refuted the charge of heresy which had been urged against me by looking my accuser freely in the face, I will pass on to the other articles of charge with which he tries to assail me. The first is that I am a scurrilous person, a detractor of every one ; that I am always snarling and biting at my predecessors. I ask him to name a single person whose reputation I have disparaged, or whom, according to an art practised by my opponent, I have galled by pretended praise. But, if I speak against ill-disposed persons, and wound with the point of my pen some Luscius Lanuvinus [2] or an Asinius Pollio of the race of the Cornelii,[3] if I repel the attacks of a man of boastful and curious spirit, and aim all my shafts at a single butt, why does he divide with others the wounds meant for him alone? And why is he so unwise as to shew, by the irritation of his answer to my attack, his consciousness that it is he alone whom the cap fits?

He brings against me the charge of perjury and sacrilege together, because, in a book written for the instruction of one of Christ's virgins, I describe the promise which I once made when I dreamed that I was before the tribunal of the Judge, that I would never again pay attention to secular literature, and that nevertheless I have sometimes made mention of the learning which I then condemned. I think that I have here lighted on the man who, under the name of Sallustianus Calpurnius, and through the letter written to me by the orator Magnus, raised a not very great question. My answer on the general subject is contained in the short treatise which I then wrote to him.[5] But at the present moment I must make answer as to the sacrilege and perjury of my dream. I said that I would thenceforward read no

secular books : it was a promise for the future, not the abolition of my memory of the past. How, you may ask me, can you retain what you have been so long without reading? I must give my answer by recurring to one of these old books : [1]

'Tis much to be inured in tender youth.

But by this mode of denial I criminate myself; for bringing Virgil as my witness I am accused by my own defender. I suppose I must weave a long web of words to prove what each man is conscious of. Which of us does not remember his infancy? I shall make you laugh though you are a man of such extreme gravity ; and you will have at last to do as Crassus did, who, Lucilius tells us, laughed but once in his life, if I recount the memories of my childhood : how I ran about among the offices where the slaves worked ; how I spent the holidays in play ; or how I had to be dragged like a captive from my grandmother's lap to the lessons of my enraged Orbilius.[2] You may still more be astonished if I say that, even now that my head is gray and bald, I often seem in my dreams to be standing, a curly youth, dressed in my toga, to declaim a controversial thesis before the master of rhetoric ; and, when I wake, I congratulate myself on escaping the peril of making a speech. Believe me, our infancy brings back to us many things most accurately. If you had had a literary education, your mind would retain what it was originally imbued with as a wine cask retains its scent. The purple dye on the wool cannot be washed out with water. Even asses and other brutes know the inns they have stopped at before, however long the journey may have been. Are you astonished that I have not forgotten my Latin books when you learnt Greek without a master? I learned the seven forms of Syllogisms in the Elements of logic ; I learned the meaning of an Axiom, or as it might be called in Latin a Determination ; I learned how every sentence must have in it a verb and a noun ; how to heap up the steps of the Sorites,[3] how to detect the clever turns of the Pseudomenos [4] and the frauds of the stock sophisms. I can swear that I never read any of these things after I left school. I suppose that, to escape from having what I learned made into a crime, I must, according to the fables of the poets, go and drink of the river

---

[1] Gal. iii, 27, 28.
[2] A rival of Terence, to whom Jerome often compares Rufinus.
[3] Asinius Pollio was a rival of Cicero. It seems that some detractor of Jerome boasted that he was of the race of the Cornelii. See Comm. on Jonah iv, 6. "A certain Cantherius, of the most ancient race of the Cornelii, or, as he boasts, of the stock of Asinius Pollio, is said to have accused me at Rome long ago for having translated 'ivy' instead of 'gourd.'"
[4] Per oratorem *Magnum* non *magnam* moverat quæstionem.
[5] Jerome, Letter LXX, c. 6. "Perhaps the question (as to Christians reading heathen books) is suggested by one who, for his love of Sallust, might go by the name of Calpurnius Lanarius."

[1] Virg. Geor. ii, 272.
[2] The name of a pedagogue recorded by Horace (Ep. ii, 1, 71), which passed into a general name for boys' tutors.
[3] The "Heap-argument," in which a number of separate arguments converge on the same point.
[4] "The Liar," another logical puzzle.

Lethe. I summon you, who accuse me for my scanty knowledge, and who think yourself a littérateur and a Rabbi, tell me how was it that you dared to write some of the things you have written, and to translate Gregory,[1] that most eloquent man, with a splendour of eloquence like his own? Whence have you obtained that flow of words, that lucidity of statement, that variety of translations, — you who in youth had hardly more than a first taste of rhetoric? I must be very much mistaken if you do not study Cicero in secret. I suspect that, being yourself so cultivated a person, you forbid me under penalties the reading of Cicero, so that you may be left alone among our church writers to boast of your flow of eloquence. I must say, however, that you seem rather to follow the philosophers, for your style is akin to that of the thorny sentences of Cleanthes[2] and the contortions of Chrysippus,[3] not from any art, for of that you say you are ignorant, but from the sympathy of genius. The Stoics claim Logic as their own, a science which you despise as a piece of fatuity; on this side, therefore, you are an Epicurean, and the principle of your eloquence is, not style but matter. For, indeed, what does it matter that no one else understands what you wish to say, when you write for your own friends alone, not for all? I must confess that I myself do not always understand what you write, and think that I am reading [4] Heraclitus; however I do not complain, nor lament for my sluggishness; for the trouble of reading what you write is not more than the trouble you must have in writing it.

31. I might well reply as I have done even if it were a question of a promise made with full consciousness. But this is a new and shameless thing; he throws in my teeth a mere dream. How am I to answer? I have no time for thinking of anything outside my own sphere. I wish that I were not prevented from reading even the Holy Scriptures by the throngs that beset this place, and the gathering of Christians from all parts of the world. Still, when a man makes a dream into a crime, I can quote to him the words of the Prophets, who say that we are not to believe dreams; for even to dream of adultery does not condemn us to hell, and to dream of the crown of martyrdom does not raise us to heaven. Often I have seen myself in dreams dead and placed in the grave: often I have flown over the earth and been carried

as if swimming through the air, over mountains and seas. My accuser might, therefore, demand that I should cease to live, or that I should have wings on my shoulders, because my mind has often been mocked in sleep by vague fancies of this kind. How many people are rich while asleep and wake to find themselves beggars! or are drinking water to cool their thirst, and wake up with their throats parched and burning! You exact from me the fulfilment of a promise given in a dream. I will meet you with a truer and closer question: Have you done all that you promised in your baptism? Have you or I fulfilled all that the profession of a monk demands? I beg you, think whether you are not looking at the mote in my eye through the beam in your own. I say this against my will; it is by sorrow that my reluctant tongue is forced into words. As to you, it is not enough for you to make up charges about my waking deeds, but you must accuse me for my dreams. You have such an interest in my actions that you must discuss what I have said or done in my sleep. I will not dwell on the way in which, in your zeal to speak against me, you have besmirched your own profession, and have done all you can by word and deed for the dishonouring of the whole body of Christians. But I give you fair warning, and will repeat it again and again. You are attacking a creature who has horns: and, if it were not that I lay to heart the words of the Apostle [1] " The evil speakers [2] shall not inherit the kingdom of God," and [3] " By hating one another you have been consumed one of another," I would make you feel what a vast discord you have stirred up after a slight and pretended reconciliation. What advantage is it to you to heap up slanders against me both among friends and strangers? Is it because I am not an Origenist, and do not believe that I sinned in heaven, that I am accused as a sinner upon earth? And was the result of our renewal of friendship to be, that I was not to speak against heretics for fear that my notice of them should be taken for an assault upon you? So long as I did not refuse to be belauded by you, you followed me as a master, you called me friend and brother, and acknowledged me as a catholic in every respect. But when I asked to be spared your praises, and judged myself unworthy to have such a great man for my trumpeter, you immediately ran your pen through what you had written, and began to abuse all that you had praised

---

[1] Nazianzen. See Prolegomena.
[2] Stoic philosopher of Assus in Lydia B. C. 300–240.
[3] Of Cilicia; disciple of Cleanthes, B. C. 280–208.
[4] Born at Ephesus B.C. 503. His philosophy was tinged with melancholy, and his style obscure.

[1] I. Cor. vi, 9. [2] Revilers. Rev. Ver. [3] Gal. v, 15.

before, and to pour forth from the same mouth both sweet and bitter words. I wish you could understand what self-repression I am exerting in not suiting my words to the boiling heat of my breast; and how I pray, like the Psalmist: [1] "Set a watch, O Lord, before my mouth, keep the door of my lips. Incline not my heart to the words of malice;" and, as he says elsewhere: [2] "While the wicked stood before me I was dumb and was humbled and kept silence even from good words;" and again: [3] "I became as a man that heareth not and in whose mouth are no reproofs." But for me the Lord the Avenger will reply, as he says through the Prophet: [4] "Vengeance is mine, I will repay, saith the Lord": and in another place: [5] "Thou satest and spakest against thy brother, and hast slandered thy mother's son. These things hast thou done, and I kept silence; thou thoughtest indeed by that I should be such an one as thyself; but I will reprove thee, and set them before thine eyes;" so that you may see yourself brought in guilty of those things which you falsely lay to another's charge.

32. I am told, to take another point, that one of his followers, Chrysogonus, finds fault with me for having said that in baptism all sins are put away,[6] and, in the case of the man who was twice married, that he had died and risen up a new man in Christ; and further that there were several such persons who were Bishops in the churches. I will make him a short answer. He and his friends have in their hands my letter, for which they take me to task. Let him give an answer to it, let him overthrow its reasoning by reasoning of his own, and prove my writings false by his writings. Why should he knit his brow and draw in and wrinkle up his nostrils, and weigh out his hollow words, and simulate among the common crowd a sanctity which his conduct belies? Let me proclaim my principles once more in his ears: That the old Adam dies completely in the laver of baptism, and a new man rises then with Christ; that the man that is earthly perishes and the man from heaven is raised up. I say this not because I myself have a special interest in this question, through the mercy of Christ; but that I made answer to my brethren when they asked me for my opinion, not intending to prescribe for others what they may think right to believe, nor to overturn their resolution by my opinion. For we who lie hid in our cells do not covet the Bishop's office. We are not like some, who, despising all humility, are eager to buy the episcopate with gold; nor do we wish, with the minds of rebels, to suppress the Pontiff chosen by God;[1] nor do we, by favouring heretics, show that we are heretics ourselves. As for money, we neither have it nor desire to have it. [2] "Having food and clothing, we are therewith content;" and meanwhile we constantly chant the words describing the man who shall ascend to the hill of the Lord: [3] "He that putteth not out his money to usury, nor taketh reward against the innocent; he who doeth these things shall not be moved eternally." We may add that he who does the opposite to these will fall eternally.

Almost every sentence in this last chapter is an insidious allusion to Rufinus. His "wrinkled-up brow" and "turned-up nose," his weighing out his words, his supposed wealth, are all alluded to in other places and especially in the satirical description of him given after his death in Jerome's letter (cxxv. c. 18) to Rusticus.

---

[1] Ps. cxli, 3, 4.   [2] Ps. xxxix, 1, 2.   [3] Ps. xxxviii, 14.
[4] Deut. xxxii, 35.   [5] Ps. l, 20.
[6] The allusion is to Jerome's letter (LXIX) to Oceanus on the case of Carterius a Spanish Bishop, who had been married before his baptism, and, his wife having died, had married again. Oceanus argued that he was to be condemned. Jerome contended in his favour, regarding his first marriage as part of the old life obliterated by baptism.

[1] The allusion is, perhaps, to Rufinus' answer to Pope Anastasius translated in this volume.
[2] I. Tim. vi, 8.   [3] Ps. xxiv, 3; xv, 5.

JEROME'S APOLOGY AGAINST RUFINUS — BOOK II.

SUMMARY OF THE CHAPTERS.

1–3. A criticism on Rufinus' Apology to Anastasius. His excuses for not coming to Rome are absurd. His parents are dead and the journey is easy. No one ever heard before of his being imprisoned or exiled for the faith.

4–8. His confession of faith is unsatisfactory. No one asked him about the Trinity, but about Origen's doctrines of the Resurrection, the origin of souls, and the salvability of Satan. As to the Resurrection and to Satan he is ambiguous. As to souls he professes ignorance.

9. What Latin! The poor souls must be tormented by his barbarisms.

10. It is not permitted to you to be ignorant of such a matter which all the churches know.

11. As to translating the Περὶ Ἀρχῶν, it is not a question, but a charge that you unjustifiably altered the book.

12, 13. Origen asserts Christ to be a creature, and maintains universal restitution. Where has he contradicted this?

14. The question is, as Anastasius says to John of Jerusalem, with what motive you translated the Περὶ Ἀρχῶν.

15. You pretend not to be Origen's defender, but you publish and enlarge the Apology for him and allege the heretics' falsification of his works.

16. Your defence gains no support from Eusebius or Didymus, who, each for his own reason, defend the Περὶ Ἀρχῶν as it stands.

17. If we may allege falsification at every turn we make a chaos of all past literature.

18. The object of Origen's letter, of which he translates only a part, is not to shew the falsification of his writings but to vituperate the Bishops who condemned him.

19. It is only in reference to a particular point in his dispute with Candidus that Origen alleges this falsification. The story of Hilary's being condemned through his writings having been falsified has no foundation.

20. That which you tell about myself in Damasus' council is mere after-dinner gossip.

21–2. The attack on Epiphanius as a plagiarist of Origen is an outrage on the Bishops generally. Origen never wrote 6000 books.

23. I ascertained at the library at Cæsarea that the Apology you quote as Pamphilus' is the work of Eusebius.

24. The letter falsely circulated in Africa as mine, and expressing regret for my translation of the Old Test. from the Hebrew bears the mark of your hand. I have always honoured the Seventy Translators.

25–32. In proof of this, I bring forward the prefaces to my Translation of the Books from Genesis to Isaiah.

33. As to Daniel, it was necessary to point out that Bel and the Dragon, and similar stories were not found in the Hebrew.

34. A vindication of the importance of the Hebrew Text of Scripture.

35. Though the LXX has been of great value, we should be grateful for fresh translations from the original.

1. Thus far I have made answer about my crimes, and indeed in defence of my crimes, which my crafty encomiast formerly urged against me, and which his disciples still constantly press. I have done so not as well as I ought but as I was able, putting a check upon my complaints, for my object has been not so much to accuse others as to defend myself. I will now come to his Apology,[1] by which he strives to justify himself to Anastasius, Bishop of the City of Rome, and, in order to defend himself, constructs a mass of calumnies against me. His love for me is like that which a man who has been carried away by the tempest and nearly drowned in deep water feels for the strong swimmer at whose foot he clutches : he is determined that I shall sink or swim with him.

2. He professes in the first place to be replying to insinuations made at Rome against his orthodoxy, he being a man most fully approved in respect both of divine faith and of charity. He says that he would have wished to come himself, were it not that he had lately returned, after thirty years' absence, to his parents, and that it would have seemed harsh and inhuman to leave them after having been so long in coming to them ; and also if he had not become somewhat less robust through his long and toilsome journey, and too infirm to begin his labours again. As he had not been able to come himself, he had sent his apology as a kind of literary cudgel which the bishop might hold in his hand and drive away the dogs who were raging against him. If he is a man approved for his divine faith and charity by all, and especially by the Bishop to whom he writes ; how is it that at Rome he is assailed and reviled, and that the reports of the attacks upon his reputation grow thicker. Further, what sort of humility is this, that a man speaks of himself as approved for his divine faith and charity? The Apostles prayed, [1]" Lord

---

[1] See this Apology translated above.

[1] Luke xvii, 5, 6.

increase our faith," and received for answer: "If ye had faith as a grain of mustard seed;" and even to Peter it is said: [1] "O thou of little faith, wherefore didst thou doubt?" Why should I speak of charity, which is greater than either faith or hope, and which Paul says he hopes for rather than assumes: without which even the blood shed in martyrdom and the body given up to the flames has no reward to crown it. Yet both of these our friend claims as his own: in such a way, however, that there still remain creatures who bark against him, and who will go on barking unless the illustrious Pontiff drives them away with his stick. But how absurd is this plea which he puts forward, of having returned to his parents after thirty years. Why, he has got neither father nor mother! He left them alive when he was a young man, and, now that he is old, he pines for them when they are dead. But perhaps, he means by "parents," what is meant in the talk of the soldiers and the common people, his kinsfolk and relations; well, he says he does not wish to be thought so harsh and inhuman as to desert them; and therefore he leaves his home [2] and goes to live at Aquileia. That most approved faith of his is in great peril at Rome, and yet he lies on his back, being a bit tired after thirty years, and cannot make that very easy journey in a carriage along that Flaminian Way. He puts forward his lassitude after his long journey, as if he had done nothing but move about for thirty years, or as if, after resting at Aquileia for two years, he was still worn out with the labour of his past travels.

3. I will touch upon the other points, and set down the actual words of his letter:

"Although my faith was proved, at the time of the persecution by the heretics, when I was living in the holy church of Alexandria, by imprisonments and exiles, to which I was subjected because of the faith."

I only wonder that he did not add [3] "The prisoner of Jesus Christ," or "I was delivered from the jaw of the lion," or "I fought with beasts at Alexandria," or "I have finished my course, I have kept the faith. Henceforth there is laid up for me a crown of righteousness." What exiles, what imprisonments are these which he describes? I blush for this open falsehood. As if imprisonment and exile would be inflicted without judicial sentences! I should like to have a list of these imprisonments and of the various provinces to which he tells us that he was forced into exile. Next there appear to have been numerous imprisonments and an infinite number of exiles; so that he might at least name one of them all. Let us have the acts of his confessorship produced, for hitherto we have been in ignorance of them; and so let us have the satisfaction of reciting his deeds with those of the other martyrs of Alexandria, and that he may be able to meet the people who bark against him with the words: [1] "From henceforth let no man trouble me, for I bear in my body the marks of our Lord Jesus Christ."

4. He goes on:

"Still, since there may be some persons, who may wish to prove my faith, or to hear and learn what it is, I will declare that I thus think of the Trinity;"

and so on. At first you said that you entrusted your faith to the Bishop as a stick with which he might fortify himself on your behalf against those barking dogs. Now you speak a little less confidently, "There may be some persons who wish to prove my faith." You begin to hesitate when the barkings which reach your ears are so numerous. I will not stop to discuss the forms of diction which you use, for these you look down upon and condemn: I will answer according to the meaning alone. You are asked about one thing, and you give account for yourself upon another. As to the doctrines of Arius, you contended against them at Alexandria a long time ago, by imprisonment and exile, not with words but with blood. But the question now relates to the heresy of Origen, and the feeling aroused against you on the subject. I should be sorry that you should trouble yourself to cure wounds which are already healed. You confess a Trinity in one Godhead. The whole world now confesses this, and I think that even the devils confess that the Son of God was born of the Virgin Mary, and took upon him the flesh and the soul belonging to human nature. But I must beg you not to think me a contentious man if I examine you a little more strictly. You say that the Son of God took the flesh and soul belonging to human nature. Well then, I would ask you not to be vexed with me but to answer this question. That soul which Jesus took upon him, did it exist before it was born of Mary? Was it created together with the body in that original Virgin nature which was begotten by the Holy Spirit? or,

---

[1] Matt. xiv. 31.
[2] This old home was at Concordia. Jer. Ep. V, 2; comp. with title of Ep. X.
[3] Expressions of St. Paul in Eph. iii, 1; 2 Tim. iv, 17; 1 Cor. xv, 32; 2 Tim. iv, 7.

[1] Gal. vi, 17.

when the body was already formed within the womb, was it made all at once, and sent down from heaven? I wish to know which one of these you choose as your opinion. If it existed before it was born from Mary, then it was not yet the soul of Jesus; and it was employed in some way, and, for a reward of its virtues, it was made his soul. If it arose by traduction,[1] then human souls, which we believe to be eternal, are subject to the same condition as those of the brutes, which perish with the body. But if it is created and sent into the body after the body has been formed, tell us so simply, and free us from anxiety.

5. None of these answers will you give us. You turn to other things, and by your tricks and shew of words prevent us from paying close attention to the question. What! you will say, was not the question about the resurrection of the flesh and the punishment of the devil? True; and therefore I ask for a brief and sincere answer. I raise no question as to your declaration that it is this very flesh in which we live which rises again, without the loss of a single member, and without any part of the body being cut off (for these are your own words). But I want to know whether you hold, what Origen denies, that the bodies rise with the same sex with which they died; and that Mary will still be Mary and John be John; or whether the sexes will be so mixed and confused that there will be neither man nor woman, but something which is both or neither; and also whether you hold that the bodies remain uncorrupt and immortal, and, as you acutely suggest after the Apostle, spiritual bodies forever; and not only the bodies, but the actual flesh, with blood infused into it, and passing by channels through the veins and bones, — such flesh as Thomas touched; or that little by little they are dissolved into nothing, and reduced into the four elements of which they were compounded. This you ought either to confess or deny, and not to say what Origen also says, but insincerely, as if he were playing upon the weakness of fools and children, " without the loss of a single member or the cutting off of any part of the body." Do you suppose that what we feared was that we might rise without noses and ears, that we should find that our genital organs would be cut off or maimed and that a city of eunuchs was built up in the new Jerusalem?

6. Of the devil he thus frames his opinion :

" We affirm also a judgment to come, in which judgment every man is to receive the due meed of his bodily life, according to that which he has done, whether good or evil. And, if in the case of men the reward is according to their works how much more will it be so in the case of the devil who is the universal cause of sin. Of the devil himself our belief is that which is written in the Gospel, namely that both he and all his angels will receive as their portion the eternal fire, and with him those who do his works, that is, who become the accusers of their brethren. If then any one denies that the devil is to be subjected to eternal fires, may he have his part with him in the eternal fire, so that he may know by experience the fact which he now denies."

I will repeat the words one by one. " We affirm also a judgment to come, in which judgment &c." I had determined to say nothing about verbal faults. But, since his disciples admire the eloquence of their master, I will make one or two strictures upon it. He had already said " a future judgment; " but, being a cautious man, he was afraid of saying simply " in which," and therefore wrote " in which judgment; " for fear that, if he had not said " judgment " a second time, we, forgetting what had gone before, might have supplied the word " ass." That which he brings in afterwards " those who become the accusers of their brethren will with him have their portion in the eternal fire," is in a style of equal beauty. Who ever heard of ' possessing ' the flames'? It would be like ' enjoying tortures.' I suppose that, being now a Greek, he had tried to translate himself, and that for the word κληρονομήσουσιν,[2] which can be rendered in Latin by the single word Hæreditabunt, he said Hæreditate potientur [3] supposing it to be something more elaborate and ornate. With such trifles and such improprieties of speech his whole discourse is teeming. But to return to the meaning of his words.

7. To proceed:

" This is a great spear with which the devil is pierced, he, ' who is the universal cause of sin,' if he is to render account of his works, like a man, and ' with his angels possess the inheritance of eternal fires.' This, no doubt, was what was lacking to him, that, having brought mankind into torment, he should himself ' possess the eternal fires ' which he had all the while been longing for."

You seem to me here to speak a little too hardly of the devil, and to assail the accuser of all with false accusations. You say ' he

---

[1] *Ex traduce*, that is, from a layer like that of the vine. This embodies the view that the soul is derived, with the body, from the parent. There is no English word for the process; and since the word Traducianism is used to express the theory, ' Traduction ' is used here to express the process.

[1] *Potiri*, rendered above ' have their portion.'
[2] *Kleronomesousin*, they shall inherit.
[3] They will enjoy the inheritance.

is the universal cause of sin;' and, while you make him the author of all crimes, you free men from fault, and take away the freedom of the will. Our Lord says that [1] 'from our heart come forth evil thoughts, murders, adulteries, fornications, thefts, false witnesses, railings,' and of Judas we read in the Gospel; [2] "After the sop Satan entered into him," that is, because he had before the sop sinned voluntarily, and had not been brought to repentance either by humbling himself or by the forbearance of the Saviour. So also the Apostle says; [3] "Such men I delivered to Satan, that they might be taught not to blaspheme." He delivered to Satan as to a torturer, with a view to their punishment, those who, before they had been delivered to him learned to blaspheme by their own will. David also draws the distinction in a few words between the faults due to his own will and the incentives of vice when he says [4] "Cleanse thou me from my secret faults," and keep back thy servant from alien sins." We read also in Ecclesiastes [5] "If the spirit of a ruler rise up against thee, leave not thy place;" from which we may clearly see that we commit sin if we give opportunity to the power which rises up, and if we fail to hurl down headlong the enemy who is scaling our walls. As to your threatening your brothers, that is, those who accuse you, with eternal fire in company with the devil, it seems to me that you do not so much drag your brethren down as raise the devil up, since he, according to you, is to be punished only with the same fires as Christian men. But you well know, I think, what eternal fires mean according to the ideas of Origen, namely, the sinners' conscience, and the remorse which galls their hearts within. These ideas he thinks are intended in the words of Isaiah: [6] "Their worm shall not die neither shall their fire be quenched." And in the words addressed to Babylon: [7] "Thou hast coals of fire, thou shalt sit upon them, these shall be thy help." So also in the Psalm it is said to the penitent; [8] "What shall be given to thee, or what shall be done more for thee against the false tongue? Sharp arrows of the mighty, with desolating coals;" which means (according to him) that the arrows of God's precepts (concerning which the Prophet says in another place, [9] "I lived in

misery while a thorn pierces me") should wound and strike through the crafty tongue, and make an end of sins in it. He also interprets the place where the Lord testifies saying: [1] "I came to send fire on the earth, and how I wish that it may burn" as meaning " I wish that all may repent, and burn out through the Holy spirit their vices and their sins; for I am he of whom it is written, [2] "Our God is a consuming fire;" it is no great thing then to say this of the devil, since it is prepared also for men." You ought rather to have said, if you wished to avoid the suspicion of believing in the salvation of the devil; [3] "Thou hast become perdition and shalt not be for ever;" and as the Lord speaks to Job concerning the devil, [4] "Behold his hope shall fail him and in the sight of all shall he be cast down. I will not arouse him as one that is cruel, for who can resist my countenance? Who has first given to me that I may return it to him? for all things beneath the heaven are mine. I will not spare him and his words that are powerful and fashioned to turn away wrath." Hence, these things may pass as the work of a plain man. Their bearing is evident enough to those who understand these matters; but to the unlearned they may wear the appearance of innocence.

8. But what follows about the condition of souls can by no means be excused. He says:

"I am next informed that some stir has been made on the question of the nature of the soul. Whether complaints on a matter of this kind ought to be entertained instead of being put aside, you must yourself decide. If, however, you desire to know my opinion upon this subject, I will state it frankly. I have read a great many writers on this question, and I find that they express divers opinions. Some of these whom I have read hold that the soul is infused together with the material body through the channel of the human seed, and of this they give such proofs as they can. I think that this was the opinion of Tertullian or Lactantius among the Latins, perhaps also of a few others. Others assert that God is every day making new souls and infusing them into the bodies which have been framed in the womb; while others again believe that the souls were all made long ago, when God made all things of nothing, and that all that he now does is to send out each soul to be born in its body as it seems good to him. This is the opinion of Origen, and of some others among the Greeks. For myself, I declare in the presence of God that, after reading each of these opinions, I am unable to hold any of them as certain and absolute: the determination of the truth in this question I leave to God and to any to whom it shall please him to reveal it. My profession on this point is, therefore, first, that these several opinions are those which I have found in books, but, secondly, that I as yet remain in ignorance on the subject, except so far as this, that the

---

[1] Matt. xv, 19.   [4] Ps. xix, 12, 13. Vulg.
[2] John xiii, 27.   [5] Eccl. x, 4.
[3] I. Tim. i, 20.   [6] Is. lxvi, 24.
[7] Is. xlvii, 14, 15. " There shall not be a coal to warm at nor fire to sit before it. Thus shall they be unto thee for whom thou hast laboured." A. V. in almost exact agreement with Vulgate. Jerome must have quoted *memoriter* from an older version.
[8] Ps. cxx, 3, 4. Vulg.
[9] Probably a loose reference to Ps. xlii, 9, 10.

[1] Luke xii, 49.   [3] Perhaps from Jer. li, 26.
[2] Deut. iv, 24, Heb. xii, 29. [4] Leviathan, Job xli, 9-12. Vulg.

Church delivers it as an article of faith that God is the creator of souls as well as of bodies."

9. Before I enter upon the subject matter of this passage, I must stand in admiration of words worthy of Theophrastus :

"I am informed, he says, that some stir has been made on the question of the nature of the soul. Whether complaints on a matter of this kind ought to be entertained instead of being put aside, you must yourself decide."

If these questions as to the origin of the soul have been stirred at Rome, what is the meaning of this complaint and murmuring on the question whether they ought to be entertained or not, a question which belongs entirely to the discretion of bishops? But perhaps he thinks that question and complaint mean the same thing, because he finds this form of speech in the Commentaries of Caper. Then he writes: "Some of those whom I have read hold that the soul is infused together with the material body through the channel of the human seed ; and of these they give such proofs as they can." What license have we here in the forms of speech! What mixing of the moods and tenses! [1] "I have read some saying — they confirmed them with what assertions they could." And in what follows: "Others assert that God is every day making new souls and infusing them into the bodies which have been framed in the womb; while others again believe that the souls were all made long ago when God made all things of nothing, and that all that he now does is to send out each soul to be born in its body as seems good to him." Here also we have a most beautiful arrangement. Some, he says, assert this and that ; some declare that the souls were made long ago, that is, when God made all things of nothing, and that He now sends them forth to be born in their own body as it pleases him. He speaks so distastefully and so confusedly that I have more trouble in correcting his mistakes than he in writing them. At the end he says: "I, however, though I have read these things;" and, while the sentence still hangs unfinished, he adds, as if he had brought forward something fresh: "I, however, do not deny that I have both read each of these things, and as yet confess that I am ignorant."

10. Unhappy souls! stricken through with all these barbarisms as with so many lances! I doubt whether they had so much

trouble when, according to the erroneous theory of Origen, they fell from heaven to earth, and were clothed in these gross bodies, as they have now in being knocked about on all sides by these strange words and sentences : not to mention that word of ill omen which says that they are infused through the channel of the human seed. I know that it is not usual in Christian writings to criticise mere faults of style ; but I thought it well to shew by a few examples how rash it is to teach what you are ignorant of, to write what you do not know : so that, when we come to the subject-matter, we may be prepared to find the same amount of wisdom. He sends a letter, which he calls a very strong stick, as a weapon for the Bishop of Rome; and on the very subject about which the dogs are barking at him he professes entire ignorance of the question. If he is ignorant on the subject for which ill-reports are current against him, what need was there for him to send an Apology, which contains no defence of himself, but only a confession of his ignorance? This course is calculated to sow a crop of suspicions, not to calm them. He gives us three opinions about the origin of souls; and his conclusion at the end is: "I do not deny that I have read each of them, and I confess that I still am ignorant." You would suppose him to be Arcesilaus [1] or Carneades [2] who declare that there is no certainty; though he surpasses even them in his cautiousness ; for they were driven by the intolerable ill-will which they aroused among philosophers for taking all truth out of human life, to invent the doctrines of probability, so that by making their probable assertions they might temper their agnosticism; but he merely says that he is uncertain, and does not know which of these opinions is true. If this was all the answer he had to make, what could have induced him to invoke so great a Pontiff as the witness of his lack of theological culture. I presume this is the lassitude about which he tells us that he is exhausted with his thirty-years' journey and cannot come to Rome. There are a great many things of which we are all ignorant; but we do not ask for witnesses of our ignorance. As to the Father, Son and Holy Ghost, as to the nativity of our Lord and Saviour, about which Isaiah cries, [3] "Who shall declare his gen-

---

[1] The words are translated literally here, so as to shew how they lend themselves to Jerome's strictures.

[1] Of Pitane in Æolia, B. C. 316-241. Founder of the Middle Academy, half-way between the Platonic idealism and the scepticism of Pyrrho.
[2] Of Cyrene, B. C. 214-124. Founder of the Third or New Academy, a disputant rather than a philosopher of fixed principles. [3] Is. liii, 8.

eration?" he speaks boldly, and a mystery of which all past ages knew nothing he claims as quite within his knowledge: this alone he does not know, the ignorance of which causes men to stumble. As to how a virgin became the mother of God, he has full knowledge; as to how he himself was born he knows nothing. He confesses that God is the maker of souls and bodies, whether souls existed before bodies or whether they came into being with the germs of bodies, or are sent into them when they are already formed in the womb. In any case we recognize God as their author. The question at issue is not whether the souls were made by God or by another, but which of the three opinions which he states is true. Of this he professes ignorance. Take care! You may find people saying that the reason for your confession of your ignorance of the three is that you do not wish to be compelled to condemn one. You spare Tertullian and Lactantius so as not to condemn Origen with them. As far as I remember (though I may be mistaken) I am not aware of having read that Lactantius spoke of the soul as planted at the same time as the body.[1] But, as you say that you have read it, please to tell me in what book it is to be found, so that you may not be thought to have calumniated him in his death as you have me in my slumber. But even here you walk with a cautious and hesitating step. You say: " I think that, among the Latins, Tertullian or Lactantius held this opinion, perhaps also some others. You not only are in doubt about the origin of souls, but you have only ' thoughts ' as to the opinion which each writer holds: yet the matter is of some importance. On the question of the soul, however, you openly proclaim your ignorance, and confess your untaught condition: as to the authors, your knowledge amounts only to ' thinking,' hardly to ' presuming.' But as to Origen alone you are quite clear. " This is Origen's opinion," you say. But, let me ask you: Is the opinion sound or not? Your reply is, " I do not know." Then why do you send me messengers and letter-carriers, who are constantly coming, merely to teach me that you are ignorant? To prevent the possibility of my doubting whether your incapacity is as great as you say, and thinking it possible that you are cunningly concealing all you know, you take an oath in the presence of God that up to the present moment you hold nothing for certain and definite on

this subject, and that you leave it to God to know what is true, and to any one to whom it may please Him to reveal it. What! Through all these ages does it seem to you that there has been no one worthy of having this revealed to him? Neither patriarch, nor prophet, nor apostle, nor martyr? Were not these mysteries made clear even to yourself when you dwelt amidst princes and exiles? The Lord says in the Gospel: [1] " Father, I have revealed thy name to men." Did he who revealed the Father keep silence on the origin of souls? And are you astonished if your brethren are scandalized when you swear that you know nothing of a thing which the churches of Christ profess to know?[2]

11. After the exposition of his faith, or rather his lack of knowledge, he passes on to another matter, and tries to make excuses for having turned the books Περὶ Ἀρχῶν into Latin. I will put down his words literally:

" I am told that objections have been raised against me because, forsooth, at the request of some of my brethren, I translated certain works of Origen from Greek into Latin. I suppose that every one sees that it is only through ill-will that this is made a matter of blame. For, if there is any offensive statement in the author, why is this to be twisted into a fault of the translator? I was asked to exhibit in Latin what stands written in the Greek text; and I did nothing more than fit Latin words to Greek ideas. If, therefore, there is anything to praise in these ideas, the praise does not belong to me: and similarly as to anything to which blame may attach."

" I hear," he says, " that thence *dispute* has arisen."[3] How clever this is, to speak of it as a dispute, when it is really an accusation against him. " That I have, at the request of my brethren, translated certain things of Origen's into Latin." Yes, but what are these " *certain things* "? Have they no name? Are you silent? Then the bills of charge brought by the accusers will speak for you. " I suppose," he says, " that every one understands that it is only through envy that these things are made matters of blame." What envy? Are people envious of your eloquence? Or have you done what no other man has ever been able to do? Here am I, who have translated many works of Origen's; yet, except you, no one shews envy towards me or calumniates me for it. " If there is any offensive statement in the author, why is it to be twisted into a fault of

---

1 John xvii, 6.
2 Though Jerome here speaks as if the question had been determined by church authority, the perusal of his correspondence with Augustin (Jerome's Letters 126, 131, 134), shows that he was in the same perplexity as Rufinus, but less ingenuous in confessing it.
3 As above, the word for word rendering is given.

the translator? I was asked to exhibit in Latin what stands written in the Greek text; and I did nothing more than fit Latin words to Greek ideas. If, therefore, there is anything to praise in these ideas, the praise does not belong to me, and similarly as to anything to which blame may attach." Can you be astonished that men think ill of you when you say of open blasphemies nothing more than, "If there are any offensive statements in the author"? What is said in those books is offensive to all men; and you stand alone in your doubt and in your complaint that this is " twisted into a fault of the translator," when you have praised it in your Preface. 'You were asked to turn it into Latin as it stood in the Greek text.' I wish you had done what you pretend you were asked. You would not then be the object of any ill will. If you had kept faith as a translator, it would not have been necessary for me to counteract your false translation by my true one. You know in your own conscience what you added, what you subtracted, and what you altered on one side or the other at your discretion; and after this you have the audacity to tell us that what is good or evil is not to be attributed to you but to the author. You shew your sense of the ill will aroused against you by again toning down your words: and as if you were walking with your steps in the air or on the tops of the ears of corn, you say, " *Whether* there is praise or blame in these opinions." You dare not defend him, but you do not choose to condemn him. Choose which of the two you please; the option is yours; if this which you have translated is good, praise it, if bad, condemn it. But he makes excuses, and weaves another artifice, He says:

" I admit that I put something of my own into the work: as I stated in my Preface, I used my own discretion in cutting out not a few passages; but only those as to which I had come to suspect that the thing had not been so stated by Origen himself, and the statement appeared to me in these cases to have been inserted by others, because in other places I had found the author state the same matter in a catholic sense." [1]

What wonderful eloquence! Varied, too, with flowers of the Attic style. " Moreover also!" [2] and " Things which came to me into suspicion!" I marvel that he should have dared to send such literary portents to Rome. One would think that the man's tongue was in fetters, and bound with

cords that cannot be disentangled, so that it could hardly break forth into human speech. However, I will return to the matter in hand.

11 (*a*). I wish to know who gave you permission to cut out a number of passages from the work you were translating? You were asked to turn a Greek book into Latin, not to correct it; to draw out another man's words, not to write a book of your own. You confess, by the fact of pruning away so much, that you did not do what you were asked. And I wish that what you curtailed had all been the bad parts, and that you had not put in many things of your own which go to support what is bad. I will take an example, from which men may judge of the rest. In the first book of the Περὶ Ἀρχῶν where Origen had uttered that impious blasphemy, that the Son does not see the Father, you supply the reasons for this, as if in the name of the writer, and translate the note of Didymus, in which he makes a fruitless effort to defend another man's error, trying to prove that Origen spoke rightly ; but we, poor simple men, like the tame creatures spoken of by Ennius, can understand neither his wisdom nor that of his translator. Your Preface, which you allege in explanation, in which you flatter and praise me so highly shows you to be guilty of the most serious faults of translation. You say that you have cut out many things from the Greek, but you say nothing of what you have put in. Were the parts cut out good or bad? Bad, I suppose. Was what you kept good or bad? Good, I presume; for you could not translate the bad. Then I suppose you cut off what was bad and left what was good? Of course. But what you have translated can be shewn to be almost wholly bad. Whatever therefore in your translation I can shew to be bad, must be laid to your account, since you translated it as being good. It is a strange thing if you are to act like an unjust censor, who is himself guilty of the crime, and are allowed at your will to expel some from the Senate and keep others in it. But you say: " It was impossible to change everything. I only thought I might cut away what had been added by the heretics." Very good. Then if you cut away all that you thought had been added by the heretics, all that you left belongs to the work which you were translating. Answer me then, are these good or bad? You could not translate what was bad, since once for all you had cut away what had been added by the heretics, that is, unless you thought it your duty to cut away the bad parts due to the heretics, while trans-

---

[1] See Rufinus' position vindicated in his treatise on the corruption of Origen's writings, translated in this volume.
[2] *Quin immo etiam,* the first words of the passage. They are literally, " Yes, moreover also."

lating the errors of Origen himself unaltered into Latin. Tell me then, why you turned Origen's heresies into Latin. Was it to expose the author of the evil, or to praise him? If your object is to expose him, why do you praise him in the Preface? If you praise him you are convicted of being a heretic. The only remaining hypothesis is that you published these things as being good. But if they are proved to be bad, then author and translator are involved in the same crime, and the Psalmist's word is fulfilled: [1] "When thou sawest a thief, thou consentedst unto him and hast been partaker with the adulterers." It is needless to make a plain matter doubtful by arguing about it. As to what follows, let him answer whence this suspicion arose in his mind of these additions by heretics. "It was," he says, "because I found the same things treated by this author in other places in a catholic sense."

12. We must consider the fact, which comes first, and so in order reach the inference, which comes after. Now I find among many bad things written by Origen the following most distinctly heretical: that the Son of God is a creature, that the Holy Spirit is a servant: that there are innumerable worlds, succeeding one another in eternal ages: that angels have been turned into human souls; that the soul of the Saviour existed before it was born of Mary, and that it is this soul which "being in the form of God thought it not robbery to be equal with God, but emptied itself and took the form of a servant;"[2] that the resurrection of our bodies will be such that we shall not have the same members, since, when the functions of the members cease they will become superfluous: and that our bodies themselves will grow aërial and spirit-like, and gradually vanish and disperse into thin air and into nothing: that in the restitution of all things, when the fulness of forgiveness will have been reached, Cherubim and Seraphim, Thrones, Principalities, Dominions, Virtues, Powers, Archangels and Angels, the devil, the demons and the souls of men whether Christians Jews or Heathen, will be of one condition and degree; and when they have come to their true form and weight, and the new army of the whole race returning from the exile of the world presents a mass of rational creatures with all their dregs left behind, then will begin a new world from a new origin, and other bodies in which the souls who fall from heaven will be clothed; so that we may have to fear that we who are

now men may afterwards be born women, and one who is now a virgin may chance then to be a prostitute. These things I point out as heresies in the books of Origen. It is for you to point out in which of his books you have found them contradicted.

13. Do not tell me that "you have found the same things treated by the same author in other places in a catholic sense," and thus send me to search through the six thousand books of Origen which you charge the most reverend Bishop Epiphanius with having read; but mention the passages with exactness: nor will this suffice; you must produce the sentences word for word. Origen is no fool, as I well know; he cannot contradict himself. The net result arising from all this calculation is, then, that what you cut out was not due to the heretics, but to Origen himself, and that you translated the bad things he had written because you considered them good; and that both the good and the bad things in the book are to be set to your account, since you approved his writings in the Prologue.

14. The next passage in this apology is as follows:

"I am neither a champion nor a defender of Origen, nor am I the first who has translated his works. Others before me have done the same thing: and I did it, the last of many, at the request of my brethren. If an order is to be given that such translations are not to be made, such an order holds good for the future, not the past: but if those are to be blamed who have made these translations before any such order was given, the blame must begin with those who took the first step."

Here at last he has vomited forth what he wanted to say, and all his inflamed mind has broken out into this malicious accusation against me. When he translates the Περὶ 'Αρχῶν, he declares that he is following me. When he is accused for having done it, he gives me as his example: whether he is in danger or out of danger, he cannot live without me. Let me tell him, therefore, what he professes not to know. No one reproaches you because you translated Origen, otherwise Hilary and Ambrose would be condemned: but because you translated a heretical work, and tried to gain support for it by praising me in the Preface. I myself, whom you criminate, translated seventy homilies of Origen, and parts of his Tomes, in order that by translating his best works I might withdraw the worst from notice: and I also have openly translated the Περὶ 'Αρχῶν to prove the falsity of your translation, so as to shew the reader what to avoid. If you wish to translate Origen into Latin, you have at hand many

---

[1] Ps. l, 18. [2] Phil. ii.

homilies and Tomes of his, in which some topic of morality is handled or some obscure passage of Scripture is opened. Translate these; give these to those who ask them of you. Why should your first labour begin with what is infamous? And why, when you were about to translate a heretical work, did you preface and support it by the supposed book of a martyr, and force upon the ears of Romans a book the translation of which threw the world into panic? At all events, if you translate such a work with the view of exhibiting the author as a heretic, change nothing from the Greek text, and make this clear in the Preface. It is this which the Pope Anastasius most wisely embodies in the letter which he has addressed to the Bishop John against you; he frees me who have done this from all blame, but condemns you who would not do it. You will perhaps deny the existence of this letter; I have therefore subjoined a copy of it; so that, if you will not listen to your brother when he advises, you may listen to the Bishop when he condemns.

15. You say that you are not the defender or the champion of Origen; but I will at once confront you with your own book of which you spoke in that notorious preface to your renowned work in these terms:

"The cause of this diversity I¹ have set forth more fully for you in the Apology which Pamphilus wrote among his treatises, adding a very short document of my own, in which I have shewn by what appear to me evident proofs, that his works have been depraved in many places by heretics and ill-disposed persons, and especially those which I am now translating, the Περὶ 'Αρχῶν."

The defence made by Eusebius, or if you will have it so, by Pamphilus, was not sufficient for you, but you must add something from your superior wisdom and learning to supply what you thought insufficient in what they had said. It would be a long business if I were to insert the whole of your book into the present treatise, and, after setting out each paragraph, to reply to each in turn, and shew what vices there are in the style, what falsehoods in the assertions, what inconsistency in the actual tissue of the language. And therefore, to avoid a redundant discussion which is distasteful to me, I will compress the verbal matter into a narrow compass, and reply to the meaning alone. As soon as he leaves the harbour he runs his ship upon a rock. He recalls the words of the Apology of the Martyr Pamphilus (which however, I have proved to be the work of Eusebius the Chief of the Arians) of which he had said, " I translated it into the Latin

tongue as best I was able and as the matter demanded;" he then adds: "It is this as to which I wish to give you a charge, Macarius, man of desires,¹ that you may feel sure that this rule of faith which I have above set forth out of his books, is such as ought to be embraced and held fast: it is clearly shewn that there is a catholic meaning in them all." Although he took away many things from the book of Eusebius, and tried to alter in a good sense the expressions about the Son and the Holy Spirit, still there are found in it many causes of offence, and even open blasphemies, which our friend cannot refuse to accept since he pronounces them to be catholic. Eusebius (or, if you please, Pamphilus) says in that book that the Son is the Servant of the Father, the Holy Spirit is not of the same substance with the Father and the Son; that the souls of men have fallen from heaven; and, inasmuch as we have been changed from the state of Angels, that in the restitution of all things angels and devils and men will all be equal; and many other things so impious and atrocious that it would be a crime even to repeat them. The champion of Origen and translator of Pamphilus is in a strange position. If there is so much blasphemy in these parts which he has corrected, what sacrilegious things must there be in the parts which, as he pretends, have been falsified by heretics! What makes him hold this opinion, as he says, is that a man who is neither a fool nor a madman could not have said things mutually repugnant; and, that we may not suppose that he had written different things at different times, and that he put forth contrary views according to the time of writing, he has added:

"What are we to say when sometimes in the same place, and, so to speak, almost in the following paragraph, a sentence with an opposite meaning is found inserted? Can we believe that, in the same work and in the same book, and sometimes, as I have said in the sentence immediately following, he can have forgotten his own words? For example, could he who had before said, we can find no passage throughout the Scriptures in which the Holy Spirit is said to be created or made, immediately add that the Holy Spirit was made among the rest of the creatures? or again, could he who defined the Father and the Son to be of one substance, that namely which is called in Greek Homoousion, say in the following portions that he was of another substance, and that he was created, when but a little before he had declared him to be born from the nature of God the Father?"

16. These are his own words, he cannot deny them. Now I do not want to be put off with such expressions as "since he

¹ Taken from Daniel x, 11, "Thou man greatly beloved" ("a man of desires").

said above" but I want to have the name of the book in which he first spoke rightly and then wrongly: in which he first says that the Holy Spirit and the Son are of the substance of God, and in what immediately follows declares that they are creatures. Do you not know that I possess the whole of Origen's works and have read a vast number of them?

> " Your trappings to the mob! I know you well;
> What lies within and on the skin I see." [1]

Eusebius who was a very learned man, (observe I say learned not catholic: you must not, according to your wont make this a ground for calumniating me) takes up six volumes with nothing else but the attempt to shew that Origen is of his way of believing, that is of the Arian perfidy. He brings out many test-passages, and effectually proves his point. In what dream in an Alexandrian prison was the revelation given to you on the strength of which you make out these passages to be falsified which he accepts as true? But possibly he being an Arian, took in these additions of the heretics to support his own error, so that he should not be thought to be the only one who had held false opinions contrary to the Church. What answer will you make, then, as to Didymus, who certainly is catholic as regards the Trinity? You know that I translated his book on the Holy Spirit into Latin. He surely could not have assented to the passages in Origen's works which were added by heretics; yet he wrote some short commentaries on the Περὶ Ἀρχῶν which you have translated; in these he never denies that what is there written was written by Origen, but only tries to persuade us simple people that we do not understand his meaning and how these passages ought to be taken in a good sense. So much on the Son and the Holy Spirit alone. But in reference to the rest of Origen's doctrines, both Eusebius and Didymus adhere to his views, and defend, as said in a catholic and Christian sense, what all the churches reprobate.

17. But let us consider what are the arguments by which he tries to prove that Origen's writings have been corrupted by the heretics.

" Clement," he says, " who was the disciple of the Apostles, and who succeeded the apostles both in the episcopate and in martyrdom, wrote the books which go by the name of Anagnorismus; that is, Recognitions. In these, though, speaking generally, the doctrine which is set forth in the name of the Apostle Peter is genuinely apostolical, yet in certain passages the doctrine of Eunomius

is brought in in such a way as that you would suppose Eunomius himself to be conducting the argument and asserting his view that the Son was created out of nothing."

And, after a passage too long to reproduce, he adds:

" What then are we to think of these facts? Must we believe that an Apostolic man wrote heresy? or is it not more likely that men of perverse mind, wishing to gain support for their own doctrines, and win easier credit for them, introduced under the names of holy men views which they cannot be believed either to have held or to have written down?"

He tells us that Clement the presbyter of Alexandria also, who was a catholic man, writes at times in his works that the Son of God is created; and that Dionysius Bishop of Alexandria, a most learned man, in the four books in which he controverted the doctrines of Sabellius, lapses into the dogma of Arius. What he aims at by quoting these instances is not to shew that Churchmen and catholics have erred, but that their writings have been corrupted by heretics, and he closes the discussion with these words:

" And when we find in Origen a certain diversity of doctrine, just as we have found it in those of whom we have spoken above, will it not be sufficient for us to believe the same in his case which we believe or understand in the case of the catholic men whom we have passed in review? Will not the same defence hold good when the case is the same?"

If, I reply, we admit that everything in a book which is offensive is corruptly inserted by others, nothing will remain belonging to the author under whose name the book passes, but everything can be assigned to those by whom it is supposed to have been corrupted. But then it will not belong to them either, since we do not know who they were: and the result will be that every book belongs to everybody and nothing to any one in particular. In this confusion which this method of defence introduces, it will be impossible to convict Marcion of error, or Manichæus or Arius or Eunomius; because, as soon as we point out a statement of their unbelief, their disciples will answer that that was not what the master wrote, but was corruptly inserted by his opponents. According to this principle, this very book of yours will not be yours nor mine. And as to this very book in which I am making reply to your accusations, whatever you find fault with in it will be held not be written by me but by you who now find fault with it. And further, while you assign everything to the heretics, there

---

will be nothing left which you can assign to churchmen as their own.

But you may ask, How is it then that in their books some false views occur? Well, if I answer that I do not know the parties whence these false views came, I must not be thought to have said that they are heretics. It is possible that they may have fallen into error unawares, or that the words bore a different meaning, or that they may have been gradually corrupted by unskilful copyists. It must be admitted that, before Arius arose in Alexandria as a demon of the south, things were said incautiously which cannot be defended against a malevolent criticism. But when glaring faults are exposed in Origen, you do not defend him but accuse others; you do not deny the faults, but summon up a host of criminals. If you were asked to name those who have been the companions of Origen in his heresies, it would be right enough to call in these others. But what you are now asked to tell us is whether those statements in the books of Origen are good or evil; and you say nothing, but bring in irrelevant matters, such as: This is what Clement says; ❧this is an error of which Dionysius is found guilty; these are the words in which the bishop Athanasius defends the error of Dionysius; in a similar way the writings of the Apostle have been tampered with: and then, while the charge of heresy is fastened upon you, you say nothing in your own defence, but make confessions about me. I make no accusations, and am content with answering for myself. I am not what you try to prove me: whether you are what you are accused of being, is for you to consider. The fact that I am acquitted of blame does not prove me innocent nor the fact that you are accused prove you a criminal.

18. After this preface as to the falsification by heretics of the apostles, of both the Clements, and of Dionysius, he at last comes to Origen; and these are his words:

"I have shewn from his own words and writings how he himself complains of this and deplores it: He explains clearly in the letter which he wrote to some of his intimate friends at Alexandria what he suffered while living here in the flesh and in the full enjoyment of his senses, by the corruption of his books and treatises, or by spurious editions of them."

He subjoins a copy of this letter; and he who imputes to the heretics the falsification of Origen's writings himself begins by falsifying them, for he does not translate the letter as he finds it in the Greek, and does not convey to the Latins what Origen states in his letter. The object of the whole letter is to assail Demetrius the Pontiff of Alexandria, and to inveigh against the bishops throughout the world, and to tell them that their excommunication of him is invalid; he says further that he has no intention of retorting their evil speaking; indeed he is so much afraid of evil speaking that he does not dare to speak evil even of the devil; insomuch that he gave occasion to Candidus an adherent of the errors of Valentinian to represent him falsely as saying that the devil is of such a nature as could be saved. But our friend takes no notice of the real purport of the letter, and makes up for Origen an argument which he does not use. I have therefore translated a part of the letter, beginning a little way below what has been already spoken of, and have appended it to the part which has been translated by him in a curtailed and disingenuous manner, so that the reader may perceive the object with which he suppressed the earlier part. He is contending, then, against the Bishops of the church generally, because they had judged him unworthy of its communion; and he continues as follows:

"Why need I speak of the language in which the prophets constantly threaten and reprove the pastors, elders, the priests and the princes? These things you can of yourselves without my aid draw out from the Holy Scriptures, and you may clearly see that it may well be the present time of which it is said [1] 'Trust not in your friends, and do not hope in princes,' and that the prophecy is now gaining its fulfilment, [2] 'The leaders of my people have not known me; my sons are fools and not wise: they are wise to do evil, but know not to do good.' We ought to pity them, not to hate them, to pray for them, not to curse them. For we have been created for blessing, not for cursing. Therefore even Michael,[3] when he disputed against the devil concerning the body of Moses, did not dare to bring a railing accusation even for so great an evil, but said; 'The Lord rebuke thee.' And we read something similar in Zachariah,[4] 'The Lord rebuke thee, O Satan; the Lord which hath chosen Jerusalem rebuke thee.' So also we desire that those who will not humbly accept the rebuke of their neighbours may be rebuked of the Lord. But, since Michael says, 'The Lord rebuke thee, O Satan,' and Zechariah says the same, the devil knows well whether the Lord rebukes him or not; and must acknowledge the manner of the rebuke."

Then, after a passage too long to insert here, he adds:

"We believe that not only those who have committed great sins will be cast out from the kingdom of heaven, such as fornicators and adulterers, and those who defile themselves with mankind, and thieves, but those also who have done evil of a less flagrant kind, since it is written; [5] 'Neither drunk-

---

[1] Mic. vii, 5.
[2] Jer. iv, 22.
[3] Jude, 9
[4] Zach. iii, 2.
[5] 1 Cor. vi, 9.

ards nor evil speakers shall inherit the kingdom of God;" and that the standard by which men will be judged is as much the goodness as the severity of God. Therefore we strive to act thoughtfully in all things, in drinking wine, and in moderation of language, so that we dare not speak evil of any man. Now, because, through the fear of God, we are careful not to utter maledictions against any one, remembering that the words 'He dared not bring against him a railing accusation,' are spoken of Michael in his dealing with the devil; as it is said also in another place, [1] 'They set at naught dominions and rail at dignities;' certain of these men who seek for matters of contention, ascribe to us and our teaching the blasphemy (as to which they have to lay to heart the words which apply to them, 'Neither drunkards nor evil speakers shall inherit the kingdom of God'), namely, that the father of wickedness and perdition of those who shall be cast out of the kingdom of God can be saved; a thing which not even a madman can say."

The rest which comes in the same letter he has [2] set down instead of the later words of Origen which I have translated: "Now, because through the fear of God we are careful not to utter maledictions against any one," and so on; he fraudulently cuts off the earlier part, on which the later depends, and begins to translate the letter, as though the former part began with this statement, and says:

"Some of those who delight in bringing complaints against their neighbours, ascribe to us and our teaching the crime of a blasphemy, which we have never spoken, (as to which they must consider whether they are willing to stand by the decree which says 'The evil speakers shall not inherit the kingdom of God,') for they say that I assert that the father of the wickedness and perdition of those who shall be cast out of the kingdom of God, that is, the devil, will be saved; a thing which no man even though he had taken leave of his senses and was manifestly insane could say."

19. Now compare the words of Origen, which I have translated word for word above, with these which by him have been turned into Latin, or rather overturned; and you will see clearly how great a discrepancy between them there is, not only of word but of meaning. I beg you not to consider my translation wearisome because it is longer; for the object I had in translating the whole passage was to exhibit the purpose which he had in suppressing the earlier part. There exists in Greek a dialogue between Origen and Candidus the defender of the heresy of Valentinian, in which I confess it seems to me when I read it that I am looking on at a fight between two Andabatian gladiators. Candidus maintains that

the Son is of the substance of the Father, falling into the error of asserting a Probolé or Production.[1] On the other side, Origen, like Arius and Eunomius, refuses to admit that He is produced or born, lest God the Father should thus be divided into parts; but he says that He was a sublime and most excellent creation who came into being by the will of the Father like other creatures. They then come to a second question. Candidus asserts that the devil is of a nature wholly evil which can never be saved. Against this Origen rightly asserts that he is not of perishable substance, but that it is by his own will that he fell and can be saved. This Candidus falsely turns into a reproach against Origen, as if he had said that the diabolical nature could be saved. What therefore Candidus had falsely accused him of, Origen refutes. But we see that in this Dialogue alone Origen accuses the heretics of having falsified his writings, not in the other books about which no question was ever raised. Otherwise, if we are to believe that all which is heretical is not due to Origen but to the heretics, while almost all his books are full of these errors, nothing of Origen's will remain, but everything must be the work of those whose names we are ignorant.

It is not enough for him to calumniate the Greeks and the men of old time, about whom the distance either of time or space gives him the power to tell any falsehood he pleases. He comes to the Latins, and first takes the case of Hilary the Confessor, whose book, he states, was falsified by the heretics after the Council of Ariminum. A question arose about him on this account in a council of bishops, and he then ordered the book to be brought from his own house. The book in its heretical shape was in his desk, though he did not know it; and when it was produced, the author of the book was condemned as a heretic and excommunicated, and left the council room. This is the story, a mere dream of his own, which he tells to his intimates; and he imagines his authority to be so great that no one will dare to contradict him when he says such things. I will ask him a few questions. In what city was the synod held by which Hilary was excommunicated? What were the names of the Bishops present? Who subscribed the sentence? Who were content, and who non-content? Who were the consuls of the year? and who was the emperor

---

[1] Jude, 8.   [2] Rufinus.

[1] A bringing forth of one thing from another, that is, according to Valentinian, of Christ as a production from another Æon.

who ordered the assembly of the council? Were the Bishops present those of Gaul alone, or of Italy and Spain as well? and for what purpose was the council called together? You tell us none of these things; yet, in order to defend Origen, you treat as a criminal and as excommunicated a man of the highest eloquence, the very clarion of the Latin tongue against the Arians. But we are in the presence of a confessor, and even his calumnies must be borne with patience. He next passes to Cyprian the illustrious martyr, and he tells us that a book by Tertullian entitled "On the Trinity" is read as one of his works by the partisans of the Macedonian heresy at Constantinople. In this charge of his he tells two falsehoods. The book in question is not Tertullian's, nor does it pass under the name of Cyprian. It is by Novatian and is called by his name; the peculiarity of the style proves the authorship of the work.

20. What nonsense is this out of which they fabricate a charge against me! It seems hardly worth while to notice it. It is a story of my own about the council held by Damasus Bishop of Rome, and I, under the name of a certain friend of his, am attacked for it. He had given me some papers about church affairs to get copied; and the story describes a trick practised by the Apollinarians who borrowed one of these, a book of Athanasius' to read in which occur the words [1] 'Dominicus homo,' and falsified it by first scratching out the words, and then writing them in again on the erasure, so that it might appear, not that the book had been falsified by them, but that the words had been added by me. I beg you, my dearest friend, that in these matters of serious interest to the church, where doctrinal truth is in question, and we are seeking for the authority of our predecessors for the wellbeing of our souls to put away silly stuff of this kind, and not take mere after-dinner stories as if they were arguments. For it is quite possible that, even after you have heard the true story from me, another who does not know it may declare that it is made up, and composed in elegant language by you like a mine of Philistion or a song of Lentulus or Marcellus.

21. To what point will not rashness reach when once the reins which check it are relaxed? After telling us of the excommunication of Hilary, the heretical book falsely bearing the name of Cyprian, the successive erasure and insertion in the work of Athanasius made while I was asleep, he

as a last effort breaks forth in.o an attack upon the pope Epiphanius: the chagrin engendered in his heart because Epiphanius in the letter which he wrote to the bishop John had called him a heretic, he pours out in his apology for Origen, and comforts himself with these words:

"The whole truth, which has been hidden, must here be laid bare. It is impossible that any man should exercise so unrighteous a judgment as to judge unequally where the cases are equal. But the fact is, the prompters of those who defame Origen are men who either make it a habit to discourse in the churches at great length or write books, the whole of which, both books and discourse are taken from Origen. To prevent men therefore from discovering their plagiarism, the crime of which can be concealed so long as they act ungratefully towards their master, they deter all simple persons from reading him. One of them, who considers himself to have a necessity laid upon him to speak evil of Origen through every nation and tongue, as if that were to preach the Gospel, once declared in the audience of a vast multitude of the brethren that he had read six thousand of his books. If he read them, as he is wont to declare, in order to know what harm there was in him, ten or twenty books, or at most thirty, would have been sufficient for that knowledge. To read six thousand books is not like one who wants to know the harm and the errors that are in him, but like one who consecrates almost his whole life to studies conducted under his tuition. How then can he claim to be listened to when he blames those who, for the sake of instruction, have read a small portion of his works, taking care to maintain whole their own system of belief and their piety?"

22. Who are these men who are wont to dispute at such great length in the churches, and to write books, and whose discourses and writings are taken wholly from Origen; these men who are afraid of their literary thefts becoming known, and shew ingratitude towards their master, and who therefore deter men of simple mind from reading him? You ought to mention them by name, and designate the men themselves. Are the reverend bishops [1]Anastasius and Theophilus, Venerius and Chromatius, and the whole council of the Catholics both in the East and in the West, who publicly denounce him as a heretic, to be esteemed to be plagiarists of his books? Are we to believe that, when they preach in the churches, they do not preach the mysteries of the Scriptures, but merely repeat what they have stolen from Origen? Is it not enough for you to disparage them all in general, but you must specially aim the spear of your pen against a reverend and eminent Bishop of the church? Who is this who considers

---

[1] "A man of the Lord," perhaps applied to Christ.

[1] Bishops respectively of Rome, Alexandria, Milan, and Aquileia.

that he has a necessity laid on him of reviling Origen, as the Gospel which he must preach among all nations and tongues? this man who proclaimed in the audience of a vast multitude of the brethren that he had read six thousand of his books? You yourself were in the very centre of that multitude and company of the brethren, when, as he complains in his letter,[1] the monstrous doctrines of Origen were enlarged upon by you. Is it to be imputed to him as a crime that he knows the Greek, the Syrian, the Hebrew, the Egyptian, and in part also the Latin language? Then, I suppose, the Apostles and Apostolic men, who spoke with tongues, are to be condemned; and you who know two languages may deride me who know three. But as for the six thousand books which you pretend that he has read, who will believe that you are speaking the truth, or that he was capable of telling such a lie? If indeed Origen had written six thousand books, it is possible that a man of great learning, who had been trained from his infancy in sacred literature might have read books alien from his own convictions, because he had an inquiring spirit and a love of learning. But how could he read what Origen never wrote? Count up the index contained in the third volume of Eusebius, in which is his life of Pamphilus: you will not find, I do not say six thousand, but not a third of that number of books. I have by me the letter of the above named Pontiff, in which he gives his answer to this calumny of yours uttered when you were still in the East; and it confutes this most manifest falsehood with the open countenance of truth.

23. After all this you dare to say in your Apology, that you are not the defender nor the champion of Origen, though you think that Eusebius and Pamphilus said all too little in his defence. I shall try to write a reply to those works in another treatise if God grants me a sufficient span of life. For the present let it suffice that I have met your assertions, and that I have set the careful reader on his guard by stating that I never saw in writing the book which was known as the work of Pamphilus till I read it in your own manuscript. It was no great concern of mine to know what was written in favour of a heretic, and therefore I always took it that the work of Pamphilus was different from that of Eusebius; but, after the question had been raised, I wished to reply to their works, and with this object I read what each of them had to say in Origen's behalf; and then I discerned clearly that the first of Eusebius' six books was the same which you had published both in Greek and Latin as the single book of Pamphilus, only altering the opinion about the Son and the Holy Spirit, which bore on their face the mark of open blasphemy. It was thus that, when my friend, Dexter, who held the office of prætorian prefect, asked me, ten years ago, to make a list for him of the writers of our faith,[1] I placed among the various treatises assigned to various authors this book as composed by Pamphilus, supposing the matter to be as it had been brought before the public by you and by your disciples. But, since Eusebius himself says that Pamphilus wrote nothing except some short letters to his friends, and the first of his six books contains the precise words which are fictitiously given by you under the name of Pamphilus, it is plain that your object in circulating this book was to introduce heresy under the authority of a martyr. I cannot allow you to make my mistake a cloak for your fraud, when you first pretend that the book is by Pamphilus and then pervert many of its passages so as to make them different in Latin from what they are in Greek. I believed the book to be by the writer whose name it bore, just as I did in reference to the Περὶ Ἀρχῶν, and many other of the works of Origen and of other Greek writers, which I never read till now, and am now compelled to read, because the question of heresy has been raised, and I wish to know what ought to be avoided and what opposed. In my youth, therefore, I translated only the homilies which he delivered in public, and in which there are fewer causes of offence; and this in ignorance and at the request of others: I did not try to prejudice men by means of the parts which they approved in favour of the acceptance of those which are evidently heretical. At all events, to cut short a long discussion, I can point out whence I received the Περὶ Ἀρχῶν, namely, from those who copied it from your manuscript. We want in like manner to know whence your copy of it came; for if you are unable to name any one else as the source from which it was derived, you will yourself be convicted of falsifying it. [2] "A good man from the good treasure of his heart bringeth forth what is good." A tree of a good stock is known by the sweetness of its fruit.

---

1 Epiphanius to John of Jerusalem. Jerome's Letters, LI, 3. See also Jerome Against John of Jerusalem, 11, 14.

1 The Catalogue of Illustrious Men translated in this volume forms the response to this request.
2 Luke vi, 45, Matt. vii, 17.

24. My brother Eusebius writes to me that, when he was at a meeting of African bishops which had been called for certain ecclesiastical affairs, he found there a letter purporting to be written by me, in which I professed penitence and confessed that it was through the influence of the press in my youth that I had been led to turn the Scriptures into Latin from the Hebrew ; in all of which there is not a word of truth. When I heard this, I was stupefied. But one witness was not enough ; even Cato was not believed on his unsupported evidence : [1] "In the mouth of two or three witnesses shall every word be established." Letters were soon brought me from many brethren in Rome asking about this very matter, whether the facts were as was stated : and they pointed in a way to make me weep to the person by whom the letter had been circulated among the people. He who dared to do this, what will he not dare to do? It is well that ill will has not a strength equal to its intentions. Innocence would be dead long ago if wickedness were always allied to power, and calumny could prevail in all that it seeks to accomplish. It was impossible for him, accomplished as he was, to copy my style and manner of writing, whatever their value may be ; amidst all his tricks and his fraudulent assumption of another man's personality, it was evident who he was. It is this same man, then, who wrote this fictitious letter of retractation in my name, making out that my translation of the Hebrew books was bad, who, we now hear, accuses me of having translated the Holy Scriptures with a view to disparage the Septuagint. In any case, whether my translation is right or wrong, I am to be condemned : I must either confess that in my new work I was wrong, or else that by my new version I have aimed a blow at the old. I wonder that in this letter he did not make me out as guilty of homicide, or adultery or sacrilege or parricide or any of the vile things which the silent working of the mind can revolve within itself. Indeed I ought to be grateful to him for having imputed to me no more than one act of error or false dealing out of the whole forest of possible crimes. Am I likely to have said anything derogatory to the seventy translators, whose work I carefully purged from corruptions and gave to Latin readers many years ago, and daily expound it at our conventual gatherings ; [2] whose version of the Psalms has so long been the subject of my meditation and my song? Was I so foolish as to wish to forget in old age what I learned in youth? All my treatises have been woven out of statements warranted by their version. My commentaries on the twelve prophets are an explanation of their version as well as my own. How uncertain must the labours of men ever be ! and how contrary at times to their own intentions are the results which men's studies reach. I thought that I deserved well of my countrymen the Latins by this version, and had given them an incitement to learning ; for it is not despised even by the Greeks now that it is retranslated into their language ; yet it is now made the subject of a charge against me ; and I find that the food pressed upon them turns upon the stomach. What is there in human life that can be safe if innocence is made the object of accusation? I am the householder [1] who finds that while he slept the enemy has sown tares among his wheat. [2] "The wild boar out of the wood has rooted up my vineyard, and the strange wild beast has devoured it." I keep silence, but a letter that is not mine speaks against me. I am ignorant of the crime laid against me, yet I am made to confess the crime all through the world. [3] "Woe is me, my mother, that thou hast borne me a man to be judged and condemned [4] in the whole earth."

25. All my prefaces to the books of the Old Testament, some specimens of which I subjoin, are witnesses for me on this point ; and it is needless to state the matter otherwise than it is stated in them. I will begin therefore with Genesis. The Prologue is as follows :

I have received letters so long and eagerly desired from my dear Desiderius [5] who, as if the future had been foreseen, shares his name with Daniel,[6] entreating me to put our friends in possession of a translation of the Pentateuch from Hebrew into Latin. The work is certainly hazardous and it is exposed to the [7] attacks of my calumniators, who maintain that it is through contempt of the Seventy that I have set to work to forge a new version to take the place of the old. They thus test ability as they do wine ; whereas I have again and again declared that I dutifully offer in the Tabernacle of God what I can, and have pointed out that the great gifts which one man brings are not marred by the inferior gifts of another. But I was stimulated to undertake the task by the zeal of Origen, who blended with the old edition Theodotion's translation and used throughout the work as distinguishing marks the

---

[1] Deut. xvii, 6.
[2] This translation has been almost wholly lost. The parts which remain are the Book of Job, the Psalms, and the Preface to the Books of Chronicles.

[1] Matt. xiii, 25. [2] Ps. lxxx, 13. [3] Jer. xv, 10 (LXX).
[4] Or examined. The Vulgate agrees with A. V. 'A man of contention.'
[5] In the original there is a play upon words — *Desiderii desideratas.*
[6] That is, *Man of desires*, Dan. ix, 23, Margin.
[7] Lit. *barkings*.

asterisk ✳ and the obelus ÷, that is the star and the spit, the first of which makes what had previously been defective to beam with light, while the other transfixes and slaughters all that was superfluous. But I was encouraged above all by the authoritative publications of the Evangelists and Apostles, in which we read much taken from the Old Testament which is not found in our manuscripts. For example, ' Out of Egypt have I called my Son' (Matt. ii. 15): ' For he shall be called a Nazarene' (*Ibid*. 23): and 'They shall look on him whom they pierced' (John xix. 37): and ' Rivers of living water shall flow out of his belly' (John vii. 38): and ' Things which eye hath not seen, nor ear heard, nor have entered into the heart of man, which God hath prepared for them that love him' (I. Cor. ii. 9), and many other passages which lack their proper context. Let us ask our opponents then where these things are written, and when they are unable to tell, let us produce them from the Hebrew. The first passage is in Hosea, (xi. 1), the second in Isaiah (xi. 1), the third in Zechariah (xii. 10), the fourth in Proverbs (xviii. 4), the fifth also in Isaiah (lxiv. 4). Being ignorant of all this many follow the ravings of the Apocrypha, and prefer to the inspired books the melancholy trash which comes to us from Spain.[1] It is not for me to explain the causes of the error. The Jews say it was deliberately and wisely done to prevent [2] Ptolemy who was a monotheist from thinking the Hebrews acknowledged two deities. And that which chiefly influenced them in thus acting was the fact that the king appeared to be falling into Platonism. In a word, wherever Scripture evidenced some sacred truth respecting Father, Son, and Holy Spirit, they either translated the passage differently, or passed it over altogether in silence, so that they might both satisfy the king, and not divulge the secrets of the faith. I do not know whose false imagination led him to invent the story of the [3] seventy cells at Alexandria, in which, though separated from each other, the translators were said to have written the same words. Aristeas,[4] the champion of that same Ptolemy, and Josephus, long after, relate nothing of the kind; their account is that the Seventy assembled in one basilica consulted together, and did not prophesy. For it is one thing to be a prophet, another to be a translator. The former through the Spirit, foretells things to come; the latter must use his learning and facility in speech to translate what he understands. It can

hardly be that we must suppose Tully was inspired with oratorical spirit when he translated Xenophon's Œconomics, Plato's Protagoras, and the oration of Demosthenes in defence of Ctesiphon. Otherwise the Holy Spirit must have quoted the same books in one sense through the Seventy Translators, in another through the Apostles, so that, whereas they said nothing of a given matter, these falsely affirm that it was so written. What then? Are we condemning our predecessors? By no means; but following the zealous labours of those who have preceded us we contribute such work as lies in our power in the name of the Lord. They translated before the Advent of Christ, and expressed in ambiguous terms that which they knew not. We after His Passion and Resurrection write not prophecy so much as history. For one style is suitable to what we hear, another to what we see. The better we understand a subject, the better we describe it. Hearken then, my rival: listen, my calumniator; I do not condemn, I do not censure the Seventy, but I am bold enough to prefer the Apostles to them all. It is the Apostle through whose mouth I hear the voice of Christ, and I read that in the classification of spiritual gifts they are placed before prophets (I. Cor. xii. 28; Eph. iv. 11), while interpreters occupy almost the lowest place. Why are you tormented with jealousy? Why do you inflame the minds of the ignorant against me? Wherever in translation I seem to you to go wrong, ask the Hebrews, consult their teachers in different towns. The words which exist in their Scriptures concerning Christ your copies do not contain. The case is different if they have [1] rejected passages which were afterward used against them by the Apostles, and the Latin texts are more correct than the Greek, the Greek than the Hebrew.

[Chapters 26 to 32 are taken up with the quotation, almost in full, of the Preface to the Vulgate translation of the books of the Old Testament. It is unnecessary to give them here. They have all the same design as the Preface to Genesis already given, namely to meet the objections of those who represented the work as a reproach to the LXX which was then supposed to have almost the authority of inspiration. The same arguments, illustrations, and even words, are reiterated. Readers who may desire to go more fully into Jerome's statements will find these Prefaces translated at length in his works, Vol. VI of this Series.]

33. In reference to Daniel my answer will be that I did not say that he was not a prophet; on the contrary, I confessed in the very beginning of the Preface that he was a prophet. But I wished to show what was the opinion upheld by the Jews; and what were the arguments on which they relied for its proof. I also told the reader that the version read in the Christian churches was not that of the Septuagint translators but that of Theodotion. It is true, I said that the Septuagint version was in this book very

---

[1] The passage is explained by Jerome's own words in the commentary on Is. lxiv. " Certain silly women in Spain, and especially in Lusitania, have been deceived into accepting as truth the marvels of Basilides and Balsaneus' treasury, and even of Barbelo and Leusiboras." Jerome goes on to add that Irenæus in explaining the origin of many heresies pointed out that the Gnostics deceived many noble women of the parts of Gaul about the Rhone, and afterwards those of Spain, framing a system partly of myths partly of immorality, and calling their folly by the name of philosophy. See also Ep. Jer. Letter 120 to Hedibia, and Com. on Amos cf. III.

[2] That is Ptolemy commonly known as the son of Lagus, but the reputed son of Philip of Macedon by Arsinoë Philip's concubine. He reigned over Egypt from B. C. 323-285. He was a great patron of learning, and, according to traditions current among the fathers, wishing to adorn his Alexandrian library with the writings of all nations, he requested the Jews of Jerusalem to furnish him with a Greek version of their Scriptures, and thus originated the Septuagint.

[3] Irenæus, Justin Martyr, Epiphanius, and Augustine among the Latins, adhere to the inspiration of the translators which Jerome here rejects.

[4] Aristeas was an officer of Ptolemy Philadelphus, son and successor of Ptolemy Lagus. The so-called letter of Aristeas to his brother Philocrates is still extant in Hody's *De Bibliorum Textibus Originalibus*, etc. (Oxon. 1705), and separately in a small volume published at Oxford 1692.

---

[1] Reading *reprobaverunt*.

different from the original, and that it was condemned by the right judgment of the churches of Christ; but the fault was not mine who only stated the fact, but that of those who read the version. We have four versions to choose from: those of Aquila, Symmachus, the Seventy, and Theodotion. The churches choose to read Daniel in the version of Theodotion. What sin have I committed in following the judgment of the churches? But when I repeat what the Jews say against the Story of Susanna and the Hymn of the Three Children, and the fables of Bel and the Dragon, which are not contained in the Hebrew Bible, the man who makes this a charge against me proves himself to be a fool and a slanderer; for I explained not what I thought but what they commonly say against us. I did not reply to their opinion in the Preface, because I was studying brevity, and feared that I should seem to be writing not a Preface but a book. I said therefore, "As to which this is not the time to enter into discussion." Otherwise from the fact that I stated that Porphyry had said many things against this prophet, and called, as witnesses of this, Methodius, Eusebius, and Apollinarius, who have replied to his folly in many thousand lines, it will be in his power to accuse me for not having written in my Preface against the books of Porphyry. If there is any one who pays attention to silly things like this, I must tell him loudly and freely, that no one is compelled to read what he does not want; that I wrote for those who asked me, not for those who would scorn me, for the grateful not the carping, for the earnest not the indifferent. Still, I wonder that a man should read the version of Theodotion the heretic and judaizer, and should scorn that of a Christian, simple and sinful though he may be.

34. I beg you, my most sweet friend, who are so curious that you even know my dreams, and that you scrutinize for purposes of accusations all that I have written during these many years without fear of future calumny; answer me, how is it you do not know the prefaces of the very books on which you ground your charges against me? These prefaces, as if by some prophetic foresight, gave the answer to the calumnies that were coming, thus fulfilling the proverb, "The antidote before the poison." What harm has been done to the churches by my translation? You bought up, as I knew, at great cost the versions of Aquila, Symmachus, and Theodotion, and the Jewish authors of the fifth and sixth translations. Your Origen, or,

that I may not seem to be wounding you with fictitious praises, our Origen, (for I may call him ours for his genius and learning, though not for the truth of his doctrines) in all his books explains and expounds not only the Septuagint but the Jewish versions. Eusebius and Didymus do the same. I do not mention Apollinarius, who, with a laudable zeal though not according to knowledge, attempted to patch up into one garment the rags of all the translations, and to weave a consistent text of Scripture at his own discretion, not according to any sound rule of criticism. The Hebrew Scriptures are used by apostolic men; they are used, as is evident, by the apostles and evangelists. Our Lord and Saviour himself whenever he refers to the Scriptures, takes his quotations from the Hebrew; as in the instance of the words [1] "He that believeth on me, as the Scripture hath said, out of his belly shall flow rivers of living water," and in the words used on the cross itself, "Eli, Eli, lama sabachthani," which is by interpretation "My God, my God, why hast thou forsaken me?" not, as it is given by the Septuagint, "My God, my God, look upon me, why hast thou forsaken me?" and many similar cases. I do not say this in order to aim a blow at the seventy translators; but I assert that the Apostles of Christ have an authority superior to theirs. Wherever the Seventy agree with the Hebrew, the apostles took their quotations from that translation; but, where they disagree, they set down in Greek what they had found in the Hebrew. And further, I give a challenge to my accuser. I have shown that many things are set down in the New Testament as coming from the older books, which are not to be found in the Septuagint; and I have pointed out that these exist in the Hebrew. Now let him show that there is anything in the New Testament which comes from the Septuagint but which is not found in the Hebrew, and our controversy is at an end.

35. By all this it is made clear, first that the version of the Seventy translators which has gained an established position by having been so long in use, was profitable to the churches, because that by its means the Gentiles heard of the coming of Christ before he came; secondly, that the other translators are not to be reproved, since it was not their own works that they published but the divine books which they translated; and, thirdly, that my own familiar friend should frankly accept from a Christian and a friend what

---

[1] John vii, 38, supposed to be taken from Prov. xviii, 4, or Is. lviii, 11.

he has taken great pains to obtain from the Jews and has written down for him at great cost. I have exceeded the bounds of a letter; and, though I had taken pen in hand to contend against a wicked heresy, I have been compelled to make answer on my own behalf, while waiting for my friend's three books, and in a state of constant mental suspense about the charges he had heaped up against me. It is easier to guard against one who professes hostility than to make head against an enemy who lurks under the guise of a friend.

JEROME'S APOLOGY IN ANSWER TO RUFINUS—BOOK III.

The two first books formed a complete whole, but it was intimated that there might be more to come when Jerome should have received Rufinus' work in full. The two first books were brought to Rufinus by the captain of a merchant-ship trading with Aquileia, together with a copy of Jerome's friendly letter which had been suppressed by Pammachius. The bearer had (as stated by Rufinus, though Jerome mocks at this as impossible) only two days to wait. Chromatius the Bishop of Aquileia urged that the strife should now cease, and prevailed so far as that Rufinus made no public reply. He wrote a private letter, however, to Jerome, which has not come down to us, and which does not seem, from the extracts given in c. 4, 6, etc., to have been of a pacific tenor. Its details may be gathered from Jerome's reply. Jerome intimates that it sought to involve him in heresy, that it renewed and aggravated the former accusations, speaking of him in language fit only for the lowest characters on the stage; and that it declared that, if its writer had been so minded, he could have produced facts which would have been the destruction of his adversary. Jerome, though receiving some expressions of the desire of Chromatius that he should not reply (perhaps also the regretful expostulation of Augustin, — Jer. Letter cx, 6, Aug. Letter 73) declared that it was impossible for him to yield. He could not refrain from defending himself from a capital charge, nor could he spare the heretics. Peace could only come by unity in the faith.

1. Your letter is full of falsehood and violence. I will try not to take the same tone.
2. Why cannot we differ as friends? Why do you, by threats of death, compel me to answer?
3, 4. Your shameful taunt that I wished to get copies of your Apology by bribing your Secretary is an imputation to me of practices which are your own.
5. Eusebius should not have accused you; but your charges against him will not stand.
6. You taunt me with boasting of my eloquence. Will you boast of your illiteracy?
7, 8. You wish first to praise, then to amend me, but both with fisticuffs; and make it impossible for me to keep silence.
9. Why cannot you join with me in condemning Origen, and so put an end to our quarrel?
10. The assertion that you had only two days for your answer is a fiction.
11. Your translation, contrariwise to my Commentaries, vouches for the soundness of Origen.
12. You try to shield Origen by falsely attributing the Apology for him to Pamphilus.
13. In my Commentaries my quotation of opposite opinions shows that neither is mine.
14. Had you translated honestly, you would not have had Origen's heresies imputed to you.
15. You say the Bishops of Italy accept your views on the Resurrection. I doubt it.
16. You rashly say that you will agree to whatever Theophilus lays down. You have to consider your friendship for Isidore now his enemy.
17, 18. You speak of the Egyptian Bishop Paul. We received him, though an Origenist, as a stranger; and he has united himself to the orthodox faith. Not only Theophilus but the Emperors condemn Origen.
19. Against Vigilantius I wrote only what was right. I knew who had stirred him up against me.
20. As to the letter of Pope Anastasius condemning you, you will find that it is genuine.
21. Siricius who is dead may have written in your favour; Anastasius who is living writes to the East against you.
22. My departure from Rome for the East had nothing blameable in it as you insinuate.
23. Epiphanius, it is true, gave you the kiss of peace; but he showed afterwards that he had come to distrust you.
24. When we parted as friends I believed you a true believer; no one was sent to Rome to injure you.
25. You swear that you did not write my pretended retractation. Your style betrays you, and I have given a full answer about my translations already.
26. You bid me beware of falsification and treachery. You warn me against yourself.
27. There is nothing inconsistent in praising a man for some things and blaming him in others. You have done it in my case.

28–31. My ignorance of many natural phenomena is no excuse for your ignorance as to the origin of souls. You ought, according to your boasting dream to know everything. The thing of most importance was forgotten in your cargo of Eastern wares.

32. Your dream was a boast: mine of which you accuse me humbled me.

33. It was not I who first disclosed your heresies, but Epiphanius long ago and Aterbius before him.

34–36. As to our translations of the Περὶ Ἀρχῶν, yours was doing harm, and mine was necessary in self-defence. You should be glad that heresy is exposed.

37. Your Apology for Origen did not save him but involved you in heresy.

38. My friendly letter was to prevent discord: the other to crush false opinions.

39, 40. Pythagoras was rightly quoted by me. I produce some of his sayings.

41, 42. You threaten me with destruction. I will not reply in the same way. Personalities should be excluded from controversies of faith.

43, 44. The way of peace is through the wisdom taught in the Book of Proverbs, and through unity in the faith.

I have read the letter[1] which you in your wisdom have written me. You inveigh against me, and, though you once praised me and called me true partner and brother, you now write books to summon me to reply to the charges with which you terrify me. I see that in you are fulfilled the words of Solomon: [2] "In the mouth of the foolish is the rod of [3] contumely," and [4] "A fool receives not the words of prudence, unless you say what is passing in his heart;" and the words of Isaiah: [5] "The fool will speak folly, and his heart will understand vain things, to practise iniquity and speak falsehood against the Lord." For what need was there for you to send me whole volumes full of accusation and malediction, and to bring them before the public, when in the end of your letter you threaten me with death if I dare to reply to your slanders — I beg pardon — to your praises? For your praises and your accusations amount to the same thing; from the same fountain proceed both sweet and bitter. I beg you to set me the example of the modesty and shamefacedness which you recommend to me; you accuse another of lying: cease to be a liar yourself. I wish to give no one an occasion of stumbling, and I will not become your accuser; for I have not to consider merely what you deserve but what is becoming in me. I tremble at our Saviour's words. [6] "Whosoever shall cause one of these little ones that believe in me to stumble, it were better for him that a great mill stone were hanged about his neck and he were drowned in the depths of the sea;" and [7] "Woe unto the world because of occasions of stumbling: for it must needs be that occasions arise; but woe to the man through whom the occasion cometh." It would have been possible for me too to pile up falsehoods against you and to say that I had heard or seen what no one had observed, so that among the ignorant my effrontery might be taken for veracity, and my violence for resolution. But far be it from me to be an imitator of you, and to do myself what I denounce in you. He who is capable of doing filthy things may use filthy words. [1] "The evil man out of the evil treasure of his heart bringeth forth that which is evil; for out of the abundance of the heart the mouth speaketh." You may count it as good fortune that one whom you once called friend but now accuse has no mind to make vile imputations against you. I say this not from any dread of the sword of your accusation, but because I prefer to be accused than to be the accuser, to suffer an injury than to do one. I know the precept of the Apostle: [2] "Dearly beloved avenge not yourselves but rather give place unto wrath: for it is written Vengeance is mine, I will repay saith the Lord. Therefore, if thine enemy hunger feed him, if he thirst give him drink; for in so doing thou shalt heap coals of fire upon his head." For he that avenges himself cannot claim the vindication of the Lord.

2. But, before I make my answer to your letter, I must expostulate with you; you who are first in age among the monks, good presbyter, follower of Christ; is it possible for you to wish to kill your brother, when even to hate him is to be a homicide? Have you learned from your Saviour the lesson that if one strike you on the one cheek you should turn to him the other also? Did not he make answer to the man who struck him, [3] "If I have spoken evil, bear witness of the evil, but if well, why smitest thou me?" You threaten me with death, which can be inflicted on us even by serpents. To die is the lot of all, to commit homicide only of the weak man. What then? If you do not kill me shall I never die? Perhaps I ought to be grateful to you

---

[1] That is, private letter, now lost, which was sent with the two books of Rufinus' Apology.
[2] Prov. xiv, 3.   [3] Pride A. V. and Vulgate.
[4] Prov. xviii, 2, as in Vulgate version.
[5] Is. xxxii, 5.   The words are not those of the Vulgate, nor of the A. V.
[6] Mark ix, 42.   [7] Matt. xviii, 7.

[1] Luke vi, 45.   [2] Rom. xii, 19, 20.   [3] John xviii, 23.

that you turn this necessity into a virtue. We read of Apostles quarrelling, namely Paul and Barnabas who were angry with each other on account of John whose surname was Mark; those who were united by the bonds of Christ's gospel were separated for a voyage; but they still remained friends. Did not the same Paul resist Peter to the face because he did not walk uprightly in the Gospel? Yet he speaks of him as his predecessor in the Gospel, and as a pillar of the church; and he lays before him his mode of preaching, '' lest he should be running, or had run in vain.' Do not children differ from parents and wives from husbands in religious matters, while yet domestic affections remain unimpaired. If you are as I am, why should you hate me? Even if you believe differently, why should you wish to kill me? Is it so, that whoever differs from you is to be slain? I call upon Jesus who will judge what I am now writing and your letter also, as a witness upon my conscience, that when the reverend bishop Chromatius begged me to keep silence, my wish was to do so, and thus to make an end of our dissensions, and to overcome evil with good. But, now that you threaten me with destruction, I am compelled to reply; otherwise, my silence will be taken as an acknowledgment of the crime, and you will interpret my moderation as the sign of an evil conscience.

3. The dilemma in which I am placed is of your making: it is brought out, not from the resources of dialectics, of which you are ignorant, but from among the tools of the murderer and with an intention like his. If I keep silence, I am held guilty: if I speak, I become an evil speaker. You at once forbid me to answer and compel me. Well, then; I must shun excess on both sides. I will say nothing that is injurious; but I must dissipate the charges made against me, for it is impossible not to be afraid of a man who is prepared to kill you. And I will do this in the order of what you have now set before me, leaving the rest as they are in those most learned books of yours which I confuted before I had read them.

You say that ' you sent your accusation against me not to the many but only to those who had been offended by what I had said; for one ought to speak to Christians not for display but for edification.' Whence then, I beg you to consider, did the report of your having written these books reach me? Who was it that sowed them broadcast through Rome and

Italy and the islands of the coast of Dalmatia? How did these charges against me ever come to my ears, if they were only lurking in your desk, and those of your friends? How can you dare to say that you are speaking as a Christian not for display but for edification when you set yourself in mature age to say things against your equal which a murderer could hardly say of a thief, or a harlot against one of her class, or a buffoon against a farce-player? You have for ever so long been labouring to bring forth these mountains of accusations against me and sharpening these swords to pierce my throat. Your cries have been as loud as Ceres' complaints[1] or a driver's shouts to his horses. Was this to make all the provinces through which they resounded read the praise you wrote of me? and recite your panegyrics upon me in every street, every corner, even in the weaving-shops of the women? This is the religious restraint and Christian edification of which you speak. Your reserve, your reticence is such that men come to me from the West, crowd upon crowd, and tell me of your abuse of me; and this, though only from memory, yet with such exact agreement that I was obliged[2] to make my answer, not to your writings which I had not then read, but to what was said to be contained in them, and to intercept with the shield of truth the missiles of mendacity which were flying about through all the world.

4. Your letter goes on:

"Pray do not trouble yourself to give a large sum of gold to bribe my secretary, as your friends did in the case of my papers containing the Περὶ Ἀρχῶν, before they had been corrected and brought to completion, so that they might more easily falsify documents which no one possessed, or at least very few. Accept the document which I send you gratis, though you would be glad to pay a large sum to buy it."

I should have thought you would be ashamed of such a beginning of your work. What! I bribe your Secretary! Is there any one who would attempt to vie with the wealth of Crœsus[3] and Darius?[3] who is there that does not tremble when he is suddenly confronted with a Demaratus[4] or a Crassus?[5] Have you become so brazen-faced, that you put your trust in lies and think lies will protect you and that we shall believe every fiction which you choose to frame? Who then was

---

[1] When she lost her daughter Proserpine and lamented her throughout the world.
[2] In the two first books of the Apology.
[3] Kings of Lydia and Persia notorious for their wealth.
[4] Father of Tarquinius Priscus, said to have been a wealthy immigrant from Corinth.
[5] The triumvir: surnamed the Rich: murdered in Persia B.C. 52.

---

it who stole that letter in which you were so highly praised, from the cell of our brother Eusebius? Whose artfulness was it, and whose accomplices, through which a certain document was found in the lodgings of that Christian woman Fabiola and of that wise man Oceanus, which they themselves had never seen? Do you think that you are innocent because you can cast upon others all the imputations which properly belong to you? Is every one who offends you, however guiltless and harmless he may be, at once held to become a criminal? You think so, I suppose, because you are possessed of that through which the chastity of Danaë[1] was broken down, that, which had more power with Gihazi than his master's sacred character, that for which Judas betrayed his Master.[2]

5. Let us understand what was the wrong done by my friend[3] who, you say ‘falsified parts of your papers when they had not yet been corrected nor carried to completion, and it was the more possible to falsify them because very few if any as yet possessed them.’[4] I have already said, and I now repeat, with protestations in the presence of God, that I did not approve his accusing you, nor of any Christian accusing another Christian; for what need is there that matters which can be corrected or set right in private should be published abroad to the stumbling and fall of many? But since each man lives for his own gullet, and a man does not by becoming your friend become master of your will, while I blame the accusing of a brother even when it is true, so also I cannot accept against a man of saintly character this accusation of falsifying your papers. How could a man who only knows Latin change anything in a translation from the Greek? Or how could he take out or put in anything in such books as the Περὶ Ἀρχῶν, in which everything is so closely knit together that one part hangs upon another, and anything that may be taken out or put in to suit your will must at once show out like a patch on a garment? What you ask me to do, it is for you to do yourself. Put on at least a small measure of natural if not of Christian modesty in your assertions; do not despise and trample upon your conscience, and imagine yourself justified by a show of words, when the facts are against you. If Eusebius bought your

uncorrected papers for money in order to falsify them, produce the genuine papers which have not been falsified: and if you can shew that there is nothing heretical in them, he will become amenable to the charge of forgery. But, however much you may alter or correct them, you will not make them out to be catholic. If the error existed only in the words or in some few statements, what is bad might be cut off and what is good be substituted for it. But, when the whole discussion[1] proceeds on a single principle, namely, the notion that the whole universe of reasonable creatures have fallen by their own will, and will hereafter return to a condition of unity: and that again from that starting point another fall will begin: what is there that you can amend, unless you alter the whole book? But if you were to think of doing this, you would no longer be translating another man's work but composing a work of your own.

However, I hardly see which way your argument tends. I suppose you mean that the papers being uncorrected and not having undergone a final revising were more easily falsified by Eusebius. Perhaps I am stupid; but the argument appears to me somewhat foolish and pointless. If the papers were uncorrected and had not undergone their final revision, the errors in them must be imputed not to Eusebius but to your sloth and delay in putting off their correction; and all the blame that can be laid upon him is that he circulated among the body of Christians writings which you had intended in course of time to correct. But if, as you assert, Eusebius falsified them, why do you put forward the allegation that they were uncorrected, and that they had gone out before the public without their final revision? For papers whether corrected or uncorrected are equally susceptible of falsification. But, No one, you say possessed these books, or very few. What contradictions this single sentence exhibits! If no one had these books, how could they be in the hands of a few? If a few possessed them, why do you state falsely that there were none? Then, when you say that a few had them, and by your own confession the statement that no one had them is overthrown, what becomes of your complaint that your secretary was bribed with money? Tell us the secretary's name, the amount of the bribe, the place, the intermediary, the recipient. Of course the traitor has been cast off from

---

[1] Jove was said to have seduced Danaë by changing himself into a shower of gold.

[2] Jerome often taunts Rufinus with being rich and luxurious. See Letter cxxv, 18.

[3] Necessarius. This no doubt applies to Eusebius of Cremona or to Paulinian, Jerome's brother, (Jer Ap. i, 21, 28.) See Ruf. Ap. i, 19, where a similar charge is made.

[4] Quoted from Rufinus' letter to Jerome, now lost.

---

[1] That is in Origen's Περὶ Ἀρχῶν.

you, and one convicted of so great a crime has been separated from all familiarity with you. Is it not more likely to be true that the copies of the work which Eusebius obtained were given him by those few friends whom you speak of, especially since these copies agree and coincide with one another so completely that there is not the difference of a single stroke. We might ask also whether it was quite wise to give a copy to others which you had not yet corrected? The documents had not received their last corrections, and yet other men possessed these errors of yours which needed correction. Do you not see that your falsehood will not hold together? Besides, what profit was there for you, at that particular moment — how would it have helped you in escaping from the condemnation of the bishops — that the book which was the subject of discussion should be open to everyone, and that you should thus be refuted by your own words? From all this it is clear, according to the epigram of the famous orator, that you have a good will for a lie, but not the art of framing it.

6. I will follow the order of your letter, and subjoin your very words as you spoke them. "I admit, that, as you say, I praised your eloquence in my Preface; and I would praise it again now were it not that contrary to the advice of your Tully, you make it hateful by excessive boastfulness." Where have I boasted of my eloquence? I did not even accept willingly the praise which you bestowed on it. Perhaps your reason for saying this is that you do not wish, yourself, to be flattered by public praise given in guile. Rest assured you shall be accused openly; you reject one who would praise you; you shall have experience of one who openly arraigns you. I was not so foolish as to criticize your illiterate style; no one can expose it to condemnation so strongly as you do whenever you write. I only wished to show your fellow-disciples who shared your lack of literary training what progress you had made during your thirty years in the East, an illiterate writer, who takes impudence for eloquence, and universal evil speaking a sign of a good conscience. I am not going to administer the ferule; I do not assume, as you put it, to apply the strokes of the leather thong to teach an aged pupil his letters. But the fact is your eloquence and teaching is so sparkling that we mere tract-writers cannot bear it, and you dazzle our eyes with the acuteness of your talents to such an extent that we must all seem to be envious of you; and we must really join in

the attempt to suppress you, for, if once you obtain the primacy among us as a writer, and stand on the summit of the rhetorical arch, all of us who profess to know anything will not be allowed to mutter a word. I am, according to you, a philosopher and an orator, grammarian, dialectician, one who knows Hebrew, Greek and Latin, a 'trilingual' man. On this estimate, you also will be 'bilingual,' who know enough Latin and Greek to make the Greek think you a Latin scholar and the Latin a Greek: and the bishop Epiphanius will be a 'pentaglossic[1] man' since he speaks in five languages against you and your favorite.[2] But I wonder at the rashness which made you dare to say to one so accomplished as you profess to think me: "You, whose accomplishments give you so many watchful eyes, how can you be pardoned if you go wrong? How can you fail to be buried in the silence of a never ending shame?" When I read this, and reflected that I must somewhere or other have made a slip in my words (for[3] "if any man does not go wrong in word, the same is a perfect man") and was expecting that he was about to expose some of my faults; all of a sudden I came upon the words: "Two days before the carrier of this letter set out your declamation against me was put into my hands." What became then of those threats of yours, and of your words: "How can you be pardoned if you go wrong? How can you fail to be covered with the silence of a never ending shame?" Yet perhaps, notwithstanding the shortness of the time, you were able to put this in order; or else you were intending to hire in one of the learned sort, who would expect to find in my works the ornaments and gems of an eloquence like yours. You wrote before this: "Accept the document which I send which you wished to buy at a great price;" but now you speak with the pretence of humility. "I intended to follow your example; but, since the messenger who was returning to you was hurrying back again I thought it better to write shortly to you than at greater length to others." In the meantime you boldly take pleasure in your illiteracy. Indeed you once confessed it, declaring that 'it was superfluous to notice a few faults of style, when it was acknowledged that there were faults in every part.' I will not therefore find fault with you for putting down that a document was acquired when you meant that it was bought; though acquiring is said of things like in kind, whereas buying implies the

---

[1] Five tongued.
[2] Amasium, sweetheart; namely, Origen.   [3] Jas. iii, 2.

counting out of money: nor for such a sentence as "as he who was returning to you was hurrying back again" which is a redundancy worthy of the poorest style of diction. I will only reply to the arguments, and will convict you, not of solæcisms and barbarisms, but of falsehood, cunning and impudence.

7. If it is true that you write a letter to me so as to admonish me, and because you wish that I should be reformed, and that you do not wish that men should have a stumbling block put in their way, and that some may be driven mad and others be put to silence; why do you write books addressed to others against me, and scatter them by your myrmidons for the whole world to read? And what becomes of your dilemma in which you try to entangle me, "Whom, best of masters, did you think to correct? If those to whom you wrote, there was no fault to find with them; if me whom you accuse, it was not to me that you wrote"? And I will reply to you in your own words: "Whom did you wish to correct, unlearned master? Those who had done no wrong? or me to whom you did not write? You think your leaders are brutish and are all incapable of understanding your subtilty, or rather your ill will, (for it was in this that the serpent was more subtile than all the beasts in paradise,) in asking that my admonition to you should be of a private character, when you were pressing an indictment against me in public. You are not ashamed to call this indictment of yours an Apology: And you complain that I oppose a shield to your poniard, and with much religiosity and sanctimoniousness you assume the mask of humility, and say: "If I had erred, why did you write to others, and not try to confute me?" I will retort on you this very point. What you complain that I did not do, why did you not do yourself? It is as if a man who is attacking another with kicks and fisticuffs, and finds him intending to shew fight, should say to him: "Do you not know the command, 'If a man smites you on the cheek, turn to him the other'?" It comes to this, my good sir, you are determined to beat me, to strike out my eye; and then, when I bestir myself ever so little, you harp upon the precept of the Gospel. Would you like to have all the windings of your cunning exposed? — those tricks of the foxes who dwell among the ruins, of whom Ezekiel writes,[1] "Like foxes in the desert, so are thy prophets, O Israel." Let me make you understand what you have done. You praised me in your Preface in such a way

that your praises are made a ground of accusation against me, and if I had not declared myself to be without any connexion with my admirer, I should have been judged as a heretic. After I repelled your charges, that is your praises, and without shewing illwill to you personally, answered the accusations, not the accuser, and inveighed against the heretics, to shew that, though defamed by you, I was a catholic; you grew angry, and raved and composed the most magnificent works against me; and when you had given them to all men to read and repeat, letters came to me from Italy and Rome and Dalmatia, shewing, each more clearly than the last, what all the encomiums were worth with which in your former laudation you had decorated me.

8. I confess, I immediately set to work to reply to the insinuations directed against me, and tried with all my might to prove that I was no heretic, and I sent these books of my Apology to those whom your book had pained, so that your poison might be followed by my antidote. In reply to this, you sent me your former books, and now send me this last letter, full of injurious language and accusations. My good friend, what do you expect me to do? To keep silence? That would be to acknowledge myself guilty. To speak? But you hold your sword over my head, and threaten me with an indictment, no longer before the church but before the law-courts. What have I done that deserves punishment? Wherein have I injured you? Is it that I have shewn myself not to be a heretic? or that I could not esteem myself worthy of your praises? or that I laid bare in plain words the tricks and perjuries of the heretics? What is all this to you who boast yourself a true man and a catholic, and who shew more zeal in attacking me than in defending yourself? Must I be thought to be attacking you because I defend myself? or is it impossible that you should be orthodox unless you prove me to be a heretic? What help can it give you to be connected with me? and what is the meaning of your action? You are accused by one set of people and you answer only by attacking another. You find an attack made on you by one man, and you turn your back upon him and attack another who was for leaving you alone.

9. I call Jesus the Mediator to witness that it is against my will, and fighting against necessity, that I come down into the arena of this war of words, and that, had you not challenged me, I would have never broken silence. Even now, let your charges against

---

[1] Ezek. xiii, 4.

me cease, and my defence will cease. For it is no edifying spectacle that is presented to our readers, that of two old men engaging in a gladiatorial conflict on account of a heretic ; especially when both of them wish to be thought catholics. Let us leave off all favouring of heretics, and there will be no dispute between us. We once were zealous in our praise of Origen ; let us be equally zealous in condemning him now that he is condemned by the whole world. Let us join hands and hearts, and march with a ready step behind the two trophy-bearers of the East and West.[1] We went wrong in our youth, let us mend our ways in our age. If you are my brother, be glad that I have seen my errors; if I am your friend, I must give you joy on your conversion. So long as we maintain our strife, we shall be thought to hold the right faith not willingly but of necessity. Our enmity prevents our affording the spectacle of a true repentance. If our faith is one, if we both of us accept and reject the same things, (and it is from this, as even Catiline testifies, that firm friendships arise), if we are alike in our hatred of heretics, and equally condemn our former mistakes, why should we set out to battle against each other, when we have the same objects both of attack and defence? Pardon me for having praised Origen's zeal for Scriptural learning in my youthful days before I fully knew his heresies ; and I will grant you forgiveness for having written an Apology for his works when your head was grey.

10. You state that my book came into your hands two days before you wrote your letter to me, and that therefore you had no sufficient leisure to make a reply. Otherwise, if you had spoken against me after full thought and preparation, we might think that you were casting forth lightnings rather than accusations. But even so veracious a person as you will hardly gain credence when you tell us that a merchant of Eastern wares whose business is to sell what he has brought from these parts and to buy Italian goods to bring over here for sale, only stayed two days at Aquileia, so that you were obliged to write your letter to me in a hurried and extempore fashion. For your books which it took you three years to put into complete shape are hardly more carefully written. Perhaps, however, you had no one at hand then to amend your sorry productions, and this is the reason why your literary journey is destitute of the aid of

Pallas, and is intersected by faults of style, as by rough places and chasms at every turn. It is clear that this statement about the two days is false ; you would not have been able in that time even to read what I wrote, much less to reply to it ; so that it is evident that either you took a good many days in writing your letter, which its elaborate style makes probable ; or, if this is your hasty style of composition, and you can write so well off-hand, you would be very negligent in your composition to write so much worse when you have had time for thought.

11. You state, with some prevarication, that you have translated from the Greek what I had before translated into Latin ; but I do not clearly understand to what you are alluding, unless you are still bringing up against me the Commentary on the Ephesians, and hardening yourself in your effrontery, as if you had received no answer on this head. You stop your ears and will not hear the voice of the charmer. What I have done in that and other commentaries is to develop both my own opinion and that of others, stating clearly which are catholic and which heretical. This is the common rule and custom of those who undertake to explain books in commentaries : They give at length in their exposition the various opinions, and explain what is thought by themselves and by others. This is done not only by those who expound the holy Scriptures but also by those who explain secular books whether in Greek or in Latin. You, however, cannot screen yourself in reference to the Περὶ Ἀρχῶν by this fact ; for you will be convicted by your own Preface, in which you undertake that the evil parts and those which have been added by heretics have been cut off but that all that is best remains ; so that all that you have written, whether good or bad, must be held to be the work, not of the author whom you are translating, but of yourself who have made the translation. Perhaps, indeed, you ought to have corrected the errors of the heretics, and to have set forth publicly what is wrong in Origen. But on this point, (since you refer me to the document itself,) I have made you my answer before reading your letter.

12. About the book of Pamphilus, what happened to me was. not comical as you call it, but perhaps ridiculous ;[1] namely that, after I had asserted it to be by Eusebius not by Pamphilus, I stated at the end of the discussion that I had for many years believed that it was by Pamphilus, and that I

---

[1] Theophilus of Alexandria — Anastasius of Rome.

[1] *non ridiculosa ut tu scribis sed ridicula.* Jerome seems to object to *ridiculosus* as bad Latin.

had borrowed a copy of this book from you. You may judge how little I fear your derision from the fact that even now I make the same statement. I took it from your manuscript as being a copy of a work of Pamphilus. I trusted in you as a Christian and as a monk: I did not imagine that you would be guilty of such a wicked imposture. But, after that the question of Origen's heresy was stirred throughout the world on account of your translation of his work, I was more careful in examining copies of the book, and in the library of Cæsarea I found the six volumes of Eusebius' Apology for Origen. As soon as I had looked through them, I at once detected the book on the Son and the Holy Spirit which you alone have published under the name of the martyr, altering most of its blasphemies into words of a better meaning. And this I saw must have been done either by Didymus or by you or some other (it is quite clear that you did it in reference to the Περὶ Ἀρχῶν) by this decisive proof, that Eusebius tells us that Pamphilus published nothing of his own. It is for you therefore to say from whence you obtained your copy; and do not, for the sake of avoiding my accusation, say that it was from some one who is dead, or, because you have no one to point to, name one who cannot answer for himself. If this rivulet has its source in your desk, the inference is plain enough, without my drawing it. But, suppose that the title of this book and the name of the author has been changed by some other lover of Origen, what motive had you for turning it into Latin? Evidently this, that, through the testimony given to him by a martyr, all should trust to the writings of Origen, since they were guaranteed beforehand by a witness of such authority. But the Apology of this most learned man was not sufficient for you; you must write a treatise of your own in his defence, and, when these two documents had been widely circulated, you felt secure in proceeding to translate the Περὶ Ἀρχῶν itself from the Greek, and commended it in a Preface, in which you said that some things in it had been corrupted by the heretics, but that you had corrected them from a study of others of Origen's writings. Then come in your praises of me for the purpose of preventing any of my friends from speaking against you. You put me forward as the trumpeter of Origen, you praise my eloquence to the skies, so that you may drag down the faith into the mire; you call me colleague and brother, and profess yourself the imitator of my works. Then, while on the one hand you cry me up as having translated seventy homilies of Origen, and some

of his short treatises on the Apostle, in which you say that I so smoothed things down that the Latin reader will find nothing in them which is discrepant from the Catholic faith; now on the other hand you brand these very books as heretical; and, obliterating your former praise, you accuse the man whom you had preached up when you thought he would figure as your ally, because you find that he is the enemy of your perfidy. Which of us two is the calumniator of the martyr? I, who say that he was no heretic, and that he did not write the book which is condemned by every one; or you, who have published a book written by a man who was an Arian and changed his name into that of the martyr? It is not enough for you that Greece has been scandalized; you must press the book upon the ears of the Latins, and dishonor an illustrious martyr as far as in you lies by your translation. Your intention no doubt was not this; it was not to accuse me but to make me serve for the defence of Origen's writings. But let me tell you that the faith of Rome which was praised by the voice of an Apostle, does not recognize tricks of this kind. A faith which has been guaranteed by the authority of an Apostle cannot be changed though an Angel should announce another gospel than that which he preached. Therefore, my brother, whether the falsification of the book proceeds from you, as many believe, or from another, as you will perhaps try to persuade us, in which case you have only been guilty of rashness in believing the composition of a heretic to be that of a martyr, change the title, and free the innocence of the Romans from this great peril. It is of no advantage to you to be the means of a most illustrious martyr being condemned as a heretic: of one who shed his blood for Christ being proud to be an enemy of the Christian faith. Take another course: say, I found a book which I believed to be the work of a martyr. Do not fear to be a penitent. I will not press you further. I will not ask from whom you obtained it; you can name some dead man if you please, or say you bought it from an unknown man in the street: for I do not wish to see you condemned, but converted. It is better that it should appear that you were in error than that the martyr was a heretic. At all events, by some means or other, draw out your foot from its present entanglement: consider what answer you will make in the judgment to come to the complaints which the martyrs will bring against you.

13. Moreover, you make a charge against

yourself which has been brought by no one against you, and make excuses where no one has accused you. You say that you have read these and in my letter: "I want to know who has given you leave, when translating a book, to remove some things, change others, and again add others." And you go on to answer yourself, and to speak against me: "I say this to you: Who I pray, has given you leave, in your Commentaries, to put down some things out of Origen, some from Apollinarius, some of your own, instead of all from Origen or from yourself or from some other?" All this while, while you are aiming at something different, you have been preferring a very strong charge against yourself; and you have forgotten the old proverb, that those who speak falsehood should have good memories. You say that I in my Commentaries have set down some things out of Origen, some from Apollinarius, some of my own. If then these things which I have set down under the names of others are the words of Apollinarius and of Origen; what is the meaning of the charge which you fasten upon me, that, when I say "Another says this," "The following is some one's conjecture," that "other" or "some one" means myself? Between Origen and Apollinarius there is a vast difference of interpretation, of style, and of doctrine. When I set down discrepant opinions on the same passage, am I to be supposed to accept both the contradictory views? But more of this hereafter.

14. Now I ask you this: Who may have blamed you for having either added or changed or taken away certain things in the books of Origen, and have put you to the question like a man on the horse-rack; [1] Are those things which you put down in your translation bad or good? It is useless for you to simulate innocence, and by some silly question to parry the force of the true inquiry. I have never accused you for translating Origen for your own satisfaction. I have done the same, and so have Victorinus, Hilary, and Ambrose; but I have accused you for fortifying your translation of a heretical work by writing a preface approving of it. You compel me to go over the same ground, and to walk in the lines I myself have traced. For you say in that Prologue that you have cut away what had been added by the heretics, and have replaced it with what is good. If you have taken out the false statement of the heretics, then what you have left or have added must be either Origen's, or yours, and you have set them down, presumably, as good. But that many of these are bad you cannot deny. "What is that," you will say, "to me?" You must impute it to Origen; for I have done no more than alter what had been added by the heretics. Tell us then for what reason you took out the bad things written by the heretics and left those written by Origen untouched. Is it not clear that parts of the false doctrines of Origen you condemned under the designation of the doctrines of heretics, and others you accepted because you judged them to be not false but true and consonant with your faith? It was these last about which I inquired whether those things which you praised in your Preface were good or bad: it was these which you confessed you have left as perfectly good when you cut out all that was worst; and I thus have placed you, as I said, on the horse-rack, so that, if you say that they are good, you will be proved to be a heretic, but if you say they are bad, you will at once be asked: "Why then did you praise these bad things in your Preface?" And I did not add the question which you craftily pretend that I asked; "Why did you by your translation bring evil doctrines to the ears of the Latins?" For to exhibit what is bad may be done at times not for the sake of teaching them but of warning men against them: so that the reader may be on his guard not to follow the error, but may make light of the evils which he knows, whereas if unknown they might become objects of wonder to him. Yet after this, you dare to say that I am the author of writings of this kind, whereas you, as a mere translator would be going beyond the translator's province if you had chosen to correct anything, but, if you did not correct anything, you acted as a translator alone. You would be quite right in saying this if your translation of the Περὶ Ἀρχῶν had no Preface; just as Hilary, when he translated Origen's homilies took care to do it so that both the good and evil of them should be imputed not to the translator but to their own author. If you had not boasted that you had cut out the worst and left the best, you would, in some way or other, have escaped from the mire. But it is this that brings to nought the trick of your invention, and keeps you bound on all sides, so that you cannot get out. And I must ask you not to have too mean an opinion of the intelligence of your readers nor to think that all who will read your writings are so dull as not to laugh at you when they see you let real

---

[1] Equuleus, the little horse, an instrument of torture.

wounds mortify while you put plasters on a healthy body.

15. What your opinions are on the resurrection of the flesh, we have already learned from your Apology. "No member will be cut off, nor any part of the body destroyed." This is the clear and open profession which you make in your innocence, and which you say is accepted by all the bishops of Italy. I should believe your statement, but that the matter of that book which is not Pamphilus' makes me doubt about you. And I wonder that Italy should have approved what Rome rejected; that the bishops should have accepted what the Apostolic see condemned.

16. You further write that it was by my letters that you had been informed that the pope Theophilus lately put forth an exposition of the faith which has not yet reached you and you promise to accept whatever he may have written. I am not aware that I ever said this, or that I sent any letters of the sort. But you consent to things of which you are still in uncertainty, and things as to which you do not know what and of what kind they will turn out to be, so that you may avoid speaking of things which you know quite well, and may not be bound by the consent you have given to them. There are two letters of Theophilus,[1] a Synodal and a Paschal letter, against Origen and his disciples, and others against Apollinarius and against Origen also, which, within the last two years or thereabouts, I have translated and given to the men who speak our language for the edification of the church. I am not aware that I have translated anything else of his. But, when you say that you assent to the opinion of the pope Theophilus in everything, you must take care not to let your masters and disciples hear you, and not to offend these numerous persons who call me a robber and you a martyr, and also not to provoke the wrath of the man[2] who wrote letters to you against the bishop Epiphanius, and exhorted you to stand fast in the truth of the faith, and not to change your opinion for any terror. This epistle in its complete form is held by those to whom it was brought. After this you say, after your manner: " I will satisfy you even when you rage against me, as I have in the matter you spoke of before." But again you say, " What do you want? have you anything

more at which you may shoot with the bow of your oratory?" And yet you are indignant if I find fault with your distasteful way of speaking, though you take up the lowest expressions of the Comedians, and in writing on church affairs adopt language fit only for the characters of harlots and their lovers on the stage.

17. Now, as to the question which you raise, when it was that I began to admit the authority of the pope Theophilus, and was associated with him in community of belief. You make answer to yourself: " Then, I suppose, when you were the supporter of Paul whom he had condemned and made the greatest effort to help him, and instigated him to recover through an imperial rescript the bishopric from which he had been removed by the episcopal tribunal." I will not begin by answering for myself, but first speak of the injury which you have here done to another. What humanity or charity is there in rejoicing over the misfortunes of others and in exhibiting their wounds to the world? Is that the lesson you have learned from that Samaritan who carried back the man that was half dead to the inn? Is this what you understand by pouring oil into his wounds, and paying the host his expenses? Is it thus that you interpret the sheep brought back to the fold, the piece of money recovered, the prodigal son welcomed back? Suppose that you had a right to speak evil of me, because I had injured you, and, to use your words, had goaded you to madness and stimulated you to evil speaking: what harm had a man who remains in obscurity done you, that you should lay bare his scars, and when they were skinned over, should tear them open by inflicting this uncalled for pain? Even if he was worthy of your reproaches, were you justified in doing this? If I am not mistaken, those whom you wish to strike at through him (and I speak the open opinion of many) are the enemies of the Origenists; you use the troubles of one of them to show your violence against both.[1] If the decisions of the pope Theophilus so greatly please you, and you think it impious that an episcopal decree should be nullified, what do you say about the rest of those whom he has condemned? And what do you say about the pope Anastasius, about whom you assert most truly that no one thinks him capable as the bishop of so great a city, of doing an injury to an innocent or an absent man? I do not say this because I

---

1 For the years 401 and 402. See Jerome Letters 96 and 98.
2 Isidore, the Origenist monk who was sent to inquire into the quarrel between Jerome and John of Jerusalem. His letter, written to John and Rufinus prejudging the case, was brought by mistake to Jerome's friend Vincentius. See Jerome Against John of Jerusalem c. 37.

1 Perhaps both Paul and Jerome.

set myself up as a judge of episcopal decisions, or wish what they have determined to be rescinded; but I say, Let each of them do what he thinks right at his own risk, it is for him alone to consider how his judgment will be judged. Our duties in our monastery are those of hospitality; we welcome all who come to us with the smile of human friendliness. We must take care lest it should again happen that Mary and Joseph do not find room in the inn, and that Jesus should be shut out and say to us, "I was a stranger and ye took me not in." The only persons we do not welcome are heretics, who are the only persons who are welcomed by you: for our profession binds us to wash the feet of those who come to us, not to discuss their merits. Bring to your remembrance, my brother, how he whom we speak of had confessed Christ: think of that breast which was gashed by the scourges: recall to mind the imprisonment he had endured, the darkness, the exile, the work in the mines, and you will not be surprised that we welcomed him as a passing guest. Are we to be thought rebels by you because we give a cup of cold water to the thirsty in the name of Christ?

18. I can tell you of something which may make him still dearer to us, though more odious to you. A short time ago, the faction of the heretics which was scattered away from Egypt and Alexandria came to Jerusalem, and wished to make common cause with him, so that as they suffered together, they might have the same heresy imputed to them. But he repelled their advances, he scorned and cast them from him: he told them that he was not an enemy of the faith and was not going to take up arms against the Church: that his previous action had been the result of vexation not of unsoundness in the faith; and that he had sought only to prove his own innocence, not to attack that of others. You profess to consider an imperial rescript upsetting an episcopal decree to be an impiety. That is a matter for the responsibility of the man who obtained it. But what is your opinion of men who, when they have been themselves condemned, haunt the palaces of the great, and in a serried column make an attack on a single man who represents the faith of Christ? However, as to my own communion with the Pope Theophilus, I will call no other witness than the very man whom you pretend that I injured.[1] His letters were always addressed to me, as you

well know, even at the time when you prevented their being forwarded to me, and when you used daily to send letter carriers to him repeating to him with vehemence that his opponent was my most intimate friend, and telling the same falsehoods which you now shamelessly write, so that you might stir up his hatred against me and that his grief at the supposed injury done him might issue in oppression against me in matters of faith. But he, being a prudent man and a man of apostolical wisdom, came through time and experience to understand both our loyalty to him and your plots against us. If, as you declare, my followers stirred up a plot against you at Rome and stole your uncorrected manuscripts while you were asleep; who was it that stirred up the pope Theophilus against the public enemy in Egypt? Who obtained the decrees of the princes against them, and the consent of the whole of this quarter of the world? Yet you boast that you from your youth were the hearer and disciple of Theophilus, although he, before he became a bishop, through his native modesty, never taught in public, and you, after he became a Bishop, were never at Alexandria. Yet you dare, in order to deal a blow at me, to say "I do not accuse, or change, my masters." If that were true it would in my opinion throw a grave suspicion on your Christian standing. As for myself, you have no right to charge me with condemning my former teachers: but I stand in awe of those words of Isaiah: [1] "Woe unto them that call evil good and good evil, that put darkness for light and light for darkness, that call bitter sweet and sweet bitter." But it is you who drink alike the honeywine of your masters and their poisons, who have fallen away from your true master the Apostle, who teaches that neither he himself or an angel, if they err in matters of faith, must not be followed.

19. You allude to Vigilantius. What dream this is that you have dreamed about him I do not know. Where have I said that he was defiled by communion with heretics at Alexandria? Tell me the book, produce the letter: but you will find absolutely no such statement. Yet with your wonted carelessness of statement or rather impudence of lying, which makes you imagine that every one will believe what you say, you add: "When you quoted a text of Scripture against him in so insulting a way that I do not dare to repeat it with my own mouth." You

---

[1] Theophilus himself.

[1] Is. v, 20.

do not dare to repeat it because you can make the charge seem worse by keeping silence; and, because your accusation has no facts to rest upon, you simulate modesty, so that the reader may imagine that you are acting from consideration towards me, although your lies show that you do not consider your own soul. What is this text of Scripture which is too shameful to proceed out of that most shameless mouth of yours? What shameful thing, indeed, can you mention in the sacred books? If you are ashamed to speak, at any rate you can write it down, and then I shall be convinced of wantonness by my own words. I might be silent on all other points, and I should still prove by this single passage how brazen is your effrontery. You know how little I fear your impeachment. If you produce the evidence with which you threaten me, all the blame which now rests on you will rest on me. I gave my reply to you when I dealt with Vigilantius; for he brought the same charges against me which you bring first in the guise of friendly eulogy, afterwards in that of hostile accusation. I am aware who it was that stirred up his ravings against me; I know your plots and vices; I am not ignorant of his simplicity which is proclaimed by every one. Through his folly your hatred against me found an outlet for its fury; and, if I wrote a letter to suppress it, so that you should not be thought to be the only one who possesses a literary cudgel, that does not justify you in inventing shameful expressions which you can find in no part of my writings whatever. You must accept and confess the fact that the same document which answered his madness aroused also your calumnies.

20. In the matter of the letter of the pope Anastasius, you seem to have come on a slippery place; you walk unsteadily, and do not see where to plant your feet. At one moment you say that it must have been written by me; at another that it ought to have been transmitted to you by him to whom it was sent. Then again you charge the writer with injustice; or you protest that it matters nothing to you whether he wrote it or not, since you hold his predecessor's testimonial, and, while Rome was begging you to give her the honor of your presence, you disdained her through love of your own little town. If you have any suspicion that the letter was forged by me, why do you not ask for it in the chartulary of the Roman See and then, when you discover that it was not written by the bishop, hold me manifestly guilty of the crime? You would

then instead of trying to bind me with cobwebs, hold me fast bound in a net of strong cords. But if it is as written by the Bishop of Rome, it is an act of folly on your part to ask for a copy of the letter from one to whom it was not sent, and not from him who sent it, and to send to the East for evidence the source of which you have in your own country. You had better go to Rome and expostulate with him as to the reproach which he has directed against you when you were both absent and innocent. You might first point out that he had refused to accept your exposition of faith, which, as you say, all Italy has approved, and that he made no use of your literary cudgel against the dogs you spoke of. Next, you might complain that he had sent to the East a letter aimed at you which branded you with the mark of heresy, and said that by your translation of Origen's books Περὶ Ἀρχῶν the Roman church which had received the work in its simplicity was in danger of losing the sincerity of faith which it had learned from the Apostle; and that he had raised yet more ill will against you by daring to condemn this very book, though it was fortified by the attestation of your Preface. It is no light thing that the pontiff of so great a city should have fastened this charge upon you or have rashly taken it up when made by another. You should go about the streets vociferating and crying over and over again, "It is not my book, or, if it is, the uncorrected sheets were stolen by Eusebius. I published it differently, indeed I did not publish it at all; I gave it to nobody, or at all events to few; and my enemy was so unscrupulous and my friends so negligent, that all the copies alike were falsified by him." This, my dearest brother, is what you ought to have done, not to turn your back upon him and to direct the arrows of your abuse across the sea against me; for how can it cure your wounds that I should be wounded? Does it comfort a man who is stricken for death to see his friend dying with him?

21. You produce a letter of Siricius[1] who now sleeps in Christ, and the letter of the living Anastasius you despise. What injury you ask, can it do you that he should have written (or perhaps not written at all) when you knew nothing of it? If he did write, still it is enough for you that you have the witness of the whole world in your favor, and that no one thinks it possible that the bishop of so great a city could have done

---

[1] Bishop of Rome in succession to Damasus. (A.D. 385–398) and succeeded by Anastasius.

an injury to an innocent man, or even to one who was simply absent. You speak of yourself as innocent, though your translation made all Rome shudder; you say you were absent, but it is only because you dare not reply when you are accused. And you so shrink from the judgment of the city of Rome that you prefer to subject yourself to an invasion of the barbarians[1] than to the opinion of a peaceful city. Suppose that the letter of last year was forged by me; who then wrote the letters which have lately been received in the East? Yet in these last the pope Anastasius pays you such compliments that, when you read them, you will be more inclined to set to work to defend yourself than to accuse me.

I should like you to consider how inevitable is the wisdom which you are shunning and the Attic Salt and the eloquence of your diction in religious writing. You are attacked by others, you are pierced through by their condemnation, yet it is against me that you toss yourself about in your fury, and say: " I could unfold a tale as to the manner of your departure from Rome; as to the opinions expressed about you at the time, and written about you afterwards, as to your oath, the place where you embarked, the pious manner in which you avoided committing perjury; all this I could enlarge upon, but I have determined to keep back more than I relate." These are specimens of your pleasant speeches. And if after this I say anything sharp in answer to you you threaten me with immediate proscription and with the sword. You are a most eloquent person, and have all the tricks of rhetoric; you pretend to be passing over things which you really reveal, so that what you cannot prove by an open charge, you may make into a crime by seeming to put it aside. All this is your simplicity; this is what you mean by sparing your friend and reserving your statements for the judicial tribunal; you spare me by heaping up a mass of charge against me.

22. If any one wishes to hear the arrangements for my journey from Rome, they were these. In the month of August,[2] when the etesian winds were blowing, accompanied by the reverend presbyter Vincentius and my young brother, and other monks who are now living at Jerusalem, I went on board ship at the port of Rome, choosing my own time, and with a very large body of the saints attending me, I arrived at Rhegium. I stood for a while on the shore of

Scylla, and heard the old stories of the rapid voyage of the versatile Ulysses, of the songs of the sirens and the insatiable whirlpool of Charybdis. The inhabitants of that spot told me many tales, and gave me the advice that I should sail not for the columns of Proteus but for the port where Jonah landed, because the former of those was the course suited for men who were hurried and flying, but the latter was best for a man who was imprisoned; but I preferred to take the course by Malea and the Cyclades to Cyprus. There I was received by the venerable bishop Epiphanius, of whose testimony to you you boast. I came to Antioch, where I enjoyed the communion of Paulinius the pontiff and confessor and was set forward by him on my journey to Jerusalem, which I entered in the middle of winter and in severe cold. I saw there many wonderful things, and verified by the judgment of my own eyes things which had before come to my ears by report. Thence I made my way to Egypt. I saw the monasteries of Nitria, and perceived the snakes[1] which lurked among the choirs of the monks. Then making haste I at once returned to Bethlehem, which is now my home, and there poured my perfume upon the manger and cradle of the Saviour. I saw also the lake of ill-omen. Nor did I give myself to ease and inertness, but I learned many things which I did not know before. As to what judgment was formed of me at Rome, or what was written afterwards, you are quite welcome to speak out, especially since you have writings to trust to; for I am not to be tried by your words which you at your will either veil in enigma or blurt out with open falsehood, but by the documents of the church. You may see how little I am afraid of you. If you can produce against me a single record of the Bishop of Rome or of any other church, I will confess myself to be chargeable with all the iniquities which I find assigned to you. It would be easy for me to tell of the circumstances of your departure, your age, the date of sailing, the places in which you lived, the company you kept. But far be it from me to do what I blame you for doing, and, in a discussion between churchmen, to make up a story worthy of the ravings of quarrelling hags. Let this word be enough for your wisdom to remember. Do not adopt a method with another which can at once be retorted on yourself.

23. As regards our reverend friend

---

[1] The Goths under Alaric passed through Aquileia to invade Italy in 401.   [2] A.D. 385.

[1] He means Origenistic heresies; but there is no trace in his early works of this detection of heresy.

Epiphanius, this is strange shuffling of yours, when you say that it was impossible for him to have written against you after his giving you the kiss and joining with you in prayer. It is as if you were to contend that he would not be dead if a short time before he had been alive, or as if it were not equally certain that he had first reproved you and then, after the kiss of peace, excommunicated you. " They went out from us," it is said,[1] " but they were not of us; otherwise they would no doubt have continued with us." The apostle bids us avoid a heretic after a first and second admonition: of course this implies that he was a member of the flock of the church before he was avoided or condemned. I confess I cannot restrain my laughter when, at the prompting of some clever person, you strike up a hymn in honour of Epiphanius. Why, this is the ' silly old man,' the ' anthropomorphite,' this is the man who boasted in your presence of the six thousand books of Origen that he had read, who ' thinks himself entrusted with the preaching of the Gospel against Origen among all nations in their own tongue' who ' will not let others read Origen for fear they should discover what he has stolen from him.' Read what he has written, and the letter, or rather letters, one of which I will adduce as a testimonial to your orthodoxy, so that it may be seen how worthy he is of your present praise. [2] " May God set you free, my brother, and the holy people of Christ which is entrusted to you, and all the brethren who are with you, and especially the Presbyter Rufinus, from the heresy of Origen, and all other heresies, and from the perdition which they bring. For if many heresies have been condemned by the Church on account of one word or of two, which are contrary to the faith, how much more must that man be counted a heretic who has invented so many perverse things, so many false doctrines! He stands forth as the enemy of God and of the church." This is the testimony which this saintly man bears to you. This is the garland of praise which he gives you to parade in. Thus runs the letter which your golden coins extracted from the chamber of our brother Eusebius, so that you might calumniate the translator of it, and might fix upon me the guilt of a most manifest crime — that of rendering a Greek word as ' dearest' which ought to have been ' honourable!' But what is all this to you who can control all events by your pru-

dent methods, and can trim your path between different possibilities, first saying, if you can find any one to believe you, that neither Anastasius nor Epiphanius ever wrote a line against you; and, secondly, when their actual letters cry out against you, and break down your audacious effrontery, despising the judgment of them both, and say it does not matter to you whether they wrote or not, since it was impossible for them to write against an innocent and an absent man.

Then again, you have no right to speak evil of that saintly man, as you do when you say " that it may be seen that he gave me peace with his words and his kiss, but kept evil and deceit in his heart" — for this is your reasoning, and it is thus that you defend yourself. That this is the letter of Epiphanius and that it is hostile to you, all the world knows: and that it came in its genuine form into your hands we can prove; and it is therefore an astounding shame or rather utter shamelessness in you to deny what you cannot doubt to be true. What! Is Epiphanius to be befouled with the imputation that he gave you the sign of peace but had deceit in his heart? Is it not much truer to believe that he first admonished you because he wished to save you from error and bring you back to the right way; and that therefore he did not reject your Judas kiss, wishing to break down by his forbearance the betrayer of the faith, — but that afterwards when he found that all his toil was fruitless, and that the leopard could not change its spots nor the Ethiopian his skin, he proclaimed in his letter what had before been only a suspicion in his mind?

24. It is somewhat the same argument which you use against the pope Anastasius, namely, that, since you hold the letters of the bishop Siricius, it was impossible that he should write against you. I am afraid you suspect that some injury has been done you. I cannot understand how a man of your acuteness and capacity can condescend to such nonsense; you suppose that your readers are foolish, but you shew that you are foolish yourself. Then after this extraordinary argumentation, you subjoin this little sentence: " Far be such conduct from these reverend persons. It is from your school that such actions proceed. You gave us all the signs of peace at our departure, and then threw missiles charged with venom from behind our backs." In this clause or rather declamatory speech, you intended, no doubt, to shew your rhetorical skill. It is true we gave you the signs of peace, but not to em-

---

[1] 1 John ii, 19.
[2] From Epiphanius' letter to John, Bishop of Jerusalem, translated by Jerome (Jer. Ep. 51 c. 6).

brace heresy; we joined hands, we accompanied you as you set forth on your journey, on the understanding that you were catholic not that we were heretical. But I want to learn what these poisoned missiles are which you complain that I threw from behind your back. I sent the presbyters, Vincentius, Paulinianus, Eusebius, Rufinus. Of these, Vincentius went to Rome long before you; Paulinianus and Eusebius set out a year after you had sailed; Rufinus two years after, for the cause of Claudius; all of them either for private reasons, or because another was in peril of his life. Was it possible for me to know that when you entered Rome, a nobleman had dreamed that a ship full of merchandise was entering with full blown sails? or that all questions about fate were being solved by a solution which should not itself be fatuous? or that you were translating the book of Eusebius as if it were Pamphilus'? or that you were putting your own cover upon Origen's poisoned dish by lending your majestic eloquence to this translation of his notorious work Περὶ Ἀρχῶν? This is a new way of calumniating a man. We sent out the accusers before you had committed the crime. It was not, I repeat, it was not by our plan, but by the providence of God, that these men, who were sent out for another reason, came to fight against the rising heresy. They were sent, like Joseph, to relieve the coming famine by the fervour of their faith.

25. To what point will not audacity burst forth when once it is freed from restraints? He has imputed to himself the charge made against another so that we may be thought to have invented it. I made a charge against some one unnamed, and he takes it as spoken against himself; he purges himself from another man's sins, being only sure of his own innocence. For he takes his oath that he did not write the letter that passed under my name to the African bishops, in which I am made to confess that I had been induced by Jewish influence to make false translations of the Scriptures; and he sends me writings which contain all these things which he declares to be unknown to him. It is remarkable to know how his subtlety has coincided with another man's malice, so that the lies which this other told in Africa, he in accord with him declared to be true; and also how that elegant style of his could be imitated by some chance and unskilled person. You alone have the privilege of translating the venom of the heretics, and of making all nations drink a draught from the cup of Babylon. You may correct the Latin Scriptures from the Greek, and may deliver to the Churches to read something different from what they received from the Apostles; but I am not to be allowed to go behind the Septuagint version which I translated after strict correction for the men of my native tongue a great many years ago, and, for the confutation of the Jews, to translate the actual copies of the Scriptures which they confess to be the truest, so that when a dispute arises between them and the Christians, they may have no place of retreat and subterfuge, but may be smitten most effectually with their own spear. I have written pretty fully on this point if I rightly remember, in many other places, especially in the end of my second book; and I have checked your popularity-hunting, with which you seek to arouse ill will against me among the innocent and the inexperienced, by a clear statement of fact. To that I think it enough to refer the reader.

26. I think it a point which should not be passed over, that you have no right to complain that the falsifier of your papers holds in my esteem the glorious position of a confessor, since you who are guilty of this very crime are called a martyr and an apostle by all the partisans of Origen, for that exile and imprisonment of yours at Alexandria. On your alleged inexperience in Latin composition I have answered you above. But, since you repeat the same things, and, as if forgetful of your former defence, again remind me that I ought to know that you have been occupied for thirty years in devouring Greek books, and therefore do not know Latin, I would have you observe that it is not a few words of yours with which I find fault, though indeed all your writing is worthy of being destroyed. What I wished to do was to shew your followers, whom you have taken so much pains in teaching to know nothing, to understand what amount of modesty there is in a man who teaches what he does not know, who writes what he is ignorant of, so that they may expect to find the same wisdom in his opinions. As to what you add " That it is not faults of words which are offensive, but sins, such as lying, calumny, disparagement, false witness, and all evil speaking, and that the mouth which speaketh lies kills the soul," and your deprecation, " Let not that ill-savour reach my nostrils;" I would believe what you say, were it not that I discover facts inconsistent with this. It is as if a fuller or a tanner in speaking to a dealer in pigments should warn him that he had better hold his nose as he passed their shops. I will do what

you recommend; I will stop my nose, so that it may not be put to the torture by the delightful odour of your truth-speaking and your benedictions.

27. In reference to your alternate praise and disparagement of me, you argue with great acuteness that you have the same right to speak good and evil of me that I have to find fault with Origen and Didymus whom I once praised. I must instruct you, then, wisest of men and chief of Roman dialecticians, that there is no fault of logic in praising a man in certain respects while you blame him in others, but only in approving and disapproving one and the same thing. I will take an example, so that, though you may not understand, the wise reader may join me in understanding the point. In the case of Tertullian we praise his great talent, but we condemn his heresy. In that of Origen we admire his knowledge of the Scriptures, but nevertheless we do not accept his false doctrine. As to Didymus, however, we extol both his powers of memory, and the purity of his faith in the Trinity, while on the other point in which he erred in trusting to Origen we withdraw from him. The vices of our teachers are not to be imitated, their virtues are. There was a man at Rome who had an African, a very learned man, as his grammar teacher; and he thought that he was rising to an equality with his teacher because he copied his strident voice and his faulty pronunciation. You in your Preface to the Περὶ Ἀρχῶν speak of me as your brother and call me your most eloquent colleague, and proclaim my soundness in the faith. From these three points you cannot draw back; carp at me on all other points as you please, so long as you do not openly contradict this testimony which you bear to me; for in calling me friend and colleague, you confess me worthy of your friendship; when you proclaim me an eloquent man, you cannot go on accusing me of ignorance; and when you confess that I am in all points a catholic, you cannot fix on me the guilt of heresy. Beyond these three points you may charge me with anything you like without openly contradicting yourself. From all this calculation the net result is that you are wrong in blaming in me what you formerly praised; but that I am not in fault when, in the case of the same men, I praise what is laudable and blame what is censurable.

28. You pass on to the origin of souls, and at great length exclaim against the smoke which you say I raise. You want to be allowed to express ignorance on a point

on which you advisedly dissemble your knowledge; and therefore begin questioning me about angels and archangels; as to the mode of their existence, the place and nature of their abodes, the differences, if there be any, existing between them; and then as to the course of the sun, the waxing and waning of the moon, the character and movements of the stars. I wonder that you did not set down the whole of the lines:[1]

Whence come the earthquakes, whence the high-swoll'n seas
Breaking their bounds, then sinking back to rest;
The Sun's eclipse, the labours of the moon;
The race of men and beasts, the storm, the fire,
Arcturus' rainy Hyads, and the Bears:
Why haste the winter's suns to bathe themselves
Beneath the wave, what stays its lingering nights.

Then, leaving things in heaven, and condescending to those on earth, you philosophize on minor points. You say: " Tell us what are the causes of the fountains, and of the wind; what makes the hail and the showers; why the sea is salt, the rivers sweet; what account is to be given of clouds and storms, thunderbolts, and thunder and lightning." You mean that if I do not know all this, you are entitled to say you know nothing about the origin of souls. You wish to balance your ignorance on a single point by mine on many. But do not you, who in page after page stir up what you call my smoke, understand that I can see your mists and whirlwinds? You wish to be thought a man of extensive knowledge, and among the disciples of Calpurnius[2] to enjoy a great reputation for wisdom, and therefore you raise up the whole physical world in front of me, as if Socrates had said in vain when he passed over to the study of Ethics: " What is above us is nothing to us." So then, if I cannot tell you why the ant, which is such a little creature, whose body is a mere point, has six feet, whereas an elephant with its vast bulk has only four to walk on; why serpents and snakes glide along on their chests and bellies; why the worm which is commonly called the millipede has such a swarming array of feet; I am prohibited from knowing anything about the origin of souls! You ask me what I know about souls, so that, when I make any statement about them, you may at once attack it. And if I say that the church's doctrine is that God forms souls every day, and sends them into the bodies of those who are born, you will at once bring out the snares your master invented, and ask, Where is God's justice if

---

[1] Virgil Georg. ii, 473, Æn. i, 746.
[2] A Latin rhetorician of the time of Hadrian and Antoninus Pius. Some of his exercises are still extant.

he grants souls to those who are born of adultery or incest? Is he not an accessory to men's sins, if he creates souls for the adulterers who make the bodies? as if, when you hear that seed corn had been stolen, you are to suppose the fault to lie in the nature of the corn, and not in the man who stole the wheat; and that therefore the earth had no business to nourish the seed in its bosom, because the hands of the sower who cast them in were unclean. Hence comes also your mysterious question, Why do infants die? since it is because of their sins, as you hold, that they received bodies. There exists a treatise of Didymus addressed to you, in which he meets this inquiry of yours, with the answer, that they had not sinned much, and therefore it was enough punishment for them just to have touched their bodily prisons. He, who was your master and mine also, when you asked this question, wrote at my request three books of comments on the prophet Hosea, and dedicated them to me. This shows what parts of his teaching we respectively accepted.

29. You press me to give my opinions about the nature of things. If there were room, I could repeat to you the views of Lucretius who follows Epicurus, or those of Aristotle as taught by the Peripatetics, or of Plato and Zeno by the Academics and the Stoics. Passing to the church, where we have the rule of truth, the books of Genesis and the Prophets and Ecclesiastes, give us much information on questions of this kind. But if we profess ignorance about all these things, as also about the origin of souls, you ought in your Apology to acknowledge your ignorance of all alike, and to ask your calumniators why they had the impudence to force you to reply on this single point when they themselves know nothing of all those great matters. But Oh! how vast was the wealth contained in that trireme[1] which had come full of all the wares of Egypt and the East to enrich the poverty of the city of Rome.

[2] " Thou art that hero, well-nam'd Maximus,
Thou who alone by writing sav'st the state."

Unless you had come from the East, that very learned man would be still sticking fast among the mathematici,[3] and all Christians would still be ignorant of what might be said against fatalism. You have a right to ply me with questions about astrology and

the cause of the sky and the stars, when you brought to land a ship full of such wares as these. I acknowledge my poverty; I have not grown rich to this extent in the East like you. You learned in your long sojourn under the shadow of the Pharos what Rome never knew: Egypt instructed you in lore which Italy did not possess till now.

30. Your Apology says that there are three opinions as to the origin of souls: one held by Origen, a second by Tertullian and Lactantius (as to Lactantius what you say is manifestly false), a third by us simple and foolish men, who do not see that, if our opinion is true, God is thereby shewn to be unjust. After this you say that you do not know what is the truth. I say, then, tell me, whether you think that outside of these three opinions any truth can be found so that all these three may be false; or whether you think one of these three is true. If there is some other possibility, why do you confine the liberty of discussion within a close-drawn line? and why do you put forward the views which are false and keep silence about the true? But if one of the three is true and the two others false, why do you include false and true in one assertion of ignorance? Perhaps you pretend not to know which is true in order that it may be safe for you, whenever you may please, to defend the false. This is the smoke, these are the mists, with which you try to keep away the light from men's eyes. You are the Aristippus[1] of our day: you bring your ship into the port of Rome full of merchandize of all kinds; you set your professorial chair on high, and represent to us Hermagoras[2] and Gorgias[3] of Leontinum: only, you were in such a hurry to set sail that you left one little piece of goods, one little question, forgotten in the East. And you cry out with reiteration that you learned both at Aquileia and at Alexandria that God is the creator of both our bodies and our souls. This then, forsooth, is the pressing question, whether our souls were created by God or by the devil, and not whether the opinion of Origen is true that our souls existed before our bodies and committed some sin because of which they have been tied to these gross bodies; or whether, again, they slept like dormice in a state of torpor and of slumber. Every one is asking this question, but you say nothing about it; nobody asks the other, but to that you direct your answer.

31. Another part of my ' smoke' which

---

[1] In Macarius' dream, see Ruf. Apol. i, 11.
[2] A parody upon the verse of Virgil and Ennius on Fabius Maximus called Cunctator because by his tactics of delay he saved Rome from the Carthaginians. "Thou art Maximus (greatest) who savedst the state by delaying (cunctando)."
[3] Astrologers or magicians.

[1] Of Cyrene. A disciple of Socrates, founder of the Cyrenaic sect, the precursors of the Epicureans.
[2] Rhetorician of Rhodes.
[3] Statesman and Sophist, came to Athens on a mission B.C. 327, and settled there.

you frequently laugh at is my pretence, as you say, to know what I do not know, and the parade I make of great teachers to deceive the common and ignorant people. You, of course, are a man not of smoke but of flame, or rather of lightning; you fulminate when you speak; you cannot contain the flames which have been conceived within your mouth, and like Barchochebas,[1] the leader of the revolt of the Jews, who used to hold in his mouth a lighted straw and blow it out so as to appear to be breathing forth flame: so you also, like a second Salmoneus,[2] brighten the whole path on which you tread, and reproach us as mere men of smoke, to whom perhaps the words might be applied, [3] " Thou touchest the hills and they smoke." You do not understand the allusion of the Prophet[4] when he speaks of the smoke of the locusts; it is no doubt the beauty of your eyes which makes it impossible for you to bear the pungency of our smoke.

32. As to your charge of perjury, since you refer me to your book; and since I have made my reply to you and Calpurnius[5] in the previous books, it will be sufficient here to observe that you exact from me in my sleep what you have never yourself fulfilled in your waking hours. It seems that I am guilty of a great crime because I have told girls and virgins of Christ, that they had better not read secular works, and that I once promised when warned in a dream not to read them. But your ship which was announced by revelation to the city of Rome, promises one thing and effects another. It came to do away with the puzzle of the mathematici: what it does is to do away with the faith of Christians. It had made its run with sails full set over the Ionian and Ægean, the Adriatic and Tyrrhenian seas, only to make shipwreck in the Roman port. Are you not ashamed of hunting up nonsense of this kind and putting me to the trouble of bringing up similar things against you? Suppose that some one had seen a dream about you such as might make you vainglorious; it would have been modest as well as wise in you not to seem to know of it, instead of boasting of other people's dreams as a serious testimony to yourself. What a difference there is between your dream and mine! Mine tells how I was humbled and repressed; yours boasts over and over again how you were

praised. You cannot say, It matters nothing to me what another man dreamed, for in those most enlightening books of yours you tell us that this was the motive which led you to make the translation; you could not bear that an eminent man should have dreamed in vain. This is all your endeavour. If you can make me out guilty of perjury, you think you will be deemed no heretic.

33. I now come to the most serious charge of all, that in which you accuse me of having been unfaithful after the restoration of our friendship. I confess that, of all the reproaches which you bring against me or threaten me with, there is none which I would so much deprecate as that of fraud, deceit and breach of faith. To sin is human, to lay snares is diabolical. What! Was it for this that I joined hands with you over the slain lamb in the Church of the Resurrection, that I might ' steal your manuscripts at Rome '? or that I might ' send out my dogs to gnaw away your papers before they were corrected '? Can any one believe that we made ready the accusers before you had committed the crime? Is it supposed that we knew what plans you were meditating in your heart? or what another man had been dreaming? or how the Greek proverb was having its fulfilment in your case, "the pig teaches Minerva"? If I sent Eusebius to bark against you, who then stirred up the passion of Aterbius and others against you? Is it not the fact that he thought that I also was a heretic because of my friendship with you? And, when I had given him satisfaction as to the heresies of Origen, you shut yourself up at home, and never dared to meet him, for fear you should have to condemn what you wished not to condemn, or by openly resisting him should subject yourself to the reproach of heresy. Do you think that he cannot be called as a witness against you because he is your accuser? Before ever the reverend bishop Epiphanius came to Jerusalem, and gave you the signs of peace by word and kiss, ' yet having evil thoughts and guile in his heart'; before I translated for him that letter[1] which was such a reproof to you, and in which he wrote you down a heretic though he had before approved you as orthodox; Aterbius was barking against you at Jerusalem, and, if he had not speedily taken himself off, would have felt not your literary cudgel but the stick you flourish in your right hand to drive the dogs away.[2]

34. "But why," you ask, "did you

[1] Son of a Star; the leader of the Jewish revolt against Hadrian, A.D. 132-5.
[2] King of Elis whom Jove destroyed for imitating thunder and lightning by his chariot and brazen bridge and torches.
[3] Ps. civ, 52.   [4] Supposed to refer to Rev. ix, 7, 17.
[5] Possibly a nick-name for one of Rufinus' friends : or ' to you even when you pose as Calpurnius.'   See above c. 28, note.

[1] Jerome Letter li.,—Epiphanius to John of Jerusalem.
[2] See Ruf. Apol. to Anastasius, 1.

accept my manuscripts which had been falsified? and why, when I had translated the Περὶ Ἀρχῶν did you dare to put your pen to the same work? If I had erred, as any man may, ought you not to summon me to reply by a private letter, and to speak smoothly to me, as I am speaking smoothly in my present letter?" My whole fault is this that, when accusations were brought against me in the guise of disingenuous praise, I tried to purge myself from them, and this without invidiously introducing your name. I wished to refer to many persons a charge which you alone had brought, not so as to retort the charge of heresy upon you, but to repel it from myself. Could I know that you would be angry if I wrote against the heretics? You had said that you had taken away the heretical passages from the works of Origen. I therefore turned my attacks not upon you but upon the heretics, for I did not believe that you were a favourer of heresy. Pardon me, if I did this with too great vehemence. I thought that I should give you pleasure. You say that it was by the dishonest tricks of those who acted for me that your manuscripts were brought out before the public, when they were kept secretly in your chamber, or were in possession only of the man who had desired to have the translation made for him. But how is this reconcilable with your former statement that either no one or very few had them? If they were kept secret in your chamber, how could they be in the possession of the man who had desired to have the translation made for him? If the one man for whom the manuscripts had been written had obtained them in order to conceal them, then they were not kept secret in your chamber, and they were not in the hands of those few who, as you now declare, possessed them. You accuse us of having stolen them away; and then again you reproach us with having bought them for a great sum of money and an immense bribe. In a single matter, and in one little letter, what a tissue of various and discordant falsehoods! You have full liberty for accusation, but I have none for defence. When you bring a charge, you think nothing about friendship. When I begin to reply, then your mind is full of the rights of friendship. Let me ask you: Did you write these manuscripts for concealment or for publication? If for concealment, why were they written? If for publication, why did you conceal them?

35. But my fault, you will say, was this, that I did not restrain your accusers who were my friends. Why, I had enough to do to answer their accusations against myself; for they charged me with hypocrisy,[1] as I could shew by producing their letters, because I kept silence when I knew you to be a heretic; and because by incautiously maintaining peace with you, I fostered the intestine wars of the Church. You call them my disciples; they suspect me of being your fellow-disciple; and, because I was somewhat sparing in my rejection of your praises, they think me to be initiated, along with you, into the mysteries of heresy. This was the service your Prologue did me; you injured me more by appearing as my friend than you would had you shewn yourself my enemy. They had persuaded themselves once for all (whether rightly or wrongly is their business) that you were a heretic. If I should determine to defend you, I should only succeed in getting myself accused by them along with you. They cast in my teeth your laudation of me, which they suppose to have been written not in craft but sincerity; and they vehemently reproach me with the very things which you always praised in me. What am I to do? To turn my disciples into my accusers for your sake? To receive on my own head the weapons which were hurled against my friend?

36. In the matter of the books Περὶ Ἀρχῶν, I have even a claim upon your gratitude. You say that you cut off anything that was offensive and replaced it by what was better. I have represented things just as they stood in the Greek. By this means both things are made to appear, your faith and the heresy of him whom you translated. The leading Christians of Rome wrote to me: Answer your accuser; if you keep silence, you will be held to have assented to his charges. All of them unanimously demanded that I should bring to light the subtle errors of Origen, and make known the poison of the heretics to the ears of the Romans to put them on their guard. How can this be an injury to you? Have you a monopoly of the translation of these books? Are there no others who take part in this work? When you translated parts of the Septuagint, did you mean to prohibit all others from translating it after your version had been published? Why, I also have translated many books from the Greek. You have full power to make a second translation of them at your pleasure; for both the good and the bad in them must be laid to the charge of their author. And this would hold in your case also, had you not said that you had cut out the heretical parts and translated only what was positively good. This is a

---

[1] See the end of the letter of Pammachius and Oceanus; Jerome Letter lxxxiii.

difficulty which you have made for yourself, and which cannot be solved, except by confessing that you have erred as all men err, and condemning your former opinion.

37. But what defence can you make in reference to the Apology which you have written for the works of Origen, or rather in reference to the book of Eusebius, though you have altered much, and translated the work of a heretic under the title of a martyr, yet you have set down still more which is incompatible with the faith of the church. You as well as I turn Latin books into Greek; can you prohibit me from giving the works of a foreigner to my own people? If I had made my answer in the case of some other work of yours in which you had not attacked me, it might have been thought that, in translating what you had already translated, I was acting in hostility to you, and wishing to prove you inaccurate or untrustworthy. But this is a new kind of complaint, when you take it amiss that an answer is made you on a point on which you have accused me. All Rome was said to have been upset by your translation; every one was demanding of me a remedy for this; not that I was of any account, but that those who asked this thought me so. You say that you who had made the translation were my friend. But what would you have had me do? Ought we to obey God or man? To guard our master's property or to conceal the theft of a fellow-servant? Can I not be at peace with you unless I join with you in committing acts which bring reproach? If you had not mentioned my name, if you had not tricked me out in your flatteries, I might have had some way of escape, and have made many excuses for not translating what had already been translated. But you, my friend, have compelled me to waste a good many days on this work, and to bring out before the public eye what should have been engulfed in Charybdis; yet still, though I had been injured, I observed the laws of friendship, and as far as possible defended myself without accusing you. It is a too suspicious and complaining temper which you shew when you take home to yourself as a reproach what was spoken against the heretics. If it is impossible to be your friend unless I am the friend of heretics, I shall more easily put up with your enmity than with their friendship.

38. You imagine that I have contrived yet another piece of falsehood, namely, that I have composed a letter to you in my own name, pretending that it was written long ago, in which I make myself appear kindly and courteous; but which you never received. The truth can easily be ascertained. Many persons at Rome have had copies of this letter for the last three years; but they refused to send it to you knowing that you were throwing out insinuations against my reputation, and making up stories of the most shameful kind and unworthy of our Christian profession. I wrote in ignorance of all this, as to a friend; but they would not transmit the letter to an enemy, such as they knew you to be, thus sparing me the effects of my mistakes and you the reproaches of your conscience. You next bring arguments to shew that, if I had written such a letter, I had no right to write another containing many reproaches against you. But here is the error which pervades all that you say, and of which I have a right to complain; whatever I say against the heretics you imagine to be said against you. What! Am I refusing you bread because I give the heretics a stone to crush their brains? But, in order to justify your disbelief in my letter, you are obliged to make out that that of pope Anastasius rests upon a similar fraud. On this point I have answered you before. If you really suspect that it is not his writing, you have the means of convicting me of the forgery. But if it is his writing, as his letters of the present year also written against you prove, you will in vain use your false reasonings to prove my letter false, since I can shew from his genuine letter that mine also is genuine.

39. In order to parry the charge of falsehood, it is your humour to become quite exacting. You are not to be called to produce the six thousand books of Origen, of which you speak; but you expect me to be acquainted with all the records of Pythagoras. What truth is there in all the boastful language, which you blurted out from your inflated cheeks, declaring that you had corrected the Περὶ Ἀρχῶν by introducing words which you had read in other books of Origen, and thus had not put in other men's words but restored his own? Out of all this forest of his works you cannot produce a single bush or sucker. You accuse me of raising up smoke and mist. Here you have smoke and mist indeed. You know that I have dissipated and done away with them; but, though your neck is broken, you do not bow it down, but, with an impudence which exceeds even your ignorance, you say that I am denying what is quite evident, so as to excuse yourself, after promising mountains of gold, for not producing even a leatherlike farthing from your treasury. I acknowledge

that your animosity against me rests on good grounds, and that your rage and passion is genuine; for, unless I made persistent demands for what does not exist, you would be thought to have what you have not. You ask me for the books of Pythagoras. But who has informed you that any books of his are extant? It is true that in my letter which you criticize these words occur: "Suppose that I erred in youth, and that, having been trained in profane literature, I at the beginning of my Christian course had no sufficient doctrinal knowledge, and that I attributed to the Apostles things which I had read in Pythagoras or Plato or Empedocles;" but I was speaking not of their books but of their tenets, with which I was able to acquaint myself through Cicero, Brutus, and Seneca. Read the short oration for [1] Vatinius, and others in which mention is made of secret societies. Turn over Cicero's dialogues. Search through the coast of Italy which used to be called Magna Græcia, and you will find there various doctrines of Pythagoras inscribed on brass on their public monuments. Whose are those Golden Rules? They are Pythagoras's; and in these all his principles are contained in a summary form. Iamblicus[2] wrote a commentary upon them, following in this, at least partly, Moderatus a man of great eloquence, and Archippus and Lysides who were disciples of Pythagoras. Of these, Archippus and Lysides held schools in Greece, that is, in Thebes; they retained so fully the precepts of their teacher, that they made use of their memory instead of books. One of these precepts is: "We must cast away by any contrivance, and cut out by fire and sword and contrivances of all kinds, disease from the body, ignorance from the soul, luxury from the belly, sedition from the state, discord from the family, excess from all things alike."[3] There are other precepts of Pythagoras, such as these. "Friends have all things in common." "A friend is a second self." "Two moments are specially to be observed, morning and evening: that is, things which we are going to do, and things which we have done." "Next to God we must worship truth, for this alone makes men akin to God." There are also enigmas which Aristotle has collated with much diligence in his works: "Never go beyond the Stater," that is, "Do not transgress the rule of justice;" "Never stir the fire with the sword," that is, "Do not provoke a man when he is angry and excited with hard

words." "We must not touch the crown," that is "We must maintain the laws of the state." "Do not eat out your heart," that is, "Cast away sorrow from your mind." "When you have started, do not return," that is, "After death do not regret this life." "Do not walk on the public road," that is, "Do not follow the errors of the multitude." "Never admit a swallow into the family," that is, "Do not admit chatterers and talkative persons under the same roof with you." "Put fresh burdens on the burdened; put none on those who lay them down;" that is, "When men are on the road to virtue, ply them with fresh precepts; when they abandon themselves to idleness, leave them alone." I said I had read the doctrines of the Pythagoreans. Let me tell you that Pythagoras was the first to discover the immortality of the soul and its transmigration from one body to another. To this view Virgil gives his adherence in the sixth book of the Æneid in these words:[1]

These, when the wheel full thousand years has turned,
God calls, a long sad line, in Lethe's stream
To drown the past, and long once more to see
The skies above, and to the flesh return.

40. Pythagoras taught, accordingly, that he had himself been originally Euphorbus, and then Callides, thirdly Hermotimus, fourthly Pyrrhus, and lastly Pythagoras; and that those things which had existed, after certain revolutions of time, came into being again; so that nothing in the world should be thought of as new. He said that true philosophy was a meditation on death; that its daily struggle was to draw forth the soul from the prison of the body into liberty: that our learning was recollection, and many other things which Plato works out in his dialogues, especially in the Phædo and Timæus. For Plato, after having formed the Academy and gained innumerable disciples, felt that his philosophy was deficient on many points, and therefore went to Magna Græcia, and there learned the doctrines of Pythagoras from Archytas of Tarentum and Timæus of Locris: and this system he embodied in the elegant form and style which he had learned from Socrates. The whole of this, as we can prove, Origen carried over into his book Περὶ Ἀρχῶν, only changing the name. What mistake, then, was I making, when I said that in my youth I had imputed to the Apostles ideas which I had found in Pythagoras, Plato and Empedocles? I did not speak, as you calumniously pretend, of what I had read in the books of Pythagoras, Plato and Empedocles, but of what I

---

[1] In the oration *against Vatinius* mention is made of his boasting himself to be a Pythagorean.
[2] Neo-Platonist of Alexandria, 4th century.
[3] This is given by Jerome both in Greek and Latin.

[1] Virg. Æn. 748-51.

had read as having existed in their writings, that is, what other men's writings shewed me to have existed in them. This mode of speaking is quite common. I might say, for instance " The opinions which I read in Socrates I believed to be true," meaning what I read as his opinions in Plato and others of the Socratic school, though Socrates himself wrote no books. So I might say, I wished to imitate the deeds which I had read of in Alexander and Scipio,[1] not meaning that they described their own deeds, but that I had read in other men's works of the deeds which I admired as done by them. Therefore, though I may not be able to inform you of any records of Pythagoras himself as being extant, and proved by the attestation of his son or daughter or others of his disciples, yet you cannot hold me guilty of falsehood, because I said not that I had read his books, but his doctrines. You are quite mistaken if you thought to make this a screen for your falsehood, and to maintain that because I cannot produce any book written by Pythagoras, you have a right to assert that six thousand books of Origen have been lost.

41. I come now to your Epilogue, (that is to the revilings which you pour upon me,) in which you exhort me to repentance, and threaten me with destruction unless I am converted, that is, unless I keep silence under your accusations. And this scandal, you say, will recoil upon my own head, because it is I who by replying have provoked you to the madness of writing when you are a man of extreme gentleness and of a meekness worthy of Moses. You declare that you are aware of crimes which I confessed to you alone when you were my most intimate friend, and that you will bring these before the public; that I shall be painted in my own colours; and that I ought to remember that I am lying at your feet, otherwise you might cut off my head with the sword of your mouth. And, after many such things, in which you toss yourself about like a madman, you draw yourself up and say that you wish for peace, but still with the intimation that I am to keep quiet for the future, that is that I am not to write against the heretics, nor to answer any accusation made by you; if I do this, I shall be your good brother and colleague, and a most eloquent person, and your friend and companion; and, what is still more, you will pronounce all the translations I have made from Origen to be orthodox. But, if I utter a word or move a step, I shall at once be unsound and a heretic, and unworthy

of all connexion with you. This is the way you trumpet forth my praises, this is the way you exhort me to peace. You do not grant me liberty for a groan or a tear in my grief.

42. It would be possible for me also to paint you in your own colours, and to meet your insanity with a similar rage; to say what I know and add what I do not know; and with a license like yours, or rather fury and madness, to keep up things false and true alike, till I was ashamed to speak and you to hear: and to upbraid you in such a way as would condemn either the accused or the accuser; to force myself on the reader by mere effrontery, make him believe that what I wrote unscrupulously I wrote truly. But far be it from the practice of Christians while offering up their lives to seek the life of others, and to become homicides not with the sword but the will. This may agree with your gentleness and innocence; for you can draw forth from the dung heap within your breast alike the odour of roses and the stench of corpses; and, contrary to the precept of the Prophet, call that bitter which once you had praised as sweet. But it is not necessary for us, in treating of Christian topics, to throw out accusations which ought to be brought before the law courts. You shall hear nothing more from me than the vulgar saying : " When you have said what you like, you shall hear what you do not like." Or if the coarse proverb seems to you too vulgar, and, being a man of culture, you prefer the words of philosophers or poets, take from me the words of Homer.[1]

" What words thou speakest, thou the like shalt hear."

One thing I should like to learn from one of such eminent sanctity and fastidiousness, (whose holiness is such that in the presence of your very handkerchiefs and aprons the devils cry out); whom do you take for your model in your writings? Has any one of the catholic writers, in a controversy of opinions, imputed moral offences to the man with whom he is arguing? Have your masters taught you to do this? Is this the system in which you have been trained, that, when you cannot answer a man, you should take off his head? that when you cannot silence a man's tongue, you should cut it out? You have nothing much to boast of, for you are doing only what the scorpions and cantharides do. This is what Fulvia[2] did to Cicero and Herodias to John. They could not bear to hear the truth, and there-

---

[1] *Gesta quæ in Alexandro et Scipione legeram.* The Latin construction will bear Jerome's meaning, but cannot be exactly or elegantly rendered in English.

[1] Iliad. xx. 250.
[2] Antony's wife who had Cicero's head brought to her, and bored through the tongue with a golden bodkin.

fore they pierced the tongue that spoke truth with the pin that parted their hair. The duty of dogs is to bark in their masters' service; why may I not bark in the service of Christ? Many have written against Marcion or Valentinus, Arius or Eunomius. By which of them was any accusation brought of immoral conduct? Did they not in each case bring their whole effort to bear upon the refutation of the heresy? It is the machination of the heretics, that is of your masters, when convicted of betrayal of the faith, to betake themselves to evil speaking. So Eustathius [1] the Bishop of Antioch was made into a father unawares. So Athanasius Bishop of Alexandria cut off a third hand of Arsenius; for, when he appeared [2] alive after having been supposed to be dead, he was found to have two. Such things also now are falsely charged against the Bishop of the same church, and the true faith is assailed by gold, which constitutes the power of yourself and your friends. But I need not speak of controversy with heretics, who, though they are really without, yet call themselves Christians. How many of our writers have contended with those most impious men, Celsus and Porphyry! but which of them has left the cause he was engaged in to busy himself with the imputation of crime to his adversary, such as ought to be set down not in church-writings but in the calendar of the judge? For what advantage have you gained if you establish a man's criminality but fail in your argument? It is quite unnecessary that in bringing an accusation you should risk your own head. If your object is revenge, you can hire an executioner, and satisfy your desire. You pretend to dread a scandal, and yet you are ready to kill a man who was once your brother, whom you now accuse, and whom you always treat as an enemy. Yet I wonder how a man like you, who knows what he is about, should be so blinded by madness as to wish to confer a benefit upon me by drawing forth my soul out of prison, [3] and should not suffer it to remain with you in the darkness of this world.

43. If you wish me to keep silence, cease from accusing me. Lay down your sword, and I will throw away my shield. To one thing only I cannot consent; that is, to spare the heretics, and not to vindicate my ortho-

doxy. If that is the cause of discord between us, I can submit to death, but not to silence. It would have been right to go through the whole of the Scriptures for answers to your ravings, and, like David playing on his harp, to take the divine words to calm your raging breast. But I will content myself with a few statements from a single book; I will oppose Wisdom to folly; for I hope if you despise the words of men you will not think lightly of the word of God. Listen, then, to that which Solomon the wise says about you and all who are addicted to evil speaking and contumely:

"Foolish men, while they desire injuries, become impious and hate wisdom.[1] Devise not evil against thy friend. Be not angry with a man without a cause. The impious exalt contumely. [2] Remove from thee the evil mouth, keep far from thee the wicked lips, the eyes of him that speaketh evil, the tongue of the unjust, the hands which shed the blood of the just,[3] the heart that deviseth evil thoughts, and the feet which hasten to do evil. He that resteth upon falsehood feedeth the winds, and followeth the flying birds. For he hath left the ways of his own vineyard, and hath made the wheels of his tillage to err. He walketh through the dry and desert places, and with his hands he gathereth barrenness.[4] The mouth of the froward is near to destruction, and [5] he who uttereth evil words is the chief of fools. Every simple man is a soul that is blessed; but a violent man is dishonourable. [6] By the fault of his lips the sinner falleth into a snare. [7] All the ways of a fool are right in his own eyes. [8] The fool showeth his anger on that very day. [9] Lying lips are an abomination to the Lord. [10] He that keepeth his lips guardeth his own soul; but he that is rash with his lips shall be a terror to himself. [11] The evil man in his violence doeth evil things, and the fool spreadeth out his folly. [12] Seek for wisdom among the evil and thou shalt not find it. [13] The rash man shall eat of the fruit of his own ways. [14] The wise man by taking heed avoideth the evil; but the fool is confident, and joins himself to it. [15] A long-suffering man is strong in his wisdom; the man of little mind is very unwise. [16] He who oppresseth the poor reproacheth his Maker. [17] The tongue of the wise knoweth good things, but the mouth of fools speaketh evil. [18] A quarrelsome man preferreth strife, and every one that lifteth up his heart is unclean before God. [19] Though hand join with hand unjustly, they shall not be unpunished. [20] He that loveth life must be sparing to his mouth. [21] Insolence goeth before bruising, and evil thoughts before a fall. [22] He who closeth his eyes speaketh perverse things, and provoketh all evil with his lips. [23] The lips of a fool lead him into evil, and the foolhardy speech calleth down death. The man of evil counsel shall suffer much loss. [24] Better is a poor man who is just than a rich man that speaketh lies. [25] It is a glory to a man to turn away from evil words; but he that is foolish bindeth himself therewith. [26] Love

---

1 Eustathius was deposed at the instigation of Eusebius the Arian bishop of Nicomedia, who brought charges both of Sabellianism and of immorality against him. Socrates, Eccl. Hist. i. 24.
2 At the Synod at Tyre in 335. See Socrates Eccl. Hist. i. 29.
3 This expression was used by the Origenists of death. This life was a prison house into which souls had fallen; Jerome imputes this opinion to Rufinus, and Rufinus to him. See Ruf. Apol. i. 26.

1 Prov. iii, 29, 30. These quotations are from the LXX.
version.

	8 xii, 16.	15 xiv, 29.	22 vi, 30.
2 iv, 24.	9 xii, 22.	16 xiv, 31.	23 xviii, 6, 7.
3 vi, 18.	10 xiii, 3.	17 xv, 12.	24 xix, 1.
4 x, 14.	11 xiii,16.	18 xv, 18.	25 xx, 3.
5 x, 18.	12 xiv, 6.	19 vi, 5.	26 xx, 13.
6 xii, 13.	13 xiv,14.	20 vi, 17.	
7 xii, 15.	14 xiv,16.	21 vi, 18.	

not detraction, lest thou be rooted out. [1] The bread of lying is sweet to a man, but afterwards his mouth shall be filled with gravel. [2] He that gaineth treasures with a lying tongue followeth vanity, and shall come into the snares of death. [3] Say thou nought in the ear of a fool, lest haply the wise mock at thy words. [4] The bludgeon and the sword and the arrow are hurtful things; [5] so is the man who beareth false witness against his friend. [6] As the birds and the sparrows fly away, so the curse shall be vain and shall not overtake him. [7] Answer not an unwise man according to his lack of wisdom, lest thou become like unto him; but answer a fool according to his folly, lest he appear to himself to be wise. [8] He who layeth wait for his friends, when he is discovered saith, I did it in sport. [9] A faggot for the coals, and wood for the fire, and a man of evil words for the tumult of strife. [10] If thine enemy ask thee aught, sparingly but with a loud voice, [11] consent thou not to him, for there are seven degrees of wickedness in his heart. [12] The stone is heavy, and the sand hard to be borne; but the anger of a fool is heavier than either; indignation is cruel, anger is sharp, and envy is impatient. [13] The impious man speaketh against the poor; and he that trusteth in the audacity of his heart is most foolish. [14] The unwise man putteth forth all his anger, but the wise dealeth it out in parts. [15] An evil son — his teeth are swords, and his grinders are as harrows, to consume the weak from off the earth, and the poor from among men."

Such are the lessons in which I have been trained; and therefore I was unwilling to return bite for bite, and to attack you by way of retaliation; and I thought it better to exorcise the madness of one who was raving, and to pour in the antidote of a single book into his poisoned breast. But I fear I shall have no success, and that I shall be compelled to sing the song of David, and to take his words for my only consolation : [1]

"The wicked are estranged from the womb, they go astray even from the belly. They have spoken lies. Their madness is like the madness of the serpent; like the deaf adder which stoppeth her ears, which will not hear the voice of the charmers, and of the magician wisely enchanting. God shall break their teeth in their mouth; the Lord shall break the great teeth of the lions. They shall come to nothing, like water that runneth away. He bendeth his bow until they be brought low. Like wax that melteth, they shall be carried away; the fire hath fallen upon them and they have not seen the sun."

And again : [2]

" The righteous shall rejoice when he seeth the vengeance upon the impious; he shall wash his hands in the blood of the sinner. And man shall say, Verily, there is a reward for the righteous; verily, there is a God that judgeth those that are on the earth."

44. In the end of your letter you say : " I hope that you love peace." To this I will answer in a few words : If you desire peace, lay down your arms. I can be at peace with one who shews kindness; I do not fear one who threatens me. Let us be at one in faith, and peace will follow immediately.

[1] Prov. xx, 17. [5] xxv, 18. [9] xxvii, 21. [13] xxviii, 25, 26.
[2] xxi, 6. [6] xxvi, 2. [10] xxvii, 14. [14] xxix, 11.
[3] xxiii, 9. [7] xxvi, 4, 5. [11] xxvi, 24, 25. [15] xxx, 14.
[4] xxv, 18. [8] xxvi, 19. [12] xxvii, 3, 4.

[1] Ps. lviii, 3–8. [2] Ps. lviii, 10, 11.

A COMMENTARY ON THE APOSTLES' CREED.

This exposition of the Creed was made at the request of Laurentius, a Bishop whose see is unknown, but is conjectured by Fontanini, in his life of Rufinus, to have been Concordia, Rufinus' birthplace.

Its exact date cannot be fixed; but from the fact that he says nothing of his difficulty in writing Latin after being so long in the East, as he does in several of his books, and from the comparative ease of the style, it is most probable that it was written in the later years of his sojourn at Aquileia, that is, about 307–309.

Its value is considerable (1) as bearing witness to the state of the Creed in local churches at the beginning of the 5th century, especially their variations. (In the church of Aquileia, in Jesu Christo. Patrem *invisibilem et impassibilem.* Resurrectio *hujus* carnis); (2) as showing the adaptation of Eastern ideas to the formation of Western theology; (3) as giving the Canon of the books of Scripture, and the Apocrypha of both the Old and New dispensations.

The exposition is clear and reasonable; and, with the exception of a very few passages, such as the argument from the Phœnix for the Virgin Birth of our Lord, is still of use to us.

We prefix the words of the creed on which Rufinus makes his commentary.

It seems desirable to give the original Latin, as well as the English version of the Creed of Aquileia. The words or letters which are peculiar to this creed are put in italics.

1. Credo in Deo Patre omnipotenti *invisibili et impassibili.*
2. Et in Jesu Christo, unico Filio ejus, Domino nostro;
3. Qui natus est de Spiritu Sancto ex Maria Virgine;

4. Crucifixus sub Pontio Pilato, et sepultus;
5. Descendit ad inferna; tertia die resurrexit a mortuis;

1. I believe in God the Father Almighty, *invisible and impassible.*
2. And in Jesus Christ, His only Son, our Lord;
3. Who was born from the Holy Ghost, of the Virgin Mary;
4. Was crucified under Pontius Pilate, and buried;
5. He descended to hell; on the third day he rose again from the dead.

6. Ascendit in cœlos; **sedet ad dexteram Patris;**

7. Inde venturus est judicare vivos et mortuos;

8. Et in Spiritu Sancto;
9. Sanctam Ecclesiam;
10. Remissionem peccatorum;
11. *Hujus* carnis resurrectionem.

6. He ascended to the heavens; he sitteth at the right hand of the Father;

7. Thence he is to come to judge the quick and the dead.

8. And in the Holy Ghost;
9. The Holy Church.
10. The remission of sins.
11. The resurrection of *this* flesh.

My mind has as little inclination for writing as sufficiency, most faithful Bishop (*Papa*) Laurentius,[1] for I well know that it is a matter of no little peril to submit a slender ability to general criticism. But, since in your letter you rashly (forgive my saying so) require me, by Christ's sacraments, which I hold in the greatest reverence, to compose something for you concerning the Faith, in accordance with the traditional and natural meaning of the Creed, although in so doing you impose a burthen upon me beyond my strength to bear (for I do not forget the opinion of the wise, which so justly says, that "to speak of God even what is true is perilous"); still, if you will aid with your prayers the necessity which your requisition has laid upon me, I will try to say something, moved rather by a reverential regard for your injunction than by presumptuous confidence in my ability. What I write, however, will hardly seem worthy of the consideration of persons of mature understanding, but suited rather to the capacity of children and young beginners in Christ.

I find, indeed, that some eminent writers have published treatises on these matters piously and briefly written. Moreover, I know that the heretic Photinus has written on the same; but with the object, not of explaining the meaning of the text to his readers, but of wresting things simply and truthfully said in support of his own dogma, while yet the Holy Spirit has taken care that in these words nothing should be set down which is ambiguous or obscure, or inconsistent with other truths: for therein is that prophecy verified, "Finishing and cutting short the word in equity: because a short word will the Lord make upon the earth."[2] It shall be our endeavour, then, first to restore and emphasize the words of the Apostles in their native simplicity; and, secondly, to supply such things as seem to have been omitted by former expositors. But that the scope of this "short word," as we have called it, may be made more plain, we will enquire from the beginning how it came to be given to the Churches.

2. Our forefathers have handed down to us the tradition, that, after the Lord's ascension, when, through the coming of the Holy Ghost, tongues of flame had settled upon each of the Apostles, that they might speak diverse languages, so that no race however foreign, no tongue however barbarous, might be inaccessible to them and beyond their reach, they were commanded by the Lord to go severally to the several nations to preach the word of God. Being on the eve therefore of departing from one another, they first mutually agreed upon a standard of their future preaching, lest haply, when separated, they might in any instance vary in the statements which they should make to those whom they should invite to believe in Christ. Being all therefore met together, and being filled with the Holy Ghost, they composed, as we have said, this brief formulary of their future preaching, each contributing his several sentence to one common summary: and they ordained that the rule thus framed should be given to those who believe.

To this formulary, for many and most sufficient reasons, they gave the name or Symbol. For Symbol (κύμβολον) in Greek answers to both "Indicium" (a sign or token) and "Collatio" (a joint contribution made by several) in Latin. For this the Apostles did in these words, each contributing his several sentence. It is called "Indicium" or "Signum," a sign or token, because, at that time, as the Apostle Paul says, and as is related in the Acts of the Apostles, many of the vagabond Jews, pretending to be apostles of Christ, went about preaching for gain's sake or their belly's sake, naming the name of Christ indeed, but not delivering their message according to the exact traditional lines. The Apostles therefore prescribed this formulary as a sign or token by which he who preached Christ truly, according to Apostolic rule, might be recognised. Finally, they say that in civil wars, since the armour of both sides is alike, and the language the same, and the custom and mode of warfare the same, each general, to guard against treachery, is wont to deliver to his soldiers a distinct symbol or watchword — in Latin "signum" or "indicium" — so that if one is met with, of whom it is doubtful to which side he belongs, being asked the sym-

---

[1] Nothing is known of this Pope Laurentius. The title "Papa," at first given to Bishops promiscuously, was not yet restricted to the Bishop of Rome. Gregory VII., in a Council held at Rome in 1073, forbade it to be given to any other.
[2] Isaiah x. 22, 23, Septuag., and so cited Rom. ix. 28.

bol (watchword), he discloses whether he is friend or foe. And for this reason, the tradition continues, the Creed is not written on paper or parchment, but is retained in the hearts of the faithful, that it may be certain that no one has learnt it by reading, as is sometimes the case with unbelievers, but by tradition from the Apostles.

The Apostles therefore, as we have said, being about to separate in order to preach the Gospel, settled upon this sign or token of their agreement in the faith; and, unlike the sons of Noah, who, when they were about to separate from one another, builded a tower of baked bricks and pitch, whose top might reach to heaven, they raised a monument of faith, which might withstand the enemy, composed of living stones and pearls of the Lord, such that neither winds might overthrow it, nor floods undermine it, nor the force of storms and tempests shake it. Right justly, then, were the former, when, on the eve of separation, they builded a tower of pride, condemned to the confusion of tongues, so that no one might understand his neighbour's speech; while the latter, who were building a tower of faith, were endowed with the knowledge and understanding of all languages; so that the one might prove a sign and token of sin, the other of faith.

But it is time now that we should say something about these same pearls, among which is placed first the fountain and source of all, when it is said,—

3. I BELIEVE IN GOD THE FATHER ALMIGHTY.

But before I begin to discuss the meaning of the words, I think it well to mention that in different Churches some additions are found in this article. This is not the case, however, in the Church of the city of Rome; the reason being, as I suppose, that, on the one hand, no heresy has had its origin there, and, on the other, that the ancient custom is there kept up, that those who are going to be baptized should rehearse the Creed publicly, that is, in the audience of the people; the consequence of which is that the ears of those who are already believers will not admit the addition of a single word. But in other places, as I understand, additions appear to have been made, on account of certain heretics, by means of which it was hoped that novelty in doctrine would be excluded. We, however, follow that order which we received when we were baptized in the Church of Aquileia.

I BELIEVE, therefore, is placed in the forefront, as the Apostle Paul, writing to the Hebrews, says, "He that cometh to God must first of all believe that He is, and that He is a rewarder of those who believe on Him."[1] The Prophet also says, "Except ye believe,[2] ye shall not understand." That the way to understand, therefore, may be open to you, you do rightly first of all, in professing that you believe; for no one embarks upon the sea, and trusts himself to the deep and liquid element, unless he first believes it possible that he will have a safe voyage; neither does the husbandman commit his seed to the furrows and scatter his grain on the earth, but in the belief that the showers will come, together with the sun's warmth, through whose fostering influence, aided by favouring winds, the earth will produce and multiply and ripen its fruits. In fine, nothing in life can be transacted if there be not first a readiness to believe. What wonder then, if, coming to God, we first of all profess that we believe, seeing that, without this, not even common life can be lived. We have premised these remarks at the outset, since the Pagans are wont to object to us that our religion, because it lacks reasons, rests solely on belief. We have shewn, therefore, that nothing can possibly be done or remain stable unless belief precede. Finally, marriages are contracted in the belief that children will be born; and children are committed to the care of masters in the belief that the teaching of the masters will be transferred to the pupils; and one man assumes the ensigns of empire, believing that peoples and cities and a well-equipped army also will obey him. But if no one enters upon any one of these several undertakings except in the belief that the results spoken of will follow, must not belief be much more requisite if one would come to the knowledge of God? But let us see what this "short word" of the Creed sets forth.

4. "I BELIEVE IN GOD THE FATHER ALMIGHTY." The Eastern Churches almost universally deliver the article thus, "I believe in ONE God the Father Almighty;" and again in the next article, where we say, "And in Christ Jesus, His only Son, our Lord," they deliver it, "And in ONE (Lord) our Lord Jesus Christ, His only Son;" confessing, that is, "one God," and "one Lord," in accordance with the authority of the Apostle Paul. But we shall return to this by-and-by. For the present, let us turn our attention to the words, "In God the Father Almighty."

"God," so far as the human mind can form an idea, is the name of that nature

---

[1] Heb. xi. 10. [2] Dan. xii. 10, or Is. vii. 9.

or substance which is above all things. "Father" is a word expressive of a secret and ineffable mystery. When you hear the word "God," you must understand thereby a substance without beginning, without end, simple, uncompounded, invisible, incorporeal, ineffable, inappreciable, which has in it nothing which has been either added or created. For He is without cause who is absolutely the cause of all things. When you hear the word "Father," you must understand by this the Father of a Son, which Son is the image of the aforesaid substance. For as no one is called "Lord" unless he have a possession or a servant whose lord he is, and as no one is called "master" unless he have a disciple, so no one can possibly be called "father" unless he have a son. This very name of "Father," therefore, shews plainly that, together with the Father there subsists a Son also.

But I would not have you discuss how God the Father begat the Son, nor intrude too curiously into the profound mystery, lest haply, by prying too eagerly into the brightness of light inaccessible, you should lose the faint glimpse which, by the gift of God, has been vouchsafed to mortals. Or, if you suppose that this is a subject to be investigated with all possible scrutiny, first propose to yourself questions which concern ourselves, and then, if you are able to deal satisfactorily with them, speed on from earthly things to heavenly, from visible to invisible. Determine first, if you can, how the mind, which is within you, generates a word, and what is the spirit of the memory which is in it; and how these, though diverse in reality and in operation, are yet one in substance or nature; and though they proceed from the mind, yet are never separated from it. And if these, though they are in us and in the substance of our own soul, yet seem to be hidden from us in proportion as they are invisible to our bodily sight, let us take for our enquiry things which are more open to view. How does a spring generate a river from itself? By what spirit is it borne into a rapidly flowing stream? How happens it that, while the river and the spring are one and inseparable, yet neither can the river be understood to be, or can be called, the spring, nor the spring the river, and yet he who has seen the river has seen the spring also? Exercise yourself first in explaining these, and explain, if you are able, things which you have under your hands; and then you may come to loftier matters. Do not think, however, that I would have you ascend all at once from the earth above

the heavens: I would first, with your leave, draw your attention to this firmament which our eyes behold, and ask you to explain, if you can, the nature of this visible luminary, —how that celestial fire generates from itself the brightness of light, how it also produces heat; and though these are three in reality, how they are yet one in substance. And if you are capable of investigating each of these, even then you must acknowledge that the mystery of the Divine generation is by so much the more diverse and the more transcendent as the Creator is more powerful than the creatures, as the artificer is more excellent than his work, as He who ever is is more noble than that which had its beginning out of nothing.

That God then is the Father of His only Son our Lord is to be believed, not discussed; for it is not lawful for a servant to dispute about the nativity of his lord. The Father hath borne witness from heaven, saying, [1] "This is My beloved Son, in Whom I am well pleased: hear Him." The Father saith that He is His Son and bids us hear Him. The Son saith, "He who seeth Me seeth the Father also," [2] and "I and the Father are one," [3] and "I came forth from God and am come into the world." [4] Where is the man who can thrust himself as a disputant between these words of Father and Son, who can divide the Godhead, separate its volition, break asunder the substance, cut the spirit in parts, and deny that what the Truth speaks is true? God then is a true Father as the Father of the Truth, not begetting extrinsically, but generating the Son from that which Himself is; that is, as the All-wise He generates Wisdom, as the Just Justice, as the Everlasting the Everlasting, as the Immortal Immortality, as the Invisible the Invisible; because He is Light, He generates Brightness, because He is Mind, He generates the Word.

5. Now whereas we said that the Eastern Churches, in their delivery of the Creed, say, "In one God [5] the Father Almighty," and "in one Lord," the "one" is not to be understood numerically but absolutely. For example, if one should say, "one man" or "one horse," here "one" is used numerically. For there may be a second man and a third, or a second horse and a third. But where a second or a third cannot be added, if we say "one" we mean one not numerically but absolutely. For example, if we say, "one Sun," here the meaning is that a second or a third cannot be added, for there is but one

---

[1] Matt. xvii. 5.   [3] John x. 30.   [5] *Deum*, not, as before, Deo.
[2] John xiv. 9.   [4] John xvi. 28.

Sun. Much more then is God, when He is said to be "one," called "one," not numerically but absolutely, that is, He is therefore said to be one because there is no other. In like manner, also, it is to be understood of the Lord, that He is one Lord, Jesus Christ, by or through Whom God the Father possesses dominion over all, whence also, in the next clause, God is called "Almighty."

God is called ALMIGHTY because He possesses rule and dominion over all things.[1] But the Father possesses all things by His Son, as the Apostle says, "By Him were created all things, visible and invisible, whether they be thrones, or dominions, or principalities, or powers."[2] And again, writing to the Hebrews, he says, "By Him also He made the worlds," and "He appointed Him heir of all things."[3] By "appointed" we are to understand "generated." Now if the Father made the worlds by Him, and all things were created by Him, and He is heir of all things, then by Him He possesses rule also over all things. Because, as light is born of light, and truth of truth, so Almighty is born of Almighty. As it is written of the Seraphim in the Revelation of John, "And they have no rest day and night, crying Holy, Holy, Holy, Lord God of Sabaoth, which was and which is and which is to come, the Almighty."[4] He then who "is to come" is called "Almighty." And what other is there who "is to come" but Christ, the Son of God?

To the foregoing is added "INVISIBLE AND IMPASSIBLE." I should mention that these two words are not in the Creed of the Roman Church. They were added in our Church, as is well known, on account of the Sabellian heresy, called by us "the Patripassian," that, namely, which says that the Father Himself was born of the Virgin and became visible, or affirms that He suffered in the flesh. To exclude such impiety, therefore, concerning the Father, our forefathers seem to have added these words, calling the Father "invisible and impassible." For it is evident that the Son, not the Father, became incarnate and was born in the flesh, and that from that nativity in the flesh the Son became "visible and passible." Yet so far as regards that immortal substance of the Godhead, which He possesses, and which is one and the same with that of the Father, we must believe that neither the Father, nor the Son, nor the Holy Ghost is "visible or passible."

But the Son, in that He condescended to assume flesh, was both seen and also suffered in the flesh. Which also the Prophet foretold when he said, "This is our God: no other shall be accounted of in comparison of Him. He hath found out all the way of knowledge, and hath given it unto Jacob His servant and to Israel His beloved. Afterward He shewed Himself upon the earth, and conversed with men."[1]

6. Next there follows, "AND IN CHRIST JESUS, HIS ONLY SON, OUR LORD." "Jesus" is a Hebrew word meaning "Saviour." "Christ" is so called from "Chrism," i.e. unction. For we read in the Books of Moses, that Auses, the son of Nave,[2] when he was chosen to lead the people, had his name changed from "Auses" to "Jesus," to shew that this was a name proper for princes and generals, for those, namely, who should "save" the people who followed them. Therefore, both were called "Jesus," both the one who conducted the people, who had been brought forth out of the land of Egypt, and freed from the wanderings of the wilderness, into the land of promise, and the other, who conducted the people, who had been brought forth from the darkness of ignorance, and recalled from the errors of the world, into the kingdom of heaven.

"Christ" is a name proper either to High Priests or Kings. For formerly both high priests and kings were consecrated with the ointment of chrism: but these, as mortal and corruptible, with material and corruptible ointment. Jesus is made Christ, being anointed with the Holy Spirit, as the Scripture saith of Him "Whom the Father hath anointed with the Holy Spirit sent down from heaven."[3] And Isaiah had prefigured the same, saying in the person of the Son, "The Spirit of the Lord is upon Me, because He hath anointed Me, He hath sent Me to preach good tidings to the poor."[4]

Having shewn them what "Jesus" is, Who saves His people, and what "Christ" is, Who is made a High Priest for ever, let us now see in what follows, of Whom these things are said, "His only Son, our Lord." Here we are taught that this Jesus, of whom we have spoken, and this Christ, the meaning of whose name we have expounded, is "the only Son of God" and "our Lord." Lest, perchance, you should think that these human names have an earthly significance,

---

[1] Compare Cyril's words, *Quod omnium teneat potentatum* — Lordship over all; ὁ παντοκράτωρ, ὁ πάντων κρατῶν, ὁ πάντων ἐξουσιάζων. (*Catech.*, 8, § 3). Rufinus evidently had St. Cyril's exposition in view here as repeatedly elsewhere.
[2] Col. i. 16.   [3] Heb. i. 2.   [4] Heb. iv. 8.

[1] Baruch iii. 35-37. Baruch is not specified by name in Rufinus's list of the Canonical books, but it is in Cyril's, as though a part of Jeremiah, "Jeremiah. with Baruch, and the Lamentations and the Epistle." (*Catech*. 4. § 36.)
[2] That is Joshua the son of Nun. It does not appear what passage is referred to.
[3] Acts x. 38.   [4] Isa. lxi. 1. Comp. Luke iv. 18.

therefore it is added that He is "the only Son of God, our Lord." For He is born One of One, because there is one brightness of light, and there is one word of the understanding. Neither does an incorporeal generation degenerate into the plural number, or suffer division, where He Who is born is in no wise separated from Him Who begets. He is "only" (unique), as thought is to the mind, as wisdom is to the wise, as a word is to the understanding, as valour is to the brave. For as the Father is said by the Apostle to be "alone wise," [1] so likewise the Son alone is called wisdom. He is then the "only Son." And, although in glory, everlastingness, virtue, dominion, power, He is what the Father is, yet all these He hath not unoriginately as the Father, but from the Father, as the Son, without beginning and equal; and although He is the Head of all things, yet the Father is the Head of Him. For so it is written, "The Head of Christ is God." [2]

7. When you hear the word "Son," you must not think of a nativity after the flesh; but remember that it is spoken of an incorporeal substance, and a simple and uncompounded nature. For if, as we said above, whether when the understanding generates a word, or the mind sense, or light brings forth brightness from itself, nothing of this sort is sought for, or any manner of weakness and imperfection imagined in this kind of generation, how much purer and more sacred ought to be our conception of the Creator of all these!

But perhaps you say, "The generation of which you speak is an unsubstantial generation. For light does not produce substantial brightness, nor the understanding generate a substantial word, but the Son of God, it is affirmed, was generated substantially." To this we reply, first, When in other things examples or illustrations are used, the resemblance cannot hold in every particular, but only in some one point for which the illustration is employed. For instance, When it is said in the Gospel, "The kingdom of heaven is like leaven, which a woman hid in three measures of meal," [3] are we to imagine that the kingdom of heaven is in all respects like leaven, so that like leaven it is palpable and perishable so as to become sour and unfit for use? Obviously the illustration was employed simply for this object — to shew how, through the preaching of God's word which seems so small a thing, men's minds could be imbued with the leaven of faith. So likewise, when it is said, "The kingdom

of heaven is like unto a net cast into the sea, which draws in fishes of every kind," [1] are we to suppose that the substance of the kingdom of heaven is likened in all respects to the nature of twine of which a net is made, and to the knots with which the meshes are tied? No; the sole object of the comparison is to shew that, as a net brings fishes to the shore from the depths of the sea, so by the preaching of the kingdom of heaven men's souls are liberated from the depth of the error of this world. From whence it is evident that examples or illustrations do not answer in every particular to the things which they are brought to exemplify or illustrate. Otherwise, if they were the same in all respects, they would no longer be called examples or illustrations, but rather would be the things themselves.

8. Then further it is to be observed that no creature can be such as its Creator. And therefore, as the divine substance or essence admits of no comparison, so neither does the Divinity. Moreover, every creature is of nothing. If therefore a spark which is so unsubstantial but yet is fire, begets of itself a creature which is of nothing, and maintains in it the essential nature of that from which it springs, (i.e. the fire of the parent spark), why could not the substance of that eternal Light, which ever has been because it has in itself nothing which is not substantial, produce from itself substantial brightness? Rightly, therefore, is the Son called "only," "unique." For He who hath been so born is "only" and "unique." That which is unique can admit of no comparison. Nor can He who made all things be like in substance to the things which He has made. This then is Christ Jesus, the only Son of God, who is also our Lord. "Only" may be referred both to Son and to Lord. For Jesus Christ is "only" both as truly Son and as one Lord. For all other sons, though they are called sons, are so called by the grace of adoption, not by verity of nature; and if there be others who are called lords, they are called so from an authority bestowed not inherent. But Christ alone is the only Son and the only Lord, as the Apostle saith, "One Lord Jesus Christ, by Whom are all things." [2] Therefore, after the Creed has in due order set forth the ineffable mystery of the nativity of the Son from the Father, it now descends to the dispensation which He vouchsafed to enter upon for man's salvation. And of Him whom just now it called the "only Son of God" and "our Lord," it now says.

---

[1] 1 Tim. i. 17.   [2] 1 Cor. xi. 3.   [3] Matt. xiii. 33.   [1] Matt. xiii. 47.   · [2] 1 Cor. viii. 6.

9. "Who was born by (*de*) the Holy Ghost of the Virgin Mary." This nativity among men is in the way of dispensation,[1] whereas the former nativity is of the divine substance; the one results from his condescension, the other from his essential nature. He is born by the Holy Ghost of the Virgin. Here a chaste ear and a pure mind is required. For you must understand that now a temple hath been built within the secret recesses of a Virgin's womb for Him of Whom erewhile you learnt that He was born ineffably of the Father. And just as in the sanctification of the Holy Ghost no thought of imperfection is to be admitted, so in the Virgin-birth no defilement is to be imagined. For this birth was a new birth given to this world, and rightly new. For He Who is the only Son in heaven is by consequence the only Son on earth, and was uniquely born, born as no other ever was or can be.

The words of the Prophets concerning Him, "A Virgin shall conceive and bring forth a Son,"[2] are known to all, and are cited in the Gospels again and again. The Prophet Ezekiel too had predicted the miraculous manner of that birth, calling Mary figuratively "the Gate of the Lord," the gate, namely, through which the Lord entered the world. For he saith, "The gate which looks towards the East shall be closed, and shall not be opened, and no one shall pass through it, because the Lord God of Israel shall pass through it, and it shall be closed."[3] What could be said with such evident reference to the inviolate preservation of the Virgin's condition? That Gate of Virginity was closed; through it the Lord God of Israel entered; through it He came forth from the Virgin's womb into this world; and the Virgin-state being preserved inviolate, the gate of the Virgin remained closed for ever. Therefore the Holy Ghost is spoken of as the Creator of the Lord's flesh and of His temple.

10. Starting from this point you may understand the majesty of the Holy Ghost also. For the Gospel witnesses of Him that when the angel said to the Virgin, "Thou shalt bring forth a Son and shalt call His name Jesus, for He shall save His people from their sins,"[4] she replied, "How shall this be, seeing I know not a man?" on which the angel said to her, "The Holy Ghost shall come upon thee, and the power of the Highest shall overshadow thee. Wherefore that holy Thing which shall be born of Thee shall be called the Son of God."[1] See here the Trinity mutually co-operating with each other. The Holy Ghost is spoken of as coming upon the Virgin, and the Power of the Highest as overshadowing her. What is the Power of the Highest but Christ Himself, Who is the Power of God and the Wisdom of God? Whose is this Power? The Power of the Highest. There is here then the Highest, there is also the Power of the Highest, there is also the Holy Ghost. This is the Trinity, everywhere latent, and everywhere apparent, distinct in names and persons, but inseparable in the substance of the Godhead. And although the Son alone is born of the Virgin, yet there is present also the Highest, there is present also the Holy Ghost, that both the conception and the bringing forth of the Virgin may be sanctified.

11. These things, since they are asserted upon the warrant of the Prophetical Scriptures, may possibly silence the Jews, infidel and incredulous though they be. But the Pagans are wont to ridicule us when they hear us speak of a Virgin-birth. We must, therefore, say a few words in reply to their cavils. Every birth, I suppose, depends upon three conditions. There must be a woman of mature age, she must have intercourse with a man, her womb must not be barren. Of these three conditions, in the birth of which we are speaking, one was wanting, the man. And this, forasmuch as He of Whose birth we speak was not an earthly but a heavenly man, was supplied by the Heavenly Spirit, the virginity of the mother being preserved inviolate. And yet why should it be thought marvellous for a virgin to conceive, when it is well known that the Eastern bird, which they call the Phœnix, is in such wise born, or born again, without the intervention of a mate, that it remains continually one, and continually by being born or born again succeeds itself?[2] That bees know no wedlock, and no bringing forth of young, is notorious. There are also other things which are found to be subject to some such law of birth. Shall it be thought incredible, then, that that was done by divine power, for the renewal and restoration of the whole world, of which instances

---

[1] Corresponding to the Greek word Economy—the "arrangement" or "plan" by which the Word became incarnate.
[2] Isa. vii. 14. [3] Ezek. xliv. 2, LXX. [4] Matt. i. 21.

[1] Luke i. 31, 34, 35.
[2] The fable of the Phœnix was very generally believed in the ancient Church, and was used as an illustration both of the Virgin-birth, as here, and of the Resurrection. Cyril of Jerusalem (xviii. 8), whom Rufinus evidently had in view, refers to it as a providentially designed confirmation of the latter. Possibly the Septuagint translation of Ps. xcii. 12, "The righteous shall flourish as a palm tree," ὡς φοῖνιξ may have been thought to sanction the fable. On the Literature connected with the Phœnix, see Bp. Jacobson's edition or the Apostolical Fathers, Clemens Romanus, Ep. i. § 25, note, p. 104.

are observed in the nativity of animals? And yet it is strange that the Gentiles should think this impossible, who believe their own Minerva to have been born from the brain of Jupiter. What is more difficult to believe, or what more contrary to nature? Here, there is a woman, the order of nature is kept, there is conception, and in due time birth; there, there is no female, but a man alone, and — birth! Why does he who believes the one marvel at the other? Again, they say that Father Bacchus was born from Jupiter's thigh. Here is another portent, yet it is believed. Venus also, whom they call Aphrodite, was born, they believe, of the foam of the sea, as her compounded name shews. They affirm that Castor and Pollux were born of an egg, the Myrmidons of ants. There are a thousand other things which, though contrary to nature, find credit with them, such as the stones thrown by Deucalion and Pyrrha, and the crop of men sprung from thence. And when they believe such myths and so many of them, does one thing seem impossible to them, that a woman of mature age, not defiled by man but impregnated by the Holy Ghost, should conceive a divine progeny? who, forsooth, if they are hard of belief, ought in no wise to have given credence to those prodigies, being, as they are, so many and so degrading; but if they do believe them, they ought much more readily to receive these beliefs of ours, so honourable and so holy, than theirs so discreditable and so vile.

12. But they say, perhaps, If it was possible to God that a virgin should conceive, it was possible also that she should bring forth, but they think it unmeet that a being of so great majesty should enter the world in such wise, that even though there had been no defilement from intercourse with man, there should yet be the unseemliness attendant upon the act of delivery. To which let us reply briefly, meeting them on their own level. If a person should see a little child in the act of being suffocated in a a quagmire, and himself, a great man and powerful, should go into the mire, just at its verge, so to say, to rescue the dying child; would you blame this man as defiled for having stepped into a little mire, or would you praise him as merciful, for having preserved the life of one that was perishing? But the case supposed is that of an ordinary man. Let us return to the nature of Him Who was born. How much, think you, is the nature of the Sun inferior to him? How much beyond doubt, the Creature to the Creator? Consider now if a ray of the

sun alights upon a quagmire, does it receive any pollution from it? or is the sun the worse for shedding his light upon foul objects? Fire, too, how far inferior is its nature to the things of which we are speaking? Yet no substance, whether foul or vile, is believed to pollute fire if applied to it. When the case is plainly thus with regard to material things, do you suppose that aught of pollution and defilement can befall that supereminent and incorporeal nature, which is above all fire and all light? Then, lastly, note this also: we say that man was created by God out of the clay of the earth. But if God is thought to be defiled in seeking to recover His own work, much more must He be thought so in making that work originally. And it is idle to ask why He passed through what is repugnant to our sense of modesty, when you cannot tell why He made what is so repugnant. And therefore it is not nature but general estimation that has made us think these things to be such. Otherwise, all things that are in the body, being formed from one and the same clay, are distinguished from one another only in their uses and natural offices.

13. But there is another consideration which we must not leave out in the solution of this question, namely, that the substance of God, which is wholly incorporeal, cannot be introduced into bodies or be received by them in the first instance, unless there be some spiritual substance as a medium, which is capable of receiving the divine Spirit. For instance, if we say that light is able to irradiate all the members of the body, yet by none of them can it be received except by the eye. For it is the eye alone which is receptive of light. So the Son of God is born of a virgin, not associated with the flesh alone in the first instance, but begotten with a soul as a medium between the flesh and God. With the soul, then, serving as a medium, and receiving the Word of God in the secret citadel of the rational spirit, God was born of the Virgin without any such disparagement as you imagine. And therefore nothing is to be esteemed base or unseemly wherein was the sanctification of the Spirit, and where the soul which was capable of God became also a partaker of flesh. Account nothing impossible where the power of the Most High was present. Have no thought of human weakness where there was the plenitude of Divinity.

14. HE WAS CRUCIFIED UNDER PONTIUS PILATE AND WAS BURIED: HE DESCENDED INTO HELL. The Apostle Paul teaches us that we ought to have " the eyes of our understand-

ing enlightened"[1] "that we may understand what is the height and breadth and depth."[2] "The height and breadth and depth" is a description of the Cross, of which that part which is fixed in the earth he calls the depth, the height that which is erected upon the earth and reaches upward, the breadth that which is spread out to the right hand and to the left. Since, therefore, there are so many kinds of death by which it is given to men to depart this life, why does the Apostle wish us to have our understanding enlightened so as to know the reason why, of all of them, the Cross was chosen in preference for the death of the Saviour. We must know, then, that that Cross was a triumph. It was a signal trophy. A triumph is a token of victory over an enemy. Since then Christ, when He came, brought three kingdoms at once into subjection under His sway (for this He signifies when he says, "That in the name of Jesus every knee should bow, of things in heaven, and things on earth, and things under the earth"),[3] and conquered all of these by His death, a death was sought answerable to the mystery, so that being lifted up in the air, and subduing the powers of the air, He might make a display of His victory over these supernatural and celestial powers. Moreover the holy Prophet says that "all the day long He stretched out His hands"[4] to the people on the earth, that He might both make protestation to unbelievers and invite believers: finally, by that part which is sunk under the earth, He signified His bringing into subjection to Himself the kingdoms of the nether world.

15. Moreover, — to touch briefly some of the more recondite topics, — when God made the world in the beginning, He set over it and appointed certain powers of celestial virtues, by whom the race of mortal men might be governed and directed. That this was so done Moses signifies in the Song in Deuteronomy, "When the Most High divided the nations, He appointed the bounds of the nations according to the number of the angels of God."[5] But some of these, as he who is called the Prince of this world, did not exercise the power which God had committed to them according to the laws by which they had received it, nor did they teach mankind to obey God's commandments, but taught them rather to follow their own perverse guidance. Thus we were brought under the bonds of sin, because, as the Prophet saith, "We were sold under our sins."[6] For every man, when he

yields to lust, is receiving the purchase-money of his soul. Under that bond then every man was held by those most wicked rulers, which same bond Christ, when He came, tore down and stripped them of this their power. This Paul signifies under a great mystery, when he says of Him, "He destroyed the hand-writing which was against us, nailing it to His cross, and led away principalities and powers, triumphing over them in Himself."[1] Those rulers, then, whom God had set over mankind, having become contumacious and tyrannical, took in hand to assail the men who had been committed to their charge and to rout them utterly in the conflicts of sin, as the Prophet Ezekiel mystically intimates when he says, "In that day angels[2] shall come forth hastening to exterminate Ethiopia, and there shall be perturbation among them in the day of Egypt; for behold He comes."[3] Having stript them then of their almighty power, Christ is said to have triumphed, and to have delivered to men the power which was taken from them, as also Himself saith to His disciples in the Gospel, "Behold I have given you power to tread upon serpents and scorpions, and upon all the might of the enemy."[4] The Cross of Christ, then, brought those who had wrongfully abused the authority which they had received into subjection to those who had before been in subjection to them. But us, that is, mankind, it teaches first of all to resist sin even unto death, and willingly to die for the sake of religion. Next, this same Cross sets before us an example of obedience, in like manner as it hath punished the contumacy of those who were once our rulers. Hear, therefore, how the Apostle would teach us obedience by the Cross of Christ: "Let this mind be in you, which was in Christ Jesus, Who, being in the form of God, thought it not robbery to be equal with God, but made Himself of no reputation, taking upon Him the form of a servant, being made in the likeness of men; and, being found in fashion as a man, He became obedient unto death, even the death of the Cross."[5] As, then, a consummate master teaches both by example and precept, so Christ taught the obedience, which good men are to render even at the cost of death, by Himself first dying in rendering it.

16. But perhaps some one is alarmed at hearing us discourse of the death of Him of Whom, a short while since, we said that

---

[1] Eph. i. 18.   [3] Phil. ii. 10.   [5] Deut. xxxii. 8, LXX.
[2] Eph. iii. 18.   [4] Isa. lxv. 2.   [6] Rom. vii. 14.

[1] Col. ii. 14, 15.   [4] Luke x. 19.
[2] Ἄγγελοι LXX, *Nuntii*, Vulg.
[3] Ezek. xxx. 9.   [5] Phil. ii. 5-8.

He is everlasting with God the Father, and that He was begotten of the Father's substance, and is one with God the Father, in dominion, majesty, and eternity. But be not alarmed, O faithful hearer. Presently thou wilt see Him of Whose death thou hearest once more immortal; for the death to which He submits is about to spoil death. For the object of that mystery of the Incarnation which we expounded just now was that the divine virtue of the Son of God, as though it were a hook concealed beneath the form and fashion of human flesh (He being, as the Apostle Paul says, "found in fashion as a man "),[1] might lure on the Prince of this world to a conflict, to whom offering His flesh as a bait, His divinity underneath might catch him and hold him fast with its hook, through the shedding of His immaculate blood. For He alone Who knows no stain of sin hath destroyed the sins of all, of those, at least, who have marked the door-posts of their faith with His blood. As, therefore, if a fish seizes a baited hook, it not only does not take the bait off the hook, but is drawn out of the water to be itself food for others, so He Who had the power of death seized the body of Jesus in death, not being aware of the hook of Divinity inclosed within it, but having swallowed it he was caught forthwith, and the bars of hell being burst asunder, he was drawn forth as it were from the abyss to become food for others. Which result the Prophet Ezekiel long ago foretold under this same figure, saying, "I will draw thee out with My hook, and stretch thee out upon the earth: the plains shall be filled with thee, and I will set all the fowls of the air over thee, and I will satiate all the beasts of the earth with thee."[2] The Prophet David also says, "Thou hast broken the heads of the great dragon, Thou hast given him to be meat to the people of Ethiopia."[3] And Job in like manner witnesses of the same mystery, for he says in the person of the Lord speaking to him, "Wilt thou draw forth the dragon with a hook, and wilt thou put thy bit in his nostrils?"[4]

17. It is with no loss or disparagement therefore of His Divine nature that Christ suffers in the flesh, but His Divine nature through the flesh descended into death, that by the infirmity of the flesh He might effect salvation; not that He might be detained by death according to the law of mortality, but that He might by Himself in his resurrection open the gates of death. It is as if

a king were to proceed to a prison, and to go in and open the doors, undo the fetters, break in pieces the chains, the bars, and the bolts, and bring forth and set at liberty the prisoners, and restore those who are sitting in darkness and in the shadow of death to light and life. The king, therefore, is said indeed to have been in prison, but not under the same condition as the prisoners who were detained there. They were in prison to be punished, He to free them from punishment.

18. They who have handed down the Creed to us have with much forethought specified the time when these things were done — "under Pontius Pilate," — lest in any respect the tradition should falter, as though vague and uncertain. But it should be known that the clause, "He descended into Hell," is not added in the Creed of the Roman Church, neither is it in that of the Oriental Churches. It seems to be implied, however, when it is said that "He was buried." But in the love and zeal for the Divine Scriptures which possess you, you say to me, I doubt not, "These things ought to be proved by more evident testimonies from the Divine Scriptures. For the more important the things are which are to be believed, so much the more do they need apt and undoubted witness." True. But we, as speaking to those who know the law, have left unnoticed, for the sake of brevity, a whole forest of testimonies. But if this also be required, let us cite a few out of many, knowing, as we do, that to those who are acquainted with the Scriptures, a very ample sea of testimonies lies open.

19. First of all, then, we must know that the doctrine of the Cross is not regarded by all in the same light. It is one thing to the Gentiles, to the Jews another, to Christians another; as also the Apostle says, "We preach Christ crucified, — to the Jews a stumbling-block, to the Gentiles foolishness, but to those who are called, both Jews and Greeks, Christ, the power of God and the wisdom of God;"[1] and, in the same place, "For the preaching of the Cross is to those who perish foolishness, but to those who are saved," that is, to us, it is "the Power of God."[2] The Jews, to whom it had been delivered out of the Law, that Christ should abide for ever, were offended by His Cross, because they were unwilling to believe His resurrection. To the Gentiles it seemed foolishness that God should have submitted to death, because they were ignorant of the mystery of the Incarnation. But Christians, who had accepted His birth and passion in

---

[1] Phil. ii. 8.
[2] Ezek. xxix. 4, 5.
[3] Ps. lxxiv. 14, LXX.
[4] Job xli. 1.

[1] 1 Cor. i. 23, 24.
[2] 1 Cor. i. 18.

the flesh and His resurrection from the dead, of course believed that it was the power of God which had overcome death.

First, therefore, hear how this very thing is prophetically declared by Isaiah, that the Jews, to whom the Prophets had foretold these things, would not believe, but that they who had never heard them from the Prophets, would believe them. "To whom He was not spoken of they shall see, and they that have not heard shall understand." [1] Moreover, this same Isaiah foretells that, while those who were engaged in the study of the Law from childhood to old age believed not, to the Gentiles every mystery should be transferred. His words are: "And the Lord of Hosts shall make a feast on this mountain unto all nations: they shall drink joy, they shall drink wine, they shall be anointed with ointment on this mountain. Deliver all these things to the nations." [2] This was the counsel of the Almighty respecting all the nations. But they who boast themselves of their knowledge of the Law will, perhaps, say to us, "You blaspheme in saying that the Lord was subjected to the corruption of death and to the suffering of the Cross." Read, therefore, what you find written in the Lamentations of Jeremiah: "The Spirit of our countenance, Christ the Lord, was taken in our [3] corruptions, of whom we said, we shall live under His shadow among the nations." [4] Thou hearest how the Prophet says that Christ the Lord was taken, and for us, that is, for our sins, delivered to corruption. Under whose shadow, since the people of the Jews have continued in unbelief, he says the Gentiles lie, because we live not in Israel, but among the Gentiles.

20. But, if it does not weary you, let me point out as briefly as possible, specific references to prophecy in the Gospels, that those who are being instructed in the first elements of the faith may have these testimonies written on their hearts, lest any doubt concerning the things which they believe should at any time take them by surprise. We are told in the Gospel that Judas, one of Christ's friends and associates at table, betrayed Him. Let me show you how this is foretold in the Psalms: "He who hath eaten My bread hath lifted up his heel against Me:" [5] and in another place; "My friends and My neighbours drew near and set themselves against Me:" [6] and again; "His words were made softer than oil and yet be they very darts." [7] What then is meant by

his words were made soft? "Judas came to Jesus and said unto Him, Hail, Master, and kissed Him." [1] Thus through the soft blandishment of a kiss he implanted the execrable dart of betrayal. On which the Lord said to him, "Judas, betrayest thou the Son of Man with a kiss?" [2] You observe that He was appraised by the traitor's covetousness at thirty pieces of silver. Of this also the Prophet speaks, "And I said unto them, If ye think good, give me my price, or if not, forbear;" and presently, "I received from them," he says, "thirty pieces of silver, and I cast them into the house of the Lord, into the foundry." [3] Is not this what is written in the Gospels, that Judas, "repenting of what he had done, brought back the money, and threw it down in the temple and departed?" [4] Well did He call it His price, as though blaming and upbraiding. For He had done so many good works among them, He had given sight to the blind, feet to the lame, the power of walking to the palsied, life also to the dead; for all these good works they paid Him death as His price, appraised at thirty pieces of silver. It is related also in the Gospels that He was bound. This also the word of prophecy had foretold by Isaiah, saying, "Woe unto their soul, who have devised a most evil device against themselves, saying, Let us bind the just One, seeing that He is unprofitable to us." [5]

21. But, says some one, "Are these things to be understood of the Lord? Could the Lord be held prisoner by men and dragged to judgment?" Of this also the same Prophet shall convince you. For he says, "The Lord Himself shall come into judgment with the elders and princes of the people." [6] The Lord is judged then according to the Prophet's testimony, and not only judged, but scourged, and smitten on the face with the palms (of men's hands), and spitted on, and suffers every insult and indignity for our sake. And because all who should hear these things preached by the Apostles would be perfectly amazed, therefore also the Prophet speaking in their person exclaims, "Lord, who hath believed our report?" [7] For it is incredible that God, the Son of God, should be spoken of and preached as having suffered these things. For this reason they are foretold by the Prophets, lest any doubt should spring up in those who are about to believe. Christ the Lord Himself therefore in His own person,

---

[1] Isa. lii. 15. Comp. Rom. xv. 21.
[2] Isa. xxv. 6.
[3] *Their corruptions*, LXX.
[4] Lamentations iv. 20.
[5] Ps. xli. 9.
[6] Ps. xxxv. 15.
[7] Ps. lv. 21.

[1] Matt. xxvi. 49.
[2] Luke xxii. 48.
[3] Zech. xi. 12, 13, LXX.
[4] Matt. xxvii. 3, 5.
[5] Isa. iii. 9, LXX.
[6] Isa. iii. 14.
[7] Isa. liii. 1.

says, "I gave My back to the scourges, and My cheeks to the palms,[1] I turned not away My face from shame and spitting."[2] This also is written among His other sufferings, that they bound Him, and led Him away to Pilate. This also the Prophet foretold, saying, "And they bound Him and conducted Him as a pledge of friendship (*xenium*) to King Jarim."[3] But some one objects, "But Pilate was not a king." Hear then what the Gospel relates next, "Pilate hearing that He was from Galilee, sent Him to Herod, who was king in Israel at that time."[4] And rightly does the Prophet add the name "Jarim," which means "a wild-vine," for Herod was not of the house of Israel, nor of that Israelitish vine which the Lord had brought out of Egypt, and "planted in a very fruitful hill,"[5] but was a wild vine, i.e. of an alien stock. Rightly, therefore, was he called "a wild-vine," because he in nowise sprung from the shoots of the vine of Israel. And whereas the Prophet used the phrase "*xenium*," "A pledge of friendship," this also corresponds, "For Herod and Pilate," as the Gospel witnesses, "from being enemies were made friends,"[6] and, as though in token of their reconciliation, each sent Jesus bound to the other. What matter, so long as Jesus, as Saviour, reconciles those who were at variance, and restores peace, and also brings back concord! Wherefore of this also it is written in Job, "May the Lord reconcile the hearts of the princes of the earth."[7]

22. It is related that when Pilate would fain have released Him all the people cried out, "Crucify Him, Crucify Him!"[8] This also the Prophet Jeremiah foretells, saying, in the person of the Lord Himself, "My inheritance is become to Me as a lion in the forest. He hath uttered his voice against Me, wherefore I have hated it. And therefore (saith He) I have forsaken and left My house."[9] And again in another place, "Against whom have ye opened your mouth, and against whom have ye let loose your tongues?"[10] When He stood before His judge, it is written that "He held His peace."[11] Many Scriptures testify of this. In the Psalms it is written, "I became as a man that heareth not, and in whose mouth are no reproofs."[12] And again, "I was as a deaf man, and heard not, and as one that is dumb and openeth not his mouth." And again another Prophet saith, "As a lamb

before her shearer, so He opened not His mouth. In His humiliation His judgment was taken away."[1] It is written that there was put on Him a crown of thorns. Of this hear in the Canticles the voice of God the Father marvelling at the iniquity of Jerusalem in the insult done to His Son: "Go forth and see, ye daughters of Jerusalem, the crown wherewith His mother hath crowned Him."[2] Moreover, of the thorns another Prophet makes mention: "I looked that she should bring forth grapes, and she brought forth thorns, and instead of righteousness a cry."[3] But that thou mayest know the secrets of the mystery, it behoved Him, Who came to take away the sins of the world, to free the earth also from the curse, which it had received through the sin of the first man, when the Lord said "Cursed be the earth in thy labours: thorns: and thistles shall it bring forth to thee."[4] For this cause, therefore, is Jesus crowned with thorns, that that first sentence of condemnation might be remitted. He is led to the cross, and the life of the whole world is suspended on the wood of which it is made. I would point out how this also is confirmed by testimony from the Prophets. You find Jeremiah speaking of it thus, "Come and let us cast wood into His bread, and crush Him out of the land of the living."[5] And again, Moses, mourning over them, says, "Thy life shall be suspended before thine eyes, and thou shalt fear day and night, and shalt not believe thy life."[6] But we must pass on, for already we are exceeding our proposed measure of brevity, and are lengthening out our "short word" by a long dissertation. Yet we will add a few words more, lest we should seem altogether to have passed over what we undertook.

23. It is written that when the side of Jesus was pierced "He shed thereout blood and water."[7] This has a mystical meaning. For Himself had said, "Out of His belly shall flow rivers of living water."[8] But He shed forth blood also, of which the Jews sought that it might be upon themselves and upon their children. He shed forth water, therefore, which might wash believers; He shed forth blood also which might condemn unbelievers. Yet it might be understood also as prefiguring the twofold grace of baptism, one that which is given by the baptism of water, the other that which is sought through martyrdom in the outpouring of blood, for both are called baptism. But if you ask

---

1 Ραπισματα, LXX.   6 Luke xxiii. 12.
2 Isa. l. 6.   7 Job xii. 24.   Διαλλάσσων, LXX.
3 Hos. x. 6.   8 Luke xxiii. 21.   11 Matt. xxvi. 63.
4 Luke xxiii. 6, 7.   9 Jer. xii. 7, 8.   12 Ps. xxxviii. 13, 14.
5 Isa. v. 1.   10 Isa. lvii. 4.

1 Isa. liii. 7, 8.   4 Gen. iii. 17, 18.   7 John xix. 34.
2 Cant. iii. 11.   5 Jer. xi. 19.   8 John vii. 38.
3 Isa. v. 4, 7.   6 Deut. xxviii. 66.

further why our Lord is said to have poured forth blood and water from His side rather than from any other member, I imagine that by the rib in the side the woman is signified. Since the fountain of sin and death proceeded from the first woman, who was the rib of the first Adam, the fountain of redemption and life is drawn from the rib of the second Adam.

24. It is written that in our Lord's passion there was darkness over the earth from the sixth hour until the ninth. To this also you will find the Prophet witnessing, "Thy Sun shall go down at mid-day."[1] And again, the Prophet Zechariah, "In that day there shall be no more light. There shall be cold and frost in one day, and that day known to the Lord; and it shall be neither day nor night, but at evening time there shall be light."[2] What plainer language could the Prophet have used for his words to seem not so much a prophecy of the future as a narrative of the past? He foretold both the cold and the frost. For Peter was warming himself at the fire because it was cold: and he was suffering cold not only in respect of the time (the early hour), but also of his faith. There is added, [2]"and that day shall be known to the Lord; and it shall be neither day nor night." What is "neither day nor night?" Did he not plainly speak of the darkness interposed in the day, and then the light afterwards restored? That was not day, for it did not begin with sun-rise, neither was it complete night, for it did not, when the day was ended, receive its due space from the beginning or prolong it to the end; but the light which had been driven away by the crime of wicked men is restored at evening time. For after the ninth hour, the darkness is driven away, and the sun is restored to the world. Again, another Prophet witnesses of the same, "The light shall be darkened upon the earth in the day-time."[3]

25. The Gospel further relates that the soldiers parted the garments of Jesus among themselves, and cast lots upon His vesture. The Holy Spirit provided that this also should be witnessed beforehand by the Prophets, for David says, "They parted my garments among them, and upon my vesture they did cast lots."[4] Nor were the Prophets silent even as to the robe, the scarlet robe, which the soldiers are said to have put upon Him in mockery. Listen to Isaiah, "Who is this that cometh from Edom, red in his garments from Bozrah? Wherefore are thy garments red, and thy raiment as

though thou hadst trodden in the wine-press?" To which Himself replies, "I have trodden the wine-press alone, O daughter of Sion."[1] For He alone it is Who hath not sinned, and hath taken away the sins of the world. For if by one man death could enter into the world, how much more by one man. Who was God also, could life be restored!

26. It is related also that vinegar was given Him to drink, or wine mingled with myrrh which is bitterer than gall. Hear what the Prophet has foretold of this: "They gave Me gall to eat, and when I was thirsty they gave Me vinegar to drink."[2] Agreeably with which Moses, even in his day, said to the people, "Their vine is of the vineyards of Sodom, and their branch of Gomorrah; their grape is a grape of gall, and their cluster a cluster of bitterness."[3] And again, the Prophet upbraiding them says, "Oh foolish people and unwise, have ye thus requited the Lord?"[4] Moreover, in the Canticles the same things are foretold, where even the garden in which the Lord was crucified is indicated: "I have come into my garden, my sister, my spouse, and have gathered in my myrrh."[5] Here the Prophet has plainly set forth the wine mingled with myrrh which the Lord has given Him to drink.

27. Next it is written that "He gave up the ghost."[6] This also had been foretold by the Prophet, who says, addressing the Father in the Person of the Son, "Into Thy hands I commend My Spirit."[7] He is related also to have been buried, and a great stone laid at the door of the sepulchre. Hear what the word of prophecy foretold by Jeremiah concerning this also, "They have cut off my life in the pit, and have laid a stone upon Me."[8] These words of the Prophet point most plainly to His burial. Here are yet others, "The righteous hath been taken away from beholding iniquity, and his place is in peace."[9] And in another place, "I will give the malignant for his burial;"[10] and yet once more, "He hath lain down and slept as a lion, and as a lion's whelp; who shall rouse Him up?"[11]

28. That He descended into hell is also evidently foretold in the Psalms, where it is said, "Thou hast brought Me also into the dust of the death."[12] And again, "What profit is there in my blood, when I shall have descended into corruption?"[13]

[1] Amos, viii. 9.   [3] Amos viii. 9.
[2] Zech. xiv. 6, 7, LXX.   [4] Ps. xxii. 18.

[1] Isa. lxiii. 1-3.   [6] Mark xv. 37.   [11] Gen. xlix. 9.
[2] Ps. lxix. 21.   [7] Ps. xxxi. 5.   [12] Ps. xxii. 15.
[3] Deut. xxxii. 32.   [8] Lam. iii. 53.   [13] Ps. xxx. 9.
[4] Deut. xxxii. 6.   [9] Isa. lvii. 1, 2.
[5] Cant. v. 1.   [10] Isa. liii. 9, LXX.

And again, "I descended into the deep mire, where there is no bottom."[1] Moreover, John says, "Art Thou He that shall come (into hell, without doubt), or do we look for another?"[2] Whence also Peter says that "Christ being put to death in the flesh, but quickened in the Spirit which dwells in Him, descended to the spirits who were shut up in prison, who in the days of Noah believed not, to preach unto them;"[3] where also what He did in hell is declared. Moreover, the Lord says by the Prophet, as though speaking of the future, "Thou wilt not leave my soul in hell, neither wilt Thou suffer Thy Holy One to see corruption."[4] Which again, in prophetic language he speaks of as actually fulfilled, "O Lord, Thou hast brought my soul out of hell: Thou hast saved me from them that go down into the pit."[5] There follows next,—

29. THE THIRD DAY HE ROSE AGAIN FROM THE DEAD. The glory of Christ's resurrection threw a lustre upon everything which before had the appearance of weakness and frailty. If a while since it seemed to you impossible that an immortal Being could die, you see now that He who has overcome death and is risen again cannot be mortal. But understand herein the goodness of the Creator, that so far as you by sinning have cast yourself down, so far has He descended in following you. And do not impute lack of power to God, the Creator of all things, by imagining his work to have ended in the fall into an abyss which He in His redemptive purpose was unable to reach. We speak of infernal and supernal, because we are bounded by the definite circumference of the body, and are confined within the limits of the region prescribed to us. But to God, Who is present everywhere and absent nowhere, what is infernal and what supernal? Notwithstanding, through the assumption of a body there is room for these also. The flesh which had been deposited in the sepulchre, is raised, that that might be fulfilled which was spoken by the Prophet, "Thou wilt not suffer Thy Holy One to see corruption."[6] He returned, therefore, a victor from the dead, leading with Him the spoils of hell. For He led forth those who were held in captivity by death, as He Himself had foretold, when He said, "When I shall be lifted up from the earth I shall draw all unto Me."[7] To this the Gospel bears witness, when it says, "The graves were opened, and many bodies of saints which slept arose, and appeared unto many,

and entered into the holy City,"[1] that city, doubtless, of which the Apostle says, "Jerusalem which is above is free, which is the Mother of us all."[2] As also he says again to the Hebrews, "It became Him, for Whom are all things, and by Whom are all things, Who had brought many sons into glory, to make the Author of their salvation perfect through suffering."[3] Sitting, therefore, on the right hand of God in the highest heavens, He placed there that human flesh, made perfect through sufferings, which had fallen to death by the lapse of the first man, but was now restored by the virtue of the resurrection. Whence also the Apostle says, "Who hath raised us up together and made us sit together in the heavenly places."[4] For He was the potter, Who, as the Prophet Jeremiah teaches, "took up again with His hands, and formed anew, as it seemed good to Him, the vessel which had fallen from His hands and was broken in pieces."[6] And it seemed good to Him that the mortal and corruptible body which He had assumed, this body raised from the rocky sepulchre and rendered immortal and incorruptible, He should now place not on the earth but in heaven, and at His Father's right hand. The Scriptures of the Old Testament are full of these mysteries. No Prophet, no Lawgiver, no Psalmist is silent, but almost every one of the sacred pages speaks of them. It seems superfluous, therefore, to linger in collecting testimonies; yet we will cite some few, remitting those who desire to drink more largely to the wellsprings of the divine volumes themselves.

30. It is said then in the Psalms, "I laid me down and slept, and rose up again, because the Lord sustained me."[6] Again, in another place, "Because of the wretchedness of the needy and the groaning of the poor, now will I arise, saith the Lord."[7] And elsewhere, as we have said above, "O Lord, thou hast brought my soul out of hell; Thou hast saved me from them that go down into the pit."[8] And in another place, "Because Thou hast turned and quickened me, and brought me out of the deep of the earth again."[9] In the 87th Psalm He is most evidently spoken of: "He became as a man without help, free among the dead."[10] It is not said "a man," but "as a man." For in that He descended into hell, He was "as a man:" but He was "free among the dead," because He could not be detained by

---

[1] Ps. lxix. 2.   [4] Ps. xvi. 10.   [6] Ps. xvi. 10.
[2] Luke vii. 20.   [5] Ps. xxx. 3.   [7] John xii. 32.
[3] 1 Pet. iii. 10-20.

[1] Matt. xxvii. 52, 53.   [5] Jerem. xviii. 4.   [9] Ps. lxxi. 10.
[2] Gal. iv. 23.   [6] Ps. iii. 5.   [10] Ps. lxxxviii. 4, 5.
[3] Heb. ii. 10.   [7] Ps. xii. 5.
[4] Eph. ii. 6.   [8] Ps. xxx. 3.

death. And therefore in the one nature the power of human weakness, in the other the power of divine majesty is exhibited. The Prophet Hosea also speaks most manifestly of the third day in this wise, " After two days He will heal us; but on the third day we shall rise and shall live in His presence." [1] This he says in the person of those who, rising with Him on the third day, are recalled from death to life. And they are the same persons who say, " On the third day we shall rise again, and shall live in His presence." But Isaiah says plainly, " Who brought forth from the earth the great Shepherd of the sheep." [2] Then, that the women were to see His resurrection, while the Scribes and Pharisees and the people disbelieved, this also Isaiah foretold in these words, " Ye women, who come from beholding, come: for it is a people that hath no understanding." [3] But as to the women who are related to have gone to the sepulchre after the resurrection, and to have sought Him without finding, as Mary Magdalene, who is related to have come to the sepulchre before it was light, and not finding Him, to have said, weeping, to the angels who were there, " They have taken away the Lord, and I know not where they have laid Him " [4] — even this is foretold in the Canticles: " On my bed I sought Him Whom my soul loveth; I sought Him in the night, and found Him not." [5] Of those also who found Him, and held Him by the feet, it is foretold, in the same book, " I will hold Him Whom my soul loveth, and will not let Him go." [6] Take these passages, a few of many; for being intent on brevity we cannot heap together more.

31. HE ASCENDED INTO HEAVEN, AND SITTETH ON THE RIGHT HAND OF THE FATHER: FROM THENCE HE SHALL COME TO JUDGE THE QUICK AND THE DEAD. These clauses follow with suitable brevity at the end of this part of the Creed which treats of the Son. What is said is plain, but the question is how and in what sense it is to be understood. For to " ascend," and to " sit," and to " come," unless you understand the words in accordance with the dignity of the divine nature, appear to point to something of human weakness. For having consummated what was to be done on earth, and having recalled souls from the captivity of hell, He is spoken of as ascending up to heaven, as the Prophet had foretold, " Ascending up on high He led captivity captive, and gave gifts unto

men," [1] those gifts, namely, which Peter, in the Acts of the Apostles, spoke of concerning the Holy Ghost, " Being therefore by the right hand of God exalted, He hath shed forth this gift which ye do see and hear." [2] He gave the gift of the Holy Ghost to men, because the captives, whom the devil had before carried into hell through sin, Christ by His resurrection from death recalled to heaven. He ascended therefore into heaven, not where God the Word had not been before, for He was always in heaven, and abode in the Father, but where the Word made flesh had not been seated before. Lastly, since this entrance within the gates of heaven seemed new to its ministers and princes, they say to one another, on seeing the nature of flesh penetrating into the secret recesses of heaven, as David full of the Holy Ghost, declares, " Lift up your gates, ye princes, and be ye lift up ye everlasting gates, and the King of glory shall enter in. Who is the King of glory? The Lord strong and mighty, the Lord mighty in battle." [3] Which words are spoken not with reference to the power of the divine nature, but with reference to the novelty of flesh ascending to the right hand of God. The same David says elsewhere, " God hath ascended jubilantly, and the Lord with the sound of the trumpet." [4] For conquerors are wont to return from battle with the sound of the trumpet. Of Him also it is said, " Who buildeth up His ascent in heaven." [5] And again, " Who hath ascended above the cherubims, flying upon the wings of the winds." [6]

32. To sit at the right hand of the Father is a mystery belonging to the Incarnation. For it does not befit that incorporeal nature without the assumption of flesh; neither is the excellency of a heavenly seat sought for the divine nature, but for the human. Whence it is said of Him, " Thy seat, O God, is prepared from thence forward; Thou art from everlasting." [7] The seat, then, whereon the Lord Jesus was to sit, was prepared from everlasting, " in whose name every knee should bow, of things in heaven and things on earth, and things under the earth; and every tongue shall confess to Him that Jesus is Lord in the glory of God the Father;" [8] of Whom also David thus speaks, " The Lord said unto my Lord, Sit Thou on my right hand until I make Thine enemies Thy footstool." [9] Referring to which words the Lord in the Gospel said to the Pharisees, " If therefore

---

[1] Hosea vi. 2. [3] Isa. xxvii. 11, LXX. [5] Cant. iii. 1.
[2] Heb. xiii. 20. [4] John xx. 13. [6] Cant. iii. 4.

[1] Ps. lxviii. 18. [4] Ps. xlviii. 5. [7] Ps. xciii. 2.
[2] Acts ii. 33. [5] Ps. lxxxix. 2. [8] Phil. ii. 10, 11.
[3] Ps. xxiv. 7, LXX. [6] Ps. xviii. 10. [9] Ps. cx. 1.

David in spirit calleth Him Lord, how is He his Son?"[1] By which He shewed that according to the Spirit He was the Lord, according to the flesh He was the Son, of David. Whence also the Lord Himself says in another place, "Verily I say unto you, henceforth ye shall see the Son of Man sitting at the right hand of the power of God."[2] And the Apostle Peter says of Christ, "Who is on the right hand of God, seated in the heavens."[3] And Paul also, writing to the Ephesians, "According to the working of the might of His power, which He wrought in Christ, when He raised Him from the dead, and seated Him on His right hand."[4]

33. That He shall come to judge the quick and the dead we are taught by many testimonies of the divine Scriptures. But before we cite what the Prophets say on this point, we think it necessary to remind you that this doctrine of the faith would have us daily solicitous concerning the coming of the Judge, that we may so frame our conduct as having to give account to the Judge who is at hand. For this is what the Prophet said of the man who is blessed, that, "He ordereth his words in judgment."[5] When, however, He is said to judge the quick and the dead, this does not mean that some will come to judgment who are still living, others who are already dead; but that He will judge both souls and bodies, where, by souls are meant "the quick," and the bodies "the dead;" as also the Lord Himself saith in the Gospel, "Fear not them who are able to kill the body, but are not able to hurt the soul; but rather fear Him who is able to destroy both soul and body in Gehenna."[6]

34. Now let us shew briefly, if you will, that these things were foretold by the Prophets. You will yourself, since you are so minded, gather together more from the ample range of the Scriptures. The Prophet Malachi says, "Behold the Lord Almighty shall come, and who shall abide the day of His coming, or who shall abide the sight of Him? For He doth come as the fire of a furnace and as fuller's soap: and He shall sit, refining and purifying as it were gold and silver."[7] But that thou mayest know more certainly Who this Lord is of Whom these things are said, hear what the Prophet Daniel also foretells: "I saw," saith he, "in the vision of the night, and, behold, One like the Son of Man coming with the clouds of heaven, and He came nigh to the

Ancient of days, and was brought near before Him; and there was given to Him dominion, and honour, and a kingdom. And all peoples, tribes, and languages shall serve Him. And His dominion is an eternal dominion which shall not pass away, and His kingdom shall not be destroyed."[1] By these words we are taught not only of His coming and judgment, but of His dominion and kingdom, that His dominion is eternal, and His kingdom indestructible, without end; as it is said in the Creed,[2] "and of His kingdom there shall be no end." So that one who says that Christ's kingdom shall one day have an end is very far from the faith. Yet it behoves us to know that the enemy is wont to counterfeit this salutary advent of Christ with cunning fraud in order to deceive the faithful, and in the place of the Son of Man, Who is looked for as coming in the majesty of His Father, to prepare the Son of Perdition with prodigies and lying signs, that instead of Christ he may introduce Antichrist into the world; of whom the Lord Himself warned the Jews beforehand in the Gospels, "Because I am come in My Father's Name, and ye received Me not, another will come in his own name, and him ye will receive."[3] And again, "When ye shall see the abomination of desolation, spoken of by Daniel the Prophet, standing in the holy place, let him that readeth understand."[4] Daniel, therefore, in his visions speaks very fully and amply of the coming of that delusion: but it is not worth while to cite instances, for we have enlarged enough already; we therefore refer any one who may wish to know more concerning these matters to the visions themselves. The Apostle also himself says, "Let no man deceive you by any means, for that day shall not come except there come a falling away first, and that man of sin be revealed, the Son of Perdition, who opposeth and exalteth himself above everything that is called God, or that is worshipped, so that he sitteth in the temple of God, shewing himself as though himself were God."[5] And soon afterwards, "Then shall that wicked one be revealed, whom the Lord Jesus shall slay with the breath of His mouth, and shall destroy with the brightness of His coming: whose coming is after the working of Satan with all power and signs and lying wonders."[6] And

---

1 Matt. xxii. 43–45
2 Matt. xxvi. 64; Luke xxii. 69.
3 1 Pet. iii. 22.
4 Eph. i. 19, 20.
5 Ps. cxii. 5.
6 Matt. x. 28.
7 Matt. iii. 1–3.

1 Dan. vii. 13, 14.
2 "The Creed" is either the Constantinopolitan, or, more probably, that of Jerusalem, with which Rufinus, as a Presbyter of that church, must have been familiar. There is no reason to suppose that the clause was in the Creed of Aquileia.
3 John v. 43.
4 Matt. xxiv. 15.
5 2 Thess. ii. 3, 4.
6 2 Thess. ii. 8, 9.

again, shortly afterwards, "And therefore the Lord shall send unto them strong delusion, that they may believe a lie, that all may be judged who have not believed the truth." [1] For this reason, therefore, is this "delusion" foretold unto us by the words of Prophets, Evangelists, and Apostles, lest any one should mistake the coming of Antichrist for the coming of Christ. But as the Lord Himself says, "When they shall say unto you, lo, here is Christ, or lo, He is there, believe it not. For many false Christs and false prophets shall come and shall seduce many." [8] But let us see how He hath pointed out the judgment of the true Christ: "As the lightning shineth from the east unto the west, so shall the coming of the Son of Man be." [2] When, therefore, the true Lord Jesus Christ shall come, He will sit and set up his throne of judgment. As also He says in the Gospel, "He shall separate the sheep from the goats," [4] that is, the righteous from the unrighteous; as the Apostle writes, "We must all stand before the judgment-seat of Christ, that every man may receive the awards due to the body, according as he hath done, whether they be good or evil." [5] Moreover, the judgment will be not only for deeds, but for thoughts also, as the same Apostle saith, "Their thoughts mutually accusing or else excusing one another, in the day when God shall judge the secrets of men." [6] But on these points let this suffice. Next follows in the order of the faith, —

35. AND IN THE HOLY GHOST. What has been delivered above somewhat at large concerning Christ relates to the mystery of His Incarnation and of His Passion, and, by thus intervening, as belonging to His Person, has somewhat delayed the mention of the Holy Spirit. Otherwise, if the divine nature alone be taken into account, as in the beginning of the Creed we say "I believe in God the Father Almighty," and afterwards, "In Jesus Christ His only Son our Lord," so in like manner we add, "And in the Holy Ghost." But all of these particulars which are spoken of above concerning Christ relate, as we have said, to the dispensation of the flesh (to His Incarnation). By the mention of the Holy Spirit, the mystery of the Trinity is completed. For as one Father is mentioned, and there is no other Father, and one only-begotten Son is mentioned, and there is no other only-begotten Son, so also there is one Holy Ghost, and there cannot be another Holy Ghost.

In order, therefore, that the Persons may be distinguished, the terms expressing relationship (the properties) are varied, whereby the first is understood to be the Father, of Whom are all things, Who Himself also hath no Father, the second the Son, as born of the Father, and the third the Holy Ghost, as proceeding from both, [1] and sanctifying all things. But that in the Trinity one and the same Godhead may be set forth, since, prefixing the preposition "in" we say that we believe "*in* God the Father," so also we say, "*in* Christ His Son," so also "*in* the Holy Ghost." But our meaning will be made more plain in what follows. For the Creed proceeds, —

36. "THE HOLY CHURCH; THE FORGIVENESS OF SIN, THE RESURRECTION OF THIS FLESH." It is not said, "*In* the holy Church," nor "*In* the forgivness of sins," nor "*In* the resurrection of the flesh." For if the preposition "in" had been added, it would have had the same force as in the preceding articles. But now in those clauses in which the faith concerning the Godhead is declared, we say "*In* God the Father," and "*In* Jesus Christ His Son," and "*In* the Holy Ghost," but in the rest, where we speak not of the Godhead but of creatures and mysteries, the preposition "in" is not added. We do not say "We believe *in* the holy Church," but "We believe the holy Church," not as God, but as the Church gathered together to God: and we believe that there is "forgiveness of sins;" we do not say "We believe *in* the forgiveness of sins;" and we believe that there will be a "Resurrection of the flesh;" we do not say "We believe *in* the resurrection of the flesh." By this monosyllabic preposition, therefore, the Creator is distinguished from the creatures, and things divine are separated from things human.

This then is the Holy Ghost, who in the Old Testament inspired the Law and the Prophets, in the New the Gospels and the Epistles. Whence also the Apostle says, "All Scripture given by inspiration of God is profitable for instruction." [2] And therefore it seems proper in this place to enumerate, as we have learnt from the tradition of the Fathers, the books of the New and of the Old Testament, which, according to the tradition of our forefathers, are believed to have been inspired by the Holy Ghost, and have been handed down to the Churches of Christ.

37. Of the Old Testament, therefore, first of all there have been handed down five

[1] Ibid. 11, 12. [3] Ibid. 27. [5] 2 Cor. v. 10.
[2] Matt. xxiv. 23, 24. [4] Matt. xxv. 32. [6] Rom. ii. 15, 16.

[1] Or, according to another reading, "from the mouth of God."
[2] 2 Tim. iii. 16.

books of Moses, Genesis, Exodus, Leviticus, Numbers, Deuteronomy; Then Jesus Nave, (Joshua the son of Nun), The Book of Judges together with Ruth; then four books of Kings (Reigns), which the Hebrews reckon two; the Book of Omissions, which is entitled the Book of Days (Chronicles), and two books of Ezra' (Ezra and Nehemiah), which the Hebrews reckon one, and Esther; of the Prophets, Isaiah, Jeremiah, Ezekiel, and Daniel; moreover of the twelve (minor) Prophets, one book; Job also and the Psalms of David, each one book. Solomon gave three books to the Churches, Proverbs, Ecclesiastes, Canticles. These comprise the books of the Old Testament.

Of the New there are four Gospels, Matthew, Mark, Luke, John; the Acts of the Apostles, written by Luke; fourteen Epistles of the Apostle Paul, two of the Apostle Peter, one of James, brother of the Lord and Apostle, one of Jude, three of John, the Revelation of John. These are the books which the Fathers have comprised within the Canon, and from which they would have us deduce the proofs of our faith.

38. But it should be known that there are also other books which our fathers call not "Canonical" but "Ecclesiastical:" that is to say, Wisdom, called the Wisdom of Solomon, and another Wisdom, called the Wisdom of the Son of Syrach, which last-mentioned the Latins called by the general title Ecclesiasticus, designating not the author of the book, but the character of the writing. To the same class belong the Book of Tobit, and the Book of Judith, and the Books of the Maccabees. In the New Testament the little book which is called the Book of the Pastor of Hermas, [and that] which is called The Two Ways,[1] or the Judgment of Peter; all of which they would have read in the Churches, but not appealed to for the confirmation of doctrine. The other writings they have named " Apocrypha." These they would not have read in the Churches.

These are the traditions which the Fathers have handed down to us, which, as I said, I have thought it opportune to set forth in this place, for the instruction of those who are being taught the first elements of the Church and of the Faith, that they may know from what fountains of the Word of God their draughts must be taken.

39. We come next in the order of belief

to the HOLY CHURCH. We have mentioned above why the Creed does not say here, as in the preceding article, " In the Holy Church." They, therefore, who were taught above to believe in one God, under the mystery of the Trinity, must believe this also, that there is one holy Church in which there is one faith and one baptism, in which is believed one God the Father, and one Lord Jesus Christ, His Son, and one Holy Ghost. This is that holy Church which is without spot or wrinkle. For many others have gathered together Churches, as Marcion, and Valentinus, and Ebion, and Manichæus, and Arius, and all the other heretics. But those Churches are not without spot or wrinkle of unfaithfulness. And therefore the Prophet said of them, " I hate the Church of the malignants, and I will not sit with the ungodly."[1] But of this Church which keeps the faith of Christ entire, hear what the Holy Spirit says in the Canticles, " My dove is one; the perfect one of her mother is one."[2] He then who receives this faith in the Church let him not turn aside in the Council of vanity, and let him not enter in with those who practise iniquity.

For Marcion's assembly is a Council of vanity in that he denies that the Father of Christ is God, the Creator, who by His Son made the world. Ebion's is a Council of vanity since he teaches that, while we believe in Christ, we are withal to observe the circumcision of the flesh, the keeping of the Sabbath, the accustomed sacrifices, and all the other ordinances according to the letter of the Law. Manichæus' is a Council of vanity in regard of his teaching; first in that he calls himself the Paraclete, then that he says that the world was made by an evil God, denies God the Creator, rejects the Old Testament, asserts two natures, one good the other evil, mutually opposing one another, affirms that men's souls are co-eternal with God, that, according to the Pythagoreans, they return through divers circles of nativity into cattle and animals and beasts, denies the resurrection of our flesh, maintains that the passion and nativity of the Lord were not in the verity of flesh, but only in appearance. It was the Council of vanity when Paul of Samosata and his successor Photinus afterwards taught, that Christ was not born of the Father before the world, but had His beginning from Mary. and believed not that being God He was born man, but that of

---

[1] It is believed that this book forms part of " The Teaching of the Twelve Apostles " lately discovered and published at Constantinople.

[1] Ps. xxvi. 5.   [2] Cant. vi. 9.

man He was made God. It was the Council of vanity when Arius and Eunomius taught as their determinate opinion that the Son of God was not born of the very substance of the Father, but was created out of nothing, and that the Son of God had a beginning, and is inferior to the Father; moreover they affirm that the Holy Ghost is not only inferior to the Son, but is also a ministering Spirit.[1] Theirs also is a Council of vanity who confess indeed that the Son is of the substance of the Father, but distinguish and separate the Holy Spirit, while yet the Saviour shews in the Gospel that the power and Godhead of the Trinity are one and the same, saying, "Baptize all nations in the Name of the Father, and of the Son, and of the Holy Ghost,"[2] and it is plainly impious for man to put asunder what God hath joined together. That also is the Council of vanity which a pertinacious and wicked contention formerly gathered together, affirming that Christ assumed human flesh indeed, but not a rational soul withal, since Christ conferred one and the same salvation on the flesh, and the animal soul, and the reason and mind of man. That also is the Council of vanity which Donatus drew together throughout Africa, by charging the Church with traditorship (delivering up the sacred books), and with which Novatus disturbed men's minds by denying the grant of repentance to the lapsed, and condemning second marriages, though contracted possibly of necessity. All of these then avoid as congregations of malignants. Those also, if such there be, who are said to assert that the Son of God does not see or know the Father, as Himself is known and seen by the Father; or that the kingdom of Christ will have an end; or that the flesh will not be raised in the complete restoration of its substance; these also who deny that there will be a just judgment of God in respect of all, and affirm that the devil will be absolved from the punishment of damnation due to him. To all these, I say, let the believer turn a deaf ear. But hold fast by the holy Church, which confesses God the Father Almighty, and His only Son, Jesus Christ our Lord, and the Holy Ghost, of one concordant and harmonious substance, believes that the Son of God was born of the Virgin, suffered for man's salvation, rose again from the dead in the same flesh in

which he was born; and, lastly, hopes that He will come the Judge of all, through Whom also both the FORGIVENESS OF SINS AND THE RESURRECTION OF THE FLESH are preached.

40. As to the FORGIVENESS OF SINS, it ought to be enough simple to believe. For who would ask the cause or the reason when a Prince grants indulgence? When the liberality of an earthly sovereign is no fit subject for discussion, shall man's temerity discuss God's largess? For the Pagans are wont to ridicule us, saying that we deceive ourselves, fancying that crimes committed in deed can be purged by words. And they say, "Can he who has committed murder be no murderer, and he who has committed adultery be accounted no adulterer? How then shall one guilty of crimes of this sort all of a sudden be made holy?" But to this, as I said, we answer better by faith than by reason. For he is King of all who hath promised it: He is Lord of heaven and earth who assures us of it. Would you have me refuse to believe that He who made me a man of the dust of the earth can of a guilty person make me innocent? And that He who when I was blind made me see, or when I was deaf made me hear, or lame walk, can recover for me my lost innocence? And to come to the witness of Nature — to kill a man is not always criminal, but to kill of malice, not by law, is criminal. It is not the deed then, in such matters, that condemns me, because sometimes it is rightly done, but the evil intention of the mind. If then my mind which had been rendered criminal, and in which the sin originated, is corrected, why should I seem to you incapable of being made innocent, who before was criminal? For if it is plain, as I have shewn, that crime consists not in the deed but in the will, as an evil will, prompted by an evil demon, has made me obnoxious to sin and death, so the will prompted by the good God, being changed to good, hath restored me to innocence and life. It is the same also in all other crimes. In this way there is found to be no opposition between our faith and natural reason, while forgiveness of sins is imputed not to deeds, which when once done cannot be changed, but to the mind, which it is certain can be converted from bad to good.

41. This last article, which affirms the RESURRECTION OF THE FLESH, concludes the sum of all perfection with succinct brevity. Although on this point also the faith of the Church is impugned, not only by Gentiles, but by heretics likewise. For

---

[1] Mittendarium, "*Mittendarii, Palatini qui in sacro Palatio militabant, et in provincias extraordinarie mittebantur, a Principe, ut eorum mandata perferrent.*" Officers attached to the Palace, who were sent into the provinces by the Emperor on extraordinary occasions, as bearers of his orders. — *Glossarium Manuale ex Magnis Glossariis Du Fresne, etc.*

[2] Matt. xxviii. 19.

Valentinus altogether denies the resurrection of the flesh, so do the Manicheans, as we shewed above. But they refuse to listen to the Prophet Isaiah when he says, "The dead shall rise, and they who are in the graves shall be raised,"[1] or to most wise Daniel, when he declares, "Then they who are in the dust of the earth shall arise, these to eternal life, but those to shame and confusion."[2] Yet even in the Gospels, which they appear to receive, they ought to learn from our Lord and Saviour, Who says, when instructing the Sadducees, "As touching the resurrection of the dead: have ye not read how He saith to Moses in the Bush, I am the God of Abraham, the God of Isaac, the God of Jacob? Now God is not the God of the dead but of the living."[3] Where in what goes before He declares what and how great is the glory of the resurrection, saying, "But in the resurrection of the dead they will neither marry or be given in marriage, but will be as the angels of God."[4] But the virtue of the resurrection confers on men an angelical state, so that they who have risen from the earth shall not live again on the earth with the brute animals but with angels in heaven — yet those only whose purer life has fitted them for this — those, namely, who even now preserving the flesh of their soul in chastity, have brought it into subjection to the Holy Spirit, and thus with every stain of sins done away and changed into spiritual glory by the virtue of santification, have been counted worthy to have it admitted into the society of angels.

42. But unbelievers cry, "How can the flesh, which has been putrified and dissolved, or changed into dust, sometimes also swallowed up by the sea, and dispersed by the waves, be gathered up again, and again made one, and a man's body formed anew out of it?" To whom our first answer is in Paul's words: "Thou fool, that which thou sowest is not quickened, except it die. And that which thou sowest, thou sowest not the body, which shall be, but bare grain of wheat or of some other seed: but God giveth it a body as seemeth good to Him."[5] Did you not believe that that which you see taking place every year in the seeds which you cast into the ground will come to pass in your flesh which by the law of God is sown in the earth? Why, pray, have you so mean an opinion of God's power that you do not believe it possible for the scattered dust of which each man's flesh was composed to be re-collected and restored to its own original

fabric? Do you refuse to admit the fact when you see mortal ingenuity search for veins of metal deeply buried in the ground, and the experienced eye discover gold where the inexperienced thinks there is nothing but earth? Why should we refuse to grant these things to Him who made man, when he whom He made can do so much? And when mortal ingenuity discovers that gold has its own proper vein, and silver another, and that a far different vein of copper, and diverse and distinct veins of iron and lead lie concealed beneath what has the appearance of earth, shall divine power be thought unable to discover and distinguish the component particles belonging to each man's flesh, even though they seem to be dispersed?

43. But let us endeavour to assist those souls which fail in their faith through reasons drawn from nature. If one should mix different sorts of seeds together and sow them indiscriminately in the earth, will not the grain of each several kind, wherever it may have been thrown, shoot forth at the proper time in accordance with its own specific nature so as to reproduce the condition of its own form and its own body.

Thus then the substance of each individual flesh, though its particles have been variously and diversely scattered, has within it an immortal principle, since it is the flesh of an immortal soul, and at the time which God in His good pleasure shall appoint, there will be collected from the earth and drawn to it, its own component particles, which will be restored to that form which death had formerly dissolved. And thus it will come to pass that to each soul will be restored, not a confused or foreign body but its own which it had when alive, in order that the flesh together with its own soul may for the conflicts of the present life either be crowned if undefiled, or punished if defiled. And accordingly our Church,[1] in teaching the faith, instead of "the Resurrection of the flesh," as the Creed is delivered in other Churches, guardedly adds the pronoun "this" — "the resurrection of *this* flesh." "Of this," that is, no doubt, of the person who rehearses the Creed, making the sign of the cross upon his forehead, while he says the word, that each believer may know that his flesh, if he have kept it clean from sin, will be a vessel of honour, useful to the Lord, prepared for every good work; but, if defiled by sins, that it will be a vessel of wrath destined to destruction.

---

[1] Is. xxvi. 19. [3] Mark xii. 26, 27. [5] 1 Cor. xv. 36–38.
[2] Dan. xii. 2. [4] Matt. xxii. 30,

[1] The Church of Aquileia.

But now, concerning the glory of the resurrection and the greatness of the promise by which God has bound Himself, if any one desires to be more fully informed, he will find notices in almost all the divine volumes, out of which, simply by way of bringing them to remembrance, we will mention a few passages in the present place, and then make an end of the work which you have enjoined. The Apostle Paul makes use of such arguments as the following in asserting that mortal flesh will rise again. " But if there be no resurrection of the dead, then is not Christ risen. And if Christ be not risen, our preaching is vain and your faith is vain."[1] And presently afterwards, " But now is Christ risen from the dead, the first-fruits of them that sleep. For since by man came death, by man came also the resurrection of the dead. For as in Adam all die, even so in Christ shall all be made alive. But every man in his own order. Christ the first-fruits, afterwards they that are Christ's at His coming, then cometh the end."[2] And afterways he adds, " Behold I shew you a mystery: We shall all rise indeed, but we shall not[3] all be changed;" or as other copies read, " We shall all sleep, indeed, but we shall not all be changed; in a moment, in the twinkling of an eye, at the last trump; for the trumpet shall sound, and the dead shall rise incorruptible, and we shall be changed."[4] However, whichever be the true text, writing to the Thessalonians, he says, " I would not have you ignorant, brethren, concerning those who are asleep, that ye sorrow not, as the others who have no hope. For if we believe that Jesus died and rose again, so those also who sleep through Jesus shall God bring with Him. For this we say unto you by the word of the Lord, that we who are alive and remain at the coming of the Lord shall not prevent them that sleep. For the Lord Himself shall descend from heaven with a shout, with the voice of the archangel, with the trump of God, and the dead who are in Christ shall rise first : then we who are alive and remain shall be caught up together with them in the clouds to meet Christ in the air, and so shall we ever be with the Lord."[5]

44. But that you may not suppose this to be a novel doctrine peculiar to Paul, I will adduce also what the Prophet Ezekiel foretold by the Holy Ghost. " Behold," saith he, " I will open your graves and bring you forth out of your graves."[1] Let me recall, further, how Job, who abounds in mystical language, plainly predicts the resurrection of the dead. " There is hope for a tree; for if it be cut down it will sprout again, and its shoot shall never fail. But if its root have waxed old in the earth, and the stock thereof be dead in the dust, yet through the scent of water it will flourish again, and put forth shoots as a young plant. But man, if he be dead, is he departed and gone? And mortal man, if he have fallen, shall he be no more?"[2] Dost thou not see, that in these words he is appealing to men's sense of shame, as it were, and saying, "Is mankind so foolish, that when they see the stock of a tree which has been cut down shooting forth again from the ground, and dead wood again restored to life, they imagine their own case to have no likeness to that of wood or trees?" But convince you that Job's words are to be read as a question, when he says, " But mortal man when he hath fallen shall he not rise again?" take this proof from what follows; for he adds immediately, " But if a man be dead, shall he live?"[3] And presently afterwards he says, " I will wait till I be made again;"[4] and afterwards he repeats the same: " Who shall raise again upon the earth my skin, which is now draining this cup of suffering?"[5]

45. Thus much in proof of the profession which we make in the Creed when we say " The resurrection of this flesh." As to the addition " this," see how consonant it is with all that we have cited from the divine books. What else does Job signify in the place which we explained above, " He will raise again my skin, which is now draining this cup of suffering," that is, which is undergoing these torments? Does he not plainly say that there will be a resurrection of this flesh, this, I mean, which is now undergoing the extremity of trials and tribulations? Moreover, when the Apostle says, " This corruptible must put on incorruption, and this mortal must put on immortality,"[6] are not his words those of one who in a manner touches his body and places his finger upon it? This body then, which is now corruptible, will by the grace of the resurrection be incorruptible, and this which is now mortal will be clothed with virtues of immortality, that, as " Christ rising from the dead dieth no more, death hath no more dominion over Him,"[7] so those who shall rise in Christ shall never again feel corruption or death,

---

[1] 1 Cor. xv. 13, 14. [4] Ibid. 51, 52.
[2] Ibid. 20-24. [5] 1 Thess. iv. 13-17.
[3] A reading current in Rufinus' time.

[1] Ezek. xxxvii. 12. [4] Ibid. [6] 1 Cor. xv. 53.
[2] Job xiv. 7-10. [5] Job xxvi. 26, 27. [7] Rom. vi. 9.
[3] Job xiv. 14.

not because the nature of flesh will have been cast off, but because its condition and quality will have been changed. There will be a body, therefore, which will rise from the dead incorruptible and immortal, not only of the righteous, but also of sinners; of the righteous that they may be able ever to abide with Christ, of sinners that they may undergo without end the punishment due to them.

46. That the righteous shall ever abide with Christ our Lord we have proved above, where we have shewn that the Apostle says, " Then we which are alive and remain shall be caught up together with them in the clouds to meet Christ in the air, and so shall we ever be with the Lord." [1] And do not marvel that the flesh of the saints is to be changed into such a glorious condition at the resurrection as to be caught up to meet God, suspended in the clouds and borne in the air, since the same Apostle, setting forth the great things which God bestows on them that love Him, says, " Who shall change our vile body that it may be made like unto His glorious body." [2] It is nowise absurd then, if the bodies of the saints are said to be raised up into the air, seeing that they are said to be renewed after the image of Christ's body, which is seated at God's right hand. But this also the holy Apostle adds, speaking either of himself or of others of his own place or merit, " He will raise us up together with Christ and make us sit together in the heavenly places." [3] Whence, since God's saints have these promises and an infinite number like them respecting the resurrection of the righteous, it will now not be difficult to believe those also which the Prophets have foretold, namely, that " the righteous shall shine as the sun and as the brightness of the firmament in the kingdom of God." [4] For who will think it difficult that they should have the brightness of the sun, and be adorned with the splendour of the stars and of this firmament, for whom the life and conversation of God's angels are being prepared in heaven, or who are represented as being hereafter to be conformed to the glory of Christ's body? In reference to which glory, promised by the Saviour's mouth, the holy Apostle says, " It is sown as an animal body; it will rise a spiritual body." [5] For if it is true, as it certainly is true, that God will vouchsafe to associate every one of the righteous and of the saints in companionship with the angels, it is cer-

tain that He will change their bodies also into the glory of a spiritual body.

47. Nor let this promise seem to you contrary to the natural structure of the body. For if we believe, according to what is written, that God took clay of the earth and made man, and that the origin of our body was this, that, by the will of God, earth was changed into flesh, why does it seem absurd to you or contrary to reason if, on the same principles on which earth is said to be advanced to an animal body, an animal body in turn should be believed to be advanced to a spiritual body? These things and many like these you will find in the divine Scriptures concerning the resurrection of the righteous. There will be given to sinners also, as we said above, a condition of incorruption and immortality at the resurrection, that, as God assigns this state to the righteous for perpetuity of glory, so He may assign the same to sinners for prolongation of confusion and punishment. For this also the Prophet's words, which we referred to above, state clearly: " Many shall rise from the dust of the earth, some to life eternal, and others to confusion and eternal shame." [1]

48. If then we have understood in what august significance God Almighty is called Father, and in what mysterious sense our Lord Jesus Christ is held to be His only Son, and with what entire perfection of meaning His Spirit is called the Holy Spirit, and how the Holy Trinity is one in substance but has distinctions of relation and of Persons, what also is the birth from a Virgin, what the nativity of the Word in the flesh, what the mystery of the Cross, what the purpose of our Lord's descent into hell, what the glory of the Resurrection, and the delivery of souls from their captivity in the infernal regions, what also His ascension into heaven, and the expected advent of the Judge ; moreover how the holy Church ought to be acknowledged as opposed to the congregations of vanity, what is the number of the sacred Volume, what conventicles of heretics ought to be avoided, and how in the forgiveness of sins there is no opposition whatever between the divine freedom and natural reason, and how not only the sacred oracles but also the example of Lord and Saviour Himself, and the conclusions of natural reason, confirm the truth of the resurrection of our flesh ; — if, I say, we have intelligently followed these in succession in accordance with the rule of the tradition hereinbefore expounded, we pray that the

---

1 1 Thess. iv. 17.   4 Matt. xiii. 43.
2 Phil. iii. 21.   5 1 Cor. xv. 44.
3 Eph. ii. 6.

1 Dan. xii, 2.

Lord will grant to us, and to all who hear these words, that having kept the faith which we have received, having finished our course, we may await the crown of righteousness laid up for us, and be found among those who shall rise again to eternal life, and be delivered from confusion and eternal shame, through Christ our Lord, through Whom to God the Father Almighty with the Holy Ghost is glory and dominion for ever and ever. Amen.

THE PREFACE TO THE BOOKS OF RECOGNITIONS OF ST. CLEMENT

Addressed to Bishop Gaudentius

(For the occasion and date [1] of this work see the Prolegomena, p. 412.)

You possess so much vigour of character, my dear Gaudentius, you who are so signal an ornament of our teachers, or as I would rather say, you have the grace of the Spirit in so large a measure, that even what you say in the way of daily conversation, or of addresses that you preach in church,[2] ought to be consigned in writing and handed down for the instruction of posterity. But I am far less quick, my native talent being but slender, and old age is already making me sluggish and slow; and this work is nothing but the payment of a debt due to the command laid upon me by the virgin Sylvia whose memory I revere. She it was who demanded of me, as you have now done by the right of heirship, to translate Clement into our language. The debt is paid at last, though after many delays. It is a part of the booty, and in my opinion no small one, which I have carried off from the libraries of the Greeks, and which I am collecting for the use and advantage of our countrymen. I have no food of my own to bring them, and I must import their nourishment from abroad. However, foreign goods are apt to appear sweeter; and sometimes they are really more useful. Moreover, almost anything which brings healing to our bodies or is a defence against disease or an antidote to poison comes from abroad. Judæa sends us the distillation of the balsam tree, Crete the leaf of the dictamnus, Arabia her aromatic flowers, and India the crop of the spikenard. These goods come to us, no doubt, in a less perfect condition than those which our own fields produce, but they preserve intact their pleasant scent and their healing power. Therefore, my friend who are as my own soul, I present to you Clement returning to Rome. I present him dressed in a Latin garb. Do not think it strange if the aspect which his eloquence presents is less bright than it might be. It makes no difference if only the meaning is felt to be the same.

These are foreign wares, then, which I am importing at a great expense of labour; and I have still to see whether our countrymen will regard with gratitude one who is bringing them the spoils (spolia) of his warfare, and who is unlocking with the key of our language a treasure house hitherto concealed, though he does it with the utmost good will. I only trust that God may look favourably on your good wishes, so that my present may not be met in any quarter by evil eyes and envious looks; and that we may not witness that extremely monstrous phenomenon, expressions of illwill on the part of those on whom the gift is conferred, while those from whom it is taken part with it ungrudgingly. It is but right that you, who have read this work in the Greek should point out to others the design of my translation — unless indeed, you feel that in some respects I have not observed the right method of rendering the original. You are, I believe well aware that there are two Greek editions of this work of Clement, his Recognitions; that there are two sets of books, which in some few cases differ from each other though the bulk of the narrative is the same. For instance, the last part of the work, that which gives an account of the transformation of Simon Magus, exists in one of these, while in the other it is entirely absent. On the other hand there are some things, such as the dissertation on the unbegotten and the begotten God, and a few others, which, though they are found in both editions, are, to say

---

[1] The date is after the Peroration to the Epistle to the Romans (see p. 568); but it seemed better not to divide the Prefaces, etc., to the translations of Origen's Commentaries.

[2] *Si quid in Ecclesia declamatur.*

the least of them, beyond my understanding; and these I have preferred to leave others to deal with rather than to present them in an inadequate manner. As to the rest, I have taken pains not to swerve, even in the slightest degree from either the sense or the diction; and this, though it makes the expression less ornate, renders it more faithful.

There is a letter in which this same Clement writing to James the Lord's brother, gives an account of the death of Peter. and says that he has left him as his successor, as ruler and teacher of the church; and further incorporates a whole scheme of ecclesiastical government. This I have not prefixed to the work, both because it is later in point of time, and because it has been previously translated and published by me. Nevertheless, there is a point which would perhaps seem inconsistent with facts were I to place the translation of it in this work, but which I do not consider to involve an impossibility. It is this. Linus and Cletus were Bishops of the city of Rome before Clement. How then, some men ask, can Clement in his letter to James say that Peter passed over to him his position as a church-teacher.[1] The explanation of this point, as I understand, is as follows. Linus and Cletus were, no doubt, Bishops in the city of Rome before Clement, but this was in Peter's life-time; that is, they took charge of the episcopal work, while he discharged the duties of the apostolate. He is known to have done the same thing at Cæsarea; for there, though he was himself on the spot, yet he had at his side Zacchæus whom he had ordained as Bishop. Thus we may see how both things may be true; namely how they stand as predecessors of Clement in the list of Bishops, and yet how Clement after the death of Peter became his successor in the teacher's chair. But it is time that we should pay attention to the beginning of Clement's own narrative, which he addresses to James the Lord's brother.

[1] *Cathedram docendi.*

PREFACE TO THE TRANSLATION OF THE SAYINGS OF XYSTUS

Composed at Aquileia about the year 307 A.D

(For the questions relating to Xystus see the Prolegomena, p. 412.)

RUFINUS TO APRONIANUS, HIS OWN FRIEND

I know that, just as the sheep come gladly when their own shepherd calls them, so in matters of religion men attend most gladly to the admonitions of a teacher who speaks their own language: and therefore, my very dear Apronianus, when that pious lady who is my daughter but now your sister in Christ, had laid her commands on me to compose for her a treatise of such a nature that its understanding should not require any great effort, I translated into Latin in a very open and plain style the work of Xystus, who is said to be the same man who at Rome is called Sixtus, and who gained the glory of being both bishop and martyr. I think that, when she reads this, she will find it expressed with such brevity that a vast meaning is unfolded in each several line, with such power that a sentence only a line long would suffice for a whole life's training, and yet with such simplicity that one who looked over the shoulder of a girl as she read it might question whether I were not quite weak in intellect. And the whole work is so concise that it would be possible for her never to let go of it. The entire book would hardly be bigger than the finger ring of one of our ancestors. And indeed it seems but right that one who has learnt through the word of God to count as dross the ornaments of the world should now receive at my hands by way of ornament a necklace of the word and of wisdom. For the present let this little book serve for a ring and be kept constantly in the hands: but it will not be long before it will penetrate into the treasure house and be wholly laid up in the heart, and bring forth from its innermost chamber the germs of instruction and of a participation in all good works. I have added further a few choice sayings addressed by a pious father to his son, but all so succinct that the whole of this little work may rightly be called in Greek the Enchiridion[1] or in Latin the Annulus.[2]

[1] A thing held in the hand.   [2] A ring.

PREFACE TO THE TWO BOOKS OF ECCLESIASTICAL HISTORY, ADDED BY RUFINUS TO HIS TRANSLATION OF EUSEBIUS

Addressed to Chromatius, Bishop of Aquileia, A.D. 401

(For the occasion of writing, and the date, see Prolegomena, p. 412.)

It is the custom, they say, of skilful physicians, when they perceive that some epidemic disease is near at hand in one of our cities, to provide some kind of medicine, whether solid or liquid, which men may use as a preventative to defend themselves from the destruction which is hanging over them. You have imitated this method of the doctors, my venerable Father, Chromatius, at the moment when the gates of Italy were broken through by Alaric the commander of the Goths, and thus a disease and plague poured in upon us, which made havoc of the fields and cattle and men throughout the land. You then sought a remedy against the cruelty and destruction, so that the minds of men which were languishing might be drawn away from the contagion of the prevailing malady, and might preserve their balance through an interest in better pursuits. This you have done by enjoining on me the task of translating into Latin the ecclesiastical history which was written in the Greek language by that most learned man, Eusebius of Cæsarea. You thought that the mind of those who heard it read to them might be so held fast by it that, in its eager desire for the knowledge of past events, it might to some extent become oblivious of their actual sufferings. I tried to excuse myself from the task, as being, through my weakness unequal to it, and as having in the lapse of years lost the use of the Latin tongue. But I reflected that your commands were not to be divaricated from your position in the Apostolic order. For, at the time when the multitude in the desert were hungering, and the Lord said to his Apostles, "Give ye them to eat," Philip who was one of them instead of bringing out the loaves which were hid in the wallet of the Apostles, said that there was a little lad there who had five loaves and two fishes. He knew that the exhibition of the divine virtue would be none the less brilliant if the ministry of some of the little ones were used in its fulfilment. He modestly excused his action by adding, "What are these among so many?" So that the divine power might be more conspicuous through tne difficult and desperate circumstances in which it acted. I felt that, since

you were a scion of the Apostolic order, you had possibly acted in remembrance of Philip's example, and that, when you saw that the time was come for the multitudes to be fed, you had engaged the services of a little lad who might be able to contribute, twice told, the five loaves[1] which he had received, but who further, to fulfil the Gospel type, might add two small fishes[2] which he had captured by his own efforts. I have therefore made the attempt to execute what you had ordered, having the assurance that the deficiency of my inexperience would be excused on account of the authority of him who gave the command.

I must point out the course I have taken in reference to the tenth book of this work. As it stands in the Greek, it has little to do with the process of events. All but a small part of it is taken up with discussions tending to the praise of particular Bishops, and adds nothing to our knowledge of facts. I have therefore left out all this superfluous matter; and, whatever in it belonged to genuine history I have added to the ninth book, with which I have made his history close. The tenth and eleventh books I have myself compiled, partly from the traditions of the former generation, partly from facts within my own memory; and these I have added to the previous books, like the two fishes to the loaves. If you bestow your approval and benediction upon them, I shall have a sure confidence that they will suffice for the multitude. The work as now completed contains the events from the Ascension of the Saviour to the present time; my own two books those from the days of Constantine when the persecution came to an end on to the death of the Emperor Theodosius.

The following note occurs at the end of the ninth book of Rufinus' Latin Version of Eusebius.

Thus far Eusebius has given us the record of the history. As to the subsequent events, as they have followed on up to the present time, as I have found them recorded in the writings of the last generation, or so far as they are covered by my own knowledge, I will add them, obeying, as best I may, in this point also the commands of our father in God.[3]

---

[1] That is, the ten books of Eusebius' History. [2] That is, the two books added by Rufinus. [3] Chromatius.

RUFINUS' PREFACE TO THE TRANSLATION OF ORIGEN'S COMMENTARY ON PSALMS 36, 37, AND 38.

Addressed to Apronianus,[1] either at Rome or at Aquileia, between A.D. 398 and A.D. 407

The whole exposition of the thirty-sixth, thirty-seventh and thirty-eighth Psalms is ethical in its character, being designed to enforce more correct methods of life; and teaches at one time the way of conversion and repentance, at another that of purification and of progress. I have therefore thought it well to translate it into Latin for you, my dearest son Apronianus, having first arranged it in nine of the short sermons which are called in Greek Homilies, and incorporated it into one whole; and thus this discourse which in all its parts aims at the correction and the advancement of the moral life, is collected into a single volume. My translation will at all events be of use so far as to put the reader without effort in posses-sion of the meaning of the author, which is here fully laid open, and to bring home to him the simplicity of life which he enjoins with clearness of thought and in simple words; and thus the voice of prophecy may reach not men alone but also god-fearing women, and lend subtlety to the minds of the simple. Yet I fear that that pious lady, who is my daughter but your sister in Christ, may think that she owes me no thanks for my work if it brings her nothing but puzzling thoughts and thorny questions: for the human body could hardly hold together if divine providence had formed it of bones and muscles alone without blending with them the ease and grace of the softer tissues.

---

[1] A Roman noble converted by Rufinus and Melania, with the latter of whom he was connected.

RUFINUS' PREFACE TO THE TRANSLATION OF ORIGEN'S COMMENTARY ON THE EPISTLE TO THE ROMANS

Addressed to Heraclius at Aquileia about A.D. 407

My intention was to press the shore of the quiet land in the little bark in which I was sailing, and to draw out a few little fishes from the pools of Greece: but you have compelled me, brother Heraclius, to give my sails to the wind and go forth into the deep sea; you persuade me to leave the work which lay before me in the translation of the homilies written by the Man of Adamant[1] in his old age, and to open to you the fifteen volumes in which he discussed the Epistle of Paul to the Romans. In these books, while he aims at representing the Apostle's thoughts, he is carried away into a sea of such depth that one who follows him into it may well be afraid of being drowned in the greatness of his thoughts as in the vastness of the waves. Then also you do not consider this, that my breath is but scanty for filling a grand trumpet of eloquence like his. And beyond all these difficulties is this, that the books themselves have been interpolated. In almost all the libraries (I grant that no one can tell how it happened) some of the volumes are absent from the body of the work, and to supply these, and to restore the continuity of the work in the Latin version is beyond my talent, but would be, as you must know when you make your demand, a special gift of God. You add, however, so that nothing may be wanting to the labour I am undertaking, that I had

---

[1] Or man of steel: (it might also be translated, The indomitable); a name given to Origen, an account of the greatness of his labours. It is said by Westcott (Dict. of Xtn. Biog. "Origen") to have been adopted by Origen himself, and to form part of his real name.

better abbreviate this whole body of fifteen volumes, which in the Greek reaches to the length of forty thousand lines or more, and bring it within moderate compass. Your injunctions are hard indeed, and might be thought to be imposed by one who did not care to consider what the burden of such a work must be. I will, however, attempt it, hoping that through your prayers, and the favour of the Lord, what seems impossible to man may become possible. But we will now, if you please, listen to the Preface which Origen himself prefixes to the work on which he was entering.

THE PERORATION OF RUFINUS APPENDED TO HIS TRANSLATION OF ORIGEN'S COMMENTARY ON THE EPISTLE TO THE ROMANS

Addressed to Heraclius at Aquileia, probably about 407

A satisfactory conclusion has now, I trust, been reached of the Commentary on the Epistle to the Romans, the writing of which has been a work of very great labour and time. I confess, my most loving brother Heraclius, that in the attempt to respond to your request I have almost forgotten the precept; "Do not lift a burden above your strength." Even in the other translations of Origen's works into Latin, which were made because you earnestly requested it, or rather exacted it as a journeyman's task, the labour was very great; for I made it my object to supplement what Origen spoke extempore in the lecture room of the church; for his aim there was the application of the subject for the sake of edification rather than the exposition of the text. This I have done in the case of the Homilies, and the short lectures on Genesis and Exodus, and especially in those on the book of Leviticus, where he spoke in a hortatory manner, whereas my translation takes the form of an exposition. This duty of supplying what was wanted I took up because I thought that the practice of agitating questions and then leaving them unsolved, which he frequently adopts in his homiletic mode of speaking, might prove distasteful to the Latin reader. The works upon Jesus Nave[1] and the book of Judges and the thirty-sixth, thirty-seventh and thirty-eighth Psalms, I translated simply as I found them, with no great labour. While then in the other cases which I have mentioned above, I employed much labour in supplying what Origen had omitted, in this work on the Epistle to the Romans the labour that fell on me for the causes described in the Preface was immense and full of complexity. But

---

[1] Joshua.

there will have been nothing but pleasure in these labours, provided only that my experience in other cases, of ill-disposed minds requiting my toils and vigils with contumely, be not repeated and that I do not gain for my studies the reward of detraction and for my labour a conspiracy to ruin me. For in dealing with these men I have to undergo a new form of accusation. They say to me; When you write these things, in which are found many pieces the composition or which is due to yourself, you should place your own name in the title, and let it run thus: 'The books of Rufinus' commentary on (for instance) the Epistle to the Romans;' for so, they say, in the case of profane writers, the name in the title is not that of the Greek author who is translated but of the Latin author who translates him. But all this complaisance, by which the works are ascribed to me, is caused not by love to me but by hatred to the author. I am much more observant of my conscience than of my reputation; it may be apparent that I have added some things to supply what was wanting; and that I have abbreviated what was too lengthy; but to steal the title from the man who laid the foundations on which the building has been reared is what I cannot think right. It must be, I grant, in the discretion of the reader, when he has examined the work, to ascribe the work to any one he thinks right; but my intention has been not to seek the applause of students but the good of those who wish to be edified.

I shall turn next to the work which was long ago imposed upon me but now is demanded with still greater vehemence by the Bishop Gaudentius, namely to turn into Latin the books called the Recognition of Clement the Bishop of Rome, the successor and companion of the Apostles. In this work I well know that, to judge by the ordinary rule, I shall have labour upon labour. In this case I will do what my friends desire, I will put my own name in the title of the work, though I shall have that of the author also. It shall be called Rufinus's Clement. If the Lord enable me to fulfil this task, I shall afterwards return to that which you desire, and say something, God willing, on the books of Numbers or of Deuteronomy (for this alone is wanting to my whole work on the Heptateuch) : or else I shall write what I can, the Lord being my guide, on the remaining epistles of the Apostle Paul.

PREFACE TO ORIGEN'S HOMILIES ON NUMBERS

Addressed to Ursacius.[1]   *Written in 410.*[2]

My dear brother, I might rightly address you in the words of the blessed master, "You do well, dearest Donatus, in reminding me of this ;" for I well remember my promise that I would collect all that Adamantius wrote in his old age on the Law of Moses, and translate it into Latin for the use of our people. But, as he says, the season was not seasonable for the fulfilment of my promise, but was full of storm and confusion. How can the pen move freely when a man is in fear of the missiles of the enemy, when he has before his eyes the devastation of cities and country, when he has to fly from dangers of the sea, and there is no safety even in exile ? As you yourself saw, the Barbarian was within sight of us ; he had set fire to the city of Rhegium, and our only protection against him was the very narrow sea which separates the soil of Italy from Sicily. In such a position, what leisure could there be for writing, and especially for translating, a work in which one's duty is not to develop one's own opinions but to express those of another? However, when there was a quiet night, and our minds were relieved from the fear of an attack by the enemy, and we got at least some little leisure for thought, I set to work, as a solace from our troubles, and to relieve the burden of our pilgrimage, together into one and arrange all that Origen had written on the book of Numbers, whether in the way of homilies or in writings such as are called Excerpts,[3] and to translate them into the Roman tongue. You urged me to do this, Ursacius, and aided me with all your might, indeed, so eager were you, that you thought the youth who acted as secretary too slow in the execution of his office. I wish, however, to point out to you, my brother, that the object of this method of studying scripture is not to deal with each clause separately, as you find done in commentaries, but to open up a path for the understanding, so that the reader may not be made negligent, but as it is written[4] may " stir up his own spirit " and draw out the meaning, and, when he has heard the good word, may add to it by his own wisdom. In this way I have tried to give all the expositions which you desired ; and now of all the writings that I have found upon the Law the short comments upon Deuteronomy alone are wanting ; these, if God so will, and if he restores my eye-sight, I hope to add to the body of the work. Indeed, my very loving son Pinianus, whose truly Christian company I have joined in their flight because of my delight in their chaste conversation, requires yet other tasks from me. But do you and he join your prayers that the Lord may be present with us, and may give peace in our time, and shew mercy to those who are in trouble, and make our work fruitful for the edification of the reader.

---

[1] Nothing more is known of Ursacius than is to be gathered from the mention of him here.
[2] The date is fixed by the burning of Rhegium by Alaric, who intended to invade Sicily, but his transports were scattered by a storm and he himself died soon after.   See Gibbon ch. xxxi.
[3] Apparently a longer style of note.   [4] Possibly from Ps. lxxvii, 7.

INDICES

THEODORET

INDEX OF SUBJECTS

Abbott, Dr. E. A., 103 n., 104 n.
Abcavius, 94 n.
Abdas, bp., 157.
Abraames, 128.
Abraham, robber of church property, 252.
Abraham the Œconomus, 288.
Abramius, 294, 296.
Abundius, bp. of Como, 347.
Acacius, bp. of Cæsarea, 70, 87, 89, 92.
Acacius, bp. of Berœa, 128, 134, 136, 149, 151, 153 n., 290, 292.
Acacius, presbyter, 289.
Acacius, bp. of Melitene, 336.
Acepsemas, 128.
Achillas, archbishop of Alexandria, 34.
Achillas, Arian deacon, 35, 38, 40, 41.
Accœmetæ, 309 n.
Adelphius, 75, 114, 115.
Adrianople, Battle of, 131.
Ædesius, 58, 154 n.
Ælia, 63, 87 n.
Æmona, 142, 149.
Æmilianus, martyr, 60 n., 97.
Aerius, 260, 269.
Æschylus, 97, 114 n., 260.
Aetius, bp. of Lydda, 41, 57, 135.
Aetius, conqueror of Attila, 293 n.
Aetius the Anomœan, 41 n., 82 n, 85, 88, 89, 90.
Agapetus, bp. of Apamea, 128, 151.
Agapius, bp., 75.
Agapius, presbyter, 266.
Agathias, 60 n.
Aïthales, 41.
Alaric, 149 n.
Alcinous, 260.
Alexander, officer of imperial household, 309 n.
Alexander, archbishop of Alexandria, 34, 35, 41, 47, 51, 52, 60, 280, 315, 332.
Alexander, bishop of Byzantium, 34, 35, 55.
Alexander, bishop of Antioch, 96, 154, 155, ?290.
Alexander, bp. of Hierapolis, 6, 341, 345, 346.
Alexander, king of Epirus, 106 n.
Alexander the coppersmith, 160.
Alexandra, 254, 286.
Alexandria, 34, 35, 89.
Alford, dean, 17, 37 n., 321 n.
Alypius, 294, 296.
Amantius, 113.

Amathus, 128 n.
Ambrosius, bp. of Milan, 41 n., 52 n., 81 n., 85 n., 110, 111, 129, 137, 141, 143, 144, 145, 146, 174, 205, 238, 315, 332, 340, 343.
Amegetius, 102.
Ammianus Marcellinus, 78 n., 91 n., 93 n., 99 n., 102 n., 104 n., 106 n., 128 n., 130 n.
Ammonius, 41, 75.
Amphilochius, bishop of Iconium, 114, 129, 136, 142, 181, 208, 239, 315, 332.
Amphion, 56.
Anagamphus, 75.
Anastasia, Church of, 136.
Anastasius, bp. of Rome, 148, 149.
Anatolius, bp. of Constantinople, 9 n.
Anatolius, the patrician, 8, 275, 284, 290, 296, 297, 307.
Ancillæ, or ministræ, in Pliny's letter, 100 n.
Ancyra, 86 n.
Andiberis, 295.
Andreas, bp. of Samosata, 259, 300 n., 336, 346.
Andreas, monk of Constantinople, 310, 345 n.
Andronicus, presbyter of Antioch, 13.
Anemius, 137.
Anthropomorphism, 114 n.
Antinoopolis, 118.
Antioch, succession of bishops at, 57.
Antioch, riots at, 145.
Antiochia Mygdonia, 91.
Antiochus, bp. of Ptolemais, 211.
Antiochus, præfect, 285.
Antiochus, presbyter, 117.
Anthony, Saint, 51 n., 91 n., 121, 128.
Antiphonal singing, 85.
Anytus, 258.
Apamea ad Orontem, 133.
Apella, 295.
Apellion, 260.
Aphthonius, 299.
Apion, 40, 52.
Aphraates, monk, 1, 127, 128.
Apollinarius, 132, 133, 138, 139, 159, 160, 182, 214, 242, 288, 294, 313, 314, 324, 327, 334, 339, 340, 344, 346.
Apollo, Shrine of, 98.
Apollo, 104 n.
Apollonia, 89 n.
Apollonius of Tyana, 106 n.
Apollonius comes Sacrarum Largitionium, 271, 287.

Apringius, 337.
Aquilinus, 248, 260, 347.
Arbogastes, 149 n.
Arcadia, 155 n.
Arcadius, 142, 126 n., 145 n., 151, 152.
Archibius, 268.
Areobindas, 259.
Ares, 106.
Ariminum, 83, 87.
Arintheus, 130.
Aristolaus, 346.
Aristophanes, 97 n.
Aristotle, 41 n., 194 n., 255 n., 329 n.
Arius, 34, 35, 38, 40, 41, 42 n., 50 n., 51, 52, 54, 56, 65, 75, 84, 92, 108, 122, 123, 135, 138, 139, 159, 258, 278, 287, 291, 295, 313, 314, 325, 326, 327, 339, 340, 342, 343, 346.
Arius the deacon, 41.
Arsacius, 332 n.
Arsenius, 62, 63, 69.
Artemas, 38.
Artemius, 102.
Ascholius, 137.
Asclepas, bp. of Gaza, 62, 67, 68, 69, 70, 77.
Asclepiades, 113.
Aspar, 308.
Asterius, bp. of Petra in Arabia, 70.
Athanasius, bp. of Anazarbus, 41.
Athanasius, archbp. of Alexandria, 41 n., 42 n., 44, 45 n., 56 n., 57 n., 58, 60, 61, 62 n., 65, 66, 67, 68, 69, 72–78, 83, 84, 86 n., 94, 95, 97, 98, 108, 120, 128, 135, 174, 178, 237, 257, 280, 315, 331 n., 332, 343.
Athanasius, bp. of Perrha, 264, 301 n., 323, 336 n.
Athanasius, orator, 259.
Athenius, 323.
Athenodorus, 75.
Atticus, bp. of Constantinople, 154, 213, 315, 332.
Attila, 156 n.
Audœus, 114.
Augustus, 96 n.
Aurelia Eusebia, 79.
Aurelianus, 60 n., 153 n.
Auxentius of Milan, 79, 81, 83, 84, 110.
Avitus, 128.
Axum, 58 n.
Ἀλλά, 169.

Babylas, martyr, 94 n., 98.

THEODORET

INDEX OF TEXTS

JEROME AND GENNADIUS.

ILLUSTRIOUS MEN

INDEX OF SUBJECTS

LIFE AND WORKS OF RUFINUS

INDEX OF SUBJECTS

Æsculapius, 458.
Alaric, 409, 410.
Albina, 407.
Alexandria, 430, 502.
Ambrose, 484.
    Defamed by Jerome, 470, 480.
Anastasius, 407 n., 409, 487, 513.
    Letter to John of Jerusalem, 432, 509, 529, 537.
    Opinions on Origen, 433.
    Rufinus' Apology to, 410, 430, 501.
    Rufinus on, 433.
Anthropomorphism, 443, 531.
Apocrypha, 558.
Apollinarius, 426.
Apostles' Creed, 541–63.
Apronianus, 407, 480, 564, 566.
Aquila, 467, 517.
Aquileia, 405, 409, 431, 432, 502.
—— Creed of, 437, 541.
Ariminum, Council of, 410, 512.
Aristotle, 452.
Arius, 558.
Aterbius, 407, 435.
Augustin, 409.

Bacurius, 406.
Barabbas, or Baranina, Jerome's Jewish teacher, 466, 476, 489.
Barcochebas, 535.
Basil, 412.
Belief, Nature of, 543, 557.
Bibliography of Rufinus' Works, 413.
Body, The, a prison, 456.
Bonosus, 405.
Bribing of Rufinus' Secretary, 520.

Canon of Scripture, 557–8.
Cerealis, 418.
Christ, Meaning of, 545; Birth of, 546–8.
Chromatius, 407, 409, 411, 430, 514.
Chronicle of Jerome, 407.
Chrysogonus, 500.
Church, opposed to heretical assemblies, 558.
Clement of Alexandria, 423, 510.
Clement of Rome, 409, 412, 417, 422–3.
—— Recognitions of, 409, 412, 422, 510, 563.
Commentator, Duty of, 490, 567–8.
Concordia, 405, 406.
Controversy may be friendly, 520, 523–4, 539–40.

Creation, 546.
Creed, The, 556.
Cross, The, a triumph, 549.
Cyprian, 425, 512.
Cyril, 406.

Damasus, 426.
Daniel, Jerome's views of, 516–7.
Demetrias, 413.
Devil, Question of salvability of, 431, 442, 454, 503.
—— Snared by Christ's death, 550.
Didymus, 458, 466, 471, 486, 510, 533.
Dionysius, 423, 510.
Donatus, 568.

Ebion, 558.
Ecclesiastical History by Rufinus, 410, 465.
Edena, 406.
Epiphanius, 406, 407, 426 n., 434, 442, 514, 522, 534, 535.
Eugenia, 413.
Eusebius of Aquileia, 436.
Eusebius of Cæsarea, 409, 411, 412, 488, 565.
Eusebius of Cremona, 407, 444, 445, 487, 515, 521, 532.
Eustochium, Jerome's letter to, 462, 465.
Evagrius Ponticus, 412.

Fabiola, 407.
Fall of men, 448.
—— the world, 448.
Fontanini on Life and Works of Rufinus, 412.
Forgiveness, ridiculed by Pagans, 559.
Frumentius, 406.

Gaudentius, 409.
Gelasius, 410.
Gennadius, 410, 412, 413.
God, as Father, 543–4; Unity of, 544; Invisible and Impassible, 545.
Greek, Knowledge of, 417, 522, 532, 537.
Gregory Nazianzen, 412, 458.

Hebrew Scriptures quoted by Christ, 517.
Heraclius, 566–7.
Hexapla of Origen, 477.
Hilary, 405, 425, 475, 512.
Homilies of Origen, 411, 412.
Homoousion, 422.

Huillus, 490.
Hylas, 405.

Incarnation, its consequences, 555.

James, the Lord's brother, 564.
Jerome, 405, 406.
    Anti-Ciceronian Dream, 462, 498.
    Apology against Rufinus, 408, 410, 411, 412, 482–541.
    Commentary on Ephesians, 446–458, 493–8.
    Defamation of Christians, 462–498.
    Departure from Rome for the East, 530.
    Friendly letter to Rufinus, 489.
    Prefaces to the Vulgate, 515.
    Reading profane literature, 464–5, 489, 498.
    Relations with Origen, 434, 445, 450, 467–470, 533.
    Story of, 426, 513.
    Supposed letter to African Bishops, 515, 532.
    Translation of Old Test., 475.
    Translator of Origen, 427, 428, 525, 536.
Jesus, Meaning of, 545.
John of Jerusalem, 406, 407, 421, 431, 432.
Jovinian, 464, 478.
Jovinus, 436.
Josephus, 413.
Judas, Prophecies of, 551.

Lactantius, 431.
Laurentius, 542.
Letters, composition and carriage of, 515, 520, 524, 532, 537.
Lightfoot on Eusebius, 411.
Logical puzzles, 498–9.

Macarius, 407, 411, 420, 421, 427, 434, 439, 444.
Manichæus, 558.
Marcella, 409, 430, 444.
Marcion, 424, 425, 485, 558.
Melania, 405, 406, 407, 471.
Middle Ages, 412.
Migne's Patrologia, 413.
Milan, Rufinus at, 444.
Minerva's Birth, 547.
Monks, Rufinus' History of, 411.
Morbus regius, 466.

LIFE AND WORKS OF RUFINUS

INDEX OF TEXTS